The People Shall Judge

The People Shall Judge

Readings in the Formation of American Policy

VOLUME II

Selected and Edited by

THE STAFF, SOCIAL SCIENCES 1

The College of the University of Chicago

"Who shall be judge whether the prince or
legislative act contrary to their trust? . . .
The people shall be judge; for who shall
be judge whether the trustee or deputy
acts well and according to the trust reposed
in him, but he who deputes him...."—LOCKE,
Second Treatise of Civil Government, chap. xix.

THE UNIVERSITY OF CHICAGO PRESS
CHICAGO · ILLINOIS

THE UNIVERSITY OF CHICAGO PRESS, CHICAGO 37
Cambridge University Press, London, N.W. 1, England
W. J. Gage & Co., Limited, Toronto 2B, Canada

PREFACE

THIS book expresses the faith of one American college in the usefulness of liberal education to American democracy. If the United States is to be a democracy, its citizens must be free. If citizens are to be free, they must be their own judges. If they are to judge well, they must be wise. Citizens may be born free; they are not born wise. Therefore, the business of liberal education in a democracy is to make free men wise. Democracy declares that "the people shall judge." Liberal education must help the people to judge well.

The teachers who have prepared this volume have been practicing the creed which is merely preached above. Insistently, they have asked themselves, "How can we help Americans to study their own past in such a way that they will grow in practical wisdom?" Their attempt to answer this question has determined both the content and the method of the course for which these teachers are responsible.

Since the wise citizen is more than the informed citizen, he needs to learn more than a summary of the facts of American history. Accordingly, these teachers have placed at the center of their course, not textbooks, but the primary materials which appear in this volume. Instead of the usual later summaries of events and controversies, the firsthand reports and original arguments of those who took part in them have been selected.

But original documents, no less than secondhand materials, might be so presented as to add to the student's information without improving his judgment. Aware of this danger, these teachers have arranged their materials problematically. They have invited the student to see how human judgments such as those he will himself have to make as citizen have been real causes in his country's history. The materials are grouped around a series of moments of decision in the American past, and they have been so selected as to present the diverse arguments and interests, the hopes and fears, the gains, losses, and compromises, of those who actively affected the character and outcome of those moments.

Yet even this open and problematic arrangement of materials could not, by itself, insure the development of practical wisdom in the citizen. Practical wisdom is an active virtue, to be acquired and perfected through exercise. It is not enough to show students how the judgments of their forefathers helped to make their nation's history. The students must themselves practice judgment. This is why the course is conducted by means of discussion classes in which the readings this volume contains and the historical decisions they illumine are subjected to critical examination. In these discussions "learning" and "thinking" advance together in so close an alliance that, in the end, what the student

v

"knows" is not what he has been told to learn but what his own active analysis of the problems of the course has led him to believe or to doubt. He and his fellow-students have been engaged not only in claiming a heritage of wisdom and achievement in the American past but in forming habits of open discussion and independent judgment which will lead to wise decisions and new achievements in the American future. Surely, a democracy should invite its citizens to learn and to think in this inquiring way. Surely, a democracy whose citizens do so learn and think will be well and freely served.

Is national improvement the final good to be expected from this undertaking? Indifferent to political frontiers, liberal education seeks a universal good; and free men, when they have also become wise, discover a concern for freedom everywhere. The college teachers who prepared this book can fairly claim that even those most general ends of education and politics are served by the kind of study of American history in which they and their students are engaged. They need

only to pursue a major American issue to its roots in order to discover that, for all its local idiom and occasion, it was and is a universal human issue, too. The protagonists in the American controversies over federation and slavery and revolution were joining Locke and Pericles, Rousseau and Gandhi, in that "great conversation" about Man and among all men which Chancellor Hutchins has recently proposed as the touchstone of civilization. This "civilization of the dialogue" may someday culminate in an hour when the great conversation will be carried on by men without a country speaking Esperanto without an accent. Pending that hour, it may well be that the most authentic citizens of the world will not be rootless cosmopolites but active citizens of those nations which have sought to liberate their people not from but through a knowledge of their own history. He who would move the world must first be given a place to stand.

F. CHAMPION WARD
Dean of the College

UNIVERSITY OF CHICAGO
November 1, 1948

INTRODUCTION

THE purpose underlying these two volumes is the promotion of intelligent citizenship. They were prepared by a teaching staff who hoped to accomplish certain definite ends by introducing their students to the political experience of the American people. This staff has three chief aims. The first is to enable the student to acquire some basic historical knowledge about American ideas and institutions. The second is to develop competence in the analysis of social issues by giving special prominence to the process of deliberation and decision through which policy is formulated. The third is to encourage the student to acquire a sense of responsibility about public issues and to examine his own standards in an atmosphere of free inquiry and discussion.

To understand the past is to know how we have come to be what we are. We learn to see ourselves as the heirs of a particular tradition, thinking, feeling, and acting along lines suggested by our previous national experience. We find that much of our political thought has revolved around an eighteenth-century creed of natural rights; that our Constitution bears the ineffaceable marks of the initial struggle with English despotism and American radicalism; that our attitude to the institution of private property is strongly affected by an experience in which the rights of property have been widely shared; that our national character reflects the exhilarations and excesses of the frontier long after the last acre of free land has disappeared. We understand why our foreign policy has often seemed to be directed from the graves of Washington and Monroe and why the names of Jefferson and Lincoln are used by party politicians to exorcise the demons in our midst. We uncover the roots of some of our problems in the Civil War; of others in the industrialism which swept away the fabric of rural society without being able to obliterate its ideas. In short, we acquire the kind of national self-knowledge—about our emotional constitution, our mental furnishings, our institutions, our established policies—which only a study of the past can give.

The first object of the editors was to find some satisfactory means of putting this general knowledge within the students' reach. This might have been done in any one of several ways. Here we have presented the historical record in a particular way because we also wanted to develop a certain kind of competence. As a citizen the student will be confronted with issues of public policy. He will join an endless debate in which these issues are perpetually arising, provoking argument, and forcing decisions on individuals, organized groups, and agencies of government. This process of deliberation and decision is the same activity in which our predecessors were involved as they faced their problems. In many cases the basic questions are the same. What is the end of man? What are the ends of government? What compromise should be sought between freedom and authority? What position should government occupy in relation to the economic system? On what principles should one nation conduct its relations with others? In all cases, however much conditions may alter, there is a certain constancy about the pattern of controversy. Interests clash; values are affirmed; argument proliferates; personality asserts itself. And all calculations have to reckon with the unknown or the unknowable. The function of intelligence in this conflict of opinion is to analyze and to clarify. If we want to develop competence in current controversies, one obvious method is to practice the same kind of talent on past controversies. And this discipline has the added advantage that, where the past is concerned, events have already passed some sort of judgment on the plans of the policy-makers.

Skill in analysis can be made to serve any scheme of values. Are the editors of these volumes, as a teaching staff, trying to promote any particular scheme? They are innocent, they hope, of any desire to indoctrinate their students with their own nostrums, but they are acting within some assumptions which ought to be made explicit. They think that their students ought to have convictions. They want them to feel responsible for the decisions which a self-governing society makes. And they believe that the beginning of wisdom is a willingness to submit all opinions to the test of free and rigorous inquiry. These considerations have led them to organize a course of study which will enable their students to feel the force of the convictions that have molded American values, to examine their own beliefs in the light of this wider world of human experience, and to accept the challenge of criticism and discussion.

Both these volumes consist of readings which might be briefly described as ideas about a public policy. They have been drawn from systematic philosophies; from opinions crystallized in law and judicial decision; from speeches or pamphlets struck off in the heat of controversy; from political and diplomatic correspondence; from sermons, lectures, and newspapers. They range from the speculative to the practical, from the nature of man and society to specific issues of political, economic, and social policy in domestic and foreign affairs. These opinions have been organized in a series of units, each corresponding with a historical situation in which the American people were encountering critical problems of government. The first unit deals with the problem of freedom and authority in the seventeenth century; the second, with the American Revolution; the third, with the organization of a federal constitution; etc. No material has been used in any of these units in which the actors or observers in the actual situation are not speaking for themselves. Their language has been modernized in spelling, in capitalization, and in punctuation; but no other labor-saving device has been inserted between the reader and the original ideas. Wherever feasible, an attempt has been made to reproduce the atmosphere of a debate rather than a monologue. Locke's views have been set side by side with those of Hobbes; Boucher's with Paine's; Jefferson's with Hamilton's; William Graham Sumner's with those of Henry Demarest Lloyd. Each unit is preceded by a brief introduction indicating the scope of the material and suggesting its significance, without prejudicing the issues involved.

These readings are not intended to supplement lectures or textbooks. They are the basic material to which lectures and textbooks are subsidiary. In any given year a selection from these readings is assigned for study, and the student is asked to prepare himself for classroom discussion by careful reading and critical analysis of the documents. This effort of his requires an exertion of historical imagination, an exercise of clear thinking, and a continuous interest in the light which past experience can shed on present problems. He begins with an argument in a particular historical setting. To understand it at all, he has to make the effort to see the problems of that age as they were seen then and to resist any superficial insinuation of his own standards. He identifies the problem which the author is facing and sees how the author defines his position; what his assumptions are, whether explicit or hidden; what alternatives he formulates; how he estimates the consequences of different courses of action. The student compares other approaches to the problem and asks himself what his

own opinion would have been in the same situation. He tries to assess the historical significance of the debate and its sequel. He then examines the arguments in their wider bearing on our own times. What has Locke's liberalism to contribute to an industrial democracy? How relevant is Adam Smith's inquiry into the wealth of nations to present-day America? What conduct would Jefferson have stigmatized as disloyal to American ideals? What can be learned by our present international society from a study of American experience under the Articles of Confederation? These are a few of the questions which might be usefully raised in the subsequent discussions.

The materials in these volumes have survived the test of considerable teaching experience. Many other readings have been tried and eliminated when they seemed unprofitable. The responsibility for this selection rests with the past and present staff of "Social Sciences 1," the first in a three-year sequence of general social science courses in the College of the University of Chicago. The basic principles of this course were first explicitly formulated and applied in 1944 by Bernard Drell, Robert E. Keohane (then chairman of the course), George Probst, Malcolm P. Sharp, Milton B. Singer, and O. Meredith Wilson. To Clarence H. Faust, Dean of the College at the time, should go the credit for convincing the staff of the possibility and desirability of this approach and for the encouragement he gave to the first efforts. Others who have contributed to the development and teaching of the course since 1945 have included Edward Banfield, Edward Bastian, Richard Birnberg, Earl Edgar, Millard Hansen, Ira Kipnis, Laurence Leamer, William Ludlow, D. Eldridge Mc-

Bride, Marvin Meyers, Edmund S. Morgan, Harvey Perloff, Kramer Rohfleisch, Lester Seligman, Alan Simpson, Ben Stephansky, Rexford Tugwell, and Jay C. Williams, Jr. Valuable advice has at various times been given by Maure E. Goldschmidt, Reuben Frodin, Maynard C. Krueger, and Gerhard E. O. Meyer.

The first printed edition of these materials has been, like the previous mimeographed and planographed editions, a cooperative staff undertaking. To Robert E. Keohane and Bernard Drell should go special mention for the time and energy they have given during the last four years to finding and modernizing texts, preparing footnotes, and otherwise making materials suitable for classroom use. They, together with Millard Hansen, George Probst, and Alan Simpson, have been responsible for the editorial direction of this edition. Mr. Simpson has prepared the final drafts of the unit introductions.

The staff is indebted to Margaret Maddox and Margaret Rosenheim for editorial assistance, to Margaret Perry for securing permissions, and to Violet A. Fogle for the art work in the Statistical Appendix. It also wishes to express its thanks to Morton Grodzins (chairman of "Social Sciences 2"), Donald Meiklejohn (chairman of "Social Sciences 3"), and Milton Singer (chairman of the Social Sciences in the College) for a critical reading of the introductions and footnotes and to F. Champion Ward, Dean of the College, for guidance and encouragement.

Publication of this volume has been aided by a grant from the Charles R. Walgreen Foundation for the Study of American Institutions of the University of Chicago.

THE STAFF, SOCIAL SCIENCES I

UNIVERSITY OF CHICAGO
May 27, 1949

TABLE OF CONTENTS

UNIT IX. SOCIAL CRITICISM IN THE INDUSTRIAL AGE, 1865–1914

UNIT X. THE POLITICS OF INDUSTRIALISM, 1865–1914

SECTION A. AGRARIAN REVOLT

SECTION B. STATE REGULATION AND THE COURTS

SECTION C. THE PROGRESSIVE MOVEMENT

SECTION D. FEDERAL EFFORTS TO MAINTAIN COMPETITION

TABLE OF CONTENTS

UNIT XI. AMERICAN FOREIGN POLICY, 1898–1920

SECTION A. A THEORY OF NATIONALISM

SECTION B. EXPANSION IN THE ORIENT

SECTION C. EXPANSION IN LATIN AMERICA

SECTION D. THE FIRST WORLD WAR

SECTION E. REJECTION OF THE LEAGUE OF NATIONS

UNIT XII. FREEDOM IN AN INDUSTRIAL SOCIETY

SECTION A. CRITERIA FOR A FREE SOCIETY

SECTION B. WHAT IS THE PROPER ROLE OF GOVERNMENT?

TABLE OF CONTENTS

TABLE OF CONTENTS

UNIT XIII. RECENT FOREIGN POLICY

SECTION A. PREWAR POLICY

SECTION B. PLANS FOR "ONE WORLD"

SECTION C. POSTWAR CONFLICT: ANALYSES AND PROPOSALS

SECTION D. OFFICIAL AMERICAN POLICY

STATISTICAL APPENDIX

UNIT IX
SOCIAL CRITICISM IN THE INDUSTRIAL AGE
1865–1914

THE Civil War divides the rural from the industrial age of American history. During the nineteenth century all the leading countries of the West were going through a similar experience at different rates of development. By the early years of the twentieth century the United States had overtaken Great Britain, the early pioneer, drawn ahead of Germany, the new power-house in Europe, and established itself as the foremost industrial nation.

Industrialism has obliged every community to absorb a sensationally new way of life. In America a swift development for the modern techniques was insured by the wealth of natural resources, the freedom of movement for capital, labor, and goods, the magnetism which attracted the immigrant, and the whole bent of the national genius for practical construction and enrichment. At the same time the very strength of the individualistic philosophy, the division in the ranks of the farmers created by the Civil War, and the difficulty of organizing labor under American conditions meant that industrialism developed here with the minimum of social restraint. The American regime of private property and free contract gave the maximum freedom to the organizers of the new forces, while their hold over the politics of the nation brought them protection from foreign competition, enormous grants of land for railway development, the reputed advantage of a hard currency, and many other privileges within the disposal of executive, legislative, or judicial officials.

The gains achieved under this system seemed to many Americans a dramatic proof of its virtues. They saw a continent spanned and peopled, production and national wealth prodigiously increased, and glittering prizes won by enterprise and initiative. Many more, while not immune from hardship and misgivings, could hardly fail to be impressed by the scale of the achievement. But, as the pattern unfolded, the feelings of disquiet and loss gathered volume. The old America, of independent farmers, small businessmen, and craftsmen, with its open frontier for the hard pressed, was rapidly disappearing. The alternation of boom and depression now affected many more than before and seemed less tolerable to an age dazzled by the potentialities of the machine. The rise of big business, concentrating economic power in fewer hands, limiting competition, corrupting politicians, and enjoying the favor of the courts, seemed to threaten America with a new tyranny. Both the farmer and the laborer were in some degree the victims of their industrial masters. Their answer was to substitute collective effort for individual self-help and to appeal to government against the oppressions which were accumulating behind the forms of freedom. To sensitive observers of the American scene it only needed such by-products of laissez faire as the sprawling squalors of the mushroom cities or the vicious looting of the national resources to complete the demand for a redefinition of social and political responsibilities.

When facts do too much violence to ideals, they provoke a re-examination of principles. This unit is devoted to the debate which developed among social theorists in the last two decades of the nineteenth century and the early years of the twentieth. The practical response to the new conditions, as it was worked out in the fields of party policy, legislative action, and judicial decision, will be the subject of the next unit.

What obligations ought to be recognized by individuals, by organized groups, and by government in this altered America? Did we need a new morality, more mutual aid and less competitive striving, a wider conception of the state's responsibility for the citizen's welfare, perhaps even a total revision of the economic system? The critics all considered themselves to be opposed to the system of public policy which is denoted by the term "laissez faire," but their analyses and prescriptions differed widely.

For Henry George the great paradox of the age was the persistence of poverty in the midst of progress—and of the deepest poverty in the greatest centers of progress. It seemed to him that American democracy, so long as it was conceived merely in terms of legal and political equality, provided no protection against a breakdown of civilized life into tyranny or anarchy. His search for the law of human progress convinced him that progress depended upon the elimination of certain forms of economic inequality, notably of monopoly in the ownership of land. It was the duty of government, he said, to destroy this monopoly through a planned program of taxation.

Henry Demarest Lloyd was shocked by the same paradox; and, like George, he believed that monopoly lay at the root of the problem. But it was not in landownership that he found the key to the puzzle. The monopolies which worried him were those combinations of capital which in his view were everywhere destroying competition and laying the foundations for a new slavery. The problem was how to "civilize" industry. He believed that it should be attempted through a new kind of industrial morality, reinforced by a considerable degree of public control.

Edward Bellamy was a social critic who used the device of a utopia, set in the future, to satirize and stimulate his contemporaries. The Americans of the year 2000, serene in their emancipation from the immorality and the inefficiency of nineteenth-century capitalism, look back on their ancestors' prejudices with a well-bred mixture of compassion and contempt.

In the writings of John A. Ryan an old philosophy comes to grips with a new situation. The social theories which have been derived from the principles of Christianity have been many and varied. Ryan stands in the tradition of Catholic thought as it was restated during these years in a papal encyclical. While determined to avoid the extremes of both individualism and socialism, he asserts the moral right of the workingman to a living wage and explains how it ought to be vindicated. Here again government is to intervene as the guarantor of claims previously left to private contract.

Socialism, in one of its many forms, has been a standard response throughout the West to the problems created by the development of industrialism within the institutions of capitalism. It is presented here in a Marxian formulation by Charles H. Vail. Vail looks forward to the eventual triumph of socialism as a result of the developing contradictions of capitalism. His blueprint envisages a co-operative commonwealth, established when the working class has seized control, in which all productive industry will be public property.

The defense of orthodoxy against these different attempts to create new responsibilities for government could often be quite safely left to the force of habit, combined with the demonstration of what successful individuals could accomplish under existing conditions. It would be a mistake to infer from the space allotted here to criticism and defense that a public opinion poll would have found Americans divided in the same proportion. However, the growing volume of protest, accompanied by proposals of the kind described, provoked certain answers. In one category is Andrew Carnegie's confidence in the laws of supply and demand as an effective safeguard against monopoly. In another is the philosophy of William Graham Sumner. Sumner's views may be considered as a variant of the "social Darwinism" which enjoyed a considerable vogue among opponents of state regulation in the latter years of the century: a comprehensive indictment of the folly of trying to cure poverty and misery through legislation.

This debate—interrupted here on the eve of World War I—still continues. The paradox of poverty in the midst of technological progress is scarcely less startling now than then. The problem of making combinations of economic force responsible to the community, which first attracted serious attention in these years, is still with us. The deities which preside over the laws of supply and demand, if somewhat neglected by the profane, still have their votaries. The conception of society as a fellowship in mutual aid continues to clash with the prudent maxims of the skeptic. As for the Marxist doctrine of Vail's pamphlet—it is echoed in the strident demands of left-wing forces throughout the world.

Perhaps one observation, among the many which could be made about the subsequent course of the debate, may be offered here. In every industrial community within the Western liberal tradition, the proposition, "That government is best which governs least," has steadily yielded ground under the pressure of conditions which have made an extension of governmental authority inescapable. America, if the freest of these communities in the lightness of its organized controls, is no exception. To that degree, modest in comparison with their hopes but impressive to the student of American ideas, the critics in this debate have had their victories.

1. THE LORDS OF INDUSTRY[1]

By HENRY DEMAREST LLOYD

EDITORS' NOTE.—Henry Demarest Lloyd (1847–1903) was one of the first of a series of outstanding journalists who viewed the development of monopoly as a threat to the continued existence of American democracy. Born in New York City of a family of pioneers and religious dissenters, Lloyd gave up the practice of law for journalism and reform politics. His articles attacking the comparatively sudden increase in trust formation began to appear in the 1880's and met with immediate success. He was an active member of the Populist party and ran unsuccessfully for Congress in 1894 as that party's candidate in one of Chicago's "corporation-controlled" districts. In the same year he published his carefully documented *Wealth against Commonwealth*, which related his concern with the growing power of corporations to his theory of community self-interest—"liberty and mo-

nopoly cannot live together" and "that which is cooperatively produced [must be] cooperatively enjoyed." The further development of this theory led him to join the Socialist party before his death in 1903.

Lloyd opposed the Populist party decision to support Bryan in 1896 on the narrow issue of free silver and for a time thereafter confined his political activities to his home suburb of Winnetka on Chicago's North Shore. He soon returned to work for national social reform, however, and in 1903 greatly impaired his health by his activity in behalf of the miners during the arbitration of the anthracite coal strike. Without allowing himself the opportunity to recover his health, Lloyd immediately plunged into the fight for municipal ownership of the Chicago street railway system. During the height of the campaign he collapsed and died.

When President Gowen, of the Reading Railroad, was defending that company in 1875 before a committee of the Pennsylvania legislature for having taken part in the combination of the coal companies to cure the evil of "too much coal" by putting up the price and cutting down the amount for sale, he pleaded that there were fifty trades in which the same thing was done. He had a list of them to show the committee. He said:

1. Henry Demarest Lloyd, "Lords of Industry," *North American Review*, CXXXVIII (June, 1884), 535–38, 541–45, 548–53.

Every pound of rope we buy for our vessels or for our mines is bought at a price fixed by a committee of the rope manufacturers of the United States. Every keg of nails, every paper of tacks, all our screws and wrenches and hinges, the boiler flues for our locomotives, are never bought except at the price fixed by the representatives of the mills that manufacture them. Iron beams for your houses or your bridges can be had only at the prices agreed upon by a combination of those who produce them. Fire-brick, gas-pipe, terra-cotta pipe for drainage, every keg of powder we buy to blast coal, are purchased under the same arrangement. Every pane of window glass in this house was bought at a scale of prices established exactly in the same manner. White lead, galvanized sheet iron, hose and belting and files are bought and sold at a rate determined in the same way. When my friend Mr. Lane was called upon to begin his speech the other day and wanted to delay because the stenographer had not arrived, I asked Mr. Collins, the stenographer of your committee, if he would not act. He said no, it was against the rules of the committee of stenographers. I said, "Well, Mr. Collins, I will pay you anything you ask. I want to get off." "Oh," said he, "prices are established by our combination, and I cannot change them." And when we come to the cost of labor, which enters more than anything else in the cost of coal, we are met by a combination there, and are often obliged to pay the price fixed by it."

Adam Smith said in 1776: "People of the same trade hardly meet together even for merriment and diversion but the conversation ends in a conspiracy against the public, or in some contrivance to raise prices." The expansive ferment of the New Industry, coming with the new science, the new land, and the new liberties of our era, broke up these "conspiracies," and for a century we have heard nothing of them; but the race to overrun is being succeeded by the struggle to divide, and combinations are re-appearing on all sides. This any one may see from the reports of the proceedings of the conventions and meetings of innumerable associations of manufacturers and dealers and even producers, which are being held almost constantly. They all do something to raise prices, or hold them up, and they wind up with banquets for which we pay.

Four years ago the Chicago Lumbermen's Exchange adopted a resolution declaring it to be "dishonorable" for any dealer to make lower prices than those published by it for the control of prices in one of the greatest lumber markets of the world. Monthly reports are required by this Exchange from dealers, so that accurate accounts may be kept of stock on hand in order to regulate prices. The price lists of the Exchange are revised and made

"honest" at monthly banquets. In February, 1883, it was found that members who ostensibly adhered to the price lists dipped into the dishonorable practice of competition on the sly by giving buyers greater than the usual discounts. This was then forbidden, and another pathway of competition closed. The effect of this price-legislation was attested by the address of a dealer of Minneapolis at one of the price-list banquets of the Exchange, who said that his firm, which made sales as far off as Manitoba and Dakota, had never sold a foot for less than the published lists. A delegation of dealers from the Mississippi River district spoke feelingly of their labors "for harmony" and their willingness that Chicago should make prices. A secret meeting of lumbermen from all parts of the West was held in Chicago, March 8, 1883, to discuss means for advancing prices, restricting production at least thirty-five per cent, and in general, in the language of one of them, putting themselves into a position like that of the coal producers of Pennsylvania, who by combination dictated the prices of coal throughout the whole country. In May, last year, the national association of lumber dealers met in Chicago. It represents over five hundred and fifty retail dealers in the West, and its principal purpose was to prevent wholesale dealers at Chicago, St. Louis, and other centers from retailing lumber to carpenters, farmers, and scalpers in the territory of the retailers. There are too many sellers, and so any wholesaler who persists in competing in this way with local dealers is, when found guilty, named to all the retailers and punished by losing their trade. . . .

Western ranch-men complain that the competition of buyers is disappearing. They declare that there exist at the Chicago stock-yards combinations of buyers who, by their ability to make large purchases and their agreement to offer but one price, get cattle at their own figures. One member of the "ring" does the buying to-day; another to-morrow, and so on. The cattle kings have combinations to defend themselves from cattle thieves, State legislatures, and other enemies, and propose to extend this category so as to include the middle-men at the stock-yards. The Stock-growers' Association of Wyoming have $100,000,000 in cattle. At the recent convention held by this body in Cheyenne, it was unanimously declared that its business had been "seriously injured by the pooling arrangements prevailing among buyers at the Chicago stock-yards," and the executive committee were instructed to obtain the fullest possible information as to the means by which cattle might be shipped direct to the European consumer.

Last July Messrs. Vanderbilt, Sloan, and one or two others out of several hundred owners of coal lands and coal railroads, met in the pleasant shadows of Saratoga to make "a binding arrangement for the control of the coal trade." "Binding arrangement" the sensitive coal presidents say they prefer to the word "combination." The gratuitous warmth of summer suggested to these men the need the public would have of artificial heat, at artificial prices, the coming winter. It was agreed to fix prices, and to prevent the production of too much of the raw material of warmth, by suspensions of mining. In anticipation of the arrival of the cold wave from Manitoba, a cold wave was sent out all over the United States, from their parlors in New York, in an order for half-time work by the miners during the first three months of this year, and for an increase of prices. These are the means this combination uses to keep down wages—the price of men, and keep up the price of coal—the wages of capital. Prices of coal in the West are fixed by the Western Anthracite Coal Association, controlled entirely by the large railroads and mine-owners of Pennsylvania. This association regulates the price west of Buffalo and Pittsburgh and in Canada. Our annual consumption of anthracite is now between 31,000,000 and 32,000,000 tons. The West takes between 5,000,000 and 6,000,000 tons. The com-

panies which compose the combination mine, transport, and sell their own coal. They are obliterating other mine-owners and the retailer. The Chicago and New York dealer has almost nothing to say about what he shall pay or what he shall charge, or what his profits shall be. The great companies do not let the little men make too much. Year by year the coal retailers are sinking into the status of mere agents of the combination, with as little freedom as the consumer. . . .

One of the sights which this coal side of our civilization has to show is the presence of herds of little children of all ages, from six years upward, at work in the coal breakers, toiling in dirt, and air thick with carbon dust, from dawn to dark, of every day in the week except Sunday. These coal breakers are the only schools they know. A letter from the coal regions in the Philadelphia "Press" declares that "there are no schools in the world where more evil is learned or more innocence destroyed than in the breakers. It is shocking to watch the vile practices indulged in by these children, to hear the frightful oaths they use, to see their total disregard for religion and humanity." In the upper part of Luzerne county, out of 22,000 inhabitants 3,000 are children, between six and fifteen years of age, at work in this way. "There is always a restlessness among the miners," an officer of one of the New York companies said, "when we are working them on half time." The latest news from the region of the coal combination is that the miners are so dissatisfied with the condition in which they are kept, by the suspension of work and the importation of competing Hungarian laborers in droves, that they are forming a combination of their own, a revival of the old Miners and Laborers' Association, which was broken up by the labor troubles of 1874 and 1875.

Combination is busy in those soft-coal districts, whose production is so large that it must be sent to competitive markets. A pool has just been formed covering the annual product of 6,000,000 tons of the mines of Ohio. Indiana and Illinois are to be brought in, and it is planned to extend it to all the bituminous coal districts that compete with each other. The appearance of Mr. Vanderbilt, last December, in the Clearfield district of Pennsylvania, at the head of a company capitalized for $5,000,-000, was the first entry of a metropolitan mind into this field. Mr. Vanderbilt's role is to be that of producer, carrier, dealer, and consumer, all in one. Until he came, the district was occupied by a number of small companies and small operators, as used to be the case in the anthracite field in the old days. But the man who works himself, with his sons, in a small mine, cutting perhaps from twenty to forty tons a day, cannot expect to survive the approach of the Manhattan capitalist. The small Clearfield producers, looking at the fate of their kind in the anthracite country, greeted Mr. Vanderbilt's arrival with the question, "What is to become of us?" "If the small operator," said one of the great man's lieutenants, "goes to the wall, that is his misfortune, not our fault." In March last the prominent Clearfield companies gave notice that wages must be reduced on the 1st of April, and immediately thereafter a union of their employés resolved that if the reduction, which they declared to be "without reason," was made they would strike.

Powerful syndicates are at work to control the coke industries of Pennsylvania, which will require from ten to fifteen millions of dollars. March 23, 1884, it was stated that the efforts of a year or more to consolidate the large and small coke-makers of the Connellsville district had succeeded. Nearly 8000 ovens joined the pool, which is under the command of the four largest firms. The smaller men agreed to shut their ovens whenever the heads of the pool ordered. It was announced, two days afterward, that one oven out of every seven had been closed "until further orders," that the price of coke would be advanced at once from ninety-five cents to $1.15 a ton, and that farther advances

would be made until the price had been raised to $1.50. In March, 1883, the St. Louis "Age of Steel" had news that a combination had been made of all the coke iron furnaces, with one exception, in Tennessee, Alabama and Georgia, to fix uniform prices and prevent indiscriminate competition and "trickery" of all kinds, which is the disrespectful language in which the coke iron economists speak of the sacred law of competition.

There has been since 1872 a national combination of the manufacturers of the stoves, into which the combination coal must be put; and its effect, the founder said, in his speech at the annual banquet in Cleveland, last February, had been to change the balance from the wrong to the right side of the ledger. Until lately, at least, combination matches lighted the fire of combination coal in these combination stoves, and it is combination oil which the cook, contrary to orders, puts on the fires to make them burn faster. The combination of match manufacturers was perfected by the experience of sixteen years of fusions, till lately it shared with the coal combination the pleasure of advancing the price of fire by proclamation on the approach of winter. It is now at war with the new companies which have gone into the manufacture since the repeal of the internal revenue tax. These it is attempting to conquer by underselling them, tactics which have hitherto never failed. The Government of the United States, before which all men are equal, helped this combination to kill off its competitors, shielding it from foreign competition by a tax of thirty-five per cent on the importation of matches from abroad, and shielding it from domestic competition, by administering the internal revenue tax so as to make its small competitors pay ten per cent more tax. This drove them into bankruptcy, or combination with the ring, at the rate of one or two every month. The railroads, like the Government, helped to transfer this business from the many to a few, by carrying the combination's matches at lower rates than were given to its little competitors.

When the house-maid strikes a combination match on the wall-paper, she leaves a mark on an article the manufacture, sale, and price of which are rigidly regulated by the American Wall Paper Manufacturers' Association. A recent writer has described this oath-bound combination which has established a wall-paper monarchy in the United States. When the cook takes the paper from the express package, the hardware, the dry-goods, the groceries, the candy, the ham, which have been sent home, she is still handling an article the price of which is fixed by private enactments. The Western Wrapping-paper Association, ever since 1880, has, with more or less success, been struggling to keep down the deluge of too much wrapping-paper, and to fix the prices of all kinds, from the paper under the carpet to that which is used in roofing. It recently failed, but was at once reorganized on a firmer footing than before, and its mills are now allowed to turn out but one-half as much as they could produce. Besides this, the wood pulp and straw paper industries have been amalgamated. The American Paper Association aims to control the prices and production of paper for newspapers and books, and for writing. The dealers in old rags and old paper formed an association in Cleveland three years ago to deal with the "old-rag" problem of how to cut down the enormous profits the women of our country are making out of the contents of their rag-bags. In January, 1883, the trade met again at Rochester, formed two "national" associations, and solemnly agreed upon the prices to be paid for mixed rags "that we gather from house to house," and for brown paper and rag carpet. "No change of price for rags or paper," runs the decree of the old-rag barons, "is to be made without consultation of every member of the executive committee." The Western Wooden Ware Association discovered, last December, that there were too many

pails, tubs, and bowls, and ordered its members to manufacture but one-fifth of their capacity. In February it gave them permission to increase this to one-half. The Western Cracker Bakers' Association met in Chicago in February to consider, among other things, "the reprehensible system of cutting prices." They first had a banquet. After their "merriment and diversion" the revelers, true to Adam Smith's description, turned to consider "some contrivance to raise prices." "The price lists were perfected," said the newspaper report, and then they adjourned.

The men who make our shrouds and coffins have formed a close corporation known as the National Burial Case Association, and held their national convention in Chicago last year. Their action to keep up prices and keep down the number of coffins was secret, lest mortality should be discouraged. The largest manufacturers of quinine in the world are the Boehringers of Milan, Mannheim, and Paris. The next largest are Powers and Weightman of Philadelphia. The latter have just leased the Boehringer factory in Mannheim. New York druggists say that these two could force up the price of quinine very high by combination, but do not believe they will do so. A pool of the seventeen leading quinine manufacturers of the world was formed last July. It included the manufacturers of America, Great Britain, and the continent of Europe. It advanced prices for a time twenty cents an ounce, but went to pieces at the beginning of 1884. The manufacturers of patent medicines organized in 1883, and the wholesale and retail druggists have followed with organizations to prevent the sale of these nostrums at cut prices, or by any persons who were not regular druggists. A "drug war" has broken out and threatens to rage over the entire Union. The combination of the wholesale druggists and that of the manufacturers have mutually agreed to divide the United States into districts, each of which shall be under a superintendent, who is to watch the druggists and report all those cutting prices, who are thereupon to be boycotted.

Every one knows about the thirty-million-dollar steel combination, which has not kept the price of rails from declining from $166 a ton in 1867 to $32 a ton in 1884, but during this decline has kept the price of rails—that is, the price of transportation, that is, the price of everything, higher in this country than anywhere else. Chairman Morrison of the Committee of Ways and Means is a witness to the fact that the chimneys of the Vulcan Mill at St. Louis stood smokeless for years, and meanwhile its owners received a subsidy reported at $400,000 a year from the other mills of the combination for not making rails, with, however, no payment to its men for not working. The steel-rail makers of England, France, Belgium, and Germany are negotiating for an international combination to keep up prices. The "Age of Steel" startled the country last January by the statement that a monster pool was to be formed of all our pig-iron manufacturers. The country was to be divided into six districts. As many furnaces were to be put out of blast as were necessary to prevent us from having too much iron, and these idle furnaces were to share, like the Vulcan Steel Mill, the profits of those that ran. This has not yet proved to be history, but it may turn out to have been prophecy. . . .

Two years ago it was found that there was too much milk in New York and Boston. The "embattled farmers"of Orange county, which supplies New York with two-thirds of its milk, declared a milk war. The New York dealers were cut off from their regular supplies. Committees of farmers waited at every railroad station, and offered to buy all the milk that was brought down for shipment by those who did not join in the combination. When bought it was spilled. When not bought it was usually spilled just the same. Two Italians with performing bears were in Goshen on the night when the first milk

was spilled. The farmers said the bears did it, and while the "milk war" lasted the spillers were known as "the bears." When the superintendent of the Lehigh and Hudson Railroad allowed milk to be shipped against the protests of the farmers, they threatened to tear up the tracks, and the sheriff of the county had to be called in to protect the road. Sheriffs' deputies, appointed to protect the shippers, helped the bears to spill the milk. At Warwick all the streets leading to the depot were barricaded by the bears with ropes. It took eight men armed with clubs, guns, and pistols to guard one man collecting milk. Peace was declared March 24, 1883. A committee of the farmers and a committee of the milkmen, representing eight hundred dealers in New York, Brooklyn, and Jersey City, agreed upon a fixed price for each month until April, 1884, ranging from two and a half to four cents a quart, according to the time of year. The organization of farmers spread until it covered Delaware, Orange, and Sullivan counties in New York, and Hunterdon and Sussex counties in New Jersey. March 22d, of this year, the farmers' committee and that of the milk dealers' organization, known to the honest farmers as the "Pump Handle Association," met again, agreed on prices for another twelve-month, and this year there will be no milk war.

The trade in milk at the point of largest consumption in the United States now rests in the hands of these combinations. The same thing is going on at other places. The New England Milk Producers' Association met in Boston, last January, for the purpose of thoroughly organizing the milk farmers. Representatives from New York who had led the farmers there were present to point out the way. The Secretary of the Massachusetts Board of Agriculture read a letter from a gentleman in which a check of one hundred dollars was inclosed, to pay for milk to be poured on the ground to help the success of the producers' cause. The membership was increased from 86 to 291. Resolutions were adopted calling upon all the farmers who supplied Boston with milk to join the association and do all in their power to solve the "milk problem." On March 22d, the day of the similar meeting in New York, the association met again in Boston, conferred with the representatives of the milk dealers, fixed the price of milk from April to October at thirty-four cents for eight and one-half quarts by a vote of 91 to 39, and adjourned. The ballot is a new force in the manufacture of prices, and one well worthy the attention of those who are curious about the developments of universal suffrage.

Other combinations, more or less successful, have been made by ice men of New York, fish dealers of Boston, Western millers, copper miners, manufacturers of sewer pipe, lamps, pottery, glass, hoop-iron, shot, rivets, sugar, candy, starch, preserved fruits, glucose, vapor stoves, chairs, lime, rubber, screws, chains, harvesting machinery, pins, salt, type, brass tubing, hardware, silk, and wire cloth, to say nothing of the railroad, labor, telegraph, and telephone pools with which we are so familiar. On the third of April the largest and most influential meeting of cotton manufacturers ever held in the South came together at Augusta to take measures to cure the devastating plague of too much cotton cloth. A plan was unanimously adopted for the organization of a Southern Manufacturers' Association for the same general purposes as the New England Manufacturers' Association. The convention recommended its members to imitate the action of the Almighty in making a short crop of cotton by making a short crop of yarns and cloth, and referred to a committee the preparation of plans for a more thorough pool.

Such are some of the pools into which our industry is eddying. They come and go, but more come than go, and those that stay grow. All are "voluntary," of course, but if the milk farmer of Orange county, the iron molder of Troy, the lumber dealer

of San Francisco, the Lackawanna Railroad, or any other individual or corporate producer, show any backwardness about accepting the invitation to join "the pool," they are whipped in with all the competitive weapons at command, from assault and battery to boycotting and conspiracy. The private wars that are ravaging our world of trade give small men their choice between extermination and vassalage. Combine or die! The little coke burner of Connellsville works or stops work, the coal dealer of Chicago raises his prices or lowers them, the type-setter takes up his stick or lays it down, as the master of the pool directs. Competitors swear themselves on the Bible into accomplices, and free and equal citizens abandon their business privacy to pool commissioners vested with absolute power, but subject to human frailties. Commerce is learning the delights of universal suffrage, and in scores of trades supply and demand are adjusted by a majority vote. In a society which has the wherewithal to cover, fatten and cheer every one, Lords of Industry are acquiring the power to pool the profits of scarcity and to decree famine. They cannot stop the brook that runs the mill, but they can chain the wheel; they cannot hide the coal mine, but they can close the shaft three days every week. To keep up gold-digging rates of dividends, they declare war against plenty. On all that keeps him alive the workman must pay them their prices, while they lock him out of the mill in which alone his labor can be made to fetch the price of life. Only society can compel a social use of its resources; the man is for himself.

On the theory of "too much of everything" our industries, from railroads to workingmen, are being organized to prevent milk, nails, lumber, freights, labor, soothing syrup, and all these other things, from becoming too cheap. The majority have never yet been able to buy enough of anything. The minority have too much of everything to sell. Seeds of social trouble germinate fast in such conditions.

Society is letting these combinations become institutions without compelling them to adjust their charges to the cost of production, which used to be the universal rule of price. Our laws and commissions to regulate the railroads are but toddling steps in a path in which we need to walk like men. The change from competition to combination is nothing less than one of those revolutions which march through history with giant strides. It is not likely that this revolution will go backward. Nothing goes backward in this country except reform. When Stephenson said of railroads that where combination was possible competition was impossible, he was unconsciously declaring the law of all industry.

Man, the only animal which forgets, has already in a century or two forgotten that the freedom, the independence of his group, of the state and even of the family, which he has enjoyed for a brief interval, have been unknown in most of the history of our race, and in all the history of most races. The livery companies of London, with their gloomy guildhalls, their wealth, their gluttony and wine-bibbing, their wretched Irish estates, exist to-day vain reminders to us of a time when the entire industry of Europe was regimented into organizations, voluntary at first, afterward adopted by the law, which did what our pools of railroads, laborers, manufacturers, and others are trying to do. Not only prices but manners were pooled. "The notion," says Cliffe Leslie, "that every man had a right to settle where he liked, to carry on any occupation he thought fit, and in whatever manner he chose, to demand the highest price he could get, or on the contrary to offer lower terms than any one else, to make the largest profit possible, and to compete with other traders without restraint, was absolutely contrary to the spirit of the ages that preceded ours." This system existed for centuries. It is so unlike our own that the contemplation of it may well shake us out of our conceit that the transitions, displacements, changes, upheavals, struggles, exterminations—from

Indians to sewing women—of the last two hundred and fifty years were the normal condition of the race.

Those were not exceptional times. Our day of free competition and free contract has been the exceptional era in history. Explorer, pioneer, protestant, reformer, captain of industry could not move in the harness of the guild brother, the vassal, the monk, and were allowed to throw away mediaeval uniforms. But now "the individual withers; the world is more and more." Society having let the individual overrun the new worlds to be conquered, is reëstablishing its lines of communication with him. Literary theorists still repeat the cant of individualism in law, politics, and morals; but the world of affairs is gladly accepting, in lieu of the liberty of each to do as he will with his own, all it can get of the liberty given by laws that let no one do as he might with his own. The dream of the French Revolution, that man was good enough to be emancipated from the bonds of association and government by the simple proclamation of Liberty, Fraternity and Equality, was but the frenzied expression of what was called Freedom of Self-interest in a quieter but not less bloody revolution, if the mortality of the factories, the mines, and the tenements be charged to its account. A rope cannot be made of sand; a society cannot be made of competitive units.

We have given competition its own way, and have found that we are not good enough or wise enough to be trusted with this power of ruining ourselves in the attempt to ruin others. Free competition could be let run only in a community where every one had learned to say and act "I am the state." We have had an era of material inventions. We now need a renaissance of moral inventions, contrivances to tap the vast currents of moral magnetism flowing uncaught over the face of society. Morals and values rise and fall together. If our combinations have no morals, they can have no values. If the tendency to combination is irresistible, control of it is imperative. Monopoly and anti-monopoly, odious as these words have become to the literary ear, represent the two great tendencies of our time: monopoly, the tendency to combination; anti-monopoly, the demand for social control of it. As the man is bent toward business or patriotism, he will negotiate combinations or agitate for laws to regulate them. The first is capitalistic, the second is social. The first, industrial; the second, moral. The first promotes wealth; the second, citizenship. These combinations are not to be waved away as fresh pictures of folly or total depravity. There is something in them deeper than that. The Aryan has proved by the experience of thousands of years that he can travel. "But travel," Emerson says, "is the fool's paradise." We must now prove that we can stay at home, and stand it as well as the Chinese have done. Future Puritans cannot emigrate from Southampton to Plymouth Rock. They can only sail from righteous-ness to righteousness. Our young men can no longer go west; they must go up or down. Not new land, but new virtue must be the outlet for the future. Our halt at the shores of the Pacific is a much more serious affair than that which brought our ancestors to a pause before the barriers of the Atlantic, and compelled them to practice living together for a few hundred years. We cannot hereafter, as in the past, recover freedom by going to the prairies; we must find it in the society of the good. In the presence of great combinations, in all departments of life, the moralist and patriot have work to do of a significance never before approached during the itinerant phases of our civilization. It may be that the coming age of combination will issue in a nobler and fuller liberty for the individual than has yet been seen, but that consummation will be possible, not in a day of competitive trade, but in one of competitive morals.

2. RELATIONS BETWEEN LABOR AND CAPITAL[1]

EDITORS' NOTE.—The efforts of labor to improve its position in the rapidly developing post–Civil War industrial economy through the organization of trade-unions and the broad Knights of Labor led the Senate in 1882 to authorize its Committee on Education and Labor "to take into consideration the subject of the relations between labor and capital." The committee attempted to obtain testimony from all interested groups and heard representatives of business, labor, the professions, and the reform movements. Whatever may have been the educational effects of the hearings on the senators, no legislation was immediately forthcoming.

With the exception of one year, Samuel Gompers (1850–1924) was president of the American Federation of Labor from its organization in 1886 until his death. Gompers was born in London of Dutch-Jewish parents and emigrated to the United States in 1863. He was a cigar-maker and in the 1870's helped build the cigar-makers' union into a financially stable unit which gave the national officers complete authority over the local unions and set high dues to provide a financial reserve for strikes and depressions. The organizational basis of that craft union was used as the pattern for the other craft unions which later associated to form the American Federation of Labor.

1. Forty-eighth Congress, Senate Committee on Education and Labor, *Report . . . upon the Relations between Labor and Capital* (Washington, 1885), I, 270–71, 293–300, 361–82; III, 3–15, 19, 22, 25, 407–12, 451–57.

A. TESTIMONY OF SAMUEL GOMPERS

NEW YORK, August 16, 1883

Samuel Gompers sworn and examined.

By the CHAIRMAN:

Question. What is your full name and where do you reside?—*Answer.* Samuel Gompers; I reside in the city of New York.

Q. What is your age?—*A.* I shall be 34 years of age next January.

Q. How long have you resided in the city of New York?—*A.* With an intermission of about ten months, over twenty years.

Q. What is your employment?—*A.* I am a cigar-maker.

Q. That has been your occupation during your life?—*A.* Yes, sir.

Q. Have you been connected with the labor movements of the country to any extent; and, if so, how closely and for how long a time?—*A.* I have; I joined the Cigar-maker's Union about eighteen years ago or a little over. . . .

Q. It would seem that your opportunities of learning the objects and scope of these labor organizations has been as good as any one's; won't you give us, therefore, a general idea of what labor organizations there are in this country, what their purposes are, and what they seem to be accomplishing as a whole. Give us an idea of the general labor movement and of those labor organizations which are leading it. Go on and open up the matter as it is in your own mind.—*A.* Then I will not start with the organizations. I would rather speak first of the general condition of labor as I find it, as I know it and believe it to be.

CONDITION OF WORKING PEOPLE

Q. Well, take up the subject in your own way, but before you get through I would like you to answer the question I have put with regard to the extent and the actual objects and results of these organizations.—*A.* Oh, certainly; I shall endeavor to give you that to the best of my ability. The condition of the working people appears to be coming to what may rightly be termed a focus. On the one hand it would be well to note the underlying motives that frequently break out in what are generally termed strikes. Strikes are the result of a condition, and are not, as is generally or frequently understood, the cause. For instance, in the State of Massachusetts they have a ten-hour law, intended to benefit the female and child operatives there, yet the employers . . . or their agents start up the mills several minutes, sometimes seven, eight, nine or ten minutes, before the time for commencing to work according to rule and law. In other instances they close them at "noon" several minutes after 12 o'clock and open them again several minutes before the hour, or half hour rather, has elapsed, closing again for the day several minutes after the rule requires. These employers are pretty well described by some of the English economists and labor advocates— not labor advocates, but men who have made economic questions a study; they call them "minute thieves."

. . . The hours of labor have been discussed by many thinkers on the labor question, and by many from different stand-points. During my attendance upon this committee I have heard a good many questions asked and answered, and in my humble opinion some of the answers were not what they ought to have been. I maintain that the hours of labor ought to be reduced. From every stand-point the hours are too long in modern industries, more especially where the individual, the worker, is but a part of the machine and is compelled to keep in motion in accordance with the velocity with which the machine turns. The production of goods is not, as many have been led to believe, lessened by a reduction of the hours of labor; but, on the contrary, the productivity of labor increases. In all countries, in all States in this country, in all factories where in certain branches of trade the experiment has been made, wherever the hours of labor have been reduced, there the productivity of labor has become greater.

By the CHAIRMAN:

Q. Absolutely, or in proportion to the time occupied?—A. Absolutely.

Q. One day with another, more goods produced?—A. More produced, one day with another. I am saying that the productivity of labor has increased; not from the desire, or probably not from the ability, of the laborer to produce more in the shorter number of hours, but as a consequence of the fact that, owing to the reduction of the hours of labor, machinery has been improved, new tools have been made, and the different industries have been divided and subdivided, so that as a consequence of the reduction of the hours there has come increased production.

Q. Then the increased productivity is the result of the improved machinery and not of the shorter hours of labor?—A. But the improved machinery is the result of the reduction of the hours of labor.

Q. But we are speaking of the direct cause; and the reduction of the hours of labor is not the direct cause of the increased production, you say, but the reduction of the hours of labor has led to invention and improved machinery, and by the machinery, combined with shorter hours of labor, more is produced?—A. Decidedly. . . .

Q. You think, then, that he [the worker] will consume more in consequence of the reduction of the hours of labor?—A. I do, positively.

Q. In a certain way he will have more time to consume in?—A. Yes, sir. And another thing: A man who goes to his work before the dawn of day requires no clean shirt to go to work in, but is content to go in an old overall or anything that will cover his members; but a man who goes to work at 8 o'clock in the morning wants a clean shirt; he is afraid his friends will see him, so he does not want to be dirty. He also requires a newspaper; while a man who goes to work early in the morning

and stays at it late at night does not need a newspaper, for he has no time to read, requiring all the time he has to recuperate his strength sufficiently to get ready for his next day's work. . . . That labor deserves a reduction of the hours of toil I believe hardly any one will dispute, unless when he is on "the other side of the house" and labor is seeking to enforce such a reduction against his interest, as he thinks. The general reduction of the hours of labor to eight per day would reach further than any other reformatory measure; it would be of more lasting benefit; it would create a greater spirit in the workingman; it would make him a better citizen, a better father, a better husband, a better man in general. The "voting cattle," so called, those whose votes are purchased on election day, are drawn from that class of our people whose life is one continuous round of toil. They cannot be drawn from workingmen who work only eight hours. A man who works but eight hours a day possesses more independence both economically and politically. It is the man who works like his machine and never knows when to stop, until in his case perpetual motion is almost arrived at—*he* is the man whose vote you can buy. The man who works longest is the first to be thrown out on the sidewalk, because his recreation is generally drink.

Q. Do you know of anybody who works only eight hours?—A. Yes, sir.

Q. Where is that system in operation? I know there are laws to that effect, but where does the eight-hour system prevail actually?—A. About twenty-six years ago, in Australia, the workingmen obtained, against the protests (because the arguments for the reduction of the hours of labor were not then understood as they are to-day)—despite the protests of the employing class, I say, the workingmen obtained the adoption of the eight-hour law, and that law is in force up to the present day, and such general satisfaction does that law give now, and the operation of it, that the 21st of April each year is observed as a national holiday almost equal to our Fourth of July here. . . .

By Mr. CALL:

Q. Let me see if I understand your idea about this eight-hour law. I understand that, in the first place, you propose a rule of action by which shall be prohibited the exaction of more than eight hours of labor daily of any one man. Now, suppose the man wants to work more than eight hours, would you favor a law prohibiting it?—A. No; I would not favor such a law. I believe that the regulation of that would easily evolve out of the organized efforts of labor and the means that would be taken to agitate the question and educate the workers to understand that it would be to their benefit, to their lasting benefit, to abstain from more than eight hours' work.

Q. You think that would become the universal custom and rule?—A. Yes, sir. . . .

NEW YORK, August 18, 1883

Samuel Gompers recalled and further examined. . . .

STRIKES

I desire to say a few words now in reference to strikes. . . . While I am in the labor movement and take a stand opposed to strikes whenever they can be avoided, I have no sympathy with, nor can I indorse or echo, the statements of many men who are too ready to condemn strikes. Strikes have their evils, but they have their good points also, and with proper management, with proper organization, strikes do generally result to the advantage of labor, and in very few instances do they result in injury to the workingmen, whether organized or unorganized.

By Mr. GEORGE:

Q. You mean ultimate injury?—A. Ultimate injury. Strikes ought to be, and in well-organized trades unions they are, the last means which workingmen resort to to protect themselves against the almost never satisfied greed of the employers. Besides this, the strike is, in many in-

stances, the only remedy within our reach as long as legislation is entirely indifferent to the interests of labor. . . . The results of organization in my own trade, cigar-making, are instructive. From the year 1873 to 1878 the cigar-makers of this country were reduced in wages systematically every *spring and every fall*. The reductions in wages were sometimes large and sometimes not quite so large, but a reduction was the order of the day at those periods. At that time the cigar-makers' organization was in a very weak and puerile condition. Further, the manufacturers of cigars throughout that period managed to introduce a system of truck or "pluck-me" payments, by which the workingmen were paid in kind, cigars, and were required to go out and sell them to any grog-shop or other place of any description where they could sell them; or they would receive store orders, or, in the case of single men, they would be required to board at certain hotels or boarding houses. In the city of Elmira, in this State, a manufacturer paid his workingmen $6 per thousand if they were taking their wages out in truck or kind, while he paid only $5 a thousand to those single men who were in boarding houses, and but $4 a thousand to those cigar-makers who wanted cash, legal tender. . . .

What I wish to show is the condition of the cigar-makers at that period when there was no organization. When our organizations commenced to emerge and reorganize throughout the country, the first year there were seventeen strikes in our trade, of which twelve or thirteen were successful. The rest were either lost or compromised. In the year following we had forty-six strikes, of which thirty-seven, I think, were successful, three lost, and six compromised. In these last two years, since which we have held no convention (we will hold one next year and we will hear the result), I am convinced that we have had over one hundred and sixty or one hundred and seventy strikes, and the strikes have been successful except in, perhaps, twenty instances, where they may have been lost or compromised. The truck system of which I spoke exists no longer in our trade. We have adopted a course of action which our experience has taught us, and that is, in certain periods of the year, when it is generally dull, not to strike for an advance of wages. Formerly, before the organization, men would probably strike for an advance of wages in the dull season, and be content that they were not reduced in the busy season. Our experience has taught us to adopt a different mode of action.

Q. You strike now when business is active?—*A.* Yes, sir; and then, when we obtain an increase of wages when times are fair, our object is to endeavor to obtain fair wages during the dull season also, and, while we have made provision not to strike for an increase of wages during those periods, we are always in a position to strike against a reduction of wages or the introduction of the truck system, or other obnoxious rules. We have found that, for the purpose of accomplishing this object, it is entirely valueless to organize a union during a strike, and that it is little better than valueless to organize just immediately before a strike. We have found that if we are desirous of gaining anything in a strike, we must prepare in peace for the turbulent time which may come. And the Cigarmakers International Union, of which I now speak especially, is an organization that has in its treasury between $130,000 and $150,000 ready to be concentrated within five days at any time at any given point. I hold in my hand a copy of the constitution of that organization. Of course I am not desirous of making a propaganda for it, but to illustrate what I have been saying I will read from it this provision: "Any union being directed by the executive board to forward money to another local union, and failing to comply within five days from date of said notice, shall be suspended." That is, in the event of a strike at a given point, the international president of the organization is directed to direct or request the nearest union to immediately send on its whole treasury if that is necessary, and the unions throughout the entire country and Canada to forward their entire treasury if necessary to be placed at the disposal of the organization that is in trouble. . . .

WHY SOME STRIKES FAIL

[Asked why a recent strike of telegraphers had failed, MR. GOMPERS replied:]

. . . *A.* My opinion is that the first few strikes that workingmen generally indulge in are lost, from the fact that their employers are unable to comprehend the idea that labor has certain rights which they ought to respect; second, because they are really unaware that the laborers who are on a strike are capable of inflicting an injury upon them; and third, that when they are once in a strike and hold out for a considerable period they do not like to weaken and accede to the terms of their employés, but prefer to make large sacrifices from their wealth or capital rather than to accede to those demands. . . .

ADVANTAGES OF TRADES UNIONS

Even in such instances, however, the organizations of labor are the conservators of the public peace; for when strikes occur among men who are unorganized, often acting upon illy-considered plans, hastily adopted, acting upon passion, and sometimes not knowing what they have gone on strike for, except possibly some fancied grievance, and hardly knowing by what means they can or may remedy their grievances, each acts upon his own account without the restraint of organization, and feels that he serves the cause of the strike best when he does something that just occurs to him; while the man who belongs to a trades union that is of some years' standing is, by the very fact of his membership of the organization and his experience there, taught to abide by the decision of the majority. Therefore, when anything of that kind I have mentioned occurs or is heard of in the organizations that are of long standing, it is condemned in the most strenuous terms and action is taken to prevent the accomplishment of any such purpose, or if it is accomplished to prevent the recurrence of it. The members of our organization are made to well understand that such a mode of warfare in strikes is not tolerated in any well-regulated or well-organized trades union. So high an authority as the Duke of Argyle, in his work, *The Reign of Law*, states that "combinations of workingmen for the protection of their labor are recommended alike by reason and experience." When we strike as organized workingmen, we generally win, and that is the reason of the trouble that our employers go to when they try to show that strikes are failures, but you will notice that they generally or always point to unorganized workers. That is one reason also why when the employers know that the workingmen are organized and have got a good treasury strikes are very frequently avoided. There are fewer strikes among organized workingmen, but when they do strike they are able to hold out much longer than the others, and they generally win. The trades unions are not what too many men have been led to believe they are, importations from Europe, if they are imported, then, as has been said, they were landed at Plymouth Rock from the Mayflower. Modern industry evolves these organizations out of the existing conditions where there are two classes in society, one incessantly striving to obtain the labor of the other class for as little as possible, and to obtain the largest amount or number of hours of labor; and the members of the other class being, as individuals, utterly helpless in a contest with their employers, naturally resort to combinations to improve their condition, and, in fact, they are forced by the conditions which surround them to organize for self-protection. Hence trades unions. Trades unions are not barbarous, nor are they the outgrowth of barbarism. On the contrary they are only possible

where civilization exists. Trades unions cannot exist in China; they cannot exist in Russia; and in all those semi-barbarous countries they can hardly exist, if indeed they can exist at all. But they have been formed successfully in this country, in Germany, in England, and they are gradually gaining strength in France. In Great Britain they are very strong; they have been forming there for fifty years, and they are still forming, and I think there is a great future for them yet in America. Wherever trades unions have organized and are most firmly organized, there are [sic] the right of the people most respected. A people may be educated, but to me it appears that the greatest amount of intelligence exists in that country or that State where the people are best able to defend their rights, and their liberties as against those who are desirous of undermining them. Trades unions are organizations that instill into men a higher motive-power and give them a higher goal to look to. The hope that is too frequently deadened in their breasts when unorganized is awakened by the trades unions as it can be by nothing else. A man is sometimes reached by influences such as the church may hold out to him, but the conditions that will make him a better citizen and a more independent one are those that are evolved out of the trades union movement. That makes him a better citizen and a better man in every particular. There are only a few who can be reached by the church so as to affect their daily walk in life compared with the numbers reached by these organizations.

TRADES UNIONS NOT COMMUNISTIC

By the CHAIRMAN:
Q. The outside public, I think, very largely confound the conditions out of which the trades union grows or is formed, with the, to the general public mind, somewhat revolutionary ideas that are embraced under the names of socialism and communism. Before you get through, won't you let us understand to what extent

the trades union is an outgrowth or an evolution of those ideas, and to what extent it stands apart from them and is based on different principles?—*A*. The trades unions are by no means an outgrowth of socialistic or communistic ideas or principles, but the socialistic and communistic notions are evolved from some of the trades unions' movements. As to the question of the principles of communism or socialism prevailing in trades unions, there are a number of men who connect themselves as workingmen with the trades union who may have socialistic convictions, yet who never gave them currency; who say, "Whatever ideas we may have as to the future state of society, regardless of what the end of the labor movement as a movement between classes may be, they must remain in the background, and we must subordinate our convictions, and our views and our acts to the general good that the trades union movement brings to the laborer." A large number of them think and act in that way. On the other hand, there are men—not so numerous now as they have been in the past—who are endeavoring to conquer the trades union movement and subordinate it to those doctrines, and in a measure, in a few such organizations that condition of things exists, but by no means does it exist in the largest, most powerful, and best organized trades unions. There the view of which I spoke just now, the desire to improve the condition of the workingmen by and through the efforts of the trades union, is fully lived up to. I do not know whether I have covered the entire ground of the question.

By Mr. GEORGE:

Q. You state, then, that the trades unions generally are not propagandists of socialistic views?—*A*. They are not. On the contrary, the endeavors of which I have spoken, made by certain persons to conquer the trades unions in certain cases, are resisted by the trades unionists; in the first place for the trades unions' sake, and even persons who have these convictions

perhaps equally as strong as the others will yet subordinate them entirely to the good to be received directly through the trades unions. These last help those who have not such convictions to resist those who seek to use the trades unions to propagate their socialistic ideas.

Q. Do you think the trades unions have impeded or advanced the spread of socialistic views?—*A*. I believe that the existence of the trades-union movement, more especially where the unionists are better organized, has evoked a spirit and a demand for reform, but has held in check the more radical elements in society. . . .

Q. Well, I did ask you a question, whether, from your standpoint, socialism was gaining control of the trades unions and becoming their actuating spirit?—*A*. I think not. Some few years ago, when the trades-union movement was down, or rather when, from the effects of the panic, the workingmen had not organized upon the present plan—had not adopted the benevolent and beneficial features, and consequently had become dispersed to a great extent—in that condition of things this element thought now was the time for them to capture the trades-union movement, and they did capture the unions in a few instances.

Q. But the general drift of the movement is conservative, merely remedial or protective to the laborer, and recognizes the existing order of society?—*A*. As I said, Mr. Chairman, the views of some individuals must not be confounded with those of whole organizations. Some of the men, of course, may not have high aspirations as to the future state of society, but, as I said, a large number of our able men, good men I believe, have convictions that the state of society under which we live, the competitive system, is not one that ought to last as the highest system of civilization that we can arrive at; yet they subordinate their theories or convictions to the general good, and many of them are regarded as very conservative, and so act.

COMPETITION TO BE DISPLACED BY COÖPERATION

Q. What would they call that condition of society, or condition of industrial trade, which they anticipate as the legitimate or desirable successor of the competitive system? What would be the term or phrase they would apply to it?—*A.* A social state.

Q. Well, "competitive" relates to the method of production. What change do they propose in that respect?—*A.* They propose a universal coöperative system to supplant and be a substitute for the competitive system.

By Mr. GEORGE:

Q. What is the feeling on the part of the laborers of the country towards their employers; is it one of confidence, unity, and goodwill, or one of distrust, suspicion, and enmity? Explain, as well as you understand it, what the feelings and sentiments of the wage-receivers are towards the wage-payers.—*A.* I think I have answered that question in my previous testimony. I have quoted a statement made by a Massachusetts manufacturer, a member of the legislature, when he said in substance, "I regard my employés the same as I would an old machine, which, when it becomes rusty, I thrust into the street."

Q. That was an expression of the feeling of the employers toward the employed. Now, I ask you about the feelings of the employed towards the employer.—*A.* Well, I think I said then, in substance, that the employed, the workingmen, believe that that is about the view generally entertained by employers as to their help, and they resent it by about the same feeling—not quite the same, but they resent it and feel it strongly.

Q. Is the present tendency of affairs to increase or intensify that feeling, or to remove it?—*A.* To intensify it. The views are gaining upon every side that the classes in society are becoming decidedly more distinct, and, as the lines are drawn, so does this feeling become intensified; in fact, I believe I can best describe that by reading from the preamble adopted by the Confederation of the Labor Unions of the United States and Canada at Pittsburg, Pa. (of which I am at present chairman), in November, 1881:

Whereas a struggle is going on in the nations of the civilized world between the oppressors and the oppressed of all countries, a struggle between capital and labor, which must grow in intensity year by year, and work disastrous results to the toiling millions of all nations, if not combined for mutual protection and benefit, for the history of the wage-workers of all countries is but the history of constant struggle and misery engendered by ignorance and disunion; and, whereas the history of the non-producers of all ages proves that a minority thoroughly organized may work wonders for good or evil, and so on.

That extract, I believe, sets forth in as few words as possible the feeling that prevails among the working classes, that there is an ever-recurring conflict between the two classes, and that the employers are ever on the watch to see whether they cannot take advantage of their employés, the same as the stock speculator looks at the ticking of the indicator to see whether he cannot take advantage of those with whom he is dealing; except that in this instance the fellow stock-broker is generally as alert to take advantage as the first, and is at the other end looking at the wire with the same object, while the workingman is not so vigilant in looking out for himself.

Q. Explain fully, if you can, the nature and extent of the social intercourse between the wage-receivers and the wage-payers.—*A.* Where the wage-payers are small manufacturers, employing one or two hands, a spirit of cordiality and friendship may exist; but as the employer engages a larger number of hands, just in proportion does he become removed from the social status of his employé. His own status is raised, and the intercourse which may have formerly existed is cut off. The ties of friendship gradually become lessened, and there is no cordiality existing between the two after that. The working-man works as well as he possibly can to retain his employment, and when he looks after the interests of his employer it is because he wishes to retain his employment, and not because he loves him.

By the CHAIRMAN:

Q. I would like to draw out your idea a little more definitely as to the exact thing that is to be accomplished before you undertake to state your remedies. All concede, I suppose, that whatever is to go to the capitalist or to the laborer must be derived from the sale of the article produced. That is so, is it not?—A. Decidedly.

Q. Now, is it or is it not your claim that, before any portion of what is produced goes to the capitalist, a full and fair remuneration to the laborer should be deducted, upon the ground that his reasonable and just claim is primary to all others. That is the main point, is it not?—A. Yes, sir.

Q. That is the first thing to be secured—that the laborer's remuneration shall take precedence, in the order of time, of any compensation to the capitalist?—A. Yes, sir.

Q. And the next thing you wish to secure is that the amount of his compensation shall be just and reasonable?—A. Yes, sir.

Q. Those are two objects that are to be attained?—A. Yes, sir. And further, the treatment of the men in the factories—not as slaves, but as men. The machinery is guarded against rust, and, when passing, if one of the arms or wheels or belts is rather lower than the other, the employer will take off his hat and pass beneath it. We do not ask the employer to take off his hat to his employés, but we do say that "good morning" will not hurt him, more especially when he is spoken to.

ARBITRATION

Q. Proceed with the statement of the remedies.—A. I would like to say a few words first with reference to arbitration. I am in favor of arbitration when that can be accomplished; but, as Mr. McGuire said here yesterday, arbitration is only possible when the workingmen have, by the power of their organization, demonstrated to the employers that they are the employers' equal. Arbitration may then be successful. But there are certain conditions in arbitration to which I wish to call attention, because, though there may appear to be a fair arbitration, yet the conditions may make it unfair to the laborer. For instance, the employer bids in the market for a contract for the production of goods. He bids lower than any other manufacturer and obtains the contract; not necessarily for the public service, but for the production of something for private consumption or use in the regular channels of commerce; for instance, the production of certain articles of clothing. Or he bids in the market, whether by contract or otherwise, and accepts an order for the production of a hundred thousand suits of clothes at a certain price, or a hundred thousand tons of pig iron at a certain price. He has calculated, "My machinery will cost so much; so much for my plant; so much for my raw material, and so much for my labor. This price will leave me a margin." He knows that he cannot get his plant cheaper; he knows he cannot get his raw material cheaper. What will he do in such a case? He will say: "There is no margin for me there, and how can I sell unless I sell somewhat cheaper than these other men, I being new in the market." So, instead of paying his laborers as much wages as they may have received in other factories, or as he may have paid them before, he says: "In consequence of my having taken this contract at this low figure, my employés will have to submit to a reduction." Now, if the employés have demonstrated their equality in power with the employer, this matter is arbitrated upon, and, if it is really a question between the employés of this man and this individual man, arbitration, even though it be a fair arbitration as between these two particular parties, will really be unfair to the workingman. The arbitrators, looking only at the particular case, will probably allow the reduction of wages; yet that will be really unfair, because if the workingmen in that case submit to the decision it will mean a general reduction of wages throughout that entire industry. Now, I hold that under such circumstances arbitration, to accomplish its true purpose, should require that this manufacturer, if he is desirous of procuring contracts or the production of goods at a lower rate than other manufacturers would produce them for, and desires to draw his profit out of the laborer, that such a man, out of regard to both the honest manufacturer and the laborer, ought to be crushed out of business. I merely wished to add that consideration to what Mr. McGuire has already stated in reference to arbitration.

By Mr. GEORGE:

Q. Suppose he was crushed out of business, what would become of his employés?—A. They would find work from another employer who would get the same order, and the business would not be undermined by this new fledgling.

By the CHAIRMAN:

Q. The trades unions, then, will have a tendency to eliminate the men from the class of employers who are not fitted to be employers either by natural qualifications or by the possession of capital or credit?—A. Yes; provided such men are desirous of having their work done cheaper than others.

Q. You do not get the point of my question. I say that the natural tendency of these trades organizations, as you understand it, is to eliminate from the class of employers those who, by lack of capacity or of credit, are really unfit to act as employers and who, if they become employers, naturally are a burden to the market?—A. Yes, sir. . . .

Q. Which do you think does the most harm in society, the man who is unfit to set up in business and who consequently

fails and produces panic and bankruptcy, or the individual laborer or professional man who undertakes to act in any given capacity without a proper preparation?— A. I think if you were to eliminate from the class of employers the incompetent men, you would not even then prevent the panics which periodically come. I think that panics come, not through those men's idiocy or incompetency, but are attributable to causes not generally understood.

REMEDIES

The remedies that I suggest, and which I think the Government can and ought to adopt, are the following:

1. Strict enforcement of the national eight-hour law. The workingmen of this country, in all their organizations where they have come together, either in private or in public, either as local, State, National, or confederated unions, have set forth that demand for the enforcement of the national eight-hour law.

2. The passage of a law by Congress giving the trades and labor unions the right to become chartered under the general laws of our Government. The laws written and now in operation to protect the property of the capitalist and the moneyed class generally are almost innumerable, yet nothing has been done to protect the property of the workingmen, the only property that they possess, their working power, their savings bank, their school, and trades union; and we ask that our existence as organizations may be legalized. . . .

3. We ask also, for the purpose of procuring information for the legislators of our country (who frequently find a very good excuse for non-action by saying that they are ignorant as to the true condition of the working people), the establishment of a national bureau of labor statistics. Such a bureau would give our legislators an opportunity to know, not from mere conjecture, but actually, the condition of our industries, our production and consumption, and what could be done by law

to improve both. Our State governments would undoubtedly follow the lead of the national Congress, and legislate in the interest of labor; but we see that so long as our national legislators have an excuse for saying that they do not know the condition of labor, there is very little chance of obtaining legislation. . . .

There are several other measures to which I might call attention and which I might suggest as remedies, but the best organized trades unions of the world are eminently practical. They are composed of men who are desirous of obtaining reforms by gradual means, and in that spirit we ask the adoption of these measures which I have set forth here, because we believe and know that they will redound to our benefit as workingmen and to the benefit of society. If the legislators of this country are desirous of acting in this matter and alleviating the distress that is too prevalent, and if they desire to assist those who are working in this cause to mount a step higher, let them adopt these measures and they will receive the thanks of the working people of the world and of all posterity. But in any event, they ought not to continue to be so indifferent to the condition of labor as they have been in the past.

Adjourned.

B. TESTIMONY OF A FACTORY MANAGER

Manchester, N.H., October 12, 1883

The committee met at 10 A.M.

Thomas L. Livermore examined. . . .

Mr. Pugh: I understand that you have been a lawyer in your time, and I wish you would now proceed, if you please, to give the committee such facts and information and such opinions as you consider pertinent to the subject of investigation as defined by that resolution, and without waiting for any special question. . . .

The Witness: I live in Manchester, N.H., and am agent in this place for the Amoskeag Manufacturing Company. I have the management of the affairs of the corporation here. I have had the management as agent for four and a half years. Before that time I practiced law in Boston for over ten years, and before that for a short time in New Hampshire. Before that time I was in the volunteer service of the United States for four years during the war of the rebellion. While practicing law I was much concerned in the trial of patent causes, and in that way became familiar with mechanical and industrial questions.

THE AMOSKEAG MANUFACTURING COMPANY
—ITS MILLS AND THEIR CAPACITY

The Amoskeag Manufacturing Company has on its pay-rolls usually from 5,500 to 6,000 people, and in the management of these people I think I have become familiar with the questions embraced in the resolution which has been shown me, so far as those questions have been developed in this place.

By Mr. Pugh:

Q. What is the capacity of the mills to manufacture, and what do they manufacture?—A. The mills under my charge use about 40,000 bales of cotton a year, and produce between 55,000,000 and 60,000,000 yards of cloth, at a cost of between $5,000,000 and $6,000,000 per annum.

Q. You mean that is the cost of the production of the cloth?—A. That is the cost of the cloth.

I should add that, in addition to manufacturing cloth, I carry on for the company the management of the water-works which run the mills in this place, and also the construction of buildings and structures relating to manufacturing establishments, and in that capacity have employed and dealt with many hundreds of laboring people.

Q. That is, outside of the number of operatives?—A. That was included in the 5,500 to 6,000. It is a varying number on that account.

The cloth manufactured by our company is mainly cloth manufactured out of yarn that has been dyed. We dye this yarn. The articles are ticks, denims, cheviots, awnings, and ginghams. Besides this we make canton flannels which are not dyed.

The cost of the labor is about 30 per cent of the total cost of the goods. That labor amounts to about $1,500,000 a year.

The amount of capital employed, and of plant in the mills, and for quick capital, is about equal to the cost of the yearly products. It takes about as much money for quick capital as it does for establishing the plant and running the mills—after our fashion of running them. As I understand it, those mills which do not have quick capital have to borrow it and pay interest upon it, in order that they may be successful.

COTTON-MILL WAGES

I have here a memorandum of the wages which we have paid, taken from the rolls of two of our large mills (embracing, the one the coarsest and the other the finest work that we make) in the month of July last, which was a fair month to make an estimate from, and is the latest month in which we have run full time, inasmuch as low water has interfered with our operations since then. Our average wages—the average wages of all employed in the mills—for the different departments are as follows: For carding, males, $1.29; females, 95 cents. For spinning, males, $1.61; females, 95 cents. For mule spinning, $1.09. For dressing, $1.28.

The average for the mule spinning and dressing is for both males and females together, as I have not been able readily to separate them. The same is the case with those that I am now about to give: For weaving, $1.34; in the cloth-room, $1.25; dye-house, $1.42; carpenters and mechanics, $1.73. This last item is of people not employed in the mills, but outside the mills, in repairs of the mills.

The average which I have given includes the wages of children as well as adults; as, for instance, some mule spinners get $1.65, and upwards per day, but the wages of the boys in the room bring down the average. So in dressing, the wages of some of the men are $1.50 per day, but the wages of the boys and women bring down the average; and so of the carpenters and mechanics. Some of them get $3 a day, but apprentices and beginners get less, and that brings down the average.

WAGES OF WOMEN AND CHILDREN

By the CHAIRMAN:
Q. What rate of prices do the women, children, and apprentices receive? It varies, no doubt, very much.—A. It varies very much. There is a wide scale, but in some of these departments women earn as much as $1.25 and $1.35 a day, and the children run all the way from 40 cents a day upwards, depending upon their age and capacity. Some of the men weavers earn as high as $1.67 a day.

COST OF NEW HAMPSHIRE LIVING OF MILL OPERATIVES

As to the cost of living, I would say that we have a pretty accurate gauge of that in our boarding-houses. The company maintains a number of substantial brick buildings which it lets to boarding-house keepers at a very low rent, upon the condition that they shall charge to women in the employ of the company fixed rates for board and lodging, which are agreed to by the company. At the present time, this rate for women is $2.25 a week for board and lodging; so that, for instance, the women in the carding and spinning departments who average 95 cents a day will earn $5.70 per week, and they are boarded and lodged for $2.25 per week, which leaves to them $3.45 a week, out of which they must pay for their clothing, which is not necessarily expensive, and the rest they can save if there are no extra calls upon them. Besides these boarding-houses, the company maintains seven hundred tenements of a substantial character for families, which it lets to its employés for about $1 a month per room. Many of these tenements have from four to six rooms, so that the rent of the families occupying them is from $48 to $72 per annum. All these boarding-houses and tenements are kept in repair and policed for sanitary purposes by the company.

By Mr. Pugh:

Q. What is about the average cost of these houses?—A. About $1,500 a tenement.

Q. That rent of them is less than 5 per cent on the price?—A. The net rent to the company, deducting repairs and taxes, is about 3 per cent.

Q. State what is the location and what are the sanitary conditions of the houses as to ventilation, cleanliness, etc.—A. These houses are situated upon good land, which is well drained. They are supplied with water from the city water works, and I think they will compare favorably with private dwellings in point of ventilation, warmth, and health generally. Of course, the cleanliness of the interior depends upon the family occupying the houses for the time being, but we endeavor to exercise an influence which will promote cleanliness on the part of the families.

The Amoskeag Company is peculiarly situated in having a large body of land in this city which is not occupied by dwellings, and which it allows its employés to cultivate for the nominal rent of $1 per annum, where they find it convenient to cultivate garden patches.

A hospital is maintained by a charitable association of ladies in the city in a building which is furnished by the company free of rent. This hospital is open to all persons who need its shelter, but the company (and I think the other corporations in the city) have contributed to its support for the purpose of securing its shelter for such of their employés as need it.

Q. What is the general health of your employés?—A. I think that the general health may be said to be good. It is the desire of the mill-managers in this part of the country, generally, I believe, to light, heat, ventilate, and care for their mills generally so as to make them as healthy and

agreeable as circumstances will allow; for other considerations not taken into account, the best mill in this respect would produce the best and the most cloth. Bad ventilation and discomfort generally has, I think, a palpable effect upon the quantity and character of product of the mill. The operative working in a well-lighted, well heated, and well ventilated mill would retain his strength and spirits to the end of the day, when one working in a mill which was not well lighted and heated and ventilated, would flag toward the end of the day, and not be at his best as a laborer.

HOURS OF MILL LABOR IN NEW HAMPSHIRE

The hours of labor in the mills here, for those who work the longest are from 6:30 A.M. to 12 and from 1 to 6:45 P.M., and on Saturday until 4 P.M.; making an average of about ten and three-quarters hours per day for each of the six working days of the week. But large numbers of the employés in the mill are enabled to finish their work sooner than the rest, and *they* average ten hours and some of them less per day.

OLD-TIME HOURS OF MILL LABOR

I am informed, and have no doubt from my investigation that it is true that forty years ago the hours of labor averaged fourteen and a half per day in the mills; that they were gradually reduced by the voluntary act of the mill managers until they reached the limit which I have given as that of to-day. I suppose this reduction was made possible, and was in a large degree due to the improvements in machinery and methods of manufacture which enabled the mills to keep up their product as time went on with reduced hours of labor.

NATIONALITY OF MILL OPERATIVES

The people employed in the mills here are of various nationalities. In the Amoskeag mills I think that nearly one-third are Canadians, perhaps one-fourth are of Irish birth or parentage, perhaps one-fifth are Yankees, and the remainder Germans, Scotch, and English. There is a considerable German element here.

Q. What seems to be the fact as to the increase or diminution of the number of Americans who go into these manufacturing industries?—*A.* Relatively to the people of other nationalities, the Americans decrease, but absolutely there are, I think, more Americans at work today in the mills of Manchester than there were thirty years ago. . . .

Q. As a rule, how long have these employés been in the service of the company you represent?—*A.* The terms have been very various. Perhaps the best illustration of the amount and frequency of changes is to be found in the fact that each month we have about 10 per cent of our people leave. . . .

POWERS OF MILL OVERSEERS

It is the system in the mills here, as I suppose it is generally in New England and elsewhere, to employ overseers—men who are skilled in the particular departments—carding, spinning, weaving, etc., to take charge, each of a given room or set of rooms, and to give to each of these overseers the privilege of hiring the people who are to work under him, and of discharging them for cause. . . .

NO LABOR UNIONS IN MANCHESTER, N.H.

Q. Have you any labor unions here? What is the fact as to the number of your employés who belong to labor unions?—*A.* I do not think that there is a labor union in this city, and I do not think that there has ever been one here which lasted. There have been several attempts to form unions since I have been here by agitators from the outside, mainly from Fall River, I think, and from one cause or another they have always failed.

STRIKES

Upon inquiry and investigation I have been led to believe that there has never been more than one general strike in this place, and that occurred about thirty years ago. I think that was a strike due to a change in the hours of labor, which was instituted by the mills, and I believe that the strike failed. Since that time there have been small strikes of detached portions of employés, but I never heard of one resulting in success. Some three or four years ago I had a strike of about one hundred of my dyers for higher wages. I thought that the strike was unreasonable and refused to accede to the demands of the strikers, and the result was that after staying away from their work about a week a large part of them—one half or more—came and asked me to take them back in the employ of the company. At that time I took pains to personally interrogate all of the men who came to me, to inquire why they had taken that means of trying to get higher wages, and I must say that with one or two exceptions they seemed to have been actuated rather by the fear of being odd and the fear of the censure of their fellow workmen than by any discontent of their situation. . . .

POWER OF ENDURANCE OF MILL OPERATIVES

By the CHAIRMAN:

Q. What is your observation as to the length of time or the hours of labor that the operative is capable of enduring without physical or other injury?—*A.* My belief is that he can work ten and three-quarter hours on an average without injury, and I may say that in a limited degree I had some experience myself as a youth, for I worked at a mechanical employment for a while; but of course my judgment must be formed mainly from my observation here. If one goes upon the main street here in the evening—Elm street—he will see the sidewalks crowded as densely as Broadway, New York, by the mill operatives who have finished their work and got their suppers and come out to promenade and see the shops and each other, and they seem to be merry and happy and laughing. I do not think that it is an exaggeration to say that you may often see on the sidewalks here in the evening thousands who have come out under those circumstances. Now, if it were the fact that they were prostrated and tired out by the hours of labor, they would not be out I think as a rule.

Q. There is another point often discussed in connection with that. It is claimed by many people that the same operatives will accomplish as much work in ten hours as they will in eleven or a longer period. What is your opinion on that point, and what your knowledge from your own observation and your intercourse with other men who have had experience in the employment of labor?—A. I do not believe that that is the fact. . . .

THE WORK IS DONE BY THE MACHINERY

Much of the work that is done by the day in the mills is such work as tending cards and the carding machinery, such as fly-frames, draw-frames, spinning-frames, etc., by women and girls. That is not labor requiring strenuous muscular exertion. They are sitting down much of the time, when a mill is running as we like to have it done. This labor requires attention. They must go to one frame or another and tie a piece of thread that is broken, or take off or put on a bobbin, or put on a spool with "roving," and that is labor which does not require muscular exertion to any considerable extent, but requires attention. That machine never tires. It does as much in the eleventh hour as it does in the first hour. It is the machine that does the work; it is the operative who keeps her eye upon it and keeps it fed with material and keeps it cleared out of the manufactured article.

By Mr. Pugh:

Q. How many mules can they run?—A. I am now speaking of spinning-frames, which girls tend. Women do not tend mules; that is the work of men. A pair of mules is a varying factor, because it may have more or may have less spindles. Some may have 1,800 spindles, for instance, sometimes.

As I was saying, it is the machine that does the labor; it is the woman or girl who gives it attention, and I really do not think she can give any closer attention in the first hour than in the eleventh hour, provided she is a healthy person, fit to work in a mill.

Q. How generally does that illustration apply to the whole labor in a mill?—A. That applies generally to perhaps a half of the operatives in the mills. There is another kind of work which requires more muscular exertion, which is done mainly by men, such as work in the dresser-rooms and in the dye-houses, where they have to do heavy lifting and hard work, and they have shorter hours of labor. Some of them work less than ten hours.

Q. How is that arranged? Do they work by the piece?—A. Part of them by the piece and part not. The fact of the matter is it regulates itself. Where we find labor too hard for more than ten hours, we stop it, and the machinery is so balanced that the slashers on which, for instance, they work ten hours, take care of the yarn that is spun in ten and three-quarters hours by the rest of the machinery. Then, there is the weaving, which is done by the piece, and it is a fact to which I think every mill manager whom you will encounter, will testify that the weavers are anxious to begin work at the earliest moment and to quit at the latest moment, and that it would not be difficult to find many of them who would be glad if we would keep the mills open longer, because the longer the mills are open the longer the looms work and the more money they make.

By Mr. Pugh:

Q. They work by the piece?—A. Yes; so many yards constitute a "cut," and they get so much more pay.

OPERATION OF LAWS LIMITING HOURS OF LABOR

By the Chairman:

Q. Suppose a system were introduced of paying, substantially, by the hour or by the piece, and it prevailed all through your entire system of work, and then the proposition was made to the operatives to absolutely limit the hours of labor to ten, nine, or eight hours. Do you think that the operatives themselves would approve of that proposition, or would they prefer to work longer and get more pay?—*A*. I do not think they would approve of it.

Q. If it were submitted to them, you think they would decide adversely?—*A*. Of course, if the operatives were persuaded that by the reduction of the hours of labor, the manufacturers would be compelled to pay more per cut, so that they could earn as much in the nine hours as they could in the eleven hours, I suppose they would willingly agree to it, but taking things as they are, with economic laws governing the prices to be paid, I do not think you would find one in a hundred who would agree to the reduction of hours under the circumstances which you suppose.

Q. Then in order to enact a ten, or say, an eight hour law—it would be a matter of indifference as to the number of hours in excess of ten—to be really enforced the compulsion would have to extend to the operatives as well as the manufacturer, would not that be so?—*A*. I see no other way.

Q. No one should be allowed by law to work more than that number of hours?—*A*. Yes. If you were to make a thing optional with the operatives, and part of the work were piece-work and part were day-work, I do not see myself how the law could result in any good, because it would either result that all operatives would agree that they wished to work eleven hours, supposing that be the number that was deemed advisable, or else part would want to work eleven and part eight or nine; and the manufacturer could not afford to supply the increased quantity of machinery to those who wished to work eight hours to keep up with those who wished to work eleven, I should think. That is something, however, that I have

never figured out, but I should suppose that that would be so.

PROBABLE EFFECT OF EIGHT-HOUR LAW WITH TWO SETS OF HANDS PER DAY

Q. How would it operate upon the interests of the manufacturer, and how upon the working people, in your judgment, if hours could be reduced so that the machinery could be employed, say, for illustration, sixteen hours a day, and two sets of hands employed, each working eight, would such a system as that be practicable, and, if so, what would be the effect upon the wages of each individual operative do you think?—*A*. I do not know whether it would be practicable. I can see objections to it, but whether they would be insuperable I am really unable now to say. The three chief objections to it which I see now are these: With two sets of hands running the same set of machinery it would be very difficult to place the responsibility for the care of the machinery upon either; that is a very important factor in maintaining a mill. Then it would be very difficult to find time to repair that machinery, and it would all have to be done in the night-time. You would have to keep a set of workmen in the night-time, which would be more expensive and troublesome. Then the risk of fire would be increased very largely by reason of the lighting of the mills at night. At the present time the insurers object to running the mills beyond 10 o'clock at night, for instance.

Q. The danger of fire increases later in the night-time, does it?—*A*. Yes, on account of the gas, and the difficulty of seeing around under the machinery for hot bearings, and all that sort of thing, which induces fire. Whether those expenses would be so great as to make it too expensive to manufacture, could only be told, I suppose, by trial.

Q. There would be this about it, that the machinery, which is perhaps the cheapest production in the mills, would work twice as long.—*A*. Not twice as long, but it would work sixteen hours a day. It would be twice as long if you worked twenty-two hours a day. Then there is this further consideration to be taken into account—whether machinery would in the course of a year do twice as much work by working twice as long. Some mechanics think that machinery needs rest; and the item of repairs of machinery is a very great item in the cost of running a mill. We read of people who make very large profits in running their mills for a year or two or three or four or five years, we will say, and then suddenly for some reason which is not obvious to the public, the mills become bankrupt, when the real reason is that they are worn out. It is not safe to calculate that you can run a mill without spending on an average of 10 per cent per annum of the value of the machinery on repairs and renewals of machinery, and that is a subject which requires very careful attention in running a mill. I know a mill which ran night and day—a cotton mill—it is the only one I think, that I ever saw do it. That is the mill at Atlanta, Ga., and they thought it succeeded, but I believe the mill was not a financial success. I think it failed. Whether the failure was due to that I do not express any opinion. . . .

Q. Do you think it would be possible to get the necessary number of laborers to supply the working interests of the country where machinery was employed largely, if more than one relay of hands was used?—A. That I do not know. . . .

THE CHAIRMAN: I asked the question because the suggestion has been made by many labor reformers, as they are termed, that even six hours, considering the increased productive power of machinery or of the human being and machinery combined, would be as long as laboring people ought to be expected to work—as long as the interests of society require that they should, and inasmuch as there are many unemployed people, a reduction of the hours of labor would give something to others to do. The question whether it could be made to work practically is the serious thing.

THE WITNESS: I do not believe at all in such theories. I think that at least in a free country like this, with thousands of miles of land to be taken up in a vast area of country which is inhabited by people occupied in industrial pursuits, and the great variety of employments to be found in this country, it is perfectly safe for at least the life-time of this generation to leave the question of how a man shall work, and how long he shall work, and where he shall work, and what wages he shall get, to himself. It is as certain that wages in a country situated as ours is, will adjust themselves to the level required by the demand and the market, as it is that water will seek its level. I do not believe that any one has ever yet seen in this country a time when distress on the part of the laboring people was universal. It has occurred in certain industries and in certain places without any question, but, every time, the tremendous field which is afforded to the laboring man in which to find employment has come to his relief, and with a little foresight, a little forehandedness, and a little energy, he has been able to find some employment in which he could earn his living and a little more.

By MR. PUGH:

Q. The complaining demand often comes for a particular kind of work in a particular place at higher wages?—A. Yes.

Q. They want to stay in the cities and do the work that they are accustomed to?—A. That is true.

Q. There is a great opposition to change; they cannot get rid of the charm of city life, although it be in tenement houses and frequently without pure air or food?—A. That is true.

CHILD LABOR IN COTTON MILLS

By the CHAIRMAN:

Q. Won't you please tell us your experience with the question of child labor; how it is, and to what extent it exists here; why it exists, and whether, as it is actually existing here, it is a hardship on a child or on a parent; or whether there is any evil in that direction that should be remedied?— *A.* There is a certain class of labor in the mills which, to put it in very common phrase, consists mainly in running about the floor—where there is not as much muscular exercise required as a child would put forth in play, and a child can do it about as well as a grown person can do it—not quite as much of it, but somewhere near it, and with proper supervision of older people, the child serves the purpose. That has led to the employment of children in the mills, I think. . . .

. . . Now, a good many heads of families, without any question in my mind, were not sufficiently considerate of the mental and physical welfare of their children, and they put them to work in the mills perhaps too early and certainly kept them there too much of the time in former years, and the legislature had to step in and protect the children against the parents by requiring that they should go to school a certain number of months or weeks in a year, or else they should not be allowed to work in the mills; and at the present time there is a very severe law in this State applicable to children—I think some under twelve and some under sixteen. I do not remember the terms of it, but the child has to have a certificate of the authorities in control of the schools that he has been to school the time required by the statute before the mill manager is able to employ him. I think the mill manager is subject to a very considerable penalty for non-compliance with that law. In this city in our mills, and as far as I know in the rest of the mills, we have been very particular to observe the statute. I do not know how it is outside of the city. I suppose that it may depend a good deal upon public sentiment. If public sentiment supports the law, it will be enforced; if it does not, it will not be. I think public sentiment does support it here to an extent, although I think it extends a little too far in prevent-ing children up to sixteen working in mills more than a given time. . . .

DANGER OF OVER-EDUCATION OF CHILDREN OF LABORERS

Now, I think that when it is provided that a child shall go to school as long as it is profitable for a workman's child (who has got to be a workingman himself) to go to school, the limit has been reached at which labor in the mills should be forbidden. There is such a thing as too much education for working people sometimes. I do not mean to say by that that I discourage education to any person on earth, or that I think that with good sense any amount of education can hurt any one, but I have seen cases where young people were spoiled for labor by being educated to a little too much refinement.

Q. You have known something of farm life, and the necessity that a boy is put under of learning to farm while he is still a boy?—*A.* Yes.

Q. Now, with reference to the acquirement of the necessary skill to earn a living, without which an education would amount to little—a man having enough knowledge to starve upon has not much advantage—do you think that the child should be withheld from the educating idea in the industrial line to so large an extent as the law now requires?—*A.* I do not.

Q. Is there danger of too much abstention from that sort of practical education which enables a child when grown to earn his living?—*A.* I think so. I will state that in our machine shops we take apprentices to learn the trade of a machinist, which is one of the best trades that any man in this country can have. We agree that if they will agree to serve three years for pay which enables them to live, we will teach them the trade of a machinist; and it is a curious illustration of the effect of very advanced common schools that our foremen prefer for apprentices boys from the country, who have worked on farms and been to a district school a little while, to boys that have been educated in the city. They say that the city boys do not stick to their work as the others do. They are a little above the employment.

Q. Is this employment that you speak about in the mills, in which children are engaged, of a character to tax their muscular or physical frame more than it ought to during their growing period?—A. No, sir; I don't know of any such employment in the mills being put upon children.

By Mr. Pugh:

Q. Do these attendants upon the machines have to stand all the time necessarily, or do they have an opportunity to sit?—A. They have the opportunity to sit, and they take advantage of that opportunity a great deal.

MILL WORK AND HOUSE WORK
FOR WOMEN CONTRASTED

By the Chairman:

Q. How about the employment of women; is the employment of a kind that is injurious to them at all?—A. I think not; most of it is employment which allows them to sit, and is not very strenuous. I never heard of any considerable number of cases of women being hurt by the employment. I have until recently had one woman who has worked in the Amoskeag mills, in one of the worst rooms that women work in, for forty years.

Q. If you gave the girls, as a rule, a chance to work in the mill or to be employed as domestics in respectable private families, which would they select?—A. My experience and observation as a housekeeper is that they would take the mills.

Q. What do you conceive to be the reason why, generally, the girl prefers the mills to domestic service? I do not refer to your own case especially.—A. I can only guess at that; I suppose the reason is a compound of two prejudices, if I may call them so; one is, she likes the independence which is the accompaniment of having fixed hours of labor, outside of which she is her own mistress, and the other is the disinclination to take upon herself what she looks upon as occupation of a menial character.

Q. You imagine that they have the impression that it is in some way a little more respectable to work in a mill than to work in a family?—A. I guess so. . . .

COTTON MILL DIVIDENDS

Q. What dividends do you declare, and how often?—A. The dividends are ordinarily declared semi-annually. The regular dividend is 5 per cent on the capital stock; 5 per cent semi-annually.

Q. That is, 10 per cent per annum?—A. Yes; but there have been during this time extra dividends, which have brought the total up to about 14 per cent per annum upon the nominal capital stock. . . .

INFLUENCE OF CHEAP LANDS ON
THE LABOR MARKET

Q. Well, will there ever be a change in the conditions of labor and capital, and of consumption and production, in this country from what they are now?—A. I think there will. When all the cheap lands are taken up so that there is no employment, like that of farming, into which the overflow of labor can pour; but I suppose that time will be a long time removed. As long, however, as the abundance of cheap lands affords the means of livelihood and of profit to all those who choose to engage in cultivating them, as is the case now, so long labor will always be in demand in this country, and will always bring a good price, I suppose.

Q. What is your judgment as to the ability of our manufacturing industries to live without the benefit of a protective tariff?—A. I do not believe that with the labor market as it is now, and as I suppose it will be until the lands are all consumed, the cotton manufacturing industries could, in general, compete with those abroad without protection. . . .

DOES THE EFFECT OF PROTECTION
FALL ON THE CONSUMER?

DOES THE EFFECT OF PROTECTION FALL ON THE CONSUMER?

By Mr. Pugh:

Q. You do not conceal the fact that whatever protection you get comes out of those who consume your fabrics. That is a necessary result, is it not?—*A.* It is, I think, when you look at it in one aspect, but when you consider that those people are the very people, for the most part, whose wages are enhanced by the profit, why, then, perhaps, their profit is greater than their loss. . . .

C. A PHYSICIAN TESTIFIES ON THE LOT OF THE WORKER

Boston, Mass., October 18, 1883
Dr. Timothy D. Stow examined.
By the Chairman:
Q. You are a physician?—*A.* Yes.
Q. You live at Fall River?—*A.* Yes.

CONDITION OF FALL RIVER OPERATIVES

Q. Won't you state how you happen to appear before the committee, what your object is in coming here, and at whose request you come; and then give us the benefit of any observations you choose to lay before us?—*A.* Mr. Robert Howard, of our city, called on me yesterday, and desired me to appear here today before your committee to give whatever testimony I could relating particularly to the physical and mental and perhaps the moral condition of the operatives and laboring classes of Fall River. I have made no notes, and I hardly know what your plan is; but I would as soon answer questions as to make any detailed statement.

The Chairman: We want to find out how the working people of Fall River are living and doing. You can tell us that in the way in which one gentleman would talk to another, the one understanding the subject and the other not understanding it. Just tell us the condition of the operatives there, in your own way, bearing in mind that we would rather have it without premeditation than as a prepared statement.

The Witness: I have been in Fall River about eleven years, though I have been one year absent during that time. As a physician and surgeon, of course, I have been brought into contact with all classes of people there, particularly the laboring classes, the operatives of the city.

THEIR PHYSICAL AND MORAL WELFARE

With regard to the effect of the present industrial system upon their physical and moral welfare, I should say it was of such a character as to need mending, to say the least. It needs some radical remedy. Our laboring population is made up very largely of foreigners, men, women, and children, who have either voluntarily come to Fall River, or who have been induced to come there by the manufacturers.

PHYSICALLY DWARFED

As a class they are dwarfed physically. Of course there are exceptions to that; some notable ones. On looking over their condition and weighing it as carefully as I have been able to, I have come to the conclusion that the character and quality of the labor which they have been doing in times past, and most of them from childhood up, has been and is such as to bring this condition upon them slowly and steadily.

THE EFFECT OF LONG HOURS AND HARD WORK

They are dwarfed, in my estimation, sir, as the majority of men and women who are brought up in factories must be dwarfed under the present industrial system; because by their long hours of indoor labor and their hard work they are cut off from the benefit of breathing fresh air, and from the sights that surround a workman outside a mill. Being shut up all day long in the noise and in the high temperature of these mills, they become physically weak.

INSUFFICIENT CLOTHING AND FOOD

Then, most of them are obliged to live from hand to mouth, or, at least, they do not have sufficient food to nourish them as they need to be nourished. Those things, together with the fact that they have to limit their clothing supply—this constant strain upon the operative—all tend to make him on the one hand uneasy and restless, or on the other hand to produce discouragement and recklessness. They make him careless in regard to his own condition. All those things combined tend to produce what we have in Fall River.

MORAL CONDITION OF FALL RIVER OPERATIVES

Now, first, as to the moral condition of the operatives of Fall River. I think so far as crime is concerned we have quite as little crime there as in any city of its size. We have a population rising on 50,000. There is a disposition at times, and under certain pressure, for some operatives to violate the law, to pilfer, or something of that kind, and I think it grows out of not what is called "pure cussedness," but a desire to relieve some physical want. For instance, a man wants a coat and has not the means of earning it, and he is out of employment, and being pinched with the cold, and with no prospect of getting employment, or of getting a coat by honest means, he steals one. Or perhaps he steals food on the same principle.

COMPARATIVELY LITTLE CRIME

But so far as crime is concerned, we have comparatively little. But what I do say, and what has been on my mind ever since I came to Fall River, with reference to operatives there, is the peculiar impress they seem to bear, a sort of dejected, tired, worn-out, discouraged appearance, growing out of the bad influences of long hours of labor, the close confinement of the mills, the din of the machinery, their exclusion from social intercourse, except at night.

CAUSES OF INTEMPERANCE

And I think we can look for a solution of the problem which the country at large is endeavoring to solve—that with reference to the intemperate habits of the laboring classes and the operatives—in those facts that I have mentioned.

LIQUOR DRUNK TO STIMULATE SOCIABILITY

I have questioned many thoughtful men and women in regard to that. I have said, "Why is it that at night particularly you frequent the dram-shops? Why is it that by day you drink; that you store enough even for the day in your houses?" The answer is, "Well, doctor, I tell you the fact is this, there is a sense of fatigue over us which we do not know how to overcome, and which we must overcome for the time being if we are to have any social qualities of an evening, and we can't do it without taking something which will bridge over the time and make us equal to the emergency of the evening or the occasion." For instance, the operative being in the mill all day long comes out at night, and it is the only time he has, unless he uses Sunday—and he uses that largely—in which to visit his friends, who are scattered here and there all over the city. Families are, of course, scattered in that way. They are either brought over here by the manufacturers or come of their own accord. One person finds a place in one mill, and another in another mill. They have no means of communication with each other except at night or on Sunday. Now, they say to themselves, "How can we fit ourselves for this social intercourse—what we deem a necessity?" The result is that a man steps into a lager-beer saloon, or often into a place where he gets stronger liquor, and he takes a glass of it, and in a few minutes he begins to feel the stimulating influence of the liquor, and it braces him up. But I have said, "How does this make you feel? You say you have been feeling fatigued in the evening and discouraged; that your future does not look bright; how do you feel when you get the liquor?" "Why," he will say, "it covers that all up; we lose all thought of that, and for the time being we feel well." And so they go on from day to day, and from night to night.

MONEY WASTED IN DRAM-SHOPS TO PRODUCE FORGETFULNESS

Now, after all, I do not know of many drunkards in Fall River, but this is true: the operative spends his 5, 10, or 15, or 25 cents a night for liquor, and it is so much lost money to him, and yet he feels impelled to it, because he does not know how otherwise to adapt himself to the circumstances of the evening. It does not seem to affect his constitution, and most of them keep up pretty well, but some succumb to it. Others who cannot succumb to the influences of lager-beer often resort to stronger liquors, such as brandy, whisky, and so on, to stimulate them more, because they require more and more to keep up the effect. Those go down to the drunkard's grave.

PAUPERS AT THIRTY-FIVE OR FORTY

I should say that the average man there who reaches that condition gets to be a pauper at thirty-five or forty. The women, particularly the English women, brew their own beer to some extent, but they buy largely of the stores and keep beer in their houses for the day. It is a common thing for these bar-keepers to peddle around beer and ale, to leave from half a dozen to a dozen bottles of ale a week at a house. Almost every Saturday some families will put in from a dozen to two dozen bottles of ale.

DRINKING TO RELIEVE MENTAL DEPRESSION

Now, it is invariably the testimony of the more intelligent men and women in answer to the question, "Why do you persist in drinking?" "It makes us feel better;

we are relieved of the *ennui* of life; we are relieved of mental depression for the time being, and after the evening's social engagements are over we get home and go to bed, and think nothing of it, and next day resume our day's work." And so it goes on from day to day.

QUALITY OF FOOD

Now, there are other things which hinge upon low wages and long hours of labor to demoralize the operative. For instance, his food. I think it is safe to say that the great mass of operatives there are forced to buy the cheapest food. They go to the meat stores and purchase joints, which, of course, made up into a soup, generally makes good food, but it does not do to have soup all the time. Then they purchase the cheapest vegetables and endeavor to make the money go as far as it possibly will to supply their wants. But all that produces this condition: they lack that sort of nutrition which is essential to an increase of fiber and flesh, and to maintain that elasticity which they ought to have for the performance of a fair amount of labor. I think if the food of the operatives could be increased it would be better.

INSUFFICIENT AS TO QUALITY AND QUANTITY

Q. You mean increased in quantity, in quality, or both?—A. I mean both.

Q. You mean that they do not have enough to eat?—A. Many of them do not; they are limited in amount. I have occasion almost every day to see the manner in which the average operative has his table spread, and certainly it seems to me eminently proper that if it be within the scope of human legislation, or within the scope of the religion which men and women profess, to alleviate the condition of the laboring classes who are our producers, it should be done. We should lift them up in the scale of humanity physically, mentally, and morally. That is the great work to be done; and I do not see under our present infernal system of political economy that any good can be reached. The whole thing must be changed.

THE TENEMENTS

Now, in regard to the tenements in which they live. Some of the corporations have very fair tenements. I would mention, as one instance, the Weetamoe corporation. The King Philip corporation, I think, has pretty fair tenements for its operatives, although many of those tenements are neglected. Whether this is because the manufacturers, or their agents, think that it is almost impossible to keep up with the destructive propensities of their tenants or not, or whether it is from sheer neglect I cannot say, but I know the defective condition of these tenements seems to be from sheer neglect in many cases.

BADLY CONSTRUCTED, UNHEALTHILY LOCATED

For instance, the Slade buildings are very badly located. The tenements were very hastily constructed, and are poorly constructed, so that the average amount of fuel which the operative has to use has to be increased—indeed, has to be nearly doubled—in order to heat these houses during the winter. The access to these houses is in many instances very bad. They are very near a swamp where the drainage is very bad; and through the summertime water and mire are steadily upon the ground within a few rods of the building. It is a noisome, disgusting place. I have noticed, on going in and out of these buildings many times, that the steps were out of repair for long periods. There were some rows of the Slade buildings where the boards of the steps were out and the children and the tenants themselves were likely to break their limbs and injure themselves seriously while going up and down those steps in the darkness of the night by falling through the loose steps. Nothing is done about it through the sheer neglect and the penuriousness of the managers of the mill. There are some corpora-

tions at Fall River that are notable exceptions in this respect, though they have not done everything that could be done, by any means.

Q. Had you not better specify some of those so as to give the good ones the benefit of their goodness?—A. I do not care to mention names, unless the committee desire, although I shall not be backward in that respect, if necessary.

CORPORATIONS WHICH FURNISH BETTER TENEMENTS

THE CHAIRMAN: I think you ought to do so.

THE WITNESS: Well, sir, so far as my observation goes, I would say that the Crescent Mills, the Weetamoe, the Mechanics, the Narragansett, the Border City (No. 1 and No. 2), the King Philip's to some extent; the Osborne (though a few of the Osborne tenements are in bad locations) are exceptions to the rule, and I hear very little complaint brought against those. On the other hand, I could name corporations there which are found fault with by the operatives, and they are marked as a general thing by those who look into these matters as not being exactly what they should be.

HIGH WAGES AND GOOD TENEMENTS PREVENT STRIKES

By MR. PUGH:

Q. In respect to those mills which you have excepted, I understand you to say that the pay is higher, and the condition of the operative better every way. Why do you except them in the remarks made?—A. Because in the King Philip's Mills they manufacture a superior quality of cloth, and I think they pay the operatives more. I have never heard of a strike in that mill, and as a general thing this applies also to the Devoll Mills. The Weetamoe corporation is a very snug one, and seem to take care of their operatives, or to give such attention as secures it. They seem to furnish them better quarters and look after their interests. I do not know that they pay their operatives any more; but they certainly do more than any other corporation to make it comfortable for their help.

NO PROSPECT OF IMPROVEMENT

Q. Are they able in the mills you have excepted to get better food? How do they manage that?—A. Well, I think as a rule, so far as food is concerned, in nearly all the mills of Fall River, with perhaps two or three or four exceptions, the food is pretty nearly the same. Those who occupy a better position, such as the overseers, and those who get better pay, because they are spinners or may be working upon a thin fabric, are enabled thereby to have more of the comforts of life; but the average operative—for instance, the average weaver—in Fall River lives just about so year in and year out, and I do not see that he can change his conditions very much on pressure. Of course, if you could instill into the minds of those who drink the necessity and duty of abandoning drink, and being at home early and sleeping as long as possible, they would be physically better, but that would be at the loss of their social ties, and they want to see their fellows of course. . . .

D. THE TESTIMONY OF AN UNEMPLOYED TEXTILE WORKER

BOSTON, MASS., October 18, 1883

Thomas O'Donnell examined.

By the CHAIRMAN:

Q. Where do you live?—A. At Fall River.

Q. How long have you lived in this country?—A. Eleven years.

Q. Where were you born?—A. In Ramsbotham, England.

Q. Have you been naturalized here?— A. No, sir.

LIFE OF A MULE-SPINNER

Q. What is your business?—A. I am a mule-spinner by trade. I have worked at it since I have been in this country— eleven years.

Q. Are you a married man?—A. Yes, sir; I am a married man; have a wife and two children. I am not very well educated. I went to work when I was young, and have been working ever since in the cotton business; went to work when I was about eight or nine years old. I was going to state how I live. My children get along very well in summertime, on account of not having to buy fuel or shoes or one thing and another. I earn $1.50 a day and can't afford to pay a very big house rent. I pay $1.50 a week for rent, which comes to about $6 a month.

Q. That is, you pay this where you are at Fall River?—A. Yes, sir.

Q. Do you have work right along?— A. No, sir, since that strike we had down in Fall River about three years ago I have not worked much more than half the time, and that has brought my circumstances down very much.

Q. Why have you not worked more than half the time since then?—A. Well, at Fall River if a man has not got a boy to act as "back-boy" it is very hard for him to get along. In a great many cases they discharge men in that work and put in men who have boys.

Q. Men who have boys of their own?— A. Men who have boys of their own capable enough to work in a mill, to earn 30 or 40 cents a day.

CHILD LABOR NECESSARY TO THE EMPLOYMENT OF PARENTS

Q. Is the object of that to enable the boy to earn something for himself?—A. Well, no; the object is this: They are doing away with a great deal of mule-spinning there and putting in ring-spinning, and for that reason it takes a good deal of small help to run this ring work, and it throws the men out of work because they are doing away with the mules and putting these ring-frames in to take their places. For that reason they get all the small help they can to run these ring-frames. There are so many men in the city to work, and whoever has a boy can have work, and whoever has no boy stands no chance. Probably he may have a few months of work in the summertime, but will be discharged in the fall. That is what leaves me in poor circumstances. Our children, of course, are very often sickly from one cause or another, on account of not having sufficient clothes, or shoes, or food, or something. And also my woman; she never did work in a mill; she was a housekeeper, and for that reason she can't help me to anything at present, as many women do help their husbands down there, by working, like themselves. My wife never did work in a mill, and that leaves me to provide for the whole family. I have two children.

HARDSHIP OF UNDERTAKERS' AND DOCTORS' BILLS UPON THE POOR

And another thing that helped to keep me down: A year ago this month I buried the oldest boy we had, and that brings things very expensive on a poor man. For instance, it will cost there, to bury a body, about $100. Now, we could have that done in England for about £5; that would not amount to much more than about $20, or something in that neighborhood. That makes a good deal of difference. Doctors' bills are very heavy—about $2 a visit; and if a doctor comes once a day for two or three weeks it is quite a pile for a poor man to pay.

Q. Will not the doctor come for a dollar a day?—A. You might get a man sometimes, and you sometimes won't, but they generally charge $2 a day.

Q. To operatives?—A. Oh, all around. You might get one for $1.50 sometimes.

Q. They charge you as much as they charge people of more means?—A. They charge as much as if I was the richest man in the city, except that some of them might be generous once in a while and put it down a little in the end; but the charge generally is $2. That makes it hard. . . .

Q. How much money have you got?—A. I have not got a cent in the house; didn't have when I came out this morning.

Q. How much money have you had within three months?—A. I have had about $16 inside of three months.

Q. Is that all you have had within the last three months to live on?—A. Yes; $16.

SUPPORTING A FAMILY ON $133 A YEAR

Q. How much have you had within a year?—A. Since Thanksgiving I happened to get work in the Crescent Mill, and worked there exactly thirteen weeks. I got just $1.50 a day, with the exception of a few days that I lost—because in following up mule-spinning you are obliged to lose a day once in a while; you can't follow it up regularly.

Q. Thirteen weeks would be seventy-eight days, and, at $1.50 a day, that would make $117, less whatever time you lost?—A. Yes. I worked thirteen weeks there and ten days in another place, and then there was a dollar I got this week, Wednesday.

Q. Taking a full year back can you tell how much you have had?—A. That would be about fifteen weeks' work. Last winter, as I told you, I got in, and I worked up to about somewhere around Fast Day, or maybe New Year's day; anyway, Mr. Howard has it down on his record, if you wish to have an exact answer to that question; he can answer it better than I can, because we have a sort of union there to keep ourselves together.

Q. Do you think you have had $150 within a year?—A. No, sir.

Q. Have you had $125?—A. Well, I could figure it up if I had time. The thirteen weeks is all I have had.

Q. The thirteen weeks and the $16 you have mentioned?—A. Yes, sir.

Q. That would be somewhere about $133, if you had not lost any time?—A. Yes, sir.

Q. That is all you have had?—A. Yes, sir.

Q. To support yourself and wife and two children?—*A.* Yes, sir.

Q. Have you had any help from outside?—*A.* No, sir.

Q. Do you mean that yourself and wife and two children have had nothing but that for all this time?—*A.* That is all. I got a couple dollars' worth of coal last winter, and the wood I picked up myself. I goes around with a shovel and picks up clams and wood.

DIGGING CLAMS TO EKE OUT AN EXISTENCE

Q. What do you do with the clams?—*A.* We eat them. I don't get them to sell, but just to eat, for the family. That is the way my brother lives, too, mostly. He lives close by us.

Q. How many live in that way down there?—*A.* I could not count them, they are so numerous. I suppose there are one thousand down there.

Q. A thousand that live on $150 a year?—*A.* They live on less.

Q. Less than that?—*A.* Yes; they live on less than I do.

Q. How long has that been so?—*A.* Mostly so since I have been married.

Q. How long is that?—*A.* Six years this month.

Q. Why do you not go West on a farm?—*A.* How could I go, walk it?

TOO POOR TO GO WEST

Q. Well, I want to know why you do not go out West on a $2,000 farm, or take up a homestead and break it and work it up, and then have it for yourself and family?—*A.* I can't see how I could get out West. I have got nothing to go with.

Q. It would not cost you over $1,500.—*A.* Well, I never saw over a $20 bill, and that is when I have been getting a month's pay at once. If someone would give me $1,500 I will go.

Q. Is there any prospect that anybody will do that?—*A.* I don't know of anybody that would.

Q. You say you think there are a thou-sand men or so with their families that live in that way in Fall River?—*A.* Yes, sir; and I know many of them. They are around there by the shore. You can see them every day; and I am sure of it because men tell me.

Q. Are you a good workman?—*A.* Yes, sir.

Q. Were you ever turned off because of misconduct or incapacity or unfitness for work?—*A.* No, sir.

Q. Or because you did bad work?—*A.* No, sir.

Q. Or because you made trouble among the help?—*A.* No, sir.

Q. Did you ever have any personal trouble with an employer?—*A.* No, sir.

Q. You have not anything now you say?—*A.* No, sir.

Q. How old are you?—*A.* About thirty.

Q. Is your health good?—*A.* Yes, sir.

Q. What would you work for if you could get work right along; if you could be sure to have it for five years, staying right where you are?—*A.* Well, if I was where my family could be with me, and I could have work every day I would take $1.50, and be glad to.

Q. One dollar and fifty cents a day, with three hundred days to the year, would make more than you make now in three or four years, would it not?

ONLY A DOLLAR'S WORTH OF COAL IN TEN MONTHS

A. Well, I would have no opportunity then to pick up clams. I have had no coal except one dollar's worth since last Christmas.

Q. When do the clams give out?—*A.* They give out in winter.

Q. You spoke of fuel—what do you have for fuel?—*A.* Wood and coal.

Q. Where does the wood come from?—*A.* I pick it up around the shore—any old pieces I see around that are not good for anything. There are many more that do the same thing.

Q. Do you get meat to live on much?—*A.* Very seldom.

Q. What kinds of meat do you get for your family?—*A.* Well, once in a while we gets a piece of pork and some clams and make a clam-chowder. That makes a very good meal. We sometimes get a piece of corn beef or something like that.

Q. Have you had any fresh beef within a month?—*A.* Yes; we had a piece of pork steak for four of us yesterday.

Q. Have you had any beef within a month?—*A.* No, sir. I was invited to a man's house on Sunday—he wanted me to go up to his house and we had a dinner of roast pork.

Q. That was an invitation out, but I mean have you had any beefsteak in your own family, of your own purchase, within a month?—*A.* Yes; there was a half a pound, or a pound one Sunday—I think it was.

Q. Have you had only a pound or a half a pound on Sunday?—*A.* That is all.

Q. A half pound of pork?—*A.* Yes. About two pounds of pork I guess we have had in the month, to make clam-chowder with, and sometimes to fry a bit.

Q. And there are four of you in the family?—*A.* Yes, sir.

Q. How many pounds of beefsteak have you had in your family, that you bought for your own home consumption within this year that we have been speaking of?—*A.* I don't think there has been five pounds of beefsteak.

Q. You have had a little pork steak? *A.* We had a half pound of pork steak yesterday; I don't know when we had any before.

Q. What other kinds of meat have you had within a year?—*A.* Well, we have had corn beef twice I think that I can remember this year—on Sunday, for dinner.

Q. Twice is all that you can remember within a year?—*A.* Yes—and some cabbage.

Q. What have you eaten?—*A.* Well, bread mostly, when we could get it; we sometimes couldn't make out to get that, and have had to go without a meal.

Q. Has there been any day in the year that you have had to go without anything to eat?—*A.* Yes, sir, several days.

Q. More than one day at a time?—*A.* No.

Q. How about the children and your wife—did they go without anything to eat too?

THE CHILDREN CRYING FOR FOOD

A. My wife went out this morning and went to a neighbor's and got a loaf of bread and fetched it home, and when she got home the children were crying for something to eat.

Q. Have the children had anything to eat to-day except that, do you think?—*A.* They had that loaf of bread—I don't know what they have had since then, if they have had anything.

Q. Did you leave any money at home?—*A.* No, sir.

Q. If that loaf is gone, is there anything in the house?—*A.* No, sir; unless my wife goes out and gets something; and I don't know who would mind the children while she goes out.

Q. Has she any money to get anything with?—*A.* No, sir.

Q. Have the children gone without a meal at any time during the year?—*A.* They have gone without bread some days, but we have sometimes got meal and made porridge of it.

Q. What kind of meal?—*A.* Sometimes Indian meal, and sometimes oatmeal.

Q. Meal stirred up in hot water?—*A.* Yes, sir.

Q. Is it cold weather down there now?—*A.* It is very cold now.

SCANT CLOTHING IN COLD WEATHER

Q. What have the children got on in the way of clothing?—*A.* They have got along very nicely all summer, but now they are beginning to feel quite sickly. One has one shoe on, a very poor one, and a slipper, that was picked up somewhere. The other has two odd shoes on, with the heel out. He has got cold and is sickly now.

Q. Have they any stockings?—*A.* He had got stockings, but his feet comes through them, for there is a hole in the bottom of the shoe.

Q. What have they got on the rest of their person?—*A.* Well, they have a little calico shirt—what should be a shirt; it is sewed up in some shape—and one little petticoat, and a kind of little dress.

Q. How many dresses has your wife got?—*A.* She has got one since she was married, and she hasn't worn that more than half a dozen times; she has worn it just going to church and coming back. She is very good in going to church, but when she comes back she takes it off, and it is pretty near as good now as when she bought it.

Q. She keeps that dress to go to church in?—*A.* Yes, sir.

Q. How many dresses aside from that has she?—*A.* Well, she got one here three months ago.

Q. What did it cost?—*A.* It cost $1 to make it and I guess about a dollar for the stuff, as near as I can tell.

Q. The dress cost $2?—*A.* Yes.

Q. What else has she?—*A.* Well, she has an undershirt that she got given to her, and she has an old wrapper, which is about a mile too big for her; somebody gave it to her.

Q. She did not buy it?—*A.* No. That is all that I know that she has.

Q. You have had $1 or $2 worth of coal last winter?—*A.* I think it was a quarter of a ton, and I believe it was $2.25 worth.

Q. Is that all you have had?—*A.* That is all I had last winter. All the rest I picked up—wood.

Q. Did you try to get work?—*A.* I was working last winter.

Q. You say that a good many others are situated just like you are?—*A.* Yes, sir; I should say as many as a thousand down in Fall River are just in the same shape, if not worse; though they can't be much worse. I have heard many women say they would sooner be dead than living. I don't know what is wrong, but something is wrong.

There is an overflow of labor in Fall River.

Q. Why do not these people go out West upon farms and go to farming?—*A.* They have not got the means. Fall River being a manufacturing place, it brings them in there; and when the mills in other places stop for want of water that brings them into Fall River. I think there are quite a lot of them that have come from Lowell and Lawrence these three or four weeks back—whatever brings them.

Q. Is there anything else that you want to say to the committee?—*A.* Well, as regards debts; it costs us so much for funeral expenses and doctors' expenses; I wanted to mention that.

THE CHAIRMAN: You have stated that. It is clear that nobody can afford either to get sick or to die there.

THE WITNESS: Well, there are plenty of them down there that are in very poor health, but I am in good health and my children generally are in fair health, but the children can't pick up anything and only get what I bring to them.

Q. Are you in debt?—*A.* Yes, sir.

Q. How much?—*A.* I am in debt for those funeral expenses now $15—since a year ago.

Q. Have you paid the rest?—*A.* Yes, sir.

Q. You live in a hired tenement?—*A.* Yes; but of course I can't pay a big rent. My rent is $6 a month. The man I am living under would come and put me right out and give me no notice either if I didn't pay my rent. He is a sheriff and auctioneer man. I don't know whether he has any authority to do it or not, but he does it with people.

Q. Do you see any way out of your troubles—what are you going to do for a living—or do you expect to have to stay right there?—*A.* Yes. I can't run around with my family.

Q. You have nowhere to go to, and no way of getting there if there was any place to go to?—*A.* No, sir; I have no means nor anything so I am obliged to remain there and try to pick up something as I can.

Q. Do the children go to school?—*A.* No, sir; they are not old enough; the oldest child is only three and a half; the youngest one is one and a half years old.

Q. Is there anything else you wanted to say?—*A.* Nothing further, except that I would like some remedy to be got to help us poor people down there in some way. Excepting the Government decides to do something with us we have a poor show. We are all, or mostly all, in good health; that is, as far as the men who are at work go.

Q. You do not know anything but mule-spinning, I suppose?—*A.* That is what I have been doing, but I sometimes do something with pick and shovel. I have worked for a man at that, because I am so put on. I am looking for work in a mill. The way they do there is this: There are about twelve or thirteen men that go into a mill every morning, and they have to stand their chance, looking for work. The man who has a boy with him he stands the best chance, and then if it is my turn or a neighbor's turn who has no boy, if another man comes in who has a boy he is taken right in, and we are left out. I said to the boss once it was my turn to go in, and now you have taken on that man; what am I to do; I have got two little boys at home, one of them three years and a half and the other one year and a half old, and how am I to find something for them to eat; I can't get my turn when I come here.

He said he could not do anything for me. I says, "Have I got to starve; ain't I to have any work?" They are forcing these young boys into the mills that should not be in mills at all; forcing them in because they are throwing the mules out and putting on ring-frames. They are doing everything of that kind that they possibly can to crush down the poor people—the poor operatives there.

3. PROGRESS AND POVERTY[1]

By Henry George

EDITORS' NOTE.—Henry George (1839–97) found the basis of corruption and inequality of opportunity in America in the open and hidden charges landowners were able to place on all economic transactions. Whereas Henry Demarest Lloyd viewed all monopoly, but particularly that in industry, as the cause of the decline of democracy, Henry George laid the blame exclusively on monopoly in land. Born in Philadelphia in a family of moderate circumstances, George was forced to leave school at fourteen. He learned the printer's trade and migrated to California, where he eventually was a liberal editor and newspaper publisher. The depression of 1873 and the seizure of large areas of the western public domain led George to write *Progress and Poverty*, in which he developed his previously formulated thesis of the evils of land monopoly. Since, as George saw it, all political and economic dislocations stemmed from the private ownership of large tracts of essential land, he suggested that the problem be solved through laying a confiscatory tax—a "single tax"—on all rent and profits accruing solely through landholding.

The book was published in 1879

1. Henry George, *Progress and Poverty* (New York, 1938), pp. 506-8, 517-20, 527-36, 540-43. (First published in 1879.) Reprinted from the Modern Library edition by permission of the Robert Schalkenbach Foundation, New York.

and, after a slow start, achieved a phenomenal sale both in America and in Europe. George moved to New York in 1881 and, with the aid of a few wealthy converts, organized the Single-Tax movement for the purpose of convincing the government of the necessity of putting his theory into operation. He participated in the movement for land nationalization in England and in 1886 ran with labor's support for mayor of New York City. He was defeated by the reform candidate the Democrats nominated in order to stop him, but he polled several thousand more votes than the Republican candidate, Theodore Roosevelt.

What, then, is the law of human progress—the law under which civilization advances?

It must explain clearly and definitely, and not by vague generalities or superficial analogies, why, though mankind started presumably with the same capacities and at the same time, there now exist such wide differences in social development. It must account for the arrested civilizations and for the decayed and destroyed civilizations; for the general facts as to the rise of civilization, and for the petrifying or enervating force which the progress of civilization has heretofore always evolved. It must account for retrogression as well as for progression; for the differences in general character between Asiatic and European civilizations; for the difference between classical and modern civilizations; for the different rates at which progress goes on; and for those bursts, and starts, and halts of progress which are so marked as minor phenomena. And, thus, it must show us what are the essential conditions of progress, and what social adjustments advance and what retard it.

It is not difficult to discover such a law. We have but to look and we may see it. I do not pretend to give it scientific precision, but merely to point it out.

The incentives to progress are the desires inherent in human nature—the desire to gratify the wants of the animal nature, the wants of the intellectual nature, and the wants of the sympathetic nature; the desire to be, to know, and to do—desires that short of infinity can never be satisfied, as they grow by what they feed on.

Mind is the instrument by which man advances, and by which each advance is secured and made the vantage ground for new advances. Though he may not by taking thought add a cubit to his stature, man may by taking thought extend his knowledge of the universe and his power over it, in what, so far as we can see, is an infinite degree. The narrow span of human life allows the individual to go but a short distance, but though each generation may do but little, yet generations, succeeding to the gain of their predecessors, may gradually elevate the status of mankind, as coral polyps, building one generation upon the work of the other, gradually elevate themselves from the bottom of the sea.

Mental power is, therefore, the motor of progress, and men tend to advance in proportion to the mental power expended in progression—the mental power which is devoted to the extension of knowledge, the improvement of methods, and the betterment of social conditions.

Now mental power is a fixed quantity—that is to say, there is a limit to the work a man can do with his mind, as there is to the work he can do with his body; therefore, the mental power which can be devoted to progress is only what is left after what is required for non-progressive purposes.

These non-progressive purposes in which mental power is consumed may be classified as maintenance and conflict. By maintenance I mean, not only the support of existence, but the keeping up of the social condition and the holding of advances already gained. By conflict I mean not merely warfare and preparation for warfare, but all expenditure of mental power in seeking the gratification of desire at the expense of others, and in resistance of such aggression.

To compare society to a boat. Her progress through the water will not depend upon the exertion of her crew, but upon the exertion devoted to propelling her. This will be lessened by any expenditure of force required for bailing, or any expenditure of force in fighting among themselves, or in pulling in different directions.

Now, as in a separated state the whole powers of man are required to maintain existence, and mental power is set free for higher uses only by the association of men in communities, which permits the division of labor and all the economies which come with the co-operation of increased numbers, association is the first essential of progress. Improvement becomes possible as men come together in peaceful association, and the wider and closer the association, the greater the possibilities of improvement. And as the wasteful expenditure of mental power in conflict becomes greater or less as the moral law which accords to each an equality of rights is ignored or is recognized, equality (or justice) is the second essential of progress.

Thus association in equality is the law of progress. Association frees mental power for expenditure in improvement, and equality, or justice, or freedom—for the terms here signify the same thing, the recognition of the moral law—prevents the dissipation of this power in fruitless struggles.

Here is the law of progress, which will explain all diversities, all advances, all halts, and retrogressions. Men tend to progress just as they come closer together, and by co-operation with each other increase the mental power that may be devoted to improvement, but just as conflict is provoked, or association develops in-

equality of condition and power, this tendency to progression is lessened, checked, and finally reversed. . . .

But the great cause of inequality is in the natural monopoly which is given by the possession of land. The first perceptions of men seem always to be that land is common property; but the rude devices by which this is at first recognized—such as annual partitions or cultivation in common—are consistent with only a low stage of development. The idea of property, which naturally arises with reference to things of human production, is easily transferred to land, and an institution which when population is sparse merely secures to the improver and user the due reward of his labor, finally, as population becomes dense and rent arises, operates to strip the producer of his wages. Not merely this, but the appropriation of rent for public purposes, which is the only way in which, with anything like a high development, land can be readily retained as common property, becomes, when political and religious power passes into the hands of a class, the ownership of the land by that class, and the rest of the community become merely tenants. And wars and conquests, which tend to the concentration of political power and to the institution of slavery, naturally result, where social growth has given land a value, in the appropriation of the soil. A dominant class, who concentraté power in their hands, will likewise soon concentrate ownership of the land. To them will fall large partitions of conquered land, which the former inhabitants will till as tenants or serfs, and the public domain, or common lands, which in the natural course of social growth are left for awhile in every country, and in which state the primitive system of village culture leaves pasture and woodland, are readily acquired, as we see by modern instances. And inequality once established, the ownership of land tends to concentrate as development goes on.

I am merely attempting to set forth the general fact that as a social development goes on, inequality tends to establish itself, and not to point out the particular sequence, which must necessarily vary with different conditions. But this main fact makes intelligible all the phenomena of petrifaction and retrogression. The unequal distribution of the power and wealth gained by the integration of men in society tends to check, and finally to counterbalance, the force by which improvements are made and society advances. On the one side, the masses of the community are compelled to expend their mental powers in merely maintaining existence. On the other side, mental power is expended in keeping up and intensifying the system of inequality, in ostentation, luxury, and warfare. A community divided into a class that rules and a class that is ruled—into the very rich and the very poor, may "build like giants and finish like jewelers"; but it will be monuments of ruthless pride and barren vanity, or of a religion turned from its office of elevating man into an instrument for keeping him down. Invention may for awhile to some degree go on; but it will be the invention of refinements in luxury, not the inventions that relieve toil and increase power. In the arcana of temples or in the chambers of court physicians knowledge may still be sought; but it will be hidden as a secret thing, or if it dares come out to elevate common thought or brighten common life, it will be trodden down as a dangerous innovator. For as it tends to lessen the mental power devoted to improvement, so does inequality tend to render men adverse to improvement. How strong is the disposition to adhere to old methods among the classes who are kept in ignorance by being compelled to toil for a mere existence, is too well known to require illustration; and on the other hand the conservatism of the classes to whom the existing social adjustment gives special advantages is equally apparent. This tendency to resist innovation, even though it be improvement, is observable in every special organization—in religion, in law,

in medicine, in science, in trade guilds; and it becomes intense just as the organization is close. A close corporation has always an instinctive dislike of innovation and innovators, which is but the expression of an instinctive fear that change may tend to throw down the barriers which hedge it in from the common herd, and so rob it of importance and power; and it is always disposed to guard carefully its special knowledge or skill.

It is in this way that petrifaction succeeds progress. The advance of inequality necessarily brings improvement to a halt, and as it still persists or provokes unavailing reactions, draws even upon the mental power necessary for maintenance, and retrogression begins.

These principles make intelligible the history of civilization. . . . There is just now a disposition to scoff at any implication that we are not in all respects progressing, and the spirit of our times is that of the edict which the flattering premier proposed to the Chinese Emperor who burned the ancient books—"that all who may dare to speak together about the She and the Shoo be put to death; that those who make mention of the past so as to blame the present be put to death along with their relatives."

Yet it is evident that there have been times of decline, just as there have been times of advance; and it is further evident that these epochs of decline could not at first have been generally recognized.

He would have been a rash man who, when Augustus was changing the Rome of brick to the Rome of marble, when wealth was augmenting and magnificence increasing, when victorious legions were extending the frontier, when manners were becoming more refined, language more polished, and literature rising to higher splendors—he would have been a rash man who then would have said that Rome was entering her decline. Yet such was the case.

And whoever will look may see that though our civilization is apparently advancing with greater rapidity than ever, the same cause which turned Roman progress into retrogression is operating now.

What has destroyed every previous civilization has been the tendency to the unequal distribution of wealth and power. This same tendency, operating with increasing force, is observable in our civilization to-day, showing itself in every progressive community, and with greater intensity the more progressive the community. Wages and interest tend constantly to fall, rent to rise, the rich to become very much richer, the poor to become more helpless and hopeless, and the middle class to be swept away.

I have traced this tendency to its cause. I have shown by what simple means this cause may be removed. I now wish to point out *how*, if this is not done, progress must turn to decadence, and modern civilization decline to barbarism, as have all previous civilizations. It is worth while to point out *how* this may occur, as many people, being unable to see how progress may pass into retrogression, conceive such a thing impossible. Gibbon, for instance, thought that modern civilization could never be destroyed because there remained no barbarians to overrun it, and it is a common idea that the invention of printing by so multiplying books has prevented the possibility of knowledge ever again being lost.

The conditions of social progress, as we have traced the law, are association and equality. The general tendency of modern development, since the time when we can first discern the gleams of civilization in the darkness which followed the fall of the Western Empire, has been toward political and legal equality—to the abolition of slavery; to the abrogation of status; to the sweeping away of hereditary privileges; to the substitution of parliamentary for arbitrary government; to the right of private judgment in matters of religion; to the more equal security in person and property of high and low, weak and strong; to the greater freedom of movement and oc-

cupation, of speech and of the press. The history of modern civilization is the history of advances in this direction—of the struggles and triumphs of personal, political, and religious freedom. And the general law is shown by the fact that just as this tendency has asserted itself civilization has advanced, while just as it has been repressed or forced back civilization has been checked.

This tendency has reached its full expression in the American Republic, where political and legal rights are absolutely equal, and, owing to the system of rotation in office, even the growth of a bureaucracy is prevented; where every religious belief or nonbelief stands on the same footing; where every boy may hope to be President, every man has an equal voice in public affairs, and every official is mediately or immediately dependent for the short lease of his place upon a popular vote. This tendency has yet some triumphs to win in England, in extending the suffrage, and sweeping away the vestiges of monarchy, aristocracy, and prelacy; while in such countries as Germany and Russia, where divine right is yet a good deal more than a legal fiction, it has a considerable distance to go. But it is the prevailing tendency, and how soon Europe will be completely republican is only a matter of time, or rather of accident. The United States are therefore, in this respect, the most advanced of all the great nations, in a direction in which all are advancing, and in the United States we see just how much this tendency to personal and political freedom can of itself accomplish.

Now, the first effect of the tendency to political equality was to the more equal distribution of wealth and power; for, while population is comparatively sparse, inequality in the distribution of wealth is principally due to the inequality of personal rights, and it is only as material progress goes on that the tendency to inequality involved in the reduction of land to private ownership strongly appears. But it is now manifest that absolute political equality does not in itself prevent the tendency to inequality involved in the private ownership of land, and it is further evident that political equality, co-existing with an increasing tendency to the unequal distribution of wealth, must ultimately beget either the despotism of organized tyranny or the worse despotism of anarchy.

To turn a republican government into a despotism the basest and most brutal, it is not necessary formally to change its constitution or abandon popular elections. It was centuries after Caesar before the absolute master of the Roman world pretended to rule other than by authority of a Senate that trembled before him.

But forms are nothing when substance has gone, and the forms of popular government are those from which the substance of freedom may most easily go. Extremes meet, and a government of universal suffrage and theoretical equality may, under conditions which impel the change, most readily become a despotism. For there despotism advances in the name and with the might of the people. The single source of power once secured, everything is secured. There is no unfranchised class to whom appeal may be made, no privileged orders who in defending their own rights may defend those of all. No bulwark remains to stay the flood, no eminence to rise above it. They were belted barons led by a mitered archbishop who curbed the Plantagenet with Magna Charta; it was the middle classes who broke the pride of the Stuarts; but a mere aristocracy of wealth will never struggle while it can hope to bribe a tyrant.

And when the disparity of condition increases, so does universal suffrage make it easy to seize the source of power, for the greater is the proportion of power in the hands of those who feel no direct interest in the conduct of government; who, tortured by want and embruted by poverty, are ready to sell their votes to the highest bidder or follow the lead of the most blatant demagogue; or who, made bitter by

hardships, may even look upon profligate and tyrannous government with the satisfaction we may imagine the proletarians and slaves of Rome to have felt, as they saw a Caligula or Nero raging among the rich patricians. Given a community with republican institutions, in which one class is too rich to be shorn of its luxuries, no matter how public affairs are administered, and another so poor that a few dollars on election day will seem more than any abstract consideration; in which the few roll in wealth and the many seethe with discontent at a condition of things they know not how to remedy, and power must pass into the hands of jobbers who will buy and sell it as the Praetorians sold the Roman purple, or into the hands of demagogues who will seize and wield it for a time, only to be displaced by worse demagogues.

Where there is anything like an equal distribution of wealth—that is to say, where there is general patriotism, virtue, and intelligence—the more democratic the government the better it will be; but where there is gross inequality in the distribution of wealth, the more democratic the government the worse it will be; for, while rotten democracy may not in itself be worse than rotten autocracy, its effects upon national character will be worse. To give the suffrage to tramps, to paupers, to men to whom the change to labor is a boon, to men who must beg, or steal, or starve, is to invoke destruction. To put political power in the hands of men embittered and degraded by poverty is to tie firebrands to foxes and turn them loose amid the standing corn; it is to put out the eyes of a Samson and to twine his arms around the pillars of national life.

Even the accidents of hereditary succession or of selection by lot, the plan of some of the ancient republics, may sometimes place the wise and just in power; but in a corrupt democracy the tendency is always to give power to the worst. Honesty and patriotism are weighted, and unscrupulousness commands success. The best gravitate to the bottom, the worst float to the top, and the vile will only be ousted by the viler. While as national character must gradually assimilate to the qualities that win power, and consequently respect, that demoralization of opinion goes on which in the long panorama of history we may see over and over again transmuting races of freemen into races of slaves.

As in England in the last century, when Parliament was but a close corporation of the aristocracy, a corrupt oligarchy clearly fenced off from the masses may exist without much effect on national character, because in that case power is associated in the popular mind with other things than corruption. But where there are no hereditary distinctions, and men are habitually seen to raise themselves by corrupt qualities from the lowest places to wealth and power, tolerance of these qualities finally becomes admiration. A corrupt democratic government must finally corrupt the people, and when a people become corrupt there is no resurrection. The life is gone, only the carcass remains; and it is left but for the plowshares of fate to bury it out of sight.

Now this transformation of popular government into despotism of the vilest and most degrading kind, which must inevitably result from the unequal distribution of wealth, is not a thing of the far future. It has already begun in the United States, and is rapidly going on under our eyes. That our legislative bodies are steadily deteriorating in standard; that men of the highest ability and character are compelled to eschew politics, and the arts of the jobber count for more than the reputation of the statesman; that voting is done more recklessly and the power of money is increasing; that it is harder to arouse the people to the necessity of reforms and more difficult to carry them out; that political differences are ceasing to be differences of principle, and abstract ideas are losing their power; that parties are passing into the control of what in general government would be oligarchies and dictator-

ships; are all evidences of political decline.

The type of modern growth is the great city. Here are to be found the greatest wealth and the deepest poverty. And it is here that popular government has most clearly broken down. In all the great American cities there is to-day as clearly defined a ruling class as in the most aristocratic countries of the world. Its members carry wards in their pockets, make up the slates for nominating conventions, distribute offices as they bargain together, and—though they toil not, neither do they spin—wear the best of raiment and spend money lavishly. They are men of power, whose favor the ambitious must court and whose vengeance he must avoid. Who are these men? The wise, the good, the learned—men who have earned the confidence of their fellow-citizens by the purity of their lives, the splendor of their talents, their probity in public trusts, their deep study of the problems of government? No; they are gamblers, saloon keepers, pugilists, or worse, who have made a trade of controlling votes and of buying and selling offices and official acts. They stand to the government of these cities as the Praetorian Guards did to that of declining Rome. He who would wear the purple, fill the curule chair, or have the fasces carried before him, must go or send his messengers to their camps, give them donatives and make them promises. It is through these men that the rich corporations and powerful pecuniary interests can pack the Senate and the bench with their creatures. It is these men who make School Directors, Supervisors, Assessors, members of the Legislature, Congressmen. Why, there are many election districts in the United States in which a George Washington, a Benjamin Franklin or a Thomas Jefferson could no more go to the lower house of a State Legislature than under the Ancient Régime a base-born peasant could become a Marshal of France. Their very character would be an insuperable disqualification.

In theory we are intense democrats.

The proposal to sacrifice swine in the temple would hardly have excited greater horror and indignation in Jerusalem of old than would among us that of conferring a distinction of rank upon our most eminent citizen. But is there not growing up among us a class who have all the power without any of the virtues of aristocracy? We have simple citizens who control thousands of miles of railroad, millions of acres of land, the means of livelihood of great numbers of men; who name the Governors of sovereign States as they name their clerks, choose Senators as they choose attorneys, and whose will is as supreme with Legislatures as that of a French King sitting in bed of justice. The undercurrents of the times seem to sweep us back again to the old conditions from which we dreamed we had escaped. The development of the artisan and commercial classes gradually broke down feudalism after it had become so complete that men thought of heaven as organized on a feudal basis, and ranked the first and second persons of the Trinity as suzerain and tenant-in-chief. But now the development of manufacture and exchange, acting in a social organization in which land is made private property, threatens to compel every worker to seek a master, as the insecurity which followed the final break-up of the Roman Empire compelled every freeman to seek a lord. Nothing seems exempt from this tendency. Industry everywhere tends to assume a form in which one is master and many serve. And when one is master and the others serve, the one will control the others, even in such matters as votes. Just as the English landlord votes his tenants, so does the New England mill owner vote his operatives.

There is no mistaking it—the very foundations of society are being sapped before our eyes, while we ask, *how* is it possible that such a civilization as this, with its railroads, and daily newspapers, and electric telegraphs, should ever be destroyed? While literature breathes but the belief that we have been, are, and for the future must be, leaving the savage state further and further behind us, there are indications that we are actually turning back again toward barbarism. Let me illustrate: One of the characteristics of barbarism is the low regard for the rights of person and of property. That the laws of our Anglo-Saxon ancestors imposed as penalty for murder a fine proportioned to the rank of the victim, while our law knows no distinction of rank, and protects the lowest from the highest, the poorest from the richest, by the uniform penalty of death, is looked upon as evidence of their barbarism and our civilization. And so, that piracy, and robbery, and slave-trading, and blackmailing, were once regarded as legitimate occupations, is conclusive proof of the rude state of development from which we have so far progressed.

But it is a matter of fact that, in spite of our laws, any one who has money enough and wants to kill another may go into any one of our great centers of population and business, and gratify his desire, and then surrender himself to justice, with the chances as a hundred to one that he will suffer no greater penalty than a temporary imprisonment and the loss of a sum proportioned partly to his own wealth and partly to the wealth and standing of the man he kills. His money will be paid, not to the family of the murdered man, who have lost their protector; not to the state, which has lost a citizen; but to lawyers who understand how to secure delays, to find witnesses, and get juries to disagree.

And so, if a man steal enough, he may be sure that his punishment will practically amount but to the loss of a part of the proceeds of his theft; and if he steal enough to get off with a fortune, he will be greeted by his acquaintances as a viking might have been greeted after a successful cruise. Even though he robbed those who trusted him; even though he robbed the widow and the fatherless; he has only to get enough, and he may safely flaunt his wealth in the eyes of day.

Now, the tendency in this direction is

an increasing one. It is shown in greatest force where the inequalities in the distribution of wealth are greatest, and it shows itself as they increase. If it be not a return to barbarism, what is it? The failures of justice to which I have alluded are only illustrative of the increasing debility of our legal machinery in every department. It is becoming common to hear men say that it would be better to revert to first principles and abolish law, for then in self-defense the people would form Vigilance Committees and take justice into their own hands. Is this indicative of advance or retrogression?

All this is matter of common observation. Though we may not speak it openly, the general faith in republican institutions is, where they have reached their fullest development, narrowing and weakening. It is no longer that confident belief in republicanism as the source of national blessings that it once was. Thoughtful men are beginning to see its dangers, without seeing how to escape them; are beginning to accept the view of Macaulay and distrust that of Jefferson. And the people at large are becoming used to the growing corruption. The most ominous political sign in the United States to-day is the growth of a sentiment which either doubts the existence of an honest man in public office or looks on him as a fool for not seizing his opportunities. That is to say, the people themselves are becoming corrupted. Thus in the United States to-day is republican government running the course it must inevitably follow under conditions which cause the unequal distribution of wealth.

Where that course leads is clear to whoever will think. As corruption becomes chronic; as public spirit is lost; as traditions of honor, virtue, and patriotism are weakened; as law is brought into contempt and reforms become hopeless; then in the festering mass will be generated volcanic forces, which shatter and rend when seeming accident gives them vent. Strong, unscrupulous men, rising up upon occasion, will become the exponents of blind popular desires or fierce popular passions, and dash aside forms that have lost their vitality. The sword will again be mightier than the pen, and in carnivals of destruction brute force and wild frenzy will alternate with the lethargy of a declining civilization.

I speak of the United States only because the United States is the most advanced of all the great nations. What shall we say of Europe, where dams of ancient law and custom pen up the swelling waters and standing armies weigh down the safety valves, though year by year the fires grow hotter underneath? Europe tends to republicanism under conditions that will not admit of true republicanism—under conditions that substitute for the calm and august figure of Liberty the petroleuse and the guillotine!

Whence shall come the new barbarians? Go through the squalid quarters of great cities, and you may see, even now, their gathering hordes! How shall learning perish? Men will cease to read, and books will kindle fires and be turned into cartridges!

It is startling to think how slight the traces that would be left of our civilization did it pass through the throes which have accompanied the decline of every previous civilization. Paper will not last like parchment, nor are our most massive buildings and monuments to be compared in solidity with the rock-hewn temples and titanic edifices of the old civilizations. And invention has given us, not merely the steam engine and the printing press, but petroleum, nitro-glycerine, and dynamite.

Yet to hint, to-day, that our civilization may possibly be tending to decline, seems like the wildness of pessimism. The special tendencies to which I have alluded are obvious to thinking men, but with the majority of thinking men, as with the great masses, the belief in substantial progress is yet deep and strong—a fundamental belief which admits not the shadow of a doubt. . . .

Whether in the present drifts of opinion and taste there are as yet any indications of retrogression, it is not necessary to inquire; but there are many things about which there can be no dispute, which go to show that our civilization has reached a critical period, and that unless a new start is made in the direction of social equality, the nineteenth century may to the future mark its climax. These industrial depressions, which cause as much waste and suffering as famines or wars, are like the twinges and shocks which precede paralysis. Everywhere is it evident that the tendency to inequality, which is the necessary result of material progress where land is monopolized, cannot go much further without carrying our civilization into that downward path which is so easy to enter and so hard to abandon. Everywhere the increasing intensity of the struggle to live, the increasing necessity for straining every nerve to prevent being thrown down and trodden under foot in the scramble for wealth, is draining the forces which gain and maintain improvements. In every civilized country pauperism, crime, insanity, and suicides are increasing. In every civilized country the diseases are increasing which come from overstrained nerves, from insufficient nourishment, from squalid lodgings, from unwholesome and monotonous occupations, from premature labor of children, from the tasks and crimes which poverty imposes upon women. In every highly civilized country the expectation of life, which gradually rose for several centuries, and which seems to have culminated about the first quarter of this century, appears to be now diminishing.

It is not an advancing civilization that such figures show. It is a civilization which in its undercurrents has already begun to recede. When the tide turns in bay or river from flood to ebb, it is not all at once; but here it still runs on, though there it has begun to recede. When the sun passes the meridian, it can be told only by the way the short shadows fall; for the heat of the day yet increases. But as sure as the turning tide must soon run full ebb; as sure as the declining sun must bring

darkness, so sure is it, that though knowledge yet increases and invention marches on, and new states are being settled, and cities still expand, yet civilization has begun to wane when, in proportion to population, we must build more and more prisons, more and more almshouses, more and more insane asylums. It is not from top to bottom that societies die; it is from bottom to top.

But there are evidences far more palpable than any that can be given by statistics, of tendencies to the ebb of civilization. There is a vague but general feeling of disappointment; an increased bitterness among the working classes; a widespread feeling of unrest and brooding revolution. If this were accompanied by a definite idea of how relief is to be obtained, it would be a hopeful sign; but it is not. Though the schoolmaster has been abroad some time, the general power of tracing effect to cause does not seem a whit improved. The reaction toward protectionism, as the reaction toward other exploded fallacies of government, shows this. And even the philosophic free-thinker cannot look upon that vast change in religious ideas that is now sweeping over the civilized world without feeling that this tremendous fact may have most momentous relations, which only the future can develop. For what is going on is not a change in the form of religion, but the negation and destruction of the ideas from which religion springs. Christianity is not simply clearing itself of superstitions, but in the popular mind it is dying at the root, as the old paganisms were dying when Christianity entered the world. And nothing arises to take its place. The fundamental ideas of an intelligent Creator and of a future life are in the general mind rapidly weakening. Now, whether this may or may not be in itself an advance, the importance of the part which religion has played in the world's history shows the importance of the change that is now going on. Unless human nature has suddenly altered in what the universal history of the race shows to be its deepest characteristics, the mightiest actions and reactions are thus preparing. Such stages of thought have heretofore always marked periods of transition. On a smaller scale and to a less depth (for I think any one who will notice the drift of our literature, and talk upon such subjects with the men he meets, will see that it is sub-soil and not surface plowing that materialistic ideas are now doing), such a state of thought preceded the French Revolution. But the closest parallel to the wreck of religious ideas now going on is to be found in that period in which ancient civilization began to pass from splendor to decline. What change may come, no mortal man can tell, but that some great change *must* come, thoughtful men begin to feel. The civilized world is trembling on the verge of a great movement. Either it must be a leap upward, which will open the way to advances yet undreamed of, or it must be a plunge downward which will carry us back toward barbarism.

4. LOOKING BACKWARD[1]

By Edward Bellamy

EDITORS' NOTE.—Edward Bellamy's *Looking Backward, 2000–1887* was the most successful of the more than forty utopian novels published in America during the last twenty years of the nineteenth century. These novels depicted life in an America which had organized its social, political, and economic structure so as to eliminate poverty, disease, and corruption. Bellamy's hero, Julian West, was a thirty-year-old Bostonian who in 1887 was contentedly living on the wealth inherited from his grandfather—"interest on investments [which] was a species of tax in perpetuity upon the product of those engaged in industry which a person possessing or inheriting money was able to levy." Since West suffered from insomnia, he was in the habit of having himself put to sleep in an underground vault in his home by a hypnotist. On May 30, 1887, while he was in a sleep-inducing trance, his house burned down above him, killing his servant who usually awakened him from the trance. Since his hypnotist had moved from the city that same day, he remained undiscovered until the year 2000. Then his body was disinterred by a Dr. Leete who was excavating on the site in order to build a laboratory. Leete brought West out of the trance which had been so deep that, despite his 113-year sleep, he was in the same physical and mental condition as on the fateful night of May 30, 1887.

Under Dr. Leete's guidance, West explores and evaluates the American utopia of the year 2000, a "nationalized" society based on "an enlightened self-interest of wholesale common sense." Bellamy's utopia was organized on a more or less military structure of industrial activity in which all were obliged to serve between the ages of twenty-one and forty-five. Officers and generals chosen by the different departments of industry formed the government, and a presi-

1. Edward Bellamy, *Looking Backward*, 2000–1887 (New York, 1888), pp. 85–98, 123, 131–33, 225–37, 239, 241–44. By permission of Houghton Mifflin and Company.

dent was selected from among the heads of departments by a vote of the men who were retired from the industrial army.

Bellamy (1850–98) was a lawyer turned newspaper editor and novelist. *Looking Backward* (1888) was his fifth novel and sold one million copies. With the success of *Looking Backward*, Bellamy devoted himself to founding and leading the Nationalist movement, which drew its inspiration from his novel. He believed that all groups in capitalist society could be persuaded as to the rationality of his utopia, and he therefore devoted himself to editing the *Nationalist* and *New Nation* magazines and to organizing Nationalist clubs. In this analysis and program he differed from the Marxian or scientific socialists who held that socialism would be gained through the struggle waged by the working class against the capitalist class. Bellamy's movement gained some political strength but soon disintegrated, with the Populist party as the chief beneficiary. In 1897 Bellamy published *Equality* as a sequel to *Looking Backward*, and this novel, too, achieved a considerable success.

CHAPTER IX

Dr. and Mrs. Leete were evidently not a little startled to learn, when they presently appeared, that I had been all over the city alone that morning, and it was apparent that they were agreeably surprised to see that I seemed so little agitated after the experience.

"Your stroll could scarcely have failed to be a very interesting one," said Mrs. Leete, as we sat down to table soon after. "You must have seen a good many new things."

"I saw very little that was not new," I replied. "But I think what surprised me as much as anything was not to find any stores on Washington Street, or any banks on State. What have you done with the merchants and bankers? Hung them all, perhaps, as the anarchists wanted to do in my day?"

"Not so bad as that," replied Dr. Leete. "We have simply dispensed with them. Their functions are obsolete in the modern world."

"Who sells you things when you want to buy them?" I inquired.

"There is neither selling nor buying nowadays; the distribution of goods is effected in another way. As to the bankers, having no money we have no use for those gentry."

"Miss Leete," said I, turning to Edith, "I am afraid that your father is making sport of me. I don't blame him, for the temptation my innocence offers must be extraordinary. But, really, there are limits to my credulity as to possible alterations in the social system."

"Father has no idea of jesting, I am sure," she replied, with a reassuring smile.

The conversation took another turn then, the point of ladies' fashions in the nineteenth century being raised, if I remember rightly, by Mrs. Leete, and it was not till after breakfast, when the doctor had invited me up to the house-top, which appeared to be a favorite resort of his, that he recurred to the subject.

"You were surprised," he said, "at my saying that we got along without money or trade, but a moment's reflection will show that trade existed and money was needed in your day simply because the business of production was left in private hands, and that, consequently, they are superfluous now."

"I do not at once see how that follows," I replied.

"It is very simple," said Dr. Leete. "When innumerable different and independent persons produced the various things needful to life and comfort, endless exchanges between individuals were requisite in order that they might supply themselves with what they desired. These exchanges constituted trade, and money was essential as their medium. But as soon as the nation became the sole producer of all sorts of commodities, there was no need of exchanges between individuals that they might get what they required. Everything was procurable from one source, and nothing could be procured anywhere else. A system of direct distribution from the national storehouses took the place of trade, and for this money was unnecessary."

"How is this distribution managed?" I asked.

"On the simplest possible plan," replied Dr. Leete. "A credit corresponding to his share of the annual product of the nation is given to every citizen on the public books at the beginning of each year, and a credit card issued him with which he procures at the public storehouses, found in every community, whatever he desires whenever he desires it. This arrangement, you will see, totally obviates the necessity for business transactions of any sort between individuals and consumers. Perhaps you would like to see what our credit-cards are like.

"You observe," he pursued as I was curiously examining the piece of pasteboard he gave me, "that this card is issued for a certain number of dollars. We have kept the old word, but not the substance. The term, as we use it, answers to no real thing, but merely serves as an algebraical symbol for comparing the values of products with one another. For this purpose they are all priced in dollars and cents, just as in your day. The value of what I procure on this card is checked off by the clerk, who pricks out of these tiers of squares the price of what I order."

"If you wanted to buy something of your neighbor, could you transfer part of your credit to him as consideration?" I inquired.

"In the first place," replied Dr. Leete, "our neighbors have nothing to sell us, but in any event our credit would not be transferable, being strictly personal. Before the nation could even think of honoring any such transfer as you speak of, it would be bound to inquire into all the circumstances of the transaction, so as to be able to guarantee its absolute equity. It would have been reason enough, had there been no other, for abolishing money, that its possession was no indication of rightful title to it. In the hands of the man who had stolen it or murdered for it, it was as good as in those which had earned it by industry. People nowadays interchange gifts and favors out of friendship, but buying and selling is considered absolutely inconsistent with the mutual benevolence and disinterestedness which should prevail between citizens and the sense of community of interest which supports our social system. According to our ideas, buying and selling is essentially anti-social in all its tendencies. It is an education in self-seeking at the expense of others, and no society whose citizens are trained in such a school can possibly rise above a very low grade of civilization."

"What if you have to spend more than your card in any one year?" I asked.

"The provision is so ample that we are more likely not to spend it all," replied Dr. Leete. "But if extraordinary expenses should exhaust it, we can obtain a limited advance on the next year's credit, though this practice is not encouraged, and a heavy discount is charged to check it. Of course if a man showed himself a reckless spendthrift he would receive his allowance monthly or weekly instead of yearly, or if necessary not be permitted to handle it all."

"If you don't spend your allowance, I suppose it accumulates?"

"That is also permitted to a certain extent when a special outlay is anticipated. But unless notice to the contrary is given, it is presumed that the citizen who does not fully expend his credit did not have occasion to do so, and the balance is turned into the general surplus."

"Such a system does not encourage saving habits on the part of citizens," I said.

"It is not intended to," was the reply. "The nation is rich, and does not wish the people to deprive themselves of any good thing. In your day, men were bound to lay up goods and money against coming failure of the means of support and for their children. This necessity made parsimony a virtue. But now it would have no such laudable object, and, having lost its utility, it has ceased to be regarded as a virtue. No man any more has any care for the morrow, either for himself or his children, for the nation guarantees the nurture, education, and comfortable maintenance of every citizen from the cradle to the grave."

"That is a sweeping guarantee!" I said. "What certainty can there be that the value of a man's labor will recompense the nation for its outlay on him? On the whole, society may be able to support all its members, but some must earn less than enough for their support, and others more; and that brings us back once more to the wages question, on which you have hitherto said nothing. It was at just this point, if you remember, that our talk ended last evening; and I say again, as I did then, that here I should suppose a national industrial system like yours would find its main difficulty. How, I ask once more, can you adjust satisfactorily the comparative wages or remuneration of the multitude of avocations, so unlike and so incommensurable, which are necessary for the service of society? In our day the market rate determined the price of labor of all sorts, as well as of goods. The employer paid as little as he could, and the worker got as much. It was not a pretty system ethically, I admit; but it did, at least, furnish us a rough and ready formula for settling a

question which must be settled ten thousand times a day if the world was ever going to get forward. There seemed to us no other practicable way of doing it."

"Yes," replied Dr. Leete, "it was the only practicable way under a system which made the interests of every individual antagonistic to those of every other; but it would have been a pity if humanity could never have devised a better plan, for yours was simply the application to the mutual relations of men of the devil's maxim, 'Your necessity is my opportunity.' The reward of any service depended not upon its difficulty, danger, or hardship, for throughout the world it seems that the most perilous, severe, and repulsive labor was done by the worst paid classes; but solely upon the strait of those who needed the service."

"All that is conceded," I said. "But, with all its defects, the plan of settling prices by the market rate was a practical plan; and I cannot conceive what satisfactory substitute you can have devised for it. The government being the only possible employer, there is of course no labor market or market rate. Wages of all sorts must be arbitrarily fixed by the government. I cannot imagine a more complex and delicate function than that must be, or one, however performed, more certain to breed universal dissatisfaction."

"I beg your pardon," replied Dr. Leete, "but I think you exaggerate the difficulty. Suppose a board of fairly sensible men were charged with settling the wages for all sorts of trades under a system which, like ours, guaranteed employment to all, while permitting the choice of avocations. Don't you see that, however unsatisfactory the first adjustment might be, the mistakes would soon correct themselves? The favored trades would have too many volunteers, and those discriminated against would lack them till the errors were set right. But this is aside from the purpose, for, though this plan would, I fancy, be practicable enough, it is no part of our system."

"How, then, do you regulate wages?" I once more asked.

Dr. Leete did not reply till after several moments of meditative silence. "I know, of course," he finally said, "enough of the old order of things to understand just what you mean by that question; and yet the present order is so utterly different at this point that I am a little at loss how to answer you best. You ask me how we regulate wages; I can only reply that there is no idea in the modern social economy which at all corresponds with what was meant by wages in your day."

"I suppose you mean that you have no money to pay wages in," said I. "But the credit given the worker at the government storehouse answers to his wages with us. How is the amount of the credit given respectively to the workers in different lines determined? By what title does the individual claim his particular share? What is the basis of allotment?"

"His title," replied Dr. Leete, "is his humanity. The basis of his claim is the fact that he is a man."

"The fact that he is a man!" I repeated, incredulously. "Do you possibly mean that all have the same share?"

"Most assuredly."

The readers of this book never having practically known any other arrangement, or perhaps very carefully considered the historical accounts of former epochs in which a very different system prevailed, cannot be expected to appreciate the stupor of amazement into which Dr. Leete's simple statement plunged me.

"You see," he said, smiling, "that it is not merely that we have no money to pay wages in, but, as I said, we have nothing at all answering to your idea of wages."

By this time I had pulled myself together sufficiently to voice some of the criticisms which, man of the nineteenth century as I was, came uppermost in my mind, upon this to me astounding arrangement. "Some men do twice the work of others!" I exclaimed. "Are the clever workmen content with a plan that ranks them with the indifferent?"

"We leave no possible ground for any complaint of injustice," replied Dr. Leete, "by requiring precisely the same measure of service from all."

"How can you do that, I should like to know, when no two men's powers are the same?"

"Nothing could be simpler," was Dr. Leete's reply. "We require of each that he shall make the same effort; that is, we demand of him the best service it is in his power to give."

"And supposing all do the best they can," I answered, "the amount of the product resulting is twice greater from one man than from another."

"Very true," replied Dr. Leete; "but the amount of the resulting product has nothing whatever to do with the question, which is one of desert. Desert is a moral question, and the amount of the product a material quantity. It would be an extraordinary sort of logic which should try to determine a moral question by a material standard. The amount of the effort alone is pertinent to the question of desert. All men who do their best, do the same. A man's endowments, however godlike, merely fix the measure of his duty. The man of great endowments who does not do all he might, though he may do more than a man of small endowments who does his best, is deemed a less deserving worker than the latter, and dies a debtor to his fellows. The Creator sets men's tasks for them by the faculties he gives them; we simply exact their fulfillment."

"No doubt that is very fine philosophy," I said; "nevertheless it seems hard that the man who produces twice as much as another, even if both do their best, should have only the same share."

"Does it, indeed, seem so to you?" responded Dr. Leete. "Now, do you know, that seems very curious to me? The way it strikes people nowadays is, that a man who can produce twice as much as another with the same effort, instead of being rewarded for doing so, ought to be punished if he does not do so. In the nineteenth century, when a horse pulled a heavier load than a goat, I suppose you rewarded him. Now, we should have whipped him soundly if he had not, on the ground that, being much stronger, he ought to. It is singular how ethical standards change." The doctor said this with such a twinkle in his eye that I was obliged to laugh.

"I suppose," I said, "that the real reason that we rewarded men for their endowments, while we considered those of horses and goats merely as fixing the service to be severally required of them, was that the animals, not being reasoning beings, naturally did the best they could, whereas men could only be induced to do so by rewarding them according to the amount of their product. That brings me to ask why, unless human nature has mightily changed in a hundred years, you are not under the same necessity."

"We are," replied Dr. Leete. "I don't think there has been any change in human nature in that respect since your day. It is still so constituted that special incentives in the form of prizes, and advantages to be gained, are requisite to call out the best endeavors of the average man in any direction."

"But what inducement," I asked, "can a man have to put forth his best endeavors when, however much or little he accomplishes, his income remains the same? High characters may be moved by devotion to the common welfare under such a system, but does not the average man tend to rest back on his oar, reasoning that it is of no use to make a special effort, since the effort will not increase his income, nor its withholding diminish it?"

"Does it then really seem to you," answered my companion, "that human nature is insensible to any motives save fear of want and love of luxury, that you should expect security and equality of livelihood to leave them without possible incentives to effort? Your contemporaries did not really think so, though they might fancy

they did. When it was a question of the grandest class of efforts, the most absolute self-devotion, they depended on quite other incentives. Not higher wages, but honor and the hope of men's gratitude, patriotism and the inspiration of duty, were the motives which they set before their soldiers when it was a question of dying for the nation, and never was there an age of the world when those motives did not call out what is best and noblest in men. And not only this, but when you come to analyze the love of money which was the general impulse to effort in your day, you find that the dread of want and desire of luxury was but one of several motives which the pursuit of money represented; the others, and with many the more influential, being desire of power, of social position, and reputation for ability and success. So you see that though we have abolished poverty and the fear of it, and inordinate luxury with the hope of it, we have not touched the greater part of the motives which underlay the love of money in former times, or any of those which prompted the supremer sorts of effort. The coarser motives, which no longer move us, have been replaced by higher motives wholly unknown to the mere wage earners of your age. Now that industry of whatever sort is no longer self-service, but service of the nation, patriotism, passion for humanity, impel the worker as in your day they did the soldier. The army of industry is an army, not alone by virtue of its perfect organization, but by reason also of the ardor of self-devotion which animates its members.

"But as you used to supplement the motives of patriotism with the love of glory, in order to stimulate the valor of your soldiers, so do we. Based as our industrial system is on the principle of requiring the same unit of effort from every man, that is, the best he can do, you will see that the means by which we spur the workers to do their best must be a very essential part of our scheme. With us, diligence in the national service is the sole and certain way to public repute, social distinction, and official power. The value of a man's services to society fixes his rank in it. Compared with the effect of our social arrangements in impelling men to be zealous in business, we deem the object-lessons of biting poverty and wanton luxury on which you depended a device as weak and uncertain as it was barbaric. The lust of honor even in your sordid day notoriously impelled men to more desperate effort than the love of money could." . . .

Chapter XII

The questions which I needed to ask before I could acquire even an outline acquaintance with the institutions of the twentieth century being endless, and Dr. Leete's good-nature appearing equally so, we sat up talking for several hours after the ladies left us. . . .

"I should not fail to mention," resumed the doctor, "that for those too deficient in mental or bodily strength to be fairly graded with the main body of workers, we have a separate grade, unconnected with the others—a sort of invalid corps, the members of which are provided with a light class of tasks fitted to their strength. . . ."

"That is a pretty idea of the invalid corps," I said. "Even a barbarian from the nineteenth century can appreciate that. It is a very graceful way of disguising charity, and must be grateful to the feelings of its recipients."

"Charity!" repeated Dr. Leete. "Did you suppose that we consider the incapable class we are talking of objects of charity?"

"Why, naturally," I said, "inasmuch as they are incapable of self-support."

But here the doctor took me up quickly.

"Who is capable of self-support?" he demanded. "There is no such thing in a civilized society as self-support. In a state of society so barbarous as not even to know family coöperation, each individual may possibly support himself, though even then for a part of his life only; but from the moment that men begin to live to-

gether, and constitute even the rudest sort of society, self-support becomes impossible. As men grow more civilized, and the subdivision of occupations and services is carried out, a complex mutual dependence becomes the universal rule. Every man, however solitary may seem his occupation, is a member of a vast industrial partnership, as large as the nation, as large as humanity. The necessity of mutual dependence should imply the duty and guarantee of mutual support; and that it did not in your day constituted the essential cruelty and unreason of your system."

"That may all be so," I replied, "but it does not touch the case of those who are unable to contribute anything to the product of industry."

"Surely I told you this morning, at least I thought I did," replied Dr. Leete, "that the right of a man to maintenance at the nation's table depends on the fact that he is a man, and not on the amount of health and strength he may have, so long as he does his best." . . .

Chapter XXII

We had made an appointment to meet the ladies at the dining-hall for dinner, after which, having some engagement, they left us sitting at table there, discussing our wine and cigars with a multitude of other matters.

"Doctor," said I, in the course of our talk, "morally speaking, your social system is one which I should be insensate not to admire in comparison with any previously in vogue in the world, and especially with that of my own most unhappy century. If I were to fall into a mesmeric sleep tonight as lasting as that other, and meanwhile the course of time were to take a turn backward instead of forward, and I were to wake up again in the nineteenth century, when I had told my friends what I had seen, they would every one admit that your world was a paradise of order, equity, and felicity. But they were a very practical people, my contemporaries, and after expressing their admiration for the moral beauty and material splendor of the system, they would presently begin to cipher and ask how you got the money to make everybody so happy; for certainly, to support the whole nation at a rate of comfort, and even luxury, such as I see around me, must involve vastly greater wealth than the nation produced in my day. Now, while I could explain to them pretty nearly everything else of the main features of your system, I should quite fail to answer this question, and failing there, they would tell me, for they were very close cipherers, that I had been dreaming; nor would they ever believe anything else. In my day, I know that the total annual product of the nation, although it might have been divided with absolute equality, would not have come to more than three or four hundred dollars per head, not very much more than enough to supply the necessities of life with few or any of its comforts. How is it that you have so much more?"

"That is a very pertinent question, Mr. West," replied Dr. Leete, "and I should not blame your friends, in the case you supposed, if they declared your story all moonshine, failing a satisfactory reply to it. It is a question which I cannot answer exhaustively at any one sitting, and as for the exact statistics to bear out my general statements, I shall have to refer you for them to books in my library, but it would certainly be a pity to leave you to be put to confusion by your old acquaintances, in case of the contingency you speak of, for lack of a few suggestions.

"Let us begin with a number of small items wherein we economize wealth as compared with you. We have no national, state, county, or municipal debts, or payments on their account. We have no sort of military or naval expenditures for men or materials, no army, navy, or militia. We have no revenue service, no swarm of tax assessors and collectors. As regards our judiciary, police, sheriffs, and jailers, the force which Massachusetts alone kept on foot in your day far more than suffices

for the nation now. We have no criminal class preying upon the wealth of society as you had. The number of persons, more or less absolutely lost to the working force through physical disability, of the lame, sick, and debilitated, which constituted such a burden on the able-bodied in your day, now that all live under conditions of health and comfort, has shrunk to scarcely perceptible proportions, and with every generation is becoming more completely eliminated.

"Another item wherein we save is the disuse of money and the thousand occupations connected with financial operations of all sorts, whereby an army of men was formerly taken away from useful employments. Also consider that the waste of the very rich in your day on inordinate personal luxury has ceased, though, indeed, this item might easily be over-estimated. Again, consider that there are no idlers now, rich or poor—no drones.

"A very important cause of former poverty was the vast waste of labor and materials which resulted from domestic washing and cooking, and the performing separately of innumerable other tasks to which we apply the coöperative plan.

"A larger economy than any of these— yes, of all together—is effected by the organization of our distributing system, by which the work done once by the merchants, traders, storekeepers, with their various grades of jobbers, wholesalers, retailers, agents, commercial travelers, and middlemen of all sorts, with an excessive waste of energy in needless transportation and interminable handlings, is performed by one-tenth the number of hands and an unnecessary turn of not one wheel. Something of what our distributing system is like you know. Our statisticians calculate that one eightieth part of our workers suffices for all the processes of distribution which in your day required one eighth of the population, so much being withdrawn from the force engaged in productive labor."

"I begin to see," I said, "where you get your greater wealth."

"I beg your pardon," replied Dr. Leete, "but you scarcely do as yet. The economies I have mentioned thus far, in the aggregate, considering the labor they would save directly and indirectly through saving of material, might possibly be equivalent to the addition to your annual production of wealth of one-half its former total. These items are, however, scarcely worth mentioning in comparison with other prodigious wastes, now saved, which resulted inevitably from leaving the industries of the nation to private enterprise. However great the economies your contemporaries might have devised in the consumption of products, and however marvelous the progress of mechanical invention, they could never have raised themselves out of the slough of poverty so long as they held to that system.

"No mode more wasteful for utilizing human energy could be devised, and for the credit of the human intellect it should be remembered that the system never was devised, but was merely a survival from the rude ages when the lack of social organization made any sort of coöperation impossible."

"I will readily admit," I said, "that our industrial system was ethically very bad, but as a mere wealth-making machine, apart from moral aspects, it seemed to us admirable."

"As I said," responded the doctor, "the subject is too large to discuss at length now, but if you are really interested to know the main criticisms which we moderns make on your industrial system as compared with our own, I can touch briefly on some of them.

"The wastes which resulted from leaving the conduct of industry to irresponsible individuals, wholly without mutual understanding or concert, were mainly four: first, the waste by mistaken undertakings; second, the waste from the competition and mutual hostility of those engaged in industry; third, the waste by periodical gluts and crises, with the consequent interruptions of industry; fourth, the waste from idle capital and labor, at all times. Any one of these four great leaks, were all the others stopped, would suffice to make the difference between wealth and poverty on the part of a nation.

"Take the waste by mistaken undertakings, to begin with. In your day the production and distribution of commodities being without concert or organization, there was no means of knowing just what demand there was for any class of products, or what was the rate of supply. Therefore, any enterprise by a private capitalist was always a doubtful experiment. The projector having no general view of the field of industry and consumption, such as our government has, could never be sure either what the people wanted, or what arrangements other capitalists were making to supply them. In view of this, we are not surprised to learn that the chances were considered several to one in favor of the failure of any given business enterprise, and that it was common for persons who at last succeeded in making a hit to have failed repeatedly. If a shoemaker, for every pair of shoes he succeeded in completing, spoiled the leather of four or five pair, besides losing the time spent on them, he would stand about the same chance of getting rich as your contemporaries did with their system of private enterprise, and its average of four or five failures to one success.

"The next of the great wastes was that from competition. The field of industry was a battlefield as wide as the world, in which the workers wasted, in assailing one another, energies which, if expended in concerted effort, as to-day, would have enriched all. As for mercy or quarter in this warfare, there was absolutely no suggestion of it. To deliberately enter a field of business and destroy the enterprises of those who had occupied it previously, in order to plant one's own enterprise on their ruins, was an achievement which never failed to command popular admiration. Nor is there any stretch of fancy in comparing this sort of struggle with actual warfare, so far as concerns the mental agony and physical suffering which attended the struggle, and the misery which overwhelmed the defeated and those dependent on them. Now nothing about your age is, at first sight, more astounding to a man of modern times than the fact that men engaged in the same industry, instead of fraternizing as comrades and co-laborers to a common end, should have regarded each other as rivals and enemies to be throttled and overthrown. This certainly seems like sheer madness, a scene from bedlam. But more closely regarded, it is seen to be no such thing. Your contemporaries, with their mutual throat-cutting, knew very well what they were at. The producers of the nineteenth century were not, like ours, working together for the maintenance of the community, but each solely for his own maintenance at the expense of the community. If, in working to this end, he at the same time increased the aggregate wealth, that was merely incidental. It was just as feasible and as common to increase one's private hoard by practices injurious to the general welfare. One's worst enemies were necessarily those of his own trade, for, under your plan of making private profit the motive of production, a scarcity of the article he produced was what each particular producer desired. It was for his interest that no more of it should be produced than he himself could produce. To secure this consummation as far as circumstances permitted, by killing off and discouraging those engaged in his line of industry, was his constant effort. When he had killed off all he could, his policy was to combine with those he could not kill, and convert their mutual warfare into a warfare upon the public at large by cornering the market, as I believe you used to call it, and putting up prices to the highest point people would stand before going without the goods. The day dream of the nineteenth century producer was to gain absolute control of the supply of some necessity of life, so that he might keep the public at the verge of starvation, and always command famine prices for what he supplied. This, Mr. West, is what was called in the nineteenth century a system of production. I will leave it to you if it does not seem, in some of its aspects, a great deal more like a system for preventing production. Some time when we have plenty of leisure I am going to ask you to sit down with me and try to make me comprehend, as I never yet could, though I have studied the matter a great deal, how such shrewd fellows as your contemporaries appear to have been in many respects ever came to entrust the business of providing for the community to a class whose interest it was to starve it. I assure you that the wonder with us is, not that the world did not get rich under such a system, but that it did not perish outright from want. This wonder increases as we go on to consider some of the other prodigious wastes that characterized it.

"Apart from the waste of labor and capital by misdirected industry, and that from the constant bloodletting of your industrial warfare, your system was liable to periodical convulsions, overwhelming alike the wise and unwise, the successful cut-throat as well as his victim. I refer to the business crises at intervals of five to ten years, which wrecked the industries of the nation, prostrating all weak enterprises and crippling the strongest, and were followed by long periods, often of many years, of so-called dull times, during which the capitalists slowly regathered their dissipated strength while the laboring classes starved and rioted. Then would ensue another brief season of prosperity, followed in turn by another crisis and the ensuing years of exhaustion. As commerce developed, making the nations mutually dependent, these crises became world-wide, while the obstinacy of the ensuing state of collapse increased with the area affected by the convulsions, and the consequent lack of rallying centres. In proportion as the industries of the world multiplied and became complex, and the volume of capital involved was increased, these business cataclysms became more frequent, till, in the latter part of the nineteenth century, there were two years of bad times to one of good, and the system of industry, never before so extended or so imposing, seemed in danger of collapsing by its own weight. After endless discussions, your economists appear by that time to have settled down to the despairing conclusion that there was no more possibility of preventing or controlling these crises than if they had been drouths or hurricanes. It only remained to endure them as necessary evils, and when they had passed over to build up again the shattered structure of industry, as dwellers in an earthquake country keep on rebuilding their cities on the same site.

"So far as considering the causes of the trouble inherent in their industrial system, your contemporaries were certainly correct. They were in its very basis, and must needs become more and more maleficent as the business fabric grew in size and complexity. One of these causes was the lack of any common control of the different industries, and the consequent impossibility of their orderly and coördinate development. It inevitably resulted from this lack that they were continually getting out of step with one another and out of relation with the demand.

"Of the latter there was no criterion such as organized distribution gives us, and the first notice that it had been exceeded in any group of industries was a crash of prices, bankruptcy of producers, stoppage of production, reduction of wages, or discharge of workmen. This process was constantly going on in many industries, even in what were called good times, but a crisis took place only when the industries affected were extensive. The markets then were glutted with goods, of which nobody wanted beyond a sufficiency at any price. The wages and profits of those making the glutted classes of goods being reduced or wholly stopped, their purchasing power as consumers of other classes of goods, of which there was no natural glut, was taken away, and, as a consequence, goods of which there was no natural glut became artificially glutted, till their prices also were broken down, and their makers thrown out of work and deprived of income. The crisis was by this time fairly under way, and nothing could check it till a nation's ransom had been wasted.

"A cause, also inherent in your system, which often produced and always terribly aggravated crises, was the machinery of money and credit. . . . It was one of your fictions that the government and the banks authorized by it alone issued money; but everybody who gave a dollar's credit issued money to that extent, which was as good as any to swell the circulation till the next crises. The great extension of the credit system was a characteristic of the latter part of the nineteenth century, and accounts largely for the almost incessant business crises which marked that period. Perilous as credit was, you could not dispense with its use, for, lacking any national or other public organization of the capital of the country, it was the only means you had for concentrating and directing it upon industrial enterprises. It was in this way a most potent means for exaggerating the chief peril of the private enterprise system of industry by enabling particular industries to absorb disproportionate amounts of the disposable capital of the country, and thus prepare disaster. Business enterprises were always vastly in debt for advances of credit, both to one another and to the banks and capitalists, and the prompt withdrawal of this credit at the first sign of a crisis was generally the precipitating cause of it.

"It was the misfortune of your contemporaries that they had to cement their business fabric with a material which an accident might at any moment turn into an explosive. They were in the plight of a man building a house with dynamite for mortar, for credit can be compared with nothing else.

"If you would see how needless were these convulsions of business which I have been speaking of, and how entirely they resulted from leaving industry to private and unorganized management, just consider the working of our system. Over-production in special lines, which was the great hobgoblin of your day, is impossible now, for by the connection between distribution and production supply is geared to demand like an engine to the governor which regulates its speed.

"Even suppose by an error of judgment an excessive production of some commodity. The consequent slackening or cessation of production in that line throws nobody out of employment. The suspended workers are at once found occupation in some other department of the vast workshop and lose only the time spent in changing, while, as for the glut, the business of the nation is large enough to carry any amount of product manufactured in excess of demand till the latter overtakes it. In such a case of over-production, as I have supposed, there is not with us, as with you, any complex machinery to get out of order and magnify a thousand times the original mistake. Of course, having not even money, we still less have credit. All estimates deal directly with the real things, the flour, iron, wood, wool, and labor, of which money and credit were for you the very misleading representatives. In our calculations of cost there can be no mistakes. Out of the annual product the amount necessary for the support of the people is taken, and the requisite labor to produce the next year's consumption provided for. The residue of the material and labor represents what can be safely expended in improvements. If the crops are bad, the surplus for that year is less than usual, that is all. Except for slight occasional effects of such natural causes, there are no fluctuations of business; the material prosperity of the nation flows on uninterruptedly from generation to generation, like an ever broadening and deepening river.

"Your business crises, Mr. West," continued the doctor, "like either of the great wastes I mentioned before, were enough, alone, to have kept your noses to the grindstone forever; but I have still to speak of one other great cause of your poverty, and that was the idleness of a great part of your capital and labor. With us it is the business of the administration to keep in constant employment every ounce of available capital and labor in the country. In your day there was no general control of either capital or labor, and a large part of both failed to find employment. 'Capital,' you used to say, 'is naturally timid,' and it would certainly have been reckless if it had not been timid in an epoch when there was a large preponderance of probability that any particular business venture would end in failure. There was no time when, if security could have been guaranteed it, the amount of capital devoted to productive industry could not have been greatly increased. The proportion of it so employed underwent constant extraordinary fluctuations, according to the greater or less feeling of uncertainty as to the stability of the industrial situation, so that the output of the national industries greatly varied in different years. But for the same reason that the amount of capital employed at times of special insecurity was far less than at times of somewhat greater security, a very large proportion was never employed at all, because the hazard of business was always very great in the best of times.

"It should be also noted that the great amount of capital always seeking employment where tolerable safety could be insured terribly embittered the competition between capitalists when a promising opening presented itself. The idleness of capital, the result of its timidity, of course meant the idleness of labor in corresponding degree. Moreover, every change in the adjustments of business, every slightest alteration in the condition of commerce or manufactures, not to speak of the innumerable business failures that took place yearly, even in the best of times, were constantly throwing a multitude of men out of employment for periods of weeks or months, or even years. A great number of these seekers after employment were constantly traversing the country, becoming in time professional vagabonds, then criminals. 'Give us work!' was the cry of an army of the unemployed at nearly all seasons, and in seasons of dullness in business this army swelled to a host so vast and desperate as to threaten the stability of the government. Could there conceivably be a more conclusive demonstration of the imbecility of the system of private enterprise as a method for enriching a nation than the fact that, in an age of such general poverty and want of everything, capitalists had to throttle one another to find a safe chance to invest their capital and workmen rioted and burned because they could find no work to do?

"Now, Mr. West," continued Dr. Leete, "I want you to bear in mind that these points of which I have been speaking indicate only negatively the advantages of the national organization of industry by showing certain fatal defects and prodigious imbecilities of the systems of private enterprise which are not found in it. These alone, you must admit, would pretty well explain why the nation is so much richer than in your day. But the larger half of our advantage over you, the positive side of it, I have yet barely spoken of. Supposing the system of private enterprise in industry were without any of the great leaks I have mentioned; that there were no waste on account of misdirected effort growing out of mistakes as to the demand, and inability to command a general view of the industrial field. Suppose, also, there were no neutralizing and duplicating of effort from competition. Suppose, also, there were no waste from business panics and crises through bankruptcy and long interruptions of industry, and also none from the idleness of capital and labor. Supposing these evils, which are essential to the conduct of industry by capital in private hands, could

all be miraculously prevented, and the system yet retained; even then the superiority of the results attained by the modern industrial system of national control would remain overwhelming.

"You used to have some pretty large textile manufacturing establishments, even in your day, although not comparable with ours. No doubt you have visited these great mills in your time, covering acres of ground, employing thousands of hands, and combining under one roof, under one control, the hundred distinct processes between, say, the cotton bale and the bale of glossy calicoes. You have admired the vast economy of labor as of mechanical force resulting from the perfect interworking with the rest of every wheel and every hand. No doubt you have reflected how much less the same force of workers employed in that factory would accomplish if they were scattered, each man working independently. Would you think it an exaggeration to say that the utmost product of those workers, working thus apart, however amicable their relations might be, was increased not merely by a percentage, but many fold, when their efforts were organized under one control? Well now, Mr. West, the organization of the industry of the nation under a single control, so that all its processes interlock, has multiplied the total product over the utmost that could be done under the former system, even leaving out of account the four great wastes mentioned, in the same proportion that the product of those mill-workers was increased by coöperation. The effectiveness of the working force of a nation, under the myriad-headed leadership of private capital, even if the leaders were not mutual enemies, as compared with that which it attains under a single head, may be likened to the military efficiency of a mob, or a horde of barbarians with a thousand petty chiefs, as compared with that of a disciplined army under one general— such a fighting machine, for example, as the German army in the time of Von Moltke."

"After what you have told me," I said, "I do not so much wonder that the nation is richer now than then, but that you are not all Croesuses."

"Well," replied Dr. Leete, "we are pretty well off. The rate at which we live is as luxurious as we could wish. The rivalry of ostentation, which in your day led to extravagance in no way conducive to comfort, finds no place, of course, in a society of people absolutely equal in resources, and our ambition stops at the surroundings which minister to the enjoyment of life. We might, indeed, have much larger incomes, individually, if we chose so to use the surplus of our product, but we prefer to expend it upon public works and pleasures in which all share, upon public halls and buildings, art galleries, bridges, statuary, means of transit, and the conveniences of our cities, great musical and theatrical exhibitions, and in providing on a vast scale for the recreations of the people. You have not begun to see how we live yet, Mr. West. At home we have comfort, but the splendor of our life is, on its social side, that which we share with our fellows. When you know more of it you will see where the money goes, as you

used to say, and I think you will agree that we do well so to expend it.

"I suppose," observed Dr. Leete, as we strolled homeward from the dining-hall, "that no reflection would have cut the men of your wealth-worshiping century more keenly than the suggestion that they did not know how to make money. Nevertheless, that is just the verdict history has passed on them. Their system of unorganized and antagonistic industries was as absurd economically as it was morally abominable. Selfishness was their only science, and in industrial production selfishness is suicide. Competition, which is the instinct of selfishness, is another word for dissipation of energy, while combination is the secret of efficient production; and not till the idea of increasing the individual hoard gives place to the idea of increasing the common stock can industrial combination be realized, and the acquisition of wealth really begin. Even if the principle of share and share alike for all men were not the only humane and rational basis for a society, we should still enforce it as economically expedient, seeing that until the disintegrating influence of self-seeking is suppressed no true concert of industry is possible." . . .

5. WEALTH AGAINST COMMONWEALTH[1]

By HENRY DEMAREST LLOYD

CHAPTER I
"THERE ARE NONE"—"THEY ARE LEGION"

Nature is rich; but everywhere man, the heir of nature, is poor. Never in this happy country or elsewhere—except in the Land of Miracle, where "they did all eat and were filled"—has there been enough of anything for the people. Never

since time began have all the sons and daughters of men been all warm, and all filled, and all shod and roofed. Never yet have all the virgins, wise or foolish, been able to fill their lamps with oil.

The world, enriched by thousands of generations of toilers and thinkers, has reached a fertility which can give every human being a plenty undreamed of even in the Utopias. But between this plenty ripening on the boughs of our civilization and the people hungering for it step the "cornerers," the syndicates, trusts, combinations, with the cry of "over-produc-

1. Henry Demarest Lloyd, *Wealth against Commonwealth* (New York, 1894), pp. 1–2, 6–8, 199–211, 494–97, 506–7, 510, 514–21, 523, 526–27, 532–33, 535–36. By permission of Harper and Brothers, publishers.

tion"—too much of everything. Holding back the riches of earth, sea, and sky from their fellows who famish and freeze in the dark, they declare to them that there is too much light and warmth and food. They assert the right, for their private profit, to regulate the consumption by the people of the necessaries of life, and to control production, not by the needs of humanity, but by the desires of a few for dividends. The coal syndicate thinks there is too much coal. There is too much iron, too much lumber, too much flour—for this or that syndicate.

The majority have never been able to buy enough of anything; but this minority have too much of everything to sell.

Liberty produces wealth, and wealth destroys liberty. "The splendid empire of Charles V," says Motley, "was erected upon the grave of liberty." Our bignesses, cities, factories, monopolies, fortunes, which are our empires, are the obesities of an age gluttonous beyond its powers of digestion. Mankind are crowding upon each other in the centres, and struggling to keep each other out of the feast set by the new sciences and the new fellowships. Our size has got beyond both our science and our conscience. The vision of the railroad stockholder is not far-sighted enough to see into the office of the General Manager; the people cannot reach across even a ward of a city to rule their rulers; Captains of Industry "do not know" whether the men in the ranks are dying from lack of food and shelter; we cannot clean our cities nor our politics; the locomotive has more man-power than all the ballot-boxes, and mill-wheels wear out the hearts of workers unable to keep up beating time to their whirl. If mankind had gone on pursuing the ideals of the fighter, the time would necessarily have come when there would have been only a few, then only one, and then none left. This is what we are witnessing in the world of livelihoods. Our ideals of livilihood are ideals of mutual deglutition. We are rapidly reaching the stage where in each province only a few are left; that is

the key to our times. Beyond the deep is another deep. This era is but a passing phase in the evolution of industrial Caesars, and these Caesars will be of a new type— corporate Caesars. . . .

What we call Monopoly is Business at the end of its journey. The concentration of wealth, the wiping out of the middle classes, are other names for it. To get it is, in the world of affairs, the chief end of man. . . .

To give the full and official history of numbers of these combinations, which are nearly identical in inspiration, method, and result, would be repetition. Only one of them, therefore, has been treated in full—the oil trust. It is the most successful of all the attempts to put gifts of nature, entire industries, and world markets under one hat. Its originators claim this precedence. It was, one of its spokesmen says, "the parent of the trust system." It is the best illustration of a movement which is itself but an illustration of the spirit of the age. . . .

CHAPTER XV
SYMPATHETICAL CO-OPERATION

Some day, perhaps, when more of our story-readers have learned that there are things in the world quite as important as the frets, follies, and loves of boys and girls half-grown, more of our story-tellers will hold their magic mirror up to the full-pulsed life with which mankind throbs through the laboring years that stretch along after the short fever of mating is over. George Rice, coming from the Green Mountains of Vermont, entered the oil business twenty-nine years ago, when he and it were young. He was one of the first comers. Beginning as a producer in the Pithole region, in the days of its evanescent glory, in 1865, he prospered. Escaping the ruin which overtook those who stayed too long in that too quick sand, he was one of the first to develop the new field at Macksburg, Ohio, and to see the advantages of Marietta, on the Ohio River, as a point for refining. Crude oil could easily be brought from Ohio and Pennsylvania by barge down the Ohio River. The field he entered was unoccupied. He drove no one out, but built a new industry in a new place. In 1876 he had risen to the dignity of manufacturer, and had a refinery of a capacity of 500 barrels a week, and later of 2000 barrels. Owning wells, he produced, himself, a part of the crude which he refined. His position gave him access to all the markets by river and rail. Everything promised him fortune. His family took hold with him in the work of breadwinning. "The executive part of the business is done altogether by my family," he says. "One daughter keeps the books, another daughter does nine-tenths of the correspondence, and my son-in-law is the general manager." One of the daughters was a witness in one of her father's cases before the Interstate Commerce Commission. "She discussed with counsel," said the New York *World*, "the knotty points involving tank-car rates, mileage, rebates, and the long and short haul as familiarly as any general freight agent present."

Several other refiners, seeing the advantages of Marietta, had settled there. They who elected themselves to be trustees of the light of the world, thus having the advantages of the place pointed out to them by practical men, determined that Marietta must be theirs. They bought up some of the refiners. Then they stopped buying. Their representative there, afterwards a member of the trust, "told me distinctly that he had bought certain refineries in Marietta, but that he would not buy any more. . . . He had another way," he said, "of getting rid of them." Of these "other ways" the independents were now to have a full exposition. In January, 1879, freight rates on oil were suddenly and without previous notice raised by the railroads leading out of Marietta, and by their connections. Some of the rates were doubled. The increase was only on oil. It was—in Ohio—only on oil shipped from Marietta; it was exacted only from the

few refiners who had not been bought, because there were "other ways of getting rid of them."

This freight-tariff attack on the independent refiners was arranged by their powerful rival and the railroad managers at a secret conference, as the latter admitted.

"Did you have any consultation or invite consultation with other manufacturers of oil at Marietta?"

"No, sir."

When the representatives of the combination in this market were taxed by a dealer with getting the benefit of this manipulation of freight, "they laughed." All the railroads took part in the surprise. Curiously enough, the minds of the managers of a dozen roads acted simultaneously and identically, over thousands of miles of country—some, as they admitted, with suggestion, and some, as they testified, without suggestion—upon so precise a detail of their business as the rates on oil at one little point. "I did it at my own instance," said the freight agent of the Baltimore and Ohio. Freight officials of railways as far apart east, west, and south, and in interest, as the Baltimore and Ohio, and the Pennsylvania, and the Lake Shore, which had no direct connection with Marietta, and reached it only over other lines, stopped their "wars" to play their part in the move by raising the rate on oil only, and, most remarkable of all, to a figure at which neither they, nor the railroad connecting them with Marietta, nor (and this was the game they were gunning for) the independent refiners could do any business. From other points than Marietta, as Cleveland, Parkersburg, Pittsburgh, and Wheeling, where the combination had refineries, but the Marietta independents had none, the railroads left the former rates unchanged.

Rice was "got rid of" at Columbus just as effectually as if Ruskin's "Money-bag Baron," successor of "the Crag Baron," stood across the road with a blunderbuss. His successful rival had but to let its

Marietta refineries lie idle, and transfer to its refineries at Wheeling its Marietta business—and Rice's too. By the pooling of the earnings and of the control of all its refineries—the essential features of the combination—its business could be transferred from one point to another without loss. One locality or another could be subjected to ruinous conditions for the extermination of competitors, and the combination, no matter how large its works there, would prosper without check. It gets the same profit as before, but the competitor by its side is ruined. All its refineries along a given railroad can be closed by high rates made to "overcome competition," but profits do not cease. Their business is done elsewhere by its other refineries, and all the profits go into a pool for the common benefit.

From Rice's point of view, Marietta was the storm-centre; but the evidence before the Ohio Legislative Investigation of 1879, before the Legislative Committee of New York of 1879, before Master in Chancery Sweitzer in Pennsylvania, and in the suit against the Lake Shore Railroad, showed that the low barometer there was part of a disturbance covering a wide area. The demonstration against the independent refiners of Marietta was only part of a wider web-spinning, in which those at all points—New York, Boston, Philadelphia, Pittsburgh, Oil City, Titusville, Buffalo, Rochester, and Cleveland—were to be forced to "come in" as dependents, or sell out, as most of them did.

That rates were not raised from points controlled by the combination is only part of the truth. At such places rates were lowered. This, like the increase of rates, was done at a secret conference with the oil combination and at its instance. Where it had refineries the rates were to be low; the high rates were for points where it had competitors to be got rid of without the expense of buying them up. The independents knew nothing of the increase of freights prepared for them by the railroad managers and their great competitor until

after, some time after, it had gone into effect.

The railroad company gave notice to their rivals what the rates were to be, but withheld that information from them. That was not all. Before the new rates were given all the old rates were cancelled. "For a few days," said an independent, "we could not obtain any rates at all. We had orders from our customers, but could not obtain any rates of freight."

As to many places the withholding of rates continued.

"There's many places we can't obtain any rates to. They just say we sha'n't ship to these other places at any price."

When the Ohio Legislature undertook to investigate, it found that the railroad men professed a higher allegiance to their corporations than to the State. They refused to answer the questions of the committee, or evaded them. "I am working under orders from the general freight agent," said one of them, "and I don't feel authorized to answer that." The arguments of the committee that the orders of an employer could not supersede the duty of a citizen to his government, or the obligations of his oath as a witness, were wasted. "I will tell you just how I feel," said the witness to these representatives of an inferior power. "I am connected with the railroad company, and get my instructions from the general agent, and I am very careful about telling anybody else anything." The Legislature accepted the rank of "anybody else" to which it was assigned, and did not compel the witness to answer.

To a question about the increase in freight: "I object," said another railroad officer, "to going into details about my own private business."

One peculiar thing about the action of the railroads was that it was an injury to themselves. The Baltimore and Ohio, for instance, by raising its rate, cut off its oil business with Marietta entirely. "What advantage is it, then?" the freight agent of the road over which the Baltimore and Ohio reached Marietta was asked.

"There is no advantage. . . . We had revenue before this increase in rates, and none since."

"What would be the inducement for her (the Baltimore and Ohio) to do it, then?"

"That is a matter I am not competent to answer."

The railroad men testified positively that the increase affected all alike at Marietta. It was supposed even by those who thought they saw to the bottom of the manoeuvre that the combination would close its Marietta works temporarily, in order to seem to be equally affected with all the rest. It could do this with no loss whatever, since, as explained, no raise in rates had been made from Wheeling, Parkersburg, Pittsburgh, Cleveland, where it was practically alone, and it could reach all its customers from those places as well as from Marietta. But the combination kept on filling orders from its refineries at Marietta at the old freight rates, while by its side the men it was hunting down sat idle because the discriminating rates of freight made it impossible for them to use the highways. It was so careless of appearances that oil ordered of its works at Parkersburg would be sent from the Marietta branch, and at the old rate of 40 cents, while the other refineries could not ship because the rate to them was 65 cents; the increase at Marietta was not enforced against it, but only against the three independents—just as planned in the South Improvement scheme.

The move was far-reaching—as far as Chicago, the rate to which was made $1.20 a barrel, instead of 90 cents a barrel.

"Then they cut you off from the Western trade as well as this State?"

"Yes, sir; almost entirely. . . . I was selling in Chicago, and it cut trade entirely off."

"Before the rates were changed did you run to your full capacity?"

"Yes, sir; about that."

At one stroke the independents lost the business which it had cost them years of work to get. As the testimony of witness after witness showed, the merchants who had been their customers in Chicago, Columbus, and other places, now had to send their orders to those for whose benefit the railroad men had raised the rates. This sweeping change was not due to any change in their desire to sell, or of their old customers to buy. They could still make oil which was still wanted. But they were the victims of a competitor who had learned the secret of a more royal road to business supremacy than making a better thing, or selling it at a better price. Their better way was not to excel but to exclude. When their "secretary" was called before the Ohio Legislature, after this freight ambuscade had transferred the bulk of the business of the independent refineries at Marietta to him and his associates, he declared that the sole cause of their success was the "large mechanical contrivances" of the combination, its "economy," and its production of the "very best oil." "With an aggregation of capital, and a business experience, and a hold upon the channels of trade such as we have, it is idle to say that the small manufacturer can compete with us; and although that is an offensive term, 'squeezing out,' yet it has never been done by the conjunction of any railroads with us."

The small manufacturer did compete and flourish until these railroad men literally switched him out of the market. He competed and got his share of the business, until the men who wanted monopoly, finding that they had no monopoly of quality or price or business ability, resorted to the "large mechanical contrivance" of inducing the managers of the railroads to derail the independent, throwing him off the track by piling impassable freight tariffs in his way. The successful men secured their supremacy by preventing their competitors from entering the market at all. Instead of winning by "better" and "cheaper," they won by preventing any competitor from coming forward to test the questions of "better" and "cheaper." Their method of demonstrating superiority has been to prevent comparisons.

All the independent refiners at Marietta, except Rice, died. "Most of those we received from have gone out of the business," a Cincinnati dealer told the Legislature. Some had fled; some had sold out. Rice set himself to do two things: the first, to drag into the light of day and the public view the secrets of these "better methods"; and the second, to get new business in the place of what he had lost. He succeeded in both. It was in January that he had notice served upon him that he could no longer go to market. In two months he had the Ohio Legislature at work investigating this extraordinary administration of the highways. This was a great public service. It did not yield the fruit of immediate reform, but it did work which is the indispensable preliminary. It roused the people who were still asleep on these new issues, and were dreaming pleasant dreams that in George III they had escaped from all tyrants forever, and that in the emancipation of the blacks they had freed all slaves forever.

Rice knew that the Legislature were planting trees for posterity, and did not wait for help from them. He set about looking up markets where the public were free to choose and buy. He could not go West or East or North. He went South. The little family kept the refinery at Marietta running, and the father travelled about establishing new agencies in the South, and studying freight tariffs, railroad routes, and terminal facilities for loading and unloading and storing. In 1880, through all the storm and stress of these days, he was able to double the capacity of his refinery. Again he succeeded in building up a livelihood, and again his success was treated as trespass and invasion. His bitter experience in Ohio in 1879 proved to be but an apprenticeship for a still sterner struggle. Rice was getting most of his crude oil from Pennsylvania, through a little pipe line which brought it to the Alleghany. The pipe line was taken up by the oil trust.

This compelled him to turn to the Macksburg, Ohio, field for most of his petroleum. He had one tank-car, and he ran this back and forth faster than ever. Then came the next blow. The railroad over which he ran his tank-car doubled his freight to 35 cents a barrel, from 17½. That was not all. The same railroad brought oil to the combination's Marietta refineries at 10 cents a barrel, while they charged him 35. That was not all. The railroad paid over to the combination 25 cents out of every 35 cents he paid for freight. If he had done all the oil business at Marietta, and his rival had put out all its fires and let its works stand empty, it would still have made 25 cents a barrel on the whole output. Rice found a just judge when he took this thing into court. "Abhorrent," "dangerous," "gross," "illegal and inexcusable abuse by a public trust," "an unparalleled wrong," are the terms in which Judge Baxter gave voice to his indignation as he ordered the removal of the receiver of the railroad who had made this arrangement with the combination, to enable it, as the judge said, "to crush Rice and his business."

In an interview, filling four columns of the New York *World* of March 29, 1890, the head of the trust which would receive this rebate is reported to have made this attempt to reverse the facts of this and similar occurrences: "The railroad company proposed to our agent," he said. But the judge who heard all the evidence and rendered the decision, which has never been reversed or impaired, declared that it "compelled" the railroad to make the arrangement, "under a threat of building a pipe line for the conveyance of its oils and withdrawing its patronage." This arrangement was negotiated by the same agent of the oil combination who engineered the similar "transfer" scheme by which the trunk-line railroads gave it, in 1878, 20 to 35 cents a barrel out of the freights paid by its competitors in Pennsylvania, as already told.

"I reluctantly acquiesced," the receiver said, writing in confidence to his lawyer, anxious lest so acquiescing he had made himself legally liable. The interview describes the arrangement as an innocent thing: "A joint agreement for the transportation of oil." It was an agreement to prevent the transportation of oil by anybody else. Judge Baxter shows that it was a joint agreement, procured by threats, for the transportation of "$25 per day, clear money," from Rice's pockets into the pockets of the members of the trust for no service rendered, and without his knowledge or consent, and with the transparent purpose of transporting his business to their own refineries. Judge Baxter called it "discrimination so wanton and oppressive it could hardly have been accepted by an honest man, and a judge who would tolerate such a wrong or retain a receiver capable of perpetrating it, ought to be impeached and degraded from his position."

This matter was also passed upon by the Select Committee of the United States Senate on Interstate Commerce. "No comment," the committee say, "is needed upon this most impudent and outrageous proposition"—by the oil company to the railroad.

"Are you going to deny that story?" a great American statesman of the latter-day type was asked by one of his friends.

"Not I," was the reply. "The story's false. When you find me taking the trouble to deny a thing, you can bet it's true!"

This "agreement for the transportation of oil" had its calculated effect. It put a stop to the transportation of oil from the Ohio field by Rice over the railroad, just as the destruction by the same hands of the pipe line to the Alleghany had cut him off from access to the Pennsylvania oil-fields. He then built his own pipe line to the Ohio field. To lay this pipe it was necessary to cross the pipe line of his great rival. Rice had the pluck to do this without asking for a consent which would never have been given. His intrepidity carried its point; for, as he foresaw, they dared not cut his pipe for fear of reprisals.

In turning to the South, after his expulsion from the Ohio and Western markets, the Marietta independent did but get out of one hornet's nest to sit down in another. His opponent was selling its oil there through a representative who, as he afterwards told Congress, "was very fortunate in competing." He thought it was "cheaper in the long-run to make the price cheap and be done with it, than to fritter away the time with a competitor in a little competition. I put the price down to the bone." Rice, in the South, ran into the embrace of this gentleman who had the "exclusive control" of that territory, and whose method of calling the attention of trespassers to his right was to cut them "to the bone." The people and the dealers everywhere in the South were glad to see Rice. He found a deep discontent among consumers and merchants alike. They perhaps felt more clearly than they knew that business feudalism was not better, but worse, because newer, than military feudalism. This representative of the combination assured Congress that "99.9 of all the first-class merchants of the South were in close sympathetical co-operation with us in our whole history"—that is, out of every hundred "first-class merchants" only one-tenth of one merchant was not with them. This is a picturesque percentage.

Rice's welcome among the people would not verify his opponent's estimate that his vassalage included all but one-tenth of one dealer in every hundred. From all parts came word of the anxiety of the merchants to escape from the power that held them fast. From Texas: "Most of our people are anxious to get clear." From Arkansas: "The merchants here would like to buy from some other." From Tennessee: "Can we make any permanent arrangement with you by which we can baffle such monopoly?" From Kentucky: "I dislike to submit to the unreasonable and arbitrary commands." From Mississippi: "It has gouged the people to such an extent that we wish to break it down and introduce some other oils." From Georgia, from different dealers: "They have the oil-dealers in this State so completely cooped in that they cannot move." "We are afraid." As Rice went about the South selling oil the agents of the cutter "to the bone" would follow, and by threats, like those revealed in the correspondence described below, would coerce the dealers to repudiate their purchases. Telegrams would pour into the discouraged office at Marietta: "Don't ship oil ordered from your agent." "We hereby countermand orders given your agent yesterday." One telegram would often be signed by all the dealers in a town, though competitors, sometimes nearly a dozen of them, showing that they were united by some outside influence they had to obey.

Where the dealers were found too independent to accept dictation, belligerent and tactical cuts in price were proclaimed, not to make oil cheap, but to prevent its becoming permanently cheaper through free competition and an open market. Rice submitted to Congress letters covering pages of the Trust Report, showing how he had been tracked through Tennessee, Missouri, Nebraska, Georgia, Kansas, Kentucky, Iowa, Mississippi, Louisiana, Texas, Arkansas, Alabama. The railroads had been got to sidetrack and delay his cars, and the dealers terrorized into refusing to buy his oils, although they were cheaper. If the merchants in any place persisted in buying his oil they were undersold until they surrendered. When Rice was driven out prices were put back. So close was the watch kept of the battle by the generals of "co-operation" that when one of his agents got out of oil for a day or two, prices would be run up to bleed the public during the temporary opportunity. "On the strength of my not having any oil to-day," wrote one of Rice's dealers, "I am told they have popped up the price 3½ cents."

The railroad officials did their best to make it true that "the poor ye have with you always." By mistake some oil meant for the combination was delivered to Rice's agent, and he discovered that it was paying only 88 cents a barrel, while he was charged $1.68, a difference of 80 cents a barrel for a distance of sixty-eight miles.

"Could you stand such competition as that?"

"No, sir. Before that I went up there and sold to every man in the place nearly. They were glad to see me in opposition. . . . I lost them, except one man who was so prejudiced that he would not buy from them."

"Your business had been on the increase up to that time?"

"Increasing rapidly. . . . I haul it in wagons now forty miles south of Manito."

"The rates against you on that railroad are so high that you can for a distance of forty miles transport your oil by wagon and meet the competition better than you can by using their own road?"

"Infinitely better."

Chapter XXXIV
THE OLD SELF-INTEREST

The corn of the coming harvest is growing so fast that, like the farmer standing at night in his fields, we can hear it snap and crackle. We have been fighting fire on the well-worn lines of old-fashioned politics and political economy, regulating corporations, and leaving competition to regulate itself. But the flames of a new economic evolution run around us, and we turn to find that competition has killed competition, that corporations are grown greater than the State and have bred individuals greater than themselves, and that the naked issue of our time is with property becoming master instead of servant, property in many necessaries of life becoming monopoly of the necessaries of life.

We are still, in part, as Emerson says, in the quadruped state. Our industry is a fight of every man for himself. The prize we give the fittest is monopoly of the necessaries of life, and we leave these winners of the powers of life and death to wield them over us by the same "self-interest" with which they took them from us. In all this we see at work a "principle" which will go into the records as one of the historic mistakes of humanity. Institutions stand or fall by their philosophy, and the main doctrine of industry since Adam Smith has been the fallacy that the self-interest of the individual was a sufficient guide to the welfare of the individual and society. Heralded as a final truth of "science" this proves to have been nothing higher than a temporary formula for a passing problem. It was a reflection in words of the policy of the day. . . .

"It is a law of business for each proprietor to pursue his own interest," said the committee of Congress which in 1893 investigated the coal combinations. "There is no hope for any of us, but the weakest must go first," is the golden rule of business. There is no other field of human associations in which any such rule of action is allowed. The man who should apply in his family or his citizenship this "survival of the fittest" theory as it is practically professed and operated in business would be a monster, and would be speedily made extinct, as we do with monsters. To divide the supply of food between himself and his children according to their relative powers of calculation, to follow his conception of his own self-interest in any matter which the self-interest of all has taken charge of, to deal as he thinks best for himself with foreigners with whom his country is at war, would be a short road to the penitentiary or the gallows. In trade men have not yet risen to the level of the family life of the animals. The true law of business is that all must pursue the interest of all. In the law, the highest product of civilization, this has long been a commonplace. The safety of the people is the supreme law. We are in travail to bring industry up to this. Our century of the caprice of the individual as the lawgiver of the common toil, to employ or disemploy, to start or stop, to open or close, to com-

pete or combine, has been the disorder of the school while the master slept. The happiness, self-interest, or individuality of the whole is not more sacred than that of each, but it is greater. They are equal in quality, but in quantity they are greater. In the ultimate which the mathematician, the poet, the reformer projects the two will coincide.

Our world, operated by individual motive, is the country of the Chinese fable, in which the inhabitants went on one leg. Yes, but an "enlightened self-interest"? The perfect self-interest of the perfect individual is an admirable conception, but it is still individual, and the world is social. The music of the spheres is not to be played on one string. Nature does nothing individually. All forces are paired like the sexes, and every particle of matter in the universe has to obey every other particle. When the individual has progressed to a perfect self-interest, there will be over against it, acting and reacting with it, a correspondingly perfect self-interest of the community. Meanwhile, we who are the creators of society have got the times out of joint, because, less experienced than the Creator of the balanced matter of earth, we have given the precedence to the powers on one side. As gods we are but half-grown. For a hundred years or so our economic theory has been one of industrial government by the self-interest of the individual. Political government by the self-interest of the individual we call anarchy. It is one of the paradoxes of public opinion that the people of America, least tolerant of this theory of anarchy in political government, lead in practising it in industry. Politically, we are civilized; industrially, not yet. Our century, given to this *laissez-faire*—"leave the individual alone; he will do what is best for himself, and what is best for him is best for all"—has done one good: it has put society at the mercy of its own ideals, and has produced an actual anarchy in industry which is horrifying us into a change of doctrines.

We have not been able to see the people

for the persons in it. But there is a people, and it is as different from a mere juxtaposition of persons as a globe of glass from the handful of sand out of which it was melted. It is becoming, socially, known to itself, with that self-consciousness which distinguishes the quick from the dead and the unborn. Every community, said Pascal, is a man, and every man, said Plato, is a community. There is a new self-interest—that of the "man called million," as Mazzini named him—and with this social motive the other, which has so long had its own way, has now to reckon. Mankind has gone astray following a truth seen only partially, but coronated as a whole truth. Many civilizations must worship good men as gods and follow the divinity of one and another before civilization sees that these are only single stars in a firmament of humanity. Our civilization has followed the self-interest of the individual to learn that it was but one of the complex forces of self-interest.

The true *laissez-faire* is, let the individual do what the individual can do best, and let the community do what the community can do best. The *laissez-faire* of social self-interest, if true, cannot conflict with the individual self-interest, if true, but it must outrank it always. What we have called "free competition" has not been free, only freer than what went before. The free is still to come. The pressure we feel is notice to prepare for it. Civilization—the process of making men citizens in their relations to each other, by exacting of each that he give to all that which he receives from all—has reached only those forms of common effort which, because most general and most vital, first demanded its harmonizing touch. Men joining in the labors of the family, the mutual sacrifices of the club or the church in the union of forces for self-defence and for the gains of co-operation on the largest scale in labors of universal concern, like letter-carrying, have come to be so far civilized. . . .

. . . The individual and society will always be wrestling with each other in a composition of forces. But to just the extent to which civilization prevails, society will be held as inviolable as the individual; not subordinate—indeed inaudible—as now in the counting-room and corporation office. We have overworked the self-interest of the individual. The line of conflict between individual and social is a progressive one of the discovery of point after point in which the two are identical. Society thus passes from conflict to harmony, and on to another conflict. Civilization is the unceasing accretion of these social solutions. We fight out to an equilibrium, as in the abolition of human slavery; then upon this new level thus built up we enter upon the struggle for a new equilibrium, as now in the labor movement. The man for himself destroys himself and all men; only society can foster him and them.

The greatest happiness of the greatest number is only the doctrine of self-interest writ large and made more dangerous by multitude. It is the self-interest of the majority, and this has written some of the unloveliest chapters of history. There have never been slaves more miserable than those of Sparta, where the State was the owner. American democracy prepares to repeat these distresses of the selfishness of the many, and gives notice to its railway employés of a new divine right—"the convenience of the public"—to which they must forego every right of manhood. No better definition of slave could be found than one who must work at the convenience of another. This is the position into which recent legal decisions and acts of the Federal executive force railway men. These speak in the name of Interstate Commerce, but their logic can be as easily applied by State judges to State commerce, and all working-men are manifestly as necessary, each in his function, to the convenience of the public as the men of the rail. The greatest happiness of all must be the formula. When Lamennais said, "I love my family more than myself, my village more than my family, my country more than my village, and mankind more than my country," he showed himself not only a good lover, but the only good arithmetician. . . .

If our civilization is destroyed, as Macaulay predicted, it will not be by his barbarians from below. Our barbarians come from above. Our great money-makers have sprung in one generation into seats of power kings do not know. The forces and the wealth are new, and have been the opportunity of new men. Without restraints of culture, experience, the pride, or even the inherited caution of class or rank, these men, intoxicated, think they are the wave instead of the float, and that they have created the business which has created them. To them science is but a never-ending répertoire of investments stored up by nature for the syndicates, government but a fountain of franchises, the nations but customers in squads, and a million the unit of a new arithmetic of wealth written for them. They claim a power without control, exercised through forms which make it secret, anonymous, and perpetual. The possibilities of its gratification have been widening before them without interruption since they began, and even at a thousand millions they will feel no satiation and will see no place to stop. They are gluttons of luxury and power, rough, unsocialized, believing that mankind must be kept terrorized. Powers of pity die out of them, because they work through agents and die in their agents, because what they do is not for themselves. . . .

Two social energies have been in conflict, and the energy of reform has so far proved the weaker. We have chartered the self-interest of the individual as the rightful sovereign of conduct; we have taught that the scramble for profit is the best method of administering the riches of earth and the exchange of services. Only those can attack this system who attack its central principle, that strength gives the strong in the market the right to destroy his neighbor. Only as we have denied

that right to the strong elsewhere have we made ourselves as civilized as we are. And we cannot make a change as long as our songs, customs, catchwords, and public opinions tell all to do the same thing if they can. Society, in each person of its multitudes, must recognize that the same principles of the interest of all being the rule of all, of the strong serving the weak, of the first being the last—"I am among you as one that serves"—which have given us the home where the weakest is the one surest of his rights and of the fullest service of the strongest, and have given us the republic in which all join their labor that the poorest may be fed, the weakest defended, and all educated and prospered, must be applied where men associate in common toil as wherever they associate. Not until then can the forces be reversed which generate those obnoxious persons—our fittest.

Our system, so fair in its theory and so fertile in its happiness and prosperity in its first century, is now, following the fate of systems, becoming artificial, technical, corrupt; and, as always happens in human institutions, after noon, power is stealing from the many to the few. Believing wealth to be good, the people believed the wealthy to be good. But, again in history, power has intoxicated and hardened its possessors, and Pharaohs are bred in counting-rooms as they were in palaces. Their furniture must be banished to the world-garret, where lie the outworn trappings of the guilds and slavery and other old lumber of human institutions.

CHAPTER XXXV

AND THE NEW

. . . Thousands of years' experience has proved that government must begin where it ends—with the people; that the general welfare demands that they who exercise the powers and they upon whom these are exercised must be the same, and that higher political ideals can be realized only through higher political forms. Myriads of experiments to get the substance of liberty out of the forms of tyranny, to believe in princes, to trust good men to do good as kings, have taught the inexorable truth that, in the economy of nature, form and substance must move together, and are as inextricably interdependent as are, within our experience, what we call matter and spirit. Identical is the lesson we are learning with regard to industrial power and property. We are calling upon their owners, as mankind called upon kings in their day, to be good and kind, wise and sweet, and we are calling in vain. We are asking them not to be what we have made them to be. We put power into their hands and ask them not to use it as power. If this power is a trust for the people, the people betrayed it when they made private estates out of it for individuals. If the spirit of power is to change, institutions must change as much. Liberty recast the old forms of government into the Republic, and it must remould our institutions of wealth into the Commonwealth.

The question is not whether monopoly is to continue. The sun sets every night on a greater majority against it. We are face to face with the practical issue: Is it to go through ruin or reform? Can we forestall ruin by reform? If we wait to be forced by events we shall be astounded to find how much more radical they are than our utopias. Louis XVI waited until 1793, and gave his head and all his investitures to the people who in 1789 asked only to sit at his feet and speak their mind. Unless we reform of our own free will, nature will reform us by force, as nature does. Our evil courses have already gone too far in producing misery, plagues, hatreds, national enervation. Already the leader is unable to lead, and has begun to drive with judges armed with bayonets and Gatling guns. History is the serial obituary of the men who thought they could drive men. . . .

Industry and monopoly cannot live together. Our modern perfection of exchange and division of labor cannot last without equal perfection of morals and sympathy. Everyone is living at the mercy of everyone else in a way entirely peculiar to our times. Nothing is any longer made by a man; parts of things are made by parts of men, and become wholes by the luck of a good-humor which so far keeps men from flying asunder. It takes a whole company to make a match. A hundred men will easily produce a hundred million matches, but not one of them could make one match. . . .

Liberty and monopoly cannot live together. What chance have we against the persistent coming and the easy coalescence of the confederated cliques, which aspire to say of all business, "This belongs to us," and whose members, though moving among us as brothers, are using against us, through the corporate forms we have given them, powers of invisibility, of entail and accumulation, unprecedented because impersonal and immortal, and, most peculiar of all, power to act as persons, as in the commission of crimes, with exemption from punishment as persons? Two classes study and practice politics and government: place hunters and privilege hunters. In a world of relativities like ours size of area has a great deal to do with the truth of principles. America has grown so big—and the tickets to be voted, and the powers of government, and the duties of citizens, and the profits of personal use of public functions have all grown so big—that the average citizen has broken down. No man can half understand or half operate the fulness of this big citizenship, except by giving his whole time to it. This the place hunter can do, and the privilege hunter. Government, therefore—municipal, State, national—is passing into the hands of these two classes, specialized for the functions of power by their appetite for the fruits of power. The power of citizenship is relinquished by those who do not and cannot know how to exercise it to those who can and do—by those who have a livelihood to make to those who make politics their livelihood.

These specialists of the ward club, the primary, the campaign, the election, and office unite, by a law as irresistible as that of the sexes, with those who want all the goods of government—charters, contracts, rulings, permits. . . . Certainly such an attempt to corner "the dear people" and the earth and the fulness thereof will break down. It is for us to decide whether we will let it go on till it breaks down of itself, dragging down to die, as a savage dies of his vice, the civilization it has gripped with its hundred hands; or whether, while we are still young, still virtuous, we will break it down, self-consciously, as the civilized man, reforming, crushes down the evil. If we cannot find a remedy, all that we love in the word America must die. It will be an awful price to pay if this attempt at government of the people, by the people, for the people must perish from off the face of the earth to prove to mankind that political brotherhood cannot survive where industrial brotherhood is denied. But the demonstration is worth even that. . . .

. . . [A]s true as that a house divided against itself cannot stand, and that a nation half slave and half free cannot permanently endure, is it true that a people who are slaves to market-tyrants will surely come to be their slaves in all else, that all liberty begins to be lost when one liberty is lost, that a people half democratic and half plutocratic cannot permanently endure.

The secret of the history we are about to make is not that the world is poorer or worse. It is richer and better. Its new wealth is too great for the old forms. The success and beauties of our old mutualities have made us ready for new mutualities. The wonder of to-day is the modern multiplication of products by the union of forces; the marvel of tomorrow will be the greater product which will follow when that which is co-operatively produced is co-operatively enjoyed. It is the spectacle of its concentration in the private fortunes of our day which reveals this wealth to its real makers—the whole people—and summons them to extend the manners and in-

stitutions of civilization to this new tribal relation.

Whether the great change comes with peace or sword, freely through reform or by nature's involuntary forces, is a mere matter of detail, a question of convenience —not of the essence of the thing. The change will come. . . .

The new self-interest will remain unenforced in business until we invent the forms by which the vast multitudes who have been gathered together in modern production can organize themselves into a people there as in government. Nothing but this institutionalization will save them from being scattered away from each other again, and it can be achieved only by such averaging and concessions and co-operations as are the price of all union. These will be gains, not losses. Soldiers become partners in invincibility by the discipline which adopts an average rate of march instead of compelling all to keep step with the fastest and stay with the strongest. Moralists tell men to love each other and the right. How, by doing what things, by leaving what undone, shall men love each other? What have the ethicals to say upon the morality of putting public highways in private hands, and of allowing these private hands to make a private and privileged use of them? If bad, will a mere "change of heart," uninstitutionalized, change them?

New freedoms cannot be operated through the old forms of slavery. The ideals of Washington and Hamilton and Adams could not breathe under kingly rule. Idle to say they might. Under the mutual dependence of the inside and outside of things their change has all through history always been dual. Change of heart is no more redemption than hunger is dinner. We must have honesty, love, justice in the heart of the business world, but for these we must also have the forms which will fit them. These will be very different from those through which the intercourse of man with man in the exchange of services now moves to such ungracious ends. Forms of Asiatic and

American government, of early institutions and to-day's, are not more different. The cardinal virtues cannot be established and kept at work in trade and on the highways with the old apparatus. In order that the spirit that gave rebates may go to stay, the rebate itself must go. If the private use of private ownership of highways is to go, the private ownership must go. There must be no private use of public power or public property. These are created by the common sacrifices of all, and can be rightfully used only for the common good of all—from all, by all, for all. All the grants and franchises that have been given to private hands for private profit are void in morals and void in that higher law which sets the copy for the laggard pens of legislatures and judges. "No private use of public powers" is but a threshold truth. The universe, says Emerson, is the property of every creature in it. . . .

The word of the day is that we are about to civilize industry. Mankind is quivering with its purpose to make men fellow-citizens, brothers, lovers in industry, as it has done with them in government and family, which are also industry. We already have on our shelves the sciences—hygienic, industrial, political, ethical—to free the world almost at a stroke from war, accidents, disease, poverty, and their flowing vices and insanities. The men of these sciences are here at call praying for employment. The people, by the books they read, show themselves to be praying to have them put at work. If we who call ourselves civilization would for one average span devote to life-dealing the moneys, armies, and genius we now give to death-dealing, and would establish over the weaker peoples a protectorate of the United States of Europe and America, we would take a long step towards settling forever the vexed question of the site of the Garden of Eden.

"Human nature," "monotony," and "individuality" are the lions which the reformer is always told will stop the way to a better world. "You cannot change human nature." There are two human natures—the human nature of Christ and of Judas; and Christ prevails. There is the human nature which seeks anonymity, secrecy, the fruits of power without its duties; and there is the human nature which rises against these and, province by province, is abolishing them from human affairs. Men have always been willing to die for their faith. The bad have died as bravely as the good, Charles I with as smooth a front as Sir Harry Vane. In this readiness to die lies folded every loyalty of life.

"You would make the world a dead level of monotony." Good society does not think it monotonous that all its women should at the same time dust the streets with long-tailed gowns, or that its men should meet every night in funereal black and identical cut, but it shrinks from the monotony of having all share in reforms which would equalize surfeit and starvation. "Good society" is still to come, and it will find some better definition of "monotony" than a fair share for all—a better definition of variety than too much for ourselves at the cost of too little for all others. Shall we choose the monotony of sharing with everyone under George III or Alexander II the denial of all right to participate in the supreme power, or shall we choose the monotony of sharing with every fellow-citizen the right to become President?—the monotony of being forbidden to enter all the great livelihoods, some syndicate blocking each way with "This business belongs to us"? Or the monotony of a democracy, where every laborer has equal rights with all other citizens to decide upon the administration of the common toil for the common welfare, and an equal right with every other to rise to be a Captain of Industry? Such are the alternatives of "monotony." We have made an historic choice in one; now for the other.

And "individuality." "You are going to destroy individuality." We can become individual only by submitting to be bound to others. We extend our freedom only by finding new laws to obey. Life outside the law is slavery on as many sides as there are disregarded laws. The locomotive off its tracks is not free. The more relations, ties, duties, the more "individual." The isolated man is the mere rudiment of an individual. But he who has become citizen, neighbor, friend, brother, son, husband, father, fellow-member, in one, is just by so many times individualized. . . .

We must either regulate, or own, or destroy, perishing by the sword we take. The possibility of regulation is a dream. As long as this control of the necessaries of life and this wealth remain private with individuals, it is they who will regulate, not we. The policy of regulation, disguise it as we may, is but moving to a compromise and equilibrium within the evil all complain of. It is to accept the principle of the sovereignty of the self-interest of the individual and apply constitutional checks to it. The unprogressive nations palter in this method with monarchy. But the wits of America are equal to seeing that as with kingship and slavery so with poverty—the weeding must be done at the roots. . . .

There is to be a people in industry, as in government. The same rising genius of democracy which discovered that mankind did not co-operate in the State to provide a few with palaces and king's-evil, is disclosing that men do not co-operate in trade for any other purpose than to mobilize the labor of all for the benefit of all, and that the only true guidance comes from those who are led, and the only valid titles from those who create. Very wide must be the emancipation of this new self-interest. If we free America we shall still be not free, for the financial, commercial, possessory powers of modern industrial life are organized internationally. If we rose to the full execution of the first, simplest, and most pressing need of our times and put an end to all private use of public powers, we should still be confronted by monopolies existing simply as private property, as in coal-mines, oil lands.

It is not a verbal accident that science is the substance of the word conscience. We must know the right before we can do the right. When it comes to know the facts the human heart can no more endure monopoly than American slavery or Roman empire. The first step to a remedy is that the people care. If they know, they will care. To help them to know and care; to stimulate new hatred of evil, new love of the good, new sympathy for the victims of power, and, by enlarging its science, to quicken the old into a new conscience, this compilation of fact has been made. Democracy is not a lie. There live in the body of the commonalty the unexhausted virtue and the ever-refreshened strength which can rise equal to any problems of progress. . . .

6. THE BUGABOO OF TRUSTS[1]

By ANDREW CARNEGIE

EDITORS' NOTE.—Andrew Carnegie (1835–1919) typified the great American dream of rags to riches through opportunity, ability, and hard work. The development of machine looms ruined his father's trade as a damask

1. Andrew Carnegie, *The Empire of Business* (New York, 1902), pp. 153–57, 159–64, 167–70. By permission of the Carnegie Corporation.

weaver and drove the Carnegie family in 1848 to migrate from Scotland to the land of opportunity, where he settled in Pittsburgh. Young Carnegie became a telegrapher and, as private operator for and protégé of an official of the Pennsylvania Railroad, found himself in a position to benefit from the many inside deals by which railroad officials were able to accumulate large fortunes with little capital and risk. Before the end of the Civil War, Carnegie had turned a salary which seldom rose over two thousand dollars a year into a fortune of well over one million dollars.

After the Civil War, Carnegie moved his activities and fortune from railroads to iron and steel on the correct assumption that America's growing industries would need prodigious quantities of those metals. By the utilization of scientific advances and astute management, he made himself the foremost independent producer of steel. When he sold his holdings to the J. P. Morgan group in 1901, he became one of the country's wealthiest men.

With his retirement from active business life, Carnegie devoted himself to championing those personal virtues which he considered responsible for his own business success and to defending the morality and inevitability of competitive capitalism. He also viewed the possession of capital as a social responsibility, which, if it did not modify the manner in which he operated his own enterprises, at least required the expenditure of some of his profits in the alleviation of want, ignorance, disease, and war.

. . . It is worth while to inquire into the appearance and growth of Trusts and learn what environments produce them. Their genesis is as follows: a demand exists for a certain article, beyond the capacity of existing works to supply it. Prices are high, and profits tempting. Every manufacturer of that article immediately proceeds to enlarge his works and increase their producing power. In addition to this the unusual profits attract the attention of his principal managers or those who are interested to a greater or less degree in the factory. These communicate the knowledge of the prosperity of the works to others. New partnerships are formed, and new works are erected, and before long the demand for the article is fully satisfied, and prices do not advance. In a short time the supply becomes greater than the demand, there are a few tons or yards more in the market for sale than required, and prices begin to fall. They continue falling until the article is sold at cost to the less favourably situated or less ably managed factory; and even until the best managed and best equipped factory is not able to produce the article at the prices at which it can be sold.

Political economy says that here the trouble will end. Goods will not be produced at less than cost. This was true when Adam Smith wrote, but it is not quite true to-day. When an article was produced by a small manufacturer, employing, probably at his own home, two or three journeymen and an apprentice or two, it was an easy matter for him to limit or even to stop production. As manufacturing is carried on today, in enormous establishments with five or ten millions of dollars of capital invested, and with thousands of workers, it costs the manufacturer much less to run at a loss per ton or per yard than to check his production. Stoppage would be serious indeed. The condition of cheap manufacture is running full. Twenty sources of expense are *fixed charges*, many of which stoppage would only increase. Therefore the article is produced for months, and in some cases that I have known for years, not only without profit or without interest upon capital, but to the impairment of the capital invested. Manufacturers have balanced their books year after year only to find their capital reduced at each successive balance. While continuing to produce may be costly, the manufacturer knows too well that stoppage would be ruin. His brother manufacturers are of course in the same situation. They see the savings of many years, as well perhaps as the capital they have succeeded in borrowing, becoming less and less, with no hope of a change in the situation. It is in soil thus prepared that anything promising relief is gladly welcomed. The manufacturers are in the position of patients that have tried in vain every doctor of the regular school for years, and are now liable to become the victims of any quack that appears. Combinations—syndicates—Trusts—they are willing to try anything. A meeting is called, and in the presence of immediate danger they decide to take united action and form a Trust. Each factory is rated as worth a certain amount. Officers are chosen, and through these the entire product of the article in question is to be distributed to the public, at remunerative prices.

Such is the genesis of "Trusts" in manufactured articles. In transportation the situation, while practically the same, differs in some particulars. Many small railways lines are built under separate charters. A genius in affairs sees that the eight or ten separate organizations, with as many different ideas of management, equipment, etc., are as useless as were the two hundred and fifty petty kings in Germany, and, Bismarck-like, he sweeps them out of existence, creates a great through line, doubles the securities or stock, the interest upon which is paid out of the saving effected by consolidation, and all is highly satisfactory, as in the case of the New York Central. Or a line is built and managed with such sagacity as distinguishes the Pennsylvania Railroad, and it succeeds in developing the resources of the State so extensively that upon a line of three hundred and fifty miles between Pittsburg and Philadelphia it nets about thirteen millions of dollars per annum. Twelve millions of dollars of this it shows upon its books. From one to two millions extra are ex-

pended in making one of the best lines in the world out of a road which was originally designed as a horse-railroad. We do not call our railroad combinations Trusts, but they are substantially such, since they aim at raising and maintaining transportation rates in certain districts. They are "combinations" or "systems" which aim at monopolies within these districts. . . .

We have given the genesis of Trusts and combinations in their several forms. The question is, Do they menace the permanent interest of the nation? Are they a source of serious danger? Or are they to prove, as many other similar forms have proved, mere passing phases of unrest and transition? To answer this question let us follow the operation of the manufacturing Trust which we have in imagination created, salt or sugar, nails, beans, or lead or copper; it is all the same. The sugar refiners, let us say, have formed a Trust after competing one with another through years of disastrous business, and all the sugar manufactured in the country in existing factories is sold through one channel at advanced prices. Profits begin to grow. Dividends are paid, and those who before saw their property vanishing before their eyes are now made happy. The dividends from that part of a man's capital invested in the sugar business yield him profit far above the capital he has invested in various other affairs. The prices of sugar are such that the capital invested in a new factory would yield enormously. He is perhaps bound not to enlarge his factory or to enter into a new factory, but his relatives and acquaintances soon discover the fresh opportunity for gain. He can advise them to push the completion of a small factory, which, of course, must be taken into the Trust. Or, even if he does not give his friends this intimation, capital is always upon the alert, especially when it is bruited about that a Trust has been formed, as in the case of sugar, and immediately new sugar manufactories spring up, as if by magic. The more successful the Trust, the surer these offshoots are to sprout. Every victory is a defeat. Every factory that the Trust buys is the sure creator of another, and so on *ad infinitum*, until the bubble bursts. The sugar refiners have tried to get more from capital in a special case than capital yields in general. They have endeavoured to raise a part of the ocean of capital above the level of the surrounding waters, and over their bulwarks the floods have burst, and capital, like water, has again found its level. It is true that to regain this level a longer or a shorter period may be required, during which the article affected may be sold to the consumer in limited quantities at a higher rate than before existed. But for this the consumer is amply recompensed in the years that follow, during which the struggle between the discordant and competitive factories becomes severer than it ever was before, and lasts till the great law of the survival of the fittest vindicates itself. Those factories and managers that can produce to the best advantage eventually close the less competent. Capital wisely managed yields its legitimate profit. After a time the growth of demand enables capital to receive an unusual profit. This in turn attracts fresh capital to the manufacture, and we have a renewal of the old struggle, the consumer reaping the benefit.

Such is the law, such has been the law, and such promises to be the law for the future; for, so far, no device has yet been devised that has permanently thwarted its operation. Given freedom of competition, and all combinations or trusts that attempt to exact from the consumer more than a legitimate return upon capital and services, write the charter of their own defeat. We have many proofs that this great law does not sleep, and that it will not be suppressed. Some time ago, as I have stated, the steel rail manufacturers of Europe formed a trust and advanced the rails to such an extent that American manufacturers were able for the first, and perhaps for the last time, to export steel rails to Canada in competition with the European. But the misunderstandings and quarrels, inseparable from these attempted unions of competitors, soon broke the Trust. With vindictive feelings, added to what was before business rivalry, the struggle was renewed, and the steel rail industry of Europe has never recovered. It was found that the advance in prices had only galvanized into life concerns which never should have attempted to manufacture rails; and so that Trust died a natural death.

During the great depression which existed for several years in this country in the steel rail trade many anxious meetings were held under circumstances described in the genesis of Trusts, and it was resolved that the plan of restricting production should be tried. Fortunately reaction soon came. A demand for rails set in before the plan went into operation, and, as a matter of fact, no restriction of product was ever attempted, and the steel rail industry was thus saved from a great error. . . .

. . . The newspapers charge that Trusts exist or have existed in wall paper, shoe laces, lumber, coal, coke, brick, screws, rope, glass, schoolbooks, insurance and hardware, and twenty more articles; but the fitting epitaph for these ephemeral creations is

> If I was so soon to be done for,
> I wonder what I was begun for!

We may exclaim with Macbeth, as he watched the shadowy descendants of Banquo filing past, "What, will the line stretch out to the crack of doom?" But as with Banquo's procession, so with Trusts, it is comforting to remember that as one approaches another disappears. They come like shadows, and so depart. . . .

The people of America can smile at the efforts of all her railway magnates and of all her manufacturers to defeat the economic laws by Trusts or combinations, or pools, or "differentials," or anything of like character. Only let them hold firmly to the doctrine of free competition. Keep the field open. Freedom for all to engage in railroad building when and where capital desires, subject to conditions open to all. Freedom for all to engage in any branch of manufacturing under like conditions.

There can be no permanent extortion of profit beyond the average return from capital, nor any monopoly, either in transportation or manufacturing. Any attempt to maintain either must end in failure, and failure ultimately disastrous just in proportion to the temporary success of the foolish effort. It is simply ridiculous for a party of men to meet in a room and attempt by passing resolutions to change the great laws which govern human affairs in the business world, and this, whether they be railway presidents, bankers or manufacturers.

The fashion of Trusts has but a short season longer to run, and then some other equally vain device may be expected to appear when the next period of depression arrives; but there is not the slightest danger that serious injury can result to the sound principles of business from any or all of these movements. The only people who have reason to fear Trusts are those foolish enough to enter into them. The Consumer and the Transporter, not the Manufacturer and the Railway owner, are to reap the harvest.

Even since the foregoing was written, a new form has appeared on the stage in the shape of "The Presidents' Agreement—an agreement among gentlemen," in which the parties engage to control, strangle and restrict the future development of our magnificent railway system under the laws of natural growth, at a time when the country requires this development as much as it ever did. These gentlemen are not going to engage in building lines which will give the public the benefit of healthy competition, or permit such to be built hereafter. It is safe to say that very soon this toy will be discarded, like its predecessors, for another, and that the very men apparently most pleased with this new rattle will then regard it with the greatest contempt, and go forward in the good work, as hitherto, developing the railway system wherever and whenever they think they see a fair chance for profit. Whenever existing railways exact from the public more than a fair return upon the actual capital invested, or upon the capital which would be required to duplicate existing lines, competing lines will be built—fortunately for the interests of the country— which is much more concerned in getting cheap transportation than it is in insuring dividends for capitalists; and whenever a percentage is to be obtained by the negotiation of railway securities, bankers will be found—also, fortunately for the best interests of the country—who will gladly find a market for them without stopping to inquire whether monopolies are to be overthrown by the new lines.

It is not in the power of man to exact for more than a brief season, and a very brief season indeed, unusual profit upon actual capital invested either in Transportation or Manufacture, so long as all are free to compete, and this freedom, it may safely be asserted, the American people are not likely to restrict.

7. THE CHALLENGE OF FACTS[1]

By WILLIAM GRAHAM SUMNER

EDITORS' NOTE.—William Graham Sumner (1840–1910), professor of sociology at Yale University, answered

1. William Graham Sumner, *The Challenge of Facts and Other Essays*, ed. Albert G. Keller (New Haven, 1914), pp. 17–18, 20–28, 30–35, 44–47, 49–52. By permission of Yale University Press.

the critics of capitalism in a manner which most capitalists themselves had neither the time, training, nor inclination to do. Sumner came from a working-class family and, after having a brilliant record as a student at Yale, trained for the ministry. He abandoned the pulpit in 1872 to accept a newly established chair of political and social science at Yale. There he furnished America's future business leaders with a philosophy which answered their need for a rationale for their future operations. Sumner combined the pursuit of self-interest theory of Adam Smith with the application of the survival of the fittest theory to human affairs of the "social Darwinists."

Unfortunately for Sumner, however, he insisted upon consistency in his opposition to government intervention in the economic and social life of the nation. His attacks on the social reform program of the Populists were coupled with similar attacks on the protective tariff, and, for the latter, businessmen demanded his dismissal on several occasions. Sumner, however, managed to keep his chair.

Socialism is no new thing. In one form or another it is to be found throughout all history. It arises from an observation of certain harsh facts in the lot of man on earth, the concrete expression of which is poverty and misery. These facts challenge us. It is folly to try to shut our eyes to them. We have first to notice what they are, and then to face them squarely.

Man is born under the necessity of sustaining the existence he has received by an onerous struggle against nature, both to win what is essential to his life and to ward off what is prejudicial to it. He is born under a burden and a necessity. Nature holds what is essential to him, but she offers nothing gratuitously. He may win for his use what she holds, if he can. Only the most meager and inadequate supply for human needs can be obtained directly from nature. There are trees which may be used for fuel and for dwellings, but labor is required to fit them for this use. There are ores in the ground, but labor is necessary to get out the metals and make tools or weapons. For any real satisfaction, labor is necessary to fit the products of nature for human use. In this struggle every individual is under the pressure of the necessities for food, clothing, shelter, fuel, and every individual brings with him more or less energy for the conflict necessary to supply his needs. The relation, therefore, between each man's needs and each man's energy,

or "individualism," is the first fact of human life.

It is not without reason, however, that we speak of a "man" as the individual in question, for women (mothers) and children have special disabilities for the struggle with nature, and these disabilities grow greater and last longer as civilization advances. The perpetuation of the race in health and vigor, and its success as a whole in its struggle to expand and develop human life on earth, therefore, require that the head of the family shall, by his energy, be able to supply not only his own needs, but those of the organisms which are dependent upon him. . . .

The next great fact we have to notice in regard to the struggle of human life is that labor which is spent in a direct struggle with nature is severe in the extreme and is but slightly productive. To subjugate nature, man needs weapons and tools. These, however, cannot be won unless the food and clothing and other prime and direct necessities are supplied in such amount that they can be consumed while tools and weapons are being made, for the tools and weapons themselves satisfy no needs directly. A man who tills the ground with his fingers or with a pointed stick picked up without labor will get a small crop. To fashion even the rudest spade or hoe will cost time, during which the laborer must still eat and drink and wear, but the tool, when obtained, will multiply immensely the power to produce. Such products of labor, used to assist production, have a function so peculiar in the nature of things that we need to distinguish them. We call them capital. A lever is capital, and the advantage of lifting a weight with a lever over lifting it by direct exertion is only a feeble illustration of the power of capital in production. The origin of capital lies in the darkness before history, and it is probably impossible for us to imagine the slow and painful steps by which the race began the formation of it. Since then it has gone on rising to higher and higher powers by a ceaseless involution, if I may use a mathematical expression. Capital is labor raised to a higher power by being constantly multiplied into itself. Nature has been more and more subjugated by the human race through the power of capital, and every human being now living shares the improved status of the race to a degree which neither he nor anyone else can measure, and for which he pays nothing.

Let us understand this point, because our subject will require future reference to it. It is the most shortsighted ignorance not to see that, in a civilized community, all the advantage of capital except a small fraction is gratuitously enjoyed by the community. For instance, suppose the case of a man utterly destitute of tools, who is trying to till the ground with a pointed stick. He could get something out of it. If now he should obtain a spade with which to till the ground, let us suppose, for illustration, that he could get twenty times as great a product. Could, then, the owner of a spade in a civilized state demand, as its price, from the man who had no spade, nineteen-twentieths of the product which could be produced by the use of it? Certainly not. The price of a spade is fixed by the supply and demand of products in the community. A spade is bought for a dollar and the gain from the use of it is an inheritance of knowledge, experience, and skill which every man who lives in a civilized state gets for nothing. What we

pay for steam transportation is no trifle, but imagine, if you can, eastern Massachusetts cut off from steam connection with the rest of the world, turnpikes and sailing vessels remaining. The cost of food would rise so high that a quarter of the population would starve to death and another quarter would have to emigrate. To-day every man here gets an enormous advantage from the status of a society on a level of steam transportation, telegraph, and machinery, for which he pays nothing.

So far as I have yet spoken, we have before us the struggle of man with nature, but the social problems, strictly speaking, arise at the next step. Each man carries on the struggle to win his support for himself, but there are others by his side engaged in the same struggle. If the stores of nature were unlimited, or if the last unit of the supply she offers could be won as easily as the first, there would be no social problem. If a square mile of land could support an indefinite number of human beings, or if it cost only twice as much labor to get forty bushels of wheat from an acre as to get twenty, we should have no social problem. If a square mile of land could support millions, no one would ever emigrate and there would be no trade or commerce. If it cost only twice as much labor to get forty bushels as twenty, there would be no advance in the arts. The fact is far otherwise. So long as the population is low in proportion to the amount of land, on a given stage of the arts, life is easy and the competition of man with man is weak. When more persons are trying to live on a square mile than it can support, on the existing stage of the arts, life is hard and the competition of man with man is intense. In the former case, industry and prudence may be on a low grade; the penalties are not severe, or certain, or speedy. In the latter case, each individual needs to exert on his own behalf every force, original or acquired, which he can command. In the former case, the average condition will be one of comfort and the population will be all nearly on the average. In the latter case, the average condition will not be one of comfort, but the population will cover wide extremes of comfort and misery. Each will find his place according to his ability and his effort. The former society will be democratic; the latter will be aristocratic.

The constant tendency of population to outstrip the means of subsistence is the force which has distributed population over the world, and produced all advance in civilization. To this day the two means of escape for an overpopulated country are emigration and an advance in the arts. The former wins more land for the same people; the latter makes the same land support more persons. If, however, either of these means opens a chance for an increase of population, it is evident that the advantage so won may be speedily exhausted if the increase takes place. The social difficulty has only undergone a temporary amelioration, and when the conditions of pressure and competition are renewed, misery and poverty reappear. The victims of them are those who have inherited disease and depraved appetites, or have been brought up in vice and ignorance, or have themselves yielded to vice, extravagance, idleness, and imprudence. In the last analysis, therefore, we come back to vice, in its original and hereditary forms, as the correlative of misery and poverty.

The condition for the complete and regular action of the force of competition is liberty. Liberty means the security given to each man that, if he employs his energies to sustain the struggle on behalf of himself and those he cares for, he shall dispose of the product exclusively as he chooses. It is impossible to know whence any definition or criterion of justice can be derived, if it is not deduced from this view of things; or if it is not the definition of justice that each shall enjoy the fruit of his own labor and self-denial, and of injustice that the idle and the industrious, the self-indulgent and the self-denying, shall share equally in the product. Aside from the *a priori* specula-

tions of philosophers who have tried to make equality an essential element in justice, the human race has recognized, from the earliest times, the above conception of justice as the true one, and has founded upon it the right of property. . . .

Private property, also, which we have seen to be a feature of society organized in accordance with the natural conditions of the struggle for existence produces inequalities between men. The struggle for existence is aimed against nature. It is from her niggardly hand that we have to wrest the satisfactions for our needs, but our fellow-men are our competitors for the meager supply. Competition, therefore, is a law of nature. Nature is entirely neutral; she submits to him who most energetically and resolutely assails her. She grants her rewards to the fittest, therefore, without regard to other considerations of any kind. If, then, there be liberty, men get from her just in proportion to their works, and their having and enjoying are just in proportion to their being and their doing. Such is the system of nature. If we do not like it, and if we try to amend it, there is only one way in which we can do it. We can take from the better and give to the worse. We can deflect the penalties of those who have done ill and throw them on those who have done better. We can take the rewards from those who have done better and give them to those who have done worse. We shall thus lessen the inequalities. We shall favor the survival of the unfittest, and we shall accomplish this by destroying liberty. Let it be understood that we cannot go outside of this alternative: liberty, inequality, survival of the fittest; not-liberty, equality, survival of the unfittest. The former carries society forward and favors all its best members; the latter carries society downwards and favors all its worst members.

For three hundred years now men have been trying to understand and realize liberty. Liberty is not the right or chance to do what we choose; there is no such liberty as that on earth. No man can do as he chooses: the autocrat of Russia or the

King of Dahomey has limits to his arbitrary will; the savage in the wilderness, whom some people think free, is the slave of routine, tradition, and superstitious fears; the civilized man must earn his living, or take care of his property, or concede his own will to the rights and claims of his parents, his wife, his children, and all the persons with whom he is connected by the ties and contracts of civilized life.

What we mean by liberty is civil liberty, or liberty under law; and this means the guarantees of law that a man shall not be interfered with while using his own powers for his own welfare. It is, therefore, a civil and political status; and that nation has the freest institutions in which the guarantees of peace for the laborer and security for the capitalist are the highest. Liberty, therefore, does not by any means do away with the struggle for existence. We might as well try to do away with the need of eating, for that would, in effect, be the same thing. What civil liberty does is to turn the competition of man with man from violence and brute force into an industrial competition under which men vie with one another for the acquisition of material goods by industry, energy, skill, frugality, prudence, temperance, and other industrial virtues. Under this changed order of things the inequalities are not done away with. Nature still grants her rewards of having and enjoying, according to our being and doing, but it is now the man of the highest training and not the man of the heaviest fist who gains the highest reward. It is impossible that the man with capital and the man without capital should be equal. To affirm that they are equal would be to say that a man who has no tool can get as much food out of the ground as the man who has a spade or a plough; or that the man who has no weapon can defend himself as well against hostile beasts or hostile men as the man who has a weapon. If that were so, none of us would work any more. We work and deny ourselves to get capital just because, other things being equal, the man who has it is superior, for

attaining all the ends of life, to the man who has it not. Considering the eagerness with which we all seek capital and the estimate we put upon it, either in cherishing it if we have it, or envying others who have it while we have it not, it is very strange what platitudes pass current about it in our society so soon as we begin to generalize about it. If our young people really believed some of the teachings they hear, it would not be amiss to preach them a sermon once in a while to reassure them, setting forth that it is not wicked to be rich, nay even, that it is not wicked to be richer than your neighbor.

It follows from what we have observed that it is the utmost folly to denounce capital. To do so is to undermine civilization, for capital is the first requisite of every social gain, educational, ecclesiastical, political, aesthetic, or other.

It must also be noticed that the popular antithesis between persons and capital is very fallacious. Every law or institution which protects persons at the expense of capital makes it easier for persons to live and to increase the number of consumers of capital while lowering all the motives to prudence and frugality by which capital is created. Hence every such law or institution tends to produce a large population, sunk in misery. All poor laws and all eleemosynary institutions and expenditures have this tendency. On the contrary, all laws and institutions which give security to capital against the interests of other persons than its owners, restrict numbers while preserving the means of subsistence. Hence every such law or institution tends to produce a small society on a high stage of comfort and well being. It follows that the antithesis commonly thought to exist between the protection of persons and the protection of property is in reality only an antithesis between numbers and quality. . . .

. . . The man who has capital possesses immeasurable advantages for the struggle of life over him who has none. The more we break down privileges of class, or industry, and establish liberty, the greater will be the inequalities and the more exclusively will the vicious bear the penalties. Poverty and misery will exist in society just so long as vice exists in human nature.

I now go on to notice some modes of trying to deal with this problem. There is a modern philosophy which has never been taught systematically, but which has won the faith of vast masses of people in the modern civilized world. For want of a better name it may be called the sentimental philosophy. It has colored all modern ideas and institutions in politics, religion, education, charity, and industry, and is widely taught in popular literature, novels, and poetry, and in the pulpit. The first proposition of this sentimental philosophy is that nothing is true which is disagreeable. If, therefore, any facts of observation show that life is grim or hard, the sentimental philosophy steps over such facts with a genial platitude, a consoling commonplace, or a gratifying dogma. The effect is to spread an easy optimism, under the influence of which people spare themselves labor and trouble, reflection and forethought, pains and caution—all of which are hard things, and to admit the necessity for which would be to admit that the world is not all made smooth and easy, for us to pass through it surrounded by love, music, and flowers.

Under this philosophy, "progress" has been represented as a steadily increasing and unmixed good; as if the good steadily encroached on the evil without involving any new and other forms of evil; and as if we could plan great steps in progress in our academies and lyceums, and then realize them by resolution. To minds trained to this way of looking at things, any evil which exists is a reproach. We have only to consider it, hold some discussions about it, pass resolutions, and have done with it. Every moment of delay is, therefore, a social crime. It is monstrous to say that misery and poverty are as constant as vice and evil passions of men! People suffer so under misery and poverty! Assuming,

therefore, that we can solve all these problems and eradicate all these evils by expending our ingenuity upon them, of course we cannot hasten too soon to do it.

A social philosophy, consonant with this, has also been taught for a century. It could not fail to be popular, for it teaches that ignorance is as good as knowledge, vulgarity as good as refinement, shiftlessness as good as painstaking, shirking as good as faithful striving, poverty as good as wealth, filth as good as cleanliness—in short, that quality goes for nothing in the measurement of men, but only numbers. Culture, knowledge, refinement, skill, and taste cost labor, but we have been taught that they have only individual, not social value, and that socially they are rather drawbacks than otherwise. In public life we are taught to admire roughness, illiteracy, and rowdyism. The ignorant, idle, and shiftless have been taught that they are "the people," that the generalities inculcated at the same time about the dignity, wisdom, and virtue of "the people" are true of them, that they have nothing to learn to be wise, but that, as they stand, they possess a kind of infallibility, and that to their "opinion" the wise must bow. It is not cause for wonder if whole sections of these classes have begun to use the powers and wisdom attributed to them for their interests, as they construe them, and to trample on all the excellence which marks civilization as an obsolete superstition.

Another development of the same philosophy is the doctrine that men come into the world endowed with "natural rights," or as joint inheritors of the "rights of man," which have been "declared" times without number during the last century. The divine rights of man have succeeded to the obsolete divine right of kings. If it is true, then, that a man is born with rights, he comes into the world with claims on somebody besides his parents. Against whom does he hold such rights? There can be no rights against nature or against God. A man may curse his fate because he is born of an inferior race, or with an hereditary disease, or blind, or, as some members of the race seem to do, because they are born females; but they get no answer to their imprecations. But, now, if men have rights by birth, these rights must hold against their fellow-men and must mean that somebody else is to spend his energy to sustain the existence of the persons so born. What then becomes of the natural rights of the one whose energies are to be diverted from his own interests? If it be said that we should all help each other, that means simply that the race as a whole should advance and expand as much and as fast as it can in its career on earth; and the experience on which we are now acting has shown that we shall do this best under liberty and under the organization which we are now developing, by leaving each to exert his energies for his own success. The notion of natural rights is destitute of sense, but it is captivating, and it is the more available on account of its vagueness. It lends itself to the most vicious kind of social dogmatism, for if a man has natural rights, then the reasoning is clear up to the finished socialistic doctrine that a man has a natural right to whatever he needs, and that the measure of his claims is the wishes which he wants fulfilled. If, then, he has a need, who is bound to satisfy it for him? Who holds the obligation corresponding to his right? It must be the one who possesses what will satisfy that need, or else the state which can take the possession from those who have earned and saved it, and give it to him who needs it and who, by the hypothesis, has not earned and saved it.

It is with the next step, however, that we come to the complete and ruinous absurdity of this view. If a man may demand from those who have a share of what he needs and has not, may he demand the same also for his wife and for his children, and for how many children? The industrious and prudent man who takes the course of labor and self-denial to secure capital, finds that he must defer marriage,

both in order to save and to devote his life to the education of fewer children. The man who can claim a share in another's product has no such restraint. The consequence would be that the industrious and prudent would labor and save, without families, to support the idle and improvident who would increase and multiply, until universal destitution forced a return to the principles of liberty and property; and the man who started with the notion that the world owed him a living would once more find, as he does now, that the world pays him its debt in the state prison.

The most specious application of the dogma of rights is to labor. It is said that every man has a right to work. The world is full of work to be done. Those who are willing to work find that they have three days' work to do in every day that comes. Work is the necessity to which we are born. It is not a right, but an irksome necessity, and men escape it whenever they can get the fruits of labor without it. What they want is the fruits, or wages, not work. But wages are capital which someone has earned and saved. If he and the workman can agree on the terms on which he will part with his capital, there is no more to be said. If not, then the right must be set up in a new form. It is now not a right to work, nor even a right to wages, but a right to a certain rate of wages, and we have simply returned to the old doctrine of spoliation again. It is immaterial whether the demand for wages be addressed to an individual capitalist or to a civil body, for the latter can give no wages which it does not collect by taxes out of the capital of those who have labored and saved.

Another application is in the attempt to fix the hours of labor *per diem* by law. If a man is forbidden to labor over eight hours per day (and the law has no sense or utility for the purposes of those who want it until it takes this form), he is forbidden to exercise so much industry as he may be willing to expend in order to accumulate capital for the improvement of his circumstances. . . .

Socialists are filled with the enthusiasm of equality. Every scheme of theirs for securing equality has destroyed liberty. The student of political philosophy has the antagonism of equality and liberty constantly forced upon him. Equality of possession or of rights and equality before the law are diametrically opposed to each other. The object of equality before the law is to make the state entirely neutral. The state, under that theory, takes no cognizance of persons. It surrounds all, without distinctions, with the same conditions and guarantees. If it educates one, it educates all—black, white, red, or yellow; Jew or Gentile; native or alien. If it taxes one, it taxes all, by the same system and under the same conditions. If it exempts one from police regulations in home, church, and occupation, it exempts all. From this statement it is at once evident that pure equality before the law is impossible. Some occupations must be subjected to police regulation. Not all can be made subject to militia duty even for the same limited period. The exceptions and special cases furnish the chance for abuse. Equality before the law, however, is one of the cardinal principles of civil liberty, because it leaves each man to run the race of life for himself as best he can. The state stands neutral but benevolent. It does not undertake to aid some and handicap others at the outset in order to offset hereditary advantages and disadvantages, or to make them start equally. Such a notion would belong to the false and spurious theory of equality which is socialistic. If the state should attempt this it would make itself the servant of envy. I am entitled to make the most I can of myself without hindrance from anybody, but I am not entitled to any guarantee that I shall make as much of myself as somebody else makes of himself.

The modern thirst for equality of rights is explained by its historical origin. The mediaeval notion of rights was that rights were special privileges, exemptions, franchises, and powers given to individuals by the king; hence each man had just so many as he and his ancestors had been able to buy or beg by force or favor, and if a man had obtained no grants he had no rights. Hence no two persons were equal in rights and the mass of the population had none. The theory of natural rights and of equal rights was a revolt against the mediaeval theory. It was asserted that men did not have to wait for a king to grant them rights; they have them by nature, or in the nature of things, because they are men and members of civil society. If rights come from nature, it is inferred that they fall like air and light on all equally. It was an immense step in advance for the human race when this new doctrine was promulgated. Its own limitations and errors need not now be pointed out. Its significance is plain, and its limits are to some extent defined when we note its historical origin.

I have already shown that where these guarantees exist and where there is liberty, the results cannot be equal, but with all liberty there must go responsibility. If I take my own way I must take my own consequences; if it proves that I have made a mistake, I cannot be allowed to throw the consequences on my neighbor. If my neighbor is a free man and resents interference from me he must not call on me to bear the consequences of his mistakes. Hence it is plain that liberty, equality before the law, responsibility, individualism, monogamy, and private property all hold together as consistent parts of the same structure of society, and that an assault on one part must sooner or later involve an assault on all the others.

To all this must be added the political element in socialism. The acquisition of some capital—the amount is of very subordinate importance—is the first and simplest proof that an individual possesses the industrial and civil virtues which make a good citizen and a useful member of society. Political power, a century ago, was associated more or less, even in the United

States, with the possession of land. It has been gradually extended until the suffrage is to all intents and purposes universal in North and South America, in Australia, and in all Europe except Russia and Turkey. On this system political control belongs to the numerical majority, limited only by institutions. It may be doubted, if the terms are taken strictly and correctly, whether the non-capitalists outnumber the capitalists in any civilized country, but in many cities where capital is most collected they certainly do. The powers of government have been abused for ages by the classes who possessed them to enable kings, courtiers, nobles, politicians, demagogues, and their friends to live in exemption from labor and self-denial, that is, from the universal lot of man. It is only a continuation of the same abuse if the new possessors of power attempt to employ it to secure for themselves the selfish advantages which all possessors of power have taken. Such a course would, however, overthrow all that we think has been won in the way of making government an organ of justice, peace, order, and security, without respect of persons; and if those gains are not to be lost they will have to be defended, before this century closes, against popular majorities, especially in cities, just as they had to be won in a struggle with kings and nobles in the centuries past.

The newest socialism is, in its method, political. The essential feature of its latest phases is the attempt to use the power of the state to realize its plans and to secure its objects. These objects are to do away with poverty and misery, and there are no socialistic schemes yet proposed, of any sort, which do not, upon analysis, turn out to be projects for curing poverty and misery by making those who have share with those who have not. Whether they are paper-money schemes, tariff schemes, subsidy schemes, internal improvement schemes, or usury laws, they all have this in common with the most vulgar of the communistic projects, and the errors of this sort in the past which have been committed in the interest of the capitalist class now furnish precedents, illustration, and encouragement for the new category of demands. . . .

It is a matter of course that a reactionary party should arise to declare that universal suffrage, popular education, machinery, free trade, and all the other innovations of the last hundred years are all a mistake. If any one ever believed that these innovations were so many clear strides towards the millennium, that they involve no evils or abuses of their own, that they tend to emancipate mankind from the need for prudence, caution, forethought, vigilance—in short, from the eternal struggle against evil—it is not strange that he should be disappointed. If any one ever believed that some "form of government" could be found which would run itself and turn out the pure results of abstract peace, justice, and righteousness without any trouble to anybody, he may well be dissatisfied. To talk of turning back, however, is only to enhance still further the confusion and danger of our position. The world cannot go back. Its destiny is to go forward and to meet the new problems which are continually arising. Under our so-called progress evil only alters its forms, and we must esteem it a grand advance if we can believe that, on the whole, and over a wide view of human affairs, good has gained a hair's breadth over evil in a century. Popular institutions have their own abuses and dangers just as much as monarchical or aristocratic institutions. We are only just finding out what they are. All the institutions which we have inherited were invented to guard liberty against the encroachments of a powerful monarch or aristocracy, when these classes possessed land and the possession of land was the greatest social power. Institutions must now be devised to guard civil liberty against popular majorities, and this necessity arises first in regard to the protection of property, the first and greatest function of government and element in civil liberty. There is no escape from any dangers involved in this or any other social struggle save in going forward and working out the development. It will cost a struggle and will demand the highest wisdom of this and the next generation. It is very probable that some nations—those, namely, which come up to this problem with the least preparation, with the least intelligent comprehension of the problem, and under the most inefficient leadership—will suffer a severe check in their development and prosperity; it is very probable that in some nations the development may lead through revolution and bloodshed; it is very probable that in some nations the consequence may be a reaction towards arbitrary power. In every view we take of it, it is clear that the general abolition of slavery has only cleared the way for a new social problem of far wider scope and far greater difficulty. It seems to me, in fact, that this must always be the case. The conquest of one difficulty will only open the way to another; the solution of one problem will only bring man face to face with another. Man wins by the fight, not by the victory, and therefore the possibilities of growth are unlimited, for the fight has no end.

The progress which men have made in developing the possibilities of human existence has never been made by jumps and strides. It has never resulted from the schemes of philosophers and reformers. . . .

The sound student of sociology can hold out to mankind, as individuals or as a race, only one hope of better and happier living. That hope lies in an enhancement of the industrial virtues and of the moral forces which thence arise. Industry, self-denial, and temperance are the laws of prosperity for men and states; without them advance in the arts and in wealth means only corruption and decay through luxury and vice. With them progress in the arts and increasing wealth are the prime conditions of an advancing civilization which is sound enough to endure. The power of the human race to-day over the conditions of prosperous and happy living are sufficient to banish poverty and misery, if it were not for folly and vice. The earth does not begin to be populated up to its power to support population on the present stage of the arts; if the United States were as densely populated as the British Islands, we should have 1,000,000,000 people here. If, therefore, men were willing to set to work with energy and courage to subdue the outlying parts of the earth, all might live in plenty and prosperity. But if they insist on remaining in the slums of great cities or on the borders of an old society, and on a comparatively exhausted soil, there is no device of economist or statesman which can prevent them from falling victims to poverty and misery or from succumbing in the competition of life to those who have greater command of capital. The socialist or philanthropist who nourishes them in their situation and saves them from the distress of it is only cultivating the distress which he pretends to cure.

8. A LIVING WAGE[1]

By John A. Ryan

EDITORS' NOTE.—The Rt. Rev. Msgr. John A. Ryan (1869–1945) taught moral theology and sociology at the Catholic University of America

1. John A. Ryan, A Living Wage (New York, 1906), pp. 43–50, 55–59, 62–66, 81–82, 99–107, 297–323. By permission of The Macmillan Company.

from 1916 until his retirement in 1939. While still in his teens he was influenced by the proposals of the Farmers' Alliance and the Populists for government regulation of industry. He also made an early acquaintance with Henry George's Progress and Poverty, and his first magazine article was a review of a book by Henry Demarest Lloyd. His Doctor's dissertation, *A Living Wage: Its Ethical and Economic Aspects*, was inspired by Pope Leo XIII's encyclical, "On the Condition of Labor," which viewed favorable legislation as a means of social reform.

CHAPTER III

THE BASIS AND JUSTIFICATION OF RIGHTS

The thesis to be maintained in this volume is that the laborer's claim to a Living Wage is of the nature of a *right*. This right is personal, not merely social: that is to say, it belongs to the individual as individual, and not as member of society; it is the laborer's personal prerogative, not his share of social good; and its primary end is the welfare of the laborer, not that of society. Again, it is a natural, not a positive right; for it is born with the individual, derived from his rational nature, not conferred upon him by a positive enactment. In brief, the right to a Living Wage is individual, natural and absolute.

A right in the moral sense of the term may be defined as an inviolable moral claim to some personal good. When this claim is created, as it sometimes is, by civil authority it is a positive or legal right; when it is derived from man's rational nature it is a natural right. All rights are means, moral means, whereby the possessor of them is enabled to reach some end. Natural rights are the moral means or opportunities by which the individual attains the end appointed to him by nature. For the present it is sufficient to say that this end is right and reasonable life. The exigencies of right and reasonable living, therefore, determine the existence, and number, and extent of man's natural rights. Just as his intellectual, volitional, sensitive, nutritive and motive faculties are the positive, or physical, agencies by which he lives and acts as a human being, so his natural rights are the *moral* faculties requisite to the same end. He cannot attain this end adequately unless he is regarded by his fellows as morally immune from arbitrary interference. They must hold themselves morally restrained from hindering him in the reasonable exercise of his faculties. His powers of intellect, will, sense, nutrition and motion will be of little use to him if his neighbors may licitly deprive him, whenever it may suit their convenience, of his external goods, or his liberty, or his members, or his life. In addition to his positive powers, he stands in need of those moral powers which give to his claim upon certain personal goods that character of sacredness which restrains or tends to restrain arbitrary interference by his fellows.

Man's natural rights are absolute, not in the sense that they are subject to no limitations—which would be absurd—but in the sense that their validity is not dependent on the will of anyone except the person in whom they inhere. They are absolute in existence but not in extent. Within reasonable limits their sacredness and binding force can never cease. Outside of these limits, they may in certain contingencies disappear. If they were not absolute to this extent, if there were no circumstances in which they were secure against *all* attacks, they would not deserve the name of rights. The matter may be made somewhat clearer by one or two examples. The right to life is said to be absolute because no human power may licitly kill an innocent man as a mere means to the realization of any end whatever. The life of the individual person is so sacred that, as long as the right thereto has not been forfeited by the perverse conduct of the subject himself, it may not be subordinated to the welfare of any other individual or any number of individuals. Not even to preserve its own existence may the State directly and deliberately put an unoffending man to death. When, however, the individual is not innocent, when by such actions as murder or attempted murder he has forfeited his right to live, he may, of course, be rightfully executed by civil authority, or killed in self-defense by his fellow man. He may also be compelled to risk his life on behalf of his country, for that is a part of his duty; and he may with entire justice be deprived of life indirectly and incidentally, as when non-combatants are unavoidably killed in a city that is besieged in time of war. Again, the right to liberty and property are not absolute in the sense that the individual may have as much of these goods as he pleases and do with them as he pleases, but inasmuch as within reasonable limits—which are always determined by the essential needs of personal development—these rights are sacred and inviolable.

With respect to their natural rights, all men are equal, because all are equal in the rational nature from which such rights are derived By nature every man is a person, that is, a rational, self-active, independent being. Every man is rational because endowed with the faculties of reason and will. His will impels him to seek the good, the end, of his being, and his reason enables him to find and adjust means to this end. Every man is self-active, inasmuch as he is master of his own faculties and able in all the essentials of conduct to direct his own actions. Every man is independent in the sense that he is morally complete in himself, is not a part of any other man, nor inferior to any man, either in the essential qualities of his being or in the end toward which he is morally bound to move. In short, every individual is an "end in himself," and has a personality of his own to develop through the exercise of his own faculties. Because of this equality in the essentials of personality, men are of equal intrinsic worth, have ends to attain that are of equal intrinsic importance, and consequently have equal natural rights to the means without which these ends cannot be achieved.

Only in the abstract, however, are men's natural rights equal. In the concrete they are unequal, just as are the concrete natures from which they spring. This is not to say that equality of rights is an empty abstraction, without any vital meaning or force or consequences in actual life. Men are equal as regards the *number* of their natural rights. The most important of these are the rights to life, to liberty, to property, to a livelihood, to marriage, to religious worship, to intellectual and moral education. These inhere in all men without distinction of person, but they have not necessarily the same *extension*, or content, in all. Indeed, proportional justice requires that individuals endowed with different powers should possess rights that vary in degree. For example, the right to a livelihood and the right to an education will include a greater amount of the means of living and greater opportunities of self-improvement in the cases of those who have greater needs and greater capacities. But in *every* case the natural rights of the individual will embrace a certain minimum of the goods to which these rights refer, which minimum is determined by the reasonable needs of personality. The rights that any person will possess in excess of this minimum will depend upon a variety of circumstances, individual and social. Hence, instead of saying that the natural rights of all men are equal in the abstract but not in the concrete, it would perhaps be more correct, or at least less misleading, to describe them as equal in kind, number and sacredness, and in extension relatively to their particular subjects; but not in quantity nor in *absolute* content.

Such in bare outline is the theory of the character, purpose, and extent of natural rights. Do they really exist? Is the individual really endowed with moral prerogatives, inviolable claims, in virtue of which it is wrong for instance, to take from him, so long as he is innocent of crime, his life or his liberty? Whence comes the validity and sacredness of these claims? The answers to these questions have already been briefly indicated in the statement of the *end* for which the claims exist. Natural rights are necessary means of right and reasonable living. They are essential to the welfare of a human being, a person. They exist and are sacred and inviolable because the welfare of the person exists— as a fact of the ideal order—and is a sacred and inviolable thing. It was Cicero who wrote: "Fine in philosophia constituto, constituta sunt omnia." In problems of philosophy, when we have established the end we have established all things else. Let us look more deeply, then, into the scope and character of this end to which natural rights are but means.

Right and reasonable life, the welfare of the person, consist in the development of man's personality through the harmonious and properly ordered exercise of his faculties. He should subordinate his sense-faculties to his rational faculties; exercise his rational faculties consistently with the claims of his Creator and the reasonable demands of his fellows; and seek the goods that minister to the senses and the selfish promptings of the spirit in subordination to the higher goods, namely, those of the intellect and of the disinterested will. In a word, the supreme earthly goal of conduct is to know in the highest degree the best that is to be known, and to love in the highest degree the best that is to be loved. These highest objects of knowledge and love are God, and, in proportion to the degrees of excellence that they possess, His creatures. To prove that these moral and spiritual values are facts, we have only to appeal to the consciousness of any normally constituted human being. The average man has an abiding conviction that the rational faculties are higher, nobler, more excellent, of greater intrinsic worth than the sense-faculties; that consequently the goods of the mind are to be preferred to those of the senses; and that among the activities of the rational powers those dictated by disinterested love are intrinsically better than those which make for selfish-

ness. These primary and general moral intuitions produce in the mind of the person who heeds them the conviction that it is not only reasonable but *obligatory* for him to pursue the path of conduct thus dimly outlined. The immediate objective basis of this obligation is the intrinsic superiority of the higher faculties, the infinite worth of God, and the essential sacredness of human personality. The ultimate source of the obligation is the Will of God; just as the ultimate source of the distinction between the higher and lower faculties, activities, and goods is the Divine Essence; and just as the ultimate source of the intuitions by which we perceive these distinctions is the Divine Reason.

Since, therefore, the individual is obliged to live a moral and reasonable life in the manner just described, the means to this end, *i.e.*, natural rights, are so necessary and so sacred that all other persons than the one in whom they reside are morally restrained from interfering with or ignoring them. The dignity of personality imposes upon the individual the duty of self-perfection; he cannot fulfil this duty adequately unless he is endowed with natural rights. Such is the immediate basis of natural rights and the proximate source of their sacredness; their ultimate source is to be found in the Reason and Will of God, who has decreed that men shall pursue self-perfection and that they shall not arbitrarily deprive one another of the means essential to this purpose. . . .

. . . Of much greater importance for our contention is the theory that all rights are positive, that is, derived from society, and conferred upon the individual primarily for the benefit of society and only secondarily for the sake of the individual. Individual rights are valid in so far as they do not hinder the social weal. "By himself," says Mackenzie, "a man has no right to anything whatever. He is a part of the social whole; and he has a right only to that which it is for the good of the whole that he should have." In this view the social organism becomes an end in itself; and its good becomes the final goal and rule of human conduct. . . .

Let us concede for the moment that society exists for its own sake, is its own highest good. All its powers, prerogatives and activities will be naturally used as a means to this end. Whenever individuals, however innocent of wrong doing, impede society's progress they are to be relentlessly blotted out of existence. Let us suppose that as a result of this social selection the general level of the race is much higher than it would have been had regard been paid to the "superstition" of natural rights. Society has been treated as an end in itself, and the result is a more excellent society.

It must be evident that the individuals who have been removed to bring about this result could not reasonably have been expected to make the sacrifice willingly. They could not have been satisfied to efface themselves for the sake of society as distinct from its members, since this would be to die for an abstraction. Nor is it likely that any considerable number of them were willing to forego existence in order that the individuals who were left behind might enjoy a more complete existence in the improved society; for the real meaning of this situation is that the former have been used as mere instruments to the welfare of the latter. It is not reasonable to expect men to devote themselves completely to any other end than their own highest good, and a superior society cannot be the highest good for those who must be annihilated as a condition of its realization. They will very naturally prefer to run the risk of securing their own welfare in a less perfect social organization. There is no duty constraining one section of the community—not simply to risk their lives, as in a just war—but to submit to be killed by the social authority, in order that the surviving citizens may have the benefit of a more efficient State. The same statement may be made concerning any other of the individual's natural and essential rights. And if the individuals whose rights are treated as non-existent are neither willing

nor bound by moral obligation to make the sacrifice, the State has certainly no right, no *moral* power, to treat them as a means pure and simple to the welfare of those of its members who are permitted to survive. For, juggle as we will with the terms "social utility" and "social welfare," talk as obscurely as we may about regarding the individual from the viewpoint of society, the true meaning of the assertion that the rights of the individual are derived from and wholly subordinate to society, is that the lives of those who are less useful to society are essentially inferior to the lives of those who are more useful. And not until those who reject natural rights have succeeded in proving that some human lives are less sacred, have less intrinsic worth, stand on a lower grade of being than others, can they indulge the hope of winning over any considerable number of thinkers to the contention that the individual—even the poorest and lowliest person that breathes—has no rights that are indestructible by society. . . .

Academic opposition to the doctrine of natural rights is directed not so much against the moderate conception of them that has always prevailed in Catholic ethical teaching, as against the exaggerated and anti-social form in which they were proclaimed by the political philosophers of France, and even by some of those of England and America, in the latter half of the Eighteenth century. . . . In the view of the Revolutionary philosophers, "nature" and "natural" referred not to what is essential and permanent in man, but to that which is primitive and unconventional. Hence they laid more stress on the "state of nature" than on the "law of nature." The natural law was merely that very simple and very primitive system of rules that would suffice for the state of nature, in which political restraints would be unknown, or at least reduced to a minimum. As the late Professor Ritchie has well said: "To the Thomist the law of nature is an ideal *for* human law; to the Rousseauist it is an ideal to be reached by getting rid of human law altogether." In the mind of the Revolutionist, therefore, to re-establish the law of nature meant to shake off the cumbersome and obstructive political regulations of the day, and get back to the simple state of nature, the semi-anarchical conditions of primitive times. This was, of course, a very inadequate interpretation of man's nature and of the natural law. No such "state of nature" ever existed or ever could exist compatibly with civilization. No valid conclusion regarding the individual's liberties, duties or rights could be deduced from his position and relations in this imaginary and irrational existence. Nevertheless, upon it were based and by it were measured men's natural rights in the Revolutionary system. As a consequence, the rights of the individual were exaggerated and the rights of society minimized. In practice this juristic liberalism has meant, and always will mean, that the State allows to the strong the legal right and power to oppress the weak. A good example of the evil is to be found in the results of the economic policy of *laissez-faire*. It is no wonder that there has been a reaction against this pernicious, anti-social and really *unnatural* theory of natural rights.

The doctrine of natural rights outlined in the foregoing pages holds, then, a middle ground between the Revolutionary and the positivistic theories of the origin and extent of the rights of the individual. It insists that the individual is endowed by nature, or rather, by God, with the rights that are requisite to a reasonable development of his personality, and that these rights are, within due limits, sacred against the power even of the State; but it insists that no individual's rights extend so far as to prevent the State from adjusting the conflicting claims of individuals and safeguarding the just welfare of all its citizens. In other words, man's natural rights must not be so widely interpreted that the strong, and the cunning, and the unscrupulous will be able, under the pretext of individual liberty, to exploit and overreach the weak, and simple, and honest majority. The formula that correctly describes the limits of individual rights is not the one enounced by Kant and Fichte, namely, that a person has a right to do everything that does not interfere with the equal liberty of others. Interpreted in one way, this formula is utterly incapable of application, since the doing of an action by one man means the limitation to that degree of the liberty of all other men. Understood in a completely subjective sense, it would justify and legalize theft, adultery and murder; for I may claim the right to steal if I am willing that others should enjoy the same liberty. The true formula is, that the individual has a right to all things that are essential to the reasonable development of his personality, consistently with the rights of others and the complete observance of the moral law. Where this rule is enforced the rights of *all* individuals, and of society as well, are amply and reasonably protected. On the other hand, if the individual's rights are given a narrower interpretation, if on any plea of public welfare they are treated by the State as non-existent, there is an end to the dignity of personality and the sacredness of human life. Man becomes merely an instrument of the State's aggrandizement, instead of the final end of its solicitude and the justification of its existence. If all rights are derived from the State, and determined by the needs of the State, the laborer has no such thing as a natural right to a Living Wage, nor any kind of right to any measure of wages, except in so far as the community would thereby be benefited. President Hadley tells us that some workers are more profitable at a low wage than at a high one, that the "economy of high wages" is not a universal law. "There are some men whose maximum efficiency per unit of food is obtained with small consumption and small output. These go into lines requiring neither exceptional strength nor exceptional skill, and remain poor because the best commercial economy in such lines is obtained by a combination of low output and low consumption." Those who would measure the rights of the individual by the social weal must logically conclude that whenever "the best commercial economy" is secured by "low consumption," in other words, by low wages, the underpaid worker, let him be never so cruelly "sweated," is not treated unjustly and has no right to a larger remuneration. Hence the importance of the doctrine of rights to the subject of this volume; for it cannot be shown that every laborer has an ethical claim to a Living Wage unless the teaching of Christianity be accepted, to-wit: "That every individual by virtue of his eternal destination is at the core somewhat holy and indestructible; that the smallest part has a value of its own, and not merely because it is part of a whole: that every man is to be regarded by the community, never as a mere instrument, but also as an end." . . .

Chapter V
THE RIGHT TO A PERSONAL LIVING WAGE

It is the purpose of this chapter to show that the workingman's right to a decent livelihood is, in the present economic and political organization of society, the right to a Living Wage. The term "workingman" is taken to describe the adult male of average physical ability who is dependent exclusively upon the remuneration that he is paid in return for his labor. And "a personal Living Wage" means that amount of remuneration that is sufficient to maintain decently the laborer himself, without reference to his family. At the close of the chapter a word will be said concerning the wage-rights of women and children.

The advocates of the Living Wage doctrine do not all reach their common conclusion by the same process of reasoning. Some of them base it on the social benefit to be derived from maintaining the workers in a condition of the highest industrial efficiency; others, on the manifest justice of giving a man sufficient to repair the energy that he expends in his labor; others,

on the "common estimate" of what constitutes a just price for work; and still others, on the personal dignity of the laborer, or his right to possess the requisites of a decent human life. . . .

. . . It has been shown in the last chapter that, on account of his sacredness as a person, every member of a community has an abstract right to a decent livelihood, and that this right becomes concrete and actual when the material goods controlled by the community are sufficient to provide such a livelihood for all, and when the individual performs a reasonable amount of useful labor. It is assumed that the first condition is verified; and it is maintained that the second is fulfilled by the man who labors for hire during a working day of normal length. His general right to as much of the earth's fruits as will furnish a decent livelihood is clear; the correlative obligation of his fellow members of the community to appropriate and use the common bounty of nature consistently with this right, ought to be equally clear. Now, the simple and sufficient reason why this general right of the laborer takes the special form of a right to a Living Wage, is that in the present industrial organization of society, there is no other way in which the right can be realized. He cannot find a part of his livelihood outside of his wages because there are no unappropriated goods within his reach. To force him to make the attempt would be to compel him to live on less than a reasonable minimum. And the obligation of paying him this amount of wages rests upon the members of the industrial community in which he lives; for they have so appropriated the resources of nature, and so distributed the opportunities and functions of industry, that he can effectively realize his natural right of access to the goods of the earth only through the medium of wages. As long, therefore, as the present organization of industry exists, the obligation of not hindering the laborer from enjoying his right to a decent livelihood will be commuted into the obligation of paying him a Living Wage.

The right to a Living Wage is asserted to be valid against "the members of the community in which the laborer lives." Whether the term "members" refers merely to the employers, or to other persons as well, or to the community in its civil capacity, that is, the State, will be fully discussed in later chapters. For the present it is sufficient to point out that the right exists, and that it holds against those who are responsible for converting the laborer's opportunity of getting a living into the opportunity of receiving wages. . . .

One of the principal reasons why the right to a Living Wage has been obscured in the minds of the many, is the complexity of modern economic life. An example or two will illustrate this contention. Let us suppose that six men settle upon a no-man's land, and proceed to divide it amongst them. Although it is capable of affording a comfortable livelihood for all six, five of them—an undoubted majority—organize a government, and divide the land in such a way that the portion allotted to the sixth will barely keep him alive. Each of the other five is thus enabled to enjoy something more than a decent livelihood. Now, it is safe to say that ninety-nine of one hundred men would condemn this proceeding as unjust. They would maintain that the right of the sixth man to the whole amount of land distributed was just as good as the right of any of the others, and that no reason, title, or justification existed for depriving him of an equal share, when that much was essential to a decent livelihood. Imagine, now, a company of fifty men taking up their abode on a territory that no man has previously visited or claimed. Instead of dividing up the land, they till it in common, and distribute its produce. Not all of them, however, labor upon the soil; there is a shoemaker, a weaver, a tailor, a carpenter, and so on; every man performs the task for which he is best fitted. But the distribution of their common product is so carried out that forty-five can live in abundance, while the remaining five have merely the means of continuing to exist and work. The services of these latter, so the other forty-five assert, are not *worth* more than this pittance. Again it is palpable that the common product of a common property has been unjustly apportioned by the arbitrary action of the majority; for the five, we assume, perform a reasonable amount of useful labor. The case is precisely the same, at least in principle, in the more complex and elaborate industrial conditions of today; the members of a community who are in control of its land and resources, violate the laborer's right to live decently out of the common bounty of nature when they so take advantage of the existing distribution of private property as to deny him a Living Wage. In exercising their right of access to the earth, they make it impossible for the laborer to exercise his as fully as is demanded by decency and justice. And they do it just as effectively, they are as truly responsible for the laborer's inability to enjoy his natural right, as the greedy and arbitrary majority in the above mentioned examples. For the laborer, generally speaking, is as little able to change his location as are the harshly treated members of those two isolated communities. A few workingmen could, indeed, find a living elsewhere, but the overwhelming majority must stay where they are, or merely exchange places with one another,—unless the whole machinery of industry is to stop, and mankind to perish off the face of the earth. The controllers of the industries and material resources of a community cannot get along without wage-workers; rather than make the attempt, they would gladly pay every one of them a Living Wage; which is a clear indication that they regard the laborer as really *worth* that amount. Hence the complexity of the present industrial system obscures, but in no way annuls, either the rights of the laborer, or the correlative obligations of his fellow citizens.

Another cause of the prevailing indifference toward these rights and obligations is ignorance and neglect of the common, or social, aspect of property. All too general is the notion sanctioned by the definitions of property in the Roman Law and in the Civil Code of France, that a man has a right to do with his own what he pleases. Such a claim is obviously absurd, since men have not a right to do as they like with their faculties, to say nothing of the bounty of nature which was created for the benefit of all. They have a right to do with their own only that which is consistent with the rights of others. The private proprietor too often forgets that his right of ownership is valid only as a means to his right of use, and that the latter is a right common to all mankind, which he is obliged to interpret and exercise within such limits that its realization shall be possible for his fellow men likewise. He forgets that when he appropriates a portion of the earth's resources for his own use and benefit he diminishes by that much the amount available for private ownership by the rest of men. He forgets that his less fortunate neighbor, among whom must be counted the laborers, have, on account of their inborn right of access to the world's material goods, some sort of claim to that part thereof which he calls his own. The exaggeration of the scope of individual ownership, and of the ability of the propertyless man to take care of himself in the competitive struggle, has converted into a maxim of business ethics the contention that employer and employee have no property rights against each other except those expressly named in the labor contract. The fact that a contract may be the *occasion* of a right which it does not explicitly provide for, is entirely overlooked. It is forgotten that the laborer enters the wage-contract as a man endowed with a natural and indestructible right to a decent livelihood, which the contract renders impossible of realization except through the medium of wages. His right to a Living Wage is merely the former right as modified and determined by the contract. In so far as it is valid against his employer, it is produced neither by his contract with the

latter nor by his right to a decent livelihood, taken separately, but by the two in conjunction.

A truer and more humane conception of the relation between the right of individual ownership and the right of use, and of the duties of the private proprietor, was developed and fostered in medieval society. The Christian doctrine that private ownership is not an absolute right, but merely a form of stewardship, according to which the individual holds his wealth from God and is obliged to administer it for the benefit of others, as well as of himself, was more frequently preached, and more generally and vitally accepted than it is to-day. In the Thirteenth century, we find Pope Clement IV permitting strangers to occupy and till the third part of any estate which the proprietor refused to put under cultivation himself. Pope Sixtus IV, in the Fifteenth century, made the same regulation with regard to domains in the Papal territory. Here we have a clear recognition of the principle that a man has not a right to do what he pleases with his own, but only that which is consistent with the right of common ownership in his needy neighbors. Every man performing a function in the medieval organization of industry, the lord of the land, the free tenant, the villein, the serf, the merchant, the master-craftsman, the journeyman, the apprentice, was regarded as rendering a *social* service. In return for this contribution to the community, the individual had a right, according to medieval theory, to security in his position or status, and to the means of living in conformity with the customs of his social rank. This, again, was merely the doctrine of man's right to a living from the bounty of the earth, applied to the conditions of medieval society. Concrete assertions of the same principle are heard today in the claim of the laborer that he has a right to work and a right to the job that he has held for a considerable time; in the conviction of the employer that his workmen commit an act of *injustice* when they arbitrarily quit work; and in the contention of the independent dealer or manufacturer that he has a right to the business of which he is deprived by the practice of temporary underselling pursued by the trust. The principle underlying all these beliefs, medieval and modern, is that formulated by Aristotle as a canon of social expediency, "it is best to have property private, but to make the use of it common"; and by Aquinas as a requirement of justice, "it is right that the ownership of goods should be private, but the use of them ought to be common, so that the owner may readily minister therefrom to the needs of others." . . .

The obligation of providing the laborer with a Living Wage has been fully outlined in its individual and class aspects. There remains only the question of the extent to which it rests upon the State. That baneful heritage of the Eighteenth century, the doctrine that a minimum of State regulation of industry means a maximum of industrial freedom for the individual, no longer counts any considerable number of adherents. It is demonstrably false in theory, and it has been completely discredited in practice. Negatively, liberty is absence of restraint; positively, it is the power to act and to enjoy. Now the restraints to action and enjoyment are not all political and legal; consequently the individual may possess the fullest immunity from governmental interference, and yet be hindered by some other restraints, such as, the strength, cunning, or selfishness of his fellows, from doing and enjoying those things that are essential to reasonable life. Whenever this happens, the absence of State intervention means the presence of insuperable obstacles to real and effective liberty. In a word, political and legal freedom are not an adequate safeguard to the welfare of the individual. As the Comte de Mun told the French Chamber of Deputies: "Liberty does not consist in a theoretical right, but in the possibility of exercising it. The power to be free, in a régime which puts the workingman's life at the mercy of supply and demand; which exposes himself, his wife,

and his children to the hardships of a competition that knows no moderation; which sets no limit to his exploitation except the interests of those who employ him,—the power to be free in such conditions, when the need of subsistence is so pressing as to permit of no waiting, no choice, no hesitation, does not exist and consequently the laborer is not free." The economic history of the Nineteenth century furnishes abundant proof of these statements, and an overwhelming refutation of the non-intervention theory. Perhaps the clearest and most logical instance is to be found in the conditions prevailing in the mines and factories of England before the passage of the Factory Acts.

Some of the opponents of State intervention in industry may be conveniently classed with the juvenile bully who resents the "interference" of parent or teacher in his relations with younger and weaker boys, and with the burglar or highwayman who objects to the activity of the policeman. These are the possessors of superior bargaining power who realize that if government will only let them alone they will be able successfully to exploit their weaker fellows. Their opposition is natural in the same sense that selfishness is natural. Those who oppose State regulation of industry on higher grounds than self-interest usually misconceive its concrete effects. From this point of view, laws may be divided into two classes: Those which actually restrict the liberty of all or a majority of the citizens; and those which limit the freedom of all potentially but of only a few actually. The first class regulates the simpler, more frequent, and more general activities of everyday life, and puts some practical restriction on the freedom of nearly every person. Yet they bring to him more freedom than they take away. For example, the ordinance forbidding a man to monopolize the street or the sidewalk curtails to that extent his liberty, but secures him the larger liberty of immunity from the inconvenience that would be produced by similar unreasonable conduct on the part of his fellows. Jevons has well said that, "the modern English citizen who lives under the burden of the revised edition of the Statutes, not to speak of innumerable municipal, railroad, sanitary, and other by-laws, is after all an infinitely freer as well as nobler creature than the savage who is always under the despotism of physical want." And the more numerous and complicated social relations become, the greater will be the necessity for regulation, and the larger will be the practical freedom that will result from wise regulation. The second class of restrictions applies theoretically to all the citizens, but practically impedes the liberty or activity of comparatively few, because it has to do with actions that are beyond the reach of the great majority. A law that forbids one hundred persons to do something that ninety-nine of them could never have done in any event, will not deprive the ninety-nine of any valuable freedom. For instance, a statute compelling all employers of railway labor to pay a certain minimum of wages, or to carry goods and passengers at certain maximum rates, would limit the freedom of all persons who owned or operated railroads; but since those who are or can hope to become employers form but a small proportion of the whole number of persons engaged in and affected by this industry, the liberty of the great majority would not be curtailed in any vital way. On the contrary, the latter section of the community would secure a wider measure of freedom in larger economic opportunities. Now, it is to this class of regulations that all the more moderate proposals for increased State intervention belong. They would enlarge the concrete freedom of the majority, and diminish that of the minority. They would affect not so much the legal independence of the individual as the distribution of economic opportunities among different groups of individuals.

As an abstract proposition, the State has both the right and the duty to compel all employers to pay a Living Wage. The function of the State is to promote the so-cial welfare. The social welfare means in practice the welfare of all individuals over whom the State has authority; and the welfare of the individual includes all those conditions that assist in the pursuit of his earthly end, namely, the reasonable development of his personality. The primary business of the State, then, is to protect men in the enjoyment of those opportunities that are essential to right and reasonable life. They may be summed up in the phrase, natural rights. In addition to this, the State is charged with the obligation of promoting social prosperity. That is to say, its task is not merely to provide men with the opportunities that are absolutely essential to right living, but also to furnish as far as practicable the conditions of wider and fuller life. Since man's capacity for progress is indefinite, the State will fail in its mission of furthering social welfare unless it does something toward securing to him the external conditions of something more than the minimum of reasonable personal development. State activity in the first sense is mainly protective and restrictive; in the second, auxiliary and co-operative. Now, a law requiring employers to pay a Living Wage would evidently be an instance of State activity in the primary sense, for it would be an attempt to protect natural rights, and to provide one of the essential conditions of reasonable human life. Even those who hold that the sole function of the State is to safeguard individuals against violence and injustice, in other words, to protect life and property, could logically admit that the enactment of such a law would not be an undue exercise of power. To compel a man to work for less than a Living Wage is as truly an act of injustice as to pick his pocket. In a wide sense it is also an attack upon his life. An ordinance prohibiting this species of oppression would, therefore, be a measure for the protection of life and property.

The question of the legal enforcement of a Living Wage is, consequently, one of expediency. It has two distinct phases. We may ask whether a universal Living Wage is economically feasible; and, supposing it to be workable, whether legal enactment could bring it about. The former inquiry does not concern itself with the productive resources of the country, since, as we have already seen, these are ample to supply all the inhabitants with the requisites of a decent livelihood, but with the consequences that might be expected to follow the establishment of a universal Living Wage in our present industrial system. The difficulties that it suggests remain substantially the same whether this condition be attained through Trade Union action, the payment of sufficiently high prices by consumers, or legal enactment.

This question is frequently answered in the negative, on the ground that if all the laborers who are at present underpaid were to receive a Living Wage, there would be such a rise in the price of the goods and services that they produce as to cause a corresponding decline in demand. Instead of insufficient wages, we should have the evil of insufficient employment. President Hadley says that society, that is, the consuming public, regards the making of a certain amount of product as worth only so much, and if compelled to pay more will diminish the quantity that it consumes. Professor Smart maintains that the decreased demand would result in the laborers being put on short time, so that their Living Wage would prove a misnomer. President Hadley's contention is true in a general way, but it is subject to two important qualifications. It implies, or at least will seem to many to imply, that the consumers look upon the low prices at which certain products sell as a full and precise equivalent of the fixed and necessary "worth" of these articles; and it easily leads to an exaggerated idea of the part taken by consumers in creating these prices. Why do consumers regard certain products of underpaid labor as worth no more than they now sell for? Because the low wages resulting from excessive competition among both employers and work-

ers have enabled these prices to become customary. As Professor Smart points out, the proposition that women's wages are low because the goods that they turn out are cheap, puts—so far as the question of primary causality is concerned—"the cart before the horse." The initiative in reducing prices comes from the producers not from the public. Once prices are down, however, the public accepts them so eagerly that to raise them and the low wages underlying them, constitutes a very difficult problem. This is the explanation of low prices and the real significance of the consumer's estimate of the "worth" of low priced goods. President Hadley would, indeed, be one of the first to subscribe to this view, but his language in the section referred to above can be construed in support of an exaggerated notion of the rigidity and significance of the evaluations made by the consumer. That society regards the prices that it pays for cheap goods as an "equivalent" of the labor expended in producing them, is true in the sense that it will not voluntarily offer to pay more; it is not necessarily true in the sense that society would not pay more for these goods rather than do without them. And this brings us to the second qualification to be made concerning President Hadley's statement, and likewise with regard to that of Professor Smart. A rise in the price of an article will always be followed by a falling off in the demand for it, *other conditions remaining unchanged*. If, however, it is accompanied by a corresponding increase in the purchasing power of consumers, actual and potential, there need be no diminution in the amount sold. The prices of most of the necessities of life have risen greatly in the last seven years, yet the effective demand for them has not decreased. The contrary has, in fact, occurred, thus exemplifying the general rule that high prices mean greater industrial activity and a smaller volume of unemployment. Whether the establishment of a Living Wage in all the industries in which it does not now exist would bring with it sufficient demand to continue or increase the number at present employed, cannot be mathematically determined beforehand. This much, however, may be confidently affirmed: of the actual and potential consumers affected, the richest section would probably buy as much as they did before prices rose; another section would certainly reduce its consumption; some of the laborers formerly underpaid would increase their consumption; and some of them would become consumers of these particular goods for the first time. Hence the effect of a rise in prices consequent upon the universal application of the Living Wage principle would be less simple as well as less serious than the statements of the above-mentioned writers seem to imply.

A second objection is drawn from the assumption that even though the higher range of prices should cause no decrease in demand or in employment, it would swallow up completely the rise in remuneration. What the laborer gained in wages he would lose in the higher cost of living. To put it technically, there would be a rise in nominal but not in real wages. Sidney and Beatrice Webb have carefully examined this contention and given a thoroughly satisfactory reply:

Mr. Herbert Spencer, in the concluding volume of his Synthetic Philosophy, naïvely makes this his one economic objection to Trade Unionism. "If," he says, "wages are forced up, the price of the article produced must presently be forced up. What then happens if, as now, Trade Unions are established among the workers in nearly all occupations, and if these Unions severally succeeded in making wages higher? All the various articles they are occupied in making must be raised in price; and each Trade Unionist, while so much the more in pocket by advanced wages, is so much the more out of pocket by having to buy them at advanced rates." But this is to assume that the wage earners purchase as consumers the whole of the commodities and services which they produce. We need not remind the reader that this is untrue. In the United Kingdom, for instance, though the wage earners number four-fifths of the population, they consume—to take the highest estimate—only between one-third and two-fifths of the annual aggregate of products and services, the remainder being enjoyed by the propertied classes and brain workers. Even if a general rise in wages, amounting to, say, fifty million sterling, produced a general rise in prices to the extent of fifty million sterling, spread equally over all products, it could not be said that the wage earners as a class would have to bear on their own purchases more than one-third to two-fifths of the additional price. If the rise in price was not spread equally over all commodities and services, but occurred only in those consumed by the other classes, the rise in wages would have been a net gain to the wage earners. Only in the impossible case of the rise occurring exclusively in the commodities consumed by the wage-earning classes—these commodities being as we have seen, only one-third to two-fifths of the whole—would that class find its action in raising wages nullified in the simple manner that Mr. Spencer imagines? Hence, it is, that even if a rise in the Standard of Life of the whole wage-earning class produces an equivalent general rise in the price of commodities, the result must nevertheless be a net gain to the wage earners.

With some difference of degree, this analysis describes the bearing of any rise in the price of their products upon that section of the American working class that is at present underpaid. They are not the sole consumers of their products; hence a part of the rise must be borne by others. Nor would these other consumers—laborers, salary-receivers, professional classes, farmers, landowners, employers and capitalists—be able to recoup by raising the price of *their* products and services to such an extent that the net gains of the heretofore underpaid workers would all be absorbed in the additional price that they would have to pay for the same amount of these products and services as they formerly consumed. The workers whose remuneration was raised to the Living Wage level would not be in the same condition of economic advantage, or disadvantage relatively to other economic classes as they were before the rise. There is no more reason for expecting this outcome than there was for the prediction, formerly made, that all the gains effected by Trade Union action would be neutralized by the higher prices that the Unionists would be obliged to pay as consumers. As a matter of fact, group after group have through organization obtained increases in wages, without suffering anything like an equivalent loss in the purchasing power of their individual dollars. Experience has shown that whenever one economic class has gained in money income at the apparent expense of other classes, a part of the gain has been not merely nominal, and a part of it has been not only in appearance but in fact at the expense of the other classes.

Thus far the discussion of both of the objections that we have been considering, has proceeded on the assumption that the rise in prices would be *fully equivalent* to the rise in wages. The assumption concedes too much. Part of the increased labor cost would come out of interest; part out of profits; part out of the saving effected through the elimination of incompetent employers; and part out of the increased efficiency of both labor and capital. Some of the employers who found it impossible to pay a Living Wage and at the same time obtain the usual rate of interest on their own capital invested in the business, would content themselves with a somewhat lower rate. They would do this rather than go out of business. Some of those who were unable to pay the old rate on borrowed capital would offer a lower rate, thereby lessening the demand for capital and exerting a downward pressure on the rate of interest. And this downward pressure would be reinforced by the action of those capitalist-employers who withdrew from business and threw their capital on the market rather than accept a smaller return from their investment. Moreover, since competition is never perfect, and since some businessmen do get money more cheaply than others in similar circumstances, some of the borrowers whom we are considering would succeed in renewing their loans at a lower rate than that which generally prevailed. Some lenders would submit to this condition in preference to the risk of faring worse elsewhere. Finally, there are some employers who would be able and willing to take a part of the added labor cost out of their personal profits. That is, they would be willing to do so rather than cease to be employers or attempt to saddle all the increased expense on the selling price of the product. To deny these general statements concerning the capitalist-employer, the loan-capitalist, and the employer in his capacity of profit receiver, is to contend that all the individuals of these three classes would absolutely refuse to accept a lower return for their money or their activity than they now obtain. It is to maintain that of all the agents of production only the laborer will ever submit to a reduction in his share of the product. Needless to say, this theory is contradicted by experience. Both interest and profits *have* fallen, and there is no good reason to think that they have already reached an irreducible minimum. On the contrary, it is practically certain that the general rate of interest must, independently of the Living Wage question, suffer a further decline. Perhaps a majority of the small employers would not, or could not, continue their present functions if their personal returns were diminished; but this is by no means the case with all. The situation in which employers who were compelled to raise the compensation of their underpaid employees to the plane of a Living Wage would find themselves, is this: the sources from which the additional wage-payments can be drawn are only three, namely, the selling price of the product, interest, and profits. Now the difficulty of raising prices to a level sufficiently high—and of maintaining them there—to provide for all the increased labor cost, is so great that many employers will find it easier and more satisfactory to secure a portion of the necessary funds from one or both of the other two sources. In the third place, some of the more competent or better situated employers at present pay substantially a Living Wage in circumstances and industries in which their competitors generally fail to do so, and could under other conditions take care of a large proportion of the business now carried on by the latter. When the Living Wage became universal they would not find it necessary to raise prices to any appreciable extent, while many of their less competent competitors would be forced to the wall. This "survival of the fittest" might proceed so far that prices would ultimately reach the old level, owing to the satisfactory profits obtained by the "survivors" through the increased volume of sales. At any rate, it is certain that a large number of incompetent employers are now able to continue their functions, not because their services are needed by the community, but because they pay a smaller wage than their competitors; and that the elimination of these from any cause whatever would reduce the total cost of production, and enable their labor force to find employment at better wages with the more competent employers. In the fourth place, a part of the increase in wages would be derived from the increased productivity of the industries in which the rise occurred. The higher wage enjoyed by the laborers would give them a higher physical and mental efficiency, and consequently a greater productive power, while the increased labor cost of production would compel business men to introduce better machinery and a better organization of industry. Most of the improvements of the last century in methods of production seem to have originated in the pressure exerted upon employers and by the demands of labor. As long as they could secure the advantages of cheap production through cheap labor, employers generally declined to undertake the exertion, risk, and expense of discovering or introducing new processes. A similar condition obtains to-day in many of the industries in which labor is underpaid, and a similar course would be adopted by many

employers if they found it no longer possible to hire workers for less than a Living Wage.

In general, it may be said that the arguments against the economic feasibility of a universal Living Wage are reducible to two. The first is that the national product of food and other articles of necessity and comfort would not be adequate; the second, that the machinery of distribution could not be so modified as to achieve the desired result. It is difficult to see how any American economist can take the former contention seriously. As pointed out in an earlier chapter, our natural resources and productive capacity are more than sufficient to furnish the entire population with the requisites of a decent livelihood. And the preceding pages of this chapter have shown that the objections based on the difficulty of obtaining the required modification of the distributive process are far from being conclusive. They can all be, and have been, urged against every effort that has ever been made, by Trade Union action or otherwise, to better the condition of any group of workers; for they all turn on the supposed evil consequences of a higher cost of production and higher prices to the consumer. If there is any difference between the economic and social effects of the gains that labor has already struggled for and secured, and those that would result from the universal application of the Living Wage principle, it is a difference only of degree. Yet experience has shown that gains in wages invariably mean a real improvement in the condition of those obtaining them, and rarely involve any hardship worth considering to other classes or to the community at large. The discussion of this point may be fitly closed with a citation from two investigators of the very highest authority.

We desire to emphasize the point that, whatever political objections there may be to the fixing by law of a National Minimum Wage, and whatever practical difficulties there may be in the way of carrying it out, the proposal, *from the point of view of abstract economics*, is open to no more objection than the fixing by law of a National Minimum of Sanitation, or a National Minimum of Leisure, both of which are, in principle, embodied in our factory legislation. Indeed, a minimum wage, since it would in no way interfere with the fullest use of machinery and plant, or otherwise check productivity, would seem to be even less open to economic criticism than a limitation of the hours of labor.

The obstacles to the legal enactment and enforcement of a Living Wage in America are great, but not necessarily insuperable. There is, in the first place, that perverse individualism which prefers irrational liberty and industrial anarchy to a legal régime of order and justice. This spirit is still sufficiently potent to render exceedingly difficult those changes in the Federal constitution and in the constitutions of the several states which would be a preliminary requisite to any such legislation. After the law had been enacted, the willingness of the unemployed, always numerous in the class affected by the new statute, to sell their labor below the legal rate through fear of not obtaining employment otherwise, would constitute a serious menace to its successful enforcement. In the case of illegal agreements entered into from this motive, both of the contracting parties would be interested in violating the law. Nevertheless there are good grounds for believing that an honest and sustained attempt to secure a Living Wage by legal enactment would meet with a fair measure of success. Public opinion is changing very rapidly in its attitude toward government regulation of industry, and especially with regard to the question of legislative repression of abuses. It is coming to see that unregulated competition has proved itself inadequate to protect the consumer against monopoly and extortionate prices, and the producer against exploitation and starvation wages. Very probably a large majority of the voters of the country agree with President Roosevelt that, if the Federal Government does not now possess the power to regulate corporations adequate-

ly, the National Constitution ought to be changed accordingly. Once an amendment of this character has been effected, constitutional modifications empowering congress and the state legislatures to pass a minimum wage law, could readily be obtained. Thus the greatest of the obstacles to a Universal Living Wage by legal enactment would have disappeared. After the law had been placed on the statute books, organized labor and a large section of the underpaid workers who were not organized would be vitally and actively interested in its enforcement. The penalties attached to its violation could be made sufficiently heavy to deter all but the boldest employers and the most reckless workingmen. Even if it were observed in the case of, say, only one-fifth of the workers previously underpaid, there would be so much gained, and according as the public came to realize the reasonableness and necessity of the new legislation, the proportion of instances in which it was violated would rapidly decrease. Owing to differences in the cost of living and other conditions, the greater part of such legislation would have to come from the several states rather than from the National congress. Its terms in detail and its enforcement could best be determined and secured through a commission, empowered to adjust it to different industries and different centres of population. Precisely the same principle is embodied in the legislation which at present authorizes state railway commissions to fix reasonable rates for the transportation of passengers and freight. Their power to lay down maximum rates on the basis of a reasonable return from investments is at bottom the power to limit, indirectly, of course, the incomes of the stockholders. The wage-commissions would attack the opposite extreme of industrial injustice by fixing a minimum rate of remuneration for the workingmen.

The principle of a Living Wage by legal enactment is already being tested in the Minimum Wage Board law of Victoria, Australia, and in the provision of the Conciliation and Arbitration act of New Zealand which empowers the court of arbitration to prescribe a minimum wage in any industry in which it makes an award. In the former region it has been found that when a fair average wage is fixed as the minimum, competition among employers to get the best possible hands for the money throws the less competent out of employment. Through fear of not obtaining work otherwise, many of the workers whose efficiency is fully up to the average represent themselves as disqualified by "age or infirmity" from earning the minimum wage, and secure a legal permit to sell their labor for less; while others contract for the legal rate, but return a part of their wages to the employer. Similar evasions of the law have been practised in New Zealand, though, it seems, in a smaller proportion of cases. Now it is obvious that any law requiring the payment of a minimum rate of wages must include some provision whereby workers of less than normal efficiency can obtain legal authorization to accept a smaller remuneration. Whenever the supply of labor is in excess of the demand at the legal rate, some of the able-bodied workers will, consequently, attempt to take advantage of the provision by unlawful practices. Illegal and secret agreements to give back a portion of the wages to the employer will likewise be inevitable. Yet the number of evasions of the law from these two causes will—if any reasonable endeavor is made to enforce it—be much smaller than the number of cases in which less than the minimum rate would be paid if the law did not exist. To put it the other way, the proportion of workers obtaining the rate fixed as the legal minimum will be much larger with the law than without it; for in the latter case there would be nothing to hinder employers from hiring the whole body of efficient laborers at a lower rate but purely economic forces, while in the former case there would be the additional obstacle set up by the legal prohibition. And the objection that some men will al-

ways evade the law by handing back a part of their pay to the employer in the form of rebate, applies with equal force to the Union scale, which is really a minimum below which the Unionist is forbidden to go; but no well-informed person rejects on this account the principle of Unionism, or denies that it has benefited the laborer. The practical question is not whether a minimum wage law would be violated—all legal enactments are violated in some degree,—but whether it would not raise to the level of decent living many who would otherwise be forced to remain in a condition of economic wretchedness. As a matter of fact, the net results of the law in both Victoria and New Zealand seem to be an ample justification of its wisdom. "A fair examination of the Victorian minimum wage law," says Dr. Victor S. Clark, "must include the statistical evidence as to its general effect upon wages and employment and the testimony as to its influence on the general condition of the worker. If nobody had been benefited by the law, it would hardly have survived nine years of amendment and legislative attack. . . . There has been a general increase in the pay of male labor equivalent to nineteen per cent, and of female labor to 17 per cent, or about 5s. 9d., and 2s. 3d. ($1.40 and $0.55) per week, respectively, in occupations under the determinations of the boards." Speaking of the arbitration law of New Zealand, an important feature of which is the provision fixing a minimum wage, the same writer says: "With all its apparent defects the act is a success beyond the expectation of many of its early supporters."

Until such time as a general Living Wage law becomes a reality, the State could apply the principle partially. The various legislative authorities, national, state, and municipal, should enact legislation providing that all adult employees in the public services, or employed by private firms on work done by contract for the public, receive a wage adequate to the decent maintenance of themselves and their families. While the number of laborers affected by the law would be comparatively small, the moral effect on public opinion and on purely private wage contracts would be very considerable. Similar legislation could without difficulty be enacted and successfully applied to all quasi-public industries of a monopolistic character, such as railroads, street railways, and telegraph, telephone and express companies. Professor T. S. Adams maintains that a compulsory arbitration law—which would necessarily include the power to determine rates of wages—covering these industries is immediately feasible. When it is recalled that in the highly prosperous year of 1903 more than three-fourths of a million adult males in steam railway occupations received less than a Living Wage, the direct benefits to be derived from this partial extension of the Living Wage principle are readily perceived.

Several indirect methods may be mentioned through which the State could extend the field in which a Living Wage would prevail. The first is legislation limiting the working day to eight hours, and fixing the minimum age at which children would be permitted to become wage earners at sixteen years. The immediate effect of these measures would be a diminution in product, and an increase in the demand for labor. An increase in the price of labor—a rise in wages—would follow necessarily. In general, the objections offered to this argument are identical with those urged against a universal Living Wage, namely, an increased cost of production and a rise in the price of the finished product. They will not be reconsidered in detail here. President Hadley and Mr. John Rae argue that if a universal eight hour régime is followed by a lessening in the per capita production of the laborer, the diminished product will but increase the number of those receiving insufficient sustenance. Mr. Rae's contention that individual wealth cannot be increased by diminishing individual production, is in one sense a mathematical truism; as an abstract and general statement, it is untrue. A smaller product may be so distributed that *some* individuals will receive more than they did when the product was larger. The curtailment of production and increase of individual profits that sometimes follow the consolidation of competing establishments into a trust, affords a familiar illustration. It cannot be too often repeated that with our present abundance of natural and industrial resources, actual and potential, the question of raising the remuneration of the underpaid is only in a very minor degree a question of production. It is almost wholly a question of distribution, of enabling one group of individuals to secure a portion of the national product that is now regularly obtained by other groups.

When machinery is replacing man and doing the heavy work of industry, it is time to get rid of the ancient prejudice that man must work ten hours a day if he is to keep the world up to the level of the comfort that it has attained. Possibly, if we clear our minds of cant, we may see that the reason why we still wish the laborer to work ten hours a day is the fear that we, the comfortable classes, may not go on receiving the lion's share of the wealth which these machines, iron and human, are turning out.

Two other methods of State action to which attention will be called are housing and old age pensions. "No problem," says a recent writer, "presents so many startling aspects as the problem of the housing of the working people." The overcrowded condition in which so many of them are forced to exist involves the "destruction of home life, weakening of parental influence, falling off of religious faith, changed relation of the sexes, absence of privacy, intrusion of strangers upon the family life, the use in common of facilities of living where propriety and decency demand the restriction to a single family, the constant sight and sound and debasing influences from which escape is impossible." The State could build dwellings and sell them to the worst off of the underpaid workers for less than cost, on condition that they be paid for in small installments without interest. The direct gain in comfort to the beneficiaries of this action is obvious; the indirect gain in the form of self-respect, self-confidence, hopefulness, and courage, ambition and ability to contend for better wages and a higher economic position, would be of even greater importance. Finally, the State ought to give every laborer who has become permanently incapacitated for work through old age, and whose wages have not been sufficient to make provision for his declining years, an annual pension. The man that has toiled faithfully during all the vigorous portion of his life has a valid claim against society for this amount. It is, in fact, a part of the Living Wage that is due him for his life work. A system of old age pensions would, moreover, afford considerable relief to many underpaid and moderately-paid workers who are now burdened with the support of relatives that are no longer able to earn their own living. Freed from this charge, many of the former would enjoy a Living Wage in the full sense of the phrase, while others would approach it much more closely than they do at present. State relief of the incapacitated has become an especially urgent problem in this machine age, when the laborer's working life comes to a close so much earlier than formerly.

These forms of State assistance would, of course, entail a heavy financial burden and increased taxation. One method of providing the required funds may be briefly touched upon because of its general bearing on the problem of distribution. A progressive tax on incomes and inheritances could be so framed as to furnish the means of carrying out the projects of housing and old age pensions on a very large scale. The rate on inheritance would naturally be higher than that on incomes. Speaking of the former method of taxation, Andrew Carnegie has written:

Of all forms of taxation, this seems to be the wisest. Men who continue hoarding great sums all their lives, the proper use of which for public ends would work good to the community, should be made to feel that the community in the form of the State, cannot be deprived of its proper share. By taxing estates heavily at death the State marks its condemnation of the selfish millionaire's unworthy life.

It is desirable that nations should go much further in this direction. Indeed, it is difficult to set bounds to the share of a rich man's estate which should go at his death to the public through the agency of the State, and by all means such taxes should be graduated, beginning at nothing upon moderate sums to dependents, and increasing rapidly as the amounts swell, until of the millionaire's hoard, as of Shylock's, at least

". . . The other half
Comes to the privy coffer of the State."

The argument for a graduated tax, increasing in rate with the size of the estate, is as valid in the case of incomes as in that of inheritance. In both, the rich man is compelled to give up to the community a larger percentage of his wealth than the man of moderate means because the richer a man is, the less hardship does he suffer when his possessions are diminished by a given fraction. If it be objected that to apply the proceeds of these forms of taxation to the purposes here advocated, is to take from the rich and give to the poor, the charge may be passed over as correct in substance. It implies, however, a false notion of the morality of the proposal. The State is bound not only to protect its citizens in the enjoyment of their natural rights to the effective opportunity of gaining a decent livelihood by their labor, but to compensate, as far as practicable, those persons for whom it has failed to provide such opportunity. For this purpose taxes must be levied, and they should be apportioned in accordance with the resources of the citizens.

9. THE SOCIALIST MOVEMENT[1]

By CHARLES H. VAIL

EDITORS' NOTE.—The American Socialist party was formed in 1901 by the amalgamation of the three-year-old Social Democratic party and a faction of the twenty-five-year-old Socialist Labor party. In its early years the Socialist party based its analysis and activities on its leaders' interpretations of the writings of Karl Marx as well as on the program and platform of the international socialist movement. It reached the height of its power in 1912, when it had about 120,000 dues-paying members and when its presidential candidate, Eugene V. Debs, polled almost a million votes.

From its inception the party was split into factions which finally grouped themselves into what were known as the right and left wings. The dominant right wing, led by Victor Berger and Morris Hillquit, gradually turned the party's program and activities into one which, while professing belief in the gradual but distant coming of socialism, bore a striking resemblance to that of the Progressive movement. The left wing, led by Eugene V. Debs and "Big Bill" Haywood, advocated a more militant program of organizing and supporting the struggles of industrial unions, which struggles were to culminate in the end of the capitalist state, the establishment of working-class power, and the construction of the co-operative commonwealth. The conflict between the two factions came to a climax in 1919, when the right-wing national leadership expelled the left-wing locals, which then apparently represented a majority of the membership. The right-wing locals continued as the Socialist party, and the left-wing locals became the basis of the new Communist party.

But in 1902, before these theories and factions reached their full development, the Reverend Charles H. Vail, as the first paid organizer for the Socialist party, attempted to state in American terms the Marxist theories which were to be implemented by the new party. His pamphlet, *The Socialist Movement*, was one of the first propaganda pieces of the party to be given national distribution.

The Socialist movement is the natural outcome of modern industrial conditions. Like most great movements, it has passed through a Utopian phase. This period began early in the eighteenth century and was characterized by the Utopian schemes of Owen, St. Simon and Fourier. These men were Socialists in that their starting point was proletarian criticism of the existing social system, and their object the overthrow of the capitalist economy and the substitution therefor of collective ownership. They were Utopians because they did not grasp the real factors of Socialism. They assumed that all that was needed to bring in the new order was enlightenment. They appealed to men as a whole, expecting that, when the matter was rightly understood, all would wish for the change,

[1]. Charles H. Vail, *The Socialist Movement* (Chicago, 1902). By permission of Charles H. Kerr and Company.

and those enjoying special privileges would divest themselves of their possessions and usher in the new order!

The Utopians ignored the class struggle and consequently failed to recognize the fact that a part of society, the ruling class, was satisfied with the existing order and desired its retention. As the Utopians repudiated the class struggle, so they repudiated all political effort. They seemed to think that the preaching of the new gospel was all that was necessary—proclaim aloud the blessings of the new order and it may come, lo! in the twinkling of an eye!

These men were truly children of their age. They did well, grandly well, considering the light they possessed, but they were not in possession of sufficient economic data to enable them to perceive the genesis of capitalist exploitation, or comprehend the law of economic evolution. They perceived the evils of our industrial order and depicted the same with clearness and satire, but it was left to the genius of Karl Marx to point out the genesis of surplus value and the law of economic determinism, and thus reduce Socialism from Utopia to science.

The discoveries of Marx placed Socialism upon a solid foundation. It is now no longer a scheme or device of anyone, but a scientific philosophy, and rests upon an historic, economic and scientific basis.

We need, however, to distinguish between Socialism as a future state of Society and the Socialist movement, which is an effort to realize that state. The Socialist movement must, of necessity, be carried on within the confines of the present social order, and so possesses several well-marked characteristics.

1. *It Is a Proletarian Movement.*

The class upon which the movement rests is the proletariat—the class of wage and salary workers. The very conditions for the existence of modern Socialism was the rise of the proletariat class. It is not my purpose here to trace the origin of this class; suffice it to say that every system has given rise to social classes and the capitalist has produced the proletariat. The history of the origin and development of the proletariat is the history of capitalism itself.

The capitalist system necessarily presupposes the rending of society into two classes—the owners of the means of production and those who have nothing but their labor-power to sell. The laboring class is thus absolutely dependent upon the capitalist class. The ideal of every proletarian movement must, necessarily, be the emancipation of the workers from this condition of dependence and servitude. Before the proletariat can make much progress toward this end it must know itself in its historic relations. A clear conception of these relations reveals the programme and tactics necessary to success.

For the working class to secure its freedom it must cease to be dependent upon the capitalist class, and this can only be accomplished by overthrowing the capitalist order. The abolition of modern capitalism can be accomplished in one of two ways: either by reversing the wheels of progress, destroying modern methods and returning to the days of handicraft and individual production, or by retaining modern methods and pushing on the organization of industry to its logical consummation, collective ownership—Socialism. The latter method is the only one to which the proletariat can attach itself, inasmuch as the proletariat class is the result of the development of the capitalist system, being necessarily associated with production on a large scale. Thus the emancipation of the proletariat must be accomplished by going forward, not backward. Collective ownership of the means of production and distribution is the only solution to the problem.

Socialism, then, naturally arises out of the economic situation of the proletariat. The proletarian movement must, of necessity, have a Socialist ideal, and Socialism must, of necessity, rest upon and receive its initiative from the proletariat class.

Socialism, then, represents the interests

of the proletariat class. A movement represents the interests of a class when it makes for the perpetuity of that class. We thus see how impossible it is for the Socialist movement to represent the interests of the capitalist class. To subserve the interests of this class would be to perpetuate the capitalist system. While Socialism does not, and can not, represent the class interests of the capitalist, it nevertheless represents the higher and truer individual interests of every member of society, for Socialism would realize a nobler civilization. But the members of the proprietary class are so blinded by prejudice and class interests that they are unable to see what would make for a higher social order and a nobler humanity. Thus while Socialism stands for the higher interests of all as human beings, as members of society, it does not represent the class interests of the capitalists, for their class interests signify such policies as make for the continuance of their class. Socialism would abolish the capitalist class and turn all mere owners into useful producers. But when we turn to the laborer we find that Socialism represents not only his personal interest but also his class interest, for the class interest of the laborer is in accord with social progress.

2. *It Points Out the Necessity of Proletarian Class Consciousness.*

Society to-day is divided into two classes—the propertied and non-propertied. Every man born into these class conditions inherits, or acquires, a classhood in addition to his manhood. True civilization can never be attained in a class-constituted society, for the members of neither class can reach their highest development in such conditions. The dominance of class interests prevents men from realizing the highest ideal. The Socialist recognizes the inevitable result of such conditions and so desires to abolish class distinctions and the class element in character, for he knows that human brotherhood must ever be Utopian in a system founded upon antagonistic interests.

While Socialists recognize the neces-

sity of abolishing classes, they nevertheless constantly endeavor to awaken the working class to a sense of class-consciousness. This appears to many inconsistent. They say, "If you wish to abolish classes, why not begin by ignoring their existence?" We answer, Ignoring classes would not alter facts. Classes exist whether we recognize them or not; we may ignore them, but they will not ignore us. Capitalists ignore the existence of classes in order that they may perpetuate them; Socialists recognize the existence of classes in order that they may abolish them. Classes will be abolished not by ignoring their existence, but by so changing our economic system that some will not be able to secure an advantage over others. To-day the possessing class, by its ownership of the means of production, is able to maintain its class character. To rid society of classes we must bring these instruments of production and distribution under collective control, for it is the private ownership of these instruments that divide society into two distinct classes. Socialize these instruments and the possessing or expropriating class will itself be expropriated, or, as Marx expresses it, expropriated of the power of expropriating, and all class distinctions will be abolished.

Now, the only class that has a direct and immediate interest in securing this end is the working class. The interests of this class are diametrically opposed to the interests of the capitalist class. As every class is moved by its material interests, it is necessary to awaken the working class to its interests; in other words, make it class conscious. This class consciousness carries with it a knowledge of the antagonism of class interests, and enables the laborers to see that their emancipation can only be achieved by abolishing the present system and establishing the Co-operative Commonwealth.

Class consciousness, then, means a consciousness of one's own interests as a member of a class, also a consciousness that his interests can best be subserved by advancing the interests of the class to which he belongs. When a laborer realizes these facts he is said to be class conscious. He then sees that his interests, and the interests of his class, are directly opposed to the interests of the capitalist class. He also apprehends the historical fact that the ruling class have always been, since the dawn of private property, the class that owns the dominant factor of production. In feudal times it was the owner of land, to-day it is the owner of the machine. Every step in the development of capitalism meant added economic power for the capitalist class, and political supremacy finally resulted from this growth of economic power. While this is true of the capitalist class, the class conscious laborer realizes that for him political supremacy cannot thus be secured, for the reason that every step in the development of capitalism has meant his greater subjection. Yet with this loss of economic power, due to the development of modern industry, there has come the possibility of political supremacy through the growth of numbers. Upon the political field the working class can become supreme. It overwhelmingly outnumbers the capitalists and its power is sure to increase.

It must be evident to all that the control of the political power is necessary to any class which would permanently improve its economic condition. The first step, then, toward the worker's emancipation is to gain this control. It is thus that Socialists, the world over, emphasize the necessity of class conscious political action upon the part of the working class.

The laborers can here learn a lesson in tactics from the capitalists. The capitalist class is thoroughly class conscious. It perceives the course of action necessary to maintain its supremacy, and it can always be relied upon to subserve its own interests.

But the laborers are, as a whole, un-class-conscious; that is, they act in direct opposition to their own interests. This they do simply because they fail to recognize the opposition of class interests, and do not see that their interests are antagonistic to those of the master class. They have been accustomed to take their economic and political ideas ready-made at the hands of their employers, and this class have seen to it that only such ideas were propagated among the workers as would result in the supremacy of capitalist class rule. Of course, as long as the workers look to their masters for guidance, they will be led like sheep to the shambles. It is to the interest of the ruling class to maintain its position, but to do this the workers must be kept in ignorance of the true situation, for if they remain in slavery it can only be by their own consent. Were it not for this systematic perversion of the egoism of the subjected class, so that they do not see what pertains to their real interests, the system could not be maintained.

The laborers are constantly deceived as to what constitutes their real interests. They are taught that the interests of laborers and capitalists are identical, that every man has an opportunity to become a capitalist and if he does not he alone is to blame, that the present system and laws are sacred and must be retained at all hazards, that workers should be meek and content with their lot and look to the future world for reward for present suffering, that the laborers are impotent to help themselves—all benefits must come from the class above, etc., etc. As the capitalist class control the means of information—the press, platform, and often the pulpit—it can bring these false conceptions to bear upon the working class and thus keep them in subjection.

The wage system in itself is admirably adapted to deceive the worker. He being paid in money, does not apprehend the manner in which he is wronged. He takes his wages, thinking it to represent the full value of his toil, when, in reality, it is far short of the value he has created. The wage system blinds him to the fact of exploitation. Of course, if he were conscious of the fact he could not help himself under the present system, for, the means of production being monopolized, he must submit to this injustice or starve. But one thing a knowledge of the evil would do, it would make him class conscious and cause him to take a stand with the class to which he belongs, and unite his efforts with other class conscious laborers in abolishing the cause of all exploitation—the capitalist system.

3. It Is Based upon the Class Struggle.

Ever since the dawn of private property in the means of production, society has been made up of classes, known at different epochs under various titles—masters and slaves, feudal lords and vassals, capitalists and proletarians—and a struggle is everywhere manifest between these classes of diverse economic interests.

The class struggle is a corollary of the struggle for existence. As the Darwinian law explains organic evolution, so the Marxian law explains social evolution. The struggle between classes, re-enacts, on the human plane, the drama of the struggle between species. It is the last form of this struggle that we are interested in to-day. The proletariat, as we have seen, is in a condition of dependence. If it becomes emancipated it must become supreme, and its supremacy can only be accomplished by a struggle. This struggle for mastery is necessarily a class struggle, a struggle between the proprietary and non-proprietary classes. The subjection of the working class, being due to the fact that the instruments of production are the private property of another class, makes the interests of these two classes antagonistic and a class struggle inevitable. The fact of this class struggle need not be argued, it is evident, on every hand, by the class legislation, and the strikes, boycotts, and lockouts which are a matter of daily occurrence.

The class struggle is the necessary outcome of class distinctions which involve class interests. The upholding of class interests naturally leads to class opposition and a class struggle.

We cannot expect those who are enjoying special privileges to willingly relinquish their advantages. It is but natural that they should strive to maintain a system that enables them to live in luxurious idleness off the labors of others. There is not an instance in history where a social class has, against its own real interests and out of altruistic motives, made any essential concessions. To suppose that through sympathy or altruism, or interest in the welfare of the whole, the capitalist class will freely divest itself of its class privileges, is to postulate greater wonders than are contained in the legends of the past. Individuals have done this, but not a whole class. This injustice will only down at the bidding of the working class. Thus a class struggle is inevitable between these two classes of opposite economic interests.

We must never lose sight of the class character of the movement. This does not mean, however, that members of other classes will not be welcome, but only that those who come should recognize the character of the movement and lend their efforts to furthering the cause, instead of, consciously or unconsciously, endeavoring to side-track the movement by efforts to introduce into its programme any middle class, reactionary measures. The Socialist movement being based upon the class struggle leaves room for no compromise.

Although the Socialist movement is based upon the class struggle, the triumph of the proletariat class means the abolition of all classes. The reason why previous revolutions resulted in the continuance of class dominance, is due to the failure to abolish class ownership in the instruments of production. But the proletariat supremacy will result in the abolition of all dependence, because the tools of production are now social and the working class cannot emancipate itself except by socializing these instruments. When these instruments are owned collectively the cause of dependence and servitude will be abolished. The abolition of private or corporate ownership, means the abolition of all class rule and all class distinctions.

The new order, then, is not merely an exchange of ruling classes, a society in which the relative positions of the two classes have been reversed, but rather a condition where classes themselves will become extinct; where the interests of one will become identical with the interests of all, and where the interests of all will be united in the social interests.

The class struggle will result in the supremacy of the working class, but when this class is exalted to power it will soon lose its present class characteristics. Out of the changed conditions a new type will arise differing from all preceding types, inasmuch as these are dominated by class conditions. Individual character is largely the child of social relations and conditions, consequently, the proletariat must necessarily bear the mark of its environment. The establishment of healthy social conditions will at once reveal itself in human conduct and character.

Thus while as militant our cause is identified with class, as triumphant it is identified with humanity. The class struggle, then, is but a means to an end—the abolition of social distinctions by abolishing class ownership of the means of production and distribution. Under Socialism all will be members of the one class—humanity, and the golden age so long dreamed will be a realization on earth.

4. *It Is a Revolutionary Movement.*

It must be perfectly clear from the foregoing that the Socialist movement is not a reform but a revolution. A reform merely proposes a readjustment of the relations within the present class organized society. It does not involve a change of economic base, but merely a change of externals. Revolution, on the other hand, involves a change from within—a change in the internal mechanism of society without which there could be no progress.

As to whether a measure is socialistic or not, depends upon its internal mechanism —upon the standpoint from which it proceeds. A measure may be apparently socialistic; that is, it may be so in outward form, while its internal working may be anti-socialistic and designed to serve the interests of some portion of the capitalist class. For example, both the reformer and Socialist want to socialize the railways, electric light plants, trolley systems, etc. The former desires to socialize them as a reform, while the latter proposes socialization as a revolution. In either case there would be a change in external form. The difference is, that the reformer would confine the change to externals, while the Socialists would cause a change in the internal mechanism. The reformer proceeds from the standpoint of middle class interests as against the interests of the plutocracy; the Socialist proceeds from the interests of the working class as against the interests of both the middle and upper class capitalists. The reformer, for instance, wishes only to abolish the railroad monopoly which is fleecing the middle class, the Socialist wishes to abolish all fleecers by abolishing the wage system. The reformers' scheme of socialization would not secure the workers emancipation—they would still be wage slaves and exploited by the capitalist government out of a portion of the wealth they produce. The scheme would undoubtedly reduce the cost of transportation, but there is no evidence that the middle class would reduce the price of their products to consumers. All they are interested in, is to transfer the large profits of the railroad magnates into their own pockets. The Socialist plan, on the other hand, proposes a change not only in the external form but in the internal mechanism. It proceeds from the proletarian point of view, and has for its object the abolition of all exploitation and the improvement in the condition of the railroad workers. To public ownership we would add democratic management.

Socialism, then, proposes a complete transformation of society—a change so radical as to constitute a Social Revolution. The term revolution is used to describe the final goal to be attained, but not the method or tactics employed in its realization. While Socialism is revolutionary in its programme, it follows the laws of evolution in its method of attainment.

But here, note, that evolution does not always proceed with regularity. At first, during the germinating period, it proceeds slowly, but it gains in rapidity and finally the decisive step is often accomplished quickly and is termed revolution. Christianity in the Roman Empire, the Reformation, the French Revolution, the abolition of Chattel Slavery, are notable examples of the working of this principle. Revolution, then, is but a form of evolution, a decisive point, and is generally the last step in a period of slow growth and preparation, although there may be many such steps, revolutions and counter revolutions, before the ultimate end is attained. In the coming transformation the final step, whether peaceful or violent, which interchanges the relations between the ruling and subject class, will constitute the Social Revolution.

Thus we see there is no contradiction between evolution and revolution, whether we employ the terms to describe methods and ideals or the different phases in the progress of the movement itself. Of course, when we speak of the movement as revolutionary, we refer to the ultimate aim and purpose. A failure to understand how scientific Socialists use this term has led to much confusion.

We are surely nearing the consummation of the industrial evolution. But this does not mean that we have nothing to do, that we are to sit quietly down and patiently wait for the transition! It is our business to take such action as will facilitate, in every way possible, the realization of our ideal.

But what action will be effective? Here the reformer again comes into evidence and argues that as Socialism cannot be completely realized at once, we should abandon our advocacy of proletarian supremacy and the ultimate aim, and concentrate all our efforts upon reform measures. This method may sound reasonable, but the fact of class government renders it impracticable. The proposition completely overlooks the fact of class rule. It fails to see that in the present class organization of society, no measure can be introduced that touches the citadel of vested rights; that is, as long as the capitalist class is in complete control of political power. Capitalists frequently permit reforms that do not interfere with their privileges, but the moment some measure is proposed that threatens their interests the tables are turned. Can we expect it to be otherwise as long as the government is in the hands of a master class? For one to imagine that he can effectually curtail the power of the privileged class, so long as that class is in possession of the machinery of government, is the height of absurdity.

It is true Socialism will not spring at once full fledged into existence—Socialists have no magic wand which will effect the social transformation in a single day—but the first step toward that end is the overthrow of the present ruling class through the mastery of the public powers. When Socialists are in control of the government they will then proceed to put their ideals into practice. It will not all be accomplished at once, but as rapidly as possible industry after industry will be socialized, until all businesses are brought under collective control.

Of course, before Socialists have captured the national government they will gain control of municipalities and states, and as fast as they gain control they will carry out, as far as possible, the principles of Socialism. But, note, the first step is to gain control—is political supremacy.

This has already been accomplished in many European municipalities, and the benefits of a Socialist administration, within the limits prescribed by the state, are now being enjoyed. It is not, however, by reform, but by revolutionary methods, that results are being realized. We do not eschew taking a step at a time, then, provided the step is in the right direction and tends toward the realization of the final ideal. To the scientific Socialist there is no contradiction between the present day work and the revolutionary agitation. The immediate results which we seek to obtain are merely means for the realization of the ultimate aim. Thus, while not losing sight of the ultimate goal, we propose taking the road that leads to the Co-operative Commonwealth and capturing en route every outpost on the way. Labor conditions will improve just in proportion as the outposts are captured by the Socialist Party. Not only this, but any temporary relief that is granted by the capitalist class will be in proportion to the fear caused the class by revolutionary agitation. If labor laws are passed it is only to pacify the proletariat, but the capitalist class will only see the need of such pacification as the proletariat organize into a class-conscious party. Even then, upon the plea of getting something now, the surest way to secure it is to build up the Socialist vote. *Revolutionary agitation and social reform go hand in hand.*

How many times the laborers have been buncoed! Measures have been passed supposedly designed to benefit labor, but afterwards were frequently found to be inadequate or ineffective, and, if not, were declared unconstitutional by the capitalist courts. The only way to secure effective labor legislation is to have it backed by a class-conscious labor party. Just in proportion as the Socialist Party gains ascendancy it will secure this end, and will also extend the public service in the interest of the working class. This will not be state Socialism or state capitalism, but rather, what has been termed the infiltration of Socialism into the State. This would result in immediate benefit to the working class. The public powers would then be an instrument in the hands of the organized proletariat to work for the betterment of social conditions. Even when we have gained complete control, the State will still be a class instrument during the period of transition from private to public owner-

ship—an instrument of the proletariat class to effect its complete emancipation. It will be the business of the Socialist Party, when in control of the State, to carry out to completeness the legislative task of transformation. But, remember, all changes that tend to leave the present class government intact are mere reforms, and no change that threatens class rule can be introduced until the present class rule itself is subverted. This can only be accomplished by the triumph of the Socialist Party.

5. It Reveals the Origin of Surplus Value.

The discovery of the source of surplus value, which reveals the secret of capitalist exploitation, we owe to Karl Marx. By surplus value is meant the excess of value in labor's product over and above what the laborer receives in return for his labor. It is the surplus value of the product of labor over the value of the labor power expended.

Labor's exploitation is due to the fact that the laborer, owing to the monopoly of the means of production, is unable to employ himself, and consequently must sell his labor power to the owning class or starve. Labor power is thus an article of merchandise and the labor market becomes a branch of the general market of commodities. The cost of labor power is determined, like the cost of any other commodity, by its cost of production. As labor power is a capacity of the individual, its production presupposes his existence, and, consequently, the production of labor power consists in the production or maintenance of the laborer.

The owner of labor power, like the possessor of any other commodity, sells its use value and receives in return its exchange value. The laborer cannot secure payment for the use value—the full productivity—of his labor power, for the means of production are owned by another class. The employer, then, can purchase labor power at its exchange value, which is determined, as we have seen, by the average cost of living. The capitalist having bought a day's labor power has use of it for the day, and all the wealth the laborer creates during this time goes to the capitalist. The capitalist returns to the laborer, in the form of wages, that which is necessary to maintain the laborer and enable him to keep up his labor power. Under present conditions this amounts to about one half the product produced. The value of labor power, then, and the value which labor power produces, are two entirely different quantities.

The peculiarity of the commodity labor power is that it imparts to the product a greater value than the cost—a value greater than the value of the labor power consumed. It is in view of this surplus that the capitalist engages in production. He buys and sells labor power, and makes the difference between its exchange value and its value in use—between what he pays for it and the value of the product it creates. He buys labor power for a certain amount of money and sells it for more money. The capitalist can make nothing in the buying and selling of the other factors of production—raw materials, machinery, etc.—their value is merely consumed in the process of manufacture and passes over and is embodied in the new product, but with no increase. It is only the living commodity, labor power, that transfers to the new product an additional value—a value in excess of its cost. This excess is called surplus value, because it is the value left after the value of the labor power consumed in the factors of production—machinery, raw and auxiliary materials, and the living labor—has been deducted. This surplus is what accrues to the capitalist class in the form of profit, interest and rent. It represents the fleecings of labor.

The only way of abolishing this exploitation is to make the means of livelihood the common, inalienable property of all the people. When the laborers own collectively the means necessary to their existence they will receive the entire product of their toil. We demand the social ownership of that which is socially used. The private ownership of social tools means the private appropriation of the product of social labor.

6. It Recognizes the Fact of Economic Determinism.

Marx's discovery of the law that economic conditions constitute the determining cause of the moral, judicial and political phenomena is one of the most important discoveries of modern times. We have here the key to the explanation of human history, and of social and moral progress.

The Socialist philosophy points out that all social advances are secured through a struggle of classes. The economic conditions, the method of wealth production of each period, produces a dominant ruling class, and this class is able, through its mastery, to determine the social laws, rules and customs. At first the interests of this class are in accord with the advance of society, but the time comes when their interests, and consequently their customs and institutions, conflict with social progress. The economic development which produces this contrast also produces a class whose interests are contrary to the ruling class and more in accord with social development. A conflict is sure to ensue between these two classes, and the class more in accord with the changed conditions is bound to triumph. In this contest for mastery both classes are actuated by material interests.

As long as the interests of the ruling class are in accord with social advance, the prevailing economic system and its ethical code are right, but when the interests of this class become opposed to social progress, then the system and its moral standard become wrong. The changed condition gives rise to a new ethical code, which, at first, is in accord with social progress and well-being. An economic system, then, and the moral code derived therefrom are right only as long as they make for the advance of society.

We see by this that there may be extant two codes of ethics at the same time—one representing the interests of the ruling class, the reflex of the established order, the other representing the interests of the new class, which the changed conditions have brought into being. This class naturally interprets right, justice and ethical precepts to uphold the system; in other words, to suit its economic interests. We may say, then, that the commonly accepted idea of morals and right conduct in any age is that which tends to the well-being of the dominant class. The ethics of each period are inspired by the interests of this class, and the subjected class is influenced in its action by an apparent egoism, that is artificially engendered in their minds through moral suasion and deception.

Every social system thus has its code of morals, which, in a class organized society, is composed of two parts: one for the masters and one for the slaves—different ideas of right and wrong always exist for the ruling and subservient classes. But the ethical systems are ever changing with the changing methods of production, which introduce new relations between men and thus give rise to new ideas of right, etc.

The validity of this philosophy becomes evident by an examination of the various stages of social evolution. In primitive times cannibalism reigned supreme. When one tribe conquered another they had no use for the captives but to roast and eat them. In this action they were following their instinct of self-interest—they knew of no more profitable way of disposing of their prisoners of war. But in the course of time certain tribes advanced, or certain members thereof became more intelligent, and turned to the cultivation of the soil for subsistence. This class soon discovered that it was more profitable to keep their captives alive and compel them to work, than it was to put them to death. The social system having now become sufficiently developed to enable them to keep their prisoners under control, cannibalism soon disappeared and was supplanted by slavery. But it was not until man found that it paid better to make his captives

slaves that he ceased to be a cannibal. This was a decided step in advance, both economically and morally, and those adopting the new method, though at first undoubtedly in the minority, secured an advantage which gave them power by which they completely overthrew the old order. From this higher material plane their moral vision enlarged, and they soon realized that it was immoral to kill and eat human beings. Here, note, it was not moral sentiment that caused the advance, but economic changes which made it to the material interests of some to preserve their captives alive. They followed this course because it was easy and advantageous. Thus cannibalism disappeared and the slave system became established.

This new system continued to exist until it became unprofitable to own human beings as chattels. This change is well illustrated in this country where history so rapidly repeats itself. When industry began to be revolutionized in the North, it was soon evident that to own the negro and care for him was too expensive. It was more profitable not to own the worker, as the ownership of the land and capital carried with it the virtual ownership of the men who must have access to these instruments or starve. So the North sold their slaves to the South and converted the propertyless workers into wage slaves. Chattel slavery, then, disappeared in the North just as soon as the introduction of machinery rendered the institution unprofitable, and it would undoubtedly have disappeared in the South ere this had not the struggle resulted in a war which summarily abolished it. The changed economic conditions rendered chattel slavery unprofitable—capitalism and the chattel system are incompatible.

The rising capitalist class at the North thus disposed of its slaves, not through sentiment or moral conviction, but purely from self-interest. But this high material plane, to which their economic development had raised them, clarified their vision, and they saw that it was wrong to own human beings as chattels. This moral conviction, however, was not general until the institution became unprofitable. The changed conditions gave rise to an ethical system in which chattel slavery was wrong, but the institution was only viewed as wrong by public opinion when modern industry found it more profitable to simply buy the labor power of men rather than buy the men themselves.

The cause of the revolution, then, was the rise of a new class whose interests were antagonistic to the old system, and more in accord with the changed economic conditions which demanded free labor. A struggle was sure to ensue between these two classes, and the class more in accord with social progress naturally survived. The transition has differed somewhat in different countries. In France, for instance, the struggle of the rising capitalist class was with the landed nobility, who had previously supplanted the slave owner. But this country passed from slavery to capitalism without going through what is usually known as the feudal stage. The colonists were freed from the oppressive restrictions on trade, which were feudal in character, by the American Revolution. Capitalism, like all preceding systems, was established by a class pursuing its material interests along the lines wrought by the industrial evolution.

Capitalism to-day rules supreme. As the laws and ethical opinions are the reflex of the prevailing economic system, it follows that the reigning morality of to-day is capitalist morality; that is, the morality that sanctions private ownership of the means of living, and the use of these means to enslave the workers. Capitalist morality, as pointed out by Loria, is made up of a series of regulations imposed by the owning class upon the laboring class, in opposition to the latter's real interests, and upon the capitalists, sometimes in opposition to their immediate interests—often masters need restraining from acts which would lead their slaves to rebel—and it is these regulations that guarantee the perpetuity of capitalist society. Were it not for the systematic perversion of the egoism of the laboring class, by which they are unable to see the line of action that subserves their real egoism, the present system could not be maintained. The working class, being thus deceived as to their real interests, are led to support a system that holds them in servitude.

The economic evolution, however, is not yet completed; the conditions have materially changed since the supremacy of the capitalist class. At first the interests of this class were in accord with social progress, but that time has long since passed. The interests of society and the interests of the capitalist class are now antagonistic. Society wants a large product, but the capitalists want high values and values are opposed to abundance. Progress and well-being are thus blocked by this antagonism between social interests, and the interests of the capitalist class. The material interests of this class and the laws, customs and institutions which they have established, are now at variance with the changed methods of production. Production to-day, based upon mechanical invention and a far-reaching division of labor, is essentially social production. This contradiction between the new form of production and the old form of appropriation is the cause of the whole social conflict. We have now reached a point where the private ownership of these tools blocks the way to further progress, consequently private ownership has now become a moral wrong. But this very economic development which has produced the contrast between the social and capitalist interests has also developed a class whose interests are more in accord with progress and well-being. This class is the proletariat—the class of wage and salary workers. An economic struggle is now on between these two classes, and the class more in accord with the changed conditions, and so in accord with the higher moral ideal, will triumph. This class is the proletariat. The interests of this rising class can only be subserved by overthrowing the ruling class, as every other class has done, and remodeling the institutions of society in accordance with its class interests. But the difference between the proletariat supremacy and that of the other classes is this: in the new regime, all society will become members of the one producing class, so that the new institutions will be advantageous to all. The triumph of the working class, as we have seen, will mean the abolition of all economic dependence, for their emancipation can only be wrought by socializing the instruments of production and distribution. By abolishing private ownership the cause of economic servitude will disappear.

The working class, then, have a mission to perform, and that mission is the abolition of wage slavery. It is perfectly natural that this class, like its predecessors, should follow its material interests and overthrow the ruling class, and establish a system in harmony with changed conditions and social progress. The self-interest of the working class will lead it to abolish capitalism and usher in the Co-operative Commonwealth, for their interests are in accord with social progress and the higher moral standard.

We see here how economic conditions determine the question of right. In the days of individual production private ownership of the tools was necessary to secure to the laborer his freedom and the full product of his toil. But when the method of production was revolutionized and the tools were transformed into social instruments, they were not capable of individual ownership on the part of the laborers. The principle of private ownership, which had hitherto been the means of securing to the laborer his full product, became now the means of his servitude and exploitation. The changed conditions rendered what was once right a decided wrong.

We need here to keep clear the fact that there exist to-day two codes of ethics—the capitalist and the proletariat or Socialist.

The interests of the capitalist class are no longer in accord with social progress—capitalism has performed its function in social advance—consequently, the capitalist code of morality is wrong. The interests of the proletariat, on the other hand, are in accord with social progress, and therefore its ethical code is right—it is the standard of the new order of society toward which we are rapidly moving.

There have been men in each period who perceived the economic changes, and so gained a glimpse of the new order then forming, and from this vantage ground were able to see clearly the incompleteness of the prevailing ethical ideas. Those of the rising class who thus gained this clear vision were lifted to a new point of view. The realization of the new conditions and their class interests raised them to a higher plane and enabled them to see the injustice of the old system. To-day those who perceive from the new standpoint realize that private property in the means of production is as wrong as private property in human beings.

And now here comes in the power of the moral idea to make for progress. Just as the old idea of right, itself the product of economic conditions, impels men to act in accord with those conditions, so the perception of the new conditions and relations gives rise to new ideas of right, which impel men to action—to labor in bringing in the new social order. It is difficult for a member of the ruling class to realize the imperfect moral standard of the present system. Here and there a capitalist may see the new moral ideal, but the great majority will have to wait until the new order is an accomplished fact before they will realize that a higher moral standard has been born. The Socialist, alone, from his standpoint, perceives the higher ideal and the ultimate morality of the final state of society.

Morality, then, has passed through a process of evolution—there has never existed a universal or permanent code of ethics. The system prevailing at any definite period was produced by the underlying economic conditions, and changed according as the conditions that produced it changed; in fact, the prevailing moral system, in common with all social institutions, has its foundation in the economic conditions and relations of men in society. Of course, we are not here considering the various ideal systems of ethics that have arisen in the minds of philosophers, but the codes that have actually existed in the different stages of social development. The moral forms are products of economic conditions. In each period the forms were considered perfect, but that which was considered moral in one period become immoral in the succeeding, because the old ideas of right, justice, etc., ceased to accord with the new conditions wrought by the industrial evolution.

We need here to note that the ethical beliefs of one system may survive for a long time (and perhaps indefinitely unless they come in direct antagonism with new conditions) after the conditions that produced them have passed away. Not only is this true in regard to the coarser ideals, but also with those high ideals of right relations of man to man, which, undoubtedly, are survivals of that early communism wherein the interests of men were identical. Beyond doubt the lofty ethical sentiments which pervade the teachings of all the ancient moral and religious leaders of the world had their origin in the economic conditions and relations of primitive communism. Mr. Louis Morgan calculated, assuming 100,000 years to cover the life of the human race on this planet, that communism existed 95,000 out of the 100,000 years. Under this form of social organization man progressed from the lowest savagery to the very frontier of civilization. In those days the means of production were owned by the gens or tribe, and the distribution was in accordance with the needs of the members of the community. Although each of these groups in the earlier stages was at war with other groups, still, within the group, perfect harmony prevailed. Kinship was the basis of connection, and out of the common interests and mutual dependence the spirit of love, brotherhood and fraternity was born. Here was first realized, although within narrow limits, the sense of man's organic unity, of their solidarity, which afterward constituted the inner, underlying meaning of all the great faiths of the past, dominating the ancient Greeks, Romans and Hebrews, and also the Christians of early times. But in these times the sense of man's organic unity was confined within narrow limits—only in the new order will the ideal be fully realized. But we find in this primitive communism the origin of the law of love and service, which is the natural outcome of the identity of economic interests. These lofty sentiments and ideals still survive, although the economic conditions that produced them have long since disappeared. This system, which bound up the interests of each with society as a whole, has left in the human mind an instinct for mutual helpfulness.

With the dawn of private property there arose a system of ethics more suitable to further the interests of individual owners. The higher ideals were rendered impracticable by the changed conditions, but the ideals have continued to exist through the various stages of social development. They are frequently referred to to-day as Utopian, as belonging only to the millennial period. These higher ideals appear so merely because they are inapplicable to the present system of industry—their economic base has been destroyed. Will the time ever come when the economic conditions will naturally accord with the highest ethical ideals? When the economic system will produce a code of perfect morality and compel men to recognize their organic unity? We believe that it will. We are nearing a point when, after our cycle of development under private property in the means of production —a cycle undoubtedly necessary to social progress as a whole—we shall complete our cycle, which, though seeming to return upon itself, always advances and ascends. The method of social evolution, to use the words of Goethe, is spiral, the concluding phase of the cycle being always higher than the starting point, and preserving all the vital conquests of the preceding period. Such is the law of all organic growths. As society began with social ownership it will again attain social ownership in its consummation, only on an infinitely higher plane. The method of production has already been socialized, and as a result a new code of ethics has arisen, which, upon examination, is found to contain all the highest ideals and sentiments that have existed through the ages. These ideals, however, will remain impracticable until the method of ownership is made to correspond with the method of operation. Social use of the means of production demands social ownership. When the means of production are collectively owned, then will be re-established, only on a higher and broader scale, the common interests of men, and out of this identity of economic interests the higher ideals—love, brotherhood and fraternity—will again be realized.

The Socialist regime, with its public functions and social co-operation, will make all conscious of their organic unity. It will restore the conviction of solidarity by establishing a system wherein the interests of all are identical. Society will then be seen to be an organism which is pursuing a definite course of development with but one destiny in view. Although human solidarity is a fact to-day, all being partakers of a common origin, a common life, and a common destiny, still men are not conscious of it, or if they are it is not a moving factor in their life. Many hold the belief in man's organic unity as a theory and preach the doctrine of human brotherhood, but it is not a vital, living truth with them. The reason they do not take their faith seriously is due to the present system of antagonistic interests. Under such conditions it is not strange that human solidarity, the brotherhood of man, even with those who have incorporated it into their creeds, is looked upon as an idle dream. This great truth can only become a vital faith in a system of social co-operation. The present class organization of society obscures the ideal. Economic solidarity is necessary to a realization of human solidarity. Men will never become conscious of the latter until they realize the former. When the means of production and distribution become the property of all the people, then the interests of all will be identical and the organic unity of men will become a recognized fact.

The realization of economic solidarity will give to life a new interpretation and realize the highest ethical ideals. The morality of individualism makes self the center, and is thus anti-Christian and anti-social. The morality of Socialism makes society the center. The realization of economic solidarity will make the interests of every man identical with the interests of every other man and with society as a whole, thus making the social welfare the ultimate good. The end of the individual, then, cannot be found in himself, but in society of which he is a part. As his interests are identical with the social interests, he can only seek and realize his own well-being through the collective well-being. In such an organization of society no one could serve his own interests without serving the interests of others, and, conversely, no one could injure others without injuring himself. The golden rule, "Whatsoever ye would that men should do unto you, do ye even so unto them," would then become a possible and natural way of living.

Egoism and altruism thus become in the new order practically identical. If I seek directly my own interests I minister to the well-being of others, and if I minister directly to their well-being I contribute to my own. Under such a system selfishness would be plucked up by the roots. Selfishness is only possible where one can gain at the expense of another. It is perfectly right for men to look out for their own interests; the trouble to-day is that they cannot perform this duty without injuring their fellows. Socialism will remove this difficulty by realizing the identity of human interests. Egoism, then, will be perfectly legitimate under the new regime; in fact, egoism and altruism will be the two sides of the moral shield. But this egoism will not be the gross egoism which results from the present system of industry. This higher egoism will care for the true self, but it will not make this the center, for it will realize that it can only care for its well-being by looking on the self as a means of forwarding the social well-being.

Under Socialism, then, morality will obtain its ultimate form. In an economic constitution which assures equality of opportunity, the personal interests of each would preclude all injurious acts, for the interests of all would be the same. Under such an economy, the free exercise of each man's egoism tends not only to the well-being of the individual but also toward social well-being. The fact that man is guided by the instinct of self-preservation, or personal egoism, does not mean that he is either bad or good. This fundamental instinct, as pointed out by Loria, is in itself undetermined in its direction; it manifests, benevolently or malevolently, in accordance with the economic relations under which it operates. Whether it impels to justice or injustice, depends entirely upon circumstances. Under present economic conditions, where one man can seek his own advantage at the expense of another, this egoism urges toward injustice; but under Socialism, where one cannot thus gain at the expense of another, this very egoism will impel toward acts of justice. The same cause which to-day leads to wickedness will then lead to goodness, for egoism, in itself, is not responsible for good or evil, but rather the condition under which it operates.

Under Socialism the highest rule of human conduct, the ethical sanction, will consist in that which makes for social well-being.

CONCLUSION

The foregoing constitutes the chief characteristics and doctrines of the modern Socialist movement. It is a movement, primarily, as we have seen, of the proletariat class to acquire possession of the means necessary to its livelihood. It appeals to the class interest of the proletariat, for its interests demand the abolition of the capitalist system. This class, as a class, is directly interested, or should be, in the establishment of the new order. But while the Socialist appeals particularly to the proletariat class, this does not mean that Socialism has nothing to offer the individual members of other classes, especially to those of the middle class. To be sure, Socialism does not subserve the class interests of the middle class; nevertheless, it offers the only hope to the individual members of this class. Unfortunately, the great majority of this class do not realize the precariousness of their position, and so do not see the advantage that would accrue to each by transforming the means of production into collective property. Through the illusions begotten by what appears to them, at least, as a privileged situation, they are unable to rise above their class prejudice, and, consequently, fail to realize their truer interests, and so strive to perpetuate the very conditions that cause their ruin. If they were alive to the situation they would join the Socialist movement, for Socialism alone can give them security. The reorganization going on to-day means their downfall. Under Socialism, the readjustment would not be accomplished by their ruin, they would merely exchange their little proprietorship, hopeless struggle and deprivations for a co-partnership in the whole productive capital of the nation, which would secure to each increased income, shorter hours of labor, freedom from worry and opportunity for development.

Socialism, then, while representing the class interests of the proletariat, represents the higher interests of all, for the emancipation of the proletariat would mean the emancipation of all and the establishment of a truer civilization. The possessing class, however, are so blinded by their class interests that they do not apprehend this fact. Of course, we expect nothing from the large exploiters, but many of the smaller owners, realizing their hopeless struggle, have seen the light and joined the forward movement. Socialism is being daily strengthened by such recruits.

The laborers, however, have no class interest to blind them—it is only by a failure to recognize their class interest that their servitude is made possible. But the laborers are becoming class conscious. All over the land, and, in fact, the whole civilized world, the working class is organizing into class conscious bodies, having for their aim the mastery of the public powers, to the end that the present system may be supplanted by the Co-operative Commonwealth.

The laborers should demand their rights and enforce that demand by the Socialist ballot. Every vote cast for Socialism is a vote against wage slavery—it brings nearer the day of human emancipation. The paramount issue is Socialism *vs.* Capitalism, and this issue will remain paramount until capitalism is abolished.

Those who have seen the light should proclaim aloud the new gospel—they should carry to their co-workers the light of Socialist teachings. The movement is worthy of our enthusiasm and zeal, for it presents to the world the only solution to the vexed problems that confront modern society. It is the evangel of human brotherhood. It maintains that every child born into this world should equally inherit with every other child the resources and opportunities for a full and free life. It wants every man, woman and child to be well housed, clothed, fed and educated. When industry is scientifically organized this can be accomplished in a few hours' daily labor, thus giving time and opportunity for mental and moral growth and development. Those who desire a realization of better conditions should join the Socialist party and aid in bringing in the higher order. Socialism will realize the golden age of peace, justice and plenty for all.

The progress of this great movement is phenomenal. It has spread with amazing rapidity until it has become international and cosmopolitan in character. The movement is co-extensive with capitalism, and is sweeping on to a world-wide victory. The sun of the Co-operative Commonwealth is already beginning to redden the eastern horizon, bringing promise of the gladsome day. Let us take new courage and press on—*the future is ours*.

All hail the kingdom of Social Justice—the Co-operative Commonwealth.

UNIT X
THE POLITICS OF INDUSTRIALISM, 1865–1914

WHAT was the reaction in the world of politics to the new industrialism? The main features of the period between the Civil War and World War I are the rise to power of the industrial interests, the revolt against their excesses, and the eventual penetration of public life by new conceptions of social expediency. The object of this unit is to present two successive phases of the revolt and to append to each a case study of certain experiments in industrial regulation.

The first phase of the revolt, culminating in the Populist movement and the presidential campaign of 1896, was primarily agrarian in origin. Farm production in these years expanded enormously under the same stimulus which was revolutionizing every other aspect of American life; but the farmer found his lot growing worse instead of better. Underlying his misfortunes was a world increase of agricultural production, helping to drive his prices steadily downward, and an irreversible trend in this country toward an urban-industrial civilization in which the American farmer would be relegated to a secondary role. But the political effects of the Civil War aggravated his position. They neutralized the fact that farmers were still a numerical majority and placed them at the mercy of industrial interests.

Wherever the interests of farmers clashed with those of city merchants, manufacturers, railroad operators, or financiers, the policy decisions within the national parties subordinated the former to the latter. Falling prices, mounting debts, the growth of tenancy, the exhaustion of soils, the dwindling of free land, he sense of victimization by the powers of organized wealth—all this combined to produce a surge of democratic protest recalling Jefferson's battles with the Federalists or Jackson's campaign against the United States Bank.

The Granger movement of the seventies was one of the early attempts at agrarian organization: part of the effort was to improve conditions through self-help, part to exert pressure for relief on the state and federal governments. This was succeeded by the Farmers Alliance, which in turn led to the formation of the Populist party. The Populists tried to reunite the farmers of all sections and to add to their power that of the urban workers, who had their own grievances against the common enemy. The Populist platform of 1892 should be studied as a mixture of the old and the new in American radicalism. The indignation seething through its preamble is an eloquent commentary on the disenchantments of the industrial age. It made the Populists the most formidable new party since the rise of the Republicans, and led the Democrats, under William Jennings Bryan, to reorient their policies in the great campaign of 1896. Bryan's crusade—which was focused on the agrarian dissatisfaction with the deflationary policy of the national government—failed to win the election; but the effort to revitalize democracy was to be carried forward into the later, and more broadly based, Progressive movement.

The significant thing about the agitation of these years was the novelty of the role envisaged for government. Over and above the demand for a change of policy within the familiar areas, the government was being asked to extend its authority into fields where it had not been active since the old days of state regulation. This demand expressed a modern conviction that the general welfare, in a highly integrated industrial society, cannot be safeguarded in any other way. The first case study will deal with attempts to use the regulative powers of the state governments; the second, with regulation by the federal government. It will be seen that the legislators, in both instances, had to reckon with the courts.

The legal basis for state regulation lay in the reserved powers of the states, which included those rights to protect the people's health, safety, and welfare which are associated under the term "police power." These powers were invoked by several states in the seventies and eighties, sometimes to protect labor, more often to protect farmers, from exploitation by industrial interests. In one area, in which the fate of state regulation of railroads was at stake, it was argued that the regulation of railroads engaged in interstate commerce was a federal province from which the state ought to be excluded. In many other areas the protection of the "due process" clause in the Fourteenth Amendment, originally drafted in the interest of Negroes, was claimed on behalf of businessmen—either as individuals or as corporations—and their employees. It was argued that attempts to regulate the freedom of industrial contracts was an unconstitutional interference with the "liberty" of the parties concerned. The series of judicial decisions ranging from the Slaughter-House cases to *Lochner* v. *New York* may serve to illustrate the pattern taken by judicial review in these crucial issues of democratic government. It will be seen that the conversion of the Court to a point of view which must have been highly gratifying to industrial business became marked in the eighties, and that by the nineties the effective powers of the state legislatures had been severely mutilated.

In the Progressive movement, which spread over the United States between the turn of the century and the outbreak of the first World War, the discontent of the earlier years developed national proportions. Broadly speaking, the efforts of muckraking journalists, socially conscious novelists, reflective historians, political reformers in city, state, and national politics, and the masses of farmers, laborers, and small businessmen who felt that something was radically wrong were all aimed in the same direction. They wanted to rebuild a democratic society. Like every great upheaval, the Progressive movement cannot be compressed into a simple statement of grievances and proposals. We may notice, however, that the concentration and irresponsibility of economic power, the problems of the new industrial cities, the breakdown of political morality, the suffocation of equality of opportunity for the mass of Americans, and the bankruptcy of laissez faire were among the targets for attack.

To many the proper remedy for the ills of democracy was more democracy—of the direct political kind from which the Founding Fathers had shrunk and of which the Jacksonians had supplied the first sweeping installments. The initiative and referendum, the recall of some elected officials, the direct primary, and the direct election of United States senators were innovations of this general type. Almost all Progressives also believed that the government would have to accept more responsibility for the economic system. There was nothing socialist about this in the minds of the great majority, if by socialism is meant a sweeping displacement of the system of private ownership. The socialists actually won more support in the election of 1912 than either before or since, but progressivism as a whole remained liberal. Some appreciation of its views

may be obtained from the materials printed here. They include extracts from the *Autobiography of Lincoln Steffens* and selections from the political literature of 1912, when Americans had a choice between two varieties of progressivism—one personified by Theodore Roosevelt and the other by Woodrow Wilson.

How did the federal government propose to deal with the growth of monopoly? By breaking up big business or by forcing it to recognize certain standards? How would the legislation be framed? What new agencies would be necessary to administer it? Could they be nullified by the political influence of organized business? How would the courts, which were busily insulating corporations from regulation in one direction, interpret this federal attempt to regulate them in another? These are questions on which the second case study should throw some light. It begins with the Sherman Antitrust Act (which preceded the Progressive movement), includes the Wilsonian program for maintaining competition, and explores once again the recesses of judicial review.

World War I diverted Americans from domestic reform into national defense, but not before the foundations had been laid for later experiments in the construction of a welfare state. The New Deal of Franklin Delano Roosevelt is the direct heir of Theodore Roosevelt's Square Deal and of Woodrow Wilson's New Freedom.

SECTION A. AGRARIAN REVOLT

1. THE SIGNIFICANCE OF THE FRONTIER IN AMERICAN HISTORY[1]

By FREDERICK JACKSON TURNER

EDITORS' NOTE.—Frederick Jackson Turner (1861–1932) was born at Portage, then a frontier-like community in Wisconsin, and was thus reared in a portion of the West about which he later wrote. He attended his state university and received a doctorate in history from the Johns Hopkins University in 1890. He taught American history, first at Wisconsin and finally at Harvard University. Turner read his essay on the significance of the frontier at the meeting of the American Historical Association that was held in conjunction with the World's Columbian Exposition to commemorate the four hundredth anniversary of the discovery of America. This paper has had more influence on American historians than any other essay of comparable length. It affected the work of a whole generation of succeeding students and led to an extensive reinterpretation of American history. Although much criticized in recent years, the Turner thesis still exercises a great deal of influence. Its location in the present volume may appropriately suggest a connection between the end of the frontier and the climax of agrarian revolt.

In a recent bulletin of the Superintendent of the Census for 1890 appear these significant words: "Up to and including 1880 the country had a frontier of settlement, but at present the unsettled area has been so broken into by isolated bodies of settlement that there can hardly be said to be a frontier line. In the discussion of its extent, its westward movement, etc., it can not, therefore, any longer have a place in the census reports." This brief official statement marks the closing of a great historic movement. Up to our own day American history has been in a large de-

gree the history of the colonization of the Great West. The existence of an area of free land, its continuous recession, and the advance of American settlement westward, explain American development.

Behind institutions, behind constitutional forms and modifications, lie the vital forces that call these organs into life and shape them to meet changing conditions. The peculiarity of American institutions is, the fact that they have been compelled to adapt themselves to the changes of an expanding people—to the changes involved in crossing a continent, in winning a wilderness, and in developing at each area of this progress out of the primitive economic and political conditions of the frontier into the complexity of city life. Said Calhoun in 1817, "We are great, and rap-

1. Frederick Jackson Turner, "The Significance of the Frontier in American History," *American Historical Association, Annual Report* (Washington, 1893), pp. 199–227. By permission of the American Historical Association.

idly—I was about to say fearfully—growing!" So saying, he touched the distinguishing feature of American life. All peoples show development; the germ theory of politics has been sufficiently emphasized.[2] In the case of most nations, however, the development has occurred in a limited area; and if the nation has expanded, it has met other growing peoples whom it has conquered. But in the case of the United States we have a different phenomenon. Limiting our attention to the Atlantic coast, we have the familiar phenomenon of the evolution of institutions in a limited area, such as the rise of representative government; the differentiation of simple colonial governments into complex organs; the progress from primitive industrial society, without division of labor, up to manufacturing civilization. But we have in addition to this a recurrence of the process of evolution in each western area reached in the process of expansion. Thus American development has exhibited not merely advance along a single line, but a return to primitive conditions on a continually advancing frontier line, and a new development for that area. American social development has been continually beginning over again on the frontier. This perennial rebirth, this fluidity of American life, this expansion westward with its new opportunities, its continuous touch with the simplicity of primitive society, furnish the forces dominating American character. The true point of view in the history of this nation is not the Atlantic coast, it is the Great West. Even the slavery struggle, which is made so exclusive an object of attention by writers like Prof. von Holst, occupies its important place in American history because of its relation to westward expansion.

In this advance, the frontier is the outer edge of the wave—the meeting point between savagery and civilization. Much has been written about the frontier from the point of view of border warfare and the

2. For an explanation of the "germ theory" see n. 4.

chase, but as a field for the serious study of the economist and the historian it has been neglected.

The American frontier is sharply distinguished from the European frontier—a fortified boundary line running through dense populations. The most significant thing about the American frontier is, that it lies at the hither edge of free land. In the census reports it is treated as the margin of that settlement which has a density of two or more to the square mile. The term is an elastic one, and for our purposes does not need sharp definition. We shall consider the whole frontier belt including the Indian country and the outer margin of the "settled area" of the census reports. This paper will make no attempt to treat the subject exhaustively; its aim is simply to call attention to the frontier as a fertile field for investigation and to suggest some of the problems which arise in connection with it.

In the settlement of America we have to observe how European life entered the continent, and how America modified and developed that life and reacted on Europe. Our early history is the study of European germs developing in an American environment. Too exclusive attention has been paid by institutional students to the Germanic origins, too little to the American factors. The frontier is the line of most rapid and effective Americanization. The wilderness masters the colonist. It finds him a European in dress, industries, tools, modes of travel, and thought. It takes him from the railroad car and puts him in the birch canoe. It strips off the garments of civilization and arrays him in the hunting shirt and the moccasin. It puts him in the log cabin of the Cherokee and Iroquois and runs an Indian palisade around him. Before long he has gone to planting Indian corn and plowing with a sharp stick; he shouts the war cry and takes the scalp in orthodox Indian fashion. In short, at the frontier the environment is at first too strong for the man. He must accept the conditions which it furnishes, or perish, and so he fits himself into the Indian clearings and follows the Indian trails. Little by little he transforms the wilderness, but the outcome is not the old Europe, not simply the development of Germanic germs, any more than the first phenomenon was a case of reversion to the Germanic mark.[3] The fact is, that here is a new product that is American. At first, the frontier was the Atlantic coast. It was the frontier of Europe in a very real sense. Moving westward, the frontier became more and more American. As successive terminal moraines result from successive glaciations, so each frontier leaves its traces behind it, and when it becomes a settled area the region still partakes of the frontier characteristics. Thus the advance of the frontier has meant a steady movement away from the influence of Europe, a steady growth of independence on American lines. And to study this advance, the men who grew up under these conditions, and the political, economic, and social results of it, is to study the really American part of our history. . . .

STATES OF FRONTIER ADVANCE

In these successive frontiers we find natural boundary lines which have served to mark and to affect the characteristics of the frontiers, namely: the "fall line"; the Alleghany Mountains; the Mississippi; the Missouri where its direction approximates north and south; the line of the arid lands, approximately the ninety-ninth meridian; and the Rocky Mountains. The "fall line" marked the frontier of the

3. The Germanic mark was an agricultural village of a type common to England and the Continent during the Middle Ages. The serfs of the manor lived in cottages that were clustered together so as to comprise a community. They went forth daily to till their fields but returned in the evening to their homes in the village. The early New England towns were laid out in similar fashion. Hence the inquiry as to whether this idea was imported from England or was native to America. In the southern colonies, on the other hand, settlers lived on their plantations rather than in villages. However, the master's house, with its adjacent servant or slave quarters, tended to comprise a community in itself.

seventeenth century; the Alleghanies that of the eighteenth; the Mississippi that of the first quarter of the nineteenth; the Missouri that of the middle of this century (omitting the California movement); and the belt of the Rocky Mountains and the arid tract, the present frontier. Each was won by a series of Indian wars.

THE FRONTIER FURNISHES A FIELD FOR COMPARATIVE STUDY OF SOCIAL DEVELOPMENT

At the Atlantic frontier one can study the germs of processes repeated at each successive frontier. We have the complex European life sharply precipitated by the wilderness into the simplicity of primitive conditions. The first frontier had to meet its Indian question, its question of the disposition of the public domain, of the means of intercourse with older settlements, of the extension of political organization, of religious and educational activity. And the settlement of these and similar questions for one frontier served as a guide for the next. The American student needs not to go to the "prim little townships of Sleswick" for illustrations of the law of continuity and development.[4] For example, he

4. Quoted, somewhat freely, from John R. Green, *History of the English People* (New York, 1881), I, 15. Green suggests that "for the fatherland of the English race we must look far away from England itself" to the Anglo-Saxon tribes of the German forests of the fifth century A.D. There, says Green, "the one country which we know to have borne the name of Angeln or England lay within the district which is now called Sleswick." As of May, 1949, this would be Schleswig, divided between Denmark and Germany, on the peninsula separating the North from the Baltic Sea. Green concludes that it was these tribes, invading Britain in the fifth century, who carried with them the institutions that later became English.

Accepting this explanation, Herbert B. Adams objected that "most writers . . . assume that New England towns are either the offspring of Puritan virtue . . . or else that they are the product of this rocky soil, which is supposed to produce free institutions spontaneously." Adams propounded, instead, the "germ theory" of history. "It is just as improbable," he declared, "that free local institutions should spring up without a germ along

may study the origin of our land policies in the colonial land policy; he may see how the system grew by adapting the statutes to the customs of the successive frontiers. He may see how the mining experience in the lead regions of Wisconsin, Illinois, and Iowa was applied to the mining laws of the Sierras, and how our Indian policy has been a series of experimentations on successive frontiers. Each tier of new States has found in the older ones material for its constitutions. Each frontier has made similar contributions to American character, as will be discussed farther on.

But with all these similarities there are essential differences, due to the place element and the time element. It is evident that the farming frontier of the Mississippi Valley presents different conditions from the mining frontier of the Rocky Mountains. The frontier reached by the Pacific Railroad, surveyed into rectangles, guarded by the United States Army, and recruited by the daily immigrant ship, moves forward at a swifter pace and in a different way than the frontier reached by the birch canoe or the pack horse. The geologist traces patiently the shores of ancient seas, maps their areas, and compares the older and the newer. It would be a work worth the historian's labors to mark these various frontiers and in detail compare one with another. Not only would there result a more adequate conception of American development and characteristics, but invaluable additions would be made to the history of society.

Loria, the Italian economist, has urged the study of colonial life as an aid in understanding the stages of European develop-

ment, affirming that colonial settlement is for economic science what the mountain is for geology, bringing to light primitive stratifications. "America," he says, "has the key to the historical enigma which Europe has sought for centuries in vain, and the land which has no history reveals luminously the course of universal history." There is much truth in this. The United States lies like a huge page in the history of society. Line by line as we read this continental page from West to East we find the record of social evolution. It begins with the Indian and the hunter; it goes on to tell of the disintegration of savagery by the entrance of the trader, the pathfinder of civilization; we read the annals of the pastoral stage in ranch life; the exploitation of the soil by the raising of unrotated crops of corn and wheat in sparsely settled farming communities; the intensive culture of the denser farm settlement; and finally the manufacturing organization with city and factory system. This page is familiar to the student of census statistics, but how little of it has been used by our historians. Particularly in eastern States this page is a palimpsest. What is now a manufacturing State was in an earlier decade an area of intensive farming. Earlier yet it had been a wheat area, and still earlier the "range" had attracted the cattle-herder. Thus Wisconsin, now developing manufacture, is a State with varied agricultural interests. But earlier it was given over to almost exclusive grain-raising, like North Dakota at the present time.

Each of these areas has had an influence in our economic and political history; the evolution of each into a higher stage has worked political transformations. But what constitutional historian has made any adequate attempt to interpret political facts by the light of these social areas and changes?

The Atlantic frontier was compounded of fisherman, fur-trader, miner, cattle-raiser, and farmer. Excepting the fisherman, each type of industry was on the march toward the West, impelled by an ir-

American shores as that English wheat should have grown here without planting. Town institutions were propagated in New England by old English and Germanic ideas, brought over by Pilgrims and Puritans, and as ready to take root in the free soil of America as would English grain which had been drying in a mummy case for thousands of years . . ." (*The Germanic Origins of New England Towns* ["Johns Hopkins University Studies in Historical and Political Science: First Series," Vol II (Baltimore, 1882)], p. 8).

resistible attraction. Each passed in successive waves across the continent. Stand at Cumberland Gap and watch the procession of civilization, marching single file—the buffalo following the trail to the salt springs, the Indian, the fur-trader and hunter, the cattle-raiser, the pioneer farmer—and the frontier has passed by. Stand at South Pass in the Rockies a century later and see the same procession with wider intervals between. The unequal rate of advance compels us to distinguish the frontier into the trader's frontier, the rancher's frontier, or the miner's frontier, and the farmer's frontier. When the mines and the cowpens were still near the fall line the traders' pack trains were tinkling across the Alleghanies, and the French on the Great Lakes were fortifying their posts, alarmed by the British trader's birch canoe. When the trappers scaled the Rockies, the farmer was still near the mouth of the Missouri.

THE INDIAN TRADER'S FRONTIER

Why was it that the Indian trader passed so rapidly across the continent? What effects followed from the trader's frontier? The trade was coeval with American discovery. The Norsemen, Vespuccius, Verrazani, Hudson, John Smith, all trafficked for furs. The Plymouth pilgrims settled in Indian cornfields, and their first return cargo was of beaver and lumber. . . . The explanation of the rapidity of this advance is connected with the effects of the trader on the Indian. The trading post left the unarmed tribes at the mercy of those that had purchased fire-arms—a truth which the Iroquois Indians wrote in blood, and so the remote and unvisited tribes gave eager welcome to the trader. . . . Every river valley and Indian trail became a fissure in Indian society, and so that society became honeycombed. . . .

. . . Thus civilization in America has followed the arteries made by geology, pouring an ever richer tide through them, until at last the slender paths of aboriginal intercourse have been broadened and interwoven into the complex mazes of modern commercial lines; the wilderness has been interpenetrated by lines of civilization growing ever more numerous. It is like the steady growth of a complex nervous system for the originally simple, inert continent. If one would understand why we are to-day one nation, rather than a collection of isolated states, he must study this economic and social consolidation of the country. In this progress from savage conditions lie topics for the evolutionist.

The effect of the Indian frontier as a consolidating agent in our history is important. From the close of the seventeenth century various intercolonial congresses have been called to treat with Indians and establish common measures of defense. Particularism was strongest in colonies with no Indian frontier. This frontier stretched along the western border like a cord of union. The Indian was a common danger, demanding united action. Most celebrated of these conferences was the Albany congress of 1754, called to treat with the Six Nations, and to consider plans of union. Even a cursory reading of the plan proposed by the congress reveals the importance of the frontier. The powers of the general council and the officers were, chiefly, the determination of peace and war with the Indians, the regulation of Indian trade, the purchase of Indian lands, and the creation and government of new settlements as a security against the Indians. It is evident that the unifying tendencies of the Revolutionary period were facilitated by the previous coöperation in the regulation of the frontier. In this connection may be mentioned the importance of the frontier, from that day to this, as a military training school, keeping alive the power of resistance to aggression, and developing the stalwart and rugged qualities of the frontiersman.

THE RANCHER'S FRONTIER

It would not be possible in the limits of this paper to trace the other frontiers across the continent. Travelers of the eighteenth century found the "cowpens" among the canebrakes and peavine pastures of the South, and "cow drivers" took their droves to Charleston, Philadelphia, and New York. Travelers at the close of the War of 1812 met droves of more than a thousand cattle and swine from the interior of Ohio going to Pennsylvania to fatten for the Philadelphia market. The ranges of the Great Plains, with ranch and cowboy and nomadic life, are things of yesterday and of to-day. The experience of the Carolina cowpens guided the ranchers of Texas. One element favoring the rapid extension of the rancher's frontier is the fact that in a remote country lacking transportation facilities the product must be in small bulk, or must be able to transport itself, and the cattle raiser could easily drive his product to market. The effect of these great ranches on the subsequent agrarian history of the localities in which they existed should be studied.

THE FARMER'S FRONTIER

The maps of the census reports show an uneven advance of the farmer's frontier, with tongues of settlement pushed forward and with indentations of wilderness. In part this is due to Indian resistance, in part to the location of river valleys and passes, in part to the unequal force of the centers of frontier attraction. Among the important centers of attraction may be mentioned the following: fertile and favorably situated soils, salt springs, mines, and army posts. . . .

LAND

The exploitation of the beasts took hunter and trader to the west, the exploitation of the grasses took the rancher west, and the exploitation of the virgin soil of the river valleys and prairies attracted the farmer. Good soils have been the most continuous attraction to the farmer's frontier. The land hunger of the Virginians drew them down the rivers into Carolina, in early colonial days; the search for soils

took the Massachusetts men to Pennsylvania and to New York. As the eastern lands were taken up migration flowed across them to the west. Daniel Boone, the great backwoodsman, who combined the occupations of hunter, trader, cattleraiser, farmer, and surveyor—learning, probably from the traders, of the fertility of the lands on the upper Yadkin, where the traders were wont to rest as they took their way to the Indians, left his Pennsylvania home with his father, and passed down the Great Valley road to that stream. Learning from a trader of the game and rich pastures, he pioneered the way for the farmers to that region. Thence he passed to the frontier of Missouri, where his settlement was long a landmark on the frontier. Here again he helped to open the way for civilization, finding salt licks, and trails, and land. His son was among the earliest trappers in the passes of the Rocky Mountains, and his party are said to have been the first to camp on the present site of Denver. His grandson, Col. A. J. Boone, of Colorado, was a power among the Indians of the Rocky Mountains, and was appointed an agent by the government. Kit Carson's mother was a Boone. Thus this family epitomizes the backwoodsman's advance across the continent.

The farmer's advance came in a distinct series of waves. In Peck's *New Guide to the West*, published in Boston in 1837, occurs this suggestive passage:

Generally, in all the western settlements, three classes, like the waves of the ocean, have rolled one after the other. First comes the pioneer, who depends for the subsistence of his family chiefly upon the natural growth of vegetation, called the "range," and the proceeds of hunting. His implements of agriculture are rude, chiefly of his own make, and his efforts directed mainly to a crop of corn and a "truck patch." The last is a rude garden for growing cabbage, beans, corn for roasting ears, cucumbers, and potatoes. A log cabin, and, occasionally, a stable and corn-crib, and a field of a dozen acres, the timber girdled or "deadened," and fenced, are enough for his occupancy. It is quite immaterial whether he ever becomes the owner of the soil. He is the occupant for the time being, pays no rent, and feels as independent as the "lord of the manor." With a horse, cow, and one or two breeders of swine, he strikes into the woods with his family, and becomes the founder of a new county, or perhaps state. He builds his cabin, gathers around him a few other families of similar tastes and habits, and occupies till the range is somewhat subdued, and hunting a little precarious, or, which is more frequently the case, till the neighbors crowd around, roads, bridges, and fields annoy him, and he lacks elbow room. The preëmption law enables him to dispose of his cabin and cornfield to the next class of emigrants; and, to employ his own figures, he "breaks for the high timber," "clears out for the New Purchase," or migrates to Arkansas or Texas, to work the same process over.

The next class of emigrants purchase the lands, add field to field, clear out the roads, throw rough bridges over the streams, put up hewn log houses with glass windows and brick or stone chimneys, occasionally plant orchards, build mills, schoolhouses, court-houses, etc., and exhibit the picture and forms of plain, frugal, civilized life.

Another wave rolls on. The men of capital and enterprise come. The settler is ready to sell out and take the advantage of the rise in property, push farther into the interior and become, himself, a man of capital and enterprise in turn. The small village rises to a spacious town or city; substantial edifices of brick, extensive fields, orchards, gardens, colleges, and churches are seen. Broadcloths, silk, leghorns, crapes, and all the refinements, luxuries, elegancies, frivolities, and fashions are in vogue. Thus wave after wave is rolling westward; the real Eldorado is still farther on.

A portion of the two first classes remain stationary amidst the general movement, improve their habits and condition, and rise in the scale of society.

The writer has traveled much amongst the first class, the real pioneers. He has lived many years in connection with the second grade; and now the third wave is sweeping over large districts of Indiana, Illinois, and Missouri. Migration has become almost a habit in the West. Hundreds of men can be found, not over 50 years of age, who have settled for the fourth, fifth, or sixth time on a new spot. To sell out and remove only a few hundred miles makes up a portion of the variety of backwoods life and manners.

Omitting those of the pioneer farmers who move from the love of adventure, the advance of the more steady farmer is easy to understand. Obviously the immigrant was attracted by the cheap lands of the frontier, and even the native farmer felt their influence strongly. Year by year the farmers who lived on soil whose returns were diminished by unrotated crops were offered the virgin soil of the frontier at nominal prices. Their growing families demanded more lands, and these were dear. The competition of the unexhausted, cheap, and easily tilled prairie lands compelled the farmer either to go west and continue the exhaustion of the soil on a new frontier, or to adopt intensive culture. Thus the census of 1890 shows, in the Northwest, many counties in which there is an absolute or a relative decrease of population. These States have been sending farmers to advance the frontier on the plains, and have themselves begun to turn to intensive farming and to manufacture. A decade before this, Ohio had shown the same transition stage. Thus the demand for land and the love of wilderness freedom drew the frontier ever onward.

Having now roughly outlined the various kinds of frontiers, and their modes of advance, chiefly from the point of view of the frontier itself, we may next inquire what were the influences on the East and on the Old World. A rapid enumeration of some of the more noteworthy effects is all that I have time for.

COMPOSITE NATIONALITY

First, we note that the frontier promoted the formation of a composite nationality for the American people. The coast was preponderantly English, but the later tides of continental immigration flowed across to the free lands. This was the case from the early colonial days. The

Scotch Irish and the Palatine Germans, or "Pennsylvania Dutch,"[5] furnished the dominant element in the stock of the colonial frontier. With these peoples were also the freed indented servants, or redemptioners, who at the expiration of their time of service passed to the frontier. Governor Spottswood of Virginia writes in 1717, "The inhabitants of our frontiers are composed generally of such as have been transported hither as servants, and, being out of their time settle themselves where land is to be taken up and that will produce the necessarys of life with little labour." Very generally these redemptioners were of non-English stock. In the crucible of the frontier the immigrants were Americanized, liberated, and fused into a mixed race, English in neither nationality or characteristics. The process has gone on from the early days to our own. Burke and other writers in the middle of the eighteenth century believed that Pennsylvania was "threatened with the danger of being wholly foreign in language, manners, and perhaps even inclinations." The German and Scotch-Irish elements in the frontier of the South were only less great. In the middle of the present century the German element in Wisconsin was already so considerable that leading publicists looked to the creation of a German state out of the commonwealth by concentrating their colonization. Such examples teach us to beware of misinterpreting the fact that there is a common English speech in America into a belief that the stock is also English.

INDUSTRIAL INDEPENDENCE

In another way the advance of the frontier decreased our dependence on England. The coast, particularly of the South, lacked diversified industries, and was dependent on England for the bulk of its supplies. In the South there was even a dependence on the Northern colonies for

5. Not from the Netherlands but from the German Rhineland area known as the Palatinate.

articles of food. Governor Glenn, of South Carolina, writes in the middle of the eighteenth century:

Our trade with New York and Philadelphia was of this sort, draining us of all the little money and bills we could gather from other places for their bread, flour, beer, hams, bacon, and other things of their produce, all which, except beer, our new townships begin to supply us with, which are settled with very industrious and thriving Germans. This no doubt diminishes the number of shipping and the appearance of our trade, but it is far from being a detriment to us.

Before long the frontier created a demand for merchants. As it retreated from the coast it became less and less possible for England to bring her supplies directly to the consumer's wharfs, and carry away staple crops, and staple crops began to give way to diversified agriculture for a time. The effect of this phase of the frontier action upon the northern section is perceived when we realize how the advance of the frontier aroused seaboard cities like Boston, New York, and Baltimore, to engage in rivalry for what Washington called "the extensive and valuable trade of a rising empire."

EFFECTS ON NATIONAL LEGISLATION

The legislation which most developed the powers of the national government, and played the largest part in its activity, was conditioned on the frontier. Writers have discussed the subjects of tariff, land, and internal improvement, as subsidiary to the slavery question. . . .

This is a wrong perspective. The pioneer needed the goods of the coast, and so the grand series of internal improvement and railroad legislation began, with potent nationalizing effects. Over internal improvements occurred great debates, in which grave constitutional questions were discussed. Sectional groupings appear in the votes, profoundly significant for the historian. Loose construction increased as the nation marched westward. But the West was not content with bringing the farm to the factory. Under the lead of Clay—"Harry of the West"—protective tariff were passed, with the cry of bringing the factory to the farm. The disposition of the public lands was a third important subject of national legislation influenced by the frontier.

THE PUBLIC DOMAIN

The public domain has been a force of profound importance in the nationalization and development of the government. The effects of the struggle of the landed and the landless States, and of the Ordinance of 1787, need no discussion. Administratively the frontier called out some of the highest and most vitalizing activities of the general government. The purchase of Louisiana was perhaps the constitutional turning point in the history of the Republic, inasmuch as it afforded both a new area for national legislation and the occasion of the downfall of the policy of strict construction. But the purchase of Louisiana was called out by frontier needs and demands. As frontier States accrued to the Union the national power grew. In a speech on the dedication of the Calhoun monument Mr. Lamar[6] explained: "In 1789 the States were the creators of the Federal Government; in 1861 the Federal Government was the creator of a large majority of the States."

When we consider the public domain from the point of view of the sale and disposal of the public lands we are again brought face to face with the frontier. The policy of the United States in dealing with its lands is in sharp contrast with the European system of scientific administration. Efforts to make this domain a source of revenue, and to withhold it from emigrants in order that settlement might be compact,

6. Lucius Quintus Cincinnatus Lamar (1825–1894), college professor, congressman, and senator, before the Civil War, in Georgia and Mississippi. Lamar served in the Confederate army and diplomatic corps but returned to Congress and the Senate after the war. He was named secretary of the interior and later appointed a Supreme Court justice by President Cleveland.

were in vain. The jealousy and the fears of the East were powerless in the face of the demands of the frontiersmen. . . .

"No subject," said Henry Clay, "which has presented itself to the present, or perhaps any preceding, Congress, is of greater magnitude than that of the public lands." When we consider the far-reaching effects of the Government's land policy upon political, economic, and social aspects of American life, we are disposed to agree with him. But this legislation was framed under frontier influences, and under the lead of Western statesmen like Benton and Jackson. Said Senator Scott of Indiana in 1841: "I consider the preëmption law merely declaratory of the custom or common law of the settlers."

NATIONAL TENDENCIES OF THE FRONTIER

It is safe to say that the legislation with regard to land, tariff, and internal improvements—the American system of the nationalizing Whig party—was conditioned on frontier ideas and needs. But it was not merely in legislative action that the frontier worked against the sectionalism of the coast. The economic and social characteristics of the frontier worked against sectionalism. The men of the frontier had closer resemblances to the Middle region than to either of the other sections. Pennsylvania had been the seed-plot of frontier emigration, and, although she passed on her settlers along the Great Valley into the west of Virginia and the Carolinas, yet the industrial society of these Southern frontiersmen was always more like that of the Middle region than like that of the tide-water portion of the South, which later came to spread its industrial type throughout the South.

The Middle region, entered by New York harbor, was an open door to all Europe. The tide-water part of the South represented typical Englishmen, modified by a warm climate and servile labor, and living in baronial fashion on great plantations; New England stood for a special English movement—Puritanism. The

Middle region was less English than the other sections. It had a wide mixture of nationalities, a varied society, the mixed town and county system of local government, a varied economic life, many religious sects. In short, it was a region mediating between New England and the South, and the East and the West. It represented that composite nationality which the contemporary United States exhibits, that juxtaposition of non-English groups, occupying a valley or a little settlement, and presenting reflections of the map of Europe in their variety. It was democratic and nonsectional, if not national; "easy, tolerant, and contented"; rooted strongly in material prosperity. It was typical of the modern United States. It was least sectional, not only because it lay between North and South, but also because with no barriers to shut out its frontiers from its settled region, and with a system of connecting waterways, the Middle region mediated between East and West as well as between North and South. Thus it became the typically American region. Even the New Englander, who was shut out from the frontier by the Middle region, tarrying in New York or Pennsylvania on his westward march, lost the acuteness of his sectionalism on the way.

The spread of cotton culture into the interior of the South finally broke down the contrast between the "tide-water" region and the rest of the State, and based Southern interests on slavery. Before this process revealed its results the western portion of the South, which was akin to Pennsylvania in stock, society, and industry, showed tendencies to fall away from the faith of the fathers into internal improvement legislation and nationalism. . . .

It was this nationalizing tendency of the West that transformed the democracy of Jefferson into the national republicanism of Monroe and the democracy of Andrew Jackson. The West of the War of 1812, the West of Clay, and Benton and Harrison, and Andrew Jackson, shut off by the Middle States and the mountains from the coast sections, had a solidarity of its own with national tendencies. On the tide of the Fathers of Waters, North and South met and mingled into a nation. Interstate migration went steadily on—a process of cross-fertilization of ideas and institutions. The fierce struggle of the sections over slavery on the western frontier does not diminish the truth of this statement; it proves the truth of it. Slavery was a sectional trait that would not down, but in the West it could not remain sectional. It was the greatest of frontiersmen who declared: "I believe this Government can not endure permanently half slave and half free. It will become all of one thing or all of the other." Nothing works for nationalism like intercourse within the nation. Mobility of population is death to localism, and the western frontier worked irresistibly in unsettling population. The effects reached back from the frontier and affected profoundly the Atlantic coast and even the Old World.

GROWTH OF DEMOCRACY

But the most important effect of the frontier has been in the promotion of democracy here and in Europe. As has been indicated, the frontier is productive of individualism. Complex society is precipitated by the wilderness into a kind of primitive organization based on the family. The tendency is antisocial. It produces antipathy to control, and particularly to any direct control. The tax-gatherer is viewed as a representative of oppression. Prof. Osgood, in an able article, has pointed out that the frontier conditions prevalent in the colonies are important factors in the explanation of the American Revolution, where individual liberty was sometimes confused with absence of all effective government. The same conditions aid in explaining the difficulty of instituting a strong government in the period of the confederacy. The frontier individualism has from the beginning promoted democracy.

The frontier States that came into the

Union in the first quarter of the century of its existence came in with democratic suffrage provisions, and had reactive effects of the highest importance upon the older States whose peoples were being attracted there. An extension of the franchise became essential. It was *western* New York that forced an extension of suffrage in the constitutional convention of that State in 1821; and it was *western* Virginia that compelled the tide-water region to put a more liberal suffrage provision in the constitution framed in 1830, and to give to the frontier region a more nearly proportionate representation with the tide-water aristocracy. The rise of democracy as an effective force in the nation came in with western preponderance under Jackson and William Henry Harrison, and it meant the triumph of the frontier—with all of its good and with all of its evil elements. An interesting illustration of the tone of frontier democracy in 1830 came from the same debates in the Virginia convention already referred to. A representative from western Virginia declared:

> But, sir, it is not the increase of population in the West which this gentleman ought to fear. It is the energy which the mountain breeze and western habits impart to those emigrants. They are regenerated, politically I mean, sir. They soon become *working politicians*; and the difference, sir, between a *talking* and a *working* politician is immense. The Old Dominion has long been celebrated for producing great orators; the ablest metaphysicians in policy; men that can split hairs in all abstruse questions of political economy. But at home, or when they return from Congress, they have Negroes to fan them asleep. But a Pennsylvania, a New York, an Ohio, or a western Virginia statesman, though far inferior in logic, metaphysics, and rhetoric to an old Virginia statesman, has this advantage, that when he returns home he takes off his coat and takes hold of the plow. This gives him bone and muscle, sir, and preserves his republican principles pure and uncontaminated.

So long as free land exists, the opportunity for a competency exists, and economic power secures political power. But the democracy born of free land, strong in selfishness and individualism, intolerant of administrative experience and education, and pressing individual liberty beyond its proper bounds, has its dangers as well as its benefits. Individualism in America has allowed a laxity in regard to governmental affairs which has rendered possible the spoils system and all the manifest evils that follow from the lack of a highly developed civic spirit. In this connection may be noted also the influence of frontier conditions in permitting lax business honor, inflated paper currency and wild-cat banking. The colonial and revolutionary frontier was the region whence emanated many of the worst forms of an evil currency. The West in the War of 1812 repeated the phenomenon on the frontier of that day, while the speculation and wild-cat banking of the period of the crisis of 1837 occurred on the new frontier belt of the next tier of States. Thus each one of the periods of lax financial integrity coincides with periods when a new set of frontier communities had arisen, and coincides in area with these successive frontiers, for the most part. The recent Populist agitation is a case in point. Many a State that now declines any connection with the tenets of the Populists, itself adhered to such ideas in an earlier stage of the development of the State. A primitive society can hardly be expected to show the intelligent appreciation of the complexity of business interests in a developed society. The continual recurrence of these areas of paper-money agitation is another evidence that the frontier can be isolated and studied as a factor in American history of the highest importance.

ATTEMPTS TO CHECK AND REGULATE THE FRONTIER

The East has always feared the result of an unregulated advance of the frontier, and has tried to check and guide it. The English authorities would have checked settlement at the headwaters of the Atlantic tributaries and allowed the "savages to enjoy their deserts in quiet lest the peltry trade should decrease." This called out Burke's splendid protest:

If you stopped your grants, what would be the consequence? The people would occupy without grants. They have already so occupied in many places. You can not station garrisons in every part of these deserts. If you drive the people from one place, they will carry on their annual tillage and remove with their flocks and herds to another. Many of the people in the back settlements are already little attached to particular situations. Already they have topped the Appalachian Mountains. From thence they behold before them an immense plain, one vast, rich, level meadow; a square of five hundred miles. Over this they would wander without a possibility of restraint; they would change their manners with their habits of life; would soon forget a government by which they were disowned; would become hordes of English Tartars; and, pouring down upon your unfortified frontiers a fierce and irresistible cavalry, become masters of your governors and your counselors, your collectors and comptrollers, and of all the slaves that adhered to them. Such would, and in no long time must, be the effect of attempting to forbid as a crime and to suppress as an evil the command and blessing of Providence, "Increase and multiply." Such would be the happy result of an endeavor to keep as a lair of wild beasts that earth which God, by an express charter, has given to the children of men.

But the English Government was not alone in its desire to limit the advance of the frontier and guide its destinies. Tidewater Virginia and South Carolina gerrymandered those colonies to insure the dominance of the coast in their legislatures. Washington desired to settle a State at a time in the Northwest; Jefferson would reserve from settlement the territory of his Louisiana purchase north of the thirty-second parallel, in order to offer it to the Indians in exchange for their settlements east of the Mississippi. "When we shall be full on this side," he writes, "we may lay off a range of States on the western bank from the head to the mouth, and so range after range, advancing compactly as we multiply." Madison went so far as to argue to the French minister that

the United States had no interest in seeing population extend itself on the right bank of the Mississippi, but should rather fear it. When the Oregon question was under debate, in 1824, Smyth, of Virginia, would draw an unchangeable line for the limits of the United States at the outer limit of two tiers of States beyond the Mississippi, complaining that the seaboard States were being drained of the flower of their population by the bringing of too much land into market. Even Thomas Benton, the man of widest views of the destiny of the West, at this stage of his career declared that along the ridge of the Rocky mountains "the western limits of the Republic should be drawn, and the statue of the fabled god Terminus should be raised upon its highest peak, never to be thrown down." But the attempts to limit the boundaries, to restrict land sales and settlement, and to deprive the West of its share of political power were all in vain. Steadily the frontier of settlement advanced and carried with it individualism, democracy, and nationalism, and powerfully affected the East and the Old World. . . .

INTELLECTUAL TRAITS

From the conditions of frontier life came intellectual traits of profound importance. The works of travelers along each frontier from colonial days onward describe certain common traits, and these traits have, while softening down, still persisted as survivals in the place of their origin, even when a higher social organization succeeded. The result is that to the frontier the American intellect owes its striking characteristics. That coarseness and strength combined with acuteness and inquisitiveness; that practical, inventive turn of mind, quick to find expedients; that masterful grasp of material things, lacking in the artistic but powerful to effect great ends; that restless, nervous energy; that dominant individualism, working for good and for evil, and withal that buoyancy and exuberance which comes with freedom— these are traits of the frontier, or traits called out elsewhere because of the existence of the frontier. Since the days when the fleet of Columbus sailed into the waters of the New World, America has been another name for opportunity, and the people of the United States have taken their tone from the incessant expansion which has not only been open but has even been forced upon them. He would be a rash prophet who should assert that the expansive character of American life has now entirely ceased. Movement has been its dominant fact, and, unless this training has no effect upon a people, the American energy will continually demand a wider field for its exercise. But never again will such gifts of free land offer themselves. For a moment, at the frontier, the bonds of custom are broken and unrestraint is triumphant. There is not *tabula rasa*. The stubborn American environment is there with its imperious summons to accept its conditions; the inherited ways of doing things are also there; and yet, in spite of environment, and in spite of custom, each frontier did indeed furnish a new field of opportunity, a gate of escape from the bondage of the past; and freshness, and confidence, and scorn of older society, impatience of its restraints and its ideas, and indifference to its lessons, have accompanied the frontier. What the Mediterranean Sea was to the Greeks, breaking the bond of custom, offering new experiences, calling out new institutions and activities, that, and more, the ever retreating frontier has been to the United States directly and to the nations of Europe more remotely. And now, four centuries from the discovery of America, at the end of a hundred years of life under the Constitution, the frontier has gone, and with its going has closed the first period of American history.

2. DECLARATION OF PURPOSE OF THE NATIONAL GRANGE, 1874[1]

EDITORS' NOTE.—That farmers were discontented with the subordinate place in the American system to which they were being relegated by the aftermath of the Civil War may be measured in part by their efforts to form a national organization of their own kind. The first of such attempts that achieved national importance was the Patrons of Husbandry, formed in 1867 under the leadership of Oliver H. Kelly. Popularly known as the Grange, this association applied the principles of the secret fraternal orders to the special needs of the farmer. For one thing, the Grangers experimented in the sale and purchase of commodities and supplies through cooperative organization. The movement was nonpolitical in the sense that it did not run candidates for office under its own name. As individuals, however, the farmers of no fewer than eleven western states formed their own independent political parties in the seventies on a state-wide basis and frequently won control of a balance of power in the state legislatures.

The farmer representatives blamed their economic difficulties upon eastern business interests. Since these groups were relatively inaccessible, the farm legislators vented their accumulated wrath upon the nearest local representatives of big business, the

1. *A Documentary History of American Industrial Society*, ed. John R. Commons and associates (Cleveland, 1911), X, 100–105. Reprinted by permission of the publishers, the Arthur H. Clark Company.

railroads and the grain elevators. In the resultant Granger Laws, passed by the states during the seventies, the nation witnessed the first extensive effort to regulate big business and restrain monopolies. The official policy of the Patrons of Husbandry may be understood from the resolutions adopted at its seventh national meeting in 1874 and reprinted below.

PREAMBLE

Profoundly impressed with the truth that the National Grange of the United States should definitely proclaim to the world its general objects, we hereby unanimously make this Declaration of Purposes of the Patrons of Husbandry:

GENERAL OBJECTS

1. United by the strong and faithful tie of agriculture, we mutually resolve to labor for the good of our Order, our country, and mankind.
2. We heartily indorse the motto: "In essentials, unity; in non-essentials, liberty; in all things, charity."

SPECIFIC OBJECTS

3. We shall endeavor to advance our cause by laboring to accomplish the following objects:

To develop a better and higher manhood and womanhood among ourselves. To enhance the comforts and attractions of our homes, and strengthen our attachments to our pursuits. To foster mutual understanding and coöperation. To maintain inviolate our laws, and to emulate each other in labor to hasten the good time coming. To reduce our expenses, both individual and corporate. To buy less and produce more, in order to make our farms self-sustaining. To diversify our crops, and crop no more than we can cultivate. To condense the weight of our exports, selling less in the bushel and more on hoof and in fleece; less in lint, and more in warp and woof. To systematize our work, and calculate intelligently on probabilities. To discountenance the credit system, the mortgage system, the fashion system, and every other system tending to prodigality and bankruptcy.

We propose meeting together, talking together, working together, buying together, selling together, and in general acting together for our mutual protection and advancement, as occasion may require. We shall avoid litigation as much as possible by arbitration in the Grange. We shall constantly strive to secure entire harmony, good-will, vital brotherhood among ourselves, and to make our order perpetual. We shall earnestly endeavor to suppress personal, local, sectional, and national prejudices, all unhealthy rivalry, all selfish ambition. Faithful adherence to these principles will insure our mental, moral, social, and material advancement.

BUSINESS RELATIONS

4. For our business interests, we desire to bring producers and consumers, farmers and manufacturers into the most direct and friendly relations possible. Hence we must dispense with a surplus of middlemen, not that we are unfriendly to them, but we do not need them. Their surplus and their exactions diminish our profits.

We wage no aggressive warfare against any other interests whatever. On the contrary, all our acts and all our efforts, so far as business is concerned, are not only for the benefit of the producer and consumer, but also for all other interests that tend to bring these two parties into speedy and economical contact. Hence we hold that transportation companies of every kind are necessary to our success, that their interests are intimately connected with our interests, and harmonious action is mutually advantageous, keeping in view the first sentence in our declaration of principles of action that "Individual happiness depends upon general prosperity."

We shall, therefore, advocate for every

state the increase in every practicable way, of all facilities for transporting cheaply to the seaboard, or between home producers and consumers, all the productions of our country. We adopt it as our fixed purpose to "open out the channels in nature's great arteries that the life-blood of commerce may flow freely."

We are not enemies of railroads, navigable and irrigating canals, nor of any corporation that will advance our industrial interests, nor of any laboring classes.

In our noble Order there is no communism, no agrarianism.

We are opposed to such spirit and management of any corporation or enterprise as tends to oppress the people and rob them of their just profits. We are not enemies to capital, but we oppose the tyranny of monopolies. We long to see the antagonism between capital and labor removed by common consent, and by an enlightened statesmanship worthy of the nineteenth century. We are opposed to excessive salaries, high rates of interests, and exorbitant per cent profits in trade. They greatly increase our burdens, and do not bear a proper proportion to the profits of producers. We desire only self-protection and the protection of every true interest of our land by legitimate transactions, legitimate trade, and legitimate profits.

EDUCATION

We shall advance the cause of education among ourselves and for our children, by all just means within our power. We especially advocate for our agricultural and industrial colleges that practical agriculture, domestic science, and all the arts which adorn the home, be taught in their courses of study.

THE GRANGE NOT PARTISAN

5. We emphatically and sincerely assert the oft-repeated truth taught in our organic law, that the Grange, National, State, or Subordinate, is not a political or party organization. No Grange, if true to its obligations, can discuss political or religious questions, nor call political conventions, nor nominate candidates, nor even discuss their merits in its meetings.

Yet the principles we teach underlie all true politics, all true statesmanship, and, if properly carried out, will tend to purify the whole political atmosphere of our country. For we seek the greatest good to the greatest number.

We must always bear in mind that no one, by becoming a Patron of Husbandry, gives up that inalienable right and duty which belongs to every American citizen, to take a proper interest in the politics of his country.

On the contrary, it is right for every member to do all in his power legitimately to influence for good the action of any political party to which he belongs. It is his duty to do all he can in his own party to put down bribery, corruption, and trickery; to see that none but competent, faithful, and honest men who will unflinchingly stand by our industrial interests, are nominated for all positions of trust; and to have carried out the principle which should always characterize every Patron, that the office should seek the man, and not the man the office.

We acknowledge the broad principle that difference of opinion is no crime, and hold that "progress toward truth is made by differences of opinion," while "the fault lies in bitterness of controversy."

We desire a proper equality, equity, and fairness; protection for the weak, restraint upon the strong; in short, justly distributed burdens and justly distributed power. These are American ideas, the very essence of American independence, and to advocate the contrary is unworthy of the sons and daughters of an American republic.

We cherish the belief that sectionalism is, and of right should be, dead and buried with the past. Our work is for the present and the future. In our agricultural brotherhood and its purposes we shall recognize no north, no south, no east, no west.

It is reserved by every Patron, as the

right of a freeman, to affiliate with any party that will best carry out his principles.

OUTSIDE COÖPERATION

6. Ours being peculiarly a farmers' institution, we cannot admit all to our ranks. Many are excluded by the nature of our organization, not because they are professional men, or artisans, or laborers, but because they have not a sufficient direct interest in tilling the soil, or may have some interest in conflict with our purposes. But we appeal to all good citizens for their cordial coöperation to assist in our efforts toward reform, that we may eventually remove from our midst the last vestige of tyranny and corruption. We hail the general desire for fraternal harmony, equitable compromises, and earnest coöperation, as an omen of our future success.

7. It shall be an abiding principle with us to relieve any of our oppressed and suffering brotherhood by any means at our command.

Last, but not least, we proclaim it among our purposes to inculcate a proper appreciation of the abilities and sphere of woman, as is indicated by admitting her to membership and position in our order.

Imploring the continued assistance of our Divine Master to guide us in our work, we here pledge ourselves to faithful and harmonious labor for all future time, to return by our united efforts to the wisdom, justice, fraternity, and political purity of our forefathers. . . .

3. THE POPULIST PLATFORM OF 1892[1]

EDITORS' NOTE.—The Patrons of Husbandry declined during the 1880's, but many farm organizations arose to take over its leadership. These groups were gradually combined into the two great Farmers' Alliances—the Northern and the Southern. By 1891 leaders of the farm movement, which was assuming many of the attributes of a crusade, repudiated the major political parties and formed a new organization, the Populist party. The Populists nominated General James B. Weaver (1833–1912) of Iowa, a former Greenbacker, for the presidency in 1892. The Populist platform of that year is reprinted below. Weaver polled over a million votes and secured twenty-two electoral votes—the first third-party candidate since the Civil War to make his mark upon the electoral college. It was significant, however, that he failed to carry the solid South. In other words, the Populists were unable, in 1892, to reunite the farmers into an independent national political party.

Assembled upon the 116th anniversary of the Declaration of Independence, the People's Party of America, in their first national convention, invoking upon their action the blessing of Almighty God, put forth in the name and on behalf of the people of this country, the following preamble and declaration of principles:

1. *The World Almanac, 1893*, pp. 83–85. By permission of the *World Almanac*. Adopted at Omaha, Nebraska, July 4, 1892.

PREAMBLE

The conditions which surround us best justify our co-operation; we meet in the midst of a nation brought to the verge of moral, political, and material ruin. Corruption dominates the ballot-box, the Legislatures, the Congress, and touches even the ermine of the bench. The people are demoralized; most of the States have been compelled to isolate the voters at the polling places to prevent universal intimidation and bribery. The newspapers are largely subsidized or muzzled, public opinion silenced, business prostrated, homes covered with mortgages, labor impoverished, and the land concentrating in the hands of capitalists. The urban workmen are denied the right to organize for self-protection, imported pauperized labor beats down their wages, a hireling standing army, unrecognized by our laws, is established to shoot them down, and they are rapidly degenerating into European conditions. The fruits of the toil of millions are boldly stolen to build up colossal fortunes for a few, unprecedented in the history of mankind; and the possessors of those, in turn, despise the Republic and endanger liberty. From the same prolific womb of governmental injustice we breed the two great classes—tramps and millionaires.

The national power to create money is appropriated to enrich bondholders; a vast public debt payable in legal tender currency has been funded into gold-bearing bonds, thereby adding millions to the burdens of the people.

Silver, which has been accepted as coin since the dawn of history, has been demonetized to add to the purchasing power of gold by decreasing the value of all forms of property as well as human labor, and the supply of currency is purposely abridged to fatten usurers, bankrupt enterprise, and enslave industry. A vast conspiracy against mankind has been organized on two continents, and it is rapidly taking possession of the world. If not met and overthrown at once it forebodes terrible social convulsions, the destruction of civilization, or the establishment of an absolute despotism.

We have witnessed for more than a quarter of a century the struggles of the two great political parties for power and plunder, while grievous wrongs have been inflicted upon the suffering people. We charge that the controlling influences dominating both these parties have permitted the existing dreadful conditions to develop without serious effort to prevent or restrain them. Neither do they now promise us any substantial reform. They have agreed together to ignore, in the coming campaign, every issue but one. They propose to drown the outcries of a plundered people with the uproar of a sham battle over the tariff, so that capitalists, corporations, national banks, rings, trusts, watered stock, the demonetization of silver and the oppressions of the usurers may all be lost sight of. They propose to sacrifice our homes, lives, and children on the altar of mammon; to destroy the multitude in order to secure corruption funds from the millionaires.

Assembled on the anniversary of the birthday of the nation, and filled with the spirit of the grand general and chief who established our independence, we seek to restore the government of the Republic to the hands of "the plain people," with which class it originated. We assert our purposes to be identical with the purposes of the National Constitution; to form a more perfect union and establish justice, insure domestic tranquillity, provide for the common defence, promote the general welfare, and secure the blessings of liberty for ourselves and our posterity.

We declare that this Republic can only endure as a free government while built upon the love of the whole people for each other and for the nation; that it cannot be pinned together by bayonets; that the civil war is over, and that every passion and resentment which grew out of it must die with it, and that we must be in fact, as we are in name, one united brotherhood of free men.

Our country finds itself confronted by conditions for which there is no precedent in the history of the world; our annual agricultural productions amount to billions of dollars in value, which must, within a few weeks or months, be exchanged for billions of dollars' worth of commodities consumed in their production; the existing currency supply is wholly inadequate to make this exchange; the results are falling prices, the formation of combines and rings, the impoverishment of the producing class. We pledge ourselves that if given power we will labor to correct these evils by wise and reasonable legislation, in accordance with the terms of our platform.

We believe that the power of government—in other words, of the people—should be expanded (as in the case of the postal service) as rapidly and as far as the good sense of an intelligent people and the teachings of experience shall justify, to the end that oppression, injustice, and poverty shall eventually cease in the land.

While our sympathies as a party of reform are naturally upon the side of every proposition which will tend to make men intelligent, virtuous, and temperate, we nevertheless regard these questions, important as they are, as secondary to the great issues now pressing for solution, and upon which not only our individual prosperity but the very existence of free institutions depend; and we ask all men to first help us to determine whether we are to have a republic to administer before we differ as to the conditions upon which it is to be administered, believing that the forces of reform this day organized will never cease to move forward until every wrong is remedied and equal rights and equal privileges securely established for all the men and women of this country.

PLATFORM

We declare, therefore—

First.—That the union of the labor forces of the United States this day consummated shall be permanent and perpetual; may its spirit enter into all hearts for the salvation of the Republic and the uplifting of mankind.

Second.—Wealth belongs to him who creates it, and every dollar taken from industry without an equivalent is robbery. "If any will not work, neither shall he eat." The interests of rural and civic labor are the same; their enemies are identical.

Third.—We believe that the time has come when the railroad corporations will either own the people or the people must own the railroads, and should the govern-

ment enter upon the work of owning and managing all railroads, we should favor an amendment to the Constitution by which all persons engaged in the government service shall be placed under a civil-service regulation of the most rigid character, so as to prevent the increase of the power of the national administration by the use of such additional government employées.

Finance.—We demand a national currency, safe, sound, and flexible, issued by the general government only, a full legal tender for all debts, public and private, and that without the use of banking corporations, a just, equitable, and efficient means of distribution direct to the people, at a tax not to exceed 2 per cent per annum, to be provided as set forth in the sub-treasury plan of the Farmers' Alliance, or a better system; also by payments in discharge of its obligations for public improvements.

1. We demand free and unlimited coinage of silver and gold at the present legal ratio of 16 to 1.

2. We demand that the amount of circulating medium be speedily increased to not less than $50 per capita.

3. We demand a graduated income tax.

4. We believe that the money of the country should be kept as much as possible in the hands of the people, and hence we demand that all State and national revenues shall be limited to the necessary expenses of the government, economically and honestly administered.

5. We demand that postal savings banks be established by the government for the safe deposit of the earnings of the people and to facilitate exchange.

Transportation.—Transportation being a means of exchange and a public necessity, the government should own and operate the railroads in the interest of the people. The telegraph, telephone, like the post-office system, being a necessity for the transmission of news, should be owned and operated by the government in the interest of the people.

Land.—The land, including all the natural sources of wealth, is the heritage of the people, and should not be monopolized for speculative purposes, and alien ownership of land should be prohibited. All land now held by railroads and other corporations in excess of their actual needs, and all lands now owned by aliens should be reclaimed by the government and held for actual settlers only.

EXPRESSION OF SENTIMENTS

Your Committee on Platform and Resolutions beg leave unanimously to report the following:

WHEREAS, Other questions have been presented for our consideration, we hereby submit the following, not as a part of the Platform of the People's Party, but as resolutions expressive of the sentiment of this Convention:

1. *Resolved*, That we demand a free ballot and a fair count in all elections, and pledge ourselves to secure it to every legal voter without Federal intervention, through the adoption by the States of the unperverted Australian or secret ballot system.

2. *Resolved*, That the revenue derived from a graduated income tax should be applied to the reduction of the burden of taxation now levied upon the domestic industries of this country.

3. *Resolved*, That we pledge our support to fair and liberal pensions to ex-Union soldiers and sailors.

4. *Resolved*, That we condemn the fallacy of protecting American labor under the present system, which opens our ports to the pauper and criminal classes of the world and crowds out our wage-earners; and we denounce the present ineffective

laws against contract labor, and demand the further restriction of undesirable emigration.

5. *Resolved*, That we cordially sympathize with the efforts of organized workingmen to shorten the hours of labor, and demand a rigid enforcement of the existing eight-hour law on Government work, and ask that a penalty clause be added to the said law.

6. *Resolved*, That we regard the maintenance of a large standing army of mercenaries, known as the Pinkerton system, as a menace to our liberties, and we demand its abolition; and we condemn the recent invasion of the Territory of Wyoming by the hired assassins of plutocracy, assisted by Federal officers.

7. *Resolved*, That we commend to the favorable consideration of the people and the reform press the legislative system known as the initiative and referendum.

8. *Resolved*, That we favor a constitutional provision limiting the office of President and Vice-President to one term, and providing for the election of Senators of the United States by a direct vote of the people.

9. *Resolved*, That we oppose any subsidy or national aid to any private corporation for any purpose.

10. *Resolved*, That this convention sympathizes with the Knights of Labor and their righteous contest with the tyrannical combine of clothing manufacturers of Rochester, and declare it to be the duty of all who hate tyranny and oppression to refuse to purchase the goods made by the said manufacturers, or to patronize any merchants who sell such goods.

4. THE REPUBLICAN PLATFORM OF 1896[1]

EDITORS' NOTE.—Economic depression prevailed throughout the second presidential term of Grover Cleveland. In the by-elections of 1894 the

1. *Republican Campaign Textbook, 1896* (Washington, 1896), pp. 251–57.

Republicans recaptured control of both houses of Congress. The country was divided as to whether the depression could be ended by inflationary monetary programs or whether more widespread and fundamental reforms were needed. As the 1896 election approached, Marcus Alonzo Hanna (1837–1904), a successful Ohio businessman, resolutely gathered support for the nomination of his fellow-Ohioan, William McKinley. So efficient were Hanna's efforts that his political protégé was nominated on the first ballot, at St. Louis, in June, 1896.

Over the protests of western Republicans, the party adopted, on June 17, what amounted essentially to high tariff and anti-inflationary money plans and stood by to allow the depression to do its political work upon the incumbent administration.

The Republicans of the United States, assembled by their representatives in national convention, appealing for the popular and historical justification of their claims to the matchless achievements of the thirty years of Republican rule, earnestly and confidently address themselves to the awakened intelligence, experience, and conscience of their countrymen in the following declaration of facts and principles:

For the first time since the civil war the American people have witnessed the calamitous consequences of full and unrestricted Democratic control of the Government. It has been a record of unparalleled incapacity, dishonor, and disaster. In administrative management it has ruthlessly sacrificed indispensable revenue, entailed an unceasing deficit, eked out ordinary current expenses with borrowed money, piled up the public debt by $262,000,000 in time of peace, forced an adverse balance of trade, kept a perpetual menace hanging over the redemption fund, pawned American credit to alien syndicates, and reversed all the measures and results of successful Republican rule.

In the broad effect of its policy it has precipitated panic, blighted industry and trade with prolonged depression, closed factories, reduced work and wages, halted enterprise, and crippled American production while stimulating foreign production for the American market. Every consideration of public safety and individual interest demands that the Government shall be rescued from the hands of those who have shown themselves incapable to conduct it

without disaster at home and dishonor abroad, and shall be restored to the party which for thirty years administered it with unequaled success and prosperity, and in this connection we heartily indorse the wisdom, patriotism, and the success of the Administration of President Harrison.

TARIFF

We renew and emphasize our allegiance to the policy of protection as the bulwark of American industrial independence and the foundation of American development and prosperity. This true American policy taxes foreign products and encourages home industry; it puts the burden of revenue on foreign goods; it secures the American market for the American producer; it upholds the American standard of wages for the American workingman; it puts the factory by the side of the farm, and makes the American farmer less dependent on foreign demand and price; it diffuses general thrift, and founds the strength of all on the strength of each. In its reasonable application it is just, fair, and impartial; equally opposed to foreign control and domestic monopoly, to sectional discrimination, and individual favoritism.

We denounce the present Democratic tariff as sectional, injurious to the public credit, and destructive to business enterprise. We demand such an equitable tariff on foreign imports which come into competition with American products as will not only furnish adequate revenue for the necessary expenses of the Government, but will protect American labor from degradation to the wage level of other lands.

We are not pledged to any particular schedules. The question of rates is a practical question, to be governed by the conditions of the time and of production; the ruling and uncompromising principle is the protection and development of American labor and industry. The country demands a right settlement, and then it wants rest.

RECIPROCITY

We believe the repeal of the reciprocity arrangements negotiated by the last Republican Administration was a national calamity, and we demand their renewal and extension on such terms as will equalize our trade with other nations, remove the restrictions which now obstruct the sale of American products in the ports of other countries, and secure enlarged markets for the products of our farms, forests, and factories.

Protection and reciprocity are twin measures of Republican policy and go hand in hand. Democratic rule has recklessly struck down both, and both must be re-established. Protection for what we produce; free admission for the necessaries of life which we do not produce; reciprocity agreements of mutual interests which gain open markets for us in return for our open markets to others. Protection builds up domestic industry and trade and secures our own market for ourselves; reciprocity builds up foreign trade and finds an outlet for our surplus.

We hopefully look forward to the eventual withdrawal of the European powers from this hemisphere, and to the ultimate union of all English-speaking parts of the continent by the free consent of its inhabitants.

SUGAR

We condemn the present Administration for not keeping faith with the sugar producers of this country. The Republican party favors such protection as will lead to the production on American soil of all the sugar which the American people use, and for which they pay other countries more than $100,000,000 annually.

WOOL AND WOOLENS

To all our products—to those of the mine and the fields as well as to those of the shop and the factory—to hemp, to wool, the product of the great industry of sheep husbandry, as well as to the finished woolens of the mills—we promise the most ample protection.

MERCHANT MARINE

We favor restoring the American policy of discriminating duties for the upbuilding of our merchant marine and the protection of our shipping in the foreign carrying trade, so that American ships—the product of American labor, employed in American shipyards, sailing under the Stars and Stripes, and manned, officered, and owned by Americans—may regain the carrying of our foreign commerce.

FINANCE

The Republican party is unreservedly for sound money. It caused the enactment of the law providing for the resumption of specie payments in 1879; since then every dollar has been as good as gold.

We are unalterably opposed to every measure calculated to debase our currency or impair the credit of our country. We are, therefore, opposed to the free coinage of silver except by international agreement with the leading commercial nations of the world, which we pledge ourselves to promote, and until such agreement can be obtained the existing gold standard must be preserved. All our silver and paper currency must be maintained at parity with gold, and we favor all measures designed to maintain inviolably the obligations of the United States and all our money, whether coin or paper, at the present standard, the standard of the most enlightened nations of the earth.

PENSIONS

The veterans of the Union Army deserve and should receive fair treatment and generous recognition. Whenever practicable they should be given the preference in the matter of employment, and they are entitled to the enactment of such laws as are best calculated to secure the fulfillment of the pledges made to them in the dark days of the country's peril. We denounce the practice in the Pension Bureau, so recklessly and unjustly carried on by the present Administration, of reducing pensions and arbitrarily dropping names from the rolls as deserving the severest condemnation of the American people.

FOREIGN RELATIONS

Our foreign policy should be at all times firm, vigorous, and dignified, and all our interests in the Western Hemisphere carefully watched and guarded. The Hawaiian Islands should be controlled by the United States, and no foreign power should be permitted to interfere with them; the Nicaraguan Canal should be built, owned, and operated by the United States; and by the purchase of the Danish islands we should secure a proper and much needed naval station in the West Indies.

ARMENIAN MASSACRES

The massacres in Armenia have aroused the deep sympathy and just indignation of the American people, and we believe that the United States should exercise all the influence it can properly exert to bring these atrocities to an end. In Turkey, American residents have been exposed to the gravest dangers and American property destroyed. There and everywhere American citizens and American property must be absolutely protected at all hazards and at any cost.

MONROE DOCTRINE

We reassert the Monroe doctrine in its full extent, and we reaffirm the right of the United States to give the doctrine effect by responding to the appeal of any American State for friendly intervention in case of European encroachment. We have not interfered and shall not interfere with the existing possessions of any European power in this hemisphere, but these possessions must not on any pretext be extended.

CUBA

From the hour of achieving their own independence the people of the United States have regarded with sympathy the struggles of other American people to free themselves from European domination. We watch with deep and abiding interest the heroic battle of the Cuban patriots against cruelty and oppression, and our best hopes go out for the full success of their determined contest for liberty.

The Government of Spain, having lost control of Cuba, and being unable to protect the property or lives of resident American citizens, or to comply with its treaty obligations, we believe that the Government of the United States should actively use its influence and good offices to restore peace and give independence to the island.

THE NAVY

The peace and security of the Republic and the maintenance of its rightful influence among the nations of the earth demand a naval power commensurate with its position and responsibility. We therefore favor the continued enlargement of the Navy and a complete system of harbor and seacoast defenses.

FOREIGN IMMIGRATION

For the protection of the quality of our American citizenship and of the wages of our workingmen against the fatal competition of low-priced labor, we demand that the immigration laws be thoroughly enforced and so extended as to exclude from entrance to the United States those who can neither read nor write.

CIVIL SERVICE

The civil-service law was placed on the statute book by the Republican party, which has always sustained it, and we renew our repeated declarations that it shall be thoroughly and honestly enforced and extended wherever practicable.

FREE BALLOT

We demand that every citizen of the United States shall be allowed to cast one free and unrestricted ballot, and that such ballot shall be counted and returned as cast.

LYNCHINGS

We proclaim our unqualified condemnation of the uncivilized and barbarous practice, well known as lynching or killing of human beings suspected or charged with crime, without process of law.

NATIONAL ARBITRATION

We favor the creation of a national board of arbitration to settle and adjust differences which may arise between employers and employees engaged in interstate commerce.

HOMESTEADS

We believe in an immediate return to the free-homestead policy of the Republican party, and urge the passage by Congress of a satisfactory free-homestead measure such as has already passed the House and is now pending in the Senate.

TERRITORIES

We favor the admission of the remaining Territories at the earliest practicable date, having due regard to the interests of the people of the Territories and of the United States. All the Federal officers appointed for the Territories should be selected from bona fide residents thereof, and the right of self-government should be accorded as far as practicable.

ALASKA

We believe the citizens of Alaska should have representation in the Congress of the United States, to the end that needful legislation may be intelligently enacted.

TEMPERANCE

We sympathize with all wise and legitimate efforts to lessen and prevent the evils of intemperance and promote morality.

RIGHTS OF WOMEN

The Republican party is mindful of the rights and interests of women. Protection of American industries includes equal opportunities, equal pay for equal work, and protection to the home. We favor the admission of women to wider spheres of usefulness, and welcome their co-operation in rescuing the country from Democratic and Populist mismanagement and misrule.

Such are the principles and policies of the Republican party. By these principles we will abide and these policies we will put into execution. We ask for them the considerate judgment of the American people. Confident alike in the history of our great party and in the justice of our cause, we present our platform and our candidates in the full assurance that the election will bring victory to the Republican party and prosperity to the people of the United States.

5. THE DEMOCRATIC PLATFORM OF 1896[1]

Editors' Note.—When the Democratic national convention assembled in Chicago in July, 1896, it soon became apparent that the silver Democrats and the money reformers were in

1. *Official Proceedings of the Democratic National Convention . . . Held in Chicago, Illinois, July . . . 1896 . . .* (Logansport, Ind., 1896), pp. 250–56. Adopted July 9, 1896.

control of the party. A platform was adopted that stood foursquare on the silver issue, demanded tariff reform, and made a bid for the labor vote.

In view of the strength of the farm movement of the day, a pertinent question for discussion could be the wisdom of making monetary reform the major issue of the campaign. At any rate, during the debate on the platform, William Jennings Bryan stampeded the convention with his "Cross of Gold" speech in favor of the unlimited coinage of silver. On the next day Bryan was nominated for the presidency. When the Populists met at St. Louis, they, too, nominated Bryan, thereby completing the coalition of the two great liberal forces. Before the campaign was over, the silver Republicans had bolted to the Democratic side, while the gold Democrats had left their party and named a separate ticket. For the first time since the Civil War party lines had been reshuffled so as to make it possible for farmers to express their views more or less independently of political tradition.

We, the Democrats of the United States in National Convention assembled, do reaffirm our allegiance to those great essential principles of justice and liberty, upon which our institutions are founded, and which the Democratic Party has advocated from Jefferson's time to our own— freedom of speech, freedom of the press, freedom of conscience, the preservation of personal rights, the equality of all citizens before the law, and the faithful observance of constitutional limitations.

During all these years the Democratic Party has resisted the tendency of selfish interests to the centralization of governmental power, and steadfastly maintained the integrity of the dual scheme of government established by the founders of this Republic of republics. Under its guidance and teachings the great principle of local self-government has found its best expression in the maintenance of the rights of the States and in its assertion of the necessity of confining the general government to the exercise of the powers granted by the Constitution of the United States.

The Constitution of the United States guarantees to every citizen the rights of civil and religious liberty. The Democratic Party has always been the exponent of political liberty and religious freedom, and it renews its obligations and reaffirms its devotion to these fundamental principles of the Constitution.

THE MONEY PLANK

Recognizing that the money question is paramount to all others at this time, we invite attention to the fact that the Federal Constitution named silver and gold together as the money metals of the United States, and that the first coinage law passed by Congress under the Constitution made the silver dollar the monetary unit and admitted gold to free coinage at a ratio based upon the silver-dollar unit.

We declare that the act of 1873 demonetizing silver without the knowledge or approval of the American people has resulted in the appreciation of gold and a corresponding fall in the prices of commodities produced by the people; a heavy increase in the burden of taxation and of all debts, public and private; the enrichment of the money-lending class at home and abroad; the prostration of industry and impoverishment of the people.

We are unalterably opposed to monometallism which has locked fast the prosperity of an industrial people in the paralysis of hard times. Gold monometallism is a British policy, and its adoption has brought other nations into financial servitude to London. It is not only un-American, but anti-American, and it can be fastened on the United States only by the stifling of that spirit and love of liberty which proclaimed our political independence in 1776 and won it in the War of the Revolution.

We demand the free and unlimited coinage of both silver and gold at the present legal ratio of 16 to 1 without waiting for the aid or consent of any other nation. We demand that the standard silver dollar shall be a full legal tender, equally with gold, for all debts, public and private, and we favor such legislation as will prevent for the future the demonetization of any kind of legal-tender money by private contract.

We are opposed to the policy and practice of surrendering to the holders of the obligations of the United States the option reserved by law to the Government of redeeming such obligations in either silver coin or gold coin.

INTEREST-BEARING BONDS

We are opposed to the issuing of interest-bearing bonds of the United States in time of peace and condemn the trafficking with banking syndicates, which, in exchange for bonds and at an enormous profit to themselves, supply the Federal Treasury with gold to maintain the policy of gold monometallism.

AGAINST NATIONAL BANKS

Congress alone has the power to coin and issue money, and President Jackson declared that this power could not be delegated to corporations or individuals. We therefore denounce the issuance of notes intended to circulate as money by National banks as in derogation of the Constitution, and we demand that all paper which is made a legal tender for public and private debts, or which is receivable for dues to the United States, shall be issued by the Government of the United States and shall be redeemable in coin.

TARIFF RESOLUTION

We hold that tariff duties should be levied for purposes of revenue, such duties to be so adjusted as to operate equally throughout the country, and not discriminate between class or section, and that taxation should be limited by the needs of the Government, honestly and economically administered. We denounce as disturbing to business the Republican threat to restore the *McKinley* law, which has twice been condemned by the people in National elections, and which, enacted under the false plea of protection to home industry, proved a prolific breeder of trusts and monopolies, enriched the few at the expense of the many, restricted trade and deprived the producers of the great American staples of access to their natural markets.

Until the money question is settled we are opposed to any agitation for further changes in our tariff laws, except such as are necessary to meet the deficit in revenue caused by the adverse decision of the Supreme Court on the income tax. But for this decision by the Supreme Court, there would be no deficit in the revenue under the law passed by a Democratic Congress in strict pursuance of the uniform decisions of that court for nearly 100 years, that court having in that decision sustained Constitutional objections to its enactment which had previously been overruled by the ablest Judges who have ever sat on that bench. We declare that it is the duty of Congress to use all the Constitutional power which remains after that decision, or which may come from its reversal by the court as it may hereafter be constituted, so that the burdens of taxation may be equally and impartially laid, to the end that wealth may bear its due proportion of the expense of the Government.

IMMIGRATION AND ARBITRATION

We hold that the most efficient way of protecting American labor is to prevent the importation of foreign pauper labor to compete with it in the home market, and that the value of the home market to our American farmers and artisans is greatly reduced by a vicious monetary system which depresses the prices of their products below the cost of production, and thus deprives them of the means of purchasing the products of our home manufactories; and as labor creates the wealth of the country, we demand the passage of such laws as may be necessary to protect it in all its rights.

We are in favor of the arbitration of differences between employers engaged in interstate commerce and their employes, and recommend such legislation as is necessary to carry out this principle.

TRUSTS AND POOLS

The absorption of wealth by the few, the consolidation of our leading railroad systems, and the formation of trusts and pools require a stricter control by the Federal Government of those arteries of commerce. We demand the enlargement of the powers of the Interstate Commerce Commission and such restriction and guarantees in the control of railroads as will protect the people from robbery and oppression.

DECLARE FOR ECONOMY

We denounce the profligate waste of the money wrung from the people by oppressive taxation and the lavish appropriations of recent Republican Congresses, which have kept taxes high, while the labor that pays them is unemployed and the products of the people's toil are depressed in price till they no longer repay the cost of production. We demand a return to that simplicity and economy which befits a Democratic Government and a reduction in the number of useless offices the salaries of which drain the substance of the people.

FEDERAL INTERFERENCE IN
LOCAL AFFAIRS

We denounce arbitrary interference by Federal authorities in local affairs as a violation of the Constitution of the United States and a crime against free institutions, and we especially object to government by injunction as a new and highly dangerous form of oppression by which Federal Judges, in contempt of the laws of the States and rights of citizens, become at

once legislators, judges and executioners; and we approve the bill passed at the last session of the United States Senate, and now pending in the House of Representatives, relative to contempts in Federal courts and providing for trials by jury in certain cases of contempt.

PACIFIC RAILROAD

No discrimination should be indulged in by the Government of the United States in favor of any of its debtors. We approve of the refusal of the Fifty-third Congress to pass the Pacific Railroad Funding bill and denounce the effort of the present Republican Congress to enact a similar measure.

PENSIONS

Recognizing the just claims of deserving Union soldiers, we heartily indorse the rule of the present Commissioner of Pensions, that no names shall be arbitrarily dropped from the pension roll; and the fact of enlistment and service should be deemed conclusive evidence against disease and disability before enlistment.

ADMISSION OF TERRITORIES

We favor the admission of the Territories of New Mexico, Arizona and Oklahoma into the Union as States, and we favor the early admission of all the Territories, having the necessary population and resources to entitle them to Statehood, and, while they remain Territories, we hold that the officials appointed to administer the government of any Territory, together with the District of Columbia and Alaska, should be bona fide residents of the Territory or District in which their duties are to be performed. The Democratic party believes in home rule and that all public lands of the United States should be appropriated to the establishment of free homes for American citizens.

We recommend that the Territory of Alaska be granted a delegate in Congress and that the general land and timber laws of the United States be extended to said Territory.

SYMPATHY FOR CUBA

The Monroe doctrine, as originally declared, and as interpreted by succeeding Presidents, is a permanent part of the foreign policy of the United States, and must at all times be maintained.

We extend our sympathy to the people of Cuba in their heroic struggle for liberty and independence.

CIVIL SERVICE LAWS

We are opposed to life tenure in the public service, except as provided in the Constitution. We favor appointments based on merit, fixed terms of office, and such an administration of the civil service laws as will afford equal opportunities to all citizens of ascertained fitness.

THIRD TERM RESOLUTION

We declare it to be the unwritten law of this Republic, established by custom and usage of 100 years and sanctioned by the examples of the greatest and wisest of those who founded and have maintained our Government that no man should be eligible for a third term of the Presidential office.

IMPROVEMENT OF WATERWAYS

The Federal Government should care for and improve the Mississippi river and other great waterways of the Republic, so as to secure for the interior States easy and cheap transportation to tide water. When any waterway of the Republic is of sufficient importance to demand aid of the Government such aid should be extended upon a definite plan of continuous work until permanent improvement is secured.

CONCLUSION

Confiding in the justice of our cause and the necessity of its success at the polls, we submit the foregoing declaration of principles and purposes to the considerate judgment of the American people. We invite the support of all citizens who approve them and who desire to have them made effective through legislation, for the relief of the people and the restoration of the country's prosperity.

6. THE CROSS OF GOLD SPEECH, 1896[1]

By William Jennings Bryan

EDITOR'S NOTE.—William Jennings Bryan (1860–1925), born at Salem, Illinois, distinguished himself as a student at Illinois College and at Union Law School in Chicago. He was admitted to the Illinois bar in 1883 but moved in 1887 to Lincoln, Nebraska. As a Democrat, Bryan showed great vote-getting power in 1890 by winning a seat to Congress from a strongly Republican district. Despite his youth he was placed on the Ways and Means Committee, where he expressed an interest in lowering the tariff and bringing about the unlimited coinage of silver. He was a leader in the contest which established the graduated income tax of 1894. When it became clear that the Republican leaders were committed to a gold standard in 1896, despite their equivocal platform statement in favor of bimetalism, Bryan became convinced that the Democrats could win the election if silver were made the issue.

Intense political passion was aroused in the campaign that followed. The agrarian forces of the South and West

1. *Speeches of William Jennings Bryan* (New York, 1913), I, 238–49. By permission of Funk and Wagnalls.

sought to unite with the debtor classes of the East to overthrow the forces that controlled the new industrialism. Bryan was defeated chiefly through failure to win the farmers of the Middle West, but the 6,300,000 votes he received were a measure of the agrarian protest as well as a tribute to his personal powers.

I would be presumptuous, indeed, to present myself against the distinguished gentlemen to whom you have listened if this were a mere measuring of abilities; but this is not a contest between persons. The humblest citizen in all the land, when clad in the armor of a righteous cause, is stronger than all the hosts of error. I come to speak to you in defense of a cause as holy as the cause of liberty—the cause of humanity.

When this debate is concluded, a motion will be made to lay upon the table the resolution offered in commendation of the administration, and also the resolution offered in condemnation of the administration. We object to bringing this question down to the level of persons. The individual is but an atom; he is born, he acts, he dies; but principles are eternal; and this has been a contest over a principle.

Never before in the history of this country has there been witnessed such a contest as that through which we have just passed. Never before in the history of American politics has a great issue been fought out as this issue has been, by the voters of a great party. On the fourth of March, 1895, a few Democrats, most of them members of Congress, issued an address to the Democrats of the nation, asserting that the money question was the paramount issue of the hour; declaring that a majority of the Democratic party had the right to control the action of the party on this paramount issue; and concluding with the request that the believers in the free coinage of silver in the Democratic party should organize, take charge of, and control the policy of the Democratic party. Three months later, at Memphis, an organization was perfected, and the silver Democrats went forth openly and courageously proclaiming their belief, and declaring that, if successful, they would crystallize into a platform the declaration which they had made. Then began the conflict. With a zeal approaching the zeal which inspired the crusaders who followed Peter the Hermit, our silver Democrats went forth from victory unto victory until they are now assembled, not to discuss, not to debate, but to enter up the judgment already rendered by the plain people of this country. In this contest brother has been arrayed against brother, father against son. The warmest ties of love, acquaintance and association have been disregarded; old leaders have been cast aside when they have refused to give expression to the sentiments of those whom they would lead, and new leaders have sprung up to give direction to this cause of truth. Thus has the contest been waged, and we have assembled here under as binding and solemn instructions as were ever imposed upon representatives of the people.

We do not come as individuals. As individuals we might have been glad to compliment the gentleman from New York (Senator Hill), but we know that the people for whom we speak would never be willing to put him in a position where he could thwart the will of the Democratic party. I say it was not a question of persons; it was a question of principle, and it is not with gladness, my friends, that we find ourselves brought into conflict with those who are now arrayed on the other side.

The gentleman who preceded me (ex-Governor Russell) spoke of the State of Massachusetts; let me assure him that not one present in all this convention entertains the least hostility to the people of the State of Massachusetts, but we stand here representing people who are the equals, before the law, of the greatest citizens in the State of Massachusetts. When you (turning to the gold delegates) come before us and tell us that we are about to disturb your business interests, we reply that you have disturbed our business interests by your course.

We say to you that you have made the definition of a business man too limited in its application. The man who is employed for wages is as much a business man as his employer, the attorney in a country town is as much a business man as the corporation counsel in a great metropolis; the merchant at the cross-roads store is as much a business man as the merchant of New York; the farmer who goes forth in the morning and toils all day—who begins in the spring and toils all summer—and who by the application of brain and muscle to the natural resources of the country creates wealth, is as much a business man as the man who goes upon the board of trade and bets upon the price of grain; the miners who go down a thousand feet into the earth, or climb two thousand feet upon the cliffs, and bring forth from their hiding places the precious metals to be poured into the channels of trade are as much business men as the few financial magnates who, in a back room, corner the money of the world. We come to speak for this broader class of business men.

Ah, my friends, we say not one word against those who live upon the Atlantic coast, but the hardy pioneers who have braved all the dangers of the wilderness, who have made the desert to blossom as the rose—the pioneers away out there (pointing to the West), who rear their children near to Nature's heart, where they can mingle their voices with the voices of the birds—out there where they have erected schoolhouses for the education of their young, churches where they praise their Creator, and cemeteries where rest the ashes of their dead—these people, we say, are as deserving of the consideration of our party as any people in this country. It is for these that we speak. We do not come as aggressors. Our war is not a war of conquest; we are fighting in the defense of our homes, our families, and posterity. We have petitioned, and our petitions have been scorned; we have entreated, and our entreaties have been disregarded; we have begged, and they have mocked when our calamity came. We beg no longer; we entreat no more; we petition no more. We defy them.

The gentleman from Wisconsin has said that he fears a Robespierre. My friends, in this land of the free you need not fear that a tyrant will spring up from among the people. What we need is an Andrew Jackson to stand, as Jackson stood, against the encroachments of organized wealth.

They tell us that this platform was made to catch votes. We reply to them that changing conditions make new issues; that the principles upon which Democracy rests are as everlasting as the hills, but that they must be applied to new conditions as they arise. Conditions have arisen, and we are here to meet these conditions. They tell us that the income tax ought not to be brought in here; that it is a new idea. They criticize us for our criticism of the Supreme Court of the United States. My friends, we have not criticized; we have simply called attention to what you already know. If you want criticisms, read the dissenting opinions of the court. There you will find criticisms. They say that we passed an unconstitutional law; we deny it. The income tax law was not unconstitutional when it was passed; it was not unconstitutional when it went before the Supreme Court for the first time; it did not become unconstitutional until one of the judges changed his mind, and we cannot be expected to know when a judge will change his mind. The income tax is just. It simply intends to put the burdens of government justly upon the backs of the people. I am in favor of an income tax. When I find a man who is not willing to bear his share of the burdens of the government which protects him, I find a man who is unworthy to enjoy the blessings of a government like ours.

They say that we are opposing national bank currency; it is true. If you will read what Thomas Benton said, you will find he said that, in searching history, he could find but one parallel to Andrew Jackson; that was Cicero, who destroyed the conspiracy of Cataline and saved Rome. Benton said that Cicero only did for Rome what Jackson did for us when he destroyed the bank conspiracy and saved America. We say in our platform that we believe that the right to coin and issue money is a function of government. We believe it. We believe that it is a part of sovereignty, and can no more with safety be delegated to private individuals than we could afford to delegate to private individuals the power to make penal statutes or levy taxes. Mr. Jefferson, who was once regarded as good Democratic authority, seems to have differed in opinion from the gentleman who has addrest us on the part of the minority. Those who are opposed to this proposition tell us that the issue of paper money is a function of the bank, and that the Government ought to go out of the banking business. I stand with Jefferson rather than with them, and tell them, as he did, that the issue of money is a function of government, and that the banks ought to go out of the governing business.

They complain about the plank which declares against life tenure in office. They have tried to strain it to mean that which it does not mean. What we oppose by that plank is the life tenure which is being built up in Washington, and which excludes from participation in official benefits the humbler members of society.

Let me call your attention to two or three important things. The gentleman from New York says that he will propose an amendment to the platform providing that the proposed change in our monetary system shall not affect contracts already made. Let me remind you that there is no intention of affecting those contracts which according to present laws are made payable in gold; but if he means to say that we cannot change our monetary system without protecting those who have loaned money before the change was made, I desire to ask him where, in law or in morals, he can find justification for not protecting the debtors when the act of 1873 was passed, if he now insists that we must protect the creditors.

He says he will also propose an amendment which will provide for the suspension of free coinage if we fail to maintain the parity within a year. We reply that when we advocate a policy which we believe will be successful, we are not compelled to raise a doubt as to our own sincerity by suggesting what we shall do if we fail. I ask him, if he would apply his logic to us, why he does not apply it to himself. He says he wants this country to try to secure an international agreement. Why does he not tell us what he is going to do if he fails to secure an international agreement? There is more reason for him to do that than there is for us to provide against the failure to maintain the parity. Our opponents have tried for twenty years to secure an international agreement, and those are waiting for it most patiently who do not want it at all.

And now, my friends, let me come to the paramount issue. If they ask us why it is that we say more on the money question than we say upon the tariff question, I reply that, if protection has slain its thousands, the gold standard has slain its tens of thousands. If they ask us why we do not embody in our platform all the things that we believe in, we reply that when we have restored the money of the Constitution all other necessary reforms will be possible; but that until this is done there is no other reform that can be accomplished.

Why is it that within three months such a change has come over the country? Three months ago, when it was confidently asserted that those who believe in the gold standard would frame our platform and nominate our candidates, even the advocates of the gold standard did not think that we could elect a President. And they had good reason for their doubt, because there is scarcely a State here to-day asking for the gold standard which is not in the absolute control of the Republican party. But note the change. Mr. McKinley was nominated at St. Louis upon a platform which declared for the maintenance of the gold standard until it can be changed into bimetalism by international agreement. Mr. McKinley was the most popular man among the Republicans, and three months ago everybody in the Republican party prophesied his election. How is it to-day? Why, the man who was once pleased to think that he looked like Napoleon—that man shudders to-day when he remembers that he was nominated on the anniversary of the battle of Waterloo. Not only that, but as he listens he can hear with ever-increasing distinctness the sound of the waves as they beat upon the lonely shores of St. Helena.

Why this change? Ah, my friends, is not the reason for the change evident to any one who will look at the matter? No private character, however pure, no personal popularity, however great, can protect from the avenging wrath of an indignant people a man who will declare that he is in favor of fastening the gold standard upon this country, or who is willing to surrender the right of self-government and place the legislative control of our affairs in the hands of foreign potentates and powers.

We go forth confident that we shall win. Why? Because upon the paramount issue of this campaign there is not a spot of ground upon which the enemy will dare to challenge battle. If they tell us that the gold standard is a good thing, we shall point to their platform and tell them that their platform pledges the party to get rid of the gold standard and substitute bimetalism. If the gold standard is a good thing, why try to get rid of it? I call your attention to the fact that some of the very people who are in this convention to-day

and who tell us that we ought to declare in favor of international bimetalism—thereby declaring that the gold standard is wrong and that the principle of bimetalism is better—these very people four months ago were open and avowed advocates of the gold standard, and were then telling us that we could not legislate two metals together, even with the aid of all the world. If the gold standard is a good thing, we ought to declare in favor of its retention and not in favor of abandoning it; and if the gold standard is a bad thing why should we wait until other nations are willing to help us to let go? Here is the line of battle, and we care not upon which issue they force the fight; we are prepared to meet them on either issue or on both. If they tell us that the gold standard is the standard of civilization, we reply to them that this, the most enlightened of all the nations of the earth, has never declared for a gold standard and that both the great parties this year are declaring against it. If the gold standard is the standard of civilization, why, my friends, should we not have it? If they come to meet us on that issue we can present the history of our nation. More than that; we can tell them that they will search the pages of history in vain to find a single instance where the common people of any land have ever declared themselves in favor of the gold standard. They can find where the holders of fixt investments have declared for a gold standard, but not where the masses have.

Mr. Carlisle said in 1878 that this was a struggle between "the idle holders of idle capital" and "the struggling masses, who produce the wealth and pay the taxes of the country"; and, my friends, the question we are to decide is: Upon which side will the Democratic party fight; upon the side of "the idle holders of idle capital" or upon the side of "the struggling masses"? That is the question which the party must answer first, and then it must be answered by each individual hereafter. The sympathies of the Democratic party, as shown by the platform, are on the side of the struggling masses who have ever been the foundation of the Democratic party. There are two ideas of government. There are those who believe that, if you will only legislate to make the well-to-do prosperous, their prosperity will leak through on those below. The Democratic idea, however, has been that if you legislate to make the masses prosperous, their prosperity will find its way up through every class which rests upon them.

You come to us and tell us that the great cities are in favor of the gold standard; we reply that the great cities rest upon our broad and fertile prairies. Burn down your cities and leave our farms, and your cities will spring up again as if by magic; but destroy our farms and the grass will grow in the streets of every city in the country.

My friends, we declare that this nation is able to legislate for its own people on every question, without waiting for the aid or consent of any other nation on earth; and upon that issue we expect to carry every State in the Union. I shall not slander the inhabitants of the fair State of Massachusetts nor the inhabitants of the State of New York by saying that, when they are confronted with the proposition, they will declare that this nation is not

able to attend to its own business. It is the issue of 1776 over again. Our ancestors, when but three millions in number, had the courage to declare their political independence of every other nation; shall we, their descendants, when we have grown to seventy millions, declare that we are less independent than our forefathers? No, my friends, that will never be the verdict of our people. Therefore, we care not upon what lines the battle is fought. If they say bimetalism is good, but that we cannot have it until other nations help us, we reply that, instead of having a gold standard because England has, we will restore bimetalism, and then let England have bimetalism because the United States has it. If they dare to come out in the open field and defend the gold standard as a good thing, we will fight them to the uttermost. Having behind us the producing masses of this nation and the world, supported by the commercial interests, the laboring interests, and the toilers everywhere, we will answer their demand for a gold standard by saying to them: You shall not press down upon the brow of labor this crown of thorns, you shall not crucify mankind upon a cross of gold.

SECTION B. STATE REGULATION AND THE COURTS

1. SLAUGHTER-HOUSE CASES[1]

EDITORS' NOTE.—In 1869 a carpet-bag legislature in Louisiana created a monopoly of the business of maintaining a slaughter-house in three parishes, including New Orleans. The monopoly covered an area of 1,154 square miles with a population of 200,000–300,000, 1,000 of whom were engaged in the animal food industry. The act provided for the inspection of animals to be slaughtered and required the slaughter-house monopoly to make its facilities available to butchers on stated terms. In the interest of public health the act also required that the slaughter-house should be maintained and animals should be delivered to it south of the city of New Orleans. It appeared that there was room below the city for others to carry on slaughter-house operations. In violation of the terms of the act, individuals and corporations conducted slaughtering operations on their own premises. An injunction prohibiting this practice was secured by the company to which the monopoly had been granted. The injunction was upheld in the state courts, and on a writ of error their decision was affirmed, in a five-to-four decision, by the Supreme Court of the United States.

Apart from the question of the need for a monopoly, the issue emerges in the form of a conflict between the freedom of the individual to conduct his business as he sees fit and the right of the community to employ what has become known as its police power for the protection of the health and welfare of its members. The case is the more noteworthy because of the effort made to invoke the Thirteenth and Fourteenth amendments on behalf of the independent businessmen. In another sense the case points up the conflict between two parts of our constitutional framework, the police power and the due-process clause, each of which developed independently, and each of which sought in its own way to enhance the rights of the individual.

The dissenting opinion of Mr. Justice Field is a classical statement of the theory of the Fourteenth Amendment which was adopted by the Court twenty-five years later in *Allgeyer* v. *Louisiana* and which, until after the great depression of 1929, served as a check on social legislation. Mr. Justice Field (1816–99) experienced in his own life some of the influences typical of American frontier individualism. His father was a New England Congregational minister. Field spent two and a half years in the Middle East with a missionary relative. After practicing law with an older brother in New York, Field went to California in 1849. In the rough conditions of the mining

1. 83 U.S. (Wall.) 36, 57, 60–62, 66–67, 71–74, 77–78, 83, 85–89, 97, 109–11 (1873).

frontier he built up a practice, served in the legislature, helped to codify the law of the state, and eventually was elected to a seat on the state supreme court.

As a pro-Union Democrat he was appointed to the Supreme Court of the United States in 1863 and served until 1897, a period slightly longer than that of Chief Justice Marshall. His sympathy toward moderate reconstruction may have influenced his dissent in the Slaughter-House cases. Perhaps it was his frontier experiences that led him to champion the individualism of the due-process clause against the implied paternalism of the police-power doctrine.

Field's position, however, was not simple. In deciding in 1877 that a corporate charter did not protect a company against state antilottery legislation, Field acknowledged that the effect of the contract clause is limited by the police power in certain areas. On the same principle the charters of brewery companies were held subject in effect to repeal by state prohibition laws. The police power, strengthened by antimonopoly arguments, was successfully invoked in 1883 to sustain later Louisiana legislation repealing the monopoly upheld in the present case. Unless one starts with the Dred Scott decision, the story of the New Orleans slaughtering-house monopoly is thus also the beginning of the process by which the due-process clause developed its subsequent importance in the American industrial economy of the twentieth century. Not the least important matter for discussion which arises out of this trend was the following paradox: on the one hand, the states created the corporations by charter; on the other hand, the courts held that the creatures of the states were not subject to control by their creators.

Mr. Justice MILLER, now, April 14th, 1873, delivered the opinion of the court. . . .

This statute is denounced not only as creating a monopoly and conferring odious and exclusive privileges upon a small number of persons at the expense of the great body of the community of New Orleans, but it is asserted that it deprives a large and meritorious class of citizens—the whole of the butchers of the city—of the right to exercise their trade, the business to which they have been trained and on which they depend for the support of themselves and their families; and that the unrestricted exercise of the business of butchering is necessary to the daily subsistence of the population of the city.

But a critical examination of the act hardly justifies these assertions. . . .

It is not, and cannot be successfully controverted, that it is both the right and the duty of the legislative body—the supreme power of the State or municipality—to prescribe and determine the localities where the business of slaughtering for a great city may be conducted. To do this effectively it is indispensable that all persons who slaughter animals for food shall do it in those places *and nowhere else*.

The statute under consideration defines these localities and forbids slaughtering in any other. It does not, as has been asserted, prevent the butcher from doing his own slaughtering. On the contrary, the Slaughter-House Company is required, under a heavy penalty, to permit any person who wishes to do so, to slaughter in their houses; and they are bound to make ample provision for the convenience of all the slaughtering for the entire city. The butcher then is still permitted to slaughter, to prepare, and to sell his own meats; but he is required to slaughter at a specified place and to pay a reasonable compensation for the use of the accommodations furnished him at that place.

The wisdom of the monopoly granted by the legislature may be open to question, but it is difficult to see a justification for the assertion that the butchers are deprived of the right to labor in their occupation, or the people of their daily service in preparing food, or how this statute, with the duties and guards imposed upon the company, can be said to destroy the business of the butcher, or seriously interfere with its pursuit.

The power here exercised by the legislature of Louisiana is, in its essential nature, one which has been, up to the present period in the constitutional history of this country, always conceded to belong to the States, however it may *now* be questioned in some of its details.

"Unwholesome trades, slaughter-houses, operations offensive to the senses, the deposit of powder, the application of steam power to propel cars, the building with combustible materials, and the burial of the dead, may all," says Chancellor Kent, "be interdicted by law, in the midst of dense masses of population, on the general and rational principle, that every person ought so to use his property as not to injure his neighbors; and that private interests must be made subservient to the general interests of the community." This is called the police power; and it is declared by Chief Justice Shaw that it is much easier to perceive and realize the existence and sources of it than to mark its boundaries, or prescribe limits to its exercise.

This power is, and must be from its very nature, incapable of any very exact definition or limitation. Upon it depends the security of social order, the life and health of the citizen, the comfort of an existence in a quickly populated community, the enjoyment of private and social life, and the beneficial use of property. "It extends," says another eminent judge, "to the protection of the lives, limbs, health, comfort, and quiet of all persons, and the protection of all property within the State; . . . and persons and property are subjected to all kinds of restraints and burdens in order to secure the general comfort, health, and prosperity of the State. Of the perfect right of the legislature to do this no question ever was, or, upon acknowledged general principles, ever can be made, so far as natural persons are concerned." . . .

It may, therefore, be considered as established, that the authority of the legislature of Louisiana to pass the present statute is ample, unless some restraint in the exercise of that power be found in the constitution of that State or in the amendments to the Constitution of the United States, adopted since the date of the decisions we have already cited.

If any such restraint is supposed to exist in the constitution of the State, the Supreme Court of Louisiana having necessarily passed on that question, it would not be open to review in this court.

The plaintiffs in error accepting this issue, allege that the statute is a violation of the Constitution of the United States in these several particulars:

That it creates an involuntary servitude forbidden by the thirteenth article of amendment;

That it abridges the privileges and immunities of citizens of the United States;

That it denies to the plaintiffs the equal protection of the laws; and,

That it deprives them of their property without due process of law; contrary to the provisions of the first section of the fourteenth article of amendment.

This court is thus called upon for the first time to give construction to these articles.

We do not conceal from ourselves the great responsibility which this duty devolves upon us. No questions so far-reaching and pervading in their consequences, so profoundly interesting to the people of this country, and so important in their bearing upon the relations of the United States, and of the several States to each other and to the citizens of the States and of the United States, have been before this court during the official life of any of its present members. We have given every opportunity for a full hearing at the bar; we have discussed it freely and compared views among ourselves; we have taken ample time for careful deliberation, and we now propose to announce the judgments which we have formed in the construction of those articles, so far as we have found them necessary to the decision of the cases before us, and beyond that we have neither the inclination nor the right to go. . . .

We repeat, then, in the light of this recapitulation of events, almost too recent to be called history, but which are familiar to us all; and on the most casual examination of the language of these amendments, no one can fail to be impressed with the one pervading purpose found in them all, lying at the foundation of each, and without which none of them would have been even suggested; we mean the freedom of the slave race, the security and firm establishment of that freedom, and the protection of the newly-made freeman and citizen from the oppressions of those who had formerly exercised unlimited dominion over him. It is true that only the fifteenth amendment, in terms, mentions the negro by speaking of his color and his slavery. But it is just as true that each of the other articles was addressed to the grievances of that race, and designed to remedy them as the fifteenth.

We do not say that no one else but the negro can share in this protection. Both the language and spirit of these articles are to have their fair and just weight in any question of construction. Undoubtedly while negro slavery alone was in the mind of the Congress which proposed the thirteenth article, it forbids any other kind of slavery, now or hereafter. If Mexican peonage or the Chinese coolie labor system shall develop slavery of the Mexican or Chinese race within our territory, this amendment may safely be trusted to make it void. And so if other rights are assailed by the States which properly and necessarily fall within the protection of these articles, that protection will apply, though the party interested may not be of African descent. But what we do say, and what we wish to be understood is, that in any fair and just construction of any section or phrase of these amendments, it is necessary to look to the purpose which we have said was the pervading spirit of them all, the evil which they were designed to remedy, and the process of continued addition to the Constitution, until that purpose was supposed to be accomplished, as far as constitutional law can accomplish it.

The first section of the fourteenth article, to which our attention is more specially invited, opens with a definition of citizenship—not only citizenship of the United States, but citizenship of the States. No such definition was previously found in the Constitution, nor had any attempt been made to define it by act of Congress. It had been the occasion of much discussion in the courts, by the executive departments, and in the public journals. It had been said by eminent judges that no man was a citizen of the United States, except as he was a citizen of one of the States composing the Union. Those, therefore, who had been born and resided always in the District of Columbia or in the Territories, though within the United States, were not citizens. Whether this proposition was sound or not had never been judicially decided. But it had been held by this court, in the celebrated Dred Scott case, only a few years before the outbreak of the civil war, that a man of African descent, whether a slave or not, was not and could not be a citizen of a State or of the United States. This decision, while it met the condemnation of some of the ablest statesmen and constitutional lawyers of the country, had never been overruled; and if it was to be accepted as a constitutional limitation of the right of citizenship, then all the negro race who had recently been made freemen, were still, not only not citizens, but were incapable of becoming so by anything short of an amendment to the Constitution.

To remove this difficulty primarily, and to establish a clear and comprehensive definition of citizenship which should declare what should constitute citizenship of the United States, and also citizenship of a State, the first clause of the first section was framed.

"All persons born or naturalized in the United States, and subject to the jurisdiction thereof, are citizens of the United States and of the State wherein they reside."

The first observation we have to make on this clause is, that it puts at rest both the questions which we stated to have been the subject of differences of opinion. It declares that persons may be citizens of the United States without regard to their citizenship of a particular State, and it overturns the Dred Scott decision by making *all persons* born within the United States and subject to its jurisdiction citizens of the United States. That its main purpose was to establish the citizenship of the negro can admit of no doubt. The phrase, "subject to its jurisdiction" was intended to exclude from its operation children of ministers, consuls, and citizens or subjects of foreign States born within the United States.

The next observation is more important in view of the arguments of counsel in the present case. It is, that the distinction between citizenship of the United States and citizenship of a State is clearly recognized and established. Not only may a man be a citizen of the United States without being a citizen of a State, but an important element is necessary to convert the former into the latter. He must reside within the State to make him a citizen of it, but it is only necessary that he should be born or naturalized in the United States to be a citizen of the Union.

It is quite clear, then, that there is a citizenship of the United States, and a citizenship of a State, which are distinct from each other, and which depend upon different characteristics or circumstances in the individual. . . .

. . . Was it the purpose of the fourteenth amendment, by the simple declaration that no State should make or enforce any law which shall abridge the privileges and immunities of *Citizens of the United States* to transfer the security and protection of all the civil rights which we have mentioned, from the States to the Federal government? And where it is declared that Congress shall have the power to enforce that article, was it intended to bring within the power of Congress the entire domain of civil rights heretofore belonging exclusively to the States?

All this and more must follow, if the proposition of the plaintiffs in error be sound. For not only are these rights subject to the control of Congress whenever in its discretion any of them are supposed to be abridged by State legislation, but that body may also pass laws in advance, limiting and restricting the exercise of legislative power by the States, in their most ordinary and usual functions, as in its judgment it may think proper on all such subjects. And still further, such a construction followed by the reversal of the judgments of the Supreme Court of Louisiana in these cases, would constitute this court a perpetual censor upon all legislation of the States, on the civil rights of their own citizens, with authority to nullify such as it did not approve as consistent with those rights, as they existed at the time of the adoption of this amendment. The argument we admit is not always the most conclusive which is drawn from the consequences urged against the adoption of a particular construction of an instrument. But when, as in the case before us, these consequences are so serious, so far-reaching and pervading, so great a departure from the structure and spirit of our institutions; when the effect is to fetter and degrade the State governments by subjecting them to the control of Congress, in the exercise of powers heretofore universally conceded to them of the most ordinary and fundamental character; when in fact it radically changes the whole theory of the relations of the State and Federal governments to each other and of both these governments to the people; the argument has a force that is irresistible, in the absence of language which expresses such a purpose too clearly to admit of doubt. . . .

Mr. Justice FIELD, dissenting:

I am unable to agree with the majority of the court in these cases, and will proceed to state the reasons of my dissent from their judgment. . . .

The substance of the averments of the plaintiffs in error is this: That prior to the passage of the act in question they were engaged in the lawful and necessary business of procuring and bringing to the parishes of Orleans, Jefferson, and St. Bernard, animals suitable for human food, and in preparing such food for market; that in the prosecution of this business they had provided in these parishes suitable establishments for landing, sheltering, keeping, and slaughtering cattle and the sale of meat; that with their association about four hundred persons were connected, and that in the parishes named about a thousand persons were thus engaged in procuring, preparing, and selling animal food. And they complain that the business of landing, yarding, and keeping, within the parishes named, cattle intended for sale or slaughter, which was lawful for them to pursue before the first day of June, 1869, is made by that act unlawful for any one except the corporation named; and that the business of slaughtering cattle and preparing animal food for market, which it was lawful for them to pursue in these parishes before that day, is made by that act unlawful for them to pursue afterwards, except in the buildings of the company, and upon payment of certain prescribed fees, and a surrender of a valuable portion of each animal slaughtered. And they contend that the lawful business of landing, yarding, sheltering, and keeping cattle intended for sale or slaughter, which they in common with every individual in the community of the three parishes had a right to follow, cannot be thus taken from them and given over for a period of twenty-five years to the sole and exclusive enjoyment of a corporation of seventeen persons or of anybody else. And they also contend that the lawful and necessary business of slaughtering cattle and preparing animal food for market, which they and all other individuals had a right to follow, cannot be thus restricted within this territory of 1154 square miles to the buildings of this corporation, or be subjected to tribute for the emolument of that body.

No one will deny the abstract justice which lies in the position of the plaintiffs in error; and I shall endeavor to show that the position has some support in the fundamental law of the country.

It is contended in justification for the act in question that it was adopted in the interest of the city, to promote its cleanliness and protect its health, and was the legitimate exercise of what is termed the police power of the State. That power undoubtedly extends to all regulations affecting the health, good order, morals, peace, and safety of society, and is exercised on a great variety of subjects, and in almost numberless ways. All sorts of restrictions and burdens are imposed under it, and when these are not in conflict with any constitutional prohibitions, or fundamental principles, they cannot be successfully assailed in a judicial tribunal. With this power of the State and its legitimate exercise I shall not differ from the majority of the court. But under the pretence of prescribing a police regulation the State cannot be permitted to encroach upon any of the just rights of the citizen, which the

Constitution intended to secure against abridgment.

In the law in question there are only two provisions which can properly be called police regulations—the one which requires the landing and slaughtering of animals below the city of New Orleans, and the other which requires the inspection of the animals before they are slaughtered. When these requirements are complied with, the sanitary purposes of the act are accomplished. In all other particulars the act is a mere grant to a corporation created by it of special and exclusive privileges by which the health of the city is in no way promoted. It is plain that if the corporation can, without endangering the health of the public, carry on the business of landing, keeping, and slaughtering cattle within a district below the city embracing an area of over a thousand square miles, it would not endanger the public health if other persons were also permitted to carry on the same business within the same district under similar conditions as to the inspection of the animals. The health of the city might require the removal from its limits and suburbs of all buildings for keeping and slaughtering cattle, but no such object could possibly justify legislation removing such buildings from a large part of the State for the benefit of a single corporation. The pretence of sanitary regulations for the grant of the exclusive privileges is a shallow one, which merits only this passing notice. . . .

The act of Louisiana presents the naked case, unaccompanied by any public considerations, where a right to pursue a lawful and necessary calling, previously enjoyed by every citizen, and in connection with which a thousand persons were daily employed, is taken away and vested exclusively for twenty-five years, for an extensive district and a large population, in a single corporation, or its exercise is for that period restricted to the establishments of the corporation, and there allowed only upon onerous conditions.

If exclusive privileges of this character can be granted to a corporation of seventeen persons, they may, in the discretion of the legislature, be equally granted to a single individual. If they may be granted for twenty-five years they may be equally granted for a century, and in perpetuity. If they may be granted for the landing and keeping of animals intended for sale or slaughter they may be equally granted for the landing and storing of grain and other products of the earth, or for any article of commerce. If they may be granted for structures in which animal food is prepared for market they may be equally granted for structures in which farinaceous or vegetable food is prepared. They may be granted for any of the pursuits of human industry, even in its most simple and common forms. Indeed, upon the theory on which the exclusive privileges granted by the act in question are sustained, there is no monopoly, in the most odious form, which may not be upheld.

The question presented is, therefore, one of the gravest importance, not merely to the parties here, but to the whole country. It is nothing less than the question whether the recent amendments to the Federal Constitution protect the citizens of the United States against the deprivation of their common rights by State legislation. In my judgment the fourteenth amendment does afford such protection, and was so intended by the Congress which framed and the States which adopted it. . . .

. . . The privileges and immunities designated are those *which of right belong to the citizens of all free governments*. Clearly among these must be placed the right to pursue a lawful employment in a lawful manner, without other restraint than such as equally affects all persons. . . .

This equality of right, with exemption from all disparaging and partial enactments, in the lawful pursuits of life, throughout the whole country, is the distinguishing privilege of citizens of the United States. To them, everywhere, all pursuits, all professions, all avocations are open without other restrictions than such as are imposed equally upon all others of the same age, sex, and condition. The State may prescribe such regulations for every pursuit and calling of life as will promote the public health, secure the good order and advance the general prosperity of society, but when once prescribed, the pursuit or calling must be free to be followed by every citizen who is within the conditions designated, and will conform to the regulations. This is the fundamental idea upon which our institutions rest, and unless adhered to in the legislation of the country our government will be a republic only in name. The fourteenth amendment, in my judgment, makes it essential to the validity of the legislation of every State that this equality of right should be respected. How widely this equality has been departed from, how entirely rejected and trampled upon by the act of Louisiana, I have already shown. And it is to me a matter of profound regret that its validity is recognized by a majority of this court, for by it the right of free labor, one of the most sacred and imprescriptible rights of man, is violated. . . .[2] That only is a free

government, in the American sense of the term, under which the inalienable right of every citizen to pursue his happiness is unrestrained, except by just, equal, and impartial laws. . . .[3]

2. "The property which every man has in his own labor," says Adam Smith, "as it is the original foundation of all other property, so it is the most sacred and inviolable. The patrimony of the poor man lies in the strength and dexterity of his own hands; and to hinder him from employing this strength and dexterity in what manner he thinks proper, without injury to his neighbor, is a plain violation of this most sacred property. It is a manifest encroachment upon the just liberty both of the workman and of those who might be disposed to employ him. As it hinders the one from working at what he thinks proper, so it hinders the others from employing whom they think proper" (Smith's *Wealth of Nations*, Book I, chap. 10, Part 2).

In the edict of Louis XVI, in 1776, giving freedom to trades and professions, prepared by his minister, Turgot, he recites the contributions that had been made by the guilds and trade companies, and says: "It was the allurement of these fiscal advantages undoubtedly that prolonged the illusion and concealed the immense injury they did to industry and their infraction of natural right. *This* illusion had extended so far that some persons asserted that the right to work was a royal privilege which the king might sell, and that his subjects were bound to purchase from him. We hasten to correct this error and to repel the conclusion. God in giving man wants and desires rendering labor unnecessary for their satisfaction, conferred the right to labor upon all men, and this property is the first, most sacred, and imprescriptible of all.". . . He, therefore, regards it "as the first duty of his justice, and the worthiest act of benevolence, to free his subjects from any restriction upon this inalienable right of humanity."—AUTHOR'S NOTE.

3. "Civil liberty, the great end of all human society and government, is that state in which each individual has the power to pursue his own happiness according to his own views of his interest, and the dictates of his conscience, unrestrained, except by equal, just, and impartial laws" (1 Sharswoods's *Blackstone*, 127, note 8).—AUTHOR'S NOTE.

2. *MUNN* v. *ILLINOIS*[1]

EDITORS' NOTE.—During the heyday of the Granger movement a number of states passed laws to regulate the middlemen who were believed by farmers to be taking too great a share of the agricultural dollar. In Chicago nine firms with thirty members controlled all the fourteen grain elevators.

Evidence was produced of price agreements among the elevator operators. Under the Granger laws these Chicago grain elevators were subjected to fixed maximum rates for the storage and handling of grain. The proprietors of one of these warehouses were convicted and sentenced for a violation of the statutory scheme. Relying on the

1. 94 U.S. 113, 123–26, 131–34 (1877).

philosophy of Mr. Justice Field's dissent in the Slaughter-House cases, which was popular with the bar and was obtaining some recognition in the state courts, lawyers attacked the Granger legislation. Again the due-process clause of the Fourteenth Amendment was invoked against the police power of the states. On a writ of error the judgment of the Illinois Supreme Court in the Munn case was upheld, and the conviction was sustained in a seven-to-two decision by the Supreme Court of the United States in 1877. Mr. Justice Field wrote a dissenting opinion in which Mr. Justice Strong concurred. At the same time another feature of the Granger laws, the effort of the states to regulate railroad rates, was also upheld, with dissents by the same two justices. Particular attention should be paid by the reader to the definition of the police power contained in the majority opinion. It is clear that the Court was aware that the police power might be abused. The student should give careful consideration to the significance of the remedy against abuse which was suggested by the concurring judges.

Mr. Chief Justice WAITE delivered the opinion of the court. . . .

When one becomes a member of society, he necessarily parts with some rights or privileges which, as an individual not affected by his relations to others, he might retain. "A body politic," as aptly defined in the preamble of the Constitution of Massachusetts, "is a social compact by which the whole people covenants with each citizen, and each citizen with the whole people, that all shall be governed by certain laws for the common good." This does not confer power upon the whole people to control rights which are purely and exclusively private . . . but it does authorize the establishment of laws requiring each citizen to so conduct himself, and so use his own property, as not unnecessarily to injure another. . . . From this source come the police powers. . . . Under these powers the government regulates the conduct of its citizens one towards another, and the manner in which each shall use his own property, when such regulation becomes necessary for the public good. In their exercise it has been customary in England from time immemorial, and in this country from its first colonization, to regulate ferries, common carriers, hackmen, bakers, millers, wharfingers, innkeepers, etc., and in so doing to fix a maximum of charge to be made for services rendered, accommodations furnished, and articles sold. To this day, statutes are to be found in many of the States upon some or all these subjects; and we think it has never yet been successfully contended that such legislation came within any of the constitutional prohibitions against interference with private property. With the Fifth Amendment in force, Congress, in 1820, conferred power upon the city of Washington "to regulate . . . the rates of wharfage at private wharves, . . . the sweeping of chimneys, and to fix the rates of fees therefor, . . . and the weight and quality of bread," 3 Stat. 587, sect. 7; and, in 1848, "to make all necessary regulations respecting hackney carriages and the rates of fare of the same, and the rates of hauling by cartmen, wagoners, carmen, and draymen, and the rates of commission of auctioneers," 9 id. 224, sect. 2.

From this it is apparent that, down to the time of the adoption of the Fourteenth Amendment, it was not supposed that statutes regulating the use, or even the price of the use, of private property necessarily deprived an owner of his property without due process of law. Under some circumstances they may, but not under all.

The amendment does not change the law in this particular: it simply prevents the States from doing that which will operate as such a deprivation.

This brings us to inquire as to the principles upon which this power of regulation rests, in order that we may determine what is within and what without its operative effect. . . . Property does become clothed with a public interest when used in a manner to make it of public consequence, and affect the community at large. When, therefore, one devotes his property to a use in which the public has an interest, he, in effect, grants to the public an interest in that use, and must submit to be controlled by the public for the common good, to the extent of the interest he has thus created. He may withdraw his grant by discontinuing the use; but, so long as he maintains the use, he must submit to the control. . . .

Under such circumstances it is difficult to see why, if the common carrier, or the miller, or the ferryman, or the innkeeper, or the wharfinger, or the baker, or the cartman, or the hackney-coachman, pursues a public employment and exercises "a sort of public office," these plaintiffs in error do not. They stand, to use again the language of their counsel, in the very "gateway of commerce," and take toll from all who pass. . . .

It is insisted, however, that the owner of property is entitled to a reasonable compensation for its use, even though it be clothed with a public interest, and that what is reasonable is a judicial and not a legislative question.

As has already been shown, the practice has been otherwise. In countries where the common law prevails, it has been customary from time immemorial for the legislature to declare what shall be a reasonable compensation under such circumstances, or, perhaps more properly speaking, to fix a maximum beyond which any charge made would be unreasonable. Undoubtedly, in mere private contracts, relating to matters in which the public has no interest, what is reasonable must be ascertained judicially. But this is because the legislature has no control over such a contract. . . .

. . . To limit the rate of charge for services rendered in a public employment, or for the use of property in which the public has an interest, is only changing a regulation which existed before. It establishes no new principle in the law, but only gives a new effect to an old one.

We know that this is a power which may be abused; but that is no argument against its existence. For protection against abuses by legislatures the people must resort to the polls, not to the courts. . . .

3. WABASH, ST. LOUIS AND PACIFIC RAILWAY CO. v. ILLINOIS[1]

EDITORS' NOTE.—While state regulation of warehouse and railroad rates was upheld as a proper exercise of state power, a serious limitation on the effectiveness of state control of railroad rates eventually was discovered by business interests in the commerce clause of the Constitution. The Wabash Railway Company charged less for the transportation of oil cake and corn from Peoria to New York City than it charged for the transportation of these commodities from Gilman, Illinois, to New York City. Gilman is about eighty-five miles nearer New York, almost in a straight line, than Peoria. This smaller charge for the longer haul, which operated to the ad-

1. 118 U.S. 557, 560, 572-73, 575-77, 588-89, 595-96 (1886).

vantage of one community at the expense of another, was the sort of practice against which Granger agitation had been particularly directed, and it was held a violation of an Illinois statute. Under the law, a shipper was permitted to recover a penalty and damages in the Illinois courts. On writ of error the decision was reversed in a six-to-three decision by the Supreme Court of the United States.

A careful reading of the commerce clause will perhaps raise some doubts whether its terms warrant any such interpretation. The history of the commerce clause, according to at least one authority, seems only to show that Congress was authorized by its action to remove state impediments to commerce among the states. The student may detect here, as elsewhere in our constitutional law, a philosophical hostility to public control of business, expressing itself in what appears on the surface to be a discussion of technical provisions regulating the organization and administration of government. The limitation on state regulation of railroad rates developed in the Wabash case led to the enactment of the Interstate Commerce Act in the following year.

Mr. Justice MILLER delivered the opinion of the court. . . .

. . . It is not the railroads themselves that are regulated by this act of the Illinois Legislature so much as the charge for transportation, and, in language just cited, if each one of the States through whose territories these goods are transported can fix its own rules for prices, for modes of transit, for times and modes of delivery, and all the other incidents of transportation to which the word "regulation" can be applied, it is readily seen that the embarrassments upon interstate transportation, as an element of interstate commerce, might be too oppressive to be submitted to. "It was," in the language of the court cited above, "to meet just such a case that the commerce clause of the Constitution was adopted."

It cannot be too strongly insisted upon that the right of continuous transportation from one end of the country to the other is essential in modern times to that freedom of commerce from the restraints which the State might choose to impose upon it, that the commerce clause was intended to secure. . . .

Let us see precisely what is the degree of interference with transportation of property or persons from one State to another which this statute proposes. A citizen of New York has goods which he desires to have transported by the railroad companies from that city to the interior of the State of Illinois. A continuous line of rail over which a car loaded with these goods can be carried, and is carried habitually, connects the place of shipment with the place of delivery. He undertakes to make a contract with a person engaged in the carrying business at the end of this route from whence the goods are to start, and he is told by the carrier, "I am free to make a fair and reasonable contract for this carriage to the line of the State of Illinois, but when the car which carries these goods is to cross the line of that State, pursuing at the same time this continuous track, I am met by a law of Illinois which forbids me to make a free contract concerning this transportation within that State, and subjects me to certain rules by which I am to be governed as to the charges which the same railroad company in Illinois may make, or has made, with reference to other persons and other places of delivery." So that while that carrier might be willing to carry these goods from the city of New York to the city of Peoria at the rate of fifteen cents per hundred pounds, he is not permitted to do so because the Illinois railroad company has already charged at the rate of twenty-five cents per hundred pounds for carriage to Gilman, in Illinois, which is eighty-six miles shorter than the distance to Peoria.

So, also, in the present case, the owner of corn, the principal product of the country, desiring to transport it from Peoria, in Illinois, to New York, finds a railroad company willing to do this at the rate of fifteen cents per hundred pounds for a carload, but is compelled to pay at the rate of twenty-five cents per hundred pounds, because the railroad company has received from a person residing at Gilman twenty-five cents per hundred pounds for the transportation of a car-load of the same class of freight over the same line of road from Gilman to New York. This is the result of the statute of Illinois, in its endeavor to prevent unjust discrimination, as construed by the Supreme Court of that State. The effect of it is, that whatever may be the rate of transportation per mile charged by the railroad company from Gilman to Sheldon, a distance of twenty-three miles, in which the loading and the unloading of the freight is the largest expense incurred by the railroad company, the same rate per mile must be charged from Peoria to the city of New York.

The obvious injustice of such a rule as this, which railroad companies are by heavy penalties compelled to conform to, in regard to commerce among the States, when applied to transportation which includes Illinois in a long line of carriage through several States, shows the value of the constitutional provision which confides the power of regulating interstate commerce to the Congress of the United States, whose enlarged view of the interests of all the States, and of the railroads concerned, better fits it to establish just and equitable rules.

Of the justice or propriety of the principle which lies at the foundation of the Illinois statute it is not the province of this court to speak. As restricted to a transportation which begins and ends within the limits of the State it may be very just and equitable, and it certainly is the province of the State legislature to determine that question. But when it is attempted to apply to transportation through an entire series of States a principle of this kind, and each one of the States shall attempt to establish its own rates of transportation, its own methods to prevent discrimination in rates, or to permit it, the deleterious influence upon the freedom of commerce among the States and upon the transit of goods through those States cannot be over estimated. That this species of regulation is one which must be, if established at all, of a general and national character, and cannot be safely and wisely remitted to local rules and local regulations, we think is clear from what has already been said. And if it be a regulation of commerce, as we think we have demonstrated it is, and as the Illinois court concedes it to be, it must be of that national character, and the regulation can only appropriately exist by general rules and principles, which demand that it should be done by the Congress of the United States under the commerce clause of the Constitution.

The judgment of the Supreme Court of Illinois is therefore

Reversed, and the case remanded to that court for further proceedings in conformity with this opinion.

Mr. Justice BRADLEY, with whom concurred the CHIEF JUSTICE and Mr. Justice GRAY, dissenting.

The CHIEF JUSTICE, Mr. Justice GRAY, and myself dissent from the opinion and judgment of the court in this case, and I am authorized to state the reasons upon which our dissent is founded. . . .

To sum up the matter in a word: we hold it to be a sound proposition of law, that the making of railroads and regulating the charges for their use is not such a regulation of commerce as to be in the remotest degree repugnant to any power given to Congress by the Constitution, so long as that power is dormant, and has not been exercised by Congress. They affect commerce, they incidentally regulate it; but they are acts in relation to the subject which the State has a perfect right to do, subject always, to the controlling power of Congress over the regulation of commerce when Congress sees fit to act.

It is only for the sake of convenience that the State lets out its railroads to private corporations. It might construct them itself. Suppose it had done so in this case: could not the State have instituted such rates of freight and fare as it pleased? Certainly it could. It might have made them uniform, as the present law requires them to be, or it might have made them discriminative between different places, and no one could have called it to account. Instructions in the form of laws, or in the form of orders made by a State board, might have been given to the superintendents of the road, acting in behalf of the State, to adopt the one course or the other. Could the agents of the State, acting under such instructions, have been interfered with by the judicial department on the ground of unconstitutionality? Certainly not; certainly not, unless discriminations were made to the prejudice of the citizens of other States, or of the products of other States.

The State of New York built and owns the Erie Canal. Did any court ever attempt to control that State in its regulation of tolls on the canal, even though made for the purpose of affecting the relative movement of goods on the canal and the railroads of the State? We presume that no such attempt was ever made, or would be successful if made. . . .

The inconveniences which it has been supposed in argument would follow from the execution of the laws of Illinois, we think have been greatly exaggerated. But if it should be found to present any real difficulty in the modes of transacting business on through lines, it is always in the power of Congress to make such reasonable regulations as the interests of interstate commerce may demand, without denuding the States of their just powers over their own roads and their own corporations.

4. *ALLGEYER* v. *LOUISIANA*[1]

EDITORS' NOTE.—In the courts the conflict over the regulation of business enterprise by the states led to many separate skirmishes and encounters. At length Chief Justice Waite of the United States Supreme Court declared in 1886: "The Court does not wish to hear argument on the question whether the provision in the Fourteenth Amendment to the Constitution, which forbids a State to deny to any person within its jurisdiction the equal protection of the laws, applies to these corporations. We are all of opinion that it does . . ." (*Santa Clara County* v.

1. 165 U.S. 578–80, 583, 589–93 (1897).

Southern Pacific Railroad Company, 118 U.S. 394, 396). This entering wedge entitled corporations to such sanctuary as might be afforded by the due-process clause. The breech was widened in 1890, when the Supreme Court ruled that the regulation of railroad rates by state legislatures was "eminently a question for judicial investigation, requiring due process of law for its determination" (*Chicago, Milwaukee and St. Paul Railway Co.* v. *Minnesota*, 134 U.S. 418, 458). This view was rejected by three justices, who insisted that the legislature rather than the courts had the right to determine who should be the final arbiter of questions involving the regulation of business. Said the dissenting opinion: "Due process of law does not always require a court. It merely requires such tribunals and proceedings as are proper to the subject in hand. . . . Injustice may take place in all tribunals. All human institutions are imperfect— courts as well as commissions and legislatures" (*ibid*., at 464–65).

This objection went unheeded. In 1897, in the quiet little commercial case of *Allgeyer* v. *Louisiana*, which might have been decided the same way under the commerce clause except

The legislature of Louisiana, in the year 1894, passed an act known as act No. 66 of the acts of that year. It is entitled "An act to prevent persons, corporations or firms from dealing with marine insurance companies that have not complied with law."

The act reads as follows: "*Be it enacted by the General Assembly of the State of Louisiana*, That any person, firm or corporation who shall fill up, sign or issue in this State any certificate of insurance under an open marine policy, or who in any manner whatever does any act in this State to effect, for himself or for another, insurance on property, then in this State, in any marine insurance company which has not complied in all respects with the laws of this State, shall be subject to a fine of one thousand dollars for each offence, which shall be sued for in any competent court by the attorney general for the use and benefit of the charity hospitals in New Orleans and Shreveport."

By reason of the provisions of this act, the State of Louisiana on the 21st of December, 1894, filed its petition in one of the courts of first instance for the parish of Orleans, and alleged, in substance, that the defendants, E. Allgeyer & Co., had violated the statute by mailing in New Or-

that at the time insurance was held not to be interstate commerce, Mr. Justice Field's radical and indeed revolutionary philosophy of the Fourteenth Amendment became part of our constitutional law. In this case the Court unanimously, and for the first time, decided that liberty of contract was protected against state legislation not justified by a limited definition of the police power. The case thus opened the way for the most serious controversies of the following thirty-five or forty years over the power of state and national legislatures to enact social legislation.

leans a letter of advice or certificate of marine insurance on the 27th of October, 1894, to the Atlantic Mutual Insurance Company of New York, advising that company of the shipment of 100 bales of cotton to foreign ports in accordance with the terms of an open marine policy, etc. The State sought to recover for three violations of the act the sum of three thousand dollars.

The defendants filed an answer, in which, among other things, they averred that the above-named act was unconstitutional in that it deprived them of their property without due process of law, and denied them the equal protection of the laws in violation of the constitution of the State of Louisiana and also of the Constitution of the United States. They also set up that the business concerning which defendants were sought to be made liable, and the contracts made in reference to such business, were beyond the jurisdiction of the State of Louisiana, and that the defendants were not amenable to any penalties imposed by its laws; that the contracts of insurance made by defendants were made with an insurance company in the State of New York, where the premiums were paid, and where the losses thereunder, if any, were also to be paid; that the contracts were New York contracts, and that under the Constitution of the United States the defendants had the right to do and perform any act or acts within the State of Louisiana which might be necessary and proper for the execution of those contracts, and that in so far as the act No. 66 of the general assembly of the State of Louisiana of the year 1894 might be construed to prevent or interfere with the execution of such contracts, the same was unconstitutional and in violation of the constitution of both the State of Louisiana and the United States.

The case was tried upon an agreed statement of facts. . . .

The court of first instance before which the trial was had ordered that plaintiff's demand be rejected and that judgment in favor of the defendants be given. An appeal was taken from that judgment to the Supreme Court of the State, which, after argument before it and due consideration, reversed the judgment of the court below and gave judgment in favor of the plaintiff for $1000, as for one violation of the statute, being the only one which was proved. *State* v. *Allgeyer*, 48 La. Ann. 104. The plaintiffs in error ask a review in this court of the judgment entered against them by directions of the Supreme Court of Louisiana. . . .

Mr. Justice PECKHAM, after stating the case, delivered the opinion of the court. . . .

The Supreme Court of Louisiana says that the act of writing within that State, the letter of notification, was an act therein done to effect an insurance on property then in the State, in a marine insurance company which had not complied with its laws, and such act was, therefore, prohibited by the statute. As so construed we think the statute is a violation of the Fourteenth Amendment of the Federal Constitution, in that it deprives the defendants of their liberty without due process of law. The statute which forbids such act does not become due process of law, because it is inconsistent with the provisions of the Constitution of the Union. The liberty mentioned in that amendment means not only the right of the citizen to be free from the mere physical restraint of his person, as by incarceration, but the term is deemed to embrace the right of the citizen to be free in the enjoyment of all his faculties; to be free to use them in all lawful ways; to live and work where he will; to earn his livelihood by any lawful calling; to pursue any livelihood or avocation, and for that purpose to enter into all contracts which may be proper, necessary and essential to his carrying out to a successful conclusion the purposes above mentioned.

It was said by Mr. Justice Bradley, in *Butchers' Union Company* v. *Crescent City Company*, 111 U.S. 746, 762, in the course of his concurring opinion in that case, that "The right to follow any of the common occupations of life is an inalienable right. It was formulated as such under the phrase 'pursuit of happiness' in the Declaration of Independence, which commenced with the fundamental proposition that 'all men are created equal, that they are endowed by their Creator with certain inalienable rights; that among these are life, liberty and the pursuit of happiness.' This right is a large ingredient in the civil liberty of the citizen." Again, on page 764, the learned justice said: "I hold that the liberty of pursuit—the right to follow any of the ordinary callings of life—is one of the privileges of a citizen of the United States." And again, on page 765: "But if it does not abridge the privileges and immunities of a citizen of the United States to prohibit him from pursuing his chosen calling, and giving to others the exclusive right of pursuing it, it certainly does deprive him (to a certain extent) of his liberty; for it takes from him the freedom of adopting and following the pursuit which he prefers; which, as already intimated, is a material part of the liberty of the citizen." It is true that these remarks were made in regard to questions of monopoly, but they well describe the rights which are covered by the word "liberty" as contained in the Fourteenth Amendment.

Again, in *Powell* v. *Pennsylvania*, 127 U.S. 678, 684, Mr. Justice Harlan, in stating the opinion of the court, said: "The main proposition advanced by the defendant is that his enjoyment upon terms of equality with all others in similar circumstances of the privilege of pursuing an ordinary calling or trade, and of acquiring, holding and selling property, is an essential part of his rights of liberty and property, as guaranteed by the Fourteenth Amendment. The court assents to this general proposition as embodying a sound principle of constitutional law." . . .

The foregoing extracts have been made for the purpose of showing what general definitions have been given in regard to the meaning of the word "liberty" as used in the amendment, but we do not intend to hold that in no such case can the State exercise its police power. When and how far such power may be legitimately exercised with regard to these subjects must be left for determination to each case as it arises.

Has not a citizen of a State, under the provisions of the Federal Constitution above mentioned, a right to contract outside of the State for insurance on his property—a right of which state legislation cannot deprive him? We are not alluding to acts done within the State by an insurance company or its agents doing business therein, which are in violation of the state statutes. Such acts come within the principle of the *Hooper case* (*supra*), and would be controlled by it. When we speak of the liberty to contract for insurance or to do an act to effectuate such a contract already existing, we refer to and have in mind the facts of this case, where the contract was made outside the State, and as such was a valid and proper contract. The act done within the limits of the State under the circumstances of this case and for the purpose therein mentioned, we hold a proper act, one which the defendants were at liberty to perform and which the state legislature had no right to prevent, at least with refer-

ence to the Federal Constitution. To deprive the citizen of such a right as herein described without due process of law is illegal. Such a statute as this in question is not due process of law, because it prohibits an act which under the Federal Constitution the defendants had a right to perform. This does not interfere in any way with the acknowledged right of the State to enact such legislation in the legitimate exercise of its police or other powers as to it may seem proper. In the exercise of such right, however, care must be taken not to infringe upon those other rights of the citizen which are protected by the Federal Constitution.

In the privileges of pursuing an ordinary calling or trade and of acquiring, holding and selling property must be embraced the right to make all proper contracts in relation thereto, and although it may be conceded that this right to contract in relation to persons or property or to do business within the jurisdiction of the State may be regulated and sometimes prohibited when the contracts or business conflict with the policy of the State as contained in its statutes, yet the power does not and cannot extend to prohibiting a citizen from making contracts of the nature involved in this case outside of the limits and jurisdiction of the State, and which are also to be performed outside of such jurisdiction; nor can the State legally prohibit its citizens from doing such an act as writing this letter of notification, even though the property which is the subject of the insurance may at the time when such insurance attaches be within the limits of the State. . . .

For these reasons we think the statute in question, No. 66 of the Laws of Louisiana of 1894, was a violation of the Federal Constitution, and afforded no justification for the judgment awarded by that court against the plaintiffs in error. That judgment must, therefore, be

Reversed, and the case remanded to the Supreme Court of Louisiana for further proceedings not inconsistent with this opinion.

5. SMYTH v. AMES[1]

EDITORS' NOTE.—In 1898, the year following the epochal decision in *Allgeyer* v. *Louisiana*, the Supreme Court finally announced another new doctrine of considerable importance. On this occasion the Court overruled an opinion expressed in *Munn* v. *Illinois* and applied a doctrine which had been anticipated in some of its opinions since 1890, designed to protect public utilities against a supposed danger of drastic rate regulation by legislative and administrative action. The decision in *Smyth* v. *Ames* has been much ridiculed for suggesting that a combination of factors should be taken into account in determining the value of a public utility's property without indicating how these factors should be weighted. It is worth noticing, however, that the factors have different effects in different phases of the business cycle and that the vagueness and flexibility of the standard suggested may be defended as giving the Court a basis for adjusting its decisions to strike a balance between investor and consumer interests under varying conditions. In particular, the emphasis

Mr. Justice HARLAN . . . delivered the opinion of the court. . . .

In view of the adjudications these principles must be regarded as settled:

1. A railroad corporation is a person within the meaning of the Fourteenth Amendment declaring that no State shall deprive any person of property without due process of law, nor deny to any person within its jurisdiction the equal protection of the laws.

1. 169 U.S. 466, 515, 526, 546–47 (1898).

given to the cost of reproduction, "the present . . . cost of construction," represented a concession to shippers' interests as they were understood during the period of unsystematic and sometimes inflated accounts and declining prices in which the case was prepared and argued. This emphasis was to this extent a victory for William Jennings Bryan, who was among the representatives of the state in the litigation. The ironical upturn in prices, which may have helped to defeat Bryan the previous year, led also to a long period in which the emphasis on reproduction cost proved favorable, not to shippers and consumers, but to investors in light and power companies, railroads, and other utilities. The decision in the case was that Nebraska legislation on intrastate railroads had resulted in the imposition of a rate structure so low as to prevent the railroad company from earning a fair return on its investment and that the company had thus been deprived of property without due process of law in violation of the Fourteenth Amendment of the Constitution.

2. A state enactment, or regulations made under the authority of a state enactment, establishing rates for the transportation of persons or property by railroad that will not admit of the carrier earning such compensations as under all the circumstances is just to it and to the public, would deprive such carrier of its property without due process of law and deny to it the equal protection of the laws, and would therefore be repugnant to the Fourteenth Amendment of the Constitution of the United States.

3. While rates for the transportation of persons and property within the limits of a State are primarily for its determination, the question whether they are so unreasonably low as to deprive the carrier of its property without such compensation as the Constitution secures, and therefore without due process of law, cannot be so conclusively determined by the legislature of the State or by regulations adopted under its authority, that the matter may not become the subject of judicial inquiry. . . .

We hold, however, that the basis of all calculations as to the reasonableness of rates to be charged by a corporation maintaining a highway under legislative sanction must be the fair value of the property being used by it for the convenience of the public. And in order to ascertain that value, the original cost of construction, the amount expended in permanent improvements, the amount and market value of its bonds and stock, the present as compared with the original cost of construction, the probable earning capacity of the property under particular rates prescribed by statute, and the sum required to meet operating expenses, are all matters for consideration, and are to be given such weight as may be just and right in each case. We do not say that there may not be other matters to be regarded in estimating the value of the property. What the company is en-titled to ask is a fair return upon the value of that which it employs for the public convenience. On the other hand, what the public is entitled to demand is that no more be exacted from it for the use of a public highway than the services rendered by it are reasonably worth. But even upon this basis, and determining the probable effect of the act of 1893 by ascertaining what could have been its effect if it had been in operation during the three years immediately preceding its passage, we perceive no ground on the record for reversing the decree of the Circuit Court. On the contrary, we are of opinion that as to most of the companies in question there would have been, under such rates as were established by the act of 1893, an actual loss in each of the years ending June 30, 1891, 1892 and 1893; and that, in the exceptional cases above stated, when two of the companies would have earned something above operating expenses, in particular years, the receipts or gains, above operating expenses, would have been too small to affect the general conclusion that the act, if enforced, would have deprived each of the railroad companies involved in these suits of the just compensation secured to them by the Constitution. Under the evidence there is no ground for saying that the operating expenses of any of the companies were greater than necessary. . . .

6. *LOCHNER* v. *NEW YORK*[1]

EDITORS' NOTE.—The reinterpretation of the due-process clause to narrow the legitimate sphere of the police power had implications that went far beyond the regulation of warehouse and railroad rates. Already a number of states had enacted measures to protect women and children in industry or to protect workers in dangerous occupations. Such laws extended to questions of hours, wages, and working conditions. In the case of *Lochner* v. *New York* the United States Supreme Court passed on the validity of a law enacted in 1897 which had limited the hours of bakers to no more than sixty per week and had also provided sanitary standards for bakeries. Under the act an employer had been fined fifty dollars for violating the maximum-hours provision. His conviction was affirmed by two New York courts before being appealed on a writ of error to the fed-

1. 198 U.S. 45, 52–66, 68–76 (1905).

eral Supreme Court. This raised the question of whether baking was a hazardous occupation requiring the especial protection of the state or whether adult males in industry must be expected to use their free bargaining power to look after their own interests. From the character of the opinions it is clear that the Court was presented not only with arguments as to the law but with a considerable body of data as to the facts of the case: Was baking a hazardous occupation? Because this approach was extensively used by Louis Brandeis, then an attorney before the Court, it became known as the "Brandeis brief."

Abiding by the principles of *Allgeyer* v. *Louisiana*, the Supreme Court held the law establishing a ten-hour day for bakers to be an unconstitutional deprivation of their freedom without due process of law. The vigorous dissents of Justices Harlan and Holmes should be examined with care. The effect of the Lochner decision was to render ineffective much of the social welfare program advocated and adopted by the states during the Progressive Era.

Mr. Justice PECKHAM. . . delivered the opinion of the court.

The indictment, it will be seen, charges that the plaintiff in error violated the one hundred and tenth section of article 8, chapter 415, of the Laws of 1897, known as the labor law of the State of New York, in that he wrongfully and unlawfully required and permitted an employé working for him to work more than sixty hours in one week. There is nothing in any of the opinions delivered in this case, either in the Supreme Court or the Court of Appeals of the State, which construes the section, in using the word "required," as referring to any physical force being used to obtain the labor of an employé. It is assumed that the word means nothing more than the requirement arising from voluntary contract for such labor in excess of the number of hours specified in the statute. There is no pretense in any of the opinions that the statute was intended to meet a case of involuntary labor in any form. All the opinions assume that there is no real distinction, so far as this question is concerned, between the words "required" and "permitted." The mandate of the statute that "no employé shall be required or permitted to work," is the substantial equivalent of an enactment that "no employé shall contract or agree to work," more than ten hours per day, and as there is no provision for special emergencies the statute is mandatory in all cases. It is not an act merely fixing the number of hours which shall constitute a legal day's work, but an absolute prohibition upon the employer, permitting, under any circumstances, more than ten hours work to be done in his establishment. The employé may desire to earn the extra money, which would arise from his working more than the prescribed time, but this statute forbids the employer from permitting the employé to earn it.

The statute necessarily interferes with the right of contract between the employer and employés, concerning the number of hours in which the latter may labor in the bakery of the employer. The general right to make a contract in relation to his business is part of the liberty of the individual protected by the Fourteenth Amendment of the Federal Constitution. *Allgeyer* v. *Louisiana*, 165 U.S. 578. Under that provision no State can deprive any person of life, liberty or property without due process of law. The right to purchase or to sell labor is part of the liberty protected by this amendment, unless there are circumstances which exclude the right. There are, however, certain powers, existing in the sovereignty of each State in the Union, somewhat vaguely termed police powers, the exact description and limitation of which have not been attempted by the courts. Those powers, broadly stated and without, at present, any attempt at a more specific limitation, relate to the safety, health, morals and general welfare of the public. Both property and liberty are held on such reasonable conditions as may be imposed by the governing power of the State in the exercise of those powers, and with such conditions the Fourteenth Amendment was not designed to interfere. *Mugler* v. *Kansas*, 123 U.S. 623;[2] *In re Kemmler*, 136 U.S. 436;[3] *Crowley* v. *Christensen*, 137 U.S. 86;[4] *In re Converse*, 137 U.S. 624.[5]

The State, therefore, has power to prevent the individual from making certain kinds of contracts, and in regard to them the Federal Constitution offers no protection. If the contract be one which the State, in the legitimate exercise of its police power, has the right to prohibit, it is not prevented from prohibiting it by the Fourteenth Amendment. Contracts in violation of a statute, either of the Federal or state government, or a contract to let one's property for immoral purposes, or to do any other unlawful act, could obtain no protection from the Federal Constitution, as coming under the liberty of person or of free contract. Therefore, when the State, by its legislature, in the assumed exercise of its police powers, has passed an act which seriously limits the right to labor or the right of contract in regard to their

2. Sustaining provisions for prohibition in a state constitution.

3. Sustaining provisions for electrocution in capital cases in state legislation.

4. Sustaining prohibition legislation.

5. Sustaining a conviction for embezzlement against a somewhat technical attack. In each case there were statements conceding the existence of private rights protected by the Fourteenth Amendment. It should be noticed that each of these cases was decided before *Allgeyer* v. *Louisiana*.

means of livelihood between persons who are *sui juris* (both employer and employé), it becomes of great importance to determine which shall prevail—the right of the individual to labor for such time as he may choose, or the right of the State to prevent the individual from laboring or from entering into any contract to labor, beyond a certain time prescribed by the State.

This court has recognized the existence and upheld the exercise of the police powers of the States in many cases which might fairly be considered as border ones, and it has, in the course of its determination of questions regarding the asserted invalidity of such statutes, on the ground of their violation of the rights secured by the Federal Constitution, been guided by rules of a very liberal nature, the application of which has resulted, in numerous instances, in upholding the validity of state statutes thus assailed. Among the later cases where the state law has been upheld by this court is that of *Holden* v. *Hardy*, 169 U.S. 366. A provision in the act of the legislature of Utah was there under consideration, the act limiting the employment of workmen in all underground mines or workings, to eight hours per day, "except in cases of emergency, where life or property is in imminent danger." It also limited the hours of labor in smelting and other institutions for the reduction or refining of ores or metals to eight hours per day, except in like cases of emergency. The act was held to be a valid exercise of the police powers of the State. A review of many of the cases on the subject, decided by this and other courts, is given in the opinion. It was held that the kind of employment, mining, smelting, etc., and the character of the employés in such kinds of labor, were such as to make it reasonable and proper for the State to interfere to prevent the employés from being constrained by the rules laid down by the proprietors in regard to labor. The following citation from the observations of the Supreme Court of Utah in that case was made by the judge writing the opinion of this court, and approved: "The law in question is confined to the protection of that class of people engaged in labor in underground mines, and in smelters and other works wherein ores are reduced and refined. This law applies only to the classes subjected by their employment to the peculiar conditions and effects attending underground mining and work in smelters, and other works for the reduction and refining of ores. Therefore it is not necessary to discuss or decide whether the legislature can fix the hours of labor in other employments."

It will be observed that, even with regard to that class of labor, the Utah statute provided for cases of emergency wherein the provisions of the statute would not apply. The statute now before this court has no emergency clause in it, and, if the statute is valid, there are no circumstances and no emergencies under which the slightest violation of the provisions of the act would be innocent. . . .

It must, of course, be conceded that there is a limit to the valid exercise of the police power by the State. There is no dispute concerning this general proposition. Otherwise the Fourteenth Amendment would have no efficacy and the legislatures of the States would have unbounded power, and it would be enough to say that any piece of legislation was enacted to conserve the morals, the health or the safety of the people; such legislation would be valid, no matter how absolutely without foundation the claim might be. The claim of the police power would be a mere pretext—become another and delusive name for the supreme sovereignty of the State to be exercised free from constitutional restraint. This is not contended for. In every case that comes before this court, therefore, where legislation of this character is concerned and where the protection of the Federal Constitution is sought, the question necessarily arises: Is this a fair, reasonable and appropriate exercise of the police power of the State, or is it an unreasonable, unnecessary and arbitrary interference with the right of the individual to his personal liberty or to enter into those contracts in relation to labor which may seem to him appropriate or necessary for the support of himself and his family? Of course the liberty of contract relating to labor includes both parties to it. The one has as much right to purchase as the other to sell labor.

This is not a question of substituting the judgment of the court for that of the legislature. If the act be within the power of the State it is valid, although the judgment of the court might be totally opposed to the enactment of such a law. But the question would still remain: Is it within the police power of the State? and that question must be answered by the court.

The question whether this act is valid as a labor law, pure and simple, may be dismissed in a few words. There is no reasonable ground for interfering with the liberty of person or the right of free contract, by determining the hours of labor, in the occupation of a baker. There is no contention that bakers as a class are not equal in intelligence and capacity to men in other trades or manual occupations, or that they are not able to assert their rights and care for themselves without the protecting arm of the State, interfering with their independence of judgment and of action. They are in no sense wards of the State. Viewed in the light of a purely labor law, with no reference whatever to the question of health, we think that a law like the one before us involves neither the safety, the morals nor the welfare of the public, and that the interest of the public is not in the slightest degree affected by such an act. The law must be upheld, if at all, as a law pertaining to the health of the individual engaged in the occupation of a baker. It does not affect any other portion of the public than those who are engaged in that occupation. Clean and wholesome bread does not depend upon whether the baker works but ten hours per day or only sixty hours a week. The limitation of the hours of labor does not come within the police power on that ground.

It is a question of which of two powers or rights shall prevail—the power of the State to legislate or the right of the individual to liberty of person and freedom of contract. The mere assertion that the subject relates though but in a remote degree to the public health does not necessarily render the enactment valid. The act must have a more direct relation, as a means to an end, and the end itself must be appropriate and legitimate, before an act can be held to be valid which interferes with the general right of an individual to be free in his person and in his power to contract in relation to his own labor. . . .

We think the limit of the police power has been reached and passed in this case. There is, in our judgment, no reasonable foundation for holding this to be necessary or appropriate as a health law to safeguard the public health or the health of the individuals who are following the trade of a baker. If this statute be valid, and if, therefore, a proper case is made out in which to deny the right of an individual, *sui juris*, as employer or employé, to make contracts for the labor of the latter under the protection of the provisions of the Federal Constitution, there would seem to be no length to which legislation of this nature might not go. The case differs widely, as we have already stated, from the expressions of this court in regard to laws of this nature, as stated in *Holden* v. *Hardy*. . . .

We think that there can be no fair doubt that the trade of a baker, in and of itself, is not an unhealthy one to that degree which would authorize the legislature to interfere with the right to labor, and with the right of free contract on the part of the individual, either as employer or employé. In looking through statistics regarding all trades and occupations, it may be true that the trade of a baker does not appear to be as healthy as some other trades, and is also vastly more healthy than still others. To the common understanding the trade of a baker has never been regarded as an unhealthy one. Very likely physicians would not recommend the exercise of that or of

any other trade as a remedy for ill health. Some occupations are more healthy than others, but we think there are none which might not come under the power of the legislature to supervise and control the hours of working therein, if the mere fact that the occupation is not absolutely and perfectly healthy is to confer that right upon the legislative department of the Government. It might be safely affirmed that almost all occupations more or less affect the health. There must be more than the mere fact of the possible existence of some small amount of unhealthiness to warrant legislative interference with liberty. It is unfortunately true that labor, even in any department, may possibly carry with it the seeds of unhealthiness. But are we all, on that account, at the mercy of legislative majorities? A printer, a tinsmith, a locksmith, a carpenter, a cabinetmaker, a dry goods clerk, a bank's, a lawyer's or a physician's clerk, or a clerk in almost any kind of business, would all come under the power of the legislature, on this assumption. No trade, no occupation, no mode of earning one's living, could escape this all-pervading power, and the acts of the legislature in limiting the hours of labor in all employments would be valid, although such limitation might seriously cripple the ability of the laborer to support himself and his family. In our large cities there are many buildings into which the sun penetrates for but a short time in each day, and these buildings are occupied by people carrying on the business of bankers, brokers, lawyers, real estate, and many other kinds of business, aided by many clerks, messengers, and other employés. Upon the assumption of the validity of this act under review, it is not possible to say that an act, prohibiting lawyers' or bank clerks, or others, from contracting to labor for their employers more than eight hours a day, would be invalid. It might be said that it is unhealthy to work more than that number of hours in an apartment lighted by artificial light during the working hours of the day; that the occupation of the bank clerk, the lawyer's clerk, the real estate clerk, or the broker's clerk in such offices is therefore unhealthy, and the legislature in its paternal wisdom must, therefore, have the right to legislate on the subject of and to limit the hours for such labor, and if it exercises that power and its validity be questioned, it is sufficient to say, it has reference to the public health; it has reference to the health of the employés condemned to labor day after day in buildings where the sun never shines; it is a health law, and therefore it is valid, and cannot be questioned by the courts.

It is also urged, pursuing the same line of argument, that it is to the interest of the State that its population should be strong and robust, and therefore any legislation which may be said to tend to make people healthy must be valid as health laws, enacted under the police power. If this be a valid argument and a justification for this kind of legislation, it follows that the protection of the Federal Constitution from undue interference with liberty of person and freedom of contract is visionary, wherever the law is sought to be justified as a valid exercise of the police power. Scarcely any law but might find shelter under such assumptions, and conduct, properly so called, as well as contract, would come under the restrictive sway of the legislature. Not only the hours of employés, but the hours of employers could be regulated, and doctors, lawyers, scientists, all professional men, as well as athletes and artisans, could be forbidden to fatigue their brains and bodies by prolonged hours of exercise, lest the fighting strength of the State be impaired. We mention these extreme cases because the contention is extreme. We do not believe in the soundness of the views which uphold this law. On the contrary, we think that such a law as this, although passed in the assumed exercise of the police power, and as relating to the public health, or the health of the employés named, is not within that power, and is invalid. The act is not, within any fair meaning of the term, a health law, but is an illegal interference with the rights of individuals, both employers and employés, to make contracts regarding labor upon such terms as they may think best, or which they may agree upon with the other parties to such contracts. Statutes of the nature of that under review, limiting the hours in which grown and intelligent men may labor to earn their living, are mere meddlesome interferences with the rights of the individual, and they are not saved from condemnation by the claim that they are passed in the exercise of the police power and upon the subject of the health of the individual whose rights are interfered with, unless there be some fair ground, reasonable in and of itself, to say that there is material danger to the public health or to the health of the employés, if the hours of labor are not curtailed. If this be not clearly the case the individuals, whose rights are thus made the subject of legislative interference, are under the protection of the Federal Constitution regarding their liberty of contract as well as of person; and the legislature of the State has no power to limit their right as proposed in this statute. All that it could properly do has been done by it with regard to the conduct of bakeries, as provided for in the other sections of the act, above set forth. These several sections provide for the inspection of the premises where the bakery is carried on, with regard to furnishing proper wash-rooms and water-closets, apart from the bake-room, also with regard to providing proper drainage, plumbing and painting; the sections, in addition, provide for the height of the ceiling, the cementing or tiling of floors, where necessary in the opinion of the factory inspector, and for other things of that nature; alterations are also provided for and are to be made where necessary in the opinion of the inspector, in order to comply with the provisions of the statute. These various sections may be wise and valid regulations, and they certainly go to the full extent of providing for the cleanliness and the healthiness, so far as possible, of the quarters in which bakeries are to be conducted. Adding to all these requirements, a prohibition to enter into any contract of labor in a bakery for more than a certain number of hours a week, is, in our judgment, so wholly beside the matter of a proper, reasonable and fair provision, as to run counter to that liberty of person and of free contract provided for in the Federal Constitution.

It was further urged on the argument that restricting the hours of labor in the case of bakers was valid because it tended to cleanliness on the part of the workers, as a man was more apt to be cleanly when not overworked, and if cleanly then his "output" was also more likely to be so. What has already been said applies with equal force to this contention. We do not admit the reasoning to be sufficient to justify the claimed right of such interference. The State in that case would assume the position of a supervisor, or *pater familias*, over every act of the individual, and its right of governmental interference with his hours of labor, his hours of exercise, the character thereof, and the extent to which it shall be carried would be recognized and upheld. In our judgment it is not possible in fact to discover the connection between the number of hours a baker may work in the bakery and the healthful quality of the bread made by the workman. The connection, if any exists, is too shadowy and thin to build any argument for the interference of the legislature. If the man works ten hours a day it is all right, but if ten and a half or eleven his health is in danger and his bread may be unhealthful and, therefore, he shall not be permitted to do it. This, we think, is unreasonable and entirely arbitrary. When assertions such as we have adverted to become necessary in order to give, if possible, a plausible foundation for the contention that the law is a "health law," it gives rise to at least a suspicion that there was some other motive dominating the legislature than the

purpose to subserve the public health or welfare.

This interference on the part of the legislatures of the several States with the ordinary trades and occupations of the people seems to be on the increase. . . .

It is manifest to us that the limitation of the hours of labor as provided for in this section of the statute under which the indictment was found, and the plaintiff in error convicted, has no such direct relation to and no such substantial effect upon the health of the employé, as to justify us in regarding the section as really a health law. It seems to us that the real object and purpose were simply to regulate the hours of labor between the master and his employés (all being men, *sui juris*), in a private business, not dangerous in any degree to morals or in any real and substantial degree, to the health of the employés. Under such circumstances the freedom of master and employé to contract with each other in relation to their employment, and in defining the same, cannot be prohibited or interfered with, without violating the Federal Constitution.

The judgment of the Court of Appeals of New York as well as that of the Supreme Court and of the County Court of Oneida County must be reversed and the case remanded to the County Court for further proceedings not inconsistent with this opinion.

Reversed

Mr. Justice HARLAN, with whom Mr. Justice WHITE and Mr. Justice DAY concurred, dissenting.

While this court has not attempted to mark the precise boundaries of what is called the police power of the State, the existence of the power has been uniformly recognized, both by the Federal and state courts.

All the cases agree that this power extends at least to the protection of the lives, the health and the safety of the public against the injurious exercise by any citizen of his own rights. . . .

Speaking generally, the State in the exercise of its powers may not unduly interfere with the right of the citizen to enter into contracts that may be necessary and essential in the enjoyment of the inherent rights belonging to every one, among which rights is the right "to be free in the enjoyment of all his faculties; to be free to use them in all lawful ways; to live and work where he will; to earn his livelihood by any lawful calling; to pursue any livelihood or avocation." This was declared in *Allgeyer* v. *Louisiana*, 165 U.S. 578, 589. But in the same case it was conceded that the right to contract in relation to persons and property or to do business, within a State, may be "regulated and sometimes prohibited, when the contracts or business conflict with the policy of the State as contained in its statutes." . . .

Granting then that there is a liberty of contract which cannot be violated even under the sanction of direct legislative enactment, but assuming, as according to settled law we may assume, that such liberty of contract is subject to such regulations as the State may reasonably prescribe for the common good and the well-being of society, what are the conditions under which the judiciary may declare such regulations to be in excess of legislative authority and void? Upon this point there is no room for dispute; for, the rule is universal that a legislative enactment, Federal or state, is never to be disregarded or held invalid unless it be, beyond question, plainly and palpably in excess of legislative power. . . .

Let these principles be applied to the present case. By the statute in question it is provided that, "No employé shall be required or permitted to work in a biscuit, bread or cake bakery or confectionery establishment more than sixty hours in any one week, or more than ten hours in any one day, unless for the purpose of making a shorter work day on the last day of the week; nor more hours in any one week than will make an average of ten hours per day for the number of days during such week in which such employé shall work."

It is plain that this statute was enacted in order to protect the physical well-being of those who work in bakery and confectionery establishments. It may be that the statute had its origin, in part, in the belief that employers and employés in such establishments were not upon an equal footing, and that the necessities of the latter often compelled them to submit to such exactions as unduly taxed their strength. Be this as it may, the statute must be taken as expressing the belief of the people of New York that, as a general rule, and in the case of the average man, labor in excess of sixty hours during a week in such establishments may endanger the health of those who thus labor. Whether or not this be wise legislation it is not the province of the court to inquire. Under our systems of government the courts are not concerned with the wisdom or policy of legislation. So that in determining the question of power to interfere with liberty of contract, the court may inquire whether the means devised by the State are germane to an end which may be lawfully accomplished and have a real or substantial relation to the protection of health, as involved in the daily work of the persons, male and female, engaged in bakery and confectionery establishments. But when this inquiry is entered upon I find it impossible, in view of common experience, to say that there is here no real or substantial relation between the means employed by the State and the end sought to be accomplished by its legislation. . . . Therefore I submit that this court will transcend its functions if it assumes to annul the statute of New York. It must be remembered that this statute does not apply to all kinds of business. It applies only to work in bakery and confectionery establishments, in which, as all know, the air constantly breathed by workmen is not as pure and healthful as that to be found in some other establishments or out of doors.

Professor Hirt in his treatise on the "Diseases of the Workers" has said: "The labor of the bakers is among the hardest and most laborious imaginable, because it has to be performed under conditions injurious to the health of those engaged in it. It is hard, very hard work, not only because it requires a great deal of physical exertion in an overheated workshop and during unreasonably long hours, but more so because of the erratic demands of the public, compelling the baker to perform the greater part of his work at night, thus depriving him of an opportunity to enjoy the necessary rest and sleep, a fact which is highly injurious to his health." Another writer says: "The constant inhaling of flour dust causes inflammation of the lungs and of the bronchial tubes. The eyes also suffer through this dust, which is responsible for the many cases of running eyes among the bakers. The long hours of toil to which all bakers are subjected produce rheumatism, cramps and swollen legs. The intense heat in the workshops induces the workers to resort to cooling drinks, which together with their habit of exposing the greater part of their bodies to the change in the atmosphere, is another source of a number of diseases of various organs. Nearly all bakers are pale-faced and of more delicate health than the workers of other crafts, which is chiefly due to their hard work and their irregular and unnatural mode of living, whereby the power of resistance against disease is greatly diminished. The average age of a baker is below that of other workmen; they seldom live over their fiftieth year, most of them dying between the ages of forty and fifty. During periods of epidemic diseases the bakers are generally the first to succumb to the disease, and the number swept away during such periods far exceeds the number of other crafts in comparison to the men employed in the respective industries. When, in 1720, the plague visited the city of Marseilles, France, every baker in the city succumbed to the epidemic, which caused considerable excitement in the neighboring cities and resulted in measures for the sanitary protection of the bakers."

In the Eighteenth Annual Report by the New York Bureau of Statistics of Labor it is stated that among the occupations involving exposure to conditions that interfere with nutrition is that of a baker (p. 52). In that Report it is also stated that "from a social point of view, production will be increased by any change in industrial organization which diminishes the number of idlers, paupers and criminals. Shorter hours of work, by allowing higher standards of comfort and purer family life, promise to enhance the industrial efficiency of the wage-working class—improved health, longer life, more content and greater intelligence and inventiveness" (p. 82).

Statistics show that the average daily working time among workingmen in different countries is, in Australia, 8 hours; in Great Britain, 9; in the United States, $9\frac{3}{4}$; in Denmark, $9\frac{3}{4}$; in Norway, 10; Sweden, France and Switzerland, $10\frac{1}{2}$; Germany, $10\frac{1}{4}$; Belgium, Italy and Austria, 11; and in Russia, 12 hours.

We judicially know that the question of the number of hours during which a workman should continuously labor has been, for a long period, and is yet, a subject of serious consideration among civilized peoples, and by those having special knowledge of the laws of health. Suppose the statute prohibited labor in bakery and confectionery establishments in excess of eighteen hours each day. No one, I take it, could dispute the power of the State to enact such a statute. But the statute before us does not embrace extreme or exceptional cases. It may be said to occupy a middle ground in respect of the hours of labor. What is the true ground for the State to take between legitimate protection, by legislation, of the public health and liberty of contract is not a question easily solved, nor one in respect of which there is or can be absolute certainty. There are very few, if any, questions in political economy about which entire certainty may be predicated. One writer on relation of the State to labor has well said: "The manner, occasion, and degree in which the State may interfere with the industrial freedom of its citizens is one of the most debatable and difficult questions of social science." [Jevons, *The State in Relation to Labour* (3d ed.), p. 34.]

We also judicially know that the number of hours that should constitute a day's labor in particular occupations involving the physical strength and safety of workmen has been the subject of enactments by Congress and by nearly all of the States. Many, if not most, of those enactments fix eight hours as the proper basis of a day's labor.

I do not stop to consider whether any particular view of this economic question presents the sounder theory. What the precise facts are it may be difficult to say. It is enough for the determination of this case, and it is enough for this court to know, that the question is one about which there is room for debate and for an honest difference of opinion. There are many reasons of a weighty, substantial character, based upon the experience of mankind, in support of the theory that, all things considered, more than ten hours' steady work each day, from week to week, in a bakery or confectionery establishment, may endanger the health, and shorten the lives of the workmen, thereby diminishing their physical and mental capacity to serve the State, and to provide for those dependent upon them.

If such reasons exist that ought to be the end of this case, for the State is not amenable to the judiciary, in respect of its legislative enactments, unless such enactments are plainly, palpably, beyond all question, inconsistent with the Constitution of the United States. We are not to presume that the State of New York has acted in bad faith. Nor can we assume that its legislature acted without due deliberation, or that it did not determine this question upon the fullest attainable information, and for the common good. We cannot say that the State has acted without reason nor ought we to proceed upon the theory that its action is a mere sham Our duty, I submit, is to sustain the statute as not being in conflict with the Federal Constitution, for the reason—and such is an all-sufficient reason—it is not shown to be plainly and palpably inconsistent with that instrument. Let the State alone in the management of its purely domestic affairs, so long as it does not appear beyond all question that it has violated the Federal Constitution. This view necessarily results from the principle that the health and safety of the people of a State are primarily for the State to guard and protect.

I take leave to say that the New York statute, in the particulars here involved, cannot be held to be in conflict with the Fourteenth Amendment, without enlarging the scope of the Amendment far beyond its original purpose and without bringing under the supervision of this court matters which have been supposed to belong exclusively to the legislative departments of the several States when exerting their conceded power to guard the health and safety of their citizens by such regulations as they in their wisdom deem best. Health laws of every description constitute, said Chief Justice Marshall, a part of that mass of legislation which "embraces everything within the territory of a State, not surrendered to the General Government; all which can be most advantageously exercised by the States themselves." *Gibbons* v. *Ogden*, 9 Wheat. 1, 203. A decision that the New York statute is void under the Fourteenth Amendment will, in my opinion, involve consequences of a far-reaching and mischievous character; for such a decision would seriously cripple the inherent power of the States to care for the lives, health and well-being of their citizens. Those are matters which can be best controlled by the States. The preservation of the just powers of the States is quite as vital as the preservation of the powers of the General Government. . . .

Mr. Justice HOLMES dissenting.

I regret sincerely that I am unable to agree with the judgment in this case, and that I think it my duty to express my dissent.

This case is decided upon an economic theory which a large part of the country does not entertain. If it were a question whether I agreed with that theory, I should desire to study it further and long before making up my mind. But I do not conceive that to be my duty, because I strongly believe that my agreement or disagreement has nothing to do with the right of a majority to embody their opinions in law. It is settled by various decisions of this court that state constitutions and state laws may regulate life in many ways which we as legislators might think as injudicious or if you like as tyrannical as this, and which equally with this interfere with the liberty to contract. Sunday laws and usury laws are ancient examples. A more modern one is the prohibition of lotteries. The liberty of the citizen to do as he likes so long as he does not interfere with the liberty of others to do the same, which has been a shibboleth for some well-known writers, is interfered with by school laws, by the Post Office, by every state or municipal institution which takes his money for purposes thought desirable, whether he likes it or not. The Fourteenth Amendment does not enact Mr. Herbert Spencer's Social Statics. The other day we sustained the Massachusetts vaccination law. *Jacobson* v. *Massachusetts*, 197 U.S. 11. United States and state statutes and decisions cutting down the liberty to contract by way of combination are familiar to this court. *Northern Securities Co.* v. *United States*, 193 U.S. 197. Two years ago we upheld the prohibition of sales of stock on margins or for future delivery in the constitution of California. *Otis* v. *Parker*, 187 U.S. 606. The decision sustaining an

eight hour law for miners is still recent. *Holden* v. *Hardy*, 169 U.S. 366. Some of these laws embody convictions or prejudices which judges are likely to share. Some may not. But a constitution is not intended to embody a particular economic theory, whether of paternalism and the organic relation of the citizen to the State or of *laissez faire*. It is made for people of fundamentally differing views, and the accident of our finding certain opinions natural and familiar or novel and even shocking ought not to conclude our judgment upon the question whether statutes embodying them conflict with the Constitution of the United States.

General propositions do not decide concrete cases. The decision will depend on a judgment or intuition more subtle than any articulate major premise. But I think that the proposition just stated, if it is accepted, will carry us far toward the end. Every opinion tends to become a law. I think that the word liberty in the Fourteenth Amendment is perverted when it is held to prevent the natural outcome of a dominant opinion, unless it can be said that a rational and fair man necessarily would admit that the statute proposed would infringe fundamental principles as they have been understood by the traditions of our people and our law. It does not need research to show that no such sweeping condemnation can be passed upon the statute before us. A reasonable man might think it a proper measure on the score of health. Men whom I certainly could not pronounce unreasonable would uphold it as a first instalment of a general regulation of the hours of work. Whether in the latter aspect it would be open to the charge of inequality I think it unnecessary to discuss.

SECTION C. THE PROGRESSIVE MOVEMENT

1. AUTOBIOGRAPHY[1]

By LINCOLN STEFFENS

EDITORS' NOTE.—Lincoln Steffens (1866–1936) is best remembered as one of the early "muckrakers"—to use the opprobrious term applied by Theodore Roosevelt to Steffens and his fellow-writers. Steffens was born in San Francisco and spent his boyhood in the Sacramento Valley of California. Upon graduation from the state university at Berkeley he joined the trek to Germany of American youth in search of the higher learning. Having acquired some education and a wife, and having lost his father's financial support, Steffens turned to newspaper work in the New York City of the

1890's. After serving an interesting apprenticeship there, Steffens (among others) wrote the articles which became *The Shame of the Cities*. On *McClure's* magazine he was a colleague of such other able muckrakers as Ida M. Tarbell, Claude H. Wetmore, and Ray Stannard Baker. World War I and the October Revolution (1917) in Russia affected his point of view significantly, so that in the later *Autobiography* his description of his earlier activities and points of view is tinctured with some skepticism of the possibilities of what may be called liberal reform and reformers.

BULLS AND BEARS[2]

When I was a boy, blacksmiths and niggers who had to handle mules and kicking horses used to tell me that the safest place to be in range was close up to the bad animals' heels, and I saw them rush in, pick up a hind leg, and hang on to it, while they shod the hard-hitting hoof. I never tried it myself on a mule, but I did on Wall Street, and there's some truth in it.

The panic of 1893, like all periods of business depression, was a dismal time of radiating destruction. But it had its bright side, inside; it was good for the bears and

for my education. The shorts rejoiced in the ruin; they made money, and they were happy. As a reporter on the side lines in the Stock Exchange I could see and hear and feel the wild joy of the bears on a day of tumbling prices, and it was a never-ending surprise to me, because everything I had read, heard, or imagined had pictured the dark depression, despair, and anguish of the losers. And of course there were sufferers, some of them on the floor, others in the banks and brokerage houses, most of all, however, far from the market, out in the country—the public. Among the brokers generally, whether "on the floor" or in their offices, an active market, whether prices are rising or falling, means that business is good; and that's what one felt, and that's what remains to be written—the joy of a panic.

1. Lincoln Steffens, *Autobiography* (New York, 1931), pp. 187–96, 365–73, 392–98, 422–29, 489–94. By permission of Harcourt, Brace and Company.

2. The chapter on "Bulls and Bears" is drawn from Steffens' experience as a financial reporter in Wall Street before he became a "muckraker."

It's like a war, a revolution, a strike—like any crisis in human affairs when men have to walk up and face the consequences of their ignorance, folly, or wickedness—the panic of '93 was a period of bad times chiefly for the innocent. The news of it, the reports printed, are "bad" because they are written by, about, and for bulls. The bears are forgotten and as friendless as the strikers are who rush gleefully forth from the factories to the cafes, or the revolutionists and army officers whose day is come. On the scene one feels the prevailing spirit of activity. It is the period of reconstruction that is gloomy and sad; it is so long, so hard, and so disappointing.

Before the panic had run its course, the regular Wall Street reporter whose place I had taken came back, and I was turned into general reporting again, politics and business, chiefly business. When the constructive work began in finance, the city editor sent me more into "the Street" to discover and report the plans making by the bankers, lawyers, and industrialists for the reorganization of bankrupt concerns and, gradually, for the organization of new corporations and new combines, even, for example, the U.S. Steel Company. These schemes began during the panic; they were compelled by the circumstances, and I heard of them, but paid no heed, while we were in that period when good news was not news. But after a year or so of failures, while the receiverships continued, good news was becoming news; not the best news, but still good, secondary news, and that was my part. I was the bull reporter, the other man was the bear. He was seeing my old conservative, more or less suffering, proper bankers who are really only money-lenders. I had to do with the private bankers who are the constructive engineering financiers.

Of these last, J. P. Morgan, Senior, was the greatest. I did not see much of him, of course; nobody did. He was in sight all the time. He sat alone in a back room with glass sides in his banking-house with his door open, and it looked as if any one could walk in upon him and ask him any question. One heard stories of the payment of large sums for an introduction to him. I could not see why the tippers with business did not come right in off the street and talk to him. They did not. My business was with his partners or associates, principally Samuel Spencer, but I noticed that these, his partners, did not go near him unless he sent for them; and then they looked alarmed and darted in like office-boys. "Nobody can answer that question except Mr. Morgan," they would tell me. Well, Mr. Morgan was there; why not go in and ask him? The answer I got was a smile or a shocked look of surprise. And once when I pressed the president of one of the Morgan banks to put to him a question we agreed deserved an answer, the banker said, "Not on your life," and when I said, "But why not?" he said, "You try it yourself and see." And I did. I went over to J. P. Morgan and Company, walked into his office, and stood before him at his flat, clean, clear desk. I stood while he examined a sheet of figures; I stood for two or three long minutes, while the whole bank seemed to stop work to watch me, and he did not look up; he was absorbed, he was sunk, in those figures. He was so alone with himself and his mind that when he did glance up he did not see me; his eyes were looking inward. He was a mathematician, you know. One of the stories told of his life was that he was so gifted in mathematics that the University of Göttingen invited him to stay there to take a lectureship that would lead up to a career in pure mathematics. I thought, as he looked at and did not see me that day, that he was doing a sum in mental arithmetic, and when he solved it he dropped his eyes back upon his sheet of figures and I slunk out.

Somebody stopped me as I was going out through the bank and laughingly asked me what had happened.

"Nothing," I said; "he didn't even see me."

"You're lucky," was the chuckling answer. "You have to call him to wake him up. If you had said, 'Mr. Morgan,' he would have come to. And then—"

"What would have happened then?" I asked.

"Oh," the partner said, "then you would have seen—an explosion."

I believed that; it was generally believed on the Street that J. P. Morgan was a dangerous man to talk to, and no doubt that made it unnecessary for him to be guarded by door men, secretaries, and stenographers. He could protect himself. I know that I came to feel, myself, what others on Wall Street felt, a vague awe of the man.

But I went through that awful circle once. I said, "Mr. Morgan." The paper received one afternoon a typewritten statement from Morgan and Company; it was some announcement about a matter of bonds that had been news for months, and the city editor called me in to read it with him. He could not make it out. It was a long complicated statement all in one sentence, and I could not read it either. "Take it down to Mr. Morgan and ask him to read it," Mr. Wright said, and I remember I was startled. I asked Wright if he knew what he was asking of me: to go and put a question to the old man himself. "Yes," said Wright, "but it has to be done." I picked up the statement, ran down to the bank, conning the sentence, and ready for the explosion, I walked into Morgan's office and right up to his desk. He saw me this time; he threw himself back in his chair so hard that I thought he would tip over.

"Mr. Morgan," I said as brave as I was afraid, "what does this statement mean?" and I threw the paper down before him.

"Mean!" he exclaimed. His eyes glared, his great red nose seemed to me to flash and darken, flash and darken. Then he roared. "Mean! It means what it says. I wrote it myself and it says what I mean."

"It doesn't say anything—straight," I blazed.

He sat back there, flashing and rum-bling; then he clutched the arms of his chair, and I thought he was going to leap at me. I was so scared that I defied him.

"Oh, come now, Mr. Morgan," I said, "you may know a lot about figures and finance, but I'm a reporter, and I know as much as you do about English. And that statement isn't English."

That was the way to treat him, I was told afterward. And it was in that case. He glared at me a moment more, the fire went out of his face, and he leaned forward over the bit of paper and said very meekly, "What's the matter with it?"

I said I thought it would be clearer in two sentences instead of one and I read it aloud so, with a few other verbal changes.

"Yes," he agreed, "that is better. You fix it."

I fixed it under his eyes, he nodded, and I, whisking it away, hurried back to the office. They told me in the bank afterward that "J. P." sat watching me go out of the office, then rapped for Spencer and asked what my name was, where I came from, and said, "Knows what he wants, and—and—gets it."

He never offered me a partnership, but when Samuel Spencer, the receiver of the Southern Railway, arranged for an interview with him a year or so later, Mr. Morgan remembered and talked to me—"not for publication"—about the south from a financial point of view. The talk was a dry, but convincing, bull prophecy of what has happened since down there, later, much later than the prophet expected; but it was a true prophecy.

Morgan was a bull. "He gets it coming and going," the Street used to say, "but he always says that for the long pull the bull side is the winning side in America. The U.S.A. is a bull country." That is to say, he made money by selling on a falling market; but he bought too on the way down and so ended, he and his bank and his "crowd," in possession of enough stock at sacrifice prices to give him the control. Then he could "reorganize" the railroad and other companies he had chosen as, in the long run, good; he could finance and direct the running of them. He made his bear profits, got his banker's commission on the reorganization, the banker's interest on money lent, the banker's profit on underwriting and floating the new stocks and bonds, and, best of all, the control. This was all common practice and common knowledge when I was in Wall Street; it was talked about as just plain business, and as I heard it all, it seemed to me to be only good business, profitable, proper, and—easy. I used to wonder why men went into any other business than Wall Street if they wanted only to make money, and I declared to myself and to my friends that when I wanted to make money I would not write, or report, or edit, or manage; I would go into Wall Street. I would quit working and—make money.

And, mind you, this was not cynicism; it was plain common sense to me. A student of ethics, I accepted it as the world does, as the business men generally, as bankers, brokers and indeed bishops accepted it as, not only the custom, but moral and wise. Many a time, I have sympathized deeply with a stock operator or a banker who was thrown into the depths of despair because he had not made the millions he had planned to make; he had not lost, he merely had not made his money. I watched men working and lying to smash a company that they were trying to get cheap, the control of it, and I rejoiced with them when they "busted" the old crowd, drove them out ruined, and got the business. I was offered the presidency of one such company. I considered taking it, and when I objected that I knew nothing of business, neither that or any other, the answer was that I did not need to; they would tell me what I was to do; in fact I must consult them. All I had to do, apparently, was to draw a good salary, occupy a fine office, and make a respectable appearance. "You'll get out of reporting and become a man of affairs." I did not grasp what this meant at the time. When I de-

clined to be lifted out of journalism up off the street into high finance with a social and financial position, I did not despise or pity as I do now the successful men who seize such opportunities. My reason was personal: business did not attract me; money was no object; I liked reporting; I did not generalize at all. I did not understand, so I did not condemn, the practices of big business. I was not thinking in those days; life was too, too interesting, the world as it was too fascinating, to stop to question anything but politics, which was all bad, just as business was all good, to me.

James B. Dill was the first man to remind me that I was an intellectual, that I might think as well as see and write. He was a masterpiece. He was the man who put through in the State of New Jersey the laws to enable the organization of trusts and combines, to free corporations, to free them to do whatever they pleased. His was a great name in Wall Street; even the big fellows spoke of James B. Dill with awe and retained him to organize their plans into going concerns. He was the man, for example, who brought Andrew Carnegie and J. P. Morgan together for the purchase and sale of the Carnegie steel properties and so laid the basis of the United States Steel Company, the biggest transaction and the biggest trust of those days. "I put Morgan in one room, Carnegie in another," he recounted, "while I took the third room in between them with my clerks and stenographers. I knew that if they met they would blow up; so I played the part of buffer and negotiator. They could express their opinions of each other to me. I could agree with both of them, sympathize with the generosity and bigness of each one, and share his contempt for the narrow meanness of the other. I was sincere, uninsultable, and true to their agreeable purposes, the one to buy, the other to sell."

Dill was a realist with insight and humor, but hardly any one knew of his humor. He was always spoken of with awe as "James B. Dill." No familiarity with him; Mr. Morgan might be "J. P."; he was called that, but James B. Dill was always and only a name, a mystery, a wonder-worker in those terrible days when the reorganization of the débris of '93 was beginning. No one but the masters ever saw him, and we, who would no more think of approaching him than we would walk in on J. P. himself, we—I thought of him as a silent, thinking, conspiring lawyer who sat still in the big back room of a great suite of offices, with an army commander's staff of almost equally great attorneys-at-law, who all joined their learning and their wits to advise, at huge fees (which rumor named), the brains of big business. He was, in brief, the great black man who showed good Business how to circumvent bad Politics and the anti-trust legislation passed to satisfy the ignorant, envious people.

For there was, at that time, a very general popular discontent, the choral accompaniment of the hard times; and the passion of the day was the anti-trust sentiment, which was a development out of the old anti-monopoly cry of the earlier period. The *Post* was not anti-trust; it was anti-Tammany; but it was for business, except now and then when there was some exceptional scandal, too outrageous to be passed by in silence. The *Post* was sincere, of course; almost everybody was, almost everybody is, sincere. I did not know it, but I can see now that what I needed then was what the world needs all the time, to find some one who was not sincere but intelligent. I found that man in James B. Dill. Bless him.

One day some morning newspaper printed a "roast" of James B. Dill, the author of the criminal New Jersey trust laws. It showed how that State had enacted statutes under which the anti-trust laws of other States could be evaded and American public opinion defied. A sovereign State, Jersey had the right to pass any laws it pleased, and if it enabled the formation of trusts in New Jersey, New York State and the other States had to recognize the creatures of the free State of New Jersey. The article declared that it was James B. Dill who had himself invented and put over this legislation, quietly, almost secretly, in New Jersey, and then it showed in some detail what was permitted: plain financial crimes.

This clipping was handed to me, with instructions to go and see Mr. James B. Dill and get his denial or correction of these charges. So! I was to see the black man! I felt as I did when I was sent to see Mr. Morgan, as an English pressman would if he were sent to interview a minister of the Crown, as a girl feels who is to be presented to the Queen. I was flattered. I was trembling with fear, I was awfully bold, as I went, hurrying and slowing up, eagerly and then dreadfully, downtown and up into the building where the silent councilor of the trusts was hidden away in—not a great suite of offices, but a small, neat set of two or three rooms. A smiling little stenographer and typist took my card, with my name and that of my paper on it, into one of the rooms, and returning instantly, swept me in to Mr. Dill, who met me with a smiling welcome on his rosy, round, happy face.

"The *Evening Post*—at last," he chuckled, and his round little body seemed to laugh as it settled back into its big chair. "I have been wondering," he said, "why you have not called on me. I have been tempted to send for you. The abuses of the Jersey Trust laws must be exposed and stopped. Yes," he added, as he glanced at the clipping I held out to him, the story that I thought would anger and drive him to a furious contradiction, "yes, all that is true, and more, much more."

And to my amazement he opened up the criminal inside of the practices under the New Jersey legislation, a picture of such chicanery and fraud, of wild license and wrong-doing, that I could not, I dared not, take it all down; I was too confused. And Dill saw that, and he laughed; his eyes twinkled and his round little belly shook with the humor of the situation.

"You are astonished?" he said. "And well you may be. But you must write what I tell you. Don't quote me. I am the founder of this legislation, and as such you may name me, but don't say I gave you these facts; it would look odd; it might be suspicious, to make me the authority for an exposure of what I am the enabling founder of, but it is your duty to describe what is done under these laws, and if your editor shows any hesitation, you may tell him to call me up on the 'phone; I will stand back of whatever you print."

I did not write all that Dill told me; not then; I never have. I could not at the time, because, as I have said, I was too imbued with the Wall Street spirit and view of things to speak as this lawyer did of the holies of the holy. Upton Sinclair learned from him; he was a socialist. I was a Wall Street man myself, unconsciously, but literally. That's how I came finally to understand what corruption is and how it gets a man, not as the Reds and the writers think, but as the Whites and the Righteous are: rogues outside, but inside, honest men. However, that's for later. When James B. Dill told me first about Wall Street and his Jersey laws, and he saw that I would not, could not, take it in, he made merry with me, laughing and quizzing and telling me ever more and more.

"Why, didn't you ever hear how they wiped out Richmond Terminal?" he would say, and he would tell me that story. "And you didn't know that? A Wall Street reporter, and you don't know that! And this—" He told me something else that I had never heard of; and then something else. "Nor that? Never knew that? What do you know?"

"I say," he said, when I rose to go after that first interview, "I must know you better. And my wife and daughter; they must know you." He invited me to his house; he took me there, and thus began a friendship that lasted as long as James B. Dill himself in the body. He had incorporated himself and his fortune under his Jersey laws as "The James B. Dill Corporation"—I think that was the title of it—he told me about it with glee, a corporation with five shares—or three, which he controlled, he laughed; one share to his wife, one for his daughter (in escrow), the rest (and the control) for him. "Avoids taxes and all sorts of troubles when I die." So "The James B. Dill Corporation" may be immortal, but my jolly little imp of a Santa Claus, my mischievous professor of financial law, my good friend James B. Dill, died, a loss, a real loss, but not till he had made me see Wall Street and Business and Politics and Law as he saw them, from the inside out; and not, of course, till he had explained to me why he, of all men, had led and inspired and provided the ammunition for the exposure of the James B. Dill laws of New Jersey.

"Why, Dr. Innocent," he said, "I was advertising my wares and the business of my State. When you and the other reporters and critics wrote as charges against us what financiers could and did actually do in Jersey, when you listed, with examples, what the trust-makers were doing under our laws, you were advertising our business—free. For financiers are dubs, as you know yourself now; don't you? They have to be told, and they have to be told plain so that they get it, and so, as I say, while I gave you the facts to roast us with, what you wrote as 'bad' struck business men all over the United States as good, and they poured in upon us to our profit to do business with us to their profit. The only drawback was that when Delaware and New York and other 'bad' political sovereigns saw what Jersey was doing and how we made money and friends out of our trust policy they copied us, and they went further than we did, or, to be exact, they tried to."

And so saying, Dill laughed and laughed and laughed; not cynically; not wickedly; but merrily, with his whole body and soul. James B. Dill was one of the "wisest,"

wisest and, yes, about the rightest man I ever met.

"Trusts are natural, inevitable growths out of our social and economic conditions," he said often. "You cannot stop them by force, with laws. They will sweep down like glaciers upon your police, courts, and States and wash them into flowing rivers. I am for clearing the way for them. Let them go, and if they cannot be brought into social use, why—then—then"—he would laugh—"then I would be for exploring their origin and dealing with —I mean closing up—their source." . . .

ST. LOUIS, A CITY INSIDE OUT

My business as a New York editor in Chicago was to call upon and draw out writers, editors, and leading citizens, to see what they were interested in, and invite some of them to write for *McClure's*. I had a list of such men. Bert Boyden, who was managing me as well as my work, gave it me, and at the end he added the name of his "brother Bill," a member of the law firm, Matz, Fisher, and Boyden. It was only as a matter of courtesy that I called finally upon William C. Boyden, and as a matter of courtesy this genial man turned his chair, his body, and his whole mind around upon my business. Had the men I had seen suggested anything for the magazine? No.

"Well, then, let's see," he said, and he went to work. "To begin here at home, there's my partner, Walter Fisher; he's undertaking to reform the city government of Chicago—"

"Reform? Chicago?" I laughed, and I must have expressed the idea that that might be news, if true, but—impossible.

"No?" said Boyden, who never argued or urged. "Well, then—let's see now. Oh, I'll tell you. Up in St. Paul there's a very quiet little old German gentleman named Weyerhäuser, who has gathered into his possession much of the timberlands of the United States. He owns wide areas of the west and northwest, and now he is acquiring the forests of the southern States.

I know about him because of a law case. He wanted to log lumber down streams so small that boats could not float on them, and he couldn't legally, because they were not 'navigable streams.' So he had the courts decide that logs were boats; a stream that navigated logs was a navigable stream; so—"

"What about him?" I asked.

"Nothing," said Boyden, "except that there is a great, effective human power of whom nothing is known, nothing is ever printed. He's one of the richest men in America, richer than some of your famous New York millionaires, and the public has never heard of him."

I went to St. Paul, found Weyerhäuser's modest, orderly office, and learned from his clerks that he always refused to be interviewed. They told me a little about him, how precise he was, how quiet, methodical, prompt. "Gets down here to the office every day at exactly 7:30." I think that was the minute; maybe it was 7:15. Anyway I was there five minutes before the hour named the next morning, and when the round, gray, smiling German arrived I asked him for an interview.

"I am never interviewed," he said. "I don't care for write-ups." He was about to go on through the swinging gate.

"I don't propose to write you up," I said. "I want to write you down."

He stopped, looked. "Come in," he invited, holding the gate open.

He led on into his private office, sat us both down, and then, without glancing at his mail, he said, "Now, then, what can I do for you?"

I told him I had learned that he had started with nothing and acquired a fortune and half the forests of America. "What did it cost you?" I asked.

He started to shake his head as if to say, "Nothing," but he was staring at me, and his intelligent-wide-open eyes saw something of my meaning. His smile vanished; his face grew serious. "You mean—"

"Yes, I mean that there are lots of able men in this country who have set out with no capital, made millions, and then tell us it cost them nothing but work, hard work. I think it cost them—something else. I think it cost them as much or more than they made. How rich are you?"

He sat still a moment, then rose and closed his office door. When he came back —all very slowly, deliberately—and sat down, he said seriously: "I don't know how rich I am. I'll ask the bank downstairs later to make an estimate for us. And I don't know what it has cost me—either. I have often wondered. You mean the things I have had to do to—to do business? Yes. I thought so. Well, that has bothered me a great deal. I have often wanted to talk it over with somebody. There was no-body—"

"Why not your pastor?"

"Oh, the clergy—they don't understand."

"They just tell you to stop it?"

"Yes, and you can't."

"Well, there's your banker, other successful business men," I suggested.

He saw my smile, but he wouldn't join in the jest. "Some of them worry, too," he protested, "but—"

He stopped, shaking his head.

"They just say to go on?"

He nodded, abstractedly. We were silent a moment; he was thinking; he wanted to talk.

"What do you have to do—?" I asked softly, and there was an immediate response. He had been looking down; his face turned up to me, and he said: "I'd like to tell you. Can I? In confidence? You can't print it, of course."

I hesitated; it wasn't fair to the magazine to take this for myself, but what could I do?

"I promise; sure," I promised.

He told me what he did to get hold of the timber, how he did it, how he got and used power in politics. And he told me, questioningly, how he justified it. He began with the ordinary practices of a business man, contributions to campaign funds. He was testing me. Did I judge? Did I

show shock? I didn't. I saw the compulsion upon him, said so, and he, encouraged, opened up more and more of the picture. We were shut in there all the forenoon, three or four hours. I did not try to help or hurt him, just listened, and he talked himself out. Toward noon he got back to his balance of profits on money and his loss in—something, and he remembered his promise. He called up the bank downstairs on the 'phone.

"There's a man here," he said, "who has asked me how rich I am. Can you make a rough estimate? No? Too long a job? All right." He hung up. "He doesn't know either, can't say offhand."

"It doesn't matter now," I said. "Does it?"

"No. That isn't the point. We've got the cost; the profits don't matter."

This he said absentmindedly, and absentmindedly he saw me to the door. I went away and back to Chicago, like Weyerhäuser, absentmindedly, thinking how much better a man can be than he thinks he is.

"Well, then," said Boyden, "if you didn't get an article out of Weyerhäuser, here's another chance. There's a man down in St. Louis; his name is Folk; he is raising the deuce of a row about bribery in the board of aldermen. We get the dust of it in the papers but no clear idea of just what it's all about. Why not go down there, see this man Folk, and have him and his findings written up plain for us who don't know St. Louis?"

That was in the line of the policy I had proposed for the magazine, a national publication: to take confused, local, serial news of the newspapers and report it all together in one long short story for the whole country. I went that night to St. Louis, and by noon the next day I was sitting with Joseph W. Folk in a quiet corner of the old Planters Hotel lobby. He had "dropped everything" to come there. He needed help, publicity.

"The local newspapers are backing me up, now, some heartily; all are printing the news. But they don't know yet what I know." He looked around as if pursued. "The ramifications of this thing, the directions the trails of evidence are taking, the character of the opposition I encounter—I'm afraid I'll soon be losing all local support. You publish in New York. You are not subject to the pulls and the threats of St. Louis. You might see me through and so set the pace for the papers published here. But I warn you that what is coming is beyond belief; I can hardly credit my own eyes and ears."

The man was dazed. Having shown thus for one little moment his inner disturbance, he smiled, put up a cool, courageous front, which he rarely lowered thereafter. He was a small man, small-boned, with a white face sharpened by thin black hair and dark eyes. A southerner from Tennessee, he came of the race of southern Puritans who have the hard, righteous traits of their New England cousins, and chivalry besides, and the pride they had put on to cover their conscience against slave-holding. Folk's hardest virtue was duty. He had had the world all pictured for him in the schools of Tennessee and in his law studies. The Bible, the English common law, the Constitution of the United States, and the charter of the City of St. Louis described things as they were—so he had believed when he came up from Tennessee to start his career as a corporation attorney. He went into politics, a bit, for the practice in public speaking, to make friends (and clients), and to prepare the way for the eloquent statesmanship which southern boys dream of. He became circuit attorney, the prosecuting officer of the St. Louis district, by chance, almost against his will. He had no interest in, he had the common horror among law students of "criminal law" (where the finest opportunities are). But the political bosses were in a tangle with their own several aspirants for the office, and there was that harmless, respectable young man Joe Folk, who was president of the harmless, respectable

Democratic Club. Ed Butler, the big Democratic boss, bade Folk stand for the election as circuit attorney.

"I'll have to do my duty," Folk warned him softly.

"Oh, sure," Butler answered; the boss had had experience of what "duty" meant to rising young men.

Now the office of the public prosecutor is a high mountain upside down, from the top of which a man with eyes to see can see all the world, the flesh, and the devil, and most observers adjust their glasses to the glare of it. Folk couldn't. Sitting there in that lobby, telling his story that day, I felt the pain he felt. His Tennessee schoolboy's picture was painted deep in fast colors. He had to believe that an American city was a government by law, and when the boss or his heelers came to the circuit attorney and told him whom to appoint as his assistants, what to do; when Ed Butler—not a judge in court, nor an officer of the law, but a one-time horse-shoer and now a representative of law-breakers—when this crook walked into Folk's office as if it were his office and said: "Joe, you will name So-and-so your first assistant, this and that man second and third, and—you will let our ballot-stuffers go and give the other bosses' repeaters the limit—"

When Folk described it thus, with startled eyes, you could see that his picture of the world was being all slashed to pieces.

"I and my office, the criminal law, was to be run by—criminals!"

He put it like that. He had imagination. He must have had, because, piecing together the fragments of his torn picture, he startled my imagination and made me make a picture, too. I was taking the single, separate facts of political corruption and joining them into a new view of a city as it is. He interrupted me.

"But that's all nothing," he said. "That's only the start of it. That's what set me inquiring into other, into all, cases."

Folk had begun to prosecute the men

who had gone about stuffing the ballot boxes for him and his party as well as for the enemy. "But they elected you, Joe," Butler remonstrated. "Without them and us you wouldn't have been where you are."

"I am doing my sworn duty," answered Folk, the Puritan.

"Well, then, we'll get you," Butler threatened.

"Not till I have first got you," the Southerner said proudly.

He discovered, however, that he had to have witnesses and evidence to win convictions; and he discovered that when a prisoner was in sight of the penitentiary he would, to save himself, peach on others. This was the practice of prosecutors—to indict and trade with peachers. Like Jerome in New York, Folk generalized; he realized that this was power. By offering leniency, he, the circuit attorney, could learn what was back of crimes; and so Folk bargained for confessions first from his ballot-stuffers whose stories were descriptions of politics; and then—

One afternoon, late in January, 1902, a newspaper reporter, known as "Red" Galvin, called Mr. Folk's attention to a ten-line newspaper item to the effect that a large sum of money had been placed in a bank for the purpose of bribing certain assemblymen to secure the passage of a street railroad ordinance. No names were mentioned, but Mr. Galvin surmised that the bill referred to was one introduced in behalf of the Suburban Railway Company. An hour later Mr. Folk sent the names of nearly one hundred persons to the sheriff, with instructions to subpoena them before the grand jury at once. The list included councilmen, members of the House of Delegates, officers and directors of the Suburban Railway, bank presidents and cashiers. Folk knew nothing, and he was not able to learn much.

Rumors he heard, but political gossip is often correct, and he had also his own judgment of the relative strength and weakness of the many men he suspected.

He picked on Charles H. Turner, president of the Suburban Railway, and Philip Stock, a lobbyist for the brewers, who, he had heard, was the legislative agent in the railway deal. He thought they would peach. He summoned them before the grand jury, and he began to bluff.

"Gentlemen," he said to them in that presence, "I have secured enough evidence to warrant the return of indictments against you for bribery, and I shall prosecute you to the full extent of the law and send you to the penitentiary unless you tell the grand jury the complete history of the corruptionist methods employed by you to secure the passage of Ordinance No. 44."

He gave them three days to decide, three days of pulls, protests, threats, tears, from them and their friends; and who were not their friends? Folk was astonished as Police Commissioner Roosevelt had been at "the prominence and respectability of the men and women who intercede for crooks." Roosevelt had yielded to some prayers, a little. Folk did his duty; he was hard, quiet, patient. Messrs. Turner and Stock broke down and confessed. They told all about this deal: names, prices, dates. They told, or they involved other men who told all about other deals by which business men, high and low, big and little, had been systematically obtaining franchises, grants, licenses, exemptions, and public properties for years and were planning to get other such privileges in the future.

As Folk told briefly, sharply, swiftly these stories of the confessions of boodling, he seemed to sink whiter and quieter into the darkness of that corner of the hotel lobby; his pinpoint eyes watched me to see (as he told me afterward) if I saw what he saw, and when I was silent, expressionless, he could not stand it. He shot forward and shouted—no, he whispered, but the way he whispered and blazed made it sound like a shout:

"It is good business men that are corrupting our bad politicians; it is good business that causes bad government—in St. Louis."

A moment he waited, then: "It is the leading citizens that are battening on our city—in St. Louis."

He waited, watching again, and when I made no response, he lay, he fell back, in his chair and said very simply: "Just as the public prosecutor and the criminal courts represent criminals, so the legislative bodies, the representative government, represents bribery and business, not the people—in St. Louis."

What Folk's mind was doing was simple, but unusual. He was sweeping all his cases of bribery together to form a truth out of his facts. He was generalizing. Instead of minding his own business and prosecuting each set of boodlers for each of the many felonies he had uncovered, he was thinking about them all together and seeing what they meant all together.

"Bribery is no mere felony," he exclaimed. "It's treason." And again, as he was rehearsing how all the confessing bribers and bribe-takers wound up by saying, "That's the way it's done, Mr. Folk; you can't do business any other way," the startled prosecutor said: "It's systematic. That *is* the way it is done. Bribery and corruption is a process of revolution, to make a democratic government represent, not the people, but a part, the worse part, of the people."

"Or—the best," I muttered, and he sprang up, echoing, "Yes, the best, the leading business men of St. Louis."

I wrote to *McClure's* that I had an article for them and that as soon as I could find a man to write it I would return to New York. Folk named over all the reporters who had been writing his revelations and suggested Claude H. Wetmore, whom I saw and instructed. He was to write an article on Folk and St. Louis. St. Louis, mind you. Wetmore, not I, was to describe the extraordinary conditions disclosed by this extraordinary circuit attorney in St. Louis. I was not yet a muckraker. I was an editor, and it never

occurred to me to write this myself. On my way home, my mind began doing what Folk's had done. I was generalizing. I thought of New York. The extraordinary conditions of St. Louis were like the extraordinary conditions of New York. The corruption I had seen in New York was of the police; that of St. Louis was of the board of aldermen, but I had read of the aldermanic corruption of New York in the Tweed days. I had heard of Philadelphia, and in the newspapers there were scrappy reports of something in Minneapolis similar to New York police corruption.

Were not the extraordinary conditions of St. Louis and New York the ordinary conditions of city government in the United States? No, not yet. I couldn't say that yet.

When Wetmore's article came in to the office, I made some changes in it. He had left out some salient facts; he had spared some very conspicuous characters; he had "gone easy" on the boss, Ed Butler, for example. I put in what I remembered of what he had omitted. He remonstrated; he could not live and work in St. Louis if the article was printed as I had edited it. When I insisted, he compromised. I must sign it with him and take the blame for my insertions. Good. Done. And so I appeared as a muckraker. But I made my bow also as a graft philosopher. I wrote the title of that article, "Tweed Days in St. Louis," and inserted a few comparisons, just enough to suggest the idea that was taking hard hold on me, the idea that Folk had expressed: that bribery is not a mere felony, but a revolutionary process which was going on in all our cities and that, if I could trace it to its source, I might find the cause of political corruption and—the cure.

But first, to make sure that the process was identical everywhere, I must go and make a study of the police corruption of Minneapolis, to compare it with that of New York. St. Louis would not do for such an inquiry. Folk said there was no such systematic corruption of the police in

St. Louis as I had described to him in New York. . . .

THE SHAMELESSNESS OF ST. LOUIS

When Circuit Attorney Folk confirmed my theory that there was organized police corruption in St. Louis as well as boodling business, I was eager to go on to another city to see if the same system of graft existed there—Chicago, for example. Enough was known of Chicago and Philadelphia to indicate that they would come up to standard, but it would not be scientific, sportsmanlike, or convincing to choose such sure things.

"Did I hear you say you were going to walk to the station?" a downtown hotel clerk asked me in Chicago one night. "Don't do it. It isn't safe. Take a cab."

Chicago was very tempting. Mr. McClure urged me to do it next, for editorial reasons. My article on Minneapolis had succeeded beyond all expectations. The newsstand sales had exhausted the printed supply; subscriptions were coming in; and the mail was bringing letters of praise, appreciation, and suggestion. "Come here to this place," they wrote from many cities, towns, and even villages; "you will find scandals that will make Minneapolis and St. Louis look like models of good government."

"Evidently," I argued with the editor-in-chief, "you could shoot me out of a gun fired at random and, wherever I lighted, there would be a story, the same way."

My mind was on my theory, but Mr. McClure's was on our business; we must increase the sensationalism of our articles if we were to hold and reap our advantage. We must find some city, like Chicago or Philadelphia, that was worse than St. Louis and Minneapolis. The disagreement became acute; it divided the office and might have caused trouble had not Miss Ida M. Tarbell made peace, as she so often did thereafter. Sensible, capable, and very affectionate, she knew each one of us and all our idiosyncrasies and troubles. She had none of her own so far as we ever heard.

When we were deadlocked we might each of us send for her, and down she would come to the office, smiling, like a tall, good-looking young mother, to say, "Hush, children." She would pick out the sense in each of our contentions, and putting them together with her own good sense, give me a victory over S. S., him a triumph over Phillips and take away from all of us only the privilege of gloating. The interest of the magazine was pointed out and we and she went back to work. In this case she saw and reminded us that there was plenty of time to decide on the next place to choose. Meanwhile St. Louis was to be done again and more thoroughly. I wanted to trace and comprehend for myself the ramifications of this typical, invisible government of the American city; the magazine wanted to publish the further revelations of Mr. Folk's later inquiries and, by the way, to help elect this man governor of Missouri. We made a vague compromise, therefore. I was to write little or nothing of my theory, stick to facts, and then, St. Louis done, we would choose almost any place I liked for our fourth city.

This was good journalism. S. S. McClure was a good journalist, one of the best I ever knew, and he knew it, and he knew why. One day when I returned to him a manuscript he had asked me to read and pass upon, he picked up, glanced at, and dropped unread into the waste-basket a long memorandum I had written. "What's this?" he demanded. "A review? I don't want your literary criticism of a manuscript. All I ask of you is whether you like it or not." Seeing that I was miffed, he explained.

"Look," he said. "I want to know if you enjoy a story, because, if you do, then I know that, say, ten thousand readers will like it. If Miss Tarbell likes a thing, it means that fifty thousand will like it. That's something to go by. But I go most by myself. For if I like a thing, then I know that millions will like it. My mind and my taste are so common that I'm the best editor." He paused, smiled, and slowly, reluctantly added, "There's only one better editor than I am, and that's Frank Munsey. If he likes a thing, then everybody will like it."

Mr. McClure was interested in facts, startling facts, not in philosophical generalizations. He hated, he feared, my dawning theory. He had his own theories, like his readers. They differed among themselves, but they were sure, every one of them. I alone did not know. I alone was not to give my theory. That was our agreement. When I entered into it, however, I made a mental reservation that while I would indeed load my new article on St. Louis with the libelous, dangerous, explosive facts in Folk's possession, I would aim them and the whole story, like a gun, at the current popular theories (including Mr. McClure's); and, I hoped, blow them out of the way for a statement later of my own diagnosis, when I was ready to frame one. I was a good shot in those days. I could write to the understanding and hit the convictions of the public because I shared or had so recently shared them.

I have told how, as the boy chum of a page in the Legislature of California, I had seen from below the machinery and bribery of politics; as a New York reporter I had seen police, political, legislative, and judicial corruption; but I did with these observations what other people do with such disturbing knowledge: I put them off in a separate compartment of the brain. I did not let them alter my conception of life. My picture of the world as it seemed to be was much the same as my readers'. It was this that made me a pretty good journalist; it is this that makes good journalism. The reporter and the editor must sincerely share the cultural ignorance, the superstitions, the beliefs, of their readers, and keep no more than one edition ahead of them. You may beat the public to the news, not to the truth.

The leading question raised in my second article on St. Louis was, "Is democracy a failure?" A trick, a political trick! I had no doubt that the people could and would govern themselves, and Folk had none. The question was put only to appeal to the pride and loyalty of the voters. Folk had shown, and I wrote, how they were herded into parties—the majority of them; how they were led to transfer to the party machines the loyalty they owed to their city, State, and the United States; how they were fooled thus, into voting straight for the nominees of a bi-partisan or a nonpartisan gang of known grafters, who controlled both machines and won elections by swinging the purchasable votes of the minority of worst citizens to the worst ticket; and how these leading grafters used their power to sell out franchises, permissions, and other valuable grants and public properties to the highest bidders, sometimes "good" local business men, sometimes "bad" New York and other "foreign" financiers. Folk had learned, and I reported, that these crooked politicians had intended to sell the Union Market, the old Court House, and the water works. Nor had they given up these plans. The water works—the water supply of the city —was estimated to be worth forty millions by the boodlers, who proposed to let it go for fifteen millions and so make a million each for the fifteen members of the ring.

"The scheme was to do it and skip," said one of the gang to me, "and if you could mix it all up with some filtering scheme, it could be done. . . . It will be done some day."

This we printed, and the facts that these very men, confessing, indicted, some of them on trial, still sat in the municipal council; that they were going on with their grafting there and fighting Folk step by step; that they were organizing the next political campaign to beat him and keep their places, their power, and carry out their piratical plans. *McClure's Magazine* "told the world" all this that St. Louis knew better and in more detail than "we" did, in the hope and in the faith that the citizens of St. Louis would rise up and vindicate the democracy which the American people, Folk, and I believed in. Yes, I too believed in political democracy even while I was observing that all political signs indicated that the boodle gang would defeat Folk if he ran for re-election as circuit attorney in St. Louis, and therefore was advising him to appeal over the heads of the people of St. Louis to the people of Missouri by running for governor! What about the mind of man that can see and think that way? My mind, for example. My brain is at least human. What sort of organ is it that can face all the facts against a belief and still stick to its belief?

Folk had his case against Ed Butler, the boss, transferred from the courts of St. Louis to Columbia, the university town of Missouri. I went there to see that trial, and I felt the sentiment for Folk. It was expressed in chiseled words over the old court house: "Oh, Justice, when driven from other habitations, make this thy dwelling-place." Folk did not attack Butler; he handled his case as if democracy and Missouri were on trial, not the boss, and his final plea, almost whispered, was for "Missouri, Missouri." The boss was convicted. The people were all right—in Missouri. But back in St. Louis they were not right. The first comment I heard there when we all returned was the obstinate declaration, everywhere repeated, that "Butler would never wear the stripes." The boss himself behaved wisely. He stayed indoors for a few weeks—till a committee of citizens from the best residence section called upon him to come out and put through the House of Delegates a bill for the improvement of a street in their neighborhood. And Butler had this done. One of the first greetings to Folk was a warning from a high source that now at length he had gone far enough. He paid no heed to this. He proceeded to the trial of other cases. One of them was of Henry Nicolaus, a rich brewer, for bribery. Mr. Nicolaus pleaded that he did not know what was to be the use of a note for

$140,000 which he had endorsed. Pretty bad? The judge immediately took the case from the jury and directed a verdict of not guilty. This was the first case Folk had lost; he won the next eight, making his record fourteen won to one lost. But the Supreme Court took up the fight. Slowly, one by one, then by wholesale, this highest court of appeal reversed the boodle cases. The machinery of justice broke down under the strain of boodle pull. And the political machinery did not break down. The bi-partisan gang with reformers and business men for backers, united on a boodle ticket, elected it, and—Boss Butler reorganized the "new" House of Delegates with his man for speaker and the superintendent of his garbage plant (in the interest of which he offered the bribe for which he was convicted) for chairman of the Sanitary Committee!

What was the matter? Folk and I asked that question many a time, without finding or framing an answer to it. And all that time we were acting upon the answer, which we must have had in our nervous system somewhere; it simply did not take the form of words in our brains. Our talks were all in the course of making up speeches for his campaign in Missouri for governor of the State, things for him to say to the people of Missouri to persuade them to save him from defeat at the hands of the people of St. Louis. We knew in our bones, and those addresses of Joe Folk to Missouri will show that we knew, that the voters of the State were in that stage of mental innocence which the voters of St. Louis were in when the disclosures of corruption began there. They thought they were innocent; they thought that bad men were deceiving and misleading them; they did not know that they themselves were involved and interested in the corruption. St. Louis found out. Missouri would find out some day, too. When that day came, as it did, then the people of the State would unite with the citizens of St. Louis to stop Folk and his interference with their business.

The people of St. Louis, like the people of Minneapolis and New York, were against bribery in the abstract and against the corruption that involved the police, vice, and petty politicians. They back reformers who attacked these petty evils. When Folk went on to discover that not only Ed Butler's garbage business but the franchises of public service corporations were linked up with garbage and gambling and prostitution, some of the people turned against Folk. They had stock or friends who held stock in these companies and so could see that they did not belong with what they called the honest citizenry. Therefore Folk had to appeal to the people of Missouri. And they elected him governor before he had gone so far that they saw that they were in it. Then Folk had the people of the United States behind him. He was a possibility for president at one time after he was governor of Missouri, when he could not have been reëlected governor of Missouri.

What did this all mean? What was this system? Folk and I could not answer this question either. Like the other question, we knew the answer, but we didn't want to face it—not clearly. I'm sure Folk didn't. One day I saw a book on his living-room table, *Social Problems* by Henry George. He saw me see it; we had just been wondering together about the nature and the cure of political corruption.

"That book explains the whole thing," Folk said.

"Have you read it?" I asked.

"No," he said. "I read into it enough to see that that man has it all sized up, and—I dropped it, as I did another book a socialist brought me."

"Why?" I demanded, astonished.

"Oh," said Folk, "if I once got socialism or any other cut-and-dried solution into my head, I'd be ruined—politically. Couldn't get anywhere. But you are not in politics. Why don't you read them?"

I gave him my reason, which was different from his, much better, I thought. My reason was that I had not only read, I had studied those books under a regular professor of political economy at college, and so knew that there was nothing in them. As Folk was to go on blundering to a career, so I was to go on "scientifically" to trace the system and see if it was the same in other cities as in St. Louis, Minneapolis, and New York. . . .

CHICAGO: AN EXAMPLE OF REFORM

My report on "Philadelphia, Corrupt and Contented," seemed to give the impression, which lasts to this day, that that beautiful old American city was the worst in the land. Not true, of course. It was only older than St. Louis and Minneapolis, and I might have shown that and put Philadelphia in its relative position, if I had gone from there to Boston or some other old town in New England; Boston was the logical next step. But my editorial associates on *McClure's* opposed my choice as they did my theory. They were for Chicago next.

My colleagues harbored, unconsciously perhaps, the theory then general among critics of government: that our political corruption was the worst in the world because we were the youngest nation. Our cities were suffering from what they called growing-pains, and as they grew older they would grow better. James Bryce, the English muckraker (of other countries), and E. L. Godkin, the Irish-English editor of my old paper, the New York *Evening Post*, taught this theory of youth, and I think they put over on Americans (and Europeans, too) the belief that England and English ideas and political practices were higher than ours; British liberalism was the ideal toward which we should strive.

Boston, Mass., and the rest of New England were a fair first test for my theory that England was our fate, not our hope. Boston, New England, was older than Philadelphia, Pa.; it was as proud as Philadelphia was contented; New England was almost as quiet, busy, rich, and aristocratic as old England. But that was the trouble. Boston and New England looked so good and sounded so quiet that we feared an investigation there might prove an anti-climax. I, too, was in doubt; indeed the respectability of Boston made me doubt my theory. I agreed, finally, that we should find something worse than Philadelphia, and Chicago would certainly be that. No doubt about it. I was sure Chicago would provide the sensationally wicked story we were looking for. And I went there with my mind made up: to expose the rough, anarchistic criminality of a wild, young western city. No one could have told me that I was to find there an example of reform, a sensible, aristocratic-democratic reform experiment.

William C. Boyden tried to. I called first on the amiable brother of my assistant managing editor. I told him I was going to "do" Chicago at last.

"Then you'd better meet my partner, Walter L. Fisher," he said.[3]

"Why?" I asked. "Isn't he the reformer you wanted me to write up the last time I was here?"

"Yes," Boyden answered, and he said no more. He didn't even smile. He seemed to fall in with my plan to go straight to the machine bosses and "get the low-down on Chicago." So I started, and right away I discovered that there was something awry. I called on Hinkey Dink and Bathhouse John. They looked their parts; they were ward leaders all right; but they would not, they could not, talk politics. They launched into tirades against the reformers who were messing up everything in Chicago. Reformers! Patiently I pressed my inquiries into the system. Who was the boss of Chicago? Nobody, they said. Who owned the mayor? Nobody. Who controlled the city council? The Voters League, a reform organization! Absurd. I could not take it from these politicians that reformers had such power anywhere,

3. Walter L. Fisher (1862–1935) was a leader of the fight for municipal reform in Chicago between 1901 and 1911 when the Municipal Voters League was at the height of its power. He served as secretary of the interior from 1911 to 1913.

to say nothing of in Chicago. There was something the matter; that I could believe. The machine existed; the system was there. My mental diagram of "the" American city fitted Chicago, but it was out of joint. The machine didn't work; the bosses were in trouble.

Turning to my own profession for guidance, I called on James N. Keeley, the managing editor of the *Tribune*. He proved to be, like me, an editor in a chair that could not hold him. A reporter at bottom, he was interested only in the news and often went out himself to get a story. He had gone as far away as Egypt once to get one. Keeley was a genius; he knew politics, his city, everything; he fascinated me, but he was no use to me. I appealed to Charles Montrose Faye, the city editor of the *Daily News*, who was reported to be "about the wisest guy" in the business. He stuttered, but he was able to express his contempt for me and a refusal to help me in any way.

"Y-you," he blazed, "you N-N-New York n-n-newspaper men, you c-come here knowing j-j-just what y-y-you'll f-f-find and nobody c-c-can tell you anything. I-I-I won't t-t-try. Go on—g-g-get it all all wrong and be damned."

Apparently he thought I was prejudiced. But I wasn't; was I? Like most men, I regarded myself as open-minded and honest at the least. In doubt of myself and in despair of Chicago, I decided to call on and consult Clarence S. Darrow, the philosopher and attorney who defended criminals and must therefore know his city from the underworld up. He might set me right. Having sent in my card, I waited in his outer office, watching his door as anxiously, as hopefully, as any client ever watched and waited. He came out, tall, hulking, absorbed; he held my card in his hand and studied it as if trying to recall where he had seen my name. He kept coming toward me till, close up, he threw back his head, looked into my face, and exclaimed: "Oh, I know. You are the man that believes in honesty!" And he laughed, and laughed, and laughed. He took and he shook my hand, but he laughed till tears came into his eyes. And he did not invite me into his office; he did not answer my questions. They only amused him the more, and I—well, I ran away. It was a year or two before I understood what Darrow meant by my belief in honesty; all I gathered at the time was that he, too, despised me as a person prejudiced by a fool conviction of some sort and not worth a moment even of his loafing time.

Humiliated and angry, I went straight to the supreme political boss of Illinois, Billy Lorimer, afterward U.S. senator. Bosses don't laugh at, they help, a fellow who is down and out, and by the time I reached his office I had whipped myself into a state of mind which expressed itself in my first question.

"What's the matter with your machine here?"

"Nothing," he answered quickly. "Why?"

"Well, it doesn't seem to run," I said. "It's the bummest political organization I have ever seen."

He defended the organization. I cited Tammany, St. Louis, Philadelphia—there were machines that worked; there were bosses that bossed. Here? Bah! He flared up and said something about the people of Chicago. "People!" I laughed at him the way Darrow had just laughed at me. He was a boss that believed in the people. He mentioned "the reformers." Reformers! I said I had seen reformers, some even of his, and they were all alike. No real boss ever suffered anything more than temporary inconvenience from reformers. He thought I'd find that Chicago reformers were different. I thought it was the Chicago politicians that were different: weak, incompetent—

"You," he charged, "with your sneers at reformers and Chicago and—all. How long have you been here? What do you know about us? What reformers have you seen?"

I laughed, and he: "Say, have you seen that son of a bitch, Fisher?"

I wilted. I feel even now that I owe it to myself to say that it was upon the authority of the big boss himself that I turned to look at Chicago as an example of reform. Chicago! The stuff was there for the other, the original story; it still is: the police graft, the traffic of authority with criminals, gamblers, prostitutes, liquor dealers, all sorts of thieves, and some sorts of murderers. The evil of Chicago was obvious, general, bold. I was warned again and again against my wanderings around in the Loop at night; the wide-openness of protected vice and crime fascinated my bulging eyes. Hinkey Dink himself said I ought not to walk home alone from his place. But I lived in a downtown club, and as a newspaper man I could not keep away from the scenes that were evidences of a great news story. How our readers would have liked the stuff I was seeing! The New York Tenderloin was a model of order and virtue compared with the badly regulated, police-paid criminal lawlessness of the Chicago Loop and its spokes. Just the same, all this was not what in newspaper parlance is called the feature of a news story of Chicago; evidently. Was it? With reluctance and doubt I acted upon the advice of the head and front of this system. I returned to Boyden's office and saw that—partner of his, Walter Fisher.

Fisher punished me with scorn for my scorn of him. Boyden must have described my attitude to him. Boyden had too much humor not to report my sure belief that Fisher and Chicago reformers in general were not worth my attention. So, though he received me politely, Fisher was short with his answers. No doubt my hangover of skepticism annoyed him. I had to acknowledge that he had some power, he and his Voters League, but how did he get it? How did he hold it? What was he doing with it?

"You are not making a very good government," I remarked sarcastically, citing the sinful scenes I had seen.

No, Fisher answered coldly. They were not out for good government, not yet. That might come later. For the present the League was fighting for representative government. The city council had been bought and owned by Yerkes, the street railway magnate, and other business men who wanted franchises, extensions, and privileges generally. Fisher and the Chicago reformers were forcing the aldermen to stand for the city, and in dealing with business men, to represent the public interest in making bargains. They were fighting first the corruption of their own class, letting the police evils of the lawless wait; they were reforming the good, not the bad, people. That might explain the popular support they had won for their movement. But just how did they manage it?

Fisher offered to this question no answer that meant anything to me. He would not generalize. He showed me files of information about candidates and politicians, such as I had seen in New York and Philadelphia. Ammunition. How was it used? He outlined in a bored tone of voice the scheme of the Municipal Voters League. No light in that. It was all incomprehensible, politically, till we happened to speak of the Seventeenth Ward, which the League carried one year for a Republican, the next year for a Democrat, the third for a Republican again. How did they do that?

Fisher came to life. His face lighted up; a keen shrewd look came into it, a twinkle in his eyes, and he told me the story. It was a story of politics. Another ward was another, different story, but it was politics. Fisher was a politician. The methods of these League reformers were the methods of politics: they dealt with each ward according to the actual situation there. They got the facts, knew the candidates, politicians, parties, grafts, and the people in a ward, and then, with this information, by publicity and by trading they swung the anonymous minority that followed the League all together to one side and one ultimate purpose.

Very practical politics, this, but was it wisdom? It was not. It was a sort of instinct, the Chicago instinct. It just happened. Walter L. Fisher was the third of the leaders of the League, which itself evolved by—accident, or instinct. Some young fellows, William Kent, the son of a millionaire; John Maynard Harlan, the son of a justice of the Supreme Court; and others of that ilk, ran for and were elected aldermen. With reporters like Finley Peter Dunne to report them, they made scenes in that "bear garden," the board of aldermen. They made informed but challenging speeches, charging their crooked colleagues with the facts, risking murder.

"Couldn't accomplish anything," said Billy Kent, whom Fisher called in to tell me the early history of the movement. "We were voted down, but we did make the meetings of the board as interesting as loud noises and bad smells could make them; we furnished the humorous reporters with 'news,' which soon got the people watching. Antics, farce, melodrama! Harlan was our orator, and he was some orator. He'd walk down in front of a boodler and call him a crook. With the details we raked up and the bad names the rest of us invented, Harlan would sock him —for Peter Dunne to hear, see, quote, describe. Some fun."

With such scenes in the limelight the people were aroused, and two hundred leading citizens met, with Lyman J. Gage, a leading banker, at their head, to do something. The two hundred appointed a committee of fifteen to find something to do. One of the fifteen drew a plan for a new municipal party—the old, old scheme. Chicago set out like any other city on the beaten path that has been proven an *impasse* over and over again. But Chicago had men who knew or felt that this was all wrong. They blocked this move. They blocked a motion to investigate conditions. "We know enough," they said; "a committee of investigation is a stall." They blocked a proposal to go to the corrupt State Legislature for a new charter, and they would not wait for the next mayoralty election to elect a good business man as mayor to give them good government. They maneuvered the big committee to seek a man, one man, to organize a league of voters to fight every fight that came up. He was not to run for office; he was to be a leader, a boss, with a minority to swing.

George E. Cole[4] was the man they chose. He was a "second-class business man" (he said to me), about five feet tall and between two and three feet across the shoulders—a fighter. He looked like a sea captain, and he worked and he talked like one. He picked a crew of nine—chosen for what they could do, not for what they represented—got rid of the big committees, and without plans, began to "let people know we were there." With his short legs apart, his weak eyes blinking, he stood on the bridge in the limelight and shouted that he was going to beat the crooks up for re-election. Chicago likes audacity and is always willing to have anybody try anything once; no matter who you are, where you come from, or what you set out to do, Chicago will give you a chance. The sporting spirit is the spirit of Chicago. When, therefore, George Cole stood up and said that he and a small, unknown committee were out to clean up the Board of Aldermen, the town looked, laughed, and asked how. "We're going to publish the records of the thieves that want to get back at the trough," said Cole, and he produced the facts, acts, votes that Kent, Harlan, and the other decent aldermen had on their indecent colleagues. Cole said that of the thirty-four retiring aldermen twenty-six were rogues; some of the rogues quit; others were beaten in their wards, each ward being handled by itself. "Old King Cole," "Boss Cole," was charged with politics, blackmail, deals—he did not care. He was as terrible with respectable candidates as he was with roughnecks; he defied the pull of leading citizens, even if they were (as they were some of them) on the old Committee of Twenty that gave the

League birth. No respecter of persons, parties, or liberal principles, he carried the League to victories and a power that amazed and amused Chicago. When his health failed he was succeeded by Billy Kent, and when Kent was exhausted he gave way to Fisher, who carried on the methods of the League, except that, having power now, he did not have to be noisy. He printed the facts quietly, made deals in the wards, got his majority of aldermen, and then organized, instructed, and pledged them right in his private office. I saw that done one night. In Fisher's office I saw him, a reform boss, perform exactly like a regular political boss, browbeat and control a various lot of (honest and dishonest) politicians, and then send them out, watched and controlled, to represent what they all knew or agreed was the best interest of the whole people of Chicago. And as boss and secretary, Walter L. Fisher dealt with the big financial interests that sought riches out of the commonwealth of Chicago and made them give some service. It was a long, slow, hard task; it lasted years, ten or twelve, and when I wrote it I described this as an example of a reform that was working. And of course, from a journalistic point of view, the exhibition of Chicago as something for other cities to imitate was a sensation; it was more astonishing "news" than the graft article which I had meant to write could possibly have been. Here was a way to do it, and other cities did follow Chicago's lead. That is to say, they set up Municipal Voters Leagues, and sure enough, some of them got results; not good government, not normal representative government, but—a temporary betterment.

Chicago failed finally; it is ripe now for either a sensational political story or a new reform movement. And I was seeing, and I noted in my report, the beginnings of the end, without realizing that those beginnings were to be the end. Walter L. Fisher, afterward in the Cabinet of President Taft and a man now with an international reputation for ability and acumen,

4. Hoyt King's *Citizen Cole of Chicago* (Chicago, 1931) tells more of this story.

was not and never has been a radical. He did not see or touch sources of privilege. All he used his great power in Chicago for was to persuade, or, if need be, force the business interests that had to come to him to get their privileges, to make open terms with and render some service to his city. It was just what big business said it wanted, a government that understands and is just to business. And they, those business men and their fellow business men, in Chicago, in New York, everywhere—they hated and fought and clamored and wriggled and bribed out of their contracts with the practical, honest, fair "reform" government of Chicago. And finally they killed it as literally as the gunmen of Chicago now kill one another, and as safely. Why? They said (to me) that what they wanted was, not this so-called representative, but good government. . . .

SOME THEORIES: BIG BUSINESS AND PRIVILEGED BUSINESS

My *Ohio: a Tale of Two Cities* must have struck some readers as valuable. Soon after it was published, Tom Johnson[5] met on a train a stranger who said he had seen the check the mayor sent me to pay for it, and the amount was large, as large as the witness. Mr. Johnson embarrassed him by remarking that "that was funny. I'll ask Steffens if he ever saw the check," he said. "For I'm Tom Johnson, and I never saw it."

The stranger choked and gradually moved away, but before he went he insisted that he had seen the check. His banker had shown it to him, and it was indorsed as received by me and as paid by the bank. Johnson may have been half persuaded, for he asked me if I had "ever seen anything like it."

By way of answer I related how I had discovered that when I wanted to get at the springs of thought and action in a man I was to write about, I should ask him about other men, and usually the witness would attribute to all others the motives and purposes which guided him. A vain man thought everybody was "after publicity," an ambitious man that his neighbors were "after office," a money-maker that we all are "after money." And just for fun, I reminded Tom Johnson that he had asked me once if Bob La Follette wasn't a demagogue. While Tom Johnson was fumbling with this half-truth, I offered him another; I rattled on about the need men felt to explain away a disturbing fact or idea to save themselves from the labor of thinking it out. Mayor Johnson, for example, had been disturbed by the appearance of Governor La Follette on the right side, and having no time to investigate, had accepted thoughtlessly of the governor the enemies' explanation of both of them. And the man who had seen the mayor's check to me had probably seen only a banker who was probably answering all the facts I put into my Ohio article by saying that probably I had been well paid by the rich mayor for reporting them. That would answer, not only those facts, but all doubts about Tom Johnson, too, and me. As the mayor knew, many people go to their bankers for advice, and not only on money matters; and they get it, too. Bankers, who have no more wisdom than they have money of their own, pay out opinions as they pay out credit, with the awe-inspiring manner of one who could pay more, much more, out of his reserves, if he liked.

Boss Cox,[6] who was most injured by the article, did not openly deny or privately resent it. He was out of power for a term, which he spent in repairing his neglected machine.

The practical politicians profited by exposure and defeat; not the reformers.

In the interval between Cox's defeat

---

5. Tom L. Johnson (1854–1911) was an inventor and street-railroad magnate. "Converted" by Henry George's *Progress and Poverty*, he led a reform movement in Cleveland, Ohio, and was elected mayor three times.

6. "Boss" George B. Cox (1853–1916) was head of the Republican "machine" of Cincinnati and dominated the city government there during most of the period between 1888 and 1910.

and his restoration to power I met him at a national convention of the Republican party. He greeted me warmly, but briefly; he made no reference to my article; he said nothing at all then. A couple of days later there was a secret session of the dominating bosses of the convention, and a group of correspondents waited outside the decisive door for hours. When Cox came out first, alone, he waved us aside. "Not a word," he said roughly, but his eye fell upon me and he added, "except to you." He drew me aside, told me "what was doing," and left me without any injunction to wait with the news till it reached the convention. I did hold it; I was not filing spot news. I took Cox's confidence as I felt he meant it, as a sign of his good will, of his appreciation of the fact that I had not made the most or the worst of the goods he knew I had on him.

The bosses and bad men generally "stood for the truth" and recognized my impersonal restraint in what I reported. It was the good men who resented the facts, partly, no doubt, because they don't know and won't recognize the truth.

Governor Myron T. Herrick of Ohio, for example, showed his indignation years later when I met him in Paris as the U.S. ambassador to France. He said I had walked into his office at Columbus and told him to his face that he was not the governor, and that he had had to put me out. Inexact. When I called on him the ex-banker was very hospitable, even confidential. He assumed that he and I were both good citizens on the same side in politics, anti-graft, for reform, but not for men who went too far, like Tom Johnson. To stop the eloquence and get down to business, I asked him who was the actual governor of his State.

"I am," he snapped.

"Good," I said; "then you can tell me the inside story of ———" and I mentioned a couple of scandalous deals of his administration, acts upon which he had said one thing and done another. He couldn't, he said, and he convinced me that he really did not himself understand what had happened. He had listened to advice, and being a reasonable man, had taken it. So I said I must find the actual governor, "your governor," I put it, "who gives you the advice you act on." He was indignant, but when I admitted his innocence and besought him to name the man who, having more power than the governor, put over those deals which I had to know about, he was placated. He soon was smiling again; we had a pleasant walk in the dusk to his residence and a talk which revealed the sweet reasonableness, the consideration for others, the wish to serve—as well as the amiable willingness to take and convey diplomatically an order from above—which made Mr. Herrick the charming, successful war- and peace-time ambassador he became. What he bore so long against me was that after our nice talk I went off and wrote that he was only the titular head of the State, who was lost and bewildered when his boss, Mark Hanna, died.

"Big business" was, and it still is, the current name of the devil, the root of all evil, political and economic. It is a blind phrase, useless; it leads nowhere. We can't abolish business, we cannot regulate big business, and we are finding that we cannot limit bigness in business, which must grow. The phrase does not cover what we mean. I know that; I must have known it, else Tom Johnson could not have told it me. As early as St. Louis I had seen and written that the big businesses which were active in political corruption were the railroads, public service corporations, banks, etc., which are "big," but also saloons, gambling and bawdy houses, which are small. And I had seen and written that what these big and little businesses all had in common was not size but the need of privileges: franchises and special legislation, which required legislative corruption; protective tariffs, interpretations of laws in their special interest or leniency or "protection" in the enforcement of laws, calling for "pulls" with judges, prosecutors, and the police. As Tom John-son said, then, it was "privilege" that was the source of the evil; it was "privileged business" that was the devil, and I had been describing and meaning this all the time I had been writing "big business." Why? My old German professor of psy-chology had taught us to distinguish be-tween perception and apperception, be-tween seeing things with the eyes and reaching out with the mind to grasp them, what the new school of *Gestalt* psychology now calls "insight." Tom Johnson was tempting me to apperceive the perception that it was privilege that hurt us. Not easy, this; it was consequential; it went to the bottom of all our moral culture of right and wrong.

If it was privilege that caused what we called evil, it was privilege that had to be dealt with, not men. Not big men, not bad men, not crooks, and not capitalists—not even the capitalist class! Punishment of in-dividuals, the class struggle and strikes, wars—all hatred, vengeance, force, were unscientific. To put in prison a man who bought government to get a street railway franchise was wrong; we should put the franchise where men can't get it. To shift our votes from one to another of two po-litical parties, both of which are organized to serve the privileged or the privilege-seekers, was folly. To throw out the ras-cals and put into office honest men without removing that which makes good men do bad things was as irrational as our experi-ence had taught us it was "unpractical." The international wars of corrupted gov-ernments for trade routes, foreign mar-kets, "empire" and the natural resources of backward countries, strikes and the class war for the conquest of economic power and advantages—these were as senseless as passing laws for reform and for peace. It's all upside down. What so-ciety does is to teach the ideal of success, set up the temptation of power and riches to men and nations—if they are brave enough to risk and able enough to escape the threats of penalties for getting caught.

These warnings keep off all but the best men, biologically best. Then when these best men succeed we honor them, and if they slip we hate and punish them. What we ought to do is to let the losers of the race go, and take down the prizes we offer to the winners.

Tom Johnson was proposing in Cleve-land to take down the prizes by wiping out privileges and all hope of privileges. His theory was that the big business men there would then come over on the city's side and be for, instead of against, good govern-ment. That was what he meant when he told his old colleagues in the street railway and other public service corporations that if he could take away their franchises they would soon be running for office in order still to have big business to do. It was his own personal experience. When he rid himself of his incentives to contribute to the political machine he quit that, became a reformer and the mayor and manager of the biggest business in Cleveland, the city's business.

His proposed method of taking over the prizes for anti-social conduct was public ownership and operation of all public serv-ice corporations and the taxation of land values, not socialism, but the Henry George plan for the closing up of all the sources of unearned wealth. His public ownership was in the interest, not only of efficiency and economy in the manage-ment of street railways, etc., but to get those businesses and those able private operators out of politics. As to his new incentive: he lost money; it cost him much more than his salary to be mayor and carry on his policy. The incentive of profit was lacking entirely, but it was obvious that his ambition to set an example in Cleveland of a solution of the universal political-eco-nomic problem of government was a stronger motive than profit in a man with imagination. I have often wondered why more men don't see that, and the answer that occurred to me came also from Tom Johnson. He thought that by removing the cause of his anti-social conduct, he changed, but he had his purpose, too, his ideal, the vision he developed out of a book. Few men have such ideals. The ideals of America, for example, the ideals that came to Ohio probably from New England and from Old England, are antiquated, dried up, contradictory; honesty and wealth, morality and success, individual achievement and respectability, privileges and democracy—these won't take us very far.

There was something wrong in our ends as well as in our beginnings, in what we are after as well as in what is after us, in American ideals as well as in American conduct and its causes.

2. THE NEW NATIONALISM[1]

By Theodore Roosevelt

EDITORS' NOTE.—Theodore Roosevelt (1858–1919), twenty-sixth President of the United States, was born in New York City and educated at Harvard. As a young man he combined a career in practical politics with the writing of history. Between 1882 and 1898 he was a member of the New York Assembly, of the United States Civil Service Commission, of the New York City Board of Police Commissioners, and assistant secretary of the Navy. From his adventures with the "Rough Riders" in Cuba he came home in 1898 to be elected governor of New York. Vice-President under William McKinley in 1900, he became President at McKinley's death, in 1901, and was elected President in 1904.

When Theodore Roosevelt spoke in 1910 on the occasion of the dedication of the John Brown Battlefield at Osawatomie, Kansas, he was not a candidate for the presidency. But this speech indicates quite cogently the union of his earlier program with the conception of using governmental power to promote a larger measure of social justice, a combination which was so important in his presidential campaign of 1912.

We come here to-day to commemorate one of the epoch-making events of the long struggle for the rights of man—the long struggle for the uplift of humanity. Our country—this great republic—means nothing unless it means the triumph of a real democracy, the triumph of popular government, and, in the long run, of an economic system under which each man shall be guaranteed the opportunity to show the best that there is in him. That is why the history of America is now the central feature of the history of the world; for the world has set its face hopefully toward our democracy; and, O my fellow citizens, each one of you carries on your shoulders not only the burden of doing well for the sake of your own country, but the burden of doing well and of seeing that this nation does well for the sake of mankind.

There have been two great crises in our country's history: first, when it was formed, and then, again, when it was perpetuated; and, in the second of these great crises—in the time of stress and strain which culminated in the Civil War, on the outcome of which depended the justification of what had been done earlier, you men of the Grand Army, you men who fought through the Civil War, not only did

1. Theodore Roosevelt, *The New Nationalism* (New York, 1910), pp. 3–5, 7–21, 23–33.

you justify your generation, not only did you render life worth living for our generation, but you justified the wisdom of Washington and Washington's colleagues. If this republic had been founded by them only to be split asunder into fragments when the strain came, then the judgment of the world would have been that Washington's work was not worth doing. It was you who crowned Washington's work, as you carried to achievement the high purpose of Abraham Lincoln.

Now, with this second period of our history the name of John Brown will be forever associated; and Kansas was the theater upon which the first act of the second of our great national life dramas was played. It was the result of the struggle in Kansas which determined that our country should be in deed as well as in name devoted to both union and freedom; that the great experiment of democratic government on a national scale should succeed and not fail. In name we had the Declaration of Independence in 1776; but we gave the lie by our acts to the words of the Declaration of Independence until 1865; and words count for nothing except in so far as they represent acts. This is true everywhere; but, O my friends, it should be truest of all in political life. A broken promise is bad enough in private life. It is worse in the field of politics. No man is worth his salt in public life who makes on the stump a pledge which he does not keep after election; and, if he makes such a pledge and does not keep it, hunt him out of public life. I care for the great deeds of the past chiefly as spurs to drive us onward in the present. I speak of the men of the past partly that they may be honored by our praise of them, but more that they may serve as examples for the future. . . .

I do not speak of this struggle of the past merely from the historic standpoint. Our interest is primarily in the application to-day of the lessons taught by the contest of half a century ago. It is of little use for us to pay lip loyalty to the mighty men of the past unless we sincerely endeavor to apply to the problems of the present precisely the qualities which in other crises enabled the men of that day to meet those crises. It is half melancholy and half amusing to see the way in which well-meaning people gather to do honor to the men who, in company with John Brown, and under the lead of Abraham Lincoln, faced and solved the great problems of the nineteenth century, while, at the same time, these same good people nervously shrink from, or frantically denounce, those who are trying to meet the problems of the twentieth century in the spirit which was accountable for the successful solution of the problems of Lincoln's time.

Of that generation of men to whom we owe so much, the man to whom we owe most is, of course, Lincoln. Part of our debt to him is because he forecast our present struggle and saw the way out. He said:—

I hold that while man exists it is his duty to improve not only his own condition, but to assist in ameliorating mankind.

And again:—

Labor is prior to, and independent of, capital. Capital is only the fruit of labor, and could never have existed if labor had not first existed. Labor is the superior of capital, and deserves much the higher consideration.

If that remark was original with me, I should be even more strongly denounced as a communist agitator than I shall be anyhow. It is Lincoln's. I am only quoting it; and that is one side; that is the side the capitalist should hear. Now, let the working-man hear his side.

Capital has its rights, which are as worthy of protection as any other rights. . . . Nor should this lead to a war upon the owners of property. Property is the fruit of labor; . . . property is desirable; is a positive good in the world.

And then comes a thoroughly Lincoln-like sentence:—

Let not him who is houseless pull down the house of another, but let him work diligently and build one for himself, thus by example assuring that his own shall be safe from violence when built.

It seems to me that, in these words, Lincoln took substantially the attitude that we ought to take; he showed the proper sense of proportion in his relative estimates of capital and labor, of human rights and property rights. Above all, in this speech, as in many others, he taught a lesson in wise kindliness and charity; an indispensable lesson to us of to-day. But this wise kindliness and charity never weakened his arm or numbed his heart. We cannot afford weakly to blind ourselves to the actual conflict which faces us to-day. The issue is joined, and we must fight or fail.

In every wise struggle for human betterment one of the main objects, and often the only object, has been to achieve in large measure equality of opportunity. In the struggle for this great end, nations rise from barbarism to civilization, and through it people press forward from one stage of enlightenment to the next. One of the chief factors in progress is the destruction of special privilege. The essence of any struggle for healthy liberty has always been, and must always be, to take from some one man or class of men the right to enjoy power, or wealth, or position, or immunity, which has not been earned by service to his or their fellows. That is what you fought for in the Civil War, and that is what we strive for now.

At many stages in the advance of humanity, this conflict between the men who possess more than they have earned and the men who have earned more than they possess is the central condition of progress. In our day it appears as the struggle of free men to gain and hold the right of self-government as against the special interests, who twist the methods of free government into machinery for defeating the popular will. At every stage, and under all circumstances, the essence of the struggle is to equalize opportunity, destroy privilege, and give to the life and citizenship of every individual the highest possible value both to himself and to the commonwealth. That is nothing new. All I ask in civil life is what you fought for in the Civil War. I ask that civil life be carried on according to the spirit in which the army was carried on. You never get perfect justice, but the effort in handling the army was to bring to the front the men who could do the job. Nobody grudged promotion to Grant, or Sherman, or Thomas, or Sheridan, because they earned it. The only complaint was when a man got promotion which he did not earn.

Practical equality of opportunity for all citizens, when we achieve it, will have two great results. First, every man will have a fair chance to make of himself all that in him lies; to reach the highest point to which his capacities, unassisted by special privilege of his own and unhampered by the special privilege of others, can carry him, and to get for himself and his family substantially what he has earned. Second, equality of opportunity means that the commonwealth will get from every citizen the highest service of which he is capable. No man who carries the burden of the special privileges of another can give to the commonwealth that service to which it is fairly entitled.

I stand for the square deal. But when I say that I am for the square deal, I mean not merely that I stand for fair play under the present rules of the game, but that I stand for having those rules changed so as to work for a more substantial equality of opportunity and of reward for equally good service. One word of warning, which, I think, is hardly necessary in Kansas. When I say I want a square deal for the poor man, I do not mean that I want a square deal for the man who remains poor because he has not got the energy to work for himself. If a man who has had a chance will not make good, then he has got to quit. And you men of the Grand Army, you want justice for the brave man who fought, and punishment for the coward who shirked his work. Is not that so?

Now, this means that our government,

national and state, must be freed from the sinister influence or control of special interests. Exactly as the special interests of cotton and slavery threatened our political integrity before the Civil War, so now the great special business interests too often control and corrupt the men and methods of government for their own profit. We must drive the special interests out of politics. That is one of our tasks to-day. Every special interest is entitled to justice—full, fair, and complete—and, now, mind you, if there were any attempt by mob violence to plunder and work harm to the special interest, whatever it may be, that I most dislike, and the wealthy man, whomsoever he may be, for whom I have the greatest contempt, I would fight for him, and you would if you were worth your salt. He should have justice. For every special interest is entitled to justice, but not one is entitled to a vote in Congress, to a voice on the bench, or to representation in any public office. The Constitution guarantees protection to property, and we must make that promise good. But it does not give the right of suffrage to any corporation.

The true friend of property, the true conservative, is he who insists that property shall be the servant and not the master of the commonwealth; who insists that the creature of man's making shall be the servant and not the master of the man who made it. The citizens of the United States must effectively control the mighty commercial forces which they have themselves called into being.

There can be no effective control of corporations while their political activity remains. To put an end to it will be neither a short nor an easy task, but it can be done.

We must have complete and effective publicity of corporate affairs, so that the people may know beyond peradventure whether the corporations obey the law and whether their management entitles them to the confidence of the public. It is necessary that laws should be passed to prohibit the use of corporate funds directly or indirectly for political purposes; it is still more necessary that such laws should be thoroughly enforced. Corporate expenditures for political purposes, and especially such expenditures by public service corporations, have supplied one of the principal sources of corruption in our political affairs.

It has become entirely clear that we must have government supervision of the capitalization, not only of public service corporations, including, particularly, railways, but of all corporations doing an interstate business. I do not wish to see the nation forced into the ownership of the railways if it can possibly be avoided, and the only alternative is thoroughgoing and effective regulation, which shall be based on a full knowledge of all the facts, including a physical valuation of property. This physical valuation is not needed, or, at least, is very rarely needed, for fixing rates; but it is needed as the basis of honest capitalization.

We have come to recognize that franchises should never be granted except for a limited time, and never without proper provision for compensation to the public. It is my personal belief that the same kind and degree of control and supervision which should be exercised over public service corporations should be extended also to combinations which control necessaries of life, such as meat, oil, and coal, or which deal in them on an important scale. I have no doubt that the ordinary man who has control of them is much like ourselves. I have no doubt he would like to do well, but I want to have enough supervision to help him realize that desire to do well.

I believe that the officers, and, especially, the directors, of corporations should be held personally responsible when any corporation breaks the law.

Combinations in industry are the result of an imperative economic law which cannot be repealed by political legislation. The effort at prohibiting all combination has substantially failed. The way out lies, not in attempting to prevent such combinations, but in completely controlling them in the interest of the public welfare. For that purpose the Federal Bureau of Corporations is an agency of first importance. Its powers, and, therefore, its efficiency, as well as that of the Interstate Commerce Commission, should be largely increased. We have a right to expect from the Bureau of Corporations and from the Interstate Commerce Commission a very high grade of public service. We should be as sure of the proper conduct of the interstate railways and the proper management of interstate business as we are now sure of the conduct and management of the national banks, and we should have as effective supervision in one case as in the other. The Hepburn Act, and the amendment to the Act in the shape in which it finally passed Congress at the last session, represent a long step in advance, and we must go yet further.

There is a widespread belief among our people that, under the methods of making tariffs which have hitherto obtained, the special interests are too influential. Probably this is true of both the big special interests and the little special interests. These methods have put a premium on selfishness, and, naturally, the selfish big interests have gotten more than their smaller, though equally selfish, brothers. The duty of Congress is to provide a method by which the interest of the whole people shall be all that receives consideration. To this end there must be an expert tariff commission, wholly removed from the possibility of political pressure or of improper business influence. Such a commission can find the real difference between cost of production, which is mainly the difference of labor cost here and abroad. As fast as its recommendations are made, I believe in revising one schedule at a time. A general revision of the tariff almost inevitably leads to log-rolling and the subordination of the general public interest to local and special interests. . . .

No man should receive a dollar unless that dollar has been fairly earned. Every dollar received should represent a dollar's worth of service rendered—not gambling in stocks, but service rendered. The really big fortune, the swollen fortune, by the mere fact of its size acquires qualities which differentiate it in kind as well as in degree from what is possessed by men of relatively small means. Therefore, I believe in a graduated income tax on big fortunes, and in another tax which is far more easily collected and far more effective—a graduated inheritance tax on big fortunes, properly safeguarded against evasion and increasing rapidly in amount with the size of the estate.

The people of the United States suffer from periodical financial panics to a degree substantially unknown among the other nations which approach us in financial strength. There is no reason why we should suffer what they escape. It is of profound importance that our financial system should be promptly investigated, and so thoroughly and effectively revised as to make it certain that hereafter our currency will no longer fail at critical times to meet our needs. . . .

Of conservation I shall speak more at length elsewhere. Conservation means development as much as it does protection. I recognize the right and duty of this generation to develop and use the natural resources of our land; but I do not recognize the right to waste them, or to rob, by wasteful use, the generations that come after us. I ask nothing of the nation except that it so behave as each farmer here behaves with reference to his own children. That farmer is a poor creature who skins the land and leaves it worthless to his children. The farmer is a good farmer who, having enabled the land to support himself and to provide for the education of his children, leaves it to them a little better than he found it himself. I believe the same thing of a nation.

Moreover, I believe that the natural resources must be used for the benefit of all our people, and not monopolized for the benefit of the few, and here again is another case in which I am accused of taking a revolutionary attitude. . . .

. . . And now a special word to the farmer. I want to see him make the farm as fine a farm as it can be made; and let him remember to see that the improvement goes on indoors as well as out; let him remember that the farmer's wife should have her share of thought and attention just as much as the farmer himself.

Nothing is more true than that excess of every kind is followed by reaction; a fact which should be pondered by reformer and reactionary alike. We are face to face with new conceptions of the relations of property to human welfare, chiefly because certain advocates of the rights of property as against the rights of men have been pushing their claims too far. The man who wrongly holds that every human right is secondary to his profit must now give way to the advocate of human welfare, who rightly maintains that every man holds his property subject to the general right of the community to regulate its use to whatever degree the public welfare may require it.

But I think we may go still further. The right to regulate the use of wealth in the public interest is universally admitted. Let us admit also the right to regulate the terms and conditions of labor, which is the chief element of wealth, directly in the interest of the common good. The fundamental thing to do for every man is to give him a chance to reach a place in which he will make the greatest possible contribution to the public welfare. Understand what I say there. Give him a chance, not push him up if he will not be pushed. Help any man who stumbles; if he lies down, it is a poor job to try to carry him; but if he is a worthy man, try your best to see that he gets a chance to show the worth that is in him. No man can be a good citizen unless he has a wage more than sufficient to cover the bare cost of living, and hours of labor short enough so that after his day's work is done he will have time and energy to bear his share in the management of the community, to help in carrying the general load. We keep countless men from being good citizens by the conditions of life with which we surround them. We need comprehensive workmen's compensation acts, both state and national laws to regulate child labor and work for women, and, especially, we need in our common schools not merely education in book learning, but also practical training for daily life and work. We need to enforce better sanitary conditions for our workers and to extend the use of safety appliances for our workers in industry and commerce, both within and between the states. Also, friends, in the interest of the workingman himself we need to set our faces like flint against mob violence just as against corporate greed; against violence and injustice and lawlessness by wage workers just as much as against lawless cunning and greed and selfish arrogance of employers. If I could ask but one thing of my fellow countrymen, my request would be that, whenever they go in for reform, they remember the two sides, and that they always exact justice from one side as much as from the other. . . . If the reactionary man, who thinks of nothing but the rights of property, could have his way, he would bring about a revolution; and one of my chief fears in connection with progress comes because I do not want to see our people, for lack of proper leadership, compelled to follow men whose intentions are excellent, but whose eyes are a little too wild to make it really safe to trust them. . . .

National efficiency has many factors. It is a necessary result of the principle of conservation widely applied. In the end it will determine our failure or success as a nation. National efficiency has to do, not only with natural resources and with men, but it is equally concerned with institutions. The state must be made efficient for the work which concerns only the people of the state; and the nation for that which concerns all the people. There must remain no neutral ground to serve as a refuge for lawbreakers, and especially for lawbreakers of great wealth, who can hire the vulpine legal cunning which will teach them how to avoid both jurisdictions. It is a misfortune when the national legislature fails to do its duty in providing a national remedy, so that the only national activity is the purely negative activity of the judiciary in forbidding the state to exercise power in the premises.

I do not ask for overcentralization; but I do ask that we work in a spirit of broad and far-reaching nationalism when we work for what concerns our people as a whole. We are all Americans. Our common interests are as broad as the continent. I speak to you here in Kansas exactly as I would speak in New York or Georgia, for the most vital problems are those which affect us all alike. The national government belongs to the whole American people, and where the whole American people are interested, that interest can be guarded effectively only by the national government. The betterment which we seek must be accomplished, I believe, mainly through the national government.

The American people are right in demanding that New Nationalism, without which we cannot hope to deal with new problems. The New Nationalism puts the national need before sectional or personal advantage. It is impatient of the utter confusion that results from local legislatures attempting to treat national issues as local issues. It is still more impatient of the impotence which springs from overdivision of governmental powers, the impotence which makes it possible for local selfishness or for legal cunning, hired by wealthy special interests, to bring national activities to a deadlock. This New Nationalism regards the executive power as the steward of the public welfare. It demands of the judiciary that it shall be interested primarily in human welfare rather than in property, just as it demands that the representative body shall represent all the people rather than any one class or section of the people.

I believe in shaping the ends of government to protect property as well as human welfare. Normally, and in the long run, the ends are the same; but whenever the alternative must be faced, I am for men and not for property, as you were in the Civil War. I am far from underestimating the importance of dividends; but I rank dividends below human character. Again, I do not have any sympathy with the reformer who says he does not care for dividends. Of course, economic welfare is necessary, for a man must pull his own weight and be able to support his family. I know well that the reformers must not bring upon the people economic ruin, or the reforms themselves will go down in the ruin. But we must be ready to face temporary disaster, whether or not brought on by those who will war against us to the knife. Those who oppose all reform will do well to remember that ruin in its worst form is inevitable if our national life brings us nothing better than swollen fortunes for the few and the triumph in both politics and business of a sordid and selfish materialism.

If our political institutions were perfect, they would absolutely prevent the political domination of money in any part of our affairs. We need to make our political representatives more quickly and sensitively responsive to the people whose servants they are. More direct action by the people in their own affairs under proper safeguards is vitally necessary. The direct primary is a step in this direction, if it is associated with a corrupt practices act effective to prevent the advantage of the man willing recklessly and unscrupulously to spend money over his more honest competitor. It is particularly important that all moneys received or expended for campaign purposes should be publicly accounted for, not only after election, but before election as well. Political action must be made simpler, easier, and freer from confusion for every citizen. I believe that the prompt removal of unfaithful or incompetent public servants should be made easy and sure in whatever way experience shall show to be most expedient in any given class of cases.

One of the fundamental necessities in a representative government such as ours is to make certain that the men to whom the people delegate their power shall serve the people by whom they are elected, and not the special interests. I believe that every national officer, elected or appointed, should be forbidden to perform any service or receive any compensation, directly or indirectly, from interstate corporations; and a similar provision could not fail to be useful within the states.

The object of government is the welfare of the people. The material progress and prosperity of a nation are desirable chiefly so far as they lead to the moral and material welfare of all good citizens. Just in proportion as the average man and woman are honest, capable of sound judgment and high ideals, active in public affairs—but, first of all, sound in their home life, and the father and mother of healthy children whom they bring up well—just so far, and no farther, we may count our civilization a success. We must have—I believe we have already—a genuine and permanent moral awakening, without which no wisdom of legislation or administration really means anything; and, on the other hand, we must try to secure the social and economic legislation without which any improvement due to purely moral agitation is necessarily evanescent. . . . No matter how honest and decent we are in our private lives, if we do not have the right kind of law and the right kind of administration of the law, we cannot go forward as a nation. That is imperative; but it must be an addition to, and not a substitution for, the qualities that make us good citizens. In the last analysis, the most important elements in any man's career must be the sum of those qualities which, in the aggregate, we speak of as character. If he has not got it, then no law that the wit of man can devise, no administration of the law by the boldest and strongest executive, will avail to help him. We must have the right kind of character—character that makes a man, first of all, a good man in the home, a good father, a good husband—that makes a man a good neighbor. You must have that, and, then, in addition, you must have the kind of law and the kind of administration of the law which will give to those qualities in the private citizen the best possible chance for development. The prime problem of our nation is to get the right type of good citizenship, and, to get it, we must have progress, and our public men must be genuinely progressive.

3. THE PROGRESSIVE PARTY PLATFORM OF 1912[1]

EDITORS' NOTE.—This platform of the "third" party which, in terms of both electoral and popular votes for President, was the second party of the country, is an interesting illustration of the thesis that, if one wants to know what the legislative reforms of the next twenty or thirty years will be, one should look at such third-party platforms. It is also significant that this promising "third" party expired four years later (although the name has twice been revived) and that most of its suggestions have since been enacted into law by members of one or both of the two major political parties.

1. *The World Almanac, 1913* (New York, 1913), pp. 693–97. By permission of the *World Almanac*.

Declaration of Principles.—The conscience of the people, in a time of grave national problems, has called into being a new party, born of the Nation's awakened sense of injustice.

We of the Progressive party here dedicate ourselves to the fulfilment of the duty laid upon us by our fathers to maintain that government of the people, by the people and for the people whose foundations they laid.

We hold with Thomas Jefferson and Abraham Lincoln, that the people are the masters of their Constitution to fulfil its purposes and to safeguard it from those who, by perversion of its intent, would convert it into an instrument of injustice. In accordance with the needs of each generation, the people must use their sovereign powers to establish and maintain equal opportunity and industrial justice, to secure which this Government was founded and without which no republic can endure.

This country belongs to the people who inhabit it. Its resources, its business, its institutions and its laws should be utilized, maintained or altered in whatever manner will best promote the general interest. It is time to set the public welfare in the first place.

The Old Parties.—Political parties exist to secure responsible government and to execute the will of the people. From these great tasks both the old parties have turned aside. Instead of instruments to promote the general welfare, they have become the tools of corrupt interests, which use them impartially to serve their selfish purposes. Behind the ostensible government sits enthroned an invisible government, owing no allegiance and acknowledging no responsibility to the people. To destroy this invisible government, to dissolve the unholy alliance between corrupt business and corrupt politics, is the first task of the statesmanship of the day.

The deliberate betrayal of its trust by the Republican party, the fatal incapacity of the Democratic party to deal with the new issues of the new time, have compelled the people to forge a new instrument of government through which to give effect to their will in laws and institutions.

Unhampered by tradition, uncorrupted by power, undismayed by the magnitude of the task, the new party offers itself as the instrument of the people to sweep away old abuses, to build a new and nobler commonwealth.

Covenant with the People.—This declaration is our covenant with the people, and we hereby bind the party and its candidates in State and Nation to the pledges made herein.

Rule of the People.—. . . In particular the party declares for direct primaries for the nomination of State and National officers, for nation-wide preferential primaries for candidates for the Presidency, for the direct election of United States Senators by the people; and we urge on the States the policy of the short ballot, with responsibility to the people secured by the initiative, referendum and recall.

Constitution Should Be Easily Amended. —The Progressive party, believing that a free people should have the power from time to time to amend their fundamental law so as to adapt it progressively to the changing needs of the people, pledges itself to provide a more easy and expeditious method of amending the Federal Constitution.

Nation and State.—Up to the limit of the Constitution, and later by amendment of the Constitution, if found necessary, we advocate bringing under effective national jurisdiction those problems which have expanded beyond reach of the individual States.

It is as grotesque as it is intolerable that the several States should by unequal laws in matter of common concern become competing commercial agencies, barter the lives of their children, the health of their women and the safety and wellbeing of their working people for the benefit of their financial interests.

The extreme insistence on States' rights

by the Democratic party in the Baltimore platform demonstrates anew its inability to understand the world into which it has survived or to administer the affairs of a union of States which have in all essential respects become one people.[2]

Social and Industrial Reform.—The supreme duty of the Nation is the conservation of human resources through an enlightened measure of social and industrial justice. We pledge ourselves to work unceasingly in State and Nation for:

Effective legislation looking to the prevention of industrial accidents, occupational diseases, overwork, involuntary unemployment, and other injurious effects incident to modern industry.

The fixing of minimum safety and health standards for the various occupations, and the exercise of the public authority of State and Nation, including the Federal control over interstate commerce and the taxing power, to maintain such standards.

The prohibition of child labor.

Minimum wage standards for working women, to provide a "living scale" in all industrial occupations.

The prohibition of night work for women and the establishment of an eight-hour day for women and young persons.

2. The plank referred to reads as follows: "Believing that the most efficient results under our system of government are to be attained by the full exercise by the States of their reserved sovereign powers, we denounce as usurpation the efforts of our opponents to deprive the States of any of the rights reserved to them, and to enlarge and magnify by indirection the powers of the Federal Government.

"We insist upon the full exercise of all the powers of the Government, both state and National, to protect the people from injustice at the hands of those who seek to make the Government a private asset in business. There is no twilight zone between the Nation and the State in which exploiting interests can take refuge from both. It is necessary that the Federal Government shall exercise the powers reserved to them, but we insist that Federal remedies for the regulation of interstate commerce and for the prevention of private monopoly shall be added to, and not substituted for, State remedies" (*ibid.*, p. 687).

One day's rest in seven for all wageworkers.

The eight-hour day in continuous twenty-four hour industries.

The abolition of the convict contract labor system; substituting a system of prison production for governmental consumption only and the application of prisoners' earnings to the support of their dependent families.

Publicity as to wages, hours and conditions of labor; full reports upon industrial accidents and diseases and the opening to public inspection of all tallies, weights, measures and check systems on labor products.

Standards of compensation for death by industrial accident and injury and trade diseases which will transfer the burden of lost earnings from the families of working people to the industry, and thus to the community.

The protection of home life against the hazards of sickness, irregular employment and old age through the adoption of a system of social insurance adapted to American use.

The development of the creative labor power of America by lifting the last load of illiteracy from American youth, and establishing continuation schools for industrial education under public control and encouraging agricultural education and demonstration in rural schools.

The establishment of industrial research laboratories to put the methods and discoveries of science at the service of American producers.

We favor the organization of the workers, men and women, as a means of protecting their interests and of promoting their progress.

Regulation of Interstate Corporations.—We believe that true popular government, justice and prosperity go hand in hand, and, so believing, it is our purpose to secure that large measure of general prosperity which is the fruit of legitimate and honest business, fostered by equal justice and by sound progressive laws.

We demand that the test of true prosperity shall be the benefits conferred thereby on all the citizens, not confined to individuals or classes, and that the test of corporate efficiency shall be the ability better to serve the public; that those who profit by control of business affairs shall justify that profit and that control by sharing with the public the fruits thereof.

We therefore demand a strong national regulation of interstate corporations. The corporation is an essential part of modern business. The concentration of modern business, in some degree, is both inevitable and necessary for National and international business efficiency. But the existing concentration of vast wealth under a corporate system, unguarded and uncontrolled by the Nation, has placed in the hands of a few men enormous, secret, irresponsible power over the daily life of the citizen—a power unsufferable in a free government and certain of abuse.

This power has been abused in monopoly of National resources, in stock watering, in unfair competition and unfair privileges, and, finally, in sinister influences on the public agencies of State and Nation. We do not fear commercial power, but we insist that it shall be exercised openly, under publicity, supervision and regulation of the most efficient sort, which will preserve its good while eradicating and preventing its evils.

To that end we urge the establishment of a strong Federal Administrative Commission of high standing, which shall maintain permanent active supervision over industrial corporations engaged in interstate commerce, or such of them as are of public importance, doing for them what the Government now does for the National banks, and what is now done for the railroads by the Interstate Commerce Commission.

Such a commission must enforce the complete publicity of those corporate transactions which are of public interest; must attack unfair competition, false capitalization and special privilege, and by continuous trained watchfulness guard and keep open equally to all the highways of American commerce. Thus the business man will have certain knowledge of the law and will be able to conduct his business easily in conformity therewith, the investor will find security for his capital, dividends will be rendered more certain and the savings of the people will be drawn naturally and safely into the channels of trade.

Under such a system of constructive regulation legitimate business, freed from confusion, uncertainty and fruitless litigation, will develop normally in response to the energy and enterprise of the American business man.

Commercial Development.—The time has come when the Federal Government should co-operate with manufacturers and producers in extending our foreign commerce. To this end we demand adequate appropriations by Congress and the appointment of diplomatic and consular officers solely with a view to their special fitness and worth, and not in consideration of political expediency. . . .

Any one who has had opportunity to study and observe first hand Germany's course in this respect must realize that their policy of co-operation between Government and business has in comparatively few years made them a leading competitor for the commerce of the world. It should be remembered that they are doing this on a National scale and with large units of business, while the Democrats would have us believe that we should do it with small units of business, which would be controlled, not by the National Government, but by forty-nine conflicting sovereignties. Such a policy is utterly out of keeping with the progress of the times and gives our great commercial rivals in Europe—hungry for international markets—golden opportunities of which they are rapidly taking advantage.

The Tariff.—We believe in a protective tariff which shall equalize conditions of competition between the United States and foreign countries, both for the farmer and the manufacturer, and which shall maintain for labor an adequate standard of living. Primarily the benefit of any tariff should be disclosed in the pay envelope of the laborer. We declare that no industry deserves protection which is unfair to labor or which is operating in violation of Federal law. We believe that the presumption is always in favor of the consuming public. . . .

We pledge ourselves to the establishment of a non-partisan scientific Tariff Commission, reporting both to the President and to either branch of Congress, which shall report first, as to the costs of production, efficiency of labor, capitalization, industrial organization and efficiency, and the general competitive position in this country and abroad of industries seeking protection from Congress. Second, as to the revenue-producing power of the tariff and its relation to the resources of government; and, thirdly, as to the effect of the tariff on prices, operations of middlemen, and on the purchasing power of the consumer. . . .

We condemn the Payne-Aldrich bill as unjust to the people. . . .

Reciprocity with Canada.—We demand the immediate repeal of the Canadian reciprocity act. . . .

Improvement of the Currency.—. . . The issue of currency is fundamentally a Government function and the system should have as basic principles soundness and elasticity. The control should be lodged with the Government and should be protected from domination or manipulation by Wall Street or any special interests.

We are opposed to the so-called Aldrich currency bill because its provisions would place our currency and credit system in private hands, not subject to effective public control.

Conservation of Natural Resources.— . . . We believe that the remaining forests, coal and oil lands, water powers and other natural resources still in State or National control (except agricultural lands) are more likely to be wisely conserved and utilized for the general welfare if held in the public hands. . . .

In particular we pledge our party to require reasonable compensation to the public for water power rights hereafter granted by the public. . . .

Waterways.—The rivers of the United States are the natural arteries of this continent. We demand that they shall be opened to traffic as indispensable parts of a great nation-wide system of transportation in which the Panama Canal will be the central link, thus enabling the whole interior of the United States to share with the Atlantic and Pacific seaboards in the benefit derived from the canal. . . .

Panama Canal.—The Panama Canal, built and paid for by the American people, must be used primarily for their benefit. We demand that the canal shall be so operated as to break the transportation monopoly now held and misused by the transcontinental railroads by maintaining sea competition with them; that ships directly or indirectly owned or controlled by American railroad corporations shall not be permitted to use the canal, and that American ships engaged in coastwise trade shall pay no tolls. . . .

Woman Suffrage.—The Progressive party, believing that no people can justly claim to be a true democracy which denies political rights on account of sex, pledges itself to the task of securing equal suffrage to men and women alike.

Corrupt Election Practices.—We pledge our party to legislation that will compel strict limitation of all campaign contributions and expenditures, and detailed publicity of both before as well as after primaries and elections.

Publicity and Public Service.—We pledge our party to legislation compelling the registration of lobbyists; publicity of committee hearings, except on foreign affairs, and recording of all votes in committee; and forbidding Federal appointees from holding office in State or National political organizations or taking part as officers or delegates in political conventions for the nomination of elective State or National officials.

Popular Review of Judicial Decisions.— The Progressive party demands such restriction of the power of the courts as shall leave to the people the ultimate authority to determine fundamental questions of social welfare and public policy. To secure this end, it pledges itself to provide:

First.—That when an act passed under the police power of the State is held unconstitutional under the State Constitution by the courts, the people, after an ample interval for deliberation, shall have an opportunity to vote on the question whether they desire the act to become law, notwithstanding such decision.

Second.—That every decision of the highest Appellate Court of a State declaring an act of the Legislature unconstitutional on the ground of its violation of the Federal Constitution shall be subject to the same review by the Supreme Court of the United States as is now accorded to decisions sustaining such legislation.

Administration of Justice.—. . . We believe that the issuance of injunctions in cases arising out of labor disputes should be prohibited when such injunctions would not apply when no labor disputes existed.

We also believe that a person cited for contempt in labor disputes, except when such contempt was committed in the actual presence of the court or so near thereto as to interfere with the proper administration of justice, should have a right to trial by jury.

A Department of Labor.—We pledge our party to establish a department of labor, with a seat in the Cabinet, and with wide jurisdiction over matters affecting the conditions of labor and living. . . .

Inheritance and Income Tax.—We believe in a graduated inheritance tax as a National means of equalizing the obligations of holders of property to Government, and we hereby pledge our party to enact such a Federal law as will tax large inheritances, returning to the States an equitable percentage of all amounts collected. We favor the ratification of the pending amendment to the Constitution giving the Government power to levy an income tax. . . .

Parcels Post.—We pledge our party to the immediate creation of a parcels post, with rates proportionate to distance and service. . . .

Supervision over Investments.—The people of the United States are swindled out of many millions of dollars every year through worthless investments. The plain people, the wage-earners and the men and women with small savings have no way of knowing the merit of concerns sending out highly colored prospectuses offering stock for sale, prospectuses that make big returns seem certain and fortunes easily within grasp.

We hold it to be the duty of the Government to protect its people from this kind of piracy. We therefore demand wise, carefully thought-out legislation that will give us such Governmental supervision over this matter as will furnish to the people of the United States this much needed protection, and we pledge ourselves thereto.

Conclusion.—On these principles and on the recognized desirability of uniting the progressive forces of the Nation into an organization which shall unequivocally represent the progressive spirit and policy, we appeal for the support of all American citizens, without regard to previous political affiliations.

4. THE NEW FREEDOM[1]

By Woodrow Wilson

EDITORS' NOTE.—(Thomas) Woodrow Wilson (1856–1924), twenty-eighth President of the United States, was born in Staunton, Virginia, and grew to manhood in Georgia and the Carolinas during the Civil War and Reconstruction periods. After his graduation from Princeton in 1879 he studied law at the University of Virginia. Unsuccessful in the practice of law, Wilson did graduate work at the Johns Hopkins University, receiving his Ph.D. there under Herbert Baxter Adams in 1886, a few years before Frederick Jackson Turner. Wilson later taught political science at Bryn Mawr, Wesleyan, and Princeton. In 1902 he became president of Princeton, where he finally lost a battle for educa-tional reform and for the democratization of social life. In 1910 he was elected governor of New Jersey and soon made a notable record as a reformer. After a long convention battle Wilson was nominated by the Democrats in 1912 to lead his party to victory over a divided Republican and Progressive opposition.

Woodrow Wilson's campaign speeches set forth the basic philosophy with which the future war President approached domestic problems in the crucial presidential campaign of 1912. The next reading, his First Inaugural, spelled out the program of progressivism for which he believed he and the Democratic party had been placed in power.

THE OLD ORDER CHANGETH

There is one great basic fact which underlies all the questions that are discussed on the political platform at the present moment. That singular fact is that nothing is done in this country as it was done twenty years ago.

We are in the presence of a new organization of society. Our life has broken away from the past. The life of America is not the life that it was twenty years ago; it is not the life that it was ten years ago. We have changed our economic conditions, absolutely, from top to bottom; and, with our economic society, the organization of our life. The old political formulas do not fit the present problems; they read now like documents taken out of a forgotten age. The older cries sound as if they belonged to a past age which men have almost forgotten. Things which used to be put into the party platforms of ten years ago would sound antiquated if put into a platform now. We are facing the necessity of fitting a new social organization, as we did once fit the old organization, to the happiness and prosperity of the great body of citizens; for we are conscious that the new order of society has not been made to fit and provide the convenience or prosperity of the average man. The life of the nation has grown infinitely varied. It does not centre now upon questions of governmental structure or of the distribution of governmental powers. It centres upon questions of the very structure and operation of society itself, of which government is only the instrument. Our development has run so fast and so far along the lines sketched in the earlier day of constitutional definition, has so

[1]. Woodrow Wilson, *The New Freedom* (New York, 1913), pp. 3–32. By permission of Doubleday and Company, Inc.

crossed and interlaced those lines, has piled upon them such novel structures of trust and combination, has elaborated within them a life so manifold, so full of forces which transcend the boundaries of the country itself and fill the eyes of the world, that a new nation seems to have been created which the old formulas do not fit or afford a vital interpretation of.

We have come upon a very different age from any that preceded us. We have come upon an age when we do not do business in the way in which we used to do business—when we do not carry on any of the operations of manufacture, sale, transportation, or communication as men used to carry them on. There is a sense in which in our day the individual has been submerged. In most parts of our country men work, not for themselves, not as partners in the old way in which they used to work, but generally as employees—in a higher or lower grade—of great corporations. There was a time when corporations played a very minor part in our business affairs, but now they play the chief part, and most men are the servants of corporations.

You know what happens when you are the servant of a corporation. You have in no instance access to the men who are really determining the policy of the corporation. If the corporation is doing the things that it ought not to do, you really have no voice in the matter and must obey the orders, and you have oftentimes with deep mortification to co-operate in the doing of things which you know are against the public interest. Your individuality is swallowed up in the individuality and purpose of a great organization.

It is true that, while most men are thus submerged in the corporation, a few, a very few, are exalted to a power which as individuals they could never have wielded. Through the great organizations of which they are the heads, a few are enabled to play a part unprecedented by anything in history in the control of the business operations of the country and in the determination of the happiness of great numbers of people.

Yesterday, and ever since history began, men were related to one another as individuals. To be sure there were the family, the Church, and the State, institutions which associated men in certain wide circles of relationship. But in the ordinary concerns of life, in the ordinary work, in the daily round, men dealt freely and directly with one another. To-day, the everyday relationships of men are largely with great impersonal concerns, with organizations, not with other individual men.

Now this is nothing short of a new social age, a new era of human relationships, a new stage-setting for the drama of life.

In this new age we find, for instance, that our laws with regard to the relations of employer and employee are in many respects wholly antiquated and impossible. They were framed for another age, which nobody now living remembers, which is, indeed, so remote from our life that it would be difficult for many of us to understand it if it were described to us. The employer is now generally a corporation or a huge company of some kind; the employee is one of hundreds or of thousands brought together, not by individual masters whom they know and with whom they have personal relations, but by agents of one sort or another. Workingmen are marshaled in great numbers for the performance of a multitude of particular tasks under a common discipline. They generally use dangerous and powerful machinery, over whose repair and renewal they have no control. New rules must be devised with regard to their obligations and their rights, their obligations to their employers and their responsibilities to one another. Rules must be devised for their protection, for their compensation when injured, for their support when disabled.

There is something very new and very big and very complex about these new relations of capital and labor. A new economic society has sprung up, and we must effect a new set of adjustments. We must not pit power against weakness. The employer is generally, in our day, as I have said, not an individual, but a powerful group; and yet the workingman when dealing with his employer is still, under our existing law, an individual.

Why is it that we have a labor question at all? It is for the simple and very sufficient reason that the laboring man and the employer are not intimate associates now as they used to be in time past. Most of our laws were formed in the age when employer and employees knew each other, knew each other's characters, were associates with each other, dealt with each other as man with man. That is no longer the case. You not only do not come into personal contact with the men who have the supreme command in those corporations, but it would be out of the question for you to do it. Our modern corporations employ thousands, and in some instances hundreds of thousands, of men. The only persons whom you see or deal with are local superintendents or local representatives of a vast organization, which is not like anything that the workingmen of the time in which our laws were framed knew anything about. A little group of workingmen, seeing their employer every day, dealing with him in a personal way, is one thing, and the modern body of labor engaged as employees of the huge enterprises that spread all over the country, dealing with men of whom they can form no personal conception, is another thing. A very different thing. You never saw a corporation, any more than you ever saw a government. Many a workingman to-day never saw the body of men who are conducting the industry in which he is employed. And they never saw him. What they know about him is written in ledgers and books and letters, in the correspondence of the office, in the reports of the superintendents. He is a long way off from them.

So what we have to discuss is, not wrongs which individuals intentionally do —I do not believe there are a great many of those—but the wrongs of a system. I want to record my protest against any discussion of this matter which would seem to indicate that there are bodies of our fellow-citizens who are trying to grind us down and do us injustice. There are some men of that sort. I don't know how they sleep o'nights, but there are men of that kind. Thank God, they are not numerous. The truth is, we are all caught in a great economic system which is heartless. The modern corporation is not engaged in business as an individual. When we deal with it, we deal with an impersonal element, an immaterial piece of society. A modern corporation is a means of co-operation in the conduct of an enterprise which is so big that no one man can conduct it, and which the resources of no one man are sufficient to finance. A company is formed; that company puts out a prospectus; the promoters expect to raise a certain fund as capital stock. Well, how are they going to raise it? They are going to raise it from the public in general, some of whom will buy their stock. The moment that begins, there is formed—what? A joint stock corporation. Men begin to pool their earnings, little piles, big piles. A certain number of men are elected by the stockholders to be directors, and these directors elect a president. This president is the head of the undertaking, and the directors are its managers.

Now, do the workingmen employed by that stock corporation deal with that president and those directors? Not at all. Does the public deal with that president and that board of directors? It does not. Can anybody bring them to account? It is next to impossible to do so. If you undertake it you will find it a game of hide and seek, with the objects of your search taking refuge now behind the tree of their individual personality, now behind that of their corporate irresponsibility.

And do our laws take note of this curious state of things? Do they even attempt to distinguish between a man's act as a corporation director and as an individual?

They do not. Our laws still deal with us on the basis of the old system. The law is still living in the dead past which we have left behind. This is evident, for instance, with regard to the matter of employers' liability for workingmen's injuries. Suppose that a superintendent wants a workman to use a certain piece of machinery which it is not safe for him to use, and that the workman is injured by that piece of machinery. Some of our courts have held that the superintendent is a fellow-servant, or, as the law states it, a fellow-employee, and that, therefore, the man cannot recover damages for his injury. The superintendent who probably engaged the man is not his employer. Who is his employer? And whose negligence could conceivably come in there? The board of directors did not tell the employee to use that piece of machinery; and the president of the corporation did not tell him to use that piece of machinery. And so forth. Don't you see by that theory that a man never can get redress for negligence on the part of the employer? When I hear judges reason upon the analogy of the relationships that used to exist between workmen and their employers a generation ago, I wonder if they have not opened their eyes to the modern world. You know, we have a right to expect that judges will have their eyes open, even though the law which they administer hasn't awakened.

Yet that is but a single small detail illustrative of the difficulties we are in because we have not adjusted the law to the facts of the new order.

Since I entered politics, I have chiefly had men's views confided to me privately. Some of the biggest men in the United States, in the field of commerce and manufacture, are afraid of somebody, are afraid of something. They know that there is a power somewhere so organized, so subtle, so watchful, so interlocked, so complete, so pervasive, that they had better not speak above their breath when they speak in condemnation of it.

They know that America is not a place of which it can be said, as it used to be, that a man may choose his own calling and pursue it just as far as his abilities enable him to pursue it; because to-day, if he enters certain fields, there are organizations which will use means against him that will prevent his building up a business which they do not want to have built up; organizations that will see to it that the ground is cut from under him and the markets shut against him. For if he begins to sell to certain retail dealers, to any retail dealers, the monopoly will refuse to sell to those dealers, and those dealers, afraid, will not buy the new man's wares.

And this is the country which has lifted to the admiration of the world its ideals of absolutely free opportunity, where no man is supposed to be under any limitation except the limitations of his character and of his mind; where there is supposed to be no distinction of class, no distinction of blood, no distinction of social status, but where men win or lose on their merits.

I lay it very close to my own conscience as a public man whether we can any longer stand at our doors and welcome all newcomers upon those terms. American industry is not free, as once it was free; American enterprise is not free; the man with only a little capital is finding it harder to get into the field, more and more impossible to compete with the big fellow. Why? Because the laws of this country do not prevent the strong from crushing the weak. That is the reason, and because the strong have crushed the weak the strong dominate the industry and the economic life of this country. No man can deny that the lines of endeavor have more and more narrowed and stiffened; no man who knows anything about the development of industry in this country can have failed to observe that the larger kinds of credit are more and more difficult to obtain, unless you obtain them upon the terms of uniting your efforts with those who already control the industries of the country; and nobody can fail to observe that any man who tries to set himself up in competition with any process of manufacture which has been taken under the control of large combinations of capital will presently find himself either squeezed out or obliged to sell and allow himself to be absorbed.

There is a great deal that needs reconstruction in the United States. I should like to take a census of the business men—I mean the rank and file of the business men—as to whether they think that business conditions in this country, or rather whether the organization of business in this country, is satisfactory or not. I know what they would say if they dared. If they could vote secretly they would vote overwhelmingly that the present organization of business was meant for the big fellows and was not meant for the little fellows; that it was meant for those who are at the top and was meant to exclude those who are at the bottom; that it was meant to shut out beginners, to prevent new entries in the race, to prevent the building up of competitive enterprises that would interfere with the monopolies which the great trusts have built up.

What this country needs above everything else is a body of laws which will look after the men who are on the make rather than the men who are already made. Because the men who are already made are not going to live indefinitely, and they are not always kind enough to leave sons as able and as honest as they are.

The originative part of America, the part of America that makes new enterprises, the part into which the ambitious and gifted workingman makes his way up, the class that saves, that plans, that organizes, that presently spreads its enterprises until they have a national scope and character—that middle class is being more and more squeezed out by the processes which we have been taught to call processes of prosperity. Its members are sharing prosperity, no doubt; but what alarms me is that they are not *originating* prosperity. No country can afford to have its prosperity originated by a small controlling class. The treasury of America does not lie in the brains of the small body of men now in control of the great enterprises that have been concentrated under the direction of a very small number of persons. The treasury of America lies in those ambitions, those energies, that cannot be restricted to a special favored class. It depends upon the inventions of unknown men, upon the originations of unknown men, upon the ambitions of unknown men. Every country is renewed out of the ranks of the unknown, not out of the ranks of those already famous and powerful and in control.

There has come over the land that un-American set of conditions which enables a small number of men who control the government to get favors from the government; by those favors to exclude their fellows from equal business opportunity; by those favors to extend a network of control that will presently dominate every industry in the country, and so make men forget the ancient time when America lay in every hamlet, when America was to be seen in every fair valley, when America displayed her great forces on the broad prairies, ran her fine fires of enterprise up over the mountain-sides and down into the bowels of the earth, and eager men were everywhere captains of industry, not employees; not looking to a distant city to find out what they might do, but looking about among their neighbors, finding credit according to their character, not according to their connections, finding credit in proportion to what was known to be in them and behind them, not in proportion to the securities they held that were approved where they were not known. In order to start an enterprise now, you have to be authenticated, in a perfectly impersonal way, not according to yourself, but according to what you own that somebody else approves of your owning. You cannot begin such an enterprise as those that have made America until you are so authenticated, until you have succeeded in obtaining the goodwill of large allied capitalists.

Is that freedom? That is dependence, not freedom.

We used to think in the old-fashioned days when life was very simple that all that government had to do was to put on a policeman's uniform, and say, "Now don't anybody hurt anybody else." We used to say that the ideal of government was for every man to be left alone and not interfered with, except when he interfered with somebody else; and that the best government was the government that did as little governing as possible. That was the idea that obtained in Jefferson's time. But we are coming now to realize that life is so complicated that we are not dealing with the old conditions, and that the law has to step in and create new conditions under which we may live, the conditions which will make it tolerable for us to live.

Let me illustrate what I mean: It used to be true in our cities that every family occupied a separate house of its own, that every family had its own little premises, that every family was separated in its life from every other family. That is no longer the case in our great cities. Families live in tenements, they live in flats, they live on floors; they are piled layer upon layer in the great tenement houses of our crowded districts, and not only are they piled layer upon layer, but they are associated room by room, so that there is in every room, sometimes, in our congested districts, a separate family. In some foreign countries they have made much more progress than we in handling these things. In the city of Glasgow, for example (Glasgow is one of the model cities of the world), they have made up their minds that the entries and the hallways of great tenements are public streets. Therefore, the policeman goes up the stairway, and patrols the corridors; the lighting department of the city sees to it that the halls are abundantly lighted. The city does not deceive itself into supposing that that great building is a unit from which the police are to keep out and the civic authority to be excluded, but it says: "These are public highways, and light is needed in them, and control by the authority of the city."

I liken that to our great modern industrial enterprises. A corporation is very like a large tenement house; it isn't the premises of a single commercial family; it is just as much a public affair as a tenement house is a network of public highways.

When you offer the securities of a great corporation to anybody who wishes to purchase them, you must open that corporation to the inspection of everybody who wants to purchase. There must, to follow out the figure of the tenement house, be lights along the corridors, there must be police patrolling the openings, there must be inspection wherever it is known that men may be deceived with regard to the contents of the premises. If we believe that fraud lies in wait for us, we must have the means of determining whether our suspicions are well founded or not. Similarly, the treatment of labor by the great corporations is not what it was in Jefferson's time. Whenever bodies of men employ bodies of men, it ceases to be a private relationship. So that when courts hold that workingmen cannot peaceably dissuade other workingmen from taking employment, as was held in a notable case in New Jersey, they simply show that their minds and understandings are lingering in an age which has passed away. This dealing of great bodies of men with other bodies of men is a matter of public scrutiny, and should be a matter of public regulation.

Similarly, it was no business of the law in the time of Jefferson to come into my house and see how I kept house. But when my house, when my so-called private property, became a great mine, and men went along dark corridors amidst every kind of danger in order to dig out of the bowels of the earth things necessary for the industries of a whole nation, and when it came about that no individual owned these mines, that they were owned by great stock companies, then all the old analogies absolutely collapsed and it became the right of the government to go down into these mines to see whether human beings were properly treated in them or not; to see whether accidents were properly safeguarded against; to see whether modern economical methods of using these inestimable riches of the earth were followed or were not followed. If somebody puts a derrick improperly secured on top of a building or overtopping the street, then the government of the city has the right to see that that derrick is so secured that you and I can walk under it and not be afraid that the heavens are going to fall on us. Likewise, in these great beehives where in every corridor swarm men of flesh and blood, it is the privilege of the government, whether of the State or of the United States, as the case may be, to see that human life is protected, that human lungs have something to breathe.

These, again, are merely illustrations of conditions. We are in a new world, struggling under old laws. As we go inspecting our lives to-day, surveying this new scene of centralized and complex society, we shall find many more things out of joint.

One of the most alarming phenomena of the time—or rather it would be alarming if the nation had not awakened to it and shown its determination to control it—one of the most significant signs of the new social era is the degree to which government has become associated with business. I speak, for the moment, of the control over the government exercised by Big Business. Behind the whole subject, of course, is the truth that, in the new order, government and business must be associated closely. But that association is at present of a nature absolutely intolerable; the precedence is wrong, the association is upside down. Our government has been for the past few years under the control of heads of great allied corporations with special interests. It has not controlled these interests and assigned them a proper place in the whole system of business; it has submitted itself to their control. As a result, there have grown up vicious systems and schemes of governmental favoritism (the most obvious being the extravagant tariff), far-reaching in effect upon the whole fabric of life, touching to his injury every inhabitant of the land, laying unfair and impossible handicaps upon competitors, imposing taxes in every direction, stifling everywhere the free spirit of American enterprise.

Now this has come about naturally; as we go on we shall see how very naturally. It is no use denouncing anybody, or anything, except human nature. Nevertheless, it is an intolerable thing that the government of the republic should have got so far out of the hands of the people; should have been captured by interests which are special and not general. In the train of this capture follow the troops of scandals, wrongs, indecencies, with which our politics swarm.

There are cities in America of whose government we are ashamed. There are cities everywhere, in every part of the land, in which we feel that, not the interests of the public, but the interests of special privileges, of selfish men, are served; where contracts take precedence over public interest. Not only in big cities is this the case. Have you not noticed the growth of socialistic sentiment in the smaller towns? Not many months ago I stopped at a little town in Nebraska, and while my train lingered I met on the platform a very engaging young fellow dressed in overalls who introduced himself to me as the mayor of the town, and added that he was a Socialist. I said, "What does that mean? Does that mean that this town is socialistic?" "No, sir," he said; "I have not deceived myself; the vote by which I was elected was about 20 per cent socialistic and 80 per cent protest." It was protest against the teachery to the people of those who led both the other parties of that town.

All over the Union people are coming to feel that they have no control over the course of affairs. I live in one of the greatest States in the union, which was at one time in slavery. Until two years ago we had witnessed with increasing concern the growth in New Jersey of a spirit of almost cynical despair. Men said: "We vote; we are offered the platform we want; we elect the men who stand on that platform, and we get absolutely nothing." So they began to ask: "What is the use of voting? We know that the machines of both parties are subsidized by the same persons, and therefore it is useless to turn in either direction."

This is not confined to some of the state governments and those of some of the towns and cities. We know that something intervenes between the people of the United States and the control of their own affairs at Washington. It is not the people who have been ruling there of late.

Why are we in the presence, why are we at the threshold, of a revolution? Because we are profoundly disturbed by the influences which we see reigning in the determination of our public life and our public policy. There was a time when America was blithe with self-confidence. She boasted that she, and she alone, knew the processes of popular government; but now she sees her sky overcast; she sees that there are at work forces which she did not dream of in her hopeful youth.

Don't you know that some man with eloquent tongue, without conscience, who did not care for the nation, could put this whole country into a flame? Don't you know that this country from one end to the other believes that something is wrong? What an opportunity it would be for some man without conscience to spring up and say: "This is the way. Follow me!"—and lead in paths of destruction!

The old order changeth—changeth under our very eyes, not quietly and equably, but swiftly and with the noise and heat and tumult of reconstruction.

I suppose that all struggle for law has been conscious, that very little of it has been blind or merely instinctive. It is the fashion to say, as if with superior knowledge of affairs and of human weakness, that every age has been an age of transition, and that no age is more full of change than another; yet in very few ages of the world can the struggle for change have been so widespread, so deliberate, or upon so great a scale as in this in which we are taking part.

The transition we are witnessing is no equable transition of growth and normal alteration; no silent, unconscious unfolding of one age into another, its natural heir and successor. Society is looking itself over, in our day, from top to bottom; is making fresh and critical analysis of its very elements; is questioning its oldest practices as freely as its newest, scrutinizing every arrangement and motive of its life; and it stands ready to attempt nothing less than a radical reconstruction, which only frank and honest counsels and the forces of generous co-operation can hold back from becoming a revolution. We are in a temper to reconstruct economic society, as we were once in a temper to reconstruct political society, and political society may itself undergo a radical modification in the process. I doubt if any age was ever more conscious of its task or more unanimously desirous of radical and extended changes in its economic and political practice.

We stand in the presence of a revolution—not a bloody revolution; America is not given to the spilling of blood—but a silent revolution, whereby America will insist upon recovering in practice those ideals which she has always professed, upon securing a government devoted to the general interest and not to special interests.

We are upon the eve of a great reconstruction. It calls for creative statesmanship as no age has done since that great age in which we set up the government under which we live, that government which was the admiration of the world until it suffered wrongs to grow up under it which have made many of our own compatriots question the freedom of our institutions and preach revolution against them. I do not fear revolution. I have unshaken faith in the power of America to keep its self-possession. Revolution will come in peaceful guise, as it came when we put aside the crude government of the Confederation and created the great Federal Union which governs individuals, not States, and which has been these hundred and thirty years our vehicle of progress. Some radical changes we must make in our law and practice. Some reconstructions we must push forward, which a new age and new circumstances impose upon us. But we can do it all in calm and sober fashion, like statesmen and patriots.

I do not speak of these things in apprehension, because all is open and aboveboard. This is not a day in which great forces rally in secret. The whole stupendous program must be publicly planned and canvassed. Good temper, the wisdom that comes of sober counsel, the energy of thoughtful and unselfish men, the habit of co-operation and of compromise which has been bred in us by long years of free government, in which reason rather than passion has been made to prevail by the sheer virtue of candid and universal debate, will enable us to win through to still another great age without violence.

5. FIRST INAUGURAL ADDRESS, 1913[1]

By WOODROW WILSON

EDITORS' NOTE.—A comparison of the program which the new President set forth here in 1913 with the legislation of the Sixty-third and Sixty-fourth Congresses is quite revealing.

It is also interesting, in the light of future events, that this speech contains no reference whatever to American foreign policy.

There has been a change of government. It began two years ago, when the House of Representatives became Democratic by a decisive majority. It has now been completed. The Senate about to assemble will also be Democratic. The offices of President and Vice President have been put into the hands of Democrats. What does the change mean? That is the question that is uppermost in our minds today. That is the question I am going to try to answer, in order, if I may, to interpret the occasion.

It means much more than the mere success of a party. The success of a party means little except when the Nation is using that party for a large and definite purpose. No one can mistake the purpose for which the Nation now seeks to use the Democratic Party. It seeks to use it to

interpret a change in its own plans and point of view. Some old things with which we had grown familiar and which had begun to creep into the very habit of our thought and of our lives, have altered their aspect as we have latterly looked critically upon them with fresh awakened eyes; have dropped their disguises and shown themselves alien and sinister. Some new things, as we look frankly upon them, willing to comprehend their real character, have come to assume the aspect of things long believed in and familiar, stuff of our own convictions. We have been refreshed by a new insight into our own life.

We see that in many things that life is very great. It is incomparably great in its material aspects, in its body of wealth, in the diversity and sweep of its energy, in the industries which have been conceived and built up by the genius of individual men and the limitless enterprise of groups of men. It is great, also, very great, in its

1. U.S., 63d Cong., Special Session, *Senate Documents* (Washington, 1913), I, No. 3 (Serial No. 6507), 3–6.

moral force. Nowhere else in the world have noble men and women exhibited in more striking forms the beauty and the energy of sympathy and helpfulness and counsel in their efforts to rectify wrong, alleviate suffering, and set the weak in the way of strength and hope. We have built up, moreover, a great system of government, which has stood through a long age as in many respects a model for those who seek to set liberty upon foundations that will endure against fortuitous change, against storm and accident. Our life contains every great thing, and contains it in rich abundance.

But the evil has come with the good, and much fine gold has been corroded. With riches has come inexcusable waste. We have squandered a great part of what we might have used, and have not stopped to conserve the exceeding bounty of nature, without which our genius for enterprise would have been worthless and impotent, scorning to be careful, shamefully prodigal as well as admirably efficient. We have been proud of our industrial achievements, but we have not hitherto stopped thoughtfully enough to count the human cost, the cost of lives snuffed out, of energies overtaxed and broken, the fearful physical and spiritual cost to the men and women and children upon whom the dead weight and burden of it all has fallen pitilessly the years through. The groans and agony of it all had not yet reached our ears, the solemn, moving undertone of our life, coming up out of the mines and factories and out of every home where the struggle had its intimate and familiar seat. With the great Government went many deep secret things which we too long delayed to look into and scrutinize with candid, fearless eyes. The great Government we loved has too often been made use of for private and selfish purposes, and those who used it had forgotten the people.

At last a vision has been vouchsafed us of our life as a whole. We see the bad with the good, the debased and decadent with the sound and vital. With this vision we approach new affairs. Our duty is to cleanse, to reconsider, to restore, to correct the evil without impairing the good, to purify and humanize every process of our common life without weakening or sentimentalizing it. There has been something crude and heartless and unfeeling in our haste to succeed and be great. Our thought has been "Let every man look out for himself, let every generation look out for itself," while we reared giant machinery which made it impossible that any but those who stood at the levers of control should have a chance to look out for themselves. We had not forgotten our morals. We remembered well enough that we had set up a policy which was meant to serve the humblest as well as the most powerful, with an eye single to the standards of justice and fair play, and remembered it with pride. But we were very heedless and in a hurry to be great.

We have come now to the sober second thought. The scales of heedlessness have fallen from our eyes. We have made up our minds to square every process of our national life again with the standards we so proudly set up at the beginning and have always carried at our hearts. Our work is a work of restoration.

We have itemized with some degree of particularity the things that ought to be altered, and here are some of the chief items: A tariff which cuts us off from our proper part in the commerce of the world, violates the just principles of taxation, and makes the Government a facile instrument in the hands of private interests; a banking and currency system based upon the necessity of the Government to sell its bonds 50 years ago and perfectly adapted to concentrating cash and restricting credits; an industrial system which, take it on all its sides, financial as well as administrative, holds capital in leading strings, restricts the liberties and limits the opportunities of labor, and exploits without renewing or conserving the natural resources of the country; a body of agricultural activities never yet given the efficiency of great business undertakings or served as it should be through the instrumentality of science taken directly to the farm, or afforded the facilities of credit best suited to its practical needs; watercourses undeveloped, waste places unreclaimed, forests untended, fast disappearing without plan or prospect of renewal, unregarded waste heaps at every mine. We have studied as perhaps no other nation has the most effective means of production, but we have not studied cost or economy as we should either as organizers of industry, as statesmen, or as individuals.

Nor have we studied and perfected the means by which government may be put at the service of humanity, in safeguarding the health of the Nation, the health of its men and its women and its children, as well as their rights in the struggle for existence. This is no sentimental duty. The firm basis of government is justice, not pity. These are matters of justice. There can be no equality or opportunity, the first essential of justice in the body politic, if men and women and children be not shielded in their lives, their very vitality, from the consequences of great industrial and social processes which they can not alter, control, or singly cope with. Society must see to it that it does not itself crush or weaken or damage its own constituent parts. The first duty of law is to keep sound the society it serves. Sanitary laws, pure-food laws, and laws determining conditions of labor which individuals are powerless to determine for themselves are intimate parts of the very business of justice and legal efficiency.

These are some of the things we ought to do, and not leave the others undone, the old-fashioned, never-to-be-neglected, fundamental safeguarding of property and of individual right. This is the high enterprise of the new day: To lift everything that concerns our life as a Nation to the light that shines from the hearthfire of every man's conscience and vision of the right. It is inconceivable that we should do this as partisans; it is inconceivable we should do it in ignorance of the facts as they are or in blind haste. We shall restore, not destroy. We shall deal with our economic system as it is and as it may be modified, not as it might be if we had a clean sheet of paper to write upon; and step by step we shall make it what it should be, in the spirit of those who question their own wisdom and seek counsel and knowledge, not shallow self-satisfaction or the excitement of excursions whither they can not tell. Justice, and only justice, shall always be our motto.

And yet it will be no cool process of mere science. The Nation has been deeply stirred, stirred by a solemn passion, stirred by the knowledge of wrong, of ideals lost, of government too often debauched and made an instrument of evil. The feelings with which we face this new age of right and opportunity sweep across our heartstrings like some air out of God's own presence, where justice and mercy are reconciled and the judge and the brother are one. We know our task to be no mere task of politics but a task which shall search us through and through, whether we be able to understand our time and the need of our people, whether we be indeed their spokesmen and interpreters, whether we have the pure heart to comprehend and the rectified will to choose our high course of action.

This is not a day of triumph; it is a day of dedication. Here muster not the forces of party, but the forces of humanity. Men's hearts wait upon us; men's lives hang in the balance; men's hopes call upon us to say what we will do. Who shall live up to the great trust? Who dares fail to try? I summon all honest men, all patriotic, all forward-looking men, to my side. God helping me, I will not fail them, if they will but counsel and sustain me!

SECTION D. FEDERAL EFFORTS TO MAINTAIN COMPETITION

1. THE SHERMAN ANTITRUST ACT, 1890[1]

EDITORS' NOTE.—The Sherman Antitrust Act of 1890 was the outcome of a decade of protest. State laws designed for the same end had proved ineffective; President Cleveland had made the issue a national one; and both major parties had inserted antitrust planks into their national platforms in 1888. Failing to define terms of the greatest importance, the Sherman Act has often been cited as an excellent illustration of a congressional attempt to satisfy public opinion by passing a law so vague that it is either unenforcible or leads to "legislation by the judiciary." For a decade it was largely unenforced; its later interpretation and amplification is illustrated by the later readings in this unit.

. . . An act to protect trade and commerce against unlawful restraints and monopolies.

Be it enacted . . .

SECTION 1. Every contract, combination in the form of trust or otherwise, or conspiracy, in restraint of trade or commerce among the several States, or with foreign nations, is hereby declared to be illegal. Every person who shall make any such contract or engage in any such combination or conspiracy, shall be deemed guilty of a misdemeanor, and, on conviction thereof, shall be punished by fine not exceeding five thousand dollars, or by imprisonment not exceeding one year, or by both said punishments, in the discretion of the court.

SEC. 2. Every person who shall monopolize, or attempt to monopolize, or combine or conspire with any other person or persons, to monopolize any part of the trade or commerce among the several States, or with foreign nations, shall be deemed guilty of a misdemeanor, and, on conviction thereof, shall be punished by fine not exceeding five thousand dollars, or by imprisonment not exceeding one year, or by both said punishments, in the discretion of the court.

SEC. 3. Every contract, combination in form of trust or otherwise, or conspiracy, in restraint of trade or commerce in any Territory of the United States or of the District of Columbia, or in restraint of trade or commerce between any such Territory and another, or between any such Territory or Territories and any State or States or the District of Columbia, or with foreign nations, or between the District of Columbia and any State or States or foreign nations, is hereby declared illegal. Every person who shall make any such contract or engage in any such combination or conspiracy, shall be deemed guilty of a misdemeanor, and, on conviction thereof, shall be punished by fine not exceeding five thousand dollars, or by imprisonment not exceeding one year, or by both said punishments, in the discretion of the court.

SEC. 4. The several circuit courts of the United States are hereby invested with jurisdiction to prevent and restrain violations of this act; and it shall be the duty of the several district attorneys of the United

1. *United States Statutes at Large* . . . (Washington, 1891), XXVI, 209–10.

States, in their respective districts, under the direction of the Attorney-General, to institute proceedings in equity to prevent and restrain such violations. Such proceedings may be by way of petition setting forth the case and praying that such violation shall be enjoined or otherwise prohibited. When the parties complained of shall have been duly notified of such petition the court shall proceed, as soon as may be, to the hearing and determination of the case; and pending such petition and before final decree, the court may at any time make such temporary restraining order or prohibition as shall be deemed just in the premises.

SEC. 5. Whenever it shall appear to the court before which any proceeding under section four of this act may be pending, that the ends of justice require that other parties should be brought before the court, the court may cause them to be summoned, whether they reside in the district in which the court is held or not; and subpoenas to that end may be served in any district by the marshal thereof.

SEC. 6. Any property owned under any contract or by any combination, or pursuant to any conspiracy (and being the subject thereof) mentioned in section one of this act, and being in the course of transportation from one State to another, or to a foreign country, shall be forfeited to the United States, and may be seized and condemned by like proceedings as those provided by law for the forfeiture, seizure, and condemnation of property imported into the United States contrary to law.

SEC. 7. Any person who shall be injured in his business or property by any other person or corporation by reason of anything forbidden or declared to be unlawful by this act, may sue therefor in any circuit court of the United States in the district in which the defendant resides or is found, without respect to the amount in controversy, and shall recover three fold the damages by him sustained, and the costs of suit, including a reasonable attorney's fee.

SEC. 8. That the word "person," or "persons," wherever used in this act shall be deemed to include corporations and associations existing under or authorized by the laws of either the United States, the laws of any of the Territories, the laws of any State, or the laws of any foreign country. . . .

2. *UNITED STATES* v. *E. C. KNIGHT AND CO.*[1]

EDITORS' NOTE.—In this case the attempt to enforce the Sherman Antitrust Act gave a conservative Supreme Court the opportunity to define very strictly the power of Congress under the commerce clause—a definition now long outmoded. A combination of sugar-refining companies operating refineries in Pennsylvania and other states comprised 98 per cent of the sugar-refining capacity of the country. Although the refineries shipped their sugar into a national market, it was held that they were engaged only in local manufacture and that the combination was not subject to the federal act, which condemned combinations in "restraint of trade or commerce among the several states," or indeed to the power of Congress under the commerce clause. Needless to say, this decision would have rendered the Sherman Act useless, except in its application to railroads and similar agencies, and the Court began to depart from the theory of the present decision within

1. 156 U.S. 1, 9, 12–13, 16–18, 32–33, 37, 42–43 (1895).

five years. While the decision has been generally discredited, Mr. Justice Harlan alone dissented. It will be recalled that he was a vigorous champion of Negro rights under the Civil War amendments, and he dissented in other cases in which it was his opinion that individual liberty was in fact being subordinated to industrial power in the name of economic freedom.

Mr. Chief Justice FULLER, after stating the case, delivered the opinion of the court. . . .

The argument is that the power to control the manufacture of refined sugar is a monopoly over a necessary of life, to the enjoyment of which by a large part of the population of the United States interstate commerce is indispensable, and that, therefore, the general government in the exercise of the power to regulate commerce may repress such monopoly directly and set aside the instruments which have created it. But this argument cannot be confined to necessaries of life merely, and must include all articles of general consumption. Doubtless the power to control the manufacture of a given thing involves in a certain sense the control of its disposition, but this is a secondary and not the primary sense; and although the exercise of that power may result in bringing the operation of commerce into play, it does not control it, and affects it only incidentally and indirectly. Commerce succeeds to manufacture, and is not a part of it. The power to regulate commerce is the power to prescribe the rule by which commerce shall be governed, and is a power independent of the power to suppress monopoly. But it may operate in repression of monopoly whenever that comes within the rules by which commerce is governed or whenever the transaction is itself a monopoly of commerce.

It is vital that the independence of the commercial power and of the police power, and the delimitation between them, however sometimes perplexing, should always be recognized and observed, for while the one furnishes the strongest bond of union, the other is essential to the preservation of the autonomy of the States as required by our dual form of government; and acknowledged evils, however grave and urgent they may appear to be, had better be borne, than the risk be run, in the effort to suppress them, of more serious consequences by resort to expedients of even doubtful constitutionality. . . .

Contracts, combinations, or conspiracies to control domestic enterprise in manufacture, agriculture, mining, production in all its forms, or to raise or lower prices or wages, might unquestionably tend to restrain external as well as domestic trade, but the restraint would be an indirect result, however inevitable and whatever its extent, and such result would not necessarily determine the object of the contract, combination, or conspiracy.

Again, all the authorities agree that in order to vitiate a contract or combination it is not essential that its result should be a complete monopoly; it is sufficient if it really tends to that end and to deprive the public of the advantages which flow from free competition. Slight reflection will show that if the national power extends to all contracts and combinations in manufacture, agriculture, mining, and other productive industries, whose ultimate result may affect external commerce, comparatively little of business operations and affairs would be left for state control.

It was in the light of well-settled principles that the act of July 2, 1890, was framed. . . . [W]hat the law struck at was combinations, contracts, and conspiracies to monopolize trade and commerce among the several States or with foreign nations; but the contracts and acts of the defendants related exclusively to the acquisition of the Philadelphia refineries and the business of sugar refining in Pennsylvania, and bore no direct relation to commerce between the States or with foreign nations. The object was manifestly private gain in the manufacture of the commodity, but not through the control of interstate or foreign commerce. . . .

Mr. Justice HARLAN, dissenting. . . .

But there is a trade among the several States which is distinct from that carried on within the territorial limits of a State. The regulation and control of the former is committed by the national Constitution of Congress. Commerce among the States, as this court has declared, is a unit, and in respect of *that* commerce this is one country, and we are one people. It may be regulated by rules applicable to every part of the United States, and state lines and state jurisdiction cannot interfere with the enforcement of such rules. The jurisdiction of the general government extends over every foot of territory within the United States. Under the power with which it is invested, Congress may remove unlawful obstructions, of whatever kind, to the free course of trade among the States. In so doing it would not interfere with the "autonomy of the States," because the power thus to protect interstate commerce is expressly given by the people of all the States. Interstate intercourse, trade, and traffic is absolutely free, except as such intercourse, trade, or traffic may be incidentally or indirectly affected by the exercise by the States of their reserved police powers. . . . It is the Constitution, the supreme law of the land, which invests Congress with power to protect commerce among the States against burdens and exactions arising from unlawful restraints by whatever authority imposed. Surely a right secured or granted by that instrument is under the protection of the government which that instrument creates. Any combination, therefore, that disturbs or unreasonably obstructs freedom in buying and selling articles manufactured to be sold to persons in other States or to be carried to other States—a freedom that cannot exist if the right to buy and sell is fettered by unlawful restraints that crush out competi-

tion—affects, not incidentally, but directly, the people of all the States; and the remedy for such an evil is found only in the exercise of powers confided to a government which, this court has said, was the government of all, exercising powers delegated by all, representing all, acting for all. . . .

In my judgment, the citizens of the several States composing the Union are entitled, of right, to buy goods in the State where they are manufactured, or in any other State, without being confronted by an illegal combination whose business extends throughout the whole country, which by the law everywhere is an enemy to the public interests, and which prevents such buying, except at prices arbitrarily fixed by it. I insist that the free course of trade among the States cannot coexist with such combinations. When I speak of trade I mean the buying and selling of articles of every kind that are recognized articles of interstate commerce. Whatever improperly obstructs the free course of interstate intercourse and trade, as involved in the buying and selling of articles to be carried from one State to another, may be reached by Congress, under its authority to regulate commerce among the States. The exercise of that authority so as to make trade among the States, in all recognized articles of commerce, absolutely free from unreasonable or illegal restrictions imposed by combinations, is justified by an express grant of power to Congress and would redound to the welfare of the whole country. I am unable to perceive that any such result would imperil the autonomy of the States, especially as that result cannot be attained through the action of any one State. . . .

While the opinion of the court in this case does not declare the act of 1890 to be unconstitutional, it defeats the main object for which it was passed. For it is, in effect, held that the statute would be unconstitutional if interpreted as embracing such unlawful restraints upon the purchasing of goods in one State to be carried to another

State as necessarily arise from the *existence* of combinations formed for the purpose and with the effect, not only of monopolizing the ownership of all such goods in every part of the country, but of controlling the prices for them in all the States. This view of the scope of the act leaves the public, so far as national power is concerned, entirely at the mercy of combinations which arbitrarily control the prices of articles purchased to be transported from one State to another State. I cannot assent to that view. In my judgment, the general government is not placed by the Constitution in such a condition of helplessness that it must fold its arms and remain inactive while capital combines, under the name of a corporation, to destroy competition, not in one State only, but throughout the entire country, in the buying and selling of articles—especially the necessaries of life—that go into commerce among the States. The doctrine of the autonomy of the States cannot properly be invoked to justify a denial of power in the national government to meet such an emergency, involving as it does that freedom of commercial intercourse among the States which the Constitution sought to attain. . . .

3. THE FEDERAL TRADE COMMISSION ACT, 1914[1]

EDITORS' NOTE.—The Federal Trade Commission was set up to maintain fair competition in interstate commerce. For the breaking-up of combinations the Antitrust Division of the Department of Justice seems to be a more effective instrument. The commission has been very useful, however, in stopping misleading advertising, misbranding of products, and other "unfair" practices. Often it has not had to use its full powers but has led to the stoppage of such practices by voluntary agreement, as will be clear from a later reading by Secretary of Commerce Herbert Hoover (p. 487). It has also been instrumental in setting up conferences with businessmen in which the differences between fair and unfair methods of competition are defined.

. . . An Act to create a Federal Trade Commission, to define its powers and duties, and for other purposes.

Be it enacted . . . That a commission is hereby created and established, to be known as the Federal Trade Commission (hereinafter referred to as the commission), which shall be composed of five commissioners, who shall be appointed by the President, by and with the advice and consent of the Senate. Not more than three of the commissioners shall be members of the same political party. The first commissioners appointed shall continue in office for terms of three, four, five, six, and seven years, respectively, from the date of the taking effect of this Act, the term of each to be designated by the President, but their successors shall be appointed for terms of seven years, except that any person chosen to fill a vacancy shall be appointed only for the unexpired term of the commissioner whom he shall succeed. The commission shall choose a chairman from its own membership. No commissioner shall engage in any other business, vocation, or employment. Any commissioner may be removed by the President for inefficiency, neglect of duty, or malfeasance in office. A vacancy in the commission

1. *United States Statutes at Large* . . . (Washington, 1915), XXXVIII, Part I, 717–21.

shall not impair the right of the remaining commissioners to exercise all the powers of the commission. . . .

Sec. 3. That upon the organization of the commission and election of its chairman, the Bureau of Corporations and the offices of Commissioner and Deputy Commissioner of Corporations shall cease to exist; and all pending investigations and proceedings of the Bureau of Corporations shall be continued by the commission. . . .

Sec. 4. That the words defined in this section shall have the following meaning when found in this Act, to wit:

"Commerce" means commerce among the several States or with foreign nations, or in any Territory of the United States or in the District of Columbia, or between any such Territory and another, or between any such Territory and any State or foreign nation, or between the District of Columbia and any State or Territory or foreign nation. . . .

Sec. 5. That unfair methods of competition in commerce are hereby declared unlawful.

The commission is hereby empowered and directed to prevent persons, partnerships, or corporations, except banks, and common carriers subject to the Acts to regulate commerce, from using unfair methods of competition in commerce.

Whenever the commission shall have reason to believe that any such person, partnership, or corporation has been or is using any unfair method of competition in commerce, and if it shall appear to the commission that a proceeding by it in respect thereof would be to the interest of the public, it shall issue and serve upon such person, partnership, or corporation a complaint stating its charges in that respect, and containing a notice of a hearing upon a day and at a place therein fixed at least thirty days after the service of said complaint. The person, partnership, or corporation so complained of shall have the right to appear at the place and time so fixed and show cause why an order should not be entered by the commission requir-

ing such person, partnership, or corporation to cease and desist from the violation of the law so charged in said complaint. . . . The testimony in any such proceeding shall be reduced to writing and filed in the office of the commission. If upon such hearing the commission shall be of the opinion that the method of competition in question is prohibited by this Act, it shall make a report in writing in which it shall state its findings as to the facts, and shall issue and cause to be served on such person, partnership, or corporation an order requiring such person, partnership, or corporation to cease and desist from using such method of competition. . . .

If such person, partnership, or corporation fails or neglects to obey such order of the commission while the same is in effect, the commission may apply to the circuit court of appeals of the United States, within any circuit where the method of competition in question was used or where such person, partnership, or corporation resides or carries on business, for the enforcement of its order. . . . Upon such filing . . . the court . . . shall have power to make and enter upon the pleadings, testimony, and proceedings set forth in such transcript a decree affirming, modifying, or setting aside the order of the commission. The findings of the commission as to the facts, if supported by testimony, shall be conclusive. . . .

Any party required by such order of the commission to cease and desist from using such method of competition may obtain a review of such order in said circuit court of appeals by filing in the court a written petition praying that the order of the commission be set aside.

Sec. 6. That the commission shall also have power—

(a) To gather and compile information concerning, and to investigate from time to time the organization, business, conduct, practices, and management of any corporation engaged in commerce, excepting banks and common carriers subject to the Act to regulate commerce, and its relation to other corporations and to individuals, associations, and partnerships.

(b) To require, by general or special orders, corporations engaged in commerce, excepting banks, and common carriers subject to the Act to regulate commerce . . . to file with the commission in such form as the commission may prescribe . . . reports or answers in writing to specific questions, furnishing to the commission such information as it may require as to the organization, business, conduct, practices, management, and relation to other corporations, partnerships, and individuals of the respective corporations filing such reports or answers in writing. . . .

(c) Whenever a final decree has been entered against any defendant corporation in any suit brought by the United States to prevent and restrain any violation of the antitrust Acts, to make investigation, upon its own initiative, of the manner in which the decree has been or is being carried out, and upon the application of the Attorney General it shall be its duty to make such investigation. It shall transmit to the Attorney General a report embodying its findings and recommendations as a result of any such investigation, and the report shall be made public in the discretion of the commission. . . .

4. THE CLAYTON ANTITRUST ACT, 1914[1]

EDITORS' NOTE.—Shortly after the Federal Trade Commission Act had been passed, the Democratic Congress supplemented the Sherman Antitrust Act of 1890 with the Clayton Antitrust Act of 1914. In this measure a number of undesirable practices of "big business" were declared illegal and an attempt was made—or seemed to be made—to relieve labor unions from prosecution under the antitrust laws.

As it turned out later, however, the ambiguity of the language of the act enabled conservative courts to retain their earlier powers to issue injunctions which often paralyzed the activities of militant unions. Only in 1932 was organized labor protected from such court interference by the Norris–La Guardia Anti-injunction Act of that year.

. . . An Act to supplement existing laws against unlawful restraints and monopolies, and for other purposes.

Be it enacted. . . .

SEC. 2. That it shall be unlawful for any person engaged in commerce, in the course of such commerce, either directly or indirectly to discriminate in price between different purchasers of commodities, which commodities are sold for use, consumption, or resale within the United States or any . . . other place under the jurisdiction of the United States, where the effect of

such discrimination may be to substantially lessen competition or tend to create a monopoly in any line of commerce. . . .

SEC. 3. That it shall be unlawful for any person engaged in commerce, in the course of such commerce, to lease or make a sale . . . of goods . . . or other commodities . . . within the United States . . . or other place under the jurisdiction of the United States, or fix a price charged therefor, or discount from, or rebate upon, such price, on the condition, agreement or understanding that the lessee or purchaser thereof shall not use or deal in the goods . . . or other commodities of a competitor or com-

1. *United States Statutes at Large* . . . (Washington, 1915), XXXVIII, Part I, 730–34, 738.

petitors of the lessor or seller, where the effect of such lease, sale, or contract for sale or such condition, agreement or understanding may be to substantially lessen competition or tend to create a monopoly in any line of commerce. . . .

SEC. 6. That the labor of a human being is not a commodity or article of commerce. Nothing contained in the antitrust laws shall be construed to forbid the existence and operation of labor, agricultural, or horticultural organizations, instituted for the purposes of mutual help, and not having capital stock or conducted for profit, or to forbid or restrain individual members of such organizations from lawfully carrying out the legitimate objects thereof; nor shall such organizations, or the members thereof, be held or construed to be illegal combinations or conspiracies in restraint of trade, under the antitrust laws.

SEC. 7. That no corporation engaged in commerce shall acquire, directly or indirectly, the whole or any part of the stock or other share capital of another corporation engaged also in commerce, where the effect of such acquisition may be to substantially lessen competition between the corporation whose stock is so acquired and the corporation making the acquisition, or to restrain such commerce in any section or community, or tend to create a monopoly of any line of commerce. . . .

This section shall not apply to corporations purchasing such stock solely for investment and not using the same by voting or otherwise to bring about, or in attempting to bring about, the substantial lessening of competition. . . .

SEC. 8. That from and after two years from the date of the approval of this Act no person shall at the same time be a director or other officer or employee of more than one bank, banking association or trust company, organized or operating under the laws of the United States, either of which has deposits, capital, surplus, and undivided profits aggregating more than

$5,000,000; and no private banker or person who is a director in any bank or trust company, organized and operating under the laws of a State, having deposits, capital, surplus, and undivided profits aggregating more than $5,000,000, shall be eligible to be a director in any bank or banking association organized or operating under the laws of the United States. . . .

That from and after two years from the date of the approval of this Act no person at the same time shall be a director in any two or more corporations, any one of which has capital, surplus, and undivided profits aggregating more than $1,000,000, engaged in whole or in part in commerce, other than banks, banking associations, trust companies and common carriers subject to the Act to regulate commerce, approved February fourth, eighteen hundred and eighty-seven, if such corporations are or shall have been theretofore, by virtue of their business and location of operation, competitors, so that the elimination of competition by agreement between them would constitute a violation of any of the provisions of any of the antitrust laws. . . .

SEC. 10. That after two years from the approval of this Act no common carrier engaged in commerce shall have any dealings in securities, supplies or other articles of commerce, or shall make or have any contracts for construction or maintenance of any kind, to the amount of more than $50,000, in the aggregate, in any one year, with another corporation, firm, partnership or association when the said common carrier shall have upon its board of directors or as its president, manager or as its purchasing or selling officer, or agent in the particular transaction, any person who is at the same time a director, manager, or purchasing or selling officer of, or who has any substantial interest in, such other corporation, firm, partnership or association, unless and except such purchases shall be made from, or such dealings shall be with, the bidder whose bid is the most favorable to such common carrier, to be ascertained by competitive bidding under regulations to be prescribed by rule or otherwise by the Interstate Commerce Commission. . . .

SEC. 11. That authority to enforce compliance with sections two, three, seven and eight of this Act by the persons respectively subject thereto is hereby vested: in the Interstate Commerce Commission where applicable to common carriers, in the Federal Reserve Board where applicable to banks, banking associations and trust companies, and in the Federal Trade Commission where applicable to all other character of commerce. . . .

SEC. 20. That no restraining order or injunction shall be granted by any court of the United States, or a judge or the judges thereof, in any case between an employer and employees, or between employers and employees, or between employees, or between persons employed and persons seeking employment, involving, or growing out of, a dispute concerning terms or conditions of employment, unless necessary to prevent irreparable injury to property, or to a property right, of the party making the application, for which injury there is no adequate remedy at law, and such property or property right must be described with particularity in the application, which must be in writing and sworn to by the applicant or by his agent or attorney.

And no such restraining order or injunction shall prohibit any person or persons, whether singly or in concert, from terminating any relation of employment, or from ceasing to perform any work or labor, or from recommending, advising, or persuading others by peaceful means so to do; or from attending at any place where any such person or persons may lawfully be, for the purpose of peacefully obtaining or communicating information, or from peacefully persuading any person to work or to abstain from working; or from ceasing to patronize or to employ any party to such dispute, or from recommending, advising, or persuading others by peaceful and lawful means so to do; or from paying or giving to, or withholding from, any person engaged in such dispute, any strike benefits or other moneys or things of value; or from peaceably assembling in a lawful manner, and for lawful purposes; or from doing any act or thing which might lawfully be done in the absence of such dispute by any party thereto; nor shall any of the acts specified in this paragraph be considered or held to be violations of any law of the United States. . . .

5. *STANDARD OIL COMPANY OF NEW JERSEY ET AL.* v. *UNITED STATES*[1]

EDITORS' NOTE.—In the famous "rule of reason" in this decision the Supreme Court adopted Theodore Roosevelt's distinction between "good" and "bad" trusts. For the application of this rule see the United States Steel case in the next reading.

In 1906 the United States government instituted a suit which sought to dissolve the Standard Oil Company as a combination in violation of the Sherman Antitrust Act. The government described three stages through which, they charged, the Standard Oil Company had perfected its combination. First, between 1870 and 1882, working through the Standard Oil Company of Ohio, Mr. Rockefeller and his associates had gained control of 90 per cent of oil production and products. Control of refineries and of pipe lines, along with agreements with railroads,

1. 221 U.S. 1, 30, 48, 50–52, 55–56, 58–60, 62, 75–77, 82–84, 98–99, 105 (1911).

were the chief means then used. In the second period (1882–99) the trustee system was used by which stockholders in the several companies put their stock into the hands of trustees, who issued them trust certificates in return. Thus a more efficient operation of the total resources of the combination could be secured without injury to one group among the stockholders of the several operating companies. In 1899 the third period began

Mr. Chief Justice WHITE delivered the opinion of the court. . . .

Duly appreciating the situation just stated, it is certain that only one point of concord between the parties is discernable, which is, that the controversy in every aspect is controlled by a correct conception of the meaning of the first and second sections of the Anti-trust Act. . . .

The debates show that doubt as to whether there was a common law of the United States which governed the subject in the absence of legislation was among the influences leading to the passage of the act. They conclusively show, however, that the main cause which led to the legislation was the thought that it was required by the economic condition of the times, that is, the vast accumulation of wealth in the hands of corporations and individuals, the enormous development of corporate organization, the facility for combination which such organizations afforded, the fact that the facility was being used, and that combinations known as trusts were being multiplied, and the widespread impression that their power had been and would be exerted to oppress individuals and injure the public generally. Although debates may not be used as a means for interpreting a statute (*United States* v. *Trans-Missouri Freight Association*, 166 U.S. 318, and cases cited) that rule in the nature of things is not violated by resorting to debates as a means of ascertaining

with the substitution of a holding company, the Standard Oil Company of New Jersey, for the trust device. The holding company maintained unified direction through control of a majority of the stock of each constituent company. The charges against the Standard Oil Company were substantially those which Henry Demarest Lloyd had publicized earlier (p. 64). In the Circuit Court the decision was in favor of the government.

the environment at the time of the enactment of a particular law, that is, the history of the period when it was adopted.

There can be no doubt that the sole subject with which the first section deals is restraint of trade as therein contemplated, and that the attempt to monopolize and monopolization is the subject with which the second section is concerned. It is certain that those terms, at least in their rudimentary meaning, took their origin in the common law, and were also familiar in the law of this country prior to and at the time of the adoption of the act in question.

We shall endeavor then, first to seek their meaning, not by indulging in an elaborate and learned analysis of the English law and of the law of this country, but by making a very brief reference to the elementary and indisputable conceptions of both the English and American law on the subject prior to the passage of the Anti-trust Act.

a. It is certain that at a very remote period the words "contract in restraint of trade" in English came to refer to some voluntary restraint put by contract by an individual on his right to carry on his trade or calling. Originally all such contracts were considered to be illegal, because it was deemed they were injurious to the public as well as to the individuals who made them. In the interest of the freedom of individuals to contract this doctrine was modified so that it was only when a restraint by contract was so general as to be coterminous with the kingdom that it was treated as void. That is to say, if the restraint was partial in its operation and was otherwise reasonable the contract was held to be valid:

b. Monopolies were defined by Lord Coke as follows: " 'A monopoly is an institution, or allowance by the king by his grant, commission, or otherwise to any person or persons, bodies politic or corporate, of or for the sole buying, selling, making, working, or using of anything, whereby any person or persons, bodies politic or corporate, are sought to be restrained of any freedom or liberty that they had before, or hindered in their lawful trade.' (3 Inst. 181, c. 85.)"

Hawkins thus defined them:

" 'A monopoly is an allowance by the king to a particular person or persons of the sole buying, selling, making, working, or using of anything whereby the subject in general is restrained from the freedom of manufacturing or trading which he had before.' (Hawk. P. C. bk. 1, c. 29.)"

The frequent granting of monopolies and the struggle which led to a denial of the power to create them, that is to say, to the establishment that they were incompatible with the English constitution is known to all and need not be reviewed. The evils which led to the public outcry against monopolies and to the final denial of the power to make them may be thus summarily stated: 1. The power which the monopoly gave to the one who enjoyed it to fix the price and thereby injure the public; 2. The power which it engendered of enabling a limitation on production; and, 3. The danger of deterioration in quality of the monopolized article which it was deemed was the inevitable resultant of the monopolistic control over its production and sale. As monopoly as thus conceived embraced only a consequence arising from an exertion of sovereign power, no express restrictions or prohibitions obtained against the creation by an individual of a monopoly as such. . . .

. . . It is remarkable that nowhere at common law can there be found a prohibition against the creation of monopoly by an individual. This would seem to manifest, either consciously or intuitively, a profound conception as to the inevitable operation of economic forces and the equipoise or balance in favor of the protection of the rights of individuals which resulted. . . .

In this country also the acts from which it was deemed there resulted a part if not all of the injurious consequences ascribed to monopoly, came to be referred to as a monopoly itself. . . .

Without going into detail and but very briefly surveying the whole field, it may be with accuracy said that the dread of enhancement of prices and of other wrongs which it was thought would flow from the undue limitation on competitive conditions caused by contracts or other acts of individuals or corporations, led, as a matter of public policy, to the prohibition or treating as illegal all contracts or acts which were unreasonably restrictive of competitive conditions, either from the nature or character of the contract or act or where the surrounding circumstances were such as to justify the conclusion that they had not been entered into or performed with the legitimate purpose of reasonably forwarding personal interest and developing trade, but on the contrary were of such a character as to give rise to the inference or presumption that they had been entered into or done with the intent to do wrong to the general public and to limit the right of individuals, thus restraining the free flow of commerce and tending to bring about the evils, such as enhancement of prices, which were considered to be against public policy. . . .

Let us consider the language of the first and second sections, guided by the principle that where words are employed in a statute which had at the time a well-known meaning at common law or in the law of this country they are presumed to have been used in that sense unless the context compels to the contrary. . . .

And as the contracts or acts embraced in the provision were not expressly defined, since the enumeration addressed itself simply to classes of acts, those classes being broad enough to embrace every conceivable contract or combination which could be made concerning trade or commerce or the subjects of such commerce, and thus caused any act done by any of the enumerated methods anywhere in the whole field of human activity to be illegal if in restraint of trade, it inevitably follows that the provision necessarily called for the exercise of judgment which required that some standard should be resorted to for the purpose of determining whether the prohibitions contained in the statute had or had not in any given case been violated. Thus not specifying but indubitably contemplating and requiring a standard, it follows that it was intended that the standard of reason which had been applied at the common law and in this country in dealing with subjects of the character embraced by the statute, was intended to be the measure used for the purpose of determining whether in a given case a particular act had or had not brought about the wrong against which the statute provided. . . .

. . . And it is worthy of observation, as we have previously remarked concerning the common law, that although the statute by the comprehensiveness of the enumerations embodied in both the first and second sections makes it certain that its purpose was to prevent undue restraints of every kind or nature, nevertheless by the omission of any direct prohibition against monopoly in the concrete it indicates a consciousness that the freedom of the individual right to contract when not unduly or improperly exercised was the most efficient means for the prevention of monopoly, since the operation of the centrifugal and centripetal forces resulting from the right to freely contract was the means by which monopoly would be inevitably prevented if no extraneous or sovereign power imposed it and no right to make unlawful contracts having a monopolistic tendency were permitted. In other words that freedom to contract was the essence of freedom from undue restraint on the right to contract. . . .

Recurring to the acts done by the individuals or corporations who were mainly instrumental in bringing about the expansion of the New Jersey corporation during the period prior to the formation of the trust agreements of 1879 and 1882, including those agreements, not for the purpose of weighing the substantial merit of the numerous charges of wrongdoing made during such period, but solely as an aid for discovering intent and purpose, we think no disinterested mind can survey the period in question without being irresistibly driven to the conclusion that the very genius for commercial development and organization which it would seem was manifested from the beginning soon begot an intent and purpose to exclude others which was frequently manifested by acts and dealings wholly inconsistent with the theory that they were made with the single conception of advancing the development of business power by usual methods, but which on the contrary necessarily involved the intent to drive others from the field and to exclude them from their right to trade and thus accomplish the mastery which was the end in view. And, considering the period from the date of the trust agreements of 1879 and 1882, up to the time of the expansion of the New Jersey corporation, the gradual extension of the power over the commerce in oil which ensued, the decision of the Supreme Court of Ohio, the tardiness or reluctance in conforming to the commands of that decision, the method first adopted and that which finally culminated in the plan of the New Jersey corporation, all additionally serve to make manifest the continued existence of the intent which we have previously indicated and which among other things impelled the expansion of the New Jersey corporation. The exercise of the power which resulted from that organization fortifies the foregoing conclusions, since the development which came, the acquisition here and there which ensued of every efficient means by which competition could have been asserted, the slow but resistless methods which followed by which means of transportation were absorbed and brought under control, the system of marketing which was adopted by which the country was divided into districts and the trade in each district in oil was turned over to a designated corporation within the combination and all others were excluded, all lead the mind up to a conviction of a purpose and intent which we think is so certain as practically to cause the subject not to be within the domain of reasonable contention.

The inference that no attempt to monopolize could have been intended, and that no monopolization resulted from the acts complained of, since it is established that a very small percentage of the crude oil produced was controlled by the combination, is unwarranted. As substantial power over the crude product was the inevitable result of the absolute control which existed over the refined product, the monopolization of the one carried with it the power to control the other, and if the inferences which this situation suggests were developed, which we deem it unnecessary to do, they might well serve to add additional cogency to the presumption of intent to monopolize which we have found arises from the unquestioned proof on other subjects. . . .

Mr. Justice HARLAN concurring in part, and dissenting in part.

A sense of duty constrains me to express the objections which I have to certain declarations in the opinion just delivered on behalf of the court.

I concur in holding that the Standard Oil Company of New Jersey and its subsidiary companies constitute a combination in restraint of interstate commerce, and that they have attempted to monopolize and have monopolized parts of such commerce—all in violation of what is known as the Anti-trust Act of 1890. . . .

All who recall the condition of the country in 1890 will remember that there was everywhere, among the people generally, a deep feeling of unrest. The Nation had been rid of human slavery—fortunately, as all now feel—but the conviction was universal that the country was in real danger from another kind of slavery sought to be fastened on the American people, namely, the slavery that would result from aggregations of capital in the hands of a few individuals and corporations controlling, for their own profit and advantage exclusively, the entire business of the country, including the production and sale of the necessaries of life. Such a danger was thought to be then imminent, and all felt that it must be met firmly and by such statutory regulations as would adequately protect the people against oppression and wrong. Congress therefore took up the matter and gave the whole subject the fullest consideration. All agreed that the National Government could not, by legislation, regulate the domestic trade carried on wholly within the several States; for, power to regulate such trade remained with, because never surrendered by, the States. But, under authority expressly granted to it by the Constitution, Congress could regulate commerce among the several States and with foreign states. Its authority to regulate such commerce was and is paramount, due force being given to other provisions of the fundamental law devised by the fathers for the safety of the Government and for the protection and security of the essential rights inhering in life, liberty and property.

Guided by these considerations, and to the end that the people, *so far as interstate commerce* was concerned, might not be dominated by vast combinations and monopolies, having power to advance their own selfish ends, regardless of the general interests and welfare, Congress passed the Anti-trust Act of 1890. . . .

After what has been adjudged, upon full consideration, as to the meaning and scope of the Anti-trust Act, and in view of the usages of this court when attorneys for litigants have attempted to reopen questions that have been deliberately decided, I confess to no little surprise as to what has occurred in the present case. . . . Now this court is asked to do that which it has distinctly declared it could not and would not do, and has now done what it then said it could not constitutionally do. It has, by mere interpretation, modified the act of Congress, and deprived it of practical value as a defensive measure against the evils to be remedied. . . .

After many years of public service at the National Capital, and after a somewhat close observation of the conduct of public affairs, I am impelled to say that there is abroad, in our land, a most harmful tendency to bring about the amending of constitutions and legislative enactments by means alone of judicial construction. As a public policy has been declared by the legislative department in respect of interstate commerce, over which Congress has entire control, under the Constitution, all concerned must patiently submit to what has been lawfully done, until the People of the United States—the source of all National power—shall, in their own time, upon reflection and through the legislative department of the Government, require a change of that policy. There are some who say that it is a part of one's liberty to conduct commerce among the States without being subject to governmental authority. But that would not be liberty, regulated by law, and liberty, which cannot be regulated by law, is not to be desired. The Supreme Law of the Land—which is binding alike upon all—upon Presidents, Congresses, the Courts and the People—gives to Congress, and to Congress alone, authority to regulate interstate commerce, and when Congress forbids *any* restraint of such commerce, in any form, all must obey its mandate. To overreach the action of Congress merely by judicial construction, that is, by indirection, is a blow at the integrity of our governmental system, and in the end will prove most dangerous to all. . . .

6. *UNITED STATES* v. *UNITED STATES STEEL CORPORATION ET AL.*[1]

EDITORS' NOTE.—The "rule of reason" established in the Standard Oil case was applied here, and later anti-trust cases came to be based upon the character of the practices engaged in rather than upon the size or power of the corporation or combination. The issue goes to the heart of the philosophy upon which the Sherman Antitrust Act was based and was important later in the New Deal and today.

Mr. Justice McKENNA delivered the opinion of the court.

Suit against the Steel Corporation and certain other companies which it directs and controls by reason of the ownership of their stock, it and they being separately and collectively charged as violators of the Sherman Anti-Trust Act.

1. 251 U.S. 417, 436–42, 444–45, 447–49, 451, 457–58, 463–66 (1920).

It is prayed that it and they be dissolved because engaged in illegal restraint of trade and the exercise of monopoly.

Special charges of illegality and monopoly are made and special redresses and remedies are prayed, among others, that there be a prohibition of stock ownership and exercise of rights under such ownership, and that there shall be such orders and distribution of the stock and other properties as shall be in accordance with equity and good conscience and "shall effectuate the purpose of the Anti-Trust Act." General relief is also prayed.

The Steel Corporation is a holding company only; the other companies are the operating ones, manufacturers in the iron and steel industry, twelve in number. There are, besides, other corporations and individuals more or less connected with the activities of the other defendants that are alleged to be instruments or accomplices in their activities and offendings; and that these activities and offendings (speaking in general terms) extend from 1901 to 1911, when the bill was filed, and have illustrative periods of significant and demonstrated illegality.

Issue is taken upon all these charges, and we see at a glance what detail of circumstances may be demanded, and we may find ourselves puzzled to compress them into an opinion that will not be of fatiguing prolixity.

The case was heard in the District Court by four judges. They agreed that the bill should be dismissed; they disagreed as to the reasons for it. 223 Fed. Rep. 55. One opinion (written by Judge Buffington and concurred in by Judge McPherson) expressed the view that the Steel Corporation was not formed with the intention or purpose to monopolize or restrain trade, and did not have the motive or effect "to prejudice the public interest by unduly restricting competition or unduly obstructing the course of trade." The corporation, in the view of the opinion, was an evolution, a natural consummation of the tendencies of the industry on account of changing conditions, practically a compulsion from "the metallurgical method of making steel and the physical method of handling it," this method, and the conditions consequent upon it, tending to combinations of capital and energies rather than diffusion in independent action. And the concentration of powers (we are still representing the opinion) was only such as was deemed necessary, and immediately

manifested itself in improved methods and products and in an increase of domestic and foreign trade. Indeed an important purpose of the organization was the building up of the export trade in steel and iron which at that time was sporadic, the mere dumping of the products upon foreign markets.

Not monopoly, therefore, was the purpose of the organization of the corporation but concentration of efforts with resultant economies and benefits.

The tendency of the industry and the purpose of the corporation in yielding to it was [*sic*] expressed in comprehensive condensation by the word "integration," which signifies continuity in the processes of the industry from ore mines to the finished product.

All considerations deemed pertinent were expressed and their influence was attempted to be assigned and, while conceding that the Steel Corporation, after its formation in times of financial disturbance, entered into informal agreements or understandings with its competitors to maintain prices, they terminated with their occasions, and, as they had ceased to exist, the court was not justified in dissolving the corporation.

The other opinion (by Judge Woolley and concurred in by Judge Hunt, 223 Fed. 161) was in some particulars, in antithesis to Judge Buffington's. The view was expressed that neither the Steel Corporation nor the preceding combinations, which were in a sense its antetypes, had the justification of industrial conditions, nor were they or it impelled by the necessity for integration, or compelled to unite in comprehensive enterprise because such had become a condition of success under the new order of things. On the contrary, that the organizers of the corporation and the preceding companies had illegal purpose from the very beginning, and the corporation became "a combination of combinations by which, directly or indirectly, approximately 180 independent concerns were brought under one business control," which, measured by the amount of production, extended to 80 per cent or 90 per cent of the entire output of the country, and that its purpose was to secure great profits which were thought possible in the light of the history of its constituent combinations, and to accomplish permanently what those combinations had demonstrated could be accomplished temporarily, and thereby monopolize and restrain trade.[2]

2. As bearing upon the power obtained and what the corporation did we give other citations from Judge Woolley's opinion as follows:

"The ore reserves acquired by the corporation at and subsequent to its organization, the relation which such reserves bear to ore bodies then existing and subsequently discovered, and their bearing upon the question of monopoly of raw materials, are matters which have been discussed in the preceding opinion, and with the reasoning as well as with the conclusion that the corporation has not a monopoly of the raw materials of the steel industry, I am in entire accord.

"Further inquiring whether the corporation inherently possesses monopolistic power attention is next given to its proportion of the manufacture and sale of finished iron and steel products of the industry. Upon this subject there is a great volume of testimony, a detailed consideration of which in an opinion would be quite inexcusable. As a last analysis of this testimony, it is sufficient to say it shows that, large as was the corporation, and substantial as was its proportion of the business of the industry, the corporation was not able in the first ten years of its history to maintain its position in the increase of trade. During that period, its proportion of the domestic business decreased from 50.1 per cent to 40.9 per cent and its increase of business during that period was but 40.6 per cent of its original volume. Its increase of business, measured by percentage, was exceeded by eight of its competitors, whose increase of business, likewise measured by percentage, ranged from 63 to 3779. This disparity in the increase of production indicates that the power of the corporation is not commensurate with its size, and that the size and the consequent power of the corporation are not sufficient to retard prosperous growth of efficient competitors.

"From the vast amount of testimony, it is conclusively shown that the Steel Corporation did not attempt to exert a power, if such it possessed, to oppress and destroy its competitors, and it is likewise disclosed by the history of the industry subsequent to the organization of the corporation that if it had made such an attempt it would have failed. It is also shown by the testimony that, act-

The organizers, however (we are still representing the opinion), underestimated the opposing conditions and at the very beginning the Corporation instead of relying upon its own power sought and obtained the assistance and the cooperation of its competitors (the independent companies). In other words the view was expressed that the testimony did "not show that the corporation in and of itself ever possessed or exerted sufficient power when acting alone to control prices of the products of the industry." Its power was efficient only when in cooperation with its competitors, and hence it concerted with them in the expedients of pools, associations, trade meetings, and finally in a system of dinners inaugurated in 1907 by the president of the company, E. H. Gary, and called "the Gary Dinners." The dinners were congregations of producers and "were nothing but trade meetings," successors of the other means of associated action and control through such action. They were instituted first in "stress of panic," but, their potency being demonstrated, they were afterwards called to control prices "in periods of industrial calm." "They were pools without penalties" and more efficient in stabilizing prices. But it was the further declaration that "when joint action was either refused or withdrawn the corporation's prices were controlled by competition."

The corporation, it was said, did not at any time abuse the power or ascendency it possessed. It resorted to none of the brutalities or tyrannies that the cases illustrate of other combinations. It did not secure freight rebates; it did not increase its profits by reducing the wages of its employés —whatever it did was not at the expense of labor; it did not increase its profits by low-

---

ing independently and relying alone upon its power and wealth, great as they were, the corporation has never been able to dominate the steel industry by controlling the supply of raw materials, restraining production of finished products, or enhancing and maintaining the prices of either."
—Author's Note.

ering the quality of its products, nor create an artificial scarcity of them; it did not oppress or coerce its competitors—its competition, though vigorous, was fair; it did not undersell its competitors in some localities by reducing its prices there below these maintained elsewhere, or require its customers to enter into contracts limiting their purchases or restricting them in resale prices; it did not obtain customers by secret rebates or departures from its published prices; there was no evidence that it attempted to crush its competitors or drive them out of the market, nor did it take customers from its competitors by unfair means, and in its competition it seemed to make no difference between large and small competitors. Indeed it is said in many ways and illustrated that "instead of relying upon its own power to fix and maintain prices, the corporation, at its very beginning sought and obtained the assistance of others." It combined its power with that of its competitors. It did not have power in and of itself, and the control it exerted was only in and by association with its competitors. Its offense, therefore, such as it was, was not different from theirs and was distinguished from "theirs only in the leadership it assumed in promulgating and perfecting the policy." This leadership it gave up and it had ceased to offend against the law before this suit was brought. It was hence concluded that it should be distinguished from its organizers and that their intent and unsuccessful attempt should not be attributed to it, that it "in and of itself is not now and has never been a monopoly or a combination in restraint of trade," and a decree of dissolution should not be entered against it.

This summary of the opinions, given necessarily in paraphrase, does not adequately represent their ability and strength, but it has value as indicating the contentions of the parties, and the ultimate propositions to which the contentions are addressed. The opinions indicate that the evidence admits of different deductions as

to the genesis of the corporation and the purpose of its organizers, but only of a single deduction as to the power it attained and could exercise. Both opinions were clear and confident that the power of the corporation never did and does not now reach to monopoly, and their review of the evidence, and our independent examination of it, enable us to elect between their respective estimates of it, and we concur in the main with that of Judges Woolley and Hunt. . . .

We have seen that the judges of the District Court unanimously concurred in the view that the corporation did not achieve monopoly, and such is our deduction, and it is against monopoly that the statute is directed, not against an expectation of it, but against its realization, and it is certain that it was not realized. The opposing conditions were underestimated. The power attained was much greater than that possessed by any one competitor—it was not greater than that possessed by all of them. Monopoly, therefore, was not achieved, and competitors had to be persuaded by pools, associations, trade meetings, and through the social form of dinners, all of them, it may be, violations of the law, but transient in their purpose and effect. They were scattered through the years from 1901 (the year of the formation of the corporation), until 1911, but, after instances of success and failure, were abandoned nine months before this suit was brought. There is no evidence that the abandonment was in prophecy of or dread of suit; and the illegal practices have not been resumed, nor is there any evidence of an intention to resume them, and certainly no "dangerous probability" of their resumption. . . .

What then can now be urged against the corporation? Can comparisons in other regards be made with its competitors and by such comparisons guilty or innocent existence be assigned it? It is greater in size and productive power than any of its competitors, equal or nearly equal to them all, but its power over prices was not and is not commensurate with its power to produce. . . .

. . . The company's officers and, as well, its competitors and customers, testified that its competition was genuine, direct and vigorous, and was reflected in prices and production. No practical witness was produced by the Government in opposition. Its contention is based on the size and asserted dominance of the Corporation—alleged power for evil, not the exertion of the power in evil. Or, as counsel put it, "a combination may be illegal because of its purpose; it may be illegal because it acquires a dominating power, not as a result of normal growth and development, but as a result of a combination of competitors." Such composition and its resulting power constitute, in the view of the Government, the offence against the law, and yet it is admitted "no competitor came forward and said he had to accept the Steel Corporation's prices." But this absence of complaint counsel urge against the corporation. Competitors, it is said, followed the corporation's prices because they made money by the imitation. Indeed the imitation is urged as an evidence of the corporation's power. "Universal imitation," counsel assert, is "an evidence of power." In this concord of action, the contention is, there is the sinister dominance of the corporation—"its extensive control of the industry is such that the others [independent companies] follow." Counsel, however, admit that there was "occasionally" some competition, but reject the suggestion that it extended practically to a war between the corporation and the independents. Counsel say: "They [the corporation is made a plural] called a few— they called 200 witnesses out of some forty thousand customers, and they expect with that customer evidence to overcome the whole train of price movement shown since the Corporation was formed." And, "movement of prices," counsel explained, "as shown by the published prices, . . . they were the ones that the competitors were maintaining all during the interval."

It would seem that "200 witnesses" would be fairly representative. Besides the balance of the "forty thousand customers" was open to the government to draw upon. Not having done so, is it not permissible to infer that none would testify to the existence of the influence that the government asserts? At any rate not one was called, but instead the opinion of an editor of a trade journal is adduced, and that of an author and teacher of economics whose philosophical deductions had, perhaps, fortification from experience as Deputy Commissioner of Corporations and as an employé in the Bureau of Corporations. His deduction was that when prices are constant through a definite period an artificial influence is indicated; if they vary during such a period it is a consequence of competitive conditions. It has become an aphorism that there is danger of deception in generalities, and in a case of this importance we should have something surer for judgment than speculation, something more than a deduction equivocal of itself even though the facts it rests on or asserts were not contradicted. If the phenomena of production and prices were as easily resolved as the witness implied, much discussion and much literature have been wasted, and some of the problems that are now distracting the world would be given composing solution. Of course, competition affects prices; but it is only one among other influences and does not, more than they, register itself in definite and legible effect.

We magnify the testimony by its consideration. Against it competitors, dealers and customers of the Corporation testify in multitude that no adventitious interference was employed to either fix or maintain prices and that they were constant or varied according to natural conditions. . . .

. . . The Corporation is undoubtedly of impressive size and it takes an effort of resolution not to be affected by it or to exaggerate its influence. But we must adhere to the law and the law does not make mere size an offence or the existence of unexerted power an offence. . . .

In conclusion we are unable to see that the public interest will be served by yielding to the contention of the Government respecting the dissolution of the company or the separation from it of some of its subsidiaries; and we do see in a contrary conclusion a risk of injury to the public interest, including a material disturbance of, and, it may be serious detriment to, the foreign trade. And in submission to the policy of the law and its fortifying prohibitions the public interest is of paramount regard.

We think, therefore, that the decree of the District Court should be affirmed.

So ordered.

Mr. Justice McREYNOLDS and Mr. Justice BRANDEIS took no part in the consideration or decision of the case.

Mr. Justice DAY dissenting.

This record seems to me to leave no fair room for a doubt that the defendants, the United States Steel Corporation and the several subsidiary corporations which make up that organization, were formed in violation of the Sherman Act. I am unable to accept the conclusion which directs a dismissal of the bill instead of following the well-settled practice, sanctioned by previous decisions of this court, requiring the dissolution of combinations made in direct violation of the law. . . .

There is no mistaking the terms of the act as they have hitherto been interpreted by this court. It was not intended to merely suppress unfair practices, but, as its history and terms amply show, it was intended to make it criminal to form combinations or engage in conspiracies or contracts in restraint of interstate trade. The remedy by injunction, at the instance of the Attorney General, was given for the purpose of enabling the courts, as the statute states, to prohibit such conspiracies, combinations and contracts, and this court interpreting its provisions has held that the proper enforcement of the act requires decrees to end combinations by dissolving them and restoring as far as possible the competitive conditions which the combinations have destroyed. . . .

Nor can I yield assent to the proposition that this combination has not acquired a dominant position in the trade which enables it to control prices and production when it sees fit to exert its power. Its total assets on December 31, 1913, were in excess of $1,800,000,000; its outstanding capital stock was $868,583,600; its surplus $151,798,428. Its cash on hand ordinarily was $75,000,000; this sum alone exceeded the total capitalization of any of its competitors, and with a single exception, the total capitalization and surplus of any one of them. That such an organization thus fortified and equipped could if it saw fit dominate the trade and control competition would seem to be a business proposition too plain to require extended argument to support it. Its resources, strength and comprehensive ownership of the means of production enable it to adopt measures to do again as it has done in the past, that is, to effectually dominate and control the steel business of the country. From the earliest decisions of this court it has been declared that it was the effective power of such organizations to control and restrain competition and the freedom of trade that Congress intended to limit and control. That the exercise of the power may be withheld, or exerted with forbearing benevolence, does not place such combinations beyond the authority of the statute which was intended to prohibit their formation, and when formed to deprive them of the power unlawfully attained. . . .

It is affirmed that to grant the Government's request for a remand to the District Court for a decree of dissolution would not result in a change in the conditions of the steel trade. Such is not the theory of the Sherman Act. That act was framed in the belief that attempted or accomplished monopolization, or combinations which suppress free competition, were hurtful to the public interest, and that a restoration of competitive conditions would benefit the public. We have here a combination in control of one-half of the steel business of the country. If the plan were followed, as in the American Tobacco Case, of remanding the case to the District Court, a decree might be framed restoring competitive conditions as far as practicable. See *United States* v. *American Tobacco Co.*, 191 Fed. 371. In that case the subject of reconstruction so as to restore such conditions was elaborated and carefully considered. In my judgment the principles there laid down if followed now would make a very material difference in the steel industry. Instead of one domi-

nating corporation, with scattered competitors, there would be competitive conditions throughout the whole trade which would carry into effect the policy of the law.

It seems to me that if this act is to be given effect, the bill, under the findings of fact made by the court, should not be dismissed, and the cause should be remanded to the District Court, where a plan of effective and final dissolution of the corporations should be enforced by a decree framed for that purpose.

Mr. Justice PITNEY and Mr. Justice CLARKE concur in this dissent.

AMERICAN FOREIGN POLICY, 1898–1920

THE end of the nineteenth century marks the beginning of a new phase in American foreign policy. A century earlier Washington's problem had been to protect the unity and independence of a precarious federation in a hemisphere still dominated by European powers. In the long interval since the end of the Napoleonic Wars this new nation had advanced across the continent by leaps and bounds in virtual freedom from serious opposition. Great Britain, the only European power in a position to inflict real injury on American interests, had been gradually converted from a one-time enemy into a peaceful neighbor by land and a valuable buffer by sea. It was in this period of continental expansion and immunity from foreign peril that the tradition of isolation from world politics had been established; but by the nineties conditions were changing. For one thing, the forces which had carried Americans across a continent were now impelling many of them to seek an empire overseas. For another, the longest peace in Europe's history was drawing to a close, and it was doubtful, in the altered condition of the world, if any great power could escape the coming conflict.

Between 1898 and 1920 the United States faced three great issues. First, should we extend our control and in-

fluence into the Orient and Latin America? Second, should we hurl our decisive industrial and military forces into the first World War? Third, should we co-operate in a League of Nations to substitute organized negotiation for armed conflict in the settlement of international disputes? The readings in this unit have been chosen to reveal some of the controversies which surrounded this new series of problems.

Admiral Mahan's writings embodied a systematic theory of imperialism which exercised great influence both at home and abroad. In Britain, Germany, and Japan his works were read with sympathetic appreciation by people who were already acting on similar principles. In America they were admired by all whose imagination had been caught by the vision of a new empire. Theodore Roosevelt described Mahan as "one of the greatest and most useful influences in American life."

Mahan made his reputation by his study of the nature of sea power. Historical in scope, it was intended to have a very practical application: he studied sea power as an instrument of national expansion. As for national expansion itself, he thought of it as a symptom of progress in the nations which pursued it and as a means of spreading progress among those who were compelled to submit to it. He preached a vast expansion of American influence in the backward regions of the Orient and Latin America, operating through suitable annexations, bases, and alliances and resting ultimately on economic and military might. Unlike the great majority of his countrymen, he was fully aware of the dependence of American security on the changing dispositions of world power.

Mahan regarded Asia as one field for the application of his principles. Here Russian power, pushing eastward over land, would encounter the power of the seafaring nations— Britain, Germany, Japan, and the United States—as they forced their influence through the coastal ports. He urged America to take a full share in this contest and to act in a broad association with the maritime powers against Russia. When the United States acquired the Philippines —an initial step which Mahan naturally considered indispensable—it seemed as if the summons to expand had been accepted. Hay's policy of the "Open Door" has a more innocent appearance than Mahan's solution for the Asian problem, but it is an interesting question to consider how far the two views really differed.

Senator Beveridge shared Mahan's enthusiasm for empire, and his eloquence was an important factor in the Senate debates; the annexation of the Philippines was adopted by a margin of only two votes. But Beveridge also personifies the problem which Americans experience in trying to reconcile

imperialism with the democratic tradition. He had to satisfy himself that neither the Declaration of Independence, the Constitution, nor any other feature of the inherited creed was inconsistent with this new departure. Bryan, the leader of the Democratic party, applied the same tests but got precisely opposite results. From his point of view, no appeal to either national security, economic enterprise, or Christian duty could prevent the annexation of the Philippines from being a flagrant betrayal of American ideals. Mr. Dooley, in his own way, felt some of the same misgivings.

The Spanish-American War opened a new phase in Latin America as well as in the Pacific. It need hardly be said that the motives for the war were not confined to the feeling, officially recorded by President McKinley, that a kindly neighbor could not stand by while the Cubans were being mistreated. Nor, apparently, was Wall Street the villain in the piece; this group, together with Mark Hanna, opposed the war. The heady wine of national expansion, the irresponsibility of the press, the righteous indignation of the public, and the peculiar virtues of the President all conspired to strike the last of her ancient dominions out of Spain's feeble grasp. As a result of this popular war, we annexed Puerto Rico, restricted the sovereignty of Cuba, and proceeded to fasten our grip on the Caribbean.

Here again a people reared in the American tradition of democracy was faced by awkward questions. One example involved the status of a colony like Puerto Rico under the American Constitution. The Supreme Court, giving their full attention to the issues raised by the growth of an American empire, discovered no grounds for the supposition that all the rights of citizenship automatically followed the flag. They held that Congress, as long as it respected certain limits, would not be prevented from governing alien peoples by methods inappropriate for Americans. Another problem—which has often led commercial nations into various forms of economic imperialism—was what to do about Latin-American republics which failed to pay their debts or to protect foreign life and property within their borders. The Roosevelt Corollary to the Monroe Doctrine was one answer to this question. Nine years later President Wilson proposed a relation of dignified equality between us and these nations, but it should be asked how far the policy of his administration really differed from that of Roosevelt's. The Mexican diplomat, Quintanilla, expresses the feelings of those numerous Latin-Americans who have suffered from an incomplete sympathy with the the North American point of view.

The vast deployment of our national energies in these years and the intensification of big-power rivalry in the world at large made little impression on one American tradition. With the exception of certain individuals, the bulk of the people believed implicitly in the wisdom of remaining aloof from European conflicts. It was this conviction which was tested in World War I and its aftermath. President Wilson proclaimed our neutrality in 1914. In time, the attacks on our shipping and the implications of the possible German domination of Europe began to change many opinions. Wilson's own decision to enter the war, which followed unsuccessful endeavors to end it by mediation, was reached during February and March, 1917. The war resolution was passed by Congress, but Senators Norris and La Follette spoke for the six senators and the fifty congressmen who opposed it. Why Wilson and they took the positions they did, and who was right, are questions which have been hotly debated.

The immense tragedy represented by this first experience of total war was a profound shock to a civilization whose controlling assumption for the past century had been a belief in the progress of man. It raised in the most drastic form the ancient, unanswered question of how peoples can live together in peace. Wilson's approach to this problem was stated with earnest eloquence in his papers and speeches. He had preached a peace without victory, a peace of freedom and mutual protection, a peace in which a league of independent nations pledged themselves to resist with the joint force of all the aggression committed by any one of them. This was the hope which an American President, from a position of unexampled authority in the world, held out in 1919; but within twenty years a second war, altogether worse than the first, was to follow. Were these principles wrong? Or was the failure due to the neglect to observe them?

The Wilsonian ideals, whatever their merits or defects, were compromised in Europe and rejected in America. After the Republican victory of 1918, Senator Lodge headed the Foreign Relations Committee of the Senate. Under his leadership, and through a maze of argument and parliamentary maneuver, the Senate rejected the Versailles Treaty, whose first article provided for a League of Nations. Wilson's effort to rouse the nation to an awareness of the issues as he saw them failed to arrest the reviving force of isolationism. Before he died in 1923 he had uttered his own bitter verdict on the refusal to follow him into the League: "I have seen fools resist Providence before and I have seen their destruction, and it will come upon these again, utter destruction and contempt. . . ."

SECTION A. A THEORY OF NATIONALISM

1. INFLUENCE OF SEA POWER[1]

By ALFRED THAYER MAHAN

EDITORS' NOTE.—Alfred Thayer Mahan (1840–1914) drew from naval and military history a systematic theory of naval warfare as a consistent part of a general philosophy of war. Mahan was the son of an army officer who was a professor at West Point. His father is said to have been the first to introduce the study of strategy, in the European sense, into the American army.

Mahan was graduated from Annapolis, served in the navy during the Civil War, and became a captain in 1885. The following year he became president of the Naval War College in Newport and taught there until 1889. His lectures appeared in 1890 as *The Influence of Sea Power upon History, 1660–1783*. These lectures received immediate recognition and were followed in 1892 by the publication of *The Influence of Sea Power upon the French Revolution and Empire, 1793–1812*. Both books developed a systematic theory of naval supremacy and economic imperialism. They were received enthusiastically in Germany, Japan, and Great Britain. Mahan received honorary degrees from Oxford and Cambridge. His works are studied intensively at Annapolis.

Mahan played a significant role as a member of the Naval War Board in charge of naval operations during the Spanish-American War. He was a very close friend of Theodore Roosevelt, who wrote him, "I speak to you with the greatest freedom, for I sympathize with your views, and I have precisely the same idea of patriotism, and of belief in and love for our country."

INTRODUCTORY

The history of Sea Power is largely, though by no means solely, a narrative of contests between nations, of mutual rivalries, of violence frequently culminating in war. The profound influence of sea commerce upon the wealth and strength of countries was clearly seen long before the true principles which governed its growth and prosperity were detected. To secure to one's own people a disproportionate share of such benefits, every effort was made to exclude others, either by the peaceful legislative methods of monopoly or prohibitory regulations, or, when these failed, by direct violence. The clash of interests, the angry feelings roused by conflicting attempts thus to appropriate the larger share, if not the whole, of the advantages of commerce, and of distant unsettled commercial regions, led to wars. On the other hand, wars arising from other causes have been greatly modified in their conduct and issue by the control of the sea. Therefore the history of sea power, while

1. Alfred Thayer Mahan, *The Influence of Sea Power upon History, 1660–1783* (8th ed.; Boston, 1894), pp. 1–2, 25–29, 50, 52–55, 57–59, 63–64, 66–67, 81–89, 225–27, 295, 324–26. By permission of Little, Brown and Company.

embracing in its broad sweep all that tends to make a people great upon the sea or by the sea, is largely a military history; and it is in this aspect that it will be mainly, though not exclusively, regarded in the following pages.

A study of the military history of the past, such as this, is enjoined by great military leaders as essential to correct ideas and to the skilful conduct of war in the future. . . .

It is doubly necessary thus to study critically the history and experience of naval warfare in the days of sailing-ships, because while these will be found to afford lessons of present application and value, steam navies have as yet made no history which can be quoted as decisive in its teaching. . . .

CHAPTER I

DISCUSSION OF THE ELEMENTS
OF SEA POWER

The first and most obvious light in which the sea presents itself from the political and social point of view is that of a great highway; or better, perhaps, of a wide common, over which men may pass in all directions, but on which some well-worn paths show that controlling reasons have led them to choose certain lines of travel rather than others. These lines of travel are called trade routes; and the reasons which have determined them are to be sought in the history of the world.

Notwithstanding all the familiar and unfamiliar dangers of the sea, both travel and traffic by water have always been easier and cheaper than by land. . . .

Under modern conditions, however, home trade is but a part of the business of a country bordering on the sea. Foreign necessaries or luxuries must be brought to its ports, either in its own or in foreign ships, which will return, bearing in exchange the products of the country, whether they be the fruits of the earth or the works of men's hands; and it is the wish of every nation that this shipping business should be done by its own ves-

sels. The ships that thus sail to and fro must have secure ports to which to return, and must, as far as possible, be followed by the protection of their country throughout the voyage.

This protection in time of war must be extended by armed shipping. The necessity of a navy, in the restricted sense of the word, springs, therefore, from the existence of a peaceful shipping, and disappears with it, except in the case of a nation which has aggressive tendencies, and keeps up a navy merely as a branch of the military establishment. As the United States has at present no aggressive purposes, and as its merchant service has disappeared, the dwindling of the armed fleet and general lack of interest in it are strictly logical consequences. When for any reason sea trade is again found to pay, a large enough shipping interest will reappear to compel the revival of the war fleet. It is possible that when a canal route through the Central-American Isthmus is seen to be a near certainty, the aggressive impulse may be strong enough to lead to the same result. This is doubtful, however, because a peaceful, gain-loving nation is not far-sighted, and far-sightedness is needed for adequate military preparation, especially in these days.

As a nation, with its unarmed and armed shipping, launches forth from its own shores, the need is soon felt of points upon which the ships can rely for peaceful trading, for refuge and supplies. . . .

In these three things—production, with the necessity of exchanging products, shipping, whereby the exchange is carried on, and colonies, which facilitate and enlarge the operations of shipping and tend to protect it by multiplying points of safety—is to be found the key to much of the history, as well as of the policy, of nations bordering upon the sea. The policy has varied both with the spirit of the age and with the character and clear-sightedness of the rulers; but the history of the seaboard nations has been less determined by the shrewdness and foresight of governments than by conditions of position, extent, configuration, number and character of their people,—by what are called, in a word, natural conditions. It must however be admitted, and will be seen, that the wise or unwise action of individual men has at certain periods had a great modifying influence upon the growth of sea power in the broad sense, which includes not only the military strength afloat, that rules the sea or any part of it by force of arms, but also the peaceful commerce and shipping from which alone a military fleet naturally and healthfully springs, and on which it securely rests.

The principal conditions affecting the sea power of nations may be enumerated as follows: I. Geographical Position. II. Physical Conformation, including, as connected therewith, natural productions and climate. III. Extent of Territory. IV. Number of Population. V. Character of the People. VI. Character of the Government, including therein the national institutions. . . .

V. *National Character.*—The effect of national character and aptitudes upon the development of sea power will next be considered.

If sea power be really based upon a peaceful and extensive commerce, aptitude for commercial pursuits must be a distinguishing feature of the nations that have at one time or another been great upon the sea. History almost without exception affirms that this is true. . . .

All men seek gain and, more or less, love money; but the way in which gain is sought will have a marked effect upon the commercial fortunes and the history of the people inhabiting a country. . . .

The English and Dutch were no less desirous of gain than the southern nations. Each in turn has been called "a nation of shopkeepers"; but the jeer, in so far as it is just, is to the credit of their wisdom and uprightness. They were no less bold, no less enterprising, no less patient. Indeed, they were more patient, in that they

sought riches not by the sword but by labor, which is the reproach meant to be implied by the epithet; for thus they took the longest, instead of what seemed the shortest, road to wealth. But these two peoples, radically of the same race, had other qualities, no less important than those just named, which combined with their surroundings to favor their development by sea. They were by nature business-men, traders, producers, negotiators. Therefore both in their native country and abroad, whether settled in the ports of civilized nations, or of barbarous eastern rulers, or in colonies of their own foundation, they everywhere strove to draw out all the resources of the land, to develop and increase them. The quick instinct of the born trader, shopkeeper if you will, sought continually new articles to exchange; and this search, combined with the industrious character evolved through generations of labor, made them necessarily producers. At home they became great as manufacturers; abroad, where they controlled, the land grew richer continually, products multiplied, and the necessary exchange between home and the settlements called for more ships. Their shipping therefore increased with these demands of trade, and nations with less aptitude for maritime enterprise, even France herself, great as she has been, called for their products and for the service of their ships. Thus in many ways they advanced to power at sea. This natural tendency and growth were indeed modified and seriously checked at times by the interference of other governments, jealous of a prosperity which their own people could invade only by the aid of artificial support—a support which will be considered under the head of governmental action as affecting sea power.

The tendency to trade, involving of necessity the production of something to trade with, is the national characteristic most important to the development of sea power. Granting it and a good seaboard, it is not likely that the dangers of the sea, or any aversion to it, will deter a people from seeking wealth by the paths of ocean commerce. Where wealth is sought by other means, it may be found; but it will not necessarily lead to sea power. . . .

The noble classes of Europe inherited from the Middle Ages a supercilious contempt for peaceful trade, which has exercised a modifying influence upon its growth, according to the national character of different countries. . . .

. . . In England the same result obtained. The nobility were proud; but in a representative government the power of wealth could be neither put down nor overshadowed. It was patent to the eyes of all, it was honored by all; and in England, as well as Holland, the occupations which were the source of wealth shared in the honor given to wealth itself. Thus, in all the countries named, social sentiment, the outcome of national characteristics, had a marked influence upon the national attitude toward trade.

In yet another way does the national genius affect the growth of sea power in its broadest sense; and that is in so far as it possesses the capacity for planting healthy colonies. . . .

Before quitting this head of the inquiry, it is well to ask how far the national character of Americans is fitted to develop a great sea power, should other circumstances become favorable.

It seems scarcely necessary, however, to do more than appeal to a not very distant past to prove that, if legislative hindrances be removed, and more remunerative fields of enterprise filled up, the sea power will not long delay its appearance. The instinct for commerce, bold enterprise in the pursuit of gain, and a keen scent for the trails that lead to it, all exist; and if there be in the future any fields calling for colonization, it cannot be doubted that Americans will carry to them all their inherited aptitude for self-government and independent growth.

VI. *Character of the Government.*—In discussing the effects upon the develop-

ment of a nation's sea power exerted by its government and institutions, it will be necessary to avoid a tendency to over-philosophizing, to confine attention to obvious and immediate causes and their plain results, without prying too far beneath the surface for remote and ultimate influences.

Nevertheless, it must be noted that particular forms of government with their accompanying institutions, and the character of rulers at one time or another, have exercised a very marked influence upon the development of sea power. The various traits of a country and its people which have so far been considered constitute the natural characteristics with which a nation, like a man, begins its career; the conduct of the government in turn corresponds to the exercise of the intelligent will-power, which, according as it is wise, energetic and persevering, or the reverse, causes success or failure in a man's life or a nation's history.

It would seem probable that a government in full accord with the natural bias of its people would most successfully advance its growth in every respect; and, in the matter of sea power, the most brilliant successes have followed where there has been intelligent direction by a government fully imbued with the spirit of the people and conscious of its true general bent. Such a government is most certainly secured when the will of the people, or of their best natural exponents, has some large share in making it; but such free governments have sometimes fallen short, while on the other hand despotic power, wielded with judgment and consistency, has created at times a great sea commerce and a brilliant navy with greater directness than can be reached by the slower processes of a free people. The difficulty in the latter case is to insure perseverance after the death of a particular despot.

England having undoubtedly reached the greatest height of sea power of any modern nation, the action of her government first claims attention. In general direction this action has been consistent, though often far from praiseworthy. It has aimed steadily at the control of the sea. . . .

. . . While England's policy thus steadily aimed at widening and strengthening the bases of her sway upon the ocean, the other governments of Europe seemed blind to the dangers to be feared from her sea growth. The miseries resulting from the overweening power of Spain in days long gone by seemed to be forgotten; forgotten also the more recent lesson of the bloody and costly wars provoked by the ambition and exaggerated power of Louis XIV. Under the eyes of the statesmen of Europe there was steadily and visibly being built up a third overwhelming power, destined to be used as selfishly, as aggressively, though not as cruelly, and much more successfully than any that had preceded it. This was the power of the sea, whose workings, because more silent than the clash of arms, are less often noted, though lying clearly enough on the surface. It can scarcely be denied that England's uncontrolled dominion of the seas, during almost the whole period chosen for our subject, was by long odds the chief among the military factors that determined the final issue. . . .

This steady keeping to a general line of policy was doubtless made specially easy for successive English governments by the clear indications of the country's conditions. Singleness of purpose was to some extent imposed. The firm maintenance of her sea power, the haughty determination to make it felt, the wise state of preparation in which its military element was kept, were yet more due to that feature of her political institutions which practically gave the government, during the period in question, into the hands of a class—a landed aristocracy. Such a class, whatever its defects otherwise, readily takes up and carries on a sound political tradition, is naturally proud of its country's glory, and comparatively insensible to the sufferings of the community by which that glory is maintained. It readily lays on the pecuniary burden necessary for preparation and for endurance of war. Being as a body rich, it feels those burdens less. Not being commercial, the sources of its own wealth are not so immediately endangered, and it does not share that political timidity which characterizes those whose property is exposed and business threatened—the proverbial timidity of capital. Yet in England this class was not insensible to anything that touched her trade for good or ill. Both houses of Parliament vied in careful watchfulness over its extension and protection, and to the frequency of their inquiries a naval historian attributes the increased efficiency of the executive power in its management of the navy. Such a class also naturally imbibes and keeps up a spirit of military honor, which is of the first importance in ages when military institutions have not yet provided the sufficient substitute in what is called *esprit-de-corps*. But although full of class feeling and class prejudice, which made themselves felt in the navy as well as elsewhere, their practical sense left open the way of promotion to its highest honors to the more humbly born; and every age saw admirals who had sprung from the lowest of the people. . . .

Since 1815, and especially in our own day, the government of England had passed very much more into the hands of the people at large. Whether her sea power will suffer therefrom remains to be seen. Its broad basis still remains in a great trade, large mechanical industries, and an extensive colonial system. Whether a democratic government will have the foresight, the keen sensitiveness to national position and credit, the willingness to insure its prosperity by adequate outpouring of money in times of peace, all which are necessary for military preparation, is yet an open question. Popular governments are not generally favorable to military expenditure, however necessary, and there are signs that England tends to drop behind. . . .

To turn now from the particular lessons drawn from the history of the past to the general question of the influence of government upon the sea career of its people, it is seen that that influence can work in two distinct but closely related ways.

First, in peace: The government by its policy can favor the natural growth of a people's industries and its tendencies to seek adventure and gain by way of the sea; or it can try to develop such industries and such sea-going bent, when they do not naturally exist; or, on the other hand, the government may by mistaken action check and fetter the progress which the people left to themselves would make. In any one of these ways the influence of the government will be felt, making or marring the sea power of the country in the matter of peaceful commerce; upon which alone, it cannot be too often insisted, a thoroughly strong navy can be based.

Secondly, for war: The influence of the government will be felt in its most legitimate manner in maintaining an armed navy, of a size commensurate with the growth of its shipping and the importance of the interests connected with it. More important even than the size of the navy is the question of its institutions, favoring a healthful spirit and activity, and providing for rapid development in time of war by an adequate reserve of men and of ships and by measures for drawing out that general reserve power which has before been pointed to, when considering the character and pursuits of the people. Undoubtedly under this second head of warlike preparation must come the maintenance of suitable naval stations, in those distant parts of the world to which the armed shipping must follow the peaceful vessels of commerce. . . .

As the practical object of this inquiry is to draw from the lessons of history inferences applicable to one's own country and service, it is proper now to ask how far the conditions of the United States involve serious danger, and call for action on the part of the government, in order to build again her sea power. It will not be too much to say that the action of the government since the Civil War, and up to this day, has been effectively directed solely to what has been called the first link in the chain which makes sea power. Internal development, great production, with the accompanying aim and boast of self-sufficingness, such has been the object, such to some extent the result. In this the government has faithfully reflected the bent of the controlling elements of the country, though it is not always easy to feel that such controlling elements are truly representative, even in a free country. However that may be, there is no doubt that, besides having no colonies, the intermediate link of a peaceful shipping, and the interests involved in it, are now likewise lacking. In short, the United States has only one link of the three.

The circumstances of naval war have changed so much within the last hundred years, that it may be doubted whether such disastrous effects on the one hand, or such brilliant prosperity on the other, as were seen in the wars between England and France, could now recur. In her secure and haughty sway of the seas England imposed a yoke on neutrals which will never again be borne; and the principle that the flag covers the goods is forever secured. The commerce of a belligerent can therefore now be safely carried on in neutral ships, except when contraband of war or to blockaded ports; and as regards the latter, it is also certain that there will be no more paper blockades. Putting aside therefore the question of defending her seaports from capture or contribution, as to which there is practical unanimity in theory and entire indifference in practice, what need has the United States of sea power? Her commerce is even now carried on by others; why should her people desire that which, if possessed, must be defended at great cost? So far as this question is economical, it is outside the scope of this work; but conditions which may entail suffering and loss on the country by war are directly pertinent to it. Granting therefore that the foreign trade of the United States, going and coming, is on board ships which an enemy cannot touch except when bound to a blockaded port, what will constitute an efficient blockade? The present definition is, that it is such as to constitute a manifest danger to a vessel seeking to enter or leave the port. This is evidently very elastic. . . .

It may be urged that, with the extensive sea-coast of the United States, a blockade of the whole line cannot be effectively kept up. No one will more readily concede this than officers who remember how the blockade of the Southern coast alone was maintained. But in the present condition of the navy, and, it may be added, with any additions not exceeding those so far proposed by the government, the attempt to blockade Boston, New York, the Delaware, the Chesapeake, and the Mississippi, in other words, the great centres of export and import, would not entail upon one of the large maritime nations efforts greater than have been made before. England has at the same time blockaded Brest, the Biscay coast, Toulon, and Cadiz, when there were powerful squadrons lying within the harbors. It is true that commerce in neutral ships can then enter other ports of the United States than those named; but what a dislocation of the carrying traffic of the country, what failure of supplies at times, what inadequate means of transport by rail or water, of dockage, of lighterage, of warehousing, will be involved in such an enforced change of the ports of entry! Will there be no money loss, no suffering, consequent upon this? And when with much pain and expense these evils have been partially remedied, the enemy may be led to stop the new inlets as he did the old. The people of the United States will certainly not starve, but they may suffer grievously. As for supplies which are contraband of war, is there not reason to fear that the United States is not now able to go alone if an emergency should arise?

The question is eminently one in which the influence of the government should make itself felt, to build up for the nation a navy which, if not capable of reaching distant countries, shall at least be able to keep clear the chief approaches to its own. The eyes of the country have for a quarter of a century been turned from the sea; the results of such a policy and of its opposite will be shown in the instance of France and of England. Without asserting a narrow parallelism between the case of the United States and either of these, it may safely be said that it is essential to the welfare of the whole country that the conditions of trade and commerce should remain, as far as possible, unaffected by an external war. In order to do this, the enemy must be kept not only out of our ports, but far away from our coasts.

Can this navy be had without restoring the merchant shipping? It is doubtful. History has proved that such a purely military sea power can be built up by a despot, as was done by Louis XIV; but though so fair seeming, experience showed that his navy was like a growth which having no root soon withers away. But in a representative government any military expenditure must have a strongly represented interest behind it, convinced of its necessity. Such an interest in sea power does not exist, cannot exist here without action by the government. How such a merchant shipping should be built up, whether by subsidies or by free trade, by constant administration of tonics or by free movement in the open air, is not a military but an economical question. Even had the United States a great national shipping, it may be doubted whether a sufficient navy would follow; the distance which separates her from other great powers, in one way a protection, is also a snare. The motive, if any there be, which will give the United States a navy, is probably now quickening in the Central American Isthmus. Let us hope it will not come to the birth too late.

Here concludes the general discussion of the principal elements which affect, favorably or unfavorably, the growth of sea power in nations. The aim has been, first to consider those elements in their natural tendency for or against, and then to illustrate by particular examples and by the experience of the past. Such discussions, while undoubtedly embracing a wider field, yet fall mainly within the province of strategy, as distinguished from tactics. The considerations and principles which enter into them belong to the unchangeable, or unchanging, order of things, remaining the same, in cause and effect, from age to age. They belong, as it were, to the Order of Nature, of whose stability so much is heard in our day; whereas tactics, using as its instruments the weapons made by man, shares in the change and progress of the race from generation to generation. From time to time the superstructure of tactics has to be altered or wholly torn down; but the old foundations of strategy so far remain, as though laid upon a rock. There will next be examined the general history of Europe and America, with particular reference to the effect exercised upon that history, and upon the welfare of the people, by sea power in its broad sense. From time to time, as occasion offers, the aim will be to recall and reinforce the general teaching, already elicited, by particular illustrations. The general tenor of the study will therefore be strategical, in that broad definition of naval strategy which has before been quoted and accepted: "Naval strategy has for its end to found, support, and increase, as well in peace as in war, the sea power of a country." In the matter of particular battles, while freely admitting that the change of details has made obsolete much of their teaching, the attempt will be made to point out where the application or neglect of true general principles has produced decisive effects; and, other things being equal, those actions will be preferred which, from their association with the names of the most distinguished officers, may be presumed to show how far just tactical ideas obtained in a particular age or a particular service. It will also be

desirable, where analogies between ancient and modern weapons appear on the surface, to derive such probable lessons as they offer, without laying undue stress upon the points of resemblance. Finally, it must be remembered that, among all changes, the nature of man remains much the same; the personal equation, though uncertain in quantity and quality in the particular instance, is sure always to be found. . . .

Chapter V

Is it meant, it may be asked, to attribute to sea power alone the greatness or wealth of any State? Certainly not. The due use and control of the sea is but one link in the chain of exchange by which wealth accumulates; but it is the central link, which lays under contribution other nations for the benefit of the one holding it, and which, history seems to assert, most surely of all gathers to itself riches. . . . What made the difference in the results? Why was France miserable and exhausted, while England was smiling and prosperous? Why did England dictate, and France accept, terms of peace? The reason apparently was the difference in wealth and credit. France stood alone against many enemies; but those enemies were raised and kept moving by English subsidies. . . .

Chapter VIII

In all other quarters of the world, after the accession of Pitt to power, the same good fortune followed the English arms, checkered only at the first by some slight reverses. It was not so on the continent, where the heroism and skill of Frederick the Great maintained with difficulty his brilliant struggle against France, Austria, and Russia. The study of the difficulties of his position, of the military and political combinations attending it, do not belong to our subject. Sea power does not appear directly in its effects upon the struggle, but indirectly it was felt in two ways—first, by the subsidies which the abundant wealth and credit of England enabled her to give Frederick, in whose thrifty and able hands they went far; and second, in the embarrassment caused to France by the attacks of England upon her colonies and her own sea-coast, in the destruction of her commerce, and in the money—all too little, it is true, and grudgingly given— which France was forced to bestow on her navy. Stung by the constant lashing of the Power of the sea, France, despite the blindness and unwillingness of the rulers, was driven to undertake something against it. With a navy much inferior, unable to cope in all quarters of the world, it was rightly decided to concentrate upon one object; and the object chosen was Great Britain itself, whose shores were to be invaded. This decision, soon apprehended by the fears of the English nation, caused the great naval operations to centre for some years around the coast of France and in the Channel. . . .

. . . Since the Treaty of Paris in 1763, the waste places of the world have been rapidly filled; witness our own continent, Australia, and even South America. A nominal and more or less clearly defined political possession now generally exists in the most forsaken regions, though to this statement there are some marked exceptions; but in many places this political possession is little more than nominal, and in others of a character so feeble that it cannot rely upon itself alone for support or protection. . . . Upon the western continents the political condition of the Central American and tropical South American States is so unstable as to cause constant anxiety about the maintenance of internal order, and seriously to interfere with commerce and with the peaceful development of their resources. So long as— to use a familiar expression—they hurt no one but themselves, this may go on; but for a long time the citizens of more stable governments have been seeking to exploit their resources, and have borne the losses arising from their distracted condition. North America and Australia still offer large openings to immigration and enter-

prise; but they are filling up rapidly, and as the opportunities there diminish, the demand must arise for a more settled government in those disordered States, for security to life and for reasonable stability of institutions enabling merchants and others to count upon the future. There is certainly no present hope that such a demand can be fulfilled from the existing native materials; if the same be true when the demand arises, no theoretical positions, like the Monroe doctrine, will prevent interested nations from attempting to remedy the evil by some measure, which, whatever it may be called, will be a political interference. Such interferences must produce collisions, which may be at times settled by arbitration, but can scarcely fail at other times to cause war. Even for a peaceful solution, that nation will have the strongest arguments which has the strongest organized force. It need scarcely be said that the successful piercing of the Central American Isthmus at any point may precipitate the moment that is sure to come sooner or later. The profound modification of commercial routes expected from this enterprise, the political importance to the United States of such a channel of communication between her Atlantic and Pacific seaboards, are not, however, the whole nor even the principal part of the question. As far as can be seen, the time will come when stable governments for the American tropical States must be assured by the now existing powerful and stable States of America or Europe. The geographical position of those States, the climatic conditions, make it plain at once that sea power will there, even more than in the case of Turkey, determine what foreign State shall predominate—if not by actual possession, by its influence over the native governments. The geographical position of the United States and her intrinsic power give her an undeniable advantage; but that advantage will not avail if there is a great inferiority of organized brute-force, which still remains the last argument of republics as of kings. Herein lies to us the great and still living interest of the Seven Years' War. In it we have seen and followed England, with an army small as compared with other States, as is still her case to-day, first successfully defending her own shores, then carrying her arms in every direction, spreading her rule and influence over remote regions, and not only binding them to her obedience, but making them tributary to her wealth, her strength, and her reputation. As she loosens the grasp and neutralizes the influence of France and Spain in regions beyond the sea, there is perhaps seen the prophecy of some other great nation in days yet to come, that will incline the balance of power in some future sea war, whose scope will be recognized afterward, if not by contemporaries, to have been the political future and the economical development of regions before lost to civilization; but that nation will not be the United States if the moment find her indifferent, as now, to the empire of the seas. . . .

2. THE PEACE CONFERENCE AND THE MORAL ASPECT OF WAR[1]

By Alfred Thayer Mahan

EDITORS' NOTE.—In 1899 Mahan served as an American delegate to the first Hague Conference. Here he took satisfaction in joining with British delegates to defeat the proposals for arbitration advanced by the Russian emperor. Mahan thought it neither sensible nor moral for sovereign nations to submit their disputes to compulsory arbitration or to renounce any of the means by which they defend themselves in war. He was responsible for the United States voting against the outlawry of gas as a weapon of warfare.

. . . Of the beneficence of the practice of arbitration, of the wisdom of substituting it, when possible, for the appeal to arms, with all the misery therefrom resulting, there can be no doubt; but it will be expected that in its application, and in its attempted development, the tendencies of the day, both good and bad, will make themselves felt. If, on the one hand, there is solid ground for rejoicing in the growing inclination to resort first to an impartial arbiter, if such can be found, when occasion for collision arises, there is, on the other hand, cause for serious reflection when this most humane impulse is seen to favor methods, which by compulsion shall vitally impair the moral freedom, and the consequent moral responsibility, which are the distinguishing glory of the rational man, and of the sovereign state.

One of the most unfortunate characteristics of our present age is the disposition to impose by legislative enactment—by external compulsion, that is—restrictions of a moral character, which are either fundamentally unjust, or at least do not carry with them the moral sense of the community, as a whole. . . .

In matters internal to a State, the bare existence of a law imposes an obligation upon the individual citizen, whatever his personal conviction of its rightfulness or its wisdom. Yet is such obligation not absolute? The primary duty, attested alike by the law and the gospel, is submission. The presumption is in favor of the law; and if there lie against it just cause for accusation, on the score either of justice or of

1. Alfred Thayer Mahan, "The Peace Conference and the Moral Aspect of War," *North American Review*, CLXIX (October, 1899), 434–42, 444–47.

expediency, the interests of the Common-wealth and the precepts of religion alike demand that opposition shall be conducted according to the methods, and within the limits, which the law of the land itself pre-scribes. But it may be—it has been, and yet again may be—that the law, however regular in its enactment, and therefore unquestionable on the score of formal au-thority, either outrages fundamental politi-cal right, or violates the moral dictates of the individual conscience. Of the former may be cited as an instance the Stamp Act, perfectly regular as regarded statutory validity, which kindled the flame of revo-lution in America. Of the second, the Fugitive Slave Law, within the memory of many yet living, is a conspicuous illustra-tion. Under such conditions, the moral right of resistance is conceded—nay, is affirmed and emphasized—by the moral consciousness of the races from which the most part of the American people have their origin, and to which, almost wholly, we owe our political and religious tradi-tions. Such resistance may be passive, ac-cepting meekly the penalty for disobedi-ence, as the martyr who for conscience' sake refused the political requirement of sacrificing to the image of the Caesar; or it may be active and violent, as when our forefathers repelled taxation without rep-resentation, or when men and women, of a generation not yet wholly passed away, re-fused to violate their consciences by ac-quiescing in the return of a slave to his bondage, resorting to evasion or to vio-lence, according to their conditions or temperaments, but in every case deriving the sanction for their unlawful action from the mandate of their personal conscience.

And let it be carefully kept in mind that it is not the absolute right or wrong of the particular act, as seen in the clearer light of a later day, that justified men, whether in the particular instances cited, or in other noteworthy incidents in the long series of steps by which the English-speaking races have ascended to their present political development. It is not the demonstrable

rightfulness of a particular action, as seen in the dispassionate light of the arbiter, posterity, that has chiefly constituted the merit of the individual rebel against the law in which he beheld iniquity; the saving salt, which has preserved the healthfulness of the body politic, has been the fidelity to Conscience, to the faithful, if passionate, arbiter of the moment, whose glorious pre-dominance in the individual or in the na-tion gives a better assurance of the highest life than does the clearest intellectual per-ception of the rightfulness, or of the ex-pediency, of a particular course. One may now see, or think that he sees, as does the writer, with Lincoln, that if slavery is not wrong, nothing is wrong. It was not so clear half a century ago; and while no honor is too great for those early heroes, who for this sublime conviction withstood obloquy and persecution, legal and illegal, it should be never forgotten that the then slave States, in their resolute determina-tion to maintain, by arms if need be, and against superior force, that which they be-lieved to be their constitutional political right, made no small contribution to the record of fidelity to conscience and to duty, which is the highest title of a nation to honor. Be it by action or be it by sub-mission, by action positive or by action negative, whatsoever is not of faith—of conviction—is sin.

The just and necessary exaltation of the law as the guarantee of true liberty, with the consequent accepted submission of the individual to it, and the recognized pre-sumption in favor of such submission, have tended to blind us to the fact that the indi-vidual, in our highest consciousness, has never surrendered his moral freedom—his independence of conscience. No human law overbears that supreme appeal, which carries the matter from the tribunal of man into the presence of God; nor can human law be pleaded at this bar as the excuse for a violation of conscience. It is a dangerous doctrine, doubtless, to preach that there may be a "higher law" than obedience to law; but truth is not to be rejected because dangerous, and the time is not long past when the phrase voiced a conviction, the forcible assertion of which brought slavery to an end forever.

The resort to arms by a nation, when right cannot otherwise be enforced, corresponds, or should correspond, precisely to the acts of the individual man which have been cited; for the old conception of an appeal to the Almighty, resembling in principle the mediaeval ordeal, is at best but a partial view of the truth, seen from one side only. However the result may afterwards be interpreted as indicative of the justice of a cause—an interpretation always questionable—a State, when it goes to war, should do so not to test the rightfulness of its claims, but because, being convinced in its conscience of that rightfulness, no other means of overcoming evil remains.

Nations, like men, have a conscience. Like men, too, the light of conscience is in nations often clouded, or misguided, by passion or by interest. But what of that? Does a man discard his allegiance to conscience, because he knows that, itself in harmony with right, its message to him is perplexed and obscured by his own infirmities? Not so. Fidelity to conscience implies not only obedience to its dictates, but earnest heartsearching, the use of every means, to ascertain its true command; yet withal, whatever the mistrust of the message, the supremacy of the conscience is not impeached. When it is recognized that its final word is spoken, nothing remains but obedience. Even if mistaken, the moral wrong of acting against conviction works a deeper injury to the man, and to his kind, than can the merely material disasters that may follow upon obedience. Even the material evils of war are less than the moral evil of compliance with wrong. . . .

. . . In the first place, compulsory arbitration stands at present no chance of general acceptance. There is but one way as yet in which arbitration can be compulsory; for the dream of some advanced thinkers, of an International Army, charged with imposing the decrees of an International Tribunal upon a recalcitrant state, may be dismissed as being outside of practical international politics, until at least the nations are ready for the intermediate step of moral compulsion, imposed by a self-assumed obligation—by a promise. Compulsory arbitration as yet means only the moral compulsion of a pledge, taken beforehand, and more or less comprehensive, to submit to arbitration questions which rest still in the unknown future; the very terms of which therefore cannot be foreseen. Although there is a certain active current of agitation in favor of such stipulations, there is no general disposition of governments to accede, except under very narrow and precise limitations, and in questions of less than secondary importance. . . .

The conviction of a nation is the conviction of the mass of the individuals thereof, and each individual has therefore a personal responsibility for the opinion he holds on a question of great national, or international, moment. Let us look, each of us—and especially each of us who fears God—into his own inner heart, and ask himself how far, in his personal life, he is prepared to accept arbitration. Is it not so that the reply must be, "In doubtful questions of moment, wherever I possibly can, knowing my necessary, inevitable proneness to one-sided views, I will seek an impartial adviser, that my bias may be corrected; but when that has been done, when I have sought what aid I can, if conscience still commands, it I must obey. From that duty, burdensome though it may be, no man can relieve me. Conscience, diligently consulted, is to the man the voice of God; between God and the man no other arbiter comes." And if this be so, a pledge beforehand is impossible. I cannot bind myself, for a future of which I as yet know nothing, to abide by the decision of any other judge than my own conscience. Much humor—less wit—has been expended upon the Emperor of Germany's supposed carefulness to reject arbitration because an infringement of his divine rights; a phrase which may well be no more than a blunt expression of the sense that no third party can relieve a man from the obligations of the position to which he is called by God, and that for the duties of that position the man can confidently expect divine guidance and help. Be that as it may, the divine right of conscience will, among Americans, receive rare challenge.

It has been urged, however, that a higher organization of the nations, the provision of a supreme tribunal issuing and enforcing judgments, settling thereby quarrels and disputed rights, would produce for the nations of the earth a condition analogous to that of the individual citizen of the State, who no longer defends his own cause, nor is bound in conscience to maintain his own sense of right, when the law decides against him. The conception is not novel, not even modern; something much like it was put forth centuries ago by the Papacy concerning its own functions. It contains two fallacies: First, the submission of the individual citizen is to force, to the constitution of which he personally contributes little, save his individual and general assent. To an unjust law he submits under protest, doubtless often silent; but he submits, not because he consents to the wrong, whether to himself personally or to others, but because he cannot help it. This will perhaps be denied, with the assertion that willing, intelligent submission to law, even when unjust, is yielded by most, for the general good. One has, however, only to consider the disposition of the average man to evade payment of taxes, to recognize how far force daily enters into the maintenance and execution of law. Nations, on the contrary, since no force exists, or without their volition can exist, to compel them to accept the institution of an authority superior to their own conscience, yield a willing acquiescence to wrong, when they so yield in obedience to an external authority imposed by themselves. The matter is not helped by the fact of a previous promise to accept such decisions. The wrong-doing of an individual, in consequence of an antecedent promise, does not relieve the conscience thus rashly fettered. The ancient rebuke still stands, "Why should thy mouth make thy flesh to sin?" For the individual or the nation, arbitration is not possible where the decision may violate conscience; it therefore can be accepted only when it is known that interest merely, not duty, will be affected by the judgment, and such knowledge cannot exist antecedent to the difficulty arising.

There is a further—a second—fallacy in the supposed analogy between the submission of individuals to law, and the advocated submission of States to a central tribunal. The law of the State, overwhelming as is its power relatively to that of the individual citizen, can neither bind nor loose in matters pertaining to the conscience. Still less can any tribunal, however solemnly constituted, liberate a State from its obligation to do right; still less, I say, because the State retains, what the individual has in great part lost, the power to maintain what it believes to be right. Many considerations may make it more right—I do not say *more expedient*—for a man or for a nation, to submit to, or to acquiesce in, wrong than to resist; but in such cases it is conscience still that decides where the balance of right turns distinctly to the side of wrong. It is, I presume, universally admitted, that occasions may arise where conscience not only justifies, but compels, resistance to law; whether it be the Christian citizen refusing to sacrifice, or the free citizen to subject himself to unconstitutional taxation, or to become the instrument of returning the slave to his master. So also for the Christian State. Existing wrong may have to be allowed, lest a greater wrong be done. Conscience only can decide; and for that very reason conscience must be kept free, that it may decide according to its sense of right, when the case is presented.

There is, therefore, the very serious

consideration attendant upon what is loosely styled "compulsory" arbitration—arbitration stipulated, that is, in advance of a question originating, or of its conditions being appreciated—that a State may thereby do that which a citizen as toward the State does not do, namely, may voluntarily assume a moral obligation to do, or to allow, wrong. And it must be remembered, also, that many of the difficulties which arise among States involve considerations distinctly beyond and higher than law, as international law now exists; whereas the advocated Permanent Tribunal, to which the ultra-organizers look, to take cognizance of all cases, must perforce be governed by law as it exists. It is not, in fact, to be supposed that nations will submit themselves to a tribunal, the general principles of which have not been crystallized into a code of some sort.

A concrete instance, however, is always more comprehensible and instructive than a general discussion. Let us therefore take the incidents and conditions which preceded our recent war with Spain. The facts, as seen by us, may, I apprehend, be fairly stated as follows. In the island of Cuba, a powerful military force—government it scarcely can be called—foreign to the island, was holding a small portion of it in enforced subjection, and was endeavoring, unsuccessfully, to reduce the remainder. In pursuance of this attempt, measures were adopted that inflicted immense misery and death upon great numbers of the population. Such suffering is indeed attendant upon war; but it may be stated as a fundamental principle of civilized warfare that useless suffering is condemned, and it had become apparent to military eyes that Spain could not subdue the island, or restore orderly conditions. The suffering was terrible, and was unavailing.

Under such circumstances, does any moral obligation lie upon a powerful neighboring State? Or, more exactly, if there is borne in upon the moral consciousness of a mighty people, that such an afflicted community as that of Cuba at their doors is like Lazarus at the gate of the rich man, and that the duty of stopping the evil rests upon them, what is to be done with such a case of conscience? Could the decision of another, whether nation or court, excuse our nation from the ultimate responsibility of its own decision? But, granting that it might have proved expedient to call in other judges, when we had full knowledge of the circumstances, what would have been our dilemma if, conscience commanding one course, we had found ourselves antecedently bound to abide by the conclusions of another arbiter? For let us not deceive ourselves. Absolutely justifiable, nay imperative, as most of us believe our action to have been, when tried at the bar of conscience, no arbitral court, acceptable to the two nations, would have decided as our own conscience did. A European diplomatist of distinguished reputation, of a small nation likeliest to be unbiased, so said to me personally, and it is known that more than one of our own ablest international lawyers held that we were acting in defiance of international law, as it now exists; just as the men who resisted the Fugitive Slave Law acted in defiance of the statute law of the land. Decision must have gone against us, so these men think, on the legal merits of the case. Of the moral question the arbiter could take no account; it is not there, indeed, that moral questions must find their solution, but in the court of conscience. Referred to arbitration, doubtless the Spanish flag would still fly over Cuba. . . .

. . . What has not "justice, with valor armed," when confronted by evil in high places, found itself compelled to effect by resort to the sword? To it was due the birth of our own nation, not least among the benefits of which was the stern experience that has made Great Britain no longer the mistress, but the mother, of her dependencies. The control, to good from evil, of the devastating fire of the French Revolution and of Napoleon was due to the sword. The long line of illustrious names and deeds, of those who bore it not in vain, has in our times culminated—if indeed the end is even yet nearly reached —in the new birth of the United States by the extirpation of human slavery, and in the downfall, but yesterday, of a colonial empire identified with tyranny. What the sword, and it supremely, tempered only by the stern demands of justice and of conscience, and the loving voice of charity, has done for India and for Egypt, is a tale at once too long and too well known for repetition here. Peace, indeed, is not adequate to all progress; there are resistances that can be overcome only by explosion. What means less violent than war would in a half-year have solved the Caribbean problem, shattered national ideas deep rooted in the prepossessions of a century, and planted the United States in Asia, face to face with the great world problem of the immediate future? What but war rent the veil which prevented the English-speaking communities from seeing eye to eye, and revealed to each the face of a brother? Little wonder that a war which, with comparatively little bloodshed, brought such consequences, was followed by the call for a Peace Conference!

Power, force, is a faculty of national life; one of the talents committed to nations by God. Like every other endowment of a complex organization, it must be held under control of the enlightened intellect and of the upright heart; but no more than any other can it be carelessly or lightly abjured, without incurring the responsibility of one who buries in the earth that which was intrusted to him for use. And this obligation to maintain right, by force if need be, while common to all States, rests peculiarly upon the greater, in proportion to their means. Much is required of those to whom much is given. So viewed, the ability speedily to put forth the nation's power, by adequate organization and other necessary preparation, according to the reasonable demands of the nation's intrinsic strength and of its posi-

tion in the world, is one of the clear duties involved in the Christian word "watchfulness"—readiness for the call that may come, whether expectedly or not. Until it is demonstrable that no evil exists, or threatens the world, which cannot be obviated without recourse to force, the obligation to readiness must remain; and, where evil is mighty and defiant, the obligation to use force—that is, war—arises. Nor is it possible, antecedently, to bring these conditions and obligations under the letter of precise and codified law, to be administered by a tribunal; while legalism, in its spirit, is marked by blemishes as real as those commonly attributed to "militarism," and not more elevated. The considerations which determine good and evil, right and wrong, in crises of national life, or of the world's history, are questions of equity often too complicated for decision upon mere rules, or even principles, of law, international or other. The instances of Bulgaria, of Armenia, and of Cuba, are entirely in point, and it is most probable that the contentions about the future of China will afford further illustration. Even in matters where the interest of nations is concerned, the moral element enters; because each generation in its day is the guardian of those which shall follow it. Like all guardians, therefore, while it has the power to act according to its best judgment, it has no right, for the mere sake of peace, to permit known injustice to be done to its wards.

The present strong feeling, throughout the nations of the world, in favor of Arbitration, is in itself a subject for congratulation almost unalloyed. It carries indeed a promise, to the certainty of which no paper covenants can pretend; for it influences the conscience by inward conviction, not by external fetter. But it must be remembered that such sentiments, from their very universality and evident laudableness, need correctives, for they bear in themselves a great danger of excess or of precipitancy. Excess is seen in the disposition, far too prevalent, to look upon war not only as an evil, but as an evil unmixed, unnecessary, and therefore always unjustifiable; while precipitancy, to reach results considered desirable, is evidenced by the wish to *impose* arbitration, to prevent recourse to war, by a general pledge previously made. Both frames of mind receive expression in the words of speakers, among whom a leading characteristic is lack of measuredness and of proportion. Thus an eminent citizen is reported to have said, "There is no more occasion for two nations to go to war, than for two men to settle their difficulties with clubs." Singularly enough, this point of view assumes to represent peculiarly Christian teaching; willingly ignorant of the truth that Christianity, while it will not force the conscience, by other than spiritual weapons, as "compulsory" arbitration might, distinctly recognizes the sword as the resister and remedier of evil in the sphere "of this world."

Arbitration's great opportunity has come in the advancing moral standards of States, whereby the disposition to deliberate wrong-doing has diminished, and consequently the occasions for redressing wrong by force are less frequent to arise. In view of recent events, however, and very especially of notorious, high-handed, oppression, initiated since the calling of the Peace Conference, and resolutely continued during its sessions in defiance of the public opinion—the conviction—of the world at large, it is premature to assume that such occasions belong wholly to the past. Much less can it be assumed that there will be no further instances of a community believing, conscientiously and entirely, that honor and duty require of it a certain course, which another community with equal integrity may hold to be inconsistent with the rights and obligations of its own members. It is quite possible, especially to one who has recently visited Holland, to conceive that Great Britain and the Boers are alike satisfied of the substantial justice of their respective claims. It is permissible most earnestly to hope that, in disputes between independent States, arbitration may find a way to reconcile peace with fidelity to conscience, in the case of both; but if, when friendly suggestion has done its best, the conviction of conscience remains unshaken, war is better than disobedience—better than acquiescence in recognized wrong. The great danger of undiscriminating advocacy of Arbitration, which threatens even the cause it seeks to maintain, is that it may lead men to tamper with equity, to compromise with unrighteousness, soothing their conscience with the belief that war is so entirely wrong that beside it no other tolerated evil is wrong. Witness Armenia and witness Crete. War has been avoided; but what of the national consciences that beheld such iniquity, and withheld the hand?

SECTION B. EXPANSION IN THE ORIENT

1. THE PROBLEM OF ASIA[1]

By ALFRED THAYER MAHAN

EDITORS' NOTE.—In 1900 Mahan backed McKinley and the American aspirations to empire in a series of articles written for *Harper's Magazine* and subsequently published in book form as *The Problem of Asia*. Here he advocated the alignment of the great sea powers, the United States and Great Britain, with the rising sea powers, Germany and Japan, together with the Mediterranean power, Italy, all to check the expansive land power, Russia, then allied with France and threatening, as he thought, to dominate the world.

By 1905 Mahan saw the realization of the policies which he had most strongly advocated. Mahan had long argued, "Whether they will or not, Americans must now begin to look outward."

Mahan viewed the Philippines as a task given by Providence to America. In conversation with certain of the British delegation at The Hague Conference, Mahan said that American in-

terests now lay in the East and the West and that America proposed to look after her Chinese markets. In 1900 Mahan's solution to the problem of Asia was that Russia would be allowed to advance into Manchuria, while the Teutonic powers—Great Britain, Germany, and the United States—acquired China proper, especially the Yangtze Valley. For this restricted area Mahan advocated cooperation among the powers and uplift of the natives. To Theodore Roosevelt, Mahan expressed his belief that neither the United States nor Great Britain, singly or jointly, could "check Russia by main force in northern China." A check on Russia appeared in the Treaty of Portsmouth of 1905 that ended the Russo-Japanese War. Theodore Roosevelt accepted the Japanese request for his good offices and was instrumental in strengthening the Japanese position in Manchuria and giving the Japanese a free hand in Korea.

CHAPTER I

. . . It would be an interesting study, but one quite apart from the object of this paper, to trace the genesis and evolution in the American people of the impulse to-

wards expansion which has recently taken so decisive a stride. To do this adequately would involve the consideration of a volume of details, in order to extricate from them the leading features which characterize and demonstrate the vital sequence in the several stages of advance. The treatment of the matter, however, would be very imperfect if it failed clearly to recognize and to state that it is but one phase of

1. Alfred Thayer Mahan, *The Problem of Asia* (Boston: Little, Brown & Co., 1900), pp. 4–18, 24–37, 55–62, 67–69, 72–75, 90–93, 96–100, 130–33, 145–46. By permission of the estate of Alfred Thayer Mahan.

a sentiment that has swept over the whole civilized European world within the last few decades, salient evidences of which are found in the advance of Russia in Asia, in the division of Africa, in the colonial ambitions of France and of Germany, in the naval growth of the latter, in the development of Japan, and in the British idea of Imperial Federation, now fast assuming concrete shape in practical combined action in South Africa. Every great state has borne its part in this common movement, the significance of which cannot be ignored. We may not know whence it comes nor whither it goes, but there it is. We see it and we hear it, and our own share in it has already radically changed our relations towards foreign states and races. Whatever its future, a future it clearly has, to read which men must lift up their hearts and strain their eyes, while at the same time they neglect not the present, but do with their might that which their hand at the moment finds to do.

A study of a particular phase of this possible future, as it appears to one man, is the object of this present paper. Before, however, proceeding with such consideration, it may be interesting, and not inappropriate, to note in briefest outline how singularly the long view and the short view have received illustration in the recent course of events. The intrinsic importance of Cuba, of the West Indies in general, and of the Isthmus of Panama, to the political, commercial, and military interests of the United States, was long ago perceived. To illustrate this by detailed account, from the words and actions of public men, would require an article—rather, perhaps, a volume—by itself; but it is easy to note, rising above the sea of incidental details, of diplomatic negotiations and governmental recommendations, a few landmarks, such as the Clayton-Bulwer Treaty, the attempt under Grant's administration to annex Santo Domingo, the abortive negotiations for the purchase of the Danish islands, our treaty with Colombia guaranteeing the transit of the Isthmus railway.

Solicitude, which traced its origin to the early years of the century, increased to conviction as the expansion of the country emphasized the consciousness of a probable destiny. Deadened temporarily by the outbreak of the Civil War, which it antedated by generations, it revived immediately upon its conclusion—the insistence upon the French withdrawal from Mexico being a first-fruits of quickened life. For the moment the long view had yielded to the imperious demands of the short; but, the emergency over, the nation again lifted its eyes and looked afar.

Meantime events had progressed and continued to progress. New factors had entered into the conditions, while the bearing and importance of old factors were seen more clearly and forcibly, for time had brought them out of the haze of distant speculation, and nearer to the decisive moment of action. The school of thought that looked to expansion became more incisive and outspoken, its ideas increasing in scope and in definiteness of expression. The long view, raising its vision gradually above the Antilles and the Isthmus, as these drew more into the foreground, saw beyond them the Pacific, Hawaii, and the beginning of momentous issues in China and Japan. There insight again was baffled; unless it may be claimed, as evidence of a wider range, that the country and the exponents of expansion, in common with the world at large, had at last aroused to consciousness of the determining influence of sea power upon the history of the world. Sea power, however, is but the handmaid of expansion, its begetter and preserver; it is not itself expansion, nor did the advocates of the latter foresee room for advance beyond the Pacific. Their vision reached not past Hawaii, which also, as touching the United States, they regarded from the point of view of defence rather than as a stepping-stone to any farther influence in the world. So far as came under the observation of the writer —and his interest in the matter dated back several years—the expansionists themselves, up to the war with Spain, were dominated by the purely defensive ideas inherited from the earlier days of our national existence. The Antilles, Cuba, the Isthmus, and Hawaii were up to that time simply outposts—positions—where it was increasingly evident that influences might be established dangerous to the United States as she then was. Such influences must be forestalled; if not by immediate action, at least by a definite policy.

It was to such a state of mind that the war with Spain came; and the result has the special interest of showing the almost instantaneous readiness with which a seed of thought germinates when it falls upon mental soil prepared already to receive it. Reflection and discussion, voice and pen, platform and press, had broken up the fallow ground left untilled by the generations which succeeded the fathers of the republic. Habit had familiarized men's minds with the idea of national power spreading beyond the bounds of this continent, and with the reasons that made it advisable, if not imperative. Though staggered for an instant by a proposition so entirely unexpected and novel as Asiatic dominion, the long view had done its work of preparation; and the short view, the action necessary at the minute, imposed primarily and inevitably by the circumstances of the instant, found no serious difficulty of acceptance, so far as concerned the annexation of the Philippines—the widest sweep, in space, of our national extension.

We have for the time being quite sufficient to occupy our activities in accommodating ourselves to these new conditions, and in organizing our duties under them. But while this is true as touching immediate action, it is not necessarily, nor equally, true as regards thought, directed upon the future. After a brief rest in contemplation of the present, effort must be resumed, not merely to note existing conditions, but to appreciate the tendencies involved in them—history in embryo—the issue of which will hereafter concern us or our descendants. Events of recent years

have substantially changed the political relations of states, and thereby have imposed such a study of these as shall give point and direction to that long view of the distant future which, uncertain though it be in its calculations, and liable to sudden disconcertment, is nevertheless essential, if sagacious and continuous guidance is to be given to the course of a nation. Such study will require an intelligent and sustained resolution; for, with the possible exception of the Monroe doctrine, the people of the United States have been by long habit indifferent to the subject of external policies. They have been so not only as the result of our particular circumstances of isolation, but by deliberate intention, inherited from a day when such abstinence was better justified than now, and depended upon a well-known, though misunderstood, warning of Washington against entangling alliances. Under changed conditions of the world, from the influence of which we cannot escape, it is imperative to arouse to the necessity of conscious effort, in order to recognize and to understand broad external problems, not merely as matters of general information or of speculative interest, but as questions in which we ourselves have, or may have, the gravest direct concern, as affecting ourselves or our children.

It is by such long views that is developed the readiness of decision, in unexpected conjunctures of international politics, which corresponds to presence of mind in common life; for ordinarily presence of mind means preparedness of mind, through previous reflection upon possible contingencies. The need of such readiness—of sustained apprehension of actual and of probable future conditions—receives the clearest demonstration from our recent experience. What more sudden or less expected, what, in a word, more illustrative of a short view resulting in decisive action, taken at a moment's notice, can be adduced than that a war begun with Spain about Cuba should result in tendering us the position of an Asiatic Power, with the consequent responsibilities and opportunities? Evidently a mind prepared by deliberation upon contemporary occurrences and tendencies is no mean equipment for prompt decision in such a case. It is in no wise a disconnected incident that the United States has been suddenly drawn out of her traditional attitude of apartness from the struggle of European states, and had a new element forced into her polity. The war with Spain has been but one of several events, nearly simultaneous, which have compelled mankind to fix their attention upon eastern Asia, and to realize that conditions there have so changed as to compel a readjustment of ideas, as well as of national policies and affiliations. Nothing is more calculated to impress the mind with the seriousness of the impending problems than the known fact that Japan, which less than four years ago notified our government of her disinclination to our annexation of Hawaii, now with satisfaction sees us in possession of the Philippines.

The altered conditions in the East have doubtless resulted—as did American expansion—from certain preparative antecedents, less obvious at the time of their occurrence, and which therefore then escaped particular notice; but the incidents that have signalized the change have been compacted into a very few years. Hence they possess the attribute of suddenness, which naturally entails for a time a lack of precise comprehension, with the necessary consequence of vagueness in opinion. Nevertheless, there they are; matters of grave international moment to those older nationalities, from whom heretofore we have held ourselves sedulously aloof. Side by side with them is our own acceptance of the Philippines, an act which we could not rightly avoid, and which carries with it opportunity. Opportunity, however, can never be severed from responsibility; for, whether utilized or neglected, a decision, positive or negative, is made, which cannot be dissociated from the imputation of moral right or wrong, of intellectual mistake or of wisdom.

It may be well here to consider for a moment the charge, now often made, that by the acceptance of the Philippines, and, still more, by any further use of the opportunities they may give us, we abandon the Monroe doctrine. The argument, if it can be allowed that name, derives such force as it has from appeal to prejudice; a word which, although it has an invidious association, does not necessarily imply more than opinion already formed, and which, if resting on solid basis, is entitled to full respect, unless, and until, it refuses to face new conditions. The Monroe doctrine, however, commits us only to a national policy, which may be comprehensively summarized as an avowed purpose to resist the extension of the European system to the American continents. As a just counterweight to this pretension, which rests in no wise upon international law, but upon our own interests as we understand them, we have adopted, as a rule of action, abstention from interference—even by suggestion, and much more by act—in questions purely European.

Of these complementary positions, neither the one nor the other possesses any legal standing, any binding force, of compact or of precedent. We are at liberty to abandon either at once, without incurring any just imputation of unlawful action. Regarded, however, purely as a matter of policy, and as such accepted as wise, by what process of reasoning is it to be established that either the one rule or the other bars us, on the ground of consistency, from asserting what we think our rights in Asia? In its inception the Monroe doctrine was, I suppose, a recognition of the familiar maxim of statesmen that geographical propinquity is a source of trouble between nations, which we, being favored by natural isolation, proposed to avert; and to this proposition the determination to keep clear of questions internal to Europe was an inevitable corollary. We took advantage, in short, of an opportunity extended to us by fortunate conditions to assure our national quiet. But there are provinces other than geographical in which the interests of nations approach and mingle, and in those we have never been deterred by the Monroe doctrine from acting as our duties or our interests demanded. It has never, that I know, been seriously wished to compass our ends by the acquisition of European territory, for it would be neither expedient nor justifiable, even if possible, to unsettle conditions the permanency of which is the secure evolution of centuries of racial and national history; but we have had no scruples of justice or of expediency as to extension of territory in this hemisphere, where no such final adjustments had been reached. Now in Asia we are confronted at this moment by questions in which our interests will probably be largely involved. There is no more inconsistency in taking there such action as the case demands than there has been in any international difference we have hitherto had with a European power; while if such action should involve use of territory, directly or incidentally, by possession or by control—sphere of influence—it will only be because decadent conditions there shall hereafter have resulted in a lack of power, either to perpetuate a present system or to resist encroachments which the progress of the world under the impulse of more virile states is sure to entail. There is certainly no desire, but rather unwillingness, on the part of the United States to undertake such an addition to her responsibilities, otherwise sufficiently great; both her traditions and her present policy are necessarily adverse to such action. Still it must be considered as a possible contingency, however deplorable, for, if life departs, a carcass can be utilized only by dissection or for food; the gathering to it of the eagles is a natural law, of which it is bootless to complain. The onward movement of the world has to be accepted as a fact, to be advantageously dealt with by guidance, not by mere opposition, still less by

unprofitable bewailing of things irretrievably past.

The Monroe doctrine has been and continues to be a good serviceable working theory, resting on undeniable conditions. But, having now a lifetime of several generations, it has acquired an added force of tradition, of simple conservatism, which has a bad as well as a good side. For tradition tends to invest accepted policy with the attribute of permanency, which only exceptionally can be predicated of the circumstances of this changing world. The principles upon which an idea rests may conform to essential, and therefore permanent, truth; but application continually varies, and maxims, rules, doctrines, not being the living breath of principles, but only their embodiment—the temporary application of them to conditions not necessarily permanent—can claim no exemption from the ebb and flow of mundane things. We should not make of even this revered doctrine a fetich, nor persuade ourselves that a modification is under no circumstances admissible.

For instance, it has become probable that, whatever our continued adherence to the doctrine itself, we may have somewhat to readjust our views of its corollary—that concerning apartness from European complications. It is not, indeed, likely, in any view that can be taken within our present horizon, that we should find reason for intervention in a dispute localized in Europe itself; but it is nevertheless most probable that we can never again see with indifference, and with the sense of security which characterized our past, a substantial, and still less a radical, change in the balance of power there. The progress of the world has brought us to a period when it is well within the range of possibilities that the declension of a European state might immediately and directly endanger our own interests; might involve us in action, either to avert the catastrophe itself or to remedy its consequences. From this follows the obvious necessity of appreciating the relations to ourselves of the power inherent in various countries, due to their available strength and to their position; what also their attitude towards us, resultant from the temper of the people, and the intelligent control of the latter by the government—two very different things, even in democratic communities. Herein, again, we only share the common fate of all nations; for not only do all touch one another more closely than of old, but—and especially in Asia—conditions external to all are drawing the regard of all towards a common centre, where as yet nothing certain is determined, where the possibilities of the future are many, and diverse, and great. . . .

Accepting provisionally the east and west belt of division as one stage in the process of analysis, we may profitably consider next the character and distribution of the forces whose northward and southward impulses constitute the primary factors in the process of change already initiated and still continuing. Upon a glance at the map one enormous fact immediately obtrudes itself upon the attention—the vast, uninterrupted mass of the Russian Empire, stretching without a break in territorial consecutiveness from the meridian of western Asia Minor, until to the eastward it overpasses that of Japan. In this huge distance no political obstacles intervene to impede the concentrated action of the disposable strength. Within the dominion of Russia only the distances themselves, and the hindrances—unquestionably great and manifold—imposed by natural conditions, place checks upon her freedom and fulness of movement. To this element of power—central position—is to be added the wedge-shaped outline of her territorial projection into central Asia, strongly supported as this is, on the one flank, by the mountains of the Caucasus and the inland Caspian Sea—wholly under her control—and on the other by the ranges which extend from Afghanistan, northeasterly, along the western frontier of China. From the latter, moreover, she as yet has no serious danger to fear.

The fact of her general advance up to the present time, most of which has been made within a generation, so that the point of the wedge is now inserted between Afghanistan and Persia, must be viewed in connection with the tempting relative facility of farther progress through Persia to the Persian Gulf, and with the strictly analogous movement, on the other side of the continent, where long strides have been made through Manchuria to Port Arthur and the Gulf of Pe-chi-li. Thus, alike in the far east and in the far west, we find the same characteristic of remorseless energy, rather remittent than intermittent in its symptoms. Russia, in obedience to natural law and race instinct, is working, geographically, to the southward in Asia by both flanks, her centre covered by the mountains of Afghanistan and the deserts of eastern Turkestan and Mongolia. Nor is it possible, even if it were desired, to interfere with the internal action, the mutual support, of the various sections of this extended line, whose length under the physical and political conditions is less an element of weakness; for the Russian centre cannot be broken. It is upon, and from, the flanks of this great line that restraint, if needed, must come; the opposition of those who, with no ill-will to Russia, no grudging of her prosperity, nevertheless think that undue predominance is an unsound condition in any body politic—in the parliament of man, if we may say so, as well as in that of a nation. In the federation of the world, if it ever come to pass, healthy politics will need an opposition of parties, drawn doubtless along national or racial lines.

As north and south are logically opposed, so it might be surmised that practically the opposition to this movement of Russia from the north would find its chief expression to the south of the broad dividing belt, between the thirtieth and fortieth parallels. In a measure this is so, but with a very marked distinction, not only in degree but in kind. In the progress of history, in which, as it unrolls, more and more of plan and of purpose seems to become evident, the great central peninsula of southern Asia, also projecting wedge-shaped far north into the middle debatable zone, has come under the control of a people the heart of whose power is far removed from it locally, and who, to the concentration of territory characteristic of Russia's geographical position, present an extreme of racial and military dispersal. India, therefore, is to Great Britain not the primary base of operations, political and military—for military action is only a specialized form of political. It is simply one of many contingent—secondary—bases, in different parts of the world, the action of which is susceptible of unification only by means of a supreme sea power. Of these many bases, India is the one best fitted, by nearness and by conformation, both for effect upon Central Asia and for operations upon either extremity of the long line over which the Russian front extends. Protected on the land side and centre by the mountains of Afghanistan and the Himalayas, its flanks, thrown to the rear, are unassailable, so long as the navy remains predominant. They constitute also frontiers, from which, in the future as in the past, expeditions may make a refreshed and final start, for Egypt on the one hand, for China on the other; and, it is needless to add, for any less distant destination in either direction.

It is not intrinsically only that India possesses the value of a base to Great Britain. The central position which she holds relatively to China and to Egypt obtains also towards Australia and the Cape of Good Hope, assisting thus the concentration upon her of such support as either colony can extend to the general policy of an Imperial Federation. Even in its immediate relations to Asiatic problems, however, India is not unsupported. On land and in the centre, the acquisition of Burmah gives a continuous extension of frontier to the east, which turns the range of the Himalayas, opening access, political

or peaceful, for influence or for commerce, to the upper valley of the Yang-tse-kiang, and to the western provinces of China proper. By sea, the Straits Settlements and Hong-kong on the one side, Aden and Egypt on the other, facilitate, as far as land positions can, maritime enterprises to the eastward or to the westward, directed in a broad sense upon the flanks of the dividing zone, or upon those of the opposing fronts of operations that mark the deployment of the northern and southern powers, which at the present time are most strongly established upon Asian territory.

The British and Russian territorial developments in Asia, as thus summarized, constitute the local bases, upon which depend not merely movement, peaceful or warlike, if such take place, but the impulse to action, defensive or offensive, felt by either nation. Were they not where they are, much that now engages their attention would pass unremarked; but, being there, there arise from the positions exterior opportunities and dangers, which neither state should nor can neglect. It becomes therefore necessary to consider, and to summarize, what those dangers and opportunities are; for they constitute the external interests, which in the political field correspond to the objectives of strategy in the Art of War.

The first law of states, as of men, is self-preservation—a term which cannot be narrowed to the bare tenure of a stationary round of existence. Growth is a property of healthful life, which does not, it is true, necessarily imply increase of size for nations, any more than it does for individuals, with whom bodily, and still more mental, development progresses long after stature has reached its limit; but it does involve the right to insure by just means whatsoever contributes to national progress, and correlatively to combat injurious action taken by an outside agency, if the latter overpass its own lawful sphere. When a difference between two states can be brought to the test of ascertained and defined right, this carries with it a strong presumption in favor of submission; but when a matter touches only advantage, not qualified by law or by prescription, and the question therefore is one of expediency, it is justly and profitably considered in the light of self-preservation. This includes the right of growth, common to both, which is not legal but natural, and consequently less capable of precise definition. It is a great gain, not only to the parties concerned, but to mankind at large, when each candidly regards in this light the claims of an opponent as well as its own, and seeks to strike a fair balance by mutual concession or impartial arbitration; but it still remains true that in such a transaction governments—and even nations— are not principals, but agents, having in charge that which is not their own, but their trust, for the generation that then is and for those which are to follow. Relinquishment, therefore, and recourse to arbitration, are conditioned by the element of trusteeship, and cannot be embraced in that spirit of simple self-sacrifice which is so admirable in the individual man dealing with what is wholly his own.

It is therefore not enough to direct attention to the security, in territorial tenure, of the two parties who at the present moment are the principal exponents of the contending impulses in Asia. There must be considered also the need and right to grow, as these may be affected either by their own opposing tendencies, or by conditions now existing in Asia itself, and localized for the most part in the dividing belt of debatable ground. Nor can the question be confined to the two most prominent disputants. The right to grow, of the world in general, and of other states in particular, is involved in these Asian problems, in the development and utilization of this vast tract, so long isolated from a share in the general order.

Growth depends upon two correlative factors; upon vigor of internal organization—which gives power to assimilate— and upon freedom of interchange with external sources of support. In the family of civilized states, the former is solely the concern of the nation itself; intervention from without, in the internal order of a community, is generally held to be permissible only when its stage of political development corresponds to that of childhood or of decay. The matter, in fact, is one properly and naturally internal, only exceptionally and accidentally one for interference from outside. It is quite different with freedom of interchange; for that, depending upon conditions external to the country, implies necessarily external acquiescence, both of the people with whom interchange is had, and of those whose interests are involved in the intervening channels of communication.

The methods of the British or Russian internal administration are therefore outside of such a discussion as this, except in so far as they indicate the probable effect upon other countries of the extension of these methods to territory desired, but not yet obtained. This is, indeed, a most serious consideration, and one that cannot fail to weigh heavily in the determination of policies. The ubiquitous tendency to territorial expansion, which is so marked a feature in European states of the period, results in a corresponding contraction of the ground free equally to all; and, as this narrows, there cannot but be increasing jealousy of every movement which carries a threat of exclusive control, whether by acquisition or by predominant influence, especially if the latter depend not upon fair commercial struggle in open markets, but upon the alien element of military or political force.

Whatever, therefore, may be the commercial possibilities involved in the application of modern methods to the further development of the countries and peoples which lie between the zones of British and Russian power in Asia, one single interest will be common to all the nations who seek by commerce—by interchange—to promote their own healthy national growth. Each alike will desire that it, individually, have its equal chance in the field, unhindered by the inimical influence of a foreign power, resting not upon fair competition, but upon force, whether exerted by open act or by secret pressure. Nothing is more dreaded, nor will be more resented—more productive of quarrel—than such interposition. In the final analysis the question is as yet essentially military. Time, much time, will be needed for the process of development; but the movement is already in progress through which, by the acquisition of new positions, and by the consolidation of power both in them and in territory already held, advantage will be gained for the exercise of control.

What has just been said applies to all the belt lying, roughly, between the thirtieth and fortieth parallels, and not to China only, although the latter, through her huge area and population, and her seeming helplessness, has naturally attracted the greater attention. The question also is, for the present, quite independent of the aggregate results of development, which not impossibly may fall very short of the rosy hopes of trade suggested by the mere words "four hundred millions of people." Those results, being so far in the future as to defy exact prediction, affect the question much as a variable quantity does a mathematical problem—that is, not at all, so far as the process of investigation is concerned, the effect being shown only when different values are assigned to it in the final expression. Be that variable quantity—the result of development—great or small, its possibilities are great, and as such it must be taken into account in discussing the political problem of obviating *now* the chance of any exclusive, or unduly preponderant, usufruct *then*.

On this account, in regarding the central zone of Asia as a source whence the nations of the world, by mutual exchange or benefit, can both invigorate their own life and that of the Asiatics, it seems quite just and reasonable to discard all attempt to estimate by detail how abundant that source may prove to be. Even if utilization be confined to the labor and capital employed in developing internal communications, the mutual effect will be great enough to merit consideration. How much more the future may hold is indifferent to the necessary forecast—the short view—of the present. The problem, into the final solution of which enter all the factors—military and naval power, military and naval positions, communications external and internal, commercial operations and benefits—is less one of proportion than of scale; and the scale will depend upon the value of that unknown and variable quantity, the potential wealth of the countries concerned, when they shall have become fully developed members of the international body.

The contribution, direct and indirect, which these regions may eventually make to the general prosperity of the world is the substantial interest which is now attracting the attention of the nations. From their aim to control or to share it, it corresponds to the objective of strategy in military operations. Accepting provisionally the conclusion just reached as to its present indeterminate value, we have next to consider the question of approaches from without, which in their turn answer to the communications that play so leading a part in the policy of war. Communications that are wholly internal fall into the category of commercial development, except where they may form sections of a great international line.

It will be apparent at once that communications—approaches from without—are of two chief kinds—by sea and by land. In these heads of division they recall the essential differences between the two European powers now most solidly settled on Asiatic soil. These concurrent facts—and factors—suggest, what will hereafter become increasingly apparent, that we have here again a fresh instance of the multiform struggle between land power and sea power. Consequently, it is not improbable that the recognition and constant recollection of this perennial contest may serve better than any other clew to guide us through this complicated inquiry, and to reach an adjustment between the two antagonists that can most certainly and most easily be maintained. Such an adjustment would be one in which the respective aggregates of power, whatever its component parts on either side, should approach equality, in amount and in disposition, while causes of friction should at the same time be minimized. If these two conditions—the smallest friction, and equality of power—be insured, there will follow from them the least disposition to break the peace. . . .

CHAPTER II

. . . It has been said that, viewing Russia as a whole, relatively to the middle zone of Asia, her advance has been, and promises still to be, by the flanks rather than by the centre. Such certainly are the present tendencies and indications. It is upon the flanks also, and upon the flanks chiefly, that opposition can be effectually made; but such opposition will be of the most forcible character, not only on account of the advantage already stated, inherent to flank attacks generally, but because it will be upon the line of the sea frontier—the seaboard—and accordingly upon the access to the sea, with which the interior, for its best welfare, requires untrammelled communication. It will be also in the hands of powers which, by the nature of their strength, and by their local positions in Asia, are essentially powers of the sea.

Let us, then, examine the conditions upon the flanks: first, as involving objects of interest—objectives of policy—control of which may be coveted; and secondly, with reference to the positions—the local tenure—of the states which may be aiming there to exert influence, whether for advance or for its prevention, and to their intrinsic strength for such purposes.

Accepting the estimates already made of Russia's position and necessary aims, her interests may be condensed into access to the sea as extensive and as free as possible: on the east by the Chinese seaboard; on the west in two directions, viz., to the Persian Gulf, by way of Persia, and to the Mediterranean, from the Black Sea, or through Asia Minor. Such plans are deducible, not from knowledge of the councils of the Russian government, but from the history of the recent past, and from the clear natural conditions indicating the lines which offer least resistance to forward movement, whether in the physical obstacles to be overcome, or in the opposition of the populations. It is allowable to add to these conjectural projects the common surmise of Russian design upon India. This, if entertained, would be an advance by the centre rather than by a flank; but even here a study of the map would seem to show that progress through Persia would not only approach the gulf, but if successful would turn—would outflank—the mountains of Afghanistan, avoiding the difficulties presented by the severe features of that country and by the character of its inhabitants. Russia would thus obtain a better position, both in itself and in its communication with the north, for beginning and sustaining operations in India itself.

Such movements as here supposed on the part of Russia, upon the two flanks, might politically affect the interests of other states in a manner to arouse decided and reasonable antagonism; for exerting which they have formidable facilities, by position and otherwise. These advantages, however, rest ultimately upon the sea, and consequently they will not, unless carefully improved, outweigh—or even equal—the predominance by land which Russia has, owing to her territorial nearness and other conditions already mentioned. Moreover, as contrasted with the political unity of Russia and her geographical continuity, the influences that can possibly be opposed to her are diverse and scattered. They find, however, a certain unifying motive in a common interest, of unfettered commerce and of transit in the regions in question. It is upon the realization of this interest, and upon the accurate appreciation of their power to protect it—and not upon artificial combinations—that correct policy or successful concert in the future must rest. Effective co-operation between nations depends upon the necessity imposed by a common interest; the more clear and general, therefore, the understanding of the interest and of attendant conditions, the more certain and abiding the co-operation.

The regions whose political and social future is in doubt, and to be determined possibly by the relative effect exerted upon their inhabitants by the contrasting powers of the land and of the sea, in the struggle of these to influence commercial conditions, constitute the objectives of policy. They are, on the east, the Chinese Empire, and more particularly China proper; on the west, Turkey in Asia and Persia. The latter two are conterminous, the line of division being marked by a lofty but not impracticable mountain chain, extending to the southeast from the ranges of Armenia nearly to the Persian Gulf. Being substantially devoid of railroads, this tract is commercially backward, judged by modern standards. Its area, omitting Arabia, is about a million square miles, distributed between two lines, roughly parallel, indicated on the south by the Mediterranean and the Persian Gulf, on the north by the Black and Caspian seas. The breadth thus bounded is about five hundred miles—one-half the distance from New York to Chicago. The interior is susceptible of great development, and, specifically, it offers opportunity for railroad communication from the Mediterranean to the head of the Persian Gulf, branching through Persia to the borders of India. From such a trunk line once in operation, lateral extensions would of course follow as improvements increase.

The question of dealing with countries such as these and China, in which governments and peoples alike are content to be stationary, neither knowing nor desiring progress, is so troublesome that it will be postponed until the day when the outside more advanced civilization has need of them; or until, as now with China, the future need is emphasized by a present consciousness of its imminence, and by a movement, more or less general, to obtain positions that can be utilized for control or influence. Whatever the nature of such influences, be they most contrary one to another, they have always this in common: they need some circumstance of advantage, in the possession of visible power and position, which alone the native occupants understand as a motive for concession. According as the relative impulses from the north and from the south compare in unmistakable force, so will they prevail. There can be, of course, no question of dispossessing the present inhabitants, that being neither practicable nor desirable. The rational object can only be to induce them to place themselves under such conditions as shall contribute to their regeneration, to their own benefit and that of the world at large. Whether this shall be effected by a gradual assumption of rule, as in India, or by actuating the government in nominal possession, as now in Egypt, is a matter of detail concerning which prediction is impossible. Results in such cases are matters less of formal preordainment than of growth—of evolution—stage by stage.

In the past the history of such changes has commonly been that private commercial enterprise leads the way, and that the incapacity of the local government permits the occurrence of abuses, which necessitate the interference of a foreign state to protect the rights of its citizens. Interference cannot be confined to mere remedy of the past and engagements for the future, but seeks prevention by guarantees, usually of such a description as to confer a certain degree of local rule. This, in turn, partaking of the vitality of its mother-country, tends to grow, as all life does. The seed, having been sown, germinates and thrives after its manner, which is not the manner of the soil; but, once planted, it is ineradicable. Whether it overspreads the land depends not upon the native resistance, but upon its meeting counteracting influence of a nature essentially akin to its own.

This process is in India a matter of past history, which had its crisis in the days when Clive and Dupleix represented the rival alien influences of Great Britain and of France; but it has received various illustrations in our own time. In Egypt its evolution is but lately complete, and there, as in India, quite contrary to what may have at first been expected, has resulted in the dominance of a single state. In China it has begun, and is still in progress. There it presents as yet only the competition of several nations; it remains to be seen whether, as has been the case in India and in Egypt, this condition will be radically modified by some sudden unanticipated event. That Asia Minor, Syria, Mesopotamia, and Persia will remain indefinitely strangers to experience of a like nature, is not to be imagined. There is no reason why they should, and there are very evident conditions which indicate that, although postponed, the first step is sure to be taken and the consequences sure to follow, although we cannot now foretell the time of the beginning nor the character of the issue. . . .

From our summary it seems evident that the four maritime states named can, by their positions on the eastern side of Asia, seriously impede advance from the north. On the western flank, embracing Persia and Asiatic Turkey, with the Levant Basin of the Mediterranean, conditions are less clear. The centre of the Russian strength is nearer, the sea power of France more at hand to support the Russian navy of the Black Sea—circumstances which favor a local predominance that for centuries has been, and still is, a leading ambition of France. As an offset, the engagements of Italy in the present state of international alliances, and her national sympathy, based upon evident interest, should prompt her active support to any combination the natural tendency of which shall be to insure the balance of power in the Mediterranean, and the consequent free use of the Suez Canal. The conspicuous political sagacity of her people cannot fail to realize that her geographical position, close to Malta and central as regards the Mediterranean Basin, enables her, by means of her powerful navy, to be a factor of decisive importance in this field, the most influential and yet most precarious link in the chain of European communications with the farther East. Neither immediate interest nor local circumstances of advantage justify either Japan or the United States in expending here any part of the energies they require for more pressing duties; and the people of the latter would certainly be loath, probably to the point of refusal, to help perpetuate the abused power of the Sultan—the more so because their traditional friendship for Russia can be alienated only by the latter promoting a policy distinctly hostile to their interests. Yet, while this is so, Americans must accept and familiarize their minds to the fact that, with their irrevocable entry into the world's polity, first by the assertion of the Monroe doctrine, and since by their insular acquisitions— above all, the Philippines—and by the interests at stake in China, they cannot divest themselves of concern, practical as well as speculative, in such a question as the balance of power in the Levant, or at the entrance of the Persian Gulf. In predominance in those quarters is involved, for the present at least, control of the shortest way from our Atlantic coast to our new possessions—that by way of the Red Sea; but still more is this road valuable to Great Britain and to Germany, whose policy in China is naturally in accord with, and therefore should be a support to our own. Consequently, what affects them in the one region necessarily affects us in the other. . . .

In order to constitute here a political

condition susceptible of durable progress, in place of the present impotent misrule, a process of development must begin from without; for it is sufficiently demonstrated that there is no internal source of regeneration under the actual tenure. Whatever shall happen, the existing populations must remain; but the fate of the government, be that near or remote, will depend upon its faculty of accommodation to the dominant, though alien, pressure. During the stages of advance, through military organization and economical administration, both comfortable to the genius of the outside force, be that Russian or Western, the fleet that there finds its territorial base of action will continue to be, not native, but that of the external power; for a navy is the most delicate, most specialized form of military institutions, and hence the latest to mature into independent life. Nevertheless, during the period of tutelage, the result upon the maritime strategic field will be the same as though the naval organization, as well as the military, were composed of the inhabitants themselves. Both embodying the genius of the educating power, the combination of the two will control in her interest this central position of the world.

It is clear, indeed, that here and in China, as well as in Egypt, and wherever a numerous population already exists, the regeneration precursory to full attainment of civilization must proceed through, and by, the inhabitants already in possession of the soil. Concerning this there can be, and should be, no dispute. It appears little less certain that these now have not, either in themselves or in their existing governments, the power to begin and to continue the necessary reformation. The question therefore is, under what impulse, under the genius of what race or of what institutions, is the movement to arise and to progress? The determination of the answer depends upon a struggle, peaceful or otherwise, between the external powers—a conflict inevitable, irrepressible, because of their opposing political institutions,

themselves the expression of the yet more vital force of contrasted national characters. Whatever the scene or the nature of the contest, whether it be decided upon the debatable ground itself or exterior to it, upon land or upon sea, by peaceful competition or by the arbitration of war, the issue depends upon a balance of force. That it is impossible of prediction is no reason for abandoning an attempt to appreciate the conditions. Quite the contrary; for, be the result what it may, there will enter into its determination not merely blind force, of numbers or of position, but intelligent direction as well, which shall be guided step by step, as emergency succeeds emergency, by informed understanding of the importance and character of the elements of the problem, and by a forecast—a long view—of the ends to be desired. This will be the more necessary on the part of the sea powers if they have the common interest that has been asserted; for, not being under a single head, community of action, without which they will be powerless, can proceed only from an accord based upon accurate comprehension of the issues at stake. . . .

Our first necessity, therefore, is to recognize that for European civilization in its turn has now arrived an important period, a day of visitation; that a process has begun which must end either in bringing the Eastern and Western civilizations face to face, as opponents who have nothing in common, or else in receiving the new elements, the Chinese especially, as factors which, however they may preserve their individuality—as is desirable, and as the Latin and the Teuton still do—have been profoundly affected by long-continued intimate contact, and in such wise assimilated that the further association may proceed quietly to work out peacefully its natural results. To effect this does not demand the merging of national characteristics, but it does require more than material development, even the indwelling of a common spirit, a gift far more slow of growth than the process of material advance. Thus as the Latin civilization at the moment of decisive confrontation with Teutonic vigor found its expression in the Roman law and the imperial idea—of which the centralized Church was the natural inheritor—our own, while embodying many diverse national types, finds its unity in the hallowing traditions of a common Christianity; which is not the unimproved inheritance of a single generation, a talent laid up in a napkin, but an ever-swelling volume of inbred spiritual convictions, transmitted habits of thought, which, by their growth from generation to generation, attest their unimpaired vitality.

Measured by this standard, the incorporation of this vast mass of beings, the fringe of which alone we have as yet touched, into our civilization, to the spirit of which they have hitherto been utter strangers, is one of the greatest problems that humanity has yet had to solve; but to us, having the light of past experience, there is concerning it no ground for doubt, much less for fear. The success with which, in our society of nations, the Latin and the Teuton types mingle, without losing their individuality or their respective spheres of manifestation and of influence, has been due mainly, if not exclusively, to that one spirit which during the critical period found its home in the hearts of each, and became the common possession of races so diverse and for so long estranged. In its sign, in truth, they conquered, for it broke down the wall of partition between them, as between the Jew and the Gentile, reconciling the antagonism of ages without impairing the permanence of type. We may be sure, therefore, that the difficulty now before us—of long estrangement, present lack of mutual comprehension, and ultimate unity to be attained—cannot be adequately regarded from the standpoint of mere commercial advantages—the short view of immediate interests. However such considerations may serve to further a policy suited to the wants of the distant future, it will be only as they are in a direction generally right, the determination

of which must be otherwise estimated. All the factors already indicated in this paper, and such others as may hereafter appear in it or elsewhere, should be contemplated not only in the light of immediate advantage, but of that great inevitable future, when, aroused to the consciousness of power, and organized by the appropriation of European methods, these peoples, and especially China, shall be able to assert an influence proportionate to their mass, and to demand their shares in the general advantage. Those who live in that day will recognize then, what our duty to them requires us to realize now, how immense the importance to the world that their development has been not merely material, but spiritual; that time shall have been secured for them to absorb the ideals which in ourselves are the result of centuries of Christian increment. . . .

CHAPTER III

The accentuating rivalry between the states of our civilization arising from the unstable conditions of China, long uneasily felt, but not formally avowed, is now approaching a moment resembling that fixed for the unveiling of a statue. The presence of the statue is no secret, the very folds of the drapery betray its outlines, yet it is as it were ignored, until the date fixed for display. From yesterday to to-morrow things continue essentially as they have been; yet we all know by experience how profound the change, the increased sense of imminence and of responsibility, when the curtain falls, and facts long dissembled are looked straight in the face. Without moving, we have traversed years of event. Action that seemed susceptible of indefinite procrastination appears now to have been too long deferred. Opportunities which might have been seized are seen to have passed irretrievably, because in heedlessness or indolence we noted not the day of visitation. But, as has been remarked, it is not China alone that lies within the debatable zone. With but slight modification of phrase, what has been said of her may be affirmed of Afghanistan, of Persia, and of Asiatic Turkey, on the other flank of the line.

In contemplating the possibilities of action, it must be repeated that consideration for the populations involved should have precedence of the interests of external nations—even of the one, or ones, taking action. This is not said as a cover or an apology for measures the originating motive of which may be national self-interest. Self-interest is not only a legitimate, but a fundamental, cause for national policy; one which needs no cloak of hypocrisy. As a principle it does not require justification in general statement, although the propriety of its application to a particular instance may call for demonstration. But as a matter of preparation, for dealing wisely and righteously with this great question, against the chance of occasion arising—a mental preparation which no government can afford to postpone—the very first element of a just and far-seeing decision must be the determination to bear in mind, and to give due precedence to, the natural rights and the future development of the peoples most directly affected. The phrase "natural rights" is chosen expressly to indicate those that result from the simple fact of being born; in this distinct from political or legal rights which depend upon other fitnesses than that of merely being a man. Thus the claim of an indigenous population to retain indefinitely control of territory depends not upon a natural right, but upon political fitness, shown in the political work of governing, administering, and developing, in such manner as to insure the natural right of the world at large that resources should not be left idle, but be utilized for the general good. Failure to do this justifies, in principles, compulsion from outside; the position to be demonstrated, in the particular instance, is that the necessary time and the fitting opportunity have arrived.

The interests of the populations in these countries is by no means necessarily identical with those of the present governments, nor with the continuance of the latter in either form or person. These are not representative, in the sense that they either embody the wishes or promote the best welfare of the subject. They represent at most the incapacity of the people to govern themselves, and in their defects are the results of generations of evolution from a false system, unmodified by healthy opposition. Being what they are, should necessity demand their discontinuance, there need be no tenderness in dealing with them as institutions, whatever consideration may be shown to the incumbents of the moment.

It is, in fact, the inefficiency of the governments that chiefly gives rise to the present uneasiness. Were they otherwise, the balance of strength which now exists between the land and the sea powers, as already indicated, and the commercial interest of the latter in the preservation of peace, would naturally and easily determine their maintenance against any aggression that overpassed the fortunes common to all states, and threatened their permanence or independence. As it is, confronted with the imminent probability of a dissolution, neither the time nor the circumstances of which can be foreseen, the result of causes either internal or external, or both, other nations are compelled to seek the preservation of their own interests, by means which may employ the existing governments, if these are equal to the task, or may supersede them. That either alternative is repugnant to the genius and traditions of the United States, it is needless to say. Under the government of no party will she willingly initiate a process so contrary to her preferences, and the grave issues of which cannot be foreseen; but equally, under no government can she stand by and see substantial injury done to the welfare of her citizens by the undue preponderance of an inimical system of occupation or of influence. . . .

The people of the United States and their successive governments have not now, nor are likely to have hereafter, in connection with the future of Asia, to consider any such complicated conditions as are presented by the surroundings of the Suez Canal and of the Levant. Our difficulty at present does not proceed from outside conditions, but from those internal to our own national habits of thought, which in the past have been distinctly averse to studying external political problems, and even to admitting their existence, until pressed home upon our consciousness by an immediate emergency. Startling as has been the effect produced upon public sentiment by the recent exigency which threw the Philippines upon our hands, it must be remembered that a mental temperament evolved and ingrained by generations of acceptance, not merely inert, but willing, must tend to revert, as passing time dulls the sharp impression and lively emotions that followed the war with Spain. Most persons have experienced that, in forming or in breaking habits, the first few days under the impulse of a recent resolve are comparatively easy, but that to them succeeds an uninteresting monotonous period of struggle, which too often issues in apathetic surrender to former conditions. With nations the tendency is the same. To resist it, where resistance is necessary, there is required a comprehension of facts, and a recognition of the duties and interests involved; for in these, distant or immediate, are to be found the only unanswerable reasons and durable motives for national policy.

The argument of these papers rests upon the assumption, now quite generally accepted, that in the wide movement of expansion which has characterized the last quarter of the closing century, the Pacific Ocean in general and eastern Asia in particular are indicated as the predominant objects of interest, common to all nations, both in the near and in the remote future. Within the home dominions of the European and the American powers no marked territorial changes are to be expected; but in the outer world, where conditions are unsettled, and towards which all eyes are turned, regions even extensive derive their present significance less from their intrinsic value than from their bearing upon access to the central objects named. South Africa, for instance, if Mr. Bryce's estimate is correct, receives from its great goldfields but a temporary importance, destined soon to disappear by their exhaustion; but as an important outpost on one of the highroads to India and the farther East it has some permanent value, which may be more or less, but in any event demands consideration.

The Isthmus of Suez, the Levant, and Persia in like manner possess inherent advantages; but it has been attempted to show that the enjoyment of these is a less pressing concern than the establishment there of political conditions which may affect the future control of the Suez route.

These, and the other factors named, by their particular values and their mutual influence, constitute the strategic features of the general world situation involved in the problem of Asia. With them nations have to deal in the light of their individual interests, checked by due respect to the rights of others, measuring the latter not exclusively by the rule of conventional ideas, essentially transitory, but by the standards of eternal justice, which human law can express only imperfectly. Nor does the mighty power of sentiment fail to find due place in such a scheme; on the contrary, when healthy in character, it receives from the considerations that have been adduced the intelligent direction which alone makes it operative for good. But a very large part of a nation's wisdom consists in reinforcing its own strength by co-operation with others, based upon a substantial identity of interests; and if such identity is found combined with community of character and tradition, fostering community of ideals, the prospect of continued and harmonious co-operation is greatly increased. From the sense of such kinship springs a sound affection, which redeems interest from much of the selfishness associated with the word. Such is the triple bond which may unite Germany, Great Britain, and the United States; not in alliance, but in solidarity of action, founded upon the rock of common interest, and cemented by the ties of blood. . . .

In conclusion a further remark may be offered. Both the signs of the times and obvious motives for action point to a probable permanent co-operation between the communities which speak the English tongue, as well as to a possible, if much less assured, coincidence of action with the empire the language and people of which come from the same stock, though differentiated by prolonged separation. But upon the horizon of the future may be described a further omen of favorable augury. Various causes have conspired during the passing century to depress the visible power and influence of the Latin communities in Europe, compared to those grouped as the Teutonic. The unification of Italy is the one conspicuous exception. To this let there be added the strategic central position of the new state in the Mediterranean, which is to Europe far more even than the Caribbean can be to America, and also the political considerations which have forced her and France into the opposite scales of the political balance.

This attitude of Italy cannot but be fully confirmed by the clear necessity, to Latin and to Teuton, to insure that predominance in the Levant which is essential to both, because, as sea powers, secure use of the Suez Canal is to them vital. The significance of this is that, by the force of circumstances, Italy, the modern representative of that which is most solid, politically, in the original Latin strain, remains in the intimacy of political attachment with the Teutonic Powers. This assures us the continued association of that Latin element which has contributed so much to the composite result of our Christian civilization; and it still more points on to the time when that element, the lineal inheritor of Roman greatness, seeing more clearly where its interests lie, shall find in Italy the centre and the pattern which shall restore it, in renewed glory, to the commonwealth of states that already owes to it so much.

NOTE.—Since concluding these papers the writer has met these recent words of Sir W. W. Hunter (introduction to *History of British India*), whose regretted death has just removed one of the most widely informed students of Asian questions: "I hail the advent of the United States in the East, as a new power for good, not alone for the island races that come under their care, but also in that great settlement of European spheres of influence in Asia, which, if we could see aright, forms a *world problem* of our day."

2. ON ANNEXATION OF THE PHILIPPINES[1]

By ALBERT J. BEVERIDGE

EDITORS' NOTE.—The United States has not been altogether innocent of designs on its neighbors, as witness the War of 1812, the Mexican War, and our middle-nineteenth-century attitude toward the Caribbean Sea and its bordering shores. In general, however, our ambitions were not flamboyantly

expressed. However, as the nineteenth century closed, the occasional phrases of a Perry or Soule were succeeded by the full-bodied arguments of Mahan. The American voting public in 1900 heard a vehement and self-conscious cry for expansion. In public debate at least one faction denied that the true mission of democracy could be consummated in peace and isolation.

1. *Congressional Record*, XXXIII, Part I (January 9, 1900), 704–5, 707.

In support of expansion, Albert Jeremiah Beveridge (1862–1927), a fiery young Indiana senator, argued from the halls of Congress for the annexation of the Philippines. Beveridge frequently allowed his nationalism to reach the pitch of jingoism. Among his phrases is included the following: "America first; not only America first but America only." He believed that only those should have self-government "who are capable of self-government!" In a notable statement he said: "The ocean does not separate us from the lands of our duty and desire—the ocean joins us, a river never

. . . MR. BEVERIDGE: I ask for the reading of the joint resolution introduced by me on Thursday last.

THE PRESIDENT pro tempore: The Chair lays before the Senate the joint resolution introduced by the Senator from Indiana, which was laid on the table subject to his call. The joint resolution will be read.

The Secretary read the joint resolution (S.R. 53) defining the policy of the United States relative to the Philippine Islands, as follows:

Be it resolved by the Senate and House of Representatives of the United States of America in Congress assembled, That the Philippine Islands are territory belonging to the United States; that it is the intention of the United States to retain them as such and to establish and maintain such governmental control throughout the archipelago as the situation may demand.

MR. BEVERIDGE: Mr. President, I address the Senate at this time because Senators and Members of the House on both sides have asked that I give to Congress and the country my observations in the Philippines and the far East, and the conclusions which those observations compel; and because of hurtful resolutions introduced and utterances made in the Senate,

to be dredged, a canal never to be repaired. Steam joins us, electricity joins us—the very elements are in league with our destiny. Cuba not contiguous? Porto Rico not contiguous? The Philippines not contiguous? Our navy will make them contiguous!" He was a Progressive Republican senator from 1899 to 1911, but in 1910 he was defeated for a third term largely because he had been too sharply critical of the old-guard Republican conservatives. As a nationalist it is fitting that his famous biographies should be about Marshall and Lincoln.

every word of which will cost and is costing the lives of American soldiers.

Mr. President, the times call for candor. The Philippines are ours forever, "territory belonging to the United States," as the Constitution calls them. And just beyond the Philippines are China's illimitable markets. We will not retreat from either. We will not repudiate our duty in the archipelago. We will not abandon our opportunity in the Orient. We will not renounce our part in the mission of our race, trustee, under God, of the civilization of the world. And we will move forward to our work, not howling out regrets like slaves whipped to their burdens, but with gratitude for a task worthy of our strength, and thanksgiving to Almighty God that He has marked us as His chosen people, henceforth to lead in the regeneration of the world.

PHILIPPINES COMMAND THE PACIFIC

This island empire is the last land left in all the oceans. If it should prove a mistake to abandon it, the blunder once made would be irretrievable. If it proves a mistake to hold it, the error can be corrected when we will. Every other progressive nation stands ready to relieve us.

But to hold it will be no mistake. Our largest trade henceforth must be with Asia. The Pacific is our ocean. More and more Europe will manufacture the most it needs, secure from its colonies the most it consumes. Where shall we turn for consumers of our surplus? Geography answers the question. China is our natural customer. She is nearer to us than to England, Germany, or Russia, the commercial powers of the present and the future. They have moved nearer to China by securing permanent bases on her borders. The Philippines give us a base at the door of all the East.

Lines of navigation from our ports to the Orient and Australia; from the Isthmian Canal to Asia; from all Oriental ports to Australia, converge at and separate from the Philippines. They are a self-supporting, dividend-paying fleet, permanently anchored at a spot selected by the strategy of Providence, commanding the Pacific. And the Pacific is the ocean of the commerce of the future. Most future wars will be conflicts for commerce. The power that rules the Pacific, therefore, is the power that rules the world. And, with the Philippines, that power is and will forever be the American Republic.

VALUE OF CHINA'S TRADE

China's trade is the mightiest commercial fact in our future. Her foreign commerce was $285,738,300 in 1897, of which we, her neighbor, had less than 9 per cent, of which only a little more than half was merchandise sold to China by us. We ought to have 50 per cent, and we will. And China's foreign commerce is only beginning. Her resources, her possibilities, her wants, all are undeveloped. She has only 340 miles of railway. I have seen trains loaded with natives and all the activities of modern life already appearing along the line. But she needs, and in fifty years will have, 20,000 miles of railway. Who can estimate her commerce, then?

That statesman commits a crime against American trade—against the American grower of cotton and wheat and tobacco, the American manufacturer of machinery and clothing—who fails to put America where she may command that trade. Germany's Chinese trade is increasing like magic. She has established ship lines and secured a tangible foothold on China's very soil. Russia's Chinese trade is growing beyond belief. She is spending the revenues of the Empire to finish her railroad into Pekin itself, and she is in physical possession of the imperial province of Manchuria. Japan's Chinese trade is multiplying in volume and value. She is bending her energy to her merchant marine, and is located along China's very coast; but Manila is nearer China than Yokahama is. The Philippines command the commercial situation of the entire East. Can America best trade with China from San Francisco or New York? From San Francisco, of course. But if San Francisco were closer to China than New York is to Pittsburgh, what then? And Manila is nearer Hongkong than Habana is to Washington. And yet American statesmen plan to surrender this commercial throne of the Orient where Providence and our soldiers' lives have placed us. When history comes to write the story of that suggested treason to American supremacy and therefore to the spread of American civilization, let her in mercy write that those who so proposed were merely blind and nothing more.

RESOURCES AND IMMENSE SIZE OF THE ISLANDS

But if they did not command China, India, the Orient, the whole Pacific for purposes of offense, defense, and trade, the Philippines are so valuable in themselves that we should hold them. I have cruised more than 2,000 miles through the archipelago, every moment a surprise at its loveliness and wealth. I have ridden hundreds of miles on the islands, every foot of the way a revelation of vegetable and mineral riches.

No land in America surpasses in fertility the plains and valleys of Luzon. Rice and coffee, sugar and cocoanuts, hemp and tobacco, and many products of the temperate as well as the tropic zone grow in various sections of the archipelago. I have seen hundreds of bushels of Indian corn lying in a road fringed with banana trees. The forests of Negros, Mindanao, Mindora, Paluan, and parts of Luzon are invaluable and intact. The wood of the Philippines can supply the furniture of the world for a century to come. At Cebu the best informed man in the island told me that 40 miles of Cebu's mountain chain are practically mountains of coal. Pablo Majia, one of the most reliable men on the islands, confirmed the statement. Some declare that the coal is only lignite; but ship captains who have used it told me that it is better steamer fuel than the best coal of Japan.

I have a nugget of pure gold picked up in its present form on the banks of a Philippine creek. I have gold dust washed out by crude processes of careless natives from the sands of a Philippine stream. Both indicate great deposits at the source from which they come. In one of the islands great deposits of copper exist untouched. The mineral wealth of this empire of the ocean will one day surprise the world. I base this statement partly on personal observation, but chiefly on the testimony of foreign merchants in the Philippines, who have practically investigated the subject, and upon the unanimous opinion of natives and priests. And the mineral wealth is but a small fraction of the agricultural wealth of these islands.

And the wood, hemp, copra, and other products of the Philippines supply what we need and can not ourselves produce. And the markets they will themselves afford will be immense. Spain's export and import trade, with the islands undeveloped, was $11,534,731 annually. Our trade with the islands developed will be $125,000,000 annually, for who believes that we can not do ten times as well as Spain?

Consider their imperial dimensions. Luzon is larger and richer than New York, Pennsylvania, Illinois, or Ohio. Mindanao is larger and richer than all New England, exclusive of Maine. Manila, as a port of call and exchange, will, in the time of men now living, far surpass Liverpool. Behold the exhaustless markets they command. It is as if a half dozen of our States were set down between Oceania and the Orient, and those States themselves undeveloped and unspoiled of their primitive wealth and resources.

Nothing is so natural as trade with one's neighbors. The Philippines make us the nearest neighbors of all the East. Nothing is more natural than to trade with those you know. This is the philosophy of all advertising. The Philippines bring us permanently face to face with the most sought-for customers of the world. National prestige, national propinquity, these and commercial activity are the elements of commercial success. The Philippines give the first; the character of the American people supply the last. It is a providential conjunction of all the elements of trade, of duty, and of power. If we are willing to go to war rather than let England have a few feet of frozen Alaska, which affords no market and commands none, what should we not do rather than let England, Germany, Russia, or Japan have all the Philippines? And no man on the spot can fail to see that this would be their fate if we retired.

PHILIPPINE CLIMATE

The climate is the best tropic climate in the world. This is the belief of those who have lived in many tropic countries, with scores of whom I have talked on this point. My own experience with tropical conditions has not been exhaustive; yet, speaking from that experience, I testify that the climate of Iloilo, Sulu, Cebu, and even of Manila, greatly surpasses that of Hongkong. And yet on the bare and burning rock of Hongkong our constructing race has built one of the noblest cities of all the world, and made the harbor it commands the focus of the commerce of the East. And the glory of that achievement illumines with a rarer splendor than that of Waterloo the flag that floats above it, for from Hongkong's heights civilization is irradiating all the Orient. If this be imperialism, its final end will be the empire of the Son of Man. . . .

CHARACTER OF THE PEOPLE—
AGUINALDO

It will be hard for Americans who have not studied them to understand the people. They are a barbarous race, modified by three centuries of contact with a decadent race. The Filipino is the South Sea Malay, put through a process of three hundred years of superstition in religion, dishonesty in dealing, disorder in habits of industry, and cruelty, caprice, and corruption in government. It is barely possible that 1,000 men in all the archipelago are capable of self-government in the Anglo-Saxon sense.

My own belief is that there are not 100 men among them who comprehend what Anglo-Saxon self-government even means, and there are over 5,000,000 people to be governed. I know many clever and highly educated men among them, but there are only three commanding intellects and characters—Arellani [sic], Mabini, and Aguinaldo. Arellano [sic], the chief justice of our supreme court, is a profound lawyer and a brave and incorruptible man. Mabini, who, before his capture, was the literary and diplomatic associate of Aguinaldo, is the highest type of subtlety and the most constructive mind that race has yet produced. Aguinaldo is a clever, popular leader, able, brave, resourceful, cunning, ambitious, unscrupulous, and masterful. He is full of decision, initiative, and authority, and had the confidence of the masses. He is a natural dictator. His ideas of government are absolute orders, implicit obedience, or immediate death. He understands the character of his countrymen. He is a Malay Sylla [sic]; not a Filipino Washington. . . .

WE WILL HOLD IT FAST, AND
HOLD IT FOREVER

Here, then, Senators, is the situation. Two years ago there was no land in all the world which we could occupy for any purpose. Our commerce was daily turning toward the Orient, and geography and trade developments made necessary our commercial empire over the Pacific. And in that ocean we had no commercial, naval, or military base. To-day we have one of the three great ocean possessions of the globe, located at the most commanding commercial, naval, and military points in the eastern seas, within hail of India, shoulder to shoulder with China, richer in its own resources than any equal body of land on the entire globe, and peopled by a race which civilization demands shall be improved. Shall we abandon it? That man little knows the common people of the Republic, little understands the instincts of our race, who thinks we will not hold it fast and hold it forever, administering just government by simplest methods. We may trick up devices to shift our burden and lessen our opportunity; they will avail us nothing but delay. We may tangle conditions by applying academic arrangements of self-government to a crude situation; their failure will drive us to our duty in the end.

MILITARY SITUATION—OTIS DEFENDED

The military situation, past, present, and prospective, is no reason for abandonment. Our campaign has been as perfect as possible with the force at hand. We have been delayed, first, by a failure to comprehend the immensity of our acquisition; and, second, by insufficient force; and, third, by our efforts for peace. In February, after the treaty of peace, General Otis had only 3,722 officers and men whom he had a legal right to order into battle. The terms of enlistment of the rest of his troops had expired, and they fought voluntarily and not on legal military compulsion. It was one of the noblest examples of patriotic devotion to duty in the history of the world.

Those who complain do so in ignorance of the real situation. We attempted a great task with insufficient means; we became impatient that it was not finished before it could fairly be commenced; and I pray we may not add that other element of disaster, pausing in the work before it is thoroughly and forever done. That is the gravest mistake we could possibly make, and that is the only danger before us. Our Indian wars would have been shortened, the lives of soldiers and settlers saved, and the Indians themselves benefited had we made continuous and decisive war; and any other kind of war is criminal because ineffective. We acted toward the Indians as though we feared them, loved them, hated them—a mingling of foolish sentiment, inaccurate thought, and paralytic purpose. Let us now be instructed by our own experience.

This, too, has been Spain's course in the Philippines. I have studied Spain's painful military history in these islands. Never sufficient troops; never vigorous action, pushed to conclusive results and a permanent peace; always treating with the rebels while they fought them; always cruel and corrupt when a spurious peace was arranged. This has been Spain's way for three hundred years, until insurrection has become a Filipino habit. Never since Magellan landed did Spain put enough troops in the islands for complete and final action in war; never did she intelligently, justly, firmly, administer government in peace.

At the outbreak of the last insurrection, in August, 1896, Spain had only 1,500 Spanish soldiers in all the Philippines, and 700 of these were in Manila. In November of that year she had only 10,000 men. The generals in command of these were criticised and assailed in Spain. It is characteristic of Spain that the people at home do not support, but criticise their generals in

the field. The Spanish method has always been a mixed policy of peace and war, a contradiction of terms, an impossible combination, rendering war ineffective and peace impossible. This was Compo's plan. It was Blanco's plan. Those who would make it our plan will inherit Blanco's fate and failure.

TRUE MILITARY POLICY

Mr. President, that must not be our plan. This war is like all other wars. It needs to be finished before it is stopped. I am prepared to vote either to make our work thorough or even now to abandon it. A lasting peace can be secured only by overwhelming forces in ceaseless action until universal and absolutely final defeat is inflicted on the enemy. To halt before every armed force, every guerrilla band, opposing us is dispersed or exterminated will prolong hostilities and leave alive the seeds of perpetual insurrection.

Even then we should not treat. To treat at all is to admit that we are wrong. And any quiet so secured will be delusive and fleeting. And a false peace will betray us; a sham truce will curse us. It is not to serve the purposes of the hour, it is not to salve a present situation, that peace should be established. It is for the tranquillity of the archipelago forever. It is for an orderly government for the Filipinos for all the future. It is to give this problem to posterity solved and settled; not vexed and involved. It is to establish the supremacy of the American Republic over the Pacific and throughout the East till the end of time.

It has been charged that our conduct of the war has been cruel. Senators, it has been the reverse. I have been in our hospitals and seen the Filipino wounded as carefully, tenderly cared for as our own. Within our lines they may plow and sow and reap and go about the affairs of peace with absolute liberty. And yet all this kindness was misunderstood, or rather not understood. Senators must remember that we are not dealing with Americans or Europeans. We are dealing with Orientals. We are dealing with Orientals who are Malays. We are dealing with Malays instructed in Spanish methods. They mistake kindness for weakness, forbearance for fear. It could not be otherwise unless you could erase hundreds of years of savagery, other hundreds of years of orientalism, and still other hundreds of years of Spanish character and custom.

OUR EFFORTS TO SECURE PEACE

Our mistake has not been cruelty; it has been kindness. . . .

The news that 60,000 American soldiers have crossed the Pacific; that, if necessary, the American Congress will make it 100,000 or 200,000 men; that, at any cost, we will establish peace and govern the islands, will do more to end the war than the soldiers themselves. But the report that we even discuss the withdrawal of a single soldier at the present time and that we even debate the possibility of not administering government throughout the archipelago ourselves will be misunderstood and misrepresented and will blow into a flame once more the fires our soldiers' blood has almost quenched.

"THE BLOOD OF OUR SOLDIERS"

Mr. President, reluctantly and only from a sense of duty am I forced to say that American opposition to the war has been the chief factor in prolonging it. Had Aguinaldo not understood that in America, even in the American Congress, even here in the Senate, he and his cause were supported; had he not known that it was proclaimed on the stump and in the press of a faction in the United States that every shot his misguided followers fired into the breasts of American soldiers was like the volleys fired by Washington's men against the soldiers of King George his insurrection would have dissolved before it entirely crystallized.

The utterances of American opponents of the war are read to the ignorant soldiers of Aguinaldo and repeated in exaggerated form among the common people. Attempts have been made by wretches claiming American citizenship to ship arms and ammunition from Asiatic ports to the Filipinos, and these acts of infamy were coupled by the Malays with American assaults on our Government at home. The Filipinos do not understand free speech, and therefore our tolerance of American assaults on the American President and the American Government means to them that our President is in the minority or he would not permit what appears to them such treasonable criticism. It is believed and stated in Luzon, Panay, and Cebu that the Filipinos have only to fight, harass, retreat, break up into small parties, if necessary, as they are doing now, but by any means hold out until the next Presidential election, and our forces will be withdrawn.

All this has aided the enemy more than climate, arms, and battle. Senators, I have heard these reports myself; I have talked with the people; I have seen our mangled boys in the hospital and field; I have stood on the firing line and beheld our dead soldiers, their faces turned to the pitiless southern sky, and in sorrow rather than anger I say to those whose voices in America have cheered those misguided natives on to shoot our soldiers down, that the blood of those dead and wounded boys of ours is on their hands, and the flood of all the years can never wash that stain away. In sorrow rather than anger I say these words, for I earnestly believe that our brothers knew not what they did.

THE FILIPINOS ARE CHILDREN, UTTERLY INCAPABLE OF SELF-GOVERNMENT

But, Senators, it would be better to abandon this combined garden and Gibraltar of the Pacific, and count our blood and treasure already spent a profitable loss, than to apply any academic arrangement of self-government to these children. They are not capable of self-government. How could they be? They are not of a self-governing race. They are Orientals, Malays, instructed by Spaniards in the latter's worst estate.

They know nothing of practical government except as they have witnessed the weak, corrupt, cruel, and capricious rule of Spain. What magic will anyone employ to dissolve in their minds and characters those impressions of governors and governed which three centuries of misrule has created? What alchemy will change the oriental quality of their blood and set the self-governing currents of the American pouring through their Malay veins? How shall they, in the twinkling of an eye, be exalted to the heights of self-governing peoples which required a thousand years for us to reach, Anglo-Saxon though we are?

Let men beware how they employ the term "self-government." It is a sacred term. It is the watchword at the door of the inner temple of liberty, for liberty does not always mean self-government. Self-government is a method of liberty—the highest, simplest, best—and it is acquired only after centuries of study and struggle and experiment and instruction and all the elements of the progress of man. Self-government is no base and common thing, to be bestowed on the merely audacious. It is the degree which crowns the graduate of liberty, not the name of liberty's infant class, who have not yet mastered the alphabet of freedom. Savage blood, oriental blood, Malay blood, Spanish example— are these the elements of self-government?

We must act on the situation as it exists, not as we would wish it. I have talked with hundreds of these people, getting their views as to the practical workings of self-government. The great majority simply do not understand any participation in any government whatever. The most enlightened among them declare that self-government will succeed because the employers of labor will compel their employees to vote as their employer wills and that this will insure intelligent voting. I was assured that we could depend upon good men always being in office because

the officials who constitute the government will nominate their successors, choose those among the people who will do the voting, and determine how and where elections will be held.

The most ardent advocate of self-government that I met was anxious that I should know that such a government would be tranquil because, as he said, if anyone criticised it, the government would shoot the offender. A few of them have a sort of verbal understanding of the democratic theory, but the above are the examples of the ideas of the practical workings of self-government entertained by the aristocracy, the rich planters and traders, and heavy employers of labor, the men who would run the government.

PEOPLE INDOLENT—NO COMPETITION WITH OUR LABOR

Example for decades will be necessary to instruct them in American ideas and methods of administration. Example, example; always example—this alone will teach them. As a race, their general ability is not excellent. Educators, both men and women, to whom I have talked in Cebu and Luzon, were unanimous in the opinion that in all solid and useful education they are, as a people, dull and stupid. In showy things, like carving and painting or embroidery or music, they have apparent aptitude, but even this is superficial and never thorough. They have facility of speech, too.

The three best educators on the island at different times made to me the same comparison, that the common people in their stupidity are like their caribou bulls. They are not even good agriculturists. Their waste of cane is inexcusable. Their destruction of hemp fiber is childish. They are incurably indolent. They have no continuity or thoroughness of industry. They will quit work without notice and amuse themselves until the money they have earned is spent. They are like children playing at men's work.

No one need fear their competition with

our labor. No reward could beguile, no force compel, these children of indolence to leave their trifling lives for the fierce and fervid industry of high-wrought America. The very reverse is the fact. One great problem is the necessary labor to develop these islands—to build the roads, open the mines, clear the wilderness, drain the swamps, dredge the harbors. The natives will not supply it. A lingering prejudice against the Chinese may prevent us from letting them supply it. Ultimately, when the real truth of the climate and human conditions is known, it is barely possible that our labor will go there. Even now young men with the right moral fiber and a little capital can make fortunes there as planters. . . .

DOMINANT NOTES OF OUR FIRST AND SECOND CENTURIES

Mr. President, self-government and internal development have been the dominant notes of our first century; administration and the development of other lands will be the dominant notes of our second century. And administration is as high and holy a function as self-government, just as the care of a trust estate is as sacred an obligation as the management of our own concerns. Cain was the first to violate the divine law of human society which makes of us our brother's keeper. And administration of good government is the first lesson in self-government, that exalted estate toward which all civilization tends.

Administration of good government is not denial of liberty. For what is liberty? It is not savagery. It is not the exercise of individual will. It is not dictatorship. It involves government, but not necessarily self-government. It means law. First of all, it is a common rule of action, applying equally to all within its limits. Liberty means protection of property and life without price, free speech without intimidation, justice without purchase or delay, government without favor or favorites. What will best give all this to the people of the Philippines—American administration, developing them gradually toward self-government, or self-government by a people before they know what self-government means?

TRUE INTERPRETATION OF DECLARATION OF INDEPENDENCE

The Declaration of Independence does not forbid us to do our part in the regeneration of the world. If it did, the Declaration would be wrong, just as the Articles of Confederation, drafted by the very same men who signed the Declaration, was found to be wrong. The Declaration has no application to the present situation. It was written by self-governing men for self-governing men.

It was written by men who, for a century and a half, had been experimenting in self-government on this continent, and whose ancestors for hundreds of years before had been gradually developing toward that high and holy estate. The Declaration applies only to people capable of self-government. How dare any man prostitute this expression of the very elect of self-governing peoples to a race of Malay children of barbarism, schooled in Spanish methods and ideas? And you, who say the Declaration applies to all men, how dare you deny its application to the American Indian? And if you deny it to the Indian at home, how dare you grant it to the Malay abroad?

PHRASE "CONSENT OF THE GOVERNED" MISUNDERSTOOD

The Declaration does not contemplate that all government must have the consent of the governed. It announces that man's "inalienable rights are life, liberty, and the pursuit of happiness; that to secure these rights governments are established among men deriving their just powers from the consent of the governed; that when any form of government becomes destructive of those rights, it is the right of the people to alter or abolish it." "Life, liberty, and the pursuit of happiness" are the important things; "consent of the governed" is one of the means to those ends.

If "any form of government becomes destructive of those ends, it is the right of the people to alter or abolish it," says the Declaration. "Any forms" includes all forms. Thus the Declaration itself recognizes other forms of government than those resting on the consent of the governed. The word "consent" itself recognizes other forms, for "consent" means the understanding of the thing to which the "consent" is given; and there are people in the world who do not understand any form of government. And the sense in which "consent" is used in the Declaration is broader than mere understanding; for "consent" in the Declaration means participation in the government "consented" to. And yet these people who are not capable of "consenting" to any form of government must be governed.

And so the Declaration contemplates all forms of government which secure the fundamental rights of life, liberty, and the pursuit of happiness. Self-government, when that will best secure these ends, as in the case of people capable of self-government; other appropriate forms when people are not capable of self-government. And so the authors of the Declaration themselves governed the Indian without his consent; the inhabitants of Louisiana without their consent; and ever since the sons of the makers of the Declaration have been governing not by theory, but by practice, after the fashion of our governing race, now by one form, now by another, but always for the purpose of securing the great eternal ends of life, liberty, and the pursuit of happiness, not in the savage, but in the civilized meaning of those terms— life according to orderly methods of civilized society; liberty regulated by law; pursuit of happiness limited by the pursuit of happiness by every other man.

If this is not the meaning of the Declaration, our Government itself denies the Declaration every time it receives the representative of any but a republican form of government, such as that of the Sultan, the Czar, or other absolute autocrats, whose governments, according to the opposition's interpretation of the Declaration, are spurious governments, because the people governed have not "consented" to them.

CONSTITUTIONAL POWER TO GOVERN
AS WE PLEASE

Senators in opposition are estopped from denying our constitutional power to govern the Philippines as circumstances may demand, for such power is admitted in the case of Florida, Louisiana, Alaska. How, then, is it denied in the Philippines? Is there a geographical interpretation to the Constitution? Do degrees of longitude fix constitutional limitations? Does a thousand miles of ocean diminish constitutional power more than a thousand miles of land?

The ocean does not separate us from the field of our duty and endeavor—it joins us, an established highway needing no repair, and landing us at any point desired. The seas do not separate the Philippine Islands from us or from each other. The seas are highways through the archipelago, which would cost hundreds of millions of dollars to construct if they were land instead of water. Land may separate men from their desire, the ocean never. Russia has been centuries in crossing Siberian wastes; the Puritans cross the Atlantic in brief and flying weeks.

If the Boers must have traveled by land, they would never have reached the Transvaal; but they sailed on liberty's ocean; they walked on civilization's untaxed highway, the welcoming sea. Our ships habitually sailed round the cape and anchored in California's harbors before a single trail had lined the desert with the whitening bones of those who made it. No! No! The ocean unites us; steam unites us; electricity unites us; all the elements of nature unite us to the region where duty and interest call us. There is in the ocean no constitutional argument against the march of the flag, for the oceans, too, are ours. With more extended coast lines than any nation of history; with a commerce vaster than any other people ever dreamed of, and that commerce as yet only in its beginnings; with naval traditions equaling those of England or of Greece, and the work of our Navy only just begun; with the air of the ocean in our nostrils and the blood of a sailor ancestry in our veins; with the shores of all the continents calling us, the Great Republic before I die will be the acknowledged lord of the world's high seas. And over them the Republic will hold dominion, by virtue of the strength God has given it, for the peace of the world and the betterment of man.

WORDS OF EMPIRE EXPRESSLY IN CONSTITUTION

No; the oceans are not limitations of the power which the Constitution expressly gives Congress to govern all territory the nation may acquire. The Constitution declares that "Congress shall have power to dispose of and make all needful rules and regulations respecting the territory belonging to the United States." Not the Northwest Territory only; not Louisiana or Florida only; not territory on this continent only, but any territory anywhere belonging to the nation. The founders of the nation were not provincial. Theirs was the geography of the world. They were soldiers as well as landsmen, and they knew that where our ships should go our flag might follow. They had the logic of progress, and they knew that the Republic they were planting must, in obedience to the laws of our expanding race, necessarily develop into the greater Republic which the world beholds today, and into the still mightier Republic which the world will finally acknowledge as the arbiter, under God, of the destinies of mankind. And so our fathers wrote into the Constitution these words of growth, of expansion, of empire, if you will, unlimited by geography or climate or by anything but the vitality and possibilities of the American people: "Congress shall have power to dispose of and make all needful rules and regulations respecting the territory belonging to the United States."

POWER IMPLIED TO GOVERN
AS WE PLEASE

The power to govern all territory the nation may acquire would have been in Congress if the language affirming that power had not been written in the Constitution. For not all powers of the National Government are expressed. Its principal powers are implied. The written Constitution is but the index of the living Constitution. Had this not been true, the Constitution would have failed. For the people in any event would have developed and progressed. And if the Constitution had not had the capacity for growth corresponding with the growth of the nation, the Constitution would and should have been abandoned as the Articles of Confederation were abandoned. For the Constitution is not immortal in itself, is not useful even in itself. The Constitution is immortal and even useful only as it serves the orderly development of the nation. The nation alone is immortal. The nation alone is sacred. The Army is its servant. The Navy is its servant. The President is its servant. This Senate is its servant. Our laws are its methods. Our Constitution is its instrument.

This is the golden rule of constitutional interpretation: The Constitution was made for the people, not the people for the Constitution. . . .

THE WHOLE QUESTION ELEMENTAL

Mr. President, this question is deeper than any question of party politics; deeper than any question of the isolated policy of our country even; deeper even than any question of constitutional power. It is elemental. It is racial. God has not been preparing the English-speaking and Teutonic peoples for a thousand years for nothing but vain and idle self-contemplation and self-admiration. No! He has made us the master organizers of the world to establish system where chaos reigns. He has given us the spirit of progress to overwhelm the forces of reaction throughout the earth. He has made us adepts in government that we may administer government among savage and senile peoples. Were it not for such a force as this the world would relapse into barbarism and night. And of all our race He has marked the American people as His chosen nation to finally lead in the regeneration of the world. This is the divine mission of America, and it holds for us all the profit, all the glory, all the happiness possible to man. We are trustees of the world's progress, guardians of its righteous peace. The judgment of the Master is upon us: "Ye have been faithful over a few things; I will make you ruler over many things."

What shall history say of us? Shall it say that we renounced that holy trust, left the savage to his base condition, the wilderness to the reign of waste, deserted duty, abandoned glory, forget our sordid profit even, because we feared our strength and read the charter of our powers with the doubter's eye and the quibbler's mind? Shall it say that, called by events to captain and command the proudest, ablest, purest race of history in history's noblest work, we declined that great commission? Our fathers would not have had it so. No! They founded no paralytic government, incapable of the simplest acts of administration. They planted no sluggard people, passive while the world's work calls them. They established no reactionary nation. They unfurled no retreating flag.

GOD'S HAND IN ALL

That flag has never paused in its onward march. Who dares halt it now— now, when history's largest events are carrying it forward; now, when we are at last one people, strong enough for any task, great enough for any glory destiny can bestow? How comes it that our first century closes with the process of consolidating the American people into a unit just accomplished, and quick upon the stroke of that great hour presses upon us our world opportunity, world duty, and world glory, which none but a people welded into an indivisible nation can achieve or perform?

Blind indeed is he who sees not the hand of God in events so vast, so harmonious, so benign. Reactionary indeed is the mind that perceives not that this vital people is the strongest of the saving forces of the world; that our place, therefore, is at the head of the constructing and redeeming nations of the earth; and that to stand aside while events march on is a surrender of our interests, a betrayal of our duty as blind as it is base. Craven indeed is the heart that fears to perform a work so golden and so noble; that dares not win a glory so immortal.

Do you tell me that it will cost us money? When did Americans ever measure duty by financial standards? Do you tell me of the tremendous toil required to overcome the vast difficulties of our task? What mighty work for the world, for humanity, even for ourselves, has ever been done with ease? Even our bread must we eat by the sweat of our faces. Why are we charged with power such as no people ever knew, if we are not to use it in a work such as no people ever wrought? Who will dispute the divine meaning of the fable of the talents?

Do you remind me of the precious blood that must be shed, the lives that must be given, the broken hearts of loved ones for their slain? And this is indeed a heavier price than all combined. And yet as a nation every historic duty we have done, every achievement we have accomplished, has been by the sacrifice of our noblest sons. Every holy memory that glorifies the flag is of those heroes who have died that its onward march might not be stayed. It is the nation's dearest lives yielded for the flag that makes it dear to us; it is the nation's most precious blood poured out for it that makes it precious to us. That flag is woven of heroism and grief, of the bravery of men and women's tears, of righteousness and battle, of sacrifice and anguish, of triumph and of glory. It is these which make our flag a holy thing. Who would tear from that sacred banner the glorious legends of a single battle where it has waved on land or sea? What son of a soldier of the flag whose father fell beneath it on any field would surrender that proud record for the heraldry of a king? In the cause of civilization, in the service of the Republic anywhere on earth, Americans consider wounds the noblest decorations man can win, and count the giving of their lives a glad and precious duty.

Pray God that spirit never fails. Pray God the time may never come when Mammon and the love of ease shall so debase our blood that we will fear to shed it for the flag and its imperial destiny. Pray God the time may never come when American heroism is but a legend like the story of the Cid, American faith in our mission and our might a dream dissolved, and the glory of our mighty race departed.

And that time will never come. We will renew our youth at the fountain of new and glorious deeds. We will exalt our reverence for the flag by carrying it to a noble future as well as by remembering its ineffable past. Its immortality will not pass, because everywhere and always we will acknowledge and discharge the solemn responsibilities our sacred flag, in its deepest meaning, puts upon us. And so, Senators, with reverent hearts, where dwells the fear of God, the American people move forward to the future of their hope and the doing of His work.

Mr. President and Senators, adopt the resolution offered, that peace may quickly come and that we may begin our saving, regenerating, and uplifting work. Adopt it, and this bloodshed will cease when these deluded children of our islands learn that this is the final word of the representatives of the American people in Congress assembled. Reject it, and the world, history, and the American people will know where to forever fix the awful responsibility for the consequences that will surely follow such failure to do our manifest duty. How dare we delay when our soldiers' blood is flowing? [Applause in the galleries.]

THE PRESIDENT *pro tempore:* Applause is not permitted in the United States Senate. . . .

3. ON ANNEXATION OF THE PHILIPPINES[1]

By WILLIAM JENNINGS BRYAN

EDITORS' NOTE.—William Jennings Bryan (p. 155) delivered the "America's Mission" and "Imperialism" addresses during the course of his campaign for the presidency in 1900. Bryan wished to make imperialism the key issue of the campaign. But Bryan's opposition to imperialism had not prevented him from urging his followers in the Senate to support the treaty that ended the Spanish-American War and acquired the Philippines. Bryan's hope was that the Filipinos would then be given their independence. The interest in peace and democracy which he displays in these speeches was later to dignify his public policy during the trying early years of World War I when he was secretary of state (1913–15) in Wilson's cabinet.

1. William Jennings Bryan, "On Annexation of the Philippines," *Speeches of William Jennings Bryan* (2 vols.; New York, 1913), II, 11–16, 19–22, 24–33, 39–49. By permission of Funk and Wagnalls.

A. AMERICA'S MISSION

. . . We have reached another crisis. The ancient doctrine of imperialism, banished from our land more than a century ago, has recrossed the Atlantic and challenged democracy to mortal combat upon American soil.

Whether the Spanish war shall be known in history as a war for liberty or as a war of conquest; whether the principles of self-government shall be strengthened or abandoned; whether this nation shall remain a homogeneous republic or become a heterogeneous empire—these questions must be answered by the American people —when they speak, and not until then, will destiny be revealed.

Destiny is not a matter of chance; it is a matter of choice; it is not a thing to be waited for, it is a thing to be achieved.

No one can see the end from the beginning, but every one can make his course an honorable one from beginning to end, by adhering to the right under all circumstances. Whether a man steals much or little may depend upon his opportunities, but whether he steals at all depends upon his own volition.

So with our nation. If we embark upon a career of conquest no one can tell how many islands we may be able to seize or how many races we may be able to subjugate; neither can any one estimate the cost, immediate and remote, to the Nation's purse and to the Nation's character, but whether we shall enter upon such a career is a question which the people have a right to decide for themselves. Unexpected events may retard or advance the Nation's growth, but the Nation's purpose determines its destiny.

What is the Nation's purpose?

The main purpose of the founders of our Government was to secure for themselves and for posterity the blessings of liberty, and that purpose has been faithfully followed up to this time. Our statesmen have opposed each other upon economic questions, but they have agreed in defending self-government as the controlling national idea. They have quarreled among themselves over tariff and finance, but they have been united in their opposition to an entangling alliance with any European power.

Under this policy our nation has grown in numbers and in strength. Under this policy its beneficent influence has encircled the globe. Under this policy the taxpayers have been spared the burden and the menace of a large military establishment and the young men have been taught the arts of peace rather than the science of war. On each returning Fourth of July our people have met to celebrate the signing of the Declaration of Independence; their hearts have renewed their vows to free institutions and their voices have praised the forefathers whose wisdom and courage and patriotism made it possible for each succeeding generation to repeat the words:

> My country, 'tis of thee,
> Sweet land of liberty,
> Of thee I sing.

This sentiment was well-nigh universal until a year ago. It was to this sentiment that the Cuban insurgents appealed; it was this sentiment that impelled our people to enter into the war with Spain. Have the people so changed within a few short months that they are now willing to apologize for the War of the Revolution and force upon the Filipinos the same system of government against which the colonists protested with fire and sword?

The hour of temptation has come, but temptations do not destroy, they merely test the strength of individuals and nations; they are stumbling blocks or stepping-stones; they lead to infamy or fame, according to the use made of them.

Benedict Arnold and Ethan Allen served together in the Continental army and both were offered British gold. Arnold yielded to the temptation and made his name a synonym for treason; Allen resisted and lives in the affections of his countrymen.

Our Nation is tempted to depart from its "standard of morality" and adopt a policy of "criminal aggression." But, will it yield?

If I mistake not the sentiment of the American people they will spurn the bribe of imperialism, and, by resisting temptation, win such a victory as has not been won since the battle of Yorktown. Let it be written of the United States: Behold a republic that took up arms to aid a neighboring people, struggling to be free; a republic that, in the progress of the war, helped distant races whose wrongs were not in contemplation when hostilities began; a republic that, when peace was restored, turned a deaf ear to the clamorous voice of greed and to those borne down by the weight of a foreign yoke spoke the welcome words, Stand up; be free—let this be the record made on history's page and the silent example of this republic, true to its principles in the hour of trial, will do more to extend the art of self-government and civilization than could be done by all the wars of conquest that we could wage in a generation.

The forcible annexation of the Philippine Islands is not necessary to make the United States a world-power. For over ten decades our Nation has been a world-power. During its brief existence it has exerted upon the human race an influence more potent for good than all the other nations of the earth combined, and it has exerted that influence without the use of sword or Gatling gun. Mexico and the republics of Central and South America testify to the benign influence of our institutions, while Europe and Asia give evidence of the working of the leaven of self-government. In the growth of democracy we observe the triumphant march of an idea—an idea that would be weighted down rather than aided by the armor and weapons proffered by imperialism.

Much has been said of late about Anglo-Saxon civilization. Far be it from me to detract from the service rendered to the world by the sturdy race whose language we speak. The union of the Angle and the Saxon formed a new and valuable type, but the process of race evolution was not completed when the Angle and the Saxon met. A still later type has appeared which is superior to any which has existed heretofore; and with this new type will come a higher civilization than any which has preceded it. Great has been the Greek, the Latin, the Slav, the Celt, the Teuton and the Anglo-Saxon, but greater than any of these is the American, in whom are blended the virtues of them all.

Civil and religious liberty, universal education and the right to participate, directly or through representatives chosen by himself, in all the affairs of government—these give to the American citizen an opportunity and an inspiration which can be found nowhere else.

Standing upon the vantage ground already gained the American people can aspire to a grander destiny than has opened before any other race.

Anglo-Saxon civilization has taught the individual to protect his own rights, American civilization will teach him to respect the rights of others.

Anglo-Saxon civilization has taught the individual to take care of himself, American civilization, proclaiming the equality of all before the law, will teach him that his own highest good requires the observance of the commandment: "Thou shalt love thy neighbor as thyself."

Anglo-Saxon civilization has, by force of arms, applied the art of government to other races for the benefit of Anglo-Saxons; American civilization will, by the influence of example, excite in other races a desire for self-government and a determination to secure it.

Anglo-Saxon civilization has carried its flag to every clime and defended it with forts and garrisons. American civilization will imprint its flag upon the hearts of all who long for freedom.

To American civilization, all hail!
Time's noblest offspring is the last!

B. IMPERIALISM

... Republicans who gloried in our independence when the Nation was less powerful now look with favor upon a foreign alliance; Republicans who three years ago condemned "forcible annexation" as immoral and even criminal are now sure that it is both immoral and criminal to oppose forcible annexation. That partizanship has already blinded many to present dangers is certain; how large a portion of the Republican party can be drawn over to the new policies remains to be seen.

For a time Republican leaders were inclined to deny to opponents the right to criticize the Philippine policy of the administration, but upon investigation they found that both Lincoln and Clay asserted and exercised the right to criticize a President during the progress of the Mexican war. ...

... When the President, supported by a practically unanimous vote of the House and Senate, entered upon a war with Spain for the purpose of aiding the struggling patriots of Cuba, the country, without regard to party, applauded.

Altho the Democrats realized that the administration would necessarily gain a political advantage from the conduct of a war which in the very nature of the case must soon end in a complete victory, they vied with the Republicans in the support which they gave to the President. When the war was over and the Republican leaders began to suggest the propriety of a colonial policy opposition at once manifested itself.

When the President finally laid before the Senate a treaty which recognized the independence of Cuba, but provided for the cession of the Philippine Islands to the United States, the menace of imperialism became so apparent that many preferred to reject the treaty and risk the ills that might follow rather than take the chance of correcting the errors of the treaty by the independent action of this country.

I was among the number of those who believed it better to ratify the treaty and end the war, release the volunteers, remove the excuse for war expenditures and then give the Filipinos the independence which might be forced from Spain by a new treaty.

In view of the criticism which my action aroused in some quarters, I take this occasion to restate the reasons given that time. I thought it safer to trust the American people to give independence to the Filipinos than to trust the accomplishment of that purpose to diplomacy with an unfriendly nation.

Lincoln embodied an argument in the question when he asked, "Can aliens make treaties easier than friends can make laws?" I believe that we are now in a better position to wage a successful contest against imperialism than we would have been had the treaty been rejected. With the treaty ratified a clean-cut issue is presented between a government by consent and a government by force, and imperialists must bear the responsibility for all that happens until the question is settled.

If the treaty had been rejected the opponents of imperialism would have been held responsible for any international complications which might have arisen before the ratification of another treaty. But whatever difference of opinion may have existed as to the best method of opposing a colonial policy, there never was any difference as to the great importance of the question and there is no difference now as to the course to be pursued. ...

Those who would have this Nation enter upon a career of empire must consider, not only the effect of imperialism on the Filipinos, but they must also calculate its effects upon our own nation. We cannot repudiate the principle of self-government in the Philippines without weakening that principle here.

Lincoln said that the safety of this Nation was not in its fleets, its armies, or its forts, but in the spirit which prizes liberty as the heritage of all men, in all lands, everywhere, and he warned his countrymen that they could not destroy this spirit without planting the seeds of despotism at their own doors.

Even now we are beginning to see the paralyzing influence of imperialism. Heretofore this Nation has been prompt to express its sympathy with those who were fighting for civil liberty. While our sphere of activity has been limited to the Western Hemisphere, our sympathies have not been bounded by the seas. We have felt it due to ourselves and to the world, as well as to those who were struggling for the right to govern themselves, to proclaim the interest which our people have, from the date of their own independence, felt in every contest between human rights and arbitrary power.

Three-quarters of a century ago, when our nation was small, the struggles of Greece aroused our people, and Webster and Clay gave eloquent expression to the universal desire for Grecian independence. In 1898 all parties manifested a lively interest in the success of the Cubans, but now when a war is in progress in South Africa, which must result in the extension of the monarchical idea, or in the triumph of a republic, the advocates of imperialism in this country dare not say a word in behalf of the Boers. . . .

Our opponents, conscious of the weakness of their cause, seek to confuse imperialism with expansion, and have even dared to claim Jefferson as a supporter of their policy. Jefferson spoke so freely and used language with such precision that no one can be ignorant of his views. On one occasion he declared: "If there be one principle more deeply rooted than any other in the mind of every American, it is that we should have nothing to do with conquest." And again he said: "Conquest is not in our principles; it is inconsistent with our government."

The forcible annexation of territory to be governed by arbitrary power differs as much from the acquisition of territory to be built up into States as a monarchy differs from a democracy. The Democratic party does not oppose expansion when expansion enlarges the area of the Republic and incorporates land which can be settled by American citizens, or adds to our population people who are willing to become citizens and are capable of discharging their duties as such.

The acquisition of the Louisiana territory, Florida, Texas and other tracts which have been secured from time to time enlarged the Republic and the Constitution followed the flag into the new territory. It is now proposed to seize upon distant territory already more densely populated than our own country and to force upon the people a government for which there is no warrant in our Constitution or our laws.

Even the argument that this earth belongs to those who desire to cultivate it and who have the physical power to acquire it cannot be invoked to justify the appropriation of the Philippine Islands by the United States. If the islands were uninhabited American citizens would not be willing to go there and till the soil. The white race will not live so near the equator. Other nations have tried to colonize in the same latitude. The Netherlands have controlled Java for three hundred years and yet today there are less than sixty thousand people of European birth scattered among the twenty-five million natives.

After a century and a half of English domination in India, less than one-twentieth of one per cent of the people of India are of English birth, and it requires an army of seventy thousand British soldiers to take care of the tax collectors. Spain had asserted title to the Philippine Islands for three centuries and yet when our fleet entered Manila bay there were less than ten thousand Spaniards residing in the Philippines.

A colonial policy means that we shall send to the Philippine Islands a few traders, a few taskmasters and a few office-holders and an army large enough to support the authority of a small fraction of the people while they rule the natives.

If we have an imperial policy we must have a great standing army as its natural and necessary complement. The spirit which will justify the forcible annexation of the Philippine Islands will justify the seizure of other islands and the domination of other people, and with wars of conquest we can expect a certain, if not rapid, growth of our military establishment.

That a large permanent increase in our regular army is intended by Republican leaders is not a matter of conjecture, but a matter of fact. In his message of December 5, 1898, the President asked for authority to increase the standing army to 100,000. In 1896 the army contained about 25,000. Within two years the President asked for four times that many, and a Republican House of Representatives complied with the request after the Spanish treaty had been signed, and when no country was at war with the United States.

If such an army is demanded when an imperial policy is contemplated, but not openly avowed, what may be expected if the people encourage the Republican party by indorsing its policy at the polls?

A large standing army is not only a pecuniary burden to the people and, if accompanied by compulsory service, a constant source of irritation, but it is ever a menace to a republican form of government.

The army is the personification of force and militarism will inevitably change the ideals of the people and turn the thoughts of our young men from the arts of peace to the science of war. The government which relies for its defense upon its citizens is more likely to be just than one which has at call a large body of professional soldiers.

A small standing army and a well-equipped and well-disciplined State militia are sufficient at ordinary times, and in an emergency the nation should in the future as in the past place its dependence upon the volunteers who come from all occupations at their country's call and return to productive labor when their services are no longer required—men who fight when the country needs fighters and work when the country needs workers.

The Republican platform assumes that the Philippine Islands will be retained under American sovereignty, and we have a right to demand of the Republican leaders a discussion of the future status of the Filipino. Is he to be a citizen or a subject? Are we to bring into the body politic eight or ten million Asiatics, so different from us in race and history that amalgamation is impossible? Are they to share with us in making the laws and shaping the destiny of this nation? No Republican of prominence has been bold enough to advocate such a proposition.

The McEnery resolution, adopted by the Senate immediately after the ratification of the treaty, expressly negatives this idea. The Democratic platform describes the situation when it says that the Filipinos cannot be citizens without endangering our civilization. Who will dispute it? And what is the alternative? If the Filipino is not to be a citizen, shall we make him a subject? On that question the Democratic platform speaks with equal emphasis. It declares that the Filipino cannot be a subject without endangering our form of government. A republic can have no subjects. A subject is possible only in a government resting upon force; he is unknown in a government deriving its just powers from the consent of the governed.

The Republican platform says that "the largest measure of self-government consistent with their welfare and our duties shall be secured to them (the Filipinos) by law." This is a strange doctrine for a government which owes its very existence to the men who offered their lives as a protest against government without consent and taxation without representation.

In what respect does the position of the Republican party differ from the position taken by the English government in 1776?

Did not the English government promise a good government to the colonists? What king ever promised a bad government to his people? Did not the English government promise that the colonists should have the largest measure of self-government consistent with their welfare and English duties? Did not the Spanish government promise to give to the Cubans the largest measure of self-government consistent with their welfare and Spanish duties? The whole difference between a monarchy and a republic may be summed up in one sentence. In a monarchy the king gives to the people what he believes to be a good government; in a republic the people secure for themselves what they believe to be a good government. . . .

. . . If, in this country where the people have a right to vote, Republican leaders dare not take the side of the people against the great monopolies which have grown up within the last few years, how can they be trusted to protect the Filipinos from the corporations which are waiting to exploit the islands?

Is the sunlight of full citizenship to be enjoyed by the people of the United States, and the twilight of semi-citizenship endured by the people of Porto Rico, while the thick darkness of perpetual vassalage covers the Philippines? . . .

What is our title to the Philippine Islands? Do we hold them by treaty or by conquest? Did we buy them or did we take them? Did we purchase the people? If not, how did we secure title to them? Were they thrown in with the land? Will the Republicans say that inanimate earth has value but that when that earth is molded by the divine hand and stamped with the likeness of the Creator it becomes a fixture and passes with the soil? If governments derive their just powers from the consent of the governed, it is impossible to secure title to people, either by force or by purchase.

We could extinguish Spain's title by treaty, but if we hold title we must hold it by some method consistent with our ideas of government. When we made allies of the Filipinos and armed them to fight against Spain, we disputed Spain's title. If we buy Spain's title we are not innocent purchasers. . . .

The principal arguments, however, advanced by those who enter upon a defense of imperialism are:

First—That we must improve the present opportunity to become a world power and enter into international politics.

Second—That our commercial interests in the Philippine Islands and in the Orient make it necessary for us to hold the islands permanently.

Third—That the spread of the Christian religion will be facilitated by a colonial policy.

Fourth—That there is no honorable retreat from the position which the nation has taken.

The first argument is addrest to the nation's pride and the second to the nation's pocket-book. The third is intended for the church member and the fourth for the partizan.

It is sufficient answer to the first argument to say that for more than a century this nation has been a world power. For ten decades it has been the most potent influence in the world. Not only has it been a world power, but it has done more to shape the politics of the human race than all the other nations of the world combined. Because our Declaration of Independence was promulgated others have been promulgated. Because the patriots of 1776 fought for liberty others have fought for it. Because our Constitution was adopted other constitutions have been adopted.

The growth of the principle of self-government, planted on American soil, has been the overshadowing political fact of the nineteenth century. It has made this nation conspicuous among the nations and given it a place in history such as no other nation has ever enjoyed. Nothing has been able to check the onward march of this idea. I am not willing that this nation shall cast aside the omnipotent weapon of truth to seize again the weapons of physical warfare. I would not exchange the glory of this Republic for the glory of all the empires that have risen and fallen since time began.

The permanent chairman of the last Republican National Convention presented the pecuniary argument in all its baldness when he said:

We make no hypocritical pretense of being interested in the Philippines solely on account of others. While we regard the welfare of those people as a sacred trust, we regard the welfare of the American people first. We see our duty to ourselves as well as to others. We believe in trade expansion. By every legitimate means within the province of government and constitution we mean to stimulate the expansion of our trade and open new markets.

This is the commercial argument. It is based upon the theory that war can be rightly waged for pecuniary advantage, and that it is profitable to purchase trade by force and violence. Franklin denied both of these propositions. When Lord Howe asserted that the acts of Parliament which brought on the revolution were necessary to prevent American trade from passing into foreign channels, Franklin replied:

To me, it seems that neither the obtaining nor retaining of any trade, howsoever valuable, is an object for which men may justly spill each other's blood; that the true and sure means of extending and securing commerce are the goodness and cheapness of commodities, and that the profits of no trade can ever be equal to the expense of compelling it and holding it by fleets and armies. I consider this war against us, therefore, as both unjust and unwise.

I place the philosophy of Franklin against the sordid doctrine of those who would put a price upon the head of an American soldier and justify a war of conquest upon the ground that it will pay. The Democratic party is in favor of the expansion of trade. It would extend our trade by every legitimate and peaceful means; but it is not willing to make merchandise of human blood.

But a war of conquest is as unwise as it is unrighteous. A harbor and coaling station in the Philippines would answer every trade and military necessity and such a concession could have been secured at any time without difficulty.

It is not necessary to own people in order to trade with them. We carry on trade today with every part of the world, and our commerce has expanded more rapidly than the commerce of any European empire. We do not own Japan or China, but we trade with their people. We have not absorbed the republics of Central and South America, but we trade with them. It has not been necessary to have any political connection with Canada or the nations of Europe in order to trade with them. Trade cannot be permanently profitable unless it is voluntary.

When trade is secured by force, the cost of securing it and retaining it must be taken out of the profits, and the profits are never large enough to cover the expense. Such a system would never be defended but for the fact that the expense is borne by all the people, while the profits are enjoyed by a few.

Imperialism would be profitable to the army contractors; it would be profitable to the ship owners, who would carry live soldiers to the Philippines and bring dead soldiers back; it would be profitable to those who would seize upon the franchises, and it would be profitable to the officials whose salaries would be fixt here and paid over there; but to the farmer, to the laboring man and to the vast majority of those engaged in other occupations it would bring expenditure without return and risk without reward.

Farmers and laboring men have, as a rule, small incomes and under systems which place the tax upon consumption pay much more than their fair share of the expenses of government. Thus the very people who receive least benefit from imperialism will be injured most by the military burdens which accompany it.

In addition to the evils which he and the farmer share in common, the laboring man will be the first to suffer if oriental subjects seek work in the United States; the first to suffer if American capital leaves our shores to employ oriental labor in the Philippines to supply the trade of China and Japan; the first to suffer from the violence which the military spirit arouses and the first to suffer when the methods of imperialism are applied to our own Government.

It is not strange, therefore, that the labor organizations have been quick to note the approach of these dangers and prompt to protest against both militarism and imperialism.

The pecuniary argument, tho more effective with certain classes, is not likely to be used so often or presented with so much enthusiasm as the religious argument. If what has been termed the "gunpowder gospel" were urged against the Filipinos only it would be a sufficient answer to say that a majority of the Filipinos are now members of one branch of the Christian church; but the principle involved is one of much wider application and challenges serious consideration.

The religious argument varies in positiveness from a passive belief that Providence delivered the Filipinos into our hands, for their good and our glory, to the exultation of the minister who said that we ought to "thrash the natives (Filipinos) until they understand who we are," and that "every bullet sent, every cannon shot and every flag waved means righteousness."

We cannot approve of this doctrine in one place unless we are willing to apply it everywhere. If there is poison in the blood of the hand it will ultimately reach the heart. It is equally true that forcible Christianity, if planted under the American flag in the far-away Orient, will sooner or later be transplanted upon American soil.

If true Christianity consists in carrying out in our daily lives the teachings of Christ, who will say that we are commanded to civilize with dynamite and proselyte with the sword? He who would declare the divine will must prove his authority either by Holy Writ or by evidence of a special dispensation.

Imperialism finds no warrant in the Bible. The command, "Go ye into all the world and preach the gospel to every creature," has no Gatling gun attachment. When Jesus visited a village of Samaria and the people refused to receive him, some of the disciples suggested that fire should be called down from Heaven to avenge the insult; but the Master rebuked them and said: "Ye know not what manner of spirit ye are of; for the Son of Man is not come to destroy men's lives, but to save them." . . .

The argument made by some that it was unfortunate for the nation that it had anything to do with the Philippine Islands, but that the naval victory at Manila made the permanent acquisition of those islands necessary, is also unsound. We won a naval victory at Santiago, but that did not compel us to hold Cuba.

The shedding of American blood in the Philippine Islands does not make it imperative that we should retain possession forever; American blood was shed at San Juan Hill and El Caney, and yet the President has promised the Cubans independence. The fact that the American flag floats over Manila does not compel us to exercise perpetual sovereignty over the islands; the American flag waves over Havana to-day, but the President has promised to haul it down when the flag of the Cuban Republic is ready to rise in its place. Better a thousand times that our flag in the Orient give way to a flag representing the idea of self-government than that the flag of this Republic should become the flag of an empire.

There is an easy, honest, honorable solution of the Philippine question. It is set forth in the Democratic platform and it is submitted with confidence to the American people. This plan I unreservedly indorse.

If elected, I will convene Congress in extraordinary session as soon as inaugurated and recommend an immediate declaration of the nation's purpose, first, to establish a stable form of government in the Philippine Islands, just as we are now establishing a stable form of government in Cuba; second, to give independence to the Filipinos as we have promised to give independence to the Cubans; third, to protect the Filipinos from outside interference while they work out their destiny, just as we have protected the republics of Central and South America, and are, by the Monroe doctrine, pledged to protect Cuba.

A European protectorate often results in the plundering of the ward by the guardian. An American protectorate gives to the nation protected the advantage of our strength, without making it the victim of our greed. For three-quarters of a century the Monroe doctrine has been a shield to neighboring republics and yet it has imposed no pecuniary burden upon us. After the Filipinos had aided us in the war against Spain, we could not honorably turn them over to their former masters; we could not leave them to be the victims of the ambitious designs of European nations, and since we do not desire to make them a part of us or to hold them as subjects, we propose the only alternative, namely, to give them independence and guard them against molestation from without.

When our opponents are unable to defend their position by argument they fall back upon the assertion that it is destiny, and insist that we must submit to it, no matter how much it violates our moral precepts and our principles of government. This is a complacent philosophy. It obliterates the distinction between right and wrong and makes individuals and nations the helpless victims of circumstance.

Destiny is the subterfuge of the invertebrate, who, lacking the courage to oppose error, seeks some plausible excuse for supporting it. Washington said that the destiny of the republican form of government was deeply, if not finally, staked on the experiment entrusted to the American people. How different Washington's definition of destiny from the Republican definition!

The Republicans say that this nation is in the hands of destiny; Washington believed that not only the destiny of our own nation but the destiny of the republican form of government throughout the world was entrusted to American hands. Immeasurable responsibility! The destiny of this republic is in the hands of its own people, and upon the success of the experiment here rests the hope of humanity. No exterior force can disturb this republic, and no foreign influence should be permitted to change its course. What the future has in store for this nation no one has authority to declare, but each individual has his own idea of the nation's mission, and he owes it to his country as well as to himself to contribute as best he may to the fulfilment of that mission.

Mr. Chairman and Gentlemen of the Committee, I can never fully discharge the debt of gratitude which I owe to my countrymen for the honors which they have so generously bestowed upon me; but, sirs, whether it be my lot to occupy the high office for which the convention has named me, or to spend the remainder of my days in private life, it shall be my constant ambition and my controlling purpose to aid in realizing the high ideals of those whose wisdom and courage and sacrifices brought this republic into existence.

I can conceive of a national destiny surpassing the glories of the present and the past—a destiny which meets the responsibilities of to-day and measures up to the possibilities of the future. Behold a republic, resting securely upon the foundation stones quarried by revolutionary patriots from the mountain of eternal truth—a republic applying in practise and proclaiming to the world the self-evident propositions that all men are created equal; that they are endowed by their Creator with inalienable rights; that governments are instituted among men to secure these rights, and that governments derive their just powers from the consent of the governed. Behold a republic in which civil and religious liberty stimulate all to earnest endeavor and in which the law restrains every hand uplifted for a neighbor's injury— a republic in which every citizen is a sovereign, but in which no one cares or dares to wear a crown. Behold a republic standing erect while empires all around are bowed beneath the weight of their own armaments—a republic whose flag is loved while other flags are only feared. Behold a republic increasing in population, in wealth, in strength and in influence, solving the problems of civilization and hastening the coming of an universal brotherhood—a republic which shakes thrones and dissolves aristocracies by its silent example and gives light and inspiration to those who sit in darkness. Behold a republic gradually but surely becoming the supreme moral factor in the world's progress and the accepted arbiter of the world's disputes—a republic whose history, like the path of the just, "is as the shining light that shineth more and more unto the perfect day."

4. REMARKS ON AMERICAN POLICY IN THE PHILIPPINES[1]

By FINLEY PETER DUNNE

EDITORS' NOTE.—Finley Peter Dunne (1867–1936), who wrote under the nom de plume of "Mr. Dooley," was able, under the protective coloration of his Irish dialect, to satirize the stuffed shirts of diplomacy as well as of domestic politics. His works were artfully constructed, filled with homespun common sense, and written in a style that both appealed to and fell within the reach of the man of the street. Most of his articles originally appeared in Chicago papers, where they became political textbooks for the urban masses. "He 'shoots folly as she flies,' and allows no humbug to remain unexposed, no cant to pass for genuine feeling." His comments were read in the cabinet meetings of at least three Presidents and had influence on public affairs. A friend of Dunne once asked him how such an inveterate enemy of poseurs was able to enjoy President Theodore Roosevelt's company, and Dunne replied that he enjoyed every minute of it, with the exception of those times when Roosevelt began to glorify war as a good in itself. Then he had to leave.

" 'Tis sthrange we don't hear much talk about th' Ph'lippeens," said Mr. Hennessy.

"Ye ought to go to Boston," said Mr. Dooley. "They talk about it there in their sleep. Th' raison it's not discussed annywhere else is that ivrything is perfectly quiet there. We don't talk about Ohio or Ioway or anny iv our other possissions because they'se nawthin' doin' in thim parts. Th' people ar-re goin' ahead, garnerin' th' products iv th' sile, sindin' their childher to school, worshipin' on Sundah in th' churches an' thankin' Hiven f'r th' blessin's iv free govermint an' th' protiction iv th' flag above thim.

"So it is in th' Ph'lippeens. I know, f'r me friend Gov'nor Taft says so, an' they'se a man that undherstands contintmint whin he sees it. Ye can' thrust th' fellows that comes back fr'm th' jools iv

1. Finley Peter Dunne, *Observations by Mr. Dooley* (New York, 1902), pp. 115–20. By permission of Mrs. Finley Peter Dunne.

th' Passyfic an' tells ye that things ar-re no betther thin they shud be undher th' shade iv th' cocoanut palm be th' blue wathers iv th' still lagoon. They mus' be satisfied with our rule. A man that isn't satisfied whin he's had enough is a glutton. They're satisfied an' happy an' slowly but surely they're acquirin' that love f'r th' govermint that floats over thim that will make thim good citizens without a vote or a right to thrile be jury. I know it. Guv'nor Taft says so.

"Says he: 'Th' Ph'lippeens as ye have been tol' be my young but speechful friend, Sinitor Bivridge, who was down there f'r tin minyits wanst an' spoke very highly an' at some lenth on th' beauties iv th' scenery, th' Ph'lippeens is wan or more iv th' beautiful jools in th' diadem iv our fair nation. Formerly our fair nation didn't care f'r jools, but done up her hair with side combs, but she's been abroad some since an' she come back with beautiful reddish goolden hair that a tiara looks well in an' that is betther f'r havin' a tiara. She is not as young as she was. Th' simple home-lovin' maiden that our fathers knew has disappeared an' in her place we find a Columbya, gintlemen, with machurer charms, a knowledge iv Euro-peen customs an' not averse to a cigareet. So we have pinned in her fair hair a diadem that sets off her beauty to advantage an' holds on th' front iv th' hair, an' th' mos' lovely pearl in this ornymint is thim sunny little isles iv th' Passyfic. They are almost too sunny f'r me. I had to come away.

" 'To shift me language suddintly fr'm th' joolry counther an' th' boodore, I will say that nawthin' that has been said even be th' gifted an' scholarly sinitor, who so worthily fills part iv th' place wanst crowded be Hendricks an' McDonald, does justice to th' richness iv thim islands. They raise unknown quantities iv produce, none iv which forchnitly can come into this counthry. All th' riches iv Cathay, all th' wealth iv Ind, as Hogan says, wud look like a second morgedge on an Apache wickeyup compared with th' untold an'

almost unmintionable products iv that gloryous domain. Me business kept me in Manila or I wud tell ye what they are. Besides some iv our lile subjects is gettin' to be good shots an' I didn't go down there f'r that purpose.

" 'I turn to th' climate. It is simply hivenly. No other wurrud describes it. A white man who goes there seldom rayturns unless th' bereaved fam'ly insists. It is jus' right. In winter enough rain, in summer plinty iv heat. Gin'rally speakin' whin that thropical sky starts rainin' it doesn't stop till it's impty, so th' counthry is not subjected to th' sudden changes that afflict more northerly climes. Whin it rains it rains; whin it shines it shines. Th' wather frequently remains in th' air afther th' sun has been shinin' a month or more, th' earth bein' a little overcrowded with juice an' this gives th' atmosphere a certain cosiness that is indescribable. A light green mould grows on th' clothes an' is very becomin'. I met a man on th' boat comin' back who said 'twas th' finest winter climate in th' wurruld. He was be profission a rubber in a Turkish bath. As f'r th' summers they are delicious. Th' sun doesn't sit aloft above th' jools iv th' Passyfic. It comes down an' mingles with th' people. Ye have heard it said th' isles was kissed be th' sun. Perhaps bitten wud be a betther wurrud. But th' timprachoor is frequently modified be an eruption iv th' neighborin' volcanoes an' th' inthraduction iv American stoves. At night a coolin' breeze fr'm th' crather iv a volcano makes sleep possible in a hammock swung in th' ice-box. It is also very pleasant to be able to cuk wan's dinner within wan.

" 'Passin' to th' pollytical situation, I will say it is good. Not perhaps as good as ye'ers or mine, but good. Ivry wanst in a while whin I think iv it, an iliction is held. Unforchnitly it usually happens that those ilicted have not yet surrindhered. In th' Ph'lippeens th' office seeks th' man, but as he is also pursooed be th' sojery, it is not always aisy to catch him an' fit it on him. Th' counthry may be divided into two parts, pollytically—where th' insurrection continues an' where it will soon be. Th' brave but I fear not altogether cheery army conthrols th' insurrected parts be martiyal law, but th' civil authorities are supreme in their own house. Th' diff'rence between civil law an' martiyal law in th' Ph'lippeens is what kind iv coat th' judge wears. Th' raysult is much th' same. Th' two branches wurruks in perfect harmony. We bag thim in th' city an' they round thim up in th' counthry.

" 'It is not always nicessary to kill a Filipino American right away. Me desire is to idjacate thim slowly in th' ways an' customs iv th' counthry. We ar-re givin' hundherds iv these pore benighted haythen th' well-known, ol'-fashioned American wather cure. Iv coorse, ye know how 'tis done. A Filipino, we'll say, niver heerd iv th' histhry iv this counthry. He is met be wan iv our sturdy boys in black an' blue iv th' Macabebee scouts who asts him to cheer f'r Abraham Lincoln. He rayfuses. He is thin placed upon th' grass an' given a dhrink, a baynit bein' fixed in his mouth so he cannot reject th' hospitality. Undher th' inflooence iv th' hose that cheers but does not inebriate, he soon warrums or perhaps I might say swells up to a ralization iv th' granjoor iv his adoptive counthry. One gallon makes him give three groans f'r th' constitchoochion. At four galloons, he will ask to be wrapped in th' flag. At th' dew pint he sings Yankee Doodle. Occasionally we run acrost a stubborn an' rebellyous man who wud sthrain at me idee iv human rights an' swallow th' Passyfic Ocean, but I mus' say mos' iv these little fellows is less hollow in their pretintions. Nachrally we have had to take a good manny customs fr'm th' Spanyard, but we have improved on thim. I was talkin' with a Spanish gintleman th' other day who had been away f'r a long time an' he said he

wudden't know th' counthry. Even th' faces iv th' people on th' sthreets had changed. They seemed glad to see him. Among th' mos' useful Spanish customs is reconcenthration. Our reconcenthration camps is among th' mos' thickly popylated in th' wurruld. But still we have to rely mainly on American methods. They are always used fin'lly in th' makin' iv a good citizen, th' garotte sildom.

" 'I have not considhered it advisable to inthrajooce anny fads like thrile be jury iv ye'er peers into me administhration. Plain sthraight-forward dealin's is me motto. A Filipino at his best has on'y larned half th' jooty iv mankind. He can be thried but he can't thry his fellow man. It takes him too long. But in time I hope to have thim thrained to a pint where they can be good men an' thrue at th' inquest.

" 'I hope I have tol' ye enough to show ye that th' stories iv disordher is greatly exaggereated. Th' counthry is progressin' splindidly, th' ocean still laps th' shore, th' mountains are there as they were in Bivridge's day, quite happy apparently; th' flag floats free an' well guarded over th' govermint offices, an' th' cherry people go an' come on their errands—go out alone an' come back with th' throops. Ivrywhere happiness, contint, love iv th' shtep-mother counthry, excipt in places where there ar-re people. Gintlemen, I thank ye.'

"An' there ye ar-re, Hinnissy. I hope this here lucid story will quite th' waggin' tongues iv scandal an' that people will let th' Ph'lippeens stew in their own happiness."

"But sure they might do something f'r thim," said Mr. Hennessy.

"They will," said Mr. Dooley. "They'll give thim a measure iv freedom."

"But whin?"

"Whin they'll sthand still long enough to be measured," said Mr. Dooley.

5. CIRCULAR LETTER, 1899[1]

By JOHN R. HAY

EDITORS' NOTE.—In a process which is similar to the inspiration of the Monroe Doctrine, the "Open Door" policy in China came into being after the English ambassador to the United States had suggested joint action to protect common interests in China. Careful consideration of our mercantile interests in the Far East and the implications of any sharp shift in the balance of power in favor of Russia or Japan made this policy seem desirable. In principle, this policy followed both the behavior and the desires of the British government during most of the nineteenth century. The specific propositions included here were written by John Hay, secretary of state, on the advice of W. W. Rockhill of the American State Department pursuant to the suggestions received from the Britishers, Lord Charles Beresford and Alfred Hippisley. In the circular note of September 6, 1899, which Secretary of State Hay sent to Japan and the leading European powers, the powers were asked to subscribe to certain common principles in governing their activities in China. The replies were evasive, but Hay, on March 20, 1900, said that the agreement of all the powers was "final and definitive."

SIR: At the time when the Government of the United States was informed by that of Germany that it had leased from His Majesty the Emperor of China the port of Kiao-chao and the adjacent territory in the province of Shantung, assurances were given to the ambassador of the United States at Berlin by the Imperial German minister for foreign affairs that the rights and privileges insured by treaties with China to citizens of the United States would not thereby suffer or be in anywise impaired within the area over which Germany had thus obtained control.

More recently, however, the British Government recognized by a formal agreement with Germany the exclusive right of the latter country to enjoy in said leased area and the contiguous "sphere of influence or interest" certain privileges, more especially those relating to railroads and mining enterprises; but as the exact nature and extent of the rights thus recognized have not been clearly defined, it is possible that serious conflicts of interest may at any time arise not only between British and German subjects within said area, but that the interests of our citizens may also be jeopardized thereby.

Earnestly desirous to remove any cause of irritation and to insure at the same time to the commerce of all nations in China the undoubted benefits which should accrue from a formal recognition by the various powers claiming "spheres of interest" that they shall enjoy perfect equality of treatment for their commerce and navigation within such "spheres," the Government of the United States would be pleased to see His German Majesty's Government give formal assurances, and lend its cooperation in securing like assurances from the other interested powers, that each, within its respective sphere of whatever influence—

First. Will in noway interfere with any treaty port or any vested interest within any so-called "sphere of interest" or leased territory it may have in China.

Second. That the Chinese treaty tariff

---

[1]. U.S. Department of State, *Papers Relating to Foreign Relations of the United States, 1899* (Washington, 1901), pp. 129-30.

of the time being shall apply to all merchandise landed or shipped to all such ports as are within said "sphere of interest" (unless they be "freeports"), no matter to what nationality it may belong, and that duties so leviable shall be collected by the Chinese Government.

Third. That it will levy no higher harbor dues on vessels of another nationality frequenting any port in such "sphere" than shall be levied on vessels of its own nationality, and no higher railroad charges over lines built, controlled, or operated within its "sphere" on merchandise belonging to citizens or subjects of other nationalities transported through such "sphere" than shall be levied on similar merchandise belonging to its own nationals transported over equal distances.

The liberal policy pursued by His Imperial German Majesty in declaring Kiaochao a free port and in aiding the Chinese Government in the establishment there of a custom-house are so clearly in line with the proposition which this Government is anxious to see recognized that it entertains the strongest hope that Germany will give its acceptance and hearty support.

The recent ukase of His Majesty the Emperor of Russia declaring the port of Ta-lien-wan open during the whole of the lease under which it is held from China to the merchant ships of all nations, coupled with the categorical assurances made to this Government by His Imperial Majesty's representative at this capital at the time and since repeated to me by the present Russian ambassador, seem to insure the support of the Emperor to the proposed measure. Our ambassador at the Court of St. Petersburg has in consequence been instructed to submit it to the Russian Government and to request their early consideration of it. A copy of my instruction on the subject to Mr. Tower is herewith inclosed for your confidential information.

The commercial interests of Great Britain and Japan will be so clearly served by the desired declaration of intentions, and the views of the Governments of these countries as to the desirability of the adoption of measures insuring the benefits of equality of treatment of all foreign trade throughout China are so similar to those entertained by the United States, that their acceptance of the propositions herein outlined and their cooperation in advocating their adoption by the other powers can be confidently expected. I inclose herewith copy of the instruction which I have sent to Mr. Choate on the subject.

In view of the present favorable conditions, you are instructed to submit the above considerations to His Imperial German Majesty's Minister for Foreign Affairs, and to request his early consideration of the subject.

Copy of this instruction is sent to our ambassadors at London and at St. Petersburg for their information. . . .

SECTION C. EXPANSION IN LATIN AMERICA

1. WAR MESSAGE, 1898[1]

By WILLIAM MCKINLEY

EDITORS' NOTE.—President McKinley in this message explained to Congress, he believed, the reasons which were purported to justify a war against Spain. Cubans had been fighting since 1895 to establish their independence, without success, and with much consequent suffering among the island's population. Whether this situation alone explained or justified our intervention must be considered in the face of two facts. A longer and bloodier revolution, 1868–78, which not only excited our sympathy but provided at least equal opportunities for intervention, had been met with a firm neutrality. When McKinley spoke, as he indicated, the Spanish government had revealed an intention to go very far toward fulfilling all our demands. The message was quickly followed by a declaration of war.

EXECUTIVE MANSION, April 11, 1898
To the Congress of the United States:

Obedient to that precept of the Constitution which commands the President to give from time to time to the Congress information of the state of the Union and to recommend to their consideration such measures as he shall judge necessary and expedient, it becomes my duty to now address your body with regard to the grave crisis that has arisen in the relations of the United States to Spain by reason of the warfare that for more than three years has raged in the neighboring island of Cuba.

I do so because of the intimate connection of the Cuban question with the state of our own Union and the grave relation the course which it is now incumbent upon the nation to adopt must needs bear to the traditional policy of our Government if it is to accord with the precepts laid down by the founders of the Republic and religiously observed by succeeding Administrations to the present day.

1. *Messages and Papers of the Presidents, 1798–1908*, ed. J. D. Richardson (New York, 1908), X, 56–57, 60–61, 64–65, 67.

The present revolution is but the successor of other similar insurrections which have occurred in Cuba against the dominion of Spain, extending over a period of nearly half a century, each of which during its progress has subjected the United States to great effort and expense in enforcing its neutrality laws, caused enormous losses to American trade and commerce, caused irritation, annoyance, and disturbance among our citizens, and, by the exercise of cruel, barbarous, and uncivilized practices of warfare, shocked the sensibilities and offended the humane sympathies of our people.

Since the present revolution began, in February, 1895, this country has seen the fertile domain at our threshold ravaged by fire and sword in the course of a struggle unequaled in the history of the island and rarely paralleled as to the numbers of the combatants and the bitterness of the contest by any revolution of modern times where a dependent people striving to be free have been opposed by the power of the sovereign state.

Our people have beheld a once prosperous community reduced to comparative want, its lucrative commerce virtually paralyzed, its exceptional productiveness diminished, its fields laid waste, its mills in ruins, and its people perishing by tens of thousands from hunger and destitution. We have found ourselves constrained, in the observance of that strict neutrality which our laws enjoin and which the law of nations commands, to police our own waters and watch our own seaports in prevention of any unlawful act in aid of the Cubans.

Our trade has suffered, the capital invested by our citizens in Cuba has been largely lost, and the temper and forbearance of our people have been so sorely tried as to beget a perilous unrest among our own citizens, which has inevitably found its expression from time to time in the National Legislature, so that issues wholly external to our own body politic engross attention and stand in the way of that close devotion to domestic advancement that becomes a self-contained commonwealth whose primal maxim has been the avoidance of all foreign entanglements. All this must needs awaken, and has, indeed, aroused, the utmost concern on the part of this Government, as well during my predecessor's term as in my own. . . .

The war in Cuba is of such a nature that, short of subjugation or extermination, a final military victory for either side seems impracticable. The alternative lies in the physical exhaustion of the one or the other party, or perhaps of both—a condition which in effect ended the ten years' war by the truce of Zanjon. The prospect of such a protraction and conclusion of the present strife is a contingency hardly to be contemplated with equanimity by the civilized world, and least of all by the United States, affected and injured as we are, deeply and intimately, by its very existence.

Realizing this, it appeared to be my duty, in a spirit of true friendliness, no less to Spain than to the Cubans, who have so much to lose by the prolongation of the struggle, to seek to bring about an immediate termination of the war. To this end I submitted on the 27th ultimo, as a result of much representation and correspondence, through the United States minister at Madrid, propositions to the Spanish Government looking to an armistice until October 1 for the negotiation of peace with the good offices of the President.

In addition I asked the immediate revocation of the order of reconcentration, so as to permit the people to return to their farms and the needy to be relieved with provisions and supplies from the United States, cooperating with the Spanish authorities, so as to afford full relief.

The reply of the Spanish cabinet was received on the night of the 31st ultimo. It offered, as the means to bring about peace in Cuba, to confide the preparation thereof to the insular parliament, inasmuch as the concurrence of that body would be necessary to reach a final result, it being, however, understood that the powers reserved by the constitution to the central Government are not lessened or diminished. As the Cuban parliament does not meet until the 4th of May next, the Spanish Government would not object for its part to accept at once a suspension of hostilities if asked for by the insurgents from the general in chief, to whom it would pertain in such case to determine the duration and conditions of the armistice.

The propositions submitted by General Woodford and the reply of the Spanish Government were both in the form of brief memoranda, the texts of which are before me and are substantially in the language above given. The function of the Cuban parliament in the matter of "preparing" peace and the manner of its doing so are not expressed in the Spanish memorandum, but from General Woodford's explanatory reports of preliminary discussions preceding the final conference it is understood that the Spanish Government stands ready to give the insular congress full powers to settle the terms of peace with the insurgents, whether by direct negotiation or indirectly by means of legislation does not appear.

With this last overture in the direction of immediate peace, and its disappointing reception by Spain, the Executive is brought to the end of his effort.

In my annual message of December last I said:

Of the untried measures there remain only: Recognition of the insurgents as belligerents; recognition of the independence of Cuba; neutral intervention to end the war by imposing a rational compromise between the contestants, and intervention in favor of one or the other party. I speak not of forcible annexation, for that can not be thought of. That, by our code of morality, would be criminal aggression. . . .

The forcible intervention of the United States as a neutral to stop the war, according to the large dictates of humanity and following many historical precedents where neighboring states have interfered to check the hopeless sacrifices of life by internecine conflicts beyond their borders, is justifiable on rational grounds. It involves, however, hostile constraint upon both the parties to the contest, as well to enforce a truce as to guide the eventual settlement.

The grounds for such intervention may be briefly summarized as follows:

First. In the cause of humanity and to put an end to the barbarities, bloodshed, starvation, and horrible miseries now existing there, and which the parties to the conflict are either unable or unwilling to stop or mitigate. It is no answer to say this is all in another country, belonging to another nation, and is therefore none of our business. It is specially our duty, for it is right at our door.

Second. We owe it to our citizens in Cuba to afford them that protection and indemnity for life and property which no government there can or will afford, and to that end to terminate the conditions that deprive them of legal protection.

Third. The right to intervene may be justified by the very serious injury to the commerce, trade, and business of our people and by the wanton destruction of property and devastation of the island.

Fourth, and which is of the utmost importance. The present condition of affairs in Cuba is a constant menace to our peace and entails upon this Government an enormous expense. With such a conflict waged for years in an island so near us and with which our people have such trade and business relations; when the lives and liberty of our citizens are in constant danger and their property destroyed and themselves ruined; where our trading vessels are liable to seizure and are seized at our very door by war ships of a foreign nation; the expeditions of filibustering that we are powerless to prevent altogether, and the irritating questions and entanglements thus arising—all these and others that I need not mention, with the resulting strained relations, are a constant menace to our peace and compel us to keep on a semi war footing with a nation with which we are at peace.

These elements of danger and disorder already pointed out have been strikingly illustrated by a tragic event which has deeply and justly moved the American people. I have already transmitted to Congress the report of the naval court of inquiry on the destruction of the battle ship *Maine* in the harbor of Havana during the night of the 15th of February. The destruction of that noble vessel has filled the national heart with inexpressible horror. Two hundred and fifty-eight brave sailors and marines and two officers of our Navy, reposing in the fancied security of a friendly harbor, have been hurled to death, grief and want brought to their homes and sorrow to the nation.

The naval court of inquiry, which, it is needless to say, commands the unqualified confidence of the Government, was unanimous in its conclusion that the destruction of the *Maine* was caused by an exterior explosion—that of a submarine mine. It did not assume to place the responsibility. That remains to be fixed.

In any event, the destruction of the

Maine, by whatever exterior cause, is a patent and impressive proof of a state of things in Cuba that is intolerable. That condition is thus shown to be such that the Spanish Government can not assure safety and security to a vessel of the American Navy in the harbor of Havana on a mission of peace, and rightfully there. . . .

The long trial has proved that the object for which Spain has waged the war can not be attained. The fire of insurrection may flame or may smolder with varying seasons, but it has not been and it is plain that it can not be extinguished by present methods. The only hope of relief and repose from a condition which can no longer be endured is the enforced pacification of Cuba. In the name of humanity, in the name of civilization, in behalf of endangered American interests which give us the right and the duty to speak and to act, the war in Cuba must stop.

In view of these facts and of these considerations I ask the Congress to authorize and empower the President to take measures to secure a full and final termination of hostilities between the Government of Spain and the people of Cuba, and to secure in the island the establishment of a stable government, capable of maintaining order and observing its international obligations, insuring peace and tranquillity and the security of its citizens as well as our own, and to use the military and naval forces of the United States as may be necessary for these purposes.

And in the interest of humanity and to aid in preserving the lives of the starving people of the island I recommend that the distribution of food and supplies be continued and that an appropriation be made out of the public Treasury to supplement the charity of our citizens.

The issue is now with the Congress. It is a solemn responsibility. I have exhausted every effort to relieve the intolerable condition of affairs which is at our doors. Prepared to execute every obligation imposed upon me by the Constitution and the law, I await your action.

Yesterday, and since the preparation of the foregoing message, official information was received by me that the latest decree of the Queen Regent of Spain directs General Blanco, in order to prepare and facilitate peace, to proclaim a suspension of hostilities, the duration and details of which have not yet been communicated to me.

This fact, with every other pertinent consideration, will, I am sure, have your just and careful attention in the solemn deliberations upon which you are about to enter. If this measure attains a successful result, then our aspirations as a Christian, peace-loving people will be realized. If it fails, it will be only another justification for our contemplated action.

2. *DOWNES* v. *BIDWELL*[1]

EDITORS' NOTE.—Downes had sued Bidwell, collector of the port of New York, for duties he had paid under protest on goods imported from Puerto Rico, and on writ of error the case came before the Supreme Court. The important issue was what relation existed between the newly acquired territory and the United States. The justices were divided five to four whether the Puerto Ricans were to be protected by the United States Constitution equally with citizens of the United States. They were not agreed about the limits of congressional authority over the island. The reader may inquire about the meaning and importance of the decision which defined Puerto Rico as belonging to the United States but not being a part of it.

1. 182 U.S. 247–51, 270–71, 276–80, 282–87, 347, 372–74 (1900).

This was an action begun in the Circuit Court by Downes, doing business under the firm name of S. B. Downes & Co., against the collector of the port of New York, to recover back duties to the amount of $659.35 exacted and paid under protest upon certain oranges consigned to the plaintiff at New York, and brought thither from the port of San Juan in the Island of Porto Rico during the month of November, 1900, after the passage of the act temporarily providing a civil government and revenues for the Island of Porto Rico, known as the Foraker act.

The District Attorney demurred to the complaint for the want of jurisdiction in the court, and for insufficiency of its averments. The demurrer was sustained, and the complaint dismissed. Whereupon plaintiff sued out this writ of error. . . .

Mr. Justice BROWN, after making the above statement, announced the conclusion and judgment of the court.

The case involves the question whether merchandise brought into the port of New York from Porto Rico since the passage of the Foraker act, is exempt from duty, notwithstanding the third section of that act, which requires the payment of "fifteen per centum of the duties which are required to be levied, collected and paid upon like articles of merchandise imported from foreign countries."

1. The exception to the jurisdiction of the court is not well taken. . . .

2. In the case of De Lima v. Bidwell, just decided, we held that upon the ratification of the treaty of peace with Spain, Porto Rico ceased to be a foreign country, and became a territory of the United States, and that duties were no longer collectible upon merchandise brought from that island. We are now asked to hold that it became a part of the United States within that provision of the Constitution which declares that "all duties, imposts and excises shall be uniform throughout the United States." Art. I, sec. 8. If Porto Rico be a part of the United States, the Foraker act imposing duties upon its products is un-

constitutional, not only by reason of a violation of the uniformity clause, but because by section 9 "vessels bound to or from one State" cannot "be obliged to enter, clear or pay duties in another."

The case also involves the broader question whether the revenue clauses of the Constitution extend of their own force to our newly acquired territories. The Constitution itself does not answer the question. Its solution must be found in the nature of the government created by that instrument, in the opinion of its contemporaries, in the practical construction put upon it by Congress and in the decisions of this court. . . .

It is sufficient to observe in relation to these three fundamental instruments [the Articles of Confederation, the Ordinance of 1787, and the Constitution] that it can nowhere be inferred that the territories were considered a part of the United States. The Constitution was created by the people of the *United States*, as a union of *States*, to be governed solely by representatives of the *States*; and even the provision relied upon here, that all duties, imposts, and excises shall be uniform "throughout the United States," is explained by subsequent provisions of the Constitution, that "no tax or duty shall be laid on articles exported from any *State*," and "no preference shall be given by any regulation of commerce or revenue to the ports of one *State* over those of another; nor shall vessels bound to or from one *State* be obliged to enter, clear or pay duties in another." In short, the Constitution deals with *States*, their people, and their representatives.

The Thirteenth Amendment to the Constitution, prohibiting slavery and involuntary servitude "within the United States, or in any place subject to their jurisdiction," is also significant as showing that there may be places within the jurisdiction of the United States that are no part of the Union. To say that the phraseology of this amendment was due to the fact that it was intended to prohibit slavery in the seceded States, under a possible interpretation that those States were no longer a part of the Union, is to confess the very point in issue, since it involves an admission that, if these States were not a part of the Union they were still subject to the jurisdiction of the United States. . . .

Eliminating, then, from the opinions of this court all expressions unnecessary to the disposition of the particular case, and gleaning therefrom the exact point decided in each, the following propositions may be considered as established:

1. That the District of Columbia and the territories are not States, within the judicial clause of the Constitution giving jurisdiction in cases between citizens of different States;

2. That territories are not States, within the meaning of Revised Statutes, sec. 709, permitting writs of error from this court in cases where the validity of a *state* statute is drawn in question;

3. That the District of Columbia and the territories are States, as that word is used in treaties with foreign powers, with respect to the ownership, disposition and inheritance of property;

4. That the territories are not within the clause of the Constitution providing for the creation of a Supreme Court and such inferior courts as Congress may see fit to establish;

5. That the Constitution does not apply to foreign countries or to trials therein conducted, and that Congress may lawfully provide for such trials before consular tribunals, without the intervention of a grand or petit jury;

6. That where the Constitution has been once formally extended by Congress to territories, neither Congress nor the territorial legislature can enact laws inconsistent therewith. . . .

To sustain the judgment in the case under consideration it by no means becomes necessary to show that none of the articles of the Constitution apply to the Island of Porto Rico. There is a clear distinction between such prohibitions as go to the very root of the power of Congress to act at all, irrespective of time or place, and such as are operative only "throughout the United States" or among the several States.

Thus, when the Constitution declares that "no bill of attainder or *ex post facto* law shall be passed," and that "no title of nobility shall be granted by the United States," it goes to the competency of Congress to pass a bill *of that description*. Perhaps, the same remark may apply to the First Amendment, that "Congress shall make no law respecting an establishment of religion, or prohibiting the free exercise thereof; or abridging the freedom of speech, or of the press; or the right of the people to peacefully assemble, and to petition the government for a redress of grievances." We do not wish, however, to be understood as expressing an opinion how far the bill of rights contained in the first eight amendments is of general and how far of local application.

Upon the other hand, when the Constitution declares that all duties shall be uniform "throughout the United States," it becomes necessary to inquire whether there be any territory over which Congress has jurisdiction which is not a part of the "United States," by which term we understand the *States* whose people *united* to form the Constitution, and such as have since been admitted to the Union upon an equality with them. Not only did the people in adopting the Thirteenth Amendment thus recognize a distinction between the United States and "any place subject to their jurisdiction," but Congress itself, in the act of March 27, 1804, c. 56, 2 Stat. 298, providing for the proof of public records, applied the provisions of the act not only to "every court and office within the United States," but to the "courts and offices of the respective territories of the United States, and countries subject to the jurisdiction of the United States," as to the courts and offices of the several States. This classification, adopted by the Eighth Congress, is carried into the Revised Statutes as follows:

"Sec. 905. The acts of the legislature of any State or Territory, or of any country subject to the jurisdiction of the United States, shall be authenticated," etc. . . .

Unless these words are to be rejected as meaningless, we must treat them as a recognition by Congress of the fact that there may be territories subject to the jurisdiction of the United States, which are not *of* the United States. . . .

Indeed, the practical interpretation put by Congress upon the Constitution has been long continued and uniform to the effect that the Constitution is applicable to territories acquired by purchase or conquest only when and so far as Congress shall so direct. . . .

We are also of opinion that the power to acquire territory by treaty implies not only the power to govern such territory, but to prescribe upon what terms the United States will receive its inhabitants, and what their *status* shall be in what Chief Justice Marshall termed the "American Empire." There seems to be no middle ground between this position and the doctrine that if their inhabitants do not become, immediately upon annexation, citizens of the United States, their children thereafter born, whether savages or civilized, are such, and entitled to all the rights, privileges and immunities of citizens. If such be their *status*, the consequences will be extremely serious. Indeed, it is doubtful if Congress would ever assent to the annexation of territory upon the condition that its inhabitants, however foreign they may be to our habits, traditions and modes of life, shall become at once citizens of the United States. . . .

It is obvious that in the annexation of outlying and distant possessions grave questions will arise from differences of race, habits, laws and customs of the people, and from differences of soil, climate and production, which may require action on the part of Congress that would be quite unnecessary in the annexation of contiguous territory inhabited only by people of the same race, or by scattered bodies of native Indians.

We suggest, without intending to decide, that there may be a distinction between certain natural rights, enforced in the Constitution by prohibitions against interference with them, and what may be termed artificial or remedial rights, which are peculiar to our own system of jurisprudence. Of the former class are the rights to one's own religious opinion and to a public expression of them, or, as sometimes said, to worship God according to the dictates of one's own conscience; the right to personal liberty and individual property; to freedom of speech and of the press; to free access to courts of justice, to due process of law and to an equal protection of the laws; to immunities from unreasonable searches and seizures, as well as cruel and unusual punishments; and to such other immunities as are indispensable to a free government. Of the latter class are the rights to citizenship, to suffrage, *Minor* v. *Happersett*, 21 Wall. 162, and to the particular methods of procedure pointed out in the Constitution, which are peculiar to Anglo-Saxon jurisprudence, and some of which have already been held by the States to be unnecessary to the proper protection of individuals.

Whatever may be finally decided by the American people as to the *status* of these islands and their inhabitants—whether they shall be introduced into the sisterhood of States or be permitted to form independent governments—it does not follow that, in the meantime, awaiting that decision, the people are in the matter of personal rights unprotected by the provisions of our Constitution, and subject to the merely arbitrary control of Congress. Even if regarded as aliens, they are entitled under the principles of the Constitution to be protected in life, liberty and property. . . . We do not desire, however, to anticipate the difficulties which would naturally arise in this connection, but merely to disclaim any intention to hold that the inhabitants of these territories are subject to an unrestrained power on the part of Congress to deal with them upon the theory that they have no rights which it is bound to respect. . . .

In passing upon the questions involved in this case and kindred cases, we ought not to overlook the fact that, while the Constitution was intended to establish a permanent form of government for the States which should elect to take advantage of its conditions, and continue for an indefinite future, the vast possibilities of that future could never have entered the minds of its framers. . . . The difficulties of bringing about a union of the States were so great, the objections to it seemed so formidable, that the whole thought of the convention centered upon surmounting these obstacles. The question of territories was dismissed with a single clause, apparently applicable only to the territories then existing, giving Congress the power to govern and dispose of them.

Had the acquisition of other territories been contemplated as a possibility, could it have been foreseen that, within little more than one hundred years, we were destined to acquire not only the whole vast region between the Atlantic and Pacific Oceans, but the Russian possessions in America and distant islands in the Pacific, it is incredible that no provision should have been made for them, and the question whether the Constitution should or should not extend to them have been definitely settled. If it be once conceded that we are at liberty to acquire foreign territory, a presumption arises that our power with respect to such territories is the same power which other nations have been accustomed to exercise with respect to territories acquired by them. If, in limiting the power which Congress was to exercise within the United States, it was also intended to limit it with regard to such territories as the people of the United States should thereafter acquire, such limitations should have been expressed. Instead of that, we find the Constitution speaking only to States, except in the terri-

torial clause, which is absolute in its terms, and suggestive of no limitations upon the power of Congress in dealing with them. . . .

. . . The liberality of Congress in legislating the Constitution into all our contiguous territories has undoubtedly fostered the impression that it went there by its own force, but there is nothing in the Constitution itself, and little in the interpretation put upon it, to confirm that impression. There is not even an analogy to the provisions of an ordinary mortgage for its attachment to after-acquired property, without which it covers only property existing at the date of the mortgage. In short, there is absolute silence upon the subject. The executive and legislative departments of the government have for more than a century interpreted this silence as precluding the idea that the Constitution attached to these territories as soon as acquired, and unless such interpretation be manifestly contrary to the letter or spirit of the Constitution, it should be followed by the judicial department. . . .

Patriotic and intelligent men may differ widely as to the desirableness of this or that acquisition, but this is solely a political question. We can only consider this aspect of the case so far as to say that no construction of the Constitution should be adopted which would prevent Congress from considering each case upon its merits, unless the language of the instrument imperatively demand it. A false step at this time might be fatal to the development of what Chief Justice Marshall called the American Empire. Choice in some cases, the natural gravitation of small bodies towards large ones in others, the result of a successful war in still others, may bring about conditions which would render the annexation of distant possessions desirable. If those possessions are inhabited by alien races, differing from us in religion, customs, laws, methods of taxation and modes of thought, the administration of government and justice, according to Anglo-Saxon principles, may for a time be impossible; and the question at once arises whether large concessions ought not to be made for a time, that, ultimately, our own theories may be carried out, and the blessings of a free government under the Constitution extended to them. We decline to hold that there is anything in the Constitution to forbid such action.

We are therefore of opinion that the Island of Porto Rico is a territory appurtenant and belonging to the United States, but not a part of the United States within the revenue clauses of the Constitution; that the Foraker act is constitutional, so far as it imposes duties upon imports from such island, and that the plaintiff cannot recover back the duties exacted in this case.

The judgment of the Circuit Court is therefore—*Affirmed.* . . .

MR. CHIEF JUSTICE FULLER (with whom concurred MR. JUSTICE HARLAN, MR. JUSTICE BREWER and MR. JUSTICE PECKHAM) dissenting. . . .

The inquiry is stated to be: "Had Porto Rico, at the time of the passage of the act in question, been incorporated into and become an integral part of the United States?" And the answer being given that it had not, it is held that the rule of uniformity was not applicable.

I submit that that is not the question in this case. The question is whether, when Congress has created a civil government for Porto Rico, has constituted its inhabitants a body politic, has given it a governor and other officers, a legislative assembly, and courts, with the right of appeal to this court, Congress can in the same act and in the exercise of the power conferred by the first clause of section eight, impose duties on the commerce between Porto Rico and the States and other territories in contravention of the rule of uniformity qualifying the power. If this can be done, it is because the power of Congress over commerce between the States and any of the territories is not restricted by the Constitution. This was the position taken by the Attorney General, with a candor and ability that did him great credit.

But that position is rejected, and the contention seems to be that if an organized and settled province of another sovereignty is acquired by the United States, Congress has the power to keep it, like a disembodied shade, in an intermediate state of ambiguous existence for an indefinite period; and, more than that, that after it has been called from that limbo, commerce with it is absolutely subject to the will of Congress, irrespective of constitutional provisions. . . .

The logical result is that Congress may prohibit commerce altogether between the States and territories, and may prescribe one rule of taxation in one territory, and a different rule in another.

That theory assumes that the Constitution created a government empowered to acquire countries throughout the world, to be governed by different rules than those obtaining in the original States and territories, and substitutes for the present system of republican government, a system of domination over distant provinces in the exercise of unrestricted power.

In our judgment, so much of the Porto Rican act as authorized the imposition of these duties is invalid, and plaintiffs were entitled to recover. . . .

3. THE PLATT AMENDMENT, 1901[1]

EDITORS' NOTE.—The congressional resolution for war on April 19, 1898,

[1]. *Treaties, Conventions, International Acts* . . . *1776–1909,* ed. W. M. Malloy (61st Cong., 2d sess.; Senate Doc., Serial No. 5646 [Washington, 1910]), I, 362–64.

contained the Teller Amendment, in which the United States stated its intention of leaving Cuba independent after the war. When a Cuban convention in 1900, however, prepared a constitution without any provision for relations between Cuba and the United States, the result was the Platt Amendment to the Army Appropriation Bill of March 2, 1901. The Cuban convention thereupon added the necessary provisions to the Cuban constitution, and these provisions were included in the treaty of 1903 between Cuba and the United States. The accord between the Teller and Platt amendments may not be immediately apparent. A new treaty with Cuba in 1934 abolished the Platt Amendment.

WHEREAS, the Congress of the United States of America, by an Act approved March 2, 1901, provided as follows:

Provided further, That in fulfillment of the declaration contained in the joint resolution approved April twentieth, eighteen hundred and ninety-eight, entitled, "For the recognition of the independence of the people of Cuba, demanding that the Government of Spain relinquish its authority and government in the island of Cuba, and to withdraw its land and naval forces from Cuba and Cuban waters, and directing the President of the United States to use the land and naval forces of the United States to carry these resolutions into effect," the President is hereby authorized to "leave the government and control of the island of Cuba to its people" so soon as a government shall have been established in said island under a constitution which, either as a part thereof or in an ordinance appended thereto, shall define the future relations of the United States with Cuba, substantially as follows:

"I. That the government of Cuba shall never enter into any treaty or other compact with any foreign power or powers which will impair or tend to impair the independence of Cuba, nor in any manner authorize or permit any foreign power or powers to obtain by colonization or for military or naval purposes or otherwise, lodgment in or control over any portion of said island."

"II. That said government shall not assume or contract any public debt, to pay the interest upon which, and to make reasonable sinking fund provision for the ultimate discharge of which, the ordinary revenues of the island, after defraying the current expenses of government shall be inadequate."

"III. That the government of Cuba consents that the United States may exercise the right to intervene for the preservation of Cuban independence, the maintenance of a government adequate for the protection of life, property, and individual liberty, and for discharging the obligations with respect to Cuba imposed by the treaty of Paris on the United States, now to be assumed and undertaken by the government of Cuba."

"IV. That all Acts of the United States in Cuba during its military occupancy thereof are ratified and validated, and all lawful rights acquired thereunder shall be maintained and protected."

"V. That the government of Cuba will execute, and as far as necessary extend, the plans already devised or other plans to be mutually agreed upon, for the sanitation of the cities of the island, to the end that a recurrence of epidemic and infectious diseases may be prevented thereby assuring protection to the people and commerce of Cuba, as well as to the commerce of the southern ports of the United States and the people residing therein."

"VI. That the Isle of Pines shall be omitted from the proposed constitutional boundaries of Cuba, the title thereto being left to future adjustment by treaty."

"VII. That to enable the United States to maintain the independence of Cuba, and to protect the people thereof, as well as for its own defense, the government of Cuba will sell or lease to the United States lands necessary for coaling or naval stations at certain specified points to be agreed upon with the President of the United States."

"VIII. That by way of further assurance the government of Cuba will embody the foregoing provisions in a permanent treaty with the United States."

WHEREAS, the Constitutional Convention of Cuba, on June twelfth, 1901, adopted a Resolution adding to the Constitution of the Republic of Cuba which was adopted on the twenty-first of February 1901, an appendix in the words and letters of the eight enumerated articles of the above cited act of the Congress of the United States;

And WHEREAS, by the establishment of the independent and sovereign government of the Republic of Cuba, under the constitution promulgated on the 20th of May, 1902, which embraced the foregoing conditions, and by the withdrawal of the Government of the United States as an intervening power, on the same date, it becomes necessary to embody the above cited provisions in a permanent treaty between the United States of America and the Republic of Cuba;

The United States of America and the Republic of Cuba, being desirous to carry out the foregoing conditions, have for that purpose appointed as their plenipotentiaries to conclude a treaty to that end,

The President of the United States of America, Herbert G. Squiers, Envoy Extraordinary and Minister Plenipotentiary at Havana,

And the President of the Republic of Cuba, Carlos de Zaldo y Beurmann, Secretary of State and Justice—who after communicating to each other their full powers found in good and due form, have agreed upon the following articles:

ARTICLE I

The Government of Cuba shall never enter into any treaty or other compact with any foreign power or powers which will impair or tend to impair the independence of Cuba, nor in any manner authorize or permit any foreign power or powers to obtain by colonization or for military or naval purposes, or otherwise, lodgment in or control over any portion of said island.

ARTICLE II

The Government of Cuba shall not assume or contract any public debt to pay the interest upon which, and to make reasonable sinking-fund provision for the ultimate discharge of which, the ordinary revenues of the Island of Cuba, after defraying the current expenses of the Government, shall be inadequate.

ARTICLE III

The Government of Cuba consents that the United States may exercise the right to intervene for the preservation of Cuban independence, the maintenance of a government adequate for the protection of life, property, and individual liberty, and for discharging the obligations with respect to Cuba imposed by the Treaty of Paris on the United States, now to be assumed and undertaken by the Government of Cuba.

ARTICLE IV

All acts of the United States in Cuba during its military occupancy thereof are ratified and validated, and all lawful rights acquired thereunder shall be maintained and protected.

ARTICLE V

The Government of Cuba will execute, and, as far as necessary, extend the plans already devised, or other plans to be mutually agreed upon, for the sanitation of the cities of the island, to the end that a recurrence of epidemic and infectious diseases may be prevented, thereby assuring protection to the people and commerce of Cuba, as well as to the commerce of the Southern ports of the United States and the people residing therein.

ARTICLE VI

The Island of Pines shall be omitted from the boundaries of Cuba specified in the Constitution, the title thereto being left to future adjustment by treaty.

ARTICLE VII

To enable the United States to maintain the independence of Cuba, and to protect the people thereof, as well as for its own defense, the Government of Cuba will sell or lease to the United States lands necessary for coaling or naval stations, at certain specified points, to be agreed upon with the President of the United States.

ARTICLE VIII

The present Convention shall be ratified by each party in conformity with the respective Constitutions of the two countries, and the ratifications shall be exchanged in the City of Washington within eight months from this date.

In witness whereof, we the respective Plenipotentiaries, have signed the same in duplicate, in English and Spanish, and have affixed our respective seals at Havana, Cuba, this twenty-second day of May, in the year nineteen hundred and three.

H. G. SQUIERS [Seal]
CARLOS DE ZALDO [Seal]

4. COROLLARY TO THE MONROE DOCTRINE, 1904, 1905[1]

By THEODORE ROOSEVELT

EDITORS' NOTE.—As Secretary of State Stimson explained in 1931 (see p. 337), the crux of our policy in the Caribbean was the security of the Panama Canal, which was completed in 1914. This security might be weakened if a European power should seize a Caribbean republic as an incident in the forcible collection of a debt. For example, in 1902 Germany, Italy, and England agreed to blockade the ports of Venezuela to collect debts which the dictator, Castro, refused to pay. President Roosevelt made a show of naval force, and the blockading powers agreed to mediation by the United States. In 1904 the Dominican Republic defaulted on its bonds, and again the danger of European intervention occurred. President Roosevelt then announced the policy which came to be called the "Roosevelt Corollary to the Monroe Doctrine" and arranged for the collection of Dominican revenues and the payment of Dominican external debts by an American naval officer. A year later, Roosevelt reiterated and expanded this doctrine. During these developments, Luis Drago, minister of foreign relations of the Argentine Republic, advocated a policy of nonintervention by creditor states for the collection of debts. A modified version of this "Drago Doctrine" became international law by a convention made at the Hague Conference of 1907. Despite this convention, the United States frequently before 1933 intervened for the collection of debts or the suppression of disorder in various Caribbean republics.

1. *Messages and Papers of the Presidents, 1798–1908*, ed. J. D. Richardson (New York, 1908), X, 831–34; XI, 1153–56.

. . . It is not true that the United States feels any land hunger or entertains any projects as regards the other nations of the Western Hemisphere save such as are for their welfare. All that this country desires is to see the neighboring countries stable, orderly, and prosperous. Any country whose people conduct themselves well can count upon our hearty friendship. If a nation shows that it knows how to act with reasonable efficiency and decency in social and political matters, if it keeps order and pays its obligations, it need fear no interference from the United States. Chronic wrongdoing, or an impotence which results in a general loosening of the ties of civilized society, may in America, as elsewhere, ultimately require intervention by some civilized nation, and in the Western Hemisphere the adherence of the United States to the Monroe Doctrine may force the United States, however reluctantly, in flagrant cases of such wrongdoing or impotence, to the exercise of an international police power. If every country washed by the Caribbean Sea would show the progress in stable and just civilization which with the aid of the Platt amendment Cuba has shown since our troops left the island, and which so many of the republics in both Americas are constantly and brilliantly showing, all question of interference by this Nation with their affairs would be at an end. Our interests and those of our southern neighbors are in reality identical. They have great natural riches, and if within their borders the reign of law and justice obtains, prosperity is sure to come to them. While they thus obey the primary laws of civilized society they may rest assured that they will be treated by us in a spirit of cordial and helpful sympathy. We would interfere with them only in the last resort, and then only if it became evident that their inability or unwillingness to do justice at home and abroad had violated the rights of the United States or had invited foreign aggression to the detriment of the entire body of American nations. It is a mere truism to say that every na-

tion, whether in America or anywhere else, which desires to maintain its freedom, its independence, must ultimately realize that the right of such independence can not be separated from the responsibility of making good use of it.

In asserting the Monroe Doctrine, in taking such steps as we have taken in regard to Cuba, Venezuela, and Panama, and in endeavoring to circumscribe the theater of war in the Far East, and to secure the open door in China, we have acted in our own interest as well as in the interest of humanity at large. There are, however, cases in which, while our own interests are not greatly involved, strong appeal is made to our sympathies. Ordinarily it is very much wiser and more useful for us to concern ourselves with striving for our own moral and material betterment here at home than to concern ourselves with trying to better the condition of things in other nations. We have plenty of sins of our own to war against, and under ordinary circumstances we can do more for the general uplifting of humanity by striving with heart and soul to put a stop to civic corruption, to brutal lawlessness and violent race prejudices here at home than by passing resolutions about wrongdoing elsewhere. Nevertheless there are occasional crimes committed on so vast a scale and of such peculiar horror as to make us doubt whether it is not our manifest duty to endeavor at least to show our disapproval of the deed and our sympathy with those who have suffered by it. The cases must be extreme in which such a course is justifiable. There must be no effort made to remove the mote from our brother's eye if we refuse to remove the beam from our own. But in extreme cases action may be justifiable and proper. What form the action shall take must depend upon the circumstances of the case; that is, upon the degree of the atrocity and upon our power to remedy it. The cases in which we could interfere by force of arms as we interfered to put a stop to intolerable conditions in Cuba are necessarily very few. Yet it is not to be expected that a people like ours, which in spite of certain very obvious shortcomings, nevertheless as a whole shows by its consistent practice its belief in the principles of civil and religious liberty and of orderly freedom, a people among whom even the worst crime, like the crime of lynching, is never more than sporadic, so that individuals and not classes are molested in their fundamental rights—it is inevitable that such a nation should desire eagerly to give expression to its horror on an occasion like that of the massacre of the Jews in Kishenef, or when it witnesses such systematic and long-extended cruelty and oppression as the cruelty and oppression of which the Armenians have been the victims, and which have won for them the indignant pity of the civilized world.

Even where it is not possible to secure in other nations the observance of the principles which we accept as axiomatic, it is necessary for us firmly to insist upon the rights of our own citizens without regard to their creed or race; without regard to whether they were born here or born abroad. It has proved very difficult to secure from Russia the right for our Jewish fellow-citizens to receive passports and travel through Russian territory. Such conduct is not only unjust and irritating toward us, but it is difficult to see its wisdom from Russia's standpoint. No conceivable good is accomplished by it. If an American Jew or an American Christian misbehaves himself in Russia he can at once be driven out; but the ordinary American Jew, like the ordinary American Christian, would behave just about as he behaves here, that is, behave as any good citizen ought to behave; and where this is the case it is a wrong against which we are entitled to protest to refuse him his passport without regard to his conduct and character, merely on racial and religious grounds. In Turkey our difficulties arise less from the way in which our citizens are sometimes treated than from the indigna-

tion inevitably excited in seeing such fearful misrule as has been witnessed both in Armenia and Macedonia.

The strong arm of the Government in enforcing respect for its just rights in international matters is the Navy of the United States. I most earnestly recommend that there be no halt in the work of upbuilding the American Navy. There is no more patriotic duty before us a people than to keep the Navy adequate to the needs of this country's position. We have undertaken to build the Isthmian Canal. We have undertaken to secure for ourselves our just share in the trade of the Orient. We have undertaken to protect our citizens from improper treatment in foreign lands. We continue steadily to insist on the application of the Monroe Doctrine to the Western Hemisphere. Unless our attitude in these and all similar matters is to be a mere boastful sham we can not afford to abandon our naval programme. Our voice is now potent for peace, and is so potent because we are not afraid of war. But our protestations upon behalf of peace would neither receive nor deserve the slightest attention if we were impotent to make them good. . . .

There are certain essential points which must never be forgotten as regards the Monroe Doctrine. In the first place we must as a Nation make it evident that we do not intend to treat it in any shape or way as an excuse for aggrandizement on our part at the expense of the republics to the south. We must recognize the fact that in some South American countries there has been much suspicion lest we should interpret the Monroe Doctrine as in some way inimical to their interests, and we must try to convince all the other nations of this continent once and for all that no just and orderly Government has anything to fear from us. There are certain republics to the south of us which have already reached such a point of stability, order, and prosperity that they themselves, though as yet hardly consciously, are among the guarantors of this doctrine. These republics we now meet not only on a basis of entire equality, but in a spirit of frank and respectful friendship, which we hope is mutual. If all of the republics to the south of us will only grow as those to which I allude have already grown, all need for us to be the especial champions of the doctrine will disappear, for no stable and growing American Republic wishes to see some great non-American military power acquire territory in its neighborhood. All that this country desires is that the other republics on this continent shall be happy and prosperous; and they cannot be happy and prosperous unless they maintain order within their boundaries and behave with a just regard for their obligations toward outsiders. It must be understood that under no circumstances will the United States use the Monroe Doctrine as a cloak for territorial aggression. We desire peace with all the world, but perhaps most of all with the other peoples of the American Continent. There are, of course, limits to the wrongs which any self-respecting nation can endure. It is always possible that wrong actions toward this Nation, or toward citizens of this Nation, in some State unable to keep order among its own people, unable to secure justice from outsiders, and unwilling to do justice to those outsiders who treat it well, may result in our having to take action to protect our rights; but such action will not be taken with a view to territorial aggression, and it will be taken at all only with extreme reluctance and when it has become evident that every other resource has been exhausted.

Moreover, we must make it evident that we do not intend to permit the Monroe Doctrine to be used by any nation on this Continent as a shield to protect it from the consequences of its own misdeeds against foreign nations. If a republic to the south of us commits a tort against a foreign nation, such as an outrage against a citizen of that nation, then the Monroe Doctrine does not force us to interfere to prevent punishment of the tort, save to see that the punishment does not assume the form of territorial occupation in any shape. The case is more difficult when it refers to a contractual obligation. Our own Government has always refused to enforce such contractual obligations on behalf of its citizens by an appeal to arms. It is much to be wished that all foreign governments would take the same view. But they do not; and in consequence we are liable at any time to be brought face to face with disagreeable alternatives. On the one hand, this country would certainly decline to go to war to prevent a foreign government from collecting a just debt; on the other hand, it is very inadvisable to permit any foreign power to take possession, even temporarily, of the custom houses of an American Republic in order to enforce the payment of its obligations; for such temporary occupation might turn into a permanent occupation. The only escape from these alternatives may at any time be that we must ourselves undertake to bring about some arrangement by which so much as possible of a just obligation shall be paid. It is far better that this country should put through such an arrangement, rather than allow any foreign country to undertake it. To do so insures the defaulting republic from having to pay debt of an improper character under duress, while it also insures honest creditors of the republic from being passed by in the interest of dishonest or grasping creditors. Moreover, for the United States to take such a position offers the only possible way of insuring us against a clash with some foreign power. The position is, therefore, in the interest of peace as well as in the interest of justice. It is of benefit to our people; it is of benefit to foreign peoples; and most of all it is really of benefit to the people of the country concerned.

This brings me to what should be one of the fundamental objects of the Monroe Doctrine. We must ourselves in good faith try to help upward toward peace and order those of our sister republics which need such help. Just as there has been a gradual growth of the ethical element in the relations of one individual to another, so we are, even though slowly, more and more coming to recognize the duty of bearing one another's burdens, not only as among individuals, but also as among nations.

Santo Domingo, in her turn, has now made an appeal to us to help her, and not only every principle of wisdom but every generous instinct within us bids us respond to the appeal. It is not of the slightest consequence whether we grant the aid needed by Santo Domingo as an incident to the wise development of the Monroe Doctrine or because we regard the case of Santo Domingo as standing wholly by itself, and to be treated as such, and not on general principles or with any reference to the Monroe Doctrine. The important point is to give the needed aid, and the case is certainly sufficiently peculiar to deserve to be judged purely on its own merits. The conditions in Santo Domingo have for a number of years grown from bad to worse until a year ago all society was on the verge of dissolution. Fortunately, just at this time a ruler sprang up in Santo Domingo, who, with his colleagues, saw the dangers threatening their country and appealed to the friendship of the only great and powerful neighbor who possessed the power, and as they hoped also the will to help them. There was imminent danger of foreign intervention. The previous rulers of Santo Domingo had recklessly incurred debts, and owing to her internal disorders she had ceased to be able to provide means of paying the debts. The patience of her foreign creditors had become exhausted, and at least two foreign nations were on the point of intervention, and were only prevented from intervening by the unofficial assurance of this Government that it would itself strive to help Santo Domingo in her hour of need. In the case of one of these nations, only the actual opening of negotiations to this end by our Government prevented the seizure of territory in Santo Domingo by a European power. Of the debts incurred some were just, while some were not of a character which really renders it obligatory on or proper for Santo Domingo to pay them in full. But she could not pay any of them unless some stability was assured her Government and people.

Accordingly, the Executive Department of our Government negotiated a treaty under which we are to try to help the Dominican people to straighten out their finances. This treaty is pending before the Senate. In the meantime a temporary arrangement has been made which will last until the Senate has had time to take action upon the treaty. Under this arrangement the Dominican Government has appointed Americans to all the important positions in the customs service, and they are seeing to the honest collection of revenues, turning over 45 per cent to the Government for running expenses and putting the other 55 per cent into a safe depository for equitable division in case the treaty shall be ratified, among the various creditors, whether European or American.

The Custom Houses offer well-nigh the only sources of revenue in Santo Domingo, and the different revolutions usually have as their real aim the obtaining of these Custom Houses. The mere fact that the Collectors of Customs are Americans, that they are performing their duties with efficiency and honesty, and that the treaty is pending in the Senate gives a certain moral power to the Government of Santo Domingo which it has not had before. This has completely discouraged all revolutionary movement, while it has already produced such an increase in the revenues that the Government is actually getting more from the 45 per cent that the American Collectors turn over to it than it got formerly when it took the entire revenue. It is enabling the poor, harassed people of Santo Domingo once more to turn their attention to industry and to be free from the cure of interminable revolutionary disturbance. It offers to all bona-fide creditors, American and European, the only really good chance to obtain that to which they are justly entitled, while it in return gives to Santo Domingo the only opportunity of defense against claims which it ought not to pay, for now if it meets the views of the Senate we shall ourselves thoroughly examine all these claims, whether American or foreign, and see that none that are improper are paid. There is, of course, opposition to the treaty from dishonest creditors, foreign and American, and from the professional revolutionists of the island itself. We have already reason to believe that some of the creditors who do not dare expose their claims to honest scrutiny are endeavoring to stir up sedition in the island and opposition to the treaty. In the meantime, I have exercised the authority vested in me by the joint resolution of the Congress to prevent the introduction of arms into the island for revolutionary purposes. . . .

5. MOBILE ADDRESS, 1913[1]

By Woodrow Wilson

EDITORS' NOTE.—In this address to the Southern Commercial Congress on October 27, 1913, President Wilson advocated a policy toward Latin America in sharp contrast with the policy proclaimed by Roosevelt and pursued by our government. Despite his words, President Wilson's administration continued the practice of intervention in the Caribbean.

. . . It is with unaffected pleasure that I find myself here to-day. I once before had the pleasure, in another southern city, of addressing the Southern Commercial Congress. I then spoke of what the future seemed to hold in store for this region, which so many of us love and toward the future of which we all look forward with so much confidence and hope. But another theme directed me here this time. I do not need to speak of the South. She has, perhaps, acquired the gift of speaking for herself. I come because I want to speak of our present and prospective relations with our neighbors to the south. I deemed it a public duty, as well as a personal pleasure, to be here to express for myself and for the Government I represent the welcome we all feel to those who represent the Latin American States.

The future, ladies and gentlemen, is going to be very different for this hemisphere from the past. These States lying to the south of us, which have always been our neighbors, will now be drawn closer to us by innumerable ties, and, I hope, chief of all, by the tie of a common understanding of each other. Interest does not tie nations together; it sometimes separates them. But sympathy and understanding does unite them, and I believe that by the new route that is just about to be opened, while we physically cut two continents asunder, we spiritually unite them. It is a spiritual union which we seek.

I wonder if you realize, I wonder if your imaginations have been filled with the significance of the tides of commerce. Your governor alluded in very fit and striking terms to the voyage of Columbus, but Columbus took his voyage under compulsion of circumstances. Constantinople had been captured by the Turks and all the routes of trade with the East had been suddenly closed. If there was not a way across

1. *Address of President Wilson . . . at Mobile, Alabama . . .* (63d Cong., 1st sess.; Senate Doc. No. 226, Serial No. 6537 [Washington, 1913]), pp. 3–6.

the Atlantic to open those routes again, they were closed forever, and Columbus set out not to discover America, for he did not know that it existed, but to discover the eastern shores of Asia. He set sail for Cathay and stumbled upon America. With that change in the outlook of the world, what happened? England, that had been at the back of Europe with an unknown sea behind her, found that all things had turned as if upon a pivot and she was at the front of Europe; and since then all the tides of energy and enterprise that have issued out of Europe have seemed to be turned westward across the Atlantic. But you will notice that they have turned westward chiefly north of the Equator and that it is the northern half of the globe that has seemed to be filled with the media of intercourse and of sympathy and of common understanding.

Do you not see now what is about to happen? These great tides which have been running along parallels of latitude will now swing southward athwart parallels of latitude, and that opening gate at the Isthmus of Panama will open the world to a commerce that she has not known before, a commerce of intelligence, of thought and sympathy between North and South. The Latin American States, which, to their disadvantage, have been off the main lines, will now be on the main lines. I feel that these gentlemen honoring us with their presence to-day will presently find that some part, at any rate, of the center of gravity of the world has shifted. Do you realize that New York, for example, will be nearer the western coast of South America than she is now to the eastern coast of South America? Do you realize that a line drawn northward parallel with the greater part of the western coast of South America will run only about 150 miles west of New York? The great bulk of South America, if you will look at your globes (not at your Mercator's projection), lies eastward of the continent of North America. You will realize that when

you realize that the canal will run southeast, not southwest, and that when you get into the Pacific you will be farther east than you were when you left the Gulf of Mexico. These things are significant, therefore, of this, that we are closing one chapter in the history of the world and are opening another, of great, unimaginable significance.

There is one peculiarity about the history of the Latin American States which I am sure they are keenly aware of. You hear of "concessions" to foreign capitalists in Latin America. You do not hear of concessions to foreign capitalists in the United States. They are not granted concessions. They are invited to make investments. The work is ours, though they are welcome to invest in it. We do not ask them to supply the capital and do the work. It is an invitation, not a privilege; and States that are obliged, because their territory does not lie within the main field of modern enterprise and action, to grant concessions are in this condition, that foreign interests are apt to dominate their domestic affairs, a condition of affairs always dangerous and apt to become intolerable. What these States are going to see, therefore, is an emancipation from the subordination, which has been inevitable, to foreign enterprise and an assertion of the splendid character which, in spite of these difficulties, they have again and again been able to demonstrate. The dignity, the courage, the self-possession, the self-respect of the Latin American States, their achievements in the face of all these adverse circumstances, deserve nothing but the admiration and applause of the world. They have had harder bargains driven with them in the matter of loans than any other peoples in the world. Interest has been exacted of them that was not exacted of anybody else, because the risk was said to be greater; and then securities were taken that destroyed the risk—an admirable arrangement for those who were forcing the terms! I rejoice in nothing so much as in the prospect that they will now be emancipated from these conditions, and we ought to be the first to take part in assisting in that emancipation. I think some of these gentlemen have already had occasion to bear witness that the Department of State in recent months has tried to serve them in that wise. In the future they will draw closer and closer to us because of circumstances of which I wish to speak with moderation and, I hope, without indiscretion.

We must prove ourselves their friends and champions upon terms of equality and honor. You cannot be friends upon any other terms than upon the terms of equality. You cannot be friends at all except upon the terms of honor. We must show ourselves friends by comprehending their interest whether it squares with our own interest or not. It is a very perilous thing to determine the foreign policy of a nation in the terms of material interest. It not only is unfair to those with whom you are dealing, but it is degrading as regards your own actions.

Comprehension must be the soil in which shall grow all the fruits and friendship, and there is a reason and a compulsion lying behind all this which is dearer than anything else to the thoughtful men of America. I mean the development of constitutional liberty in the world. Human rights, national integrity, and opportunity as against material interests—that, ladies and gentlemen, is the issue which we now have to face. I want to take this occasion to say that the United States will never again seek one additional foot of territory by conquest. She will devote herself to showing that she knows how to make honorable and fruitful use of the territory she has, and she must regard it as one of the duties of friendship to see that from no quarter are material interests made superior to human liberty and national opportunity. I say this, not with a single thought that anyone will gainsay it, but merely to fix in our consciousness what our real relationship with the rest of

America is. It is the relationship of a family of mankind devoted to the development of true constitutional liberty. We know that that is the soil out of which the best enterprise springs. We know that this is a cause which we are making in common with our neighbors, because we have had to make it for ourselves.

Reference has been made here to-day to some of the national problems which confront us as a nation. What is at the heart of all our national problems? It is that we have seen the hand of material interest sometimes about to close upon our dearest rights and possessions. We have seen material interests threaten constitutional freedom in the United States. Therefore we will now know how to sympathize with those in the rest of America who have to contend with such powers, not only within their borders but from outside their borders also.

I know what the response of the thought and heart of America will be to the program I have outlined, because America was created to realize a program like that. This is not America because it is rich. This is not America because it has set up for a great population great opportunities of material prosperity. America is a name which sounds in the ears of men everywhere as a synonym with individual opportunity because a synonym of individual liberty. I would rather belong to a poor nation that was free than to a rich nation that had ceased to be in love with liberty. But we shall not be poor if we love liberty, because the nation that loves liberty truly sets every man free to do his best and be his best, and that means the release of all the splendid energies of a great people who think for themselves. A nation of employees cannot be free any more than a nation of employers can be.

In emphasizing the points which must unite us in sympathy and in spiritual interest with the Latin American peoples we are only emphasizing the points of our own life, and we should prove ourselves untrue to our own traditions if we proved ourselves untrue friends to them. Do not think, therefore, gentlemen, that the questions of the day are mere questions of policy and diplomacy. They are shot through with the principles of life. We dare not turn from the principle that morality and not expediency is the thing that must guide us and that we will never condone iniquity because it is most convenient to do so. It seems to me that this is a day of infinite hope, of confidence in a future greater than the past has been, for I am fain to believe

that in spite of all the things that we wish to correct the nineteenth century that now lies behind us has brought us a long stage toward the time when, slowly ascending the tedious climb that leads to the final uplands, we shall get our ultimate view of the duties of mankind. We have breasted a considerable part of that climb and shall presently—it may be in a generation or two—come out upon those great heights where there shines unobstructed the light of the justice of God.

6. AMERICAN POLICY IN THE CARIBBEAN[1]

By HENRY L. STIMSON

EDITORS' NOTE.—This essay by Secretary of State Stimson is a candid explanation of our policy of intervention in the Caribbean and the reasons which were believed to justify it. Written in 1931, it serves as a summary of a policy which was supplanted in the next administration by the Good-Neighbor policy.

Henry L. Stimson was born in 1867 in New York, educated at Yale and

Harvard, and began law practice in 1891. In 1893 he joined, and in 1897 became a partner in, a law firm of which Elihu Root was the senior member. Stimson, a loyal and active Republican, held many public offices. He was United States district attorney (1906–9), secretary of war (1911–13), governor-general of the Philippines (1927–29), secretary of state (1929–33), and secretary of war (1940–45).

... During the past two years widespread economic depression and consequent unemployment have brought instability and unrest to many of the countries of the Western Hemisphere. Since March 1929, there have been Revolutions in no less than seven Latin American republics, resulting in the forcible overthrow in six of them of the existing governments. These changes, and the armed contests by which some of them have been accompanied, have presented to the State Department of this country a rapid succession of critical problems for decision. It was inevitable in such a situation that criticism

of our decisions should be excited, and it has been.

Therefore, this evening, I shall place before you from the standpoint of the State Department a brief statement of the facts as well as of the underlying principles and reasons upon which some of these recent decisions have been based. In particular, I shall discuss the principles by which we have been guided in the recognition of the new governments which have arisen and also the principles which have underlain our action in the regulation of the sale and transportation of arms and munitions to the countries which have been involved in strife.

As a background for this discussion a brief review of the general policy of the United States towards the other republics

1. Henry L. Stimson, "The United States and Other Latin American Republics," *Foreign Affairs*, IX (1931), i–xiv. By permission of *Foreign Affairs*.

of their hemisphere during the past century is pertinent. That policy, in its general conception, has been a noble one. From the beginning we have made the preservation of individual independence of these nations correspond with our own interest. This was announced in the Monroe Doctrine and has been maintained ever since. That doctrine, far from being an assertion of suzerainty over our sister republics, was an assertion of their individual rights as independent nations. It declared to the world that their independence was so vital to our own safety that we would be willing to fight for it against an aggressive Europe. The Monroe Doctrine was a declaration of the United States versus Europe—not of the United States versus Latin America.

In taking this position in the Western Hemisphere, our policy has coincided with the basic conception of international law, namely, the equal rights of each nation in the family of nations. The law justly regards this conception as the chief protection of weak nations against oppression. Our people led in the recognition of the independence of those countries with an instinctive readiness which was based upon their sympathy with the doctrine upon which that independence rested. In the language of John Quincy Adams, Secretary of State at the time:

the principles upon which the right of independence has been maintained by the South American patriots have been proved not only as identical with those upon which our own independence was asserted and achieved, but as involving the whole theory of government on the emphatically American foundation of the sovereignty of the people and the unalienable rights of men. To a cause reposing upon this basis the people of this country never could be indifferent, and their sympathies have accordingly been, with great unanimity and constancy, enlisted in its favor.

I am not forgetful of the fact that the foreign policy of every nation is devoted primarily to its own interest. It also rises and falls with the character and wisdom of the individuals or groups who from time to time are in power. I do not close my eyes to the occasional dark spots which have been charged to that record, particularly seventy-five or eighty years ago. But the actions which were the foundation for the most serious of these charges were directly attributable to the influence of slavery in this country, then at the height of its political power, and that influence has long since been wiped out in the blood of a great Civil War. They no more reflected the democratic idealism which has generally characterized our foreign policy at its best than the Fugitive Slave Act fairly reflected our domestic social policy.

In spite of these and all other aberrations, it is a very conservative statement to say that the general foreign policy of the United States during the past century toward the republics of Latin America has been characterized by a regard for their rights as independent nations, which, when compared with current international morality in the other hemisphere, has been as unusual as it has been praiseworthy.

People are sometimes prone to forget our long and honorable fulfilment of this policy towards our younger sister nations. It was our action which obtained the withdrawal of French imperialism from Mexico. It was our influence which provided for the return from Great Britain of the Bay Islands to Honduras, and the Mosquito Coast, including Greytown, to Nicaragua. It was our pressure which secured the arbitration of the boundary dispute between Great Britain and Venezuela and which later secured by arbitration the solution of serious disputes between Venezuela, Germany, and Italy. Between the republics themselves, our influence has constantly been exerted for a friendly solution of controversies which might otherwise mar their independent and peaceful intercourse. To speak only of recent matters, I may refer to the long-standing Tacna-Arica dispute between Chile and Peru, and the open clash between Bolivia and Paraguay. During the past seven years our good offices have resulted in the settlement of eight boundary disputes between eleven countries of this hemisphere.

In our successive Pan American conferences, as well as in the Pan American Union, the fundamental rule of equality, which is the mainstay of independence, has been unbroken. Action is taken only by unanimous consent. No majority of states can conclude a minority, even of the smallest and weakest. This is in sharp contrast to the practice which prevailed in the former Concert of Europe, where only the great powers were admitted on a basis of equality. It was also at variance with the original organization of the Covenant of the League of Nations, where it was proposed that a majority of the seats in the Council should be permanently occupied by the Great Powers.

While such recognition of their equal rights and national independence has always been the basic foundation upon which our policy toward these republics has rested, there is another side of the picture which must be borne in mind. This basic principle of equality in international law is an ideal resting upon postulates which are not always and consistently accurate. For independence imposes duties as well as rights. It presupposes ability in the independent nation to fulfil the obligations towards other nations and their nationals which are prescribed and expected to exist in the family of nations. The hundred years which have ensued since the announcement of our policy towards these republics have contained recurring evidence of how slow is the progress of mankind along that difficult highway which leads to national maturity and how difficult is the art of popular self-government. Years and decades of alternations between arbitrary power at one time and outbreaks of violence at another have pointed out again and again how different a matter it is in human affairs to have the vision and to achieve the reality.

Furthermore, the difficulties which have beset the foreign policy of the United States in carrying out these principles cannot be understood without the comprehension of a geographical fact. The very locality where the progress of these republics has been most slow; where the difficulties of race and climate have been greatest; where the recurrence of domestic violence has most frequently resulted in the failure of duty on the part of the republics themselves and the violation of the rights of life and property accorded by international law to foreigners within their territory, has been in Central America, the narrow isthmus which joins the two Americas, and among the islands which intersperse the Caribbean Sea adjacent to that isthmus. That locality has been the one spot external to our shores which nature has decreed to be most vital to our national safety, not to mention our prosperity. It commands the line of the great trade route which joins our eastern and western coasts. Even before human hands had pierced the isthmus with a seagoing canal, that route was vital to our national interest. Since the Panama Canal has become an accomplished fact, it has been not only the vital artery of our coastwise commerce but, as well, the link in our national defense which protects the defensive power of our fleet. One cannot fairly appraise American policy toward Latin America or fully appreciate the standard which it has maintained without taking into consideration all of the elements of which it is the resultant.

Like the rocks which mark the surface of a steady river current, the facts and circumstances which I have outlined have produced ripples in the current of our steady policy towards the Latin American republics. Some of them have resulted in temporary intrusions into the domestic affairs of some of those countries, which our hostile critics have not hesitated to characterize as the manifestation of a selfish American imperialism. I am clear that a calm historical perspective will refute that criticism and will demonstrate that the international practice of this Government in the Western Hemisphere has been asserted with a much readier recognition of the legal rights of all the countries with which we have been in contact than has been the prevalent practice in any other part of the world. The discussion of the particular topics which I am bringing before you this evening will, I hope, help to develop the character, trend, and uniformity of this policy.

The recognition of a new state has been described by writers on international law as the assurance given to it that it will be permitted to hold its place and rank in the character of an independent political organism in the society of nations. The recognition of a new government within a state arises in practice only when a government has been changed or established by revolution or by a *coup d'état*. No question of recognition normally arises, for example, when a king dies and his heir succeeds to the throne, or where as the result of an election in a republic a new chief executive constitutionally assumes office. The practice of this country as to the recognition of new governments has been substantially uniform from the days of the administration of Secretary of State Jefferson in 1792 to the days of Secretary of State Bryan in 1913. There were certain slight departures from this policy during the Civil War, but they were manifestly due to the exigencies of warfare and were abandoned immediately afterwards. This general policy, as thus observed, was to base the act of recognition not upon the question of the constitutional legitimacy of the new government but upon its *de facto* capacity to fulfil its obligations as a member of the family of nations. This country recognized the right of other nations to regulate their own internal affairs of government and disclaimed any attempt to base its recognition upon the correctness of their constitutional action.

Said Mr. Jefferson in 1792:

We certainly cannot deny to other nations that principle whereon our own Government is founded, that every nation has a right to govern itself internally under what forms it pleases, and to change these forms at its own will; and externally to transact business with other nations through whatever organ it chooses, whether that be a king, convention, assembly, committee, president, or whatever it be.

In these essentials our practice corresponded with the practice of the other nations of the world.

The particular considerations upon which our action was regularly based were well stated by Mr. Adee, long the trusted Assistant Secretary of State of this Government, as follows:

Ever since the American Revolution entrance upon diplomatic intercourse with foreign states has been *de facto*, dependent upon the existence of three conditions of fact: the control of the administrative machinery of the state; the general acquiescence of its people; and the ability and willingness of their government to discharge international and conventional obligations. The form of government has not been a conditional factor in such recognition; in other words, the *de jure* element of legitimacy of title has been left aside.

With the advent of President Wilson's administration this policy of over a century was radically departed from in respect to the Republic of Mexico, and, by a public declaration on March 11, 1913, it was announced that

Coöperation [with our sister republics of Central and South America] is possible only when supported at every turn by the orderly processes of just government based upon law, not upon arbitrary or irregular force. We hold, as I am sure that all thoughtful leaders of republican government everywhere hold, that just government rests always upon the consent of the governed, and that there can be no freedom without order based upon law and upon the public conscience and approval. We shall look to make these principles the basis of mutual intercourse, respect, and helpfulness between our sister republics and ourselves.

Mr. Wilson's government sought to put this new policy into effect in respect to the recognition of the then Government of Mexico held by President Victoriano Huerta. Although Huerta's government was in *de facto* possession, Mr. Wilson refused to recognize it, and he sought through the influence and pressure of his great office to force it from power. Armed conflict followed with the forces of Mexico, and disturbed relations between us and that republic lasted until a comparatively few years ago.

In his sympathy for the development of free constitutional institutions among the people of our Latin American neighbors, Mr. Wilson did not differ from the feelings of the great mass of his countrymen in the United States, including Mr. Jefferson and Mr. Adams, whose statements I have quoted; but he differed from the practice of his predecessors in seeking actively to propagate these institutions in a foreign country by the direct influence of this Government and to do this against the desire of the authorities and people of Mexico.

The present administration has declined to follow the policy of Mr. Wilson and has followed consistently the former practice of this Government since the days of Jefferson. As soon as it was reported to us, through our diplomatic representatives, that the new governments in Bolivia, Peru, Argentina, Brazil, and Panama were in control of the administrative machinery of the state, with the apparent general acquiescence of their people, and that they were willing and apparently able to discharge their international and conventional obligations, they were recognized by our Government. And, in view of the economic depression, with the consequent need for prompt measures of financial stabilization, we did this with as little delay as possible in order to give those sorely pressed countries the quickest possible opportunities for recovering their economic poise.

Such has been our policy in all cases where international practice was not affected or controlled by preëxisting treaty. In the five republics of Central America, Guatemala, Honduras, Salvador, Nicaragua, and Costa Rica, however, an entirely different situation exists from that normally presented under international law and practice. As I have already pointed out, those countries geographically have for a century been the focus of the greatest difficulties and the most frequent disturbances in their earnest course towards competent maturity in the discharge of their international obligations. Until some two decades ago, war within and without was their frequent portion. No administration of their government was long safe from revolutionary attack instigated either by factions of its own citizens or by the machinations of another one of the five republics. Free elections, the cornerstone upon which our own democracy rests, had been practically unknown during the entire period. In 1907 a period of strife, involving four of the five republics, had lasted almost without interruption for several years. In that year, on the joint suggestion and mediation of the Governments of the United States and Mexico, the five republics met for the purpose of considering methods intended to mitigate and, if possible, terminate the intolerable situation. By one of the conventions which they then adopted, the five republics agreed with one another as follows:

The Governments of the high contracting parties shall not recognize any other government which may come into power in any of the five republics as a consequence of a *coup d'état*, or of a revolution against the recognized government, so long as the freely elected representatives of the people thereof have not constitutionally reorganized the country.

Sixteen years later, in 1923, the same five republics, evidently satisfied with the principle they had thus adopted and desiring to reinforce it and prevent any future evasions of that principle, met again, reënacted the same covenant, and further promised each other that even after a revolutionary government had been constitutionally reorganized by the representatives of the people, they would not recognize it if its president should have been a leader in the preceding revolution or related to such a leader by blood or marriage, or if he should have been a cabinet officer or held some high military command during the accomplishment of the revolution. Some four months thereafter, our own Government, on the invitation of these republics, who had conducted their meeting in Washington, announced, through Secretary Hughes, that the United States would in its future dealings with those republics follow out the same principle which they had thus established in their treaty. Since that time we have consistently adhered to this policy in respect to those five republics.

We followed that policy in Guatemala in the case of a recent revolution in which some fifty-seven people were killed. General Orellano, the leader of the revolt, set himself up as the provisional president of that republic on December 16, 1930. On December 22, 1930, we notified him that in accordance with the policy established by the 1923 treaty he would not be recognized by us. No recognition was granted him by any of the other four republics. Following this, he tendered his resignation and retired from office; and on January 2, 1931, through the constitutional forms provided in the Guatemalan Constitution, Señor Reina Andrade was chosen provisional president by the Guatemalan Congress and immediately called a new election for a permanent president. Thereupon this country and the other four republics recognized the government of Señor Reina Andrade.

Since the adoption by Secretary Hughes, in 1923, of the policy of recognition agreed upon by the five republics in their convention, not one single revolutionary government has been able to maintain itself in any of those five republics. Twice, once in Nicaragua and once in the case of Guatemala, just described, a revolutionary leader has succeeded in grasping the reins of government for a brief period. But in each case the failure to obtain recognition has resulted in his prompt resignation, on account of his inability to borrow money in the international markets. Several times within the same period a contemplated revolution has been abandoned by its conspirators on the simple reminder by a minister from this country or one of the other republics that, even if they were successful, their government would not be recognized; and undoubtedly in many more cases has the knowledge of the existence of the policy prevented even the preparation for a revolution or *coup d'état*. In every one of these cases the other four republics have made common cause in the efforts of the United States to carry out their policy and maintain stability. When one compares this record with the blood stained history of Central America before the adoption of the treaty of 1923, I think that no impartial student can avoid the conclusion that the treaty and the policy which it has established in that locality has been productive of very great good. . . .

I will now pass to the subject of the policy of this Government in respect to the export of arms and munitions to countries which are engaged in civil strife. Twice during the present Administration we have had to make important decisions and take important action in respect to this subject. The first of these occasions was in March, 1929, when a military insurrection broke out in the Republic of Mexico. This insurrection was of serious nature and extent. It involved disturbances in many of the Mexican provinces and much fighting and bloodshed. Acting under a joint resolution of our Congress, adopted in 1922, this Government maintained an embargo upon the exportation of all arms and munitions which might reach the rebels. At the same time, it permitted the sale and itself sold arms and ammunition to the established government of Mexico, with which we were then and had been for a number of years in diplomatic relations. In about three months the insurrection was suppressed, and I think it can be fairly said that it is due in no slight degree to our action in this matter that the feelings of hostility on the part of Mexico to the United States which had existed ever since the intervention of President Wilson against Huerta in 1913 were finally ended and the relations of the two countries became friendly and cordial. . . .

Under the law of nations the duty of neutrality does not arise until the insurgents have assumed the status of a belligerent power between whom and the mother country other governments must maintain impartiality. This occurs when a condition of belligerency is recognized either by the parent state itself or by the governments of other nations. Such a situation arose in our Civil War when the Confederate States, having occupied exclusively a portion of the territory of the United States and having set up their own

capital at Richmond, were recognized as belligerents by the nations of Europe. . . .

Until belligerency is recognized and the duty of neutrality arises, all the humane predispositions towards stability of government, the preservation of international amity, and the protection of established intercourse between nations are in favor of the existing government. This is particularly the case in countries where civil strife has been as frequent, as personal, and as disastrous as it has been in some sections of Central and South America during the past century. The law of nations is not static. It grows and develops with the experience of mankind, and its development follows that same line of human predispositions and experiences to which I have referred.

7. U.S. AGAINST US[1]

By Luis Quintanilla

EDITORS' NOTE.—The preceding readings of this section are concerned with our policy toward the Caribbean from the point of view of the interests of the United States. The subject appears in a new light when it is seen from the viewpoint of an inhabitant of the region. Luis Quintanilla, Mexican diplomat and writer, was born in 1900 in Paris and educated at the Sorbonne, where he received both the B.S. and the M.A. degrees. He spent much of his time from 1922 to 1945 in the diplo-

matic service of the Republic of Mexico in several Latin-American states, France, and the United States, and as ambassador to Russia (1943–45). He has taught languages and political science at both the University of Mexico and the George Washington University, Washington, D.C. In addition to *A Latin American Speaks*, from which this reading is taken, he has written books on aviation, radio, the theater, and the controversy over the church in Mexico.

At the time of its enunciation, the Monroe Doctrine was intended to be, essentially, a policy toward Europe; not a policy for the Hemisphere. It was a toothless warning indeed, but one definitely aimed at Europe. As such, there is nothing that

we can hold against it. To reject its original intention would be tantamount to accepting the right of Europe to meddle with the nations of our Hemisphere: and that, no Latin American wants.

It is only by virtue of later interpretations—or rather "misinterpretations"—that the momentous Message was gradually fashioned into a Machiavellian policy

1. Luis Quintanilla, *A Latin American Speaks* (New York, 1943), pp. 111–19, 122–24, 129–30. Copyright 1943 by the Macmillan Company and used with their permission.

for *intra*-Hemisphere consumption. From a candid but commendable United States gesture against European interference, the Doctrine was turned into a ruthless axiom, utilized by Washington administrations to suit the interests of what is known as "*Yankee Imperialism.*" Because the Doctrine—certainly through no fault of its victims—was perverted to the point of being invoked as a justification for attacks against the sovereignty of the nations which it claimed to protect, it bulks large today as a stumbling block in the way of inter-American relations. "Paramount Interests," "Manifest Destiny," "Big-Stick Policy," "Watchful Waiting," "Dollar Diplomacy," "Paternalism," "Protectionism"—in short, "Yankee Imperialism"—those slogans have become irrevocably connected, in the minds of Latin Americans, with the two words, "*Monroe Doctrine.*"

Yes, it may be said that historically there are *two* Monroe Doctrines: the one, promulgated by the President; and the other, the distorted Doctrine of the Corollaries. But the authentic one has been pushed into the background. Today people have not in mind the mild offering of the fifth President of the United States, but the subsequent concoction into which entered all the imperialistic ingredients added by more voracious occupants of the White House, among whom Theodore Roosevelt —twenty-sixth President of the United States of America—stands out conspicuously.

"The Monroe Doctrine, first enunciated by President Monroe in 1823," writes Professor Schuman, "was a warning to the European powers to keep out of the American Hemisphere and, by implications and successive reinterpretations, an assertion of the hegemony of the United States over the American continents." That is precisely the point! The Doctrine has come to mean "an assertion of the hegemony of the United States over the American continents": a policy of bloody military occu-

pation and outright diplomatic intervention.

Practically any Spanish American could put forward an impressive list of perfectly legitimate reasons why he rejects vehemently the Monroe Doctrine. A striking sample of genuine Latin American attitude in this respect, can be found in Gaston Nerval's book, significantly entitled *Autopsy of the Monroe Doctrine*.

"Autopsy" is perhaps wishful thinking. The *original* Doctrine is not dead. The Axis has given it a shot in the arm. To handle the *original* Doctrine as if it were dead would be not "autopsy" but vivisection. It is not dead, yet the weight of its additions places it beyond redemption. The Corollaries have become an intrinsic part of it. We cannot and must not forget them. No historical or diplomatic surgeon could sever the Doctrine from the acts of aggression committed in its name; not even Professor Perkins, family doctor of Monroe's troublesome child, nor official interpreter Reuben Clark and his authoritative Memorandum. After all, a political Doctrine should not be judged by its intent only, but also by its results. Scores of charges can be leveled at the Monroe Doctrine by a Latin American. For the sake of clearness, I will limit the counts of my indictment to five:

1) It is *unilateral*.
2) It proved *inefficient*.
3) It was *perverted*.
4) It is *unpopular*.
5) It has become *outmoded*.

1) There can be no argument concerning the first count. Practically all historians, Anglo-Saxon as well as Latin, agree on that. Even Dr. Perkins writes: "The Monroe Doctrine was not, and was not intended to be, anything else than a unilateral declaration of policy. From that day to this American statesmen have insisted upon its purely American character, upon the right of the United States to interpret it in its own fashion, and on the basis of its own interests." That point is so incontro-

vertible that we find, for once, Gaston Nerval and Dr. Perkins completely in accord. Nerval writes: "If there is anything at all upon which the statesmen of the United States, from Monroe to our day, agree in their views of the Monroe Doctrine, it is on the unilateral, nationalistic nature of the Doctrine." Even so unbiased a critic as Stephen Duggan acknowledges that "the Monroe Doctrine is a unilateral statement made by, maintained by, and interpreted by, the United States alone, without consultation with any other country." Also Reuben Clark, most unbiased *official* United States interpreter, writes: "The United States determines *when* and *if* the principles of the Doctrine are violated, and when and if violation is threatened. We *alone* determine what measures, if any, shall be taken to vindicate the principles of the Doctrine, and *we* of necessity determine when the principles have been vindicated. No *other* power in the world has *any* relationship to, or voice in, the implementing of the principles which the Doctrine contains. It is *our* Doctrine, to be by *us* invoked and sustained, held in abeyance, or abandoned as *our* high international policy or vital national interest shall seem to *us*, and to *us alone*, to demand." Here again, I have italicized some words to bring out the point. There is nothing the matter with a *unilateral* policy. But its interpreters have no right to make it multilateral. The Monroe Doctrine was never meant to be anything but a one-sided policy. To pretend otherwise, is to commit historical heresy. It is not saving the Monroe Doctrine but rather confessing, by implication, that it has ceased to exist.

The Doctrine was a *monologue*, not a dialogue. It assumed, after the Theodore Roosevelt Corollary, an order of things entirely created and maintained by a self-appointed *guardian;* not one agreed to by equal partners. Why speak of "Americanization" or "continentalization"? Whatever rabbits Monroeist magicians pull out of their hats, that thing called Pan Americanism will never come out of it!

The Doctrine was unilateral not only in its proclamation, definition, and application, but also in its original motive, which was not the safety of the Hemisphere, but the security of the United States. So well known an authority as Professor Charles Edward Chapman, states: "The benevolent feature never was, and is not, the primary purpose of the doctrine. Its fundamental idea has always been *the security of the United States*. In this all-important respect, the Monroe Doctrine has not 'changed,' as so often alleged." The security of the United States: again, there is nothing the matter with that. Pan Americanism also includes it—but does not stop there. It cares not only for the security of the United States but for that of all and each of the American Republics. *Good-Neighbor Pan Americanism is a joint enterprise freely undertaken by partners with equal rights and mutual obligations.* And that is precisely what the Monroe Doctrine is not!

2) *The Doctrine proved inefficient.* To be accurate, one should say that it was created impotent. It was the expression of a wish: to remove from the Western Hemisphere the threat of European military or political interference. But there was never mention of specific measures to be taken, should that wish go unheeded. Every North American statesman made it clear that the Doctrine never implied the slightest pledge by the United States actually to fight for the sovereignty of any American Republic. The man who as Secretary of State is credited with the drafting of the Message read by President Monroe to Congress—John Quincy Adams—said in a Message to the Senate December 26, 1825, after he had become President of his country: "An agreement between all the parties represented at the meeting that each will guard *by its own means* against the establishment of any future European colony within its border may be found advisable. This was more than two years since announced by my predecessor." It could not be clearer: *"each by its own means."* From

the outset and from the lips of the statesmen who played the principal parts in the elaboration of the Doctrine, the world was advised that it was up to every country by its own means to uphold Monroe's recommendation, with the inference that, should any European nation violate such recommendation, the United States would not consider itself obligated to act; nor, of course, the other American republics. The Monroe Doctrine was too platonic to be effective. Later on, President Adams' Secretary of State, Henry Clay, in his instructions to the United States delegates—who did not reach Panama in time for Bolivar's Congress—made a similar statement: "The President wishes you to propose a joint declaration of the several American states, each, however, acting for and binding only itself, that within the limits of their respective territories no new European colony will hereafter be allowed to be established." *Each* by its *own* territory, binding only *itself:* that is the only type of Pan Americanism which legitimately could be built on the foundation of the real Monroe Doctrine. That, again, is as different from our modern concept of Pan Americanism as anything we can think of. A policy along those lines is precisely what our Pan Americanism does not want to be! In the same document, Secretary Clay goes further: "It is not intended to commit the parties . . . to the support of the particular boundaries . . . nor is it proposed to commit them to a *joint* resistance against any future attempt to plant a new European colony." Here again we find the genuine expression of what Monroe's Message originally meant: a commendable but timid admonition. When there is no sanction, any transgressor is willing to take the risk. To consider European infringements as "the manifestation of an unfriendly disposition toward the United States," was not enough. Monroe did not say "act of hostility" but simply "unfriendly disposition." Little wonder that European interventions, of all kinds, took place from 1823 on.

The Doctrine was appealed to in vain by some Latin American countries because of optimistic misinterpretations (improving the essence of the Message, not perverting it). The Doctrine did not bind the United States to any joint resistance against Europe. It never placed upon the United States the heavy burden of protecting the Hemisphere. The Corollaries of the Doctrine tended in that direction, but Monroe and the original Monroeists took pains to make it clear that it made no promise as to the international action of the United States.

It was appealed to in vain by Colombia in 1824; by Venezuela, Peru, and Ecuador, in 1846; by Nicaragua in 1848; again by Nicaragua, plus Honduras and El Salvador in 1849; by Mexico in 1862; by Venezuela, on five occasions (1876, 1880, 1881, 1884, 1887); by the Dominican Republic in 1905; and by Argentina in 1902–1903. Although impressive, this record is far from complete. I quote from Professor Perkins: "We must not imagine, however, that, speaking broadly, the United States, in the period with which we are dealing, pursued a consistent policy looking to the discouragement of a show of force against American republics by the states of the Old World. The recurrent chastisement of the Haitians, for example, never seems to have been regarded with much emotion in Washington. France in 1869, Spain in 1871, Germany in 1872, Great Britain in 1877, France, Spain, and Great Britain in concert in 1883, Russia in 1885, Great Britain again in 1887, resorted to force or the threat of force against the black politicians of Port-au-Prince without a word of protest from the State Department. The British in 1874, the Germans in 1878, the French in 1882, made minatory gestures against the Nicaraguans without arousing any concern in the United States. The Italians had a short-lived brawl with Colombia in 1886 which awakened no mention of the Monroe Doctrine. The French used coercive measures against the Dominican Republic in 1893 without the lifting of a hand at Washington." There were other violations, treated in detail by Nerval in a chapter significantly entitled "Violations Wholesale":

"In 1833, the United States did not prevent, nor even oppose, the seizure of the Argentine Islas Malvinas, or Falkland Islands, by Great Britain." Two years later, "the United States failed to support the government of Central America against the colonization which England was carrying on in Honduras Bay." "In 1838 France, and in 1845 France and England jointly, intervened by armed force in the Rio de la Plata." "New British encroachments on territory of Central America occurred in 1838, when the Bay Islands, of which the most important was Ruatán, were seized by the authorities of British Honduras." "In 1837, a British squadron, in reprisal for alleged indignities heaped upon a British consul, proclaimed the closing of the ports of New Granada (Colombia) and actually blockaded the main port of Cartagena." In 1838 again French naval forces blockaded the Mexican port of Veracruz, "in order to insure the collection of private claims of French citizens from the Mexican government." In 1850 the United States and Great Britain signed the Clayton-Bulwer treaty which "provided for construction of a ship canal from the Atlantic to the Pacific Ocean by way of the San Juan River and the lakes of Managua and Nicaragua." "Thus," writes Nerval, "intervention by a European power in Latin America was not only accepted, but, in this case, invited and solemnly sanctioned by the country which had given the Monroe Doctrine to the world." In the same year "the government of the United States, after confidential conversations in Washington between the Secretary of State and the British and French Ministers, agreed to join France and England in a mediation to bring about the conclusion of the war between the Dominican Republic and Haiti." "In 1861, Spain, following several years of open intermeddling with the domestic affairs of

the Dominican Republic, finally proclaimed its annexation to the Spanish Crown." "In 1864, the greatest violation of the Monroe Doctrine, and by far the most famous one, was consummated. This was the overthrow of the republican form of government in Mexico by French troops, and the enthronement of the Archduke Maximilian of Austria as the Emperor of Mexico."

These are the ten major violations of the original Monroe Doctrine. Nerval mentions "secondary" violations: "the invitation by the United States to England and France, in 1862, to aid in insuring the free transit through the Panama Isthmus and in restoring internal order in Colombia; the seizure of the Chincha Islands by Spain as a reprisal against the Peruvian government, in 1864; the bombardment of Valparaiso, major Chilean port, by Spanish naval forces, in 1866, as a coercive measure; the collective intervention of the United States and certain European powers, suggested by the former though never materialized, during the Cuban insurrection of 1868–78; the retrocession of the Island of St. Bartholomew by Sweden to France, in 1877; the refusal of the United States to prevent German military action against Haiti, in the controversy of 1897; etc., etc." . . .

3) *The Doctrine was perverted.* Originally it meant, "America not for Europe," but the Corollaries made it say, "America for the U.S.A." Cuba, Puerto Rico, Panama, the Dominican Republic, Haiti, Nicaragua —six United States "protectorates" in less than fifteen years. Outright interventions, with Marines landing, occupying territories, setting up governments and running the country: in Cuba from 1898 to 1903, then from 1906 to 1909, again in 1912, and finally from 1917 to 1922; in the Dominican Republic, from 1916 to 1924; in Nicaragua, from 1912 to 1933, practically without interruption; in Haiti, from 1915 to 1934. We can mention these facts because they represent a policy which belongs to the past. We *must* mention them

because, since they cannot be forgotten, we expect the United States at least to admit them and never to minimize their historical significance. Wrongs belong to the past only when you are able to talk about them and still be friends. That is precisely our attitude today: do not keep wrongs bottled up inside. Friendship is a positive, driving force. Frustrated rancor cannot be taken for love. Not to fear is necessary but not sufficient. Friendship is not restraint but forward impulse.

The Monroe Doctrine is guilty—not only because it did not prevent but because it even was invoked to justify manifestations of imperialism. Rather, not the original Message, but its inglorious additions. There are a good many Corollaries. I will mention the most significant ones:

In 1825, Secretary of State Clay declared that the United States could not consent to the occupation of Cuba and Puerto Rico, by "any other power than Spain." The idea was good, as is often the case in the history of Monroe's Problem Doctrine. It is better known today as the "No transfer" principle, reiterated by Van Buren in 1829, Forsyth in 1840, Webster in 1843, and consecrated at the Habana 1940 Conference. Yet the timely warning did not apply to the United States, which, for too many years, made of Cuba a virtual Protectorate. Until 1936, when Franklin D. Roosevelt's Administration renounced the right of intervention granted to its country by the well known Platt Amendment, Cuba was freed from Spain but remained subjugated to the U.S.A.

In 1845, President Polk—of whom Abraham Lincoln said, "He feels the blood of this [Mexican] war, like the blood of Abel crying to heaven against him"— added his Corollary, intended to justify the annexation of Texas. Said he: "We can never consent that European powers shall interfere to prevent such a union [of Texas and the United States] because it might disturb the 'balance of power,' which they [European countries] may desire to maintain upon this continent." So, having promulgated the Doctrine to redress and maintain the balance of power *in Europe*, a North American President claimed that Europe, in turn, had no right to be concerned over changes in the balance of power of the Western Hemisphere. . . .

The Monroe Doctrine, with its imperialistic connotations, is loaded with the kind of explosive that endangers the Pan American structure. That explains why United States Presidents sincerely concerned with their neighbors' feelings, from Abraham Lincoln to Franklin D. Roosevelt, have found no need to mention the Monroe Doctrine. Not even during the meeting of foreign ministers of the Americas, held at Rio de Janeiro in January, 1942, did the skillful United States delegate, Sumner Welles, mention the name of that unhappy Doctrine which for the last fifty years has been the greatest stumbling block in the way of genuine inter-Americanism. And there is no doubt that the situation discussed at the Rio Conference was one which, had the Message of 1823 not been perverted, would have fallen within the jurisdiction of the original Doctrine. But, right or wrong, the delegates knew that the emotional connotations of the words "Monroe Doctrine" were such that they could not be pronounced without stirring up legitimate ill feelings. *The moment Monroe's distorted shadow enters a Pan American Conference, the Good Neighbors disband.* The silence made around the Monroe Doctrine at the historical meeting at Rio is more eloquent than any indictment ever uttered against it.

5) Finally, in the light of authentic, genuine Pan Americanism *à la* Bolivar or *à la* F. D. Roosevelt, it is obvious that the Doctrine seems completely *outmoded*. The days in which a single country—however powerful—could claim the exclusive right to behave, on the world stage, as a "rugged individualist," are gone forever. Ask Napoleon, ask the Kaiser, or ask Hitler! Civilized order is a joint enterprise, freely accepted by all partners. Mankind does not allow gangsters, be they individuals or na-

tions. Order was established, first among the members of the family, then among the residents of the community, later among the citizens of a nation. Finally the day is near when a cooperative international order will be established among the nations of the earth. That order, whether local or national, continental or international, can be conceived only as a joint enterprise. America was the first continent in history to struggle for the establishment of such order. There can be no room in this continent for a doctrine which, even at its best

and in its original intention, rests essentially on the arbitrary decision of one self-appointed "leader." The hour of selfish nationalism is past. There is no room for anarchy in organized society. Because the welfare of the many must prevail over that of the few, Monroeist Pan Americanism has been gradually but irrevocably displaced by democratic Pan Americanism.

The Monroe Doctrine may not be dead, but there is little use for it today. And there certainly will be less room for it in the world of tomorrow.

SECTION D. THE FIRST WORLD WAR

1. APPEAL FOR NEUTRALITY, 1914[1]

By Woodrow Wilson

EDITORS' NOTE.—The first official response of this country to World War I was this reaffirmation of the traditional neutrality of the United States toward the politics and wars of Europe. The assumption underlying the policy was candidly revealed in the sentence: "The effect of the war upon the United States will depend upon what American citizens say and do." The adequacy of this assumption should be tested by reading President Wilson's war message of 1917.

My Fellow Countrymen:

I suppose that every thoughtful man in America has asked himself, during these last troubled weeks, what influence the European war may exert upon the United States, and I take the liberty of addressing a few words to you in order to point out that it is entirely within our own choice what its effects upon us will be and to urge very earnestly upon you the sort of speech and conduct which will best safeguard the Nation against distress and disaster.

The effect of the war upon the United States will depend upon what American citizens say and do. Every man who really loves America will act and speak in the true spirit of neutrality, which is the spirit of impartiality and fairness and friendliness to all concerned. The spirit of the Nation in this critical matter will be determined largely by what individuals and society and those gathered in public meetings do and say, upon what newspapers and magazines contain, upon what ministers utter in their pulpits, and men proclaim as their opinions on the street.

The people of the United States are drawn from many nations, and chiefly

1. Woodrow Wilson, *Appeal for Neutrality* (63d Cong., 2d sess.; Senate Doc. No. 566; Serial No. 6596 [Washington, 1914]), pp. 3–4.

from the nations now at war. It is natural and inevitable that there should be the utmost variety of sympathy and desire among them with regard to the issues and circumstances of the conflict. Some will wish one nation, others another, to succeed in the momentous struggle. It will be easy to excite passion and difficult to allay it. Those responsible for exciting it will assume a heavy responsibility, responsibility for no less a thing than that the people of the United States, whose love of their country and whose loyalty to its Government should unite them as Americans all, bound in honor and affection to think first of her and her interests, may be divided in camps of hostile opinion, hot against each other, involved in the war itself in impulse and opinion if not in action.

Such divisions among us would be fatal to our peace of mind and might seriously stand in the way of the proper performance of our duty as the one great nation at peace, the one people holding itself ready to play a part of impartial mediation and speak the counsels of peace and accommodation, not as a partisan, but as a friend.

I venture, therefore, my fellow countrymen, to speak a solemn word of warning to you against that deepest, most subtle, most essential breach of neutrality which may spring out of partisanship, out of passionately taking sides. The United States must be neutral in fact as well as in name during these days that are to try men's souls. We must be impartial in thought as well as in action, must put a curb upon our sentiments as well as upon every transaction that might be construed as a preference of one party to the struggle before another.

My thought is of America. I am speaking, I feel sure, the earnest wish and purpose of every thoughtful American that this great country of ours, which is, of course, the first in our thoughts and in our hearts, should show herself in this time of peculiar trial a Nation fit beyond others to exhibit the fine poise of undisturbed judgment, the dignity of self-control, the efficiency of dispassionate action; a Nation that neither sits in judgment upon others nor is disturbed in her own counsels and which keeps herself fit and free to do what is honest and disinterested and truly serviceable for the peace of the world.

Shall we not resolve to put upon ourselves the restraints which will bring to our people the happiness and the great and lasting influence for peace we covet for them?

2. WAR MESSAGE, 1917[1]

By Woodrow Wilson

EDITORS' NOTE.—In contrast to the neutrality of 1914, the United States in 1917 had clearly linked its sympathy and interest with the Allied Powers. At the same time the United States insisted upon its neutral rights on the seas and defined unrestricted submarine warfare by the Germans as an inhumane act of war against us. The German Imperial War Council on January 9, 1917, decided to resume the submarine attacks as the only means left to break the stalemate on the Western Front. To the statement of the Foreign Office that such action would bring the United States into the war against Germany, Admiral Von Tirpitz replied that the submarines would defeat the Allies before the United States would have time enough to make any significant contribution to the struggle. The German decision was communicated to the United States on February 1, 1917; diplomatic relations were broken on February 3; when several United States ships had been attacked by German submarines, President Wilson requested a declaration of war. On the morning of April 6 the war resolution was passed by a vote of 86 to 6 in the Senate and 373 to 50 in the House.

Gentlemen of the Congress:

I have called the Congress into extraordinary session because there are serious, very serious, choices of policy to be made, and made immediately, which it was neither right nor constitutionally permissible that I should assume the responsibility of making.

1. Woodrow Wilson, *War Message* (65th Cong., 1st sess.; Senate Doc. No. 5, Serial No. 7264 [Washington, 1917]), pp. 3–8.

On the third of February last I officially laid before you the extraordinary announcement of the Imperial German Government that on and after the first day of February it was its purpose to put aside all restraints of law or of humanity and use its submarines to sink every vessel that sought to approach either the ports of Great Britain and Ireland or the western coasts of Europe or any of the ports controlled by the enemies of Germany within the Mediterranean. That had seemed to be the object of the German submarine warfare earlier in the war, but since April of last year the Imperial Government had somewhat restrained the commanders of its undersea craft in conformity with its promise then given to us that passenger boats should not be sunk and that due warning would be given to all other vessels which its submarines might seek to destroy, when no resistance was offered or escape attempted, and care taken that their crews were given at least a fair chance to save their lives in their open boats. The precautions taken were meagre and haphazard enough, as was proved in distressing instance after instance in the progress of the cruel and unmanly business, but a certain degree of restraint was observed. The new policy has swept every restriction aside. Vessels of every kind, whatever their flag, their character, their cargo, their destination, their errand, have been ruthlessly sent to the bottom without warning and without thought of help or mercy for those on board, the vessels of friendly neutrals along with those of belligerents. Even hospital ships and ships carrying relief to the sorely bereaved and stricken people of Belgium, though the latter were provided with safe conduct through the proscribed areas by the German Government itself and were distinguished by unmistakable marks of identity, have been sunk with the same reckless lack of compassion or of principle.

I was for a little while unable to believe that such things would in fact be done by any government that had hitherto subscribed to the humane practices of civilized nations. International law had its origin in the attempt to set up some law which would be respected and observed upon the seas, where no nation had right of dominion and where lay the free highways of the world. By painful stage after stage has that law been built up, with meagre enough results, indeed, after all was accomplished that could be accomplished, but always

with a clear view, at least, of what the heart and conscience of mankind demanded. This minimum of right the German Government has swept aside under the plea of retaliation and necessity and because it had no weapons which it could use at sea except these which it is impossible to employ as it is employing them without throwing to the winds all scruples of humanity or of respect for the understandings that were supposed to underlie the intercourse of the world. I am not now thinking of the loss of property involved, immense and serious as that is, but only of the wanton and wholesale destruction of the lives of non-combatants, men, women, and children, engaged in pursuits which have always, even in the darkest periods of modern history, been deemed innocent and legitimate. Property can be paid for; the lives of peaceful and innocent people cannot be. The present German submarine warfare against commerce is a warfare against mankind.

It is a war against all nations. American ships have been sunk, American lives taken, in ways which it has stirred us very deeply to learn of, but the ships and people of other neutral and friendly nations have been sunk and overwhelmed in the waters in the same way. There has been no discrimination. The challenge is to all mankind. Each nation must decide for itself how it will meet it. The choice we make for ourselves must be made with a moderation of counsel and a temperateness of judgment befitting our character and our motives as a nation. We must put excited feeling away. Our motive will not be revenge or the victorious assertion of the physical might of the nation, but only the vindication of right, of human right, of which we are only a single champion.

When I addressed the Congress on the twenty-sixth of February last I thought that it would suffice to assert our neutral rights with arms, our right to use the seas against unlawful interference, our right to keep our people safe against unlawful violence. But armed neutrality, it now appears, is impracticable. Because submarines are in effect outlaws when used as the German submarines have been used against merchant shipping, it is impossible to defend ships against their attacks as the law of nations has assumed that merchantmen would defend themselves against privateers or cruisers, visible craft giving chase upon the open sea. It is common prudence in such circumstances, grim necessity indeed, to endeavour to destroy them before they have shown their own intention. They must be dealt with upon sight, if dealt with at all. The German Government denies the right of neutrals to use arms at all within the areas of the sea which it has proscribed, even in the defense of rights which no modern publicist has ever before questioned their right to defend. The intimation is conveyed that the armed guards which we have placed on our merchant ships will be treated as beyond the pale of law and subject to be dealt with as pirates would be. Armed neutrality is ineffectual enough at best; in such circumstances and in the face of such pretensions it is worse than ineffectual: it is likely only to produce what it was meant to prevent; it is practically certain to draw us into the war without either the rights or the effectiveness of belligerents. There is one choice we cannot make, we are incapable of making: we will not choose the path of submission and suffer the most sacred rights of our nation and our people to be ignored or violated. The wrongs against which we now array ourselves are no common wrongs; they cut to the very roots of human life.

With a profound sense of the solemn and even tragical character of the step I am taking and of the grave responsibilities which it involves, but in unhesitating obedience to what I deem my constitutional duty, I advise that the Congress declare the recent course of the Imperial German Government to be in fact nothing less than war against the government and people of the United States; that it formally accept the status of belligerent which has thus been thrust upon it; and that it take immediate steps not only to put the country in a more thorough state of defense but also to exert all its power and employ all its resources to bring the Government of the German Empire to terms and end the war.

What this will involve is clear. It will involve the utmost practicable cooperation in counsel and action with the governments now at war with Germany, and, as incident to that, the extension to those governments of the most liberal financial credits, in order that our resources may so far as possible be added to theirs. It will involve the organization and mobilization of all the material resources of the country to supply the materials of war and serve the incidental needs of the nation in the most abundant and yet the most economical and efficient way possible. It will involve the immediate full equipment of the navy in all respects but particularly in supplying it with the best means of dealing with the enemy's submarines. It will involve the immediate addition to the armed forces of the United States already provided for by law in case of war at least five hundred thousand men, who should, in my opinion, be chosen upon the principle of universal liability to service, and also the authorization of subsequent additional increments of equal force so soon as they may be needed and can be handled in training. It will involve also, of course, the granting of adequate credits to the Government, sustained, I hope, so far as they can equitably be sustained by the present generation, by well conceived taxation. . . .

I shall take the liberty of suggesting, through the several executive departments of the Government, for the consideration of your committees, measures for the accomplishment of the several objects I have mentioned. I hope that it will be your pleasure to deal with them as having been framed after very careful thought by the branch of the Government upon which the responsibility of conducting the war and safeguarding the nation will most directly fall.

While we do these things, these deeply momentous things, let us be very clear, and make very clear to all the world what our motives and our objects are. My own thought has not been driven from its habitual and normal course by the unhappy events of the last two months, and I do not believe that the thought of the nation has been altered or clouded by them. I have exactly the same things in mind now that I had in mind when I addressed the Senate on the twenty-second of January last; the same that I had in mind when I addressed the Congress on the third of February and on the twenty-sixth of February. Our object now, as then, is to vindicate the principles of peace and justice in the life of the world as against selfish and autocratic power and to set up amongst the really free and self-governed peoples of the world such a concert of purpose and of action as will henceforth ensure the observance of those principles. Neutrality is no longer feasible or desirable where the peace of the world is involved and the freedom of its peoples, and the menace to that peace and freedom lies in the existence of autocratic governments backed by organized force which is controlled wholly by their will, not by the will of their people. We have seen the last of neutrality in such circumstances. We are at the beginning of an age in which it will be insisted that the same standards of conduct and of responsibility for wrong done shall be observed among nations and their governments that are observed among the individual citizens of civilized states.

We have no quarrel with the German people. We have no feeling towards them but one of sympathy and friendship. It was not upon their impulse that their government acted in entering this war. It was not with their previous knowledge or approval. It was a war determined upon as wars used to be determined upon in the old, unhappy days when peoples were nowhere consulted by their rulers and

wars were provoked and waged in the interest of dynasties or of little groups of ambitious men who were accustomed to use their fellow men as pawns and tools. Self-governed nations do not fill their neighbour states with spies or set the course of intrigue to bring about some critical posture of affairs which will give them an opportunity to strike and make conquest. Such designs can be successfully worked out only under cover and where no one has the right to ask questions. Cunningly contrived plans of deception or aggression, carried, it may be, from generation to generation, can be worked out and kept from the light only within the privacy of courts or behind the carefully guarded confidences of a narrow and privileged class. They are happily impossible where public opinion commands and insists upon full information concerning all the nation's affairs.

A steadfast concert for peace can never be maintained except by a partnership of democratic nations. No autocratic government could be trusted to keep faith within it or observe its covenants. It must be a league of honour, a partnership of opinion. Intrigue would eat its vitals away; the plottings of inner circles who could plan what they would and render account to no one would be a corruption seated at its very heart. Only free peoples can hold their purpose and their honour steady to a common end and prefer the interests of mankind to any narrow interest of their own.

Does not every American feel that assurance has been added to our hope for the future peace of the world by the wonderful and heartening things that have been happening within the last few weeks in Russia? Russia was known by those who knew it best to have been always in fact democratic at heart, in all the vital habits of her thought, in all the intimate relationships of her people that spoke their natural instinct, their habitual attitude towards life. The autocracy that crowned the summit of her political structure, long as it had stood and terrible as was the reality of its power, was not in fact Russian in origin, character, or purpose; and now it has been shaken off and the great, generous Russian people have been added in all their naïve majesty and might to the forces that are fighting for freedom in the world, for justice, and for peace. Here is a fit partner for a League of Honour.

One of the things that has served to convince us that the Prussian autocracy was not and could never be our friend is that from the very outset of the present war it has filled our unsuspecting communities and even our offices of government with spies and set criminal intrigues everywhere afoot against our national unity of counsel, our peace within and without, our industries and our commerce. Indeed it is now evident that its spies were here even before the war began; and it is unhappily not a matter of conjecture but a fact proved in our courts of justice that the intrigues which have more than once come perilously near to disturbing the peace and dislocating the industries of the country have been carried on at the instigation, with the support, and even under the personal direction of official agents of the Imperial Government accredited to the Government of the United States. Even in checking these things and trying to extirpate them we have sought to put the most generous interpretation possible upon them because we knew that their source lay, not in any hostile feeling or purpose of the German people towards us (who were, no doubt as ignorant of them as we ourselves were), but only in the selfish designs of a Government that did what it pleased and told its people nothing. But they have played their part in serving to convince us at last that that Government entertains no real friendship for us and means to act against our peace and security at its convenience. That it means to stir up enemies against us at our very doors the intercepted note to the German Minister at Mexico City is eloquent evidence.

We are accepting this challenge of hostile purpose because we know that in such a government, following such methods, we can never have a friend; and that in the presence of its organized power, always lying in wait to accomplish we know not what purpose, there can be no assured security for the democratic governments of the world. We are now about to accept gauge of battle with this natural foe to liberty and shall, if necessary, spend the whole force of the nation to check and nullify its pretensions and its power. We are glad, now that we see the facts with no veil of false pretence about them, to fight thus for the ultimate peace of the world and for the liberation of its peoples, the German peoples included: for the rights of nations great and small and the privilege of men everywhere to choose their way of life and of obedience. The world must be made safe for democracy. Its peace must be planted upon the tested foundations of political liberty. We have no selfish ends to serve. We desire no conquest, no dominion. We seek no indemnities for ourselves, no material compensation for the sacrifices we shall freely make. We are but one of the champions of the rights of mankind. We shall be satisfied when those rights have been made as secure as the faith and the freedom of nations can make them.

Just because we fight without rancour and without selfish object, seeking nothing for ourselves but what we shall wish to share with all free peoples, we shall, I feel confident, conduct our operations as belligerents without passion and ourselves observe with proud punctilio the principles of right and of fair play we profess to be fighting for.

I have said nothing of the governments allied with the Imperial Government of Germany because they have not made war upon us or challenged us to defend our right and our honour. The Austro-Hungarian Government has, indeed, avowed its unqualified endorsement and acceptance of the reckless and lawless submarine warfare adopted now without disguise by the Imperial German Government, and it has therefore not been possible for this Government to receive Count Tarnowski, the Ambassador recently accredited to this Government by the Imperial and Royal Government of Austria-Hungary; but that Government has not actually engaged in warfare against citizens of the United States on the seas, and I take the liberty, for the present at least, of postponing a discussion of our relations with the authorities at Vienna. We enter this war only where we are clearly forced into it because there are no other means of defending our rights.

It will be all the easier for us to conduct ourselves as belligerents in a high spirit of right and fairness because we act without animus, not in enmity towards a people or with the desire to bring any injury or disadvantage upon them, but only in armed opposition to an irresponsible government which has thrown aside all considerations of humanity and of right and is running amuck. We are, let me say again, the sincere friends of the German people, and shall desire nothing so much as the early re-establishment of intimate relations of mutual advantage between us—however hard it may be for them, for the time being, to believe that this is spoken from our hearts. We have borne with their present government through all these bitter months because of that friendship—exercising a patience and forbearance which would otherwise have been impossible. We shall, happily, still have an opportunity to prove that friendship in our daily attitude and actions towards the millions of men and women of German birth and native sympathy who live amongst us and share our life, and we shall be proud to prove it

towards all who are in fact loyal to their neighbours and to the Government in the hour of test. They are, most of them, as true and loyal Americans as if they had never known any other fealty or allegiance. They will be prompt to stand with us in rebuking and restraining the few who may be of a different mind and purpose. If there should be disloyalty, it will be dealt with with a firm hand of stern repression; but, if it lifts its head at all, it will lift it only here and there and without countenance except from a lawless and malignant few.

It is a distressing and oppressive duty, Gentlemen of the Congress, which I have performed in thus addressing you. There are, it may be, many months of fiery trial and sacrifice ahead of us. It is a fearful thing to lead this great peaceful people into war, into the most terrible and disastrous of all wars, civilization itself seeming to be in the balance. But the right is more precious than peace, and we shall fight for the things which we have always carried nearest our hearts—for democracy, for the right of those who submit to authority to have a voice in their own governments, for the rights and liberties of small nations, for a universal dominion of right by such a concert of free peoples as shall bring peace and safety to all nations and make the world itself at last free. To such a task we can dedicate our lives and our fortunes, everything that we are and everything that we have, with the pride of those who know that the day has come when America is privileged to spend her blood and her might for the principles that gave her birth and happiness and the peace which she has treasured. God helping her, she can do no other.

3. OPPOSITION TO WILSON'S WAR MESSAGE[1]

By Robert M. La Follette

EDITORS' NOTE.—Senator Robert M. La Follette of Wisconsin (1855–1925) was one of the six senators who voted against the declaration of war. His opposition was widely regarded as pro-German, a movement arose to expel him from the Senate, and his action was censured by the legislature and the university of his state. The mood of the nation had changed, however, by 1922, when La Follette was easily re-elected to the Senate. Born and educated in Wisconsin, La Follette was admitted to the bar in 1880. His principal interest was politics rather than a legal practice, however, and in that year he was elected county district attorney. He was a Republican member of the House of Representatives from 1885 to 1891, when he was defeated by the popular hostility to the high McKinley tariff, which he had helped write. In private life for a decade, La Follette developed his progressive reform ideas, many of which he established after 1900 as governor of Wisconsin. He was a member of the Senate from 1905 until his death. In 1912 he was deprived of the Progressive presidential nomination by Theodore Roosevelt, and in 1924 he was nominated for the presidency by another progressive party and received nearly five million votes (see p. 435).

Mr. President, I had supposed until recently that it was the duty of Senators and Representatives in Congress to vote and act according to their convictions on all public matters that came before them for consideration and decision.

1. STANDING BACK OF THE PRESIDENT

Quite another doctrine has recently been promulgated by certain newspapers, which unfortunately seems to have found considerable support elsewhere, and that is the doctrine of "standing back of the President," without inquiring whether the President is right or wrong. For myself I have never subscribed to that doctrine and never shall. I shall support the President in the measures he proposes when I believe them to be right. I shall oppose measures proposed by the President when I believe them to be wrong. The fact that the matter which the President submits for consideration is of the greatest importance is only an additional reason why we should be sure that we are right and not to be swerved from that conviction or intimidated in its expression by any influence of power whatsoever. If it is important for us to speak and vote our convictions in matters of internal policy, though we may unfortunately be in disagreement with the President, it is infinitely more important for us to speak and vote our convictions when the question is one of peace or war, certain to involve the lives and fortunes of many of our people and, it may be, the destiny of all of them and of the civilized world as well. If, unhappily, on such momentous questions the most patient research and conscientious consideration we could give to them leave us in disagreement with the President, I know of no course to take except to oppose, regretfully but not the less firmly, the demands of the Executive. . . .

Mr. President, many of my colleagues

[1] *Congressional Record*, LV, Part 1 (April 5, 1917), 223–28, 231, 233–35.

on both sides of this floor have from day to day offered for publication in the *Record* messages and letters received from their constituents. I have received some 15,000 letters and telegrams. They have come from 44 States in the Union. They have been assorted according to whether they speak in criticism or commendation of my course in opposing war.

Assorting the 15,000 letters and telegrams by States in that way, 9 out of 10 are an unqualified indorsement of my course in opposing war with Germany on the issue presented. . . .

Do not these messages indicate on the part of the people a deep-seated conviction that the United States should not enter the European war? The armed-ship bill meant war. Senators who opposed its being forced through Congress in the closing hours of the session were rebuked by the President. It is highly important, therefore, to note at this time that the President in his address on the 2d of this month takes the same view of arming merchant ships that was entertained by at least some of the Senators, including myself, when the armed-ship bill was before us for consideration. In his address of April 2 the President said: "It is impossible to defend ships against their (submarine) attacks as the law of nations has assumed that merchantmen would defend themselves against privateers or cruisers, visible craft giving chase on the open sea."

He says in the same address: "It [arming merchant ships] is practically certain to draw us into the war without either the rights or the effectiveness of belligerents."

I take satisfaction in noting that this is exactly what I stated in an editorial in my magazine, which was published a short time after the armed-ship bill discussion.

I will read just a paragraph or two from that editorial:

The armed ship bill was not only unconstitutional, it was, in my judgment, foolish and inadequate. It pleased the supporters of this bill to assume that it was only necessary to place guns on merchant ships in order to defend them successfully against submarine attack. There was no evidence before Congress that would warrant the conclusion that arming these ships would afford protection.

1. The available evidence points to the futility of such armament. The *Laconia* was armed, but she was torpedoed twice and sunk without a chance to fire a shot. Merchant ships of the allies are armed. Their great loss of tonnage is conclusive evidence that guns planted on merchant ships are ineffectual in warding off submarine attack. It is criminal to lure from our harbors our merchant ships with passengers, crew, and freight to embark on a voyage fraught with such imminent peril in the belief that they may resist attack.

I venture to read two or three more paragraphs:

2. The first question we should ask ourselves, before we enter on this war with our armed merchantmen or our Navy for the express purpose of maintaining our right to the seas, is: What will happen to our ships? If it is so easy to clear the trans-Atlantic lanes of submarines, why is not the British Admiralty keeping them open and free for our commerce—since our carrying trade across the Atlantic now consists of supplies for the allies—food and ammunition? From all we can learn it appears that the British Navy is not attempting this perilous task, but is keeping inside carefully guarded harbors.

What assurance have we that we can clear the German war zone with armed merchantmen or with battleships as convoys or with any of the so-called "submarine chasers"?

Manifestly it is an undertaking which the British Admiralty declines for good and sufficient reason.

The American public is being woefully deceived. We are derided for hiding behind the British Navy. Moving pictures portray our fleet firing on submarines that instantly go to the bottom. The daily papers are filled with stuff that would lead us to believe that we need only declare war, order out our fleet to scour the seas, and the war is ended and won.

It is admitted that the submarine discharges its torpedo with deadly accuracy at a range of 2 to 4 miles.

It is admitted that the submarine, with its hull submerged several feet below the surface and exposing nothing but its periscope, can discharge its torpedo with equal chance to achieve its purpose.

The periscope furnishes a target no larger than a sailor's cap for merchant and naval gunners to fire at.

I have the best authority for the statement that the chances of hitting a target of that size at the distance of 2 miles, or of damaging a submarine so submerged, would in a hundred shots be practically zero.

WAR-MAD PRESS BREEDS INTOLERANCE

It is unfortunately true that a portion of the irresponsible and war-crazed press, feeling secure in the authority of the President's condemnation of the Senators who opposed the armed-ship bill, have published the most infamous and scurrilous libels on the honor of the Senators who opposed that bill. It was particularly unfortunate that such malicious falsehoods should fill the public press of the country at a time when every consideration for our country required that a spirit of fairness should be observed in the discussions of the momentous questions under consideration.

A member of the British Parliament is visiting in this country. He has had some opportunity to observe this new spirit of intolerance that has been bred in the press and through the press in the United States within the last few months that challenges the right of any man to utter his independent judgment on a question vital, sir, to the people of this Nation; vital to the interests of this Government. It has led him to institute some comparisons between the conditions that prevail in Great Britain, a part of that war-torn territory of Europe, and the conditions that prevail here, where we still have peace. I have this comment of his upon it. I am not permitted to use his name, though he may be within the sound of my voice. He said:

In England we feel that the theory of democracy requires the fullest and frankest discussion of every measure. We feel that the minority has a right to a respectful hearing. This is the only way you can carry on a democracy, and keep it a democracy.

Another strange thing I find is that in America you seem to expect that when the minority is beaten it will at once capitulate, declare it has been in the wrong, and join the majority. This is not democracy either. In England during the Boer War and this war, but especially in the Boer War, there was an organized minority in Parliament—there always has been in time of war. In the Boer War this minority was led by no less a person than David Lloyd-George.

If you make it an American policy that when the majority has once spoken, the right and duty of the minority to express itself and fight for what it believes in ends, you have lost your democracy. There is no safety or wisdom in trying to suppress thought or to force men to silence. . . .

V. GERMANY'S WARFARE IS AGAINST MANKIND

The President in his message of April 2 says: "The present German warfare against commerce is a warfare against mankind. It is a war against all nations."

Again referring to Germany's warfare he says: "There has been no discrimination. The challenge is to all mankind."

Is it not a little peculiar that if Germany's warfare is against all nations the United States is the only nation that regards it necessary to declare war on that account? If it is true, as the President says, that "there has been no discrimination," that Germany has treated every neutral as she has treated us, is it not peculiar that no other of the great nations of the earth seem to regard Germany's conduct in this war as a cause for entering into it? Are we the only nation jealous of our rights? Are we the only nation insisting upon the protection of our citizens? Does not the strict neutrality maintained on the part of all the other nations of the earth suggest that possibly there is a reason for their action, and that that reason is that Germany's conduct under the circumstances does not merit from any nation which is determined to preserve its neutrality a declaration of war?

Norway, Sweden, the Netherlands, Switzerland, Denmark, Spain, and all the great Republics of South America are quite as interested in this subject as we are, and yet they have refused to join with us in a combination against Germany. I venture to suggest also that the nations named, and probably others, have a somewhat better right to be heard than we, for by refusing to sell war material and munitions to any of the belligerents they have placed themselves in a position where the suspicion which attaches to us of a desire for war profits can not attach to them. . . .

VIII. THIS IS A WAR OF DEMOCRACY

Just a word of comment more upon one of the points in the President's address. He says that this is a war "for the things which we have always carried nearest to our hearts—for democracy, for the right of those who submit to authority to have a voice in their own government." In many places throughout the address is this exalted sentiment given expression.

It is a sentiment peculiarly calculated to appeal to American hearts and, when accompanied by acts consistent with it, is certain to receive our support; but in this same connection, and strangely enough, the President says that we have become convinced that the German Government as it now exists—"Prussian autocracy" he calls it—can never again maintain friendly relations with us. His expression is that "Prussian autocracy was not and could never be our friend," and repeatedly throughout the address the suggestion is made that if the German people would overturn their Government it would probably be the way to peace. So true is this that the dispatches from London all hailed the message of the President as sounding the death knell of Germany's Government.

But the President proposes alliance with Great Britain, which, however liberty-loving its people, is a hereditary monarchy, with a hereditary ruler, with a hereditary House of Lords, with a hereditary landed system, with a limited and restricted suffrage for one class and a multiplied suffrage power for another, and with grinding industrial conditions for all the wageworkers. The President has not suggested that we make our support of Great Britain conditional to her granting home rule to Ireland, or Egypt, or India. We rejoice in the establishment of a democracy in Russia, but it will hardly be contended that if Russia was still an autocratic Government, we would not be asked to enter this alliance with her just the same. Italy and the lesser powers of Europe, Japan in the Orient; in fact, all of the countries with whom we are to enter into alliance, except France and newly revolutionized Russia, are still of the old order— and it will be generally conceded that no one of them has done as much for its people in the solution of municipal problems and in securing social and industrial reforms as Germany.

Is it not a remarkable democracy which leagues itself with allies already far overmatching in strength the German nation and holds out to such beleaguered nation the hope of peace only at the price of giving up their Government? I am not talking now of the merits or demerits of any government, but I am speaking of a profession of democracy that is linked in action with the most brutal and domineering use of autocratic power. Are the people of this country being so well represented in this war movement that we need to go abroad to give other people control of their governments? Will the President and the supporters of this war bill submit it to a vote of the people before the declaration of war goes into effect? Until we are willing to do that, it illy becomes us to offer as an excuse for our entry into the war the unsupported claim that this war was forced upon the German people by their Government "without their previous knowledge or approval."

Who has registered the knowledge or approval of the American people of the course this Congress is called upon to take in declaring war upon Germany? Submit the question to the people, you who support it. You who support it dare not do it, for you know that by a vote of more than ten to one the American people as a body would register their declaration against it.

In the sense that this war is being forced upon our people without their knowing why and without their approval, and that wars are usually forced upon all peoples in the same way, there is some truth in the statement; but I venture to say that the response which the German people have made to the demands of this war shows that it has a degree of popular support which the war upon which we are entering has not and never will have among our people. The espionage bills, the conscription bills, and other forcible military measures which we understand are being ground out of the war machine in this country is the complete proof that those responsible for this war fear that it has no popular support and that armies sufficient to satisfy the demand of the entente allies can not be recruited by voluntary enlistments. . . .

OUR NEUTRAL RIGHTS SET ASIDE

Now, I want to repeat: It was our absolute right as a neutral to ship food to the people of Germany. That is a position that we have fought for through all of our history. The correspondence of every Secretary of State in the history of our Government who has been called upon to deal with the rights of our neutral commerce as to foodstuffs is the position stated by Lord Salisbury, just quoted. He was in line with all of the precedents that we had originated and established for the maintenance of neutral rights upon this subject.

In the first days of the war with Germany, Great Britain set aside, so far as her own conduct was concerned, all these rules of civilized naval warfare.

According to the declaration of London, as well as the rules of international law, there could have been no interference in trade between the United States and Holland or Scandinavia and other countries, except in the case of ships which could be proven to carry absolute contraband, like arms and ammunition, with ultimate German destination. There could have been no interference with the importation into Germany of any goods on the free list, such as cotton, rubber, and hides. There could have properly been no interference with our export to Germany of anything on the conditional contraband list, like flour, grain, and provisions, unless it could be proven by England that such shipments were intended for the use of the German Army. There could be no lawful interference with foodstuffs intended for the civilian population of Germany, and if those foodstuffs were shipped to other countries to be reshipped to Germany, no question could be raised that they were not intended for the use of the civilian population.

It is well to recall at this point our rights as declared by the declaration of London and as declared without the declaration of London by settled principles of international law, for we have during the present war become so used to having Great Britain utterly disregard our rights on the high seas that we have really forgotten that we have any, as far as Great Britain and her allies are concerned.

Great Britain, by what she called her modifications of the declaration of London, shifted goods from the free list to the conditional contraband and contraband lists, reversed the presumption of destination for civilian population, and abolished the principle that a blockade to exist at all must be effective.

Edwin J. Clapp, professor of economics of the New York University, in his book, *Economic Aspects of the War*, describes the situation aptly. It is supported by all the authorities, but I quote from him:

The modifications [of the declaration of London] were subversive of the principles of the declaration to which they were attached. These modifications supplemented by an unexampled extension of the British contraband list and finally by what our Government calls an illegal blockade, have been England's method of exercising economic pressure upon Germany and, necessarily, upon all neutral nations that trade with her.

Again the same author says:

This action stopped our direct trade with Germany. It might appear that goods on the free list could still move. Some of them did move, from free to contraband. People feared to ship the others lest they should be so listed while ships were on the ocean, and the goods made subject to seizure. Practically nothing has been shipped to Germany from this country but cotton, and it was not shipped until December. In belated response to the insistence of southern Senators and of American business interests which had found themselves gravely embarrassed by the cessation of cotton shipments, Great Britain finally made a clear statement that this particular commodity would not be considered contraband.

So much for direct trade with Germany. There was still a method by which we should have been able to export our goods and discharge our neutral obligations to trade with Germany as with England. We might have carried on this trade via neutral ports like Rotterdam or Copenhagen, from which the goods might have been shipped to Germany. The declaration of London allows a belligerent to interfere with a shipment between two neutral ports only when it consists of absolute contraband for enemy territory. Conditional contraband so moving may not even be suspected. The order in council changed this. It extended the new intention of capturing conditional contraband to goods moving to Germany even through a neutral port. And, as explained, conditional contraband was seizable if destined to anyone in Germany; it was not conditional but absolute.

The British action, besides stopping our trade with Germany, barring only a certain amount of indirect trade carried on with much difficulty and danger, subjected to grave peril our commerce with other neutrals. The British contraband lists were extended so rapidly that soon almost no important article of commerce with neutrals was free from seizure by England, who suspected everything on these lists as being of possible German destination. By these methods England proposed to starve the civilian population of Germany and destroy neutral trade. . . .

WE SUBMIT TO ENGLAND'S WAR ZONE

The only reason why we have not suffered the sacrifice of just as many ships and just as many lives from the violation of our rights by the war zone and the submarine mines of Great Britain, as we have through the unlawful acts of Germany in making her war zone in violation of our neutral rights, is simply because we have submitted to Great Britain's dictation. If our ships had been sent into her forbidden high-sea war zone, as they have into the proscribed area Germany marked out on the high seas as a war zone, we would have had the same loss of life and property in the one case as in the other; but because we avoided doing that in the case of England, and acquiesced in her violation of law, we have not only a legal but a moral responsibility for the position in which Germany has been placed by our collusion and cooperation with Great Britain. By suspending the rule with respect to neutral rights in Great Britain's case, we have been actively aiding her in starving the civil population of Germany. We have helped to drive Germany into a corner, her back to the wall, to fight with what weapons she can lay her hands on to prevent the starving of her women and children, her old men and babes. . . .

WE HAVE NOT BEEN NEUTRAL

Jefferson asserted that we could not permit one warring nation to curtail our neutral rights if we were not ready to allow her enemy the same privileges, and that any other course entailed the sacrifice of our neutrality.

That is the sensible, that is the logical position. No neutrality could ever have commanded respect if it was not based on that equitable and just proposition; and we from early in the war threw our neutrality to the winds by permitting England to make a mockery of it to her advantage against her chief enemy. Then we expect to say to that enemy, "You have got to respect my rights as a neutral." What is the answer? I say Germany has been patient with us. Standing strictly on her rights, her answer would be, "Maintain your neutrality; treat these other Governments warring against me as you treat me if you want your neutral rights respected." . . .

The best and clearest exposition of the exact question, however, was made long ago by one of the greatest of Democrats and statesmen of this country—Thomas Jefferson. Mr. Jefferson, then Secretary of State, in writing to Thomas Pinckney, United States minister to Great Britain regarding England's stoppage of our food shipments to France, with whom England was then at war, dealt with precisely the same situation that confronts President Wilson in the war between Germany and England, but Secretary Jefferson dealt with the situation in precisely the opposite manner from that adopted by President Wilson. In this letter, under date of September 7, 1793, Secretary Jefferson said:

The first article of it [the British order] permits all vessels laden wholly or in part with corn, flour, or meal, bound to any port in France, to be stopped and sent into any British port, to be purchased by that Government or to be released only on the condition of security given by the master that he will proceed to dispose of his cargo in the ports of some country in amity with his majesty.

This article is so manifestly contrary to the law of nations that nothing more would seem necessary than to observe that it is so.

How much less was it obnoxious to the law of nations than mining the great area of the North Sea.

Reason and usage have established that when two nations go to war those who choose to live in peace, retain their neutral right to pursue their agriculture, manufactures, and other ordinary vocations; to carry the produce of their industry, for exchange, to all nations, belligerent or neutral, as usual; to go, and come freely without injury or molestation, and, in short, that the war among others shall be, for them, as if it did not exist. One restriction on those mutual rights has been submitted to by nations at peace; that is to say, that of not furnishing to either party implements merely of war, for the annoyance of the other, nor anything whatever to a place blockaded by its enemy.

This act, too, tends directly to draw us from that state of peace in which we are wishing to remain. It is an essential character of neutrality to furnish no aids (not stipulated by treaty) to one party which we are not equally ready to furnish to the other. If we permit corn to be sent to Great Britain and her friends, we are equally bound to permit it to France. To restrain it would be a partiality which might lead to war with France, and, between restraining it ourselves and permitting her enemies to restrain it unrightfully is no difference. She would consider this as a mere pretext, of which she would not be the dupe; and on what honorable ground could we otherwise explain it? Thus we should see ourselves plunged by this unauthorized act of Great Britain into a war, with which we meddle not and which we wish to avoid, if justice to all parties, and from all parties, will enable us to avoid it.

In the same letter Jefferson says:

The loss of our produce destined for foreign markets or that loss which would result from an arbitrary restraint of our markets is a tax too serious for us to acquiesce in. It is not enough for a nation to say, "We and our friends will buy your produce." We have a right to answer that it suits us better to sell to their enemies as well as their friends.

We have a right to judge for ourselves what market best suits us, and they have none to forbid to us the enjoyment of the necessaries and comforts which we may obtain from any other independent country.

Further, he says:

Were we to withhold from her [France] supplies of provisions, we should in like manner be bound to withhold them from her enemies also and thus shut to ourselves all the ports of Europe where corn is in demand or make ourselves parties in the war. This is a dilemma which Great Britain has no right to force upon us, and for which no pretext can be found in any part of our conduct. She may, indeed, feel the desire of starving an enemy nation, but she can have no right of doing it at our loss nor of making us the instruments of it.

And with a firmness which it would have been well had the present administration emulated, it is said:

It is with concern, however, I am obliged to observe that so marked has been the inattention of the British court to every application which has been made to them on any subject by this Government (not a single answer, I believe, having ever been given to one of them, except in the act of exchanging a minister) that it may become unavoidable in certain cases, where an answer of some sort is necessary, to consider their silence as an answer.

IF WE WERE NEUTRAL, WE WOULD NOT NOW FACE WAR

Had the plain principle of international law announced by Jefferson been followed by us, we would not be called on to-day to declare war upon any of the belligerents. The failure to treat the belligerent nations of Europe alike, the failure to reject the unlawful "war zones" of both Germany and Great Britain, is wholly accountable for our present dilemma. We should not seek to hide our blunder behind the smoke of battle, to inflame the mind of our people by half truths into the frenzy of war, in order that they may never appreciate the real cause of it until it is too late. I do not believe that our national honor is served by such a course. The right way is the honorable way.

One alternative is to admit our initial blunder to enforce our rights against Great Britain as we have enforced our rights against Germany; demand that both those nations shall respect our neutral rights upon the high seas to the letter; and give notice that we will enforce those rights from that time forth against both belligerents and then live up to that notice.

The other alternative is to withdraw our commerce from both. The mere suggestion that food supplies would be with-held from both sides impartially would compel belligerents to observe the principle of freedom of the seas for neutral commerce.

MR. WILLIAMS:[2] Mr. President, if immortality could be attained by verbal eternity, the Senator from Wisconsin would have approximated immortality. We have waited and have heard a speech from him which would have better become Herr Bethmann-Hollweg, of the German Parliament, than an American Senator. In fact, he has gone much further than Herr Bethmann-Hollweg ever dared to go. Herr Bethmann-Hollweg said that the use of submarines, in the manner in which they are being used now, could be justified only by "military necessity." The Senator from Wisconsin has put their use upon the same footing as the use by Great Britain of ships to enforce a blockade. I fully expected before he took his seat to hear him defend the invasion of Belgium—the most absolutely barbarous act that ever took place in the history of any nation anywhere. I heard from him a speech which was pro-German, pretty nearly pro-Goth, and pro-Vandal, which was anti-American President and anti-American Congress, and anti-American people. I heard his eulogy of the German Government. I heard his justification of its barbarous methods in war. I heard his surly, contemptuous criticism of the entente powers. The American people will read a part of it. I fancy that it is the speech that the Senator from Wisconsin prepared to deliver upon the neutrality bill in the last Congress. We are better prepared to re-

2. The temper of La Follette's opponents is illustrated in this brief excerpt of the speech immediately following that of Senator La Follette. Senator John S. Williams of Mississippi (1854–1932) was born in Tennessee, educated at the University of Virginia and at Heidelberg, and began his law practice in Mississippi in 1878. He was a member of the House of Representatives (1893–1909), the minority leader (1905–9), and a senator (1911–23). He wrote *Thomas Jefferson, His Permanent Influence on American Institutions* (1913).

ceive it now than we were then, because we have grown a little bit older and a little bit more patient and perhaps a little bit more submissive to wrong.

The Senator from Wisconsin, while he was pronouncing a eulogy upon the German people, might have pronounced a eulogy upon a people very much greater, very much more intelligent, and very much more moral—the American people. His speech was absolutely worthy of Bethmann-Hollweg in the Reichstag, if Bethmann-Hollweg had had the audacity to make it there; but Bethmann-Hollweg did not have the audacity, and he had too much knowledge and common sense to have attempted to make that particular speech, even in the Reichstag.

4. OPPOSITION TO WILSON'S WAR MESSAGE[1]

By George Norris

EDITORS' NOTE.—Senator George W. Norris of Nebraska (1861–1944) was another of the six senators who voted against the declaration of war. Like La Follette, Norris was a progressive Republican whose constituency included many persons of German origin. His speech against the war shows some of the economic reasons for the position. Norris was born in Ohio, educated there and in Indiana, and admitted to the bar in 1883. He moved to Nebraska in 1885, which he represented in Congress from 1903 to 1913 in the House of Representatives and from 1913 to 1943 in the Senate. His important legislative contributions include the anti-injunction act to protect labor unions, the Tennessee Valley Authority, and the structural changes made by the Twentieth Amendment to the United States Constitution and the establishment in Nebraska of a unicameral legislature.

. . . There are a great many American citizens who feel that we owe it as a duty to humanity to take part in this war. Many instances of cruelty and inhumanity can be found on both sides. Men are often biased in their judgment on account of their sympathy and their interests. To my mind, what we ought to have maintained from the beginning was the strictest neutrality. If we had done this I do not believe we would have been on the verge of war at the present time. We had a right as a nation, if we desired, to cease at any time to be neutral. We had a technical right to respect the English war zone and to disregard the German war zone, but we could not do that and be neutral. I have no quarrel to find with the man who does not desire our country to remain neutral. While many such people are moved by selfish motives and hopes of gain, I have no doubt but that in a great many instances, through what I believe to be a misunderstanding of the real condition, there are many honest, patriotic citizens who think we ought to engage in this war and who are behind the President in his demand that we should declare war against Germany. I think such people err in judgment and to a great extent have been misled as to the real history and the true facts by the almost unanimous demand of the great combination of wealth that has a direct financial interest in our participation in the war. We have loaned many hundreds of millions of dollars to the allies in this controversy. While such action was legal and countenanced by international

1. *Congressional Record*, LV, Part 1 (April 4, 1917), 213–14.

law, there is no doubt in my mind but the enormous amount of money loaned to the allies in this country has been instrumental in bringing about a public sentiment in favor of our country taking a course that would make every bond worth a hundred cents on the dollar and making the payment of every debt certain and sure. Through this instrumentality and also through the instrumentality of others who have not only made millions out of the war in the manufacture of munitions, etc., and who would expect to make millions more if our country can be drawn into the catastrophe, a large number of the great newspapers and news agencies of the country have been controlled and enlisted in the greatest propaganda that the world has ever known, to manufacture sentiment in favor of war. It is now demanded that the American citizens shall be used as insurance policies to guarantee the safe delivery of munitions of war to belligerent nations. The enormous profits of munition manufacturers, stockbrokers, and bond dealers must be still further increased by our entrance into the war. This has brought us to the present moment, when Congress, urged by the President and backed by the artificial sentiment, is about to declare war and engulf our country in the greatest holocaust that the world has ever known.

In showing the position of the bondholder and the stockbroker I desire to read an extract from a letter written by a member of the New York Stock Exchange to his customers. This writer says:

Regarding the war as inevitable, Wall Street believes that it would be preferable to this uncertainty about the actual date of its commencement. Canada and Japan are at war, and are more prosperous than ever before. The popular view is that stocks would have a quick, clear, sharp reaction immediately upon outbreak of hostilities, and that then they would enjoy an old-fashioned bull market such as followed the outbreak of war with Spain in 1898. The advent of peace would force a readjustment of commodity prices and would probably mean a postponement of new enterprises. As peace negotiations would be long drawn out,

the period of waiting and uncertainty for business would be long. If the United States does not go to war it is nevertheless good opinion that the preparedness program will compensate in good measure for the loss of the stimulus of actual war.

Here we have the Wall Street view. Here we have the man representing the class of people who will be made prosperous should we become entangled in the present war, who have already made millions of dollars, and who will make many hundreds of millions more if we get into the war. Here we have the cold-blooded proposition that war brings prosperity to that class of people who are within the viewpoint of this writer. He expresses the view, undoubtedly, of Wall Street, and of thousands of men elsewhere, who see only dollars coming to them through the handling of stocks and bonds that will be necessary in case of war. "Canada and Japan," he says, "are at war, and are more prosperous than ever before."

To whom does war bring prosperity? Not to the soldier who for the munificent compensation of $16 per month shoulders his musket and goes into the trench, there to shed his blood and to die if necessary; not to the broken-hearted widow who waits for the return of the mangled body of her husband; not to the mother who weeps at the death of her brave boy; not to the little children who shiver with cold; not to the babe who suffers from hunger; nor to the millions of mothers and daughters who carry broken hearts to their graves. War brings no prosperity to the great mass of common and patriotic citizens. It increases the cost of living of those who toil and those who already must strain every effort to keep soul and body together. War brings prosperity to the stock gambler on Wall Street—to those who are already in possession of more wealth than can be realized or enjoyed. Again this writer says that if we can not get war, "it is nevertheless good opinion that the preparedness program will compensate in good measure for the loss of the stimulus of actual war." That is, if we can not get war, let us go as far in that direction as possible. If we can not get war, let us cry for additional ships, additional guns, additional munitions, and everything else that will have a tendency to bring us as near as possible to the verge of war. And if war comes do such men as these shoulder the musket and go into the trenches?

Their object in having war and in preparing for war is to make money. Human suffering and the sacrifice of human life are necessary, but Wall Street considers only the dollars and the cents. The men who do the fighting, the people who make the sacrifices, are the ones who will not be counted in the measure of this great prosperity that he depicts. The stock brokers would not, of course, go to war, because the very object they have in bringing on the war is profit, and therefore they must remain in their Wall Street offices in order to share in that great prosperity which they say war will bring. The volunteer officer, even the drafting officer, will not find them. They will be concealed in their palatial offices on Wall Street, sitting behind mahogany desks, covered up with clipped coupons—coupons soiled with the sweat of honest toil, coupons stained with mothers' tears, coupons dyed in the lifeblood of their fellow men.

We are taking a step to-day that is fraught with untold danger. We are going into war upon the command of gold. We are going to run the risk of sacrificing millions of our countrymen's lives in order that other countrymen may coin their lifeblood into money. And even if we do not cross the Atlantic and go into the trenches, we are going to pile up a debt that the toiling masses that shall come many generations after us will have to pay. Unborn millions will bend their backs in toil in order to pay for the terrible step we are now about to take. We are about to do the bidding of wealth's terrible mandate. By our act we will make millions of our countrymen suffer, and the consequences of it may well be that millions of our brethren must shed their lifeblood, millions of broken-hearted women must weep, millions of children must suffer with cold, and millions of babes must die from hunger, and all because we want to preserve the commercial right of American citizens to deliver munitions of war to belligerent nations. . . .

SECTION E. REJECTION OF THE LEAGUE OF NATIONS

1. PEACE WITHOUT VICTORY, 1917[1]

By Woodrow Wilson

EDITORS' NOTE.—President Wilson made this speech advocating peace without victory on the eve of the American declaration of war. A year earlier his representative, Edward House, had sought an agreement with Britain to end the war by negotiation and, should this fail, probably to put the strength of the United States into the struggle against Germany. Britain did not enter into this agreement. In December, 1916, the German government asked for direct negotiations to end the war. Britain and the Allies refused the invitation because Germany failed to state the terms of the negotiation. Wilson's appeal for a negotiated peace was made too late, for twelve days earlier Germany had decided to undertake renewed unrestricted submarine attacks.

Gentlemen of the Senate:

On the eighteenth of December last I addressed an identic note to the governments of the nations now at war requesting them to state, more definitely than they had yet been stated by either group of belligerents, the terms upon which they would deem it possible to make peace. I spoke on behalf of humanity and of the rights of all neutral nations like our own, many of whose most vital interests the war puts in constant jeopardy. The Central Powers united in a reply which stated merely that they were ready to meet their antagonists in conference to discuss terms of peace. The Entente Powers have replied much more definitely and have stated, in general terms, indeed, but with sufficient definiteness to imply details, the arrangements, guarantees, and acts of reparation which they deem to be the indispensable conditions of a satisfactory settlement. We are that much nearer a definite discussion of the peace which shall end the present war. We are that much nearer the discussion of the international concert which must thereafter hold the world at peace. In every discussion of the peace that must end this war it is taken for granted that that peace must be followed by some definite concert of power which will make it virtually impossible that any such catastrophe should ever overwhelm us again. Every lover of mankind, every sane and thoughtful man must take that for granted.

I have sought this opportunity to address you because I thought that I owed it to you, as the council associated with me in the final determination of our international obligations, to disclose to you without reserve the thought and purpose that have been taking form in my mind in regard to the duty of our Government in the days to come when it will be necessary to lay afresh and upon a new plan the foundations of peace among the nations.

It is inconceivable that the people of the United States should play no part in that great enterprise. To take part in such a service will be the opportunity for which they have sought to prepare themselves by

1. Woodrow Wilson, *Peace without Victory Address* (64th Cong., 2d sess.; Senate Doc. No. 2685, Serial No. 7125 [Washington, 1917]), pp. 3–8.

the very principles and purposes of their polity and the approved practices of their Government ever since the days when they set up a new nation in the high and honourable hope that it might in all that it was and did show mankind the way to liberty. They cannot in honour withhold the service to which they are now about to be challenged. They do not wish to withhold it. But they owe it to themselves and to the other nations of the world to state the conditions under which they will feel free to render it.

That service is nothing less than this, to add their authority and their power to the authority and force of other nations to guarantee peace and justice throughout the world. Such a settlement cannot now be long postponed. It is right that before it comes this Government should frankly formulate the conditions upon which it would feel justified in asking our people to approve its formal and solemn adherence to a League for Peace. I am here to attempt to state those conditions.

The present war must first be ended; but we owe it to candour and to a just regard for the opinion of mankind to say that, so far as our participation in guarantees of future peace is concerned, it makes a great deal of difference in what way and upon what terms it is ended. The treaties and agreements which bring it to an end must embody terms which will create a peace that is worth guaranteeing and preserving, a peace that will win the approval of mankind, not merely a peace that will serve the several interests and immediate aims of the nations engaged. We shall have no voice in determining what those terms shall be, but we shall, I feel sure, have a voice in determining whether they shall be made lasting or not by the guarantees of a universal covenant; and our judgment upon what is fundamental and essential as a condition precedent to permanency should be spoken now, not afterwards when it may be too late.

No covenant of cooperative peace that does not include the peoples of the New World can suffice to keep the future safe against war; and yet there is only one sort of peace that the peoples of America could join in guaranteeing. The elements of that peace must be elements that engage the confidence and satisfy the principles of the American governments, elements consistent with their political faith and with the practical convictions which the peoples of America have once for all embraced and undertaken to defend.

I do not mean to say that any American government would throw any obstacle in the way of any terms of peace the governments now at war might agree upon, or seek to upset them when made, whatever they might be. I only take it for granted that mere terms of peace between the belligerents will not satisfy even the belligerents themselves. Mere agreements may not make peace secure. It will be absolutely necessary that a force be created as a guarantor of the permanency of the settlement so much greater than the force of any nation now engaged or any alliance hitherto formed or projected that no nation, no probable combination of nations could face or withstand it. If the peace presently to be made is to endure, it must be a peace made secure by the organized major force of mankind.

The terms of the immediate peace agreed upon will determine whether it is a peace for which such a guarantee can be secured. The question upon which the whole future peace and policy of the world depends is this: Is the present war a struggle for a just and secure peace, or only for a new balance of power? If it be only a struggle for a new balance of power, who will guarantee, who can guarantee, the stable equilibrium of the new arrangement? Only a tranquil Europe can be a stable Europe. There must be, not a balance of power, but a community of power; not organized rivalries, but an organized common peace.

Fortunately we have received very explicit assurances on this point. The statesmen of both of the groups of nations now arrayed against one another have said, in terms that could not be misinterpreted, that it was no part of the purpose they had in mind to crush their antagonists. But the implications of these assurances may not be equally clear to all—may not be the same on both sides of the water. I think it will be serviceable if I attempt to set forth what we understand them to be.

They imply, first of all, that it must be a peace without victory. It is not pleasant to say this. I beg that I may be permitted to put my own interpretation upon it and that it may be understood that no other interpretation was in my thought. I am seeking only to face realities and to face them without soft concealments. Victory would mean peace forced upon the loser, a victor's terms imposed upon the vanquished. It would be accepted in humiliation, under duress, at an intolerable sacrifice, and would leave a sting, a resentment, a bitter memory upon which terms of peace would rest, not permanently, but only as upon quicksand. Only a peace between equals can last. Only a peace the very principle of which is equality and a common participation in a common benefit. The right state of mind, the right feeling between nations, is as necessary for a lasting peace as is the just settlement of vexed questions of territory or of racial and national allegiance.

The equality of nations upon which peace must be founded if it is to last must be an equality of rights; the guarantees exchanged must neither recognize nor imply a difference between big nations and small, between those that are powerful and those that are weak. Right must be based upon the common strength, not upon the individual strength, of the nations upon whose concert peace will depend. Equality of territory or of resources there of course cannot be; nor any other sort of equality not gained in the ordinary peaceful and legitimate development of the peoples themselves. But no one asks or expects anything more than an equality of rights.

Mankind is looking now for freedom of life, not for equipoises of power.

And there is a deeper thing involved than even equality of right among organized nations. No peace can last, or ought to last, which does not recognize and accept the principle that governments derive all their just powers from the consent of the governed, and that no right anywhere exists to hand peoples about from sovereignty to sovereignty as if they were property. I take it for granted, for instance, if I may venture upon a single example, that statesmen everywhere are agreed that there should be a united, independent, and autonomous Poland, and that henceforth inviolable security of life, of worship, and of industrial and social development should be guaranteed to all peoples who have lived hitherto under the power of governments devoted to a faith and purpose hostile to their own.

I speak of this, not because of any desire to exalt an abstract political principle which has always been held very dear by those who have sought to build up liberty in America, but for the same reason that I have spoken of the other conditions of peace which seem to me clearly indispensable—because I wish frankly to uncover realities. Any peace which does not recognize and accept this principle will inevitably be upset. It will not rest upon the affections or the convictions of mankind. The ferment of spirit of whole populations will fight subtly and constantly against it, and all the world will sympathize. The world can be at peace only if its life is stable, and there can be no stability where the will is in rebellion, where there is not tranquility of spirit and a sense of justice, of freedom, and of right.

So far as practicable, moreover, every great people now struggling towards a full development of its resources and of its powers should be assured a direct outlet to the great highways of the sea. Where this cannot be done by the cession of territory, it can no doubt be done by the neutralization of direct rights of way under the general guarantee which will assure the peace itself. With a right comity of arrangement no nation need be shut away from free access to the open paths of the world's commerce.

And the paths of the sea must alike in law and in fact be free. The freedom of the seas is the *sine qua non* of peace, equality, and cooperation. No doubt a somewhat radical reconsideration of many of the rules of international practice hitherto thought to be established may be necessary in order to make the seas indeed free and common in practically all circumstances for the use of mankind, but the motive for such changes is convincing and compelling. There can be no trust or intimacy between the peoples of the world without them. The free, constant, unthreatened intercourse of nations is an essential part of the process of peace and of development. It need not be difficult either to define or to secure the freedom of the seas if the governments of the world sincerely desire to come to an agreement concerning it.

It is a problem closely connected with the limitation of naval armaments and the cooperation of the navies of the world in keeping the seas at once free and safe. And the question of limiting naval armaments opens the wider and perhaps more difficult question of the limitation of armies and of all programmes of military preparation. Difficult and delicate as these questions are, they must be faced with the utmost candour and decided in a spirit of real accommodation if peace is to come with healing in its wings, and come to stay. Peace cannot be had without concession and sacrifice. There can be no sense of safety and equality among the nations if great preponderating armaments are henceforth to continue here and there to be built up and maintained. The statesmen of the world must plan for peace and nations must adjust and accommodate their policy to it as they have planned for war and made ready for pitiless contest and rivalry. The question of armaments, whether on land or sea, is the most immediately and intensely practical question connected with the future fortunes of nations and of mankind.

I have spoken upon these great matters without reserve and with the utmost explicitness because it has seemed to me to be necessary if the world's yearning desire for peace was anywhere to find free voice and utterance. Perhaps I am the only person in high authority amongst all the peoples of the world who is at liberty to speak and hold nothing back. I am speaking as an individual, and yet I am speaking also, of course, as the responsible head of a great government, and I feel confident that I have said what the people of the United States would wish me to say. May I not add that I hope and believe that I am in effect speaking for liberals and friends of humanity in every nation and of every programme of liberty? I would fain believe that I am speaking for the silent mass of mankind everywhere who have as yet had no place or opportunity to speak their real hearts out concerning the death and ruin they see to have come already upon the persons and the homes they hold most dear.

And in holding out the expectation that the people and Government of the United States will join the other civilized nations of the world in guaranteeing the permanence of peace upon such terms as I have named I speak with the greater boldness and confidence because it is clear to every man who can think that there is in this promise no breach in either our traditions or our policy as a nation, but a fulfilment, rather, of all that we have professed or striven for.

I am proposing, as it were, that the nations should with one accord adopt the doctrine of President Monroe as the doctrine of the world: that no nation should seek to extend its polity over any other nation or people, but that every people should be left free to determine its own polity, its own way of development, unhindered, unthreatened, unafraid, the little along with the great and powerful.

I am proposing that all nations henceforth avoid entangling alliances which would draw them into competitions of power, catch them in a net of intrigue and selfish rivalry, and disturb their own affairs with influences intruded from without. There is no entangling alliance in a concert of power. When all unite to act in the same sense and with the same purpose all act in the common interest and are free to live their own lives under a common protection.

I am proposing government by the consent of the governed; that freedom of the seas which in international conference after conference representatives of the United States have urged with the eloquence of those who are the convinced disciples of liberty; and that moderation of armaments which makes of armies and navies a power for order merely, not an instrument of aggression or of selfish violence.

These are American principles, American policies. We could stand for no others. And they are also the principles and policies of forward looking men and women everywhere, of every modern nation, of every enlightened community. They are the principles of mankind and must prevail.

2. THE FOURTEEN POINTS, 1918[1]

By Woodrow Wilson

Editors' Note.—In the winter of 1918 the morale of the Allied peoples was low, and there was great and justified fear that Russia under Lenin would withdraw from the war. President Wilson's announcement of the Fourteen Points, a series of principles which should guide the postwar settlement, was designed to encourage the sagging Allied morale, to exhibit to the Russians the just and satisfactory results to be expected of Allied victory, and at the same time to suggest to the German people that to stop fighting might be better than continuation until complete destruction by arms. The Fourteen Points are Wilson's central program for a postwar settlement to provide permanent justice and safety for the nations of the world.

Gentlemen of the Congress:

Once more, as repeatedly before, the spokesmen of the Central Empires have indicated their desire to discuss the objects of the war and the possible bases of a general peace. Parleys have been in progress at Brest-Litovsk between Russian representatives and representatives of the Central Powers to which the attention of all the belligerents has been invited for the purpose of ascertaining whether it may be possible to extend these parleys into a general conference with regard to terms of peace and settlement. The Russian representatives presented not only a perfectly definite statement of the principles upon which they would be willing to conclude peace but also an equally definite programme of the concrete application of those principles. The representatives of the Central Powers, on their part, presented an outline of settlement which, if much less definite, seemed susceptible of liberal interpretation until their specific programme of practical terms was added. That programme proposed no concessions at all either to the sovereignty of Russia or to the preferences of the populations with whose fortunes it dealt, but meant, in a

1. Woodrow Wilson, *The Fourteen Points* (65th Cong., 2d sess.; House Doc. No. 765, Serial No. 7443 [Washington, 1918]), pp. 3–7.

word, that the Central Empires were to keep every foot of territory their armed forces had occupied—every province, every city, every point of vantage—as a permanent addition to their territories and their power. It is a reasonable conjecture that the general principles of settlement which they at first suggested originated with the more liberal statesmen of Germany and Austria, the men who have begun to feel the force of their own peoples' thought and purpose, while the concrete terms of actual settlement came from the military leaders who have no thought but to keep what they have got. The negotiations have been broken off. The Russian representatives were sincere and in earnest. They cannot entertain such proposals of conquest and domination.

The whole incident is full of significance. It is also full of perplexity. With whom are the Russian representatives dealing? For whom are the representatives of the Central Empires speaking? Are they speaking for the majorities of their respective parliaments or for the minority parties, that military and imperialistic minority which has so far dominated their whole policy and controlled the affairs of Turkey and of the Balkan states which have felt obliged to become their associates in this war? The Russian representatives have insisted, very justly, very wisely, and in the true spirit of modern democracy, that the conferences they have been holding with the Teutonic and Turkish statesmen should be held within open, not closed, doors, and all the world has been audience, as was desired. To whom have we been listening, then? To those who speak the spirit and intention of the resolutions of the German Reichstag of the ninth of July last, the spirit and intention of the liberal leaders and parties of Germany, or to those who resist and defy that spirit and intention and insist upon conquest and subjugation? Or are we listening, in fact, to both, unreconciled and in open and hopeless contradiction? These are very serious and pregnant questions. Upon the answer

to them depends the peace of the world.

But, whatever the results of the parleys at Brest-Litovsk, whatever the confusions of counsel and of purpose in the utterances of the spokesmen of the Central Empires, they have again attempted to acquaint the world with their objects in the war and have again challenged their adversaries to say what their objects are and what sort of settlement they would deem just and satisfactory. There is no good reason why that challenge should not be responded to, and responded to with the utmost candor. We did not wait for it. Not once, but again and again, we have laid our whole thought and purpose before the world, not in general terms only, but each time with sufficient definition to make it clear what sort of definitive terms of settlement must necessarily spring out of them. Within the last week Mr. Lloyd George has spoken with admirable candor and in admirable spirit for the people and Government of Great Britain. There is no confusion of counsel among the adversaries of the Central Powers, no uncertainty of principle, no vagueness of detail. The only secrecy of counsel, the only lack of fearless frankness, the only failure to make definite statement of the objects of the war, lies with Germany and her Allies. The issues of life and death hang upon these definitions. No statesman who has the least conception of his responsibility ought for a moment to permit himself to continue this tragical and appalling outpouring of blood and treasure unless he is sure beyond a peradventure that the objects of the vital sacrifice are part and parcel of the very life of Society and that the people for whom he speaks think them right and imperative as he does.

There is, moreover, a voice calling for these definitions of principle and of purpose which is, it seems to me, more thrilling and more compelling than any of the many moving voices with which the troubled air of the world is filled. It is the voice of the Russian people. They are prostrate and all but helpless, it would seem, before the grim power of Germany, which has hitherto known no relenting and no pity. Their power, apparently, is shattered. And yet their soul is not subservient. They will not yield either in principle or in action. Their conception of what is right, and what it is humane and honorable for them to accept, has been stated with a frankness, a largeness of view, a generosity of spirit, and a universal human sympathy which must challenge the admiration of every friend of mankind; and they have refused to compound their ideals or desert others that they themselves may be safe. They call to us to say what it is that we desire, in what, if in anything, our purpose and our spirit differ from theirs; and I believe that the people of the United States would wish me to respond, with utter simplicity and frankness. Whether their present leaders believe it or not, it is our heartfelt desire and hope that some way may be opened whereby we may be privileged to assist the people of Russia to attain their utmost hope of liberty and ordered peace.

It will be our wish and purpose that the processes of peace, when they are begun, shall be absolutely open and that they shall involve and permit henceforth no secret understandings of any kind. The day of conquest and aggrandizement is gone by; so is also the day of secret covenants entered into in the interest of particular governments and likely at some unlooked-for moment to upset the peace of the world. It is this happy fact, now clear to the view of every public man whose thoughts do not still linger in an age that is dead and gone, which makes it possible for every nation whose purposes are consistent with justice and the peace of the world to avow now or at any other time the objects it has in view.

We entered this war because violations of right had occurred which touched us to the quick and made the life of our own people impossible unless they were corrected and the world secured once for all against their recurrence. What we demand in this war, therefore, is nothing peculiar to ourselves. It is that the world be

made fit and safe to live in; and particularly that it be made safe for every peace-loving nation which, like our own, wishes to live its own life, determine its own institutions, be assured of justice and fair dealing by the other peoples of the world as against force and selfish aggression. All the peoples of the world are in effect partners in this interest, and for our own part we see very clearly that unless justice be done to others it will not be done to us. The programme of the world's peace, therefore, is our programme; and that programme, the only possible programme, as we see it, is this:

I. Open covenants of peace, openly arrived at, after which there shall be no private international understandings of any kind but diplomacy shall proceed always frankly and in the public view.

II. Absolute freedom of navigation upon the seas, outside territorial waters, alike in peace and in war, except as the seas may be closed in whole or in part by international action for the enforcement of international covenants.

III. The removal, so far as possible, of all economic barriers and the establishment of an equality of trade conditions among all the nations consenting to the peace and associating themselves for its maintenance.

IV. Adequate guarantees given and taken that national armaments will be reduced to the lowest point consistent with domestic safety.

V. A free, open-minded, and absolutely impartial adjustment of all colonial claims, based upon a strict observance of the principle that in determining all such questions of sovereignty the interests of the populations concerned must have equal weight with the equitable claims of the government whose title is to be determined.

VI. The evacuation of all Russian territory and such a settlement of all questions affecting Russia as will secure the best and freest cooperation of the other nations of the world in obtaining for her an unhampered and unembarrassed opportunity for the independent determination of her own political development and national policy and assure her of a sincere welcome into the society of free nations under institutions of her own choosing; and, more than a welcome, assistance also of every kind that she may need and may herself desire. The treatment accorded Russia by her sister nations in the months to come will be the acid test of their good will, of their comprehension of her needs as distinguished from their own interests, and of their intelligent and unselfish sympathy.

VII. Belgium, the whole world will agree, must be evacuated and restored, without any attempt to limit the sovereignty which she enjoys in common with all other free nations. No other single act will serve as this will serve to restore confidence among the nations in the laws which they have themselves set and determined for the government of their relations with one another. Without this healing act the whole structure and validity of international law is forever impaired.

VIII. All French territory should be freed and the invaded portions restored, and the wrong done to France by Prussia in 1871 in the matter of Alsace-Lorraine, which has unsettled the peace of the world for nearly fifty years, should be righted, in order that peace may once more be made secure in the interest of all.

IX. A readjustment of the frontiers of Italy should be effected along clearly recognizable lines of nationality.

X. The peoples of Austria-Hungary, whose place among the nations we wish to see safeguarded and assured, should be accorded the freest opportunity of autonomous development.

XI. Rumania, Serbia, and Montenegro should be evacuated; occupied territories restored; Serbia accorded free and secure access to the sea; and the relations of the several Balkan states to one another determined by friendly counsel along historically established lines of allegiance and nationality; and international guarantees of the political and economic independence

and territorial integrity of the several Balkan states should be entered into.

XII. The Turkish portions of the present Ottoman Empire should be assured a secure sovereignty, but the other nationalities which are now under Turkish rule should be assured an undoubted security of life and an absolutely unmolested opportunity of autonomous development, and the Dardanelles should be permanently opened as a free passage to the ships and commerce of all nations under international guarantees.

XIII. An independent Polish state should be erected which should include the territories inhabited by indisputably Polish populations, which should be assured a free and secure access to the sea, and whose political and economic independence and territorial integrity should be guaranteed by international covenant.

XIV. A general association of nations must be formed under specific covenants for the purpose of affording mutual guarantees of political independence and territorial integrity to great and small states alike.

In regard to these essential rectifications of wrong and assertions of right we feel ourselves to be intimate partners of all the governments and peoples associated together against the Imperialists. We cannot be separated in interest or divided in purpose. We stand together until the end.

For such arrangements and covenants we are willing to fight and to continue to fight until they are achieved; but only because we wish the right to prevail and desire a just and stable peace such as can be secured only by removing the chief provocations to war, which this programme does remove. We have no jealousy of German greatness, and there is nothing in this programme that impairs it. We grudge her no achievement or distinction of learning or of pacific enterprise such as have made her record very bright and very enviable. We do not wish to injure her or to block in any way her legitimate influence or power. We do not wish to fight her either with arms or with hostile arrangements of trade if she is willing to associate herself with us and the other peace-loving nations of the world in covenants of justice and law and fair dealing. We wish her only to accept a place of equality among the peoples of the world—the new world in which we now live—instead of a place of mastery.

Neither do we presume to suggest to her any alteration or modification of her institutions. But it is necessary, we must frankly say, and necessary as a preliminary to any intelligent dealings with her on our part, that we should know whom her spokesmen speak for when they speak to us, whether for the Reichstag majority or for the military party and the men whose creed is imperial domination.

We have spoken now, surely, in terms too concrete to admit of any further doubt or question. An evident principle runs through the whole programme I have outlined. It is the principle of justice to all peoples and nationalities, and their right to live on equal terms of liberty and safety with one another, whether they be strong or weak. Unless this principle be made its foundation no part of the structure of international justice can stand. The people of the United States could act upon no other principle; and to the vindication of this principle they are ready to devote their lives, their honor, and everything that they possess. The moral climax of this the culminating and final war for human liberty has come, and they are ready to put their own strength, their own highest purpose, their own integrity and devotion to the test.

3. COVENANT OF THE LEAGUE OF NATIONS[1]

EDITORS' NOTE.—The Covenant of the League of Nations was the first article of the Versailles Treaty between Germany and the twenty-seven nations which had broken relations or been at war with her. The treaty was drafted from January to June, 1919, and represented primarily the convictions of the three principal powers present —France, Britain, and the United States—each represented during most of the conference by its head of state, Clemenceau, Lloyd George, and Wilson. The other nations ratified the treaty and created the League of Nations, which was the cornerstone of Wilson's program for settlement and permanent peace. The United States Senate refused to ratify the treaty. A separate peace with Germany was made by congressional resolution on July 2, 1921.

THE HIGH CONTRACTING PARTIES,

In order to promote international cooperation and to achieve international peace and security

by the acceptance of obligations not to resort to war,

by the prescription of open, just and honourable relations between nations,

by the firm establishment of the understandings of international law as the actual rule of conduct among Governments, and

by the maintenance of justice and a scrupulous respect for all treaty obligations in the dealings of organised peoples with one another,

Agree to this Covenant of the League of Nations.

1. Secretariat of the League of Nations, *The Aims, Methods, and Activity of the League of Nations* (Geneva, 1935), pp. 196–209.

ARTICLE 1

The original Members of the League of Nations shall be those of the Signatories which are named in the Annex to this Covenant and also such of those other States named in the Annex as shall accede without reservation to this Covenant. Such accession shall be effected by a Declaration deposited with the Secretariat within two months of the coming into force of the Covenant. Notice thereof shall be sent to all other Members of the League.

Any fully self-governing State, Dominion or Colony not named in the Annex may become a Member of the League if its admission is agreed to by two-thirds of the Assembly, provided that it shall give effective guarantees of its sincere intention to observe its international obligations, and shall accept such regulations as may be prescribed by the League in regard to its military, naval and air forces and armaments.

Any Member of the League may, after two years' notice of its intention so to do, withdraw from the League, provided that all its international obligations and all its obligations under this Covenant shall have been fulfilled at the time of its withdrawal.

ARTICLE 2

The action of the League under this Covenant shall be effected through the instrumentality of an Assembly and of a Council, with a permanent Secretariat.

ARTICLE 3

The Assembly shall consist of Representatives of the Members of the League.

The Assembly shall meet at stated intervals and from time to time as occasion may require at the Seat of the League or at such other place as may be decided upon.

The Assembly may deal at its meetings with any matter within the sphere of action of the League or affecting the peace of the world.

At meetings of the Assembly each Member of the League shall have one vote, and may have not more than three Representatives.

ARTICLE 4

The Council shall consist of Representatives of the Principal Allied and Associated Powers, together with Representatives of four other Members of the League. These four Members of the League shall be selected by the Assembly from time to time in its discretion. Until the appointment of the Representatives of the four Members of the League first selected by the Assembly, Representatives of Belgium, Brazil, Spain and Greece shall be members of the Council.

With the approval of the majority of the Assembly, the Council may name additional Members of the League whose Representatives shall always be members of the Council; the Council with like approval may increase the number of Members of the League to be selected by the Assembly for representation on the Council.

The Council shall meet from time to time as occasion may require, and at least once a year, at the Seat of the League, or at such other place as may be decided upon.

The Council may deal at its meetings with any matter within the sphere of action of the League or affecting the peace of the world.

Any Member of the League not represented on the Council shall be invited to send a Representative to sit as a member at any meeting of the Council during the consideration of matters specially affecting the interests of that Member of the League.

At meetings of the Council, each Member of the League represented on the Council shall have one vote, and may have not more than one Representative.

ARTICLE 5

Except where otherwise expressly provided in this Covenant or by the terms of the present Treaty, decisions at any meeting of the Assembly or of the Council shall require the agreement of all the Members of the League represented at the meeting.

All matters of procedure at meetings of the Assembly or of the Council, including the appointment of Committees to investigate particular matters, shall be regulated by the Assembly or by the Council and may be decided by a majority of the Members of the League represented at the meeting.

The first meeting of the Assembly and the first meeting of the Council shall be summoned by the President of the United States of America.

ARTICLE 6

The permanent Secretariat shall be established at the Seat of the League. The Secretariat shall comprise a Secretary-General and such secretaries and staff as may be required.

The first Secretary-General shall be the person named in the Annex; thereafter the Secretary-General shall be appointed by the Council with the approval of the majority of the Assembly.

The secretaries and staff of the Secretariat shall be appointed by the Secretary-General with the approval of the Council.

The Secretary-General shall act in that capacity at all meetings of the Assembly and of the Council.

ARTICLE 7

The Seat of the League is established at Geneva.

The Council may at any time decide that the Seat of the League shall be established elsewhere.

All positions under or in connection with the League, including the Secretariat, shall be open equally to men and women.

Representatives of the Members of the League and officials of the League when engaged on the business of the League shall enjoy diplomatic privileges and immunities.

The buildings and other property occu-pied by the League or its officials or by Representatives attending its meetings shall be inviolable.

ARTICLE 8

The Members of the League recognise that the maintenance of peace requires the reduction of national armaments to the lowest point consistent with national safety and the enforcement by common action of international obligations.

The Council, taking account of the geographical situation and circumstances of each State, shall formulate plans for such reduction for the consideration and action of the several Governments.

Such plans shall be subject to reconsideration and revision at least every ten years.

After these plans have been adopted by the several Governments, the limits of armaments therein fixed shall not be exceeded without the concurrence of the Council.

The Members of the League agree that the manufacture by private enterprise of munitions and implements of war is open to grave objections. The Council shall advise how the evil effects attendant upon such manufacture can be prevented, due regard being had to the necessities of those Members of the League which are not able to manufacture the munitions and implements of war necessary for their safety.

The Members of the League undertake to interchange full and frank information as to the scale of their armaments, their military, naval and air programmes and the condition of such of their industries as are adaptable to warlike purposes.

ARTICLE 9

A permanent Commission shall be constituted to advise the Council on the execution of the provisions of Articles 1 and 8 and on military, naval and air questions generally.

ARTICLE 10

The Members of the League undertake to respect and preserve as against external aggression the territorial integrity and existing political independence of all Members of the League. In case of any such aggression or in case of any threat or danger of such aggression the Council shall advise upon the means by which this obligation shall be fulfilled.

ARTICLE II

Any war or threat of war, whether immediately affecting any of the Members of the League or not, is hereby declared a matter of concern to the whole League, and the League shall take any action that may be deemed wise and effectual to safeguard the peace of nations. In case any such emergency should arise, the Secretary-General shall on the request of any Member of the League forthwith summon a meeting of the Council.

It is also declared to be the friendly right of each Member of the League to bring to the attention of the Assembly or of the Council any circumstance whatever affecting international relations which threatens to disturb international peace or the good understanding between nations upon which peace depends.

ARTICLE 12

The Members of the League agree that if there should arise between them any dispute likely to lead to a rupture they will submit the matter either to arbitration or to inquiry by the Council, and they agree in no case to resort to war until three months after the award by the arbitrators or the report by the Council.

In any case under this Article the award of the arbitrators shall be made within a reasonable time, and the report of the Council shall be made within six months after the submission of the dispute.

ARTICLE 13

The Members of the League agree that whenever any dispute shall arise between them which they recognise to be suitable for submission to arbitration and which cannot be satisfactorily settled by diplomacy, they will submit the whole subject-matter to arbitration.

Disputes as to the interpretation of a treaty, as to any question of international law, as to the existence of any fact which, if established, would constitute a breach of any international obligation, or as to the extent and nature of the reparation to be made for any such breach, are declared to be among those which are generally suitable for submission to arbitration.

The Members of the League agree that they will carry out in full good faith any award that may be rendered, and that they will not resort to war against a Member of the League which complies therewith. In the event of any failure to carry out such an award, the Council shall propose what steps should be taken to give effect thereto.

ARTICLE 14

The Council shall formulate and submit to the Members of the League for adoption plans for the establishment of a Permanent Court of International Justice. The Court shall be competent to hear and determine any dispute of an international character which the parties thereto submit to it. The Court may also give an advisory opinion upon any dispute or question referred to it by the Council or by the Assembly.

ARTICLE 15

If there should arise between Members of the League any dispute likely to lead to a rupture, which is not submitted to arbitration in accordance with Article 13, the Members of the League agree that they will submit the matter to the Council. Any party to the dispute may effect such submission by giving notice of the existence of the dispute to the Secretary-General, who will make all necessary arrangements for a full investigation and consideration thereof.

For this purpose the parties to the dispute will communicate to the Secretary-General, as promptly as possible, statements of their case with all the relevant facts and papers, and the Council may forthwith direct the publication thereof.

The Council shall endeavour to effect a settlement of the dispute, and if such efforts are successful, a statement shall be made public giving such facts and explanations regarding the dispute and the terms of settlement thereof as the Council may deem appropriate.

If the dispute is not thus settled, the Council either unanimously or by a majority vote shall make and publish a report containing a statement of the facts of the dispute and the recommendations which are deemed just and proper in regard thereto.

Any Member of the League represented on the Council may make public a statement of the facts of the dispute and of its conclusions regarding the same.

If a report by the Council is unanimously agreed to by the members thereof other than the Representatives of one or more of the parties to the dispute, the Members of the League agree that they will not go to war with any party to the dispute which complies with the recommendations of the report.

If the Council fails to reach a report which is unanimously agreed to by the members thereof, other than the Representatives of one or more of the parties to the dispute, the Members of the League reserve to themselves the right to take such action as they shall consider necessary for the maintenance of right and justice.

If the dispute between the parties is claimed by one of them, and is found by the Council, to arise out of a matter which by international law is solely within the domestic jurisdiction of that party, the Council shall so report, and shall make no recommendation as to its settlement.

The Council may in any case under this Article refer the dispute to the Assembly. The dispute shall be so referred at the request of either party to the dispute provided that such request be made within fourteen days after the submission of the dispute to the Council.

In any case referred to the Assembly, all the provisions of this Article and of Article 12 relating to the action and powers of the Council shall apply to the action and powers of the Assembly, provided that a a report made by the Assembly, if concurred in by the Representatives of those Members of the League represented on the Council and of a majority of the other Members of the League, exclusive in each case of the Representatives of the parties to the dispute, shall have the same force as a report by the Council concurred in by all the members thereof other than the Representatives of one or more of the parties to the dispute.

ARTICLE 16

Should any Member of the League resort to war in disregard of its covenants under Articles 12, 13 or 15, it shall *ipso facto* be deemed to have committed an act of war against all other Members of the League, which hereby undertake immediately to subject it to the severance of all trade or financial relations, the prohibition of all intercourse between their nationals and the nationals of the covenant-breaking State, and the prevention of all financial, commercial or personal intercourse between the nationals of the covenant-breaking State and the nationals of any other State, whether a Member of the League or not.

It shall be the duty of the Council in such case to recommend to the several Governments concerned what effective military, naval or air force the Members of the League shall severally contribute to the armed forces to be used to protect the covenants of the League.

The Members of the League agree, further, that they will mutually support one another in the financial and economic measures which are taken under this Article, in order to minimise the loss and inconvenience resulting from the above measures, and that they will mutually support one another in resisting any special measures aimed at one of their number by the covenant-breaking State, and that they will take the necessary steps to afford passage through their territory to the forces of any of the Members of the League which are co-operating to protect the covenants of the League.

Any Member of the League which has violated any covenant of the League may be declared to be no longer a Member of the League by a vote of the Council concurred in by the Representatives of all the other Members of the League represented thereon.

ARTICLE 17

In the event of a dispute between a Member of the League and a State which is not a Member of the League, or between States not Members of the League, the State or States not Members of the League shall be invited to accept the obligations of membership in the League for the purposes of such dispute, upon such conditions as the Council may deem just. If such invitation is accepted, the provisions of Articles 12 to 16 inclusive shall be applied with such modifications as may be deemed necessary by the Council.

Upon such invitation being given the Council shall immediately institute an inquiry into the circumstances of the dispute and recommend such action as may seem best and most effectual in the circumstances.

If a State so invited shall refuse to accept the obligations of membership in the League for the purposes of such dispute, and shall resort to war against a Member of the League, the provisions of Article 16 shall be applicable as against the State taking such action.

If both parties to the dispute when so invited refuse to accept the obligations of membership in the League for the purposes of such dispute, the Council may take such measures and make such recommendations as will prevent hostilities and will result in the settlement of the dispute.

ARTICLE 18

Every treaty or international engagement entered into hereafter by any Member of the League shall be forthwith registered with the Secretariat and shall, as soon as possible, be published by it. No such treaty or international engagement shall be binding until so registered.

ARTICLE 19

The Assembly may from time to time advise the reconsideration by Members of the League of treaties which have become inapplicable and the consideration of international conditions whose continuance might endanger the peace of the world.

ARTICLE 20

The Members of the League severally agree that this Covenant is accepted as abrogating all obligations or understandings *inter se* which are inconsistent with the terms thereof, and solemnly undertake that they will not hereafter enter into any engagements inconsistent with the terms thereof.

In case any Member of the League shall, before becoming a Member of the League, have undertaken any obligations inconsistent with the terms of this Covenant, it shall be the duty of such Member to take immediate steps to procure its release from such obligations.

ARTICLE 21

Nothing in this Covenant shall be deemed to affect the validity of international engagements, such as treaties of arbitration or regional understandings like the Monroe doctrine, for securing the maintenance of peace.

ARTICLE 22

To those colonies and territories which as a consequence of the late war have ceased to be under the sovereignty of the States which formerly governed them and which are inhabited by peoples not yet able to stand by themselves under the strenuous conditions of the modern world, there should be applied the principle that the well-being and development of such peoples form a sacred trust of civilisation and that securities for the performance of this trust should be embodied in this Covenant.

The best method of giving practical effect to this principle is that the tutelage of such peoples should be entrusted to advanced nations who by reason of their resources, their experience or their geographical position, can best undertake this responsibility, and who are willing to accept it, and that this tutelage should be exercised by them as Mandatories on behalf of the League.

The character of the mandate must differ according to the stage of the development of the people, the geographical situation of the territory, its economic conditions and other similar circumstances.

Certain communities formerly belonging to the Turkish Empire have reached a stage of development where their existence as independent nations can be provisionally recognised subject to the rendering of administrative advice and assistance by a Mandatory until such time as they are able to stand alone. The wishes of these communities must be a principal consideration in the selection of the Mandatory.

Other peoples, especially those of Central Africa, are at such a stage that the Mandatory must be responsible for the administration of the territory under conditions which will guarantee freedom of conscience and religion, subject only to the maintenance of public order and morals, the prohibition of abuses such as the slave trade, the arms traffic and the liquor traffic, and the prevention of the establishment of fortifications or military and naval bases and of military training of the natives for other than police purposes and the defence of territory, and will also secure equal opportunities for the trade and commerce of other Members of the League.

There are territories, such as South West Africa and certain of the South Pacific Islands, which, owing to the sparseness of their population, or their small size, or their remoteness from the centres of civilisation, or their geographical contiguity to the territory of the Mandatory, and other circumstances, can be best administered under the laws of the Mandatory as integral portions of its territory, subject to the safeguards above mentioned in the interests of the indigenous population.

In every case of mandate, the Mandatory shall render to the Council an annual report in reference to the territory committed to its charge.

The degree of authority, control or administration to be exercised by the Mandatory shall, if not previously agreed upon by the Members of the League, be explicitly defined in each case by the Council.

A permanent Commission shall be constituted to receive and examine the annual reports of the Mandatories and to advise the Council on all matters relating to the observance of the mandates.

ARTICLE 23

Subject to and in accordance with the provisions of international conventions existing or hereafter to be agreed upon, the Members of the League:

(*a*) will endeavour to secure and maintain fair and humane conditions of labour for men, women and children, both in their own countries and in all countries to which their commercial and industrial relations extend, and for that purpose will establish and maintain the necessary international organisations;

(*b*) undertake to secure just treatment of the native inhabitants of territories under their control;

(*c*) will entrust the League with the general supervision over the execution of agreements with regard to the traffic in women and children, and the traffic in opium and other dangerous drugs;

(*d*) will entrust the League with the general supervision of the trade in arms and ammunition with the countries in which the control of this traffic is necessary in the common interest;

(e) will make provision to secure and maintain freedom of communications and of transit and equitable treatment for the commerce of all Members of the League. In this connection, the special necessities of the regions devastated during the war of 1914–1918 shall be borne in mind;

(f) will endeavour to take steps in matters of international concern for the prevention and control of disease.

ARTICLE 24

There shall be placed under the direction of the League all international bureaux already established by general treaties if the parties to such treaties consent. All such international bureaux and all commissions for the regulation of matters of international interest hereafter constituted shall be placed under the direction of the League.

In all matters of international interest which are regulated by general conventions but which are not placed under the control of international bureaux or commissions, the Secretariat of the League shall, subject to the consent of the Council

and if desired by the parties, collect and distribute all relevant information and shall render any other assistance which may be necessary or desirable.

The Council may include as part of the expenses of the Secretariat the expenses of any bureau or commission which is placed under the direction of the League.

ARTICLE 25

The Members of the League agree to encourage and promote the establishment and co-operation of duly authorised voluntary national Red Cross organisations having as purposes the improvement of health, the prevention of disease and the mitigation of suffering throughout the world.

ARTICLE 26

Amendments to this Covenant will take effect when ratified by the Members of the League whose Representatives compose the Council and by a majority of the Members of the League whose Representatives compose the Assembly.

No such amendment shall bind any Member of the League which signifies its dissent therefrom, but in that case it shall cease to be a Member of the League.

4. PUEBLO SPEECH ON THE LEAGUE, 1919[1]

By Woodrow Wilson

EDITORS' NOTE.—President Wilson submitted the Versailles Treaty to the Senate for ratification in July, 1919. To counter the strong opposition in the Senate to the League of Nations, Wilson toured the country in September to arouse a popular demand for the League which he hoped the Senate would be unable to ignore. The last

and most impassioned speech of this trip was given at Pueblo, Colorado, on September 25. Wilson fell ill the next day, returned hurriedly to Washington, and, partially paralyzed, was largely inactive during the crucial struggle resulting in the American rejection of the Versailles Treaty.

. . . The chief pleasure of my trip has been that it has nothing to do with my per-

1. *Congressional Record*, LVIII, Part 7 (October 6, 1919), 6424–27.

sonal fortunes, that it has nothing to do with my personal reputation, that it has nothing to do with anything except great principles uttered by Americans of all sorts and of all parties which we are now trying to realize at this crisis of the affairs of the world. But there have been unpleasant impressions as well as pleasant impressions, my fellow citizens, as I have crossed the continent. I have perceived more and more that men have been busy creating an absolutely false impression of what the treaty of peace and the covenant of the league of nations contain and mean. I find, moreover, that there is an organized propaganda proceeded from which threatened this country here and there with disloyalty, and I want to say—I cannot say too often—any man who carries a hyphen about with him carries a dagger that he is ready to plunge into the vitals of this Republic whenever he gets ready. If I can catch any man with a hyphen in this great contest I will know that I have got an enemy of the Republic. My fellow citizens, it is only certain bodies of foreign sympathies, certain bodies of sympathy with foreign nations that are organized against this great document which the American representatives have brought back from Paris. Therefore, in order to clear away the mists, in order to remove the impressions, in order to check the falsehoods that have clustered around this great subject, I want to tell you a few very simple things about the treaty and the covenant.

Do not think of this treaty of peace as merely a settlement with Germany. It is that. It is a very severe settlement with Germany, but there is not anything in it that she did not earn. Indeed, she earned more than she can ever be able to pay for, and the punishment exacted of her is not a punishment greater than she can bear, and it is absolutely necessary in order that no other nation may ever plot such a thing against humanity and civilization. But the treaty is so much more than that. It is not merely a settlement with Germany; it is a readjustment of those great injustices which underlie the whole structure of European and Asiatic society. This is only the first of several treaties. They are all constructed upon the same plan. The Austrian treaty follows the same lines. The treaty with Hungary follows the same lines. The treaty with Bulgaria follows the same lines. The treaty with Turkey, when it is formulated, will follow the same lines. What are those lines? They are based upon the purpose to see that every government dealt with in this great settlement is put in the hands of the people and taken out of the hands of coteries and of sovereigns who had no right to rule over the people. It is a people's treaty, that accomplishes by a great sweep of practical justice the liberation of men who never could have liberated themselves, and the power of the most powerful nations has been devoted not to their aggrandizement but to the liberation of people whom they could have put under their control if they had chosen to do so. Not one foot of territory is demanded by the conquerors, not one single item of submission to their authority is demanded by them. The men who sat around that table in Paris knew that the time had come when the people were no longer going to consent to live under masters, but were going to live the lives that they chose themselves, to live under such governments as they chose themselves to erect. That is the fundamental principle of this great settlement.

And we did not stop with that. We added a great international charter for the rights of labor. Reject this treaty, impair it, and this is the consequence to the laboring men of the world, that there is no international tribunal which can bring the moral judgments of the world to bear upon the great labor questions of the day. What we need to do with regard to the labor questions of the day, my fellow countrymen, is to lift them into the light, is to lift them out of the haze and distraction of passion, of hostility, out into the calm spaces where men look at things without passion. The more men you get into a great discussion the more you exclude passion. Just so soon as the calm judgment of the world is directed upon the question of justice to labor, labor is going to have a forum such as it never was supplied with before, and men everywhere are going to see that the problem of labor is nothing more nor less than the problem of the elevation of humanity. We must see that all the questions which have disturbed the world, all the questions which have eaten into the confidence of men toward their governments, all the questions which have disturbed the processes of industry, shall be brought out where men of all points of view, men of all attitudes of mind, men of all kinds of experience, may contribute their part to the settlement of the great questions which we must settle and can not ignore.

At the front of this great treaty is put the covenant of the league of nations. It will also be at the front of the Austrian treaty and the Hungarian treaty and the Bulgarian treaty and the treaty with Turkey. Every one of them will contain the covenant of the league of nations, because you can not work any of them without the covenant of the league of nations. Unless you get the united, concerted purpose and power of the great Governments of the world behind this settlement, it will fall down like a house of cards. There is only one power to put behind the liberation of mankind, and that is the power of mankind. It is the power of the united moral forces of the world, and in the covenant of the league of nations the moral forces of the world are mobilized. For what purpose? Reflect, my fellow citizens, that the membership of this great league is going to include all the great fighting nations of the world, as well as the weak ones. It is not for the present going to include Germany, but for the time being Germany is not a great fighting country. All the nations that have power that can be mobilized are going to be members of this league, including the United States. And what do they unite for? They enter into a solemn promise to one another that they will never use their power against one another for aggression; that they never will impair the territorial integrity of a neighbor; that

they never will interfere with the political independence of a neighbor; that they will abide by the principle that great populations are entitled to determine their own destiny and that they will not interfere with that destiny; and that no matter what differences arise amongst them they will never resort to war without first having done one or the other of two things—either submitted the matter of controversy to arbitration, in which case they agree to abide by the result without question, or submitted it to the consideration of the council of the league of nations, laying before that council all the documents, all the facts, agreeing that the council can publish the documents and the facts to the whole world, agreeing that there shall be six months allowed for the mature consideration of those facts by the council, and agreeing that at the expiration of the six months, even if they are not then ready to accept the advice of the council with regard to the settlement of the dispute, they will still not go to war for another three months. In other words, they consent, no matter what happens, to submit every matter of difference between them to the judgment of mankind, and just so certainly as they do that, my fellow citizens, war will be in the far background, war will be pushed out of the foreground of terror in which it has kept the world for generation after generation, and men will know that there will be a calm time of deliberate counsel. The most dangerous thing for a bad cause is to expose it to the opinion of the world. The most certain way that you can prove that a man is mistaken is by letting all his neighbors know what he thinks, by letting all his neighbors discuss what he thinks, and if he is in the wrong you will notice that he will stay at home, he will not walk on the street. He will be afraid of the eyes of his neighbors. He will be afraid of their judgment of his character. He will know that his cause is lost unless he can sustain it by the arguments of right and of justice. The same law that applies to individuals applies to nations.

But, you say, "We have heard that we might be at a disadvantage in the league of nations." Well, whoever told you that either was deliberately falsifying or he had not read the covenant of the league of nations. I leave him the choice. I want to give you a very simple account of the organization of the league of nations and let you judge for yourselves. It is a very simple organization. The power of the league, or rather the activities of the league, lie in two bodies. There is the council, which consists of one representative from each of the principal allied and associated powers—that is to say, the United States, Great Britain, France, Italy, and Japan—along with four other representatives of smaller powers chosen out of the general body of the membership of the league. The council is the source of every active policy of the league, and no active policy of the league can be adopted without a unanimous vote of the council. That is explicitly stated in the covenant itself. Does it not evidently follow that the league of nations can adopt no policy whatever without the consent of the United States? The affirmative vote of the representative of the United States is necessary in every case. Now, you have heard of six votes belonging to the British Empire. Those six votes are not in the council. They are in the assembly, and the interesting thing is that the assembly does not vote. I must qualify that statement a little, but essentially it is absolutely true. In every matter in which the assembly is given a voice, and there are only four or five, its vote does not count unless concurred in by the representatives of all the nations represented on the council, so that there is no validity to any vote of the assembly unless in that vote also the representative of the United States concurs. That one vote of the United States is as big as the six votes of the British Empire. I am not jealous for advantage, my fellow citizens, but I think that is a perfectly safe situation. There is no validity in a vote, either by the council or the assembly, in which we do not concur. So much for the statements about the six votes of the British Empire.

Look at it in another aspect. The assembly is the talking body. The assembly was created in order that anybody that purposed anything wrong should be subjected to the awkward circumstance that everybody could talk about it. This is the great assembly in which all the things that are likely to disturb the peace of the world or the good understanding between nations are to be exposed to the general view, and I want to ask you if you think it was unjust, unjust to the United States, that speaking parts should be assigned to the several portions of the British Empire? Do you think it unjust that there should be some spokesman in debate for that fine little stout Republic down in the Pacific, New Zealand? Do you think it was unjust that Australia should be allowed to stand up and take part in the debate—Australia, from which we have learned some of the most useful progressive policies of modern time, a little nation only five million in a great continent, but counting for several times five in its activities and in its interest in liberal reform? Do you think it unjust that that little Republic down in South Africa, whose gallant resistance to being subjected to any outside authority at all we admired for so many months and whose fortunes we followed with such interest, should have a speaking part? Great Britain obliged South Africa to submit to her sovereignty, but she immediately after that felt that it was convenient and right to hand the whole self-government of that colony over to the very men whom she had beaten. The representatives of South Africa in Paris were two of the most distinguished generals of the Boer Army, two of the realest men I ever met, two men that could talk sober counsel and wise advice, along with the best statesmen in Europe. To exclude General Botha and General Smuts from the right to stand up in the parliament of the world and say something concerning the affairs of mankind would be absurd. And what about Canada? Is not Canada a good neighbor? I ask you, Is not Canada more likely to agree with the United States than with Great Britain? Canada has a speaking part. And then, for the first time in the history of the world, that great voiceless multitude, that throng hundreds of millions strong in India, has a voice, and I want to testify that some of the wisest and most dignified figures in the peace conference at Paris came from India, men who seemed to carry in their minds an older wisdom than the rest of us had, whose traditions ran back into so many of the unhappy fortunes of mankind that they seemed very useful counselors as to how some ray of hope and some prospect of happiness could be opened to its people. I for my part have no jealousy whatever of those five speaking parts in the assembly. Those speaking parts can not translate themselves into five votes that can in any matter override the voice and purpose of the United States.

Let us sweep aside all this language of jealousy. Let us be big enough to know the facts and to welcome the facts, because the facts are based upon the principle that America has always fought for, namely, the equality of self-governing peoples, whether they were big or little—not counting men, but counting rights, not counting representation, but counting the purpose of that representation. When you hear an opinion quoted, you do not count the number of persons who hold it; you ask, "Who said that?" You weigh opinions, you do not count them, and the beauty of all democracies is that every voice can be heard, every voice can have its effect, every voice can contribute to the general judgment that is finally arrived at. That is the object of democracy. Let us accept what America has always fought for, and accept it with pride that America showed the way and made the proposal. I do not mean that America made the proposal in this particular instance; I mean that the principle was an American principle, proposed by America.

When you come to the heart of the covenant, my fellow citizens, you will find it in article 10, and I am very much interested to know that the other things have been blown away like bubbles. There is nothing in the other contentions with regard to the league of nations, but there is something in article 10 that you ought to realize and ought to accept or reject. Article 10 is the heart of the whole matter. What is article 10? I never am certain that I can from memory give a literal repetition of its language, but I am sure that I can give an exact interpretation of its meaning. Article 10 provides that every member of the league covenants to respect and preserve the territorial integrity and existing political independence of every other member of the league as against external aggression. Not against internal disturbance. There was not a man at that table who did not admit the sacredness of the right of self-determination, the sacredness of the right of any body of people to say that they would not continue to live under the Government they were then living under, and under article 11 of the covenant they are given a place to say whether they will live under it or not. For following article 10 is article 11, which makes it the right of any member of the league at any time to call attention to anything, anywhere, that is likely to disturb the peace of the world or the good understanding between nations upon which the peace of the world depends. I want to give you an illustration of what that would mean.

You have heard a great deal—something that was true and a great deal that was false—about that provision of the treaty which hands over to Japan the rights which Germany enjoyed in the Province of Shantung in China. In the first place, Germany did not enjoy any rights there that other nations had not already claimed. For my part, my judgment, my moral judgment, is against the whole set of concessions. They were all of them unjust to China, they ought never to have been exacted, they were all exacted by duress from a great body of thoughtful and ancient and helpless people. There never was any right in any of them. Thank God, America never asked for any, never dreamed of asking for any. But when Germany got this concession in 1898, the Government of the United States made no protest whatever. That was not because the Government of the United States was not in the hands of high-minded and conscientious men. It was. William McKinley was President and John Hay was Secretary of State—as safe hands to leave the honor of the United States in as any that you can cite. They made no protest because the state of international law at that time was that it was none of their business unless they could show that the interests of the United States were affected, and the only thing that they could show with regard to the interests of the United States was that Germany might close the doors of Shantung Province against the trade of the United States. They, therefore, demanded and obtained promises that we could continue to sell merchandise in Shantung. Immediately following that concession to Germany there was a concession to Russia of the same sort, of Port Arthur, and Port Arthur was handed over subsequently to Japan on the very territory of the United States. Don't you remember that when Russia and Japan got into war with one another the war was brought to a conclusion by a treaty written at Portsmouth, N.H., and in that treaty, without the slightest intimation from any authoritative sources in America that the Government of the United States had any objection, Port Arthur, Chinese territory, was turned over to Japan? I want you distinctly to understand that there is no thought of criticism in my mind. I am expounding to you a state of international law. Now, read articles 10 and 11. You will see that international law is revolutionized by putting morals into it. Article 10 says that no member of the league, and that includes all these nations that have demanded these things unjustly of China, shall impair

the territorial integrity or the political independence of any other member of the league. China is going to be a member of the league. Article 11 says that any member of the league can call attention to anything that is likely to disturb the peace of the world or the good understanding between nations, and China is for the first time in the history of mankind afforded a standing before the jury of the world. I, for my part, have a profound sympathy for China, and I am proud to have taken part in an arrangement which promises the protection of the world to the rights of China. The whole atmosphere of the world is changed by a thing like that, my fellow citizens. The whole international practice of the world is revolutionized.

But you will say, "What is the second sentence of article 10? That is what gives very disturbing thoughts." The second sentence is that the council of the league shall advise what steps, if any, are necessary to carry out the guaranty of the first sentence, namely, that the members will respect and preserve the territorial integrity and political independence of the other members. I do not know any other meaning for the word "advise" except "advise." The council advises, and it can not advise without the vote of the United States. Why gentlemen should fear that the Congress of the United States would be advised to do something that it did not want to do I frankly can not imagine, because they can not even be advised to do anything unless their own representative has participated in the advice. It may be that that will impair somewhat the vigor of the league, but, nevertheless, the fact is so, that we are not obliged to take any advice except our own, which to any man who wants to go his own course is a very satisfactory state of affairs. Every man regards his own advice as best, and I dare say every man mixes his own advice with some thought of his own interest. Whether we use it wisely or unwisely, we can use the vote of the United States to make impossible drawing the United States into any enterprise that she does not care to be drawn into.

Yet article 10 strikes at the taproot of war. Article 10 is a statement that the very things that have always been sought in imperialistic wars are henceforth forgone by every ambitious nation in the world. I would have felt very lonely, my fellow countrymen, and I would have felt very much disturbed if, sitting at the peace table in Paris, I had supposed that I was expounding my own ideas. Whether you believe it or not, I know the relative size of my own ideas; I know how they stand related in bulk and proportion to the moral judgments of my fellow countrymen, and I proposed nothing whatever at the peace table at Paris that I had not sufficiently certain knowledge embodied the moral judgment of the citizens of the United States. I had gone over there with, so to say, explicit instructions. Don't you remember that we laid down 14 points which should contain the principles of the settlement? They were not my points. In every one of them I was conscientiously trying to read the thought of the people of the United States, and after I uttered those points I had every assurance given me that could be given me that they did speak the moral judgment of the United States and not my single judgment. Then when it came to that critical period just a little less than a year ago, when it was evident that the war was coming to its critical end, all the nations engaged in the war accepted those 14 principles explicitly as the basis of the armistice and the basis of the peace. In those circumstances I crossed the ocean under bond to my own people and to the other governments with which I was dealing. The whole specification of the method of settlement was written down and accepted beforehand, and we were architects building on those specifications. It reassures me and fortifies my position to find how before I went over men whose judgment the United States has often trusted were of exactly the same opinion that I went abroad to express. Here is something

I want to read from Theodore Roosevelt:

"The one effective move for obtaining peace is by an agreement among all the great powers in which each should pledge itself not only to abide by the decisions of a common tribunal but to back its decisions by force. The great civilized nations should combine by solemn agreement in a great world league for the peace of righteousness; a court should be established. A changed and amplified Hague court would meet the requirements, composed of representatives from each nation, whose representatives are sworn to act as judges in each case and not in a representative capacity." Now there is article 10. He goes on and says this: "The nations should agree on certain rights that should not be questioned, such as territorial integrity, their right to deal with their domestic affairs, and with such matters as whom they should admit to citizenship. All such guarantee each of their number in possession of these rights."

Now, the other specification is in the covenant. The covenant in another portion guarantees to the members the independent control of their domestic questions. There is not a leg for these gentlemen to stand on when they say that the interests of the United States are not safeguarded in the very points where we are most sensitive. You do not need to be told again that the covenant expressly says that nothing in this covenant shall be construed as affecting the validity of the Monroe doctrine, for example. You could not be more explicit than that. And every point of interest is covered, partly for one very interesting reason. This is not the first time that the Foreign Relations Committee of the Senate of the United States has read and considered this covenant. I brought it to this country in March last in a tentative, provisional form, in practically the form that it now has, with the exception of certain additions which I shall mention immediately. I asked the Foreign Relations committees of both Houses to come to the White House and we spent a long evening in the frankest discussion of every portion that they wished to discuss. They made certain specific suggestions as to what should be contained in this document when it was to be revised. I carried those suggestions to Paris, and every one of them was adopted. What more could I have done? What more could have been obtained? The very matters upon which these gentlemen were most concerned were, the right of withdrawal, which is now expressly stated; the safeguarding of the Monroe doctrine, which is now accomplished; the exclusion from action by the league of domestic questions, which is now accomplished. All along the line, every suggestion of the United States was adopted after the covenant had been drawn up in its first form and had been published for the criticism of the world. There is a very true sense in which I can say this is a tested American document.

I am dwelling upon these points, my fellow citizens, in spite of the fact that I dare say to most of you they are perfectly well known, because in order to meet the present situation we have got to know what we are dealing with. We are not dealing with the kind of document which this is represented by some gentlemen to be; and inasmuch as we are dealing with a document simon-pure in respect of the very principles we have professed and lived up to, we have got to do one or other of two things—we have got to adopt it or reject it. There is no middle course. You can not go in on a special-privilege basis of your own. I take it that you are too proud to ask to be exempted from responsibilities which the other members of the league will carry. We go in upon equal terms or we do not go in at all; and if we do not go in, my fellow citizens, think of the tragedy of that result—the only sufficient guaranty to the peace of the world withheld! Ourselves drawn apart with that dangerous pride which means that we shall be ready to take care of ourselves, and that means that we shall maintain great standing armies and an irresistible navy; that means we shall have the organization of a military nation; that

means we shall have a general staff, with the kind of power that the general staff of Germany had, to mobilize this great manhood of the Nation when it pleases, all the energy of our young men drawn into the thought and preparation for war. What of our pledges to the men that lie dead in France? We said that they went over there, not to prove the prowess of America or her readiness for another war but to see to it that there never was such a war again. It always seems to make it difficult for me to say anything, my fellow citizens, when I think of my clients in this case. My clients are the children; my clients are the next generation. They do not know what promises and bonds I undertook when I ordered the armies of the United States to the soil of France, but I know, and I intend to redeem my pledges to the children; they shall not be sent upon a similar errand.

Again and again, my fellow citizens, mothers who lost their sons in France have come to me and, taking my hand, have shed tears upon it not only, but they had added, "God bless you, Mr. President!" Why, my fellow citizens, should they pray God to bless me? I advised the Congress of the United States to create the situation that led to the death of their sons. I ordered their sons oversea. I consented to their sons being put in the most difficult parts of the battle line, where death was certain, as in the impenetrable difficulties of the forest of Argonne. Why should they weep upon my hand and call down the blessings of God upon me? Because they believe that their boys died for something that vastly transcends any of the immediate and palpable objects of the war. They believe, and they rightly believe, that their sons saved the liberty of the world. They believe that wrapped up with the liberty of the world is the continuous protection of that liberty by the concerted powers of all civilized people. They believe that this sacrifice was made in order that other sons should not be called upon for a similar gift—the gift of life, the gift of all that died—and if we did not see this thing through, if we fulfilled the dearest present wish of Germany and now dissociated ourselves from those alongside whom we fought in the war, would not something of the halo go away from the gun over the mantelpiece, or the sword? Would not the old uniform lose something of its significance? These men were crusaders. They were not going forth to prove the might of the United States. They were going forth to prove the might of justice and right, and all the world accepted them as crusaders, and their transcendent achievement has made all the world believe in America as it believes in no other nation organized in the modern world. There seems to me to stand between us and the rejection or qualification of this treaty the serried ranks of those boys in khaki, not only these boys who came home, but those dear ghosts that still deploy upon the fields of France.

My friends, on last Decoration Day I went to a beautiful hillside near Paris, where was located the cemetery of Suresnes, a cemetery given over to the burial of the American dead. Behind me on the slopes was rank upon rank of living American soldiers, and lying before me upon the levels of the plain was rank upon rank of departed American soldiers. Right by the side of the stand where I spoke there was a little group of French women who had adopted those graves, had made themselves mothers of those dear ghosts by putting flowers every day upon those graves, taking them as their own sons, their own beloved, because they had died in the same cause—France was free and the world was free because America had come! I wish some men in public life who are now opposing the settlement for which these men died could visit such a spot as that. I wish that the thought that comes out of those graves could penetrate their consciousness. I wish that they could feel the moral obligation that rests upon us not to go back on those boys, but to see the thing through, to see it through to the end and make good their redemption of the world. For nothing less depends upon this decision, nothing less than the liberation and salvation of the world.

You will say, "Is the league an absolute guaranty against war?" No; I do not know any absolute guaranty against the errors of human judgment or the violence of human passion; but I tell you this: With a cooling space of nine months for human passion, not much of it will keep hot. I had a couple of friends who were in the habit of losing their tempers, and when they lost their tempers they were in the habit of using very unparliamentary language. Some of their friends induced them to make a promise that they never would swear inside the town limits. When the impulse next came upon them, they took a street car to go out of town to swear, and by the time they got out of town they did not want to swear. They came back convinced that they were just what they were, a couple of unspeakable fools, and the habit of getting angry and of swearing suffered great inroads upon it by that experience. Now, illustrating the great by the small, that is true of the passions of nations. It is true of the passions of men however you combine them. Give them space to cool off. I ask you this: If it is not an absolute insurance against war, do you want no insurance at all? Do you want nothing? Do you want not only no probability that war will not recur, but the probability that it will recur? The arrangements of justice do not stand of themselves, my fellow citizens. The arrangements of this treaty are just, but they need the support of the combined power of the great nations of the world. And they will have that support. Now that the mists of this great question have cleared away, I believe that men will see the truth, eye to eye and face to face. There is one thing that the American people always rise to and extend their hand to, and that is the truth of justice and of liberty and of peace. We have accepted that truth and we are going to be led by it, and it is going to lead us, and through us the world, out into pastures of quietness and peace such as the world never dreamed of before. . . .

5. THE LODGE RESERVATIONS, 1919[1]

EDITORS' NOTE.—The chairman of the Senate Foreign Relations Committee, Henry Cabot Lodge (1850–1924) of Massachusetts, submitted these reservations to the Versailles Treaty. It is not clear whether his intention was to defeat the League of Nations by these parliamentary tactics or whether he wished to join a League of Nations modified in the ways suggested. The reservations were accepted by majority vote of the Senate.

Senator Lodge belonged to a rich Boston family. He received the B.A. degree from Harvard University in 1871, was graduated in 1874 from the Harvard Law School, and in 1876 received one of the first Ph.D.'s in political science awarded by Harvard. His literary and historical work included the assistant editorship, under Henry Adams, of the *North American Review* from 1873 to 1876, a lectureship at Harvard from 1876 to 1879, and biographies of Hamilton, Webster, and Washington. He entered state politics in 1879, was a member of the United States House of Representatives from 1887 to 1893, and served in the United States Senate (1893–1924).

RESOLVED (*two-thirds of the Senators present concurring therein*), That the Senate advise and consent to the ratification of the treaty of peace with Germany concluded at Versailles on the 28th day of June, 1919, subject to the following reservations and understandings, which are hereby made a part and condition of this resolution of ratification, which ratification is not to take effect or bind the United States until the said reservations and understandings adopted by the Senate have been accepted by an exchange of notes as a part and a condition of this resolution of ratification by at least three of the four principal allied and associated powers, to wit, Great Britain, France, Italy, and Japan:

1. The United States so understands and construes article 1 that in case of notice of withdrawal from the league of nations, as provided in said article, the United States shall be the sole judge as to whether all its international obligations and all its obligations under the said covenant have been fulfilled, and notice of withdrawal by the United States may be given by a concurrent resolution of the Congress of the United States.

2. The United States assumes no obligation to preserve the territorial integrity or political independence of any other country or to interfere in controversies between nations—whether members of the league or not—under the provisions of article 10, or to employ the military or naval forces of the United States under any article of the treaty for any purpose, unless in any particular case the Congress, which, under the Constitution, has the sole power to declare war or authorize the employment of the military or naval forces of the United States, shall by act or joint resolution so provide.

3. No mandate shall be accepted by the United States under article 22, part 1, or any other provision of the treaty of peace with Germany, except by action of the Congress of the United States.

4. The United States reserves to itself exclusively the right to decide what questions are within its domestic jurisdiction and declares that all domestic and political questions relating wholly or in part to its internal affairs, including immigration, la-

1. *Congressional Record*, LVIII, Part 9 (November 19, 1919), 8777–78.

bor, coastwise traffic, the tariff, commerce, the suppression of traffic in women and children, and in opium and other dangerous drugs, and all other domestic questions, are solely within the jurisdiction of the United States and are not under this treaty to be submitted in any way either to arbitration or to the consideration of the council or of the assembly of the league of nations, or any agency thereof, or to the decision or recommendation of any other power.

5. The United States will not submit to arbitration or to inquiry by the assembly or by the council of the league of nations, provided for in said treaty of peace, any questions which in the judgment of the United States depend upon or relate to its long-established policy, commonly known as the Monroe doctrine; said doctrine is to be interpreted by the United States alone and is hereby declared to be wholly outside the jurisdiction of said league of nations and entirely unaffected by any provision contained in the said treaty of peace with Germany.

6. The United States withholds its assent to articles 156, 157, and 158, and reserves full liberty of action with respect to any controversy which may arise under said articles between the Republic of China and the Empire of Japan.

7. The Congress of the United States will provide by law for the appointment of the representatives of the United States in the assembly and the council of the league of nations, and may in its discretion provide for the participation of the United States in any commission, committee, tribunal, court, council, or conference, or in the selection of any members thereof and for the appointment of members of said commissions, committees, tribunals, courts, councils, or conferences, or any other representatives under the treaty of peace, or in carrying out its provisions, and until such participation and appointment have been so provided for and the powers and duties of such representatives have been defined by law, no person shall represent the United States under either said league of nations or the treaty of peace with Germany or be authorized to perform any act for or on behalf of the United States thereunder, and no citizen of the United States shall be selected or appointed as a member of said commissions, committees, tribunals, courts, councils, or conferences except with the approval of the Senate of the United States.

8. The United States understands that the reparation commission will regulate or interfere with exports from the United States to Germany, or from Germany to the United States, only when the United States by act or joint resolution of Congress approves such regulation or interference.

9. The United States shall not be obligated to contribute to any expenses of the league of nations, or of the secretariat, or of any commission, or committee, or conference, or other agency, organized under the league of nations or under the treaty or for the purpose of carrying out the treaty provisions, unless and until an appropriation of funds available for such expenses shall have been made by the Congress of the United States.

10. If the United States shall at any time adopt any plan for the limitation of armaments proposed by the council of the league of nations under the provisions of article 8, it reserves the right to increase such armaments without the consent of the council whenever the United States is threatened with invasion or engaged in war.

11. The United States reserves the right to permit, in its discretion, the nationals of a covenant-breaking State, as defined in article 16 of the covenant of the league of nations, residing within the United States or in countries other than that violating said article 16, to continue their commercial, financial, and personal relations with the nationals of the United States.

12. Nothing in articles 296, 297, or in any of the annexes thereto or in any other article, section, or annex of the treaty of peace with Germany shall, as against citi-

zens of the United States, be taken to mean any confirmation, ratification, or approval of any act otherwise illegal or in contravention of the rights of citizens of the United States.

13. The United States withholds its assent to Part XIII (articles 387 to 427, inclusive) unless Congress by act or joint resolution shall hereafter make provision for representation in the organization established by said Part XIII, and in such event the participation of the United States will be governed and conditioned by the provisions of such act or joint resolution.

14. The United States assumes no obligations to be bound by any election, decision, report, or finding of the council or assembly in which any member of the league and its self-governing dominions, colonies, or parts of empire, in the aggregate have cast more than one vote, and assumes no obligation to be bound by any decision, report, or finding of the council or assembly arising out of any dispute between the United States and any member of the league if such member, or any self-governing dominion, colony, empire, or part of empire united with it politically has voted. . . .

6. SENATE DEBATE ON THE LEAGUE, NOVEMBER 19, 1919[1]

EDITORS' NOTE.—This excerpt from the Senate debates on the League of Nations exhibits the principal positions and arguments. Three votes were taken on November 19, 1919. The first, Wilson supporters voting in the negative, was 39 for and 55 against. The second, on the treaty with five reservations proposed by Democratic Senator Hitchcock, was 41 for and 51 against. The third, for the treaty without reservations, was 38 for and 53 against. The treaty with the Lodge reservations was put to a vote again on March 19, 1920, and was again rejected by a vote of 49 for—which was less than the required two-thirds—and 35 against.

MR. LODGE: Mr. President, I have received from the press a copy of a letter which has been given out, I understand, and which I think, as the Senator from Nebraska [MR. HITCHCOCK] has not offered it, should be read at this time before we vote.

THE VICE-PRESIDENT: Is there objection? The Chair hears none, and the Secretary will read.

MR. LODGE: It can be read in my time. The Secretary read as follows:

THE WHITE HOUSE
WASHINGTON, 18 November, 1919

MY DEAR SENATOR:

You were good enough to bring me word that the Democratic Senators supporting the treaty expected to hold a conference before the final vote on the Lodge resolution of ratification and that they would be glad to receive a word of counsel from me.

I should hesitate to offer it in any detail, but I assume that the Senators only desire my judgment upon the all-important question of the final vote on the resolution containing the many reservations by Senator LODGE. On that I can not hesitate, for, in my opinion, the resolution in that form does not provide for ratification but, rather, for the nullification of the treaty. I sincerely hope that the friends and supporters of the treaty will vote against the Lodge resolution of ratification.

I understand that the door will probably then be open for a genuine resolution of ratification.

I trust that all true friends of the treaty will refuse to support the Lodge resolution.

Cordially and sincerely, yours,

[Signed] WOODROW WILSON

HON. G. M. HITCHCOCK
United States Senate

1. *Congressional Record*, LVIII, Part 9 (November 19, 1919), 8768–69, 8781–84.

MR. LODGE: Mr. President, I think comment is superfluous, and I shall make none.

MR. THOMAS: Mr. President, the conclusion which I have reached regarding the pending resolution was reached long before I was made acquainted with the contents of the letter which has just been read to the Senate.

I shall vote against the ratification of the treaty. The reasons which animate me to that end I have so frequently stated upon the floor of the Senate that it is not necessary for me to say more at this time.

MR. ROBINSON:[2] Mr. President, for reasons very different from those asserted by the Senator from Pennsylvania [MR. KNOX], it is my purpose to vote against the pending resolution of ratification incorporating reservations adopted by a majority of Senators.

During several months, to the exclusion of nearly all other important business, the Senate has had under consideration the treaty of peace with Germany. It now seems probable, unless the advocates of unqualified ratification and so-called reservation Senators reconcile differences, that the result of our labors may be failure. The Senate is about to vote on an alleged resolution of ratification, a resolution which, it seems to me, does not ratify, but which in fact and in legal effect, constitutes a rejection of this treaty.

All Senators recognize the importance of the vote soon to be taken. This vote invites the judgment of the people of this country, and, indeed, the judgment of all mankind, upon the policy implied in the resolution of ratification incorporating reservations agreed to by the majority.

Many of us are convinced that the adoption of the pending resolution, as I have already stated, will accomplish no

2. Senator Joseph T. Robinson (1872–1937) was a strong supporter of the Wilson administration. Born and educated in Arkansas, he began the practice of law there in 1895. He was a member of the House of Representatives from 1903 to 1913 and of the Senate from 1913 to 1937.

useful purpose. The Senator from Massachusetts [MR. LODGE] has had read into the *Record* a letter issued by the President, in which that officer, representing a part of the treaty-making power, declares that the pending resolution of ratification can not accomplish ratification; that it is in fact rejection of the treaty; and therefore it is futile to adopt the resolution.

The statement that the resolution of ratification will in fact defeat the treaty will occasion no regret to the Senators who from the beginning have advocated its rejection. They have apparently succeeded, temporarily at least, in accomplishing indirectly what could not be done openly and frankly. Through alleged reservations, which will not likely be accepted by other parties to the treaty, they seek to exclude the United States from fellowship with her late allies and from membership in the league of nations. In almost every line of the reservations is implied antagonism of Senators toward the President. Suspicion and mistrust of the nations associated with this Government in the recent war are reflected by the reservations, sometimes poorly concealed, often clearly evinced.

The avowed purpose is to completely repudiate every obligation of this Government to encourage and sustain the new and feeble States separated, by our assistance during the war, from their former sovereignties by withholding from them the moral and military power of the United States.

To me it seems regrettable beyond expression that Senators who desire to improve the treaty and who desire also that it shall become effective should lend their assistance to a course in which the avowed enemies of the league of nations must find unbounded gratification and pleasure. Is it not unpardonable for friends of the treaty to couple with the resolution of ratification conditions designed to deprive the Executive of his constitutional functions? It is worse than idle—it seems to me hypocritical—to impose terms and conditions which make the exchange of ratifications impracticable, if not impossible.

Membership in the league of nations is treated, in the reservations, with so little dignity and as of such slight importance as to authorize its termination by the passage of a mere concurrent resolution of Congress. This attempt to deny to the President participation in withdrawal by this Government from the league and to vest that authority solely in the two Houses of Congress in disregard of the plain provision of the Constitution displays a spirit of narrow opposition to the Executive unworthy of the subject and unworthy of the Senate of the United States.

The requirement that before ratification by the United States shall become effective the reservations adopted by the Senate must be approved by three of the four principal allied powers is designed to make difficult the exchange of ratifications. Mr. President, it can have no other purpose; it can accomplish no other end.

The reservation respecting article 10 nullifies the most vital provision in the league of nations contract. It absolves the United States from any obligation to assist in enforcing the terms of peace, an obligation that the leader of the majority, in his speech to this body on the 23d day of August, 1918, and again in December of the same year, asserted as one which the United States can not without dishonor avoid or escape.

No Senator can doubt that the repudiation by the United States of the undertaking in article 10 to respect and preserve the territorial integrity and political independence of the other members of the league weakens, if it does not destroy, one of the principal agencies or means provided by the league for the prevention of international war.

The reservation withholding the agreement of the United States to the arrangement in the treaty respecting Japanese rights in Shantung, and reserving for this Government freedom of action in case of controversy between China and Japan re-garding the subject, admittedly will not be accepted by Japan, and probably it will not be accepted by either France or Great Britain. In making this declaration, I repeat the statement made in the Senate a day or two ago by the Senator from North Dakota [Mr. McCumber], and I make the inquiry how any friend of the treaty who wants it ratified, and who realizes that under these reservations our ratification can not become effective unless it is approved by three of the four principal allied powers—I make the inquiry now how a Senator who takes that view of the subject and wants the treaty ratified can support the pending resolution?

It may be, Mr. President, that the friends of this treaty have made a mistake. Undoubtedly the friends of the treaty, and not its enemies, should dictate the policy of the Senate concerning ratification. The Senators who have opposed ratification from the beginning have imposed upon an overwhelming majority of the Senate, by their power and influence, their views respecting the resolution of ratification.

As the measure now comes before the Senate it comes with the open declaration of the Executive, who is the sole agency through whom this Government may exchange ratifications, that that act will not be accomplished. It comes with the recognition of the fact by the Senators who favor the treaty that the reservations are of such a nature that they will not be accepted by other nations.

Make no mistake about it. The Senate should either ratify this treaty unqualifiedly or upon such terms and conditions as will justify the Executive and enable him speedily to conclude peace by an exchange of ratifications.

The resolution of the Senator from Massachusetts incorporating the reservations as agreed upon will probably result in the refusal of the Executive to attempt to procure the consent and approval of three of the four principal allied powers. If he should make the attempt, it is plain that our self-respecting allies will not accept the terms and conditions which we seek to impose by these reservations. Why, then, Mr. President, should the resolution proposed by the Senator from Massachusetts be agreed to? Every Senator knows that it can not effectuate peace. The Senator from Massachusetts himself on last Sunday issued a statement to the press in which he declared that "The treaty is dead."

I call now upon the friends of the treaty to take charge of the corpse. By their action they can revitalize it. The enemies of the treaty, Senators who do not favor its ratification, have controlled the proceedings of the Senate heretofore. It is time now that those of us who favor the treaty, and we have the necessary number, should get together and ratify it.

MR. SHERMAN:[3] Mr. President, I turn for solace and for guidance to Holy Writ and quote from the Book of Job: "Shall not the multitude of words be answered? And shall a man full of talk be justified?"

I felicitate myself on this occasion, Mr. President, as, for the first time since the armistice was signed, finding myself in accord and voting with the administration. [Laughter in the galleries.]

THE VICE-PRESIDENT: It may just as well be understood now as at any time that occupants of the galleries must keep order or the doorkeepers will remove the offending visitors.

MR. SHERMAN: I, too, shall vote against the treaty and the reservations attached to the resolution, much as I regret to part company with some of my beloved associates on both sides of this Chamber.

The future of this measure is shrouded in uncertainty. Perchance it sleepeth only and waits for our all-wise Executive to rouse it from its torpor and again threaten us with its pristine beauty and excellence.

It may be pleasingly arrayed in alliterative phrase and sonorous periods cunningly placed to obscure the selfish, boiling hell of the original text. Every ambush to the military man who is caught thereby looks mild until it starts into action. Beware of future reservations that do not reserve. . . .

MR. BORAH:[4] Mr. President, I am not misled by the debate across the aisle into the view that this treaty will not be ratified. I entertain little doubt that sooner or later—and entirely too soon—the treaty will be ratified with the league of nations in it, and I am of the opinion with the reservations in it as they are now written. There may possibly be some change in verbiage in order that there may be a common sharing of parentage, but our friends across the aisle will likely accept the league of nations with the reservations in substance as now written. I think, therefore, this moment is just as appropriate as any other for me to express my final views with reference to the treaty and the league of nations. It is perhaps the last opportunity I shall have to state, as briefly as I may, my reasons for opposing the treaty and the league.

Mr. President, after Mr. Lincoln had been elected President before he assumed the duties of the office and at a time when all indications were to the effect that we would soon be in the midst of civil strife, a friend from the city of Washington wrote him for instructions. Mr. Lincoln wrote back in a single line, "Entertain no compromise; have none of it." That states the position I occupy at this time and which I have, in an humble way, occupied from the first contention in regard to this proposal.

My objections to the league have not been met by the reservations. I desire to state wherein my objections have not been

3. Senator Lawrence Y. Sherman (1858–1939) was born in Ohio but was taken next year by his family to Illinois, where he was educated and practiced law. He was a member of the state legislature (1897–1905), was lieutenant-governor (1905–9), and served in the Senate (1913–21).

4. Senator William E. Borah (1865–1940), Republican, was born in Illinois, graduated from the University of Kansas, and after one year's law practice in Kansas moved in 1891 to Idaho. He was a United States senator from 1907 to 1940, serving from 1924 to 1932 as chairman of the Foreign Relations Committee.

met. Let us see what our attitude will be toward Europe and what our position will be with reference to the other nations of the world after we shall have entered the league with the present reservations written therein. With all due respect to those who think that they have accomplished a different thing and challenging no man's intellectual integrity or patriotism, I do not believe the reservations have met the fundamental propositions which are involved in this contest.

When the league shall have been formed, we shall be a member of what is known as the council of the league. Our accredited representative will sit in judgment with the accredited representatives of the other members of the league to pass upon the concerns not only of our country but of all Europe and all Asia and the entire world. Our accredited representatives will be members of the assembly. They will sit there to represent the judgment of these 110,000,000 people—more then—just as we are accredited here to represent our constituencies. We can not send our representatives to sit in council with the representatives of the other great nations of the world with mental reservations as to what we shall do in case their judgment shall not be satisfactory to us. If we go to the council or to the assembly with any other purpose than that of complying in good faith and in absolute integrity with all upon which the council or the assembly may pass, we shall soon return to our country with our self-respect forfeited and the public opinion of the world condemnatory.

Why need you gentlemen across the aisle worry about a reservation here or there when we are sitting in the council and in the assembly and bound by every obligation in morals, which the President said was supreme above that of law, to comply with the judgment which our representative and the other representatives finally form? Shall we go there, Mr. President, to sit in judgment, and in case that judgment works for peace join with our allies, but in case it works for war withdraw our cooperation? How long would we stand as we now stand, a great Republic commanding the respect and holding the leadership of the world, if we should adopt any such course?

So, sir, we not only sit in the council and in the Assembly with our accredited representatives, but bear in mind that article 11 is untouched by any reservation which has been offered here; and with article 11 untouched and its integrity complete, article 10 is perfectly superfluous. If any war or threat of war shall be a matter of consideration for the league, and the league shall take such action as it deems wise to deal with it, what is the necessity of article 10? Will not external aggression be regarded as a war or threat of war? If the political independence of some nation in Europe is assailed will it be regarded as a war or threat of war? Is there anything in article 10 that is not completely covered by article 11?

It remains complete, and with our representatives sitting in the council and the assembly, and with article 11 complete, and with the assembly and the council having jurisdiction of all matters touching the peace of the world, what more do you need to bind the United States if you assume that the United States is a Nation of honor?

We have said, Mr. President, that we would not send our troops abroad without the consent of Congress. Pass by now for a moment the legal proposition. If we create executive functions, the Executive will perform those functions without the authority of Congress. Pass that question by and go to the other question. Our members of the council are there. Our members of the assembly are there. Article 11 is complete, and it authorizes the league, a member of which is our representative, to deal with matters of peace and war, and the league through its council and its assembly deals with the matter, and our accredited representative joins with the others in deciding upon a certain course, which involves a question of sending troops. What will the Congress of the United States do? What right will it have left, except the bare technical right to refuse, which as a moral proposition it will not dare to exercise? Have we not been told day by day for the last nine months that the Senate of the United States, a coordinate part of the treaty-making power, should accept this league as it was written because the wise men sitting at Versailles had so written it, and has not every possible influence and every source of power in public opinion been organized and directed against the Senate to compel it to do that thing? How much stronger will be the moral compulsion upon the Congress of the United States when we ourselves have indorsed the proposition of sending our accredited representatives there to vote for us?

Ah, but you say that there must be unanimous consent, and that there is vast protection in unanimous consent.

I do not wish to speak disparagingly; but has not every division and dismemberment of every nation which has suffered dismemberment taken place by unanimous consent for the last 300 years? Did not Prussia and Austria and Russia by unanimous consent divide Poland? Did not the United States and Great Britain and Japan and Italy and France divide China and give Shantung to Japan? Was that not a unanimous decision? Close the doors upon the diplomats of Europe, let them sit in secret, give them the material to trade on, and there always will be unanimous consent.

How did Japan get unanimous consent? I want to say here, in my parting words upon this proposition, that I have no doubt the outrage upon China was quite as distasteful to the President of the United States as it is to me. But Japan said: "I will not sign your treaty unless you turn over to me Shantung, to be turned back at my discretion," and you know how Japan's discretion operates with reference to such things. And so, when we are in the league,

and our accredited representatives are sitting at Geneva, and a question of great moment arises, Japan, or Russia, or Germany, or Great Britain will say, "Unless this matter is adjusted in this way I will depart from your league." It is the same thing, operating in the same way, only under a different date and under a little different circumstances.

Mr. President, if you have enough territory, if you have enough material, if you have enough subject peoples to trade upon and divide, there will be no difficulty about unanimous consent.

Do our Democratic friends ever expect any man to sit as a member of the council or as a member of the Assembly equal in intellectual power and in standing before the world with that of our representative at Versailles? Do you expect a man to sit in the council who will have made more pledges, and I shall assume made them in sincerity, for self-determination and for the rights of small peoples, than had been made by our accredited representative? And yet, what became of it? The unanimous consent was obtained nevertheless.

But take another view of it. We are sending to the council one man. That one man represents 110,000,000 people.

Here, sitting in the Senate, we have two from every State in the Union, and over in the other House we have Representatives in accordance with population, and the responsibility is spread out in accordance with our obligations to our constituency. But now we are transferring to one man the stupendous power of representing the sentiment and convictions of 110,000,000 people in tremendous questions which may involve the peace or may involve the war of the world.

However you view the question of unanimous consent, it does not protect us.

What is the result of all this? We are in the midst of all of the affairs of Europe. We have entangled ourselves with all European concerns. We have joined in alliance with all the European nations which have thus far joined the league, and all nations which may be admitted to the league. We are sitting there dabbling in their affairs and intermeddling in their concerns. In other words, Mr. President—and this comes to the question which is fundamental with me—we have forfeited and surrendered, once and for all, the great policy of "no entangling alliances" upon which the strength of this Republic has been founded for 150 years.

My friends of reservations, tell me where is the reservation in these articles which protects us against entangling alliances with Europe?

Those who are differing over reservations, tell me what one of them protects the doctrine laid down by the Father of his Country. That fundamental proposition is surrendered, and we are a part of the European turmoils and conflicts from the time we enter this league.

Let us not underestimate that. There has never been an hour since the Venezuelan difficulty that there has not been operating in this country, fed by domestic and foreign sources, a powerful propaganda for the destruction of the doctrine of no entangling alliances.

Lloyd-George is reported to have said just a few days before the conference met at Versailles that Great Britain could give up much, and would be willing to sacrifice much, to have America withdraw from that policy. That was one of the great objects of the entire conference at Versailles, so far as the foreign representatives were concerned. Clemenceau and Lloyd-George and others like them were willing to make any reasonable sacrifice which would draw America away from her isolation and into the internal affairs and concerns of Europe. This league of nations, with or without reservations, whatever else it does or does not do, does surrender and sacrifice that policy; and once having surrendered and become a part of the European concerns, where, my friends, are you going to stop?

You have put in here a reservation upon the Monroe doctrine. I think that, in so far

as language could protect the Monroe doctrine, it has been protected. But as a practical proposition, as a working proposition, tell me candidly, as men familiar with the history of your country and of other countries, do you think that you can intermeddle in European affairs; and, secondly, never to permit Europe to.

When Mr. Monroe wrote to Jefferson, he asked him his view upon the Monroe doctrine, and Mr. Jefferson said, in substance, our first and primary obligation should be never to interfere in European affairs; and, secondly, never to permit Europe to interfere in our affairs.

He understood, as every wise and practical man understands, that if we intermeddle in her affairs, if we help to adjust her conditions, inevitably and remorselessly Europe then will be carried into our affairs, in spite of anything you can write upon paper.

We can not protect the Monroe doctrine unless we protect the basic principle upon which it rests, and that is the Washington policy. I do not care how earnestly you may endeavor to do so, as a practical working proposition your league will come to the United States. Will you permit me to digress long enough to read a paragraph from a great French editor upon this particular phase of the matter, Mr. Stephen Lausanne, editor of *Le Matin*, of Paris?

When the executive council of the league of nations fixes "the reasonable limits of the armament of Peru"; when it shall demand information concerning the naval program of Brazil; when it shall tell Argentina what shall be the measure of the "contribution to the armed forces to protect the signatories of the social covenant"; when it shall demand the immediate registration of the treaty between the United States and Canada at the seat of the league; it will control, whether it wills or no, the destinies of America. And when the American States shall be obliged to take a hand in every war or menace of war in Europe (art. II), they will necessarily fall afoul of the fundamental principle laid down by Monroe, which was that Americans should never take part in a European war.

If the league takes in the world, then Europe must mix in the affairs of America; if only Europe is included, then America will violate of necessity her own doctrine by intermixing in the affairs of Europe.

If the league includes the affairs of the world, does it not include the affairs of all the world? Is there any limitation of the jurisdiction of the council or of the assembly upon the question of peace or war? Does it not have now, under the reservations, the same as it had before, the power to deal with all matters of peace or war throughout the entire world? How shall you keep from meddling in the affairs of Europe or keep Europe from meddling in the affairs of America?

Mr. President, there is another and even a more commanding reason why I shall record my vote against this treaty. It imperils what I conceive to be the underlying, the very first principles of this Republic. It is in conflict with the right of our people to govern themselves free from all restraint, legal or moral, of foreign powers. It challenges every tenet of my political faith. If this faith were one of my own contriving, if I stood here to assert principles of government of my own evolving, I might well be charged with intolerable presumption, for we all recognize the ability of those who urge a different course. But I offer in justification of my course nothing of my own save the deep and abiding reverence I have for those whose policies I humbly but most ardently support. I claim no merit save fidelity to American principles and devotion to American ideals as they were wrought out from time to time by those who built the Republic and as they have been extended and maintained throughout these years. In opposing the treaty I do nothing more than decline to renounce and tear out of my life the sacred traditions which throughout 50 years have been translated into my whole intellectual and moral being. I will not, I can not, give up my belief that America must, not alone for the happiness of her own people, but for the moral guidance and greater contentment of the world, be permitted to live her own life. Next to the tie which binds a man to his God is the tie which binds a man to his country, and all schemes, all plans, however ambitious and fascinating they seem in their proposal, but which would embarrass or entangle and impede or shackle her sovereign will, which would compromise her freedom of action, I unhesitatingly put behind me.

Sir, since the debate opened months ago those of us who have stood against this proposition have been taunted many times with being little Americans. Leave us the word American, keep that in your presumptuous impeachment, and no taunt can disturb us, no gibe discompose our purposes. Call us little Americans if you will, but leave us the consolation and the pride which the term American, however modified, still imparts. Take away that term and though you should coin in telling phrase your highest eulogy we would hurl it back as common slander. We have been ridiculed because, forsooth, of our limited vision. Possibly that charge may be true. Who is there here that can read the future? Time, and time alone, unerring and remorseless, will give us each our proper place in the affections of our countrymen and in the esteem and commendation of those who are to come after us. We neither fear nor court her favor. But if our vision has been circumscribed it has at all times within its compass been clear and steady. We have sought nothing save the tranquillity of our own people and the honor and independence of our own Republic. No foreign flattery, no possible world glory and power have disturbed our poise or come between us and our devotion to the traditions which have made us a people or the policies which have made us a Nation, unselfish and commanding. If we have erred we have erred out of too much love for those things which from childhood you and we together have been taught to revere—yes, to defend even at the cost of limb and life. If we have erred it is because we have placed too high an estimate upon the wisdom of Washington and Jefferson, too exalted an opinion upon the patriotism of the sainted Lincoln. And blame us not therefore if we have, in our limited vision, seemed sometimes bitter and at all times uncompromising, for the things for which we have spoken, feebly spoken, the things which we have endeavored to defend, have been the things for which your fathers and our fathers were willing to die.

Senators, even in an hour so big with expectancy we should not close our eyes to the fact that democracy is something more, vastly more, than a mere form of government by which society is restrained into free and orderly life. It is a moral entity, a spiritual force, as well. And these are things which live only and alone in the atmosphere of liberty. The foundation upon which democracy rests is faith in the moral instincts of the people. Its ballot boxes, the franchise, its laws, and constitutions are but the outward manifestations of the deeper and more essential thing—a continuing trust in the moral purposes of the average man and woman. When this is lost or forfeited your outward forms, however democratic in terms, are a mockery. Force may find expression through institutions democratic in structure equal with the simple and more direct processes of a single supreme ruler. These distinguishing virtues of a real republic you can not commingle with the discordant and destructive forces of the Old World and still preserve them. You can not yoke a government whose fundamental maxim is that of liberty to a government whose first law is that of force and hope to preserve the former. These things are in eternal war, and one must ultimately destroy the other. You may still keep for a time the outward form, you may still delude yourself, as others have done in the past, with appearances and symbols, but when you shall have committed this Republic to a scheme of world control based upon force, upon the combined military force of the four great nations of the world, you will have soon destroyed the atmosphere of freedom, of confidence in the self-governing capacity of the masses, in which alone a democracy may thrive. We may become one of the four dictators of the world, but we shall no longer be master of our own spirit. And what shall it profit us as a Nation if we shall go forth to the dominion of the earth and share with others the glory of world control and lose that fine sense of confidence in the people, the soul of democracy?

Look upon the scene as it is now presented. Behold the task we are to assume, and then contemplate the method by which we are to deal with this task. Is the method such as to address itself to a Government "conceived in liberty and dedicated to the proposition that all men are created equal"? When this league, this combination, is formed four great powers representing the dominant people will rule one-half of the inhabitants of the globe as subject peoples—rule by force, and we shall be a party to the rule of force. There is no other way by which you can keep people in subjection. You must either give them independence, recognize their rights as nations to live their own life and to set up their own form of government, or you must deny them these things by force. That is the scheme, the method proposed by the league. It proposes no other. We will in time become inured to its inhuman precepts and its soulless methods, strange as this doctrine now seems to a free people. If we stay with our contract, we will come in time to declare with our associates that force—force, the creed of the Prussian military oligarchy—is after all the true foundation upon which must rest all stable governments. Korea, despoiled and bleeding at every pore; India, sweltering in ignorance and burdened with inhuman taxes after more than a hundred years of dominant rule; Egypt, trapped and robbed of her birthright; Ireland, with 700 years of sacrifice for independence—this is the task, this is the atmosphere, and this is the creed in and under which we are to keep alive our belief in the moral purposes and self-governing capacity of the people, a belief without which the Republic must disintegrate and die. The maxim of liberty will soon give way to the rule of blood and iron. We have been pleading here for our Constitution. Conform this league, it has been said, to the technical terms of our charter, and all will be well. But I declare to you that we must go further and conform to those sentiments and passions for justice and freedom which are essential to the existence of democracy. You must respect not territorial boundaries, not territorial integrity, but you must respect and preserve the sentiments and passions for justice and for freedom which God in His infinite wisdom has planted so deep in the human heart that no form of tyranny however brutal, no persecution however prolonged, can wholly uproot and kill. Respect nationality, respect justice, respect freedom, and you may have some hope of peace, but not so if you make your standard the standard of tyrants and despots, the protection of real estate regardless of how it is obtained.

Sir, we are told that this treaty means peace. Even so, I would not pay the price. Would you purchase peace at the cost of any part of our independence? We could have had peace in 1776—the price was high, but we could have had it. James Otis, Sam Adams, Hancock, and Warren were surrounded by those who urged peace and British rule. All through that long and trying struggle, particularly when the clouds of adversity lowered upon the cause, there was a cry of peace—let us have peace. We could have had peace in 1860; Lincoln was counseled by men of great influence and accredited wisdom to let our brothers— and, thank Heaven, they are brothers— depart in peace. But the tender, loving Lincoln, bending under the fearful weight of impending civil war, an apostle of peace, refused to pay the price, and a reunited country will praise his name forevermore —bless it because he refused peace at the price of national honor and national integrity. Peace upon any other basis than national independence, peace purchased at the cost of any part of our national integrity, is fit only for slaves, and even when purchased at such a price it is a delusion, for it can not last.

But your treaty does not mean peace— far, very far, from it. If we are to judge the future by the past it means war. Is there any guaranty of peace other than the guaranty which comes of the control of the war-making power by the people? Yet what great rule of democracy does the treaty leave unassailed? The people in whose keeping alone you can safely lodge the power of peace or war nowhere, at no time and in no place, have any voice in this scheme for world peace. Autocracy which has bathed the world in blood for centuries reigns supreme. Democracy is everywhere excluded. This, you say, means peace.

Can you hope for peace when love of country is disregarded in your scheme, when the spirit of nationality is rejected, even scoffed at? Yet what law of that moving and mysterious force does your treaty not deny? With a ruthlessness unparalleled your treaty in a dozen instances runs counter to the divine law of nationality. Peoples who speak the same language, kneel at the same ancestral tombs, moved by the same traditions, animated by a common hope, are torn asunder, broken in pieces, divided, and parceled out to antagonistic nations. And this you call justice. This, you cry, means peace. Peoples who have dreamed of independence, struggled and been patient, sacrificed and been hopeful, peoples who were told that through this peace conference they should realize the aspirations of centuries, have again had their hopes dashed to earth. One of the most striking and commanding figures in this war, soldier and statesman, turned away from the peace table at Versailles declaring to the world, "The promise of the new life, the victory of the great humane ideals for which the peoples have shed their blood and their treasure without stint, the fulfillment of their aspirations toward a new international order and a fairer and better world, are not written into the treaty." No; your treaty means injustice. It means slavery. It means war. And to all this you ask this Republic to become a party. You ask it to abandon the creed under which it has grown to power and accept the creed of autocracy, the creed of repression and force.

Mr. President, I turn from this scheme based upon force to another scheme, planned 143 years ago in old Independence Hall, in the city of Philadelphia, based upon liberty. I like it better. I have become so accustomed to believe in it that it is difficult for me to reject it out of hand. I have difficulty in subscribing to the new creed of oppression, the creed of dominant and subject peoples. I feel a reluctance to give up the belief that all men are created equal —the eternal principle in government that all governments derive their just powers from the consent of the governed. I can not get my consent to exchange the doctrine of George Washington for the doctrine of Frederick the Great translated into mendacious phrases of peace. I go back to that serene and masterful soul who pointed the way to power and glory for the new and then weak Republic, and whose teachings and admonitions even in our majesty and dominance we dare not disregard.

I know well the answer to my contention. It has been piped about of late from a thousand sources—venal sources, disloyal sources, sinister sources—that Washington's wisdom was of his day only and that his teachings are out of fashion—things long since sent to the scrap heap of history—that while he was great in character and noble in soul he was untrained in the arts of statecraft and unlearned in the science of government. The puny demagogue, the barren editor, the sterile professor now vie with each other in apologizing for the temporary and commonplace expedients which the Father of his Country felt constrained to adopt in building a republic!

What is the test of statesmanship? Is it the formation of theories, the utterance of abstract and incontrovertible truths, or is it the capacity and the power to give to a people that concrete thing called liberty, that vital and indispensable thing in human happiness called free institutions, and to establish over all and above all the blessed and eternal reign of order and law? If this be the test, where shall we find another whose name is entitled to be written beside the name of Washington? His judgment and poise in the hour of turmoil and peril, his courage and vision in times of adversity, his firm grasp of fundamental principles, his almost inspired power to penetrate the future and read there the result, the effect of policies, have never been excelled, if equaled, by any of the world's commonwealth builders. Peter the Great, William the Silent, and Cromwell the Protector, these and these alone perhaps are to be associated with his name as the builders of States and the founders of governments. But in exaltation of moral purpose, in the unselfish character of his work, in the durability of his policies, in the permanency of the institutions which he more than anyone else called into effect, his service to mankind stands out separate and apart in a class by itself. The works of these other great builders, where are they now? But the work of Washington is still the most potent influence for the advancement of civilization and the freedom of the race.

Reflect for a moment over his achievements. He led the Revolutionary Army to victory. He was the very first to suggest a union instead of a confederacy. He presided over and counseled with great wisdom the convention which framed the Constitution. He guided the Government through its first perilous years. He gave dignity and stability and honor to that which was looked upon by the world as a passing experiment, and finally, my friends, as his own peculiar and particular contribution to the happiness of his countrymen and to the cause of the Republic, he gave us his great foreign policy under which we have lived and prospered and strengthened for nearly a century and a half. This policy is the most sublime confirmation of his genius as a statesman. It was then, and it now is, an indispensable part of our whole scheme of government. It is to-day, a vital, indispensable element in our entire plan, purpose, and mission as a nation. To abandon it is nothing less than a betrayal of the American people. I say betrayal deliberately, in view of the suffering and the sacrifice which will follow in the wake of such a course.

But under the stress and strain of these extraordinary days, when strong men are being swept down by the onrushing forces of disorder and change, when the most sacred things of life, the most cherished hopes of a Christian world seem to yield to the mad forces of discontent—just such days as Washington passed through when the mobs of Paris, wild with new liberty and drunk with power, challenged the established institutions of all the world, but his steadfast soul was unshaken—under these conditions come again we are about to abandon this policy so essential to our happiness and tranquillity as a people and our stability as a Government. No leader with his commanding influence and his unquailing courage stands forth to stem the current. But what no leader can or will do experience, bitter experience, and the people of this country in whose keeping, after all, thank God, is the Republic, will ultimately do. If we abandon his leadership and teachings, we will go back. We will return to this policy. Americanism shall not, can not, die. We may go back in sackcloth and ashes, but we will return to the faith of the fathers. America will live her own life. The independence of this Republic will have its defenders. Thousands have suffered and died for it, and their sons and daughters are not of the breed who will be betrayed into the hands of foreigners. The noble face of the Father of his Country, so familiar to every boy and girl, looking out from the walls of the Capitol in stern reproach, will call those who come here for public service to a reckoning. The people of our beloved country will finally speak, and we will return to the policy which we now abandon. America disenthralled and free in spite of all these things will continue her mission in the cause of peace, of freedom, and of civilization. . . .

UNIT XII
FREEDOM IN AN INDUSTRIAL SOCIETY

THE earlier impact of industrialism on American life has been examined in a previous unit. It was seen then how the whole structure of society was being extensively modified. The forms of production were changing; the capacity to produce was doubled and redoubled; population was being concentrated in urban centers; Americans were exchanging their relative isolation, severally as individuals and jointly as a nation, for a growing involvement in the processes of an international market and an interdependent world. In brief, a new order of economic and social relationships, within nations and between nations, was establishing itself—an order characterized by the mutual dependence of its component parts and by a high potentiality for both constructive and destructive performance. And under these conditions—which have become alternately the wonder and the despair of modern man—Americans were being forced to undertake a re-examination of their basic values and institutions.

In the last generation this process has continued. It has been accompanied by prodigies of productive invention, by violent cycles of war and peace, boom and bust, and by the convergence on the political agencies of human societies of irresistible pressures for relief or reform. All industrial nations are involved in the same gigantic process of readjustment, and all have acknowledged that none of them can work out its salvation alone. But the search for adequate solutions is plagued both by the dissidence within national states and by the profound differences between them.

The American response to these problems, like that of every other community, has been conditioned by our location in the world, by our resources, and by our traditions. In particular, there has been a continuing effort to preserve the substance of a "free society" as defined with different degrees of emphasis by such representatives of the liberal tradition as Locke, Smith, Jefferson, Lincoln, and Wilson. This tradition, once the dominant theme among the secular values of western Europe, has been more resistant to change in this country than elsewhere. In many states it has been repudiated by various forms of authoritarian government; in others the modification of its basic individualism in the effort to come to grips with the industrial order has gone much further than here. But even here it has been necessary to invest the state with responsibilities which far exceed the limits to which the action of government was once confined. The retreat from laissez faire was vigorously opposed in the early days of progressivism, when a doctrine of state help first began to graft itself onto a doctrine of self-help. Since then the central controversy in domestic history has been between the opponents and the proponents of the "positive state."

The object of this unit is to review some of the principles which have guided our decisions in these years. It begins with a statement written in 1945 by Henry Simons. The problems before him were a mixture of old and new. How should we deal with concentration of power in business and labor? With the demand for agricultural subsidies? With the old and the new features of economic nationalism? With the demand for state intervention in health, housing, and education? With the growth of bureaucracy at the various levels of government? With the need to build supranational institutions? Simons wrote this essay to explain the presuppositions which determined his approach to such questions. It is a political credo which acknowledges its debt to the liberal tradition while demanding a freedom for experimentation which obscures many of the popular distinctions between liberalism and democratic socialism. In its definition of a good society as a free society built and rebuilt through discussion, experimentation, and compromise; in its anxiety to keep power dispersed in order that freedom may may flourish; in its preference for a multiplicity of voluntary associations existing side by side in healthy rivalry; in its pragmatic approach to the prob-

lems of world government—it is an affirmation of the principles which have generally appealed to Americans as the secret of political wisdom. Yet Simons' proposals would be strenuously controverted by many who consider themselves no less concerned with the goals of freedom and equality. It is suggested that this essay be used as a stimulus to an examination of first principles and as a standard of comparison for the assumptions which are either explicit or implicit in the subsequent readings.

The economist with his philosophic probings is followed by a succession of political leaders, ranging from Wilson and La Follette through Hoover and Roosevelt to Thomas, Taft, and Truman. They are dealing in their speeches with the place which government ought to occupy in relation to the economic system. One method of measuring the interval which separates Wilson from Truman is to recall that, whereas the former hoped that authoritarianism might be discredited by a universal victory for liberal institutions, the latter has seen totalitarianism, in its Fascist or Communist forms, engulf immense areas of the civilized world. A second is to recall that about half of these speeches precede, while the other half follow, the onset of the most shattering event in the domestic history of twentieth-century America—the depression. Perhaps a third might be added. Modern war provides a dramatic example of social planning, and it is always less easy to dismantle wartime controls than it is to assemble them. There was one war behind Wilson when he made this speech; there are two behind us.

All the spokesmen in this series consider themselves committed to "free institutions" and, they might add— Norman Thomas excepted—"capitalistic institutions." Some want more governmental intervention, some less; but it is noticeable that those who want less today have already accepted far more than those who wanted less twenty years ago would have thought credible. A contemporary enumeration of the state's responsibilities—each of which would be interpreted differently but none of which could be denied some title to exist—would include the following: a responsibility to avert a repetition of the events of 1929–32; to maintain the income of farmers; to provide for social security in terms of minimum wages, minimum standards of health, housing, and unemployment insurance; to manage the resource development of at least one great physical region; to control the production of nuclear fuels; to rehabilitate foreign countries through financial aid and appropriate commercial policies. This list, far from exhaustive, is composed of items which are either entirely new or so transformed as to be virtually new. Many people, while reluctantly treading this path, are gravely disturbed by the risks they see in it; others acclaim the enlargement of the state power as the only means through which American ideals can be made effective.

From this review of policy statements at the broadest level of generality we pass to an examination of the alternatives offered within three major areas of the economy—business, labor, and agriculture.

In a previous unit we studied the impact of the corporation on the American economy and the adoption of a federal program to maintain competition through antitrust enforcement. In the subsequent years the relation of government to business has been reviewed in the light of the successive emergencies which have confronted our economic institutions. They have passed through the war mobilization of World War I, the boom years of postwar expansion, the bust of the early thirties, the recession of 1937, the second period of war mobilization, and the current years of postwar inflation. One organizational change which has persisted throughout these years is the progressive displacement of individualistic activity by collectivist activity and the domination of American business by the great corporation. This last feature has been the focus of much analysis and controversy, especially since the depression. Who controls these immense aggregations of economic power? How do they discharge their responsibilities to the investor, the smaller competitor, the consumer, and the laborer? How far has their enterprise had the effect of superseding a competitive economy by a managed economy? What standards should they be required to observe—or are they incompatible in their present form with the requirements of a free society?

To these questions, others have been added: Should government abandon its traditional detachment from the life of business and enter the national economy as an active partner of management and labor? Should it assume powers to regulate the volume of investment, to share in the making of the key industrial decisions, to institute programs of public works adjusted to emergencies, or to produce certain goods and services on a permanent basis? And if it is to enlarge its functions in any of these ways, through what kind of agencies should it act, and under what safeguards against the abuse of power?

Several aspects of this controversy are illustrated here: the pre-1929 phase of benevolent neutrality; the NRA phase of industrial self-government under federal supervision; the criticism that the NRA programs merely aggravated the worst features of monopoly and the discovery that this experiment in federal planning was unconstitutional; the revival of confidence in the antitrust policy; the revelation of the extent of concentration in industry and the proposal to impose conditions on the conduct of corporations through a national licensing system. Finally, there is an explanation and justification of TVA by the administrator who has since exchanged the leadership of that public corporation for an even bigger one—the Atomic Energy Commission.

Any policy for business must involve a policy for labor. The incentive to radical change was supplied by the depression, in which the masses of laboring men were naturally among the worst victims. The New Deal adopted a deliberate policy of promoting labor, both as an insurance against depressions and as a belated instalment of social justice. It was in this context that the first phase developed between 1932 and 1939. In these years the basic issue was the right of labor to organize and to bargain collectively without disturbance from legal injunctions or from the impediments which employers had put in their way. The injunction issue was largely solved by the Norris–La Guardia Act of 1932, and the employer tactics by the Wagner Act of 1935. The Supreme Court, which might conceivably have visited the same censures on this policy as it had done on others, was pleased to uphold it. Thus a long period of governmental indifference or hostility to labor unions was succeeded by an ardent and prolific honeymoon.

It was the spectacular growth of labor unionism which raised the next question. What should be done about a movement which was no longer small and weak but large and powerful—and which was now exhibiting several features once regarded as the peculiar sins of business monopolies? The reaction was vehemently exploited by all those employer interests which have never been reconciled to unions. It began before the war, was revived after it, and reached a climax in the passage by a Republican Congress of the Taft-Hartley Act. According to its sponsors, this act corrects the partiality of the Wagner Act and protects the legitimate interests of the employer, the community, and the individual workman, while still preserving the collective bargaining process. According to its opponents, it substitutes "government dictation" for true collective bargaining and inhibits the reasonable freedom of labor to fulfil its economic, social, and political aspirations.

The reversal of tradition which marked the New Deal approach to business and labor also applied to agriculture. The complaints of the farmer —who never shared in the boom of the twenties—had fallen on deaf ears. When he attempted to obtain unconventional assistance from an administration presided over by a purist of business orthodoxy, he received a typical chastisement in the Coolidge veto of the McNary-Haugen Bill. We print this message as one standard of comparison for the later legislation. A competitive industry, exposed to the rigors of unfavorable markets and handicapped by an accumulation of ills which are explored in these readings, was caught defenseless by the depression and only rescued after an immense salvage operation. As a result of this experience both the farmer's status in the community and the responsibilities of the government which helps to support him have been sensationally altered. The rationale of this instructive history may be studied in the documents defending the first and second Agricultural Adjustment Acts.

Perhaps the New Deal philosophy of the welfare state is nowhere more characteristically suggested than in President Roosevelt's proposals of 1944 for an economic bill of rights. These reflect the conviction, per-

sistently expressed since the Commonwealth Club address and fortified by the experience of planning for war, that the mission of America is now to pioneer in "economic democracy" as it once pioneered in "political democracy." The scope of this program is indicated by a speech made by Henry Wallace before a committee of the United States Senate in January, 1945. The text of the Full Employment Bill —one effort to implement the ideal— has been added, together with a criticism from the conservative standpoint of Senator Robert A. Taft.

In the individualistic age freedom of economic enterprise was closely associated in American minds with the same freedom from governmental action which safeguarded civil rights. While the former has contracted, what has happened to the latter?

Opponents of the New Deal, the Fair Deal, and of democratic socialism would undoubtedly hold that the foundations of civil rights are being undermined. One of their arguments would be that economic, political, and civil liberty flourished in unison and are bound to languish in unison: what injures one injures all. This is denied by the above parties, who conceive of themselves as effecting a fruitful reconciliation between the permanent claims of the old individualism and the new obligations of a positive state.

This argument is one consideration which enters into the current controversies over civil rights, but they have also been stirred by many other factors: the claims of military security during and after the war; the aspirations for a juster conception of human rights which led Wendell Willkie to stigmatize the mocking paradoxes in our American life; the effort to reanimate the New Deal in a period of Republican victory; the civil rights program of President Truman and the revolt of the Dixiecrats; and the world-wide conflict between the Russian and American systems. This last has produced the most violent crosscurrents in American opinion. To some it acts as a challenge to demonstrate our faith in freedom by enlarging the content of civil liberties and by preserving our immunity from the kind of hysteria which disfigured our conduct after World War I. To others it seems a compelling reason for protecting our institutions from Communist infection by the methods of the purge and the quarantine.

If a firm grasp of principle should inform our approach to these problems, it is nonetheless true that they yield to no simple solution. They have to be examined in their particulars. What tests should be applied in given cases when we try to determine the limits of free speech? How should the relations between the citizens of a democratic country and the military power be organized under specific conditions of emergency? How should the rights of racial and religious mi-norities be safeguarded in their effort to secure voting privileges, educational opportunities, homes in restricted areas, or the equal use of public services? Should Communists be permitted to teach, to work in government departments, to hold office in labor unions, to travel freely, to organize a political party or a political club on a university campus? And what is a "Communist"? The readings which terminate this section do not settle these questions, but they do something to illuminate them. The spirit in which they may be read was well expressed by Wendell Willkie in *One World*:

"For now more than ever, we must keep in the forefront of our minds the fact that whenever we take away the liberties of those whom we hate, we are opening the way to loss of liberty for those we love.

"Our way of living together in America is a strong but delicate fabric. It is made up of many threads. It has been woven over many centuries by the patience and sacrifice of countless liberty-loving men and women. It serves as a cloak for the protection of poor and rich, of black and white, of Jew and gentile, of foreign- and native-born.

"Let us not tear it asunder. For no man knows, once it is destroyed, where or when man will find its protective warmth again."

SECTION A. CRITERIA FOR A FREE SOCIETY

1. A POLITICAL CREDO[1]

By HENRY C. SIMONS

EDITORS' NOTE.—"A Political Credo" is a cogent reaffirmation in the twentieth century of continued confidence in the modern applicability of the essential principles of Locke, Smith, and Tocqueville. Its pertinence lies in its criticism of both "right" and "left"—of those who would reinstate the liberal tradition through recourse to laissez faire and those who would seek to preserve liberal values by moving toward a planned welfare state. It has the added pertinence of being a clear formulation of the fundamental values of a free society.

Its author, Henry C. Simons (1899–1946), was a University of Chicago economist who tried to elaborate for his fellow-economists the conditions for the suitable functioning of the free market system and an equitable tax policy. In 1934 he issued the pamphlet for which he is best known—*A Positive Program for Laissez Faire*. "A Political Credo" was written in 1945 as an effort to formulate specifically the political philosophy implicit in his work. Both of these essays are included in a collection of his major works entitled *Economic Policy for a Free Society*.

The other essays of this volume deal mainly with special problems of economic policy. Inviting readers' attention to such discussion, one may offer at the start a candid statement of the more general or ancillary persuasions which inform that discussion and in awareness of which the reader may, whether with agreement or dissent, best understand it.

A good Introduction would expound a coherent scheme of practical ethics, a political-economic philosophy, or, if you please, a clear-cut ideological position. Limitations of space and of competence, however, permit only rather naked display of fragmentary ideas and opinions. I hope that they are fragments of one intelligible general position and that they do con-

sistently inform or underlie the argument of the other essays.

The underlying position may be characterized as severely libertarian or, in the English-Continental sense, liberal. The intellectual tradition is intended to be that of Adam Smith, Herrmann, Thünen, Mill, Menger, Brentano, Sidgwick, Marshall, Fetter, and Knight, and of Locke, Hume, Bentham, Humboldt, Tocqueville, Burckhardt, Acton, Dicey, Barker, and Hayek.

The distinctive feature of this tradition is emphasis upon liberty as both a requisite and a measure of progress. Its liberty or freedom, of course, comprises or implies justice, equality, and other aspectual qualities of the "good society." Its society, however, is no mere aggregate of reified aspects but a living, functioning organization or "organism"; and its good society is no static conception but is essentially so-

1. Henry C. Simons, *Economic Policy for a Free Society* (Chicago, 1948), pp. 1–39. By permission of the University of Chicago Press.

cial process whose goodness is progress—and progress not only in terms of prevailing criteria but also in the criteria themselves. Liberalism is thus largely pragmatic as regards the articulation or particularization of its values; but its ethics, if largely pragmatic, also gives special place to liberty (and nearly co-ordinate place to equality) as a "relatively absolute absolute."

Liberalism involves a theory of history or of human progress; and it offers a generalized prescription or working hypothesis for policy—in terms of both what and how. Its claims, however, may well be limited to certain societies or cultures, if not to certain latitudes or climates. It may offer clues to why societies become progressive; but proponents need claim only a limited relevance or applicability. It purports only to tell something of how progress has occurred and of how it may be sustained in advanced nations. How unfree societies may start toward freedom; how the accumulation of knowledge may be made to prevail against the intrenchment of superstition; how economic progress may be made to prevail against inordinate birth rates—these are social problems for which Western liberalism offers no clear or simple answers, only dubious conjectures and earnest hopes. It would serve mankind mainly by sustaining progress in areas already blessed with forward momentum (i.e., in western European civilization and its outposts)—which is perhaps the largest possible contribution to progress elsewhere. Despotisms of superstition may be dissipated by external contacts; despotisms of authorities may be mitigated or disciplined by the slow osmosis of moral-political ideas and standards; and despotisms of hopelessness may be relaxed by adventitious bursts of prosperity which check population increase instead of accelerating it. An optimistic view of our own civilization thus becomes, in long perspective, an optimistic view of the whole world.

THE "INVISIBLE HAND"

Liberalism is an optimistic view of man and society. It surveys recent centuries and calls them mainly good, each better than the one before, each achieving greatly and bequeathing enlarged potentialities. Modern history testifies to the virtues of liberty; it shows man acquiring freedom and, in the process, acquiring ever larger capacity for freedom. Two frightful, global wars may now undermine our faith; but they doubtless loom overlarge to a contemporary view and well may mark the beginnings of modern world organization. They may eventually be viewed as the death struggle of aggressive, self-centered nationalism, whose growth in turn marked the demise of a despotic church and of feudal, aristocratic government.

Liberalism implicitly postulates some "invisible hand"—as does any optimistic view of man's fate or potentialities. Its beneficent force may be identified as social process in a free society. The libertarian policy prescription calls essentially for planning to sustain freedom. It argues that, if advanced nations can remain substantially free, other goods will be added unto them and gradually unto other peoples. It demands that every policy problem be examined as, in part, a problem of sustaining the vital, creative processes of a free society and that all proposals to sacrifice freedom on behalf of other ends (notably, security) be examined under a presumption of error.

POLITICAL VERSUS VOLUNTARY ASSOCIATION

A free society must be organized largely through voluntary associations. Freedom to associate or to dissociate, to belong or not to belong, especially in economic activities, is an essential liberty—and will remain so, short of the millennial "economy of abundance." Man will continue indefinitely to be occupied, even in the richest nations, mainly in "making a living"; and his other liberties are unlikely to be or to remain larger than the liberty he enjoys in such central activity.

Freedom of association, of course, implies also coercive association, that is, strong government and an elaborate, stable, confining structure of law. Liberals exalt the "rule of the law" and hold that, as the antithesis of the rule of men or authority, it is attainable only within an economy of (largely) voluntary association.

Freedom to belong or not to belong also implies multitudes of similar associations among which one may choose and move, as worker, as investor, as customer, etc. Likewise it implies effective freedom to initiate new associations, that is, free enterprise. Economics properly stresses competition among organizations as a means to proper resource allocation and combination and to commutative justice. But effective competition is also requisite to real freedom of association—and to real power dispersion. All monopolies, and all very large organizations of sellers (or buyers), are impairment of that freedom and, unless transitory or unsubstantial, must tend to be governmentalized, not only because they involve exploitation (departure from commutative justice) and diseconomies, but also because adequately strong government cannot tolerate usurpation of its coercive powers.

At the bottom of any structure of voluntary associations, of course, is the family. Perhaps the hardest problems of libertarian policy concern the division of responsibilities between the family and the government. Liberal ideals include equality of opportunity—or steadily diminishing inequality. This and other purposes doubtless require governmental assumption of responsibilities once largely or exclusively those of families, notably as regards the health and education of children, and, also, substantial restriction on family accumulation of wealth. In either case, limitation on the freedom of families is involved; and hard questions arise of how and how rapidly egalitarian measures may be pursued

without undermining the structure of voluntary associations at its foundation.

COMMUTATIVE AND DISTRIBUTIVE JUSTICE

The norm in all voluntary economic association is commutative justice. Such justice connotes exchange of equal values, as measured objectively by organized markets. It is an obvious or "natural" basis of co-operation among strangers or persons not members of the same "primary" groups, and especially among communities, enterprises, and nations. It dictates that each shall receive according as he (or it) contributes to organized, co-operative, joint production or, in technical economic language, according to the productivity of his property, capital, or capacity (including personal capacity).

Commutative justice simply takes for granted an existing distribution of capital, among persons, families, communities, regions, and nations. Large-scale organization, and supranational organization especially, must start from a status quo. All participants will, generally speaking, be far better off with co-operative production, division of labor, and exchange. A few, to be sure, may prosper by altering the distribution of existing possessions, that is, by theft, robbery, or war. But every violent or arbitrary redistribution impedes or disrupts the elaborate, co-operative production on which all depend; and no large group anywhere can possibly gain enough from redistributing wealth to compensate for its probable income losses from the consequent disorganization of production. Economic co-operation, like supranational organization, must largely accept possessions as facts.

A free society must be organized, not wholly but basically or primarily, around voluntary, free exchange of goods and services. The alternative is no large organization at all. A little understanding of interregional trade suggests, moreover, that supranational organization is nearly impossible save among areas, communities, or nations in which substantially free exchange prevails.

To stress commutative justice is not to ignore distributive justice, or the real problem of inequality, but merely to urge that two problems be distinguished in analysis, discussion, and action. It is a virtue of a free-exchange society that it invites separation of these problems. But it also involves and permits progressive mitigation of inequality; indeed, it affords the largest possibilities of substantial equality. However, our primary problem is production. The common man or average family has a far greater stake in the size of our aggregate income than in any possible redistribution of income. Large and efficient production requires close approximation to the norm of commutative justice. Achieving or approaching that instrumental end, we may and properly do sharply modify the distributional results of free exchange and, in the long view, may further modify them almost indefinitely. What is important, for libertarians, is that we preserve the basic processes of free exchange and that egalitarian measures be superimposed on those processes, effecting redistribution afterward and not in the immediate course of production and commercial transactions.

Commutative justice assures no one a livelihood. It is almost entirely superseded within families or primary groups and is radically modified in all societies, especially free-exchange societies, by private charity and governmental outlays at the bottom and, notably, by taxation at the top. Even extreme collectivism, by the way, must sharply distinguish, if only for purposes of planning and accounting, between payments for services and mere transfers of income. Moreover, the best mitigation of inequality will involve progressive equalization of personal or family contributions to the social income, not increasing disparity between contributions and receipts. The good society is not one that achieves substantial or increasing equality by extensive redistribution or manipulation of incomes but one that enjoys such equality on the basis of commutative justice. Sound meliorative measures must yield not mere leveling of incomes but leveling accretions of capacity, capital, and possessed power.

Equality of opportunity is an ideal that free societies should constantly pursue, even at much cost in terms of other ends. Freedom without power, like power without freedom, has no substance or meaning. The practical problem of freedom now is one of dispersing or redistributing power among organizations. Inequality, on the other hand, is overwhelmingly a problem of investment in human capacity, that is, in health, education, and skills; it can hardly be scratched by possible redistributions of wealth.

Freedom and equality convey, among libertarians, similar and complementary meanings. Both imply responsible individuals or families, the rule of law, and great dispersion of power. An equality imposed from above, or by remote authority, is a negation not only of freedom but of equality as well. Progress connotes ever enlarged human capacity for responsible freedom. Such capacity is power; and its future enlargement must mean mass accumulation of the private capital in, mainly, personal capacities. Save as the bride of liberty, equality is pale and deadly dull, if not revolting. But the ultimate liberty obviously is that of men equal in power.

DISCUSSION AND CONSENSUS

An essential ingredient of good social process is organized, free discussion. The virtues of freedom in the pursuit of scientific truth are obvious and undisputed. It is now unthinkable that any question of physics or biology should be answered by appeal to force, to political authority, or to soothsayers or that any scientist should seek to establish a thesis by deliberate fraud. The modern test of truth is simply voluntary rational consensus, and the moral standards of scientific discussion or controversy are a priceless human achievement. These standards tend to elevate all discussion, to discipline all controversy, and to subordinate mere persuasion to co-operative discovery of the best answers, in matters of morals as well as in natural science.

If the social process of free discussion is essential to the progress of scientific knowledge, it is even more obviously essential to moral progress; and, to repeat, truth-seeking is itself a matter of moral standards. The good, progressive moral order must rest on intelligent consensus and on much the same kind of free, critical discussion as is involved in scientific inquiry. A moral order imposed by force or fraud, by authorities, or by threats of punishment in this world or the next is a contradiction in terms. Moral individual conduct is meaningful only within a range of responsible freedom; and social morality is, like truth, a matter of voluntary consensus. The libertarian recognizes no test of moral truth or moral wisdom save such consensus. Society is always right—provided it is the right kind of society. The social processes of a free society are, if not infallible, the only reliable means to moral truth and the best means to security under law.

DEMOCRACY AS GOVERNMENT BY DISCUSSION

Democracy, as viewed by libertarians, is basically a process of government by free, intelligent discussion. It is a means for promoting discussion of obtrusive social problems and for achieving continuous improvement of the moral order through experimental action-out-of-discussion. Such a process implies an elaborate structure of political institutions and conventions, including constitutions, legislatures, executives or ministries, courts, and parties. It implies an inclusive electorate, if not universal adult suffrage, and moral, intelligent electors—although qualitative selection for suffrage, with universal eligibility to qualify, should not be hastily ruled out. It also implies, at best, a con-

tinuing process of relevant discussion and inquiry among professional truth-seekers or academic problem-solvers, who, though scrupulously detached from active politics and from factional affiliations, subtly and unobtrusively guide or arbitrate political debate by their own discussions. Effective discussion presupposes an elaborate division of labor—between agitators and dispassionate students, between debaters and inquirers, between specialists and philosophers, between political tacticians and statesmen; and, at the highest levels, it presupposes hierarchies of competence, based on the standards of many intellectual disciplines, with groups shifting from the status of arbiter-authorities to that of laymen as different problems arise for discussion.

The democratic process rests proximately upon representative, deliberative assemblies. It contemplates agitation, discussion of problems, proposals for dealing with them, examination of such proposals, continuous compromise and revision of bills, and eventual enactments of legislation. At best, such final enactments will mainly not involve close votes or sharp dissent; discussion and compromise should usually eventuate in substantial legislative consensus. Occasionally, however, there will be "agreements to disagree" which afford the proper issues at general elections, especially under two-party systems of an organized "government" or ministry and a similarly organized "opposition" or alternative "government."

With good government, the discussion of problems is more important than the action to which it immediately leads. It tends to define areas of large agreement (if only by neglecting or ignoring) as well as of small disagreement and thus to enlarge or to deepen that consensus which is the moral basis of order. All legislative acts are provisional, experimental changes in the moral code, subject to repeal or to progressive modification. They may rest initially on mere majorities and thus remain controversial, in which case compromise will probably continue on the basis of experience until the legislation really becomes law, that is, until dissent from the majority decree is dissipated and mature consensus realized. Acts, like bills, are primarily discussion projects, focusing controversy upon important problems and inducing continuous redefinition or rearticulation of what is beyond serious dispute.

CONTINUITY AS REQUISITE TO DEMOCRATIC PROCESS

Sound democracy must continuously reaffirm faith in its own processes. There must be implicit agreement to preserve the process of action through deliberative discussion and continued compromise. This means agreement to proceed slowly and to avoid radical, irreversible experiments. In this respect, democracy is inherently conservative, as our radicals lament. It can try short cuts but only by abdication, that is, only by imposing discontinuity, which is the negation of its process.

Democracy is properly conservative in guarding liberty and in protecting itself against zealous power-seekers, megalomaniacs, and fools. In highly undemocratic societies revolution may permit movement toward freedom or displacement of worse authorities by better ones. Given a functioning democratic process, however, revolution means abandonment of government by discussion in favor of authorities, claiming a mandate for "temporary" dictatorship. It means grand innovations consolidated without benefit of compromise or of experimental gradualism. No really democratic government of the day, however large its electoral or legislative majority, may grossly impair the prerogatives of future governments; no legislature may closely bind future legislatures to continue particular innovations, to disregard experience, to avoid compromise, or to ignore strong persisting dissent; and no dominant faction may properly act in a way that requires revolution to undo its acts. Given substantial political freedom, there are no worthy institutional changes which preclude gradual, tentative, experimental measures—and, in any case, no "leaders" who may be trusted either to conceive or to execute schemes that involve prompt burning of bridges back. To believe otherwise is to trust grand revelations instead of tedious experiment and to trust men, cults, or mobs instead of society and free societal process.

Radical, imaginative societal constructs, as construct goals of slow, orderly changes, are invaluable for informing discussion of immediate policy problems. Everyone should try to judge particular measures in terms of the kinds of total systems toward which they lead. Radical factional differences in the long-term objectives that inform current proposals may jeopardize democracy. But, adhering to gradualist measures, a nation may sustain large consensus in its step-by-step actions, in spite of sharp ideological controversy; and sharp ideological differences may themselves be effectively compromised and gradually disintrenched in the process. (The conflict between socialists and libertarians, in a good future, will afford a striking case in point.) Democratic action, however, must never defy or impugn dissent; it must not run far ahead of general, fundamental consensus or squander opportunities for reconciling opposition; it must recognize its basic task as ever that of recreating and enlarging moral consensus among free men.

Strong, organized opposition is of the essence of responsible government—and its most fragile element. It may be lost in the too-strong government of the one-party system or, along with properly strong government, in the multiplication of parties and factions. The golden mean between these evil extremes is again a matter of underlying consensus, between "government" and "opposition" and, in only slightly larger measure, within each organization. In these circumstances agreements to disagree are powerful weapons on both sides; and the pressure for tolerant, salutary compromise is then effective.

Elections may then be contested in terms of discrete, discussable issues; debate may be disciplined by intellectual standards; and controversy may involve genuine political education. Factions may contest without seeking or desiring to destroy one another; the "government" and the "opposition" may change places without serious discontinuity and without much shift of power; and the community as voters may be required to answer only questions which men can and must be trusted to answer, namely, along what lines particular, tentative, *experimental* changes in laws or institutions shall proceed. Such millennial conditions have never prevailed and doubtless will never be closely approached. But they have in fact always been approached wherever democracy functioned well; they may always be brought nearer by closer observance of the proper rules of democratic process; and continued departure from such conditions can only impair or destroy such freedom as men have won.

LIBERALISM AND FEDERALISM

Traditional liberalism commends constitutional federalism. It calls for a political structure in which organization becomes looser and more flexible, and functions narrower and more negative, as one moves from local bodies to counties, to provinces or states, to the central, national government, and on to supranational or world government. Its good state is instrumental, subordinate to society, and so constructed as to minimize the dangers of power concentration, that is, the danger that governmental power may be usurped by armies, factions, or majorities and used to dominate society rather than to implement free societal process and social-moral development.

Good political structure should be closely similar to the informal organization or federation of large societies, cultures, or civilizations. The range and kind of governmental activities and legislation at different levels should reflect the different range and kind of consensus, attained or attainable. As one moves from primary groups through small to large communities and on to inclusive society, the range of moral consensus becomes narrower and its content at once more fundamental or abstract and more vague or ambiguous. Government in a free society must, at different levels, adapt itself to the existing hierarchy of moral consensus and try to build, or to facilitate society's building, a strong, bottom-heavy moral structure.

CENTRAL VERSUS LOCAL GOVERNMENTS

Individualism and collectivism are usually discussed largely in terms of political (coercive) versus voluntary (free) association and of governmental-monopolistic versus private-competitive organizations. The range of aggregate governmental activities, however, is hardly more important, as a policy problem, than their distribution between small and large, local and central, governments. Extensive local socialization need not be incompatible with, or very dangerous to, a free society. Local bodies are themselves largely voluntary associations; people have much freedom to choose and to move among them; they are substantially competitive and, even if permitted to do so, rarely could much restrain trade. The libertarian argument against "too much government," consequently, relates mainly to national governments, not to provincial or local units—and to great powers rather than to small nations.

Democratic process is an invention of local bodies. It has been extended upward and may be extended gradually toward world organization. In any case, modern democracy rests upon free, responsible local government and will never be stronger than this foundation. Free, responsible local bodies correspond, in the political system, to free, responsible individuals or families and voluntary associations in the good society. A people wisely conserving its liberties will seek ever to enlarge the range and degree of local freedom and responsibility. In so doing, it may sacrifice possible proximate achievements. Doing specific good things by centralization will always be alluring. It may always seem easier to impose "progress" on localities than to wait for them to effect it for themselves—provided one is not solicitous about the basis or sources of progress. A community imposing good local government from above may seem to get ahead rapidly for a time. Likewise, a community may temporarily raise its economic scale of life by living up its capital. And the analogy seems closely in point. Progress to which local freedom, responsibility, and experimentation have pointed the way may be accelerated for a time and effected more uniformly by the short cut of central action. But such short-cutting tends to impair or to use up the roots of progress in order to obtain a briefly luxuriant bloom.

The inefficiency and corruption of local government are recognized evils—which make us unduly complacent or enthusiastic about centralization. It is generally supposed that almost any function will be more efficiently and more honestly discharged by a larger unit of government. So, we readily accept increase of central responsibility, through supervision or outright transfer of functions or both. As regards corruption, the prevailing view is simply wrong—unless one sticks to a narrow, legalistic definition. Our federal government (I venture) is far more corrupt in its best years than municipal government at its worst, if one judges by the proportion of outlays (activities) which serve the common interest as against the proportion spent in vote-buying, that is, in serving special interests against the common interest. Municipal machines at worst divert a modest tribute; their graft and patronage are small fractions of the value of public services actually rendered. Our national government typically spends freely on behalf of organized, logrolling minorities, tossing in some general welfare outlays for good measure. For decades the subsidies appropriated in the form of protective tariffs probably amounted to more than the total of all other federal outlays, including silver subsidies.

The notion that large governmental units are more efficient than small ones is equally wrong but hard to attack, because efficiency is far more ambiguous or deceptive in meaning than is corruption. Large administrative units may seem more efficient than small ones, if only because they contain so many people employed to increase efficiency rather than to produce substantive services. But administrative efficiency in government, at best, is a false god and a dangerously static good. Large governments, like giant business corporations, may effectively mobilize existing technology, realizing fully its current potentialities. In a shortsighted view they are instruments of progress; but they lack the creative powers of a multiplicity of competitive smaller units. They are, to repeat, at best only means for "forcing" the plant—for enriching the present at the expense of the future. The French genius for *administration* would appear to have been purchased dearly in terms of capacity of *government*. Free government is always worth some cost in terms of "good" or efficient government.

The political agnostic or specialized reformer would transfer control or responsibility upward whenever proximate gains seemed thus attainable. Libertarians would counsel a bolder scheme of improving local government by enlarging local freedom and removing the props of central control—and they would join in recommending central measures for facilitating proper discharge of local responsibilities.

CENTRAL GOVERNMENT FUNCTIONS: WAR

The most obvious central function is that of external defense. In the ultimate federalism this function disappears, and only at or near this limit can libertarian democracy be securely attained. Total war, actual or imminent, demands extreme centralization, that is, a unitary, military, collectivist state which is the antithesis of a free society. It involves moral, economic, and governmental mobilization in which all freedom may be subordinated to one overriding, concrete purpose. And such mobilization is hard to undo after the emergency is past, for it brings its own other "emergencies" and invites retention for all manner of worthy purposes. The emotional experience of war and the impressive achievements of mobilization leave us ill prepared for the prosaic processes of a free society and for renewed faith in any "invisible hand."

Fortunately, however, even the demands of external defense are ambivalent. If wars are frequent, victories will probably accrue to those who remain mobilized. Otherwise, planning for peace may also be the best planning for war. If there are vital, creative forces to be released by demobilization—by return to a free society—the nation may thereby gain enough strength to compensate handsomely for the risks involved. Victories may consistently accrue to those who bet on peace; and progress toward world order may continue secularly in spite of disastrous retrogressions.

This a libertarian must believe, for war is the great threat to his kind of society. There is simply no democratic answer to the problem of external defense, save indefinite extension of federalism, first, into a predominantly powerful supranational federation, and then gradually into inclusive world organization of all nations capable of responsible participation. Here the important next steps must be taken in the field of commercial policies; and the next conspicuous institutional innovation will be an international court with compulsory jurisdiction, albeit only among some Western democracies at the start. Libertarian democracy can survive without world order but not without secular movement toward such order.

OTHER CENTRAL FUNCTIONS

The basic function of central government is to sustain domestic peace. Internal order is prerequisite to external defense and, of course, is the essence of world federation. The good central government will represent a monopoly of violence; it must sustain that monopoly against both its constituent political units and all extra-governmental bodies. It must promote all kinds of peaceful intercourse, intellectual and commercial. It must articulate the prevailing moral consensus and promote enlargement of that consensus by organized, free discussion and legislative-judicial experimentation.

Two more definite central government functions are stressed by libertarians: first, the maintenance of free trade and, second, the provision of a stable currency. The central government, retaining its monopoly of violence, must either itself conduct trade or prevent any other organization from exercising effective control. A federation which is not at least a customs union is hardly a federation. The central government must deny to its constituent units the power to engage in economic warfare among themselves. It must prevent them from arbitrarily restraining commerce or from blocking national economic integration. It must systematically prevent, destroy, or control all artificial private monopoly, that is, all extra-governmental organizations with power to restrain trade. Such organizations are not merely an economic evil; they are also an impairment or usurpation of the state monopoly of coercion and, to repeat, of individual freedom of association.

Stabilization of the currency is a function implicit in federal monopoly of currency issue and in federal fiscal powers. Legal-tender money, stable in value, is almost indispensable to orderly internal commerce and to economic development. Monetary stabilization, moreover, affords an invaluable guide for fiscal policy and a salutary, quasi-constitutional rule limiting the abuse of fiscal powers by particular legislatures or governing factions. Its obvious virtue is that of requiring "governments" to pay for the political blessings of expenditure with appropriately heavy taxation.

SERVICE FUNCTIONS AND THE RULE OF LAW

Beyond these specifications it is difficult to indicate concretely a proper distribution of powers or functions among grades or levels of government. Two general prescriptions, however, may be suggested, although they are largely reducible one to the other.

First, the service functions or community-housekeeping activities of government should be concentrated at the bottom of the scale and not ordinarily or permanently intruded at the upper levels. Larger units may properly do all manner of things to facilitate local discharge of service responsibilities. They may conduct research, formulate standards, publicize relevant information, offer training for local personnel, and even contribute funds, provided that assistance is not (long?) combined with positive, direct control and that local responsibility remains essentially unimpaired. This means, in terms of one obtrusive issue, that all grants of funds from above should be (tend to become) bloc grants and largely unconditional. Grants should involve a minimum of central control and should not (permanently) be made for special purposes. Moreover, all federal grants should be made to and through the states, even when intended for local bodies—and, again, unconditionally.

These prescriptions require, to be sure, some qualifications. Disciplinary action against communities is occasionally admissible, as against criminals or irresponsible persons. But such intervention must be confined to extreme cases of persistent departure from moderate, accepted standards. Moreover, conditional and special-purpose grants, even with substantial control from above, may sometimes be defensible as temporary subsidies to particular local experimentation, provided they are clearly recognized as temporary expedients and as deliberate aberrations from an accepted general policy. The same may perhaps be said, more cautiously, of more extreme measures of centralization.

Second, the older strictures about the rule of law should be interpreted more and more severely as one moves up through the governmental hierarchy. Extensive delegations of power to executive or administrative officers should be largely confined to local bodies. At higher levels such delegations of legislative discretion should be severely economized and, when invoked, should be regarded as a temporary or transitional expedient. National government should be government by law, by legislative rules, and by legislation which follows clear, announced rules of policy. A national legislature should bind administration by closely confining rules, enforcible by an independent judiciary; and it should, at least as "government" and "opposition," also bind itself by confining rules of policy (platforms) which preclude sheer opportunism or tactical nose-following.

This prescription largely repeats the first prescription about service functions but is perhaps more fundamental. Local government, as a service-rendering agency, must be largely a government of men. Legislation and administration are almost indistinguishable; and responsible administration, closely confined by legislative rules, is unthinkable in education, health, police, fire protection, and other local utilities. Local government is largely a collection of business or service enterprises that must be run as such. The proper function of state, and especially federal, governments, on the other hand, is largely not that of providing services but that of providing the framework within which business, local-public and private, may effectively be conducted. This framework may, of course, include a vast amount of services, provided they are not final services but services rendered primarily to enterprises.

THE RULE OF LAW AND GOVERNMENT BY DISCUSSION

If such prescriptions are followed, government by discussion and consensus is facilitated and strengthened thereby. At higher levels, and especially at the highest level, political discussion should be focused on clear-cut, general rules of law and policy. It is such discussion that feeds the growth and diffusion of the basic moral consensus. Only from slow action out of such discussion may a nation build solidly and progressively the principles and working rules which afford political security and economic stability. Only by adherence to the rule of law and to announced rules of policy may a people have strong government without granting inordinate, arbitrary power to ruling parties, factions, or majorities of the moment. Only thus may it assure the use of governmental power in the common interest or avoid the degradation of government by logrolling, patronage-seeking, special-interest groups. Only thus may freedom be protected against large-government power and, to repeat, large-scale discussion focused on questions that can be fruitfully discussed or usefully settled by discussion.

The alternative is "plebicitary democracy," the antithesis of libertarian government. Elections then merely choose among leaders or factions. Campaigns are mere contests for power—slogan-mongering, promising everything to all minorities save the scapegoats, absurd eulogies and vilifications. Platforms are unprincipled in themselves and binding, if at all, only during the campaign. Parties are simply organizations for promising and dispensing patronage, standing for nothing but unlimited prerogative of tactical opportunism, either as "government" or as "opposition" (if any). Such, at all events, is the meaning of government by men as the antithesis of government by law and policy rules.

These prescriptions in terms of service functions (concentrated at the bottom) and the rule of law (severely adhered to at the top) are, like federalism itself, designed to assure minimal dispersion or decentralization of power. Executive-administrative discretion in large governments is an ominous thing—as is *ad hoc* legislation on behalf of particular areas, industries, producers, or pressure groups. Constitutional rules, enforced by courts, are one means for limiting the exercise of power implicit in central government. But constitutional provisions are no stronger than the moral consensus that they articulate. At best, they can only check abuse of power until moral pressure is mobilized; and their check must become ineffective if often overtly used.

Protective tariffs and silver subsidies are instructive cases in point. They fall outside any seriously discussable rule of policy. If any party proposed to subsidize uniformly all domestic production, all domestic enterprises, it would only expose itself to ridicule. If anyone undertook to formulate rules which are or should be implicit in a system of highly differential subsidies, that is, rules determining how the differentials are or should be fixed, he would soon abandon the undertaking. Here, then, are dispensations which follow no rule or principle whatever and, consequently, can continuously be manipulated as patronage or vote-buying and fixed by the procedures of logrolling. Moreover, since there is no rule of policy, there is no issue to discuss or to debate usefully and no possibility of intelligent electoral decision or significant consensus. Campaign discussion, like legislation, stresses the special interests of each community or producer group; and the basic policy problem is obfuscated and ignored. The virtue of bad rules as against no rules, by the way, is evident in the case of agricultural subsidies. The "parity principle," if not very confining, is amenable to discussion—which leaves farm subsidies in a much weaker political position than the analogous worse subsidies of our tariff. The parity principle is inherently ridiculous;

people can see what it would mean if generalized, that is, applied to all commodities; but protective tariffs are strongly intrenched simply because they involve no principle whatever and admit of discussion not as a policy but only as an unintelligible mass of expedients.

FEDERALISM AND INTERNATIONAL ORGANIZATION

A great virtue of extreme federalism or decentralization in great nations is that it facilitates their extension toward world organization or their easy absorption into still larger federations. If central governments were, as they should be, largely repositories of unexercised powers, held simply to prevent their exercise by constituent units or extra-governmental organizations, then supranational organization would be easy if not almost gratuitous. Indeed, such great-nation decentralization or deorganization is both end and means of international organization.

War is a collectivizing process, and large-scale collectivism is inherently warlike. If not militarist by national tradition, highly centralized states must become so, by the very necessities in sustaining at home an inordinate, "unnatural" power concentration, by the threat of their governmental mobilization as felt by other nations, and by their almost inevitable transformation of commercial intercourse into organized economic warfare among great economic-political blocs. There can be no real peace or solid world order in a world of a few great, centralized powers.

To count on early breakup of Russia or the United States is fantastic, desirable as it would be for the world in both cases. But it is not fantastic to contemplate steady decentralization within both these nations. One may be slightly encouraged by several facts. The third world power is, at the top level, almost the ideal federation, so decentralized that the central government can hardly be said to exist. Its major constituent, to be sure, has recently been rushing into extreme centralization;

but this Continentalizing of Great Britain may be a passing aberration and might be rapidly undone in an orderly, prosperous world. The Dominions have also been moving the same way; but there would seem to be great obstacles, constitutional and other, to rapid or extreme centralization in Canada or Australia. Second, the tradition or memory of federalism is still honored in the United States, and the substance may still be resurrected. Third, Russia, having fulfilled the great purpose of its new centralization, namely, erasure of disgraceful defeat and destruction of German power, may consolidate its domestic achievements by rapid, orderly decentralization. It has already made grand gestures toward constitutional democracy and democratic federalism. With all skepticism about their immediate significance, one may recognize these formal commitments as evidence of genuine aspirations, and of national purposes which, with an orderly world outside, might steadily be realized.

DECENTRALIZATION AND PEACE

Collectivism is a name for an extreme form of governmental centralization or power concentration. To the student of society, it must seem wholly unnatural and utterly unstable. It may serve useful purposes for a time; but it is not itself a viable social or political order. Its order is synthetic and fragile; its order is imposed from above, while real social order is a growth or building-upward. A highly centralized world government is nearly unthinkable—save as a hysterical imputation of evil purpose in an enemy power. It could be the imposition only of a predominant, militarized nation and, in the modern world, would be the most precarious basis of peace—if it is not the antithesis of peace—in any discerning apprehension of meanings.

If order were not merely a quality or aspect of a substantial, functioning society, if it could be reified, synthesized, and poured on the world like manna or DDT, the application would surely induce (mean?) rapid, radical decentralization and deorganization of power among men. Centralization is a product of disorder. In advanced societies it is retrogression, induced by disasters. The obvious case is, of course, war or prospect of war, when everyone naturally looks to the largest available organization and demands mobilized concentration of power—which assures the war if it is still only a fear. But the economic disasters of depression and deflation work the same way. Indeed, it may reasonably be said that economic disaster was the crucial proximate cause of World War II—that it caused a governmental mobilization, or reversal of the gradual demobilization from World War I, and that this in turn precipitated the conflict.

To recognize that an orderly world would be highly decentralized (if only by definition) is to see something of how durable peace may wisely be sought. If we can apprehend fragments or aspects of an organized world, we apprehend something of how the firm substance may gradually be realized.

"POWER ALWAYS CORRUPTS"

Traditional liberalism, to repeat, is an optimistic faith in the potentialities of free men and free societal process. By vulgar repute, however, it is a narrow, negative, and pessimistic doctrine perhaps by association with "the dismal science." The charge of pessimism is valid as regards "Malthusian" societies, notably India. Moreover, all positive or optimistic prescriptions necessarily have their negative corollaries. And one of these, while implicit above, may properly be stressed in passing.

A cardinal tenet of libertarians is that no one may be trusted with much power— no leader, no faction, no party, no "class," no majority, no government, no church, no corporation, no trade association, no labor union, no grange, no professional association, no university, no large organization of any kind. They must forever repeat with Lord Acton: "Power always corrupts"—and not merely those who exercise it but those subject to it and the whole society. The only good power is that of law based on overwhelming voluntary consensus of free men and built and rebuilt by gradual experimentation, organized discussion, and tolerant compromise. They do not deny that concentrated power may occasionally serve human progress as a temporary or transitional expedient. They do deny its uses in advanced nations, save in the gravest military emergencies and then only until the peak of crisis has been passed—and any libertarian who cries wolf easily or frequently is automatically disqualified.

LIBERALISM AND COMMERCIAL POLICY

Liberalism is also notorious for its uncompromising opposition to governmental restraint or manipulation of foreign trade. This "negative" aspect of liberalism, that is, its categorical free-trade prescription, perhaps merits a few remarks in connection with world problems.

The main content of centralization in the modern world has been control of foreign trade. It was this aspect of mercantilism that Adam Smith mainly attacked; and this same aspect of government remains, or has again become, the proper first concern of libertarians. Commercial policy is not only the hard core of bad national centralization; it is also the necessary basis or prerequisite of bad centralization in other manifestations. Bad central planning begins historically in commercial policy and, in all major aspects, involves or requires arbitrary restrictions on foreign trade. Free foreign trade would largely frustrate all major enterprises in economic centralization or in direct federal control of relative prices, wages, or production. To specify that central economic planning or regulation should proceed with a framework of free external trade is to suggest perhaps the most useful distinction between good and bad "planning." To achieve free trade would be to realize, directly and indirectly, most of the decentralization that libertarians propose.

Nationalism, as imposition of internal free trade, is a means to prosperity and peace. As imposed control of trade, external and then internal, it is mobilization for war, which immediately jeopardizes world order and, in the longer view, also undermines the moral basis of internal peace.

The proximate future of libertarian democracy depends crucially on the future of commercial policy, especially in the United States. This country cannot long have free internal trade without free or much freer trade across its borders; and, be that as it may, this country cannot maintain a libertarian political-economic system as an isolated island surrounded by increasingly antithetical systems. On the other hand, its power is adequate to re-establish a libertarian trend among its friends and neighbors; and, so re-established, libertarian democracy may then resume its gradual, peaceful "conquest" of the world.

Recent decades have witnessed a steady resurgence of protectionism, culminating during the great depression in disastrous economic warfare. The subtle, substantial international organization implicit in mutual self-denying ordinances, under the rule of equal treatment or nondiscrimination, was suddenly swept away in an orgy of bilateralism, quota restrictions, clearing agreements, and exchange control. Blame for this disaster may be placed largely on the United States—on its supid tariff legislation, on its impardonable devaluation, and primarily on its failure, as custodian of the dominant or world currency, to prevent a long and deep deflation. Whosesoever the blame for what is past, this country alone can lead the world back to decent commercial policies.

We may negotiate all manner of nobly vague resolutions and paper organizations of sovereign great powers. Much ultimate good may come from such beginnings. But the substance of supranational order will in the near future be achieved, if at all, largely in the field of commercial relations. Here organization, though subtle and obscure, is a matter of almost continuous, daily national actions; it grows or is cut away with every political decision, legislative and administrative, affecting world trade and finance. Thus commercial policies become more or less discriminatory, more or less restrictive, more or less collectivist, more or less informed by narrow national or bloc interests in relative power; and thus commercial intercourse becomes more or less subject to arbitrary controls, more or less governmental, and less or more free.

Whether such changes cause or reflect changes in the degree of international organization and stability is mainly a question of intellectual fashions among contemplators of "first causes"—a question of what abstractions are commonly hypostatized, of whether one set of "causes" is prevailingly translated into another or conversely. The prospect is that world commercial, productional, financial organization will mainly lead the way, or manifest the basic direction of change, during the next decade. Major national issues in commercial policy seem certain to obtrude themselves; momentous decisions are likely to be made; and these decisions will either fill or empty the synthetic forms of political structure.

Free trade is an essential feature of stable federation. Real international organization, removing sovereign national prerogatives of trade manipulation, must come slowly out of discussion, experiment, and compromise. The proximate means toward abolition of the prerogatives is gradual abandonment of the practices, under the venturesome leadership of the nation which is at once most influential, best able to risk the venture and likely to gain most by its success.

International organization must be pursued opportunistically on every front which offers opportunity for substantial institutional growth. Beyond the immediate problems of the enemy nations and a political *modus vivendi* lie the persistent problems of economic instability and commercial warfare. Toward progressive mitigation of economic nationalism, blocism, and commercial separatism, America might offer almost irresistible leadership. We should dismantle our tariff. We should assure the world a dollar currency highly stable in purchasing power and enlist cooperation in its stabilization. We should eschew all preferential treatment of our exports in our colonies and dependencies. We should abandon "tied" foreign lending, save possibly as loans are tied to reduction of trade barriers and discrimination in the borrowing nations. Along these lines, we might lead wisely toward an ordered world and toward a Western world economy compatible with libertarian political-economic institutions in the United States. Such bold investment of our national power offers fabulous returns to us and to the world.

PRIVATE PROPERTY

It seems necessary here to say something about "private property" because of its conspicuous place in ideological controversy. "The institution of property" is a kind of shorthand notation for an infinitely complicated political-economic system and, indeed, for almost any possible alternative system. Meaning both nothing and everything, it naturally is the subject of much loose talk and impassioned rhetoric, among both stupid reactionaries and romantic radicals. To say that liberal democracy rests on private property is almost pure tautology. To discuss policy problems of "property" would be to discuss almost all economic-policy problems of our society. Only a few discursive remarks on the subject are here in order.

Private property in the instruments of production is an institutional device both for dispersing power and for securing effective organization of production. The only simple property system is that of a slave society with a single slaveowner—which, significantly, is the limiting case of despotism and of monopoly. Departure from such a system is a fair measure of human progress. The libertarian good society lies at an opposite extreme, in the maximum dispersion of property compatible with effective production or, as process, in progressive reconciliation of conflicts between equality and efficiency. Such process involves increasing dispersion both of wealth among persons or families and of proximate productional control among enterprises or firms.

Basic to liberty are property rights in labor or personal capacities. The abolitions of slavery and serfdom are the great steps toward freedom—and, by the way, are striking reconciliations of apparent conflict between productional and distributional considerations. Property in one's own services, however, is a secure, substantial right only where there are many possible buyers. It thus implies private property in other resources and freedom of independent sellers of labor to choose and to move among autonomous, independent organizations or firms. It also implies a distinctively modern institutional achievement, namely, the separation or dissociation of the economic and the political—a political order that sustains formal rights and a largely separate economic order that gives them substance. Otherwise, freedom to contract for one's services is merely an anomalous, synthetic, administrative construct, resting on "platforms" or on "administrative law," that is, freedom to contract with a single buyer or to choose among the offers of a single ultimate authority.

It is advisable, for most practical purposes, to avoid or to minimize categorical distinction between "inalienable" or "personal" capital and "external" property—to regard all property rights as integral aspects of personal capacity. Both kinds of property are the result of investment; both are largely inherited and hence are bound up with the family; both are largely acquired by luck; and each is subject to deliberate transfer from parents to children and transmutable into the other for that purpose. There is no obvious tendency, at any particular income level, toward excessive relative investment in either kind of property; and it certainly is doubtful whether any social gain would result if the more fortunate families endowed their children with access to political power instead of with "material" property. It is no accident that income taxes represent the substantial modern institutional achievement among taxes; that property taxes serve a narrow special purpose unrelated to personal inequality; and that inheritance taxes should remain inelegant, inequitable, ineffective, and chock-full of ineradicable anomalies.

A society based on free, responsible individuals or families must involve extensive rights of property. The economic responsibilities of families are an essential price of their freedom and, like the inseparable moral responsibilities, are necessary to moral development. Family property, in the occidental sense of the primary family, moreover, is largely the basis of preventive checks on population and of the effort to increase personal capacity from generation to generation, that is, to raise a few children hopefully and well or to sacrifice numbers to quality in family reproduction.

Private property is practically indispensable, if only as an administrative device, in modern large-scale organization of production. This organization is national and supranational; it requires wide delegation or dispersion of managerial control, and freedom and opportunity responsibly to initiate new undertaking. Responsible control of managerial units or firms implies property against which responsibility may be enforced; and responsibility for costs implies rights to revenues, especially if there is to be venturesome enterprise and progress.

LIBERTARIAN SOCIALISM

Modern socialism has been deeply sobered by the first meager efforts to become something more than a negative, revolutionary movement. Its intellectuals have finally begun to face the task of drafting positive proposals and an intelligible platform for action beyond the revolution. Their positive prescriptions are usefully and paradoxically epitomized in the name "decentralized socialism."

A revolutionary movement is naturally sobered by the possibility of acquiring power without revolution. Socialists have largely ceased to be revolutionary, and socialism has thus almost ceased to be a distinctive ideology. In a world obviously plagued by excessive nationalism, it must speak cautiously about the extreme nationalism of its own centralization, about the military implications of its governmental mobilization, and especially about its implication for international commercial policy. It is senseless to talk about world socialism and almost senseless to talk about order among national state socialisms. Socialists are thus in an awful dilemma, being deeply internationalist in sentiment and irredeemably nationalist in their economic program—just as they must be at once syndicalist in tactics and antisyndicalist in strategy or principle.

Socialism, of necessity, has been deeply corrupted by liberalism and conversely, for they have been contemporaries in a world of free discussion and have been catalyzed by the same evils and guided by much the same aspirations. Indeed, it is now hard to see how socialists and libertarians can long sustain substantial intellectual differences, save by avoiding all discussion.

Modern socialism is avowedly concerned mainly about inequalities of wealth (and power?) and about industrial monopoly—both major concerns of libertarians. Inequality, in the sense of too much at the top, is admittedly a matter of taxation; but taxation presents no issues which need divide socialists from libertarians—if socialist interest in the subject or its problems ever becomes substantial and informed. On monopoly problems there is at least a tactical difference: socialists talk much about enterprise monopolies; libertarians talk much about both enterprise monopolies and labor monopolies. Real difference appears only in the respective policy prescriptions for "basic industries." Socialists would "cure" monopoly problems by extending, consolidating, and "politicalizing" monopolies, that is, by abolishing competition in areas where it is relatively "impure." Libertarians would directly regulate or governmentalize only a small group of intractable "natural monopolies," leaving them largely to local bodies, and then seek, by innumerable policy devices, partly direct but mainly indirect, to render competition more and more effective everywhere else.

When socialists begin to talk about decentralization, however, even this difference promises to become empty and nominal. "Decentralized socialism" has perhaps great merit as vicarious, intellectual experimentation. It may be fruitful of insights to ask what government should do if a basic industry, paralyzed by administrative disorganization, were simply dropped in its lap. The first step, of course, would be to impose organization from above, perhaps by putting the army quartermasters in charge. Vicarious experimentation, intelligently pursued, probably would lead to a financial-administrative organization in which the administrative units, if autonomous enterprises, would be numerous enough to assure effective competition. Properly decentralized in administration, a socialized industry would probably be completely ripe for alienation; indeed, alienation would be necessary to implement the administrative decentralization. Wise central control would surely come to rely more and more on competition among numerous, similar administrative units, if only to set standards. The administrative devices necessary to sustain such competition would probably transform the central authority gradually from a proprietor to a bondholder or prior claimant. At this stage the public administrative units would become private enterprises, but with the worst possible financial structures. The next obvious step would be to liquidate the government's fixed claims from the proceeds of common-stock issues—and thus to reduce the government debt.

"Decentralized socialism" may thus be regarded as a very roundabout kind of antitrust policy—and as a stimulating approach to both economic and political theory. As social experimentation, however, it is not likely to be well conducted unless it is purely vicarious. Socialist rules regarding outputs, prices, wages, and marginal cost could hardly be implemented against the inevitable pressure-group demands; no governing faction could be expected to eschew the enormous available patronage; and the desirable administrative decentralization would be blocked by central appetites for power and jobs. At best, however, the experiment would turn out to be not one of abolishing private property but one of contriving new property arrangements. If, out of such vicarious experiment, one is able better to apprehend the good property arrangements, one may attain a sound directional sense for actual experimentation and see more clearly the promising routes from here and now. The more intelligently socialists plan for decentralization, the more does socialism fall into line with an orderly, gradual, libertarian process of dispersing property and of continuous, experimental development in the institution of property itself.

PROGRESS AND SECURITY OF PROPERTY

As in the case of the democratic political process, the importance of continuity in property arrangements can hardly be overstressed. Property must be secure in advanced nations, if production is to sustain living standards and if real social wealth is to be conserved or accumulated. Insecurity of property means diversion of production toward precious metals and jewels, that is, high valuation of assets that permit of concealment and can be securely possessed at the price of serviceless possession. Security of property means production of highly useful things, especially improved instruments of production. In the one case, property means withdrawal of resources from socially useful production and accumulation of assets in socially useless forms; in the other, property releases resources from merely protecting possession and promotes their accumulation in forms which augment both currently useful output and the progressive accumulation of capacity.

Economic progress requires that property be secure. Otherwise, those who hold it—governments, organizations, or individuals—must or will use property (and personal capacity) largely to protect property. Such use may involve either the concealment of oriental hoarding or the gross social abuse of property in rivalrous military organization. A telling objection to collectivism is that it locates property where it is least secure and aggravates total insecurity thereby. Its extreme national centralization, if only by threatening other nations, aggravates world insecurity and, in turn, commends external threats as indispensable to domestic order. An unnatural concentration of property affords, at best, only momentary, relative external security, at the cost of greater insecurity for everyone outside; and its only real protection against either the *coup d'état* or divisive civil war is unremitting fear of external attack.

Security of property, moreover, implies a flexible institution of property and persistent, progressive resolution of problems as they obtrude themselves into the democratic discussion process. Radical movements may impair economic organization and disturb economic processes by their direct threat to security of property; on the other hand, they may mainly serve merely to keep us properly busy with the small, manageable problems which are the grist of the democratic mill. Whether radicalism is excessive or inadequate at any period is not for contemporaries to judge with confidence. Whatever the balance of benefits and costs, however, the main cost now lies in the diversion of intellectual and political talents away from urgent small problems and the dull business of particularist discussion, compromise, legislation, and experimentation. Radicals jeopardize the security of property less by attacking the institution than by neglecting it. There is nothing more insidious than the notion that big, rapid changes are easier or more fruitful than small, slow changes; it leads to talk without action, to action without talk, and perhaps to collapse of democracy under a mass of accumulated, neglected routine business. The way to multiply big problems is to neglect small ones. There is nothing seriously wrong with our institution of property or our institutional system save our proclivity to waste time in attacking or defending it and to neglect proper tasks of changing it continuously by wise collective experimentation.

DEMOCRACY VERSUS SYNDICALISM

Effective competition is indispensable for adequate dispersion of power within industries and functional groups. The antithesis of a competitive economy is not socialism but syndicalism. It is, to repeat, one of the deep anomalies of socialism that its political strength derives mainly from highly syndicalist labor organizations. Syndicalist organization is equally incompatible with democratic socialism and libertarian democracy and, indeed, inherently incompatible with order. It bars both concentration and dispersion of power.

All monopoly or bargaining power implies special privilege to limit production, to restrict entry into industries or occupations, and thereby to levy tribute upon the whole community. As an actual present evil, it involves a concentration of power that has little relation to the concentration of personal wealth.

In one aspect it is a matter of uncontrolled corporate imperialism and giant enterprise aggregations. The profligate dispensation of privileges under incorporation laws may have accelerated the industrialization of America. Existing corporation laws may have been somewhat appropriate to an agricultural nation bent on rapid change. They may, by their extravagances, have accelerated progress. But they are surely ill designed to sustain progress or tolerable operation of the economy they promoted. Turned loose with inordinate powers, corporations have vastly overorganized most industries. Having perhaps benefited briefly by corporate organization, America might now be better off if the corporate form had never been invented or never made available to private enterprise.

A heritage of excessive centralization may be a necessary or reasonable price to pay for rapid maturing of new industries and new technology—and the same may be true of some desirable new governmental functions or services. In any case, America should face now an urgent task of deorganizing industry and deconcentrating industrial control. Some direct dismantling of corporate empires seems indispensable. The main concern of policy, however, should be that of facilitating new enterprise and multiplication of moderate-sized firms. There are grave productional diseconomies in giant enterprises; but these are compensated by larger artificial, private "economies" which wise public policy may and should cut away. Notable are the "economies" of national advertising and vast sales organizations (a problem of consumer education, consumer-goods standards, and technical information), of differential access to technical knowledge (patent-pooling and research), and differential access to new capital funds (inordinate centralization of securities markets). All these merely private advantages of great, monopolistic size present challenges

which can be met. Reasonable access to markets, to technology, and to capital funds, on the part of new and moderate-sized firms, would mean an end of serious enterprise monopoly.

Industrial monopolies are not yet a serious evil. Their organization is largely superficial; their powers, with rare exceptions, are very limited and precariously held; they tend to fall apart, though too slowly, in spite of policy. Their menace remains largely potential and complementary. In a community bent on preserving libertarian democracy, enterprise monopolies, standing alone, would be diagnosed as a simple skin disease and easily remedied.

The hard monopoly problem is labor organization. Here are monopolies, actual and imminent, with really great power, economic, political, and military. Once grown large, they cannot easily be taken apart like enterprise aggregations. Like corporations and up to about the same size or scale, unions have real social uses— which may outweigh abuses. But their size potentials and their appetites for power exceed even those of business corporations. Organized like armies rather than like businesses, and encountering no productional diseconomies of size because they produce nothing, they tend to absorb all competitors and to use power zealously and overtly while any eligible workers remain outside. Their size tendencies, moreover, are almost unamenable to the check of law or governmental policy. There would appear to be no stable or attainable happy mean. Strong labor organizations either die aborning or grow into intolerable monopolies. Moreover, labor monopolies and enterprise monopolies are ominously complementary; each tends to foster and to strengthen the other, fighting together to maximize joint exactions from the public while also fighting each other over division of the spoils.

Libertarians can offer no specific for the affliction of labor monopoly. They may propose to deal intelligently with other problems, in the hope that this one may somehow be mitigated or rendered less intractable by progress on other fronts.

An awful question here, as in the case of tariffs and other producer subsidies, is the capacity of democracy to protect the common interest or general welfare against organized minorities. Labor organization presents the hardest of the tests which democracy must meet. It can hardly meet this severest test unless it improves its record in dealing with other minorities as beneficiaries of promiscuous vote-buying and as usurpers of the coercion which all private restraint of trade involves. The old easy tests were matters of obvious corruption—government buying off groups with votes to sell. The hard test ahead involves all this plus a contest for power with organizations whose capacity for violence and coercion rivals that of the state itself. Under modern division of labor, any one of many large organizations of workers can stop or seriously disrupt the whole production process; such coercive power, resting fundamentally on violence, is an abuse (indeed, a negation) of freedom of association, which freedom must be limited by prohibition of monopoly as well as by prohibition of private armies. Here is the perennial problem of pressure groups developing into threat of civil war—the state monopoly of violence so impaired that no remedy compatible with democratic government is readily available.

INEQUALITY AND SYNDICALISM

The modern problem of inequality largely and progressively ceases to be a problem of ordinary property or personal wealth. Already it is overwhelmingly a problem of acquired status within organizations—parties, factions, civil service, giant corporations, labor unions, and farm organizations—and of differential access to high salaries and power. Only deorganization of extra-governmental, functional "states," along with decentralization of government, offers solution for such inequality. Otherwise, our society must offer superlative rewards of power and income to those few whose task it is to hold together organizations that should not exist—and that draw its ablest or most aggressive citizens into essentially antisocial activities. Libertarian society, with its multitude of small organizations, offers a field for millions of leaders and the prospect of moderate power differences among officials within organizations. It places a premium on personal qualities and skills which are, at worst, not grossly unbecoming to men and may properly be cultivated in the good society. It protects men from the corruption of great power by dispersing power, by avoiding large organizations outside government, and by limiting severely the exercise of power by large governmental units. In government the power of men may be limited by constitutional-conventional rules; outside, the power of men within organizations may be limited by keeping organizations loose or small. The best single device, in business organization, is to limit the power of officials by keeping their organizations under the severe discipline of competition. Moreover, wars apart, the need for exercise of central-government power varies progressively with the size and power of extra-governmental organizations. Extreme federalism becomes easiest when there are no strong extra-governmental "states."

PROSPECTIVE CHANGES IN "PROPERTY"

Libertarian policy contemplates a scheme of property law which is both stable and flexible and which, even with prompt excision of archaic elements, becomes more and more complex. There is, and always will be, obvious need for substantial changes. Our progressive personal taxes remain needlessly crude, full of loopholes, and inequitable among persons in similar real circumstances. They can easily be made more equitable, more effective in curtailing inequality of income and opportunity, and at the same time less injurious to desirable incentives. There is need for new arrangements regarding property in fugacious materials, notably oil; for reconsideration of property rights in knowledge, technology, and names; for wise experiments with laws concerning farm tenancy and urban housing; etc.

The time is more than ripe for undoing most of the complexity in property that modern corporations, and finance corporations especially, have imposed. In the good society private property would consist almost exclusively of claims against government (money and consols), unincumbered titles to tangible assets, and homogeneous equities in enterprises—together with the inevitable minimum of accounts in process of (quick) collection and of interpersonal debts. Interest-bearing government debt should be issued, if at all, only in consol form, should rise only during grave war emergencies, and should be retired rapidly thereafter. Net returns from personal wealth normally should accrue only to owners of tangible assets and to pure proprietors, partners, and common shareholders in riskful enterprises.

The problem here, to repeat, is mainly one of corporation finance, of corporate issue powers, and of financial corporations, notably banks. The recent trend in business finance has turned sharply and surely in the right direction and largely in spite of government policy. The policy task is thus a fairly simple one, first, of getting out of the way (e.g., by tax reform) and, second, of guiding and accelerating a trend already well established. The goal, while wisely attainable only by gradualist measures, is fairly clear: an economy where the securities or private corporations consist exclusively of common stocks, where financial corporations exist only as pure investment trusts (highly localized as to both portfolios and shareholders), and where only pure investment-trust corporations are permitted to own securities of other corporations.

Libertarian policy also calls for a currency of stable purchasing power, that is, for firm, conventional rules of fiscal policy calculated to prevent aberrations of inflation or deflation. No advanced nation has ever had a good monetary system or the financial structure and institutions necessary to stable employment and orderly economic progress. Only with firm monetary stabilization and minimal monetary uncertainty can the best potentialities of the libertarian political-economic system be released; and, incidentally, stabilization of our currency is perhaps the largest single contribution America can make to the progress of international organization. Here, however, as in the paragraph just above, we touch fiscal problems which are the central subject of other chapters.

SECTION B. WHAT IS THE PROPER ROLE OF GOVERNMENT?

1. THE ROAD AWAY FROM REVOLUTION[1]

By WOODROW WILSON

EDITORS' NOTE.—Woodrow Wilson (see p. 224) lived until 1924, long enough to witness the sordid scandals of the Harding administration. In this final article written during his retirement, Wilsonian liberalism stands out in sharp contrast to the prevailing doctrines of Harding "normalcy."

In these doubtful and anxious days, when all the world is at unrest and, look which way you will, the road ahead seems darkened by shadows which portend dangers of many kinds, it is only common prudence that we should look about us and attempt to assess the causes of distress and the most likely means of removing them.

There must be some real ground for the universal unrest and perturbation. It is not to be found in superficial politics or in mere economic blunders. It probably lies deep at the sources of the spiritual life of our time. It leads to revolution; and perhaps if we take the case of the Russian Revolution, the outstanding event of its kind in our age, we may find a good deal of instruction for our judgment of present critical situations and circumstances.

What gave rise to the Russian Revolution? The answer can only be that it was the product of a whole social system. It was not in fact a sudden thing. It had been gathering head for several generations. It was due to the systematic denial to the great body of Russians of the rights and privileges which all normal men desire and must have if they are to be contented and within reach of happiness. The lives of the great mass of the Russian people contained no opportunities, but were hemmed in by

barriers against which they were constantly flinging their spirits, only to fall back bruised and dispirited. Only the powerful were suffered to secure their rights or even to gain access to the means of material success.

It is to be noted as a leading fact of our time that it was against "capitalism" that the Russian leaders directed their attack. It was capitalism that made them see red; and it is against capitalism under one name or another that the discontented classes everywhere draw their indictment.

There are thoughtful and well-informed men all over the world who believe, with much apparently sound reason, that the abstract thing, the system, which we call capitalism, is indispensable to the industrial support and development of modern civilization. And yet everyone who has an intelligent knowledge of social forces must know that great and widespread reactions like that which is now unquestionably manifesting itself against capitalism do not occur without cause or provocation; and before we commit ourselves irreconcilably to an attitude of hostility to this movement of the time, we ought frankly to put to ourselves the question, Is the capitalistic system unimpeachable? which is another way of asking, Have capitalists generally used their power for the benefit of the countries in which their capital is employed and for the benefit of their fellow men?

1. Woodrow Wilson, "The Road Away from Revolution," *Atlantic Monthly*, CXXXII (August, 1923), 145–46. Reprinted by permission of the *Atlantic Monthly*.

Is it not, on the contrary, too true that capitalists have often seemed to regard the men whom they used as mere instruments of profit, whose physical and mental powers it was legitimate to exploit with as slight cost to themselves as possible, either of money or of sympathy? Have not many fine men who were actuated by the highest principles in every other relationship of life seemed to hold that generosity and humane feeling were not among the imperative mandates of conscience in the conduct of a banking business, or in the development of an industrial or commercial enterprise?

And, if these offenses against high morality and true citizenship have been frequently observable, are we to say that the blame for the present discontent and turbulence is wholly on the side of those who are in revolt against them? Ought we not, rather, to seek a way to remove such offenses and make life itself clean for those who will share honorably and cleanly in it?

The world has been made safe for democracy. There need now be no fear that any such mad design as that entertained by the insolent and ignorant Hohenzollerns and their counselors may prevail against it. But democracy has not yet made the world safe against irrational revolution. That supreme task, which is nothing less than the salvation of civilization, now faces democracy, insistent, imperative. There is no escaping it, unless everything we have built up is presently to fall in ruin about us; and the United States, as the greatest of democracies, must undertake it.

The road that leads away from revolution is clearly marked, for it is defined by the nature of men and of organized society. It therefore behooves us to study very carefully and very candidly the exact nature of the task and the means of its accomplishment.

The nature of men and of organized society dictates the maintenance in every field of action of the highest and purest standards of justice and of right dealing; and it is essential to efficacious thinking in this critical matter that we should not entertain a narrow or technical conception of justice. By justice the lawyer generally means the prompt, fair, and open application of impartial rules; but we call ours a Christian civilization, and a Christian conception of justice must be much higher. It must include sympathy and helpfulness and a willingness to forgo self-interest in order to promote the welfare, happiness, and contentment of others and of the community as a whole. This is what our age is blindly feeling after in its reaction against what it deems the too great selfishness of the capitalistic system.

The sum of the whole matter is this, that our civilization cannot survive materially unless it be redeemed spiritually. It can be saved only by becoming permeated with the spirit of Christ and being made free and happy by the practices which spring out of that spirit. Only thus can discontent be driven out and all the shadows lifted from the road ahead.

Here is the final challenge to our churches, to our political organizations, and to our capitalists—to everyone who fears God or loves his country. Shall we not all earnestly coöperate to bring in the new day?

2. THE LA FOLLETTE PLATFORM OF 1924[1]

EDITORS' NOTE.—Senator Robert Marion La Follette (p. 357) devoted the greater part of his career to keeping alive the progressive movement in American politics. It was at La Follette's home in Washington, D.C., and with La Follette as one of the organizers, that a group of Republicans, revolting against Taft's reversion to conservatism, formed the National Progressive Republican League. It was La Follette again who, in 1924, organized and as presidential nominee led the Progressive party in that presidential campaign. The nearly five million votes that La Follette received had a triple significance: First, it kept alive the progressive opposition to both Republican and Democratic conservatism. Second, the size of the La Follette vote was concrete evidence that the country was far from converted to the Republican "normalcy" under business sovereignty. And, third, the character of the Progressive platform foreshadowed the New Deal philosophy of a decade later. It was the La Follette–led movement of 1924 that established the historical continuity between the Populists of the 1890's, the progressives of the next decade, and the New Deal.

The great issue before the American people today is the control of government and industry by private monopoly.

For a generation the people have struggled patiently, in the face of repeated betrayals by successive administrations, to free themselves from this intolerable power which has been undermining representative government.

Through control of government, monopoly has steadily extended its absolute dominion to every basic industry.

In violation of law, monopoly has crushed competition, stifled private initiative and independent enterprise, and without fear of punishment now exacts extortionate profits upon every necessity of life consumed by the public.

The equality of opportunity proclaimed by the Declaration of Independence and asserted and defended by Jefferson and Lincoln as the heritage of every American citizen has been displaced by special privilege for the few, wrested from the government of the many.

FUNDAMENTAL RIGHTS IN DANGER

. . . The usurpation in recent years by the federal courts of the power to nullify laws duly enacted by the legislative branch of the government is a plain violation of the Constitution. Abraham Lincoln, in his first inaugural address, said: "The candid citizen must confess that if the policy of the government, upon vital questions affecting the whole people, is to be irrevocably fixed by decisions of the Supreme Court, the people will have ceased to be their own rulers, having to that extent practically resigned their government into the hands of that eminent tribunal." The Constitution specifically vests all legislative power in the Congress, giving that body power and authority to override the veto of the president. The federal courts are given no authority under the Constitution to veto acts of Congress. Since the federal courts have assumed to exercise such veto power, it is essential that the Constitution shall give to the Congress the right to override such judicial veto, otherwise the Court will make itself master over the other coordinate branches

1. National Party Platforms, ed. Kirk H. Porter (New York, 1924), pp. 516–22. By permission of The Macmillan Company.

of the government. The people themselves must approve or disapprove the present exercise of legislative power by the federal courts.

DISTRESS OF AMERICAN FARMERS

The present condition of American agriculture constitutes an emergency of the gravest character. The Department of Commerce report shows that during 1923 there was a steady and marked increase in dividends paid by the great industrial corporations. The same is true of the steam and electric railways and practically all other large corporations. On the other hand, the Secretary of Agriculture reports that in the fifteen principal wheat growing states more than 108,000 farmers since 1920 have lost their farms through foreclosure or bankruptcy; that more than 122,000 have surrendered their property without legal proceedings, and that nearly 375,000 have retained possession of their property only through the leniency of their creditors, making a total of more than 600,000 or 25 per cent of all farmers who have virtually been bankrupted since 1920 in these fifteen states alone.

Almost unlimited prosperity for the great corporations and ruin and bankruptcy for agriculture is the direct and logical result of the policies and legislation which deflated the farmer while extending almost unlimited credit to the great corporations; which protected with exorbitant tariffs the industrial magnates, but depressed the prices of the farmers' products by financial juggling while greatly increasing the cost of what he must buy; which guaranteed excessive freight rates to the railroads and put a premium on wasteful management while saddling an unwarranted burden on to the backs of the American farmer; which permitted gambling in the products of the farm by grain speculators to the great detriment of the farmer and to the great profit of the grain gambler.

A COVENANT WITH THE PEOPLE

Awakened by the dangers which menace their freedom and prosperity the American people still retain the right and courage to exercise their sovereign control over their government. In order to destroy the economic and political power of monopoly, which has come between the people and their government, we pledge ourselves to the following principles and policies: . . .

NATURAL RESOURCES

2. . . . We favor public ownership of the nation's water power and the creation and development of a national superwater-power system, including Muscle Shoals, to supply at actual cost light and power for the people and nitrate for the farmers, and strict public control and permanent conservation of all the nation's resources, including coal, iron and other ores, oil and timber lands, in the interest of the people.

RAILROADS

3. . . . We declare for public ownership of railroads with definite safeguards against bureaucratic control, as the only final solution of the transportation problem.

TAX REDUCTION

4. . . . We . . . favor a taxation policy providing for immediate reductions upon moderate incomes, large increases in the inheritance tax rates upon large estates to prevent the indefinite accumulation by inheritance of great fortunes in a few hands; taxes upon excess profits to penalize profiteering, and complete publicity, under proper safeguards, of all Federal tax returns.

THE COURTS

5. We favor submitting to the people, for their considerate judgment, a constitutional amendment providing that Congress may by enacting a statute make it effective over a judicial veto. . . .

THE FARMERS

6. ... We advocate the calling of a special session of Congress to pass legislation for the relief of American agriculture. We favor such further legislation as may be needful or helpful in promoting and protecting cooperative enterprises. We demand that the Interstate Commerce Commission proceed forthwith to reduce by an approximation to pre-war levels the present freight rates on agricultural products, including live stock, and upon the materials required upon American farms for agricultural purposes.

LABOR

7. We favor abolition of the use of injunctions in labor disputes and declare for complete protection of the right of farmers and industrial workers to organize, bargain collectively through representatives of their own choosing, and conduct without hindrance cooperative enterprises.

We favor prompt ratification of the Child Labor amendment, and subsequent enactment of a Federal law to protect children in industry. ...

GREAT LAKES TO SEA

10. We favor a deep waterway from the Great Lakes to the sea. The government should, in conjunction with Canada, take immediate action to give the northwestern states an outlet to the ocean for cargoes, without change in bulk, thus making the primary markets on the Great Lakes equal to those of New York.

POPULAR SOVEREIGNTY

11. ... We favor such amendments to the Federal Constitution as may be necessary to provide for the direct nomination and election of the President, to extend the initiative and referendum to the federal government, and to insure a popular referendum for or against war except in cases of actual invasion.

3. RUGGED INDIVIDUALISM[1]

By Herbert Hoover

EDITORS' NOTE.—Herbert Hoover (1874———) appropriately closed his 1928 campaign for the presidency with this speech. It was appropriate in that in it he summarized his economic views gained by varied experience as engineer, as food administrator during the first World War, and as Secretary of Commerce (1921–29). It was also appropriate in that it expressed a view of the proper relation of the government to the economy that was widely

accepted in the prosperous twenties, especially in Republican circles, and which is still approved by many.

But October, 1928, proved to be an unfortunate time for such a pronouncement, for one year later, almost to the day, the stock market crashed, initiating the great depression. Causes and their effects are often obscure, but even the most rugged of individualists, when sinking into the economic abyss that followed, must have asked whether his philosophy was not to blame.

1. Herbert Hoover, "Rugged Individualism," *New York Times*, October 23, 1928. Reprinted by permission of the *New York Times*.

This campaign now draws near a close. The platforms of the two parties defining principles and offering solutions of various national problems have been presented and are being earnestly considered by our people. . . .

In my acceptance speech I endeavored to outline the spirit and ideals by which I would be guided in carrying that platform into administration. Tonight, I will not deal with the multitude of issues which have been already well canvassed. I intend rather to discuss some of those more fundamental principles and ideals upon which I believe the Government of the United States should be conducted. . . .

But in addition to this great record of contributions of the Republican Party to progress, there has been a further fundamental contribution—a contribution underlying and sustaining all the others—and that is the resistance of the Republican Party to every attempt to inject the Government into business in competition with its citizens.

After the war, when the Republican Party assumed administration of the country, we were faced with the problem of determination of the very nature of our national life. During 150 years we have builded up a form of self-government and a social system which is peculiarly our own. It differs essentially from all others in the world. It is the American system. It is just as definite and positive a political and social system as has ever been developed on earth. It is founded upon a particular conception of self-government in which decentralized local responsibility is the very base. Further than this, it is founded upon the conception that only through ordered liberty, freedom and equal opportunity to the individual will his initiative and enterprise spur on the march of progress. And in our insistence upon equality of opportunity has our system advanced beyond all the world.

During the war we necessarily turned to the Government to solve every difficult economic problem. The Government hav-ing absorbed every energy of our people for war, there was no other solution. For the preservation of the State the Federal Government became a centralized despotism which undertook unprecedented responsibilities, assumed autocratic powers, and took over the business of citizens. To a large degree we regimented our whole people temporarily into a socialistic state. However justified in time of war, if continued in peace time it would destroy not only our American system but with it our progress and freedom as well.

When the war closed, the most vital of all issues both in our own country and throughout the world was whether Governments should continue their wartime ownership and operation of many instrumentalities of production and distribution. We were challenged with a peace-time choice between the American system of rugged individualism and a European philosophy of diametrically opposed doctrines—doctrines of paternalism and state socialism. The acceptance of these ideas would have meant the destruction of self-government through centralization of government. It would have meant the undermining of the individual initiative and enterprise through which our people have grown to unparalleled greatness.

The Republican Party from the beginning resolutely turned its face away from these ideas and these war practices. A Republican Congress cooperated with the Democratic Administration to demobilize many of our war activities. At that time the two parties were in accord upon that point. When the Republican Party came into full power it went at once resolutely back to our fundamental conception of the State and the rights and responsibilities of the individual. Thereby it restored confidence and hope in the American people, it freed and stimulated enterprise, it restored the Government to its position as an umpire instead of a player in the economic game. For these reasons the American people have gone forward in progress while the rest of the world has halted, and some countries have even gone backward. If any one will study the causes of retarded recuperation in Europe, he will find much of it due to the stifling of private initiative on one hand, and overloading of the Government with business on the other.

There has been revived in this campaign, however, a series of proposals which, if adopted, would be a long step toward the abandonment of our American system and a surrender to the destructive operation of governmental conduct of commercial business. Because the country is faced with difficulty and doubt over certain national problems—that is, prohibition, farm relief and electrical power—our opponents propose that we must thrust government a long way into the businesses which give rise to these problems. In effect, they abandon the tenets of their own party and turn to State socialism as a solution for the difficulties presented by all three. It is proposed that we shall change from prohibition to the State purchase and sale of liquor. If their agricultural relief program means anything, it means that the Government shall directly or indirectly buy and sell and fix prices of agricultural products. And we are to go into the hydro-electric power business. In other words, we are confronted with a huge program of government in business.

There is, therefore, submitted to the American people a question of fundamental principle. That is: shall we depart from the principles of our American political and economic system, upon which we have advanced beyond all the rest of the world, in order to adopt methods based on principles destructive of its very foundations? And I wish to emphasize the seriousness of these proposals. I wish to make my position clear; for this goes to the very roots of American life and progress.

I should like to state to you the effect that this projection of government in business would have upon our system of self-government and our economic system. That effect would reach to the daily life of every man and woman. It would impair the very basis of liberty and freedom not only for those left outside the fold of expanded bureaucracy but for those embraced within it.

Let us first see the effect upon self-government. When the Federal Government undertakes to go into commercial business it must at once set up the organization and administration of that business, and it immediately finds itself in a labyrinth, every alley of which leads to the destruction of self-government.

Commercial business requires a concentration of responsibility. Self-government requires decentralization and many checks and balances to safeguard liberty. Our government to succeed in business would need become in effect a despotism. There at once begins the destruction of self-government.

The first problem of the Government about to adventure in commercial business is to determine a method of administration. It must secure leadership and direction. Shall this leadership be chosen by political agencies or shall we make it elective? The hard practical fact is that leadership in business must come through the sheer rise in ability and character. That rise can only take place in the free atmosphere of competition. Competition is closed by bureaucracy. Political agencies are feeble channels through which to select able leaders to conduct commercial business.

Government, in order to avoid the possible incompetence, corruption and tyranny of too great authority in individuals entrusted with commercial business, inevitably turns to boards and commissions. To make sure that there are checks and balances, each member of such boards and commissions must have equal authority. Each has his separate responsibility to the public, and at once we have the conflict of ideas and the lack of decision which would ruin any commercial business. . . .

Bureaucracy is ever desirous of spreading its influence and its power. You cannot extend the mastery of the Government over the daily working life of a people without at the same time making it the master of the people's souls and thoughts. Every expansion of Government in business means that Government in order to protect itself from the political consequences of its errors and wrongs is driven irresistibly without peace to greater and greater control of the nation's press and platform. Free speech does not live many hours after free industry and free commerce die.

It is a false liberalism that interprets itself into the Government operation of commercial business. Every step of bureaucratizing of the business of our country poisons the very roots of liberalism—that is, political equality, free speech, free assembly, free press and equality of opportunity. It is the road not to more liberty but to less liberty. Liberalism should be found not striving to spread bureaucracy but striving to set bounds to it. True liberalism seeks all legitimate freedom, first in the confident belief that without such freedom the pursuit of all other blessings and benefits is vain. That belief is the foundation of all American progress, political as well as economic.

Liberalism is a force truly of the spirit, a force proceeding from the deep realization that economic freedom cannot be sacrificed if political freedom is to be preserved. Even if governmental conduct of business could give us more efficiency instead of less efficiency, the fundamental objection to it would remain unaltered and unabated. It would destroy political equality. It would increase rather than decrease abuse and corruption. It would stifle initiative and invention. It would undermine the development of leadership. It would cramp and cripple the mental and spiritual energies of our people. It would extinguish equality and opportunity. It would dry up the spirit of liberty and progress. For these reasons primarily it must be resisted. For a hundred and fifty years liberalism has found its true spirit in the American system, not in the European systems.

I do not wish to be misunderstood in this statement. I am defining a general policy. It does not mean that our Government is to part with one iota of its national resources without complete protection to the public interest. I have already stated that where the Government is engaged in public works for purposes of flood control, of navigation, of irrigation, of scientific research or national defense, or in pioneering a new art, it will at times necessarily produce power or commodities as a by-product. But they must be a by-product of the major purpose, not the major purpose itself.

Nor do I wish to be misinterpreted as believing that the United States is free-for-all and devil-take-the-hindmost. The very essence of equality of opportunity and of American individualism is that there shall be no domination by any group or combination in this Republic, whether it be business or political. On the contrary, it demands economic justice as well as political and social justice. It is no system of laissez faire.

I feel deeply on this subject because during the war I had some practical experience with governmental operation and control. I have witnessed not only at home but abroad the many failures of Government in business. I have seen its tyrannies, its injustices, its destructions of self-government, its undermining of the very instincts which carry our people forward to progress. I have witnessed the lack of advance, the lowered standards of living, the depressed spirits of people working under such a system. My objection is based not upon theory or upon a failure to recognize wrong or abuse, but I know the adoption of such methods would strike at the very roots of American life and would destroy the very basis of American progress.

Our people have the right to know whether we can continue to solve our great problems without abandonment of our American system. I know we can. We have demonstrated that our system is responsive enough to meet any new and intricate development in our economic and business life. We have demonstrated that we can meet any economic problem and still maintain our democracy and master in its own house and that we can at the same time preserve equality of opportunity and individual freedom. . . .

And what have been the results of our American system? Our country has become the land of opportunity to those born without inheritance, not merely because of the wealth of its resources and industry, but because of this freedom of initiative and enterprise. Russia has natural resources equal to ours. Her people are equally industrious, but she has not had the blessings of 150 years of our form of government and of our social system.

By adherence to the principles of decentralized self-government, ordered liberty, equal opportunity and freedom to the individual our American experiment in human welfare has yielded a degree of well-being unparalleled in all the world. It has come nearer to the abolition of poverty, to the abolition of fear of want, than humanity has ever reached before. Progress of the past seven years is the proof of it. This alone furnishes the answer to our opponents who ask us to introduce destructive elements into the system by which this has been accomplished.

Let us see what this system has done for us in our recent years of difficult and trying reconstruction and let us then solemnly ask ourselves if we now wish to abandon it.

As a nation we came out of the war with great losses. We made no profits from it. The apparent increases in wages were at that time fictitious. We were poorer as a nation when we emerged from the war. Yet during these last eight years we have recovered from these losses and increased our national income by over one-third, even if we discount the inflation of the dollar. That there has been a wide diffusion of our gain in wealth and income is marked by a hundred proofs. I know of no better test of the improved conditions of the average family than the combined increase in assets of life and industrial insur-

ance, building and loan associations, and savings deposits. These are the savings banks of the average man. These agencies alone have in seven years increased by nearly 100 per cent to the gigantic sum of over fifty billions of dollars, or nearly one-sixth of our whole national wealth. We have increased in home ownership, we have expanded the investments of the average man.

In addition to these evidences of larger savings, our people are steadily increasing their spending for higher standards of living. Today there are almost nine automobiles for each ten families, where seven and a half years ago only enough automobiles were running to average less than four for each ten families. The slogan of progress is changing from the full dinner pail to the full garage. Our people have more to eat, better things to wear and better homes. We have even gained in elbow room, for the increase of residential floor space is over 25 per cent, with less than 10 per cent increase in our number of people. Wages have increased, the cost of living has decreased. The job to every man and woman has been made more secure. We have in this short period decreased the fear of poverty, the fear of unemployment, the fear of old age; and these are fears that are the greatest calamities of human kind. . . .

I have endeavored to present to you that the greatness of America has grown out of a political and social system and a method of control of economic forces distinctly its own—our American system— which has carried this great experiment in human welfare further than ever before in all history. We are nearer today to the ideal of the abolition of poverty and fear from the lives of men and women than ever before in any land. And I again repeat that the departure from our American system by injecting principles destructive to it which our opponents propose will jeopardize the very liberty and freedom of our people, will destroy equality of opportunity, not alone to ourselves but to our children. . . .

4. NO ONE HAS STARVED[1]

EDITORS' NOTE.—In September, 1932, the editors of *Fortune* surveyed the conditions of the American economy as it affected individuals in the late summer of that year. Their findings, reproduced in part below, were presented under the heading: " 'No One Has Starved' . . . which is not true. 'Twenty-five Millions in Want'— which may be true before the winter is over. 'America Faces the Facts'— which is true today for the first time, as a result of the Federal Relief Act of 1932. Under these headlines *Fortune* presents the whole story of unemployment relief: the story of an industrial problem which charity has attempted unsuccessfully to solve."

It is against this fact of potential unemployment and its consequences that the policy proposals of Herbert Hoover and of Franklin Roosevelt should be read. The Statistical Appendix (Nos. 13, 15–18) may aid in making the facts of unemployment more meaningful.

Dull mornings last winter the sheriff of Miami, Florida, used to fill a truck with homeless men and run them up to the county line. Where the sheriff of Fort Lauderdale used to meet them and load them into a second truck and run them up to *his* county line. Where the sheriff of Saint Lucie's would meet them and load them into a third truck and run them up to *his* county line. Where the sheriff of Brevard County would *not* meet them. And whence they would trickle back down the roads to Miami. To repeat.

It was a system. And it worked. The only trouble was that it worked too well. It kept the transients transient and it even increased the transient population in the process. But it got to be pretty expensive, one way or another, if you sat down and figured it all out—trucks and gas and time and a little coffee. . . .

That was last winter.

Next winter there will be no truck. And there will be no truck, not because the transients will have disappeared from Miami: if anything, there will be more blistered Fords with North Dakota licenses and more heel-worn shoes with the Boston trade-mark rubbed out next winter than there were last. But because the sheriff of Miami, like the President of the U.S., will next winter think of transients and unemployed miners and jobless mill workers in completely different terms.

The difference will be made by the Emergency Relief Act. Or rather by the fact that the Emergency Relief Act exists. For the Act itself with its $300,000,000 for direct relief loans to the states is neither an adequate nor an impressive piece of legislation. But the passage of the Act, like the green branch which young Mr. Ringling used to lay across the forks of the Wisconsin roads for his circus to follow, marks a turning in American political history. And the beginning of a new chapter in American unemployment relief. It constitutes an open and legible acknowledgment of governmental responsibility for the welfare of the victims of industrial unemployment. And its ultimate effect must be the substitution of an ordered, realistic, and intelligent relief program for the wasteful and uneconomic methods (of which the Miami truck is an adequate symbol) employed during the first three years of the depression.

1. "No One Has Starved," *Fortune*, IV (September, 1932), 19–28, 80. Reprinted by special permission of the Editors; copyright Time, Inc.

There can be no serious question of the failure of those methods. For the methods were never seriously capable of success. They were diffuse, unrelated, and unplanned. The theory was that private charitable organizations and semi-public welfare groups, established to care for the old and the sick and the indigent, were capable of caring for the casuals of a world-wide economic disaster. And the theory in application meant that social agencies manned for the service of a few hundred families, and city shelters set up to house and feed a handful of homeless men, were compelled by the brutal necessities of hunger to care for hundreds of thousands of families and whole armies of the displaced and the jobless. And to depend for their resources upon the contributions of communities no longer able to contribute, and upon the irresolution and vacillation of state Legislatures and municipal assemblies long since in the red on their annual budgets. The result was the picture now presented in city after city and state after state—heterogeneous groups of official and semi-official and unofficial relief agencies struggling under the earnest and untrained leadership of the local men of affairs against an inertia of misery and suffering and want they are powerless to overcome.

But the psychological consequence was even worse. Since the problem was never honestly attacked as a national problem, and since the facts were never frankly faced as facts, people came to believe that American unemployment was relatively unimportant. They saw little idleness and they therefore believed there was little idleness. It is possible to drive for blocks in the usual shopping and residential districts of New York and Chicago without seeing a breadline or a food station or a hungry mob or indeed anything else much more exciting than a few casuals asleep on a park bench. And for that reason, and because their newspapers played down the subject as an additional depressant in depressing times, and because they were bored with relief measures anyway, the great American public simply ignored the whole thing. They would still ignore it today were it not that the committee hearings and the Congressional debate and the Presidential veto of relief bills this last June attracted their attention. And that the final passage of the Emergency Relief and Construction Act of 1932 has committed their government and themselves to a policy of affirmative action which compels both it and them to know definitely and precisely what the existing situation is. . . .

The following minimal statements may be accepted as true—with the certainty that they underestimate the real situation:

(1) Unemployment has steadily increased in the U.S. since the beginning of the depression and the rate of increase during the first part of 1932 was more rapid than in any other depression year.

(2) The number of persons totally unemployed is now at least 10,000,000.

(3) The number of persons totally unemployed next winter will, at the present rate of increase, be 11,000,000.

(4) Eleven millions unemployed means better than one man out of every four employable workers.

(5) This percentage is higher than the percentage of unemployed British workers registered under the compulsory insurance laws (17.1 per cent in May, 1932, as against 17.3 per cent in April and 18.4 per cent in January) and higher than the French, the Italian, and the Canadian percentages, but lower than the German (43.9 per cent of trade unionists in April, 1932) and the Norwegian.

(6) Eleven millions unemployed means 27,500,000 whose regular source of livelihood has been cut off.

(7) Twenty-seven and a half millions without regular income includes the families of totally unemployed workers alone. Taking account of the numbers of workers on part time, the total of those without adequate income becomes 34,000,000 or

better than a quarter of the entire population of the country.

(8) Thirty-four million persons without adequate income does not mean 34,000,000 in present want. Many families have savings. But savings are eventually dissipated and the number in actual want tends to approximate the number without adequate income. How nearly it approximates it now or will next winter no man can say. But it is conservative to estimate that the problem of next winter's relief is a problem of caring for approximately 25,000,-000 souls. . . .

But it is impossible to think or to act in units of 25,000,000 human beings. Like the casualty lists of the British War Office during the Battle of the Somme, they mean nothing. They are at once too large and too small. A handful of men and women and children digging for their rotten food in the St. Louis dumps are more numerous, humanly speaking, than all the millions that ever found themselves in an actuary's column. The 25,000,000 only become human in their cities and their mill towns and their mining villages. And their situation only becomes comprehensible in terms of the relief they have already received.

That is to say that the general situation can only be judged by the situation in the particular localities. But certain generalizations are possible. Of which the chief is the broad conclusion that few if any of the industrial areas have been able to maintain a minimum decency level of life for their unemployed. Budgetary standards as set up by welfare organizations, public and private, after years of experiment have been discarded. Food only, in most cases, is provided and little enough of that. Rents are seldom paid. Shoes and clothing are given in rare instances only. Money for doctors and dentists is not to be had. And free clinics are filled to overflowing. Weekly allowances per family have fallen as low as $2.39 in New York with $3 and $4 the rule in most cities and $5 a high figure. And even on these terms funds budgeted for a twelve-month period have been

exhausted in three or four. While city after city has been compelled to abandon a part of its dependent population. "We are merely trying to prevent hunger and exposure," reported a St. Paul welfare head last May. And the same sentence would be echoed by workers in other cities with such additions as were reported at the same time from Pittsburgh where a cut of 50 per cent was regarded as "inevitable," from Dallas where Mexicans and Negroes were not given relief, from Alabama where discontinuance of relief in mining and agricultural sections was foreseen, from New Orleans where no new applicants were being received and 2,500 families in need of relief were receiving none, from Omaha where two-thirds of the cases receiving relief were to be discontinued, from Colorado where the counties had suspended relief for lack of funds . . . from Scranton . . . from Cleveland . . . from Syracuse. . . . But the individual localities present their own picture:

About 1,000,000 out of New York City's 3,200,000 working population are unemployed. Last April 410,000 were estimated to be in dire want. Seven hundred and fifty thousand in 150,000 families were receiving emergency aid while 160,000 more in 32,000 families were waiting to receive aid not then available. Of these latter families—families which normally earn an average of $141.50 a month—the average income from all sources was $8.20. Of families receiving relief, the allowance has been anything from a box of groceries up to $60 a month. In general, New York relief, in the phrase of Mr. William Hodson, executive director of the New York Welfare Council, has been on "a disaster basis." And the effects have been disaster effects. It is impossible to estimate the number of deaths in the last year in which starvation was a contributing cause. But ninety-five persons suffering directly from starvation were admitted to the city hospitals in 1931, of whom twenty died; and 143 suffering from malnutrition, of whom twenty-five died.

While visiting nurses and welfare workers report a general increase in malnutrition, and the clinics and medical relief agencies are so overcrowded they can give adequate relief to no one, although 75 per cent of persons applying to one relief agency had some form of illness. Housing is, of course, with the general lowering of standards and the doubling-up of families, worse even than it was during the boom. Relief expenditures for 1930 were something over $6,000,000; for 1931, more than $25,000,-000; and for the first four months of 1932 over $20,000,000, or $5,000,000 per month. But large as this latter figure is it must be compared with the wage and salary loss by reason of unemployment, which is at least $100,000,000 per month. . . .

The situation in Philadelphia was described by its Community Council in July, 1932, as one of "slow starvation and progressive disintegration of family life. . . ." Of the city's 445,000 families with employable workers 210,000 had workers unemployed or on part time, about one in four had no worker employed on full time, and 12 per cent had *no* worker employed. Even the average person unemployed had been out of work for thirty-seven weeks and had had only a little over one week of casual or relief work during the period. . . . The Governor of the state estimated that 250,000 persons in Philadelphia "faced actual starvation." Over the state at large the same conditions held. In June, 1931, 919,000 or 25 per cent of the normally employed in the state were unemployed, according to the "secret" report then submitted to the Governor, and the number had risen to 1,000,000 by December and to 1,250,000 in August, 1932. One hundred and fifty thousand children were in need of charity. Malnutrition had increased in forty-eight counties—27 per cent of school children being undernourished. . . . New patients in the tuberculosis clinics had doubled. And the general death rate and disease rate had risen. Only nine counties were well organized. Fifty-

five gave cause for grave concern and nineteen were listed as distressed counties in dire need. Moreover, relief allowances have steadily dropped. Last December 43,000 of the 56,000 families in Philadelphia where no one was employed were receiving relief at the rate of $4.39 per week for families averaging 4.8 persons. By May the number of families receiving relief had risen to 55,000 and the amount of relief had dropped to $4.23, of which $3.93 was for food, being two-thirds of the minimum required for health. No provision is made for rents and the result is that the landlords of Philadelphia, like the landlords of the country at large, are compelled to choose between throwing their tenants into the streets or providing from their own pockets the shelter required. Outside of Philadelphia the weekly grant to a family is $3 or less in thirteen counties, and $3 to $4 in six more, while in some of the small steel towns it may be even lower. Funds in the counties are either exhausted or will be exhausted before November. . . .

Unemployed in Chicago number . . . 40 per cent of its employable workers while the number for the state at large is about one in three of the gainfully employed. . . . The minimum relief budget has been $2.40 per week for an adult and $1.50 per week for a child for food, with $22 to $23 per month to a family. But these figures have since been cut to $2.15 weekly for a man, $1.10 for a child. And persons demanding relief must be completely destitute to receive it. Rents are not paid by the relief agencies and housing is, in certain sections, unspeakably bad. While the situation of city employees is tragic. Teachers in May, 1932, had had only five months cash for the last thirteen months, 3,177 of them had lost $2,367,000 in bank failures, 2,278 of them had lost $7,800,000 in lapsed policies, 805 had borrowed $232,000 from loan sharks at rates adding up to 42 per cent a year, and 759 had lost their homes. (The city at one time undertook to sell for tax default the houses of its employees unable to pay taxes because of its own default in wages.) . . .

In St. Louis 125,000 of the city's 330,000 employable persons were unemployed last December, one-eighth of the population was estimated to face eviction and starvation, three-fourths of the families under care presented one or more medical problems each, and relief campaigners published full-page advertisements pointing to the number of hungry men and women rifling garbage buckets for their food. Starvation is reported as a contributory cause in several deaths. And even so the relief agencies were forced by lack of funds to drop 8,000 families on July 1 and 5,000 more on July 15. Since these cuts were made, large numbers of the destitute have been living in refuse dumps along the river where they build shacks and dig in the dump for food. The city's Board of Estimate and Apportionment has petitioned the Governor to apply for a $2,000,000 loan from the federal government but the amount will not suffice to carry the city through the winter.

. . . In Youngstown, due to the local optimism, no united relief was undertaken until January, 1931. Meantime homeless men slept in the garbage in the municipal incinerator to keep warm. In January an abandoned police station was made into a flophouse. Attempts of Communists to organize the flophouseholders failed and a bond issue was eventually floated. Men in desperate need get two days work a week. As ex-Mayor Heffernan puts it: "If a man owned a small home, if a young couple possessed furniture, if a woman had a good coat or her husband a presentable suit, these things had to be sacrificed first. Not until they had drained every other resource was official charity able to do anything for them." . . .

Obviously, however, urban figures give an incomplete picture of the whole industrial situation, for they do not include such areas as the industrial area of New Jersey. In Passaic County, for example, 23,749 persons, heads of families, representing 90,699 of the county's 300,000 population, have applied for relief. The authorities have been forced to pick 12,171 families, about half, and give them relief amounting to about $9 a month per family. And in Paterson 8,500 of the registered 12,000 unemployed are without relief of any kind. Moreover, the situation in the textile areas of the state is complicated by the fact that certain employers have taken advantage of the necessity of their employees to reëstablish sweatshop conditions. Under such circumstances the employed as well as the unemployed become a burden upon the community. But elsewhere in the textile mill towns even the pretense of a living wage has been dropped. North Carolina has 100,000 unemployed textile workers with another 100,000 on the payrolls of closed plants, most of whom are begging on the roads, having long ago exhausted their savings from the low wage paid them before the depression. And those employed on part time are hardly better off since the full-time wage now averages about $6.50. In Georgia, in the Piedmont Mill Village of Egan Park, fifteen families have banded together to keep alive on a total weekly income of $10. And similar stories come from other towns in the region. While some of the small steel towns are almost as badly off. At Donora, Pennsylvania, there were in March 277 workers out of a population of 13,900 while 2,500 others performed "made work" at $3.50 per week and 2,000 others "seem to have disappeared." It is hardly necessary to add that malnutrition, undernourishment, rickets, tuberculosis, and other diseases increase under such conditions. And that relief in these areas is badly organized or nonexistent.

The story of factory unemployment is, however, only part of the story. In *agriculture* and in *mining*, particularly soft-coal mining, the depression is not in its fourth year but in its eighth or tenth or twelfth. It is estimated that there is a destitute coal-mining population of 1,200,000 souls dependent upon some 240,000 unemployed and distressed bituminous miners, most of whom live in six states in regions where coal mining is the only important enterprise, where merchants are bankrupt, banks closed, schools without funds, and once wealthy residents in actual want. And this situation is of many years' standing for even in the boom years of 1928 and 1929 the industry as a whole lost a total of $41,000,000. The American Friends Service Committee, which has worked with children in Kentucky, West Virginia, and Williamson and Franklin counties, Illinois, estimates that of the 500,000 soft-coal workers making a living in 1928 only 300,000 are now employed and on wages often as low as $8 a week. Over the entire area from 20 per cent to 99 per cent of the children are found to be underweight and the probability is that 20,000 children and 20,000 adults will shortly be in actual and pressing want.

Kentucky conditions have been well aired as a result of the Fascist policy pursued by the local authorities, particularly in Harlan County. Miners in that county who work at all work one to one and a half days a week with payment in scrip from which the company deducts an average of $11.80 monthly for rent, medical attention, power and caps, and insurance. To pay this deduction, a man must mine forty-five tons a month, which means that he must work nine days. Most of them work a total of six days and the result is a load of debt with no balance for food. As a consequence, pellagra—a deficiency disease of the nerve centers finally causing insanity—is common. In Pineville, Kentucky, 157 children are fed one meal a day at a soup kitchen—the meal consisting of boiled potatoes, boiled beans, and cornbread, an ideal pellagra-breeding diet. Most of the miners attempt to farm but the land is poor and jars for canning are too expensive for a community in which cash is practically nonexistent. Moreover, there was last year a severe drought in this district, and a great many miners' crops were

destroyed by sun and pests—a fact which must be compared with the September, 1931, statement of Executive-Director Croxton of the President's Organization on Unemployment Relief to the effect that the unemployment situation in West Virginia and Kentucky would be alleviated by the "bountiful crops."

The state of Franklin and Williamson counties in Illinois is, if anything, worse. All mines in the counties were closed by April, 1932. A cross section of twelve homes in the town of Benton showed no money, worn-out clothing, houses bare of "unnecessary" furniture, dishes made of flour, emaciated parents, undernourished children, unpaid rentals, and an average family indebtedness for groceries and doctors' bills of $300. Twenty-five thousand persons in the two counties were either in want last spring or rapidly approaching it. . . .

So it goes from one city to another and out into the mill towns and the mine villages and on beyond into the farms where the hides of a carload of cattle will hardly buy a pair of shoes and alfalfa costing $12 a ton to raise sells at $2.50 and the tractors rust in the fields. The difficulty with such facts is that in mass they cease to have meaning. And the reiteration of the statement that hundreds of thousands of people have faced or are facing starvation with inadequate doles to support them merely produces skepticism. "They haven't starved yet," remarks the reader. "They get along somehow."

It is true they get along somehow. But just how they get along is another matter. There were eleven days in Philadelphia last April when private funds had run out and public funds were not yet available. During that period, the relief organizations studied ninety-one families to see just how people get along under those circumstances. They found out. One woman borrowed fifty cents, bought stale bread at three and one half cents a loaf, and the family lived on it for eleven days. Another put the last food order into soup stock and vegetables and made a soup. When a member of the family was hungry, he ate as little as he could. Another picked up spoiled vegetables along the docks and except for three foodless days, the family ate them. Another made a stew with her last food order, which she cooked over and over daily to keep it from spoiling. Another family lived on dandelions. Another on potatoes. Another had no food for two and one-half days. And one in ten of the women were pregnant and one in three of the children of nursing age. And they "got along."

Such is the problem created by three years of increasing unemployment and two years of hand-to-mouth relief: city after city attempting to feed a half or a third or a quarter of its citizens upon gifts made from the reduced earnings, or from taxes levied on the over-appraised homes of the other half or the other two-thirds or the other three-quarters; city after city maintaining the lives but not the health of its unemployed on a survival ration; city after city where the whole mechanism of relief has failed or is about to fail or has survived only by abandoning a major part of its task; and beyond the cities the mill towns and the coal mines and the cropper farms where relief is merely a name.

But the depression, along with its misery, has produced its social curiosities, not the least of which is the wandering population it has spilled upon the roads. Means of locomotion vary but the objective is always the same—somewhere else. No one has yet undertaken to estimate the number of hitch-hikers whose thumbs jerk onward along the American pike, nor the number of spavined Fords dragging destitute families from town to town in search of a solvent relative or a generous friend. But the total migratory population of the country has been put at 600,000 to 1,000,000. . . .

The presence of these wandering groups is curious and significant. It has long been recognized that the population of the U.S. was becoming increasingly migratory in character. But it was not until the depression that the meaning of the phenomenon was made clear. When millions of people have no relation to the land and are able at the same time to find cheap transportation, the effect of an economic crisis is not to fix them in one place but to drive them elsewhere. And the consequence, as regards these groups, is a complete failure of local relief. The destitute families of the Fords and the homeless men of the flat cars are entitled to relief in no city. As the history of the Bonus Expeditionary Force after its ouster from Washington makes clear.

So far at least the phenomenon of migration is the only important social consequence of the depression, and the Communistic outbreaks foreseen by extremists in both directions have not taken place. The unemployed of Passaic County, New Jersey, may be and doubtless are in ugly temper. And the state of mind of the idle miners in Harlan County, Kentucky, may have been such as to justify, through fear, the otherwise unjustifiable repressive measures adopted by the local authorities. But by and large there has been extraordinarily little unrest. The two major manifestations of the year, the January hunger march of Father Cox's army to Washington and the later Bonus Expeditionary Force, were notoriously and avowedly anti-revolutionary, and contrasted remarkably in number with the feeble 1,500 produced for the Communist hunger march of last December. And most of the food riots reported from various cities—or not reported—have so far been bloodless, the only fatalities having occurred in the mismanaged resistance to a job march upon the Ford factories in Dearborn in March, when four were killed and fifty wounded, the July attempt of St. Louis police to prevent a mob of 300 from rushing the City Hall where the Board of Aldermen was considering (and thereupon promptly passing) special tax bills for relief, the demonstration of 400 against the employment of non-union men on public works in Marseilles, Illinois, in the same month in which one man was killed and twenty-two wounded, and the Battle of Pennsylvania Avenue. Other and milder disturbances occurred in New York in January (a riot before the Home Relief Bureau Office), in Chicago in February (a demonstration of 20,000 said to have been led by Communists), in Boston in May (a hunger march of 500), in Philadelphia in May (a demonstration before the City Hall in which twenty people were beaten), in Charleston, West Virginia, in June (a hunger seige of 500 around the State House), in Clinton, Massachusetts, in July (a demonstration for food by 300 men, women, and crying children), in Sioux City, Iowa, in July (a demonstration of 500 unemployed against the use of a steam shovel on a post-office site), in North Carolina in July (a demonstration of 5,000 textile workers against a wage cut, resulting in the forced closing of the mills of five towns), and in Olympia, Washington, in July (a concentration of jobless upon the State Capitol demanding relief). But the tension has naturally increased in the industrial communities as time has passed. Indiana has recently offered the spectacle of striking miners besieging strike breakers in violation of an anti-picketing injunction with the purpose of either inviting their own arrest so that they might be fed in jail, or starving out their enemies. And it is not necessary to appeal, as Mayor Cermak did last winter, to class fear in order to point out that there is a limit beyond which hunger and misery become violent.[2]

5. THE COMMONWEALTH CLUB ADDRESS, 1932[1]

By FRANKLIN D. ROOSEVELT

EDITORS' NOTE.—Franklin Delano Roosevelt (1882–1945) and the Democratic party in 1932 succeeded in convincing the nation that after four years of Hoover "rugged individualism" and three years of deepening depression it was time for a change of administration and for a change in policy. Like most parties seeking to recover the presidency, the Democrats were much clearer about the need for changes of policy than they were about the nature of this change.

Roosevelt's education for political leadership had included the positions of assistant secretary of the navy (1913–20), of Democratic vice-presidential candidate in 1920, and of governor of New York (1929–33).

The following address, delivered before the Commonwealth Club at San Francisco on September 23, 1932, is often cited as Roosevelt's clearest campaign expression of his general economic and political views.

2. Two years later (October, 1934) *Fortune* again surveyed unemployment in America, this time under the revealing title: "On the Dole, 17,000,000." Most significant was the impact which the depression and the New Deal had made on the editors of *Fortune.* "Although no one has yet succeeded," they wrote, "in bringing much economic order out of the economic chaos that unemployment has produced, we have at least abandoned one hypocrisy: the hypocrisy of believing that unemployment could be cured by ignoring it. . . . The depression seems to have crystallized one notion in the mind of America and the notion is that the right to work is a social right. The relief millions have set their jaws in demanding it. And it is pretty safe to say that by one means or another, and under whatever administration you like, the nation in the future will enforce that right. It will not be easy. It will change the pattern of life for everyone. But the nation will do it because, in the words that Woodrow Wilson used on a less worthy occasion, 'God helping her, she can do no other.' "

1. Franklin Delano Roosevelt, *Public Papers and Addresses* (New York, 1938), I, 742–56. By permission of Random House.

New conditions impose new requirements upon government and those who conduct government.

. . . I want to speak not of politics but of Government. I want to speak not of parties, but of universal principles. They are not political, except in that larger sense in which a great American once expressed a definition of politics, that nothing in all of human life is foreign to the science of politics.

I do want to give you, however, a recollection of a long life spent for a large part in public office. Some of my conclusions and observations have been deeply accentuated in these past few weeks. I have traveled far—from Albany to the Golden Gate. I have seen many people, and heard many things, and today, when in a sense my journey has reached the half-way mark, I am glad of the opportunity to discuss with you what it all means to me.

Sometimes, my friends, particularly in years such as these, the hand of discouragement falls upon us. It seems that things are in a rut, fixed, settled, that the world has grown old and tired and very much out of joint. This is the mood of depression, of dire and weary depression.

But then we look around us in America, and everything tells us that we are wrong. America is new. It is in the process of change and development. It has the great potentialities of youth, and particularly is this true of the great West, and of this coast, and of California.

I would not have you feel that I regard this as in any sense a new community. I have traveled in many parts of the world, but never have I felt the arresting thought of the change and development more than here, where the old, mystic East would seem to be near to us, where the currents of life and thought and commerce of the whole world meet us. This factor alone is sufficient to cause man to stop and think of the deeper meaning of things, when he stands in this community.

But more than that, I appreciate that the membership of this club consists of men who are thinking in terms beyond the immediate present, beyond their own immediate tasks, beyond their own individual interests. I want to invite you, therefore, to consider with me in the large, some of the relationships of Government and economic life that go deeply into our daily lives, our happiness, our future and our security.

The issue of Government has always been whether individual men and women will have to serve some system of Government or economics, or whether a system of Government and economics exists to serve individual men and women. This question has persistently dominated the discussion of Government for many generations. On questions relating to these things men have differed, and for time immemorial it is probable that honest men will continue to differ.

The final word belongs to no man; yet we can still believe in change and progress. Democracy, as a dear old friend of mine in Indiana, Meredith Nicholson, has called it, is a quest, a never-ending seeking for better things, and in the seeking for these things and the striving for them, there are many roads to follow. But, if we map the course of these roads, we find that there are only two general directions.

When we look about us, we are likely to forget how hard people have worked to win the privilege of Government. The growth of the national Governments of Europe was a struggle for the development of a centralized force in the Nation, strong enough to impose peace upon ruling barons. In many instances the victory of the central Government, the creation of a strong central Government, was a haven of refuge to the individual. The people preferred the master far away to the exploitation and cruelty of the smaller master near at hand.

But the creators of national Government were perforce ruthless men. They were often cruel in their methods, but they did strive steadily toward something that Society needed and very much wanted, a strong central State able to keep the peace, to stamp out civil war, to put the unruly nobleman in his place, and to permit the bulk of individuals to live safely. The man of ruthless force had his place in developing a pioneer country, just as he did in fixing the power of the central Government in the development of Nations. Society paid him well for his services and its development. When the development among the Nations of Europe, however, had been completed, ambition and ruthlessness, having served their term, tended to overstep their mark.

There came a growing feeling that Government was conducted for the benefit of a few who thrived unduly at the expense of all. The people sought a balancing—a limiting force. There came gradually, through town councils, trade guilds, national parliaments, by constitution and by popular participation and control, limitations on arbitrary power.

Another factor that tended to limit the power of those who ruled, was the rise of the ethical conception that a ruler bore a responsibility for the welfare of his subjects.

The American colonies were born in this struggle. The American Revolution was a turning point in it. After the Revolution the struggle continued and shaped itself in the public life of the country. There were those who because they had seen the confusion which attended the years of war for American independence surrendered to the belief that popular Government was essentially dangerous and essentially unworkable. They were honest people, my friends, and we cannot deny that their experience had warranted some measure of fear. The most brilliant, honest and able exponent of this point of view was Hamilton. He was too impatient of slow-moving methods. Fundamentally he believed that the safety of the republic lay in the autocratic strength of its Government, that the destiny of individuals was to serve that Government, and that fundamentally a great and strong group of central institutions, guided by a small group of able and public spirited citizens, could best direct all Government.

But Mr. Jefferson, in the summer of 1776, after drafting the Declaration of Independence turned his mind to the same problem and took a different view. He did not deceive himself with outward forms. Government to him was a means to an end, not an end in itself; it might be either a refuge and a help or a threat and a danger, depending on the circumstances. We find him carefully analyzing the society for which he was to organize a Government. "We have no paupers. The great mass of our population is of laborers, our rich who cannot live without labor, either manual or professional, being few and of moderate wealth. Most of the laboring class possess property, cultivate their own lands, have families and from the demand for their labor, are enabled to exact from the rich and the competent such prices as enable them to feed abundantly, clothe above mere decency, to labor moderately and raise their families."

These people, he considered, had two sets of rights, those of "personal competency" and those involved in acquiring and possessing property. By "personal competency" he meant the right of free thinking, freedom of forming and expressing opinions, and freedom of personal living, each man according to his own lights. To insure the first set of rights, a Government must so order its functions as not to interfere with the individual. But even Jefferson realized that the exercise of the property rights might so interfere with the rights of the individual that the Government, without whose assistance the property rights could not exist, must intervene, not to destroy individualism, but to protect it.

You are familiar with the great political duel which followed; and how Hamilton, and his friends, building toward a dominant centralized power were at length defeated in the great election of 1800, by Mr. Jefferson's party. Out of that duel came the two parties, Republican and Democratic, as we know them today.

So began, in American political life, the new day, the day of the individual against the system, the day in which individualism was made the great watchword of American life. The happiest of economic conditions made that day long and splendid. On the Western frontier, land was substantially free. No one, who did not shirk the task of earning a living, was entirely without opportunity to do so. Depressions could, and did, come and go; but they could not alter the fundamental fact that most of the people lived partly by selling their labor and partly by extracting their livelihood from the soil, so that starvation and dislocation were practically impossible. At the very worst there was always the possibility of climbing into a covered wagon and moving west where the untilled prairies afforded a haven for men to whom the East did not provide a place. So great were our natural resources that we could offer this relief not only to our own people, but to the distressed of all the world; we could invite immigration from Europe, and welcome it with open arms. Traditionally, when a depression came a new section of land was opened in the West; and even our temporary misfortune served our manifest destiny.

It was in the middle of the nineteenth century that a new force was released and a new dream created. The force was what is called the industrial revolution, the advance of steam and machinery and the rise of the forerunners of the modern industrial plant. The dream was the dream of an economic machine, able to raise the standard of living for everyone; to bring luxury within the reach of the humblest; to annihilate distance by steam power and later by electricity, and to release everyone from the drudgery of the heaviest manual toil. It was to be expected that this would necessarily affect Government. Heretofore, Government had merely been called upon to produce conditions within which people could live happily, labor peacefully, and rest secure. Now it was called upon to aid in the consummation of this new dream. There was, however, a shadow over the dream. To be made real, it required use of the talents of men of tremendous will and tremendous ambition, since by no other force could the problems of financing and engineering and new developments be brought to a consummation.

So manifest were the advantages of the machine age, however, that the United States fearlessly, cheerfully, and, I think, rightly, accepted the bitter with the sweet. It was thought that no price was too high to pay for the advantages which we could draw from a finished industrial system. The history of the last half century is accordingly in large measure a history of a group of financial Titans, whose methods were not scrutinized with too much care, and who were honored in proportion as they produced the results, irrespective of the means they used. The financiers who pushed the railroads to the Pacific were always ruthless, often wasteful, and frequently corrupt; but they did build railroads, and we have them today. It has been estimated that the American investor paid for the American railway system more than three times over in the process; but despite this fact the net advantage was to the United States. As long as we had free land; as long as population was growing by leaps and bounds; as long as our industrial plants were insufficient to supply our own needs, society chose to give the ambitious man free play and unlimited reward provided only that he produced the economic plant so much desired.

During this period of expansion, there was equal opportunity for all and the business of Government was not to interfere but to assist in the development of industry. This was done at the request of business men themselves. The tariff was originally imposed for the purpose of "fostering our infant industry," a phrase I think the older among you will remember as a political issue not so long ago. The railroads were subsidized, sometimes by grants of money, oftener by grants of land; some of the most valuable oil lands in the United States were granted to assist the financing of the railroad which pushed through the Southwest. A nascent merchant marine was assisted by grants of money, or by mail subsidies, so that our steam shipping might ply the seven seas. Some of my friends tell me that they do not want the Government in business. With this I agree; but I wonder whether they realize the implications of the past. For while it has been American doctrine that the Government must not go into business in competition with private enterprises, still it has been traditional, particularly in Republican administrations, for business to ask the Government to put at private disposal all kinds of Government assistance. The same man who tells you that he does not want to see the Government interfere in business—and he means it, and has plenty of good reasons for saying so—is the first to go to Washington and ask the Government for a prohibitory tariff on his product. When things get just bad enough, as they did two years ago, he will go with equal speed to the United States Government and ask for a loan; and the Reconstruction Finance Corporation is the outcome of it. Each group has sought protection from the Government for its own special interests, without realizing that the function of Government must be to favor no small group at the expense of its duty to protect the rights of personal freedom and of private property of all its citizens.

In retrospect we can now see that the turn of the tide came with the turn of the century. We were reaching our last frontier; there was no more free land and our industrial combinations had become great uncontrolled and irresponsible units of power within the State. Clear-sighted men saw with fear the danger that opportunity would no longer be equal; that the growing corporation, like the feudal baron of old, might threaten the economic freedom of individuals to earn a living. In that hour, our anti-trust laws were born. The cry was raised against the great corporations. Theodore Roosevelt, the first great Republican Progressive, fought a Presidential campaign on the issue of "trust busting" and talked freely about malefactors of great wealth. If the Government had a policy it was rather to turn the clock back, to destroy the large combinations and to return to the time when every man owned his individual small business.

This was impossible; Theodore Roosevelt, abandoning the idea of "trust busting," was forced to work out a difference between "good" trusts and "bad" trusts. The Supreme Court set forth the famous "rule of reason" by which it seems to have meant that a concentration of industrial power was permissible if the method by which it got its power, and the use it made of that power were reasonable.

Woodrow Wilson, elected in 1912, saw the situation more clearly. Where Jefferson had feared the encroachment of political power on the lives of individuals, Wilson knew that the new power was financial. He saw, in the highly centralized economic system, the despot of the twentieth century, on whom great masses of individuals relied for their safety and their livelihood, and whose irresponsibility and greed (if they were not controlled) would reduce them to starvation and penury. The concentration of financial power had not proceeded so far in 1912 as it has today; but it had grown far enough for Mr. Wilson to realize fully its implications. It is interesting, now, to read his speeches. What is called "radical" today (and I have reason to know whereof I speak) is mild compared to the campaign of Mr. Wilson. "No man can deny," he said, "that the lines of endeavor have more and more narrowed and stiffened; no man who knows anything about the development of industry in this country can have failed to observe that the larger kinds of credit are more and more difficult to obtain unless you obtain them upon terms of uniting your efforts with those who already control the industry of the country, and nobody can fail to observe that every man who tries to set himself up in competition with any process of manufacture which has taken place under the control of large combinations of capital will presently find himself either squeezed out or obliged to sell and allow himself to be absorbed." Had there been no World War—had Mr. Wilson been able to devote eight years to domestic instead of to international affairs—we might have had a wholly different situation at the present time. However, the then distant roar of European cannon, growing ever louder, forced him to abandon the study of this issue. The problem he saw so clearly is left with us as a legacy; and no one of us on either side of the political controversy can deny that it is a matter of grave concern to the Government.

A glance at the situation today only too clearly indicates that equality of opportunity as we have known it no longer exists. Our industrial plant is built; the problem just now is whether under existing conditions it is not overbuilt. Our last frontier has long since been reached, and there is practically no more free land. More than half of our people do not live on the farms or on lands and cannot derive a living by cultivating their own property. There is no safety valve in the form of a Western prairie to which those thrown out of work by the Eastern economic machines can go for a new start. We are not able to invite the immigration from Europe to share our endless plenty. We are now providing a drab living for our own people.

Our system of constantly rising tariffs has at last reacted against us to the point of closing our Canadian frontier on the north, our European markets on the east, many of our Latin-American markets to the south, and a goodly proportion of our Pacific markets on the west, through the retaliatory tariffs of those countries. It has forced many of our great industrial institutions which exported their surplus produc-

tion to such countries, to establish plants in such countries, within the tariff walls. This has resulted in the reduction of the operation of their American plants, and opportunity for employment.

Just as freedom to farm has ceased, so also the opportunity in business has narrowed. It still is true that men can start small enterprises, trusting to native shrewdness and ability to keep abreast of competitors; but area after area has been preempted altogether by the great corporations, and even in the fields which still have no great concerns, the small man starts under a handicap. The unfeeling statistics of the past three decades show that the independent business man is running a losing race. Perhaps he is forced to the wall; perhaps he cannot command credit; perhaps he is "squeezed out," in Mr. Wilson's words, by highly organized corporate competitors, as your corner grocery man can tell you. Recently a careful study was made of the concentration of business in the United States. It showed that our economic life was dominated by some six hundred odd corporations who controlled two-thirds of American industry. Ten million small business men divided the other third. More striking still, it appeared that if the process of concentration goes on at the same rate, at the end of another century we shall have all American industry controlled by a dozen corporations, and run by perhaps a hundred men. But plainly, we are steering a steady course toward economic ogligarchy, if we are not there already.

Clearly, all this calls for a reappraisal of values. A mere builder of more industrial plants, a creator of more railroad systems, an organizer of more corporations, is as likely to be a danger as a help. The day of the great promoter or the financial Titan, to whom we granted anything if only he would build, or develop, is over. Our task now is not discovery or exploitation of natural resources, or necessarily producing more goods. It is the soberer, less dramatic business of administering resources and plants already in hand, of seeking to reestablish foreign markets for our surplus production, of meeting the problem of underconsumption, of adjusting production to consumption, of distributing wealth and products more equitably, of adapting existing economic organizations to the service of the people. The day of enlightened administration has come.

Just as in older times the central Government was first a haven of refuge, and then a threat, so now in a closer economic system the central and ambitious financial unit is no longer a servant of national desire, but a danger. I would draw the parallel one step farther. We did not think because national Government had become a threat in the 18th century that therefore we should abandon the principle of national Government. Nor today should we abandon the principle of strong economic units called corporations, merely because their power is susceptible of easy abuse. In other times we dealt with the problem of an unduly ambitious central Government by modifying it gradually into a constitutional democratic Government. So today we are modifying and controlling our economic units.

As I see it, the task of Government in its relation to business is to assist the development of an economic declaration of rights, an economic constitutional order. This is the common task of statesman and business man. It is the minimum requirement of a more permanently safe order of things.

Happily, the times indicate that to create such an order not only is the proper policy of Government, but it is the only line of safety for our economic structures as well. We know, now, that these economic units cannot exist unless prosperity is uniform, that is, unless purchasing power is well distributed throughout every group in the nation. That is why even the most selfish of corporations for its own interest would be glad to see wages restored and unemployment ended and to bring the Western farmer back to his ac-customed level of prosperity and to assure a permanent safety to both groups. That is why some enlightened industries themselves endeavor to limit the freedom of action of each man and business group within the industry in the common interest of all; why business men everywhere are asking a form of organization which will bring the scheme of things into balance, even though it may in some measure qualify the freedom of action of individual units within the business.

The exposition need not further be elaborated. It is brief and incomplete, but you will be able to expand it in terms of your own business or occupation without difficulty. I think everyone who has actually entered the economic struggle—which means everyone who was not born to safe wealth—knows in his own experience and his own life that we have now to apply the earlier concepts of American Government to the conditions of today.

The Declaration of Independence discusses the problem of Government in terms of a contract. Government is a relation of give and take, a contract, perforce, if we would follow the thinking out of which it grew. Under such a contract rulers were accorded power, and the people consented to that power on consideration that they be accorded certain rights. The task of statesmanship has always been the redefinition of these rights in terms of a changing and growing social order. New conditions impose new requirements upon Government and those who conduct Government.

I held, for example, in proceedings before me as Governor, the purpose of which was the removal of the Sheriff of New York, that under modern conditions it was not enough for a public official merely to evade the legal terms of official wrongdoing. He owed a positive duty as well. I said in substance that if he had acquired large sums of money, he was when accused required to explain the sources of such wealth. To that extent this wealth was colored with a public interest. I said that in financial matters, public servants should, even beyond private citizens, be held to a stern and uncompromising rectitude.

I feel that we are coming to a view through the drift of our legislation and our public thinking in the past quarter century that private economic power is, to enlarge an old phrase, a public trust as well. I hold that continued enjoyment of that power by any individual or group must depend upon the fulfillment of that trust. The men who have reached the summit of American business life know this best; happily, many of these urge the binding quality of this greater social contract.

The terms of that contract are as old as the Republic, and as new as the new economic order.

Every man has a right to life; and this means that he has also the right to make a comfortable living. He may by sloth or crime decline to exercise that right; but it may not be denied him. We have no actual famine or dearth; our industrial and agricultural mechanism can produce enough and to spare. Our Government formal and informal, political and economic, owes to everyone an avenue to possess himself of a portion of that plenty sufficient for his needs, through his own work.

Every man has a right to his own property; which means a right to be assured, to the fullest extent attainable, in the safety of his savings. By no other means can men carry the burdens of those parts of life which, in the nature of things, afford no chance of labor; childhood, sickness, old age. In all thought of property, this right is paramount; all other property rights must yield to it. If, in accord with this principle, we must restrict the operations of the speculator, the manipulator, even the financier, I believe we must accept the restriction as needful, not to hamper individualism but to protect it.

These two requirements must be satisfied, in the main, by individuals who claim and hold control of the great industrial and financial combinations which dominate so large a part of our industrial life. They have undertaken to be, not business men, but princes of property. I am not prepared to say that the system which produces them is wrong. I am very clear that they must fearlessly and competently assume the responsibility which goes with the power. So many enlightened business men know this that the statement would be little more than a platitude, were it not for an added implication.

This implication is, briefly, that the responsible heads of finance and industry instead of acting each for himself, must work together to achieve the common end. They must, where necessary, sacrifice this or that private advantage; and in reciprocal self-denial must seek a general advantage. It is here that formal Government—political Government, if you choose—comes in. Whenever in the pursuit of this objective the lone wolf, the unethical competitor, the reckless promoter, the Ishmael or Insull whose hand is against every man's, declines to join in achieving an end recognized as being for the public welfare, and threatens to drag the industry back to a state of anarchy, the Government may properly be asked to apply restraint. Likewise, should the group ever use its collective power contrary to the public welfare, the Government must be swift to enter and protect the public interest.

The Government should assume the function of economic regulation only as a last resort, to be tried only when private initiative, inspired by high responsibility, with such assistance and balance as Government can give, has finally failed. As yet there has been no final failure, because there has been no attempt; and I decline to assume that this nation is unable to meet the situation.

The final term of the high contract was for liberty and the pursuit of happiness. We have learned a great deal of both in the past century. We know that individual liberty and individual happiness mean nothing unless both are ordered in the sense that one man's meat is not another man's poison. We know that the old "rights of personal competency," the right to read, to think, to speak, to choose and live a mode of life, must be respected at all hazards. We know that liberty to do anything which deprives others of those elemental rights is outside the protection of any compact; and that Government in this regard is the maintenance of a balance, within which every individual may have a place if he will take it; in which every individual may find safety if he wishes it; in which every individual may attain such power as his ability permits, consistent with his assuming the accompanying responsibility.

All this is a long, slow task. Nothing is more striking than the simple innocence of the men who insist, whenever an objective is present, on the prompt production of a patent scheme guaranteed to produce a result. Human endeavor is not so simple as that. Government includes the art of formulating a policy, and using the political technique to attain so much of that policy as will receive general support; persuading, leading, sacrificing, teaching always, because the greatest duty of a statesman is to educate. But in the matters of which I have spoken, we are learning rapidly, in a severe school. The lessons so learned must not be forgotten, even in the mental lethargy of a speculative upturn. We must build toward the time when a major depression cannot occur again; and if this means sacrificing the easy profits of inflationist booms, then let them go; and good riddance.

Faith in America, faith in our tradition of personal responsibility, faith in our institutions, faith in ourselves demand that we recognize the new terms of the old social contract. We shall fulfill them, as we fulfilled the obligation of the apparent Utopia which Jefferson imagined for us in 1776, and which Jefferson, Roosevelt and Wilson sought to bring to realization. We must do so, lest a rising tide of misery, engendered by our common failure, engulf us all. But failure is not an American habit; and in the strength of great hope we must all shoulder our common load.

6. THE FUTURE: SOCIALISM?[1]

By NORMAN THOMAS

EDITORS' NOTE.—At a time in which conservatives were labeling the New Deal experiment as "socialistic," Norman Thomas (1884——), who has been the perennial Socialist candidate for the presidency, was just as vehemently arguing that it was not. The following chapter from his volume entitled *After the New Deal, What?* was written in the earlier stages of the 1936 presidential campaign. It may be viewed both as a campaign document

1. Norman Thomas, *After the New Deal, What?* (New York, 1936), pp. 156–85. By permission of The Macmillan Company.

and as a more careful Socialist statement as to the desirable direction for policy.

Norman Thomas was educated for the ministry, held several Protestant pulpits from 1910 to 1918, and thereafter served in various political editorial capacities and engaged in politics as a member of the Socialist party. He has been Socialist candidate for the presidency in each campaign from 1928 to 1948, and in only the 1932 campaign did he receive as many as 1 per cent of the total popular votes.

To this bleak future of the suicide of western civilization in a new cycle of wars, general chaos, or the organized tyranny of fascism, the Socialist has an answer. He does not trust to kind fortune, vague optimism, or any inevitable victory of good over evil without effort and purpose of man. Of the disintegration of the capitalist system he is sure; it is already far advanced. The victory of socialism is not equally sure. But it must be burned into the conscience of this generation and the next not only that we *can* have new dark ages, but that we *will* have new dark ages unless there is a conscious and creative purpose of building a federation of cooperative commonwealths in an interdependent world. Socialism, we believe, is the reasonable and the only reasonable way of life and social organization in an age of interdependence and collectivism such as power-driven machinery has imposed. Socialism in this day and generation is the condition of true democracy. It is the fulfillment of the prophet's dream of brotherhood. But although socialism is the reasonable form of organization in a machine age and the desirable fulfillment of the dream of prophets, patriots, and sages, it does not follow that it is inevitable. To establish socialism requires struggle and intelligent struggle. It requires the development of new and nobler loyalties. The socialist society is not for fools or cowards. There is no foreordained assurance that man will have the wisdom to use for the social good the machinery which he had the intelligence to invent.

But half the battle for socialism will be won when men understand two things: First, that there is not room for plenty, peace or freedom in the present disintegrating social order; and second, that socialism in itself is a thing infinitely desirable. So far we have been concerned primarily to develop the first argument; now we must turn to the second. Socialism is first of all a reasoned conviction that plenty and peace, freedom and fellowship, lie within the grasp of men. It is the assertion that our failure to conquer poverty in the midst of potential abundance is due to an acceptance of a system which is based on relative scarcity, and upon the exploitation of the masses by an owning class. Socialism believes that men may be free by making power-driven machinery the slave of mankind. It believes in planned production for the use of all rather than an unplanned production for the profit of an owning class. It asserts that this type of production for use requires social ownership of land, natural resources and the principal means of production and distribution, including, of course, the entire system of money, banking and credit. In the name of social ownership of land and tools it does not propose to house men in public barracks or to take from a worker his favorite hammer, violin or typewriter, or anything else which he uses without exploiting others. Socialism does intend to end absentee landlordism, but it intends to make men more, not less, secure in the occupancy and use of homes in which they live.

Because men will be more secure against the loss of their homes and their jobs there will be more real liberty. The statement that socialism will take from men civil and religious liberty is born either of malice or complete misunderstanding of the subject of socialism.

American Socialism has expressly recognized a man's right to the religion of his choice. Many socialists would go farther and quote approvingly the statement I heard a young socialist make to a woman perturbed that if she accepted socialism she would lose her religion. "Madam," said he, "one does not have to be a Christian to be a socialist, but I cannot understand how you can be a true Christian in these times and not be a socialist."

Social ownership of the great means of production and distribution is necessary for planning. It is the only basis on which we can end the dominion of profit. Even under capitalism social ownership has had an encouraging degree of success. Witness for instance such a list of publicly owned enterprises as schools, roads, parks, the post office, the Panama Canal, city water and sewer systems, power plants, and the like. They are supplemented, too, by the success of consumers' cooperatives carried on for the benefit of the consumers who are members of them and not for the private profit of any group of individuals.

It takes custom derived from a long historic development to explain how anything as utterly absurd as the legal control of private enterprises by absentee stockholders could come into existence. These stockholders know nothing about the conduct of the steel mills, electric power systems, railroads or banks which legally they own. They are concerned only with the profit they get. Their enterprises would fail disastrously except for the hired brains and hands employed by boards of directors to run them, not for the use of all, but for the profit of these same absentee stockholders. There was some rhyme and reason to the old individualistic capitalism where the capitalist assumed definite responsibility. In this age when the engineer, the technician, the manager, are the key to productive enterprise there is no reason under the sun why they should not work for society rather than for absentee owners. Logically they could do a much better job because the fact is that the interest of the absentee owners is by no means identical with the interest of the consumers, still less with the interest of the workers. So far is it from being true that the profit system puts the most advanced science and the more advanced inventions automatically to work, that, on the contrary, a great many inventions are kept off the market by the monopolists or semi-monopolists who can control them in order to protect profit. There is no reason to doubt that the engineers who have given us the modern automobile could also have added to the skill of their performance engines which would use less gasoline, but that would not suit powerful financial interests. Progress in railroad travel was held back for years by the belief, probably the mistaken belief, of directors that profits would not be increased by further improvements.

We have already accepted the estimate of experts that it would be possible to provide every American family on the average with an income equivalent to that now enjoyed by those with between $4,000 and $5,000 a year. Or, from a different angle, we have accepted the estimate of those experts who say that we could establish a minimum income for each American worker of between $2,000 and $2,500 a year without notably reducing higher incomes, except the swollen fortunes of the very rich. Economic machinery ought to be operated to make this great possibility a reality. It is hard to imagine any single thing which could do so much to end physical misery, mental anguish, frustration, yes, crime, as the certainty that every family worth holding together at all, every family where breadwinners are willing to work, would be guaranteed a minimum of $2,500 a year.

Above that level, at least during the transition period and the earlier stages of socialism, it would be well to reward men according to deed. Common sense and the Russian experience unite to convince us that it is better to attract men to difficult jobs, or to jobs for which well-trained workers are scarce than to try to conscript them. One of the ways to attract men is to remunerate them according to deed. There is no such thing as perfect justice in rewarding them according to deed. Differentials in reward, particularly in the earlier stages of socialist transition, will have something to do with traditional holdovers and with the kind of pressure which different groups can exert. Nevertheless, socialism can rapidly apply three principles to the incalculable benefit of mankind: (1) No income for any able-bodied adult without work; no long search for work in vain; (2) a minimum standard of decent living for all; (3) above the minimum an approximation to reward according to deed, far more just than that which prevails in our gamblers' world.

It will be almost the first business of a socialist society to get rid of the ugliness as well as the discomfort of the slums and shacks which now disgrace America. Even more surely, it will be the first business of socialism to see that every boy and girl born into the world shall receive food necessary for physical health, training to enable him to do the work for which he is best fitted, a chance when he comes to working age to do that work, and to do it under conditions which give him both security and leisure.

It is logically possible today to house all our people in comfort and beauty; to feed them amply; to help them through a socialized medical service to get well and stay well; to provide them economic security against the vissicitudes of life; and to substitute for the present alternation between long hours of monotonous, ill-rewarded toil and bitter unemployment a shorter working week and enriched leisure.

To establish and maintain all this Socialists do not depend upon an omnipotent and omniscient state. They regard the state as the principal instrument that must be used for the establishment of a new social order. It is the business of workers with hand and brain to gain control of government in order to accomplish this great change. Between the fascist conception of the totalitarian state as an end in itself, and the socialist conception of the state as something to be used to establish the co-operative commonwealth, there is the difference between darkness and light. A socialist does not believe that the state is the only form of social organization which should be allowed to exist. It has no divine right. Its powers will have to be vigorously asserted and effectively used in a transition period, but as the habit of co-operation and functional self-government grows the coercive state should wither away. It should become a true common-

wealth. In this connection it is encouraging that the new Soviet Constitution shows progress toward democracy and civil liberty—a decided contrast with the unchanging emphasis on dictatorship in Germany and other fascist countries. The power of the state will be necessary to effect the transfer from private to public ownership, but it should not supersede or crush consumers' cooperatives. They would admirably supplement it.

A society which is in a way to achieve a socialist revolution with a minimum of disorder and strife could well afford, as part of the price of achieving it, to offer some compensation to expropriated owners. There would be a certain equity in this as between certain classes of owners because probably certain key industries would be taken first. Such key industries as the public utilities are precisely those in which the savings of the little men are invested. For these reasons, as I have elsewhere explained at more length, socialists generally would offer compensation plus taxation, taxation that would amount to expropriation in the higher brackets. Besides income and inheritance taxes a socialist government should use what has been called a capital levy; that is a tax upon wealth in private hands. It could be paid in money, in bonds, which would be retired, thus lessening the burden of debt, or in stocks of those enterprises which the government is ready to socialize anyway. Even under capitalism such a levy is the best way to deal with the crushing burden of debt. It would be less destructive than wholesale inflation or deflation. It is a way, however, that a capitalist society finds it psychologically impossible to take.

Of course an owning class which stubbornly and blindly resists socialism and which resorts to violence against it, cannot expect compensation. On the other hand, if the day ever comes when, as it were, over night, a smooth-running socialist society should be put into operation it would be better to cut the Gordian knot of vested right and property privilege than to try any kind of compensation. Under such a society, all except the very wealthy would be materially better off than they can ever be under any form of private ownership of the great machinery of production. And even the very wealthy might find new health to their souls!

To carry out a socialist program it is necessary that at least the key industries be taken over under a concerted plan. For example, good as publicly owned electric plants may be, it will be found unsatisfactory to try to carry on a socialized or partially socialized power industry under the capitalist economy. T.V.A. is now doing a remarkably good job. Its success is an encouragement for the future. It is worth while as a yardstick and much more than a yardstick. But the yardstick theory, or any other theory of piecemeal socialization within the confines of capitalism, has its disadvantages in waste and confusion. Socialism is much more than the sum total of certain socialized industries. It involves a general plan impossible on the yardstick theory. It involves also a way of life to which strife between government-owned industry and its privately owned rivals offers more of disadvantage than advantage. There may be a kind of socialist emulation between publicly or cooperatively owned enterprises, but scarcely satisfactory competition between enterprises operating on a different basis and with an appeal to different ideals.

Let us assume, then, that the state has taken over the key industries; that it itself is under the control of workers with hand and brain, well organized on both the industrial and economic fronts; that its activities are supplemented by the activities of consumers' cooperatives—under what plan will it control industry? It will put each socialized industry under the administrative direction of a governing authority representing the two permanent interests which always must exist in our economic life. They are the interests of man as consumer and as producer. They are not necessarily in opposition, but they are not identical. A coal miner or a textile worker has a peculiar set of interests in regard to the industry in which he invests his life. He has another set of the interests as a consumer. The interest of the workers as consumers should be dominant. Men work to live, not live to work. It is essential for managing a world where technological advance is rapid that the primary emphasis should not be on the vested rights of workers in one particular trade, but rather on the vested rights of men to enjoy what well-managed work can create. Sidney and Beatrice Webb assert that part of the success of the Russian planned economy is due to "placing the control in the hands of representatives, not of any organizations of producers, but organizations representing the consumers." That general principle should be followed with consumers' interest dominant in the new set-up. Nevertheless the unique interest of the worker in his own industry should be recognized under administration by a board on which there is representation of the general consuming interest and the particular interests of the various categories of workers employed in it. The precise form may vary in different industries. Labor unions will have a function even in a socialist society as an expression and protection of the interests of different groups of producers. They should no longer be organized consciously or subconsciously in terms of the class conflict since society or the mass of workers themselves will be the owners.

Socialized industries, each a law unto itself, cannot plan for work, leisure, security, and abundance for all unless there is over them a general economic planning council to prepare the master plan. This council is the general staff in the war against poverty. It is the expert arm of government, subject to general decisions of Congress or the electorate as to policy, but free from interference in detail. It should be composed of men and women chosen from panels suggested by engineering societies and various industrial and agricultural groups. It must make the most efficient possible use of expert skills in engineering and accounting.

It will be seen that the plan which I have outlined offers as a safeguard against bureaucratic centralization functional self-administration. It may also offer some degree of decentralization through regional machinery of government and of economic planning. That regional machinery cannot conform to present state lines or accept the dogma of states' rights because state lines have no intelligent relation to economic geography. The plan which I have suggested conserves democracy in its truest sense. It permits choices of policy and leadership to be made by those concerned in them. It recognizes that no one organization can express or carry out all a man's interests. It realizes to the full the usefulness of the expert, the engineer, and the technician, and the principle that those engaged in special tasks should have special voice in the way those tasks are carried out.

Agriculture offers somewhat greater difficulties in the earlier stages of socialization than such industries as steel, textiles, coal, or the railroads. That is partly because agriculture is in process of a delayed mechanization. The coming of the mechanical cotton picker will revolutionize hundreds of thousands of lives for better or for worse. The farmer under any kind of social order must reckon not only with new machinery and new methods but also the possibility that for his products there may be substituted the synthetic products of the chemical industry.

Mr. O. F. Wilcox, an authority on intensive agriculture, states in his book, *Reshaping Agriculture*, that it would be comparatively easy to eliminate four out of five farmers and four out of five acres under cultivation, if the best known practices of farming were adopted today. Messrs. Wayne W. Parish and Harold F. Clark, commenting on such statements as this, go on to add: "Virtually all food from wheat and corn to meat have been made in the laboratory." An engineer with more than national reputation told me recently that he doubted if cotton would be commercially grown on any important scale in America twenty years from now because cheaper ways would be found to produce cloth out of cellulose, which will supplant cotton more effectively than rayon has supplanted silk. (Incidentally, when I quoted this opinion to another high authority in the field of chemical industry he expressed great doubt of it.) At even the most moderate estimate the contrast between what is and what might be is startling. Consider, for instance, Dr. Wilcox's statement that four-fifths of the farmers may become superfluous in contrast to the fact that under present agricultural practices we need the product of forty-one million acres more than are now in cultivation. The inevitable displacement of farm workers means that they must be absorbed in industry. There is a limit to man's need or desire for food much more rigid than the limit to his desire for other material things. It follows that socialism which will plan for a whole economy is in a far better position to handle the difficult situation than capitalism which can do nothing but subsidize scarcity in order to protect the farmers.

Socialist plans in America most assuredly do not call for the forcible elimination of a man who farms his own land. Rather he would be protected against the vicissitudes which have brought it to pass that in the fertile central valleys of California something like 35 per cent of the land, I was recently told, is corporation farmed. One practical method of protection is to be found in crop insurance. A socialist government would socialize the machinery of marketing both what the farmer buys and what he sells. By taxation and otherwise it would abolish absentee landlordism. It would substitute collectives for great privately owned plantations, and train the workers in the democratic management of those collectives or cooperatives. It would enlist the farmers themselves in planning for the conservation and best use of soil. It would guide excess farm workers from the fields into other occupations. There is no inexorable limitation to employment if we set out to meet human needs rather than to preserve private profits. We can then control the rate of introduction of machinery or new technological processes according to our ability to increase production and shorten working hours.

I am still convinced, as I have often said, that the outstanding difficulty for socialism on the theoretical side is not to draw up plans for the operation of socialism within a great country like the United States, but to draw up plans for the operation of socialism throughout the world. Every year gives new proof that the great problem for socialism is nationalism. We have to begin where we are. That means that we must begin in a world divided into national states, each claiming absolute sovereignty. There are certain variations of national culture and traditions which make it both impossible and undesirable to impose so rigid a mould on all nations as the Communists once thought to impose. On the other hand, no nation is economically or culturally self-sufficient. Prosperity as well as peace depends upon international cooperation. Rather, both depend on a world-wide cooperation which does not emphasize the nation as the ultimate unit, fixed and unchangeable. There must be machinery for such cooperation. How shall we set up that machinery and develop the ideals which will make it function effectively? The League of Nations has not even tried to do this fundamental task. It is something yet to be done. How to do it is the most difficult single question which Socialists and all lovers of peace have to face. It is a task which will be easier as Socialists come to power within each nation. But socialism achieved on a national scale will not automatically answer the question. One answer might well be a league of Socialist states, a federation of cooperative commonwealths, not primarily for military defense but rather for economic cooperation. Another answer, not necessarily inconsistent with the first, is an effort after organized world-wide controls of such fundamentals as the allocation of raw materials, a uniform fiscal system or the relation of fiscal systems to one another, universal minimum standards for workers, and the effective limitation of armaments. This, as we have said in Chapter V, is part of the price of peace. Every effort toward it will be worth while, but its satisfactory attainment is incompatible with capitalist nationalism.

Some such precedents for international economic organization may be found in what was done by the Allied Powers and the United States in the control of such essentials as wheat, wool, sugar, etc. Arrangements for giving to all peoples greater economic opportunity will certainly include the removal of the barriers to trade established in the interest of capitalist nationalism. It is not likely that the nations can work that out successfully by practicing the laissez-faire free trade preached by Richard Cobden a century ago. Such unqualified free trade would serve to continue and strengthen some of the industrial and economic inequalities set up under the reign of capitalist nationalism. It would leave most of Asia and Africa comparatively non-industrialized, a source of supply for raw materials, and a market for finished goods to be more or less exploited by the industrialized nations. There is no evidence at all that this is the best economic arrangement in a well-planned world. Yet it is the sort of arrangement that unqualified free trade as the only change in a capitalist-nationalist set-up would perpetuate.

Our solution of the problem of world organization cannot proceed as if nationalism did not exist. It exists, and exists with power. It represents at its best a certain cultural variety which enriches the world. For colonial peoples nationalism is an expression, however inadequate, of a determination to break an economic yoke imposed by imperialism. The process of education in world loyalty which is essential under socialism is consistent with the patriotism which would put each country first in the service that it renders its own citizens and the contribution that it makes to mankind. But there is no education in this sort of patriotism except as it deliberately cultivates the loyalties, and builds the organizations, which cross national and racial lines. There never will be the right sort of League of Nations until workers, farmers, and professional men build real international organizations with strength and wisdom and an understanding of national differences consistent with world interdependence.

There was a time when the vision of freedom, peace and plenty to be achieved through a federation of cooperative commonwealths was not only held to be fantastic but unnecessary. Capitalism, it was argued, could bring general prosperity; its abolition was by no means necessary for peace. That sort of argument today is connected in the public mind with Mr. Herbert Hoover's unfortunately timed remark about the American system which was to give us two cars in every garage and a chicken in every pot. (Why the ratio of two cars to one chicken I have never understood!) Today, if one hears that sort of optimism at all, it is voiced in terms of vague hope, not of confidence. A capitalist defense is mostly an attack upon socialism. In so far as that attack is not born out of ignorance, fear, and a raw rationalization of class interest, it falls under two heads: First, in the name of economics, human nature, or what have you, it is argued that a planned economy of a socialist sort cannot and will not work. Second, in the name of the dignity of the individual and democracy, and the Stars and Stripes forever, it is argued that socialism is incompatible with American liberty which depends upon the ownership of property. Socialism, say these critics, if possible at all, is possible only under a servile state.

The argument that we cannot plan successfully is based in its superficial form on a simple denial of the ability of men to manage for their own good the complicated machinery which they have invented. It is rarely accompanied by an attempt to prove that we can use modern power-driven machinery and the collectivism which it entails without plan. It is simply an assertion that the job is too difficult. It ignores, or passes over far too lightly, such partial examples of successful planning as the economic planning of the World War afforded, to say nothing of the success of the Five-Year Plan in Soviet Russia.

In particular the critics of planning are fond of proclaiming the impossibility of planning for agriculture because of the uncertainty of the weather and other conditions which make farming, they say, the world's greatest gamble. Here the critics are on fairly sound ground if they confine their remarks to a planning in terms of profit dependent on relative scarcity. Such planning will always cut its margin too fine. It will always think in terms of the profit of a great many individual farmers rather than in terms of the best use of land for the common good. Agricultural planning under socialism must put to the forefront the accumulation of reserves in order to maintain an economy of abundance against drouth and disaster. If this is done it is absurd to say that all agricultural planning must fail. A great deal is known about the proper use of soil, how much land should be restored to buffalo grass and how much to forests here in America. A great deal is known about the average amount of foodstuff necessary for a well-fed population. Under these conditions agricultural planning becomes necessary, desirable, and by no means impossible in a true commonwealth in which the predominant idea is the production and sharing of abundance.

One superficial argument against planning asserts that without the stimulus of future profit there would be no savings, no investment for new enterprises, and hence no "progress." Such a contention overlooks the fact that already we are dependent upon the initiative of the engineer, not the entrepreneur. Great corporations maintain laboratories for invention. They set aside reserves and do not trust much to private savings to provide for their future. The Steel Trust is not dependent for capital for expansion on speculation in the stock market with its stocks. Society can provide its own experimental laboratories and its own working capital at least as well as the Steel Trust or the A.T. and T.

There is a statement of the argument against the possibility of planning which goes deeper and raises some real problems. Certain orthodox economists, of whom Hayek is perhaps the ablest, assert that planned economy not only tends to produce a sort of paralysis by removing any effective consumers' choice, but also that it makes any real cost accounting impossible. In other words, that it strips us of any mechanism by which to judge the way in which the productive resources of the community may most efficiently be used. In *The Nation* (April 22, 1936), Dr. Abram Harris thus summarizes this argument. "They [the orthodox economists] maintain . . . that the whole market mechanism with which capitalist profits are connected serves properly to allocate the resources of the community through the medium of the relation between cost of production and market prices. From their argument it follows that in a social economy not simply profits but this entire mechanism is destroyed. There is no way of determining the most economic employment of labor and capital. A planned Socialist economy is therefore without administrative guidance and must ultimately fall down in hopeless confusion."

To some extent Sidney and Beatrice Webb have successfully refuted this argument in their discussion of planning in Soviet Russia and the success of the Five-Year Plan. I think they have done a rather better job at it than Dr. Harris allows, but it is true, as he points out, that the Webbs do not sufficiently take into account the position of the orthodox economists on the

Five-Year Plan in Russia. On the whole the critics admit its success, but say that it is due to the fact that it is a plan to industrialize a country insufficiently industrialized, and that when that job is done the unemployment and business cycle problems will again emerge. Dr. Harris goes on to state that what the Webbs have not done to meet this argument the economist Gourevich and others have done on the basis of a theoretical analysis of the functioning of costs and prices in the Soviet economy.

Some things are clear. There is nothing scientifically infallible about the determination of costs in our capitalist economy. The cost of producing cotton cloth as compared to the cost of producing automobiles is based on no natural laws. It is based on the historic tradition which has brought it to pass that cotton is grown by half-starved serf labor and made into cloth by underpaid textile workers. The cost accounting of the orthodox economist takes no account of the social cost of this kind of a system. Under our present capitalist economy, the increase of monopoly control, and the steady march of mass advertising certainly interfere with any scientific cost accounting resting on consumers' choice and the free working of the market. Difficulties of cost accounting under a planned economy may be great but they can scarcely be as great as the difficulties which exist today, and make cost accounting in any true sense so weak a defense against recurring crises and continuous waste.

As a general answer to those who assert, rather than prove, that planned economy requires complete loss of consumers' choice, the rationing of goods, and the conscription of workers, it may be pointed out that this would be true only if one were to conceive of the world as a beleaguered garrison with limited supplies. On the contrary, ours is a world with ever-expanding ability to produce not only necessities but luxuries. It can produce them so generously that what might be regarded as waste in a beleaguered garrison would be justified in order to make possible consumers' choice. A study of the incomes now possible in America shows that there would be a wide margin of what might be called free income over and above what is necessary for subsistence. Experts can calculate on the basis of known facts and observed tendencies the probable direction of consumers' choice. That calculation is no more likely to be equivalent to the rationing which exists among a beleaguered garrison than is the calculation of the average expectancy of life equivalent to a sentence of death to the individual at the expiration of that period. The probable trends of human demands and industrial improvements, the kinds of jobs therefore likely to be open, are matters known to other experts who can then help young men and women to find the type of work for which they are most fit. That is not conscription but guidance, far more compatible with real freedom than the haphazard whims of chance and the need to live which now confine thousands of workers to blind-alley occupations regardless of their temperaments and abilities. Again we stress the significant fact that Russia with all her industrial backwardness has not, generally speaking, conscripted workers into given tasks but has attracted them, using to that end wage differentials.

In Russia there is increasing freedom of workers' choice of jobs and consumers' choice of goods. The latter was at first impaired by a broken-down industrial plant. There is encouragement not only in Russian progress but in remembering that consumers' cooperatives give plenty of room for effective consumers' choice. Their patrons do not all have to buy corned beef one day and ham another. They make use of a price mechanism divorced from private profit. Some such mechanism may be worked out in the interest of consumers' choice under a socialist economy of abundance.

The second argument, that socialism is incompatible with civil and religious liberty, is more popular and in some statements of it weightier. The Liberty League or *Saturday Evening Post* version of it need not greatly concern us. It comes close to pure hypocrisy in the mouths of men who are not really concerned about liberty, but only about profit. Their liberty means not justice for Mooney and Billings, the share-croppers of Alabama and Arkansas, or the workers whose employers arm themselves with machine guns and poison gas. It means the right to get all you can and keep all you get. It is true in practical experience that liberty rests upon tolerance. Tolerance is not and cannot be the chief of virtues to men engaged in the tremendous enterprise of setting up a new social order. But even the tolerance of skepticism or indifference is a virtue against brutality and oppression. Historically, intolerance has often killed or wounded the thing it sought to protect. Even in a transition society the Jeffersonian principle that the state should act only to punish overt acts may be found to minister to social well-being no less than to individual liberty.

But the chief argument of those who say that socialism and liberty are incompatible is not a theory which is confined to the exigencies of the transition period. That argument has been well stated in the April issue of the *International Journal of Ethics* by H. Gomperz of Vienna: "*I think it was the tragic error of democratic socialism to think that men could be deprived of their economic independence and yet maintain independence of thought.* Loyalty to one's convictions requires an economic prop; where this is lacking the former has no permanence . . . the pillars of spiritual—more especially of religious, but also of political, liberty have everywhere been, first of all the higher and the lower aristocracy; further the burgesses, who if not actually wealthy were at least not without property; occasionally, too, here and there, the yeomen."

Before we come to the heart of this contention certain preliminary things must be said. Liberty, in the sense in which Mr.

Gomperz is considering it, has always been the possession of the comparatively few. It is, I forget who first said it, an aristocratic virtue. This will always be true unless and until it can be planted and made to flourish in the soil of economic justice and equality. For years I have been insisting to deaf ears that if and when the time comes when the masses feel that they must choose between liberty and economic security they will take economic security. Fascism in Europe expressed open scorn of liberty and fascism won. A great many men like to be told what to do. It saves them the trouble of thinking, and when the dictator's commands can be sweetened by an emotional appeal to nationalism or by a promise of bread they are doubly acceptable.

Liberty in the sense of assured justice for the individual or of Milton's "right to know, to utter, and to argue freely according to conscience" exists most imperfectly even in the bourgeois democracies of our day, as Mr. Gomperz admits. Very few there are even in America who have the economic independence which he considers necessary to independence of thought. He overlooks the fact that many workers have won through their unions a degree of security which gives them an independence of thought greater than members of the middle class display. The upper middle class despite its economic independence is not free. Its members are bound by prejudice, fear, and desire for social prestige into a herd of their own. Historically, it is some sense of security rather than private ownership of property which has furthered freedom of thought. Indeed there has been an interaction between liberty and economic security or well-being. Sometimes men have come to understand that independence of thought is necessary to the successful working of a society which may provide material security.

Moreover, the possession of great property enables the possessor not only to exploit the labor of his fellows but to corrupt their liberties. Mr. Gomperz admits that

it is not a true or desirable freedom of the press which gives a William Randolph Hearst the power to use his fortune to play upon men's passions to satisfy his own lust for power or profit. Freedom and peace are both jeopardized by a system which gives to the ambitious man of fortune such power over the press. The jeopardy is increased when the demagogue is able to buy a great deal of time on the radio and use it for mass propaganda, unchecked by hecklers or unanswered by argument.

However the socialist who believes in liberty as a necessary condition of the good life cannot be content to resort merely to the *tu quoque* argument, or in less classical language, to reply "So's your old man." The problem of liberty in human society is difficult. It will not be solved automatically by any theory. Every generation must struggle for true liberty. The conditions of it are likely to be of major concern for a long while to come. The political controversies of the future will arise largely out of the problem of the relation of the individual to society and the way to carry out in practice the noble ideal of a fellowship of free men.

This we may affirm with confidence: Socialism, by providing a wider security to men, provides a better basis for liberty. It is not animated by the ideals of the totalitarian or servile state. In a genuine socialist society industries will not be administered by political appointees of a dominant party. They will be functionally self-governed. Workers will be protected by an improved civil service and by their own industrial organizations. If, temporarily, they should lose their jobs they will not starve but will be automatically eligible to whatever provisions may be made for temporary unemployment. They will have protection against old age. They will have an income over and above what it costs them to exist which they can use in association with their fellows to support the kind of papers they like and societies in which they have confidence. There has never been a distribution of property which gave to the masses the economic security necessary to independence of thought on the same scale on which socialism can provide it. It would be a sorry outlook if liberty, civil or religious, were dependent on the right and power of the "free" man to exploit his fellows by private ownership of production goods. The contrary is true.

What is necessary for the increase of freedom in the socialist society is that it put in the forefront a conscious recognition of the value of liberty to the individual and to society. It is possible for a man to believe something intensely and yet to believe that he must justify his faith by winning conviction, not by repression. There may be a stage in social revolution when it will be necessary to deprive recalcitrant enemies of the new order of the right to sabotage it under pretext of democracy. There certainly will be a stage of the social revolution which will call for a firm hand against counter revolution. But even in the transition years, in America with our traditions, the ideal to be held up is not the ideal of dictatorship but of workers' democracy. Such workers' democracy is not psychologically or practically equivalent to the dictatorship of the proletariat. Recent events have made the very word "dictatorship" obnoxious to lovers, I shall not say of freedom, but of human decency. To accept the idea of dictatorship means to accept tyranny and oppression. The dictatorship of the proletariat in Russia was not as Communists have sometimes claimed, equivalent to workers' democracy. It was the dictatorship of a particular party. The two are not the same.

We cannot settle all the problems of freedom and cooperation for the future. We can rejoice that some of them, once socialism has triumphed, will automatically grow less difficult. No William Randolph Hearst of the future will be allowed to have a fortune of $220,000,000 which he can use to corrupt public opinion and public taste in the name of freedom of the press.

A new society may also find a way short of censorship to enforce certain standards of factual truth and to prevent the libelling not only of individuals but of races and nations. Liberty should not mean the right to foment wars by lies and slander. On this difficult question I do not dogmatize. Problems of liberty cannot be solved offhand by a formula.

They can be solved if we remember that liberty is a necessity of the good life, that without it society will stagnate and men will be less than men. To hold high the torch of freedom is essential to defense against the brutality and the obscurantism of a Mussolini or a Hitler. Socialism will be untrue to itself if ever it forgets that its purpose is not merely to bring prosperity and peace, but freedom to mankind.

7. THE FAIR DEAL, 1949[1]
By HARRY S. TRUMAN

EDITORS' NOTE.—The Republican party's prospects of a return to power in 1948 seemed very bright to Republican candidate Dewey and the pollsters. Harry S. Truman (1884——), Democratic senator from Missouri (1935–45), Vice-President of the United States (January–April, 1945), and President

since the death of Franklin D. Roosevelt on April 12, 1945, thought otherwise. His surprise victory by means of a hard campaign he interpreted as a mandate for a new postwar version of the Roosevelt program. The program with which he responded—his "Fair Deal" —he outlined to the new Congress in the following message of January, 1949.

1. *Congressional Record*, XCV (January 20, 1949), 490–92.

Mr. Vice President, Mr. Chief Justice, and fellow citizens, I accept with humility the honor which the American people have conferred upon me. I accept it with a resolve to do all that I can for the welfare of this Nation and for the peace of the world.

In performing the duties of my office, I need the help and prayers of every one of you. I ask for your encouragement and for your support. The tasks we face are difficult. We can accomplish them only if we work together.

Each period of our national history has had its special challenges. Those that confront us now are as momentous as any in the past. Today marks the beginning not only of a new administration, but of a period that will be eventful, perhaps decisive, for us and for the world.

It may be our lot to experience, and in a large measure bring about, a major turning point in the long history of the human race. The first half of this century has been marked by unprecedented and brutal attacks on the rights of man, and by the two most frightful wars in history. The supreme need of our time is for men to learn to live together in peace and harmony.

The peoples of the earth face the future with grave uncertainty, composed almost equally of great hopes and great fears. In this time of doubt, they look to the United States as never before for good will, strength, and wise leadership.

It is fitting, therefore, that we take this occasion to proclaim to the world the essential principles of the faith by which we live, and to declare our aims to all peoples.

The American people stand firm in the faith which has inspired this Nation from the beginning. We believe that all men have a right to equal justice under law and equal opportunity to share in the common good. We believe that all men have the right to freedom of thought and expression. We believe that all men are created equal because they are created in the image of God.

From this faith we will not be moved.

The American people desire, and are determined to work for, a world in which all nations and all peoples are free to govern themselves as they see fit and to achieve a decent and satisfying life. Above all else, our people desire, and are determined to work for, peace on earth—a just and lasting peace—based on genuine agreement freely arrived at by equals.

In the pursuit of these aims, the United States and other like-minded nations find themselves directly opposed by a regime with contrary aims and a totally different concept of life.

That regime adheres to a false philosophy which purports to offer freedom, security, and greater opportunity to mankind. Misled by that philosophy, many peoples have sacrificed their liberties only to learn to their sorrow that deceit and mockery, poverty and tyranny, are their reward.

That false philosophy is communism.

Communism is based on the belief that man is so weak and inadequate that he is unable to govern himself, and therefore requires the rule of strong masters.

Democracy is based on the conviction that man has the moral and intellectual capacity, as well as the inalienable right, to govern himself with reason and justice.

Communism subjects the individual to arrest without lawful cause, punishment without trial, and forced labor as a chattel of the state. It decrees what information he shall receive, what art he shall produce, what leaders he shall follow, and what thoughts he shall think.

Democracy maintains that government is established for the benefit of the individual, and is charged with the responsibility of protecting the rights of the individual and his freedom in the exercise of his abilities.

Communism maintains that social wrongs can be corrected only by violence.

Democracy has proved that social justice can be achieved through peaceful change.

Communism holds that the world is so

widely divided into opposing classes that war is inevitable.

Democracy holds that free nations can settle differences justly and maintain a lasting peace.

The differences between communism and democracy do not concern the United States alone. People everywhere are coming to realize that what is involved is material well-being, human dignity, and the right to believe in and worship God.

I state these differences, not to draw issues of belief as such, but because the actions resulting from the Communist philosophy are a threat to the efforts of free nations to bring about world recovery and lasting peace.

Since the end of hostilities, the United States has invested its substance and its energy in a great constructive effort to restore peace, stability, and freedom to the world.

We have sought no territory; we have imposed our will on none. We have asked for no privileges we would not extend to others.

We have constantly and vigorously supported the United Nations and related agencies as a means of applying democratic principles to international relations. We have consistently advocated and relied upon peaceful settlement of disputes among nations.

We have made every effort to secure agreement on effective international control of our most powerful weapon, and we have worked steadily for the limitation and control of all armaments.

We have encouraged, by precept and example, the expansion of world trade on a sound and a fair basis.

Almost a year ago, in company with sixteen free nations of Europe, we launched the greatest cooperative economic program in history. The purpose of that unprecedented effort is to invigorate and strengthen democracy in Europe, so that the free people of that continent can resume their rightful place in the forefront of civilization and can contribute once

more to the security and welfare of the world.

Our efforts have brought new hope to all mankind. We have beaten back despair and defeatism. We have saved a number of countries from losing their liberty. Hundreds of millions of people all over the world now agree with us that we need not have war—that we can have peace.

The initiative is ours.

We are moving on with other nations to build an even stronger structure of international order and justice. We shall have as our partners countries which, no longer solely concerned with the problem of national survival, are now working to improve the standards of living of all their people. We are ready to undertake new projects to strengthen a free world.

In the coming years, our program for peace and freedom will emphasize four major courses of action.

First, we will continue to give unfaltering support to the United Nations and related agencies, and we will continue to search for ways to strengthen their authority and increase their effectiveness. We believe that the United Nations will be strengthened by the new nations which are being formed in lands now advancing toward self-government under democratic principles.

Second, we will continue our programs for world economic recovery.

This means, first of all, that we must keep our full weight behind the European recovery program. We are confident of the success of this major venture in world recovery. We believe that our partners in this effort will achieve the status of self-supporting nations once again.

In addition, we must carry out our plans for reducing the barriers to world trade and increasing its volume. Economic recovery and peace itself depend on increased world trade.

Third, we will strengthen freedom-loving nations against the dangers of aggression.

We are working out with a number of

countries a joint agreement designed to strengthen the security of the North Atlantic area. Such an agreement would take the form of a collective defense arrangement within the terms of the United Nations Charter.

We have already established such a defense pact for the Western Hemisphere by the Treaty of Rio de Janeiro.

The primary purpose of these agreements is to provide unmistakable proof of the joint determination of the free countries to resist armed attack from any quarter. Every country participating in these arrangements must contribute all it can to the common defense.

If we can make it sufficiently clear, in advance, that any armed attack affecting our national security will be met with overwhelming force, the armed attack may never occur.

I hope soon to send to the Senate a treaty respecting the North Atlantic security plan.

In addition, we will provide military advice and equipment to free nations which will cooperate with us in the maintenance of peace and security.

Fourth, we must embark on a bold new program for making the benefits of our scientific advances and industrial progress available for the improvement and growth of underdeveloped areas.

More than half the people of the world are living in conditions approaching misery. Their food is inadequate. They are victims of disease. Their economic life is primitive and stagnant. Their poverty is a handicap and a threat both to them and to more prosperous areas.

For the first time in history, humanity possesses the knowledge and skill to relieve the suffering of these people.

The United States is preeminent among the nations in the development of industrial and scientific techniques. The material resources which we can afford to use for the assistance of other peoples are limited. But our imponderable resources in technical knowledge are constantly growing and are inexhaustible.

I believe that we should make available to peace-loving peoples the benefits of our store of technical knowledge in order to help them realize their aspirations for a better life. And, in cooperation with other nations, we should foster capital investment in areas needing development.

Our aim should be to help the free peoples of the world, through their own efforts, to produce more food, more clothing, more materials for housing, and more mechanical power to lighten their burdens.

We invite other countries to pool their technological resources in this undertaking. Their contributions will be warmly welcomed. This should be a cooperative enterprise in which all nations work together through the United Nations and its specialized agencies whenever practicable. It must be a world-wide effort for the achievement of peace, plenty, and freedom.

With the cooperation of business, private capital, agriculture, and labor in this country, this program can greatly increase the industrial activity in other nations and can raise substantially their standards of living.

Such new economic developments must be devised and controlled to benefit the peoples of the areas in which they are established. Guaranties to the investor must be balanced by guaranties in the interest of the people whose resources and whose labor go into these developments.

The old imperialism—exploitation for foreign profit—has no place in our plans. What we envisage is a program of development based on the concepts of democratic fair-dealing.

All countries, including our own, will greatly benefit from a constructive program for the better use of the world's human and natural resources. Experience shows that our commerce with other countries expands as they progress industrially and economically.

Greater production is the key to

prosperity and peace. And the key to greater production is a wider and more vigorous application of modern scientific and technical knowledge.

Only by helping the least fortunate of its members to help themselves can the human family achieve the decent, satisfying life that is the right of all people.

Democracy alone can supply the vitalizing force to stir the peoples of the world into triumphant action, not only against their human oppressors, but also against their ancient enemies—hunger, misery, and despair.

On the basis of these four major courses of action we hope to help create the conditions that will lead eventually to personal freedom and happiness for all mankind.

If we are to be successful in carrying out these policies, it is clear that we must have continued prosperity in this country and we must keep ourselves strong.

Slowly but surely we are weaving a world fabric of international security and growing prosperity.

We are aided by all who wish to live in freedom from fear—even by those who live today in fear under their own governments.

We are aided by all who want relief from the lies of propaganda—who desire truth and sincerity.

We are aided by all who desire self-government and a voice in deciding their own affairs.

We are aided by all who long for economic security—for the security and abundance that men in free societies can enjoy.

We are aided by all who desire freedom of speech, freedom of religion, and freedom to live their own lives for useful ends.

Our allies are the millions who hunger and thirst after righteousness.

In due time, as our stability becomes manifest, as more and more nations come to know the benefits of democracy and to participate in growing abundance, I believe that those countries which now oppose us will abandon their delusions and join with the free nations of the world in a just settlement of international differences.

Events have brought our American democracy to new influence and new responsibilities. They will test our courage, our devotion to duty, and our concept of liberty.

But I say to all men, what we have achieved in liberty, we will surpass in greater liberty.

Steadfast in our faith in the Almighty, we will advance toward a world where man's freedom is secure.

To that end we will devote our strength, our resources, and our firmness of resolve. With God's help, the future of mankind will be assured in a world of justice, harmony, and peace.

8. THE REPUBLIC PARTY[1]

By ROBERT A. TAFT

EDITORS' NOTE.—The fifth consecutive Republican defeat in 1948 caused many loyal followers of the "Grand Old Party" to ask: Was the Republican party through, as Democrats were prone to suggest? Had it failed because it adhered to its historic principles or

because it lacked principles capable of gaining the support of the American public? An answer is provided by Robert A. Taft (1889——), son of former President William H. Taft, Republican senator from Ohio since 1939, and Republican leader in the Senate, who wrote the following reaffirmation of faith in the principles of the Republican party.

1. Robert A. Taft, "The Republican Party," *Fortune*, April, 1949, pp. 108–10, 112, 114, 116–18. Reprinted by special permission of the editors; copyright Time, Incorporated.

Some Republicans are discouraged to-day, because for five successive elections the Republican party has met defeat. Yet it lost by very narrow margins in 1940, 1944, and 1948. Nearly half of the voters voted for it in the recent election. And its organization is strong in many states throughout the nation. It is therefore short-sighted and cowardly to give way to despair. Political parties have a strong will to live. Indeed, the only parties that have died are those that have forgotten or abandoned the principles on which they were founded.

A party can live only if it represents a great principle or a set of great principles. The two-party system is based on the theory that a large number of men who think differently on many subjects unite in the belief that certain principles are vital to the welfare of their country, and that differences on less important questions must be reconciled or forgotten in the common effort to secure those basic principles. A political party is not just an organization in which men of completely different points of view join because their parents or their friends belong to that party, or because they became members through youthful and forgotten prejudices.

No one who has been in Congress during the past ten years can doubt that the Republican party is a party of principles. Moreover, I believe that there is basic agreement among Republicans concerning these principles, even though there are wide differences of opinion on the application of them to the complex problems of our modern world. The principles of a great party are not made by its leaders, nor by the National Committee, nor by Congress itself, but by the great bulk of the party members throughout the country. They are interpreted by the votes cast in Congress; Senators and Congressmen vote the way they do because they know they are reflecting the philosophy of their constituents, and because they are imbued with the same philosophy themselves. It is Congress that is forced to apply, by actual voting, the principles of the party to particular measures, and so the record made by Congress becomes the practical expression of the philosophy of the party. If the party does not control the executive, it must run on the record made by Congress, plus the promises made at a national convention covering those measures on which Congress has not yet acted.

The defeats of the Republican party have not been due to its principles, but to its failure to present those principles effectively to the people. They are not principles that interpret themselves easily into higher prices for the farmer, higher wages for the workingman, more profits for the businessman, and government handouts from the cradle to the grave. The enemies of the party have been clever, particularly in their conversion to New Deal philosophy of columnists, editors, commentators, and other writers who have an influence on public opinion. They have obscured and confused American thinking on the very basic principles which this nation was founded to secure. They have convinced many that there are no principles involved in the position of the two parties; from which the only conclusion can be that the party making the greatest promises must receive popular approval. In the general state of public opinion, I believe it is remarkable that the Republican party has adhered to its principles as it has. Its life depends on that adherence.

The Republican party will continue to live and will take over the administration of the government if it dedicates itself again to the principles for which it was founded, and if it presents those principles to the people in the most forceful and effective manner, not only in elections but at all times during the next four years.

I. HUMAN LIBERTY

What is the Republican philosophy? First, and before all, it is the same philosophy of human liberty that created the United States of America. Every American today still pays lip service to the term "liberty." But he does not feel it as he did for a hundred years, when the idea of liberty inspired all Americans and they boasted of it until it became tiresome to every visiting foreigner. The examples of America and of France spread the idea throughout the world, and the philosophy of free government was accepted in nearly all sections of the globe, even where the thing itself did not really exist. But today many Americans and most people throughout the world have forgotten what it means. The limitations on liberty have grown until in many totalitarian states the substance of liberty has completely disappeared. The totalitarian theory that government must plan and direct and control dominates the thinking of today throughout the world, and has made great headway here in the U.S. without a realization of the fact that it means the end of individual liberty.

What is liberty? It is freedom of speech and of the press, as the President said in his inaugural—but it is much more. It is the freedom of the individual to choose his own work and his life occupation, to spend his earnings as he desires to spend them, to choose the place where he desires to live, to take the job that fits him whether some union official is willing that he get it or not. It is the freedom of the local community to work out its own salvation when it has the power to do so. It is the freedom of cities, of counties, of school districts; the freedom to educate one's own children as one thinks best. It is the freedom of thought and experiment in academic institutions. It is the freedom of men in industry to run their businesses as they think best so long as they do not interfere with the rights of others to do the same. Certainly, there are limitations that must be imposed by the state to protect the liberty of others, more and more as our economy becomes complex. But a party that believes in liberty will impose such limitations only to the extent that they are absolutely necessary.

As we look back through history, we see brief periods in which liberty has pre-vailed, but in the major part of historical time it has been suppressed by emperors and kings, by oligarchies, by plutocracies, by so-called democracies and proletarian majorities. It is hard to gain and easy to lose—unless it is kept alive by an aggressive determination that it shall not perish from the earth. Today the battle between liberty and totalitarian government permeates every problem of life. It lies at the base of our battle with Fascism and Naziism and Communism. The American people believe in liberty, but the totalitarian creed we face abroad has insinuated itself into the philosophy of many of our labor unions and of the Democratic party. If it prevails it must ultimately destroy liberty here at home.

It is tragic that our people in recent elections have tended to support the theory that the government should be the source of all planning, of all control, and of bread and circuses for the multitude. It is tragic, because at this very moment we see the magnificent success of a system of liberty in the U.S. as contrasted with the comparative poverty and dissatisfaction of many foreign nations. Liberty has succeeded in the U.S. in developing original thinking, original methods, and new ideas. It has succeeded in giving a wide distribution of property and income to our people. It has succeeded in building up a tremendous production of material things and a standard of living higher than has ever been seen before in the history of the world. A man from Mars who studied the world today would of necessity come to the conclusion that only the free can solve the problems of production.

There are many other aims besides liberty to be sought by political policy and party principle, but every policy must be justified either as an affirmative policy to secure liberty or as a policy of human progress making no sacrifice to the god of the totalitarian state.

There may be many differences among Republicans as to the application of the principle of liberty to different situations.

I can only explain how my belief in the vital need of liberty has led me to certain conclusions on the issues now before Congress. In my opinion the President's program, if enacted in full, would destroy great areas of freedom without even accomplishing his stated purposes. Economic freedom would be destroyed by price control, wage control, allocation control, rationing, and government operation of business as suggested in the new controlled-economy bill. So-called health insurance would socialize and nationalize medical service and the medical profession and bring the daily life of every family under the supervision of a government bureau. The tremendous burden of taxation proposed would reduce the freedom of the people, because it takes from them the right to spend the money they have earned by the sweat of their brows and spends it for something that the government thinks is good for them, whether they want it or not. Universal compulsory military training would take from a boy and his family the right to choose his own education and occupation and would impose a year of training and indoctrination determined by so-called experts in Washington.

We have many alternative programs to accomplish some of the purposes sought in this legislation, but in its present form it utterly disregards the whole principle of liberty.

2. HIGHER STANDARDS OF LIVING

Every party, of course, believes in the maintenance of full production, full employment, and a higher standard of living for all the people, and the Republican party is no exception. In fact, in its full-dinner-pail campaign in 1900 it not only made that the issue, but it convinced the workingman that prosperity could be achieved only by sound fiscal principles. In recent years the American people, or perhaps only the politicians, have almost forgotten the essential principles necessary for character and happiness in their search for more material welfare. The ideal of prosperity and material welfare is not peculiar to liberty or a free state—in fact, every dictator claims that he can provide it more effectively than a free government, and maintains his power to some extent by government stimulation of consumer welfare. Nevertheless, a reasonable prosperity is essential if the people are to enjoy the advantages of liberty. Prevention of hardship and poverty is necessary, because those who suffer them have no real freedom to determine their own lives.

Fortunately for the cause of liberty, liberty itself has constituted the most active agent in bringing about increased prosperity. It is unquestionably owing to our free economy that we have become the most productive country in the world, to which all other countries look for assistance and support. We have come where we are because the American has still the right to keep the proceeds of his efforts. There has been a constant incentive to redouble those efforts because of the reward given in material welfare. The Socialists overlook the tremendous importance of that incentive—the fact that most men do not like to work unless there is something to be gained. Lethargy has been the greatest enemy of progress in many sections of the world.

We are concerned that the government keep the economic machine running at a high rate of speed with as little friction and intermission as possible. We believe this can be brought about by sound fiscal policies, by balancing the budget, by a sound currency and proper control of credit. We believe in incentive rewards for workingmen for good work done, such as those our system gives to the man who risks his time and money in new enterprise. To this end government should keep competition alive and prevent the destruction of freedom; it should not kill incentive. On these grounds, I am opposed to price and wage control; to the prohibition of strikes even if collective bargaining has failed; to allocation controls; and, in general, to all attempts to substitute government planning for the normal forces of competition.

To this end also I favor lower government expenses, a lower burden to taxation on the economic machine to which we look for the production of taxes themselves. Already taxation is taking more than 25 per cent of our national income. Already it is discouraging the development of private industry in some fields. Already the choking effect of the tax burden on productive activity is discouraging the very energy that produces the taxes; and once a buyers' market prevents the passing on of so much of the tax burden to the consumer, the situation will be infinitely worse.

I was in Europe in December. There I observed that every European country is hamstrung by government controls, by taxation, by black markets, by the planners who forget human nature. Every country with controls is looking to the U.S. to share some part of the products of our liberty with those to whom liberty is denied.

3. TO PREVENT HARDSHIP AND POVERTY

We believe that government has the obligation to promote better education, better health, better housing, better security for our people, and equality of opportunity. Equality of opportunity for the children is an essential element of true liberty. These tasks are primarily the job of our states and local governments, and while federal aid is often necessary in order that they may be properly done, particularly in the poorer states, there should be no federal control or concentration of power in Washington. I believe the American people are convinced that with the tremendous productivity of our free country we can prevent extreme hardship and poverty in the U.S. today, that we can maintain a minimum floor under education, health, housing, and food. We have recognized that obligation in the past, but the job has not been systematically done. With federal aid it can be done, but there are plenty of pitfalls and dangers to liberty in the *way* in which it is done.

There are many respects in which we can promote better health and welfare for the whole population, but our efforts should not include direct or indirect subsidy to the bulk of the people or giving men something for nothing, except where we do face problems of extreme hardship. Nothing can so quickly kill the incentive and reduce the production of the people as to encourage them to look to government as their benefactor and supporter.

Aid to those in the lowest income class is necessary. But a policy of government handouts to all would impose an intolerable tax burden, would sap the energy and liberty of the people, and would destroy the American character. No people as a whole can get something for nothing. They can only be fooled into such a hope. The idea that people can get their medical care from the government without paying even a greater price than they pay today is fantastic. To the extent that we do support those at the lowest end of the income field by aid or subsidy, they can only be supported by the other four-fifths of the population; and the burden must not be so great as to discourage that four-fifths from the magnificent job they are doing today.

I favor federal aid to the states and local governments to enable them to extend medical care to all those who are unable to pay for it, but I am strenuously opposed to the system of socialized and nationalized medicine outlined in the Murray-Wagner-Dingell bill. Organized charity or free government welfare service to the whole population can destroy the freedom and also the character of the people to whom it is extended. It can increase the power of the central government in Washington until Washington bureaus govern the daily lives of every family in the U.S. Incentive and initiative can be paralyzed. We will be ruled by people who take no personal risks and create no jobs. The people will be taxed without realizing it, through a deduction from payroll, and perhaps get some part of those taxes back in the form of government services and activity, which they may or may not want. There is real danger to liberty in the welfare state.

As in the case of federal aid to states for medical care, I believe that federal aid should be extended to enable local communities to provide decent public housing for those unable to pay the rents charged for privately owned homes of decent character. I favor the extension of federal aid to states, particularly the poorer states, so that they may provide adequate primary and secondary education for children, no matter how poor the state or community in which they live. I favor the extension of the old-age pension plan to all those employees not now included. And there are other fields of social welfare in which the federal government can be of assistance if the proper safeguards are observed. But I cannot emphasize too strongly that these programs must be devised in such a way that they do not substitute a welfare state for a free government and a free people.

4. EQUAL JUSTICE UNDER LAW

Equal justice under law is a necessary corollary to liberty, for there can be no liberty if the life and property of men are subject to the arbitrary will of others.

Those who would destroy freedom in any country make the courts a tool of the government, as they are in Russia. Modern totalitarian government cannot admit the right of any court to balk its policies. Of course the Communists go further. They do not admit that such a thing as real justice can exist, or that any tribunal can be truly impartial or decide cases on their merits. My objection to the Nürnberg trials was that, while clothed with the forms of justice, they were in fact an instrument of government policy, determined months before at Tehran and Yalta. Those who wrote the original draft of the United Nations Charter at Dumbarton Oaks completely forgot the ideal of justice, and even today the charter is subject to serious criticism because it gives the Security Council power to act on grounds of expediency unrestrained by justice. Fortunately, when the issue is clearly presented the American people feel deeply that we must have free and impartial courts. They reacted violently to the New Deal attempt to swamp the Supreme Court. We must oppose the powerful forces that today are still attempting to take from the courts the power to interpret the Constitution.

The New Deal and the present Administration still seek the solution of every problem by the creation of boards and commissions, with power to make regulations having the force of law, with power to file prosecutions, try the alleged culprits and condemn them, practically without recourse to the courts. Of course, in our complicated modern system there must be some control by administrative law, as in the fields of radio and air traffic, but it should be imposed in such a way as to preserve the maximum amount of freedom for those regulated; and it should subject the administrative boards to definite principles laid down by Congress on which an appeal can be taken to the courts.

Perhaps the greatest miscarriages of justice that have ever occurred in the U.S. occurred under the National Labor Relations Board in interpreting the Wagner Act. Yet today President Truman is trying to get Congress to restore the one-sided and unrestrained power of that board. The Republican party should stand today, as it has stood in the past, for a rule of law instead of the rule of arbitrary men.

5. EQUALITY AND NO SPECIAL PRIVILEGE

In our defense of liberty, while today the primary threat is from totalitarian government seeking arbitrary power, we are equally determined to protect the individual from the oppression of private privilege and private power.

The Republican party enacted the Sherman Act to prevent the economic power of monopoly. People often say that it is ineffective. My judgment is that it has an effect on all business thinking in the U.S., and has done more to maintain freedom in the economic field than any other measure ever enacted. The contrast today between conditions here and those brought about in Europe by the cartel system is striking and conclusive.

On the other hand, we have favored the increase of the minimum wage to protect the unorganized worker against the oppression of employers unrestrained by the proper power of labor unions.

Liberty may be ended by the tyranny of a majority of the people as well as by the tyranny of special groups. We are concerned that minorities shall receive fair treatment, the same rights to vote, to work, and to live their own lives as the majority. We are concerned that the economic system shall not work to the unfair disadvantage of any group, either large or small, that the small businessman shall be able to prosper if he deserves it, that the general level of farm prices and farmers' income be not out of line with the level of industrial prices, that taxation fall with substantial equality on all the people in accordance with their ability to pay. Therefore, the Republican Eightieth Congress enacted last year a bill directing the government to maintain the price of farm products in reasonable relation to other prices—the concept of parity. We enacted a fair tax-reduction bill removing seven million of the lowest-income taxpayers from the income-tax rolls. And the Republicans have sought repeatedly to enact anti-poll-tax and anti-lynching laws.

In all this kind of legislation, from the Sherman Act to the anti-lynching laws, the exact form of the statute must be such as to infringe as little as possible on the freedom of the individual and the local community. We should inject federal power only where it is absolutely necessary and we should subject any authorized action to review by impartial courts.

PEACE

Finally, the Republican party believes that peace must be the ultimate aim of our foreign policy and that no object is more important, except the liberty of this nation itself. The wars into which we have been plunged are evidence of the failure of our foreign policy, not of its success. There can be no greater tragedy than war, even for the victorious nation. No nation can really win a modern war. While war is justified only as a means of preserving liberty, it is likely to destroy the very liberty it is designed to preserve by making necessary restrictions on that liberty at home, which may be permanently fastened on the people. Horrible as have been the death and destruction caused by war in the past, they will be still worse in the future.

Of course the affairs of different nations have become so interwoven that it is not easy to keep our mind on the ultimate purposes of foreign policy, liberty, and peace. Unquestionably, we must join with other nations in any international organization that can effectively keep the peace. We have done so in the United Nations. Because the United Nations organization itself is defective, and because of the attitude of Russia, we are justified in joining other groups with a more limited membership to keep the peace within the area of their jurisdiction.

In order to protect our liberty and also to discourage others from attacking us, we have to maintain armed forces completely adequate for defense. Personally, I think in modern times defense is adequate only if we have an Air Force able to dominate the air over this country and for quite a long distance beyond our boundaries. But here again, the very instrument necessary to maintain liberty must not be one that can itself destroy liberty. Obviously, if we want absolutely airtight protection, our military establishment would cost from $50 billion to $100 billion a year; but this would end liberty at home and prevent the very improvement of civilian standards of living that should be the result of liberty. The size of our armed forces must be a question for decision by civilians representing the entire people and must be based on a calculated risk.

Under the present-day conditions, I believe we should continue our assistance to many nations to restore their economies from the disruption arising from the war, because that disruption leads to the spread of Communism and encourages Russia to end the peace and threaten the freedom of America. We can well interest ourselves in giving economic assistance to undeveloped areas of the world to relieve extreme human misery, which may lead to war. But we must realize first that in the long run a country can maintain only that standard of living justified by its own production and cannot live on the bounty of another nation. Our aid should be confined to special fields where it can clearly be of exceptional value to the country receiving the aid. If we promise a millennium we cannot deliver, if we make other people think that they can get something for nothing, our failure will create resentment and do more harm to peace than good.

Furthermore, let us not slip quietly into using our economic power to assume political power. We have to make certain conditions on any aid that we give, and yet such conditions are soon likely to be resented and involve us in disputes that constitute a threat to peace. It is easy to slip into an attitude of imperialism and to entertain the idea that we know what is good for other people better than they know themselves. From there, it is an easy step to the point where war becomes an instrument of public policy rather than the last resort to maintain our own liberty.

CONCLUSION

I have tried to outline what I conceive to be the basic principles of the Republican party—the maintenance of liberty, equal justice under law, equality without special privilege, and the preservation of peace. There was a time when these were the principles of all American parties, while they differed on less consequential matters. Today the Democratic party gives lip service to these principles, but its policies are certain to destroy them.

The Republican party has not done a very good job of explaining its principles or the principles of American history and government. They are the principles in which the great majority of the American people still believe today. When their liberties have been directly affected by regulation, as were those of the farmers in 1938 and the housewives in 1946, they have risen up with indignation against the party of government controls. But they have not always realized the steady reduction of liberty that is resulting from the steady advance of totalitarian methods and concepts propounded by the Democrats; nor do they yet realize the threat contained in the program that is now presented by the Democratic party. That program, if fulfilled, would soon bring a federal-tax burden of $60 billion, subject all business to detailed controls, extend the federal welfare bureaus into every home, and extend actual government operation of business into the larger industries. It would subject America to a totalitarian government. The Republican party will survive and prevail, because it is in fact the Party of American Principles.

479

SECTION C. GOVERNMENT POLICY FOR BUSINESS

1. THE MODERN CORPORATION[1]

By Gardiner C. Means

EDITORS' NOTE.—As the American economy turned from the "prosperous twenties" to the "depressed thirties," A. A. Berle, Jr. (1895———), and Gardiner C. Means (1896———), professor of corporate law and economist, respectively, in Columbia University, were doing research on Thorstein Veblen's view that a new controlling class was emerging as a result of the growth of modern corporate enterprise. In 1932 Berle and Means published the results of their empirical findings in *The Modern Corporation and Private Property*, a volume which became one of the most widely discussed books of the thirties on economic matters. That its ideas would have a distinct influence on governmental policy was assured when both authors, shortly after its publication, became influential advisers to Franklin D. Roosevelt—Berle as a member of the so-called "Brain Trust" and Means as an economic adviser to the administration in various capacities. The following article by Gardiner C. Means, which was published in 1931, was a presentation of the essential argument of *The Modern Corporation and Private Property*. The Statistical Appendix (No. 34) should prove useful in understanding this article.

The ownership of industrial wealth and the control over that wealth are coming to lie less and less in the same hands. Through the mechanism of the corporation, control over industrial wealth can be and is being exercised with a modicum of ownership interest. Conceivably it can be exercised without any such interest. Ownership of wealth without appreciable control, and control of wealth without appreciable ownership, appear to be the logical outcome of present corporate development.

This separation of function suggests that "control" as something apart from ownership on the one hand and from management on the other should be introduced as a major economic concept. It is the purpose of this article, first, to examine the nature of "control," giving some measure of definition to the concept, second, to examine various types of control situations and the extent to which they involve a separation of ownership and control, and third, to present evidence tending to indicate the degree to which ownership and control have become separated in American corporations.

THE CONCEPT "CONTROL"

In discussing problems of enterprise, the economist has distinguished between two groups of individuals, owners and managers, and it is necessary to examine

1. Gardiner C. Means, "The Separation of Ownership and Control in American Industry," *Quarterly Journal of Economics*, XLVI (November, 1931), 68–77, 80–84, 86–87, 94. Reprinted by permission of the *Quarterly Journal of Economics*.

the functions of these groups before seeking to develop the concept "control." The owners appear to have been distinguished primarily by the fact that they were *in a position* both to manage an enterprise or delegate its management and to receive any profits or benefits which might accrue. The managers on the other hand *operated* an enterprise, presumably in the interests of the owners. The difference between ownership and management is thus in part one between position and action. An owner who remained completely quiescent towards his enterprise would nevertheless remain an owner. His title is not applied because he acts or is expected to act. Indeed, when the owner acts, as for instance in hiring a manager or giving him directions, to that extent the owner manages his own enterprise. His acts with respect to it are acts of management. On the other hand, it is difficult to think of applying the title "manager" to an individual who had been entirely quiescent. It is because he acts or is expected to act that he receives his name.

When the customary idea of ownership is further examined it becomes apparent that it involves both a set of legal and factual *interests* in the enterprise and a set of legal and factual *powers* over the enterprise. These two functions, interest and power, have not customarily been distinguished in discussions of ownership since they have usually been exercised by the same persons. There is no necessity, however, that they should lie in the same hands. A legal minor may have almost no power over a business of which he is the owner and in which he has very important interests. At the same time his guardian may have very great powers over the business with relatively few interests therein. It is customary to say that the minor owns the enterprise and that the guardian controls it. The essential characteristic of ownership appears, therefore, to consist of having interests in an enterprise while the essential characteristic of control consists of having powers over the enterprise. The

two functions, even when combined in the hands of a single individual, are as essentially separate functions as either is from management.

With the development of the modern corporation, interests and powers have come to be attached to separate groups and the term "ownership" has in practice been applied to the group with interests in the enterprise whether or not that group has powers over it. The group with powers may be termed "the control." Instead, therefore, of discussing in the traditional manner, the two functions, ownership and management, we should use three distinct concepts: ownership or interest, control or power, and management or action. . . .

CORPORATE CONTROL

In examining the separation of ownership and control in the modern corporation, it is apparent that we are dealing with a separation of the major powers over an enterprise from the major interests therein. One group of individuals, the owners, hold the major interests while a second group, no longer identical with the first, holds the major powers. Since the latter are usually made effective through the corporate management and in particular through the board of directors, "control" may be said for practical purposes to lie in the hands of the individual or group who have the actual power to select the board of directors (or its majority), either by mobilizing the legal right to choose them —"controlling" a majority of the votes directly or through some legal device—or by exerting pressure which influences their choice. Occasionally the major elements of control are made effective not through the selection of directors, but through dictation to the management, as where a bank determines the policy of a corporation seriously indebted to it. In most cases, however, if one can determine who does actually have the power to select the directors, one has located the group of individuals who for practical purposes may be regarded as "the control."

When control is thus defined a wide variety of kinds and conditions of control situations can be found—forms derived wholly or in part from ownership, forms which depend on legal devices, and forms which are extra-legal in character.

Five major types can be distinguished, tho no sharp dividing line separates type from type. These include (1) control through almost complete ownership, (2) majority control, (3) control through a legal device without majority ownership, (4) minority control, and (5) management control. Of these, the first three are forms of control resting on a legal base and revolve about the right to vote a majority of the voting stock. The last two, minority and management control, are extra-legal, resting on a factual rather than a legal base.

1. *Control through almost complete ownership.*—The first of these is found in what may be properly called the private corporation in which a single individual or small group of associates own all or practically all the outstanding stock. They are presumably in a position of control, not only having the legal powers of ownership, but also being in a position to make use of them and, in particular, being in a position to elect and dominate the management. Of this type is the Ford Motor Company, completely owned by Henry Ford and his family, with Mr. Ford able to exercise the full functions of ownership, control and ultimate management. In such an enterprise, ownership and control are combined in the same hands.

2. *Majority control.*—Majority control, the first step in the separation of ownership and control, involves ownership of a majority of the outstanding stock. In the case of a simple corporate structure, the ownership of a majority of the stock by a single individual or small group gives to this group virtually all the legal powers of control which would be held by a sole owner of the enterprise and in particular the power to select the board of directors. Certain powers of control such as the power to amend the charter or to discontinue the enterprise may require more than a simple majority vote and to that extent the majority exercises less control than a sole owner. Furthermore, the powers of control may be to a slight extent curbed by the existence of a compact minority which is ready to question the policy or acts of the majority both directly, at stockholders' meetings, and in the courts. Where all stock except that held by the majority interest is widely scattered, on the other hand, majority ownership (in the absence of a "legal device") means undiminished actual control. At the same time, the concentrating of control in the hands of a majority means that the minority have lost most of the powers of control over the enterprise of which they are part owners. For them, at least, the separation of ownership and control is well nigh complete, tho for the majority the two functions are combined.

Among the largest corporations, however, the separation of ownership and control has passed far beyond the separation represented in majority control. In a truly large corporation, the investment necessary for majority ownership is so considerable as to make such control extremely expensive. Among such companies majority control is conspicuous more by its absence than by its presence. More often control is maintained with a relatively small proportion of ownership.

3. *Control through legal device.*—In the effort to maintain control of a corporation without ownership of a majority of its stock, various legal devices have been developed. Of these, the most important among the very large companies is the device of "pyramiding." This involves the owning of a majority of the stock of one corporation which in turn holds a majority of the stock of another—a process which can be repeated a number of times. An interest equal to slightly more than a quarter or an eighth or a sixteenth or an even smaller proportion of the ultimate property to be controlled is by this method

legally entrenched. By issuing bonds and non-voting preferred stock of the intermediate companies the process can be accelerated. By the introduction of two or three intermediate companies, each of which is legally controlled through ownership of a majority of its stock by the company higher in the series, complete legal control of a large operating company can be maintained by an ownership interest equal to a fraction of one per cent of the property controlled. The owner of a majority of the stock of the company at the apex of a pyramid can have almost as complete control of the entire property as a sole owner, even tho his ownership interest is a small fraction of the whole. . . .

A second legal device for retaining control with a small investment is the use of non-voting stock. This is a comparatively new device, but one which has received so much comment as to be thoroughly familiar. It consists in so arranging the rights attached to different classes of stock that most of the stock is disfranchised, and only a very small class, or a class representing a very small investment, is permitted to vote. Ownership of just over half of this privileged class is sufficient to give legal control and virtually all the powers of majority ownership. For many years it has been possible in certain states to issue non-voting preferred stock. This has frequently been done but without causing serious objections, presumably in part because the issue of common stock is as a rule very much larger than the corresponding issue of preferred stock and in part because the self interest of the common stockholders has been regarded as ample protection for the interests of the preferred holders. . . .

A similar device is, however, being employed which may perhaps be considered a variant of the non-voting stock. This consists of issuing to the controlling group a very large number of shares of a class of stock having excessive voting power, *i.e.*, voting power out of proportion to the capital invested. A striking use has been made of this device in the case of the Cities Service Company. In 1929 this corporation sold to H. L. Doherty & Co. one million shares of a $1 par preferred stock. Each share of this stock was entitled to one vote in the election of directors. Yet each share of common stock outstanding was entitled to only 1/20 vote per share. Twenty-seven per cent of the votes could be cast by the million shares of preferred. Since the other classes of stock were widely distributed (81,470 holders of preferred and 377,988 holders of common stock on June 15, 1930) the excessive voting power given to this cheap stock practically nullified the voting privilege of the regular stockholders. By the use of this device a million dollar par value of stock held virtual control over assets of approximately a billion dollars. . . .

In the typical large corporation, however, control does not rest upon legal status. In these companies control is more often factual, depending upon a strategic position secured through a measure of ownership, a share in management or an external circumstance important to the conduct of the enterprise. Such control is less clearly defined than the legal forms, is more precarious, and more subject to accident and change. It is, however, none the less actual. It may be maintained over a long period of years, and as a corporation becomes larger and its ownership more widespread, it tends towards a position of security comparable to that of legal control, a position from which it can be dislodged only by a virtual revolution.

As in the case of legal control, factual control apart from legal control may involve varying degrees of ownership, tho never more than 50 per cent of the voting stock. Factual control may rest to a very considerable extent on the ownership of a large minority stock interest, or, when stock ownership is widely distributed, it may lie in the hands of the management. No sharp dividing line exists between these two situations, but so far as they can be distinguished, they may properly be referred to as minority control and management control.

4. *Minority control.*—Minority control may be said to exist when an individual or small group holds a sufficient minority stock interest to be in a position to dominate a corporation *through their stock interest.* Such a group is often said to have "working control" of the company. In general their control rests upon their ability to attract from scattered owners proxies sufficient when combined with their substantial minority interest to control a majority of the votes at the annual elections. Conversely this means that no other stock holding is sufficiently large to act as a nucleus around which to gather a majority of the votes. Where a corporation is comparatively small and the number of stockholders is not great, minority control appears to be comparatively difficult to maintain. A rival group may be able to purchase a majority of the stock, or perhaps a minority large enough to attract the additional votes necessary to obtain control in a proxy fight. The larger the company and the wider the distribution of its stock, the more difficult it appears to be to dislodge a controlling minority. As a financial operation it would be practically impossible for an outside interest to purchase a majority of the stock of the General Motors Corporation; even a Rockefeller would think twice before endeavoring to purchase a majority ownership of the Standard Oil Company of Indiana. Likewise the cost of mobilizing the votes of tens or hundreds of thousands of stockholders by circularizing them and perhaps conducting a publicity campaign, must be such as to prevent any but the most wealthy from seeking this method of seizing control from an existing minority. This is especially the case because the existing control can charge to the corporation the costs of its fight to maintain its position.

There is, however, a serious limitation on minority control in the possibility that the management may be antagonistic. So long as the affairs of the corporation run smoothly, minority control may be quietly maintained over a period of years. In time of crisis, however, or where a conflict of interest between the control and the management arises, the issue may be drawn and a proxy fight to determine control may demonstrate how far dependent upon its appointed management the controlling group has become.

In recent years the most striking illustration of this fight for control was occasioned by the open warfare between Mr. John D. Rockefeller, Jr., and the management of the Standard Oil Company of Indiana. Mr. Rockefeller actually held 14.5 per cent of the voting stock. He had been in substantial control of the company for years. Colonel Stewart, the chairman of the board of directors and undeniably the driving force behind much of that company's activity, displeased Mr. Rockefeller in connection with certain transactions which were the subject of discussion during the administration of President Harding. He asked Colonel Stewart to resign; Stewart refused and did not grant to Mr. Rockefeller the use of the proxy machinery at the following annual election of directors. Thereupon Mr. Rockefeller waged a most dramatic proxy battle against him. He circularized the stockholders at considerable expense, asking for proxies. He engaged the most eminent legal talent to guard against any "technical mistakes." He brought to bear the tremendous influence of his standing in the community. The Wall Street Journal pointed out at the time that the fight marked the first time the Rockefeller domination in a large Standard Oil unit "had been really in question." In opposition, Colonel Stewart obtained the full support of the existing board of directors and sought the support of the 16,000 employees who were stockholders. At this most opportune moment the company declared a 50 per cent stock dividend. The issue was for long in grave doubt. Four days previous to the election both sides are reported to have claimed the support of a majority, the one of votes and the other of stockholders. In the final election of directors, Mr. Rockefeller won, 59 per cent of the votes outstanding or 65 per cent of the votes cast being in favor of his candidates. Control may be said to have remained in his hands. Colonel Stewart's connection with the company was brought to a close.

This case has been described in detail because it probably marks the dividing line between minority control and management control. If Mr. Stewart had won the fight we could say that management without appreciable ownership was in the saddle. As it is, we may say that Mr. Rockefeller is in control, to a considerable degree, through his ownership of a minority interest of 14.5 per cent and in part through less tangible factors. Could other men with less prestige and financial power have retained control with but a 15 per cent ownership? Could Mr. Rockefeller have retained control if his ownership had been appreciably less? Here would seem to be control based on the minimum of ownership which would allow it to be held separate from the titular management.

5. *Management control.*—The fifth type of control is that in which ownership is so widely distributed that no individual or small group has even a minority interest large enough to dominate the affairs of the company. When the largest single interest amounts to but a fraction of one per cent, as in the case of several of the largest American corporations, no stockholder is in the position through his holdings alone to place important pressure upon the management or to use his holdings as a considerable nucleus for the accumulation of the majority of votes necessary to control. . . .

In such companies where does control lie? To answer this question, it is necessary to examine in greater detail the conditions surrounding the election of the board of directors. Ordinarily, at an election, the stockholder has three alternatives. He can refrain from voting, he can attend the annual meeting and personally vote his stock, or he can sign a proxy transferring his voting power to certain individuals selected by the management of the corporation, the proxy committee. As his personal vote will count for little or nothing at the meeting unless he has a very large block of stock, the stockholder is practically reduced to the alternative of not voting at all or else of *handing over his vote to individuals over whom he has no control and in whose selection he did not participate.* In neither case will he be able to exercise any measure of control. Rather, control will tend to be in the hands of those who select the proxy committee by whom, in turn, the election of directors for the ensuing period may be made. Since this committee is appointed by the existing management, the latter can virtually dictate their own successors. Where ownership is sufficiently subdivided, the management can thus become a self-perpetuating body even though its share in the ownership is negligible. This form of control can properly be called "management control."

Such control, though resting on no legal foundation, appears to be comparatively secure where the stock is widely distributed. Even here, however, there is always the possibility of revolt. A group outside the management may seek control. If the company has been seriously mismanaged, a protective committee of stockholders may combine a number of individual owners into a group which can successfully contend with the existing management and replace it by another which in turn can be ousted only by revolutionary action. . . .

. . . [L]et us examine the type of control exercised over the 42 railroads, the 52 public utilities, and the 106 industrials which compose the list of 200 largest companies at the end of 1929. Of these companies *ultimate control* appeared to be.

	By Number	By Wealth
Management control......	44%	58%
Legal device............	21	22
Minority control.........	23	14
Majority ownership......	5	2
Private ownership........	6	4
In hands of receiver....	1	Negligible
	100%	100%

485

CONCLUSION

It is apparent that, with the increasing dispersion of stock ownership in the largest American corporations, a new condition has developed with regard to their control. No longer are the individuals in control of most of these companies, the dominant owners. Rather, there are no dominant owners, and control is maintained in large measure separate from ownership. As has been indicated, control as something apart from ownership on one hand and from management on the other is a new concept ill defined in practice. It deals with a condition which exists only relatively and one on which information is of the most approximate character. Probably the condition of "joint control" which appears only rarely on the above list is more characteristic of the big corporation than is indicated, control in fact being not a single clearly defined phenomenon local to an individual or small group, but an element in the organization of industry which is broken up and appears in various forms. Like sovereignty, its counterpart in the political field, it may be held to a greater or less extent by a wide variety of individuals. We are justified, however, in treating it here as a single factor; because whether whole or divided, whether dependent upon proxy machinery, legal device, a measure of ownership, or a strategic position astride the management, it has in very considerable extent become separate from ownership. Formerly assumed to be merely a function of ownership, control now appears as a clearly distinguishable factor.

This separation of ownership and control involves a change in the organization of enterprise almost as revolutionary as that which occurred in the industrial revolution. The corporate system is now bringing a change in the position of capital much as the factory system changed that of labor. As the factory system divorced control from labor so the corporate system is divorcing control from ownership. The one brought the labor of a multitude of workers under a single control, the other is bringing the wealth of countless owners under the same unified control. The limits to the size of the business unit have thus been extended far beyond the bounds of the wealth of the individual or partnership, as they were before extended beyond the bounds of the labor of a single worker and his apprentices. The economic areas within which production can be conducted on a rational coördinated basis become limited only by the ability of a few individuals to administer successfully the huge organization of workers and of wealth which can be brought under their control. At the same time, the corporate system creates a vast class of individuals dependent, in so far as their wealth is concerned, on the action of others just as the factory system created a vast class of dependent workers.

To the economist, this new revolution presents a challenge. As the work of Adam Smith, "the first great theorist of that stage of capitalistic enterprise which we call the domestic system," had to be reconstructed during the nineteenth century to fit an economy dominated by the factory system, so must the modern economist redescribe economic relations in terms of an economy dominated by a relatively few huge enterprises in which both laborer and owner are separated from control. The individualism of Adam Smith's private enterprise has in large measure given way to the collective activity of the modern corporation, and economic theory must shift its emphasis from analysis in terms of competition to analysis in terms of control.

2. UNFAIR COMPETITION AND BUSINESS ETHICS[1]

By HERBERT HOOVER

EDITORS' NOTE.—Herbert Hoover, as Secretary of Commerce (1921–28), had tried to put into practice parts of the view he later expressed in his "Rugged Individualism" speech. He invited trade associations (i.e., organizations of businessmen engaged in a single trade) to Washington to prepare codes to be voluntarily accepted by their members for the elimination of "unfair" business practices and for the establishment and enforcement of high standards of business ethics. The assistance of the Federal Trade Commission was secured by having them refrain from antitrust prosecutions which might otherwise arise out of such "business co-operation" and by having them use these codes as the standard for fair business practice to be enforced by the Commission.

Wilbur and Hyde, commenting upon this new conception of the proper relation of government to business, said: "He brought into these associations a new purpose—to use them not alone for economic advancement but for moral improvement." The same writers, contrasting the later NRA experiments with codes of fair competition, wrote: "The attempt of the NRA to make these codes of ethics compulsory at once lost the moral lift."

The following is from an address delivered by Secretary of Commerce Herbert Hoover at Cleveland, Ohio, in 1924.

The advancement of science and our increasing population require constantly new standards of conduct and breed an increasing multitude of new rules and regulations. The basic principles laid down in the Ten Commandments and the Sermon on the Mount are as applicable today as when they were declared, but they require a host of subsidiary clauses. The ten ways to evil in the time of Moses have increased to ten thousand now.

A whole host of rules and regulations are necessary to maintain human rights with this amazing transformation into an industrial era. Ten people in a whole country, with a plow apiece, did not elbow each other very much. But when we put 7,000,000 people in a county with the tools of electric, steam, thirty-floor build-

1. Ray Lyman Wilbur and Arthur Mastick Hyde, *The Hoover Policies* (New York, 1937), pp. 301–4. By permission of Charles Scribner's Sons.

ings, telephones, miscellaneous noises, street-cars, railways, motors, stock exchanges, and what not, then we do jostle each other in a multitude of directions. Thereupon our lawmakers supply the demand by the ceaseless piling up of statutes.

... Moreover, with increasing education our senses become more offended and our moral discriminations increase; for all of which we discover new things to remedy. In one of our states over 1000 laws and ordinances have been added in the last eight months. It is also true that a large part of them will sleep peacefully in the statute book.

The question we need to consider is whether these rules and regulations are to be developed solely by government or whether they cannot be in some large part developed out of voluntary forces in the nation. In other words, can the abuses which give rise to government in business be eliminated by the systematic and voluntary action of commerce and industry itself? . . .

National character cannot be built by law. It is the sum of the moral fibre of its individuals. When abuses which rise from our growing system are cured by live individual conscience, by initiative in the creation of voluntary standards, then is the growth of moral perceptions fertilized in every individual character.

No one disputes the necessity for constantly new standards of conduct in relation to all these tools and inventions. Even our latest great invention—radio—has brought a host of new questions. No one disputes that much of these subsidiary additions to the Ten Commandments must be made by legislation. Our public utilities are wasteful and costly unless we give them a privilege more or less monopolistic. At once when we have business affected with monopoly we must have regulation by law. Much of even this phase might have been unnecessary had there been a higher degree of responsibility to the public, higher standards of business practice among those who dominated these agencies in years gone by. . . .

When legislation penetrates the business world it is because there is abuse somewhere. A great deal of this legislation is due rather to the inability of business hitherto to so organize as to correct abuses than to any lack of desire to have it done. Sometimes the abuses are more apparent than real, but anything is a handle for demagoguery. In the main, however, the public acts only when it has lost confidence in the ability or willingness of business to correct its own abuses.

Legislative action is always clumsy—it is incapable of adjustment to shifting needs. It often enough produces new economic currents more abusive than those intended to be cured. Government too often becomes the persecutor instead of the regulator.

The thing we all need to searchingly consider is the practical question of the method by which the business world can develop and enforce its own standards and thus stem the tide of governmental regulation. The cure does not lie in mere opposition. It lies in the correction of abuse. It lies in an adaptability to changing human outlook.

The problem of business ethics as a prevention of abuse is of two categories: Those where the standard must be one of individual moral perceptions, and those where we must have a determination of standards of conduct for a whole group in order that there may be a basis for ethics.

The standards of honesty, of a sense of mutual obligation, and of service, were determined two thousand years ago. They may require at times to be recalled. And the responsibility for them increases infinitely in high places either in business or government, for there rests the high responsibility for leadership in fineness of moral perception. Their failure is a blow at the repute of business and at confidence in government itself.

The second field and the one which I am primarily discussing is the great area of indirect economic wrong and unethical practices that spring up under the pressures of competition and habit. There is also the great field of economic waste through destructive competition, through strikes, booms, and slumps, unemployment, through failure of our different industries to synchronize, and a hundred other causes which directly lower our productivity and employment. Waste may be abstractly unethical, but in any event it can only be remedied by economic action.

If we are to find solution to these collective issues outside of government regulation we must meet two practical problems:

First, there must be organization in such form as can establish the standards of conduct in this vast complex of shifting invention, production, and use. There is no existing basis to check the failure of service or the sacrifice of public interest. Some one must determine such standards. They must be determined and held flexibly in tune with the intense technology of trade.

Second, there must be some sort of enforcement. There is the perpetual difficulty of a small minority who will not play the game. They too often bring disrepute upon the vast majority; they drive many others to adopt unfair competitive methods which all deplore; their abuses give rise to public indignation and clamor which breed legislative action.

I believe we now for the first time have the method at hand for voluntarily organized determination of standards and their adoption. I would go further; I believe we are in the presence of a new era in the organization of industry and commerce in which, if properly directed, lie forces pregnant with infinite possibilities of moral progress. I believe that we are, almost unnoticed, in the midst of a great revolution—or perhaps a better word, a transformation in the whole super-organization of our economic life. We are passing from a period of extremely individualistic action into a period of associational activities.

Practically our entire American working world is now organized into some form of economic association. We have trade associations and trade institutes embracing particular industries and occupations. We have chambers of commerce embracing representatives of different industries and commerce. We have the labor unions representing the different crafts. We have associations embracing all the different professions—law, engineering, medicine, banking, real estate, and what not. We have farmers' associations, and we have the enormous growth of farmers' co-operatives for actual dealing in commodities. Of indirect kin to this is the great increase in ownership of industries by their employees, and customers, and again we have

a tremendous expansion of mutualized insurance and banking.

Associational activities are, I believe, driving upon a new road where the objectives can be made wholly and vitally of public interest. . . .

Three years of study and intimate contact with associations of economic groups whether in production, distribution, labor, or finance, convince me that there lies within them a great moving impulse toward betterment.

If these organizations accept as their primary purpose the lifting of standards, if they will co-operate together for voluntary enforcement of high standards, we shall have proceeded far along the road of the elimination of government from business. . . .

The test of our whole economic and social system is its capacity to cure its own abuses. New abuses and new relationships to the public interest will occur as long as we continue to progress. If we are to be wholly dependent upon government to cure these abuses we shall by this very method have created an enlarged and deadening abuse through the extension of bureaucracy and the clumsy and incapable handling of delicate economic forces. . . .

American business needs a lifting purpose greater than the struggle of materialism. Nor can it lie in some evanescent, emotional, dramatic crusade. It lies in the higher pitch of economic life, in a finer regard for the rights of others, a stronger devotion to obligations of citizenship that will assure an improved leadership in every community and the nation; it lies in the organization of the forces of our economic life so that they may produce happier individual lives, more secure in employment and comfort, wider in the possibilities of enjoyment of nature, larger in its opportunities of intellectual life.

3. RUGGED INDIVIDUALISM VERSUS BALANCED ECONOMY[1]

By HUGH S. JOHNSON

EDITORS' NOTE.—The New Deal answer, at first, to the problem of the proper relation of the government to business was largely embodied in the National Industrial Recovery Act (better known as the NRA). President Roosevelt described the machinery of this act in these terms: "The administrative instrumentality for the operation . . . of this statute consisted of codes of fair competition drawn up for separate trades or industries by associations or groups, which under the statute had to be truly representative of such trades or industries, with no inequitable restrictions on admission. An express provision of the Act required that the codes should not promote monopolies or eliminate or oppress small enterprises. The codes had to be approved by the President or his representative. . . . A code once approved was to become binding upon the entire industry to which it applied, and was to be enforceable in court." The student should compare this experiment with that of Secretary of Commerce Hoover.

On June 16, 1935, when the NRA became law, General Hugh S. Johnson (1882–1942) was made its administrator. The following chapters are taken from Johnson's review of the sixteen-month NRA experiment in his *The Blue Eagle from Egg to Earth.*

Hugh Johnson's "education" for this responsibility is of particular interest. His administrative qualities and his general economic philosophy were perhaps the product of his military training, of his rise in World War I to brigadier general, of his service in that war as chief of the Purchase and Supply Bureau of the Army General Staff and as a member of the War Industries Board. After the war General Johnson completed his "business education" by becoming general counsel and assistant general manager of the Moline Plow Company and later (1925–29) the organizer and chairman of the board of directors of the Moline Implement Company. The Statistical Appendix (Nos. 13, 15, 23, 24, 29) may be useful in understanding General Johnson's argument.

There is something about this depression that doesn't speak well for what we call our common sense. We have suffered for five years. And for what? The fields are just as green and fruitful, the skies are just as blue as they were in the 1929 boom, when everybody was going to get rich and poverty was to be no more in the land.

The birds and the beasts seem to be faring about as well as ever—except those in care of men—and, so far as one can see just riding through, there is nothing much the matter with the country—until we get to the Lords of Creation—the vaunted human race.

If we saw a squirrel starving to death in a knot hole in his nut-filled hollow tree, we wouldn't believe it. And yet here are 125,000,000 people—granaries full, factories shut—but with millions of workers

1. Hugh S. Johnson, *The Blue Eagle from Egg to Earth* (Garden City, N.Y., 1935), pp. 158–64, 172–79, 188. Reprinted by permission of Doubleday, Doran and Company, Inc.

idle and hungry and shabby and afraid of the future and of everything and everybody about them—and money galore in banks and depositories. It just doesn't make sense. It is too much like a dark huddle of jungle savages dying, by swarms, of Asiatic cholera, because nobody ever told them to wash their hands before eating. It is a shocking thing.

Although tariffs and selective taxes and Adamson Acts and many other devices affect the natural laws of supply and demand, yet during the depression and up to March 4, 1933, few legislative steps were tried and the argument was "Let things alone and they will get all right because they always did, and because you cannot interfere with natural laws." That is the same philosophy that kills the savages. It is the philosophy that opposes vaccination for smallpox or the use of a parachute when you jump out of a balloon. We can and do daily interfere with natural laws. It is fair to say that if we had let things alone for a few weeks longer we *would* have had to call somebody in—the undertaker and the riot squad.

We have mechanized our industries and specialized our people. Families are no longer self-contained, economic units that can be put on wheels and trundled into a new environment to start things over again. Our nineteenth century safety valve of cheap or free new lands and a constantly expanding country has ceased to exist. The old order of our frontier days is gone forever and by no man's designing. All this has brought benefits, but it has also brought great griefs. The roaring, clacking engine of our industry and commerce has become a vast and highly active machine of which no individual is more than an integrated part. Each performs a specialized function. In most cases living income comes as a matter of determination by a power with whom there is no bargaining in any true sense. The individual worker accepts the wage scales decreed by employers and is thankful, and his separation from the particular ratchet in which

he revolves may be a tragedy. At his doorway there is no longer an open road to high adventure in a new and brighter country, and even if there were such a road, his specialization has unfitted him to take it.

In March, 1933, we had almost achieved economic collapse. Of the credit and product and hoarded reserve of domestic industry and labor and agriculture (indeed of all our people) *too much had been concentrated on production—too little on distribution and consumption.* The people's financial resources were thus squandered, either through their own unwise investment or the equal madness of their bankers. The results were a grotesque speculative structure of values; an elephantine production and service plant; a creeping paralysis of consumption and employment which began as far back as 1926; a decay of agriculture which began even further back in 1921; and an interior cavity in domestic absorptive and resisting power which started coincident with this diversion and impairment of the proper income of all people, but which was concealed until 1929 by an expansion of all kinds of credit—an expansion like a bubble—the skin of which became so tenuous and thin in 1929 that no power on earth could have saved it.

If you want to know where the consuming power of America went, you need only look around you and see it congealed in icebergs of unnecessary building and un-needed plants—and in the dead leaves of the worthless securities which financed them, and our fatuous foreign loans. Suppose that, instead of so freezing such vast sums a prudent part of them had been distributed in wages and dividends or conserved in cushions of credit invested in more stable securities—does anybody doubt that we would never have suffered this Gethsemane? . . .

Up to 1933, we thought that both our industry and our agriculture could depend on foreign markets to sell their products. We did not admit that, if only we could give the agricultural half of our population a fair price for its products, we could create—in our own backyard—one of the richest markets for industry in the whole world. We did not fully realize that, if only we could see to it that the working segments of our population—employees of all classes and grades—get a fair wage for their labor, we could create in our own country the best market for our farm products that we could expect if we combed the whole round earth.

We did not concede that we must try to balance production and consumption and that the best way to increase both is to *push them up together*. The way to do that is to try to balance and correlate the income of great groups. We must not let too much of profit and the people's credit and savings run into unwise speculative obligations of debt for the purpose of increasing production. We should try to direct more of it toward the uses of distribution and consumption, so that farmers and workers and *all* producers can constantly consume more and more in order that there may be more employment, more business, more profit, and that the people of this bountiful country can enjoy to the full the fruit of their own labor and the resources which are now locked away from them. We did not act on the principle that *it is the distressed and backward economic areas which topple the structure of prosperity, make depressions, and that the exploitation of any class is a downward drag on the progress of the whole people.*

If we could have perfect balance among all producing segments—agriculture, capital, industry, workers in industry, the services, and the segment engaged in transportation and distribution, there would be almost no limit to our consuming capacity. Of course, that is Utopia and can never be attained. My only point is that all law, all administration, and all popular effort should be directed toward that goal instead of away from that goal. I think that the *essence of the New Deal is to point toward that balance*. I think that the *essence of what preceded the New Deal was to point away from that balance.*

Savage wolfish competition without any direction whatever, has proved to be one of the most destructive forces in our economic life. When it got savage and wolfish enough it began immediately to gnaw upon the living standards of wage and salary earners and hence of farmers, and that happens to include over 85 per cent of our population. When times are fabulously good the great prosperity of the few filters down to the many and tends to obscure this tendency. But in normal times and especially when depression such as that which began five years ago comes upon us like a blight and millions of men begin tramping the streets, looking for any kind of work that will afford a crust of bread for their families, the whole aspect changes.

Plants finding a scant market for their products begin frantically to seek for any possible method of reducing prices and the most obvious methods of all are to reduce wages, speed up machines to produce more in a shorter time, and extend the hours of work to the limit. Most humane employers do not want to do this—but a single great competitor can force it, and, like a rotten apple spoiling a whole barrel, one plant or one locality which adopts this method can bring it eventually to a whole industry. . . .

Another thing—apart from savage competition—too great a share of prosperity went to too few people. Just because a man has a million dollars he doesn't actually consume very much more than a man who has a thousand dollars. The very rich do not buy forty dollars' worth of ham and eggs for breakfast. If we want to preserve economic activity we must find a way to let everybody buy at least a half-dollar's worth of ham and eggs. This is the same old theory that 1,000 men with ten dollars each are a better market for any product than one man with ten thousand dollars and 999 men with nothing at all, or even than 500 men with five dollars apiece, and 500 with fifteen dollars each. This is a point of vital importance, which the Old Deal advocates persistently overlooked.

That does not argue any effort to distribute wealth. When you try that you only distribute poverty. It does mean an effort *to distribute opportunity*.

When the President's Recovery Program finally got under way, employment and wages in this country were at a low point. Fierce competition and disproportions among great segments of consuming power were starving us in plenty, freezing us in warmth, and destroying us behind bulwarks of financial strength.

There is no virtue in sitting and taking all this and never striking back. Even the good Lord only mentioned turning one cheek and, when he found men in the court of the Temple fattening on the faith of a distressed people, he used the knotted end of a rope. This country had tried sitting and taking it for five years, and now it is trying to do something about it. That is the reason for NRA, AAA, PWA and all the loan and fiscal acts. We are here concerned only with NRA.

The most obvious, immediate way to erase the effect of the depression on wages and hours was the NRA project to decrease hours, to speed work and to increase wages to maintain purchasing power. The whole idea of shortening hours and raising wages has been attacked on this argument:

The principal element of cost in any article is the labor cost. Increases in that cost by higher payments to those benefited simply increases price to the whole people whose capacity to buy is already so limited, that it may be assumed that they are buying all they can. The result can only be reduction in the tonnage of consumption and hence of manufacture and hence of net employment.

There is no doubt in the world that there is much here to give us pause. Dr. Sachs and I considered it prayerfully when we blocked out the NRA program. We relied, however, on PWA to activate the heavy industries at once and thus increase the *total number of available purchasers*. We relied on AAA to increase farm purchasing power immediately and thus still further add to the *number of purchasers*. These added to NRA additions would so far increase *volume* that we thought (and I still think) the increased labor cost could be absorbed without much increase in price. The president specifically asked industry to take this gamble. But we also relied on the principle just mentioned, that many men with a little each is a far better market than one man with much, and all the rest with nothing. . . .

Before going further with this narrative, it will be well to consider briefly the evolution of the philosophy on which NRA was based.

Before the war, American business was a honeycomb of water-tight industrial compartments. Each cell was jealously guarded. There was a maximum of competition and a minimum of coöperation. Ruthless and untempered competition was decreed by the Sherman and Clayton acts. The war changed that. The world went mad. The nations entered a contest to see which could pour the greatest mass of its young manhood and the largest amount of its money and property into the fire in the shortest space of time. That was the way to win the war.

The old honeycomb machine of the United States couldn't produce things fast enough in this race to destroy everything. We had to scrap it. And in the short period between April, 1917, and November, 1918, we literally tore it apart and put it together again. On the call of government and under the pressure of patriotism the old individualist battlers royal became an organized squad—all marching toward the sound of the guns.

We did not repeal the Anti-Trust Acts. *We simply ignored them.* Competitors pooled their resources, their trade secrets, their facilities. Industries organized themselves into groups and figures with the speed and almost the precision of a highly drilled chorus on a musical comedy stage and government took charge of both production and consumption and to a large extent, prices. It worked. It poured forth

493

such a flood of production for the uses of war as the world had never seen in one country. It won the war. . . .

. . . There was a "let-us-alone" gang then also, but we swept them into the ash can and there was no longer any sentiment for the old slogan of "Let-us-alone" because all knew that government intervention was the sole salvation. When that pressure was gone, "Let-us-alone" rebounded into light and became the guiding principle of government administration from the depths of 1921 to the giddy peaks of 1929.

"Let-us-alone" and unhampered individualism worked well enough during the formative days of individual pioneering—nothing else would have worked—but it did not work when we had to meet the war crisis and after-the-war reorganization of trade and industry. It had become a relic of old days and, as things turned out, a very dangerous one. . . .

There is now much talk about the desirability of a return to the good old Anti-Trust Acts and the safety of the Federal Trade Commission. They talk about the mild control of NRA, as encouraging monopoly, oppressing small enterprise, and thus threatening people with economic serfdom. We shall discuss some of these things in detail later; here it is enough to say that *NRA will have to move on a broad front and at terrific speed if it can beat that record of the destruction of individual enterprise made under the full force of the Anti-Trust Acts, the negative powers of the Federal Trade Commission, and the most active business period in our history.*

It is black on the record that the unchecked competitive plan under the Anti-Trust Acts was destroying small enterprise of every kind at a most astonishing rate. It is a shorter record but equally certain the NRA has exactly reversed this killing process. Competition down to reasonable cost is still as free as air but the public does not want and cannot afford competition of bankrupt stocks and it is now protected against the flim-flam of

being enticed into a store by a window display of some popular product being sold for half its cost and then inveigled into buying other things at a good fat profit. There is a curious—almost maddening—confusion in terms when superficial observers begin using the words "monopoly," "price fixing," "anti-trust acts," etc.

The Anti-Trust Acts prohibit combinations in restraint of trade. But NRA specifically permits such combinations with government sanction and supervision. *There is not one single Code that is not a combination in restraint of trade*, and if Codes are not permitted so to restrain trade then NIRA ought to be repealed tomorrow. It doesn't mean a thing.

But both NIRA and the Anti-Trust Acts do prohibit monopoly—there is no question about that. The only real question that has been raised comes from the assertion that price agreements and combinations in restraint of trade *are of themselves* monopolistic. *That is the very heart of the question that plagues NRA.*

Of course price control *can* be used as a weapon of monopoly. It has frequently been so used and that use of it was the very reason for the Anti-Trust Acts themselves. But that was price control *downward* in an effort to destroy competition and practiced by powerful combinations for the specific and determined purpose of oppressing and wiping out small enterprise and individual initiative, and transforming all business in the country into a gigantic corporate cluster under private control—an unthinkable and intolerable result. No such thing exists or is attempted or could exist or be attempted under any code. NRA price stabilizations are all for exactly the reverse purpose—to prevent cutthroat and monopolistic price slashing, to maintain small industry, to continue employment, to abolish economic murder. There is only a fragmentary element of cases where this is not true—i.e., cases in which small industries can pay code wages and actually undersell large ones and whenever and as often as this happens relief is given at once. There was never a more ghastly, nonsensical, and destructive anomaly than the charge that price controls under NRA tend toward monopoly. The trend is in precisely the reverse direction. So far as that particular argument is concerned it is a silly sophistry inimical to the public welfare. . . .

Of course there are two other aspects of this subject which are rarely mentioned but which are really matter for grave concern. In the first place there are parts of industries which have been built up on *low prices derived from sweated labor*—such as sweat shops, dependents on home piecework and child labor, and other cases which will be described at another place. When *they* are forced by NRA to pay living wages, they cannot continue to exist. They say, therefore, that NRA *oppresses* them. But as to this the President, in giving NRA its marching orders, took the bull by the horns. He said that *no industry which depends for existence on less than living wages has a right to continue to exist*. And on that phase of my administration I stand or fall. These were not only my orders—they were also my convictions. I will concede that all the regional differentials under NRA are not scientifically worked out. I know there is a wide field where readjustment is necessary. But that is no argument for permitting the return of the scandalous labor conditions revealed by NRA.

The second question is *whether the consumer has a right to the lowest prices that any kind of competition can provide*. The Anti-Trust Acts say yes. NIRA says no. And there is the white-hot center of the dispute. Everybody is a consumer. Nearly everybody depends on *some* enterprise in the competitive field. Consumers are not entitled to low prices achieved by the degradation of human labor and if they were entitled to them they would be fatuous to accept them, because once the principle is admitted it applies to all human labor and all human labor consumes. Nor are consumers wise in seeking the low prices of

economic slaughter—especially at a time like this when explosive and disruptive changes in the existing structure throw more and more people out of work.

On all these considerations, NRA came as a blessed alleviation of the dog-eat-dog rule of the Anti-Trust Acts. This does not mean that there is no competition or even any improper limitation of competition under NRA. It means only that competition must keep its blows above the belt, and that there can be no competition at the expense of decent living. The only price limitations in NRA outside of three (or at most four) special cases, are limitations against making a practice of selling at less than cost of production for the purpose of destroying competition or of preventing competition based on the degradation of human labor. . . .

You can't have recovery without amending the Anti-Trust Acts because you must prevent a repetition of 1922–1929. You can't do that without control and you can't have that control under Anti-Trust legislation. Those Acts have failed in every crisis. They had to be forgotten during the war to enable the country to defend itself. When they came back to memory in 1919, they set the stage for what happened up to 1929. They contributed to the boom and they were helpless in the crash. Without amendment, following the principles of NIRA, they will go on (as they did) to create the very condition of monopoly and erasure of individualism which they were conceived to prevent and in the future, as in the past, they will have to be abandoned in any crisis economic or military. Unless so amended, they have no place in the mechanized, highly organized and integrated civilization in which we live. *There is no more vital and fundamental issue before the country than whether we are going to control modern scientific and industrial development to our use or suffer it to our destruction.*

The only forces that *can* control it are industrial self-government under Federal supervision and the only plan that has ever been presented through which that control can be applied is NRA. If we scrap NRA, it will be just like releasing on a roomful of school children a flock of mechanical man-eating Frankensteins—irresistible and ravenous. If we follow and develop and perfect NRA, it will be like harnessing them, putting brains into their brazen skulls and driving them in a powerful team to pull us out of the mud of this morass.

4. TOWARD STABILITY[1]

EDITORS' NOTE.—The following editorial appeared in *Business Week* shortly after President Roosevelt had asked Congress to enact the National Industrial Recovery Act, though a month before its actual passage. In this early period many businessmen were prepared by industrial stagnation to welcome any recovery formula, especially one which promised to rescue them from the insecurity of competition.

Two main conclusions emerge from the wide discussion of the revolutionary proposal to set up governmental control of industry on a scale never before seriously proposed in the United States.

The first is that there is a surprising unanimity among business men in favor of the general theory. The second, that every business man believes it would be extraordinarily difficult to set up regulations for his particular industry.

The American business man at this moment is utterly weary of the ruthless competitive struggle. It has been too much for him; he has survived so far, but he is spent. He is willing, he feels just now, to surrender some part of his freedom of action to achieve a degree of stability.

Reduced to lowest terms, his support of the general ideas is based on the thought that he would be willing to pay higher wages for shorter hours if he could be assured that every competitor would be on the same footing, and if he could be sure a fair price level would be enforced. On the higher plane, he recognizes the broad truth that business exists for the satisfaction of human needs; essentially it has no other excuse for being. Among the greatest of human needs is safety, stability of employ-ment and of earnings. But what can one business concern do of itself, and alone? Again the need for protection from the unscrupulous.

There is general agreement among the leading business men who have appeared before the Congressional hearings that something must be done to regulate hours, pay, production, and prices. Even more convincing are the results of a questionnaire conducted by Cornell. Most of the leading business men questioned felt that the times demand a drastic reorganization, designed to reduce to a minimum the effects of the business cycle, to increase the stability of employment, and to insure adequate purchasing power. A minimum wage is necessary to prevent the unscrupulous from exploiting labor. Any plan devised to reach these ends must have in mind raising the standard of living of the country as a whole.

But, and this brings us back to the beginning, the incredible complexity of our industrial structure creates myriad special problems. It seems impossible to conceive of general legislation rigid enough to achieve the desired ends, flexible enough to meet thousands of special cases.

It is to be feared that because of these detailed objections, the Black bill [thirty-hour-week bill] may be rejected—which

1. *Business Week,* May 10, 1933, p. 32. By permission of *Business Week.*

will be no loss—and nothing put in its place, which will be a real tragedy.

Tremendous issues are before this special session of Congress. There is too much to be done. Some things must be postponed. But no issue can be much more important than this one. The Administration believes it can launch a business recovery. If it does not at the very inception of recovery lay plans for its control, we predict that we shall run straight through wild boom to ghastly depression with a speed hitherto unprecedented.

It will take some pains to work out details. But the solution is not impossible and it is worth all the pains and time it may cost. Let industry formulate its own codes of practice. Each industry knows its own special needs, its own problems. Let the government supervise these self-formulated codes, first to see that they are fair to the public, second, to see that they are enforced on the unscrupulous fringe who will never cooperate voluntarily with the majority, and who, under the present system of free competition, can undo the progressive work of all the rest.

Limit this, if you like, to the period of the emergency. Once tried we predict the system never will be abandoned.

5. REPORT OF THE NATIONAL RECOVERY REVIEW BOARD[1]

EDITORS' NOTE.—The circumstances of the creation of the National Recovery Review Board, perhaps better known as the Darrow Board, after the name of its chairman, Clarence Darrow (1857–1938), a well-known labor and criminal lawyer, are perhaps best described by NRA Administrator Hugh S. Johnson:

I recognized, as NRA progressed, the necessity for a court of industrial appeals from the codes to look into particular cases, grant exceptions, and make recommendations for code changes. . . . We . . . worked out an idea of an independent Court and, in what now seems a moment of total aberration, *I myself suggested Clarence Darrow!* . . . I did not know him personally although I had always admired his consistent intransigeance and his barnyard philosophy. . . .

When Clarence came I think he meant to do everything he could do to help. He told me that his idea was to hear every

complaint, come to a conclusion, and then bring it over to NRA to see what he could do to right any wrong and relieve any hardship he might discover. He volunteered the suggestion that he was not there to start any newspaper trial of cases or to put boulders in our stony path but only to be helpful.

But Clarence is not so young as once he was. He brought in a younger man named Mason and another named Thompson and they had political ideas. . . . A newspaper campaign to knock NRA into a cocked hat was to be started at once, based on any dirt the Darrow Board could dig up—and lots and lots of other things.

But for some reason the press did not come up to these expectations. But Bloody Old Jefferies at the Assizes never conducted any hearings to equal those for cavalier disposal of cases. They condemned codes in a half-hour "hearing" upon which the men who had made the code and the NRA officials who had approved it had spent weeks of investigation, agreement and compromise, and they refused to allow any explanation and appearance from these men. It was a Cave of Adullun to which every man who had a grievance, real or fancied, could come to

1. National Recovery Review Board, *First Report to the President of the United States*, pp. 10–14; *Second Report to the President of the United States*, pp. 43–47; *Third Report to the President of the United States*, pp. 9–12, 19–21, 35–39.

the wailing wall and have his complaints avidly encouraged and promptly under-written without the slightest inquiry into its merits. Little was called for from the files of the NRA and it was only too apparent that many of the codes passed upon and condemned had not even been used by the Board. No codes were sent back to NRA for correction. Instead a "Report to the President" was made and given to the press. The eminent socialist Charles Edward Russell had been called to write it and its principal recommendation was that the government forthwith adopt Communism as the only solution of its difficulties.

We promptly announced that, as far as NRA was concerned, we would pay no more attention to the Board and its reports than if neither existed.

RETAIL SOLID FUEL

The dominating power in this industry is the National Retail Coal Dealers Association. The code was made and the Code Authority chosen by members of this Association without due representation of coal dealers that were not members. The operation of the Code thus made and administered tends to oppress the small enterprise. The Code requires certain confidential business information to be disclosed, which constitutes a perilous practice and one liable to abuse. Power is given to Divisional Code Authorities to prohibit the marketing of "blends," a prohibition that seems unnecessary and is the occasion for complaint. It is in these particulars that the small enterprise seems most oppressed. The evil can and should be remedied by amending the Code and by giving fair representation to the dealers not members of the Association.

STEEL

Monopolistic conditions have long existed in this industry, due to its absolute control by the larger companies. This control is assured through the American Iron and Steel Institute, supposed to represent both large and small enterprises, but wherein as a matter of fact, the voting arrangements really leave the small enterprise at the mercy of the large. Each member has one vote for each $500,000 of invoiced product for the year. The total number of votes is reported to be approximately fifteen thousand, of which the five largest companies have 7,688.

By this system of voting the Board of Directors of the Iron and Steel Institute is chosen. Since this same Board of Directors was constituted the Code Authority for the Steel Industry, and this authority made the Code and now administers it in the interest of the larger companies in control of the Iron and Steel Institute it is obvious that we have here a body not only perfectly equipped to exercise monopolistic control but is endowed with extraordinary powers incompatible with the ideals heretofore entertained in a free country.

One of these powers, exercised in a way that has produced many and bitter complaints from small enterprises, is that of arbitrarily fixing prices for the advantage of the large companies. Another is a rule that forbids the enlarging of the producing capacity of any unit in the industry.

Both of these conditions seem to us harmful, monopolistic and oppressive, and in both respects the Code has operated to augment the evils previously existing.

The Federal Trade Commission recently made an exhaustive study of the Steel Industry and presented a report that held it to be essentially monopolistic and unfairly conducted. At the outset of the hearing by this Board, April 4, this report of the Federal Trade Commission on the Steel Industry was offered in evidence and admitted.

On April 17, the chief counsel of this Board was called on the long distance telephone from New York by the chief counsel of the Code Authority (Directorate of the Iron and Steel Institute) who protested against the inclusion in our evidence of the Federal Trade Commission Report on the ground that it was "a tissue of falsehoods," and demanded opportunity to appear before this board and demonstrate the falsity of the Commission's findings. This was accorded and the Board held hearings on April 19 and 20 for the purpose of allowing counsel for the Code Authority (Directorate of the Iron and Steel Institute) to disclose wherein the Commission's findings were unfounded.

The first day was consumed by counsel in readings from the Code, a copy of which lay before each member of the Board, in explications of the obvious and in dissertations upon the insignificant. No witness was examined nor evidence presented. At the second day's hearings, this course being pursued through an apparently endless maze of verbiage, counsel for the Board objected and asked that some facts be presented. The Chairman ruled that every opportunity be given to counsel for the Code Authority (Directorate of the Iron and Steel Institute) to present the case for the industry but that at the rate of progress so far achieved, years would be consumed in apparently fruitless discussion. Counsel for the Code Authority protested at each step but finally called a witness that he questioned. The nature of the questions and their long drawn out and dilatory answerings strengthened the impression that the Code Authority was merely seeking to consume time. When the hearing adjourned at 5 P.M., the only witness summoned by the counsel for the Authority was still on the stand and his cross-examination by the counsel for the Board was hardly begun.

It was agreed that the hearing should proceed on Tuesday, April 24, but on April 23, the counsel for the Board received a letter from the chief counsel for the Authority (Directorate of the Iron and Steel Institute) saying that as the Board was manifestly unwilling to grant to the Authority sufficient time to make a proper presentation of its cause, his clients had instructed him to withdraw from the case.

No further hearings have been held in this industry. The Board requested the counsel for the Authority to allow the cross-examination interrupted on April 20 to be resumed and continued, but this request was not complied with. It also sent a representative to the office of the Authority in New York with a request that this representative be allowed to examine the minutes and records of the Authority but this effort again was unsuccessful.

No conclusion was left to the Board except that the industry (which is controlled by the Iron and Steel Institute, the Directorate of which in turn constitutes the Code Authority) did not answer the charges of the Federal Trade Commission because no answer was possible and the dilatory proceedings before this Board were but play-acting for the purpose of creating the impression that the Board was unjust.

At the hearings held by the Board, it was impossible to escape the conclusions from the testimony offered that the misfortunes of the small enterprise in this industry were multiplied by the grotesque absurdities of what is called the "basing point" system or phantom freight rates. The origin of this huge evil was the insane practice of the railroads in wrenching freight rates out of their normal relations to obtain competitive shipments or favor competitive enterprises, but the present extent of the disease is far beyond railroad medication. It plagues many industries and from the testimony before us we conclude that the people of the country must be paying annually many millions of dollars for pretended freight rates that are purely fictitious. . . .

WOOD CASED LEAD PENCILS

Monopolistic practices and the oppression of the small enterprise are conspicuous in this industry, due primarily to its domination by four large companies which together produce more than seventy per cent of the total domestic output. From

1929 to the present year, this control was exercised by the Lead Pencil Institute, an arrangement frequently to be encountered in industries similarly controlled. The Institute was supposed to represent the entire trade but as voting in it was arranged upon the basis of one vote for every fifty persons employed, the supremacy of the four leading companies was complete and unassailable.

The Code for this industry was made by the Institute which means that it was made by the four great companies. When it went into effect the Institute virtually became the authority for the administration of the Code that it had made.

The Executive Secretary of the Institute became the secretary of the Code Authority at the same salary of $25,000 a year, although it was testified to that he combined the duties of his office with the practice of law. Of the six members of the Code Authority, four are representatives of the four great companies that overshadow the business.

These companies have their factories in or near New York City. Five smaller units operating in competition with these, are planted in small towns in Tennessee, where the wage levels have always been much lower than in the metropolitan area.

The Code provides a minimum wage against which complaint was made on the ground that the changes it effected increased the advantage of the large and the disabilities of the small manufacturer. Before the adoption of the Code a differential in wages between North and South had come to be recognized. According to a survey made in June, 1933, and not disputed, the average wage of men working in this industry was in the North 42.2 cents an hour for men and 36.8 an hour for women. In the South the average in this industry was 23.1 for men and 15.1 for women. The Code established a general minimum of 36 cents an hour for men and $32\frac{1}{2}$ cents for women, except that for plants in the state of Tennessee a minimum

of 30 cents an hour was fixed for men and women.

The contention of the complainants, who were representatives of the small units in Tennessee, was that this provision compelled them to increase heavily their wage costs, being an increase of close to 100 per cent in the case of women's wages, while it enabled the larger companies to reduce some of their labor expenditures. It was testified that in the northern factories 60 per cent of the employees were women and in the southern only 50 per cent. The Code provides for equal pay for men and women where they do the same class of work but this is not as significant as might be thought since instances where women are doing exactly the same class of work as men do are comparatively rare.

There is a bad provision of the Code to the effect that where shipments are of 100 pounds or more the manufacturer is to pay the freight charges. This works in two ways to the disadvantage of the small unit. As the business is less in bulk and orders it receives are usually smaller, it has less chance to attain to 100 pound shipments. Between forty and fifty gross of lead pencils are required to make 100 pounds and few small enterprises ever ship so much as forty and fifty gross of lead pencils in one consignment. Again, the small enterprise deals in pencils only, whereas the large companies supply also pens, penholders, erasers, and other articles, so that it is much easier for them to reach the 100 pound limit and therefore to hold out to buyers the allurement of the free delivery of their orders.

The assessments levied upon members of the industry to defray the expenses of the Code administration seem grossly unfair. They were arranged on the basis of 1 cent for each gross of pencils sold, a manifest injustice since it was clearly established that the small enterprises make chiefly the cheaper grades of pencils, whereas the larger companies make the more expensive brands upon which the profit is much greater. Yet, on a gross of pencils for which the small manufacturer would receive $1.19 he must pay the same assessment as the large company pays on a gross that would net it $2.40.

The complainants averred also that the provisions of the Code in regard to price fixing bore more heavily upon them than upon the larger companies. For example, prices are not fixed on pencils made to retail at more than five cents each, but are definitely fixed upon the cheap grades. A small manufacturer testified that less than one per cent of his sales were of the five cent variety, while 95 per cent were of pencils that retailed at less than three cents. The large companies specialize in pencils to be sold at five cents or more and on these there is no price limitation.

The price list in force compels rubber tipped and metal feruled pencils to be sold at $1.68 a gross and another pencil without tip or ferule to be sold at $2.16 when the $1.68 pencil costs no less to make than the $2.16 kind.

The restrictions of the Code about the coloring of pencil casing seem arranged to give another advantage to the larger company. For some unexplained reason yellow is by far the most popular color. It appears that certain kinds of pencils of the cheaper grade, made by the small enterprises are strictly forbidden to wear the coveted yellow while costlier grades made by the larger companies enjoy to the full their natural liberty about tints. But as this matter is to be settled by the Bureau of Standards of the Department of Commerce it need not be passed upon here.

As an instructive illumination of the true nature of many complaints we found that several withdrew their pleas and one of them retracted a statement made the day before. It appeared from the testimony subsequently introduced that this change of attitude had been brought about by the granting of certain concessions to these two complainants that were not made to the rest of the trade—a fact that seems to bear its own comment.

One point raised at this hearing remains unanswered because there is no answer to it. The differences in labor costs due to geographical location are beyond adjustment. Labor is not only cheaper in the warmer regions; it is also less productive. If a differential is allowed on the basis of this undeniable fact, the producers in regions with a higher level of productive efficiency complain of unfairness; if no differential is allowed, the regions at a productive disadvantage complain of excessive labor costs. This is true and will remain true, whatever efforts may be made to reach the ground of common agreement that does not exist. . . .

GRAPHIC ARTS

Monopolistic practices are rank and intolerable in this industry and the oppression of the small enterprise is carried with a high hand.

In this instance, as in so many others that have come before the Board, the root of all evil is the inordinate greed and unbridled power of the larger units, by whom the Code was prepared and by whom it is administered.

The Graphic Arts industry is divided into four groups, based upon the printing process employed in each. The Commercial Relief Printing Group embraces the establishments of what are called job printers, from which have come the more urgent of the complaints reaching this Board. The Code provides that the Authority for the Commercial Relief Printing shall be the United Typothetae of America with whose charter and by-laws the proceedings of the Authority must conform.

When the Code was to be made, the printing industry was invited to come to a meeting in Chicago, but so few of the owners of small enterprises were able to attend that the meeting consisted virtually of members of the Typothetae who framed the Code and placed in it the provision by which their own organization became the Authority to enforce the Code they had framed.

The Typothetae is a guild of master printers and owners of printing establishments. It is dominated by its larger units and what is called its Administrative agency is like the Institute in other industries. That is to say, the Agency is an executive committee of the larger interests by which they register and have their will.

To be a member of the Code, as to be a member of the Typothetae, one must submit a schedule of wages paid in one's establishment for the last year previous to the application. This makes for small enterprises a barrier extremely difficult to overcome. The average small enterprise has no system of accounting that will meet the requirements affirmed by the Code Authority nor could it without great difficulty supply the lack. But if the small enterprise could not join the Typothetae it could not join the Code and if it could not join the Code it might as well retire from business. This seems to have been indeed the end aimed at in formulating these breath-taking arrangements. What more an autocratic and high-riding monopoly could have done to assure such an exodus is not easily imagined.

The accounting requirements involved still another practical hardship for small enterprises. They must in their cost accounting observe carefully a division of labor costs among the different activities in their establishment. To large units this was no difficulty because in such units there is no overlapping of employments; a compositor does not do press work and a binder does not set type. But in small shops with but a few employees the case was wholly different. There, the same man might have two or three lines of work and to assort his time at each would be a puzzling task. Hardly could it be done at all without a time clock and a second employee to follow and record the movements of the first. The same man might work for a time at a type case and then on the press and then on a stitcher.

The basic price fixed by the Code seemed to have no relation to ascertained costs of production but to represent a bald application to printing of the practice once familiar in railroad banditries as "what the traffic will bear." In this instance it must have somewhat overstepped even these generous boundaries, for we are informed of a decline in the printing industry because of the unreasonably high prices charged under the Code. But this again is more of an injury to the small enterprise than to the large. The small shop has lived chiefly because, having smaller expenses, it could make lower rates. On the same scale of prices it could hardly expect to meet the competition of the large unit.

The book of prices prepared for the trade by the Authority thus constituted contains something like five thousand items and seems abnormally, if not preposterously, high in its levels. In some instances, the profit provided is from 200 to 600 per cent. "A customer came to me this week," writes one of the complainants, a small enterprise man in a small city, "to buy 500 sheets of legal size typewriting paper (blank), which cost me less than $1. I had to charge him $3.20 for the blank paper when $1.50 or $2 would have been enough profit. These are only a few samples of the prices we must charge and you can readily see that customers with limited means cannot and will not pay them. Consequently, the small printer is facing ruin in the very near future."

To sum up then, the gentlemen of the Typothetae, finding themselves clothed with arbitrary and irresponsible power concluded to use that power to their own great advantage and the accelerated exit of the small competitor. . . .

STEEL

As an illustration of the practical workings of the basing point swindle, this Board cites the case of a manufacturer of Duluth, Minnesota, organized in the making of tools and other small articles of steel. He buys as raw material chiefly two kinds of steel, merchant bars and billets. All this steel he obtains in his own city from a subsidiary of the United States Steel Corporation, which manufactures the steel on the spot from ore dug sixty miles away. Yet it appeared that from the date of the inauguration of the original Steel Code, this manufacturer had been charged for his steel bars $45.00 a ton, which was $39 a ton, the normal price, plus $6.00 a ton phantom freight rates from Chicago or had ever been outside of Duluth. The manufacturer was charged for steel billets $37.25 a ton, which was $34 a ton normal price plus $3.25 a ton phantom freight rates from Chicago to Duluth, although the only transportation these billets had ever known was a haul in a truck part way across the city of Duluth. Because of these inexcusable extortions, the manufacturer was confronted with the imminent necessity of closing his factory and the discharge of three hundred employees.

The gouging in this case was so manifest and so raw that general indignation was aroused by the publication of the facts. When the "Revised Steel Code" was announced it was noted with satisfaction that Duluth was to be made a "basing point," which it was believed, would eliminate the "phantom freight rates" and give the manufacturer a chance for his life. The news was widely printed and widely applauded. What was not printed although equally true and much more significant, was that effective June 11, the day the alleged "Revised Code" went into effect and the basing points were multiplied, the Steel Trust advanced the price of merchant steel bars in the Duluth area from $39 a ton to $42 a ton plus 50 cents switching charges and the price of steel billets from $34 to $37 a ton plus 30 cents switching charges.

The net result of all the far-famed revision of the Steel Code therefore is to leave the manufacturer much as he was before. When the phantom freight rate could no longer be extorted the monopoly merely slapped an additional price upon steel. Tweedledee, tweedledum.

The full measure of this proceeding can be grasped only when we remember that Duluth is now paying $3 a ton more for steel bars and steel billets than Chicago or Gary, although it is hundreds of miles nearer to the ore and has a lower labor cost.

Of this gesture of cool insolence, therefore, the significance can hardly be overlooked. We have had before in the history of corporations in America instances of an overweening assumption of autocratic power, but not many marked by an equal appearance of purposed contempt. Nothing seems lacking except that the order of the Steel Company establishing these increases should end with the historic question, "What are you going to do about it?" . . .

CONCLUSIONS

Submitting thus our third report we feel constrained to emphasize certain conclusions that seem to us of grave moment.

1. In virtually all the codes we have examined, one condition has been persistent, undeniable and apparent to any impartial observation. It is this, that the code has offered an opportunity for the more powerful and more profitable Interests to seize control of an industry or to augment and extend a control already obtained.

In industry after industry, the larger units, sometimes through the agency of what is called an "Institute," sometimes by other means, have for their own advantage written the codes, and then, in effect and for their own advantage, assumed the administration of the code they have framed. Thus privilege has exerted itself to gather more privilege. Little else indeed has been considered in these operations. The interests of the nation and of the consuming public have been utterly ignored in all too many instances. Profit making power has been multiplied for the one purpose of gathering more profits that will mean still more power for still more profits.

The nation's need, sternly revealed by

the depression, was for a better distribution of wealth. In the respects we have specified in these reports, the Recovery Act has failed to meet this need. Nor has it been merely negative in its reactions. However beneficent may have been its intents, its practice has increased an evil fraught with grave dangers to the Republic. It has not discouraged but in the ways we have pointed out it has fostered and fortified those practices and systems under which one per cent of the nation's population has been enabled to possess itself of sixty per cent of the nation's wealth. In this respect it has become not the foe but the adjunct of depression. For of what use would it be to win the hectic and delusive prosperity when close beside wait the conditions that will inevitably produce another and greater disaster?

2. This Board was created to ascertain if the codes permitted monopolistic practices and the oppression of small enterprises. Our investigations have shown that in the instances mentioned the codes do not only permit but foster monopolistic practices and the small enterprise is not only oppressed but in many cases its exit is accelerated from the field of business. We, therefore, report what we have found.

3. It is ominous and disquieting to have to note that although these evil conditions have been demonstrated and are well known to exist, nothing has been done to remove or even to restrain them. On the contrary, there seems a sinister purpose to entrench them still more securely in the processes of the act, to make still more unquestioned the monopolistic sway of the Great Interest. Thousands upon thousands of small enterprises in many lines of business have petitioned for relief. The answer has been to drive the car of suppression still more relentlessly upon them.

4. If monopolistic business combinations in this country could have everything ordered to their wish they could not order anything better for themselves than to have the anti-trust laws suspended, industry put into their unlimited mastery and the means provided to silence, suppress, eliminate or ignore their complaining small competitors. And exactly this is the situation in most of the codes we have examined.

5. Further observations should be made concerning the control of industry by trade associations, known as "institutes," or by similarly constituted bodies. In many instances this has been plainly revealed as an evil having many aspects. In general it is obtained by a voting arrangement whereby the larger interests win unfairly to an autocratic sway. But the principles of democracy must apply to industry no less than to politics. So long as men are coerced by institutions or powers in which they have no share in this country at least they will resent their servitude, and the efficiency of production and distribution will fall short. We are, therefore, forced to the conclusion that the present method of setting up code authorities is sadly defective and that the cost of administration is, in many cases, expensive and sometimes heavily burdensome to the smaller interests of the industry. Our candid and unbiased belief is that every member of an industry subject to the provisions of a code should be guaranteed a voice in the selection of the governing body known as the code authority. We are concerned, further, that all administrative members of the code authority should be selected with an eye single to their fitness and qualifications for the duties to be assumed; they should be entitled to vote upon all questions; they should be paid out of government funds.

6. The basing point system of price making is a potent instrument to protect and further monopolistic practices and to increase the oppression of small enterprises. It should be eliminated from all industry.

7. While "stop loss" provisions in the codes are desirable and in harmony with the purposes of the National Recovery

Act, nevertheless, the attempt to fix prices was an error and should be abandoned as soon as possible.

8. Too many codes were attempted. Most of the codes covering small industries were worse than superfluous; they were inexcusable interferences with business enterprises conducted in the main as well as is possible.

9. The codes were too drastic and attempted too much. To abolish child labor was a most worthy object; to establish labor's right to bargain collectively was most salutary. To shorten the hours of la-

bor was well. But to deliver industry into the hands of its greatest and most ruthless units when the protection of the anti-trust laws had been withdrawn was a grave error. It may safely be said that not in many years have monopolistic tendencies in industry been so forwarded and strengthened as they have been through the perversion of an act excellently intended to restore prosperity and promote the general welfare. These are the facts, and we believe that the sooner they are frankly recognized and bravely dealt with the better for the nation and its people.

6. *SCHECHTER POULTRY CORPORATION* v. *UNITED STATES*[1]

EDITORS' NOTE.—In May, 1935, the Supreme Court, by the following decision, declared the NRA unconstitutional and thereby brought to a sudden close this two-year-old experiment in industrial self-rule. Even many New Deal admirers were relieved by this court decision, which thereby eliminated the necessity of action to alter

or terminate in part an economic experiment which seemed increasingly to be breaking down. However, certain aspects of the NRA which seemed to the administration to be worthy of salvage were reinstituted in constitutional fashion in the Wagner Act of July, 1935, and in the Wages and Hours Act of 1938.

Mr. Chief Justice HUGHES delivered the opinion of the Court.

Petitioners were convicted in the District Court of the United States for the Eastern District of New York on eighteen counts of an indictment charging violations of what is known as the "Live Poultry Code," and on an additional count for conspiracy to commit such violations. By demurrer to the indictment and appropriate motions on the trial, the defendants contended (1) that the Code had been adopted pursuant to an unconstitutional delegation by Congress of legislative power; (2) that it attempted to regulate intrastate transactions which lay outside the authority of Congress; and (3) that in

certain provisions it was repugnant to the due process clause of the Fifth Amendment. . . .

The defendants are slaughterhouse operators of the latter class. A. L. A. Schechter Poultry Corporation and Schechter Live Poultry Market are corporations conducting wholesale poultry slaughterhouse markets in Brooklyn, New York City. Joseph Schechter operated the latter corporation and also guaranteed the credits of the former corporation which was operated by Martin, Alex and Aaron Schechter. Defendants ordinarily purchase their live poultry from commission men at the West Washington Market in New York City or at the railroad terminals serving the City, but occasionally they purchase from commission men in Philadelphia. They buy the poultry for slaughter

1. *Schechter Poultry Corporation* v. *United States,* 295 U.S. 495, 519–25, 527–29, 534–35, 537–39, 541–44, 546–51.

and resale. After the poultry is trucked to their slaughterhouse markets in Brooklyn, it is there sold, usually within twenty-four hours, to retail poultry dealers and butchers who sell directly to consumers. The poultry purchased from the defendants is immediately slaughtered, prior to delivery, by shochtim in defendants' employ. Defendants do not sell poultry in interstate commerce.

The "Live Poultry Code" was promulgated under §3 of the National Industrial Recovery Act. That section—the pertinent provisions of which are set forth in the margin—authorizes the President to approve "codes of fair competition." Such a code may be approved for a trade or industry, upon application by one or more trade or industrial associations or groups, if the President finds (1) that such associations or groups "impose no inequitable restrictions on admission to membership therein and are truly representative," and (2) that such codes are not designed "to promote monopolies or to eliminate or oppress small enterprises and will not operate to discriminate against them, and will tend to effectuate the policy" of Title I of the Act. Such codes "shall not permit monopolies or monopolistic practices." As a condition of his approval, the President may "impose such conditions (including requirements for the making of reports and the keeping of accounts) for the protection of consumers, competitors, employees, and others, in furtherance of the public interest, and may provide such exceptions to and exemptions from the provisions of such code as the President in his discretion deems necessary to effectuate the policy herein declared." Where such a code has not been approved, the President may prescribe one, either on his own motion or on complaint. Violation of any provision of a code (so approved or prescribed) "in any transaction in or affecting interstate or foreign commerce" is made a misdemeanor punishable by a fine of not more than $500 for each offense, and each

day the violation continues is to be deemed a separate offense.

The "Live Poultry Code" was approved by the President on April 13, 1934. Its divisions indicate its nature and scope. The Code has eight articles entitled (1) purposes, (2) definition, (3) hours, (4) wages, (5) general labor provisions, (6) administration, (7) trade practice provisions, and (8) general.

The declared purpose is "To effect the policies of title I of the National Industrial Recovery Act." The Code is established as "a code of fair competition for the live poultry industry of the metropolitan area in and about the City of New York." That area is described as embracing the five boroughs of New York City, the counties of Rockland, Westchester, Nassau and Suffolk in the State of New York, the counties of Hudson and Bergen in the State of New Jersey, and the county of Fairfield in the State of Connecticut.

The "industry" is defined as including "every person engaged in the business of selling, purchasing for resale, transporting, or handling and/or slaughtering live poultry, from the time such poultry comes into the New York metropolitan area to the time it is first sold in slaughtered form," and such "related branches" as may from time to time be included by amendment. Employers are styled "members of the industry," and the term employee is defined to embrace "any and all persons engaged in the industry, however compensated," except "members."

The Code fixes the number of hours for work-days. It provides that no employee, with certain exceptions, shall be permitted to work in excess of forty (40) hours in any one week, and that no employee, save as stated, "shall be paid in any pay period less than at the rate of fifty (50) cents per hour." The article containing "general labor provisions" prohibits the employment of any person under sixteen years of age, and declares that employees shall have the right of "collective bargaining," and freedom of choice with respect to labor organizations, in the terms of §7(a) of the Act. The minimum number of employees, who shall be employed by slaughterhouse operators, is fixed, the number being graduated according to the average volume of weekly sales.

Provision is made for administration through an "industry advisory committee," to be selected by trade associations and members of the industry, and a "code supervisor" to be appointed, with the approval of the committee, by agreement between the Secretary of Agriculture and the Administrator for Industrial Recovery. The expenses of administration are to be borne by the members of the industry proportionately upon the basis of volume of business, or such other factors as the advisory committee may deem equitable, "subject to the disapproval of the Secretary and/or Administrator."

The seventh article, containing "trade practice provisions," prohibits various practices which are said to constitute "unfair methods of competition." The final article provides for verified reports, such as the Secretary or Administrator may require, "(1) for the protection of consumers, competitors, employees, and others, and in furtherance of the public interest, and (2) for the determination by the Secretary or Administrator of the extent to which the declared policy of the act is being effectuated by this code." The members of the industry are also required to keep books and records which "will clearly reflect all financial transactions of their respective businesses and the financial condition thereof," and "to submit weekly reports showing the range of daily prices and volume of sales" for each kind of produce. . . .

Of the eighteen counts of the indictment upon which the defendants were convicted, aside from the count for conspiracy, two counts charged violation of the minimum wage and maximum hour provisions of the Code, and ten counts were for violation of the requirement (found in the "trade practice provisions")

of "straight killing." This requirement was really one of "straight" selling. The term "straight killing" was defined in the Code as "the practice of requiring persons purchasing poultry for resale to accept the run of any half coop, coop, or coops, as purchased by slaughterhouse operators, except for culls." The charges in the ten counts, respectively, were that the defendants in selling to retail dealers and butchers had permitted "selections of individual chickens taken from particular coops and half coops."

Of the other six counts, one charged the sale to a butcher of an unfit chicken; two counts charged the making of sales without having the poultry inspected or approved in accordance with regulations or ordinances of the City of New York; two counts charged the making of false reports or the failure to make reports relating to the range of daily prices and volume of sales for certain periods; and the remaining count was for sales to slaughterers or dealers who were without licenses required by the ordinances and regulations of the city of New York.

First. Two preliminary points are stressed by the Government with respect to the appropriate approach to the important questions presented. We are told that the provision of the statute authorizing the adoption of codes must be viewed in the light of the grave national crisis with which Congress was confronted. Undoubtedly, the conditions to which power is addressed are always to be considered when the exercise of power is challenged. Extraordinary conditions may call for extraordinary remedies. But the argument necessarily stops short of an attempt to justify action which lies outside the sphere of constitutional authority. Extraordinary conditions do not create or enlarge constitutional power. The Constitution established a national government with powers deemed to be adequate, as they have proved to be both in war and peace, but these powers of the national government are limited by the constitutional grants.

Those who act under these grants are not at liberty to transcend the imposed limits because they believe that more or different power is necessary. Such assertions of extra-constitutional authority were anticipated and precluded by the explicit terms of the Tenth Amendment—"The powers not delegated to the United States by the Constitution, nor prohibited by it to the States, are reserved to the States respectively, or to the people."

The further point is urged that the national crisis demanded a broad and intensive cooperative effort by those engaged in trade and industry, and that this necessary cooperation was sought to be fostered by permitting them to initiate the adoption of codes. But the statutory plan is not simply one for voluntary effort. It does not seek merely to endow voluntary trade or industrial associations or groups with privileges or immunities. It involves the coercive exercise of the law-making power. The codes of fair competition which the statute attempts to authorize are codes of laws. If valid, they place all persons within their reach under the obligation of positive law, binding equally those who assent and those who do not assent. Violations of the provisions of the codes are punishable as crimes.

Second. The question of the delegation of legislative power. . . .

For a statement of the authorized objectives and content of the "codes of fair competition" we are referred repeatedly to the "Declaration of Policy" in section one of Title I of the Recovery Act. Thus, the approval of a code by the President is conditioned on his finding that it "will tend to effectuate the policy of this title." §3(a). The President is authorized to impose such conditions "for the protection of consumers, competitors, employees, and others, and in furtherance of the public interest, and may provide such exceptions to and exemptions from the provisions of such code as the President in his discretion deems necessary to effectuate the policy herein declared." *Id.* The "policy herein declared" is manifestly that set forth in section one. That declaration embraces a broad range of objectives. Among them we find the elimination of "unfair competitive practices." . . .

. . . We think the conclusion is inescapable that the authority sought to be conferred by §3 was not merely to deal with "unfair competitive practices" which offend against existing law, and could be the subject of judicial condemnation without further legislation, or to create administrative machinery for the application of established principles of law to particular instances of violation. Rather, the purpose is clearly disclosed to authorize new and controlling prohibitions through codes of laws which would embrace what the formulators .would propose, and what the President would approve, or prescribe, as wise and beneficient measures for the government of trades and industries in order to bring about their rehabilitation, correction and development, according to the general declaration of policy in section one. Codes of laws of this sort are styled "codes of fair competition."

We find no real controversy upon this point and we must determine the validity of the Code in question in this aspect. . . .

The question, then, turns upon the authority which §3 of the Recovery Act vests in the President to approve or prescribe. If the codes have standing as penal statutes, this must be due to the effect of the executive action. But Congress cannot delegate legislative power to the President to exercise an unfettered discretion to make whatever laws he thinks may be needed or advisable for the rehabilitation and expansion of trade or industry. . . .

Accordingly we turn to the Recovery Act to ascertain what limits have been set to the exercise of the President's discretion. *First*, the President, as a condition of approval, is required to find that the trade or industrial associations or groups which propose a code, "impose no inequitable restrictions on admission to membership" and are "truly representative." That condition, however, relates only to the status of the initiators of the new laws and not to the permissible scope of such laws. *Second*, the President is required to find that the code is not "designed to promote monopolies or to eliminate or oppress small enterprises and will not operate to discriminate against them." And, to this is added a proviso that the code "shall not permit monopolies or monopolistic practices." But these restrictions leave virtually untouched the field of policy envisaged by section one, and, in that wide field of legislative possibilities, the proponents of a code, refraining from monopolistic designs, may roam at will and the President may approve or disapprove their proposals as he may see fit. . . .

Nor is the breadth of the President's discretion left to the necessary implications of this limited requirement as to his findings. As already noted, the President in approving a code may impose his own conditions, adding to or taking from what is proposed, as "in his discretion" he thinks necessary "to effectuate the policy" declared by the Act. Of course, he has no less liberty when he prescribes a code on his own motion or on complaint, and he is free to prescribe one if a code has not been approved. The Act provides for the creation by the President of administrative agencies to assist him, but the action or reports of such agencies, or of his other assistants—their recommendations and findings in relation to the making of codes —have no sanction beyond the will of the President, who may accept, modify or reject them as he pleases. Such recommendations or findings in no way limit the authority which §3 undertakes to vest in the President with no other conditions than those there specified. And this authority relates to a host of different trades and industries, thus extending the President's discretion to all the varieties of laws which he may deem to be beneficial in dealing with the vast array of commercial and industrial activities throughout the country.

Such a sweeping delegation of legisla-

tive power finds no support in the decisions upon which the Government especially relies. . . .

To summarize and conclude upon this point: Section 3 of the Recovery Act is without precedent. It supplies no standards for any trade, industry or activity. It does not undertake to prescribe rules of conduct to be applied to particular states of fact determined by appropriate administrative procedure. Instead of prescribing rules of conduct, it authorizes the making of codes to prescribe them. For that legislative undertaking, §3 sets up no standards, aside from the statement of the general aims of rehabilitation, correction and expansion described in section one. In view of the scope of that broad declaration, and of the nature of the few restrictions that are imposed, the discretion of the President in approving or prescribing codes, and thus enacting laws for the government of trade and industry throughout the country, is virtually unfettered. We think that the code-making authority thus conferred is an unconstitutional delegation of legislative power.

Third. The question of the application of the provisions of the Live Poultry Code to intrastate transactions. Although the validity of the codes (apart from the question of delegation) rests upon the commerce clause of the Constitution, §3(a) is not in terms limited to interstate and foreign commerce. From the generality of its terms, and from the argument of the Government at the bar, it would appear that §3(a) was designed to authorize codes without that limitation. But under §3(f) penalties are confined to violations of a code provision "in any transaction in or affecting interstate or foreign commerce." This aspect of the case presents the question whether the particular provisions of the Live Poultry Code, which the defendants were convicted for violating and for having conspired to violate, were within the regulating power of Congress.

These provisions relate to the hours and wages of those employed by defendants in their slaughterhouses in Brooklyn and to the sales there made to retail dealers and butchers.

(1) Were these transactions *"in"* interstate commerce? Much is made of the fact that almost all the poultry coming to New York is sent there from other States. But the code provisions, as here applied, do not concern the transportation of the poultry from other States to New York, or the transactions of the commission men or others to whom it is consigned, or the sales made by such consignees to defendants. When defendants had made their purchases, whether at the West Washington Market in New York City or at the railroad terminals serving the City, or elsewhere, the poultry was trucked to their slaughterhouses in Brooklyn for local disposition. The interstate transactions in relation to that poultry then ended. Defendants held the poultry at their slaughterhouse markets for slaughter and local sale to retail dealers and butchers who in turn sold directly to consumers. Neither the slaughtering nor the sales by defendants were transactions in interstate commerce. . . .

The undisputed facts thus afford no warrant for the argument that the poultry handled by defendants at their slaughterhouse markets was in a *"current"* or *"flow"* of interstate commerce and was thus subject to congressional regulation. The mere fact that there may be a constant flow of commodities into a State does not mean that the flow continues after the property has arrived and has become commingled with the mass of property within the State and is there held solely for local disposition and use. So far as the poultry here in question is concerned, the flow in interstate commerce had ceased. The poultry had come to a permanent rest within the State. It was not held, used, or sold by defendants in relation to any further transactions in interstate commerce and was not destined for transportation to other States. Hence, decisions which deal with a stream of interstate commerce—

where goods come to rest within a State temporarily and are later to go forward in interstate commerce—and with the regulations of transactions involved in that practical continuity of movement, are not applicable here. . . .

(2) Did the defendants' transactions directly *"affect"* interstate commerce so as to be subject to federal regulation? The power of Congress extends not only to the regulation of transactions which are part of interstate commerce, but to the protection of that commerce from injury. . . .

In determining how far the federal government may go in controlling intrastate transactions upon the ground that they "affect" interstate commerce, there is a necessary and well-established distinction between direct and indirect effects. The precise line can be drawn only as individual cases arise, but the distinction is clear in principle. Direct effects are illustrated by the railroad cases we have cited, as *e.g.*, the effect of failure to use prescribed safety appliances on railroads which are the highways of both interstate and intrastate commerce, injury to an employee engaged in interstate transportation by the negligence of an employee engaged in an intrastate movement, the fixing of rates for intrastate transportation which unjustly discriminates against interstate commerce. But where the effect of intrastate transactions upon interstate commerce is merely indirect, such transactions remain within the domain of state power. If the commerce clause were construed to reach all enterprises and transactions which could be said to have an indirect effect upon interstate commerce, the federal authority would embrace practically all the activities of the people and the authority of the State over its domestic concerns would exist only by sufferance of the federal government. Indeed, on such a theory, even the development of the State's commercial facilities would be subject to federal control. . . .

The distinction between direct and indirect effects has been clearly recognized in the application of the Anti-Trust Act. Where a combination or conspiracy is formed, with the intent to restrain interstate commerce or to monopolize any part of it, the violation of the statute is clear. . . . But where that intent is absent, and the objectives are limited to intrastate activities, the fact that there may be an indirect effect upon interstate commerce does not subject the parties to the federal statute, notwithstanding its broad provisions. . . .

While these decisions related to the application of the federal statute, and not to its constitutional validity, the distinction between direct and indirect effects of intrastate transactions upon interstate commerce must be recognized as a fundamental one, essential to the maintenance of our constitutional system. Otherwise, as we have said, there would be virtually no limit to the federal power and for all practical purposes we should have a completely centralized government. We must consider the provisions here in question in the light of this distinction.

The question of chief importance relates to the provisions of the Code as to the hours and wages of those employed in defendants' slaughterhouse markets. It is plain that these requirements are imposed in order to govern the details of defendants' management of their local business. The persons employed in slaughtering and selling in local trade are not employed in interstate commerce. Their hours and wages have no direct relation to interstate commerce. The question of how many hours these employees should work and what they should be paid differs in no essential respect from similar questions in other local businesses which handle commodities brought into a State and there dealt in as a part of its internal commerce. This appears from an examination of the considerations urged by the Government with respect to conditions in the poultry trade. Thus, the Government argues that hours and wages affect prices; that slaughterhouse men sell at a small margin above operating costs; that labor represents 50 to 60 per cent of these costs; that a slaughterhouse operator paying lower wages or reducing his cost by exacting long hours of work, translates his saving into lower prices; that this results in demands for a cheaper grade of goods; and that the cutting of prices brings about a demoralization of the price structure. Similar conditions may be adduced in relation to other businesses. The argument of the Government proves too much. If the federal government may determine the wages and hours of employees in the internal commerce of a State, because of their relation to cost and prices and their indirect effect upon interstate commerce, it would seem that a similar control might be exerted over other elements of cost, also affecting prices, such as the number of employees, rents, advertising, methods of doing business, etc. All the processes of production and distribution that enter into cost could likewise be controlled. If the cost of doing an intrastate business is in itself the permitted object of federal control, the extent of the regulation of cost would be a question of discretion and not of power.

The Government also makes the point that efforts to enact state legislation establishing high labor standards have been impeded by the belief that unless similar action is taken generally, commerce will be diverted from the States adopting such standards, and that this fear of diversion has led to demands for federal legislation on the subject of wages and hours. The apparent implication is that the federal authority under the commerce clause should be deemed to extend to the establishment of rules to govern wages and hours in intrastate trade and industry generally throughout the country, thus overriding the authority of the States to deal with domestic problems arising from labor conditions in their internal commerce.

It is not the province of the Court to consider the economic advantages or disadvantages of such a centralized system. It is sufficient to say that the Federal Constitution does not provide for it. Our growth and development have called for wide use of the commerce power of the federal government in its control over the expanded activities of interstate commerce, and in protecting that commerce from burdens, interferences, and conspiracies to restrain and monopolize it. But the authority of the federal government may not be pushed to such an extreme as to destroy the distinction, which the commerce clause itself establishes, between commerce "among the several States" and the internal concerns of a State. The same answer must be made to the contention that is based upon the serious economic situation which led to the passage of the Recovery Act—the fall in prices, the decline in wages and employment, and the curtailment of the market for commodities. Stress is laid upon the great importance of maintaining wage distributions which would provide the necessary stimulus in starting "the cumulative forces making for expanding commercial activity." Without in any way disparaging this motive, it is enough to say that the recuperative efforts of the federal government must be made in a manner consistent with the authority granted by the Constitution.

We are of the opinion that the attempt through the provisions of the Code to fix the hours and wages of employees of defendants in their intrastate business was not a valid exercise of federal power. . . .

On both the grounds we have discussed, the attempted delegation of legislative power, and the attempted regulation of intrastate transactions which affect interstate commerce only indirectly, we hold the code provisions here in question to be invalid and that the judgment of conviction must be reversed. . . .

[Justice CARDOZO delivered a concurring opinion with which Justice STONE concurred.]

7. THE MAKING OF INDUSTRIAL POLICY[1]

By GARDINER C. MEANS

EDITORS' NOTE.—American history of the interwar period, including as it did a major economic collapse, has been productive of proposals of varied political roads to economic reconstruction and stability. Herbert Hoover, Hugh Johnson, Senator O'Mahoney, and David Lilienthal have described several of these roads. The diversity of these proposals has also produced several significant efforts to study the alternative roads for government in dealing with the economy with the aim of clarifying their similarities and differences so that the people may judge more wisely.

1. Senate Document No. 13, Serial No. 9909 (74th Cong., 1st sess.), pp. 9–13.

Gardiner C. Means, who has already been introduced as co-author of *The Modern Corporation and Private Property* (p. 480), was one of the major writers in the government service seeking to fulfil this role. His experiences from 1933 to 1935 as a member of the Consumers' Advisory Board of the NRA, which tried to protect consumer interests in the framing of the codes, and as economic adviser on finance to the Secretary of Agriculture contributed to his report of January, 1935, reproduced in part below, on "The Making of Industrial Policy."

The following year, with Caroline F. Ware, his wife, he published *The Modern Economy in Action*, an effort to make economic issues understandable to the general reader. In 1939 and 1940 the National Resources Committee published *The Structure of the American Economy*, Volume I of which presented a comprehensive description of the basic characteristics of our economy of the interwar period and Volume II of which included analyses of our future policy alternatives. Gardi-

ner C. Means was the director in charge of its preparation. Since 1943 Means has been associated with the Committee for Economic Development, an independent, nonpolitical organization established by American businessmen to promote clear thinking on economic policy. The Statistical Appendix (Nos. 15, 30, 31) should prove useful in following Means's discussion.

I. THE BASIC CAUSE FOR THE FAILURE OF A LAISSEZ FAIRE POLICY

1. The National Recovery Administration and Agricultural Adjustment Administration were created in response to an overwhelming demand from many quarters that certain elements in the making of industrial policy (including agriculture as an industry) should no longer be left to the market place and the price mechanism but should be placed in the hands of administrative bodies—code authorities, crop control committees, etc. This demand is not only a product of emergency conditions, but is also a reflection of more basic dissatisfactions with the results of laissez faire, such as are reflected in the demands for weakening the antitrust laws, strengthening labor organization, intervening aid to farmers, and for such economic reorganization as will bring the higher standard of living made possible by modern technology.

2. The whole trend of social development both in this country and abroad has been to recognize the failure of a complete laissez faire policy.

3. The basic cause for the failure of a laissez faire policy is to be found in the very same forces which have made possible a high standard of living for all, namely, the gradual, century-long shift from market to administrative coordination of economic activity which has resulted in modern industrial organization and modern technology. This shift to administration has brought a new type of

competition and inflexible administered prices which disrupt the workings of the market.

4. A century ago the great bulk of economic activity in the United States was conducted on an atomistic basis by individuals or families—as is most of agriculture today—while the actions of the separate individuals were coordinated by the market. The individual produced for sale and his activity was geared to and in part controlled by flexible market prices. Balance between the actions of individuals was maintained—insofar as it was maintained—by the impersonal forces of the market and the law of supply and demand. Through the market, the apparently unrelated activities of individuals were thus made to mesh into a single coordinated whole and industrial policy was made by the market as a result. The policy of laissez faire has rested on the assumption that the market would continue to make industrial policy and would remain a satisfactory coordinating mechanism.

5. But gradually more and more of economic coordination has been accomplished administratively. Great numbers of individuals have been drawn into large factories or business organizations and their activities have come to be coordinated within the separate enterprises by administrative action. In a single factory the separate activities of thousands of workers are coordinated by the factory management so as to mesh into a single producing organization. Within single corporate enter-

prises, tens and even hundreds of thousands of individuals have their economic activity coordinated by administrative direction. In 1929 the activity of over 400,-000 workers was meshed into a great communication system by the management of the American Telephone & Telegraph Co. Contrast the coordination and balance among this group of workers with that among 400,000 separate farmers whose action in producing more or less of each product is controlled and balanced only by the market. In the first, we have the extreme of administrative coordination; in the second, the extreme of market coordination.

6. The shift from market to administrative coordination has gone so far that a major part of American economic activity is now carried on by great administrative units—our great corporations. More than half of all manufacturing activity is carried on by 200 big corporations while big corporations dominate the railroad and public-utility fields and play an important role in the fields of construction and distribution.

7. This development of administrative coordination has made possible tremendous increases in the efficiency of industrial production within single enterprises. The large number of workers brought into a single organization has allowed a high degree of subdivision of labor and the use of complicated series of machines so that the volume of production has been expanded way beyond the capacity of the same number of workers operating independently. Organization has made for rapid and extensive development of technology and the improving technology in turn has increased the advantages of administrative coordinating. The telephone, the automobile, modern plumbing, are the joint product of technology and administration. The possibility of a high standard of living for all rests on these two interrelated factors.

8. But the very concentration of economic activity which brought increased productivity has by its nature destroyed the free market and disrupted the operations of the law of supply and demand in a great many industries and for the economy as a whole.

9. Evidence of this disruption is to be found in the administrative character and relative inflexibility of price in a great many industries and the fact that on the whole prices during the depression have tended to go down least where the drop in demand has been greatest.

10. The failure of prices to adjust is perfectly familiar to business men in nearly every industry. But the implications of this familiar fact for the economy as a whole have not been recognized.

11. In a large part of industry, the market is not equating supply and demand through a flexible price mechanism, but is bringing an adjustment of production to demand at administratively determined prices. Thus, General Motors may set the f.o.b. price of a 1934 Chevrolet at $500 and produce the half million cars demanded at that price, yet be willing and eager to produce and sell a million cars at that price if only there were buyers.

12. The presence of administered prices, while it does not indicate monopoly, does mean that the number of concerns competing in the market has been reduced to the point that the individual concern has a significant power to choose within limits between changing its prices and changing its volume of production or sales. When any small drop in demand occurs, it is in a position to hold its price and reduce its production without losing all its business. As a result it tends to hold up price and reduce volume of production for the industry as a whole.

13. But this means that individuals have a direct power over industrial policy which they exercise in making business policy for their own enterprise.

14. The distinction drawn here between industrial policy and business policy is of the greatest importance.

15. According to laissez faire principles, industrial policy was supposed to result

from the interaction in the market of the business policies of a large number of independent units, no one of which had any significant power. In the truly atomistic economy to which the principles of laissez faire applied, no individual buyer or seller alone had any significant power over either price or total volume of production for the industry. Prior to A.A.A., agricultural products, such as wheat and cotton, were produced and marketed under these conditions.

16. Where the number of competing units in a particular industry have been reduced to a relatively small handful, industrial policy is no longer made wholly by the market but in part by individuals. Industrial policy becomes subject to administrative control even though there is no monopoly or collusion between the separate enterprises.

17. But when the business man has the power to affect industrial policy, he almost necessarily makes wrong industrial decisions. The very position, experience and training of the business man which lead him to make the correct decisions on business policy tend to force him to make the wrong decisions on industrial policy in spite of the utmost public spirit which he, as an individual, may seek to exercise. The fact that his decisions are wrong from the point of view of the public interest is no necessary reflection on either his character or his intelligence, but arises from the nature of the situation within which he operates and the functions which he performs.

18. The business man is expected to make business policy in a way to maximize the profits of his own enterprise. When he has the power to choose between lowering price and lowering production, good business policy frequently requires him in the presence of falling demand to hold price and curtail his production even though this means idle men and idle machines. The amount by which he can count on increasing his sales by lowering price is usually so small that the whole balance of his interest as a business man points toward a restriction of production. The fact that he can lay off his workers enables him to cut production without having to carry the burden of idle workers as he does that of idle machines. His interest dictates lowering price only when he is able to squeeze his costs, particularly his labor costs. At best, it is an even choice whether he will choose to maintain profits or minimize losses by seeking a relatively large profit margin on a reduced volume or a small margin on a maintained volume of sales, and in such a situation the easier device, and the one involving the lesser risk, is the device of holding price and accepting curtailed volume. It is only because this holding of prices has become widespread and customary that the term "price chiseler" could be a term of opprobrium in an economy supposed to be coordinated through flexible prices.

19. The net effect of business control over industrial policy is, therefore, to aggravate any fluctuations in economic activity and prevent any necessary readjustments. An initial drop in demand would result, not in price readjustment, but in maintained prices and curtailment of production, thus throwing workers and machines out of employment, reducing money income and spending power, and further reducing demand. The inflexible administered prices resulting from the shift from market to administration thus act as a disrupting factor in the economy and could cause an initial small drop in demand to become a national disaster.

20. Only as the business man was willing to go directly counter to the interests of his enterprise as a profit-making concern and against business tradition would he make the kind of decisions which, if made throughout industry, would keep the economy functioning and would serve the fundamental interests of business itself. If during the depression individual business men throughout the economy had been persuaded to lower their prices, thus making decisions which appeared by all the standards available to them to be adverse

to their interests, the result would actually have been in their interest since it would have reduced the severity of the breakdown.

21. So long, therefore, as concentration exists and important powers over industrial policy are exercised in the guise of business policy and result in inflexible administered prices, the market cannot be expected to coordinate and balance economic activity under a policy of laissez faire.

22. Thus, administrative coordination —the very thing that has made modern technology and a high standard of living possible—has destroyed the effectiveness of the market as an overall coordinator by the inflexible administered prices which are inherent in the reduction of competing units it has produced.

23. It is the effects of this failure of the market mechanism which have brought the overwhelming demand from many quarters for governmental intervention in economic matters. This inflexibility has impeded the balancing of trade between nations, disrupted the workings of monetary policy, brought the banking system to its knees, obstructed the full use of human and material resources, disorganized the flow of savings into useful equipment, brought an unbalanced national budget and greatly increased economic insecurity.

II. THE BASIC CHOICE IN SOCIAL POLICY

1. Since the administrative coordination which promises a high standard of living carries with it inflexible administered prices which destroy the effectiveness of the market as an overall coordinator, it is necessary to choose between two alternatives if an effectively functioning economy is to be established—either (1) atomize the administrative units to the point where inflexible administered prices disappear and the free market can become an effective coordinator, or (2) supplement the market mechanism with institutional arrangements (N.R.A., A.A.A., money system, etc.) sufficient to allow the economy to

function effectively in the presence of and in spite of inflexible prices.

2. The first road would require the breaking up of large corporate units into a very great number of separate and wholly independent competing enterprises with the loss in efficiency which it would entail. Few realize the extent to which it would be necessary to pulverize industry. Each of the big automobile companies would probably have to be made into a hundred or more independent concerns; the big chemical companies would have to be broken into very much smaller units; and even after the breakup of the unregulated part of industry, the inflexible prices in the railroad and utility fields would impede economic adjustment, unless they also were broken up and made competitive. In order to make a laissez faire policy truly effective, productive efficiency would have to be greatly impaired and a lower standard of living accepted than is made possible by modern industrial organization and modern technology.

3. The second road, while employing the market as a major instrument, would seek to supplement the market at the points where it tends to fail. Many have held that this would require Government ownership or dictatorship since they can see no other alternative to a laissez faire policy.

4. Actually, the choice does not lie between private ownership and Government ownership because the problem is primarily the distribution of controls, not the locus of ownership.

5. Nor does the choice lie between the atomization of industry and an economic dictatorship, since it is only necessary to set up an institutional framework through which certain key industrial decisions are made and within which private or corporate enterprise and initiative can function effectively.

6. If inflexible administered prices are to be accepted as an inevitable product of modern technology and modern industrial organization, the following lines of action

would be called for to prevent them from being a disrupting influence and to allow the optimum use of human and material resources.

a) First, all pressure making for a general revision of prices either upward or downward would have to be eliminated from the economy, since any development requiring a general change in the inflexible prices would result in a change in production and economic unbalance. This would mean that a monetary policy would have to be adopted which aimed to keep the flexible prices as a group approximately in line with inflexible prices as a group and that a mechanism for the adjustment of international trade balances through general changes in price would have to be replaced.

b) Second, new techniques of control would have to be worked out for establishing the necessary elements of industrial policy so that the self-interest of individuals working through the market but limited by the framework of policy established would tend to produce the optimum use of human and material resources.

c) Finally, violent dislocations in the flow of savings into capital goods would have to be minimized.

The remainder of this report will be devoted to the problems of making industrial policy.

III. THE PROBLEM OF MAKING INDUSTRIAL POLICY

1. The National Recovery Administration and the Agricultural Adjustment Administration are in part a product of the economic break-down resulting from inflexible administered prices. The major task ahead of them, if they are to facilitate the functioning of the economy, is to participate in the making of industrial policy where the market cannot produce satisfactory results.

2. The basic problem of both N.R.A. and A.A.A. is, therefore, to devise techniques of control for establishing the necessary elements of industrial policy.

3. Until this is recognized as the basic function of N.R.A. and A.A.A. the economic policies of these two agencies tend to be contradictory and confused; once the true function of these bodies has been recognized, the organization and policy implicit in this function will clarify much of their economic activity.

4. In establishing certain elements of industrial policy, the purpose of N.R.A. and A.A.A. should be to set up a framework within which the actions of individuals or groups, operating on their own initiative and in their own interest, will result in a fully functioning economy. The objective should be to accomplish what the market is supposed to accomplish, namely, a balance of the interests of the various interest groups which constitute industry so as to produce the most effective use of human and material resources.

5. To do this it is only necessary to find key decisions for each industry which, if made right, would so condition the other elements of industrial policy that the latter could be left to the actions of individuals and the operation of the market. Thus, in the peach canning industry, the single act of setting the number of cases of peaches to be packed is said to be a sufficient supplement to the market to establish all the other elements of policy in the industry. Because of market forces, the fixing of the size of the pack is said to determine within fairly narrow limits—

a) The price to and the money receipts of peach growers.

b) The profits of the peach canners.

c) The amount of employment given to labor in picking, packing and transporting peaches, making tin cans, etc. (wage rates are mostly determined by other factors).

d) The amount of peaches received (at wholesale) for a consumer's dollar.

6. The setting of key elements of industrial policy by administrative bodies to facilitate economic functioning is a new technique.

a) Earlier interventions of government in industry have been essentially different.

(1) Anti-trust legislation tried to maintain competition and the market as the maker of industrial policy and failed because it confused the absence of monopoly with the existence of a free market. The market break-down is not a matter of monopoly (as the courts have interpreted the term), but of the making of industrial policy by private individuals.

(2) Public-utility regulation establishes a major element of industrial policy—namely rates—but, because it is focused on the interests of property and not on balancing the interests of investors, workers, and consumers, it tends to aggravate the faults inherent in business decisions—witness the efforts to increase railroad rates during the depression. It has neither tackled the problem of getting service to the public under optimum conditions nor has it taken account of the problem of price rigidity introduced by the process of rate making.

(3) Government ownership and operation has involved taking on the whole job of industrial and business operation instead of simply the key industrial decisions. Government has here had to determine not only industrial policy but also business policy as well, with all the centralization which this involves.

b) Collective bargaining has been a technique for establishing certain elements of industrial policy, but it tends to place the whole emphasis on the division of the spoils and loses sight of the other major aspects of industrial policy having to do with increasing the spoils to be divided.

7. In determining industrial policy by the making of key decisions, the essential problems are, first, to discover, industry by industry, what, if any, elements of industrial policy need to be established administratively, and, second, to set up a mechanism which will get those key decisions made "right."

a) Finding key decisions is a highly technical matter of applied economics and should become increasingly effective with experience.

b) Getting the right decisions made is primarily a matter of: (1) adequate research and planning; and (2) appropriate organization to obtain the adoption of policies worked out as a joint product of the research staff and the various interests in the industry.

c) "Right" decisions are those which will achieve the results that the market has been supposed to produce, i.e., if the "right" decisions are made throughout all industries, the net effect will be the smooth functioning of the economic machine, the full use of human and material resources, and a balance of interest among individuals and groups. The "right" decisions are thus "ipso facto" in the public interest. In a depression, the decisions in each industry could only tend in the direction of fuller utilization of human and material resources, but as each industry utilized its resources to a fuller extent its expansion would allow other industries to expand further so that the making of the "right" decisions throughout all industries would gradually lead to full utilization. (When the decisions are made to maximize profit, they tend in the reverse direction, or in a manner to minimize the impetus toward recovery coming from other directions.)

IV. POSSIBLE TECHNIQUES FOR MAKING INDUSTRIAL POLICY

1. If the N.R.A. and A.A.A. are to develop a partnership technique wherein government and industry are in some way combined to establish the necessary elements of industrial policy, the location and division of power and responsibility in making decisions will importantly affect the likelihood that key decisions will be made "right." Four different methods of distributing responsibility appear to be within the realm of immediate possibility.

a) Decisions could be made by a body (code authority or control committee) made up of business men (or farmers) with the Government acting as a rubber stamp, reserving its veto power for extreme cases. This is the method which the

N.R.A. and, to a lesser extent, the A.A.A. employed for the most part during their first year.

b) The Government might undertake to make these decisions and impose them on industry, using Research and Planning Division to determine what would be "right," perhaps using the code authorities and control committees as channels for carrying out the decisions, supplemented by some method of enforcement.

c) The code authorities and control committees might constitute a balanced partnership between government and business in which government represented not only the public interest but also the specific interests of other groups in industry, i.e., labor and consumers.

d) The several interests might jointly be represented in making the key decisions with the Government, in possession of all the necessary factual data, exercising a veto power and responsible for seeing that the interactions of the several interests produced a balance in the public interest.

2. A body of business men constituting a code authority will almost necessarily make the wrong decisions on industrial policy for their industry for the same reasons that in an individual enterprise power over industrial policy leads to harmful industrial decisions. As has been indicated, this is due not primarily to lack of business foresight and intelligence but to the fact situation with which each industrial authority has to deal. Partly because of the particular interest which the business men have in the industrial policy established, and partly because the experience and training of business men have been primarily in the exercise of business judgment, the decisions on industrial policy inevitably tend to be made in terms of business policy. The result for each industry is comparable to the result when individual business men make elements of industrial policy through their own, strongly situated enterprises. The pressure to create values by establishing higher prices and lower production will persist. In each in-

dustry, the only sound business answer to falling demand is to restrict production so as to hold prices. The fact situation does not allow of any other business decision, even though the business interests of each industry would ultimately be better served if all industries lowered prices in the presence of falling demand.[2]

It is thus apparent that sound industrial policy cannot be expected if left to business groups alone, whether because in making industrial policy they act in their own business interest or simply because they exercise sound business judgment. When the lumber code authority raised prices, thus impeding recovery, it was acting according to sound business policy in the interests of the business men in the industry. To blame the lumber code authority for not establishing an effective industrial policy is to place the blame where it does not belong. It should rest on those who would place such a responsibility upon business men alone on the assumption that business policy, which aims to create values, and industrial policy, which aims to get things to people, are the same, and that those who are familiar with and interested in the one can be expected to accomplish the other. Only as business men failed to act as business men and failed to follow their business judgment would their decisions on industrial policy result in a properly functioning economy.

3. If the Government took on the whole job of making industrial decisions, it would be better equipped with the information necessary to the making of sound decisions

2. Even if in a particular case all other industries had lowered prices, it would not be sound business policy for a particular industry to lower its prices but rather to reap the benefits at the old prices of the increased volume of activity resulting from the actions of other industries. Only if the lowering of prices on the part of all other industries were dependent on the action of the particular industry would sound business policy call for a lowering of price, and even then sound business policy would mean attempting to force other industries to lower prices as much as possible while the particular industry lowers its prices as little as possible.

than would anyone else; it is committed to the public interest as the basis for those decisions; and it commands the powers of enforcement.

On the other hand, it is doubtful whether the Government could effectively exercise the whole function of making industrial policy without using almost dictatorial methods. It would inevitably become the focus of group pressures vastly more vigorous and disruptive than those now existing; it would expose itself to political attack as dictatorial, and errors in detail would be used against it as political ammunition; industrial policy making by Government itself would call for a very high degree of centralization.

4. The third possibility—joint action of Government and business, with the Government representing not only the public interest, but also the specific interests of labor and consumer groups—would probably provide the most effective available method for getting the interests of the non-dominant economic groups represented in the immediate future.

On the other hand, the Government would thereby be placed in the position of playing a dual role. In behalf of the public interest it should act as arbiter between conflicting interests; as representative of labor and consumer interests it should play a partisan role. It would be most difficult for the Government to perform this partisan role, for it would be constantly under pressure from business, the strongest of the economic interest groups, to act at least equally in its behalf; democratic government rests upon the philosophy that it is an impartial rather than a partisan body; and even if this present administration, or any other particular administration, succeeded in acting on behalf of the non-dominant groups, there is neither guaranty nor likelihood that the political commitments of future administrations would permit them so to act.

5. In the fourth possibility, that of having the several interests impinge upon each other under Government supervision, the Government would be placed in a favorable position to influence the decisions in the direction of the public interest as it would not have to play a partisan role and it would not have to thrust industrial policy upon those who had not shared directly in the making of that policy. Most of the conflict between economic interests would take place between representatives of these interests rather than focusing upon a representative of Government.[3]

The introduction of the other interests besides those of business would tend to push the decisions in the direction of the balance of interests which the market is supposed to achieve and whereby it is supposed to produce the optimum functioning of the economy. The pressure from labor representatives to maintain or increase employment and from consumer representatives to lower price and maintain the fullest use of labor and machines would be set against the business man's normal tendency to establish higher prices and lower production than the public interest demands.

Thus, in the case of canned peaches, the size of the peach pack was actually decided by a control committee composed of growers and canners, with the Secretary of Agriculture exercising a veto power over the decision. The figure finally fixed was probably not as large as the public interest demanded. The growers wanted a somewhat larger pack, the canners a smaller pack. Both consumers and picking and canning labor would have been better served by a larger pack. If consumer and labor representatives had also participated in making the decision, it is probable that the size finally set would have been somewhat larger. At the same time, if the consumers and workers had attempted to increase the size of pack too far, the growers

3. This principle was made use of in the NRA when the advisory council was set up composed of representatives from the three advisory boards (business, labor, and consumer), thereby removing from the administrators the impact of conflict among the advisory boards.

would have shifted sides and joined the canners in resisting further increase since too large a pack would have been just as much against their interests as too small a pack.

It would be essential for the consumer interest to be represented as well as those of business and labor, for labor cannot always be relied upon to counteract the inclination of business to create value by restricting production. Too often labor representatives, by focusing their attention on the division of the spoils, would be persuaded to join business in using the scarcity technique in return for higher money wages. This is indicated by the experience of some of the German cartels in which business and labor combined to exploit the consumers—i.e., the owners and workers in other industries—and of some American cities where organized labor and organized business in the building industry have combined for similar exploitation. The inclusion of consumer representatives along with those of business and labor would insure a direct pressure for the full use of resources.[4]

The chief disadvantages of such a set-up would be (1) that the diverse interests are not equally strong as pressure groups, so that the greater and more effective organization of business would make business interests still dominant; and (2) that the veto power in the hands of the government and the necessity of getting agreement on the part of conflicting groups may lead to stalemates in particular situations—a disadvantage which might also present itself if the government represented the nondominant groups in a partnership with business.

6. Whichever method of determining the key elements of industrial policy is adopted, problems distinctive to each solution must be met.

4. Determination of industrial policy by either labor or consumer groups alone, or by a combination of the two, is not a realistic possibility in America at present, short of a violent revolution.

(1) If the Government is to do the whole job, an effective enforcement machinery must be developed; it would be essential to secure public acceptance of the idea that government should exercise such power over industry; the problems inherent in centralization would have to be solved. The direct impact of conflicting groups upon the Government could be minimized by the creation of an advisory body for each industry within which the conflicting interests were represented.

(2) If the Government is to represent the nondominant economic groups, the problem becomes that of pitting the political power of these groups against the economic power of the business group. This would call for a definite realinement of political parties on the basis of economic interests.

(3) If the interests are to impinge on each other, labor and consumer interests must be strengthened as pressure groups, presumably through the building up of their organizations. Such organizations would gain a status which they do not now have by being given a constructive roll [sic] to play in the making of industrial policy, and the Government might properly take positive steps to encourage their growth, just as it did in the case of business organizations in the first year of N.R.A. and in the case of farmers through the encouragement of farm cooperatives and the farm-extension service. As the interest groups became more nearly equal in power, their decisions would tend increasingly to be in the public interest.

The danger of stalemate is inherent in any solution which contains the element of democracy and which avoids both a positive dictatorship and the complete atomization of industry necessary to make laissez faire operate effectively. By shifting the major emphasis in industrial relations from the division of the spoils to making the economic machine work—a shift which is basic to the whole technique here described—a chief reason for stalemate would automatically be removed.

7. The choice among these possible ways of determining key elements of industrial policy should be made with reference to the basic requirements for a satisfactory American program. It should be geared to the conditions established by modern technology; it should leave existing economic and governmental organization intact as far as possible; it should provide the minimum centralization compatible with necessary coordination, and avoid as far as possible bureaucracy and political influence; it should secure industrial decisions in the direction of the optimum use of human and material resources and a balance of economic interest among various groups; it should meet the traditional American demands for liberty, opportunity, and democracy as far as the need to provide security will permit, and it must be compatible with the Constitution.

8. THE TEMPORARY NATIONAL ECONOMIC COMMITTEE[1]

EDITORS' NOTE.—Franklin D. Roosevelt, on April 29, 1938, sent the following message to Congress recommending that a study be undertaken on the concentration of economic power which should aim at offering "a program to preserve private enterprise for profit by keeping it free enough to be able to utilize our resources of capital and labor at a profit." As a result, the Temporary National Economic Committee was created, with Joseph C. O'Mahoney (1884——), Democratic senator from Wyoming since 1934, as its chairman.

After several years of hearings (1938–41), Senator O'Mahoney presented his final statement, one which summarizes some of the major findings and which suggests governmental policies to deal with industrial concentration. The coming of the war diverted the President from carrying out these recommendations. Since the war Senator O'Mahoney has resumed his efforts to bring about the adoption of his program. The Statistical Appendix (Nos. 32–35) may assist in making this reading clear.

A. MESSAGE TO CONGRESS ON CONCENTRATION OF ECONOMIC POWER, 1938

By FRANKLIN D. ROOSEVELT

To the Congress of the United States:

Unhappy events abroad have retaught us two simple truths about the liberty of a democratic people.

The first truth is that the liberty of a democracy is not safe if the people tolerate the growth of private power to a point where it becomes stronger than their dem-

1. *Final Report and Recommendations of the Temporary National Economic Committee* (Washington, D.C., 1941), pp. 11–17, 672–75, 677–83, 686–87.

ocratic state itself. That, in its essence, is fascism—ownership of government by an individual, by a group, or by any other controlling private power.

The second truth is that the liberty of a democracy is not safe, if its business system does not provide employment and produce and distribute goods in such a way as to sustain an acceptable standard of living.

Both lessons hit home.

Among us today a concentration of private power without equal in history is growing.

This concentration is seriously impairing the economic effectiveness of private enterprise as a way of providing employment for labor and capital and as a way of assuring a more equitable distribution of income and earnings among the people of the Nation as a whole.

I. THE GROWING CONCENTRATION OF ECONOMIC POWER

Statistics of the Bureau of Internal Revenue reveal the following amazing figures for 1935:

Ownership of corporate assets: Of all corporations reporting from every part of the Nation, one-tenth of 1 percent of them owned 52 percent of the assets of all of them.

And to clinch the point: Of all corporations reporting, less than 5 percent of them owned 87 percent of all the assets of all of them.

Income and profits of corporations: Of all the corporations reporting from every part of the country, one-tenth of 1 percent of them earned 50 percent of the net income of all of them.

And to clinch the point: Of all the manufacturing corporations reporting, less than 4 percent of them earned 84 percent of all the net profits of all of them.

The statistical history of modern times proves that in times of depression concentration of business speeds up. Bigger business then has larger opportunity to grow still bigger at the expense of smaller competitors who are weakened by financial adversity.

The danger of this centralization in a handful of huge corporations is not reduced or eliminated, as is sometimes urged, by the wide public distribution of their securities. The mere number of security holders gives little clue to the size of their individual holdings or to their actual ability to have a voice in the management. In fact, the concentration of stock ownership of corporations in the hands of a tiny minority of the population matches the concentration of corporate assets.

The year 1929 was a banner year for distribution of stock ownership.

But in that year three-tenths of 1 percent of our population received 78 percent of the dividends reported by individuals. This has roughly the same effect as if, out of every 300 persons in our population, one person received 78 cents out of every dollar of corporate dividends, while the other 299 persons divided up the other 22 cents between them.

The effect of this concentration is reflected in the distribution of national income.

A recent study by the National Resources Committee shows that in 1935–36—

Forty-seven percent of all American families and single individuals living alone had incomes of less than $1,000 for the year; and at the other end of the ladder a little less than 1½ percent of the Nation's families received incomes which in dollars and cents reached the same total as the incomes of the 47 percent at the bottom.

Furthermore, to drive the point home, the Bureau of Internal Revenue reports that estate-tax returns in 1936 show that—

Thirty-three percent of the property which was passed by inheritance was found in only 4 percent of all the reporting estates. (And the figures of concentration would be far more impressive, if we included all the smaller estates which, under the law, do not have to report.)

We believe in a way of living in which political democracy and free private enterprise for profit should serve and protect each other—to insure a maximum of human liberty, not for a few, but for all.

It has been well said that, "The freest government, if it could exist, would not be long acceptable if the tendency of the laws were to create a rapid accumulation of property in few hands and to render the great mass of the population dependent and penniless."

Today many Americans ask the uneasy question: Is the vociferation that our liberties are in danger justified by the facts?

Today's answer on the part of average men and women in every part of the country is far more accurate than it would have been in 1929 for the very simple reason that during the past nine years we have been doing a lot of common-sense thinking. Their answer is that if there is that danger, it comes from that concentrated private economic power which is struggling so hard to master our democratic government. It will not come, as some (by no means all) of the possessors of that private power would make the people believe—from our democratic government itself.[2]

2. There is considerable evidence of growing industrial concentration during and since World War II. At least two-thirds of all prime war supply contracts were handled by only a hundred corporations. The resulting growth of these larger firms as compared with the smaller largely explains the fact that the two hundred largest manufacturing corporations in 1944 accounted for 43 per cent of the total manufacturing sales as compared with 39 per cent in 1939.

The government policy of sale of its war plants to large corporations, in the opinion of some, further increased industrial concentration. The merging of business units, which historically has been the major way of circumventing Section 7 of the Clayton Antitrust Act, has been again accelerated. Thus from 1940 through 1946 more than 1,800 formerly independent firms in manufacturing and mining, with assets amounting to nearly 5 per cent of the total asset value of all manufacturing, disappeared. And significantly, in contrast with the earlier merger movements, the present one has been characterized principally by big firms buying smaller ones rather than by combinations of big corporations.

It should be added, however, that economists are not in agreement as to whether industrial concentration has actually been associated with increase in monopoly. First, they often point out that *both* increase and decline in industrial concentration have been very real facts in the American economy. For example, whereas the famed sugar trust

II. FINANCIAL CONTROL OVER INDUSTRY

Even these statistics I have cited do not measure the actual degree of concentration of control over American industry.

Close financial control, through interlocking spheres of influence over channels of investment and through the use of financial devices like holding companies and strategic minority interests, creates close control of the business policies of enterprises which masquerade as independent units.

That heavy hand of integrated financial and management control lies upon large and strategic areas of American industry. The small businessman is unfortunately being driven into a less and less independent position in American life. You and I must admit that.

Private enterprise is ceasing to be free enterprise and is becoming a cluster of private collectivisms; masking itself as a system of free enterprise after the American model, it is in fact becoming a concealed cartel system after the European model. . . .

III. THE DECLINE OF COMPETITION AND ITS EFFECTS ON EMPLOYMENT

In output per man or machine we are the most efficient industrial nation on earth.

In the matter of complete mutual employment of capital and labor we are among the least efficient.

Our difficulties of employing labor and capital are not new. We have had them since good, free land gave out in the West at the turn of the century. They were old

---

of the E. C. Knight Case controlled 90 per cent of all refining in 1893, today the figure has dropped to 28 per cent. Second, fewness of producers in an industry or even the largeness of a single producer is not in itself proof of the actual practice of monopoly. For example, to cite the extreme case, it is said that even a single producer for an entire industry would have to compete against related products and indeed against any other product, however remote, which competes for the consumer's dollar.

before we undertook changes in our tax policy or in our labor and social legislation. They were caused not by this legislation but by the same forces which caused the legislation. The problem of bringing idle men and idle money together will not be solved by abandoning the forward steps we have taken to adjust the burdens of taxation more fairly and to attain social justice and security.

If you believe with me in private initiative, you must acknowledge the right of well-managed small business to expect to make reasonable profits. You must admit that the destruction of this opportunity follows concentration of control of any given industry into a small number of dominating corporations.

One of the primary causes of our present difficulties lies in the disappearance of price competition in many industrial fields, particularly in basic manufacture where concentrated economic power is most evident—and where rigid prices and fluctuating pay rolls are general.

Managed industrial prices mean fewer jobs. It is no accident that in industries like cement and steel where prices have remained firm in the face of a falling demand pay rolls have shrunk as much as 40 and 50 percent in recent months. Nor is it mere chance that in most competitive industries where prices adjust themselves quickly to falling demand, pay rolls and employment have been far better maintained. By prices we mean, of course, the prices of the finished articles and not the wages paid to workers.

When prices are privately managed at levels above those which would be determined by free competition, everybody pays.

The contractor pays more for materials; the homebuilder pays more for his house; the tenant pays more rent; and the worker pays in lost work.

Even the Government itself is unable, in a large range of materials, to obtain competitive bids. It is repeatedly confronted with bids identical to the last cent.

Our housing shortage is a perfect example of how ability to control prices interferes with the ability of private enterprise to fill the needs of the community and provide employment for capital and labor.

On the other hand, we have some lines of business, large and small, which are genuinely competitive. Often these competitive industries must buy their basic products from monopolistic industry, thus losing, and causing the public to lose, a large part of the benefit of their own competitive policy. Furthermore, in times of recession, the practices of monopolistic industries make it difficult for business or agriculture, which is competitive and which does not curtail production below normal needs, to find a market for its goods even at reduced prices. For at such times a large number of customers of agriculture and competitive industry are being thrown out of work by those noncompetitive industries which choose to hold their prices rather than to move their goods and to employ their workers.

If private enterprise left to its own devices becomes half-regimented and half-competitive, half-slave, and half-free, as it is today, it obviously cannot adjust itself to meet the needs and the demands of the country.

Most complaints for violations of the antitrust laws are made by businessmen against other businessmen. Even the most monopolistic businessman disapproves of all monopolies but his own. We may smile at this as being just an example of human nature, but we cannot laugh away the fact that the combined effect of the monopolistic controls which each business group imposes for its own benefit inevitably destroys the buying power of the Nation as a whole.

IV. COMPETITION DOES NOT MEAN EXPLOITATION

Competition, of course, like all other good things, can be carried to excess. Competition should not extend to fields where it has demonstrably bad social and economic consequences. The exploitation of child labor, the chiseling of workers' wages, the stretching of workers' hours, are not necessary, fair, or proper methods of competition. I have consistently urged a Federal wages-and-hours bill to take the minimum decencies of life for the working man and woman out of the field of competition.

It is, of course, necessary to operate the competitive system of free enterprise intelligently. In gaging the market for their wares, businessmen, like farmers, should be given all possible information by government and by their own associations so that they may act with knowledge, and not on impulse. Serious problems of temporary over-production can and should be avoided by disseminating information that will discourage the production of more goods than the current markets can possibly absorb or the accumulation of dangerously large inventories for which there is obvious need.

It is, of course, necessary to encourage rises in the level of those competitive prices, such as agricultural prices, which must rise to put our price structure into more workable balance and make the debt burden more tolerable. Many such competitive prices are now too low.

It may at times be necessary to give special treatment to chronically sick industries which have deteriorated too far for natural revival, especially those which have a public or quasi-public character.

But generally over the field of industry and finance we must revive and strengthen competition if we wish to preserve and make workable our traditional system of free private enterprise.

The justification of private profit is private risk. We cannot safely make America safe for the businessman who does not want to take the burdens and risks of being a businessman. . . .

VI. A PROGRAM

The traditional approach to the problems I have discussed has been through the antitrust laws. That approach we do not propose to abandon. On the contrary, although we must recognize the inadequacies of the existing laws, we seek to enforce them so that the public shall not be deprived of such protection as they afford. To enforce them properly requires thorough investigation not only to discover such violations as may exist but to avoid hit-and-miss prosecutions harmful to business and government alike. To provide for the proper and fair enforcement of the existing antitrust laws I shall submit, through the Budget, recommendations for a deficiency appropriation of $200,000 for the Department of Justice.

But the existing antitrust laws are inadequate—most importantly because of new financial economic conditions with which they are powerless to cope.

The Sherman Act was passed nearly forty years ago. The Clayton and Federal Trade Commission Acts were passed over twenty years ago. We have had considerable experience under those acts. In the meantime we have had a chance to observe the practical operation of large-scale industry and to learn many things about the competitive system which we did not know in those days.

We have witnessed the merging-out of effective competition in many fields of enterprise. We have learned that the so-called competitive system works differently in an industry where there are many independent units, from the way it works in an industry where a few large producers dominate the market.

We have also learned that a realistic system of business regulation has to reach more than consciously immoral acts. The community is interested in economic results. It must be protected from economic as well as moral wrongs. We must find practical controls over blind economic forces as well as over blindly selfish men.

Government can deal and should deal with blindly selfish men. But that is a comparatively small part—the easier part

—of our problem. The larger, more important and more difficult part of our problem is to deal with men who are not selfish and who are good citizens, but who cannot see the social and economic consequences of their actions in a modern economically interdependent community. They fail to grasp the significance of some of our most vital social and economic problems because they see them only in the light of their own personal experience and not in perspective with the experience of other men and other industries. They therefore fail to see these problems for the Nation as a whole.

To meet the situation I have described, there should be a thorough study of the concentration of economic power in American industry and the effect of that concentration upon the decline of competition. There should be an examination of the existing price system and the price policies of industry to determine their effect upon the general level of trade, upon employment, upon long-term profits, and upon consumption. The study should not be confined to the traditional antitrust field. The effects of tax, patent, and other Government policies cannot be ignored.

The study should be comprehensive and adequately financed. I recommend an appropriation of not less than $500,000 for the conduct of such comprehensive study by the Federal Trade Commission, the Department of Justice, the Securities and Exchange Commission, and such other agencies of government as have special experience in various phases of the inquiry. . . .

B. THE PRESERVATION OF ECONOMIC FREEDOM

By Joseph C. O'Mahoney

The unalienable rights of life, liberty, and the pursuit of happiness, the preservation of which was described in the Declaration of Independence as the primary reason why governments are instituted among men, belong to people and may not be taken away from people by any institution which man creates. This principle we must recognize as the cornerstone of our economic as well as of our political structure, for without it all freedom is endangered.

We must make it clear, therefore, if the work of this committee is to be successful, that we have no purpose of trying to cure the evils which have resulted from private restriction of individual opportunity by setting up any system of public restriction to take its place. The recommendations which we shall make will be designed not only to keep government free and responsive to the people, but to keep business free also. Our efforts are directed toward the maintenance of the traditional American system which regards the opportunity to labor and to possess the fruits of labor as an essential and inseparable element of the democratic system. . . .

The danger to democracy does not proceed from the propaganda of those who believe in the authoritarian state, but from our own failure to comprehend the causes of economic instability and to proceed immediately to democratic remedies. . . .

. . . We need a program which will set free for productive enterprise the unimagined energies of the most progressive people which ever inhabited this globe.

Before that task can be accomplished, however, we must first discover the underlying causes of the economic maladjustment with which we have been struggling and to mitigate which, because there was no other alternative, the Government at Washington has been compelled to engage upon a program of deficit-spending which arouses the fears even of those who authorize it.

Everyone acknowledges that in America industrial progress of a most remarkable character has been accomplished. The

American standard of living exceeds that of any other nation or of any other era. The rank and file of the people of this country enjoy luxuries which were denied to the wealthiest and most powerful only a few years ago. Yet while this is true, it is also clear, upon the other hand, that the standard of living today is much more unstable than it was in the time of our grandfathers. A much larger proportion of the people of our time are dependent for their livelihood upon conditions, agencies, and tools over which they have no control than at any time in our history.

In the beginning our commercial and industrial system, like our political system, was essentially local in almost all its aspects. The means of livelihood, the instruments of production and distribution were all readily commended by each community. So far as commerce was concerned, the functions of the National Government were directed chiefly to that which was carried on with foreign nations. With the passing years, however, local and State boundaries began to mean less and less so far as business was concerned and as this change took place the powers of the National Government began to grow. . . .

Certainly this did not come about because the people of America wanted to surrender local powers to Washington. It came about solely because people in every community found themselves dealing with new economic agencies to cope with which their traditional local governments were inadequate. Year by year business became increasingly national in scope and the new organizations by which this national business was carried on became steadily more important in the every day existence of all people in all States and in all localities.

The modern industrial system produced geographical concentration of productive enterprise before it produced the concentration of economic power and wealth which this committee has been studying. As all observers know, when manufacturing was moved from the home to the fac-tory a new era began. It was a natural and in most aspects a wholly desirable development. It was the very development which has provided the present generation with all the marvelous tools which make available the amazing convenience and luxuries in which we take so much pride, but it almost completely robbed commerce of its local aspect and made it a national phenomenon with wholly national effects and national significance. Geographical boundaries have lost most of their importance so far as commerce is concerned.

The inevitable result has been the expansion of national law. Throughout the long period during which this change has been taking place, Congress was reluctant to impose national regulations in the place of local regulations and it made changes but slowly. This generation needs no instruction to understand that commerce among the states is the most important element of our modern economic activity, but the Congress which confronted this problem for the first time more than fifty years ago thought of interstate commerce in terms of railroad transportation only and when it set up the Interstate Commerce Commission it had no thought of "interfering with private enterprise," as the phrase goes, except with respect to the railroads. That Commission was set up to regulate the railroads only because the railroad industry had grown to such an extent and had expanded so far beyond the powers of the states to regulate in the public interest that Congress had no other recourse. From that day to this there has been a steady growth of the government establishment at Washington, but let no one make the mistake of assuming that this growth has taken place because "politicians" have wanted to take business over. It has grown solely because commerce must be regulated by government in the public interest and because in this country there is no agency except the federal government which is capable of such regulation. The duty of regulating national commerce was imposed on Congress when the Constitution was adopted. It is a power which has been exercised throughout the history of our Government and its expansion is solely the result of the growth of business and not the result of the desire of Government to throttle private enterprise.

But private enterprise is threatened indeed, it has been undermined to an appalling degree not by Government and not so much by business itself, for all the monopolistic practices which have so frequently been condemned, but by a general failure to comprehend the change that has taken place and a failure properly to coordinate Government and business in their relation to people. This failure, it has seemed to me, is principally due to the fact that we seem not to realize that modern business is no longer the activity of individuals, but is the activity of organizations of individuals and we have permitted these organizations to grow so large that people are actually helpless before them. We have persisted in treating these organizations as though they were clothed with natural human rights instead of having only the rights which the people, acting through their Government, see fit to bestow upon them. It will be impossible even to begin the task of adjusting Government to business until we realize that the modern business organization has grown to such proportions that neither the people, as individuals, nor through their local governments are able to cope with it. Local business, little business, private enterprise and local government, even the government of the states themselves, are in truth and in fact submerged by modern business organizations. . . .

It may be observed that there are only ten sovereign states which have within their respective borders property valued at more than the assets of either the Metropolitan Life Insurance Company or the American Telegraph and Telephone Company. Stated in another way, each of these two corporations is richer than any

one of thirty-eight sovereign states. At the other end of the scale there are eighteen states, the taxable wealth of each of which is less than the total assets of the smallest of the thirty "billion dollar" corporations. Of these eighteen states which rank so low among the sisterhood in property values and far below the smallest of the billion dollar giants, some have been particularly active in creating interstate corporations, large and small, to carry on this national commerce upon which the economic life of the nation depends, although none of the states has the constitutional power to regulate the activities of the artificial agencies they launch upon the sea of national commerce.

Among the great corporations . . . are banks, insurance companies and industrials. In the popular discussion they are regarded as "private enterprise." But how private is such enterprise after all? The American Telephone and Telegraph Company, like Commonwealth and Southern, is a public utility and although in recent years there has been a tendency in certain circles to drop the word "public" when referring to such utilities, it is nevertheless quite clear that each of them is just as public as the thousands of municipal corporations which are likewise chartered by the several states. They are different, however, from municipal corporations in that the latter operate within the borders of the states which create them while the modern interstate corporation operates throughout the length and breadth of the land and in the land and in the field of commerce "with foreign nations and among the states," the power to regulate which was exclusively committed by the Federal Constitution to the Congress of the United States. When one considers the number of policyholders who are the owners of mutual life insurance companies like Metropolitan and Prudential, wholly national in their operation and effect, the number of stockholders and employees of a utility like American T & T, or of an industrial like General Motors and the stockholders, employees, and natural resources of industrials like the Standard Oil of New Jersey and United States Steel it becomes immediately clear that there is no justification whatsoever for thinking of these units or of dealing with them as though they were natural persons clothed with the rights which are guaranteed to flesh-and-blood persons by the Constitution of the United States.

It also becomes clear from this comparison why during the past fifty years the local aspects of commerce have been constantly decreasing in importance and the national aspects increasing. If it be said that these thirty giants fall into an unusual category and that the corporate system as a whole should not be judged by their wealth and power, it is only necessary to point out, as was shown in the hearings of this committee, that the share of all our business which is done by corporations has been steadily increasing. It was estimated, for example, by Doctor Willard L. Thorp of the Bureau of Foreign and Domestic Commerce . . . that corporations now do from 60 to 65% of the total volume of business in the United States. Few of these, of course, are to be classed with the billion dollar giants, but the fact that they do so large a proportion of the business of the country is conclusive demonstration of the all important fact that we have passed from an individual economy to a corporate economy. The position of the individual business man in all types of American industry has been steadily growing less and less important while the position of the large corporation has been growing more and more important. The computations presented by Doctor Thorp . . . show that communication and the manufacture and distribution of electric light, power and gas are 100% corporate activities. That is to say, there is no such thing as individual private enterprise left in communication or in the utility business.

In the early days of our country mining was carried on by the pioneer and it was the prospector operating usually on a grubstake who placed the riches of the western mountains at the disposal of the people. Today, 96% of all mining is carried on by corporations leaving only 4% for individual enterprise. In transportation, all but 11% of the business is carried on by corporations and in manufacturing, which produces 24% of the total national income, all but 8% is carried on by the corporate unit.

Agriculture remains today the sole industry which is still carried on for the most part by private individuals in their individual capacity. 93% of all the agricultural business of the United States is done by individuals, only 7% by corporations, but the total share of agriculture in the national income amounts to only 8.9%. The service industry is one of which one naturally thinks as a private individual activity, yet the amazing fact is that 30% of this business is carried on by corporations. Thus it becomes clear that the individual has been relegated to a position of ever lessening importance in the structure of our modern economy. The man has been losing out to the organizations of men.

GREAT CONCENTRATION OF WEALTH

It is not surprising, therefore, to find from the cold examination of the facts that organized enterprise is obtaining an increasingly larger proportion not only of national income, but of all savings and of all wealth. It was estimated by Berle and Means in their notable volume, "The Modern Corporation and Private Property," which though published in 1932, is still regarded as the primary authority in this field, that 78% of all business wealth in this country is owned by corporations. Every student of the subject paints the same picture, not only that the corporations have gained the great bulk of industrial and commercial assets and income, but that within the corporate structure itself the concentration is progressing. . . .

It might have been imagined that with

the change from the individual to the corporate economy there would probably be a large distribution of corporate ownership among individuals. The fact, however, seems to be that this amazing concentration of the corporate ownership of wealth has been accompanied by a similar concentration of dividend distribution. The great and powerful business organizations which dominate the economic scene are owned by a numerically insignificant proportion of the total population. In this study prepared by the Securities and Exchange Commission for this committee on the "Distribution of Ownership in Two Hundred Largest Non-financial Corporations" . . . it is indicated that fully one-half of all corporate stock dividends are received by less than 75,000 persons of the 130,000,000 who inhabit the United States. That is to say, less than 1% of all American corporate stockholders are the beneficiaries of one-half of all the dividends paid in this country.

The degree of concentration is even more striking when one reviews the material assembled in Monograph No. 12 on "Profits, Productive Activity and New Investment" in which it is stated that only one family out of every 6 pays an income [sic] and that of these income tax-paying families only ¼ receive corporate dividends. In 1928 . . . 96.6% of all the dividends reported by taxpayers that year were received by less than ⅕ of the persons who made income tax returns. Thus it appears that the great bulk of the wealth and income of the country is owned by corporations, that the overwhelming percentage of this is owned by comparatively few corporations, that the stock ownership of these corporations is not substantially distributed among the people of the country and, finally, that the dividends paid by these corporations go to a very small proportion of the population.

CONCENTRATION OF SAVINGS

It is only natural that with such concentration of the ownership of business wealth and income there should likewise exist a similar concentration of savings, for, obviously, only those who own sufficient property and receive an income greater than is necessary for day to day living are able to save. . . .

The natural and inevitable result is an increasing trend toward a further concentration of investment in government. Between 1921 and 1938 government obligations held by the Federal Reserve System increased from 11% of the total loans and investments to 40%. The same trend is observable in the investments of all other institutions and particularly of the life insurance companies.Whereas the 26 largest legal reserve life insurance companies on December 31, 1929, held $302,000,000 worth of United States government bonds, in 1938 they held $4,525,000,000 of these securities. Holdings of public utility bonds had increased only from $1,300,-000,000 to $2,900,000,000 while the holdings of railroad bonds had fallen off. Thus slowly as the concentration proceeds, the flow turns away even from organized business to government. Surely the moral is clear. The inevitable and inescapable result of continued concentration in big business is the final triumph of big government and the destruction of what we call the private enterprise system.

If we are agreed, and we all seem to be agreed at least here in the United States, that we want to preserve free enterprise it becomes apparent that we had better get about the task and a good way to begin, it seems to me, would be to make up our minds exactly what we want to do about our problem instead of trying to blame one another for its existence. The representatives of business, as well as the representatives of government, those who are engaged in agriculture, those who are engaged in industry, all are vitally concerned and it must be perfectly clear that any remedy which does not stop the steady progress of concentration will be utterly futile and will end only in an all-powerful government. If we want to remedy these obvious ills, we'd better stop scolding one another and begin to cooperate.

Business leaders who object to any government action overlook the plain fact that there is no possible way of bringing about the coordination which we need except through government action. To refuse to cooperate means only to accentuate the present drift toward centralism which has produced the authoritarian government in Europe and brought the democratic nations of the old world to the very brink of disaster. It is more important to business than to any other group to cooperate in the reestablishment to free individual, local, private enterprise and full employment if it desires to remain free from complete government control.

NATIONAL CHARTERS FOR NATIONAL BUSINESS

The first and most necessary step is to recognize that we must have a national rule for national business. We must be able to differentiate between that business which is naturally and properly national in scope and that business which is naturally and properly local in scope. If we desire to have business carried on by collective units, and it must be carried on thus in the modern world, then we must find the way to make these units thoroughly democratic. Economic freedom and political freedom go hand in hand. Neither can survive without the other, and since it must be acknowledged that in a republic the government of all the people must be able to speak for all the people then we have no recourse except to have that government define the rights, duties and responsibilities of the organized agencies which conduct and control the commerce on which its citizens depend for employment and income.

It is idle to think that the huge collective institutions which carry on our modern business can continue to operate without more definite responsibility toward all the people of the Nation than they now have. To do this it will be necessary, in my judgment, to have a national charter system for all national corporations. Whether this system should operate through licenses or through direct charters seems to me to be of little importance. One thing is certain: We cannot hope to stop the processes of concentration if we are willing to continue to allow the States to create agencies through and by which the concentration has been brought about.

I am aware that many businessmen, fortunately not so many now as formerly, look upon this plan for Federal charters as merely another step in the growth of all-powerful government. That is an error. It is only through a charter system that the growth of government can be prevented. For fifty years, Federal regulation and, in some instances, even Federal control of business has been steadily increasing. It is unnecessary to recite here the laws by which, during the past generation, new bureaus and commissions have been established in Washington. Without regard to which political party happened to be in power, one bureau after another has been created and, necessarily so, because without them the public interest would have been completely neglected. Businessmen have resisted every such law, but once a new agency has been created it has never been abandoned. From the establishment of the Interstate Commerce Commission down to the establishment of the Securities and Exchange Commission the same story has been told and although each in its turn has been roundly denounced by the organized agencies which were to be regulated, the necessity of the regulation has always been recognized by most of those affected and no political leader has ever dared to propose the abolition of such a commission after its establishment and the restoration of the conditions that existed before its creation.

But these bureaus and boards have been unable to solve the problem. Concentration has proceeded without interruption because those who wish to avoid the objectives of regulation in the public interest were always able through the corporate charter of some state to find a way around the law. The Insulls and the Hopsons, the Coster-Musicas, have been able to prey upon the economic system of all the people solely because they were able to secure the separate states charters which enabled them to engage in national commerce although their creators had neither the desire nor the governmental power to regulate the commerce in which they were engaged.

I see no other way to avoid the continued expansion of government debt and the continued expansion of government control over private business except through a national charter system. Such a system would make unnecessary the creation of new boards and commissions because it could be used to define so clearly the responsibilities and the duties of all national corporations that discretionary regulation would be unnecessary.

Over and over again it ought to be asserted that a corporate charter is a contract between individuals who want the privilege of doing business in corporate form and a government which speaks, or ought to speak, for all the people. Here in the United States the separate states do not have the constitutional power to speak in the public interest. Only the Federal Government has that power so far as interstate and foreign commerce is concerned. If we believe that the framers of the Constitution acted wisely when they gave to the Federal Congress the power to regulate interstate and foreign commerce, then we cannot fail to acknowledge that the Federal Congress should exercise that power by insisting upon writing the contracts which call into existence the corporations which carry on that commerce. Until that is done there can be no effective regulation except by piecemeal through the continued multiplication of government boards and commissions. That system will inevitably be accompanied by continued evasions, continued abuse, con-

tinued concentration, and continued expansions of government.

The maintenance of free private enterprise demands first of all that small enterprise should be effectively protected against attack by what we call monopoly. The big company which crushes its small competitor by underselling, that is to say, by selling at a loss, commits the unforgivable economic sin. That is not competition. That is economic war. The national oil company, for example, which enters a little community and builds a filling station across the street from an independent dealer and, by selling at a loss, forces him to sell out or suspend, destroys the very basis of a free economy. The monopolistic practices which kill free enterprise and which are without justification are so well known that they need not be restated here, but certainly the great crisis which the world now faces in the conflict of democracy and dictatorship should be enough to convince every business executive, as well as every government spokesman, that the time has come to outlaw all such practices in a way that will be effective.

That such practices exist in the United States in violation of well known law is demonstrated by the anti-trust record of the Department of Justice under the direction of one of the members of this committee. The defendants who have been charged with violations of the anti-trust law in the past three years have, for the most part, walked into court and pleaded guilty. The cases were so clear that there was no resistance. That the practices of which they were accused should not be tolerated in any society which even pretends to believe in free private enterprise no one can possibly deny, yet it is perfectly evident that the Sherman Anti-trust Law can be effectively enforced only so long as we have an Attorney General who is disposed to enforce it and a Congress that is willing to make the appropriations necessary to maintain a sufficient staff. That such a staff has not been maintained during the past fifty years except under

Thurman Arnold is one of the reasons why the concentration of economic power and wealth so clearly demonstrated by the hearings and publications of this committee has not been prevented.

It would not be difficult so to draft a national charter law as to reduce materially not only the possibilities of evasion of the antitrust law, but the difficulties of its enforcement. A charter law which, for example, would make corporate directors trustees in fact as well as in law and, at the same time, make them personally liable for violations of the antitrust law which they themselves conceived and directed, a law which would clearly define the fields into which a corporation might enter through subsidiaries and one which would standardize intercorporate financing would not only tend to prevent some of the worst infractions of both ethics and law, which have contributed to the creation of our dilemma, but would also tend to open new fields for small enterprise. . . .

The discussion I have undertaken today was not intended to be all-inclusive. I have ventured merely to point to the alternative which is now squarely presented to the people of the United States—free private enterprise or government planning.

For two generations, the concentration of economic power and wealth has proceeded at such a pace that the welfare of the masses in agriculture and industry has been seriously jeopardized. Small business has been swallowed up by big business and big business is now confronted with the danger of being swallowed up by government. The way to reverse this trend is not to be found in further expanding the powers of government, nor releasing big business from so-called "government interference." The only remedy to save a democratic economy is to be found in making the economy democratic. If we are to avoid an all-powerful central government,

we have no recourse but to reestablish and encourage free private enterprise, that is to say, private enterprise which will be free from the arbitrary control of private organizations as well as of public organization.

Therefore, I recommend:

1. National charters for national corporations, in order that these agencies may have a definite and a free place in our economy and local business may be differentiated and protected from national business;

2. The effective and thorough enforcement of the antitrust laws to maintain competition and to prevent all combinations and agreements that destroy business;

3. The encouragement of new business and small enterprise by revision of the tax laws for the purpose of encouraging new employment and new industry;

4. A national conference called by Congress of the various organizations representative of business, labor, agriculture, and consumers which have for years been working on diverse phases of this central problem might concentrate public thought and action on the objectives on which there is general agreement instead of, as now, on the objectives concerning which there is only misunderstanding, suspicion, and disagreement.

In an hour of political uncertainty one hundred and fifty-three years ago, the Continental Congress called a national convention to draft a national political constitution. That conference of American leaders was successful beyond the dreams of any of those who authorized it. Our need today is a national economic constitution which shall abolish the economic uncertainties which seem to threaten even our political system. I have an abiding faith that the patriotism and ability of the people of America is equal to the task.

In defense of democracy we must find the way to maintain and defend economic freedom for all.

9. TVA—DEMOCRACY ON THE MARCH[1]

By David E. Lilienthal

EDITORS' NOTE.—Passage of the Tennessee Valley Act of 1933 opened one of the earliest, and perhaps the most significant, of New Deal experiments in the use of positive government—an experiment which wrought vital changes in the lives of some four and one-half million people in the Tennessee River Valley.

Twice before 1933 the Congress, under the leadership of a distinguished Republican senator from Nebraska, George W. Norris, had passed bills for the public ownership and operation of certain government-built dams and nitrogen plants at Muscle Shoals on the Tennessee River. Following an earlier veto by President Coolidge, President Herbert Hoover in 1931 again defeated the plan with this warning: "I am firmly opposed to the Government entering into any business the major purpose of which is competition with our citizens . . . for the Federal Government deliberately to go out to build up and expand an occasion to the major purpose of a power and manufacturing business is to break down the initiative and enterprise of the American people; it is destruction of equality of opportunity of our people; it is the negation of the ideals upon which our civilization has been based."

The production and distribution of electric power by the government was then, and continues to be, the center of controversy over the Tennessee Valley Authority; and critics hardly feel that their case has been closed by the Supreme Court's 1936 decision, upholding the constitutionality of these governmental functions (*Ashwander et al.* v. *Tennessee Valley Authority*, 297 U.S. 288).

For David Lilienthal, former chairman of the Tennessee Valley Authority and present head of the Atomic Energy Commission, TVA is far more than a public power project. His enthusiastic defense of the agency's record rests upon a philosophy of regional planning—an attempt to join freedom and control in a new synthesis.

6. A NEW WAY—AN OLD TASK

A new chapter in American public policy was written when Congress in May of 1933 passed the law creating the TVA. For the first time since the trees fell before the settlers' ax, America set out to command nature not by defying her, as in that wasteful past, but by understanding and acting upon her first law—the oneness of men and natural resources, the unity that binds together land, streams, forests, minerals, farming, industry, mankind. . . .

For fifteen years before TVA came into being Congressional and public debate centered largely on a single potential resource of the Tennessee River, a hydroelectric power. For long years there had been determined efforts to dispose of the government dam and power plant at

[1]. David E. Lilienthal, *TVA—Democracy on the March* (New York, 1944), pp. 52–55, 65–67, 84–99, 119–20, 124–25, 138–41, 148–49, 152, 165–66, 171–72, 193–96, 199–200, 202–17, 233, 242. Reprinted by permission of Pocket Books, Inc.

Muscle Shoals in Alabama, built with public funds for World War I, as if it were like any other of the flotsam left over from that war—the trucks and shoes and trench shovels—to be knocked down to the highest bidder. It was simply regarded as a power plant, either to be dealt with as such a plant in the hands of a private operator would be, or, if continued under public control, to be limited to the sale of generated power for distribution at a profit by private industry. . . .

. . . The message of President Roosevelt urging approval of the Norris bill (which became a law with his signature on May 18, 1933) boldly proposed a new and fundamental change in the development of our country's resources. . . .

It is clear [the message read] that the Muscle Shoals development is but a small part of the potential public usefulness of the entire Tennessee River. Such use, if envisioned in its entirety, transcends mere power development: it enters the wide fields of flood control, soil erosion, afforestation, elimination from agricultural use of marginal lands, and distribution and diversification of industry. In short, this power development of war days leads logically to national planning for a complete river watershed involving many states and the future lives and welfare of millions. It touches and gives life to all forms of human concerns. . . .

To a single agency, the TVA, these potentialities of the river for good and evil were entrusted. But the river was to be seen as part of the larger pattern of the region, one asset of the many that in nature are interwoven: the land, the minerals, the waters, the forests—and all of these as one—in their relation to the lives of the valley's people. It was the total benefit to all that was to be the common goal and the new agency's responsibility. . . .

It was the methods of the past which the Act creating TVA deliberately repudiated. For in this major characteristic—the unified approach—TVA was a definite break with government tradition. There was, however, nothing particularly novel about the individual tasks entrusted for execution to this new agency. There were long-established precedents for government activity in flood control and navigation, in forestry and agriculture, and in research. Public power systems were not an innovation. The new thing about the TVA was that one agency was entrusted with responsibility for them all, and that no one activity could be considered as an end in itself. Constructing dams or rebuilding soil, whatever the activity, it had to be treated as an inseparable part of a general program to promote the well-being of all the men and women of the region, whether they worked in offices, in factories, or in the crossroads stores, in kitchens or in the fields.

ONE JOB—ONE AGENCY

The jurisdiction of the TVA cut across existing lines of federal bureaus and departments. A single agency, instead of half a dozen, was to design and build the dams, buy the land, construct transmission lines, and market the power the river produced. One agency was to "envision in its entirety" the potentialities of the whole river system, for navigation, for power, for flood control, and for recreation. The contrast between such an administrative scheme for the Tennessee River and the plans on other rivers is illustrated by a contrasting instance, where one set of men designed a dam, another agency actually built it, a third group of men then took over the operation and maintenance of one part of the dam, still a fourth group another part, a fifth disposes of one share of the output—each acting under separate direction and policies, with the power of decision for the several parts of the task centered in different hands in distant places.

Each TVA dam is a project of several purposes. TVA's engineers have designed it not only to give navigation depth to the river and the greatest possible protection from floods, but to assure every other benefit, of which power production is only one. And every dam is part of a system for the whole river, from headwaters to mouth. The location, the size, the operation of each dam is determined in relation to all the others, so that the total potential value of the entire river may be realized.

It makes a great difference in the way a job is done when responsibility is as broad as that of the TVA, when the welfare of the region is the direct objective, when the construction of a dam or a series of them is seen as only one means to that end. Each task must be carried out in such a way as to contribute to that total result, to salvage every possible benefit. With this range of responsibility in mind, the Board of the TVA decided at the beginning to build the dams by "force account"—that is, that the TVA should directly select, hire, train, and supervise the workmen and be responsible for the policies governing wages and conditions of work. The almost universal federal practice is otherwise. Government construction projects are generally "let out to contract"—that is, a contractor agrees to do the job, to buy the materials, select and pay the employees, and turn over a finished job for a price. With a few minor exceptions, for work of a special and temporary nature, such as tunnel building or the raising of a bridge, every man who has worked on these Tennessee Valley projects has been employed directly by his government. All were recruited and employed by the TVA.

Building the dams has been not only a matter of digging foundations and pouring concrete so that the river might be controlled. It has also afforded an opportunity to the men of the region to learn new skills, skills that will be badly needed as industry develops in the South. As a result of apprentice training, sharecroppers have become skilled craftsmen in these ten years, and tenant farmers have learned to be mechanics. In this way the TVA has helped to add to the reservoir of trained workmen, white and Negro, who are ready to help process the raw materials of the area. . . .

DEMOCRACY AT THE GRASS ROOTS

People are the most important fact in resource development. Not only is the welfare and happiness of individuals its true purpose, but they are the means by which that development is accomplished; their genius, their energies and spirit are the instruments; it is not only "for the people" but "by the people."

The purpose of resource development must be more than the mere physical welfare of the greatest number of human beings. It is true that we cannot be starving and cold and still be happy. But an abundance of food, the satisfaction of elementary physical needs alone, is not enough. A man wants to feel that he is important. He wants to be able not only to express his opinion freely, but to know that it carries some weight; to know that there are some things that he decides, or has a part in deciding, and that he is a needed and useful part of something far bigger than he is. . . .

Resource development need not be held fast by the dehumanizing forces of modern life that whittle down the importance of the individual. Surely it should be freed of their grip, for they are the very negation of democracy. . . .

It is the unique strength of democratic methods that they provide a way of stimulating and releasing the individual resourcefulness and inventiveness, the pride of workmanship, the creative genius of human beings whatever their station or function. A world of science and great machines is still a world of men; our modern task is more difficult, but the opportunity for democratic methods is greater even than in the days of the ax and the hand loom.

A method of organizing the modern task of resource development that not only will be based upon the principle of unity but can draw in the average man and make him a part of the great job of our time, in

537

the day-to-day work in the fields and factories and the offices of business, will tap riches of human talent that are beyond the reach of any highly centralized, dictatorial, and impersonal system of development based upon a remote control in the hands of a business, a technical, or a political elite.

It is just such widespread and intimate participation of the people in the development of their valley that has gone on here in these ten years past.

The spiritual yield of democratic methods, a renewed sense that the individual counts, would be justification enough. But there is yet another reason, a practical one, for seeking at every turn to bring people actively into the task of building a region's resources; there is, I think, really no other way in which the job can be done. The task of harmonizing and from time to time adjusting the intricate, detailed maze of pieces that make up the unified development of resources in a world of technology is something that simply cannot be done effectively from some remote government or business headquarters.

The people must be in on that job. The necessities of management make it mandatory. Efficiency, in the barest operating sense, requires it. There is nothing in my experience more heartening than this: that devices of management which give a lift to the human spirit turn out so often to be the most "efficient" methods. Viewed in any perspective there is no other way. No code of laws or regulations can possibly be detailed enough to direct the precise course of resource development. No district attorney or gestapo could, for long, hope to enforce such a regime. No blueprints or plans can ever be comprehensive enough, or sufficiently flexible, as a matter of management, for so ever-changing an enterprise. It is the people or nothing. . . .

. . . In telling how these ideas have been put in practice, I have chosen to begin with the story of how TVA has applied grass-roots democracy to the job of rebuilding the land.

The farmers—there are about 225,000 farms in the watershed of the Tennessee River, with 1,350,000 people living on them—have long seen that their lands were in trouble. They knew, almost all of them, what they wanted. They knew that what was needed was to increase the productivity of their lands, to heal the gullies, to keep water on the land, and to prevent the soil from washing away. Like almost everyone else they were reluctant to change their habits of doing things. They wanted to have a say-so about changes, they had to be "shown"; but when their confidence had been earned they were enthusiastic, and they were generous of spirit.

The farm experts, both in the Department of Agriculture's scientific bureaus in Washington and in the state agencies of the Tennessee Valley, had known most of the technical answers to the *separate* problems of soils, of fertilizer, of terracing, and had known them for a good many years. They were competent in their special fields, and devoted to their work. Nevertheless farm income in the valley as in the whole Southeast continued at a low ebb; in some counties the average cash income for a farm *family* was less than $150 a year. Soil losses were appalling. Farm tenantry increased. Changes in farming favored by the technicians, away from cotton and corn, for example, did occur, but the pace was so slow that the direction on the whole continued downward. Entire rural counties, the towns included, were without a single telephone, a mile of farm electric line, a public library, a newspaper, a hospital, a single public health officer. . . .

What was needed was not alone more technical information, but that *on the farm itself* there should be a unification of all the available knowledge and skills. The technical knowledge of all kinds available at the various state university agricultural experiment farms had somehow to be moved to thousands of valley farms, actual farms. What happened at a beautifully equipped experiment station or in a laboratory was one thing; what would happen on a man's farm was quite another. The laboratory had to be taken to the farm; the whole farm as a business was the farmer's problem.

Furthermore, as TVA saw it, and as the agricultural colleges were quick to confirm, the individual farmer was the only one who could *apply* all this available expertness. He must therefore become the center of the scheme of education in new methods. We did not want a method of restoring soil whereby the farmer would be ordered; he would learn *by doing*, on his own place; his neighbors would learn by watching him and adapting what "worked out." Nor did we want a mere false front, using the outward form of voluntary and educational methods to disguise actual coercion, or "uplift," or narrow political purposes.

After some searching the method that was worked out, with state, local, and federal agencies as co-operating parties, centered about "whole farm demonstrations" on tens of thousands of dirt farms. . . . On the land of these demonstration farmers two ideas met and were combined in action: the idea of unity, and the democratic idea that much of the planning and execution of resource development must be in the hands of the people. . . .

The demonstration farm program of the Tennessee Valley began, back in 1935, in this way: The farmers in a community, called together by their county agricultural agent, selected several of their own number who were willing to have their farms serve as a "demonstration" for the rest. Later on it became apparent to farmers and technicians that all the farms in a community usually constituted a more useful unit for demonstration than one farm or a scattered few. As a consequence what are called "area demonstrations" were set up by the farmers' associations. . . .

. . . Once selected, the first step was to map and inventory this farm schoolroom. These maps and inventories are not "documents," built up by questionnaires from a distance, nor are they "professional."

They are made by the farmer and the committee of his neighbors. Then the farmer, the technicians, and the county agent and his demonstration assistant, "talk over" that map. They walk over the place, map and inventory in hand, often several times, still talking it over. A new management plan for the farm is the result, reduced to writing. . . .

Most demonstration farmers have succeeded in increasing their capital resources, many have increased their income in cash received or in a rising family living standard; at the same time they have conserved and revitalized their soil. This is important because this method, being voluntary with no powers of enforcement in anyone, depends upon hitching together the farmer's self-interest and the general public interest in the basic resource of the soil. The individual has made himself one with the common purpose which the TVA idea holds for all individuals, the development of the resources upon which all stand. Self-interest here has served that public interest. . . .

. . . The demonstration farms became places to visit, to study, to emulate. The greatest effect in spreading new farming practices has been among those who have never been selected as demonstrators at all. Hundreds of farmers, non-demonstrators, will spend a day going from one of these farm schoolrooms to another.

A report from Virginia shows that large proportions of the "students" went home and adopted some or all the changes on their own farms. I have attended some of these all-day meetings where scores of farmers gathered in the fields, earnestly observing, asking questions, arguing, prodding the "experts" for an answer to this difficulty or the "why" of this or that.

Thomas Jefferson, also a Virginia farmer, saw that education is the foundation of a democratic nation; what was true in the eighteenth century is doubly true when technology of a hundred kinds must be at the hand of every citizen. At these meetings one man steps up and tells his experience; then another adds his story. One man's planning is compared with another's. The "lessons" learned are taken back to be tested at home. . . .

In the Tennessee Valley the effect of working together, building a fertile soil, and finding ways to protect it and keep it strong is not merely a matter of men's livelihood. Revitalizing the soil has done things to the people and their institutions quite as much as to the land. Schools have been painted, lighted, or rebuilt, church and community activities stimulated; the effect is felt in a score of people's activities which they share in common. Only cynics will find this surprising. To those with faith in humankind it is natural enough that when men adopt a common purpose so deep and broad as that of working with nature to build a region's resources there ensue inevitable consequences to the spirit of men. These indeed may be the most important result of all. . . .

PRIVATE INDUSTRY AND THE PUBLIC INTEREST

With the eyes of industry now upon this valley (as they are indeed upon many valleys the world over) planning a considerable industrial expansion here after the war, there is an opportunity to plan and to build so that our resources will endure, our natural beauty be spared despoliation. Here there is a chance to see to it that human well-being in city and town will not, through lack of ingenuity and foresight, be needlessly sacrificed. Shall we succeed? Is the only choice one between pastoral poverty and industrial slums? Can private industry utilize these resources, at a profit, and yet sustain their vigor and longevity? Can business and the common weal both be served? To be able to make an affirmative reply is a matter of the greatest moment.

In the Tennessee Valley the answers will turn to some extent upon how successful the TVA is in its efforts to weld a union of the public interest and the private interests of businessmen. We appear to be

uncovering and developing in this valley principles and practices for effecting a jointure of public interests with private, by methods that are voluntary and noncoercive. Our actual experience is unpretentious as measured by the scope of the problem, but it is definitely encouraging and of not a little significance for industry and the people of the country generally. . . .

What the TVA, in specific ways, has sought to do can be simply stated: to accept an obligation to harmonize the private interest in earning a return from resources, with the dominant public interest in their unified and efficient development. The method—and this is the distinctive part of the experiment—is to bring to bear at the grass roots the skills of public experts and administrators not for negative regulation but *to make affirmative action in the public interest both feasible and appealing to private industry*. By public interest I mean the interest of people—people as human beings—not "the people" in their institutional roles as wage earners or investors or voters or consumers. "Underneath all, individuals," men and women and children. . . .

. . . In most cases industry has joined with us actively and with ingenuity in seeking in specific cases a way by which its own limited but important business interest could be furthered by a use of resources that is in the broad public interest. A comprehensive and unique contract between the TVA and the Aluminum Company of America illustrates how far businessmen, even those whose point of view is generally widely different from that of the TVA, will go in this direction.

The Aluminum Company has long owned several dams at the headwaters of the Little Tennessee River, a tributary of the Tennessee. Those dams, lying above the many dams of the TVA, if operated as part of the TVA system of dams, would result in greater public benefits both in power and flood control than if they continued to operate independently. The purpose of the years of study and negotiations that resulted in the contract was to find a way whereby the maximum public usefulness of the river's water resource could be secured without reducing the power available to the company from its dams or increasing its cost. Under the contract, signed in 1941, the Aluminum Company agreed to turn over to the TVA, indefinitely, the right to direct just how Alcoa's dams should function, that is, when water should be stored from hour to hour, and when released through power turbines or sluice gates. The contract's effect (without any change in Alcoa's title to its property) is to unify the control of water of the entire watershed, and thereby increase the public benefits accruing in power, flood control, and navigation. The added power benefits created by the arrangements are divided between the parties to the contract by a formula which both sides believe advantageous. A strategic power site, long owned by the company, is also turned over to TVA, and upon it Fontana Dam has been constructed.

The Aluminum Company of America and TVA are organizations widely apart in their purposes. And yet by keeping their attention on the physical facts—that the river could be made more productive if Alcoa's private dams and TVA's public ones were operated as a unit—agreement was reached in a complex situation. . . .

13. GOVERNMENT IN THE OPEN AIR

The unified development of resources requires the broadest coalition of effort. This is a job not only for all the people, but for all of the people's institutions. The purpose is national, but the task is one that calls for a partnership of *every* agency of government, state and local as well as federal, that can further the common purpose. Therefore the grass-roots policy of drawing in private organizations and individuals—such as those of farmers, workers, and businessmen, discussed in preceding chapters—has in like manner been applied by TVA, a *federal* organization, so

that the governmental agencies of *local* communities and of the *states* of the Tennessee Valley have become TVA's active and responsible partners.

CO-OPERATION WITH LOCAL AGENCIES

Decentralizing the administration of government functions that are clearly national has been carried so far in this valley that it is literally true (I can think of no exceptions) that, whenever there is a state or a local institution which can perform part of the task that has been assigned by law to the TVA, we have sought to have that non-federal agency do it. This way of getting results is an exacting test of managerial skill in defining functions clearly and in securing a union of effort. Legalistic arguments about "states' rights" or "federal supremacy" have faded into irrelevance.

There is therefore nothing in this region's experience to support the genuine fears or the partisan outcry of ten years ago that setting up a federal regional agency would mean the undermining and ultimate destruction of state government and local communities. The contrary has been the case. It is indisputable from the record that state government is stronger in the Tennessee Valley today than it was ten years ago and has more functions to perform. It is notably true that local community government and functions are more vigorous. I know of no other place in the United States of which this can be said with equal basis in performance. . . .

The device for effecting this widespread partnership relation with local and state government has been the written contract. There are now hundreds of such formal contracts between the TVA and every manner of public institution in the valley, ranging all the way from county library boards to state universities and the highway and conservation commissions. . . .

Most of the activities thus carried on under these contracts by a community or state agency *could have been done by the TVA alone*, if the matter were viewed as a narrow issue of TVA's "prerogatives" or "jurisdiction." But dynamic decentralization is not concerned with the abstract issue of whether the national government under the Constitution has a superior "right" in a particular field from which it may exclude state and local action. TVA is charged with a broad national responsibility. Its function is that of leadership, stimulus, guidance: planning in the broadest sense.

In calling upon a state or local agency to share responsibility instead of setting up a TVA organization to do a specific job alone, and in negotiating the contracts upon which such joint efforts rest, we have deliberately tried to "start something" that local forces might later carry on, on their own. We have tried to place each new activity into the stream of the region's life, in the hands of local agencies to be continued when the initial federal support is withdrawn. Grass-roots methods, decentralization as here applied, are therefore not simply the making of "grants-in-aid" to state or local bodies, and the "matching of federal funds" technique. . . .

THE POWER SYSTEM

The most far-reaching instance of a grass-roots partnership between local agencies and the TVA is afforded by the valley's power system. Now one of the largest power producers in the world, it presents the picture of a joint enterprise of the federal government and hundreds of local communities in six states, and the reliance for power of more than four million people. These communities range from small farming centers and mountain villages to a major city of a third of a million people.

Centralized large-scale production combined with decentralized, grass-roots local responsibility: this formula may prove of considerable importance in a number of other fields of business and of domestic and international governmental affairs.

Electricity, like the land, touches the everyday lives of people, directly and intimately. And yet the business of generating, transmitting, and distributing electricity is one of the most highly centralized industries in the United States. What TVA has done in decentralizing the service of this vital necessity of modern life may throw light not only upon public administration but also on how grass-roots methods may serve in a serious problem facing business generally.

Nowhere is the fear of bigness for bigness' sake and distrust of control from a far-off place better exemplified. People want not only government but also such essential services as electricity as close to them as possible.

A degree of centralization in a power system produces certain economies which cannot be effected in any other way. For some years I have been convinced, however, that a substantial measure of decentralized administration can be achieved with distinct social gains and without impairing the efficiency of the service. The power program of the Tennessee Valley constitutes the first large-scale demonstration by which the country can judge. Power generation and transmission require size and technical and physical integration to achieve economies. Here those responsibilities alone are centralized: the powerhouses and high-tension transmission network are operated directly by the TVA itself.

But the same principles of economy do not apply to the retail distribution of this "bulk electricity." And in the valley system the ownership and management of the *distribution* systems are decentralized. The decision to enter into a contract for wholesale power supply with TVA, and thereby to participate in the region-wide power program, was made voluntarily by each community, after public discussion, council meetings, referenda. Responsibility for those municipal and co-operative systems which deliver the power directly to the consumers who live in the cities, on the farms, and in the villages is lodged with the people themselves. . . .

... *National* standards laid down by Congress in TVA's Act are maintained by means of provisions in the Authority's wholesale power contracts. In this way substantial uniformity of policy among its retail electricity distributors prevails in such important matters as rates, accounting, distribution of surplus revenues, and payments in lieu of taxes. But the ownership and control of the local electricity distribution systems are vested in the people themselves, usually through boards of trustees composed of local citizens. . . .

. . . These boards are made up of men with every kind of background and interest: there are several bank presidents, a stockbroker, a labor leader, many farmers, lawyers, a druggist. They have an opportunity to take an active role in the entire development undertaking, of which this electricity operation in their town is a part. Not a few of the power boards have thus become a center of community initiative in industrial development, community planning, public recreation, post-war planning, and so on. . . .

15. Regional Pillars of Decentralization

You cannot, of course, decentralize the functions of the federal government if the whole nation is the operating unit for the carrying out of national powers. Obviously some smaller area than the whole country must be used. In the case of the TVA, Congress and the President determined that in the development of resources that smaller unit should be based upon the natural region; this region is described in the language of the 1933 enactment as "the Tennessee River drainage basin and . . . such adjoining territory as may be related to or materially affected by the development consequent to this Act. . . ."

The use of the region as an autonomous unit of development was a deliberate "experiment." The results of this departure in national policy were to be reported to the nation and become the object of study as to its effectiveness. It was anticipated at the time that if the experiment commended itself by its results the method might be followed or adapted to other regions. The idea that the Tennessee Valley region was set up as a kind of testing ground for the nation has been often expressed, and appears in the President's original message: "If we are successful here," he said, "we can march on, step by step, in a like development of other great natural territorial units within our borders." . . .

Modern regionalism . . . rests squarely upon the supremacy of the *national* interest. It admits that there are problems and resources common to areas larger than any single state—a river basin, for example. It recognizes that certain points of view develop in some portions of the country and are not shared by the nation as a whole. It affirms and insists, however, that the solution of regional problems and the development of regional resources are *matters of concern to the whole country*. It proposes to harmonize regional advancement with the national welfare. That concern for and supremacy of the national interest distinguishes "regionalism" from "sectionalism." Under the banner of sectionalism, states throughout our history have combined to support or to oppose federal action. Under the modern concept of regionalism, the federal government acts to meet regional needs to the end that the entire nation may profit.

The organization of the Tennessee Valley Authority is an example of this modern idea of regionalism. To create it seven states did not unite to demand special privileges to distinguish them from the country as a whole, regardless of the ensuing consequences to the national welfare. The federal legislature itself created an independent regional agency whose basic objective was to conserve the natural resources lying in the valley of the Tennessee and to develop those resources *in conformity with broad national objectives and policies*. This is the very opposite—indeed it is the antidote—of "Balkanization." . . .

17. WHAT ABOUT "POLITICS"?

Can politics be kept out of TVA?

This is a question that is often asked and has been extensively debated. By "politics" people mean nothing vague nor abstract. They mean such things as these: the appointment of engineers, land buyers, and workmen because they (or their friends or relatives) have helped to elect certain men to office; the preparation of specifications in a way that will favor the bid of some manufacturer who is politically "right"; the location of dams where they will win the most votes; in short, the use of TVA for partisan political purposes. . . .

A river has no politics. Whether an engineer is a Democrat or a Republican, a conservative or a liberal, or indeed whether he has any interest in or knowledge of political matters at all, is entirely unrelated to his ability to design a dam. In this sense, experts as well as rivers have no politics. But the question of whether a river should be developed *is* a political question, and hence a proper subject of "politics." Whether a series of dams should provide only navigation, or instead should serve all the unified purposes to which the river can be put—this *is* a political question, and should be decided by Congress. The TVA Act is filled with such broad political decisions, made, as they should and must be made, by the elected representatives of the whole people. The decision to develop resources as a unified whole was a political one; the opportunity afforded for regional decentralization, the fixing of responsibility on a single agency in a region, even the decision that TVA must keep politics out of the selection of personnel—all these were political decisions.

Facts and experienced judgment, not political views, are the foundation of dependable technical decisions and action. Whether the rock at a particular site is a safe dam foundation or whether a certain kind of truck or transmission tower is best fitted for a job—these are not political questions and should not be decided politically or by political bodies. And, conversely, experts and administrators should not directly or by indirection decide political issues; moreover it is vital that they be held strictly answerable for their performance to prevailing public opinion, as expressed from time to time through democratic political methods.

Are these compatible principles? *Can science and politics live together* without one dominating the other? Can experts and managers be kept accountable to the public despite the great power over the lives of all of us that technical knowledge puts in their hands?

CAN SCIENCE AND POLITICS MIX?

The TVA has, of course, inevitably faced these fundamental questions many times in the past ten years. The answers thus far have been in the affirmative. It is quite generally conceded that a high standard of technical and managerial competence has been maintained, and that the TVA has been guided by public policies laid down by Congress. It has remained responsive to the wishes of the people it serves, who warmly support TVA's resistance to political interference. . . .

No broad conclusions about politics in its relation to technology, however, should be drawn from TVA's successful course in this respect in its first ten years. It is always within the power of Congress to change the policy of keeping politics out of TVA. As a matter of fact the proposal condemned by Senator Bankhead did pass the Senate in June, 1943, but it was not accepted by the House of Representatives. Later the same proposal was attached by the Senate as a rider to the Appropriations Bill relating to TVA. The House rejected the rider by an overwhelming vote. Nevertheless, the issue, even as to TVA, may never be safely deemed as "settled."

Public understanding is the only possible safeguard against the mixing of politics and technology, and against the parallel evil of lack of accountability of administrators to the people. Considerations of theory will hardly determine whether the policy thus far successful in the TVA will be applied and followed in other comparable fields of public technical and managerial activities. Such public understanding must be constantly refreshed by concrete instances of the wisdom of the right course and the high cost of the wrong one.

This is no abstract question of "political science." In the immediate future America will be faced with major decisions that involve this very issue—questions, for example, concerning the disposition of government-owned plane factories, aluminum, rubber, chemical and steel works, shipyards, and the like—investments running into many billions of dollars. Will the many technical questions be decided by political methods? On the other hand, will experts and industrial managers seek to disguise underlying policy questions by calling them "technical" or "economic," and thereby themselves decide political issues? Will these problems be dealt with in a kind of free-for-all fight between politics and managerial and technical judgment? The light of TVA's analogous experience is here of not a little practical importance. . . .

POLITICS AND POLITICS

Now there are of course all kinds of "politics." Administrators and technicians, however high-minded their purposes may seem to them, cannot piously abjure party politics, and then indulge in their own variety. "Taking care of the boys" is an evil in any guise, whether it is on the basis of personal friendship, business or social ties, or some amateur political notion about an "elite of brains" (self-selected), a kind of Phi Beta Kappa version of Tammany Hall.

The usual forthrightness of Congressmen is wholesome compared with the "holier-than-thou" attitude toward politicians of those who occasionally practice their own personal brand of politics. I was reminded of this hypocrisy a few years ago, when I read a signed magazine editorial which denounced the political patronage system, in the most righteous terms. The writer of this piece is a man who in 1933 had been a powerful figure in the government. When TVA was first created this Galahad sent word to our Board that we must put one of his relatives on our pay roll. A jaunty young satellite brought us the message. We made the same reply that we had been giving to similar requests from Members of Congress: Let the relative file his application and be judged along with other applicants. The messenger tried to wave all this aside. He had been told (he said) to let us know that such rules about examinations were not intended to apply to men of such high social purposes! Both of these men have long since discredited themselves and are out of public service, but before this happened they had done not a little damage to the reputation for disinterestedness of all public administrators.

The employment of relatives is a form of personal politics; one of TVA's first actions was to establish a strong policy against the practice of nepotism. And then there are those businessmen who come into the government to perform a technical job of war production who find nothing incongruous in injecting into a conference a partisan attack on the President or Members of Congress, or who even use a government post to further a particular political candidacy—these too are men who surely fail to comprehend the harm they are doing to public confidence in technicians in public affairs. There are all kinds of politics; administrators and experts must see to it that they keep out of all varieties.

Congress itself determined to keep its kind of politics out of TVA's technical administration. It was, in turn, our responsibility as administrators to keep TVA out of political matters. Accordingly TVA in 1936 adopted a policy forbidding political activity by anyone connected with the

TVA, even in municipal affairs. No TVA employee could be a candidate for any office, or be active in elections of any kind, except of course, to vote. This was a number of years before the Hatch Act placed similar but less extensive limits upon political activity of all federal employees. It is arguable that the TVA's policy is too extreme in that it forbids thousands of citizens living in the Tennessee Valley from useful participation in strictly community governmental affairs, but on balance we feel this restriction is justified by the dangers it averts. . . .

"NO POLITICS IS GOOD POLITICS"

It is accurate to say that TVA has demonstrated to the satisfaction of those most directly affected that the task of getting resources developed should be kept nonpolitical. It is now "good politics" for political leaders themselves, in the Tennessee Valley, to urge that politics be kept out of TVA. Probably the most thoughtful and informed leadership on the basic issues of the valley's development is coming from a group of its younger political leaders and elected officials. They know that their support of TVA will not be rewarded by jobs or favors, and have long since ceased to think in those terms. If TVA does a good job, one that the valley and the country judges to be competent, that constitutes their political reward. And to the surprise of many "realistic" people, it turns out that helping to keep politics out of TVA is a political asset to candidates for public office in the valley. It is another case where "no politics is good politics." As long as the people these elected officials represent have confidence in the TVA idea and the technical and managerial craftsmanship behind it, the danger of politics in administration is not great; whenever that is lost, the injection of political decisions and methods is not far off.

ACCOUNTABILITY TO THE PUBLIC

But it would not be safe or wise to give to the administrators of the TVA such broad independence of action in carrying out political decisions made by Congress unless they were held strictly accountable for results. (And what is true of TVA seems to me applicable to managers and experts generally.) Moreover, TVA's freedom from interference in carrying out policies determined by Congress makes it imperative that the policies themselves be under constant control and review by Congress as the instrument of politics. When managers and technicians, in business or in government, are permitted to use the leverage of their authority and expert knowledge to lodge irresponsible power in themselves, the foundation of democracy is threatened at once.

Accountability begins with a full report of results. The TVA each year makes several such reports, public documents with a wide circulation. The Authority's regular report of its activities, made annually to Congress, is in great detail. Reports on special subjects are made from time to time. Financial reporting is comprehensive; it embodies the most progressive business methods: detailed unit cost accounting; a monthly and annual financial statement, including balance sheet and income account; an audit not only by the Comptroller General of the United States, but in addition by a leading firm of commercial accountants, whose report attached to TVA's annual financial reports is in much the same language as the certification the same firm appends to the financial statements of some of America's largest private concerns. An elaborate accounting of results is also made each year before the Appropriations Committees of both Houses of Congress, as well as to the President through the Bureau of the Budget. Such reports as these have been the occasion of extensive debate over TVA in Congress, in the press, and in other public forums. . . .

It has been demonstrated by these and other instances that it is entirely feasible to hold this public enterprise to strict accountability and responsibility without resort to political controls of the details of operation from the floor of Congress. But it is in far less formal ways that the most effective responsibility to the people is established. *Working at the grass roots is the surest guarantee of that day-to-day adjustment to the needs and aspirations of the people which is the liveliest form of public accountability.* When the managers and the experts are close to the people and their problems, it does not ordinarily take the formality of a Congressional hearing to determine whether the program undertaken is succeeding or needs adjustment, whether staff members are alive to their opportunities or are arrogant and self-seeking.

Decentralization is a kind of mirror in which one can see, each day and each hour, how well or how badly the work responds to its broad purpose. Because it is a regional agency, doing its work and making its decisions in the valley, TVA cannot escape the sight of its mistakes or irresponsibly turn its back upon the stream of daily life. Success can come only through a technical leadership in which the people, not in the mysterious aura of distance but under the revealing and commonplace light of proximity and familiarity, have confidence. At the grass roots a new kind of accountability is born, more significant than reports, reviews, criticism by Congress. It is the day-to-day accountability of working partner to working partner. . . .

18. PLANNING AND PLANNERS

TVA is supposed to be a planning agency for this region. Yet nowhere on your organization chart do I find a Department of Social Planning; and when I ask for a copy of the TVA Plan no one can produce it: Some such comment has been made to us many times by friendly and earnest students of TVA.

The reason the TVA Plan is not available is that there is no such document. Nor is there one separate department set off by itself, where planners exercise their brains. To one who has read thus far in this account, it is evident this does not constitute our idea of planning.

The TVA *is* a planning agency, the first of its kind in the United States. The great change going on in this valley is an authentic example of modern democratic planning; this was the expressed intent of Congress, by whose authority we act. But through the years we have deliberately been sparing in the use of the terminology of "plans" and "planning" within TVA and outside, and those terms have hardly appeared thus far in this book. For the term "planning" has come to be used in so many different senses that the nomenclature has almost lost usefulness, has even come to be a source of some confusion.

It is necessary, however, to translate the ideas of this book into the terminology of planning and the language that planners employ. For planning ideas are widely discussed these days. To some the content of the word "planning" has been pared down until it means merely ordinary foresight, and thereby the term has lost any broad significance. Others have gone to the other extreme; they approve or violently condemn "planning" because to them it means a complete reconstitution of our social system, comprehensive state socialism, and the like. Some discerning and broad-gauge industrialists urge widespread "planning" for the post-war period; by this they mean a way of assuring the future of "free enterprise" or "democratic capitalism"— phrases that also have come by loose handling to be as foggy in their meaning as "planning" itself.

The term "planning," however, is here to stay; but, since it has apparently come to mean all things to all men, I have avoided using the term until I had set out specifically, as I have done in preceding chapters, just what I have in mind in using the word, and what planning means to us in this valley. "Unified development" as I have described the idea in action is, in substance, the valley's synonym for "planning."

547

EARLY AMERICAN "PLANS"

We have always made plans in America. The question for us is not: Shall we plan? but: *What kind of plans* should we make? What kind of planners? What method of "enforcement of plans"? On these matters what has transpired in the Tennessee Valley, as I have tried to describe it, casts the light of actual experience. . . .

Great as were some of the accomplishments of public planners in the past, we know that we suffer today from the consequences of some of those plans. The state of our natural resources has become a national emergency, grave and critical. Some of the public land policies embodied in such planning as the Homestead laws we now realize were short-sighted and costly. Such piecemeal planning for the immediate year-to-year demands of particular groups of constituents we now know was not wise planning. Catastrophic floods, denuded forests, soil exhaustion—these are part of the price we are paying. For a generation now a change in those plans has been urged. Overtones prophetic of President Roosevelt's message to Congress concerning TVA were heard, faintly it is true, as early as 1909 when President Theodore Roosevelt's Conservation Commission made this recommendation:

Broad plans should be adopted providing for a system of waterway improvement extending to all uses of the waters and benefits to be derived from their control, including the clarification of the water and abatement of floods for the benefit of navigation; the extension of irrigation; the development and application of power; the prevention of soil wash; the purification of streams for water supply; and the drainage and utilization of the waters of swamp and overflow lands.

INDUSTRIAL PLANNING

Discussion of industrial planning to enable America to grasp the opportunities of the post-war period is now much in the public prints, led by some of our ablest men of private business. Here again, as in the case of planning by public men, we should remember that when businessmen become planners they are not venturing into new and strange fields. Long-range planning is a familiar and established practice of progressive business. Perhaps the best-known example is that of the American Telephone and Telegraph Company. This vast communication service has expended large sums of money in continuous and intensive study of the future, and on the basis of such study develops plans five years, ten years, and even longer in advance—plans for new construction, for the revision of its exchanges, for the building of additional capacity. In other businesses there has long been comparable economic planning with substantial organizations devoted to the task. Surveys are made of the market, financial trends, technological changes, all the complex factors which will affect the future activities of a great business enterprise.

Planning by businessmen, often under some other name, is recognized as necessary to the conduct of private enterprise. It has the virtue of a single and direct objective, one that can be currently measured, that is, the making of a profit. A plan that is impressive in the form of a report but which does not work, as judged by the financial reports of the company, is an unsuccessful plan. It has been just as simple as that. The business planner has rarely felt it necessary to complicate his problem by trying to determine whether the making of profit under his plan benefits the whole of society, or injures it. And, as I have said, it is not often that a single business or even an entire industry is in a position to decide such a question.

This is admittedly a grave defect of planning by the businessman. For his legitimate object, namely a profitable business, is not necessarily consistent with the object of society, that is, a prosperous and happy people. The plans of the A. T. & T. and of the small manufacturer may both be quite effective within those enterprises. But factors affecting the plans of the A. T. & T. and the small manufacturer go far beyond their businesses. Over this multitude of external factors the businessman has no effective control. As this and a thousand valleys demonstrate so tragically, private planning, even when temporarily sound from the viewpoint of a particular enterprise, has often resulted in great injury to many other enterprises, and therefore to the public welfare.

THE PUBLIC INTEREST

The idea of unified resource development is based upon the premise that by democratic planning the individual's interest, the interest of private undertakings, can increasingly be made one with the interest of all of us, i.e., the community interest. By and large, things are working out that way in the Tennessee Valley. The income of the private business of farming has increased, largely as a result of a program of aiding the region's soil. Sales by private fertilizer companies have increased more rapidly than at any other time in their history as a result of TVA's production and the demonstration of new fertilizer products designed to further the over-all public interest in the land. Promotion of education in forest-fire protection and scientific cutting methods has furthered conservation and at the same time aided the private business of lumbering. Community planning has made towns more attractive and pleasant for everyone, and at the same time increased land values for individual owners. These results and many others I have described have been in the general public interest; all have furthered the interest of particular business enterprises.

Effective planners must understand and believe in people. The average man is constantly in the mind of the effective planning expert. Planners, whether they are technicians or administrators, must recognize that they are not dealing with philosophical abstractions, or mere statistics or engineering data or legal principles, and that planning is not an end in itself.

In the last analysis, in democratic planning it is human beings we are concerned with. Unless plans show an understanding and recognition of the aspirations of men and women, they will fail. Those who lack human understanding and cannot share the emotions of men can hardly forward the objectives of realistic planning. Thurman Arnold, in *The Symbols of Government*, has well described this type of earnest but unrealistic person:

They usually bungle their brief opportunities in power because they are too much in love with an ideal society to treat the one actually before them with skill and understanding. Their constant and futile cry is reiterated through the ages: "Let us educate the people so that they can understand and appreciate us."

A great Plan, a moral and indeed a religious purpose, deep and fundamental, is democracy's answer both to our own homegrown would-be dictators and foreign anti-democracy alike. In the unified development of resources there is such a Great Plan: the Unity of Nature and Mankind. Under such a Plan in our valley we move forward. True, it is but a step at a time. But we assume responsibility not simply for the little advance we make each day, but for that vast and all-pervasive end and purpose of all our labors, the material well-being of all men and the opportunity for them to build for themselves spiritual strength.

Here is the life principle of democratic planning—an awakening in the whole people of a sense of this common moral purpose. Not one goal, but a direction. Not one plan, once and for all, but *the conscious selection by the people of successive plans.* It was Whitman the democrat who warned that "the goal that was named cannot be countermanded."

If this conception of planning is sound, as I believe, then it is plain that in a democracy we always must rest our plans upon "here and now," upon "things as they are." How many are the bloody casualties of liberal efforts to improve the lot of man, how bitter the lost ground and disillusionment because of failure to understand so simple and yet so vital an issue of human strategy. So frequently have men sought an escape from the long task of education, the often prosaic day-by-day steps to "do something about it," by pressing for a plan—usually in the form of a law—without considering whether the people understand the reason for the law's plan, or how they are to benefit by it.

An unwillingness to start from where you are ranks as a fallacy of historic proportions; present-day planning, anywhere in the world for that matter, will fall into the same pit if it makes the same gigantic error. It is because the lesson of the past seems to me so clear on this score, because the nature of man so definitely confirms it, that there has been this perhaps tiresome repetition throughout this record: the people must be in on the planning; their existing institutions must be made part of it; self-education of the citizenry is more important than specific projects or physical changes.

And it is because of this same conviction that the TVA has never attempted by arbitrary action to "eliminate" or to force reform upon those factors or institutions in the valley's life which are vigorously antagonistic to a plan for unified development. . . .

THINKING AND DOING

The TVA idea of planning sees action and planning not as things separate and apart, but as one single and continuous process. In the President's message to the Congress in 1933, this fact was stressed. The words bear repetition here: The TVA, he said, "should be charged with the broadest duty of planning for the proper use, conservation, and development of the natural resources of the Tennessee River drainage basin and its adjoining territory for the general social and economic welfare of the Nation." Then follows this sentence: "This Authority should also be clothed with the necessary power to carry these plans into effect." And the law enacted this principle.

This is fundamental. And yet it is here that much of the disagreement with TVA has arisen from outside, and in its first years internal disagreement as well. The idea that planning and responsibility for action may and should be divorced—the maker of plans having little or nothing to do with their execution—follows the analogy of the planning of a house, an office building, any fixed structure. But the analogy is a mistaken one. For the development of a region is a course of action; it has no arbitrary point of beginning and goes on and on with no point of completion. The individual acts that make up regional development are the day-to-day activities of plowing a particular field, harvesting timber from a particular tract, the building of a factory, a church, a house, a highway. TVA's purpose was not the making of plans but that a valley be developed.

Plans had to be made, of course, many of them. But plans and action are part of one responsibility. TVA is responsible not alone for plans but for results. Those results depend chiefly upon the people's participation. Getting that participation was to be almost wholly on a voluntary basis. To get a job done in this way was a unique assignment, one that required the invention of new devices and new methods. If TVA had been a "planning agency" in the sense that its responsibility had been limited to the making of plans—the usual meaning of the term—those plans would probably have met the fate of so many other plans: brochures decorating bookshelves, adornments of the bibliography of a sterile learning.

In *The Coming Victory of Democracy*, Thomas Mann put his finger on this deeplying error of intellectualism that treats planning apart from action. His words are moving, for they tell much of the causes beneath the catastrophe of European culture:

Democracy is thought; but it is thought related to life and action. . . . No intellectual of the pre-democratic era ever thought of action, nor of what kind of action would result if his thinking were put into practice. It is characteristic of undemocratic or of democratically uneducated nations that their thinking goes on without reference to reality, in pure abstraction, in complete isolation of the mind from life itself, and without the slightest consideration for the realistic consequences of thought.

In the TVA the merging of planning and responsibility for the carrying out of those plans forces our technicians to make them a part of the main stream of living in the region or community; this it is that breathes into plans the breath of life. For in the Tennessee Valley the expert cannot escape from the consequences of his planning, as he can and usually does where it is divorced from execution. This has a profound effect on the experts themselves. Where planning is conceived of in this way, the necessity that experts should be close to the problems with which they are dealing is evident.

In my opinion the idea of planning is still struggling for popular support in America largely for this reason: that the most spectacular plans have been drawn by men who did not have the responsibility for carrying them out. They did not have the salutary discipline which the experts of this valley had who have had to ask themselves: "Is this a plan that I can take responsibility for seeing carried out? Will the people understand it, will the people help to make it effective? Will they make the plan their own?"

In the work of the TVA we have taken to heart and sought to put into practice what seems to me one of the most profound utterances upon the problem of freedom through democracy. They are the words of John Dewey.

The conflict as it concerns the democracy to which our history commits us [he wrote] is *within* our own institutions and attitudes. It can be won only by extending the application of democratic methods, methods of consultation, persuasion, negotiation, communication, co-operative intelligence, in the task of making our own politics, industry, education, our cultures generally, a servant and an evolving manifestation of democratic ideas. . . .

. . . democratic ends demand democratic methods for their realization. . . . Our first defense is to realize that democracy can be served only by the slow day-by-day adoption and contagious diffusion in every phase of our common life of methods that are identical with the ends to be reached. . . . An American democracy can serve the world only as it demonstrates in the conduct of its own life the efficacy of plural, partial, and experimental methods in securing and maintaining an ever-increasing release of the powers of human nature, in service of a freedom which is co-operative and a co-operation which is voluntary.

What of the enforcement of economic and social plans in this valley? In the building of dams and other structures, TVA of course has the power which even private utilities and railroads have, to take property of landowners who are unwilling to sell, at a price fixed by court proceedings. But, beyond that, in no significant particular is TVA planning for the development of this region enforceable by law. And this we have not found to be a handicap.

This is not to say dogmatically that there is never any justification whatever for regulatory measures, or that voluntary methods have not resulted in a good many mistakes and waste that good planning would have avoided, if the people who made those decisions had been persuaded to make different ones. It is pointed out to us constantly that the course of education and voluntary action is too slow, that only the force of law will meet the crisis of depletion. Our critics, admitting that not a little progress has been made by our methods, point to the many farmers who still persist in plowing higher and higher on their hills, planting more corn and cotton, destroying more and more land; to the timber interests which continue to spurn the advice of forest technicians that would sustain the yield of lumber; to the manufacturers who still pollute the streams with waste and show scant interest in technical means of ending this contamination. More than once industries have been located at points where it seemed clear to us that sound planning should discourage industrial location.

This lack of power to enforce plans has disturbed a good many observers and students of the enterprise, especially in the early years, and still mystifies and even angers some of them. But we have continued to rely wholly upon the methods described in this book, the ways of contract, persuasion, incentives, encouragement, methods based on the people's confidence in TVA's comprehension, its good faith, and the quality of its technical leadership. I feel strongly that the admitted limitations of voluntary methods, distressing and tragic as their consequences sometimes are, do not invalidate the wisdom of a *minimum of coercion* in carrying out plans for resource development. For coercion is insatiable. In whatever guise, once coercion becomes the accepted reliance for making planning effective, more and more coercion is needed. I am deeply persuaded that high as the price of voluntary methods may be, in delays and errors, in the end the price of arbitrary enforcement of planning is nothing less than our freedom. . . .

In this one of the thousand valleys of the earth the physical setting of men's living has improved. Each day the change becomes more pronounced. The river is productive, the land more secure and fruitful, the forests are returning, factories and workshops and new houses and electric lines have put a different face upon the Tennessee Valley. . . .

I share with many of my neighbors in the Tennessee Valley a deep conviction that it can be done, the modern job of building our resources and making the machine work for all men. And because of our experience together we believe that it can be done by such methods and with such purposes as will enrich the things of the spirit. This experience convinces me that science and invention can be consciously and deliberately directed to achieving the kind of world that people want. If it is decentralized industry men want, "family farming," or pleasant cities not too large, an end to smoke and congestion and filth—there are modern tools which can be turned to just such ends. The people, working through their private enterprises and public institutions which are democratic in spirit, can get substantially the kind of community and country they want. . . .

SECTION D. GOVERNMENT POLICY FOR LABOR

1. *NLRB v. JONES AND LAUGHLIN STEEL CORPORATION*[1]

EDITORS' NOTE.—As one of a group of court cases that tested the constitutionality of the National Labor Relations Act of 1935, the Jones and Laughlin case reflects the reasoning of the United States Supreme Court, which supported the New Deal's enterprises of protecting labor's right to organize, especially against certain stipulated employer "unfair labor practices" threatening that right.

Section 7a of the National Industrial Recovery Act (June, 1933) granted labor "the right to organize and bargain collectively free from the interference, restraint, or coercion by employers." Despite two tribunals established to enforce Section 7a, the National Labor Board of 1933, and its successor, the first National Labor Relations Board of 1934, still employer resistance sapped much of the effectiveness of this "magna charta" for labor. In May, 1935, the Supreme Court in the Schechter case declared the NIRA unconstitutional, but in June of the same year the experience of the two labor boards which had administered Section 7a was cast into the National Labor Relations Act, under which was established the second National Labor Relations Board. For the following twelve years this act (known as the Wagner Act) constituted the national labor policy. This was the act that was the subject matter of the Jones and Laughlin case.

Mr. Chief Justice HUGHES delivered the opinion of the Court.

In a proceeding under the National Labor Relations Act of 1935, the National Labor Relations Board found that the respondent, Jones & Laughlin Steel Corporation, had violated the Act by engaging in unfair labor practices affecting commerce. The proceeding was instituted by the Beaver Valley Lodge No. 200, affiliated with the Amalgamated Association of Iron, Steel and Tin Workers of America, a labor organization. The unfair labor practices charged were that the corporation was discriminating against members of the union with regard to hire and tenure of employment, and was coercing and intimidating its employees in order to interfere with their self-organization. The discriminatory and coercive action alleged was the discharge of certain employees.

The National Labor Relations Board, sustaining the charge, ordered the corporation to cease and desist from such discrimination and coercion, to offer reinstatement to ten of the employees named, to make good their losses in pay, and to post for thirty days notices that the corporation would not discharge or discriminate against members, or those desiring to become members, of the labor union. As the corporation failed to comply, the Board petitioned the Circuit Court of Appeals to enforce the order. The court denied the petition, holding that the order lay beyond the range of federal power. . . . We granted certiorari.

1. *National Labor Relations Board v. Jones and Laughlin Steel Corp.*, 301 U.S. 1, 22–37, 40–49, 76, 97–101 (1937).

The scheme of the National Labor Relations Act . . . is too long to be quoted in full. . . . The first section sets forth findings with respect to the injury to commerce resulting from the denial by employers of the right of employees to organize and from the refusal of employers to accept the procedure of collective bargaining. There follows a declaration that it is the policy of the United States to eliminate these causes of obstruction to the free flow of commerce.[2] The Act then de-

2. This section is as follows:

"Section 1. The denial by employers of the right of employees to organize and the refusal by employers to accept the procedure of collective bargaining lead to strikes and other forms of industrial strife or unrest, which have the intent or the necessary effect of burdening or obstructing commerce by (a) impairing the efficiency, safety, or operation of the instrumentalities of commerce; (b) occurring in the current of commerce; (c) materially affecting, restraining, or controlling the flow of raw materials or manufactured or processed goods from or into the channels of commerce, or the prices of such materials or goods in commerce; or (d) causing diminution of employment and wages in such volume as substantially to impair or disrupt the market for goods flowing from or into the channels of commerce.

"The inequality of bargaining power between employees who do not possess full freedom of association or actual liberty of contract, and employers who are organized in the corporate or other forms of ownership association substantially burdens and affects the flow of commerce and tends to aggravate recurrent business depressions, by depressing wage rates and the purchasing power of wage earners in industry and by preventing the stabilization of competitive wage rates and working conditions within and between industries.

"Experience has proved that protection by law of the right of employees to organize and bargain collectively safeguards commerce from injury, impairment, or interruption, and promotes the flow of commerce by removing certain recognized sources of industrial strife and unrest, by encouraging practices fundamental to the friendly adjustment of industrial disputes arising out of differences as to wages, hours, or other working conditions, and by restoring equality of bargaining power between employers and employees.

"It is hereby declared to be the policy of the United States to eliminate the causes of certain substantial obstructions to the free flow of commerce and to mitigate and eliminate these obstructions when they have occurred by encouraging the

fines the terms it uses, including the terms "commerce" and "affecting commerce." . . . The labor union filed with the Board its verified charge. The Board thereupon issued its complaint against the respondent alleging that its action in discharging the employees in question constituted unfair labor practices affecting commerce within the meaning of § 8, subdivisions (1) and (3), and § 2, subdivisions (6) and (7) of the Act. Respondent, appearing specially for the purpose of objecting to the jurisdiction of the Board, filed its answer. Respondent admitted the discharges, but alleged that they were made because of inefficiency or violation of rules or for other good reasons and were not ascribable to union membership or activities. As an affirmative defense respondent challenged the constitutional validity of the statute and its applicability in the instant case. . . The Board received evidence upon the merits and at its close made its findings and order.

Contesting the ruling of the Board, the respondent argues (1) that the Act is in reality a regulation of labor relations and not of interstate commerce; (2) that the Act can have no application to the respondent's relations with its production employees because they are not subject to regulation by the federal government; and (3) that the provisions of the Act violate § 2 of Article III and the Fifth and Seventh Amendments of the Constitution of the United States.

The facts as to the nature and scope of the business of the Jones & Laughlin Steel Corporation have been found by the Labor Board and, so far as they are essential to the determination of this controversy, they are not in dispute. The Labor Board has found: The corporation is organized under

practice and procedure of collective bargaining and by protecting the exercise by workers of full freedom of association, self-organization, and designation of representatives of their own choosing, for the purpose of negotiating the terms and conditions of their employment or other mutual aid or protection."

the laws of Pennsylvania and has its principal office at Pittsburgh. It is engaged in the business of manufacturing iron and steel in plants situated in Pittsburgh and nearby Aliquippa, Pennsylvania. It manufactures and distributes a widely diversified line of steel and pig iron, being the fourth largest producer of steel in the United States. With its subsidiaries—nineteen in number—it is a completely integrated enterprise, owning and operating ore, coal and limestone properties, lake and river transportation facilities and terminal railroads located at its manufacturing plants. It owns or controls mines in Michigan and Minnesota. It operates four ore steamships on the Great Lakes, used in the transportation of ore to its factories. It owns coal mines in Pennsylvania. It operates towboats and steam barges used in carrying coal to its factories. It owns limestone properties in various places in Pennsylvania and West Virginia. It owns the Monongahela connecting railroad which connects the plants of the Pittsburgh works and forms an interconnection with the Pennsylvania, New York Central and Baltimore and Ohio Railroad systems. It owns the Aliquippa and Southern Railroad Company which connects the Aliquippa works with the Pittsburgh and Lake Erie, part of the New York Central system. Much of its product is shipped to its warehouses in Chicago, Detroit, Cincinnati and Memphis,—to the last two places by means of its own barges and transportation equipment. In Long Island City, New York, and in New Orleans it operates structural steel fabricating shops in connection with the warehousing of semi-finished materials sent from its works. Through one of its wholly-owned subsidiaries it owns, leases and operates stores, warehouses and yards for the distribution of equipment and supplies for drilling and operating oil and gas wells and for pipe lines, refineries and pumping stations. It has sales offices in twenty cities in the United States and a wholly-owned subsidiary which is devoted exclusively to distributing its product in Canada. Approximately 75 per cent of its product is shipped out of Pennsylvania.

Summarizing these operations, the Labor Board concluded that the works in Pittsburgh and Aliquippa "might be likened to the heart of a self-contained, highly integrated body. They draw in the raw materials from Michigan, Minnesota, West Virginia, Pennsylvania in part through arteries and by means controlled by the respondent; they transform the materials and then pump them out to all parts of the nation through the vast mechanism which the respondent has elaborated." . . .

Practically all the factual evidence in the case, except that which dealt with the nature of respondent's business, concerned its relations with the employees in the Aliquippa plant whose discharge was the subject of the complaint. These employees were active leaders in the labor union. Several were officers and others were leaders of particular groups. Two of the employees were motor inspectors; one was a tractor driver; three were crane operators; one was a washer in the coke plant; and three were laborers. Three other employees were mentioned in the complaint but it was withdrawn as to one of them and no evidence was heard on the action taken with respect to the other two.

While respondent criticises the evidence and the attitude of the Board, which is described as being hostile toward employers and particularly toward those who insisted upon their constitutional rights, respondent did not take advantage of its opportunity to present evidence to refute that which was offered to show discrimination and coercion. In this situation, the record presents no ground for setting aside the order of the Board so far as the facts pertaining to the circumstances and purpose of the discharge of the employees are concerned. Upon that point it is sufficient to say that the evidence supports the findings of the Board that respondent discharged these men "because of their union activity and for the purpose of discouraging membership in the union." We turn to the questions of law which respondent urges in contesting the validity and application of the Act.

First. The scope of the Act.—The Act is challenged in its entirety as an attempt to regulate all industry, thus invading the reserved powers of the States over their local concerns. It is asserted that the references in the Act to interstate and foreign commerce are colorable at best; that the Act is not a true regulation of such commerce or of matters which directly affect it but on the contrary has the fundamental object of placing under the compulsory supervision of the federal government all industrial labor relations within the nation. The argument seeks support in the broad words of the preamble (section one) and in the sweep of the provisions of the Act, and it is further insisted that its legislative history shows an essential universal purpose in the light of which its scope cannot be limited by either construction or by the application of the separability clause.

If this conception of terms, intent and consequent inseparability were sound, the Act would necessarily fall by reason of the limitation upon the federal power which inheres in the constitutional grant, as well as because of the explicit reservation of the Tenth Amendment. . . . The authority of the federal government may not be pushed to such an extreme as to destroy the distinction, which the commerce clause itself establishes, between commerce "among the several States" and the internal concerns of a State. That distinction between what is national and what is local in the activities of commerce is vital to the maintenance of our federal system.

But we are not at liberty to deny effect to specific provisions, which Congress has constitutional power to enact, by superimposing upon them inferences from general legislative declarations of an ambiguous character, even if found in the same statute. The cardinal principle of statutory construction is to save and not to destroy. We have repeatedly held that as between

two possible interpretations of a statute, by one of which it would be unconstitutional and by the other valid, our plain duty is to adopt that which will save the Act. Even to avoid a serious doubt the rule is the same. . . .[3]

We think it clear that the National Labor Relations Act may be construed so as to operate within the sphere of constitutional authority. The jurisdiction conferred upon the Board, and invoked in this instance, is found in § 10(a), which provides:

SEC. 10(a). The Board is empowered, as hereinafter provided, to prevent any person from engaging in any unfair labor practice (listed in section 8) affecting commerce.

The critical words of this provision, prescribing the limits of the Board's authority in dealing with the labor practices, are "affecting commerce." The Act specifically defines the "commerce" to which it refers (§ 2[6]):

The term "commerce" means trade, traffic, commerce, transportation, or communication among the several States, or between the District of Columbia or any Territory of the

3. Compare this observation of the Court with the Court's comment in *United States* v. *Butler et al.* decided the previous year (297 U.S. 1 [1936]): "There should be no misunderstanding as to the function of this court in such a case. It is sometimes said that the court assumes a power to overrule or control the action of the people's representatives. This is a misconception. The Constitution is the supreme law of the land ordained and established by the people. All legislation must conform to the principles it lays down. When an act of Congress is appropriately challenged in the courts as not conforming to the constitutional mandate the judicial branch of Government has only one duty—to lay the article of the Constitution which is invoked beside the statute which is challenged and to decide whether the latter squares with the former. All the court does, or can do, is to announce its considered judgment upon the question. The only power it has, if such it may be called, is the power of judgment. This court neither approves nor condemns any legislative policy. Its delicate and difficult office is to ascertain and declare whether the legislation is in accordance with, or in contravention of, the provisions of the Constitution; and having done that, its duty ends."

United States and any State or other Territory, or between any foreign country and any State, Territory, or the District of Columbia, or within the District of Columbia or any Territory, or between points in the same State but through any other State or any Territory or the District of Columbia or any foreign country.

There can be no question that the commerce thus contemplated by the Act (aside from that within a Territory or the District of Columbia) is interstate and foreign commerce in the constitutional sense. The Act also defines the term "affecting commerce" (§ 2[7]):

The term "affecting commerce" means in commerce, or burdening or obstructing commerce or the free flow of commerce, or having led or tending to lead to a labor dispute burdening or obstructing commerce or the free flow of commerce.

This definition is one of exclusion as well as inclusion. The grant of authority to the Board does not purport to extend to the relationship between all industrial employees and employers. Its terms do not impose collective bargaining upon all industry regardless of effects upon interstate or foreign commerce. It purports to reach only what may be deemed to burden or obstruct that commerce and, thus qualified, it must be construed as contemplating the exercise of control within constitutional bounds. It is a familiar principle that acts which directly burden or obstruct interstate or foreign commerce, or its free flow, are within the reach of the congressional power. Acts having that effect are not rendered immune because they grow out of labor disputes. . . . It is the effect upon commerce, not the source of the injury, which is the criterion. . . . Whether or not particular action does affect commerce in such a close and intimate fashion as to be subject to federal control, and hence to lie within the authority conferred upon the Board, is left by the statute to be determined as individual cases arise. We are thus to inquire whether in the instant case the constitutional boundary has been passed.

Second. The unfair labor practices in question.—The unfair labor practices found by the Board are those defined in § 8, subdivisions (1) and (3). These provide:

SEC. 8. It shall be an unfair labor practice for an employer—

(1) To interfere with, restrain, or coerce employees in the exercise of the rights guaranteed in section 7.

(3) By discrimination in regard to hire or tenure of employment or any term or condition of employment to encourage or discourage membership in any labor organization: . . .

Section 8, subdivision (1), refers to § 7, which is as follows:

SEC. 7. Employees shall have the right to self-organization, to form, join, or assist labor organizations, to bargain collectively through representatives of their own choosing, and to engage in concerted activities, for the purpose of collective bargaining or other mutual aid or protection.

Thus, in its present application, the statute goes no further than to safeguard the right of employees to self-organization and to select representatives of their own choosing for collective bargaining or other mutual protection without restraint or coercion by their employer.

That is a fundamental right. Employees have as clear a right to organize and select their representatives for lawful purposes as the respondent has to organize its business and select its own officers and agents. Discrimination and coercion to prevent the free exercise of the right of employees to self-organization and representation is a proper subject for condemnation by competent legislative authority. Long ago we stated the reason for labor organizations. We said that they were organized out of the necessities of the situation; that a single employee was helpless in dealing with an employer; that he was dependent ordinarily on his daily wage for the maintenance of himself and family; that if the employer refused to pay him the wages that he thought fair, he was nevertheless unable to leave the employ and resist arbitrary and unfair treatment; that union was essential to give laborers opportunity to deal on an equality with their employer. . . . We reiterated these views when we had under consideration the Railway Labor Act of 1926. Fully recognizing the legality of collective action on the part of employees in order to safeguard their proper interests, we said that Congress was not required to ignore this right but could safeguard it. Congress could seek to make appropriate collective action of employees an instrument of peace rather than of strife. We said that such collective action would be a mockery if representation were made futile by interference with freedom of choice. Hence the prohibition by Congress of interference with the selection of representatives for the purpose of negotiation and conference between employers and employees, "instead of being an invasion of the constitutional right of either, was based on the recognition of the rights of both." . . .

Third. The application of the Act to employees engaged in production.—The principle involved.—Respondent says that whatever may be said of employees engaged in interstate commerce, the industrial relations and activities in the manufacturing department of respondent's enterprise are not subject to federal regulation. The argument rests upon the proposition that manufacturing in itself is not commerce. . . .

The Government distinguishes these cases. The various parts of respondent's enterprise are described as interdependent and as thus involving "a great movement of iron ore, coal and limestone along well-defined paths to the steel mills, thence through them, and thence in the form of steel products into the consuming centers of the country—a definite and well-understood course of business." It is urged that these activities constitute a "stream" or "flow" of commerce, of which the Aliquippa manufacturing plant is the focal point, and that industrial strife at that point would cripple the entire movement.

Reference is made to our decision sustaining the Packers and Stockyards Act. . . . The Court found that the stockyards were but a "throat" through which the current of commerce flowed and the transactions which there occurred could not be separated from that movement. . . .

Respondent contends that the instant case presents material distinctions. Respondent says that the Aliquippa plant is extensive in size and represents a large investment in buildings, machinery and equipment. The raw materials which are brought to the plant are delayed for long periods and, after being subjected to manufacturing processes, "are changed substantially as to character, utility and value." The finished products which emerge "are to a large extent manufactured without reference to pre-existing orders and contracts and are entirely different from the raw materials which enter at the other end." Hence respondent argues that "If importation and exportation in interstate commerce do not singly transfer purely local activities into the field of congressional regulation, it should follow that their combination would not alter the local situation." . . .

We do not find it necessary to determine whether these features of defendant's business dispose of the asserted analogy to the "stream of commerce" cases. . . . The congressional authority to protect interstate commerce from burdens and obstructions is not limited to transactions which can be deemed to be an essential part of a "flow" of interstate or foreign commerce. Burdens and obstructions may be due to injurious action springing from other sources. The fundamental principle is that the power to regulate commerce is the power to enact "all appropriate legislation" for "its protection and advancement" . . . to adopt measures "to promote its growth and insure its safety" . . . "to foster, protect, control and restrain." . . . Although activities may be intrastate in character when separately considered, if they have such a close and substantial relation to interstate commerce that their control is essential or appropriate to protect that commerce from burdens and obstructions, Congress cannot be denied the power to exercise that control. . . . Undoubtedly the scope of this power must be considered in the light of our dual system of government and may not be extended so as to embrace effects upon interstate commerce so indirect and remote that to embrace them, in view of our complex society, would effectually obliterate the distinction between what is national and what is local and create a completely centralized government. *Id.* The question is necessarily one of degree. . . .

It is thus apparent that the fact that the employees here concerned were engaged in production is not determinative. The question remains as to the effect upon ininterstate commerce of the labor practice involved. . . .

Fourth. Effects of the unfair labor practice in respondent's enterprise.—Giving full weight to respondent's contention with respect to a break in the complete continuity of the "stream of commerce" by reason of respondent's manufacturing operations, the fact remains that the stoppage of those operations by industrial strife would have a most serious effect upon interstate commerce. In view of respondent's far-flung activities, it is idle to say that the effect would be indirect or remote. It is obvious that it would be immediate and might be catastrophic. We are asked to shut our eyes to the plainest facts of our national life and to deal with the question of direct and indirect effects in an intellectual vacuum. Because there may be but indirect and remote effects upon interstate commerce in connection with a host of local enterprises throughout the country, it does not follow that other industrial activities do not have such a close and intimate relation to interstate commerce as to make the presence of industrial strife a matter of the most urgent national concern. When industries organize themselves on a national scale, making their re-lation to interstate commerce the dominant factor in their activities, how can it be maintained that their industrial labor relations constitute a forbidden field into which Congress may not enter when it is necessary to protect interstate commerce from the paralyzing consequences of industrial war? We have often said that interstate commerce itself is a practical conception. It is equally true that interferences with that commerce must be appraised by a judgment that does not ignore actual experience.

Experience has abundantly demonstrated that the recognition of the right of employees to self-organization and to have representatives of their own choosing for the purpose of collective bargaining is often an essential condition of industrial peace. Refusal to confer and negotiate has been one of the most prolific causes of strife. This is such an outstanding fact in the history of labor disturbances that it is a proper subject of judicial notice and requires no citation of instances. . . . But with respect to the appropriateness of the recognition of self-organization and representation in the promotion of peace, the question is not essentially different in the case of employees in industries of such a character that interstate commerce is put in jeopardy from the case of employees of transportation companies. And of what avail is it to protect the facility of transportation, if interstate commerce is throttled with respect to the commodities to be transported!

These questions have frequently engaged the attention of Congress and have been the subject of many inquiries. The steel industry is one of the great basic industries of the United States, with ramifying activities affecting interstate commerce at every point. The Government aptly refers to the steel strike of 1919–1920 with its far-reaching consequences. The fact that there appears to have been no major disturbance in that industry in the more recent period did not dispose of the possibilities of future and like dangers to interstate commerce which Congress was entitled to foresee and to exercise its protective power to forestall. It is not necessary again to detail the facts as to respondent's enterprise. Instead of being beyond the pale, we think that it presents in a most striking way the close and intimate relation which a manufacturing industry may have to interstate commerce and we have no doubt that Congress had constitutional authority to safeguard the right of respondent's employees to self-organization and freedom in the choice of representatives for collective bargaining.

Fifth. The means which the Act employs.—Questions under the due process clause and other constitutional restrictions.— Respondent asserts its right to conduct its business in an orderly manner without being subjected to arbitrary restraints. What we have said points to the fallacy in the argument. Employees have their correlative right to organize for the purpose of securing the redress of grievances and to promote agreements with employers relating to rates of pay and conditions of work. . . . Restraint for the purpose of preventing an unjust interference with that right cannot be considered arbitrary or capricious. The provisions of § 9(a) that representatives, for the purpose of collective bargaining, of the majority of the employees in an appropriate unit shall be the exclusive representatives of all the employees in that unit, imposes upon the respondent only the duty of conferring and negotiating with the authorized representatives of its employees for the purpose of settling a labor dispute. . . .

The Act does not compel agreements between employers and employees. It does not compel any agreement whatever. It does not prevent the employer "from refusing to make a collective contract and hiring individuals on whatever terms" the employer "may by unilateral action determine." The Act expressly provides in § 9(a) that any individual employee or a group of employees shall have the right at any time to present grievances to their em-

ployer. The theory of the Act is that free opportunity for negotiation with accredited representatives of employees is likely to promote industrial peace and may bring about the adjustments and agreements which the Act in itself does not attempt to compel. . . . The Act does not interfere with the normal exercise of the right of the employer to select its employees or to discharge them. The employer may not, under cover of that right, intimidate or coerce its employees with respect to their self-organization and representation, and, on the other hand, the Board is not entitled to make its authority a pretext for interference with the right of discharge when that right is exercised for other reasons than such intimidation and coercion. The true purpose is the subject of investigation with full opportunity to show the facts. It would seem that when employers freely recognize the right of their employees to their own organizations and their unrestricted right of representation there will be much less occasion for controversy in respect to the free and appropriate exercise of the right of selection and discharge.

The Act has been criticised as one-sided in its application; that it subjects the employer to supervision and restraint and leaves untouched the abuses for which employees may be responsible; that it fails to provide a more comprehensive plan,— with better assurances of fairness to both sides and with increased chances of success in bringing about, if not compelling, equitable solutions of industrial disputes affecting interstate commerce. But we are dealing with the power of Congress, not with a particular policy or with the extent to which policy should go. We have frequently said that the legislative authority, exerted within its proper field, need not embrace all the evils within its reach. The Constitution does not forbid "cautious advance, step by step," in dealing with the evils which are exhibited in activities within the range of legislative power. . . . The question in such cases is whether the legislature, in what it does prescribe, has gone beyond constitutional limits.

The procedural provisions of the Act are assailed. But these provisions, as we construe them, do not offend against the constitutional requirements governing the creation and action of administrative bodies. . . . The Act establishes standards to which the Board must conform. There must be complaint, notice and hearing. The Board must receive evidence and make findings. The findings as to the facts are to be conclusive, but only if supported by evidence. The order of the Board is subject to review by the designated court, and only when sustained by the court may the order be enforced. Upon that review all questions of the jurisdiction of the Board and the regularity of its proceedings, all questions of constitutional right or statutory authority, are open to examination by the court. We construe the procedural provisions as affording adequate opportunity to secure judicial protection against arbitrary action in accordance with the well-settled rules applicable to administrative agencies set up by Congress to aid in the enforcement of valid legislation. It is not necessary to repeat these rules which have frequently been declared. None of them appears to have been transgressed in the instant case. Respondent was notified and heard. It had opportunity to meet the charge of unfair labor practices upon the merits, and by withdrawing from the hearing it declined to avail itself of that opportunity. The facts found by the Board support its order and the evidence supports the findings. Respondent has no just ground for complaint on this score.

The order of the Board required the reinstatement of the employees who were found to have been discharged because of their "union activity" and for the purpose of "discouraging membership in the union." That requirement was authorized by the Act. . . .

Respondent complains that the Board not only ordered reinstatement but directed the payment of wages for the time lost by the discharge, less amounts earned by the employee during that period. This part of the order was also authorized by the Act, § 10(c). It is argued that the requirement is equivalent to a money judgment and hence contravenes the Seventh Amendment with respect to trial by jury. The Seventh Amendment provides that "In suits at common law, where the value in controversy shall exceed twenty dollars, the right of trial by jury shall be preserved." The Amendment thus preserves the right which existed under the common law when the Amendment was adopted. . . . Thus it has no application to cases where recovery of money damages is an incident to equitable relief even though damages might have been recovered in an action at law. . . . It does not apply where the proceeding is not in the nature of a suit at common law. . . .

The instant case is not a suit at common law or in the nature of such a suit. The proceeding is one unknown to the common law. It is a statutory proceeding. Reinstatement of the employee and payment for time lost are requirements imposed for violation of the statute and are remedies appropriate to its enforcement. The contention under the Seventh Amendment is without merit.

Our conclusion is that the order of the Board was within its competency and that the Act is valid as here applied. The judgment of the Circuit Court of Appeals is reversed and the cause is remanded for further proceedings in conformity with this opinion.

Reversed.

Mr. Justice McReynolds delivered the following dissenting opinion in the cases preceding:

Mr. Justice Van Devanter, Mr. Justice Sutherland, Mr. Justice Butler and I are unable to agree with the decisions just announced. . . .

We are told that Congress may protect the "stream of commerce" and that one who buys raw material without the state, manufactures it therein, and ships the output to another state is in that stream. Therefore it is said he may be prevented from doing anything which may interfere with its flow.

This, too, goes beyond the constitutional limitations heretofore enforced. If a man raises cattle and regularly delivers them to a carrier for interstate shipment, may Congress prescribe the conditions under which he may employ or discharge helpers on the ranch? The products of a mine pass daily into interstate commerce; many things are brought to it from other states. Are the owners and the miners within the power of Congress in respect to the miners' tenure and discharge? May a mill owner be prohibited from closing his factory or discontinuing his business because so to do would stop the flow of products to and from his plant in interstate commerce? May employees in a factory be restrained from quitting work in a body because this will close the factory and thereby stop the flow of commerce? May arson of a factory be made a Federal offense whenever this would interfere with such flow? If the business cannot continue with the existing wage scale, may Congress command a reduction? If the ruling of the Court just announced is adhered to these questions suggest some of the problems certain to arise.

And if this theory of a continuous "stream of commerce" as now defined is correct, will it become the duty of the Federal Government hereafter to suppress every strike which by possibility may cause a blockade in that stream? . . . Moreover, since Congress has intervened, are labor relations between most manufacturers and their employees removed from all control by the state? . . .

There is no ground on which reasonably to hold that refusal by a manufacturer, whose raw materials come from states other than that of his factory and whose products are regularly carried to other states, to bargain collectively with employees in his manufacturing plant, directly affects interstate commerce. In such business there is not one but two distinct movements or streams in interstate transportation. The first brings in raw material and there ends. Then follows manufacture, a separate and local activity. Upon completion of this, and not before, the second distinct movement or stream in interstate commerce begins and the products go to other states. Such is the common course for small as well as large industries. It is unreasonable and unprecedented to say the commerce clause confers upon Congress power to govern relations between employers and employees in these local activities. . . .

It is gravely stated that experience teaches that if an employer discourages membership in "any organization of any kind" "in which employees participate, and which exists for the purpose in whole or in part of dealing with employers concerning grievances, labor disputes, wages, rates of pay, hours of employment or conditions of work," discontent may follow and this in turn may lead to a strike, and as the outcome of the strike there may be a block in the stream of interstate commerce. Therefore Congress may inhibit the discharge! Whatever effect any cause of discontent may ultimately have upon commerce is far too indirect to justify Congressional regulation. Almost anything—marriage, birth, death—may in some fashion affect commerce.

That Congress has power by appropriate means, not prohibited by the Constitution, to prevent direct and material interference with the conduct of interstate commerce is settled doctrine. But the interference struck at must be direct and material, not some mere possibility contingent on wholly uncertain events; and there must be no impairment of rights guaranteed. A state by taxation on property may indirectly but seriously affect the cost of transportation; it may not lay a direct tax upon the receipts from interstate transportation. The first is an indirect effect, the other direct. . . .

Section 13 of the Labor Act provides—
"Nothing in this Act shall be construed so
as to interfere with or impede or diminish
in any way the right to strike." And yet it
is ruled that to discharge an employee in a
factory because he is a member of a labor
organization (any kind) may create discontent which may lead to a strike and
this may cause a block in the "stream of
commerce"; consequently the discharge
may be inhibited. Thus the Act exempts
from its ambit the very evil which counsel

insist may result from discontent caused
by a discharge of an association member,
but permits coercion of a non-member to
join one.

The things inhibited by the Labor Act
relate to the management of a manufacturing plant—something distinct from commerce and subject to the authority of the
state. And this may not be abridged because of some vague possibility of distant
interference with commerce. . . .

2. COLLECTIVE BARGAINING[1]

By Selig Perlman

Editors' Note.—No phase of the
New Deal's program was more significant for future social developments
than its active promotion of labor's
right to self-organization. In the article
reproduced below Selig Perlman outlines and interprets the larger historical perspective of labor's great
achievement under the New Deal: a
large and significant share of the social
sovereignty (see Statistical Appendix,
Nos. 9, 11–13).

The historical character of this
achievement is yet to unfold. In 1947
there occurred an interruption to this
process of labor's rise to power—the
passage of the Taft-Hartley Act. The

intensity of the regulatory scheme introduced by this law, which is summarized elsewhere in these readings
(p. 569), induces speculation as to
whether the United States has begun
a process of "absorption" of the labor
movement, in the sense described by
Perlman.

Selig Perlman (1888——), at present
professor of economics at the University of Wisconsin, is noted for his
extensive historical writings on the
American labor movement. He is perhaps best known for his *Theory of
the Labor Movement*, first published in
1928 and republished in 1948.

Collective bargaining is not just a
means of raising wages and improving conditions of employment. Nor is it merely
democratic government in industry. It is
above all a technique whereby an inferior
social class or group carries on a never
slackening pressure for a bigger share in

1. Selig Perlman, "The Principle of Collective
Bargaining," *Annals of the American Academy of
Political and Social Sciences*, CLXXXIV (March,
1936), 154–60. Reprinted by permission of the
Academy of Political and Social Sciences.

the social sovereignty as well as for more
welfare, security, and liberty for its individual members. As such it is not confined
to a single arena, the industrial one, where
employers and labor unions meet directly,
but manifests itself equally in politics, legislation, court litigation, government administration, religion, education, and propaganda. Nor is collective bargaining only
a phenomenon of modern society. On the
contrary, its clearest and most comprehen-

sive manifestation was shown by the urban communities in the Middle Ages—the boroughs and the guilds in the struggle against feudal lords.

Collective bargaining as a technique of the rise of a new class is quite different from the class struggle of the Marxians. It is nominalist instead of realist. It is pragmatic and concrete instead of idealist and abstract. It is much less concerned with algebraic formulae summing up basic economic trends than with the problems of building discipline in organization and of training leadership. It derives its emotional impetus not from the desire to displace or "abolish" the "old ruling class," but from the wish to bring one's own class abreast of the superior class; to gain equal rights as a class and equal consideration for the members of that class with the members of that other class; to acquire an exclusive jurisdiction in that sphere where the most immediate interests, both material and spiritual, are determined, and a shared jurisdiction with the older class or classes in all the other spheres.

THE MEDIEVAL GUILDS

As said above, the early medieval urban communities practiced collective bargaining thus defined. England, then a backward country away from the main trade routes, shows most clearly the technique of the rise of this "under dog." Starting as communities of petty traders, to which craftsmen groups came to be added, these communities were tiny "cells" built on the fellowship principle, in the midst of a huge organism dominated by feudalism. Assuming that they had come into existence through trade activities as a result of an economic differentiation from the original agricultural manorial communities, they inherited from their own manorial background a communal organization of a kind, around the manorial court, resembling the modern company union.

However, the new ambition of these communities required "recognition" from the lord or overlord—the right of the chosen leaders to act as their collective spokesmen and to stand between the lord and their own individual members. For, as long as the lord or his appointee could reach into these communities and seize an individual member for the purpose of discipline in a remote court, or assess his taxes at will, a basis was lacking for a real communal organization and life—for a real "unionism." Recognition came with the borough charter, which granted the payment of taxes in lump sum, as well as a judicial and administrative autonomy. Thenceforth there was no individual bargaining and no need for the individual to kowtow to the outside power; his loyalty went to the "union."

But civil rights and protection from burdensome and discriminatory taxation were not enough to set up these aspiring communities. Conscious of the limitation of their economic opportunity in a world of scant purchasing power, they demanded and obtained the "closed market," or the right to treat the sum total of market opportunity as their own preserves, a species of "economic territory." The geographical territory of the town supported as many economic territories as there were guilds. Each guild administered its own economic territory and made its own "rules of occupancy and tenure" of opportunity for the individual.

The main objective was the literal *commune*, "communism of opportunity"—an enforced sharing of opportunity to assure to each member a chance to earn a livelihood. Profit seeking was condemned as antisocial and as destructive of solidarity. Also, the allotment of market opportunity to individuals was often guided by the seniority principle. With recognition as a starting point and with solidarity assured by the communal administration of the economic opportunity, these communities were equipped to continue bargaining collectively for more liberties in the political, administrative, judicial, and economic spheres.

The early democratic master workman's guild later became the capitalist-dominated Elizabethan corporation, and the original working rules looking to communism of opportunity became sabotaged and distorted to serve business rather than manual labor. But this hardly affected the collective bargaining technique of the rising class. The guild capitalism of the towns and the "free" capitalism of the open country, though divided by clashing interests, on the whole presented a united front, pressing for the incorporation of the customs or working rules of their class into the law of the land.

However, when wage labor began to employ the same collective bargaining technique through its early trade unions, the triumphant business class, instead of feeling flattered by such imitation, however humble, saw in it nothing but rebellion calling for suppression. The rise of the labor under dog had to begin from a lower depth.

GUILDS AND UNIONS COMPARED

Unionism . . . is, at bottom, labor's instrument for collective bargaining in the wider sense of the term, namely, to effect a rise to a fuller recognition in every sphere of social activity.

While it is not the lineal successor of the guilds, unionism shares with the latter the problems of establishing discipline in its own ranks and of obtaining recognition. And animated by the identical psychology of the scarcity of economic opportunity—job opportunity in this instance, not market opportunity—unionism is equally bent upon extending its control over the sum total of extant opportunity, in other words upon obtaining job control. Just as the guild owned its market territory, so the union considers itself the sole owner of its job territory; and, as with the guild, the union's guiding objective is administration of its job territory upon a principle approaching communism of opportunity, to give each member . . . a reasonable chance to earn a livelihood. This is coupled with the protection of the individual in his own particular opportunity holding, his job, and is frequently combined with seniority preference.

Since the union cannot prevent contact between its individual members and the employer, in the manner in which the guild prevented contact of its members and the lord, it does the next best thing and prevents *individual bargaining* by enforcing union conditions of employment, the union's rules of occupancy and tenure of the job opportunity. But wherever possible, the union tries to be the unquestioned administrator of the job opportunities as in union print shops, where the union sits alone in judgment over the foreman who has discharged an employee, and confines its bargains with the employer to wages and hours.

ATTITUDES OF PUBLIC AUTHORITY

The employer, however, is only one of the powers with whom the union has to make terms. Public authority is the other one, and during crucial stages, even the more important of the two. Generally speaking, the attitude of the public authority towards labor's collective bargaining has passed through the stages of suppression, grudging toleration, benevolent toleration, promotion, and (lately in countries ruled by dictatorship) absorption.

Suppression.—The stage of suppression existed in England prior to 1824. As the mercantilist state assumed the obligation to find for labor regular employment at wages adequate for its customary though low standard of living, the conclusion seemed logical and unavoidable that the trade union form of self-help was unnecessary and contrary to law. The flaw in the logic was disclosed with time, when the protective portion of the Elizabethan labor code had fallen into desuetude, while the prohibitive portion remained. In Germany the stage of suppression lasted down to the sixties of the nineteenth century. . . . But it was in Russia where, lasting as it did down to the fall of the monarchy, the socio-political effects of trade union suppression were clearest. At the show-down between communism and capitalism in 1917–1918, Russia, unlike Germany in the same predicament a year later, lacked the influence for a conservatism of a mature and sure-footed unionism.

Grudging toleration.—The next stage, that of grudging toleration, lasted in England from 1825 to 1875, in Germany to the fall of the monarchy or possibly only to the Auxiliary Labor Law of 1916, and in the United States, in some regards, has gone on almost to the present. In this stage the union is no longer illegal per se, but in effect can remain legal only on condition that it is satisfied with a state of animated suspension. In England and America the restrictions on union action came mainly from the court doctrines of criminal and civil conspiracy; in Germany from statutory law and police regulations. Nevertheless, during this stage unions not only managed to build up national organizations and an internal discipline, but also to impose a network of restrictive shop rules upon the employers. The objectives of these shop rules comprised protection of the standard of living and of health, security of the job, including freedom from discrimination, and invulnerability of the union to attack.

The long duration of this stage in the United States goes back to the structure of American government. When, in the seventies and eighties of the past century, the executive branch of the government proved incompetent to control the enormous amount of violence in industrial disputes, the courts were brought in to effect through the injunction what the vote-minded sheriffs and governors had failed to accomplish by standard police methods. But invoking the courts to do the policeman's job has effected not only a freezing of the legal rights of unions, since the courts justified their own interference by principles which became embedded in the law of the land, but also stimulated further restrictions through the extension of the same principles, as in the treatment of the

so-called "yellow-dog contract." Hence, to all practical intents and purposes, in America, the stage of grudging toleration virtually overlapped what in England became the next stage, the stage of benevolent toleration.

Benevolent toleration.—Benevolent toleration showed in the sweeping away of the charge of criminal conspiracy against unions, in their right to obtain court protection for their funds against dishonest officials, and in the privilege of legal invisibility when the employer brought them into court to levy for strike damages upon their treasuries. . . .

In Germany the war in 1914 put an end to the policy of pin pricks and worse, and in 1916 it was the High Military Command that forced the arrogant heavy industry to give the unions standing.

In the United States the intermittent and half-hearted "benevolence" of the legislative and the executive branches of the government, as shown in the Clayton Act of 1914 and in the earlier attempts to outlaw anti-union discrimination by employers, proved of little avail in the face of the superior position of the court.

Promotion.—The stage of promotion arrives when public authority endeavors to make the union the sole spokesman for the individual wage earners. In Australia, where labor's collective bargaining takes place on the legal arena, as litigation before an industrial court, the individual worker has no standing before that court. Hence Australian labor is the best organized labor of all countries outside Soviet Russia. And under the Australian procedure the key customs of labor—the living wage and the standard wage, the eight-hour day, and preference to union men where the employer has shown discrimination—have been incorporated in the law of the land.

Promotion is also present when the government extends the terms of a collective bargain over the unorganized portion of an industry or trade. Finally, promotion operates where the law makes a special effort to insure the independence of the union from undue employer influence. The laws of the German Republic and of the Commonwealth of Australia charge the proper tribunals to establish such independence before a union is given standing.

In America the stage of promotion arrived with the New Deal, with an adumbration as regards railway labor and the "yellow-dog" contract in the two preceding administrations. Although the National Industrial Recovery Act and the National Labor Relations Act both failed to compel employers to conclude bargains with unions, they went beyond the mere freeing of the unions from their earlier legal shackles—acts characteristic of the stage of benevolent toleration—and attempted to shackle the employer as a would-be organizer of company unions.

Absorption.—The stage of absorption or assimilation comes with political dictatorship, whether communist or fascist. Dictatorship excludes collective bargaining, both the direct kind and the indirect one, through legislation, politics, and propaganda. Under a dictatorship, unionism ceases to be the true expression of the labor group and becomes the mere creature of an outside power, either a communist intelligentsia or a middle-class fascist semi-intelligentsia. Under a dictatorship it is wholly immaterial whether unionism is compulsory or voluntary, or even whether it is limited to wage earners or admits employers. Therefore, forewarned of its fate under dictatorship, unionism is today the mainstay of democracy.

DEVELOPMENT OF LABOR STRATEGY

The stages in the evolution of the attitude of public authority towards labor's collective bargaining roughly accord with the stages in the development of labor strategy. The revolutionary stage coincides with the period of the unions' illegality and with the more intolerant portion of the stage of grudging toleration. Russian labor in 1904–1906 and 1917, British labor at the time of the Grand Consolidated Trades' Union and of the Chartist movement, German labor under the anti-socialist laws, and American labor in the eighties and nineties when the labor injunction made its debut—amply demonstrate that revolutionary correlation. In Russia, due to the absence in her body politic of the centers of resistance which in the countries of the Western pattern had been built up in the course of their more organic developments, labor, molded by professional revolutionaries from among the intellectuals, won a complete victory virtually by default. With that victory, collective bargaining as defined here came to an end in Russia. Elsewhere, the onrush of revolutionary labor shattered itself against the defenses of the established order.

Thereupon labor, making the best of the arrived grudging toleration by public authority, turned to a strategy of trench warfare on innumerable craft fronts, and of pounding its way inch by inch into the employer's field of prerogative. This campaign of opportunistic pressure on the many economic fronts, by means of strikes and union working rules, was supplemented by an equally opportunistic tactic on the political, legislative, and propaganda fronts. It was during this stage of many small wars, wars without formal truces, that the physiognomy of job-conscious unionism took its definite and hard shape—a hard-hitting unionism capable of great endurance but aspiring towards no millennium, only towards recognition as a legitimate partner in industrial government.

INDUSTRIAL GOVERNMENT

In fact, industrial government is labor's outstanding contribution to capitalist society. In America it began in a large way with the agreement system, erected in 1898, between the United Mine Workers and the operators in the Central Competitive Field. That agreement system became a school in which labor taught the employers the art of peaceably sharing their market opportunity instead of the former cutthroat competition. This was implemented through an elaborate wage rate structure aiming to equalize competitive costs notwithstanding geological and geographical inequalities.

The union, of course, was inspired by no philanthropy towards the employers. It merely felt that for the realization of its own objective of job conservation and job sharing, it was necessary that the operators as competitors be trained in economic good manners and sportsmanship. This industrial government of the mining industry disregarded the ideology of competitive capitalism, as well as the gospel of scientific management; it advanced the economic life of the weak and it increased the costs to the consumer. But it did so in the name of humanity to the producer, the job holder, and the operator alike.

In the agreement system in the men's clothing industry, established in Chicago in 1911 between Hart Shaffner and Marx and the union led by Sidney Hillman, industrial government avoided conflict with efficiency, and, in time, developed a governing apparatus which should be the delight of catholic-minded political scientists. In the industrial government under that agreement there are clearly discernible the legislative, executive, and judicial branches of government, and also the "administrative commission" which combines features of all three. The "constitution," elaborated by their own subsequent judicial interpretation, also contains a "bill of rights" safeguarding the employer, the employee, and the union. For instance, the employer is guaranteed against "stoppages"—economic "riots" as it were; the employee is protected by economic "habeas corpus" proceedings against the loss of his job either through discriminatory discharge or from technological change; and the union is upheld as a vigorous bargaining agency by the grant of "parlia-

mentary immunity" to the "shop chairmen"—namely, protection from discharge except with the preliminary consent of the impartial "court"—and through union preference in employment. Under this agreement system, efficiency, or progress, far from being blocked, has been encouraged, and since 1925 perhaps somewhat unduly so in this age of technological unemployment.

However, both varieties of industrial government, in bituminous coal and in men's clothing, require, for survival, an extension over each entire industry of the standards fixed by the collective bargain. And the implication, as far as the attitude of public authority is concerned, is that collective bargaining has entered into the stage of promotion rather than that of mere toleration, however benevolent.

DANGERS OF PROMOTION

But such promotion holds its dangers, especially in this country, with its labor movement unevenly developed and in many basic industries virtually lacking; for it is the rare governmental promoter of collective bargaining who will resist the temptation to try to impose his own views of what is rational and good for the labor movement.

In practice, of course, it is extremely difficult to draw the line between the genuine "organicism" of the labor movement, vital to its existence and vigor, and stubborn conservatism rooted in vested rights and selfishness. Especially in a time like the present, apparently a *Sturm und Drang* period in the American labor movement, union building from a blueprint, will seem to many a matter of public duty. For these the fate of Joseph II of Austria should hold a restraining lesson. Genuine reform, even in the labor movement, can come only from within.

3. ANALYSIS OF THE TAFT-HARTLEY ACT[1]

By the BUREAU OF NATIONAL AFFAIRS

EDITORS' NOTE.—Attending the spectacular growth of labor unions in the late 1930's was a growing reaction, the expression of which was delayed by the advent of World War II. A comprehensive bill, drastically altering the Wagner Act, had passed the House and had been sent to the Senate two days before Pearl Harbor. With the declaration of war, consideration of this labor legislation was suspended in favor of an emergency labor-management conference out of which emerged the wartime national labor policy.

After the war there again appeared the signs of an anxiety about labor's growth, undoubtedly intensified by the fact of continued increase in labor union membership during the war. In 1946 the Ball-Burton-Hatch Bill, strikingly similar to the bill which had passed the House in 1941, was widely debated; however, it was not until the character of the Congress was altered in the congressional elections of 1946 that the reaction was consummated in the form of the Labor Management Relations Act of 1947 (known also as the Taft-Hartley Act), passed in the late spring of 1947 over President Truman's veto.

The new law, complex and far-reaching in character, repealed the Wagner Act of 1935, thus overhauling extensively a national labor policy of twelve years' standing. The purpose of the Taft-Hartley Act is set forth in Section 1 as follows: "It is the purpose and policy of this Act, in order to promote the full flow of commerce, to prescribe the legitimate rights of both employees and employers in their relations affecting commerce, to provide orderly and peaceful procedures for preventing the interference by either with the legitimate rights of the other, to protect the rights of individual employees in their relations with labor organizations whose activities affect commerce, to define and proscribe practices on the part of labor and management which affect commerce and are inimical to the general welfare, and to protect the rights of the public in connection with labor disputes affecting commerce." The topical summary below pulls together all the provisions dealing with each of the law's major topics.

I. STRIKES

Compulsory arbitration is avoided, even in labor disputes of a national emergency character, but the problem of reducing work stoppages is tackled from a number of angles.

[1]. Bureau of National Affairs, *The Labor-Management Relations Act of 1947* (Washington, D.C., 1947), pp. 2–6. Reprinted by permission of the Bureau of National Affairs, Inc.

A. *Cooling-off Periods.* Any party to a bargaining contract desiring to negotiate a change in terms on expiration must give 60 days advance notice. The status quo must be maintained during the 60-day period or until the contract expires, whichever is the longer period. Employees who strike during the period forfeit their Wagner Act rights unless and until they are reemployed.

B. *Unlawful Strikes and Boycotts*. Outlawed are strikes and boycotts for the following purposes:

1. To force an employer or a self-employed person to join a labor or employer organization.

2. To force a business to cease dealing with another company or to cease using, selling, handling, or transporting its products. (Secondary boycotts.)

3. To force *another employer* (not the employer of the striking or boycotting employees) to recognize a union which has not been certified as the bargaining agent of his employees.

4. To force *any* employer to recognize one union if another union has been certified as bargaining agent.

5. To force an employer to assign particular work to one union rather than another, unless the employer is disregarding a certification of the Labor Relations Board. (Jurisdictional strikes and boycotts.)

A union which engages in or encourages employees to engage in strikes and boycotts of these kinds is guilty of an unfair labor practice. When charges are filed and NLRB, after a preliminary investigation, has reason to believe they are true, it is required to go to court immediately and seek an injunction or temporary restraining order against the union. In the case of jurisdictional strikes, NLRB is to give the unions 10 days in which to work out some basis for settlement of their dispute, failing which NLRB itself is to decide the dispute which led to the strike.

In addition, strikes or boycotts in these categories are made unlawful and anyone injured as a result may go into federal court and claim damages from the union.

C. *Strikes in Violation of Contract*. In addition to barring strikes in the 60-day waiting period prior to termination of a contract, the Act throws open the federal courts to suits by employers for breach of contract. Where the contract contains a no-strike clause which is alleged to have been violated, the employer would seem to be free to seek both damages and an injunction against the strike.

D. *National Emergency Strikes*. Strikes of an industry-wide or substantially industry-wide character which are found to imperil the national health or safety are subject to injunction for a maximum period of 80 days. Injunction proceedings are instituted by the Attorney General at the direction of the President. The President is advised by a specially-appointed board of inquiry which makes a preliminary investigation prior to the time an injunction is sought and turns in a final report after the injunction has been in effect for 60 days. If the dispute is still unsettled, NLRB polls employees as to whether they want to accept the employer's final offer and reports the results to the President. Then, if the dispute is still unsettled, the injunction is dissolved and the case is dropped in the lap of Congress.

E. *Mediation and Conciliation*. To speed the settlement of all disputes, the government's conciliation functions are expanded and placed under the direction of a new independent agency, the Federal Mediation and Conciliation Service, headed by a Director appointed by the President. Halfway through the 60-day cooling-off period required prior to the expiration of a contract, the Mediation Service must be notified if no agreement on a new contract has been reached. The Service may on its own motion step into any dispute which appears to threaten a substantial interruption of commerce.

Reinforcing the conciliation machinery is what amounts to a code of ethics for management and labor. Employers, employees, and their representatives are directed: (1) to exert every reasonable effort to make and maintain agreements; (2) to meet promptly on request of the other party and try to settle any dispute arising over the terms or application of an existing agreement; and (3) failing settlement of a dispute by conference, to participate fully and promptly in any conciliation efforts undertaken by the Mediation Service.

II. SUBJECTS OF COLLECTIVE BARGAINING

Some of the most far-reaching provisions of the law are those which regulate the terms of certain standard subjects of collective bargaining, including union security, the checkoff, and employee benefits. In most instances, but not all, existing contracts are not affected until expiration or renewal.

A. *Union Security*. By a tightening of the Wagner Act's so-called closed shop proviso, closed shop contracts and other agreements which require hiring through the union or hiring of union members only are effectively outlawed. The maximum form of union security permitted is a contract which requires, as a condition of employment, membership in the union 30 days after the date of employment or the effective date of the contract, whichever is the later. Even then—

1. The union must be the employees' lawful bargaining representative and must have received no assistance from the employer.

2. A majority of all employees in the unit (not merely of those voting) must have signified their approval of the negotiation of a union shop contract in a secret ballot election conducted by NLRB.

3. The contract may not be applied to penalize an employee who (*a*) was denied union membership on the same terms and conditions applicable to other union members or (*b*) was denied membership or expelled from the union for any reason other than failure to tender the regular dues and initiation fees.

Discrimination against an employee which goes beyond these bounds is an unfair labor practice on the part of the employer, and action by a union to cause or attempt to cause discrimination by an employer is an unfair labor practice on its part. Where charges of such discrimination are sustained, NLRB may assess back pay for the employee against either the employer or the union, whichever it finds responsible.

At any time beyond one year after employees have voted to authorize a union shop contract, 30 percent or more of the employees may petition NLRB for a new election.

State legislation placing greater restrictions on union security contracts is recognized in the law, and nothing in the Taft-Hartley Act would nullify such state laws.

B. *Checkoff*. Deductions from employees' wages for payment of union dues are permitted only in respect to employees who have given their employer a written assignment. The authorization must be revocable by the employee after one year or the termination of the contract, whichever is earlier. Existing checkoff agreements must be brought into conformity on expiration or by July 1, 1948, whichever date occurs first.

C. *Featherbedding*. The bill makes it an unfair labor practice for a union "to cause or attempt to cause an employer to pay or deliver any money or other thing of value in the nature of an exaction for services which are not performed or not to be performed." While this provision will require considerable litigation before its meaning becomes clear, it would appear to prohibit a union from demanding contract clauses which obligate the employer to employ standby workers.

D. *Health and Welfare Funds* are surrounded by elaborate restrictions. Any such arrangement must provide for a trust fund established for the sole benefit of employees, their families and dependents. The purposes for which payments may be made out of the trust are limited. Except for plans established before January 1, 1946, any plan must be set out fully in writing and must provide for bipartisan administration with some arrangement for a neutral person to break deadlocks. Payments intended to be used for purchasing pensions or annuities for employees must be made into a separate trust which cannot be used for any other purpose.

E. *Other Payments by an Employer* to a union or a representative of the employees, except for services rendered as an employee, are virtually forbidden. It is not clear from the law's language whether this would affect contract clauses requiring compensation for time spent in grievance activity.

F. *No-Strike Clauses* assume added significance in negotiations in view of the opening of federal courts to suits for violation of contract.

III. THE COLLECTIVE BARGAINING PROCESS

The obligation continues on employers to bargain with the duly designated representative of employees, and a parallel obligation to bargain with the employer is placed on the employee representative. Added is a definition of what the legal obligation to bargain means. This includes meeting at reasonable times and conferring with the other party and conferring in good faith with respect to terms and conditions of employment, and the execution, on request, of a written contract incorporating any agreement reached.

The obligation to bargain does not compel either party to agree to a proposal or to make a concession, nor does it require either party to discuss or agree to any modification of a fixed term agreement to take effect before the contract can properly be reopened.

The employer, like the employees, is free to select his own representative for purposes of collective bargaining. This provision is generally understood to mean that an employer may not be forced by a union to bargain through an association if he chooses to bargain individually.

Grievance handling is more carefully distinguished from collective bargaining. It is made clear that employees are free if they choose to take up their grievances and have them settled directly with management, provided (*a*) the settlement does not undercut the union contract and (*b*) the collective bargaining representative is allowed to be present.

IV. THE COLLECTIVE BARGAINING REPRESENTATIVE

As in the Wagner Act, the union designated by a majority of employees in the bargaining unit is the exclusive bargaining representative. *But:* (1) the opportunity to challenge a union's bargaining status is broadened considerably and (2) the discretion of NLRB in establishing the bargaining unit is narrowed.

A. *Decertification.* Petitions from employees for decertification of a union as their bargaining agent must be treated by NLRB in the same manner as union petitions for certification. An employer may petition the Board for an election if *one or more* unions claims the right to bargain for his employees, and such petitions must likewise be given equal treatment.

B. *Elections.* No election, other than a runoff, is to be held in the bargaining unit within a year of the last election. Runoff elections must provide for selection between the two choices (one of which may be "no union") receiving the largest number of votes in the original election. Where there is only one union seeking to organize employees, the employer cannot force the union into an election before it is ready for it, since the employer may ask for an election only if the union has claimed the right to represent employees. A secret election is the only means NLRB may employ to determine the bargaining representative.

C. *Bargaining Units.* NLRB's discretion is hedged in these respects:

1. *Craft groups* may, as a general rule, be set up only as separate units unless a majority in the unit votes against separate representation.

2. *Professional employees* may be set up only as separate units unless a majority votes for inclusion in a larger unit.

3. *Guards* must not only be set up as separate units, but also may be represented only by a union which is unaffiliated with any organization admitting other classes of employees to membership.

4. *Supervisors* must be excluded from all units.

5. *The extent of organization* of employees is not to be taken as the controlling factor in establishing bargaining units.

V. UNION CONDUCT

In addition to the restrictions on strikes and on the subjects of collective bargaining described above, the Act affects the operations of labor unions in these important respects:

A. *Organizing Activity*. Employees are held to be free to refrain from collective activity, except to the extent they are limited by a valid union shop contract. Restraint or coercion of employees in the exercise of this right is a union unfair labor practice, but this does not mean that the union cannot prescribe its own membership rules.

B. *Union Registration*. Protection of the Wagner Act is denied to unions unless they file with the Secretary of Labor reports which show, among other things: names, compensation, and method of selection of officers; dues and initiation fees; procedure for the conduct of internal union affairs; and full financial data. This information must be kept up to date annually, and the report on the union's finances must also be distributed to all members. An affidavit must also be filed with NLRB by each officer of the union stating that he is not a Communist.

C. *Initiation Fees* must not be excessive or discriminatory. NLRB is made the judge.

D. *Suits against Unions*. Unions are made suable in the federal courts as entities, and they are held bound by the acts of their agents. Both for purposes of suit and for purposes of the National Labor Relations Act, the term "agent" is given a broad meaning. A money judgment against a union is enforceable only against the organization's assets, not against those of individual members.

E. *Political Activity* by unions is restricted by a ban on contributions or expenditures in connection with a national election or a primary.

F. *Picketing*. The right of unions and of employees to recognize a picket line around another employer's plant is expressly preserved where the strike is one which has been ratified by the authorized bargaining agent.

VI. EMPLOYER CONDUCT

The five employer unfair labor practices proscribed by the Wagner Act remain unchanged in language, but with some modifications as a result of amendments to other sections of the Act. These modifications include the new restrictions on union security contracts and the new definition of collective bargaining discussed above. In addition—

A. *Views, Arguments, and Opinions* which contain no threats of reprisal and no promises of benefits are not to be considered evidence of an unfair labor practice.

B. *Reinstatement and Back Pay* are not to be ordered by NLRB for any employee who was suspended or discharged for cause.

VII. LABOR RELATIONS BOARD PROCEDURE

In addition to acquiring two new members, NLRB gets a number of new duties, including the conduct of "union shop" elections and elections to determine whether employees involved in a national emergency dispute want to accept the employer's last offer; the determination of jurisdictional disputes; and appraisal of the reasonableness of union initiation fees. The Board's former procedure also is altered in the following respects:

A. *Judicial and Prosecuting Functions* are further separated by an increase in the responsibility and independence of the Board's General Counsel, who has final authority over investigation of charges, issuance of complaints, and prosecution of unfair labor practice cases before the Board. He is appointed by the President.

B. *The Review Division of the Board* is abolished and several other steps are taken with the idea of insuring that final decisions of the Board represent the independent judgment of the Board members.

C. *Evidence.* The Board is instructed to observe, so far as practicable, the rules of evidence applicable in the United States district courts under the rules of civil procedure. In reviewing decisions of the Board, the courts are to treat the Board's findings as to questions of fact as conclusive "if supported by substantial evidence on the record considered as a whole."

D. *Injunctions.* The Board is given new authority to go into court and seek a temporary restraining order, or other appropriate relief, at the time it issues a complaint of unfair labor practices. This gives it power to act quickly where the delay attendant on hearings and final decision would prejudice full enforcement of the Act.

E. *Independent Unions.* The Board is directed to draw no distinction in its treatment of unaffiliated and affiliated unions with regard either to complaints of company-domination or to elections.

F. *Other Changes* in procedure limit the Board's discretion in the issuance of subpoenas, and require in complaint cases that the report and recommendations of

the trial examiner be served on the parties and, if no exceptions are taken within 20 days, become the final order of the Board.

VIII. COVERAGE

Major change in coverage is the exclusion of supervisors in businesses affecting commerce from the protection, not only of the National Labor Relations Act, but of any other federal or state law relating to collective bargaining. Nothing in the bill would prevent a supervisor from joining a union or an employer from bargaining with a foreman's union, but there is no compulsion on the employer to do so.

"*Employee*," as redefined for purposes of the NLRA, also excludes persons having the status of independent contractors and employees of businesses subject to the Railway Labor Act. This last exclusion is intended, according to the Senate Labor Committee, to make the new union unfair labor practice provisions inapplicable as regards employees under the Railway Labor Act.

Additional Employer Groups excluded from the NLRA are Federal Reserve Banks, wholly-owned government corporations, and nonprofit hospitals.

4. ON THE TAFT-HARTLEY ACT[1]

By Robert A. Taft

Mr. President, why is a labor bill necessary? Why is it demanded today by an overwhelming proportion of public opinion? Of course, on the surface it is due to the fact that we have had a large number of strikes, inconveniencing the public, even threatening their safety and welfare. I think even more, the widespread demand for some correction of the existing labor legislation arises because of many injustices which have developed in labor relations, injustices which are perfectly clear to all the people who come in contact with particular disputes which in effect are

without remedy in the courts under present laws.

I myself feel that the larger employers can well look after themselves, but throughout the United States there are hundreds of thousands of smaller employers, smaller businessmen, who, under the existing statutes, have come gradually to be at the mercy of labor-union leaders, either labor-union leaders attempting to organize their employees, or labor-union leaders interfering with the conduct of their business for one reason or for another.

Mr. President, originally, before the passage of any of these laws, the employer

1. *Congressional Record*, XCIII, Part 3 (April 23, 1947), 3834–40.

undoubtedly had an advantage in dealing with his employees. He was one man; the employees might be thousands; and he could deal with them one at a time. In negotiations of that character he had such a superior advantage that Congress came to feel that it must legislate specifically in order to correct that situation and bring about a balance. Congress passed the Clayton Act and the Norris–LaGuardia Act in order to limit legal actions against unions. Congress passed the Wagner National Labor Relations Act in order that the employees of a single employer might act as one in dealing with the one employer, in order that they might be on a sound and an equal basis, a principle which I think no one can question, and which certainly is not questioned in the pending bill.

The difficulty with the Clayton Act and the Norris–LaGuardia Act is that they went at the situation with a meat ax. They practically eliminated all legal remedy against unions for any action taken by them. In effect they provide—as construed by the courts, at least—that any action by a union taken in order to advance its own interests is proper, and there is no legal recourse against the union. The laws referred to do not discriminate between strikes for justifiable purposes and strikes for wholly illegal and improper purposes. They do not distinguish between strikes for higher wages and hours and better working conditions, which are entirely proper and which throughout this bill are recognized as completely proper strikes, and strikes in the nature of secondary boycotts, jurisdictional strikes, and strikes of the racketeering variety. The acts simply eliminated all remedy against any union, leaving the union leaders free, practically without any control even by their members, to order strikes and boycotts and various kinds of actions that interfered, I believe certainly unlawfully under common law, with the activities of many other persons who were entirely innocent.

The National Labor Relations Act was enacted for a proper purpose, but the result of the actual administration of that act has been completely one-sided. It was simply for the one purpose of equalizing, or permitting a large number of employees to act as one; in effect to compel them to act as one if the majority desired such action.

Of course, it was one-sided, and the first board that was appointed, I believe, established a method of procedure which was completely prejudiced and completely on the side of labor unions. In 1939 I sat through the hearings for nearly 6 months on the operation of the National Labor Relations Board up to that time, and I do not think I have ever heard, certainly in America, such a series of miscarriages of justice as occurred under the first National Labor Relations Board.

The members of that board were gradually dismissed by President Roosevelt, the protests being so violent against their acts. As their terms expired other men were appointed to take their place, and they disappeared from the picture. The most violent testimony we had in that particular hearing that I remember came from the A.F. of L. unions themselves, from Mr. Green and Mr. Padway, who took the position, as I think correctly, that the board regarded themselves not as a judicial board to determine rights under the law in a lawful manner, but as crusaders to put the CIO union in every plant in the United States. In every way they could warp the law to accomplish that purpose, they did so.

Since then they have been succeeded by others who have proved to be much more judicial and who today I think constitute a very fair board. Yet much of the personnel that was appointed under the original law remains. Many of the precedents which were established by the original board still exist, and the result is that in the administration of that law, as testified to before our committee, there were so many injustices that it seemed impossible to correct them without legislation.

The greater part of the bill which is now before the Senate is a revision and amendment of the Wagner Labor Relations Act, which is rewritten from the first section to the last, with amendments dealing with particular injustices which were called to our attention, and which we believe can be corrected by an amendment of the law. These various injustices have been frozen into the law by the fact that for 8 years since the hearings in 1939 there has been no labor bill, no comprehensive consideration of the problem, and nothing for action by the Senate except the Case bill of last year, which was only a partial approach to the problem, and which was vetoed by the President.

Mr. President, the interpretations not only of the laws themselves but of the administrative regulations and the administrative rulings, and the decisions of the Supreme Court itself—holding in effect that there was no way in which any court could revise injustices perpetrated by the National Labor Relations Act—resulted in gradually building up the power of the labor leaders, so that today, in my opinion, the weight in collective bargaining negotiations is all on the side of the labor leaders, except perhaps against the very largest companies in the United States. In particular I believe that in dealing with small business, with farmers, and even with the workers themselves, the labor-union leaders have acquired a power which today the people resent and which inevitably has been abused. Many of our labor leaders are just as judicial and as fair as anyone could wish them to be, but extreme power, unreasonable power, cannot be granted to any group of men without a large number of them being willing to exercise it to accomplish ends which are not reasonable. Polls taken today show that union members themselves resent the power of labor-union leaders. Even on the question of the closed shop, which the union leaders are most vigorously defending, the polls show that more than half their men are actually opposed to the position the leaders are taking, because apparently they feel that today they are at a great disadvantage in dealing with union leaders, and that the power given to the leaders by existing legislation is so great that the individual is unable to exercise their right to free speech, his right to work as he pleases, and their general right to live as he pleases.

As to the proper method of correcting the situation, certainly there is no panacea. I have been interested in talking with employers. A group of employers will say, "This situation must be corrected." When asked, "What is the most important thing?" one man will say one thing, another man will say another thing, and a third man will say something else, because those are the matters that have come to their attention in dealing with labor unions.

The problem is infinitely complicated. I suppose there are at least fifty amendments to the present law in the pending bill. Wherever we found an injustice we tried to correct it; and, of course, the net result of correcting a number of injustices is incidentally to decrease some of the power of the labor-union leaders. It seems to me that our aim should be to get back to the point where, when an employer meets with his employees, they have substantially equal bargaining power, so that neither side feels that it can make an unreasonable demand and get away with it. If neither side feels that it can get away with certain demands, I do not believe that the demands will ever be made. If there is reasonable equality at the bargaining table, I believe that there is much more hope for labor peace. That is the method pursued by the bill which is now before the Senate. It is not an antilabor bill. It is not a bill inspired by a desire to wreak vengeance on anyone because of what he may have done. It simply proposes to deal with the causes of labor trouble and the injustices and inequities of the present law.

Basically, I believe that the committee feels, almost unanimously, that the solution of our labor problems must rest on a free economy and on free collective bargaining. The bill is certainly based upon that proposition. That means that we recognize freedom to strike when the question involved is the improvement of wages, hours, and working conditions, when a contract has expired and neither side is bound by a contract. We recognize that right in spite of the inconvenience, and in some cases perhaps danger, to the people of the United States which may result from the exercise of such right. In the long run, I do not believe that that right will be abused. In the past few disputes finally reached the point where there was a direct threat to and defiance of the rights of the people of the United States.

We have considered the question whether the right to strike can be modified. I think it can be modified in cases which do not involve the basic question of wages, prices, and working conditions. But if we impose compulsory arbitration, or if we give the Government power to fix wages at which men must work for another year or for two years to come, I do not see how in the end we can escape a collective economy. If we give the Government power to fix wages, I do not see how we can take from the Government the power to fix prices; and if the Government fixes wages and prices, we soon reach the point where all industry is under Government control, and finally there is a complete socialization of our economy.

I feel very strongly that so far as possible we should avoid any system which attempts to give to the Government this power finally to fix the wages of any man. Can we do so constitutionally? Can we say to all the people of the United States, "You must work at wages fixed by the Government?" I think it is a long step from freedom and a long step from a free economy to give the Government such a right.

It is suggested that we might do so in the case of public utilities; and I suppose the argument is stronger there, because we fix the rates of public utilities, and we might, I suppose, fix the wages of public-utility workers. Yet we have hesitated to embark even on that course, because if we once begin a process of the Government fixing wages, it must end in more and more wage fixing and finally Government price fixing. It may be a popular thing to do. To-day people seem to think that all that it is necessary to do is to forbid strikes, fix wages, and compel men to continue working, without consideration of the human and constitutional problems involved in that process.

If we begin with public utilities, it will be said that coal and steel are just as important as public utilities. I do not know where we could draw the line. So far as the bill is concerned, we have proceeded on the theory that there is a right to strike and that labor peace must be based on free collective bargaining. We have done nothing to outlaw strikes for basic wages, hours, and working conditions after proper opportunity for mediation.

On page 48 of the bill we have provided for the delay of national emergency strikes. We have provided that when a threatened or actual strike or lock-out affecting substantially an entire industry engaged in trade, commerce, transportation, transmission, or communication among the several States, if permitted to occur or to continue, would imperil the national health or safety, the Attorney General may appoint a board of inquiry to inquire into the issues and make a statement of the issues and report back to him as promptly as he may direct. He may then seek from the court an injunction against striking for a period of 60 days, during which time the Government has another opportunity, through the Mediation Board, to try to bring about an agreement between employers and employees which will prevent a Nation-wide strike.

If such mediation should fail, then at the end of 60 days it is provided that there shall be an election by the employees to determine whether or not they accept the last offer made by the employer. If they vote to accept it, of course the strike is terminated. If they vote not to accept it, the injunction is dissolved and they are free to strike. The bill provides that when that happens the Attorney General shall submit to the President a full and comprehensive report of the proceedings, and that the President shall transmit such report, together with such recommendations as he may see fit to make, to the Congress for consideration and appropriate action.

If there finally develops a complete national emergency threatening the safety and health of the people of the United States, Congress can pass an emergency law to cover the particular emergency.

We did not feel that we should put into the law, as a part of the collective-bargaining machinery, an ultimate resort to compulsory arbitration, or to seizure, or to any other action. We feel that it would interfere with the whole process of collective bargaining. If such a remedy is available as a routine remedy, there will always be pressure to resort to it by whichever party thinks it will receive better treatment through such a process than it would receive in collective bargaining, and it will back out of collective bargaining. It will not make a bona-fide attempt to settle if it thinks it will receive a better deal under the final arbitration which may be provided.

We have felt that perhaps in the case of a general strike, or in the case of other serious strikes, after the termination of every possible effort to resolve the dispute, the remedy might be an emergency act by Congress for that particular purpose.

I have had in mind drafting such a bill, giving power to seize the plants, and other necessary facilities, to seize the unions, their money, and their treasury, and requisition trucks and other equipment; in fact, to do everything that the British did in their general strike of 1926. But while such a bill might be prepared, I should be unwilling to place such a law on the books until we actually face such an emergency, and Congress applies the remedy for the particular emergency only. Eighty days will provide plenty of time within which to consider the possibility of what should be done; and we believe very strongly that there should not be anything in this law which prohibits finally the right to strike.

I have dealt with this question, Mr. President, because it is one of perhaps greater interest and one which affects more the fundamental philosophy of the bill than the other provisions. It is contained in title 3 as part of the mediation procedure.

But of course the injunctive process does not deal with the main causes of labor trouble, the injustices, and the inequalities of the present law. The bill seeks to restore equality of bargaining power and imposes on the unions the responsibility to balance the power which they have acquired. The bill is not inspired by a mere theory or by any hostility to unions. It is based on specific testimony of specific wrongs.

I shall try to summarize the changes which have been made. They are important. They make a substantial step forward toward the furnishing of equal bargaining power.

The bill provides that foremen shall not be considered employees under the National Labor Relations Act. They may form unions if they please, or join unions, but they do not have the protection of the National Labor Relations Act. They are subject to discharge for union activity, and they are generally restored to the basis which they enjoyed before the passage of the Wagner Act.

It is felt very strongly by management that foremen are part of management; that it is impossible to manage a plant unless the foremen are wholly loyal to the management. We tried various inbetween steps, but the general conclusion was that they must either be a part of management or a part of the employees. It was proposed that there be separate foremen's unions not affiliated with the men's unions, but it was found that that was almost impossible; that there was always an affiliation of some sort; that foremen, in order to be successful in a strike, must have the support of the employees' union. A plant can promote other men to be foremen if necessary. The tie-up with the employees is inevitable. The committee felt that foremen either had to be a part of management and not have any rights under the Wagner Act, or be treated entirely as employees, and it was felt that the latter course would result in the complete disruption of discipline and productivity in the factories of the United States.

The definition of foremen is applied to persons who are strictly foremen. We have not extended it to timekeepers or guards or any of the others about whom controversy has arisen.

For many years the National Labor Relations Board held that, under the existing amendment of the National Labor Relations Act, foremen were not employees. By a two-to-one vote that was changed, and it was held that they were employees and that decision as an interpretation of the existing law was upheld by the Supreme Court by a vote of 5 to 4. The legal question in the past has been whether they are included as employees under the existing law but we felt that on the questions of theory and of intention of the law, and on the considerations which I have submitted, foremen should be excluded from the operations of the National Labor Relations Act.

Some other changes have been made in the method of classifying employees, particularly professional employees. Professional employees are defined to be those who are strictly professional, men with highly specialized professional qualifications, who may, if they desire, vote themselves out of a plant unit and establish a special union for professional employees. Such a union would have the protection of the Wagner Act. It is not a situation similar to that of foremen. It would mean that the Board could not include professional employees with nonprofessional employees if the majority of the professional employees in a plant did not desire to be in the general union.

In the third place we have provided further protection for craft unions. Today the situation is that when a new plant is organized the Board ordinarily permits the craft members of that plant to vote as to whether they will have a special craft union or join a general plant union. The Board has followed the desires of the craft unit on that question. But if at the time of the first certification a craft unit is not organized, or if no action is taken, and if by default they are all included in a plant union which is certified to the Board, the Board has taken the position that after 1 year of such bargaining no craft union will be recognized or given an opportunity to be heard in connection with establishing a craft unit.

All this bill does is to provide that such a previous finding shall not have that effect, and that if a year later the craft people want to form a separate union they shall have the same consideration at that time as they would have had if they had taken that action when the plant was first organized. In effect I think it gives greater power to the craft units to organize separately. It does not go the full way of giving them an absolute right in every case; it simply provides that the Board shall have discretion and shall not bind itself by previous decision, but that the subject shall always be open for further consideration by the Board.

The provisions of the bill regarding the closed shop are found on pages 12, 13, and 14. They present a substantial change in the present law. They present, I think, so far as I have been able to study the House bill, very much the same change as has been made in the House bill. They do not abolish the union shop. They do abolish the so-called closed shop. A closed shop is a shop in which the employer binds himself not to employ anyone unless he is a member of the union at that time. A union shop is defined as a shop in which the employer binds himself not to continue anyone in employment after the first 30 days unless he joins the union. In other words, an employer may employ anyone whom he chooses to employ, but after 30 days such employee has to join the union or else the employer can no longer employ him. . . .

In the first place, Mr. President, the bill does not abolish the closed shop. Perhaps that is best exemplified by the so-called hiring halls on the west coast, where shipowners cannot employ anyone unless the union sends him to them. That has produced a situation, certainly on the ships going to Alaska, as the testimony before our committee showed clearly, where there is no discipline. A man may be discharged one day and may be hired the next day, either for the same ship or for another ship. Such an arrangement gives the union tremendous power over the employees; furthermore, it abolishes a free labor market. A man cannot get a job where he wants to get it. He has to go to the union first; and if the union says that he cannot get in, then he is out of that particular labor field. Under such circumstances there is no freedom of exchange in the labor market, but all labor opportunities are frozen.

As a matter of fact, most of the so-called closed shops in the United States are union shops; there are not very many closed shops. If in a few rare cases the employer wants to use the union as an employment agency, he may do so; there is nothing to prohibit his doing so. But he cannot make a contract in advance that he will only take the men recommended by the union.

There are two conditions which we have imposed even on the union shop. In the first place, the men must vote that they wish to have such a union shop provided for in the contract with the employer, and the vote must carry by a majority of all the men in the unit not just a majority of

those voting, but a majority of all the men in the unit. That follows, in a somewhat reduced form, the bill introduced by the junior Senator from Indiana [Mr. Jenner]. Certainly it seems clear to me that unless a majority of the men in the unit want a union shop, they should not have to have a union shop imposed upon them by some agreement made by their leaders, thus giving the leaders increased power over their men.

In the second place, we have proposed a proviso in the case where a man is refused admittance to a union, when an employer employs a nonunion man, and during the first 30 days of his employment he goes to the union and says, "I want to join the union," but the union refuses to take him. It is provided that in such case the employer shall not be compelled to discharge the man simply because the union will not let him join the union on the same terms and conditions as any other member. In effect, we say, "if you are going to have a union shop, then you must have an open union. You cannot say to people, 'We have a closed union shop, and we are not going to let you in under any circumstances.'"

The bill further provides that if the man is admitted to the union, and subsequently is fired from the union for any reason other than nonpayment of dues, then the employer shall not be required to fire that man. In other words, what we do, in effect, is to say that no one can get a free ride in such a shop. That meets one of the arguments for the union shop. The employee has to pay the union dues. But on the other hand, if the union discriminates against him and fires him from the union, the employer shall not be required to fire him from the job. During the testimony we heard of a case in which a union member saw a shop steward hit a foreman. That union member was called to testify in court, and he testified that he saw the shop steward hit the foreman. Subsequently, the union called him before their board for discipline, and said that for him to testify as he did was unfair to the union, although he had been subpoenaed to testify in court and sworn. Thereupon he was fired from the union, and under the union agreement the employer would have to fire him. Under this bill the employer would not have to fire that man unless he did not pay his union dues.

I think the justice of such an arrangement should be clear. As I have said, either we should have an open shop or we should have an open union. I do not believe we should permit the complete exclusion from any industry of a man who wants to work in that industry, and whom the employer wants to employ, and who is perfectly competent to work there, simply because the union says, "We do not want you and we will not let you in" or "We are going to fire you from the union because we do not like the way you act."

Mr. President, I have hesitated to support the complete outlawing of the union shop, because the union shop has been in force in many industries for many years, and to upset it today probably would destroy relationships of long standing and probably would bring on more strikes than it would cure. I think there are abuses. I mentioned three or four during the course of the hearings. With respect to abuses of that kind, we have attempted to deal with them by this proviso.

Mr. President, on page 16 the bill contains a provision guaranteeing free speech to employers. That provision in effect carries out approximately the present rule laid down by the Supreme Court of the United States. It freezes that rule into the law itself, rather than to leave employers dependent upon future decisions. That is one of the matters which has been most widely discussed, and I believe that we deal with it in this section with reasonable adequacy.

We have completely revised the nature of the National Labor Relations Board. That is required for the reason that we have created a number of unfair labor practices on the part of unions. The Senate is aware that in the past there have only been unfair

labor practices on the part of employers. All action taken has been against employers. The Board has been given a necessary bias because the Board's only job has been to act against employers and to take action in the case of wrongs which it has been alleged that employers have committed. This bill designates a number of unfair labor practices on the part of employees and labor unions as being unfair. I shall describe those later. The result is that it changes the nature of the Board; it gives it more work to do, and we have increased the number of the members of the Board from 3 to 7, in order that they may sit in two panels, with 3 members on each panel, and accordingly may accomplish twice as much in the way of the number of hearings held. Today the Board is behind in its work, and of course this bill will impose a considerably greater volume of work upon the Board.

We have attempted to deal with the obvious fault, in the early days, that the Board not only prosecuted a man or initiated the prosecution of a man, but also judged the fairness of its own prosecution, almost completely free from any review by the courts. That has offended certainly my sense of justice and it has offended every principle of Anglo-Saxon law. We have tried in various ways to assure that there shall be a separation of those functions. We have not provided for a complete separation, because the Board itself, as time has passed since 1939, has gradually separated those functions in most respects, and a good many of the really serious abuses which occurred previously could not occur today. We have abolished the Review Section, so that this Board will act more as a court; the cases will go directly to the Board, and must be heard by the Board; and each member of the Board is to be given attorneys to work for him, just as each Justice of the Supreme Court has attorneys working for him. So the policy of the Board will not be determined by some anonymous Review Section, but will be determined by the Board itself.

It is provided that when a trial examiner makes a report he shall not then enter into secret meetings with the Board in an attempt to persuade the Board that he is right, after the hearing has been held. His point of view is to be presented in open hearings, and the other side of the matter is to be heard in open hearings. Thereafter, it will not be possible for the trial examiner to have a private or secret meeting with the Board, to argue against a possible reversal of his opinion, just as it is not permissible for a United States district judge to have a private meeting with the judges of a circuit court of appeals, after a hearing has been held before that court to determine whether the district judge's opinion shall be reversed.

If exceptions are taken in representation matters, the hearing officer, who is in effect in the prosecuting end of the job, shall make no recommendations; he shall simply pass on the hearing to the Board, and the Board itself shall pass on the question of representation, and shall do so on the basis of the facts that are shown in the hearing.

The general attempt is to separate those functions, so that we do not have the confusion which has existed and which has operated unfairly against those prosecuted by the Board.

I think the very fact that we specify unfair labor practices on the part of labor unions, as well as on the part of employers, will necessarily restore the Board to a more judicial attitude of mind. I think that in itself may eliminate much of the difficulty which has arisen.

What are the new unfair labor practices on the part of unions? The provision starts on page 14 of the bill. First, it is provided that—

It shall be an unfair labor practice for a labor organization or its agents—

1. To interfere with, restrain, or coerce an employer in the selection of his representatives for the purposes of collective bargaining or the adjustment of grievances.

Last night David Lawrence, in a completely puerile analysis of the bill, referred to that as not meaning anything, and being something to fool the public.

This unfair labor practice referred to is not perhaps of tremendous importance, but employees cannot say to their employer, "We do not like Mr. X, we will not meet Mr. X. You have to send us Mr. Y." That has been done. It would prevent their saying to the employer, "You have to fire Foreman Jones. We do not like Foreman Jones, and therefore you have to fire him, or we will not go to work." This is the only section in the bill which has any relation to Nation-wide bargaining. Under this provision it would be impossible for a union to say to a company, "We will not bargain with you unless you appoint your national employers' association as your agent so that we can bargain nationally." Under the bill the employer has a right to say, "No, I will not join in national bargaining. Here is my representative, and this is the man you have to deal with." I believe the provision is a necessary one, and one which will accomplish substantially wise purposes. . . .

Secondly, it is made an unfair labor practice for a union to try to get an employer to discharge a man who has been improperly fired from the union. That is supplemental to the provisions I have dealt with relating to the closed shop.

In the third place, it is made an unfair labor practice for a union to refuse to bargain collectively with an employer. Up to this time the obligation to bargain collectively has been solely on the employer. Now it is on both the employer and the employee.

The fourth unfair labor practice is an extremely important one. It is made an unfair labor practice for any union to engage in a secondary boycott. That is subdivision (4) (i).

It is made an unfair labor practice for any union to engage in an indirect organizational strike. That is to say, the teamsters cannot go to a store and say, "Unless you sign up with the clerks' union, we are going to boycott your store," unless the clerks' union has been certified as a bargaining agent by the National Labor Relations Board.

The third type of strike which is made an unfair labor practice is the strike in which one union is certified by the National Labor Relations Board and another union strikes against the decision of the National Labor Relations Board.

The fourth type of unfair labor practice is the ordinary jurisdictional strike, in which two unions compete for work on a particular job.

I think the committee all agreed that those types of strikes are in effect racketeering strikes. They are strikes which are not direct strikes to settle questions of wages or hours or better working conditions. They are strikes which are, in effect, attempts to bring indirect pressure on third parties, to get third parties to work in some way to bring about a result which may ultimately be favorable to the one initiating the pressure, which has no direct relation to the work except perhaps with regard to the question of power.

As to the secondary boycott, I shall later describe that type of strike, but I ran into one over the last week end. The plant of a manufacturer of neon signs in Connecticut, I think in Hartford, or near Hartford, had not been organized, and finally his men were organized by a CIO union. The result was that the A.F. of L. sign hangers' union refused to hang this man's signs before any store. Almost the same type of case occurred in Ohio. In Lima, Ohio, a small manufacturer of neon signs was forced out of business because he recognized under the provisions of the act, the union which the National Labor Relations Board compelled him to recognize. Yet he could not get his signs hung. If the stores were able to get them hung, they were broken by stones. They are particularly vulnerable objects, of course. This man was driven out of business. The man

from Hartford told me he had lost $100,000 in the last three months, and that he would be bankrupt in another three days and out of business, so far as he was concerned. That is an example of the secondary boycott, the A.F. of L. sign hangers' union boycotting an employer using certain material because it was made by a CIO union. Senators have heard of other instances. I cite this one only as a type of that kind of action.

The bill provides that that type of strike is an unfair labor practice. When a strike occurs, the man who is damaged by it is to go to the National Labor Relations Board and file a charge, and they give him a hearing. If he can persuade them to do so the Board can go to court and get a temporary injunction against further operation of the strike while the National Labor Relations Board is hearing the question as to whether it is an illegal strike or not, and deciding whether it will issue a permanent injunction against that particular strike.

Mr. President, I think what is provided in the bill is a substantial step forward. The provision is a most important one. At a later time I shall state why I think there should be a more direct remedy than is given, in this type of strike. The members of the committee who favored the method set out have provided the best possible means by which to get action if it is necessary to go to the National Labor Relations Board at all. The same remedy applies to organisational strikes and one type of jurisdictional strike.

Finally, violation of a contract by a union or an employer is also made an unfair labor practice which may be enjoined by the Board.

Mr. President, one of the matters which created the greatest complaint in the early days, and still does, is conduct of elections by the National Labor Relations Board. An election under present law may be sought only by a union. In the early days the Board exercised its discretion in favor of particular unions. It would not order an election until the union told it conditions were favorable, and it might win. Many of the greatest abuses on the part of unions occurred in the use of that discretionary power by the Board in the early days.

Today an employer is faced with this situation. A man comes into his office and says, "I represent your employees. Sign this agreement, or we strike tomorrow." Such instances have occurred all over the United States. The employer has no way in which to determine whether this man really does represent his employees or does not. The bill gives him the right to go to the Board under those circumstances, and say, "I want an election. I want to know who is the bargaining agent for my employees." Certainly I do not think any-one can question the fairness of such a proposal.

We provide, further, that there may be an election asked by the men to decertify a particular union. Today if a union is once certified, it is certified forever; there is no machinery by which there can be any de-certification of that particular union. An election under this bill may be sought to decertify a union and go back to a non-union status, if the men so desire.

It is provided that where there is a ballot having three proposals on it, the A.F. of L. union, the CIO union, and no union at all, the two highest shall be certified in the run-off. Under existing conditions if, we will say, the A.F. of L. has the highest number but not a majority, the no-union has next, and the CIO union, third, the Board says that since the A.F. of L. and CIO together had a majority of the total, therefore the men want a union, and they do not put on the ballot the no-union pro-posal which was second in number of votes cast, they simply put the A.F. of L. and the CIO on it.

This bill requires them to pursue the policy that has been pursued in every run-off election I know of—the two highest have to be certified in the run-off. The bill also provides that elections shall be held only once a year, so that there shall not be a constant stirring up of excitement by continual elections. The men choose a bargaining agent for 1 year. He remains the bargaining agent until the end of that year.

The bill provides further that in these elections, and otherwise, there shall be equal treatment of independent unions. Today the Board refuses as a rule to cer-tify an independent union. Most of the independent unions had some cloud on their original formation.

Originally, perhaps they were a com-pany union, or they had some aid from the company. The Board has taken the posi-tion that if those facts are once shown, they never will certify such a union, al-though it may have purged itself of that connection for the last ten or fifteen years. The telephone union was originally a company union. Now, nobody can ques-tion it is bona fide.

If there be an A.F. of L. or CIO af-filiate union which is company dominated, but which affiliates itself with the national A.F. of L. union, then the Board will per-mit it to purge itself promptly and will certify it as bargaining agent.

This bill provides that it must give inde-pendent unions, under those circum-stances, the same treatment that would be given a union affiliated with the A.F. of L. or the CIO. Numerous representatives of independent unions appeared before the committee who told us how unfairly they had been treated. It was felt that theirs was a good case.

The bill provides, that in elections, one shall not have the right to vote if he has no right to be reinstated in his employment. In the Redwood case, in California, the men in a particular sawmill company plant, struck, and walked out. They have been out now for eighteen months, and gradually they have been replaced, mostly by returning veterans, until there is a full force working in the plant, and the men who were formerly employed are out, working on other jobs; and yet, when an election is held, the old men still vote, still select the bargaining agent; and there is no possible way for the employer to stop the strike or stop the picketing, that still continues, because he can deal only with the union which is represented by men who are no longer there. The men who are in the plant cannot be strikebreakers, they cannot be men who are given more money than the ordinary employee; but under present decisions if the new men are standard replacements, men willing to work, and taken on for permanent work, then they take the jobs of men who are striking and the former workers are not entitled to have their jobs back. This bill provides in that case that the former employee cannot vote in the election, so that the new men can form a union and can make finally an agreement, an effective legal agreement with their employer.

Mr. President, the bill provides that unions must file financial reports on forms certified by the Secretary of Labor, and furnish the reports to all their members, and file a copy with the Secretary of Labor. Such reports are not open to the public, any more than corporation reports are open to the public; but they are open to inspection by the members, and they are also open to proper Government officials. There is no special provision, but they are not specifically provided to be open to the public.

The filing of such report is a condition of certification as bargaining agent under the law, and is also a condition of the right to file any charges under the National Labor Relations Act. One of the most important things, I think, that the public feel should be done, is to make unions responsible. This bill provides that such reports shall be made. They are made in many unions today. Many unions favored the proposal. No man may longer conduct a union as his private concern and conceal from his members the salary he receives or the methods by which he disposes of their funds.

The bill makes a change in the provision regarding court review of National Labor Relations Board decisions. The present rule in the law is simply that any decision supported by evidence shall be final as to the facts, and the result has been that as a practical matter it is almost impossible for a court to reverse the National Labor Relations Board.

Under this proposal, it is said that the finding of the Board with respect to questions of fact, if supported by substantial evidence on the record considered as a whole, shall be conclusive.

In the first place, the evidence must be substantial; in the second place, it must still look substantial when viewed in the light of the entire record. That does not go so far as saying that a decision can be reversed on the weight of the evidence. It does not go quite so far as the power given to a circuit court of appeals to review a district-court decision, but it goes a great deal further than the present law, and gives the court greater opportunity to reverse an obviously unjust decision on the part of the National Labor Relations Board.

Mr. President, title III of the bill, on page 53, makes unions suable in the Federal courts for violation of contract. As a matter of law unions, of course, are liable in theory on their contracts today, but as a practical matter it is difficult to sue them. They are not incorporated; they have many members; in some States all the members must be served; it is difficult to know who is to be served. But the pending bill provides they can be sued as if they were corporations and if a judgment is found against the labor organization, even though it is an unincorporated association, the liability is on the labor union and the labor-union funds, and it is not on the individual members of the union, where it has fallen in some famous cases to the great financial distress of the individual members of labor unions.

Finally, Mr. President, the bill provides for a joint committee to study and report on basic problems affecting friendly labor relations and productivity. We have not had time to study a good many fundamental questions relating to labor relations. There are various subjects which were not covered by the testimony, and we felt that there should be a more fundamental study leading to better relations between employer and employee, leading to better productivity on the part of the individual workman, with his willingness and consent, because, after all, his standard of living depends ultimately on his particular productivity.

We see today what has happened in England where the productivity of workmen has for one reason or other steadily decreased.

The committee is to study, first, a means by which permanent friendly cooperation between employers and employees and stability of labor relations may be secured throughout the United States.

Second, the means by which the individual employee may achieve a greater productivity and higher wages, including plans for guaranteed annual wages, incentive profit-sharing and bonus systems. There are many such plans proposed as solutions of the labor problem, and we believe all of them should have a hearing and that they should be studied by Congress;

Third, the labor relations policies and practices of employers and associations of employees;

Fourth, the coordination of welfare funds with the social-security system.

We have an amendment to offer later which will deal with the question of holding up the formation of wide open welfare funds until this study is made but in any event, a study should be made of the relationship between the security funds of special corporations and industries and the social-security plan, whether they can exist alongside, whether they should be coordinated, and what the relationship should be.

Finally, the methods and procedures for best carrying out the collective-bargaining processes, with special attention to the effects of industry-wide or regional bargaining upon the national economy, and such other problems as the committee sees

fit to study. That committee is to be composed of seven members of the Senate Committee on Labor and Public Welfare and seven members of the House Committee on Education and Labor, a total of fourteen, which is given the usual power of joint committees.

Mr. President, I did not mention the fact that the bill proposes to revise the Federal Mediation Service. The revision, which occurs in the section dealing with the emergency injunction process, provides for a single Director of Mediation, who is not to be under the jurisdiction of the Labor Department but is made an independent agency, for the reason that it was felt that the Labor Department was formed to represent the interests of labor, and that a conciliation service should be absolutely impartial between labor and employer. . . .

I might say that in this mediation procedure we have provided greater power for the Mediation Service. We hope that the prestige which it acquires may lead to more successful mediation than there has been.

We have provided in the revision of the collective-bargaining procedure, in connection with the mediation process, that before the end of any contract, whether it contains such a provision or not, either party who wishes to open the contract may give 60 days' notice in order to afford time for free collective bargaining, and then for the intervention of the Mediation Service. If such notice is given, the bill provides for no waiting period except during the life of the contract itself. If, however, either party neglects to give such notice and waits, let us say, until 30 days before the end of the contract to give the notice, then there is a waiting period provided during which the strike is an unlawful labor practice for 60 days from that time, or to the end of the contract and 30 days beyond that time. In that case there is a so-called waiting period during which a strike is illegal, but it is only brought about by the failure of the union itself to give the notice which the bill requires shall be given. So it seems to me to be no real limitation of the rights of labor unions.

Mr. President, I have covered the bill. I shall be glad to answer any questions dealing with it today or at any other time. I feel that the bill makes an extraordinary reversal along the right lines toward the equalizing of the power of labor unions and employers. It is certainly a substantial step forward. There are four other things that I think ought to be added to it, but they are in no way inconsistent with the bill itself. I hope very much that the Senate will proceed to a consideration of the bill and will act upon it promptly.

I do not think that labor can claim that any of its legitimate rights are interfered with, but if anyone can point out language which seems to be broader than the legitimate purposes shown to be necessary by the hearings we have held, certainly we shall be glad to modify such language.

I think I can say that I support wholeheartedly the bill which is here presented, and I believe it will deal with a majority of the serious problems which now exist in the relations between employers and employees; that it will impose upon unions a responsibility more equal to the power which they have acquired, and that it will tend to bring about industrial peace in the United States.

5. FOR A NEW LABOR LAW—A BASIC ANALYSIS[1]

By WILLIAM M. LEISERSON

EDITORS' NOTE.—In the presidential election of 1948 the Taft-Hartley Act was a primary issue. President Truman followed his campaign promise to attempt repeal of this law that had created so much controversy since its adoption in the spring of 1947 by a Republican Congress over his veto. In February, 1949, new legislation was introduced designed to repeal the Taft-Hartley Law and to re-enact (with a few changes) the Wagner Act of 1935.

One of those who commented on the nation's experience with the Taft-

Hartley Law and advocated the law's repeal was William M. Leiserson (1883———). Now visiting professor and director of labor organization study at Johns Hopkins University, Leiserson has had a long career in industrial relations, including chairmanship of the Railway Labor Mediation Board, of the National Mediation Board, and member of the National Labor Relations Board. In the following article he discusses foundations for a new labor policy to take into account changes that have occurred since the passage of the Wagner Act in 1935.

A good way to begin thinking about a new labor law, now taking shape in Congressional hearings, is to compare the policy pronouncements of the Taft-Hartley Act and the Wagner Act.

1. William M. Leiserson, "For a New Labor Law—a Basic Analysis," *New York Times Magazine*, February 6, 1949. By permission of the *New York Times*.

The Taft-Hartley Act says: "It is the purpose and policy of this act to prescribe the legitimate rights of both employes and employers, to (prevent) interference by either with the legitimate rights of the other, to protect the rights of individual employes in their relations with labor organizations . . . , to define and proscribe practices (inimical to general welfare) on the part of labor and management, and to protect the rights of the public. . . .''

Quite different was the purpose of the Wagner Act. It declared the policy of the United States to be "encouraging the practice and procedure of collective bargaining . . . , protecting the exercise by workers of full freedom of association, self-organization, and designation of representatives of their own choosing for the purpose of negotiating terms and conditions of their employment or other mutual aid or protection.''

The two laws approached the problems of employer-employe relations differently, and they went off in different directions to find solutions. The Wagner Act put its faith in collective bargaining; but, while the Taft-Hartley Act paid lip service to the principle of collective bargaining, its insistence on "legal rights" encouraged individual bargaining and, to an even greater extent, Government determination of the labor bargain.

The act's attempt to pursue three incompatible labor policies at the same time could result only in confusion.

The confusion was soon reflected in the administration of the law—the NLRB and its coordinate general counsel being unable to agree as to its intentions. Apparently the voters sensed the act was working at cross-purposes, and returned to office the President over whose veto it was adopted, with a Congress dominated by the party whose platform called for its repeal.

No one is in a position to say precisely what the mandate is as to the kind of a new labor law that should be adopted. But we shall not go far astray if we assume that the public wants a law based on a clear-cut labor policy that it can understand, with specific provisions reasonably calculated to carry out the policy. Making a definite choice among possible national labor policies is in any case an indispensable preliminary requirement for drafting a workable law to govern so emotion-filled and explosive a subject as labor and management relationships.

But what are the possible choices? Broadly speaking, there are only the three: (1) individual bargaining; (2) collective bargaining; (3) Government dictation. The first leaves labor relations to be governed by individual contracts of employment. This means, as the Supreme Court said as far back as 1898, "The proprietors lay down the rules and the laborers are practically constrained to obey them"; in other words, management dictation. The second policy requires the rules to be made jointly by representatives of managements and the workers, and embody them in collective agreements. The third is the policy by which the Government determines the rules or terms of employment, or both.

The Taft-Hartley Act favors this third policy. Although it did not venture to fix wages, it did decide by Congressional fiat vital issues of rules and working conditions involved in labor contracting, under the guise of determining "legitimate rights." In doing this it purported to further the policy of collective bargaining, but its concern that "strikes and other forms of industrial unrest or concerted activities (shall not) impair the interest of the public" led it to prescribe "rights" which had the effect of determining disputed issues and removing them from the field of bargaining. Incidentally, in encouraging individual bargaining the act in effect stipulated for employes a right to refrain from collective bargaining.

The Wagner Act, on the other hand, clearly chose the collective bargaining policy as a middle ground between the two extremes of management dictation and Government dictation. But it did not carry this forward to completion. It restricted itself to equalizing bargaining power and making sure that employers recognized and dealt with unions as authorized representatives of the employes. It did not concern itself with the eventuality of collective negotiations ending in disagreement. Nor did it consider the possibility that unions might refuse to bargain collectively.

In these respects the Wagner Act's collective bargaining policy was incomplete. As a consequence, "the friendly adjustment of industrial disputes arising out of differences as to wages, hours or other working conditions" to which it looked forward was far from achieved, although it was quite successful in gaining its other objectives.

What, then, shall be the national labor policy on which a new labor relations law is to be based? The answer seems obvious. There can be no going back to individual bargaining under our present industrial system of corporate enterprises. The American people, most of whom are wage-earners and salaried employes, will not permit it. So long as corporate enterprise remains predominantly private enterprise, and is not supplanted by Government corporations, the American people are not likely to support a national policy by which public authorities fix either the rules or the terms of the labor contract.

The collective bargaining policy is the only one suitable to American conditions as a basis for labor relations legislation.

The Wagner Act went a long way toward working out a law based on this policy. But it did not go far enough. It stopped, as the traditional novel ends, at the point where management and labor are joined in a vow to bargain collectively, as if they were going to live happily ever afterward. We know, when we are not bemused by an exciting story of conflict and tribulation, that marriage is a beginning, not an ending.

So is collective bargaining. Its story too goes on, often with discord removed by "friendly adjustment," but frequently, also, through conciliation, mediation, arbitration, fact-finding and subsequent negotiations to come to reasonable adjustment. All are part of the practice and procedure of collective bargaining. The act dealt with none of these aids to contract negotiation. As a result, when disputes broke into open conflict—as strikes or lockouts—the collective bargaining policy of the law was blamed rather than the failure to provide the mediatory measures necessary to complete the bargaining process.

Ironically, it was the Taft-Hartley Act that contributed most toward remedying this deficiency. Title II of the law declares "that the settlement of issues between employers and employes through collective bargaining may be advanced by making available full and adequate governmental facilities for conciliation, mediation and voluntary arbitration. . . ." It set up, for the first time on a statutory basis, a Federal Mediation and Conciliation Service with appropriate functions and responsibilities.

However, the preoccupation of the authors of the law with "legitimate rights" and "suits by and against labor organizations" led them to include in the mediation procedures court injunctions and a compulsory vote of employes on the employers' last offer when disputes may or do "imperil national health and safety."

The first problem to be faced in devising a workable new law is the so-called unfair labor practices. Here it is important to bear in mind that the Government cannot reach all unfair, unjust or oppressive conduct of either industrial managements or labor organizations. Even if it could, few would agree that such paternalism is desirable in a democratic country. That is why collective bargaining is favored to provide joint or impartial grievance machinery for handling abuses of both parties.

What kind of unfair practices, then, should a labor relations law undertake to suppress? The Wagner Act answered this question by prohibiting a few well-known activities of employers directed toward obstructing, preventing or destroying collective bargaining. To these, but to no other unfair, unjust or reprehensible conduct of employers and their managerial staffs it gave the legal name "unfair labor practices." It conceived the collective bargaining policy to require that obstructions to the working of the policy should be removed, but other wrongs should be dealt with by the management and labor representatives.

Many people were misled by the legal term "unfair practice," however, thinking it covered much more than it actually did. These and others, too, felt that the act was one-sided, since it did not prohibit similar practices by labor organizations. The Taft-Hartley Act reflected this feeling, and it undertook to bring the law into balance. But because its approach was to define rights rather than to encourage voluntary adjustments by mutual consent, it did not confine itself to proscribing only those unfair practices of unions which, like the employers' similar practices, hampered or blocked collective bargaining.

The Taft-Hartley Act went much further. It attempted to prohibit by law other unjust conduct by labor unions, quite like that which is common in management organizations, which the Wagner policy left for voluntary adjustment by collective bargaining. But it did not extend the same proscriptions to management misconduct.

For example, the Taft-Hartley Act undertook "to protect the rights of individual employes in their relations with labor organizations." It made no such provision, however, for protecting individuals in their relations with the management organizations which employ them. Indeed, the Taft-Hartley Law even restricted the legal right of supervisory employes to bargain collectively with the management about common injustices imposed on them. Except for union activity, these enterprises and their managements are legally free to fire workers for any or no reason, to discriminate and play favorites among employes, to overwork, underpay or otherwise mistreat them.

On the other hand, similar conduct by labor organizations, no more reprehensible when practiced by them, are prohibited by the act. "Featherbedding," defined as pay for services not rendered, was prohibited as an unfair labor practice. But not so the employers' counterpart practice known as the "stretch out," which means additional work or services for which no pay is rendered. Management may require a plumber to do an electrician's work, or a machinist to work at a carpenter's job; but a union commits a legal offense in "requiring any employer to assign particular work to employes in a particular labor organization or in a particular trade."

Again, a corporation may freely cease buying the products of an employer whose plant is unionized or pays higher wages; but if the union tries to get the employer to cease buying the products of the lower-wage nonunion corporation, its efforts are unfair practices condemned by the law.

These are but examples of the inequities created by the Taft-Hartley Act in its attempts to deal with injustices in labor relations by prescribing "legitimate rights."

The problems are real, however, and the question is whether wrongful conduct on the part of both management and labor is not more effectively and speedily removed by the processes of collective bargaining. The success of such a program, however, depends upon keeping the bargaining power of employers and workers reasonably equal.

The shrill cries of employers who are hurt by union arbitrariness, for example, must not deafen us to the less vocal complaints of employes who have no unions to protect them against employer artibrariness. We must not forget that millions of workers are still unorganized, and their employers' power is still supreme. There are many weak unions not effective as bargaining agents, and there is need for more unions among those who still have to bargain individually.

The Wagner Act became law when labor was generally the weaker party, and its success in increasing labor's bargaining power has been spectacular. Sixteen million workers are now in organizations capable of bargaining on an equality with employers, and collective agreements govern labor relations in all the major industries of the country. This makes many employers feel abused, and in some instances their feeling is justified; some of them are now the weaker party.

The remedy, however, is not to weaken unionism but rather to strengthen the bargaining power of employers in the same way that the Wagner Act did for employes; namely, by subjecting unions to the same bargaining responsibilities that this law imposes on managements.

The normal union bargains collectively, for that is its reason for existence. But some unions have grown so strong that they do not want collective bargaining, as so many employers don't. They prefer to dictate terms or, as someone has said, to collect first and bargain afterward.

Experience having shown that unions as well as employers may obstruct and tend to destroy collective bargaining, it is clear that a requirement that unions shall not refuse to bargain is as necessary as the provision that employers shall not so refuse. The Taft-Hartley Law made such refusal by a union an unfair labor practice, and there can be no reasonable objection to it. The national labor policy is furthered, not retarded, by such a requirement.

Similarly, when a union is chosen by a majority of the employes to represent them as bargaining agent, the minority union that lost the election sometimes tries to force the employer to deal with it. The employer would be guilty of an unfair practice if he acceded to such a demand, and a union which tries to force it should be held equally unfair. Adding such a provision to the Wagner Act would also further the collective bargaining policy.

On the other hand, giving the employer the right to petition for an election, as the Taft-Hartley Law does, when there is no dispute as to whether the employes want any union to bargain for them, freezes individual bargaining. Unions must present signatures from at least 30 per cent of the workers before they can have an election. A similar showing that it is the employes and not he that wants an election should be required of the employer. This can be done by requiring the employer to show that a union, or two unions each claiming a majority, is demanding recognition from him.

Then there is the question of jurisdictional disputes. Such disputes are not as wholly unjustified as they appear. They require delicate handling because involved in them is freedom of workers to form unions with fellow employes in their own occupations, crafts or industries. Conflicts naturally arise when the work habitually done by a class of employes belonging to one union is assigned by an employer to men of a different occupation belonging to another union.

Sometimes, too, a union invades the jurisdiction of another regardless of whether the work is the same or different. Such disputes are common also where the workers have no unions. So long as the disputes do not seriously interrupt production and inconvenience the public there is no more wisdom in legislating on the subject than there would be if the Government tried to decide disputes between man and wife as to who should do the dishes. Most such disputes are adjusted somehow without strikes. "The Taft Act's ban on jurisdictional strikes was seldom invoked during the law's first year, and was the subject of no definitive ruling," according to the Bureau of National Affairs.

Such strikes are dramatic when they do occur, however, and attract unusual attention. They are better handled by conciliation and mediation, and because they often result from different interpretations of collective agreements, a provision that such disputes be arbitrated, if not otherwise settled, would be appropriate to a collective bargaining policy.

Related to this question is the problem of "secondary boycotts." This is an ambiguous legal term which is often used to include primary boycotts that are wholly justified. A union that is engaged in a lawful strike obviously will tell its members not to work on the "struck work." But commonly employers whose men are on strike try to get their work done by other employers where members of the same union are employed. If the men refuse to do this work, they are apparently violating the secondary boycott prohibition of the Taft-Hartley Law, according to the general counsel of the NLRB and at least one court decision. This is hardly equal protection of legitimate rights of both labor and management.

On the other hand, some unions boycott the use of materials made in plants by men belonging to other unions. This is using collective action not to bargain but rather to prevent another union from bargaining. Obviously, such interference with the collective bargaining policy needs to be prevented. A simple provision making it an unfair practice to refuse to work on materials made by employers dealing with other bona fide unions would accomplish this.

But what about the closed shop? This has been a traditional policy of American trade unionism ever since it began about 150 years ago. The Taft-Hartley Act outlawed it but made a questionable distinction between this and a union shop, which, contrary to the intent of its authors, had the effect of extending union membership as a condition of employment far beyond anything that had previously prevailed. By a vote of a majority of the employes, it is made legal for an employer to require all his employes to be union members. This is the form of closed shop that industrial unions prefer.

The only difference between this "union shop" and the outlawed "closed shop" is that the latter requires workers to be members before they are hired. The justification for the compulsory membership is the same in both. Nonmembers enjoy the benefits of union bargaining, but they refuse to pay its costs. They want their grievances adjusted either free by the machinery the union provides, or they want

to handle them by individual bargaining with the employer. Nonmembers thus tend to undermine both the collective agreement and the union's position in the shop or plant. Hence it is "union security" that unions seek under either form of closed shop.

If the effectiveness of unions and their security are adequately protected by a collective bargaining law, the closed shop issue might well be left to unions and managements to work out in their contract negotiations. But a new problem in union relations is created by a national collective bargaining law which organized labor itself has largely overlooked. This is the threat to union security not from "freeriders" or "no-bills," as nonmembers are dubbed, but from other unions equally enfolded in the American labor movement and devoted to its aims and principles.

Thus in elections conducted by the NLRB to select bargaining agents the employes increasingly find on their ballots that they must choose between two AFL unions or two CIO unions, or between an AFL and a CIO union. In such cases, when one union wins a closed shop contract from another, the members who have been working under it, though they may constitute 49 per cent of the employes, must renounce allegiance to their organization and join the union that won the election. This neither promotes security for unionism nor for collective bargaining.

How then shall a labor law deal with the closed shop problem in the light of its rapidly changing nature? A suggestion might be taken from the way in which nations treat aliens in their midst who might endanger the state. The aliens are not compelled to become citizens, but they are required to obey the laws and to pay taxes. Let all the employes whose wages and working conditions are determined by a collective bargaining agreement be obligated to abide by its terms, rules and procedures, and also to pay their fair share of the expenses of negotiations and administering the agreement.

In other words, let nonmembers be governed by collective labor contracts exactly as members are, and require them to pay the equivalent of union dues to the union that negotiates the contract and is responsible for carrying it out; but let no one be compelled to join any particular labor organization. Neither employers nor organized labor is likely to take to this suggestion, but some provision of this kind will be needed in a labor relations law if union security continues to be endangered not only by nonmembers, but by competing unions as well.

But protecting collective bargaining against practices which tend to obstruct or weaken it is only the negative side of such a national labor policy. The positive side is equally indispensable. This requires encouragement, aid and ever-ready mediation machinery to help representatives of labor and management reach agreement when negotiations end in deadlock. Moreover, this positive aid must be made available *before*, not after, the deadlock brings on a strike or lockout.

Labor disputes are often confused with strikes. It is important to keep them distinguished. Disputes are normally healthy; they show that both parties are free and able to maintain their positions without one being able to suppress the other. But strikes or lockouts measure the failure of peaceful methods. They are like a resort to war to settle international differences.

Where the disputants are equal as sovereign states are, and labor and management ought to be, consultation and then mediation by a third party are the primary methods of peaceful settlement. As already indicated, the Wagner Act was incomplete because, though it required consultation and negotiation, it was not accompanied by an adequate mediation policy or administrative organization. Obviously, when the Wagner Act freed workers to organize and equalized their bargaining power with management, this was bound to bring more disputes as well as more agreements. But the only mediation machinery available,

until Title II of the Taft-Hartley Law was adopted, was a meagerly financed and staffed conciliation service maintained by the Department of Labor under the general powers vested in the Secretary who headed the department.

The NLRB, which administered the negative part of collective bargaining, covered the country with twenty-two regional offices, some sub-offices and a thousand employes or more. The conciliation service needed to be expanded correspondingly to make available the positive help needed to resolve disagreements. The present Federal Mediation and Conciliation Service is still far from meeting this need. It has only about 300 employes.

There are two distinctly different kinds of disagreements about which collective bargaining may become deadlocked. One involves differences about terms to be included in new or renewed labor contracts; the other is about questions as to the meaning or requirements of contracts already made. As to controversies of the first kind, the mediation and voluntary arbitration principles and procedures provided in the Taft-Hartley Act are soundly designed to facilitate peaceful settlements. These need to be retained in any new labor relations law. They might well be strengthened, however, by the establishment of a National Arbitration Tribunal, with panels of expert arbitrators, to decide such disputes when both parties are agreeable to doing this. Such a tribunal is needed to stimulate voluntary arbitration.

But, as already mentioned, the act attempted to distinguish disputes affecting national health and safety, and to provide special measures for these. The distinction is a dubious one, for almost any important strike endangers health and safety to some extent. Moreover, injunctions prohibiting strikes for eighty days are brought into the procedures, and this turns the labor dispute into a court controversy about rights which have little relation to the industrial issues involved.

True, a board of inquiry is appointed to

find the facts in the case, but it is restricted to reporting facts without drawing conclusions from them, or expressing any opinion as to what they indicate in relation to the merits of the issues in dispute. Instead a vote of the employees is required on the employer's last offer, thus implying that there is more merit in what he offers than in what the employes ask. Regardless of the outcome, however, the injunction must be lifted after the vote, and then the employes are free to strike.

This is a clumsy and undesirable substitute for the customary method of fact-finding which is the final step in the mediation process developed from the practice of collective bargaining itself and often used to secure settlements by mutual agreement. It is common in any major labor dispute, whether it appears to affect public health and safety or not, when direct negotiations between the parties and mediatory efforts both fail and they cannot agree on arbitration, for a board to investigate positions of the parties and the facts in the case and then to recommend an equitable settlement.

Such recommendations form the basis on which the parties usually reach agreement. This procedure takes time, but a provision in the law that neither party shall change the conditions out of which the dispute arose for a period of sixty days is now generally acceptable to both labor and management. There is no need to resort to injunctions and court procedures to secure maintenance of the status quo pending a fact-finding investigation.

The second kind of disputes—those about agreements that have already been reached and embodied in contracts—are best settled by adjudication rather than mediation, if the parties themselves cannot adjust them. The agreement settled their disputes when it was signed, and both are bound until it expires. But differences arise as to interpretation of what was agreed to. Such differences need to be adjudicated when they cannot be other-

wise settled, like any other disagreements about contracts.

Pursuant to its legal rights policy the Taft-Hartley Act authorized United States District Courts to entertain suits by either party charging violation of collective agreements. It also declared it to be desirable that such disputes ought to be settled by a method agreed upon by the parties. But it did not act on this suggestion, though court procedures are about as helpful in securing friendly adjustments in cases of this kind as divorce suits are between man and wife.

Most agreements do provide their own methods, usually requiring arbitration as a last resort by permanent umpires in some cases, more frequently by temporary referees or tripartite boards. This being a common practice developed by the process of collective bargaining itself, a labor relations law should extend it to cover all disputes about the meaning of agreements. Every such dispute arises out of an alleged or threatened violation. Instead of sending the parties to the courts, the law should require all collective contracts to include provisions for settling disputes about its meaning by arbitration, if they are not otherwise adjusted. Failure to do so, however, should not be punishable at law.

A better method is to authorize the National Arbitration Tribunal previously mentioned, or arbitrators appointed by it, to make final decisions in such cases on request of either party. Other democratic countries have so provided with good effects, and it is required by our own Railway Labor Act. Arbitration of this kind, strictly bound by the terms of the agreements, would merely facilitate carrying out the intent of collective contracts. It would not, like compulsory arbitration, fix what terms labor and management must agree to by Government fiat.

The program here outlined will not abolish strikes, even those which might imperil national health and safety. Only a police state can do that. The injunction procedures of the Taft-Hartley Law postponed strikes for eighty days but did not prohibit them. The Railway Labor Act postpones them too, and for much longer periods, but does not authorize court injunctions.

During the latter part of the war we adopted what was substantially a system of compulsory arbitration, yet in 1944 we had the greatest number of strikes on record up to that time, and the number of workers involved was almost at the record peak. Both individual and collective bargaining were all but done away with in war industries, and the War Labor Board was authorized by Congress to fix terms of employment. Nevertheless, strikes continued to bedevil the war effort on a scale greater than in the previous peacetime years. One study showed that 37 per cent of these strikes were directed not against employers but against actions of the Government.

No country which values free labor can abolish strikes in any industry, however affected with public interest, so long as the employers are private persons or corporations. A free Government does better not to expose its own impotence.

Ample experience has demonstrated, then, that compulsory arbitration is less successful in preventing strikes or reducing their number and extent than a national collective bargaining law, such as here outlined, with safeguards against unfair practices that tend to obstruct or undermine it, and with adequate mediation facilities for aiding positively in the process of settling labor differences by mutual agreement.

SECTION E. GOVERNMENT POLICY FOR AGRICULTURE

1. VETO OF THE McNARY-HAUGEN BILL, 1928[1]

By Calvin Coolidge

EDITORS' NOTE.—The American farmer did not share the prosperity of the twenties. This fact together wth the political strength of the so-called "farm bloc" accounts for the numerous and varied proposals which were advanced to aid the farmer. From 1922 to 1928 the McNary-Haugen Bill was the most prominent of these proposals. Twice it passed Congress; twice it was vetoed (February, 1927, and May, 1928). The second of these veto messages is reprinted below. Since the McNary-Haugen Bill was a forerunner of similar New Deal and "Fair Deal" agricultural policies, President Coolidge's veto may also appropriately be read as a criticism of the principles for agricultural policy of the subsequent decades.

To the Senate:

Senate bill 3555, called the surplus control act, is in some respects an improvement over Senate bill 4808 of the last Congress. It includes several provisions, which, if unencumbered by objectionable features, would form a basis for a measure that should do much to develop stronger business organizations in agriculture. But the present bill contains not only the so-called equalization fee and other features of the old measure prejudicial, in my opinion, to sound public policy and to agriculture, but also new and highly objectionable provisions. In its entirety it is little less undesirable than the earlier measure. The bill still is unconstitutional. This position is supported by the opinion of the Attorney General, which is hereto attached.

In its essentials the objectionable plan proposed here is the stimulation of the price of agricultural commodities and products thereof by artificially controlling the surpluses so that there will be an apparent scarcity on the market. This is to be done by means of a board having supposedly adequate powers and adequate funds to accomplish such purpose through various agencies, governmental and private. The surpluses of the different selected commodities so accumulated by the board are then to be sold by export and otherwise directly or through such agencies at whatever loss is necessary in making the disposition. The fund to pay the losses and other costs while at first furnished by the Government is ultimately to be replaced and thereafter replenished from time to time by means of a tax or fee charged against the product. The theory is that the enhanced price of the commodity would enable the producer to pay the equalization fee and still reap a profit.

The recurring problem of surpluses in farm products has long been a subject of deep concern to the entire Nation, and any economically sound, workable solution of it would command not only the approval but the profound gratitude of our people. The present measure, however, falls far short of that most desirable objective; indeed, although it purports to provide farm relief by lessening the cares of our greatest industry, it not only fails to accomplish that purpose but actually heaps even higher

1. Calvin Coolidge, *McNary-Haugen Veto* (70th Cong., 1st sess.; Senate Miscellaneous Docs., II, No. 141, Serial No. 8871 [Washington, 1928]), pp. 1–7, 9–10.

its burdens of political control, of distribution costs, and of foreign competition. It embodies a formidable array of perils for agriculture which are all the more menacing because of their being obscured in a maze of ponderously futile bureaucratic paraphernalia. In fact, in spite of the inclusion in this measure of some constructive steps proposed by the administration, it renews most of the more vicious devices which appeared in the bill that was vetoed last year. This document is much altered from its previous form but its substance, particularly as to its evident ultimate effect of tending to delude the farmer with a fantastic promise of unworkable governmental price regulation, is still as repugnant as ever to the spirit of our institutions, both political and commercial.

A detailed analysis of all of the objections to the measure would involve a document of truly formidable proportions. However, its major weaknesses and perils may be summarized under six headings:

I. Its attempted price-fixing fallacy.
II. The tax characteristics of the equalization fee.
III. The widespread bureaucracy which it would set up.
IV. Its encouragement to profiteering and wasteful distribution by middlemen.
V. Its stimulation of overproduction.
VI. Its aid to our foreign agricultural competitors.

These topics by no means exhaust the list of fallacious and indeed dangerous aspects of the bill, but they afford ample ground for its emphatic rejection.

I. *Price fixing.*—This measure is as cruelly deceptive in its disguise as governmental price-fixing legislation and involves quite as unmistakably the impossible scheme of attempted governmental control of buying and selling of agricultural products through political agencies as any of the other so-called surplus control bills. In fact, in certain respects it is much broader and more flagrant in its scope. The heights to which price lifting might be

promised are freed from the limitations fixed in previous measures. The bill carefully avoids any direct allusion to such price-fixing functions, but there can be no doubt about its intentions and authorizations to the Federal farm board in this respect. There is apparently no change in the import of the bill in the resolution to impose upon the farmer and upon the consumers of farm produce a régime of futile, delusive experiments with price fixing, with indirect governmental buying and selling, and with a nation-wide system of regulatory policing, intolerable espionage, and tax collection on a vast scale.

These provisions would disappoint the farmer by naïvely implying that the law of supply and demand can thus be legislatively distorted in his favor. Economic history is filled with the evidences of the ghastly futility of such attempts. Fiat prices match the folly of fiat money.

The board would be compelled to arrive in some way at the premium on the domestic price which would be demanded from the consumer, and this figure would have to be fixed in the contracts which it would make with the millers, packers, canners, spinners, and other processors. Such prices and other terms fixed in the contracts would be used by the board to calculate the losses upon which it will base the size of the equalization fee. This procedure is the very essence of price fixing no matter how cumbersome and crudely camouflaged it may be. By throwing the very large resources of the Government into this operation the present bill gives the widest latitude for the most vicious temptations adherent in autocratic authority in complete command of vast industries and trades.

In previous bills definite yardsticks have been determined by which prices were to be established by the Government. They are omitted from this bill, which thereby leaves almost no restraint whatever upon the discretion of the board in this respect. The present measure, therefore, has even less merit than its predecessors in this regard since it carries no limitation as to the extent of price inflation which it can undertake.

II. *The equalization fee*, which is the kernel of this legislation, is a sales tax upon the entire community. It is in no sense a mere contribution to be made by the producers themselves, as has been represented by supporters of the measure. It can be assessed upon the commodities in transit to the consumer and its burdens can often unmistakably be passed on to him.

Furthermore, such a procedure would certainly involve an extraordinary relinquishment of the taxing power on the part of Congress, because the tax would not only be levied without recourse to legislative authority but its proceeds would be expended entirely without the usual safeguards of congressional control of appropriations. This would be a most dangerous nullification of one of the essential checks and balances which lie at the very foundation of our Government.

Incidentally, this taxation or fee would not be for purposes of revenue in the accepted sense but would simply yield a subsidy for the special benefit of particular groups of processors and exporters. It would be a consumption or sales tax on the vital necessities of life, regulated not by the ability of the people to pay but only by the requirements and export losses of various trading intermediaries. It would be difficult indeed to conceive of a more flagrant case of the employment of all of the coercive powers of the Government for the profit of a small number of specially privileged groups.

It has been alleged that these operations would be inaugurated only as a last resort, but this would be scanty assurance indeed, since no board would be able to resist the pressure of the political forces which could be mustered in behalf of every staple commodity to demand that the Government should undertake the responsibility of attempting to legislate its prices above those fixed in the normal operations of the law of supply and demand.

III. *Widespread bureaucracy.*—A bureaucratic tyranny of unprecedented proportions would be let down upon the backs of the farm industry and its distributors throughout the Nation in connection with the enforcement of this measure. Thousands of contracts involving scores of different grades, quantities, and varieties of products would have to be signed by the board with the 4,400 millers, the 1,200 meat-packing plants, the 3,000 or more cotton and woolen mills, and the 2,700 canners. If this bill had been in operation in 1925 it would have involved collections upon an aggregate of over 16,000,000,000 units of wheat, corn, and cotton.

The bill undertakes to provide insurance against loss, but presumably only against reasonable and unavoidable loss. Just what this might be would involve judgment on the part of Government employees upon tens of thousands of transactions running into billions of dollars. This is bureaucracy gone mad. Cooperative associations, flour-mills, packing plants, and grain elevators will cease to be private and become public agencies. If there is any conclusion that we can announce as final with regard to governmental business operations, particularly after the bitter and excessively costly war-time experiences with such enterprises, it is that we can not maintain a bureaucracy of such vast proportions engaged in buying and selling without constant danger of corruption, mismanagement, and prodigious tax burdens. No private agency of so gigantic and complex a character attempting to juggle with profound economic principles in such fashion could survive under such circumstances, and the chances for a governmental trading organization would be even less.

Swarms of inspectors, auditors, disbursers, accountants, and regulatory officers would be let loose throughout the land to enforce the terms of these contracts and to curb the inevitable attempts at evasion of the equalization fee. This plague of petty officialdom would set up an intolerable tyranny over the daily lives and operations of farmers and of every individual and firm engaged in the distribution of farm products, intruding into every detail of their affairs, setting up thousands of prohibitory restrictions and obnoxious inspections.

Such autocratic domination over our major industry, its dependent trades, and the every-day activities of hundreds of thousands of our citizens would indeed be profoundly repugnant to every instinct of our institutions. It would undermine individual initiative, place a premium upon evasion and dishonesty, and poison the very well-springs of our national spirit of providing abundant rewards for thrift and for open competitive effort.

The arbitrary powers in the hands of the 12 members of the board are almost incredible. But even more extraordinary would be the veto power over the board which this measure places in the hands of the commodity advisory councils.

Acting with the board, these men could throw the entire machinery of the Government into an attempt to raise or lower domestic prices at will. Even though such efforts would ultimately be doomed to certain failure, these men would meanwhile, during the course of costly experiment, hold in their hands the fate of vast industries using farm products employing millions of persons and of great cooperatives with thousands of farmer members. They could disrupt the settled channels of trade and commerce; they could alter at will the cost of living, influence wage levels in all lines of industry, and affect conditions of business in every part of the country. The mere enumeration of such powers is the complete answer to the proposal that they be granted.

IV. *Encouragement to profiteering and wasteful distribution by middlemen.*—As was pointed out in the veto last year, it seems almost incredible that the farmers in this country are being offered this scheme of legislative relief in which the only persons who are guaranteed to benefit are the exporters, packers, millers, canners, spinners, and other processors. Their profits are definitely assured. They have, in other words, no particular incentive toward careful operation, since each of them holding a contract, no matter how unscrupulous, wasteful, or inefficient his operations may have been, would be fully reimbursed for all of his losses.

This would be bound to encourage wholesale profiteering at the expense of the farmer and of the consumer. Every one of these processors could charge what he chose to his domestic trade and recoup the loss incurred on any one of his products thus made unsalable at home through excessive prices by dumping it at reduced rates in foreign markets. With such a complete guaranty of profit these concerns would be entirely without restraint or limitation as to profiteering and as to slovenly and wasteful processing and selling operations.

Surely there could be no more direct means of destroying the very germ of American commercial genius which is so frankly envied by our foreign rivals—the tireless search for better and more efficient business methods, the competitive zeal for superior service and for adequate returns through large sales of better merchandise at lower prices.

The packers could be commanded by the board to buy hogs enough to create a near shortage at home and then raise the prices to a fixed level. The unsalable surplus would then be dumped abroad at a loss, which would thereupon be made good out of the pockets of all taxpayers, including the farmers. The operations would involve an impenetrable maze of contracts between the board and hundreds of packers and provisioners. The result would be a bewildering snarl of entangled accounting problems because packing houses buy one kind of product and sell a wide range of highly differentiated specialties. To "equalize" the losses on these would indeed be a task of overwhelming difficulty.

These objections were raised against

the previous measure and apparently an attempt has been made to meet them by broadening the discretionary powers of the board so as to escape the necessity of describing its functions and limiting its authority. The result, however, has been entirely the reverse from that which was intended. The board is endowed with vast powers over our basic industry, but unlike every other agency in the Government it would not be limited by congressional control over its appropriations since it would have within itself the power to raise funds without limit by means of the compulsory equalization fee.

V. *Stimulation of overproduction.*—The bill runs counter to an economic law as well settled as the law of gravitation. Increased prices decrease consumption; they also increase production. These two conditions are the very ones that spell disaster to the whole program. The vaguely drawn clause in the measure to meet this obvious danger merely amounts to moral suasion and as a last resort the withdrawal of the equalization fee. Thus if 90 per cent of the growers of a given commodity heed the admonitions of the board and refrain from production, they will, nevertheless, be punished because of the evasions of the remaining 10 per cent who have ignored the board's requests. In other words, no farmer will be safe in directing his planning upon his individual judgment, for should the result be a stimulation of an increased yield the board will be likely to withdraw the support which encouraged the surpluses and allow the prices to collapse under the weight of that artificially created excess. The annals of the industrial and agricultural world are replete with the catastrophes that have come in the wake of such attempted distortions of one of the most fundamental principles of commercal relations.

VI. *Aid to our foreign agricultural competitors.*—This measure continues, as did its predecessor, to give substantial aid to the foreign competitors of American agriculture and industry. It continues the amazing proposal to supply foreign workers with cheaper food than those of the United States, and this at the expense of the American farm industry, thereby encouraging both the foreign peasant, whose produce is not burdened with the costs of any equalization fees, and also affording through reduced food prices the means of cutting the wage rates paid by foreign manufacturers. The latter step would promptly impair the prosperity of our manufacturing population, which is by far the leading and most profitable market for our farm produce. It is nonsense to say that our farmers are not interested in such a development, which can only result in unemployment and in consequent decreases in food consumption in the great industrial districts. It is surely poor business to transfer the farmer's market from an employed American workman to the latter's competitor in the low wage scale countries across the seas, whose potential buying power and standards of living even at best are far below those of this country.

This is indeed an extraordinary process of economic reasoning, if such it could be called. Certainly it is a flagrant case of direct, insidious attack upon our whole agricultural and industrial strength.

By the inevitable stimulation of production the bill can only mean an increase of exportable surplus to be dumped in the world market. This in turn will bring about a constantly decreasing world price, which will soon reach so low a figure that a wholesale curtailment of production in this country with its attendant demoralization and heavy losses would be certain. Where is the advantage of dragging our farmers into such folly?

Furthermore, as the board undertakes to dump the steadily mounting surplus into foreign countries at the low-cost figures, it will come into direct conflict with the dumping and similar trade laws of many foreign lands which are interested in the maintenance of their own agricultural industries. We might, therefore, expect immediately a series of drastic, retaliatory discriminations on the part of these consumer countries. This will drive our surplus into narrower market channels and force even further price reductions with consequent increases in the burdens of the equalization tax.

Lastly, and most important, in connection with this aspect of the bill as an aid to our foreign competitors, the measure will inevitably devastate many of our important farm areas. For instance, the board is expected to obtain higher prices for the American farmer for corn by removing the surplus from the home market and dumping it over our borders at a lower level of prices. In other words, the hog grower in Ontario, Canada, may buy American corn at a very much lower level than the hog grower in the State of Ohio. Both being situated equally as to the European market for their pork products, we shall see immediately the migration of the Ohio hog industries across the border into Canada with consequent losses to our pork industry by this Canadian competition.

Likewise the dumping of cheaper American feeds for Dutch and Scandinavian producers of dairy products further subsidizes them in direct competition with the American industry. In other words, the framers of this measure naïvely submit a proposal to save the American livestock grower and dairyman by supplying his overseas rival with abundant feedstuffs at reduced rates. It would be difficult indeed to conceive of a more preposterous economic and commercial fallacy.

To take another illustration, our cotton-manufacturing industry, which now has some 18,400,000 spindles in the cotton-growing States and 16,400,000 in the New England States, has been in a precarious condition for several years. Further handicaps imposed upon it by this bill might spell its ruin and the consequent serious crippling of our entire cotton-growing belt. Under this bill it would be quite conceivable that foreign mills could obtain American cotton for prices substantially less than those paid by domestic mills.

Foreign mills could ship cotton goods to this country in spite of the tariff since the equalization fee in this measure is not applied to cotton fabrics. Furthermore, foreign mills would undoubtedly capture our existing export markets for the 600,000,-000 square yards which we ship abroad annually, valued at over $75,000,000. The very serious hardships thus inflicted upon the nearly 500,000 wage earners in the cotton-manufacturing industries and the consequent impairment of their consumption of farm produce, as well as of the raw cotton in the mills, would be indeed a tragic, if not disastrous, episode.

All of this assumes that the foreign countries will permit the carrying out of the plan, but many of those countries are interested in the production of their own agricultural industries and will not hesitate to impose higher tariff duties or anti-dumping laws to prevent such undue depression of their own markets. Furthermore, they would be inclined to institute discriminatory measures in favor of our competitors by way of retaliation. The markets for our surpluses would thus be limited if not fatally obstructed. To stake the future prosperity of American agriculture upon the course of action to be taken by foreign governments acting under such hostile impulses is altogether too hazardous. . . .

The real objective of the plan in this bill is to raise domestic prices to artificially high levels by governmental price fixing and to dump the surplus abroad.

While agriculture has been distressed in many countries since the World War, the severity of the agricultural depression in the United States must not be underestimated. It is true there has been an increase in prices and purchasing power of agricultural products. Many important farm products have increased rapidly in price in recent months. Nor should we overlook the fact that our farmers have made noteworthy progress since 1921 both in the purchasing power of their products and in the output per worker in agriculture. The latter is the result of improved methods and equipment, and is in keeping with the fundamental cause of American prosperity—high productivity per worker. Moreover, we should avoid the error of seeking in laws the cause of the ills of agriculture. This mistake leads away from a permanent solution, and serves only to make political issues out of fundamental economic problems that can not be solved by political action.

In conclusion, if the measure is enacted one would be led to wonder how long it would be before producers in other lines would clamor for similar "equalizing" subsidies from the public coffers. The lobbies of Congress would be filled with emissaries from every momentarily distressed industry demanding similar relief of a burdensome surplus at the expense of the Treasury. Once we plunged into the futile sophistries of such a system of wholesale commercial doles for special groups of middlemen and distributors at the expense of farmers and other pro-

ducers, it is difficult to see what the end might be.

I have believed at all times that the only sound basis for further Federal Government action in behalf of agriculture would be to encourage its adequate organization to assist in building up marketing agencies and facilities in the control of the farmers themselves. I want to see them undertake, under their own management, the marketing of their products under such conditions as will enable them to bring about greater stability in prices and less waste in marketing, but entirely within unalterable economic laws. Such a program, supported by a strong protective tariff on farm products, is the best method of effecting a permanent cure of existing agricultural ills. Such a program is in accordance with the American tradition and the American ideal of reliance on and maintenance of private initiative and individual responsibility, and the duty of the Government is discharged when it has provided conditions under which the individual can achieve success. . . .

2. SELECTIONS FROM *DEMOCRACY REBORN*[1]

By Henry A. Wallace

Editors' Note.—The Wallaces had long been practical farmers and critics of Herbert Hoover's views on agricultural policy. Henry A. Wallace's father served as Secretary of Agriculture (1921–24) under Harding and Coolidge and in this position had clashed with Secretary of Commerce Hoover. Back in Iowa young Henry A. Wallace (1888——) was editing the family's farm paper, pursuing his researches in plant genetics, and disliking more and more the farm policy

1. Henry A. Wallace, *Democracy Reborn*, ed. Russell Lord (New York, 1944), pp. 43–46, 78–80, 103–6. Reprinted by permission of Reynal and Hitchcock.

of his family's political party, the Republicans.

Motivated especially by Hoover's farm and tariff policies, Wallace left the party and soon described President Hoover as "an honest, earnest man who doesn't know what it's all about." But, with the election of Franklin D. Roosevelt, Henry Wallace had his turn; for he was Secretary of Agriculture (1933–41), was Vice-President of the United States (1941–45), and was Secretary of the Department of Commerce (1945–46) in which Hoover had earlier distinguished himself.

On May 12, 1933, President Roosevelt's new farm act was passed, and on the following evening Wallace presented on the radio his explanatory message, "The Declaration of Interdependence." The general philosophy of this act and the view of economics back of it were spelled out in Wallace's pamphlet of 1934 entitled *America Must Choose*, part of which is reproduced here, and in his speech on "Pigs and Pig Iron" given on November 12, 1935.

His 1938 *Report of the Secretary of Agriculture* is of especial significance, for it follows the passage of the Agricultural Adjustment Act of February, 1938, in which the government shifted from emergency policy (such as had characterized the earlier Agricultural Adjustment Act) to provision of a comprehensive permanent agricultural program. In addition to its use in indicating the new direction for policy, the student will find a useful diagnosis of the long-run problem of agriculture —a diagnosis against which he should evaluate the "cure" provided by Wallace. The Statistical Appendix (Nos. 14, 15, 19, 25) will be useful in helping to understand this problem.

A. THE DECLARATION OF INTERDEPENDENCE

The new Farm Act, which the President signed yesterday, initiates a program for a general advance of buying power. It is not an isolated advance in a restricted sector; it is part of a large attack on the whole problem of depression.

Agriculture and tradesmen must make their way together out of a wilderness of economic desolation and waste. This new machinery will not work itself. The farmers and the distributors of foodstuffs must use it, and make it work. The government can help map lines of march, and can see that the interest of no one group is advanced out of line with the interest of all. But government officials cannot and will not go out and work for private businesses. A farm is a private business; so is a farmers' cooperative; and so are all the great links in the food distributing chain. Government men cannot and will not go out and plow down old trails for agriculture, or build for the distributing industries new roads out of the woods. The growers, the processors, the carriers and sellers of food must do that for themselves. Following trade agreements, openly and democratically arrived at, with the consumer repre-

sented and protected from gouging, these industries must work out their own salvation. This emergency Adjustment Act makes it lawful and practical for them to get together and do so. It provides for a control of production to accord with actual need, and for an orderly distribution of essential supplies.

In the end, we envision programs of planned land use; and we must turn our thought to this end immediately; for many thousands of refugees from urban pinch and hunger are turning, with little or no guidance, to the land. A tragic number of city families are reoccupying abandoned farms, farms on which born farmers, skilled, patient, and accustomed to doing with very little, were unable to make a go of it. In consequence of this back-flow there are now thirty-two million people on the farms of the United States, the greatest number ever recorded in our history. Some of those who have returned to farming will find their place there, but most of them, I fear, will not. I look to a day when men and women will be able to do in the country the work that they have been accustomed to doing in the city; a day when we shall have more industrial workers out in the open where there is room to live. I look to a decentralization of industry; but in this respect we shall have to make haste slowly. We do not need any more farmers out in the country now. We do need there more people with some other means of livelihood, buying, close at hand, farm products; enriching and making more various the life of our open-country and village communities.

The Act authorizes the Secretary of Agriculture to apply excise taxes on the processing of these products, and to pay the money thus derived to farmers who agree to enter upon programs of planned production, and who abide by that agreement. These processing taxes will be put on gradually. Few, if any, will be levied before fall; and then we shall make them as light as we can and yet bring about the required reduction in acreage. In no case will taxes be levied on products purchased for the unemployed.

What it amounts to is an advance toward higher prices all along the line. Current proposals for government cooperation with industry are really at one with this Farm Act. Unless we can get re-employment going, lengthen pay rolls, and shorten breadlines, no effort to lift prices can last very long. Our first effort as to agriculture will be to adjust production downward, with safe margins to provide enough food for all. This effort we shall continue until such time as diminishing stocks raise prices to a point where the farmer's buying power will be as high as it was in the pre-war years, 1909 to 1914.

The reason that we chose that period is because the prices farmers got for their crops, in those years, and the prices they paid for manufactured goods and urban services most nearly approached an equitable relationship. There was thus a balance between our major producing groups. At that time there was not the terrific disparity between rural and urban purchasing power which now exists and which is choking the life out of all forms of American business.

We do not propose to reduce agricultural production schedules to a strictly domestic basis. Our foreign trade has dwindled to a mere trickle; but we still have some foreign customers for cotton, tobacco, and certain foodstuffs; we want to keep that trade and to get more foreign trade, if we can. The immediate job is to organize American agriculture to reduce its output to domestic need plus that amount which we can export at a profit. If the world tide turns and world trade revives, we still can utilize to excellent advantage our crop adjustment and controlled distribution setup. We can find out how much they really want over there, and at what price; and then we can take off the brakes and step on the gas.

The first sharp downward adjustment is necessary because during the past years we have defiantly refused to face an overwhelming reality. In consequence, changed world conditions bear down on us so heavily as to threaten our national life.

Ever since 1920, hundreds of thousands of farm families have had to do without civilized goods and services which in normal times they were glad and eager to buy. Since 1929, millions of farm people have had to patch their garments, store their cars and tractors, deprive their children of educational opportunities, and cease, as farmers, to improve their practices and their property. They have been forced to let their homes and other buildings stand bare and unpainted, eaten by time and the weather. They have been driven toward peasant, or less than peasant, standards; they have been forced to adopt frontier methods of bare sustenance at a time when, in the old surging, unlimited sense of the word, we have no longer a frontier.

When the farmer gets higher prices, he will start spending. He will have to. He needs things. He needs new shoes and clothing for all the family, so that his children can go to school in any weather with dry feet, protected bodies, and a decent

American feeling of equality and pride. He needs paint and roofing, fencing, machinery and so on, endlessly.

To reorganize agriculture, co-operatively, democratically, so that the surplus lands on which men and women now are toiling, wasting their time, wearing out their lives to no good end, shall be taken out of production—that is a tremendous task. The adjustment we seek calls first of all for a mental adjustment, a willing reversal, of driving, pioneer opportunism and ungoverned *laissez-faire*. The ungoverned push of rugged individualism perhaps had an economic justification in the days when we had all the West to surge upon and conquer; but this country has filled up now, and grown up. There are no more Indians to fight. No more land worth taking may be had for the grabbing. We must experience a change of mind and heart.

The frontiers that challenge us now are of the mind and spirit. We must blaze new trails in scientific accomplishment, in the peaceful arts and industries. Above all, we must blaze new trails in the direction of a controlled economy, common sense, and social decency.

There have been delays in the passage of this Act. Meanwhile the planting season has advanced, and our assigned task of adjusting production to effective demand has become infinitely more difficult. We cannot proceed as if this were the middle of winter. Perhaps our wisest course will be to concentrate on those commodities most in need of adjustment, and on which the adjustment decided upon, this late in the season, can be practical and effective.

To help us in these determinations, we shall have here in Washington within a few days representatives of agriculture and representatives of the processing and distributing trades. Bearing their recommendations in mind, we shall decide just what action to take, and when to take it. As each decision is made we shall get it out directly and publicly to the farmers affected, and launch organization efforts throughout the Nation.

Unless as we lift farm prices we also unite to control production, this plan will not work for long. The only way we can effectively control production for the long pull is for you farmers to organize, and stick, and do it yourselves. This Act offers you promise of a balanced abundance, a shared prosperity, and a richer life. It will work, if you will make it yours, and make it work. I hope that you will come to see in this Act, as I do now, a Declaration of Interdependence, a recognition of our essential unity and of our absolute reliance one upon another. . . .

B. AMERICA MUST CHOOSE

Much as we all dislike them, the new types of social control that we have now in operation are here to stay and to grow on a world or national scale. We shall have to go on doing all these things we do not want to do. The farmer dislikes production control instinctively. He does not like to see land idle and people hungry. The carriers dislike production control because it cuts down loadings. The processors dislike it because of the processing tax. The consumer dislikes it because it adds to the price of food. Practically the entire population dislikes our basic program of controlling farm production; and they will do away with it unless we can reach the common intelligence and show the need of continuing to plan. We must show that need of continuing if we are to save in some part the institutions which we prize.

Enormously difficult adjustments confront us, whatever path we take. There are at least three paths: internationalism, nationalism, and a planned middle course. We cannot take the path of internationalism unless we stand ready to import nearly a billion dollars more goods than we did in 1929. What tariffs should we lower? What goods shall we import? Tariff adjustments involve planning just as certainly as internal adjustments do. Even foreign loans might involve a certain amount of planning. When we embarked on our terrific postwar expansion of foreign loans, we did not plan. We plunged in blindly, and soon any reasonable observer could predict that the whole thing was bound to blow up.

We did not then in our boisterous youth have the same view that England had after the Napoleonic Wars. Rather consciously Great Britain placed its loans with a long-time program of imports and an exchange of goods in view. Our own adventure was only from the short-time profit consideration. What tariffs to lower? What goods to accept? How readjust our own farming operations and industrial operations to the planned inflow of foreign goods? We scarcely gave such things a thought.

I shall here try to sketch the probable price—in terms of the actual and psychological pain of readjustment—of following the national, the international, or a rigorously planned middle trail out of the woods.

As a foundation and framework of a new American design, we have undertaken to put our farmland into better order. What we have done has been frankly experimental and emergency in nature, but we are working on something that is going to be permanent.

If we finally go the whole way toward nationalism, it may be necessary to have compulsory control of marketing, licensing of plowed land, and base and surplus quotas for every farmer. Every plowed field would have its permit sticking up on its post.

I have raised the question whether we as a people have the patience and fortitude to go through with an international program when the world seems with varying degrees of panic to be stampeding the other way. It is quite as serious a question whether we have the resolution and staying power to swallow all the words and deeds of our robust, individualistic past, and submit to a completely armylike, nationalist discipline in peacetime.

Our own maneuvers of social discipline to date (1934) have been mildly persuasive and democratic. I want to see things go on that way. I would hate to live in a country where individual thought is punished or stifled, and where speech is no longer free. Even if the strictest nationalist discipline reared for us here at home, exclusively, a towering physical standard of living, I would consider the spiritual price too high. I think, too, that this would be pretty much the temper of the rest of the country; but there is no telling. Regimentation without stint might, indeed, I sometimes think, go farther and faster here than anywhere else, if we once took the bit in our teeth and set out for a 100 percent American conformity in everything. The American spirit as yet knows little of moderation, whichever way it turns.

A surprising number of farmers, after a year of voluntary production control, are writing me letters insisting that hereafter the co-operation of all farmers be compelled absolutely; and that every field, cotton gin, cow, and chicken be licensed; and that the strictest sort of controls be applied to transportation and marketing. I believe they mean it, but I wonder very seriously whether they are ready for such measures, and if they really know what they are asking for.

The middle path between economic internationalism and nationalism is the path we shall probably take in the end. We need not go the whole way on a program involving an increase of a billion dollars a year in imports. There are intermediate points between internationalism and nationalism, and I do not think we can say just where we are headed yet. We shall be under increasing difficulties, no matter which way we tend, as our people become more and more familiar with the discomforts of the procedure.

My own bias is international. It is an inborn attitude with me. I have very very deeply the feeling that nations should be naturally friendly to each other and express that friendship in international trade. At the same time we must recognize as realities that the world at the moment is ablaze with nationalist feeling, and that with our own tariff impediments it is highly unlikely that we shall move in an international direction very fast in the next few years.

There is still another trail—I mean the back trail, letting things drift, trusting to luck, plunging on toward internationalism as sellers and trying at the same time to huddle behind nationalist barriers as buyers. Even this, probably the most painful trail of all, is worth mentioning, for thousands of our people vociferously yearn to head that way; and the number of such people is likely to increase rather than diminish, I am afraid, in the next few years.

Whether we are prepared at this time to engage in a genuinely scientific nation-wide discussion of the tariff, as it affects agriculture and other elements in a long-time plan for the whole nation, I have little means of knowing; but I suspect that the desperateness of the situation has done a great deal to make realists of us all. And I have faith that we can arouse from the ranks of our democracy, in city and country alike, a leadership that will address itself to fundamentals, and not simply blow off in the empty and prejudiced emotional bombast which has characterized such discussions in the past.

I lean to the international solution. But it is no open-and-shut question. It needs study, and above all dispassionate discussion. I want to see the whole question examined by our people in a new spirit. . . .

C. PIGS AND PIG IRON

People are still interested in the six million pigs that were killed in September of 1933. In letters I have received following these radio talks, the pigs are mentioned more often than any one thing except potatoes. One letter says:

"It just makes me sick all over when I think how the government has killed millions and millions of little pigs, and how that has raised pork prices until today we poor people cannot even look at a piece of bacon."

It is common belief that pork is high today because the little pigs were killed in 1933. As a matter of fact, there is more pork now and the price is lower because these pigs were killed two years ago. Let me tell the story:

For eighteen months before August, 1933, farmers had been selling hogs for an average of $3.42 a hundredweight. Such a price was ruinous to farmers. The average hog grower suffered from low hog prices during this period one thousand times more than the average consumer has suffered from high hog prices during the past few months. Hog prices in August of 1933 were intolerably low, and the northwestern Corn Belt was suffering from drought. There was every reason to expect prices to continue low because there had been an increase in the spring pig crop, and because the foreign market, which formerly had absorbed the product of as many as twelve million hogs from this country, had largely disappeared because of tariffs and quotas.

So six million little pigs were killed in September of 1933. They were turned into one hundred million pounds of pork. That pork was distributed for relief. It went to feed the hungry. Some very small pigs could not be handled as meat by the packers. These were turned into grease and tankage for fertilizer.

If those six million pigs had grown up they would have been marketed in January, February, and March of 1934. They probably would have brought around $2.50 a hundredweight. Instead of that the price of hogs at that time averaged $3.60. In January, February, and March of 1934, the consumers of the United States, in spite of the absence of the little pigs which would have come to market at that time, had their customary quantity of pork. Hogs at $3.60 made it possible for farmers to buy more city products and so put more city people back to work.

If those little pigs had grown up to normal weight they would have eaten about seventy-five million bushels of corn. The pork made out of these seventy-five million bushels of corn would have been consumed by August, 1934. But because of the emergency pig marketing program those seventy-five million bushels of corn were not eaten in early 1934. You remember that in 1934 we had the most terrible drought in our history. The corn crop was a billion bushels short. In that situation we had on hand those seventy-five million bushels of corn produced the year before, and that corn was used to make pork in late 1934 and early 1935. It gave us more pork this year than we would have had without it. Had it been fed in early 1934 the oversupply of pork would have been terrific then and the price would have been $2.50 a hundredweight instead of $3.60. But this year there would have been even fewer hogs and even higher prices than we have had.

As long as we have our program of Agricultural Adjustment we shall never again need to slaughter little pigs to keep hog prices from going to zero. We have the machinery to furnish consumers a normal, balanced supply.

I suppose it is a marvelous tribute to the humanitarian instincts of the American people that they sympathize more with little pigs which are killed than with full-grown hogs. Some people may object to killing pigs at any age. Perhaps they think that farmers should run a sort of old-folks home for hogs and keep them around indefinitely as barnyard pets. But we have to think about farmers as well as hogs. And we must think about consumers and try to get a uniform supply of pork from year to year at a price which is fair to farmer and consumer alike.

The drought of 1934, which cut the supply of feed grain by twice as much as any previous drought, is chiefly responsible for high pork prices today. The slaughter of little pigs in 1933 gave us more pork and lower prices this year than we would have had if they had been allowed to live and eat those seventy-five million bushels of corn. Those who hold to the contrary are misinformed.

Beef prices are high now because of the same drought. We have never had an A.A.A. production-control program in beef. Thousands of cattle were on the point of starvation in the West in 1934. Should we have allowed them to starve? Because we had the machinery of the Agricultural Adjustment Administration, we were able to step in promptly, buy those cattle, slaughter them and can them. The government has thus been able to distribute hundreds of millions of pounds of meat for relief that would otherwise have been wasted.

Strange to say, I find myself in strong sympathy with the attitude of many folks who held up their hands in horror about the killing of little pigs. I will go further than most of them in condemning scarcity economics. We want an economy of abundance, but it must be balanced abundance of those things we really want. The pig-iron reduction control of the big steel companies in 1933 was in principle one thousand times as damnable as the pig-reduction campaign of 1933. Pig-iron production in 1932 was about twenty percent of that in 1929. Pig production in 1933 in pounds was ninety-seven percent of that of 1929. In 1934 pig-iron production was forty-five percent of that of 1929. Pig production in 1934, the drought year, was eighty percent of that of 1929. In other words, farmers cut pig production three percent when steel companies cut pig-iron production eighty percent. That sort of industrial reduction program plowed millions of workers out into the streets. It is because of that industrial reduction program that we have to spend billions for relief to keep the plowed-out workers from starvation. I hope industry in future reduction programs will not find it desirable to plow millions of workers out of their jobs. People are more important than pigs.

Great corporations should not finance people to attack Agricultural Adjustment. They are too vulnerable. Instead they should co-operate with agriculture to bring about increased, balanced production of those things which the American people really want at a price which they can afford to pay, but at a price high enough to keep the production coming without undue speculative gain. If industry were as productive as it knows how to be, the increased home market for fruit, vegetables, meat, and dairy products would be truly surprising. But this market cannot come to pass until industry ceases its reduction control program.

My attention has been called to a statement by a minister out in the Corn Belt before the district conference of his faith. Concerning the actions of the New Deal he says: ". . . some of them are downright sinful as the destruction of foodstuffs in the face of present want."

I have been used to statements of this sort by partisans, demagogues, politicians, and even newspaper columnists. To men of this sort I pay no attention, because I know that their interest in a cause makes it impossible for them to distinguish truth from falsehood. But when a minister of the gospel makes a statement, we expect it to be the truth. Just what food does he think this administration has destroyed? We would like to know the specific in-

stances. If he is merely referring to acreage control which enabled us to keep out of use in 1935 some thirty million of the fifty million acres which have produced in the past for markets in foreign countries, I would say, "Yes we are guilty of acreage control and, depending on variations in weather, we shall continue to be until foreign purchasing power is restored by the breaking down of tariff and quota barriers."

We have not destroyed foodstuffs. We do not contemplate destroying them. However, foodstuffs *were* destroyed back in 1932 by farmers who found it profitable to burn their corn for fuel rather than to sell it for ten cents a bushel (which amounted to $3.33 a ton). It was cheaper for many farmers in the northwest Corn Belt to burn food for fuel at those pitiful prices than to burn coal.

People who believe that we ordered the destruction of food are merely the victims of their prejudices and the misinformation that has been fed to them by interested persons. What we actually did was to stop the destruction of foodstuffs by making it worth while for farmers to sell them rather than to destroy them.

Agricultural Adjustment of the past two years has been a million times as warranted as the industrial reduction policy of the past five years. Why does not the minister attack the industrial reduction which was made possible by corporate and tariff laws? It was this reduction by industry that created the *unemployment* and destroyed the farmers' markets. Might it not be better for all of us to do what is possible to build up on the part of both agriculture and industry a situation which will result in greatly increased balanced output of those things which we really want?

3. SOURCES OF AGRICULTURAL MALADJUSTMENT AND THE AGRICULTURAL ADJUSTMENT ACT OF 1938[1]

FARM EXPANSION AND SPECIALIZATION

It is the past, of course, that shapes the present, and largely determines what we must do now. Until less than a century ago the agricultural conquest of this continent was a slow-moving procession through one of the largest and densest forests in the world. Then came the rapid settlement of the grasslands. This was a movement, in general, to better soils. It promoted farm proprietorship by farm operators, retarded tenancy, and increased production vastly. Along with the agricultural expansion westward went an increasing specialization of farm functions.

Many farmers a century ago were also artisans, merchants, teachers, doctors, and lawyers. Gradually they surrendered various functions to the cities. Science and invention revolutionized the agricultural technique. Indeed, the revolution continues. Our farmers now pay the city people something like about $1,500,000,000 annually for power and power machinery; whereas, before the World War, they sold power to the cities in the form of work animals worth several hundred million dollars annually. This specialization and mechanization of agriculture, along with the building of railroads, made agriculture increasingly commercial. In 1929, for example, products sold or traded constituted 87 percent of our farm production.

Meantime, our population increased prodigiously. We had a large excess of births over deaths and also heavy immigration. Before the Civil War population doubled each quarter century. After the Civil War the rate of increase diminished but the actual number increased, until between 1920 and 1930 the increase exceeded 16,000,000—a number almost equal to the total population of Canada and Australia.

[1]. *Report of the Secretary of Agriculture, 1938* (Washington, D.C., 1938), pp. 2–11, 13, 20–21, 25–33.

This increase went largely to the cities. By the close of the World War migration to the West, except to the Pacific Coast States, had practically ceased.

Europe's population likewise increased rapidly in the nineteenth century. We imported capital from Europe as well as immigrants. Growth of population in Europe and the necessity to repay with interest the capital that we had borrowed gave us a rapidly expanding market for agricultural products. American agriculture responded with a rapidly increasing production, which aided the further growth of urban populations in both hemispheres.

OUTPUT PER MAN INCREASED

In the last hundred years the production per worker engaged in agriculture in the United States has increased threefold. In crop production the increase per worker was probably 25 percent from 1850 to 1860, probably 50 percent from 1850 to 1900, and probably 30 percent between 1900 and 1930. In the post-war decade, 1920–29, the crop production per worker increased less than 10 percent; but the total agricultural production per worker, including livestock and livestock products, increased about 25 percent. Between 1910 and 1930 the increase in agricultural production per worker was about 41 percent.

Moreover, mechanical power largely supplanted horses and mules and released the feed from 35,000,000 to 40,000,000 acres of crops for meat and milk animals. Also, the farmers shifted their livestock classes from the less productive to the more productive animals per unit of feed consumed; notably, from beef cattle to dairy cattle, hogs and chickens. They improved their feeding and breeding practices, and greatly reduced the mortality of their livestock. In 1930 the average American farmer, after providing for himself, for

3 other persons in his family, and for a hired laborer, produced food and fibers for 12 people in American cities or elsewhere than on farms, and for 2 more persons in foreign countries. Full use of the available acreage, agriculture science, and machinery would have enabled him to support still more people.

Until after the World War the national and world economy encouraged this growing productivity. Europe took our products liberally, and the market at home expanded. Moreover, the farm population declined relatively to the total population. Only 21 percent of the American people who were gainfully employed were in agriculture in 1930, as compared with about 70 percent a century ago. The proportion now is probably about 25 percent. A similar proportion of the occupied population are engaged in manufacturing and mechanical trades. The proportion of the gainfully employed in distribution has practically doubled in 50 years. Trade and transportation, including associated clerks, now employ almost as many people as do the manufacturing and mechanical trades combined. Over one-fourth of the gainfully employed are in the services—clerical, domestic, personal, public, and professional. From one-fourth to one-half of the farm youth left the farms for the cities each decade between 1870 and 1930. This transference of personnel from farm to nonfarm occupations helped greatly to keep agriculture in balance with industry.

PROFOUND CHANGES AFTER WORLD WAR

Suddenly we became aware of profound changes in some of these factors: Notably, the rate of growth declined in the domestic population; immigration ceased; the cities became unable to absorb rural youth as they had previously done; depression and unemployment reduced the buying power of wage earners; there were no more frontiers; and foreign countries became unable, for various reasons, to maintain their purchases of American farm products. American agriculture entered an era of

resistance to its further expansion. It became intensely concerned with marketing.

As a partial remedy it has been suggested that we should diminish our imports of agricultural commodities. These consist mostly of noncompetitive things such as silk, rubber, bananas, tea, and coffee. Among the competing products that we import the most important are sugar, flaxseed, and wool, which can be produced on the whole more cheaply in foreign countries than in the United States. All told, however, we import, of crops that could be grown in the United States, the equivalent of the production of only 10,000,000 to 15,000,000 American acres. Our exports-producing acreage is much greater. Any further restriction of our agricultural imports would react adversely on our exports. What we import enables foreign countries to buy our exports; if they could not sell and buy here they would sell and buy elsewhere.

More important to us is the trend in our farm exports, which has been declining almost steadily since the early 1920's. In the peak year of the 1920's our farm exports required the production of over 80,000,000 acres. They required the production of about 70,000,000 acres during the 5 years before the depression. Since then they have required only the production of from 20,000,000 to 50,000,000 acres, mostly of cotton. The export demand may even decline further.

RELATION TO WORLD MARKET

American agriculture grew up to supply the world market as well as the home market. When its production for export cannot be sold, or can be sold only at a very low price, crops produced for the domestic market drop in price too. It is then impossible, without special remedial measures, to prevent ruinous disparities between farm and nonfarm incomes. Appeasement in European politics may moderately improve the situation. Even then, however, the outlook will be less favorable than it was before the depression, though it may be better than it is now.

Our trade-agreement program, and the work of various semiofficial and private agencies, are gradually improving the outlook for trans-Atlantic trade. But we cannot expect the restoration of our trade with Europe to predepression levels. No other area can absorb our crops in quantities sufficient to make up for the European reduction. It is virtually certain that in one way or another we shall have to limit our production for export and take steps to guard the domestic market from the influence upon it of bargain-counter prices abroad. . . .

CONSUMPTION IN THE UNITED STATES

Turning to the domestic market, we see changes in food consumption—in kind rather than in aggregate per capita quantity. The consumption of cereals, for example, has declined notably in the last few decades, while the consumption of sugar, of green vegetables, and of citrus fruits has increased. The trend of total consumption per capita has been stationary or slightly downward. Even the depression did not greatly change the diet of the American people, though the per capita consumption of milk, including milk products, dropped 2 percent between 1929 and 1933. With farm production still abundant, the domestic consumption continued in almost predepression quantities. But the growth of population is slowing down. The domestic market now requires only about half as much annual increase in production as it required 10 to 15 years ago. Only a small increase in our harvested acreage will be necessary to provide for the probable future increases in population, even if the demand for exports remains undiminished. Should the export demand decline, or if mechanization continues to supplant horses and mules, or if technological improvement continues, no increase in cropland may be necessary before the Nation's population becomes stationary. . . .

RATIO OF RURAL TO URBAN POPULATION

Another aspect of the population problem that affects American agriculture greatly is the distribution of the population between town and country. In depression years, the outlook is for a less rapid increase in urban than in rural population; and in cities, where deaths exceed births, as is the case in several large cities at present, a decrease in population may occur. During the recent depression more than 1,000,000 young farm people remained on farms who would normally have gone to the cities. They could not get work in the cities.

Approximately 6,000,000 persons, mostly of farm origin, moved back to the farms. They sought food and shelter with relatives and friends or started little farms of their own. The agricultural census reported 2,000,000 of these people still on the land in 1935. Apparently, New York, Detroit, and Chicago declined in population during the depression. Migration from the farms to the cities, which declined to about 600,000 net during the years 1930–34 as compared with 3,000,000 in the preceding five-year period, doubtless will revive in periods of prosperity; but there are no signs as yet of a sufficient increase in urban work to absorb the excess rural manpower. It is wholly improbable that the trend in the twentieth century will resemble that of the nineteenth. Agriculture may find itself with an increasing personnel, rather than an increasing market.

Another tendency should be noticed in the prevailing agricultural situation. Along with the growing congestion in the rural population in many parts of the Nation goes a decline in farm ownership by farmers. . . .

OPERATORS' STAKE IN FARMS AND BUILDINGS

The proportion of the farm land and buildings in the Nation really owned by farm operators has fallen from nearly two-thirds to less than two-fifths in 55 years. The decline has been about 4 points each 10 years, in periods of prosperity as well as of depression. Continued at the same rate for another half century the decline would reduce the farm operators' share of farm real estate to one-sixth. The other five-sixths would belong to absentees. In the Corn Belt this proportion is approaching rapidly. Farm operators in Illinois and Iowa in 1935 owned, above mortgage debt, only 28 and 24 percent, respectively, of the value of all farm land and buildings. In the wheat regions the equity of farm operators in the farm real estate ranged from 20 percent in South Dakota to 35 in Montana. Farmers have been much more successful in retaining the ownership of land in the Dairy Belt.

Declining farm ownership is an important cause of soil erosion and soil depletion. Tenants and farm operators with only small equities have small incentive to practice conservation and are often almost forced by rent or interest payments to plant the most productive crops, notably corn and cotton, which, being intertilled, facilitate erosion. Soil erosion in the United States has seriously impoverished approximately 282 million acres of land. From an additional 775 million acres erosion has stripped away from one-fourth to three-fourths of the fertile topsoil. Considering only cropland, erosion has ruined about 50 million acres for further practical cultivation. Another 50 million acres of cropland are bordering on the same condition. Nearly 100 million acres more, still largely in cultivation, have been severely damaged by the loss of from one-half to all of the topsoil. On at least another 100 million acres of cropland erosion is getting actively under way.

NEED FOR GOVERNMENT ACTION

These conditions necessitate governmental action. There is no way for the farmers individually to deal effectively with the partial loss of the export market, the rapid approach of stationary populations, and the increasing rural congestion in many areas that results from industrial depression and unemployment. Nor is there any individual remedy for the fact that technology increases farm production per agricultural worker, while other forces contract the market. Some people believe agriculture should decommercialize itself and become more self-sufficient. That would be a backward step. Moreover, the resulting reduced purchasing power of farmers would force some urban people into subsistence farming. Agriculture needs to get back on a business footing, and well-conceived national programs must help it to do so.

There is no escaping the necessity to adjust the farm output through measures that will not drive farmers from their farms. There is no escaping the further necessity of finding new outlets or of providing marketing controls to deal with surpluses when they accumulate unavoidably. Also, we must arrest the increase of tenancy and increase the equities of owner operators. Left uncontrolled, the prevailing trends will tremendously increase these evils. With farm youth backed up on farms and with the urban unemployed flocking to the country in periods of depression, land hunger is likely to produce absentee landlordism. These problems constitute an obvious national responsibility.

This Department and its action agencies carry only part of the responsibility, for the problem is urban as well as rural. It involves our whole economy. It will help us to understand the specific agricultural requirements if we bear in mind the historical and economic developments above described. No one who understands them can propose a mere let-alone policy. It is absolutely impossible for the Government to stand aside. The debate narrows down to what the Government should do. Let us consider, therefore, what it has done in recent years and more particularly in 1938. This will give us a basis for considering what further steps should be taken.

Evolution of the Ever-Normal Granary

Against this background of history and economics let us examine the farm program that we have in operation. We are now in the middle of the first year's operation of a new Agricultural Adjustment Act. It is timely to glance at what the act contains, to indicate the origins and application of its more important principles, and to notice some of the difficulties involved. The act is a coordinating and integrating measure based on our experience during the period 1933–37, first with the Agricultural Adjustment Act of 1933 and then with the Soil Conservation and Domestic Allotment Act of 1936. It represents the main stream of our developing agricultural policy. It embodies principles hammered out in nearly two decades of Nation-wide discussion on the farms, in the cities, and in Congress. Indeed, to a considerable extent it includes principles unwittingly championed as substitute proposals. In short, the Agriculture Adjustment Act of 1938, and the programs in operation under it, are the Nation's well-matured answer to the challenge of an undisputed need for profound agricultural readjustments. . . .

ADDITIONAL REQUIREMENTS RECOGNIZED

In the first emergency, the A.A.A. programs envisaged primarily crop curtailment, with soil conservation as a byproduct. They protected individual cultivators from eviction, and saved thousands of farms from neglect and deterioration, and that was all to the good. There was a direct immediate benefit to the cities. In keeping the farmers on the land, while at the same time helping them to reduce the farm output, the early A.A.A. programs reduced the national unemployment total, directly by preventing an undue exodus of population from the country to the town and indirectly by enabling farmers to re-enter the market for industrial commodities. Also, they checked the drift into so-called subsistence farming and rural poverty. But the first steps in crop adjustment took out of production efficient and inefficient acres indiscriminately. It became necessary to take longer views, and to plan the agricultural adjustment for additional ends. There was an equal need for better land use, balanced farming, and soil conservation.

With world trade throttled by tariffs, import quotas, bilateral trade restrictions, and exchange controls, there was no practical alternative to the American farm-adjustment policy. Geared to production for an abnormal market that was vanishing, and with land, labor, and capital far in excess of the domestic requirement, our agriculture had urgent need to prevent its export surpluses from beating down the prices of all its products. Later, other requirements emerged. As the adjustment went along and the early surpluses diminished, it became necessary to consider the occasional lean year, and to combine production for a lessened world demand with precautions against crop failure. Exceptional weather conditions emphasized the necessity to maintain adequate crop reserves.

In its developed form, therefore, the adjustment policy becomes the ever-normal granary. This term is a good short description of the whole process. As the words imply, it covers far more than the concept of the first emergency period, when the predominant purpose was adjustment to the fact of a smaller world market. It promotes jointly the interest of producer and consumer through means that protect both parties—namely, the reciprocal action of acreage adjustment and crop storage. In the ever-normal-granary program there is room, as occasion requires, for expansion of the farm output. It rejects the notion that farm welfare always requires acreage reduction and looks instead to the production of different crops in the proper amounts and proportions. Moreover, it looks toward the stabilization of supplies through the conservation of soil and soil productivity. It does not waste land following seasons of overproduction but devotes it through conservational activities to the uses of the future.

Combining acreage adjustment, soil care, and protection for the consumer, the ever-normal granary compares with our first experiment in agricultural adjustment as the modern automobile compares with the horseless carriage. The program calls for production equal to the normal domestic consumption plus probable export requirements, and it makes also an allowance for a rise in the domestic consumption per capita. It provides the maximum abundance possible for commercial agriculture under the rules of the commercial game. The new act provides for parity payments on the normal production of the basic commodities when funds are available so that farmers have a direct incentive to meet all the requirements of the domestic market. . . .

HAZARDS OF COMMODITY LOANS

The machinery of the ever-normal granary provides for commodity loans under certain specified conditions of supply and price, and these loans involve certain hazards. The best protection against these hazards is a clear grasp of the purposes the loans should fulfill.

Obviously, since the ever-normal granary exists to carry surpluses from fat to lean years, the commodity loans should finance the storage and measurably stabilize the price of the stored commodities from one season to the next.

In terms of prices for commodities stored, the result should be a higher price level than would otherwise prevail in the big-crop years and a lower price level than would otherwise prevail in the short-crop years. In other words, the true function of the ever-normal-granary type of loan is to counteract fluctuations in market supplies and prices. It is not its function to maintain an average price level above that warranted by basic demand and supply factors. . . .

PRESENT PROGRAM OFFERS BETTER APPROACH

Our present many-sided agricultural program . . . provides a rational approach to conservation and good farming. Acreages of the major depleting and conserving crops, and desirable soil-building and conserving practices, can be distributed geographically so as to combine conservation with efficient farming and bring about balanced production. With acreages of the major crops kept within individual, county, State, and national allotments and goals, farmers have an assurance in years of ordinary weather of production in line with market requirements. If yields are above the average, they can take a second step under the act. They can store their crops and get a commodity loan on them from the Government. If, in spite of these measures, the granary overflows, they can take a third step and vote marketing quotas on themselves and bring supplies in line with normal requirements. Conversely, the act through its ever-normal-granary feature avoids scarcity in years of drought.

Each of these steps is in the true spirit of self-government by the farmers. The first two are completely voluntary, in that the individual farmer can choose whether to come into the soil conservation program or stay out, and can choose whether or not to put his corn, wheat, or cotton in storage and take a Government loan. The third step, the use of marketing quotas, is an emergency step. It will not be taken unless two-thirds of the producers concerned vote for it in a referendum.

Under this act, at a time when factory production and pay rolls have been cut by a third and a recurrence of serious depression has been temporarily threatened, farm cash income has been sustained at a level only 12 percent less than a year ago. Income this year will be around $7,500,-000,000 compared with $8,600,000,000 a year ago. Undoubtedly the stability in farm income has been an important factor in keeping business in general from going into a downward spiral similar to that which followed 1929. . . .

For the promotion of our agricultural export trade the measure authorizes the use of funds derived from customs duties. Our reciprocal trade agreements program offers the most hope in this direction. But in periods of emergency, such as now exist with respect to wheat, it may be necessary temporarily to adopt limited export-subsidy measures in order to retain our fair share of the world market. If all nations used export-subsidy measures simultaneously as a general policy, these measures would be mutually self-defeating. They would mean international price cutting. Price wars in international trade are as disastrous as in private business. There is urgent need for an international understanding on the matter. Meantime, until the situation improves, we must take steps to keep our place in the world market and to expand the market for our farm products. Our Government is doing what it can to persuade other wheat-exporting nations to join in what might be called an international ever-normal-granary plan; in a plan to stabilize the amounts of wheat offered on the world markets by each nation year after year. . . .

LAW PROMOTES ABUNDANCE AND DEMOCRACY

In a democracy such as ours economic legislation must promote certain noneconomic ends. Besides encouraging the production of wealth, it must maintain the freedom of the individual and of the community. The object cannot be exclusively material.

Man needs both bread and freedom; it is a calamity when he must barter one for the other, and the result may be the breakdown of civilization. To promote abundance, both material and spiritual, at the same time and by the same means is not easy. Increased production calls for economic and social organization, with increasing interdependence and cooperation among different economic groups. How can we achieve this and at the same time preserve freedom and democracy?

This is a complex and delicate task, which depends for its accomplishment on a blend of physical and economic science with social justice. It requires, moreover, the support of public opinion. Everything done must enlist the informed and willing cooperation of the Nation as a whole; otherwise it will not be truly democratic. Efficient social cooperation without coercion is the formula, which may not be abandoned on pain of grave social disturbance.

In the Agricultural Adjustment Act of 1938 we have an important instrument for promoting the twofold objective. On the economic side the law expresses the unity of interest among different groups in agriculture and safeguards the consumer through provisions for the maintenance of a continuous and stable supply of agricultural commodities at fair prices. On the social side it applies the principle of democracy. It is a new charter of economic and political freedom for both producer and consumer. Abundance and democracy are the twin foundations. Few people doubt that, as we may infer from the majorities which the measure received in Congress, and also from the general support it obtained throughout the country. Nevertheless, both before and after the enactment of the measure, it came under certain amount of fire. . . .

There is still some feeling that the law may promote scarcity and not abundance and regimentation as distinguished from democracy. A minority refuses to believe it will promote both abundance and democracy. Unless it does the Nation will condemn it. There can be no true freedom without abundance and no satisfying abundance without freedom. There must be widespread understanding and approval of the principles involved; otherwise programs really democratic in conception will not have the necessary public support and will have to be dropped or modified. Moreover, the support required is urban as well as rural.

The present farm act, like its predecessor of 1933, provides in certain circumstances for the limitation of farm production. With respect to corn, wheat, cotton, tobacco, and rice it authorizes the establishment of national acreage allotments divided up among the farmers. These allotments contemplate production sufficient for the domestic and export markets, and for the provision of above-average carry-overs. Also, the measure authorizes marketing quotas for use when the granaries overflow as a means of supporting prices. The quotas regulate the movement of crops to market. Superficially, these regulations may seem opposed to the idea of abundance. Actually, they promote it by smoothing out the fluctuations of supply and price from year to year. Controlled stable production means more production in the long run than would result from uncontrolled mass swings from high to low production. . . .

AGRICULTURE AIDS URBAN PRODUCTION

Stable production in agriculture means more production in urban industry likewise. For one thing, it meshes better with the rest of the economic system. Stable production in agriculture is an important contribution to stability in the whole economy. Activity in many urban businesses, particularly in those that depend directly on agriculture for supplies, varies directly with the production of agriculture. For example, railroads, elevator companies, ginners, exporters, and other handlers of farm commodities get more out of big crops than out of small. Widely fluctuating farm production, however, obliges them to maintain a plant sufficient to carry the peak loads, and this means heavy overhead. Gain to agriculture through stability is gain to them, and gives them ultimately a larger and more profitable business.

Industries for which agriculture is pri-marily a market, rather than a source of supplies, find themselves in a different position. They depend on agriculture's buying power. Ordinarily, when farm production soars farm income drops; whereupon sales of agricultural implements, fertilizer, farm building materials, farm furnishings, and other goods decline. This type of urban industry, equally with the type that looks to agriculture as a source of supplies, stands to benefit from a better regulation of farm production and a more even level of farm income. Gains and economies effected in agriculture through regulated production tend to be reflected throughout the industrial system, which has increased and more uniform activity.

There is a saving to industry both in capital investment, which need not be so large for the occasional boom, and in labor. Frequent and extreme changes in the employment of labor are notoriously wasteful. They increase the labor turnover and diminish the individual efficiency. Moreover, lay-offs crowd the relief rolls and burden industry with taxes. Farming and industry, including mining, comprise the base for practically the whole economic system. Each carries a superstructure of financial, technical, scientific, and legal institutions, but the taproots are fairly concentrated. Hence, increasing stability in the agricultural half of the system means increasing stability in the other, and ultimately greater production. When the historian describes this epoch, he may report that it largely bridged the gap between scarcity and abundance, through the use of the ever-normal granary in agriculture and the resulting evening out of the business cycle.

ECONOMIC PLANNING AND DEMOCRACY

Acknowledging that the Agricultural Adjustment Act truly promotes abundance and not scarcity, we come now to its methods. Are they compatible with our democracy? They introduce governmental planning into matters formerly not subject to governmental guidance, and place the power of the Government behind the necessary action programs. Opponents call this regimentation; they say it is not consistent with our traditions and principles. Manifestly, however, this begs the question, because it assumes that the scope of democracy has long since been established once for all. It sets up mere custom as the arbiter. In a constantly changing and evolving economic and social environment, the basic political principle must be capable of change and development likewise, or it will die and give place to something with life in it. We cannot condemn the farm legislation in terms of democracy merely on the ground that it is an innovation; many things in our economic and political system, things that no one dreams of calling undemocratic nowadays, were innovations not so long ago. Among the familiar examples are the Federal income tax, the Federal Reserve System, Federal regulation of the railroads, regulation of public utilities, meat inspection, and Federal food and drug legislation. Nor can we say that the democratic principle should not apply to economic matters. There are too many accepted instances to the contrary, from the tariff to urban zoning and market supervision.

Every American has his own definition of democracy, and the definitions vary widely. There is a mistaken view that it means freedom for every man to do just as he likes with his property, regardless of how his actions may affect the general welfare. In countless instances the courts have said he may not. Every democratic right has its limitations, even the right of free speech, which may not be blasphemous, seditious, or defamatory. Another obviously mistaken view is that democracy enjoins public agencies from doing anything that might conceivably be left to private initiative, and frowns on public enterprises like mail distribution, education, forestry, water-works, irrigation, drainage, crop reporting, and road building. Democracy is not just laissez faire; it includes the protection and the constructive

advancement of public as well as of private interests. In proof we may note the progress of democracy in this and other countries side by side with a great extension of public works and services. We cannot define democracy in negative terms, and make of it a mere system of prohibitions. It is a positive doctrine that authorizes positive programs with regard to any issue of pressing national concern. Not to admit that is to condemn democracy to impotence.

SAFEGUARDS OF DEMOCRACY IN FARM ACT

In the Agricultural Adjustment Act the first safeguard of democracy is the authority of Congress, which enacted and may amend or repeal the measure. The second is the injunction to use democratic processes in working out and administering the farm programs. Our farmers have been experimenting with economic democracy for the last 5 years; they began in 1933 under the original Agricultural Adjustment Act. Subsequently, under the Soil Conservation and Domestic Allotment Act, they elected committees in 25,000 agricultural communities. These community committees assist the county committee, cooperate with county agents and with State and Federal officials in working out desirable changes in cropping systems, and actually administer local aspects of the crop adjustment and soil conservation work. This system continues under the new law. County committeemen supervise the programs, hold discussion meetings, inquire into complaints, transmit recommendations from farmers to the State committees, check the compliance with requirements, and acquaint farmers with the world facts and conditions that determine agricultural policy. Such methods enable millions of farmers to understand and influence the programs.

When the granaries fill, farmers themselves decide through democratic processes whether marketing quotas enforced by penalties shall go into effect. Under the first Agricultural Adjustment Act the A.A.A. applied this principle as a matter of administrative discretion. Now the principle has the specific mandate of Congress. Not just a simple majority of the interested producers, but a favorable vote by a two-thirds majority of the votes cast, is necessary before the quota provision can be set in motion. Moreover, the principle can be invoked only when substantial surpluses exist. This requirement has a twofold justification. It prevents the coercion of large minorities, and tends to delay the resort to the quota principle. Obviously, since production costs vary from farm to farm, prices must usually drop very low before two-thirds of the farmers will want to store their crops. As the prices rise, the proportion of the farmers who can get by will increase, and with it the reluctance to use quotas. Hence, the two-thirds rule protects both the consumer and the farmer from hasty or ill-considered action.

Some might insist that nonfarmers as well as farmers should be entitled to vote on proposals for marketing restrictions, since the decision may affect prices. This would be true were the restrictions likely to create shortages. They can never do that. The national crop goals provide for abundance. They call for the production of plenty for domestic requirements and for export trade and carry-overs as well. Not until the granaries overflow may farmers invoke the quota principle for the limitation of excessive marketing supplies. Only as a last resort, through a two-thirds majority vote, may the farmers claim this protection. There is no consumer interest in jeopardy or even in question. As a matter of fact, the situations in which the quota principle may be invoked give the consumer a temporary advantage. Farmers cannot injure consumers by utilizing the marketing-control sections of the Agricultural Adjustment Act, though conceivably they may injure consumers by not doing so. As already indicated, consumers as well as farmers have an interest in the control of the surpluses. It is entirely democratic to take marketing referenda among farmers only, because the situation itself as well as the enabling legislation amply protects the consumer. . . .

DEMOCRACY THE HEART OF SCIENCE AND INVENTION

Another issue connected with the farm law in its relation to democracy goes deeper. Some critics admit that the law may promote abundance, and that it utilizes democratic processes. They contend, however, that the final result will be anti-democratic, because it will involve the growing intervention of the Government in economic life. Extension of governmental power over economic matters they regard as synonymous with the growth of regimentation and dictatorship. This is a very serious charge. If it could be proved, it would warrant our dropping the whole agricultural program, and letting agriculture go back to unrestricted individual competition, with whatever penalties that may involve in wildly fluctuating prices and recurrent overproduction. Indeed, it is essential to preserve democracy even for material reasons. It is the heart of science and invention, and it is therefore a great economic power. Modern productivity is largely the result of it and of the mental freedom it implies, and the decay of democracy would be followed eventually by a decline in material well-being. Economic planning through public agencies must promote democracy as well as production or we cannot afford it.

Fortunately, economic planning is wholly compatible with democracy, and widens the scope of it. There is no need to dread it as a cause of dictatorship. It may or may not accompany dictatorship. There is no cause-and-effect relationship. Numerous dictatorships in the past have done little economic planning, while many democratic nations have done much. Quite other things are the real essence of dictatorship. Among them are the censorship of speech and of the press, the subjection of science and learning to the Government, the destruction of parliaments and of independent political parties and trade unions, and the concentration of authority in a single individual or in a small group. Often there is another sinister development—the mobilization of men and of industry for aggression. Nations thus controlled inevitably do considerable economic planning, but this is not their vital characteristic. What is vital in them is the substitution of a concentrated for a diffused political power.

This concentration of political power, with the consequent destruction of individual liberty, is quite different from the purely administrative centralization of various governmental tasks. It is important to keep the distinction well in mind. Concentration of political power means the total extinction of the voter's rights, whereas mere administrative centralization leaves the rights of the voter unimpaired. It is the concentration of law making rather than of law administration, and of policy rather than of procedure, that distinguishes the totalitarian from the democratic governments. Efficiency obliges all governments to centralize many administrative operations, such as defense, diplomacy, customs collections, mail distribution, and the regulation of transport and communications. As long as the deciding voice with regard to policy in these matters rests with the voter, the administrative function remains the servant of the legislative power, which in turn is the reflection of the national will. In a democracy political power belongs to the voters, and the popular sovereignty can delegate administrative jobs to central agencies without the slightest danger to itself. Responsible people never contend, for example, that Federal road construction, Federal control of the traffic in food and drugs, or Federal supervision of the great commodity markets is inconsistent with democracy in the United States. . . .

In times like these economic planning is the savior rather than the destroyer of democracy. It substitutes order for chaos, and appeasement for disaffection. In this way it averts dictatorship, which indeed cannot arise until orderly government has broken down and the masses are in revolt. Ancient and modern history testify to that. With unemployment unrelieved, and with agriculture in ruins, we should be in real danger of dictatorship. There would be bread riots in the cities and mortgage strikes in the country; it would be impossible to maintain order without the use of force. From that point to dictatorship the descent would be swift. Instead, we have domestic peace, increasing economic justice, and firm reliance on government by discussion. All this has come about through employment relief, agricultural adjustment, and enlightened social legislation—in short through precisely the instrumentalities that some people take to be the germs of totalitarianism. Confusion as to the true sequence of events indicates a willful blindness. Perhaps those who object to economic planning dislike what it costs them, and call it dictatorship because they want to hide their real objection. Impartial minds will clearly distinguish the remedy from the disease, and will regard it as a sign of health and vigor in our democracy when it deals efficiently with our economic maladjustments.

APPLICATIONS OF SCIENCE THROUGH DEMOCRATIC PROCEDURES

As we look back over the last few centuries, we can trace a large part of our economic progress to science, and that means to freedom and democracy; for there is no science without freedom. Science must be free to investigate everything, the problems of ethics, politics, religion, and philosophy, as well as the practical affairs of industry and agriculture. Otherwise it cannot advance broadly; the practical applications suffer along with the so-called pure research. It is a commonplace that many important uses of science, particularly in chemistry and biology, began in studies that seemed at first to concern chiefly religion and philosophy. Science and democracy are correlatives; for it is impossible to make science free, which means to democratize it, without simultaneously emancipating other legitimate interests as well. Obviously, therefore, the natural home of science is the democratic society, which puts a premium rather than a penalty on the discovery and publication of knowledge. The present conflict between the powers of production and the limitations of the market need not change this relationship. It calls simply for new applications of science through democratic processes and Government agencies.

Our problem is to conserve the democracy that has given us our progress, while at the same time adapting it to the new conditions of which it is in part the cause. In short, we must control the economic powers our democracy has developed, and not let them become a Frankenstein. What the democracy produced it can manage, without going outside itself for the means, and without stultifying its own

nature. That is not a mere assertion; it is an inference from the strong probability that progress and freedom are interdependent. It has yet to be proved that progress can continue anywhere without freedom for the individual to offer new proposals and to challenge established ways. Obviously, if progress and democracy go together, there is no question of preferring one to the other. It is both or neither. This condemns experimentation with undemocratic procedures. There is no point in controlling production by means that eventually may kill the production. The problem is to achieve by common consent whatever is necessary, with the springs of information running free and clear, with decisions arrived at through democratic processes, and with full freedom at all times for full discussion. This assumes that what is necessary is reasonable, and that whatever is decided by the electorate to be reasonable is democratic. It is a fair assumption.

SECTION F. AN ECONOMIC BILL OF RIGHTS?

1. AN ECONOMIC BILL OF RIGHTS[1]

By HENRY A. WALLACE

EDITORS' NOTE.—In an appearance before the Senate committee considering the Full Employment Bill of 1945, Henry A. Wallace (p. 602) elaborates the "Economic Bill of Rights" which President Roosevelt advocated as post- war economic goals for the United States in his message to Congress in 1944. In this context Mr. Wallace discussed the "right to a job" as he sees its meaning embodied in the Full Employment Bill of 1945.

For the second time in twenty-five years America has proved her capacity to meet the challenge of total war. Twice in twenty-five years we have amazed the whole world—and ourselves—with our daring conception of what America could do when forced to war. We have astonished a grateful world by the stupendous number of planes, tanks and guns rolling off our assembly lines; with the bridge of ships we have erected across the oceans; by the overwhelming force with which America has turned the scales of battle.

Thus has America met the challenge of war—with boldness, courage and determination. Thus has America become the symbol—the world over—for the dynamic force of a free people fighting for a free world.

But what of the peacetime problems here at home which will follow the successful conclusion of this war? Is America prepared to meet the challenge of these peacetime problems as it has twice met the challenge of war? Shall we approach the problems of peace with the same boldness of conception, the same courage and determination as we have approached the problems of war?

In the answer to these questions lies the future of America. To anyone who has

faith in America the answer is clear. The American people are prepared to meet the problems of peace in the same inspiring way that they have met the problems of war. The American people are resolved that we shall insure that the youth of this nation will never again be called upon to fight in another war.

And the American people are equally resolved that when our boys return home from this war they shall come back to the brightest possible, the freest possible, the finest possible place on the face of this earth—to a place where all persons, regardless of race, color, creed or place of birth, shall live in peace, honor and dignity—free from want and free from fear.

To do otherwise would betray the faith of every soldier, every worker, every business man, every farmer in this country, who is giving his best for America.

In determining the course of action we should pursue after the war it is well for America to pause and take stock of her capacities. For America's capacities should be the measure of America's future.

America's known capacities are not difficult to calculate. We are now producing goods and services to the gigantic total of $200,000,000,000 a year with 52,000,000 workers and 12,000,000 soldiers. In simple language that means that today America is producing nearly twice as much as she had

1. *New York Times*, January 26, 1945.

ever produced before the war. But an enormous part of the goods and services we are producing today does not find its way into the American home. No, it represents the ships, the guns, the planes and tanks we are using to fight this war.

But I know, and you know, that if we can produce a huge flow of ships and guns and planes and tanks, we can also produce an abundance of houses and cars and clothing and provide education and recreation and the other good things of life for all Americans.

And I know, and you know, that when our boys return home from the war and are again able to put their power into the stream of peacetime production, America's capacity to produce will be even greater than it is today. Yes, much greater than today, even when we remember that some of our returning soldiers will prefer to resume their education; that some older people will begin a retirement, delayed to participate in war work, and that many women will give up their jobs in favor of homemaking.

Making full allowance for these groups, the fact remains that America will have the capacity after the war for producing houses, cars, clothing, education, recreation and all of the other good things of life on a scale that staggers the imagination. That is what America can and will do if we have the courage and vision to give her the chance.

But to accomplish this task of utilizing our full productive capacity year after year, it is childish to think that this can be accomplished by a small segment of business and finance, even though that small segment consists of the giants of industry and the tycoons of American finance.

Nor can this be accomplished by throwing crumbs to 20,000 business enterprises out of a total of over 3,000,000 struggling small businesses in the United States. Why, an America geared to that limited conception of our capacity will find itself faced with millions of unemployed. The same people who set their sights too low

for war are now asking the American people to set their sights too low for prosperity. They do not grasp the strength and the spirit of America.

Nor do any of us think for a minute that there is any quack remedy or cure-all that can be automatically applied. The sober facts are that genuine progress will be achieved only through concrete plans and a real effort.

In the President's message to Congress last year and this year he set forth eight self-evident economic truths as representing a second Bill of Rights under which a new basis of security and prosperity can be established for all—regardless of station, race or creed.

America led the world in establishing political democracy. It must lead the world once more in strengthening and extending political democracy by firmly establishing economic democracy. Let us not forget the painful lessons of the rise of fascism. Let us remember that political democracy is at best insecure and unstable without economic democracy. Fascism thrives on domestic economic insecurity, as well as on lack of or divided resistance to external aggression. Fascism is not only an enemy from without, it is also potentially an enemy from within.

We now must establish an economic bill of rights, not only out of common decency, but also to insure the preservation of our political freedoms. We must accord to this economic bill of rights the same dignity—the same stature—in our American tradition as that we have accorded to the original Bill of Rights.

Let us therefore affirm this economic bill of rights—and keep affirming it—until it is as familiar and real to us as our political bill of rights.

The economic bill of rights as embodied in the President's message to Congress last January is:

The right to a useful and remunerative job in the industries or shops or farms or mines of the nation;

The right to earn enough to provide

adequate food and clothing and recreation;

The right of every farmer to raise and sell his products at a return which will give him and his family a decent living;

The right of every business man, large and small, to trade in an atmosphere of freedom from unfair competition and domination by monopolies at home or abroad;

The right of every family to a decent home;

The right to adequate medical care and the opportunity to achieve and enjoy good health;

The right to adequate protection from the economic fears of old age, sickness, accident and unemployment;

The right to a good education.

But the achievement of this American economic bill of rights will not come of itself. These rights will not come to those who merely sit and wait. Nor will they come through merely pious repetition. Our forefathers had to struggle for our political Bill of Rights, we will have to struggle for our economic bill of rights. If we are going to make those rights a living reality we must map out a vigorous and concerted course. We must set as our goal the implementation and fulfillment of the eight self-evident truths which together constitute our economic bill of rights.

The key to making this economic bill of rights a part of the American way of life is as self-evident as are the rights themselves. The key is the wholehearted recognition by all our people of the simple fact that in America the future of the American worker lies in the well-being of American private enterprise; and the future of American private enterprise lies in the well-being of the American worker. The greatest single thing that this war has demonstrated on the home front is that when the American worker and the American business man and the American farmer work together as one team, there are no limits on what America can accomplish.

But to work together as a team, how-

ever, there must be a common goal. In this war that goal has been the defeat of our enemies in the shortest possible period of time. In the peace to come the goal must be the well-being of America.

I am now going to outline to you the type of program which I think would make each of these economic rights a part of our way of life.

In your consideration of this program you will note this striking fact, namely, that to the extent that private enterprise grows in strength, the economic bill of rights grows in reality—and to the extent that the economic bill of rights grows in reality, American private enterprise grows in strength. Thus, all the measures which are suggested in this program for the implementation of the economic bill of rights are at the same time designed to make American capitalism and private enterprise work in the same great manner in peace as it has worked in war.

And I also want to emphasize what the implementation of these rights will mean to our service men and women. They have given America the opportunity to work out its destiny as a free nation in a free world. The America to which they return must be a land of economic opportunity in which they will find not only jobs but a chance for economic advancement and independent enterprise in industry, commerce, agriculture and the professions.

A grateful nation can do no less for her returning service men and women. The G.I. Bill of Rights, which became law in June of last year, following a series of recommendations which the President made to the Congress, is only designed to fulfill the special needs of our men and women in the service. The economic bill of rights is designed to fulfill the needs which they value most—yes, the needs which they value more than life itself—the needs of America.

The first economic right is "the right to a useful and remunerative job in the industries, or shops, or farms, or mines of the nation."

To assure the full realization of this right to a useful and remunerative job, an adequate program must provide America with sixty million productive jobs. We must have more jobs than workers; not more workers than jobs. Only with more jobs than workers can every man be guaranteed a job with good wages and decent working conditions. This requires private enterprise working at expanded capacity.

This necessary expansion of our peacetime productive capacity will require new facilities, new plants and new equipment.

It will require large outlays of money which should be raised through normal investment channels. But while private capital should finance this expansion program, the Government should recognize its responsibility for sharing part of any special or abnormal risk of loss attached to such financing.

Therefore I propose that the Government guarantee the lender against the special and abnormal risks which may be involved in achieving our objective. This will provide new and expanding industry with plenty of private credit at reasonable interest rates. Through this program we shall merely be extending to the financing of old and new business the principles which have proved so successful in our experience with the V loans, T loans and the Federal Housing Administration loans.

A comprehensive investment program dedicated to expanding the peacetime productive capacity of America is the very essence of the American way of raising our standard of living. We build the plants for greater production so that all of us may share in their greater output. But greater output is not our only benefit from this plant expansion.

In fact, our benefits also include the wages paid to the labor employed in building these plants, in constructing the machinery to be used in the plants and in operating the plants after they are erected. These payments as wages all contribute to the nation's buying power, so that as a nation we shall have more money with

which to buy the goods produced by these expanded plants.

As a matter of fact, a comprehensive investment program of this character could make possible $20,000,000,000 of new private investment each year. Why, just the job of building these plants and the machinery for them would give America 5,000,000 more jobs a year than we had in this work before the war. And this does not include the workers who would be needed to operate these plants after they are built.

In a nutshell, then, if we are going to have remunerative jobs for all, we must have an expanded private industry capable of hiring millions more men. I propose that the Government do its part in helping private enterprise finance this expansion of our industrial plant. It will be privately owned, privately operated and privately financed, but the Government will share with the private investor the unusual and abnormal financial risks which may be involved in getting started.

But, in providing jobs for everyone, we shall not only have to increase demand for our industrial and agricultural production here at home but also abroad. Some parts of our industrial and agricultural production demand a high level of foreign trade to be efficient and prosperous.

This is particularly true in our heavy equipment industries whose output will be needed. The foreign demand for such farm commodities as cotton, tobacco and wheat will also be great if other countries have the opportunity to buy. We therefore must take steps, in cooperation with other countries, to see that international trade and investment is resumed promptly on a sound basis.

This Administration has pioneered in the direction of international economic collaboration with its reciprocal trade program and the establishment of the export-import bank. It has again taken the lead in suggesting international monetary stabilization and sound international investment measures—measures that are a fundamental prerequisite to healthy foreign trade and commerce.

It was for the purpose of working out concrete measures of this character that the President convened the United Nations monetary and financial conference at Bretton Woods last summer. At the Bretton Woods conference forty-four countries agreed upon plans for an international monetary fund and an international bank for reconstruction and development.

The international monetary fund, when approved by Congress, will aid the nations of the world in establishing sound currencies. It will clear the channels of foreign trade of discriminatory restrictions and controls so that there can be a genuine expansion of world trade.

With the help of the international bank, American capital can play a great constructive role—and a profitable role—in the development of the economies of other countries. It will provide us with enormous post-war foreign markets. For our greatest markets are in prosperous, industrialized countries.

But America will not be merely a seller of goods abroad. A truly prosperous America—an America with jobs for all—will be a tremendous buyer of raw materials and products abroad. It will be an America constantly enlarging the scope of our reciprocal trade agreements. It will be an America with the time and money to spend on tourist travel, abroad as well as at home. It will be an America from which other countries can afford to buy more because they are selling more.

With Congressional approval of this program and with our program of jobs for all in this country—the foreign trade of the United States can be trebled after the war. This increase in our foreign trade should mean 3,000,000 more jobs after the war than we had before the war.

Nor are the benefits of increased foreign trade and investment confined to increasing our prosperity. I want to emphasize that such cooperative measures for expanding international trade and investment are at the same time the economic foundation for a lasting peace. A prosperous world will be a world free of both economic and political aggression.

There is one further phase of this program of providing jobs for all which must be made an integral part of any long-range program. That is the task of seeing to it that there are not just jobs for all next year—or for the year after that. No, we are talking about jobs for all as a permanent part of our American way of life.

But it is inevitable, however, that an economy of free enterprise like ours will have some fluctuation in the number of jobs it can provide. Adjustments in employment are an essential part of an expanding free economy, and for these minor fluctuations, we provide unemployment insurance. But we must not allow such fluctuations ever to deteriorate into panic or depression. We cannot again be caught in that vicious downward spiral of unemployment, wage cuts and stagnated business.

Whenever the number of gainfully employed in this country falls below 57,000,000 our Government should take prompt steps to see that new jobs are made available to keep the total from falling significantly below that figure. This is the floor below which we must not allow employment to fall.

The basic function of your Government in taking care of any such slack in jobs is to see to it that private enterprise is assisted until it can absorb this slack. This is entirely possible. During the war the Federal, State and local Governments have found it necessary to put aside the construction of roads, buildings and public facilities to the value of many billions of dollars. We have a need, too, for vast programs of the type exemplified by TVA.

Some of this construction will have to be undertaken immediately after the war. A good deal of it, however, can be postponed so that its construction could be timed with periods when the volume of employment that industry, commerce and agriculture can offer begins to fall. We must have a reservoir of planned and approved Federal, State and local projects ready to be tapped. And when employment falls below this floor of 57,000,000 jobs, this reservoir of planned and approved public works should be opened up to provide more jobs and take up the slack.

Such useful and essential public works should not produce Government or "relief" jobs, however. No, they should produce private jobs. This is possible if we insist that this construction be done by private firms under contract with the Government; private firms employing labor at the prevailing rate of wages and under standard labor conditions.

This assurance of a reserve of private jobs through constructive public works when needed to take up the slack will have a profound effect on the whole direction of our economy. In fact, the knowledge that Government accepts this responsibility of maintaining a floor under jobs will act as an immense stabilizing force on the whole economy.

The second economic right is "the right to earn enough to provide food and clothing and recreation."

America must remain pre-eminently the land of high wages and efficient production. Every job in America must provide enough for a decent living.

During the war we have been compelled to hold down wage increases that might have provoked runaway inflation. With all the arms and war materials we were producing, there was only a limited amount of consumption goods available. Increasing wages without increasing the amount of goods available to the consumer would have been an open invitation to inflation.

However, the end of the war, even the end of the war in Europe, will change this picture. Then there will be more goods available for America to buy, and it is only good common sense to see that the workman is paid enough to buy these goods.

The gains made by labor during the war must be retained in full. After the last war, as part of the process of returning to "normalcy," the slogan "Labor must be deflated" was adopted. This must not happen again. This time we must make sure that wage rates are not reduced when the wartime demand for labor is diverted into peacetime channels. We must make sure that the labor market is not broken by unemployment and wage slashes.

American labor should be assured that there are not going to be any wage cuts after this war. What is even more important—when the worker's hours are cut back to peacetime levels a real attempt must be made to adjust wage rates upward.

And wages should be constantly increased as the productivity of industry is increased. An expanding American economy can continue to expand only if the increased productivity is divided equitably between business and the worker. In fact —you know, and I know, that unless the worker does get his share of America's increased production in the form of increased wages and unless business gets its share in the form of increased profits— neither will prosper and all, business men, wage-earners and farmers, will lose.

But an increase in wages is not the only benefit the American worker should secure from increased productivity. He should also benefit in the form of shorter hours of work, in the form of increased leisure and opportunities for healthful recreation. Thus increased wages and shorter hours go hand-in-hand in solving the prosperity problem the American way.

There is one further aspect of the wage-earner's problem that I would like to comment on. That is his aspiration for an annual wage or guaranteed annual income from his job. It is a terribly important part of any real attempt to implement America's economic bill of rights. The size of the wage-earner's pay envelope is important—vitally important to American prosperity. But we all know that it is equally important to know how many pay envelopes he gets during a year. I would like to see him get a guaranteed minimum annual wage and I think the time has come for America to begin tackling this most difficult problem.

Now this goal cannot be attained overnight. It cannot be achieved in a manner to harm business. Nor can it be achieved with the same speed in every business.

But we can start on the job of giving labor an annual wage. We can do a lot if we all will only agree that it is a problem business and labor must solve and if we all approach the problem with a genuine desire to succeed. And Government must do its part too. It must aid business in stabilizing its labor needs so that the burden of an annual wage will not be uneconomical. This, in my opinion, is the American way to bring about the annual wage, and I have confidence in the American way of doing things.

The third economic right is "the right of every farmer to raise and sell his products at a rate which will give him and his family a decent living."

American farmers now have by far the largest farm income in history. This is their due reward for the greatest agricultural production in history. We must assure the farmers that there will always be a market for all their output at good prices.

Concretely we should maintain an adequate floor on farm prices and thereby assure the farmer against the dangers of falling prices for his products. Our farm program must be one of expansion rather than curtailment. With jobs for all at good wages and with foreign markets greatly expanded, the farmer will be able to sell at good prices all that he can raise.

But this is not all. The farmer's income must have stability. To that end there should be established a comprehensive Federal crop insurance program which will secure the farmer against the hazards of crop failure.

To this must be added concrete steps to raise the standards of living on the farm and in the rural areas. We need a complete program of new and modernized homes and farm buildings. We must press forward with rural electrification and improvement. Only in this way can we bring to the rural communities modern facilities for decent and healthful living.

The fourth economic right is "the right of every business man, large and small, to trade in an atmosphere of freedom from unfair competition and domination by monopolies at home and abroad."

Our economic bill of rights, like our political Bill of Rights, is based on freedom of enterprise—freedom of enterprise not merely and exclusively for the few, but broadly and inclusively for the many. The political Bill of Rights insured the destruction of special prerogatives and privileges. The economic bill of rights will insure the destruction of special economic prerogatives and privileges.

No special class of business deserves to be the spoiled darling of Government. The American people have no interest in preserving the vested interests and monopolistic privileges of greedy big business. The interest of the American people lies in using the resources of the country to achieve a prosperous America, prosperous for all business, large and small, and for all the people.

We must break through the barriers of monopoly and international cartels that stand in the way of a healthy expansion of free enterprise.

We must overcome the monopolistic frame of mind which thinks of business in terms of restricted output at high prices per unit. We must pass on to workers and consumers the benefits of technological progress and large-scale production. Free enterprise in the American tradition can flourish only by doing a large volume of business at a small profit per unit.

We must protect free enterprise against monopolies and cartels through continued vigorous enforcement of the anti-trust laws. Private enterprise yields its full advantage to the consuming public and to other business only when it is genuinely free and competitive. He is a sinister enemy of free enterprise who pays lip-service to competition but also labels every anti-trust prosecution a "persecution."

Our economy has important new expanding sectors in air transport, frequency modulation, television, and fibers, plastics and many other fields. These new expanding business areas in particular must be kept free of the constricting hand of monopoly. There must be a place in these new business areas—as everywhere in our economy—for enterprising small firms. It is from these new and small firms that the great industries of the future will grow. We need new industries and new firms to have industrial progress and we must not permit them to be stifled by monopoly.

The fifth economic right is "the right of every family to a decent home."

Concretely, we should adopt a housing program looking toward the construction, through private enterprise of 2,000,000 housing units a year and ridding this country of its urban and rural slums. We need to build at least 15,000,000 new housing units if we are to eliminate all our slums and substandard dwellings. The right to a home is meaningless when that home is a hovel. We cannot afford slums.

A well-housed America must have modern homes—homes with all the latest electrical and mechanical equipment which will eliminate the drudgery of houshold work. To the fullest extent possible we must be a land of home owners, and to that end we must assure every family an opportunity for home ownership by making certain that there is available private credit on terms which will reduce the down payment and cut by one-third the monthly cost of buying homes.

New residential construction and the modernization of America's homes alone can provide jobs for 4,000,000 people a year. This is 2,000,000 more than the maximum amount engaged in such work prior to the war.

The sixth economic right is "the right to adequate medical care and the opportunity to achieve and enjoy good health."

As Selective Service has revealed, too large a proportion of our younger men now fall below reasonable health standards. This is a warning signal to America with respect to that state of health of all segments of our population. This condition calls for immediate and drastic action.

We cannot permit the health of our people to be impaired by poverty or lack of medical and hospital facilities. I say to you that your Federal and State Governments have just as much responsibility for the health of their people as they have for providing them with education and police and fire protection. Health and adequate medical and hospital care are not luxuries. They are basic necessities to which all are entitled.

We must see that medical attention is available to all the people. But this health program must be achieved in the American way. Every person should have the right to go to the doctor and hospital of their own choosing. The Federal and State Governments should work hand in hand in making health insurance an integral part of our Social Security program just as old age and unemployment benefits are today.

We need more hospitals and doctors. We should make sure that such facilities are available and that we build hospitals in every community, rural and urban, that does not now have such facilities for all of its people.

Never again can we afford the waste of poor health in America because of poverty or inadequate facilities. And I say to you now that this program will prove in the long run to be a saving to America.

We must not be content to provide medical attention for people after they become sick. We must implement and extend our knowledge of maximum health as well as preventions of sickness. The Government should appropriate needed funds to finance a greatly expanded program of medical research in private and public institutions.

The seventh economic right is "the right to adequate protection from the economic fears of old age, sickness, accident and unemployment."

We must assure people who are disabled and temporarily unemployed that they will be taken care of adequately. We must assure them that they will not be in want because of loss of income during this period of compulsory unemployment. We cannot neglect these groups without incurring serious dangers to the stability of our whole economy.

A broader Social Security program will be needed after the war. Old Age Insurance should be adequate to provide all of our older men and women with the means for decent living. Our present old age benefits are definitely inadequate. A decent, self-respecting old age Social Security program should be deemed to be a right, not a charity, a right springing from the years of service each person delivers to the sum total of a better America.

An adequate Social Security program will, of itself, by adding to the spendable purchasing power available to the people and by placing a floor on consumption, add more than 2,000,000 jobs a year.

The eighth economic right is "the right to a good education."

We must have an educated and informed America. Even now most of our rural areas and some of our urban areas are poorly provided with schools. Our teachers are underpaid. Our schools are badly understaffed. We need more schools and at least 500,000 more teachers.

Through Federal aid to poorer communities for the development of locally controlled educational programs we propose to equalize and extend educational opportunities through the land. We propose to provide facilities for technical and higher education for all qualified young men and women without regard to their financial means. In this America, the pioneer of free education, the right to technical and higher education should be as universal as the right to a secondary school education.

This is the kind of program that can provide jobs, economic security and rising standards of living for all Americans—regardless of race, color or creed. Our democracy can be a living force only if it means the good life for all the people.

The millions of productive jobs that this program will bring are jobs in private enterprise. They are jobs based on the expanded demand for the output of our economy for consumption and investment. And this program need place no real burden on the Federal budget, notwithstanding the reduction in taxes which must come after the war.

On the contrary, a program of this character can provide America with a national income of such a size that it will be possible to reduce the tax rates still further on personal incomes, on business profits and on consumption, and still collect enough tax revenues to meet the needs of the Government, including orderly retirement of the national debt.

These should be our immediate goals, once final victory over our enemies has been achieved.

Now there are those who say that these goals are the dream of a "man willing to jeopardize the country's future with untried ideas and idealistic schemes." These people think they are the realists.

Actually, these are the persons of limited vision and stunted imagination. These people are of the same breed as these "sound business men" who haggled over pennies in the purchase of strategic stockpiles before the war, only to leave the materials for the Japs to use against us. Those are people who will fight against enemies, waging total war, by pinching pennies. These people think the same as those who said the President was dreaming when he declared in 1940 that the American people would produce 50,000 planes in one year. Do these Monday-morning quarterbacks have that great faith in the American people, and in their way of life, which is required in order to understand the meaning of America?

I am confident, however, that the great majority of the American people share the same great faith in America and in the American way of doing things which I have expressed here. We know our way and the road ahead is straight and broad, although there are many hills which we must climb. The program which I have set forth is only the first milestone, for the capacity of the American way of life in the years to come is beyond the vision of man. The American system of free enterprise is the best the world has ever known, and through it we can obtain, God willing, the best that this world has to offer. . . .

2. FULL EMPLOYMENT BILL OF 1945[1]

EDITORS' NOTE.—The issue of full employment emerged as a primary question immediately after World War II for at least three reasons. First, there was the memory of the long depression of the 1930's, which many believed was in part responsible for the outbreak of the war. Second, there was the fact of full employment and unparalleled production during World War II and the general reaction that if war could produce full employment, certainly peace deserved full utilization of resources for recovery and general well-being. The third reason was, as a Manchester economist, John Jewkes, observed in his book, *Ordeal by Planning*, published in 1948: "Who would have anticipated in 1925 that, within twenty years, the Keynesian economic doctrines offering us a route towards the maintenance of full employment within a free society would have been so generally accepted?"

The Full Employment Bill of 1945 was a kind of statutory version of the economic doctrines of J. M. Keynes (1883–1946), outstanding British economist who influenced world economic thought during the depression of the 1930's with his *General Theory of Employment, Interest and Money* (1936) and who gave form and popularity to the doctrine of government expenditure to insure full employment. A careful reading of the bill's provisions will disclose the methods designed to derive the "full employment budget," and the kinds of policies to be pursued by the government in the event that estimates of employment were below those required to employ the full labor force.

Although introduced and extensively considered, the Full Employment Bill of 1945 was not passed. Instead, the Employment Act of 1946 was passed in the following year, sharply curtailing the proposed governmental functions embodied in the 1945 bill. The 1946 act did, however, provide for semiannual economic reports to Congress and the people through the President, which have come to be known as the "President's Economic Reports." In these reports there has been developed a scheme of "national bookkeeping" of great value in the economics of full employment (see the Statistical Appendix Nos. 7–10, 13, and 20).

1. Senate Bill No. 380 (79th Cong., 1st sess.), introduced January 22, 1945.

A bill to establish a national policy and program for assuring continuing full employment in a free competitive economy, through the concerted efforts of industry, agriculture, labor, State and local governments, and the Federal Government.

Be it enacted by the Senate and House of Representatives of the United States of America in Congress assembled,

SECTION 1. This Act may be cited as the "Full Employment Act of 1945."

DECLARATION OF POLICY

SEC. 2. The Congress hereby declares that—

(a) It is the policy of the United States to foster free competitive enterprise and the investment of private capital in trade and commerce and in the development of the natural resources of the United States;

(b) All Americans able to work and seeking work have the right to useful, remunerative, regular, and full-time employment, and it is the policy of the United States to assure the existence at all times of sufficient employment opportunities to enable all Americans who have finished their schooling and who do not have full-time housekeeping responsibilities freely to exercise this right;

(c) In order to carry out the policies set forth in subsections (a) and (b) of this section, and in order to (1) promote the general welfare of the Nation; (2) foster and protect the American home and the American family as the foundation of the American way of life; (3) raise the standard of living of the American people; (4) provide adequate employment opportunities for returning veterans; (5) contribute to the full utilization of our national resources; (6) develop trade and commerce among the several States and with foreign nations; (7) preserve and strengthen competitive private enterprise, particularly small business enterprise; (8) strengthen the national defense and security; and (9) contribute to the establishment and maintenance of lasting peace among nations, it is essential that continuing full employment be maintained in the United States;

(d) In order to assist industry, agriculture, labor, and State and local governments in achieving continuing full employment, it is the responsibility of the Federal Government to pursue such consistent and openly arrived at economic policies and programs as will stimulate and encourage the highest feasible levels of employment opportunities through private and other non-Federal investment and expenditure;

(e) To the extent that continuing full employment cannot otherwise be achieved, it is the further responsibility of the Federal Government to provide such volume of Federal investment and expenditure as may be needed to assure continuing full employment; and

(f) Such investment and expenditure by the Federal Government shall be designed to contribute to the national wealth and well-being, and to stimulate increased employment opportunities by private enterprise.

THE NATIONAL PRODUCTION AND EMPLOYMENT BUDGET

SEC. 3. (a) The President shall transmit to Congress at the beginning of each regular session the National Production and Employment Budget (hereinafter referred to as the "National Budget"), which shall set forth in summary and detail, for the ensuing fiscal year or such longer period as the President may deem appropriate—

(1) the estimated size of the labor force, including the self-employed in industry and agriculture;

(2) the estimated aggregate volume of investment and expenditure by private enterprises, consumers, State and local governments, and the Federal Government, required to produce such volume of the gross national product, at the expected level of prices, as will be necessary to provide employment opportunities for such labor force (such dollar volume being hereinafter referred

to as the "full employment volume of production"); and

(3) the estimated aggregate volume of prospective investment and expenditure by private enterprises, consumers, State and local governments, and the Federal Government (not taking into account any increased or decreased investment or expenditure which might be expected to result from the programs set forth in such Budget).

The estimates and information herein called for shall take account of such foreign investments and expenditure for exports and imports as affect the volume of the gross national product.

(b) The extent, if any, by which the estimated aggregate volume of prospective investment and expenditure for any fiscal year or other period, as set forth in the National Budget in accordance with paragraph (a) (3) of this section, is less than the estimated aggregate volume of investment and expenditure required to assure a full employment volume of production, as set forth in the National Budget in accordance with paragraph (a) (2) of this section, shall for the purposes of this title be regarded as a prospective deficiency in the National Budget. When there is a prospective deficiency in the National Budget for any fiscal year or other period, the President shall set forth in such Budget a general program for encouraging such increased non-Federal investment and expenditure, particularly investment and expenditure which will promote increased employment opportunities by private enterprise, as will prevent such deficiency to the greatest possible extent. The President shall also include in such Budget such recommendations for legislation relating to such program as he may deem necessary or desirable. Such program may include, but need not be limited to, current and projected Federal policies and activities with reference to banking and currency, monopoly and competition, wages and working conditions, foreign trade and investment, agriculture, taxation, social se-

curity, the development of natural resources, and such other matters as may directly or indirectly affect the level of non-Federal investment and expenditure.

(c) To the extent, if any, that such increased non-Federal investment and expenditure as may be expected to result from actions taken under the program set forth in accordance with subsection (b) of this section are deemed insufficient to provide a full employment volume of production, the President shall transmit a general program for such Federal investment and expenditure as will be sufficient to bring the aggregate volume of investment and expenditure by private business, consumers, State and local government, and the Federal Government, up to the level required to assure a full employment volume of production. Such program shall be designed to contribute to the national wealth and well-being, and to stimulate additional non-Federal investment and expenditure. Any of such programs calling for the construction of public works by the Federal Government shall provide for the performance of the necessary construction work by private concerns under contracts awarded in accordance with applicable laws, except where the performance of such work by some other method is necessary by reason of special circumstances or is authorized by other provisions of law.

(d) If the estimated aggregate volume of prospective investment and expenditure for any fiscal year or other period, as set forth in the National Budget in accordance with paragraph (a) (3) of this section, is more than the estimated aggregate volume of investment and expenditure required to assure a full employment volume of production, as set forth in the National Budget in accordance with paragraph (a) (2) of this section, the President shall set forth in such Budget a general program for preventing inflationary economic dislocations, or diminishing the aggregate volume of investment and expenditure to the level required to assure a full employment volume of production, or both.

(e) The programs referred to in subsections (b), (c), and (d) of this section shall include such measures as may be necessary to assure that monopolistic practices with respect to prices, production, or distribution, or other monopolistic practices, will not interfere with the achievement of the purposes of this Act.

(f) The National Budget shall include a report on the distribution of the national income during the preceding fiscal year, or such longer period as the President may deem appropriate, together with an evaluation of the effect upon the distribution of the national income of the programs set forth in such Budget.

(g) The President may from time to time transmit to Congress such supplemental or revised estimates, information, programs, or legislative recommendations as he may deem necessary or desirable in connection with the National Budget.

PREPARATION OF NATIONAL BUDGET

Sec. 4. (a) The National Budget shall be prepared in the Executive Office of the President under the general direction and supervision of the President, and in consultation with the members of his Cabinet and other heads of departments and establishments.

(b) The President shall transmit to the several departments and establishments such preliminary estimates and other information as will enable them to prepare such plans and programs as may be needed during the ensuing or subsequent fiscal years to help achieve a full employment volume of production.

(c) The President may establish such advisory boards or committees composed of representatives of industry, agriculture, labor, and State and local governments, and others, as he may deem advisable for the purpose of advising and consulting on methods of achieving the objectives of this Act.

JOINT COMMITTEE ON THE NATIONAL BUDGET

Sec. 5. (a) There is hereby established a Joint Committee on the National Budget, to be composed of the chairmen and ranking minority members of the Senate Committees on Appropriations, Banking and Currency, Education and Labor, and Finance, and seven additional Members of the Senate, to be appointed by the President of the Senate; and the chairmen and ranking minority members of the House Committees on Appropriations, Banking and Currency, Labor, and Ways and Means, and seven additional Members of the House of Representatives to be appointed by the Speaker of the House of Representatives. The party representation of the Joint Committee shall reflect the relative membership of the majority and minority parties in the Senate and the House of Representatives.

(b) It shall be the function of the Joint Committee—

(1) to make a study of the National Budget transmitted to Congress by the President in accordance with section 3 of this Act; and

(2) to report to the Senate and the House of Representatives, not later than March 1 of each year, its findings and recommendations with respect to the National Budget, together with a joint resolution setting forth for the ensuing fiscal year a general policy with respect to such National Budget to serve as a guide to the several committees of Congress dealing with legislation relating to such National Budget. . . .

RATE OF EXPENDITURES

Sec. 6. (a) The President shall review quarterly all Federal investment and expenditure for the purpose of ascertaining the extent to which the current and anticipated level of non-Federal investment and expenditure warrants any change in the volume of such Federal investment and expenditure.

(b) Subject to such principles and standards as may be set forth in applicable appropriation Acts and other statutes, the rate of Federal investment and expenditure may be varied to whatever extent and in whatever manner the President may determine to be necessary for the purpose of assisting in assuring continuing full employment, with due consideration being given to current and anticipated variations in savings and in investment and expenditure by private business, consumers, State and local governments, and the Federal Government. . . .

INTERPRETATION

SEC. 8. Nothing contained herein shall be construed as calling for or authorizing—

(a) the operation of plants, factories, or other productive facilities by the Federal Government;

(b) the use of compulsory measures of any type whatsoever in determining the allocation or distribution of manpower;

(c) any change in the existing procedures on appropriations; or

(d) the carrying out of, or any appropriation for, any program set forth in the National Budget, unless such program shall have been authorized by provisions of law other than this Act.

3. ON THE GOVERNMENTAL GUARANTEE OF FULL EMPLOYMENT[1]

By ROBERT A. TAFT

EDITORS' NOTE.—Addressing himself to the Full Employment Bill of 1945 as well as to President Roosevelt's "Economic Bill of Rights," Senator Robert A. Taft (p. 472) analyzes the meaning of a guarantee of a right to a job by the federal government. His analysis carries him into some aspects of the "economics of full employment" as involved in the Full Employment Bill. Mr. Taft attempts to draw the line between legitimate and dangerous action on the part of government in creating the conditions for full employment.

Ladies and gentlemen of the National Industrial Conference Board:

It is a great pleasure to appear again before your Board, which for so many years has conducted a sound impartial survey of economic problems and set an example now followed by many organizations. I am sure that none has investigated questions with a more realistic and impartial approach, and I am quite sure that none has more successfully assembled the basic facts on which every sound economic policy must be based.

In the last year or two we have seen the announcement of a new theory of government or economics, that every man is entitled to a full-time job at good wages, just as he is entitled to police protection and the possession of his own home. The necessary corollary has followed that the government must guarantee him a full-time job at good wages. This is an attractive and plausible theory, and it has made substantial headway throughout the United States with very little critical examination of its soundness. Your purpose here this evening is to examine the basis for this new theory.

1. Robert A. Taft, "Shall the Government Guarantee Employment?" an address to the National Industrial Conference Board, New York, January 18, 1945. Reprinted with permission from a copy of the speech supplied by Senator Taft.

We can all agree that full employment at good wages for every man and every woman who wishes to work in the United States is a goal devoutly to be wished. It is an ideal to be strenuously sought, and no questioning of its existence as a legal right in any way detracts from the desire of the questioner to attain the ideal. "Good wages" means perhaps $2,500 a year. Obviously a goal of $5,000 a year apiece, or $25,000, is even more desirable. Even the most hardheaded realists have agreed that Utopia itself is a proper goal to seek.

The distinction is between an ideal or a hope, and a right which can be conferred by law. Thus we can agree on the desirability of the principles of the Atlantic Charter and the Four Freedoms, but even the President today admits that these are merely a hope and not something to be guaranteed by a world government. This proposed new legal right certainly goes far beyond the Declaration of Independence which mentions only the rights to "life, liberty and the *pursuit* of happiness." The Constitution while promising to *secure* the blessing of liberty, only proposes to *promote* the general welfare. It seems impossible to me to assert the legal duty of our government to guarantee full-time employment. It may take many steps toward that goal and adopt many methods which are more likely to secure it than others.

The means by which we have raised our standard of living to a higher average than any other country in the history of the world, and in a shorter time, have been the application of freedom to individual activity, not the guarantee to anybody of anything other than freedom. The economic machine of America created out of that freedom has made this country the most powerful in the world. That freedom can be qualified so that it does not include the freedom to throw monkey wrenches in the machine. The economic machinery can be oiled and speeded up and improved. But a guarantee of work by the government to every individual is wholly inconsistent with the very freedom which has produced the machine which provides jobs at good wages.

Just what is this theory of a government guarantee of employment? My attention was first called to it in the National Resources Planning Board Report of January 1, 1943, in which that Board stated its belief that it should be the declared policy of the United States Government to underwrite full employment for the unemployable, and guarantee a job for every man released from the armed forces or the war industries with fair pay and working conditions. The whole report of that Board was based on that theory, without the slightest consideration of cost or taxation. It proposed a vast spending program for the United States Government as a means of producing prosperity. The government was not only to underwrite full employment but it was to "underwrite effective demand for goods and services" and "underwrite the attainment of high production."

President Roosevelt adopted the so-called economic bill of rights of the Board in his address to Congress in January, 1944, and reaffirmed his position this year, saying that "of these rights the most fundamental, and one on which the fulfillment of the others in large degree depends, is the right to a useful and remunerative job in the industries or shops or farms or mines of the nation." He says that the full employment means not only jobs, but productive jobs at standard wages.

The C.I.O. P.A.C. platform of January, 1944, commends the President's new bill of rights and says that the full employment program must "be guaranteed by the Government with a prepared program of jobs at useful work, with standard wages and working conditions, if and to the extent that private industry falls short of the guarantee."

The Kilgore Subcommittee of the Senate Military Affairs Committee, largely dominated by the Political Action Committee thinking, proposed the enactment of this theory into law. This bill would require the President each year to inform Congress as to the prospects of employment and national production and, if his estimate fell short of full employment, to recommend a specific program of Federal expenditure to fill the gap. The policy crystallizes into a proposal that the United States Government shall guarantee sixty million jobs at $2,500 a year.

The whole policy sounds so easy and attractive that it has been thoughtlessly accepted by many without analysis. Even the Committee of Economic Development, made up of hardheaded business-men, has rather undertaken to assume for industry the responsibility of guaranteeing from fifty-three to fifty-seven million jobs. A guarantee of employment by private enterprise of course is even more difficult than one by government, because there are millions of employers wholly unable to employ more men than economic conditions permit, and wholly without the power to combat nation-wide economic forces. The danger is that if employers undertake the responsibility and fail in any degree because of conditions beyond their control, it would certainly open the door for the claim that the government must step into the breach with the complete guarantee.

The first question that arises is whether it is necessary or wise to provide, or try to provide, sixty million or even fifty-three million full-time jobs. There are only thirty-five million families in the United States, and this would provide two jobs for many million families. Should there be an obligation to provide a full-time job for every woman who wants to work when perhaps her husband or other member of the family is perfectly able and willing to support her? Is it perhaps not better to keep boys and girls longer in school, and retire the aged at a lower age? How can we say that there must be sixty million jobs when perhaps fifty million workers can do all the work of the nation?

In analyzing the soundness of this new doctrine, a good many questions arise as to its exact meaning. What is full employment and what is a good wage? Is this to be a guarantee of any job a man wants in any industry, or is it to be such a job as the government chooses to provide? Who is to decide what a good wage is? Men have a way of overestimating their own ability, and few are going to be satisfied with the wage the government thinks adequate. Is the government going to guarantee a flat wage for all, or a wage having some relation to the amount or quality of work that a man does? Who will decide when his wages are to be raised?

The President says every man has the right to a job in the "industries or shops or farms or mines of the nation." The total number of men employed in these categories is only thirty million. How can they be increased and why should they be? Millions are employed in other types of service. The census of 1940 showed 9,758,-000 employees and home-account workers, including farmers. How will the government guarantee this kind of a job, or guarantee that they can make a living wage? Some 2,300,000 people are listed as in domestic service. Is the provision of such a job going to be a performance of the government guarantee or not?

It is clear to me that any direct guarantee of full-time jobs at good wages would involve the Government in the placement of every man and woman in the country, and ultimately the assignment by the government of every man and woman to the job selected by the government. This is exactly the system pursued in Russia today, as anyone can see by reading the recent articles in the *Readers' Digest* by William L. White. It is in contradiction of the whole American tradition and is bound to destroy the very freedom for which our Armies fight throughout the world. It is obvious to me that the proponents of the theory would very quickly back away from any literal interpretation of the supposed guarantee. They would quickly disown the theory that the right to work is one which can be ordered by the government and protected by court decree.

How then is this guarantee to be carried out? The Political Action Committee suggests that it is to be done by direct government employment of all those not employed by private industry. The unthinking popular view is that the jobs are to be guaranteed by the planning and execution of public works. The President says that full employment means employment in productive jobs and therefore the public works must not be makeshift or make-work projects, but must be real public works. I have yet to hear of the most ardent New Dealer who has devised a system of spending more than five billion dollars a year on productive public works.

A billion dollars a year for public housing is about the largest single proposal for the expenditure of public money. We passed a public road bill proposing the expenditure of approximately half a billion dollars a year of Federal money, and I doubt if it will all be spent. We passed a billion-dollar flood control bill but it will certainly take five years to carry it out, so that it only provides two hundred million a year. Rivers and harbors expenditure is likely to be even less. Supposing we can find five billion dollars a year of worthwhile projects for the expenditure of Federal funds, that would mean about two and one-half million jobs. But we are trying to provide sixty million jobs. We can get many more jobs by tuning up the private economic machine by ten percent, than by the largest public works program anyone has conceived.

We found in the great depression that the employment of a man on public works cost three times the amount expended on work relief programs per man, and six times the cost of direct relief. Furthermore, public works are only a stopgap, because most such works cost money to maintain after they are constructed. The construction of a factory may give employment to many men year after year. But a courthouse or a new road or a new school costs more to maintain and more taxes than before. Of course, there are some productive public works, but most of them produce no permanent jobs.

The lack of public works available to meet mass unemployment suggests to those who advocate direct government employment that the government would have to go into many fields of nongovernment activity. Most employment in any nation must be in the making of goods and the furnishing of service. The government could take over factories and make clothing, food, and other necessities to be given away to the low-income groups. We saw a start in that direction in the thirties. The difficulty is that the moment the government enters such a field, private capital is afraid to go ahead. You hamper and discourage the recovery of the very economic machine on which you are relying to produce prosperity. No individual can successfully compete with the government. Constant government experimentation and interference in the thirties delayed recovery far beyond the time required in foreign countries, or in past depressions in this country. The expenditure by the government of thirty or forty billion dollars a year to give direct employment on a full-time basis and good wages to, say fifteen million men would add that sum to the public debt, and certainly discourage any attempt at real recovery.

When the difficulty of direct employment, and the limitations of any public works program, are pointed out, the proponents of the guarantee theory turn to another policy which they probably intended to follow all the time.

Public works shall be only one branch of the means by which jobs are to be guaranteed. The other branches are set forth in the President's recent budget message of January 3, most of which passed unnoticed in the excitement of the war and foreign relations.

That message proposes many different methods of additional Government spending after the war. The borrowing authority of the Farm Security Administration is to be increased sixty million dollars for rural rehabilitation. The Commodity Credit Corporation is to spend two billions more in the purchase of crops. The Federal Government is to give aid to all common-school and high-school education, leading ultimately, according to the plan of the National Resources Planning Board, to a Federal expenditure of three billion dollars. Federal loans and guarantees are recommended to stimulate private construction after the war. Federal salary rates are to be increased. Taxes on consumers are all to be reduced while there is no indication that progressive income taxes on high incomes are to be changed. Rather they are to be increased. Unemployment compensation payment rates are to be increased. Six billion dollars is to be turned over to the proposed international monetary fund and the proposed international bank. This aid to foreign countries is to be supplemented by further loans extended by the Export-Import Bank, not only to cover short- and medium-term commitments to finance exporters, but in the form of long-term loans for reconstruction and development. Finally, the President's program is to include provision for extended social security, including medical care; for better education, health and nutrition; for the improvement of our homes, cities and farms; and for the development of transportation facilities and river valleys.

When we add to all these proposals the expenditure of six billion dollars for interest on the public debt, five or six billion dollars for the postwar Army and Navy, over two and a half billion dollars for compulsory military training, and the expenditures already authorized for veterans, we find a Federal budget which may well amount to fifty billion dollars a year. Many of these expenditures are frankly urged as a means of guaranteeing full employment. It is said that we have had full employment during the war because of vast Government spending and the only way we can fulfill the new guarantee is to continue this Government spending in time of peace. In this form the supposed guarantee of employment merges into the same old Government spending theory advocated by Keynes and Hansen—the theory that a nation can spend itself into prosperity, that deficits are a blessing in disguise, that we need have no concern about our public debt because we owe it to ourselves.

We tried it in the thirties, and it left us with a large debt and ten million unemployed. Any huge spending, whether for direct employment, or to prime the pump for indirect employment, leads to the same result. The postwar budget of the government will be at least twenty billion dollars for expenses that we cannot escape, four times our prewar budget. It may be just possible to find a tax system that will produce this much income in time of peace without discouraging all initiative. If we add the additional government spending proposed by the guarantee theory, we will run the budget up to forty or fifty billion dollars. Either a tax system must be imposed at even higher rates than the war system now in force, or we must increase the debt by somewhere between fifteen and thirty billion dollars a year. Either of these alternatives would destroy the economic machine upon which our prosperity has been based. Either would destroy the system of private enterprise to which the advocates of this new theory, even Earl Browder, give lip service.

If the present tax rates on business are continued, there will be no incentive to anyone either to put his money into new business or to expand old business. If the present rates on individual incomes are continued, there will be little incentive to any man to exert himself to build up his income with the hope of providing a better living for himself and a better education for his children or a better provision for his family after death. The incentive created by the American system of rewards for genius, initiative and daring will disappear, and it is vain to hope that the expansion of private industry will continue. One industry after another will become unprofitable, just as the railroads became unprofitable before the war. The government will have to finance necessary expansion and will gradually absorb one industry after another.

The advocates of the theory, however, do not really contemplate any such tax system. They are disciples of the Keynesian theory that the public debt can be indefinitely increased. To me it is obvious that this can only end in extreme inflation. Because of government deficits, we have had an increase in the cost of living of approximately thirty percent during the war, in spite of the most rigid price and wage controls. In my opinion, while controls of this kind can be enforced to some extent in wartime, in peacetime in America they would suffer the fate of prohibition. A steady increase in prices would force increases of wages and a cycle of rising costs which could not be checked while government deficits continued.

Such an inflation would lead to more government interference and more government expense and finally a complete breakdown of the financial and banking structure upon which our commerce, business and currency are based. It would mean the destruction of the private industry system. We could point out that it had been sabotaged by its enemies, but I am afraid it would be like Humpty Dumpty, and, once fallen, all the king's horses and all the king's men could not put it together again. We would have to reconstruct our business and price system completely and that would only be done on the basis of 100% government control and operation. In my opinion the more radical wing of those who advocate the spending theory, and this government guarantee of full employment, really look forward with pleasure to that result. It is the best and surest method of destroying the system which they detest.

One interesting phase of the full employment program and the spending the-

ory is the plan to lend money abroad in large sums. It is frequently said, and generally accepted without analysis of any kind, that we cannot provide full employment without a tremendous increase in our export trade. We are exporting about twelve billion dollars worth of goods a year, about eighty percent under Lease-Lend. It is said that that volume must continue even though we have to lend all the money to continue it.

Of course, in the immediate postwar period it will be necessary to lend money for humanitarian reasons, and perhaps in an amount sufficient to enable the foreign countries to set their economic machinery in motion, but continued government lending can only have the same effect which we saw in the twenties with private lending. Sooner or later it becomes glaringly apparent that the loans will never be repaid. Thereupon the lending stops and the employment created thereby comes to a sudden and disastrous end, producing or accentuating a depression; and the debt is added to our own debt and our citizens pay the interest on it. Obviously it can be of no advantage to our workers to produce goods and give them away, and that is what foreign trade means if it is created only by large loans which cannot be repaid. Like the other forms of spending, it will produce full employment at the cost of ultimately destroying all employment and all freedom with it.

The sounder advocates of a stimulated foreign trade realize that we must import goods if the trade is to be of any advantage to us. But if those imports reduce employment in our home industries, why is there any net increase in employment, except a very small advantage comparatively in buying the imports cheaper? The theory is that by manufacturing goods and shipping them abroad, we create an additional purchasing power in the workers who produce these exports which can be used to pay for imported goods without interfering with our own industries. Since, however, it is admitted that exports are of no use unless paid for by imports, and that an American market must be created for those imports, why isn't it just as easy to create an additional home market for home goods as it is to create an American market for imported goods?

The truth probably lies between the two extremes. Some additional market can be created for imported goods which is not available for domestic production. But the idea that foreign trade can produce any tremendous increase in employment, unless we are going to give away our products at the expense of the taxpayer, is a mirage. And one thing is certainly clear. There can be no sound expansion of employment by the Government guaranteeing expanded exports, but on the gradual building-up by hard work of a foreign trade based on mutual advantage in the exchange of certain types of goods. Tariffs can be lower, but they cannot be reduced so as to destroy established industries in this country.

So also the path to prosperity and happiness at home cannot be solved by any panacea of public spending or a government guarantee of full employment. It can only be achieved by the gradual speeding up of the great private economic machinery upon which our prosperity depends. That is an infinitely delicate machine. To secure the best results prices must bear the right relation to wages and wages to prices. There must be an accurate adjustment between the production of capital goods and consumers goods. There must be incentive to save and invest and work and open up new fields. There must be continued reward for hard work and ability and the willingness to take a chance. There must be a free choice of employment so that every man may choose that profession or calling to which he is best suited. The progress which we have achieved under the American system in the last 150 years at least suggests that we had better rely on it a while longer. It has the advantage of being based on freedom of the individual as no other economic system is based. Let us not give up our guarantee of freedom for a spurious guarantee of employment.

For the spending theory on which the legal guarantee of full employment is based is a false god. It is fatal to the very prosperity which it seeks to attain. It is fatal to sound government because the spending of money becomes its own justification regardless of the soundness of the project for which it is spent. It teaches the people that they can obtain something for nothing and that every man is entitled to the same living from the government whether his ability and willingness to produce justify it or not; and therefore it is fatal to the character of the people who fall down and worship it.

SECTION G. CIVIL LIBERTIES AND LOYALTY SINCE 1919

1. *GITLOW* v. *NEW YORK*[1]

EDITORS' NOTE.—Although this opinion is dated 1925, the original action against Benjamin Gitlow was taken in 1919. The specter of communism was haunting all America in the days following World War I. Radicals, and especially those who declared allegiance to the principles and program of the successful Russian Revolution, were the objects of a feverish "red hunt" conducted by such state and national authorities as the Lusk Committee in New York and United States Attorney-General A. Mitchell Palmer. Many states adopted or revived "criminal syndicalism" laws; and under one such measure, New York's old Criminal Anarchy Act of 1902, Benjamin Gitlow was arrested. The precise circumstances of the case are stated in the text below.

Gitlow later became a severe critic of communism.

Gitlow v. *New York* was one in a series of civil rights cases which raised the important constitutional question whether the due-process clause of the Fourteenth Amendment prohibited interference with freedom of speech by the states. Some of the more important cases were: *Schenck* v. *United States* (1919); *Abrams* v. *United States* (1919); *Schaefer* v. *United States* (1920); and *Whitney* v. *California* (1927). Speaking for a unanimous Court in the Schenck case, Justice Holmes first formulated his standard for judging abridgments of free speech, the "clear-and-present-danger" doctrine. Diverse as have been the interpretations of "clear and present danger," the principle itself remains a towering landmark in the civil rights field.

Mr. Justice SANFORD delivered the opinion of the Court.

Benjamin Gitlow was indicted in the Supreme Court of New York, with three others, for the statutory crime of criminal anarchy. New York Penal Laws, §§ 160, 161. He was separately tried, convicted, and sentenced to imprisonment. The judgment was affirmed by the Appellate Division and by the Court of Appeals. . . . The case is here on writ of error to the Supreme Court, to which the record was remitted. . . .

The contention here is that the statute,

by its terms and as applied in this case, is repugnant to the due process clause of the Fourteenth Amendment. Its material provisions are:

§ 160. *Criminal anarchy defined*. Criminal anarchy is the doctrine that organized government should be overthrown by force or violence, or by assassination of the executive head or of any of the executive officials of government, or by any unlawful means. The advocacy of such doctrine either by word of mouth or writing is a felony.

§ 161. *Advocacy of criminal anarchy*. Any person who:

1. By word of mouth or writing advocates, advises or teaches the duty, necessity or propri-

1. *Gitlow* v. *New York*, 268 U.S. 652, 654–59, 661, 664–70, 672–73 (1925).

ety of overthrowing or overturning organized government by force or violence, or by assassination of the executive head or of any of the executive officials of government, or by any unlawful means; or,

2. Prints, publishes, edits, issues or knowingly circulates, sells, distributes or publicly displays any book, paper, document, or written or printed matter in any form, containing or advocating, advising or teaching the doctrine that organized government should be overthrown by force, violence or any unlawful means. . . .

Is guilty of a felony and punishable, by imprisonment or fine or both.

The indictment was in two counts. The first charged that the defendant had advocated, advised and taught the duty, necessity and propriety of overthrowing and overturning organized government by force, violence and unlawful means, by certain writings therein set forth entitled "The Left Wing Manifesto"; the second that he had printed, published and knowingly circulated and distributed a certain paper called "The Revolutionary Age," containing the writings set forth in the first count advocating, advising and teaching the doctrine that organized government should be overthrown by force, violence and unlawful means.

The following facts were established in the trial by undisputed evidence and admissions: The defendant is a member of the Left Wing Section of the Socialist Party, a dissenting branch or faction of that party formed in opposition to its dominant policy of "moderate Socialism." . . . The Left Wing Section was organized nationally at a conference in New York City in June, 1919, attended by ninety delegates from twenty different States. The conference elected a National Council, of which the defendant was a member, and left to it the adoption of a "Manifesto." This was published in The Revolutionary Age, the official organ of the Left Wing. The defendant was on the board of managers of the paper and was its business manager. He arranged for the printing of the paper and took to the printer the manuscript of the first issue which contained the Left Wing Manifesto, and also a Communist Program and a Program of the Left Wing that had been adopted by the conference. . . .

Extracts from the Manifesto are set forth in the margin. Coupled with a review of the rise of Socialism, it condemned the dominant "moderate Socialism" for its recognition of the necessity of the democratic parliamentary state; repudiated its policy of introducing Socialism by legislative measures; and advocated, in plain and unequivocal language, the necessity of accomplishing the "Communist Revolution" by a militant and "revolutionary Socialism," based on "the class struggle" and mobilizing the "power of the proletariat in action," through mass industrial revolts developing into mass political strikes and "revolutionary mass action," for the purpose of conquering and destroying the parliamentary state and establishing in its place, through a "revolutionary dictatorship of the proletariat," the system of Communist Socialism. The then recent strikes in Seattle and Winnipeg were cited as instances of a development already verging on revolutionary action and suggestive of proletarian dictatorship, in which the strike-workers were "trying to usurp the functions of municipal government"; and revolutionary Socialism, it was urged, must use these mass industrial revolts to broaden the strike, make it general and militant, and develop it into mass political strikes and revolutionary mass action for the annihilation of the parliamentary state. . . .

The court, among other things, charged the jury, in substance, that they must determine what was the intent, purpose and fair meaning of the Manifesto; that its words must be taken in their ordinary meaning, as they would be understood by people whom it might reach; that a mere statement or analysis of social and economic facts and historical incidents, in the nature of an essay, accompanied by prophecy as to the future course of events, but with no teaching, advice or advocacy of action, would not constitute the advocacy, advice or teaching of a doctrine for the overthrow of government within the meaning of the statute; that a mere statement that unlawful acts might accomplish such a purpose would be insufficient, unless there was a teaching, advising and advocacy of employing such unlawful acts for the purpose of overthrowing government; and that if the jury had a reasonable doubt that the Manifesto did teach, advocate or advise the duty, necessity or propriety of using unlawful means for the overthrowing of organized government, the defendant was entitled to an acquittal.

... The sole contention here is, essentially, that as there was no evidence of any concrete result flowing from the publication of the Manifesto or of circumstances showing the likelihood of such result, the statute as construed and applied by the trial court penalizes the mere utterance, as such, of "doctrine" has no quality of incitement, without regard either to the circumstances of its utterance or to the likelihood of unlawful sequences; and that, as the exercise of the right of free expression with relation to government is only punishable "in circumstances involving likelihood of substantive evil," the statute contravenes the due process clause of the Fourteenth Amendment. The argument in support of this contention rests primarily upon the following propositions: 1st, That the "liberty" protected by the Fourteenth Amendment includes the liberty of speech and of the press; and 2nd, That while liberty of expression "is not absolute," it may be restrained "only in circumstances where its exercise bears a causal relation with some substantive evil, consummated, attempted or likely," and as the statute "takes no account of circumstances," it unduly restrains this liberty and is therefore unconstitutional.

The precise question presented, and the only question which we can consider under this writ of error, then is, whether the statute, as construed and applied in this case by the state courts, deprived the defendant of his liberty of expression in violation of the due process clause of the Fourteenth Amendment.

The statute does not penalize the utterance or publication of abstract "doctrine" or academic discussion having no quality of incitement to any concrete action. It is not aimed against mere historical or philosophical essays. It does not restrain the advocacy of changes in the form of government by constitutional and lawful means. What it prohibits is language advocating, advising or teaching the overthrow of organized government by unlawful means. These words imply urging to action. Advocacy is defined in the Century Dictionary as: "1. The act of pleading for, supporting, or recommending; active espousal." It is not the abstract "doctrine" of overthrowing organized government by unlawful means which is denounced by the statute, but the advocacy of action for the accomplishment of that purpose. It was so construed and applied by the trial judge, who specifically charged the jury that: "A mere grouping of historical events and a prophetic deduction from them would neither constitute advocacy, advice or teaching of a doctrine for the overthrow of government by force, violence or unlawful means. [And] if it were a mere essay on the subject, as suggested by counsel, based upon deductions from alleged historical events, with no teaching, advice or advocacy of action, it would not constitute a violation of the statute. . . ."

The Manifesto, plainly is neither the statement of abstract doctrine nor, as suggested by counsel, mere prediction that industrial disturbances and revolutionary mass strikes will result spontaneously in an inevitable process of evolution in the economic system. It advocates and urges in fervent language mass action which shall progressively foment industrial disturbances and through political mass strikes and revolutionary mass action overthrow and destroy organized parliamentary government. It concludes with a call to action in these words: "The proletariat revolution and the Communist reconstruction of society—*the struggle for these*—is now indispensable. . . . The Communist International calls the proletariat of the world to the final struggle!" This is not the expression of philosophical abstraction, the mere prediction of future events; it is the language of direct incitement. . . .

. . . That the jury were warranted in finding that the Manifesto advocated not merely the abstract doctrine of overthrowing organized government by force, violence and unlawful means, but action to that end, is clear.

For present purposes we may and do assume that freedom of speech and of the press—which are protected by the First Amendment from abridgment by Congress —are among the fundamental personal rights and "liberties" protected by the due process clause of the Fourteenth Amendment from impairment by the States. . . .

It is a fundamental principle, long established, that the freedom of speech and of the press which is secured by the Constitution does not confer an absolute right to speak or publish, without responsibility, whatever one may choose, or an unrestricted and unbridled license that gives immunity for every possible use of language and prevents the punishment of those who abuse this freedom. . . .

That a State in the exercise of its police power may punish those who abuse this freedom by utterances inimical to the public welfare, tending to corrupt public morals, incite to crime, or disturb the public peace, is not open to question. . . .

And, for yet more imperative reasons, a State may punish utterances endangering the foundations of organized government and threatening its overthrow by unlawful means. These imperil its own existence as a constitutional State. Freedom of speech and press, said Story . . . does not protect disturbances to the public peace or the attempt to subvert the government. It does

not protect publications or teachings which tend to subvert or imperil the government or to impede or hinder it in the performance of its governmental duties. . . . It does not protect publications prompting the overthrow of government by force; the punishment of those who publish articles which tend to destroy organized society being essential to the security of freedom and the stability of the State. . . . And a State may penalize utterances which openly advocate the overthrow of the representative and constitutional form of government of the United States and the several States, by violence or other unlawful means. . . . In short this freedom does not deprive a State of the primary and essential right of self preservation; which, so long as human governments endure, they cannot be denied. . . .

By enacting the present Statute the state has determined, through its legislative body, that utterances advocating the overthrow of organized government by force, violence and unlawful means, are so inimical to the general welfare and involve such danger of substantive evil that they may be penalized in the exercise of its police power. That determination must be given great weight. Every presumption is to be indulged in favor of the validity of the statute. . . . That utterances inciting to the overthrow of organized government by unlawful means, present a sufficient danger of substantive evil to bring their punishment within the range of legislative discretion, is clear. Such utterances, by their very nature, involve danger to the public peace and to the security of the State. They threaten breaches of the peace and ultimate revolution. And the immediate danger is none the less real and substantial, because the effect of a given utterance cannot be accurately foreseen. The State cannot reasonably be required to measure the danger from every such utterance in the nice balance of a jeweler's scale. A single revolutionary spark may kindle a fire that, smouldering for a time, may burst into a sweeping and destructive conflagration. It cannot be said that the State is acting arbitrarily or unreasonably when in the exercise of its judgment as to the measures necessary to protect the public peace and safety, it seeks to extinguish the spark without waiting until it has enkindled the flame or blazed into the conflagration. It cannot reasonably be required to defer the adoption of measures for its own peace and safety until the revolutionary utterances lead to actual disturbances of the public peace or imminent and immediate danger of its own destruction; but it may, in the exercise of its judgment, suppress the threatened danger in its incipiency. . . .

We cannot hold that the present statute is an arbitrary or unreasonable exercise of the police power of the State unwarrantably infringing the freedom of speech or press; and we must and do sustain its constitutionality.

. . . In other words, when the legislative body has determined generally, in the constitutional exercise of its discretion, that utterances of a certain kind involve such danger of substantive evil that they may be punished, the question whether any specific utterance coming within the prohibited class is likely, in and of itself, to bring about the substantive evil, is not open to consideration. It is sufficient that the statute itself be constitutional and that the use of the language comes within its prohibition. . . .

And finding, for the reasons stated, that the statute is not in itself unconstitutional, and that it has not been applied in the present case in derogation of any constitutional right, the judgment of the Court of Appeals is

Affirmed.

Mr. Justice HOLMES, dissenting.

Mr. Justice BRANDEIS and I are of opinion that this judgment should be reversed. The general principle of free speech, it seems to me, must be taken to be included in the Fourteenth Amendment, in view of the scope that has been given to the word "liberty" as there used, although perhaps it may be accepted with a somewhat larger latitude of interpretation than is allowed to Congress by the sweeping language that governs or ought to govern the laws of the United States. If I am right, then I think that the criterion sanctioned by the full Court in *Schenck* v. *United States* . . . applies. "The question in every case is whether the words used are used in such circumstances and are of such a nature as to create a clear and present danger that they will bring about the substantive evils that [the State] has a right to prevent." . . . If what I think the correct test is applied, it is manifest that there was no present danger of an attempt to overthrow the government by force on the part of the admittedly small minority who shared the defendant's views. It is said that this manifesto was more than a theory, that it was an incitement. Every idea is an incitement. It offers itself for belief and if believed it is acted on unless some other belief outweighs it or some failure of energy stifles the movement at its birth. The only difference between the expression of an opinion and an incitement in the narrower sense is the speaker's enthusiasm for the result. Eloquence may set fire to reason. But whatever may be thought of the redundant discourse before us it had no chance of starting a present conflagration. If in the long run the beliefs expressed in proletarian dictatorship are destined to be accepted by the dominant forces of the community, the only meaning of free speech is that they should be given their chance and have their way.

If the publication of this document had been laid as an attempt to induce an uprising against government at once and not at some indefinite time in the future it would have presented a different question. The object would have been one with which the law might deal, subject to the doubt whether there was any danger that the publication could produce any result, or in other words, whether it was not futile and too remote from possible consequences. But the indictment alleges the publication and nothing more.

2. *WEST VIRGINIA BOARD OF EDUCATION* v. *BARNETTE*[1]

EDITORS' NOTE.—In the Gitlow case the Court had agreed that the rights protected by the First Amendment from abridgment by Congress were among the "liberties" protected by the due-process clause of the Fourteenth Amendment from impairment by the states. This reasoning was again applied in the Barnette case.

Often in its history the Court had adjudicated disputes involving limitations which the Fourteenth Amendment placed upon the exercise of the "police power" by the states (Vol. I, p. 284). By locating the "police-power" issue in the domain not of business regulation but of intellectual and religious freedom, the Barnette case adds a new dimension to an old problem.

Mr. Justice JACKSON delivered the opinion of the Court.

Following the decision by this Court on June 3, 1940, in *Minersville School District* v. *Gobitis*, . . . the West Virginia legislature amended its statutes to require all schools therein to conduct courses of instruction in history, civics, and in the Constitutions of the United States and of the State "for the purpose of teaching, fostering and perpetuating the ideals, principles and spirit of Americanism, and increasing the knowledge of the organization and machinery of the government." Appellant Board of Education was directed, with advice of the State Superintendent of Schools, to "prescribe the courses of study covering these subjects" for public schools. The Act made it the duty of private, parochial and denominational schools to prescribe courses of study "similar to those required for the public schools."

The Board of Education on January 9, 1942, adopted a resolution containing recitals taken largely from the Court's *Gobitis* opinion and ordering that the salute to the flag become "a regular part of the program of activities in the public schools," that all teachers and pupils "shall be required to participate in the salute honoring the Nation represented by the Flag; provided, however that refusal to salute the Flag be regarded as an act of in-

subordination, and shall be dealt with accordingly."

The resolution originally required the "commonly accepted salute to the Flag" which it defined. Objections to the salute as "being too much like Hitler's" were raised by the Parent and Teachers Association, the Boy and Girl Scouts, the Red Cross, and the Federation of Women's Clubs. Some modification appears to have been made in deference to these objections, but no concession was made to Jehovah's Witnesses. What is now required is the "stiff-arm" salute, the saluter to keep the right hand raised with palm turned up while the following is repeated: "I pledge allegiance to the Flag of the United States of America and to the Republic for which it stands; one Nation, indivisible, with liberty and justice for all."

Failure to conform is "insubordination" dealt with by expulsion. Readmission is denied by statute until compliance. Meanwhile the expelled child is "unlawfully absent" and may be proceeded against as a delinquent. His parents or guardians are liable to prosecution, and if convicted are subject to fine not exceeding $50 and jail term not exceeding thirty days.

Appellees, citizens of the United States and of West Virginia, brought suit in the United States District Court for themselves and others similarly situated asking its injunction to restrain enforcement of these laws and regulations against Jehovah's Witnesses. The Witnesses are an unincorporated body teaching that the ob-

1. *West Virginia Board of Education* v. *Barnette*, 319 U.S. 624, 625–35, 638–44, 646–52, 664–67 (1943).

ligation imposed by law of God is superior to that of laws enacted by temporal government. Their religious beliefs include a literal version of Exodus, Chapter 20, verses 4 and 5, which says: "Thou shalt not make unto thee any graven image, or any likeness of anything that is in heaven above, or that is in the earth beneath, or that is in the water under the earth; thou shalt not bow down thyself to them nor serve them." They consider that the flag is an "image" within this command. For this reason they refuse to salute it.

Children of this faith have been expelled from school and are threatened with exclusion for no other cause. Officials threaten to send them to reformatories maintained for criminally inclined juveniles. Parents of such children have been prosecuted and are threatened with prosecutions for causing delinquency.

The Board of Education moved to dismiss the complaint setting forth these facts and alleging that the law and regulations are an unconstitutional denial of religious freedom, and of freedom of speech, and are invalid under the "due process" and "equal protection" clauses of the Fourteenth Amendment to the Federal Constitution. The cause was submitted on the pleadings to a District Court of three judges. It restrained enforcement as to the plaintiffs and those of that class. The Board of Education brought the case here by direct appeal.

This case calls upon us to reconsider a precedent decision, as the Court throughout its history often has been required to do. Before turning to the *Gobitis* case, however, it is desirable to notice certain characteristics by which this controversy is distinguished.

The freedom asserted by these appellees does not bring them into collision with rights asserted by any other individual. It is such conflicts which most frequently require intervention of the State to determine where the rights of one end and those of another begin. But the refusal of these persons to participate in the ceremony does not interfere with or deny rights of others to do so. Nor is there any question in this case that their behavior is peaceable and orderly. The sole conflict is between authority and rights of the individual. The State asserts power to condition access to public education on making a prescribed sign and profession and at the same time to coerce attendance by punishing both parent and child. The latter stand on a right of self-determination in matters that touch individual opinion and personal attitude. . . .

There is no doubt that, in connection with the pledges, the flag salute is a form of utterance. Symbolism is a primitive but effective way of communicating ideas. The use of an emblem or flag to symbolize some system, idea, institution, or personality is a short cut from mind to mind. Causes and nations, political parties, lodges and ecclesiastical groups seek to knit the loyalty of their followings to a flag or banner, a color or design. The State announces rank, function, and authority through crowns and maces, uniforms and black robes; the church speaks through the Cross, the Crucifix, the altar and shrine, and clerical raiment. Symbols of State often convey political ideas just as religious symbols come to convey theological ones. Associated with many of these symbols are appropriate gestures of acceptance or respect: a salute, a bowed or bared head, a bended knee. A person gets from a symbol the meaning he puts into it, and what is one man's comfort and inspiration is another's jest and scorn. . . .

It is also to be noted that the compulsory flag salute and pledge requires affirmation of a belief and an attitude of mind. It is not clear whether the regulation contemplates that pupils forego any contrary convictions of their own and become unwilling converts to the prescribed ceremony or whether it will be acceptable if they simulate assent by words without belief and by a gesture barren of meaning. It is now a commonplace that censorship or suppression of expression of opinion is tolerated by our Constitution only when the expression presents a clear and present danger of action of a kind the State is empowered to prevent and punish. It would seem that involuntary affirmation could be commanded only on even more immediate and urgent grounds than silence. But here the power of compulsion is invoked without any allegation that remaining passive during a flag salute ritual creates a clear and present danger that would justify an effort even to muffle expression. To sustain the compulsory flag salute we are required to say that a Bill of Rights which guards the individual's right to speak his own mind, left it open to public authorities to compel him to utter what is not in his mind.

Whether the First Amendment to the Constitution will permit officials to order observance of ritual of this nature does not depend upon whether as a voluntary exercise we would think it to be good, bad or merely innocuous. Any credo of nationalism is likely to include what some disapprove or to omit what others think essential, and to give off different overtones as it takes on different accents or interpretations. If official power exists to coerce acceptance of any patriotic creed, what it shall contain cannot be decided by courts, but must be largely discretionary with the ordaining authority, whose power to prescribe would no doubt include power to amend. Hence validity of the asserted power to force an American citizen publicly to profess any statement of belief or to engage in any ceremony of assent to one, presents questions of power that must be considered independently of any idea we may have as to the utility of the ceremony in question.

Nor does the issue as we see it turn on one's possession of particular religious views or the sincerity with which they are held. While religion supplies appellees' motive for enduring the discomforts of making the issue in this case, many citizens who do not share these religious views hold such a compulsory rite to infringe constitutional liberty of the individual. It is not necessary to inquire whether nonconformist beliefs will exempt from the duty to salute unless we first find power to make the salute a legal duty. . . .

The very purpose of a Bill of Rights was to withdraw certain subjects from the vicissitudes of political controversy, to place them beyond the reach of majorities and officials and to establish them as legal principles to be applied by the courts. One's right to life, liberty, and property, to free speech, a free press, freedom of worship and assembly, and other fundamental rights may not be submitted to vote; they depend on the outcome of no elections.

In weighing arguments of the parties it is important to distinguish between the due process clause of the Fourteenth Amendment as an instrument for transmitting the principles of the First Amendment and those cases in which it is applied for its own sake. The test of legislation which collides with the Fourteenth Amendment, because it also collides with the principles of the First, is much more definite than the test when only the Fourteenth is involved. Much of the vagueness of the due process clause disappears when the specific prohibitions of the First become its standard. The right of a State to regulate, for example, a public utility may well include, so far as the due process test is concerned, power to impose all of the restrictions which a legislature may have a "rational basis" for adopting. But freedoms of speech and of press, of assembly, and of worship may not be infringed on such slender grounds. They are susceptible of restriction only to prevent grave and immediate danger to interests which the State may lawfully protect. It is important to note that while it is the Fourteenth Amendment which bears directly upon the State it is the more specific limiting principles of the First Amendment that finally govern this case.

Nor does our duty to apply the Bill of Rights to assertions of official authority depend upon our possession of marked competence in the field where the invasion of rights occurs. True, the task of translating the majestic generalities of the Bill of Rights, conceived as part of the pattern of liberal government in the eighteenth century, into concrete restraints on officials dealing with the problems of the twentieth century, is one to disturb self-confidence. These principles grew in soil which also produced a philosophy that the individual was the center of society, that his liberty was attainable through mere absence of governmental restraints, and that government should be entrusted with few controls and only the mildest supervision over men's affairs. We must transplant these rights to a soil in which the *laissez-faire* concept or principle of non-interference has withered at least as to economic affairs, and social advancements are increasingly sought through closer integration of society and through expanded and strengthened governmental controls. These changed conditions often deprive precedents of reliability and cast us more than we would choose upon our own judgment. But we act in these matters not by authority of our competence but by force of our commissions. We cannot, because of modest estimates of our competence in such specialties as public education, withhold the judgment that history authenticates as the function of this Court when liberty is infringed. . . .

National unity as an end which officials may foster by persuasion and example is not in question. The problem is whether under our Constitution compulsion as here employed is a permissible means for its achievement.

Struggles to coerce uniformity of sentiment in support of some end thought essential to their time and country have been waged by many good as well as by evil men. Nationalism is a relatively recent phenomenon but at other times and places the ends have been racial or territorial security, support of a dynasty or regime, and particular plans for saving souls. As first and moderate methods to attain unity have failed, those bent on its accomplishment must resort to an ever-increasing severity. As governmental pressure toward unity becomes greater, so strife becomes more bitter as to whose unity it shall be. Probably no deeper division of our people could proceed from any provocation than from finding it necessary to choose what doctrine and whose program public education officials shall compel youth to unite in embracing. Ultimate futility of such attempts to compel coherence is the lesson of every such effort from the Roman drive to stamp out Christianity as a disturber of its pagan unity, the Inquisition, as a means to religious and dynastic unity, the Siberian exiles as a means to Russian unity, down to the fast failing efforts of our present totalitarian enemies. Those who begin coercive elimination of dissent soon find themselves exterminating dissenters. Compulsory unification of opinion achieves only the unanimity of the graveyard.

It seems trite but necessary to say that the First Amendment to our Constitution was designed to avoid these ends by avoiding these beginnings. There is no mysticism in the American concept of the State or of the nature or origin of its authority. We set up government by consent of the governed, and the Bill of Rights denies those in power any legal opportunity to coerce that consent. Authority here is to be controlled by public opinion, not public opinion by authority.

The case is made difficult not because the principles of its decision are obscure but because the flag involved is our own. Nevertheless, we apply the limitations of the Constitution with no fear that freedom to be intellectually and spiritually diverse or even contrary will disintegrate the social organization. To believe that patriotism will not flourish if patriotic ceremonies are voluntary and spontaneous instead of a compulsory routine is to make an unflattering estimate of the appeal of our institutions to free minds. We can have intellectual individualism and the rich cultural diversities that we owe to exceptional minds only at the price of occasional eccentricity and abnormal attitudes. When they are so harmless to others or to the State as those we deal with here, the price is not too great. But freedom to differ is not limited to things that do not matter much. That would be a mere shadow of freedom. The test of its substance is the right to differ as to things that touch the heart of the existing order.

If there is any fixed star in our constitutional constellation, it is that no official, high or petty, can prescribe what shall be orthodox in politics, nationalism, religion, or other matters of opinion or force citizens to confess by word or act their faith therein. If there are any circumstances which permit an exception, they do not now occur to us.

We think the action of the local authorities in compelling the flag salute and pledge transcends constitutional limitations on their power and invades the sphere of intellect and spirit which it is the purpose of the First Amendment to our Constitution to reserve from all official control.

The decision of this Court in *Minersville School District* v. *Gobitis* and the holdings of those few *per curiam* decisions which preceded and foreshadowed it are overruled, and the judgment enjoining enforcement of the West Virginia Regulation is

Affirmed.

Mr. Justice ROBERTS and Mr. Justice REED adhere to the views expressed by the Court in *Minersville School District* v. *Gobitis*, 310 U.S. 586, and are of the opinion that the judgment below should be reversed.

Mr. Justice BLACK and Mr. Justice DOUGLAS, concurring:

We are substantially in agreement with the opinion just read, but since we originally joined with the Court in the *Gobitis* case, it is appropriate that we make a brief statement of reasons for our change of view.

Reluctance to make the Federal Constitution a rigid bar against state regulation of conduct thought inimical to the public welfare was the controlling influence which moved us to consent to the *Gobitis* decision. Long reflection convinced us that although the principle is sound, its application in the particular case was wrong. . . . We believe that the statute before us fails to accord full scope to the freedom of religion secured to the appellees by the First and Fourteenth Amendments.

The statute requires the appellees to participate in a ceremony aimed at inculcating respect for the flag and for this country. The Jehovah's Witnesses, without any desire to show disrespect for either the flag or the country, interpret the Bible as commanding, at the risk of God's displeasure, that they not go through the form of a pledge of allegiance to any flag. The devoutness of their belief is evidenced by their willingness to suffer persecution and punishment, rather than make the pledge.

No well-ordered society can leave to the individuals an absolute right to make final decisions, unassailable by the State, as to everything they will or will not do. The First Amendment does not go so far. Religious faiths, honestly held, do not free individuals from responsibility to conduct themselves obediently to laws which are either imperatively necessary to protect society as a whole from grave and pressingly imminent dangers or which, without any general prohibition, merely regulate time, place or manner of religious activity. Decision as to the constitutionality of particular laws which strike at the substance of religious tenets and practices must be made by this Court. The duty is a solemn one, and in meeting it we cannot say that a failure, because of religious scruples, to assume a particular physical position and to repeat the words of a patriotic formula creates a grave danger to the nation. Such a statutory exaction is a form of test oath, and the test oath has always been abhorrent in the United States.

Words uttered under coercion are proof of loyalty to nothing but self-interest. Love of country must spring from willing hearts and free minds, inspired by a fair administration of wise laws enacted by the people's elected representatives within the bounds of express constitutional prohibitions. These laws must, to be consistent with the First Amendment, permit the widest toleration of conflicting viewpoints consistent with a society of free men.

Neither our domestic tranquillity in peace nor our martial effort in war depend on compelling little children to participate in a ceremony which ends in nothing for them but a fear of spiritual condemnation. If, as we think, their fears are groundless, time and reason are the proper antidotes for their errors. The ceremonial, when enforced against conscientious objectors, more likely to defeat than to serve its high purpose, is a handy implement for disguised religious persecution. As such, it is inconsistent with our Constitution's plan and purpose. . . .

Mr. Justice FRANKFURTER, dissenting:

One who belongs to the most vilified and persecuted minority in history is not likely to be insensible to the freedoms guaranteed by our Constitution. Were my purely personal attitude relevant I should wholeheartedly associate myself with the general libertarian views in the Court's opinion, representing as they do the thought and action of a lifetime. But as judges we are neither Jew nor Gentile, neither Catholic nor agnostic. We owe equal attachment to the Constitution and are equally bound by our judicial obligations whether we derive our citizenship from the earliest or the latest immigrants to these shores. As a member of this Court I am not justified in writing my private notions of policy into the Constitution, no matter how deeply I may cherish them or how mischievous I may deem their disregard. The duty of a judge who must decide which of two claims before the Court shall prevail, that of a State to enact and enforce laws within its general competence

or that of an individual to refuse obedience because of the demands of his conscience, is not that of the ordinary person. It can never be emphasized too much that one's own opinion about the wisdom or evil of a law should be excluded altogether when one is doing one's duty on the bench. The only opinion of our own even looking in that direction that is material is our opinion whether legislators could in reason have enacted such a law. In the light of all the circumstances, including the history of this question in this Court, it would require more daring than I possess to deny that reasonable legislators could have taken the action which is before us for review. Most unwillingly, therefore, I must differ from my brethren with regard to legislation like this. I cannot bring my mind to believe that the "liberty" secured by the Due Process Clause gives this Court authority to deny to the State of West Virginia the attainment of that which we all recognize as a legitimate legislative end, namely, the promotion of good citizenship, by employment of the means here chosen.

Not so long ago we were admonished that "the only check upon our own exercise of power is our own sense of self-restraint. For the removal of unwise laws from the statute books appeal lies not to the courts but to the ballot and to the processes of democratic government." *United States* v. *Butler*, 297 U.S. 1, 79 (dissent). We have been told that generalities do not decide concrete cases. But the intensity with which a general principle is held may determine a particular issue, and whether we put first things first may decide a specific controversy.

The admonition that judicial self-restraint alone limits arbitrary exercise of our authority is relevant every time we are asked to nullify legislation. The Constitution does not give us greater veto power when dealing with one phase of "liberty" than with another, or when dealing with grade school regulations than with college regulations that offend conscience, as was the case in *Hamilton* v. *Regents.* . . . In neither situation is our function comparable to that of a legislature or are we free to act as though we were a super-legislature. Judicial self-restraint is equally necessary whenever an exercise of political or legislative power is challenged. There is no warrant in the constitutional basis of this Court's authority for attributing different rôles to it depending upon the nature of the challenge to the legislation. Our power does not vary according to the particular provision of the Bill of Rights which is invoked. The right not to have property taken without just compensation has, so far as the scope of judicial power is concerned, the same constitutional dignity as the right to be protected against unreasonable searches and seizures, and the latter has no less claim than freedom of the press or freedom of speech or religious freedom. In no instance is this Court the primary protector of the particular liberty that is invoked. This court has recognized, what hardly could be denied, that all the provisions of the first ten Amendments are "specific" prohibitions, *United States* v. *Carolene Products Co.* . . . But each specific Amendment, in so far as embraced within the Fourteenth Amendment, must be equally respected, and the function of this Court does not differ in passing on the constitutionality of legislation challenged under different Amendments.

When Mr. Justice Holmes, speaking for this Court, wrote that "it must be remembered that legislatures are ultimate guardians of the liberties and welfare of the people in quite as great a degree as the courts," *Missouri, K. & T. Ry. Co.* v. *May,* 194 U.S. 267, 270, he went to the very essence of our constitutional system and the democratic conception of our society. He did not mean that for only some phases of civil government this Court was not to supplant legislatures and sit in judgment upon the right or wrong of a challenged measure. He was stating the comprehensive judicial duty and rôle of this Court in our constitutional scheme when-

ever legislation is sought to be nullified on any ground, namely, that responsibility for legislation lies with legislatures, answerable as they are directly to the people, and this Court's only and very narrow function is to determine whether within the broad grant of authority vested in legislatures they have exercised a judgment for which reasonable justification can be offered.

The framers of the federal Constitution might have chosen to assign an active share in the process of legislation to this Court. They had before them the well-known example of New York's Council of Revision, which had been functioning since 1777. After stating that "laws inconsistent with the spirit of this constitution, or with the public good, may be hastily and unadvisedly passed," the state constitution made the judges of New York part of the legislative process by providing that "all bills which have passed the senate and assembly shall, before they become laws," be presented to a Council of which the judges constituted a majority, "for their revisal and consideration." Art. III, New York Constitution of 1777. Judges exercised this legislative function in New York for nearly fifty years. See Art. I, § 12, New York Constitution of 1821. But the framers of the Constitution denied such legislative powers to the federal judiciary. They chose instead to insulate the judiciary from the legislative function. They did not grant to this Court supervision over legislation.

The reason why from the beginning even the narrow judicial authority to nullify legislation has been viewed with a jealous eye is that it serves to prevent the full play of the democratic process. The fact that it may be an undemocratic aspect of our scheme of government does not call for its rejection or its disuse. But it is the best of reasons, as this Court has frequently recognized, for the greatest caution in its use. . . .

Under our constitutional system the legislature is charged solely with civil concerns of society. If the avowed or intrinsic legislative purpose is either to promote or to discourage some religious community or creed, it is clearly within the constitutional restrictions imposed on legislatures and cannot stand. But it by no means follows that legislative power is wanting whenever a general non-discriminatory civil regulation in fact touches conscientious scruples or religious beliefs of an individual or a group. Regard for such scruples or beliefs undoubtedly presents one of the most reasonable claims for the exertion of legislative accommodation. It is, of course, beyond our power to rewrite the State's requirement, by providing exemptions for those who do not wish to participate in the flag salute or by making some other accommodations to meet their scruples. That wisdom might suggest the making of such accommodations and that school administration would not find it too difficult to make them and yet maintain the ceremony for those not refusing to conform, is outside our province to suggest. Tact, respect, and generosity toward variant views will always commend themselves to those charged with the duties of legislation so as to achieve a maximum of good will and to require a minimum of unwilling submission to a general law. But the real question is, who is to make such accommodations, the courts or the legislature?

This is no dry, technical matter. It cuts deep into one's conception of the democratic process—it concerns no less the practical differences between the means for making these accommodations that are open to courts and to legislatures. A court can only strike down. It can only say "This or that law is void." It cannot modify or qualify, it cannot make exceptions to a general requirement. And it strikes down not merely for a day. At least the finding of unconstitutionality ought not to have ephemeral significance unless the Constitution is to be reduced to the fugitive importance of mere legislation. When we are dealing with the Constitution of the United States, and more particularly with the great safeguards of the Bill of Rights, we are dealing with principles of liberty and justice "so rooted in the traditions and conscience of our people as to be ranked as fundamental"— something without which "a fair and enlightened system of justice would be impossible." . . . If the function of this Court is to be essentially no different from that of a legislature, if the considerations governing constitutional construction are to be substantially those that underlie legislation, then indeed judges should not have life tenure and they should be made directly responsible to the electorate. There have been many but unsuccessful proposals in the last sixty years to amend the Constitution to that end. . . .

. . . [E]very Justice—thirteen in all— who has hitherto participated in judging this matter has at one or more times found no constitutional infirmity in what is now condemned. Only the two Justices sitting for the first time on this matter have not heretofore found this legislation inoffensive to the "liberty" guaranteed by the Constitution. And among the Justices who sustained this measure were outstanding judicial leaders in the zealous enforcement of constitutional safeguards of civil liberties—men like Chief Justice Hughes, Mr. Justice Brandeis, and Mr. Justice Cardozo, to mention only those no longer on the Court.

One's conception of the Constitution cannot be severed from one's conception of a judge's function in applying it. The Court has no reason for existence if it merely reflects the pressures of the day. Our system is built on the faith that men set apart for this special function, freed from the influences of immediacy and from the deflections of worldly ambition, will become able to take a view of longer range than the period of responsibility entrusted to Congress and legislatures. We are dealing with matters as to which legislators and voters have conflicting views. Are we as judges to impose our strong convictions on where wisdom lies? That which three years ago had seemed to five successive

Courts to lie within permissible areas of legislation is now outlawed by the deciding shift of opinion of two Justices. What reason is there to believe that they or their successors may not have another view a few years hence? Is that which was deemed to be of so fundamental a nature as to be written into the Constitution to endure for all times to be the sport of shifting winds of doctrine? Of course, judicial opinions, even as to questions of constitutionality, are not immutable. As has been true in the past, the Court will from time to time reverse its position. But I believe that never before these Jehovah's Witnesses cases (except for minor deviations subsequently retracted) has this Court overruled decisions so as to restrict the powers of democratic government. Always heretofore, it has withdrawn narrow views of legislative authority so as to authorize what formerly it had denied.

In view of this history it must be plain that what thirteen Justices found to be within the constitutional authority of a state, legislators cannot be deemed unreasonable in enacting. Therefore, in denying to the states what heretofore has received such impressive judicial sanction, some other tests of unconstitutionality must surely be guiding the Court than the absence of a rational justification for the legislation. But I know of no other test which this Court is authorized to apply in nullifying legislation.

In the past this Court has from time to time set its views of policy against that embodied in legislation by finding laws in conflict with what was called the "spirit of the Constitution." Such undefined destructive power was not conferred on this Court by the Constitution. Before a duly enacted law can be judicially nullified, it must be forbidden by some explicit restriction upon political authority in the Constitution. Equally inadmissible is the claim to strike down legislation because to us as individuals it seems opposed to the "plan and purpose" of the Constitution. That is too tempting a basis for finding in one's personal views the purposes of the Founders.

The uncontrollable power wielded by this Court brings it very close to the most sensitive areas of public affairs. As appeal from legislation to adjudication becomes more frequent, and its consequences more far-reaching, judicial self-restraint becomes more and not less important, lest we unwarrantably enter social and political domains wholly outside our concern. I think I appreciate fully the objections to the law before us. But to deny that it presents a question upon which men might reasonably differ appears to me to be intolerance. And since men may so reasonably differ, I deem it beyond my constitutional power to assert my view of the wisdom of this law against the view of the State of West Virginia.

Jefferson's opposition to judicial review has not been accepted by history, but it still serves as an admonition against confusion between judicial and political functions. As a rule of judicial self-restraint, it is still as valid as Lincoln's admonition. For those who pass laws not only are under duty to pass laws. They are also under duty to observe the Constitution. And even though legislation relates to civil liberties, our duty of deference to those who have the responsibility for making the laws is no less relevant or less exacting. And this is so especially when we consider the accidental contingencies by which one man may determine constitutionality and thereby confine the political power of the Congress of the United States and the legislatures of forty-eight states. The attitude of judicial humility which these considerations enjoin is not an abdication of the judicial function. It is a due observance of its limits. Moreover, it is to be borne in mind that in a question like this we are not passing on the proper distribution of political power as between the states and the central government. We are not discharging the basic function of this Court as the mediator of powers within the federal system. To strike down a law like this is to deny a power to all government. . . .

3. *KOREMATSU* v. *UNITED STATES*[1]

EDITORS' NOTE.—The Korematsu case was one of three cases which arose out of the problem created by the presence in the United States and especially on the West Coast of Americans of Japanese descent, both citizens and noncitizens, at the time of the Japanese attack on Pearl Harbor. Like *Ex parte Milligan* (Vol. I, pp. 772–78) after the Civil War, the Korematsu case is concerned with the fundamental question of the position of the military power in our public life and, more specifically, with the relationship between constitutional guaranties and security measures taken by the military in a wartime situation.

Mr. Justice BLACK delivered the opinion of the Court.

The petitioner, an American citizen of Japanese descent, was convicted in a federal district court for remaining in San Leandro, California, a "Military Area," contrary to Civilian Exclusion Order No. 34 of the Commanding General of the Western Command, U.S. Army, which directed that after May 9, 1942, all persons of Japanese ancestry should be excluded from that area. No question was raised as to petitioner's loyalty to the United States. The Circuit Court of Appeals affirmed, and the importance of the constitutional question involved caused us to grant certiorari.

It should be noted, to begin with, that all legal restrictions which curtail the civil rights of a single racial group are immediately suspect. That is not to say that all such restrictions are unconstitutional. It is to say that courts must subject them to the most rigid scrutiny. Pressing public necessity may sometimes justify the existence of such restrictions; racial antagonism never can.

In the instant case prosecution of the petitioner was begun by information charging violation of an Act of Congress, of March 21, 1942, 56 Stat. 173, which provides that:

... whoever shall enter, remain in, leave, or commit any act in any military area or military zone prescribed, under the authority of an Executive order of the President, by the Secretary of War, or by any military commander designated by the Secretary of War, contrary to the restrictions applicable to any such area or zone or contrary to the order of the Secretary of War or any such military commander, shall, if it appears that he knew or should have known of the existence and extent of the restrictions or order and that his act was in violation thereof, be guilty of a misdemeanor and upon conviction shall be liable to a fine of not to exceed $5,000 or to imprisonment for not more than one year, or both, for each offense.

Exclusion Order No. 34, which the petitioner knowingly and admittedly violated, was one of a number of military orders and proclamations, all of which were substantially based upon Executive Order No. 9066, 7 Fed. Reg. 1407. That order, issued after we were at war with Japan, declared that "the successful prosecution of the war requires every possible protection against espionage and against sabotage to national-defense material, national-defense premises, and national-defense utilities. . . ."

One of the series of orders and proclamations, a curfew order, which like the exclusion order here was promulgated pursuant to Executive Order 9066, subjected all persons of Japanese ancestry in prescribed West Coast military areas to remain in their residences from 8 P.M. to 6 A.M. As is the case with the exclusion order here, that prior curfew order was designed as a "protection against espio-

1. *Korematsu* v. *United States*, 323 U.S. 214–26, 228–46, 248 (1944).

nage and against sabotage." In *Hirabayashi v. United States*, 320 U.S. 81, we sustained a conviction obtained for violation of the curfew order. The Hirabayashi conviction and this one thus rest on the same 1942 Congressional Act and the same basic executive and military orders, all of which orders were aimed at the twin dangers of espionage and sabotage.

The 1942 Act was attacked in the *Hirabayashi* case as an unconstitutional delegation of power; it was contended that the curfew order and other orders on which it rested were beyond the war powers of the Congress, the military authorities and of the President, as Commander in Chief of the Army; and finally that to apply the curfew order against none but citizens of Japanese ancestry amounted to a constitutionally prohibited discrimination solely on account of race. To these questions, we gave the serious consideration which their importance justified. We upheld the curfew order as an exercise of the power of the government to take steps necessary to prevent espionage and sabotage in an area threatened by Japanese attack.

In the light of the principles we announced in the *Hirabayashi* case, we are unable to conclude that it was beyond the war power of Congress and the Executive to exclude those of Japanese ancestry from the West Coast war area at the time they did. True, exclusion from the area in which one's home is located is a far greater deprivation than constant confinement to the home from 8 P.M. to 6 A.M. Nothing short of apprehension by the proper military authorities of the gravest imminent danger to the public safety can constitutionally justify either. But exclusion from a threatened area, no less than curfew, has a definite and close relationship to the prevention of espionage and sabotage. The military authorities, charged with the primary responsibility of defending our shores, concluded that curfew provided inadequate protection and ordered exclusion. They did so, as pointed out in our *Hira-*

bayashi opinion, in accordance with Congressional authority to the military to say who should, and who should not, remain in the threatened areas.

In this case the petitioner challenges the assumptions upon which we rested our conclusions in the *Hirabayashi* case. He also urges that by May 1942, when Order No. 34 was promulgated, all danger of Japanese invasion of the West Coast had disappeared. After careful consideration of these contentions we are compelled to reject them.

Here, as in the *Hirabayashi* case, ". . . we cannot reject as unfounded the judgment of the military authorities and of Congress that there were disloyal members of that population, whose number and strength could not be precisely and quickly ascertained. We cannot say that the warmaking branches of the government did not have ground for believing that in a critical hour such persons could not readily be isolated and separately dealt with, and constituted a menace to the national defense and safety, which demanded that prompt and adequate measures be taken to guard against it."

Like curfew, exclusion of those of Japanese origin was deemed necessary because of the presence of an unascertained number of disloyal members of the group, most of whom we have no doubt were loyal to this country. It was because we could not reject the finding of the military authorities that it was impossible to bring about an immediate segregation of the disloyal from the loyal that we sustained the validity of the curfew order as applying to the whole group. In the instant case, temporary exclusion of the entire group was rested by the military on the same ground. The judgment that exclusion of the whole group was for the same reason a military imperative answers the contention that the exclusion was in the nature of group punishment based on antagonism to those of Japanese origin. That there were members of the group who retained loyalties to Japan has been confirmed by investigations made subsequent to the exclusion. Approximately five thousand American citizens of Japanese ancestry refused to swear unqualified allegiance to the United States and to renounce allegiance to the Japanese Emperor, and several thousand evacuees requested repatriation to Japan.

We uphold the exclusion order as of the time it was made and when the petitioner violated it. . . . In doing so, we are not unmindful of the hardships imposed by it upon a large group of American citizens. . . . But hardships are part of war, and war is an aggregation of hardships. All citizens alike, both in and out of uniform, feel the impact of war in greater or lesser measure. Citizenship has its responsibilities as well as its privileges, and in time of war the burden is always heavier. Compulsory exclusion of large groups of citizens from their homes, except under circumstances of direst emergency and peril, is inconsistent with our basic governmental institutions. But when under conditions of modern warfare our shores are threatened by hostile forces, the power to protect must be commensurate with the threatened danger. . . .

. . . It is now argued that the validity of the exclusion order cannot be considered apart from the orders requiring him, after departure from the area, to report and to to remain in an assembly or relocation center. The contention is that we must treat these separate orders as one and inseparable; that, for this reason, if detention in the assembly or relocation center would have illegally deprived the petitioner of his liberty, the exclusion order and his conviction under it cannot stand.

We are thus being asked to pass at this time upon the whole subsequent detention program in both assembly and relocation centers, although the only issues framed at the trial related to petitioner's remaining in the prohibited area in violation of the exclusion order. Had petitioner here left the prohibited area and gone to an assembly center we cannot say either as a matter of fact or law that his presence in

that center would have resulted in his detention in a relocation center. Some who did report to the assembly center were not sent to relocation centers, but were released upon condition that they remain outside the prohibited zone until the military orders were modified or lifted. This illustrates that they pose different problems and may be governed by different principles. The lawfulness of one does not necessarily determine the lawfulness of the others. This is made clear when we analyze the requirements of the separate provisions of the separate orders. These separate requirements were that those of Japanese ancestry (1) depart from the area; (2) report to and temporarily remain in an assembly center; (3) go under military control to a relocation center there to remain for an indeterminate period until released conditionally or unconditionally by the military authorities. Each of these requirements, it will be noted, imposed distinct duties in connection with the separate steps in a complete evacuation program. Had Congress directly incorporated into one Act the language of these separate orders, and provided sanctions for their violations, disobedience of any one would have constituted a separate offense. . . . There is no reason why violations of these orders, insofar as they were promulgated pursuant to Congressional enactment, should not be treated as separate offenses.

The *Endo* case . . . graphically illustrates the difference between the validity of an order to exclude and the validity of a detention order after exclusion has been effected.

Since the petitioner has not been convicted of failing to report or to remain in an assembly or relocation center, we cannot in this case determine the validity of those separate provisions of the order. It is sufficient here for us to pass upon the order which petitioner violated. To do more would be to go beyond the issues raised, and to decide momentous questions not contained within the framework of the pleadings or the evidence in this case. It will be time enough to decide the serious constitutional issues which petitioner seeks to raise when an assembly or relocation order is applied or is certain to be applied to him, and we have its terms before us.

Some of the members of the Court are of the view that evacuation and detention in an Assembly Center were inseparable. After May 3, 1942, the date of Exclusion Order No. 34, Korematsu was under compulsion to leave the area not as he would choose but via an Assembly Center. The Assembly Center was conceived as a part of the machinery for group evacuation. The power to exclude includes the power to do it by force if necessary. And any forcible measure must necessarily entail some degree of detention or restraint whatever method of removal is selected. But whichever view is taken, it results in holding that the order under which petitioner was convicted was valid.

It is said that we are dealing here with the case of imprisonment of a citizen in a concentration camp solely because of his ancestry, without evidence or inquiry concerning his loyalty and good disposition towards the United States. Our task would be simple, our duty clear, were this a case involving the imprisonment of a loyal citizen in a concentration camp because of racial prejudice. Regardless of the true nature of the assembly and relocation centers—and we deem it unjustifiable to call them concentration camps with all the ugly connotations that term implies—we are dealing specifically with nothing but an exclusion order. To cast this case into outlines of racial prejudice, without reference to the real military dangers which were presented, merely confuses the issue. Korematsu was not excluded from the Military Area because of hostility to him or his race. He *was* excluded because we are at war with the Japanese Empire, because the properly constituted military authorities feared an invasion of our West Coast and felt constrained to take proper

security measures, because they decided that the military urgency of the situation demanded that all citizens of Japanese ancestry be segregated from the West Coast temporarily and finally, because Congress, reposing its confidence in this time of war in our military leaders—as inevitably it must—determined that they should have the power to do just this. There was evidence of disloyalty on the part of some, the military authorities considered that the need for action was great and time was short. We cannot—by availing ourselves of the calm perspective of hindsight—now say that at that time these actions were unjustified.

Affirmed

Mr. Justice FRANKFURTER, concurring.

. . . I join in the opinion of the Court, but should like to add a few words of my own.

The provisions of the Constitution which confer on the Congress and the President powers to enable this country to wage war are as much part of the Constitution as provisions looking to a nation at peace. And we have had recent occasion to quote approvingly the statement of former Chief Justice Hughes that the war power of the Government is "the power to wage war successfully." . . . Therefore, the validity of action under the war power must be judged wholly in the context of war. That action is not to be stigmatized as lawless because like action in times of peace would be lawless. To talk about a military order that expresses an allowable judgment of war needs by those entrusted with the duty of conducting war as "an unconstitutional order" is to suffuse a part of the Constitution with an atmosphere of unconstitutionality. The respective spheres of action of military authorities and of judges are of course very different. But within their sphere, military authorities are no more outside the bounds of obedience to the Constitution than are judges within theirs. . . . To recognize that military orders are "reasonably expedient military precautions" in time of war and yet to deny them constitutional legitimacy makes of the Constitution an instrument for dialectic subleties not reasonably to be attributed to the hard-headed Framers, of whom a majority had had actual participation in war. If a military order such as that under review does not transcend the means appropriate for conducting war, such action by the military is as constitutional as would be any authorized action by the Interstate Commerce Commission within the limits of the constitutional power to regulate commerce. And being an exercise of the war power explicitly granted by the Constitution for safeguarding the national life by prosecuting war effectively, I find nothing in the Constitution which denies to Congress the power to enforce such a valid military order by making its violation an offense triable in the civil courts. . . .

Mr. Justice ROBERTS.

I dissent, because I think the indisputable facts exhibit a clear violation of Constitutional rights.

This is not a case of keeping people off the streets at night as was *Hirabayashi* v. *United States* . . . nor a case of temporary exclusion of a citizen from an area for his own safety or that of the community, nor a case of offering him an opportunity to go temporarily out of an area where his presence might cause danger to himself or to his fellows. On the contrary, it is the case of convicting a citizen as a punishment for not submitting to imprisonment in a concentration camp, based on his ancestry, and solely because of his ancestry, without evidence or inquiry concerning his loyalty and good disposition towards the United States. If this be a correct statement of the facts disclosed by this record, and facts of which we take judicial notice, I need hardly labor the conclusion that Constitutional rights have been violated.

The Government's argument, and the opinion of the court, in my judgment, erroneously divide that which is single and

indivisible and thus make the case appear as if the petitioner violated a Military Order, sanctioned by Act of Congress, which excluded him from his home, by refusing voluntarily to leave and, so, knowingly and intentionally, defying the order and the Act of Congress.

The petitioner, a resident of San Leandro, Alameda County, California, is a native of the United States of Japanese ancestry who, according to the uncontradicted evidence, is a loyal citizen of the nation. . . .

March 21, 1942, Congress enacted that anyone who knowingly "shall enter, remain in, leave, or commit any act in any military area or military zone prescribed . . . by any military commander . . . contrary to the restrictions applicable to any such area or zone or contrary to the order of . . . any such military commander" shall be guilty of a misdemeanor. This is the Act under which the petitioner was charged. . . .

March 27, 1942, by Proclamation No. 4, the General recited that "it is necessary, in order to provide for the welfare and to insure the orderly evacuation and resettlement of Japanese *voluntarily migrating* from Military Area No. 1, to restrict and regulate such migration"; and ordered that, as of March 29, 1942, "all alien Japanese and persons of Japanese ancestry who are within the limits of Military Area No. 1, be and they are hereby prohibited from leaving that area for any purpose until and to the extent that a future proclamation or order of this headquarters shall so permit or direct." . . .

May 3, 1942, General De Witt issued Civilian Exclusion Order No. 34 providing that, after 12 o'clock May 8, 1942, all persons of Japanese ancestry, both alien and non-alien, were to be excluded from a described portion of Military Area No. 1, which included the County of Alameda, California. . . .

The predicament in which the petitioner thus found himself was this: He was forbidden, by Military Order, to leave the zone in which he lived; he was forbidden, by Military Order, after a date fixed, to be found within that zone unless he were in an Assembly Center located in that zone. General De Witt's report to the Secretary of War concerning the programme of evacuation and relocation of Japanese makes it entirely clear, if it were necessary to refer to that document—and, in the light of the above recitation, I think it is not—that an Assembly Center was a euphemism for a prison. No person within such a center was permitted to leave except by Military Order.

In the dilemma that he dare not remain in his home, or voluntarily leave the area, without incurring criminal penalties, and that the only way he could avoid punishment was to go to an Assembly Center and submit himself to military imprisonment, the petitioner did nothing.

June 12, 1942, an Information was filed in the District Court for Northern California charging a violation of the Act of March 21, 1942, in that petitioner had knowingly remained within the area covered by Exclusion Order No. 34. A demurrer to the information having been overruled, the petitioner was tried under a plea of not guilty and convicted. Sentence was suspended and he was placed on probation for five years. We know, however, in the light of the foregoing recitation, that he was at once taken into military custody and lodged in an Assembly Center. We further know that, on March 18, 1942, the President had promulgated Executive Order No. 9102 establishing the War Relocation Authority under which so-called Relocation Centers, a euphemism for concentration camps, were established pursuant to cooperation between the military authorities of the Western Defense Command and the Relocation Authority, and that the petitioner has been confined either in an Assembly Center, within the zone of which he had lived or has been removed to a Relocation Center where, as the facts disclosed in *Ex parte Endo* . . . demonstrate, he was illegally held in custody.

The Government has argued this case as if the only order outstanding at the time the petitioner was arrested and informed against was Exclusion Order No. 34 ordering him to leave the area in which he resided, which was the basis of the information against him. That argument has evidently been effective. The opinion refers to the *Hirabayashi* case . . . to show that this court has sustained the validity of a curfew order in an emergency. The argument then is that exclusion from a given area of danger, while somewhat more sweeping than a curfew regulation, is of the same nature—a temporary expedient made necessary by a sudden emergency. This, I think, is a substitution of an hypothetical case for the case actually before the court. I might agree with the court's disposition of the hypothetical case. The liberty of every American citizen freely to come and to go must frequently, in the face of sudden danger, be temporarily limited or suspended. The civil authorities must often resort to the expedient of excluding citizens temporarily from a locality. The drawing of fire lines in the case of a conflagration, the removal of persons from the area where a pestilence has broken out, are familiar examples. If the exclusion worked by Exclusion Order No. 34 were of that nature the *Hirabayashi* case would be authority for sustaining it. But the facts above recited, and those set forth in *Ex parte Endo*, . . . show that the exclusion was but a part of an over-all plan for forceable detention. This case cannot, therefore, be decided on any such narrow ground as the possible validity of a Temporary Exclusion Order under which the residents of an area are given an opportunity to leave and go elsewhere in their native land outside the boundaries of a military area. To make the case turn on any such assumption is to shut our eyes to reality.

As I have said above, the petitioner, prior to his arrest, was faced with two diametrically contradictory orders given sanction by the Act of Congress of March

21, 1942. The earlier of those orders made him a criminal if he left the zone in which he resided; the later made him a criminal if he did not leave.

I had supposed that if a citizen was constrained by two laws, or two orders having the force of law, and obedience to one would violate the other, to punish him for violation of either would deny him due process of law. And I had supposed that under these circumstances a conviction for violating one of the orders could not stand.

We cannot shut our eyes to the fact that had the petitioner attempted to violate Proclamation No. 4 and leave the military area in which he lived he would have been arrested and tried and convicted for violation of Proclamation No. 4. The two conflicting orders, one which commanded him to stay and the other which commanded him to go, were nothing but a cleverly devised trap to accomplish the real purpose of the military authority, which was to lock him up in a concentration camp. The only course by which the petitioner could avoid arrest and prosecution was to go to that camp according to instructions to be given him when he reported at a Civil Control Center. We know that is the fact. Why should we set up a figmentary and artificial situation instead of addressing ourselves to the actualities of the case?

These stark realities are met by the suggestion that it is lawful to compel an American citizen to submit to illegal imprisonment on the assumption that he might, after going to the Assembly Center, apply for his discharge by suing out a writ of habeas corpus, as was done in the *Endo* case. . . . The answer, of course, is that where he was subject to two conflicting laws he was not bound, in order to escape violation of one or the other, to surrender his liberty for any period. Nor will it do to say that the detention was a necessary part of the process of evacuation, and so we are here concerned only with the validity of the latter.

Again it is a new doctrine of constitutional law that one indicted for disobedience to an unconstitutional statute may not defend on the ground of the invalidity of the statute but must obey it though he knows it is no law and, after he has suffered the disgrace of conviction and lost his liberty by sentence, then, and not before, seek, from within prison walls, to test the validity of the law.

Moreover, it is beside the point to rest decision in part on the fact that the petitioner, for his own reasons, wished to remain in his home. If, as is the fact, he was constrained so to do, it is indeed a narrow application of constitutional rights to ignore the order which constrained him, in order to sustain his conviction for violation of another contradictory order.

I would reverse the judgment of conviction.

Mr. Justice MURPHY, dissenting.

This exclusion of "all persons of Japanese ancestry, both alien and non-alien," from the Pacific Coast area on a plea of military necessity in the absence of martial law ought not to be approved. Such exclusion goes over "the very brink of constitutional power" and falls into the ugly abyss of racism.

In dealing with matters relating to the prosecution and progress of a war, we must accord great respect and consideration to the judgments of the military authorities who are on the scene and who have full knowledge of the military facts. The scope of their discretion must, as a matter of necessity and common sense, be wide. And their judgments ought not to be overruled lightly by those whose training and duties ill-equip them to deal intelligently with matters so vital to the physical security of the nation.

At the same time, however, it is essential that there be definite limits to military discretion, especially where martial law has not been declared. Individuals must not be left impoverished of their constitutional rights on a plea of military necessity that has neither substance nor support. Thus, like other claims conflicting with the asserted constitutional rights of the individual, the military claim must subject itself to the judicial process of having its reasonableness determined and its conflicts with other interests reconciled. "What are the allowable limits of military discretion, and whether or not they have been overstepped in a particular case, are judicial questions." *Sterling* v. *Constantin.* . . .

The judicial test of whether the Government, on a plea of military necessity, can validly deprive an individual of any of his constitutional rights is whether the deprivation is reasonably related to a public danger that is so "immediate, imminent, and impending" as not to admit of delay and not to permit the intervention of ordinary constitutional processes to alleviate the danger. . . . Civilian Exclusion Order No. 34, banishing from a prescribed area of the Pacific Coast "all persons of Japanese ancestry, both alien and non-alien," clearly does not meet that test. Being an obvious racial discrimination, the order deprives all those within its scope of the equal protection of the laws as guaranteed by the Fifth Amendment. It further deprives these individuals of their constitutional rights to live and work where they will, to establish a home where they choose and to move about freely. In excommunicating them without benefit of hearings, this order also deprives them of all their constitutional rights to procedural due process. Yet no reasonable relation to an "immediate, imminent, and impending" public danger is evident to support this racial restriction which is one of the most sweeping and complete deprivations of constitutional rights in the history of this nation in the absence of martial law.

It must be conceded that the military and naval situation in the spring of 1942 was such as to generate a very real fear of invasion of the Pacific Coast, accompanied by fears of sabotage and espionage in that area. The military command was therefore justified in adopting all reasonable means necessary to combat these dangers. In ad-

judging the military action taken in light of the then apparent dangers, we must not erect too high or too meticulous standards; it is necessary only that the action have some reasonable relation to the removal of the dangers of invasion, sabotage and espionage. But the exclusion, either temporarily or permanently, of all persons with Japanese blood in their veins has no such reasonable relation. And that relation is lacking because the exclusion order necessarily must rely for its reasonableness upon the assumption that *all* persons of Japanese ancestry may have a dangerous tendency to commit sabotage and espionage and to aid our Japanese enemy in other ways. It is difficult to believe that reason, logic or experience could be marshalled in support of such an assumption.

That this forced exclusion was the result in good measure of this erroneous assumption of racial guilt rather than bona fide military necessity is evidenced by the Commanding General's Final Report on the evacuation from the Pacific Coast area. In it he refers to all individuals of Japanese descent as "subversive," as belonging to "an enemy race" whose "racial strains are undiluted," and as constituting "over 112,000 potential enemies . . . at large today" along the Pacific Coast. In support of this blanket condemnation of all persons of Japanese descent, however, no reliable evidence is cited to show that such individuals were generally disloyal, or had generally so conducted themselves in this area as to constitute a special menace to defense installations or war industries, or had otherwise by their behavior furnished reasonable ground for their exclusion as a group.

Justification for the exclusion is sought, instead, mainly upon questionable racial and sociological grounds not ordinarily within the realm of expert military judgment, supplemented by certain semi-military conclusions drawn from an unwarranted use of circumstantial evidence. Individuals of Japanese ancestry are condemned because they are said to be "a large, unassimilated, tightly knit racial group, bound to an enemy nation by strong ties of race, culture, and religion." They are claimed to be given to "emperor worshipping ceremonies" and to "dual citizenship." Japanese language schools and allegedly pro-Japanese organizations are cited as evidence of possible group disloyalty, together with facts as to certain persons being educated and residing at length in Japan. It is intimated that many of these individuals deliberately resided "adjacent to strategic points," thus enabling them "to carry into execution a tremendous program of sabotage on a mass scale should any considerable number of them have been inclined to do so." The need for protective custody is also asserted. The report refers without identity to "numerous incidents of violence" as well as to other admittedly unverified or cumulative incidents. From this, plus certain other events not shown to have been connected with the Japanese Americans, it is concluded that the "situation was fraught with danger to the Japanese population itself" and that the general public "was ready to take matters into its own hands." Finally, it is intimated, though not directly charged or proved, that persons of Japanese ancestry were responsible for three minor isolated shellings and bombings of the Pacific Coast area, as well as for unidentified radio transmissions and night signalling.

The main reasons relied upon by those responsible for the forced evacuation, therefore, do not prove a reasonable relation between the group characteristics of Japanese Americans and the dangers of invasion, sabotage and espionage. The reasons appear, instead, to be largely an accumulation of much of the misinformation, half-truths and insinuations that for years have been directed against Japanese Americans by people with racial and economic prejudices—the same people who have been among the foremost advocates of the evacuation. A military judgment based upon such racial and sociological considerations is not entitled to the great weight ordinarily given the judgments based upon strictly military considerations. Especially is this so when every charge relative to race, religion, culture, geographical location, and legal and economic status has been substantially discredited by independent studies made by experts in these matters.

The military necessity which is essential to the validity of the evacuation order thus resolves itself into a few intimations that certain individuals actively aided the enemy, from which it is inferred that the entire group of Japanese Americans could not be trusted to be or remain loyal to the United States. No one denies, of course, that there were some disloyal persons of Japanese descent on the Pacific Coast who did all in their power to aid their ancestral land. Similar disloyal activities have been engaged in by many persons of German, Italian and even more pioneer stock in our country. But to infer that examples of individual disloyalty prove group disloyalty and justify discriminatory action against the entire group is to deny that under our system of law individual guilt is the sole basis for deprivation of rights. Moreover, this inference, which is at the very heart of the evacuation orders, has been used in support of the abhorrent and despicable treatment of minority groups by the dictatorial tyrannies which this nation is now pledged to destroy. To give constitutional sanction to that inference in this case, however well-intentioned may have been the military command on the Pacific Coast, is to adopt one of the cruelest of the rationales used by our enemies to destroy the dignity of the individual and to encourage and open the door to discriminatory actions against other minority groups in the passions of tomorrow.

No adequate reason is given for the failure to treat these Japanese Americans on an individual basis by holding investigations and hearings to separate the loyal from the disloyal, as was done in the case of persons of German and Italian ancestry. . . . It is asserted merely that the loyalties of this group "were unknown and time was of the essence." Yet nearly four months elapsed after Pearl Harbor before the first exclusion order was issued; nearly eight months went by until the last order was issued; and the last of these "subversive" persons was not actually removed until almost eleven months had elapsed. Leisure and deliberation seem to have been more of the essence than speed. And the fact that conditions were not such as to warrant a declaration of martial law adds strength to the belief that the factors of time and military necessity were not as urgent as they have been represented to be.

Moreover, there was no adequate proof that the Federal Bureau of Investigation and the military and naval intelligence services did not have the espionage and sabotage situation well in hand during this long period. Nor is there any denial of the fact that not one person of Japanese ancestry was accused or convicted of espionage or sabotage after Pearl Harbor while they were still free, a fact which is some evidence of the loyalty of the vast majority of these individuals and of the effectiveness of the established methods of combatting these evils. It seems incredible that under these circumstances it would have been impossible to hold loyalty hearings for the mere 112,000 persons involved —or at least for the 70,000 American citizens—especially when a large part of this number represented children and elderly men and women. Any inconvenience that may have accompanied an attempt to conform to procedural due process cannot be said to justify violations of constitutional rights of individuals.

I dissent, therefore, from this legalization of racism. Racial discrimination in any form and in any degree has no justifiable part whatever in our democratic way of life. It is unattractive in any setting but it is utterly revolting among a free people who have embraced the principles set forth in the constitution of the United States. All residents of this nation are kin in some way by blood or culture to a foreign land. Yet they are primarily and necessarily a part of the new and distinct civilization of the United States. They must accordingly be treated at all times as the heirs of the American experiment and as entitled to all the rights and freedoms guaranteed by the Constitution.

Mr. Justice JACKSON, dissenting.

Korematsu . . . has been convicted of an act not commonly a crime. It consists merely of being present in the state whereof he is a citizen, near the place where he was born, and where all his life he has lived. . . .

A citizen's presence in the locality, however, was made a crime only if his parents were of Japanese birth. . . .

Now, if any fundamental assumption underlies our system, it is that guilt is personal and not inheritable. Even if all of one's antecedents had been convicted of treason, the Constitution forbids its penalties to be visited upon him, for it provides that "no attainder of treason shall work corruption of blood, or forfeiture except during the life of the person attainted." But here is an attempt to make an otherwise innocent act a crime merely because this prisoner is the son of parents as to whom he had no choice, and belongs to a race from which there is no way to resign. If Congress in peace-time legislation should enact such a criminal law, I should suppose this Court would refuse to enforce it.

But the "law" which this prisoner is convicted of disregarding is not found in an act of Congress, but in a military order. Neither the Act of Congress nor the Executive Order of the President, nor both together, would afford a basis for this conviction. It rests on the orders of General De Witt. And it is said that if the military commander had reasonable military grounds for promulgating the orders, they are constitutional and become law, and the Court is required to enforce them. There are several reasons why I cannot subscribe to this doctrine.

It would be impracticable and dangerous idealism to expect or insist that each specific military command in an area of probable operations will conform to conventional tests of constitutionality. When an area is so beset that it must be put under military control at all, the paramount consideration is that its measures be successful, rather than legal. The armed services must protect a society, not merely its Constitution. The very essence of the military job is to marshal physical force, to remove every obstacle to its effectiveness, to give it every strategic advantage. Defense measures will not, and often should not, be held within the limits that bind civil authority in peace. No court can require such a commander in such circumstances to act as a reasonable man; he may be unreasonably cautious and exacting. Perhaps he should be. But a commander in temporarily focusing the life of a community on defense is carrying out a military program; he is not making law in the sense the courts know the term. He issues orders, and they may have a certain authority as military commands, although they may be very bad as constitutional law.

But if we cannot confine military expedients by the Constitution, neither would I distort the Constitution to approve all that the military may deem expedient. That is what the Court appears to be doing, whether consciously or not. I cannot say, from any evidence before me, that the orders of General De Witt were not reasonably expedient military precautions, nor could I say that they were. But even if they were permissible military procedures, I deny that it follows that they are constitutional. If, as the Court holds, it does follow, then we may as well say that any military order will be constitutional and have done with it.

The limitation under which courts always will labor in examining the necessity for a military order are illustrated by this case. How does the Court know that these orders have a reasonable basis in necessity? No evidence whatever on that subject has been taken by this or any other court. There is sharp controversy as to the credibility of the De Witt report. So the Court, having no real evidence before it, has no choice but to accept General De Witt's own unsworn, self-serving statement, untested by any cross-examination, that what he did was reasonable. And thus it will always be when courts try to look into the reasonableness of a military order.

In the very nature of things, military decisions are not susceptible of intelligent judicial appraisal. They do not pretend to rest on evidence, but are made on information that often would not be admissible and on assumptions that could not be proved. Information in support of an order could not be disclosed to courts without danger that it would reach the enemy. Neither can courts act on communications made in confidence. Hence courts can never have any real alternative to accepting the mere declaration of the authority that issued the order that it was reasonably necessary from a military viewpoint.

Much is said of the danger to liberty from the Army program for deporting and detaining these citizens of Japanese extraction. But a judicial construction of the due process clause that will sustain this order is a far more subtle blow to liberty than the promulgation of the order itself. A military order, however unconstitutional, is not apt to last longer than the military emergency. Even during that period a succeeding commander may revoke it all. But once a judicial opinion rationalizes such an order to show that it conforms to the Constitution, or rather rationalizes the Constitution to show that the Constitution sanctions such an order, the Court for all time has validated the principle of racial discrimination in criminal procedure and of transplanting American citizens. The principle then lies about like a loaded weapon ready for the hand of any authority that can bring forward a plausible claim of an urgent need. Every repetition imbeds that principle more deeply in our law and thinking and expands it to new purposes. All who observe the work of courts are familiar with what Judge Cardozo described as "the tendency of a principle to expand itself to the limit of its logic." A military commander may overstep the bounds of constitutionality, and it is an incident. But if we review and approve, that passing incident becomes the doctrine of the Constitution. There it has a generative power of its own, and all that it creates will be in its own image. Nothing better illustrates this danger than does the Court's opinion in this case. . . .

Of course the existence of a military power resting on force, so vagrant, so centralized, so necessarily heedless of the individual, is an inherent threat to liberty. But I would not lead people to rely on this Court for a review that seems to me wholly delusive. The military reasonableness of these orders can only be determined by military superiors. If the people ever let command of the war power fall into irresponsible and unscrupulous hands, the courts wield no power equal to its restraint. The chief restraint upon those who command the physical forces of the country, in the future as in the past, must be their responsibility to the political judgments of their contemporaries and to the moral judgments of history.

My duties as a justice as I see them do not require me to make a military judgment as to whether General De Witt's evacuation and detention program was a reasonable military necessity. I do not suggest that the courts should have attempted to interfere with the Army in carrying out its task. But I do not think they may be asked to execute a military expedient that has no place in law under the Constitution. I would reverse the judgment and discharge the prisoner.

4. "TO SECURE THESE RIGHTS"[1]

By the PRESIDENT'S COMMITTEE ON CIVIL RIGHTS

EDITORS' NOTE.—Harry S. Truman emerged from the traditional obscurity of the vice-presidency by a chance event, the death of President Franklin D. Roosevelt in April, 1945. By the end of 1947 the new President had underwritten a bold and comprehensive civil rights program, an action which defied the powerful southern interests in the Democratic party. One southern counterstroke, the Dixiecrat revolt of 1948, failed to defeat Truman at the polls. A second, the resort to filibustering tactics in the Senate, has proved at least temporarily effective in blocking federal civil rights legislation.

"To Secure These Rights" is the report issued late in 1947 by the President's Committee on Civil Rights. The findings and recommendations of the committee in part form the basis for pending legislation. An earlier controversy over federal action in this field may be found in the civil rights cases of 1883 (Vol. I, p. 787).

THE ESSENTIAL RIGHTS

The men who founded our Republic, as those who have built any constitutional democracy, faced the task of reconciling personal liberty and group authority, or of establishing an equilibrium between them.

In a democratic state we recognize that the common interests of the people must

1. "To Secure These Rights": The Report of the President's Committee on Civil Rights (Washington, 1947), pp. 5–9, 20, 23–25, 29–30, 35–36, 39–40, 53, 55–57, 74–75, 77–78, 81–83, 87, 99–104, 151, 153–63, 166–70, 172–73.

be managed by laws and procedures established by majority rule. But a democratic majority, left unrestrained, may be as ruthless and tyrannical as were the earlier absolute monarchs. Seeing this clearly, and fearing it greatly, our forefathers built a constitutional system in which valued personal liberties, carefully enumerated in a Bill of Rights, were placed beyond the reach of popular majorities. Thus the people permanently denied the federal government power to interfere with certain personal rights and freedoms.

Freedom, however, as we now use the term, means even more than the traditional "freedoms" listed in our Bill of Rights —important as they are. . . .

Four basic rights have seemed important to this Committee and have influenced its labors. We believe that each of these rights is essential to the well-being of the individual and to the progress of society.

1. *The right to safety and security of the person.*—Freedom can exist only where the citizen is assured that his person is secure against bondage, lawless violence, and arbitrary arrest and punishment. Freedom from slavery in all its forms is clearly necessary if all men are to have equal opportunity to use their talents and to lead worthwhile lives. Moreover, to be free, men must be subject to discipline by society only for commission of offenses clearly defined by law and only after trial by due process of law. Where the administration of justice is discriminatory, no man can be sure of security. Where the threat of violence by private persons or mobs exists, a cruel inhibition of the sense of freedom of activity and security of the person inevitably results. Where a society permits private and arbitrary violence to be done to its members, its own integrity is inevitably corrupted. It cannot permit human beings to be imprisoned or killed in the absence of due process of law without degrading its entire fabric.

2. *The right to citizenship and its privileges.*—Since it is a purpose of govern-ment in a democracy to regulate the activity of each man in the interest of all men, it follows that every mature and responsible person must be able to enjoy full citizenship and have an equal voice in his government. Because the right to participate in the political process is customarily limited to citizens there can be no denial of access to citizenship based upon race, color, creed, or national origin. Denial of citizenship for these reasons cheapens the personality of those who are confined to this inferior status and endangers the whole concept of a democratic society.

To deny qualified citizens the right to vote while others exercise it is to do violence to the principle of freedom and equality. Without the right to vote, the individual loses his voice in the group effort and is subjected to rule by a body from which he has been excluded. Likewise, the right of the individual to vote is important to the group itself. Democracy assumes that the majority is more likely as a general rule to make decisions which are wise and desirable from the point of view of the interests of the whole society than is any minority. Every time a qualified person is denied a voice in public affairs, one of the components of a potential majority is lost, and the formation of a sound public policy is endangered.

To the citizen in a democracy, freedom is a precious possession. Accordingly, all able-bodied citizens must enjoy the right to serve the nation and the cause of freedom in time of war. Any attempt to curb the right to fight in its defense can only lead the citizen to question the worth of the society in which he lives. A sense of frustration is created which is wholly alien to the normal emotions of a free man. In particular, any discrimination which, while imposing an obligation, prevents members of minority groups from rendering full military service in defense of their country is for them a peculiarly humiliating badge of inferiority. The nation also suffers a loss of manpower and is unable to marshal maximum strength at a moment when such strength is most needed.

3. *The right to freedom of conscience and expression.*—In a free society there is faith in the ability of the people to make sound, rational judgments. But such judgments are possible only where the people have access to all relevant facts and to all prevailing interpretations of the facts. How can such judgments be formed on a sound basis if arguments, viewpoints, or opinions are arbitrarily suppressed? How can the concept of the marketplace of thought in which truth ultimately prevails retain its validity if the thought of certain individuals is denied the right of circulation? The Committee reaffirms our tradition that freedom of expression may be curbed by law only where the danger to the well-being of society is clear and present.

Our forefathers fought bloody wars and suffered torture and death for the right to worship God according to the varied dictates of conscience. Complete religious liberty has been accepted as an unquestioned personal freedom since our Bill of Rights was adopted. We have insisted only that religious freedom may not be pleaded as an excuse for criminal or clearly anti-social conduct.

4. *The right to equality of opportunity.*—It is not enough that full and equal membership in society entitles the individual to an equal voice in the control of his government; it must also give him the right to enjoy the benefits of society and to contribute to its progress. The opportunity of each individual to obtain useful employment, and to have access to services in the fields of education, housing, health, recreation and transportation, whether available free or at a price, must be provided with complete disregard for race, color, creed, and national origin. Without this equality of opportunity the individual is deprived of the chance to develop his potentialities and to share the fruits of society. The group also suffers through the loss of the contributions which might have been made by persons excluded from the main channels of social and economic activity. . . .

THE CONDITION OF OUR RIGHTS[2]

THE CRIME OF LYNCHING . . .

While available statistics show that, decade by decade, lynchings have decreased, this Committee has found that in the year 1947 lynching remains one of the most serious threats to the civil rights of Americans. It is still possible for a mob to abduct and murder a person in some sections of the country with almost certain assurance of escaping punishment for the crime. The decade from 1936 through 1946 saw at least 43 lynchings. No person received the death penalty, and the majority of the guilty persons were not even prosecuted.

The communities in which lynchings occur tend to condone the crime. Punishment of lynchers is not accepted as the responsibility of state or local governments in these communities. Frequently, state officials participate in the crime, actively or passively. Federal efforts to punish the crime are resisted. Condonation of lynching is indicated by the failure of some local law enforcement officials to make adequate efforts to break up a mob. It is further shown by failure in most cases to make any real effort to apprehend or try those guilty. If the federal government enters a case, local officials sometimes actively resist the federal investigation. Local citizens often combine to impede the effort to apprehend the criminals by convenient "loss of memory"; grand juries refuse to indict; trial juries acquit in the face of overwhelming proof of guilt.

The large number of attempted lynchings highlights, even more than those which have succeeded, the widespread

2. "The Committee's first task was the interpretation of its assignment. We were not asked to evaluate the extent to which civil rights have been achieved in our country. We did not, therefore, devote ourselves to the construction of a balance sheet which would properly assess the great progress which the nation has made, as well as the shortcomings in the record. Instead, we have almost exclusively focused our attention on the bad side of our record—on what might be called the civil rights frontier."

readiness of many communities to resort to mob violence. Thus, for seven of the years from 1937 to 1946 for which statistics are reported, the conservative estimates of the Tuskegee Institute show that 226 persons were rescued from threatened lynching. Over 200 of these were Negroes. . . .

The devastating consequences of lynchings go far beyond what is shown by counting the victims. When a person is lynched and the lynchers go unpunished, thousands wonder where the evil will appear again and what mischance may produce another victim. And every time lynchers go unpunished, Negroes have learned to expect other forms of violence at the hands of private citizens or public officials. In describing the thwarted efforts of the Department of Justice to identify those responsible for one lynching, J. Edgar Hoover stated to the Committee: "The arrogance of most of the white population of that county was unbelievable, and the fear of the Negroes was almost unbelievable."

The almost complete immunity from punishment enjoyed by lynchers is merely a striking form of the broad and general immunity from punishment enjoyed by whites in many communities for less extreme offenses against Negroes. Moreover, lynching is the ultimate threat by which his inferior status is driven home to the Negro. As a terrorist device, it reinforces all the other disabilities placed upon him. The threat of lynching always hangs over the head of the southern Negro; the knowledge that a misinterpreted word or action can lead to his death is a dreadful burden. . . .

INVOLUNTARY SERVITUDE

Slavery was abolished in this country nearly a century ago, and in its traditional form has disappeared. But the temptation to force poor and defenseless persons, by one device or another, into a condition of virtual slavery, still exists. As recently as 1944, in the case of *Pollock* v. *Williams*, the

Supreme Court struck down as a violation of the Thirteenth Amendment to the Constitution an Alabama statute which enabled employers to force employees, in debt on account of advanced wage payments, to continue to work for them under threat of criminal punishment. This is one of the more subtle devices for securing forced labor. More direct is the practice whereby sheriffs in some areas free prisoners into the custody of local entrepreneurs who pay fines or post bonds. The prisoners then work for their "benefactors" under threat of returning to jail. Sometimes the original charge against the prisoners is trumped up for the purpose of securing labor by this means. In still other instances persons have been held in peonage by sheer force or by threats of prosecution for debt. . . .

Where large numbers of people are frightened, uneducated, and underprivileged, the dangers of involuntary servitude remain. If economic conditions deteriorate, a more general recurrence of peonage may be anticipated. . . .

THE RIGHT TO VOTE

The right of all qualified citizens to vote is today considered axiomatic by most Americans. To achieve universal adult suffrage we have carried on vigorous political crusades since the earliest days of the Republic. In theory the aim has been achieved, but in fact there are many backwaters in our political life where the right to vote is not assured to every qualified citizen. The franchise is barred to some citizens because of race; to others by institutions or procedures which impede free access to the polls. Still other Americans are in substance disfranchised whenever electoral irregularities or corrupt practices dissipate their votes or distort their intended purpose. Some citizens— permanent residents of the District of Columbia—are excluded from political representation and the right to vote as a result of outmoded national traditions. As a result of such restrictions, all of these citizens are limited, in varying degrees, in their opportunities to seek office and to influence the conduct of government on an equal plane with other American citizens.

The denial of the suffrage on account of race is the most serious present interference with the right to vote. Until very recently, American Negro citizens in most southern states found it difficult to vote. Some Negroes have voted in parts of the upper South for the last twenty years. In recent years the situation in the deep South has changed to the point where it can be said that Negroes are beginning to exercise the political rights of free Americans. In the light of history, this represents progress, limited and precarious, but nevertheless progress. . . .

Until 1944, the white primary, by which participation in the Democratic primary is limited to white citizens, was used in Texas, Alabama, Arkansas, Georgia, Louisiana, and Mississippi as the most effective modern "legal" device for disfranchising Negroes. While some southern Negroes succeeded in spite of various obstacles in voting in general elections, almost none voted in the Democratic primaries. Since the Democratic primary is the only election of any significance, the device of the white primary resulted in exclusion of Negroes from government in these states. Over a period of time, advocates of white supremacy had refined this device to the point where it seemed to be constitutionally foolproof. The command of the Fifteenth Amendment, prohibiting states from abridging suffrage because of race or color, was circumvented by purporting to vest the power to exclude Negroes in the political party rather than in the state.

But in 1944, the United States Supreme Court in the case of *Smith* v. *Allwright* overruled an earlier decision and held the Texas white primary illegal. It declared that the exclusion rules of the Texas Democratic Party were in effect the rules of the state and were therefore forbidden by the Fifteenth Amendment.

Some states adapted their primary laws to the Supreme Court ruling, others resisted, first, by refusing to open white primaries to Negroes until further litigation made the Texas ruling applicable to them, then, by devising other methods of depriving Negroes of the ballot. Today the effort to preserve the pure white electoral system in these states is continuing. . . .

The poll tax—another important legal obstacle to full suffrage in some southern states—limits white as well as Negro suffrage. The poll tax has frequently had an unequal racial effect, since, like the "understand and explain" clauses, it has been administered in a discriminatory manner. It has been very effective as an anti-Negro device. A poll tax simply places the payment of a fee between the voter and the ballot box. In some states it is cumulative; taxes not paid in years when the voter does not go to the polls pile up and he must pay more than one year's tax before he can vote. The poll tax has curtailed the size of the entire electorate, white and Negro. Seven states—Alabama, Arkansas, Mississippi, South Carolina, Tennessee, Texas, and Virginia—still maintain this tax as a prerequisite to voting. Since 1921 four other states have abandoned the poll tax. These are North Carolina, Louisiana, Florida, and Georgia.

It was estimated on the floor of the House of Representatives on July 21, 1947, that:

In the Presidential elections of 1944, 10 percent of the potential voters voted in the seven poll-tax states, as against 49 percent in the free-vote states. In the congressional elections of 1946, the figures are 5 percent for the poll-tax states as compared with 33 percent for the free-voting states. . . .

In addition to formal, legal methods of disfranchisement, there are the long-standing techniques of terror and intimidation, in the face of which great courage is required of the Negro who tries to vote. In the regions most characterized by generalized violence against Negroes, little more than "advice" is often necessary to frighten them away from the polls. They have learned, through the years, to discover threats in mood and atmosphere. In one case in a deep southern state, a middle-class Negro who had courageously attempted to vote and to complain to the Department of Justice when he was refused access to the polls, subsequently became so afraid of reprisal that he indicated uncertainty whether he would be willing to testify in court. He asked, if he should decide to testify, to be given ample notice of the date so that he could first move his family out of the region. . . .

THE RIGHT TO EMPLOYMENT

A man's right to an equal chance to utilize fully his skills and knowledge is essential. The meaning of a job goes far beyond the paycheck. Good workers have a pride in the organization for which they work and feel satisfaction in the jobs they are doing. A witness before a congressional committee has recently said:

Discrimination in employment damages lives, both the bodies and the minds, of those discriminated against and those who discriminate. It blights and perverts that healthy ambition to improve one's standard of living which we like to say is peculiarly American. It generates insecurity, fear, resentment, division and tension in our society. . . .

Discrimination is most acutely felt by minority group members in their inability to get a job suited to their qualifications. Exclusions of Negroes, Jews, or Mexicans in the process of hiring is effected in various ways—by newspaper advertisements requesting only whites or gentiles to apply, by registration or application blanks on which a space is reserved for "race" or "religion," by discriminatory job orders placed with employment agencies, or by the arbitrary policy of a company official in charge of hiring. . . .

Discrimination in hiring has forced many minority workers into low-paying and often menial jobs such as common laborer and domestic servant. This has done much to bring about the situation re-

ported by the Bureau of the Census in 1940—

Striking differences between the occupations of whites and Negroes were shown in 1940 census statistics. Farmers, farm laborers, and other laborers constituted 62.2 percent of all employed Negro men and only 28.5 percent of all employed white men. Only about 5 percent of all employed Negro men, compared with approximately 30 percent of employed white men, were engaged in professional, semiprofessional, proprietary, managerial, and clerical or sales occupations. Skilled craftsmen represented 15.6 percent of employed white men and only 4.4 percent of employed Negro men. More than half of the Negro craftsmen were mechanics, carpenters, painters, plasterers and cement finishers, and masons. . . .

THE RIGHT TO PUBLIC SERVICES
AND ACCOMMODATIONS

Services supplied by the government should be distributed in a non-discriminatory way. Activities financed by the public treasury should serve the whole people; they cannot, in consonance with the democratic principle, be used to advance the welfare of a portion of the population only. Moreover, many privately-owned and operated enterprises should recognize a responsibility to sell to all who wish to buy their services. They cannot be permitted to confine their benefits to a selected clientele. This is particularly true of those private businesses which hold franchises from the state or enjoy a monopoly status. Even when no franchise has been granted, and competition exists, certain private businesses because of the essential character of the services they render should serve all comers. It has been made clear to the Committee that unfortunately, many public services, supplied by both government and private business, do not reach all persons on an equality of access basis. . . .

Eighteen states have statutes prohibiting discrimination in places of public accommodation. These states prohibit discrimination in restaurants, and usually in other eating places. Most of them prohibit discrimination in public conveyances of all types, and over half of them, in theaters and barber shops. All include some general phrase, such as "and all other places of public accommodation." The courts, however, have tended to limit this general phrasing by the list of specific places. The statutes can be enforced by criminal action or by a civil suit for damages.

At the other extreme, 20 states by law compel segregation in one way or another. The remaining 10 states have no laws on the subject. In the states with compulsory segregation laws Negroes are usually separated from whites in all forms of public transportation, and in hotels, restaurants, and places of amusement. . . .

In the states which do legally secure the right of access, practice does not necessarily conform to the law. One prominent Negro has stated that it is difficult to find a meal or a hotel room in the downtown areas of most northern cities. The display of "whites only" signs may sometimes go unchallenged. When laws guaranteeing equal access to places of public accommodation are enforced, the penalty is usually small and the chance of being prosecuted or sued a second time is slight.

Devices to get around the law are more common than direct violation of the law. Unwanted customers are discouraged from patronizing places by letting them wait indefinitely for service, charging higher prices, giving poor service, and publicly embarrassing them in various ways. . . .

SEGREGATION RECONSIDERED . . .

. . . Segregation has become the cornerstone of the elaborate structure of discrimination against some American citizens. Theoretically this system simply duplicates educational, recreational and other public services, according facilities to the two races which are "separate but equal." In the Committee's opinion this is one of the outstanding myths of American history for it is almost always true that while indeed separate, these facilities are far from equal. Throughout the segregated public institutions, Negroes have been denied an equal share of tax-supported services and facilities. So far as private institutions are concerned, there is no specific legal disability on the right of Negroes to develop equal institutions of their own. However, the economic, social, and indirect legal obstacles to this course are staggering. . . .

. . . In any event we believe that not even the most mathematically precise equality of segregated institutions can properly be considered equality under the law. No argument or rationalization can alter this basic fact: a law which forbids a group of American citizens to associate with other citizens in the ordinary course of daily living creates inequality by imposing a caste status on the minority group.

If reason and history were not enough to substantiate the argument against segregation, recent experiences further strengthen it. For these experiences demonstrate that segregation is an obstacle to establishing harmonious relationships among groups. They prove that where the artificial barriers which divide people and groups from one another are broken, tension and conflict begin to be replaced by cooperative effort and an environment in which civil rights can thrive. . . .

More than 400 merchant seamen were asked a series of indirect questions which were then built into an "Index of Prejudice Against Negroes." The results reported by Ira N. Brophy in the *Public Opinion Quarterly*, Winter, 1945–46, were surprising. They demonstrated that whether a man had been born in the North or the South was not important in determining whether he was prejudiced against Negroes. The extent of his education and the jobs he had held before he went to sea were not important. What was important was whether the men were members of unions with tolerant policies toward Negroes; how many trips to sea a man had made; how many times he had been under enemy fire; and how many times he had been to sea with Negroes. Here again what determined whether a white man was prejudiced against Negroes was the kind and amount of experience he had had with them. Where there was contact with Negroes on an equal footing in a situation of mutual dependence and common effort prejudice declined. . . .

The Committee is not convinced that an end to segregation in education or in the enjoyment of public services essential to people in a modern society would mean an intrusion upon the private life of the individual. In a democracy, each individual must have freedom to choose his friends and to control the pattern of his personal and family life. But we see nothing inconsistent between this freedom and a recognition of the truth that democracy also means that in going to school, working, participating in the political process, serving in the armed forces, enjoying government services in such fields as health and recreation, making use of transportation and other public accommodation facilities, and living in specific communities and neighborhoods, distinctions of race, color, and creed have no place. . . .

GOVERNMENT'S RESPONSIBILITY
SECURING THE RIGHTS

The National Government of the United States must take the lead in safeguarding the civil rights of all Americans. We believe that this is one of the most important observations that can be made about the civil rights problem in our country today. We agree with words used by the President, in an address at the Lincoln Memorial in Washington in June, 1947:

We must make the Federal Government a friendly, vigilant defender of the rights and equalities of all Americans. . . . Our National Government must show the way.

It is essential that our rights be preserved against the tyrannical actions of public officers. Our forefathers saw the need for such protection when they gave

us the Bill of Rights as a safeguard against arbitrary government. But this is not enough today. We need more than protection of our rights against government; we need protection of our rights against private persons or groups, seeking to undermine them. In the words of the President:

We cannot be content with a civil liberties program which emphasizes only the need of protection against the possibility of tyranny by the Government. . . . We must keep moving forward, with new concepts of civil rights to safeguard our heritage. The extension of civil rights today means not protection of the people against the Government, but protection of the people by the Government.

There are several reasons why we believe the federal government must play a leading role in our efforts as a nation to improve our civil rights record.

First, many of the most serious wrongs against individual rights are committed by private persons or by local public officers. In the most flagrant of all such wrongs— lynching—private individuals, aided upon occasion by state or local officials, are the ones who take the law into their own hands and deprive the victim of his life. The very fact that these outrages continue to occur, coupled with the fact that the states have been unable to eliminate them, points clearly to a strong need for federal safeguards.

Second, it is a sound policy to use the idealism and prestige of our whole people to check the wayward tendencies of a part of them. It is true that the conscience of a nation is colored by the moral sense of its local communities. Still, the American people have traditionally shown high national regard for civil rights, even though the record in many a community has been far from good. We should not fail to make use of this in combating civil rights violations. The local community must be encouraged to set its own house in order. But the need for leadership is pressing. That leadership is available in the national government and it should be used. We cannot afford to delay action until the most backward community has learned to prize civil liberty and has taken adequate steps to safeguard the rights of every one of its citizens.

Third, our civil rights record has growing international implications. These cannot safely be disregarded by the government at the national level which is responsible for our relations with the world, and left entirely to government at the local level for proper recognition and action. Many of man's problems, we have been learning, are capable of ultimate solution only through international cooperation and action. The subject of human rights, itself, has been made a major concern of the United Nations. It would indeed be ironical if in our own country the argument should prevail that safeguarding the rights of the individual is the exclusive, or even the primary concern of local government.

A lynching in a rural American community is not a challenge to that community's conscience alone. The repercussions of such a crime are heard not only in the locality, or indeed only in our own nation. They echo from one end of the globe to the other, and the world looks to the American national government for both an explanation of how such a shocking event can occur in a civilized country and remedial action to prevent its recurrence.

Similarly, interference with the right of a qualified citizen to vote locally cannot today remain a local problem. An American diplomat cannot forcefully argue for free elections in foreign lands without meeting the challenge that in many sections of America qualified voters do not have free access to the polls. Can it be doubted that this is a right which the national government must make secure?

Fourth, the steadily growing tendency of the American people to look to the national government for the protection of their civil rights is highly significant. This popular demand does not by itself prove the case for national government action. But the persistent and deep-felt desire of the American citizen for federal action safeguarding his civil rights is neither a request for spoils by a selfish pressure group, nor is it a shortsighted and opportunistic attempt by a temporary majority to urge the government into a dubious or unwise course of action. It is a demand rooted in the folkways of the people, sound in instinct and reason, and impossible to ignore. The American people are loyal to the institutions of local self-government, and distrust highly centralized power. But we have never hesitated to entrust power and responsibility to the national government when need for such a course of action has been demonstrated and the people themselves are convinced of that need.

Finally, the national government should assume leadership in our American civil rights program because there is much in the field of civil rights that it is squarely responsible for in its own direct dealings with millions of persons. It is the largest single employer of labor in the country. More than two million persons are on its payroll. The freedom of opinion and expression enjoyed by these people is in many ways dependent upon the attitudes and practices of the government. By not restricting this freedom beyond a point necessary to insure the efficiency and loyalty of its workers, the government, itself, can make a very large contribution to the effort to achieve true freedom of thought in America. By scrupulously following fair employment practices, it not only sets a model for other employers to follow, but also directly protects the rights of more than two million workers to fair employment.

The same is true of the armed forces. Their policies are completely determined by the federal government. That government has the power, the opportunity and the duty to see that discrimination and prejudice are completely eliminated from the armed services, and that the American soldier or sailor enjoys as full a measure of civil liberty as is commensurate with military service.

The District of Columbia and our dependent areas are under the immediate authority of the national government. By safeguarding civil rights in these areas, it can protect several million people directly, and encourage the states and local communities throughout the country to do likewise. Finally, through its extensive public services, the national government is the largest single agency in the land endeavoring to satisfy the wants and needs of the consumer. By making certain that these services are continuously available to all persons without regard to race, color, creed or national origin, a very important step toward the elimination of discrimination in American life will have been taken.

Leadership by the federal government in safeguarding civil rights does not mean exclusive action by that government. There is much that the states and local communities can do in this field, and much that they alone can do. The Committee believes that Justice Holmes' view of the states as 48 laboratories for social and economic experimentation is still valid. The very complexity of the civil rights problem calls for much experimental, remedial action which may be better undertaken by the states than by the national government. Parallel state and local action supporting the national program is highly desirable. It is obvious that even though the federal government should take steps to stamp out the crime of lynching, the states cannot escape the responsibility to employ all of the powers and resources available to them for the same end. Or again, the enactment of a federal fair employment practice act will not render similar state legislation unnecessary.

In certain areas the states must do far more than parallel federal action. Either for constitutional or administrative reasons, they must remain the primary protectors of civil rights. This is true of governmental efforts to control or outlaw racial or religious discrimination practiced by privately supported public-service institutions such as schools and hospitals, and of places of public accommodation such as hotels, restaurants, theaters, and stores.

Furthermore, government action alone, whether federal, state, local, or all combined, cannot provide complete protection of civil rights. Everything that government does stems from and is conditioned by the state of public opinion. Civil rights in this country will never be adequately protected until the intelligent will of the American people approves and demands that protection. Great responsibility, therefore, will always rest upon private organizations and private individuals who are in a position to educate and shape public opinion. The argument is sometimes made that because prejudice and intolerance cannot be eliminated through legislation and government control we should abandon that action in favor of the long, slow, evolutionary effects of education and voluntary private efforts. We believe that this argument misses the point and that the choice it poses between legislation and education as to the means of improving civil rights is an unnecessary one. In our opinion, both approaches to the goal are valid, and are, moreover, essential to each other.

It may be impossible to overcome prejudice by law, but many of the evil discriminatory practices which are the visible manifestations of prejudice can be brought to an end through proper government controls. At the same time, it is highly desirable that efforts be made to understand more fully the causes of prejudice and to stamp them out. These efforts will necessarily occupy much time and can in many instances best be made by private organizations and individuals. . . .

The Committee rejects the argument that governmental controls are themselves necessarily threats to liberty. This statement overlooks the fact that freedom in a civilized society is always founded on law enforced by government. Freedom in the absence of law is anarchy.

Because it believes there is need for

leadership by the national government, the Committee has not hesitated to recommend increased action by that government in support of our civil rights. At the same time, it has not overlooked the many possibilities for remedial action by the states, nor the benefits to be derived from private efforts in the never-ending struggle to make civil liberty more secure in America. Certain of the Committee's recommendations look in each of these directions. . . .

THE COMMITTEE'S RECOMMENDATIONS

I. *To strengthen the machinery for the protection of civil rights, the President's Committee recommends:*

1. The reorganization of the Civil Rights Section of the Department of Justice to provide for:

    The establishment of regional offices;

    A substantial increase in its appropriation and staff to enable it to engage in more extensive research and to act more effectively to prevent civil rights violation;

    An increase in investigative action in the absence of complaints;

    The greater use of Civil sanctions;

    Its elevation to the status of a full division in the Department of Justice. . . .

2. The establishment within the FBI of a special unit of investigators trained in civil rights work. . . .

3. The establishment by the state governments of law enforcement agencies comparable to the federal Civil Rights Section. . . .

4. The establishment of a permanent Commission on Civil Rights in the Executive Office of the President, preferably by Act of Congress; and the simultaneous creation of a Joint Standing Committee on Civil Rights in Congress. . . .

5. The establishment by the states of permanent commissions on civil rights to parallel the work of the federal Commission at the state level. . . .

6. The increased professionalization of state and local police forces. . . .

II. *To strengthen the right to safety and security of the person, the President's Committee recommends:* . . .

4. The enactment by Congress of a new statute, to supplement Section 52, [of Title 18, U.S. Code] specifically directed against police brutality and related crimes. . . .

5. The enactment by Congress of an anti-lynching act. . . .

6. The enactment by Congress of a new criminal statute on involuntary servitude, supplementing Sections 443 and 444 of Title 18 of the United States Code. . . .

7. A review of our wartime evacuation and detention experience looking toward the development of a policy which will prevent the abridgment of civil rights of any person or groups because of race or ancestry. . . .

8. Enactment by Congress of legislation establishing a procedure by which claims of evacuees for specific property and business losses resulting from wartime evacuation can be promptly considered and settled. . . .

III. *To strengthen the right to citizenship and its privileges, the President's Committee recommends:*

1. Action by the states or Congress to end poll taxes as a voting prerequisite. . . .

2. The enactment by Congress of a statute protecting the right of qualified persons to participate in federal primaries and elections against interference by public officers and private persons. . . .

3. The enactment by Congress of a statute protecting the right to qualify for, or participate in, federal or state primaries or elections against discriminatory action by state officers based on race or color, or depending on any other unreasonable classification of persons for voting purposes. . . .

4. The enactment by Congress of legislation establishing local self-government for the District of Columbia; and the amendment of the Constitution to extend suffrage in presidential elections, and representation in Congress to District residents. . . .

5. The granting of suffrage by the States of New Mexico and Arizona to their Indian citizens. . . .

6. The modification of the federal naturalization laws to permit the granting of citizenship without regard to the race, color, or national origin of applicants. . . .

7. The repeal by the states of laws discriminating against aliens who are ineligible for citizenship because of race, color, or national origin. . . .

8. The enactment by Congress of legislation granting citizenship to the people of Guam and American Samoa. . . .

9. The enactment by Congress of legislation, followed by appropriate administrative action, to end immediately all discrimination and segregation based on race, color, creed, or national origin, in the organisation and activities of all branches of the Armed Services. . . .

10. The enactment by Congress of legislation providing that no member of the armed forces shall be subject to discrimination of any kind by any public authority or place of public accommodation, recreation, transportation, or other service or business. . . .

V. *To strengthen the right to equality of opportunity, the President's Committee recommends:*

1. In general:

The elimination of segregation, based on race, color, creed or national origin, from American life. . . .

The conditioning by Congress of all federal grants-in-aid and other forms of federal assistance to public or private agencies for any purpose on the absence of discrimination and segregation based on race, color, creed, or national origin. . . .

2. For employment:

The enactment of a federal Fair Employment Practice Act prohibiting all forms of discrimination in private employment, based on race, color, creed, or national origin. . . .

The enactment by the states of similar laws. . . .

The issuance by the President of a mandate against discrimination in government employment and the creation of adequate machinery to enforce this mandate. . . .

3. For education:

Enactment by the state legislatures of fair educational practice laws for public and private educational institutions, prohibiting discrimination in the admission and treatment of students based on race, color, creed, or national origin. . . .

4. For housing:

The enactment by the states of laws outlawing restrictive covenants;

Renewed court attack, with intervention by the Department of Justice, upon restrictive covenants. . . .

5. For health services:

The enactment by the states of fair health practice statutes forbidding discrimination and segregation based on race, creed, color, or national origin, in the operation of public or private health facilities. . . .

6. For public services:

The enactment by Congress of a law stating that discrimination and segregation, based on race, color, creed, or national origin, in the rendering of all public services by the national government is contrary to public policy;

The enactment by the states of similar laws. . . .

The establishment by act of Congress or executive order of a unit in the federal Bureau of the Budget to review the execution of all government programs, and the expenditures of all government funds, for compliance with the policy of nondiscrimination. . . .

The enactment by Congress of a law prohibiting discrimination or segregation, based on race, color, creed, or national origin, in interstate transportation and all the facilities thereof, to apply against both public officers and the employees of private transportation companies. . . .

The enactment by the states of laws guaranteeing equal access to places of public accommodation, broadly defined, for persons of all races, colors, creeds, and national origins. . . .

8. The enactment by Congress of legislation ending the system of segregation in the Panama Canal Zone. . . .

VI. *To rally the American people to the support of a continuing program to strengthen civil rights, the President's Committee recommends:*

A long term campaign of public education to inform the people of the civil rights to which they are entitled and which they owe to one another. . . .

5. RESTRICTIVE COVENANT CASES

EDITORS' NOTE.—Discriminatory housing agreements by private owners (called "restrictive covenants") have been used widely, North and South, to bar Negroes from certain residential areas. Here for the first time the Court interprets the Fourteenth Amendment as a prohibition upon the legal enforcement of such private agreements.

A long history of litigation under the "due-process" clause of the Fourteenth Amendment had almost obscured the original design of the article: equal citizenship for the Negro in such cases as the civil rights cases (Vol. I, p. 787) and *Plessy* v. *Ferguson* (Vol. I, p. 792). The Court in *Shelley* v. *Kraemer* does something to restore that purpose.

A. *SHELLEY* v. *KRAEMER*[1]

Mr. Chief Justice VINSON delivered the opinion of the Court.

These cases present for our consideration questions relating to the validity of court enforcement of private agreements, generally described as restrictive covenants, which have as their purpose the exclusion of persons of designated race or color from the ownership or occupancy of real property. Basic constitutional issues of obvious importance have been raised.

1. 334 U.S. 1, 4–16, 18–23 (1947).

The first of these cases comes to this Court on certiorari to the Supreme Court of Missouri. On February 16, 1911, thirty out of a total of thirty-nine owners of property fronting both sides of Labadie Avenue between Taylor Avenue and Cora Avenue in the city of St. Louis, signed an agreement, which was subsequently recorded, providing in part:

. . . the said property is hereby restricted to the use and occupancy for the term of Fifty (50) years from this date, so that it shall be a condition all the time and whether recited and referred to as [sic] not in subsequent conveyances and shall attach to the land as a condition precedent to the sale of the same, that hereafter no part of said property or any portion thereof shall be, for said term of Fifty-years, occupied by any person not of the Caucasian race, it being intended hereby to restrict the use of said property for said period of time against the occupancy as owners or tenants of any portion of said property for resident or other purpose by people of the Negro or Mongolian Race.

The entire district described in the agreement included fifty-seven parcels of land. The thirty owners who signed the agreement held title to forty-seven parcels, including the particular parcel involved in this case. At the time the agreement was signed, five of the parcels in the district were owned by Negroes. One of those had been occupied by Negro families since 1882, nearly thirty years before the restrictive agreement was executed. The trial court found that owners of seven out of nine homes on the south side of Labadie Avenue, within the restricted district and "in the immediate vicinity" of the premises in question, had failed to sign the restrictive agreement in 1911. At the time this action was brought, four of the premises were occupied by Negroes, and had been so occupied for periods ranging from twenty-three to sixty-three years. A fifth parcel had been occupied by Negroes until a year before this suit was instituted.

On August 11, 1945, pursuant to a contract of sale, petitioners Shelley, who are Negroes, for valuable consideration received from one Fitzgerald a warranty deed to the parcel in question. The trial court found that petitioners had no actual knowledge of the restrictive agreement at the time of the purchase.

On October 9, 1945, respondents, as owners of other property subject to the terms of the restrictive covenant, brought suit in the Circuit Court of the city of St. Louis praying that petitioners Shelley be restrained from taking possession of the property and that judgment be entered divesting title out of petitioners Shelley and revesting title in the immediate grantor or in such other person as the court should direct. The trial court denied the requested relief on the ground that the restrictive agreement, upon which respondents based their action, had never become final and complete because it was the intention of the parties to that agreement that it was not to become effective until signed by all property owners in the district, and signatures of all the owners had never been obtained.

The Supreme Court of Missouri sitting en banc reversed and directed the trial court to grant the relief for which respondents had prayed. That court held the agreement effective and concluded that enforcement of its provisions violated no rights guaranteed to petitioners by the Federal Constitution. At the time the court rendered its decision, petitioners were occupying the property in question.

The second of the cases under consideration comes to this Court from the Supreme Court of Michigan. The circumstances presented do not differ materially from the Missouri case. In June, 1934, one Ferguson and his wife, who then owned the property located in the city of Detroit which is involved in this case, executed a contract providing in part:

This property shall not be used or occupied by any person or persons except those of the Caucasian race.

It is further agreed that this restriction shall not be effective unless at least eighty percent of the property fronting on both sides of the street in the block where our land is located is subjected to this or a similar restriction. . . .

By deed dated November 30, 1944, petitioners, who were found by the trial court to be Negroes, acquired title to the property and thereupon entered into its occupancy. On January 30, 1945, respondents, as owners of property subject to the terms of the restrictive agreement, brought suit against petitioners in the Circuit Court of Wayne County. After a hearing, the court entered a decree directing petitioners to move from the property within ninety days. Petitioners were further enjoined and restrained from using or occupying the premises in the future. On appeal, the Supreme Court of Michigan affirmed, deciding adversely to petitioners' contentions that they had been denied rights protected by the Fourteenth Amendment.

Petitioners have placed primary reliance on their contentions, first raised in the state courts, that judicial enforcement of the restrictive agreements in these cases has violated rights guaranteed to petitioners by the Fourteenth Amendment of the Federal Constitution and Acts of Congress passed pursuant to that Amendment. Specifically, petitioners urge that they have been denied the equal protection of the laws, deprived of property without due process of law, and have been denied privileges and immunities of citizens of the United States. We pass to a consideration of those issues. . . .

It is well, at the outset, to scrutinize the terms of the restrictive agreements involved in these cases. In the Missouri case, the covenant declares that no part of the affected property shall be "occupied by any person not of the Caucasian race, it being intended hereby to restrict the use of said property . . . against the occupancy as owners or tenants of any portion of said property for residential or other purpose by people of the Negro or Mongolian Race." Not only does the restriction seek to proscribe use and occupancy of the affected properties by members of the excluded class, but as construed by the Missouri courts, the agreement requires that title of any person who uses his property in violation of the restriction shall be divested. The restriction of the covenant in the Michigan case seeks to bar occupancy by persons of the excluded class. It provides that "This property shall not be used or occupied by any person or persons except those of the Caucasian race."

It should be observed that these covenants do not seek to proscribe any particular use of the affected properties. Use of the properties for residential occupancy, as such, is not forbidden. The restrictions of these agreements, rather, are directed toward a designated class of persons and seek to determine who may and who may not own or make use of the properties for residential purposes. The excluded class is defined wholly in terms of race or color; "simply that and nothing more."

It cannot be doubted that among the civil rights intended to be protected from discriminatory state action by the Fourteenth Amendment are the rights to acquire, enjoy, own and dispose of property. Equality in the enjoyment of property rights was regarded by the framers of that Amendment as an essential precondition to the realization of other basic civil rights and liberties which the Amendment was intended to guarantee. Thus, § 1978 of the Revised Statutes, derived from § 1 of the Civil Rights Act of 1866 which was enacted by Congress while the Fourteenth Amendment was also under consideration, provides:

All citizens of the United States shall have the same right, in every State and Territory, as is enjoyed by white citizens thereof to inherit, purchase, lease, sell, hold, and convey real and personal property.

This Court has given specific recognition to the same principle. *Buchanan* v. *Warley*, 245 U.S. 60 (1917).

It is likewise clear that restrictions on the right of occupancy of the sort sought to be created by the private agreements in these cases could not be squared with the requirements of the Fourteenth Amendment if imposed by state statute or local ordinance. . . .

But the present cases . . . do not involve action by state legislatures or city councils. Here the particular patterns of discrimination and the areas in which the restrictions are to operate, are determined, in the first instance, by the terms of agreements among private individuals. Participation of the State consists in the enforcement of the restrictions so defined.

The crucial issue with which we are here confronted is whether this distinction removes these cases from the operation of the prohibitory provisions of the Fourteenth Amendment.

Since the decision of this Court in the *Civil Rights Cases*, 109 U.S. 3 (1883), the principle has become firmly embedded in our constitutional law that the action inhibited by the first section of the Fourteenth Amendment is only such action as may fairly be said to be that of the States. That Amendment erects no shield against merely private conduct, however discriminatory or wrongful.

We conclude, therefore, that the restrictive agreements standing alone cannot be regarded as violative of any rights guaranteed to petitioners by the Fourteenth Amendment. So long as the purposes of those agreements are effectuated by voluntary adherence to their terms, it would appear clear that there has been no action by the State and the provisions of the Amendment have not been violated. Cf. *Corrigan* v. *Buckley, supra*.

But here there was more. These are cases in which the purposes of the agreements were secured only by judicial enforcement by state courts of the restrictive terms of the agreements. The respondents urge that judicial enforcement of private agreements does not amount to state action; or, in any event, the participation of the State is so attenuated in character as not to amount to state action within the meaning of the Fourteenth Amendment. Finally, it is suggested, even if the States in these cases may be deemed to have acted in the constitutional sense, their action did not deprive petitioners of rights guaranteed by the Fourteenth Amendment. We move to a consideration of these matters.

That the action of state courts and judicial officers in their official capacities is to be regarded as action of the State within the meaning of the Fourteenth Amendment, is a proposition which has long been established by decisions of this Court. That principle was given expression in the earliest cases involving the construction of the terms of the Fourteenth Amendment. Thus, in *Virginia* v. *Rives*, 100 U.S. 313, 318 (1880), this Court stated: "It is doubtless true that a State may act through different agencies—either by its legislative, its executive, or its judicial authorities; and the prohibitions of the amendment extend to all action of the State denying equal protection of the laws, whether it be action by one of these agencies or by another." In *Ex parte Virginia*, 100 U.S. 339, 347 (1880), the Court observed: "A State acts by its legislative, its executive, or its judicial authorities. It can act in no other way." In the *Civil Rights Cases*, 109 U.S. 3, 11, 17 (1883), this Court pointed out that the Amendment makes void "State action of every kind" which is inconsistent with the guaranties therein contained, and extends to manifestations of "State authority in the shape of laws, customs, or judicial or executive proceedings." Language to like effect is employed no less than eighteen times during the course of that opinion. . . .

One of the earliest applications of the prohibitions contained in the Fourteenth Amendment to action of state judicial officials occurred in cases in which Negroes had been excluded from jury service in criminal prosecutions by reason of their race or color. These cases demonstrate, also, the early recognition by this Court that state action in violation of the Amendment's provisions is equally repugnant to the constitutional commands whether directed by state statute or taken by a judicial official in the absence of statute. Thus, in *Strauder* v. *West Virginia*, 100 U.S. 303 (1880), this Court declared invalid a state statute restricting jury service to white persons as amounting to a denial of the equal protection of the laws to the colored defendant in that case. In the same volume of the reports, the Court in *Ex parte Virginia, supra*, held that a similar discrimination imposed by the action of a state judge denied rights protected by the Amendment, despite the fact that the language of the state statute relating to jury service contained no such restrictions. . . .

The short of the matter is that from the time of the adoption of the Fourteenth Amendment until the present, it has been the consistent ruling of this Court that the action of the States to which the Amendment has reference includes action of state courts and state judicial officials. Although, in construing the terms of the Fourteenth Amendment, differences have from time to time been expressed as to whether particular types of state action may be said to offend the Amendment's prohibitory provisions, it has never been suggested that state court action is immunized from the operation of those provisions simply because the act is that of the judicial branch of the state government.

Against this background of judicial construction, extending over a period of some three-quarters of a century, we are called upon to consider whether enforcement by state courts of the restrictive agreements in these cases may be deemed to be the acts of those States; and, if so, whether that action has denied these petitioners the equal protection of the laws which the Amendment was intended to insure.

We have no doubt that there has been state action in these cases in the full and complete sense of the phrase. The undisputed facts disclose that petitioners were willing purchasers of properties upon which they desired to establish homes. The owners of the properties were willing sellers; and contracts of sale were accordingly consummated. It is clear that but for the active intervention of the state courts, supported by the full panoply of state power, petitioners would have been free to occupy the properties in question without restraint.

These are not cases, as has been suggested, in which the States have merely abstained from action, leaving private individuals free to impose such discrimina-
tions as they see fit. Rather, these are cases in which the States have made available to such individuals the full coercive power of government to deny to petitioners, on the grounds of race or color, the enjoyment of property rights in premises which petitioners are willing and financially able to acquire and which the grantors are willing to sell. The difference between judicial enforcement and non-enforcement of the restrictive covenants is the difference to petitioners between being denied rights of property available to other members of the community and being accorded full enjoyment of those rights on an equal footing.

The enforcement of the restrictive agreements by the state courts in these cases was directed pursuant to the common-law policy of the States as formulated by those courts in earlier decisions. In the Missouri case, enforcement of the covenant was directed in the first instance by the highest court of the State after the trial court had determined the agreement to be invalid for want of the requisite number of signatures. In the Michigan case, the order of enforcement by the trial court was affirmed by the highest state court. The judicial action in each case bears the clear and unmistakable imprimatur of the State. We have noted that previous decisions of this Court have established the proposition that judicial action is not immunized from the operation of the Fourteenth Amendment simply because it is taken pursuant to the state's common-law policy. Nor is the Amendment ineffective simply because the particular pattern of discrimination, which the State has enforced, was defined initially by the terms of a private agreement. State action, as that phrase is understood for the purposes of the Fourteenth Amendment, refers to exertions of state power in all forms. And when the effect of that action is to deny rights subject to the protection of the Fourteenth Amendment, it is the obligation of this Court to enforce the constitutional commands.

We hold that in granting judicial enforcement of the restrictive agreements in these cases, the States have denied petitioners the equal protection of the laws and that, therefore, the action of the state courts cannot stand. We have noted that freedom from discrimination by the States in the enjoyment of property rights was among the basic objectives sought to be effectuated by the framers of the Fourteenth Amendment. That such discrimination has occurred in these cases is clear. Because of the race or color of these petitioners they have been denied rights of ownership or occupancy enjoyed as a matter of course by other citizens of different race or color. The Fourteenth Amendment declares "that all persons, whether colored or white, shall stand equal before the laws of the States, and, in regard to the colored race, for whose protection the amendment was primarily designed, that no discrimination shall be made against them by law because of their color." . . .

The problem of defining the scope of the restrictions which the Federal Constitution imposes upon exertions of power by the States has given rise to many of the most persistent and fundamental issues which this Court has been called upon to consider. That problem was foremost in the minds of the framers of the Constitution, and, since that early day, has arisen in a multitude of forms. The task of determining whether the action of a State offends constitutional provisions is one which may not be undertaken lightly. Where, however, it is clear that the action

of the State violates the terms of the fundamental charter, it is the obligation of this Court so to declare.

The historical context in which the Fourteenth Amendment became a part of the Constitution should not be forgotten. Whatever else the framers sought to achieve, it is clear that the matter of primary concern was the establishment of equality in the enjoyment of basic civil and political rights and the preservation of those rights from discriminatory action on the part of the States based on considerations of race or color. Seventy-five years ago this Court announced that the provisions of the Amendment are to be construed with this fundamental purpose in mind. Upon full consideration, we have concluded that in these cases the States have acted to deny petitioners the equal protection of the laws guaranteed by the Fourteenth Amendment. Having so decided, we find it unnecessary to consider whether petitioners have also been deprived of property without due process of law or denied privileges and immunities of citizens of the United States.

For the reasons stated, the judgment of the Supreme Court of Missouri and the judgment of the Supreme Court of Michigan must be reversed.

Reversed

Mr. Justice REED, Mr. Justice JACKSON, and Mr. Justice RUTLEDGE took no part in the consideration or decision of these cases.

B. *HURD* v. *HODGE*[2]

Mr. Chief Justice VINSON delivered the opinion of the Court.

These are companion cases to *Shelley* v. *Kraemer* and *McGhee* v. *Sipes*, *ante*, p. 1, and come to this Court on certiorari to the United States Court of Appeals for the District of Columbia.

In 1906, twenty of thirty-one lots in the 100 block of Bryant Street, Northwest, in

the City of Washington, were sold subject to the following covenant: ". . . that said lot shall never be rented, leased, sold, transferred or conveyed unto any Negro or colored person, under a penalty of Two Thousand Dollars ($2,000), which shall be a lien against said property." The covenant imposes no time limitation on the restriction. . . .

These cases involve seven of the twenty

2. 334 U.S. 24, 26–28, 30–36 (1947).

lots which are subject to the terms of the restrictive covenants. In No. 290, petitioners Hurd, found by the trial court to be Negroes, purchased one of the restricted properties from the white owners. In No. 291, petitioner Urciolo, a white real estate dealer, sold and conveyed three of the restricted properties to the Negro petitioners Rowe, Savage, and Stewart. Petitioner Urciolo also owns three other lots in the block subject to the covenants. In both cases, the Negro petitioners are presently occupying as homes the respective properties which have been conveyed to them.

Suits were instituted in the District Court by respondents, who own other property in the block subject to the terms of the covenants, praying for injunctive relief to enforce the terms of the restrictive agreements. The cases were consolidated for trial, and after a hearing, the court entered a judgment declaring null and void the deeds of the Negro petitioners; enjoining petitioner Urciolo and one Ryan, the white property owners who had sold the houses to the Negro petitioners, from leasing, selling or conveying the properties to any Negro or colored person; enjoining the Negro petitioners from leasing or conveying the properties and directing those petitioners "to remove themselves and all of their personal belongings" from the premises within sixty days.

The United States Court of Appeals for the District of Columbia, with one justice dissenting, affirmed the judgment of the District Court. The majority of the court was of the opinion that the action of the District Court was consistent with earlier decisions of the Court of Appeals and that those decisions should be held determinative in these cases.

Petitioners have attacked the judicial enforcement of the restrictive covenants in these cases on a wide variety of grounds. Primary reliance, however, is placed on the contention that such governmental action on the part of the courts of the District of Columbia is forbidden by the due process clause of the Fifth Amendment of the Federal Constitution. . . .

Upon full consideration, however, we have found it unnecessary to resolve the constitutional issue which petitioners advance; for we have concluded that judicial enforcement of restrictive covenants by the courts of the District of Columbia is improper for other reasons hereinafter stated.

Section 1978 of the Revised Statutes, derived from § 1 of the Civil Rights Act of 1866, provides: "All citizens of the United States shall have the same right, in every State and Territory, as is enjoyed by white citizens thereof to inherit, purchase, lease, sell, hold, and convey real and personal property."

All petitioners in these cases, as found by the District Court, are citizens of the United States. We have no doubt that, for the purposes of this section, the District of Columbia is included within the phrase "every State and Territory." Nor can there be doubt of the constitutional power of Congress to enact such legislation with reference to the District of Columbia.

We may start with the proposition that the statute does not invalidate private restrictive agreements so long as the purposes of those agreements are achieved by the parties through voluntary adherence to the terms. The action toward which the provision of the statute under consideration is directed is governmental action. Such was the holding of *Corrigan* v. *Buckley, supra.*

In considering whether judicial enforcement of restrictive covenants is the kind of governmental action which the first section of the Civil Rights Act of 1866 was intended to prohibit, reference must be made to the scope and purposes of the Fourteenth Amendment; for that statute and the Amendment were closely related both in inception and in the objectives which Congress sought to achieve.

Both the Civil Rights Act of 1866 and the joint resolution which was later adopted as the Fourteenth Amendment were passed in the first session of the Thirty-ninth Congress. Frequent references to the Civil Rights Act are to be found in the record of the legislative debates on the adoption of the Amendment. It is clear that in many significant respects the statute and the Amendment were expressions of the same general congressional policy. Indeed, as the legislative debates reveal, one of the primary purposes of many members of Congress in supporting the adoption of the Fourteenth Amendment was to incorporate the guaranties of the Civil Rights Act of 1866 in the organic law of the land. Others supported the adoption of the Amendment in order to eliminate doubt as to the constitutional validity of the Civil Rights Act as applied to the States.

The close relationship between § 1 of the Civil Rights Act and the Fourteenth Amendment was given specific recognition by this Court in *Buchanan* v. *Warley*, *supra* at 79. There, the Court observed that, not only through the operation of the Fourteenth Amendment, but also by virtue of the "statutes enacted in furtherance of its purpose," including the provisions here considered, a colored man is granted the right to acquire property free from interference by discriminatory state legislation. In *Shelley* v. *Kraemer*, *supra*, we have held that the Fourteenth Amendment also forbids such discrimination where imposed by state courts in the enforcement of restrictive covenants. That holding is clearly indicative of the construction to be given to the relevant provisions of the Civil Rights Act in their application to the Courts of the District of Columbia.

Moreover, the explicit language employed by Congress to effectuate its purposes leaves no doubt that judicial enforcement of the restrictive covenants by the courts of the District of Columbia is prohibited by the Civil Rights Act. That statute, by its terms, requires that all citizens of the United States shall have the same right "as is enjoyed by white citizens . . . to inherit, purchase, lease, sell, hold, and convey real and personal property." That the Negro petitioners have been denied that right by virtue of the action of the federal courts of the District is clear. The Negro petitioners entered into contracts of sale with willing sellers for the purchase of properties upon which they desired to establish homes. Solely because of their race and color they are confronted with orders of court divesting their titles in the properties and ordering that the premises be vacated. White sellers, one of whom is a petitioner here, have been enjoined from selling the properties to any Negro or colored person. Under such circumstances, to suggest that the Negro petitioners have been accorded the same rights as white citizens to purchase, hold, and convey real property is to reject the plain meaning of language. We hold that the action of the District Court directed against the Negro purchasers and the white sellers denies rights intended by Congress to be protected by the Civil Rights Act and that, consequently, the action cannot stand.

But even in the absence of the statute, there are other considerations which would indicate that enforcement of restrictive covenants in these cases is judicial action contrary to the public policy of the United States, and as such should be corrected by this Court in the exercise of its supervisory powers over the courts of the District of Columbia. The power of the federal courts to enforce the terms of private agreements is at all times exercised subject to the restrictions and limitations of the public policy of the United States as manifested in the Constitution, treaties, federal statutes, and applicable legal precedents. Where the enforcement of private agreements would be violative of that policy, it is the obligation of courts to refrain from such exertions of judicial power.

We are here concerned with action of federal courts of such a nature that if taken by the courts of a State would violate the prohibitory provisions of the Fourteenth Amendment. *Shelley* v. *Kraemer*, *supra*. It is not consistent with the public policy of the United States to permit federal courts in the Nation's capital to exercise general equitable powers to compel action denied the state courts where such state action has been held to be violative of the guaranty of the equal protection of the laws. We cannot presume that the public policy of the United States manifests a lesser concern for the protection of such basic rights against discriminatory action of federal courts than against such action taken by the courts of the States.

Reversed

Mr. Justice REED, Mr. Justice JACKSON, and Mr. Justice RUTLEDGE took no part in the consideration or decision of these cases.

6. WHO IS LOYAL TO AMERICA?[1]

By HENRY STEELE COMMAGER

EDITORS' NOTE.—The question of national loyalty takes on great urgency in periods of crisis, when the necessities—real or imagined—seem to require obedience and conformity at the expense of liberty and variety. Henry Steele Commager (1902———), writing in an atmosphere charged with the tensions of the "cold war," reaches back into the American past for a principle of loyalty which will at once strengthen the nation and extend individual freedom. The validity of this principle, as applied by Professor Commager to the stormy issue of civil rights for Communists, has been challenged from several sides. For one expression of sharp dissent see the report of Representative Mundt (pp. 701–5).

The author is a distinguished American historian, whose works include a study of *Majority Rule and Minority Rights* (1943).

On May 6 a Russian-born girl, Mrs. Shura Lewis, gave a talk to the students of the Western High School of Washington, D.C. She talked about Russia—its school system, its public health program, the position of women, of the aged, of the workers, the farmers, and the professional classes—and compared, superficially and uncritically, some American and Russian social institutions. The most careful examination of the speech—happily reprinted for us in the *Congressional Record*—does not disclose a single disparagement of anything American unless it is a quasi-humorous reference to the cost of having a baby and of dental treatment in this country. Mrs. Lewis said nothing that had not been said a thousand times, in speeches, in newspapers, magazines, and books. She said nothing that any normal person could find objectionable.

Her speech, however, created a sensation. A few students walked out on it. Others improvised placards proclaiming their devotion to Americanism. Indignant mothers telephoned their protests. Newspapers took a strong stand against the outrage. Congress, rarely concerned for the political or economic welfare of the citizens of the capital city, reacted sharply when its intellectual welfare was at stake. Congressmen Rankin and Dirksen thundered and lightened; the District of Columbia Committee went into a huddle; there were demands for housecleaning in the whole school system, which was obviously shot through and through with Communism.

1. Henry Steele Commager, "Who Is Loyal to America?" *Harper's*, CXCV (September, 1947), 193–99. Reprinted with permission of Henry Steele Commager.

All this might be ignored, for we have learned not to expect either intelligence or understanding of Americanism from this element in our Congress. More ominous was the reaction of the educators entrusted with the high responsibility of guiding and guarding the intellectual welfare of our boys and girls. Did they stand up for intellectual freedom? Did they insist that high-school children had the right and the duty to learn about other countries? Did they protest that students were to be trusted to use intelligence and common sense? Did they affirm that the Americanism of their students was staunch enough to resist propaganda? Did they perform even the elementary task, expected of educators above all, of analyzing the much-criticized speech?

Not at all. The District Superintendent of Schools, Dr. Hobart Corning, hastened to agree with the animadversions of Representatives Rankin and Dirksen. The whole thing was, he confessed, "a very unfortunate occurrence," and had "shocked the whole school system." What Mrs. Lewis said, he added gratuitously, was "repugnant to all who are working with youth in the Washington schools," and "the entire affair contrary to the philosophy of education under which we operate." Mr. Danowsky, the hapless principal of the Western High School, was "the most shocked and regretful of all." The District of Columbia Committee would be happy to know that though he was innocent in the matter, he had been properly reprimanded!

It is the reaction of the educators that makes this episode more than a tempest in a teapot. We expect hysteria from Mr. Rankin and some newspapers; we are shocked when we see educators, timid before criticism and confused about first principles, betray their trust. And we wonder what can be that "philosophy of education" which believes that young people can be trained to the duties of citizenship by wrapping their minds in cotton-wool.

Merely by talking about Russia, Mrs. Lewis was thought to be attacking Americanism. It is indicative of the seriousness of the situation that during this same week the House found it necessary to take time out from the discussion of the labor bill, the tax bill, the International Trade Organization, and the world famine, to meet assaults upon Americanism from a new quarter. This time it was the artists who were undermining the American system, and members of the House spent some hours passing around reproductions of the paintings which the State Department had sent abroad as part of its program for advertising American culture. We need not pause over the exquisite humor which congressmen displayed in their comments on modern art: weary statesmen must have their fun. But we may profitably remark the major criticism which was directed against this unfortunate collection of paintings. What was wrong with these paintings, it shortly appeared, was that they were un-American. "No American drew those crazy pictures," said Mr. Rankin. Perhaps he was right. The copious files of the Committee on Un-American Activities were levied upon to prove that of the forty-five artists represented "no less than twenty were definitely New Deal in various shades of Communism." The damning facts are specified for each of the pernicious twenty; we can content ourselves with the first of them, Ben-Zion. What is the evidence here? "Ben-Zion was one of the signers of a letter sent to President Roosevelt by the United American Artists which urged help to the USSR and Britain after Hitler attacked Russia." He was, in short, a fellow-traveler of Churchill and Roosevelt.

The same day that Mr. Dirksen was denouncing the Washington school authorities for allowing students to hear about Russia ("In Russia equal right is granted to each nationality. There is no discrimination. Nobody says, you are a Negro, you are a Jew") Representative Williams of Mississippi rose to denounce the *Survey-*

Graphic magazine and to add further to our understanding of Americanism. The *Survey-Graphic*, he said, "contained 129 pages of outrageously vile and nauseating anti-Southern, anti-Christian, un-American, and pro-Communist tripe, ostensibly directed toward the elimination of the custom of racial segregation in the South." It was written by "meddling un-American purveyors of hate and indecency."

All in all, a busy week for the House. Yet those who make a practice of reading their *Record* will agree that it was a typical week. For increasingly Congress is concerned with the eradication of disloyalty and the defense of Americanism, and scarcely a day passes that some congressman does not treat us to exhortations and admonitions, impassioned appeals and eloquent declamations, similar to those inspired by Mrs. Lewis, Mr. Ben-Zion, and the editors of the *Survey-Graphic*. And scarcely a day passes that the outlines of the new loyalty and the new Americanism are not etched more sharply in public policy.

And this is what is significant—the emergence of new patterns of Americanism and of loyalty, patterns radically different from those which have long been traditional. It is not only the Congress that is busy designing the new patterns. They are outlined in President Truman's recent disloyalty order; in similar orders formulated by the New York City Council and by state and local authorities throughout the country; in the programs of the D.A.R., the American Legion, and similar patriotic organizations; in the editorials of the Hearst and the McCormick-Patterson papers; and in an elaborate series of advertisements sponsored by large corporations and business organizations. In the making is a revival of the red hysteria of the early 1920's, one of the shabbiest chapters in the history of American democracy; and more than a revival, for the new crusade is designed not merely to frustrate Communism but to formulate a positive definition of Americanism, and a positive concept of loyalty.

What is the new loyalty? It is, above all, conformity. It is the uncritical and unquestioning acceptance of America as it is—the political institutions, the social relationships, the economic practices. It rejects inquiry into the race question or socialized medicine, or public housing, or into the wisdom or validity of our foreign policy. It regards as particularly heinous any challenge to what is called "the system of private enterprise," identifying that system with Americanism. It abandons evolution, repudiates the once popular concept of progress, and regards America as a finished product, perfect and complete.

It is, it must be added, easily satisfied. For it wants not intellectual conviction nor spiritual conquest, but mere outward conformity. In matters of loyalty it takes the word for the deed, the gesture for the principle. It is content with the flag salute, and does not pause to consider the warning of our Supreme Court that "a person gets from a symbol the meaning he puts into it, and what is one man's comfort and inspiration is another's jest and scorn." It is satisfied with membership in respectable organizations and, as it assumes that every member of a liberal organization is a Communist, concludes that every member of a conservative one is a true American. It has not yet learned that not everyone who saith Lord, Lord, shall enter into the kingdom of Heaven. It is designed neither to discover real disloyalty nor to foster true loyalty.

What is wrong with this new concept of loyalty? What, fundamentally, is wrong with the pusillanimous retreat of the Washington educators, the barbarous antics of Washington legislators, the hysterical outbursts of the D.A.R., the gross and vulgar appeals of business corporations? It is not merely that these things are offensive. It is rather that they are wrong—morally, socially, and politically.

The concept of loyalty as conformity is a false one. It is narrow and restrictive, denies freedom of thought and of conscience, and is irremediably stained by private and selfish considerations. "Enlightened loyalty," wrote Josiah Royce, who made loyalty the very core of his philosophy, "means harm to no man's loyalty. It is at war only with disloyalty, and its warfare, unless necessity constrains, is only a spiritual warfare. It does not foster class hatreds; it knows of nothing reasonable about race prejudices; and it regards all races of men as one in their need of loyalty. It ignores mutual misunderstandings. It loves its own wherever upon earth its own, namely loyalty itself, is to be found." Justice, charity, wisdom, spirituality, he added, were all definable in terms of loyalty, and we may properly ask which of these qualities our contemporary champions of loyalty display.

Above all, loyalty must be to something larger than oneself, untainted by private purposes or selfish ends. But what are we to say of the attempts by the NAM and by individual corporations to identify loyalty with the system of private enterprise? Is it not as if officeholders should attempt to identify loyalty with their own party, their own political careers? Do not those corporations which pay for full-page advertisements associating Americanism with the competitive system expect, ultimately, to profit from that association? Do not those organizations that deplore, in the name of patriotism, the extension of government operation of hydro-electric power expect to profit from their campaign?

Certainly it is a gross perversion not only of the concept of loyalty but of the concept of Americanism to identify it with a particular economic system. This precise question, interestingly enough, came before the Supreme Court in the Schneiderman case not so long ago—and it was Wendell Willkie who was counsel for Schneiderman. Said the Court:

Throughout our history many sincere people whose attachment to the general Constitutional scheme cannot be doubted have, for various and even divergent reasons, urged differing degrees of governmental ownership and control of natural resources, basic means of production, and banks and the media of exchange, either with or without compensation. And something once regarded as a species of private property was abolished without compensating the owners when the institution of slavery was forbidden. Can it be said that the author of the Emancipation Proclamation and the supporters of the Thirteenth Amendment were not attached to the Constitution?

There is, it should be added, a further danger in the willful identification of Americanism with a particular body of economic practices. Many learned economists predict for the near future an economic crash similar to that of 1929. If Americanism is equated with competitive capitalism, what happens to it if competitive capitalism comes a cropper? If loyalty and private enterprise are inextricably associated, what is to preserve loyalty if private enterprise fails? Those who associate Americanism with a particular program of economic practices have a grave responsibility, for if their program should fail, they expose Americanism itself to disrepute.

The effort to equate loyalty with conformity is misguided because it assumes that there is a fixed content to loyalty and that this can be determined and defined. But loyalty is a principle, and eludes definition except in its own terms. It is devotion to the best interests of the commonwealth, and may require hostility to the particular policies which the government pursues, the particular practices which the economy undertakes, the particular institutions which society maintains. "If there is any fixed star in our Constitutional constellation," said the Supreme Court in the Barnette case, "it is that no official, high or petty, can prescribe what shall be orthodox in politics, nationalism, religion, or other matters of opinion, or force citizens to confess by word or act their faith therein. If there are any circumstances which permit an exception they do not now occur to us."

True loyalty may require, in fact, what appears to the naïve to be disloyalty. It may require hostility to certain provisions of the Constitution itself, and historians have not concluded that those who subscribed to the "Higher Law" were lacking in patriotism. We should not forget that our tradition is one of protest and revolt, and it is stultifying to celebrate the rebels of the past—Jefferson and Paine, Emerson and Thoreau—while we silence the rebels of the present. "We are a rebellious nation," said Theodore Parker, known in his day as the Great American Preacher, and went on: "Our whole history is treason; our blood was attained before we were born; our creeds are infidelity to the mother church; our constitution, treason to our fatherland. What of that? Though all the governors in the world bid us commit treason against man, and set the example, let us never submit."

Those who would impose upon us a new concept of loyalty not only assume that this is possible, but have the presumption to believe that they are competent to write the definition. We are reminded of Whitman's defiance of the "never-ending audacity of elected persons." Who are those who would set the standards of loyalty? They are Rankins and Bilbos, officials of the D.A.R. and the Legion and the NAM, Hearsts and McCormicks. May we not say of Rankin's harangues on loyalty what Emerson said of Webster at the time of the Seventh of March speech: "The word honor in the mouth of Mr. Webster is like the word love in the mouth of a whore."

What do men know of loyalty who make a mockery of the Declaration of Independence and the Bill of Rights, whose energies are dedicated to stirring up race and class hatreds, who would straitjacket the American spirit? What indeed do they know of America—the America of Sam Adams and Tom Paine, of Jackson's defiance of the Court and Lincoln's celebra-tion of labor, of Thoreau's essay on Civil Disobedience and Emerson's championship of John Brown, of the America of the Fourierists and the Come-Outers, of cranks and fanatics, of socialists and anarchists? Who among American heroes could meet their tests, who would be cleared by their committees? Not Washington, who was a rebel. Not Jefferson, who wrote that all men are created equal and whose motto was "rebellion to tyrants is obedience to God." Not Garrison, who publicly burned the Constitution; or Wendell Phillips, who spoke for the underprivileged everywhere and counted himself a philosophical anarchist; not Seward of the Higher Law or Sumner of racial equality. Not Lincoln, who admonished us to have malice toward none, charity for all; or Wilson, who warned that our flag was "a flag of liberty of opinion as well as of political liberty"; or Justice Holmes, who said that our Constitution is an experiment and that while that experiment is being made "we should be eternally vigilant against attempts to check the expression of opinions that we loathe and believe to be fraught with death."

There are further and more practical objections against the imposition of fixed concepts of loyalty or tests of disloyalty. The effort is itself a confession of fear, a declaration of insolvency. Those who are sure of themselves do not need reassurance, and those who have confidence in the strength and the virtue of America do not need to fear either criticism or competition. The effort is bound to miscarry. It will not apprehend those who are really disloyal, it will not even frighten them; it will affect only those who can be labeled "radical." It is sobering to recall that though the Japanese relocation program, carried through at such incalculable cost in misery and tragedy, was justified to us on the ground that the Japanese were potentially disloyal, the record does not disclose a single case of Japanese disloyalty or sabotage during the whole war. The warning sounded by the Supreme Court in the Barnette flag-salute case is a timely one:

Ultimate futility of such attempts to compel obedience is the lesson of every such effort from the Roman drive to stamp out Christianity as a disturber of pagan unity, the Inquisition as a means to religious and dynastic unity, the Siberian exiles as a means to Russian unity, down to the fast-failing efforts of our present totalitarian enemies. Those who begin coercive elimination of dissent soon find themselves exterminating dissenters. Compulsory unification of opinion achieves only the unanimity of the graveyard.

Nor are we left to idle conjecture in this matter; we have had experience enough. Let us limit ourselves to a single example, one that is wonderfully relevant. Back in 1943 the House Un-American Activities Committee, deeply disturbed by alleged disloyalty among government employees, wrote a definition of subversive activities and proceeded to apply it. The definition was admirable, and no one could challenge its logic or its symmetry:

Subversive activity derives from conduct intentionally destructive of or inimical to the Government of the United States—that which seeks to undermine its institutions, or to distort its functions, or to impede its projects, or to lessen its efforts, the ultimate end being to overturn it all.

Surely anyone guilty of activities so defined deserved not only dismissal but punishment. But how was the test applied? It was applied to two distinguished scholars, Robert Morss Lovett and Goodwin Watson, and to one able young historian, William E. Dodd, Jr., son of our former Ambassador to Germany. Of almost three million persons employed by the government, these were the three whose subversive activities were deemed the most pernicious, and the House cut them off the payroll. The sequel is familiar. The Senate concurred only to save a wartime appropriation; the President signed the bill under protest for the same reason. The Supreme Court declared the whole business a "bill of attainder" and therefore unconstitutional. Who was it, in the end, who engaged in "subversive activities"—Lovett, Dodd, and Watson, or the Congress which flagrantly violated Article One of the Constitution?

Finally, disloyalty tests are not only futile in application, they are pernicious in their consequences. They distract attention from activities that are really disloyal, and silence criticism inspired by true loyalty. That there are disloyal elements in America will not be denied, but there is no reason to suppose that any of the tests now formulated will ever be applied to them. It is relevant to remember that when Rankin was asked why his Committee did not investigate the Ku Klux Klan he replied that the Klan was not un-American, it was American!

Who are those who are really disloyal? Those who inflame racial hatreds, who sow religious and class dissensions. Those who subvert the Constitution by violating the freedom of the ballot box. Those who make a mockery of majority rule by the use of the filibuster. Those who impair democracy by denying equal educational facilities. Those who frustrate justice by lynch law or by making a farce of jury trials. Those who deny freedom of speech and of the press and of assembly. Those who press for special favors against the interest of the commonwealth. Those who regard public office as a source of private gain. Those who would exalt the military over the civil. Those who for selfish and private purposes stir up national antagonisms and expose the world to the ruin of war.

Will the House Committee on Un-American Activities interfere with the activities of these? Will Mr. Truman's disloyalty proclamation reach these? Will the current campaigns for Americanism convert these? If past experience is any guide, they will not. What they will do, if they are successful, is to silence criticism, stamp out dissent—or drive it underground. But if our democracy is to flourish it must have criticism, if our government is to function it must have dissent. Only totalitarian governments insist upon conformity and they—as we know—do so at their peril. Without criticism abuses will go unrebuked; without dissent our dynamic system will become static. The American people have a stake in the maintenance of the most thorough-going inquisition into American institutions. They have a stake in nonconformity, for they know that the American genius is nonconformist. They have a stake in experimentation of the most radical character, for they know that only those who prove all things can hold fast that which is good.

It is easier to say what loyalty is not than to say what it is. It is not conformity. It is not passive acquiescence in the status quo. It is not preference for everything American over everything foreign. It is not an ostrich-like ignorance of other countries and other institutions. It is not the indulgence in ceremony—a flag salute, an oath of allegiance, a fervid verbal declaration. It is not a particular creed, a particular version of history, a particular body of economic practices, a particular philosophy.

It is a tradition, an ideal, and a principle. It is a willingness to subordinate every private advantage for the larger good. It is an appreciation of the rich and diverse contributions that can come from the most varied sources. It is allegiance to the traditions that have guided our greatest statesmen and inspired our most eloquent poets —the traditions of freedom, equality, democracy, tolerance, the tradition of the higher law, of experimentation, co-operation, and pluralism. It is a realization that America was born of revolt, flourished on dissent, became great through experimentation.

Independence was an act of revolution; republicanism was something new under the sun; the federal system was a vast experimental laboratory. Physically Americans were pioneers; in the realm of social and economic institutions, too, their tradition has been one of pioneering. From the beginning, intellectual and spiritual diversity have been as characteristic of America as racial and linguistic. The most distinctively American philosophies have been transcendentalism—which is the philosophy of the Higher Law—and pragmatism —which is the philosophy of experimentation and pluralism. These two principles are the very core of Americanism: the principle of the Higher Law, or of obedience to the dictates of conscience rather than of statutes, and the principle of pragmatism, or the rejection of a single good and of the notion of a finished universe. From the beginning Americans have known that there were new worlds to conquer, new truths to be discovered. Every effort to confine Americanism to a single pattern, to constrain it to a single formula, is disloyalty to everything that is valid in Americanism.

7. MUNDT-NIXON BILL AND REPORT, 1948

EDITORS' NOTE.—The present Communist party of the United States traces its origins to the left-wing group which split away from the Socialist party in 1919. Measured by membership figures or election returns, the movement has never in the following thirty years attained the dimensions of a major political force, comparable to the Populists or the La Follette movement of 1924. Few in numbers, the Communists have nevertheless appeared to many a dangerous threat to the established order in America. Charges of disloyalty and conspiracy have been provoked by their advocacy of proletarian revolution and by their alignment with an international combination of Communist organizations anchored in the Soviet Union.

This widely held view of the character of American communism—reinforced perhaps by a generalized hostility toward radicalism—has furnished support for a series of public measures designed to limit and regulate the exercise of civil rights by Communists. The Mundt Bill and report are indexes of a domestic anti-Communist policy which has grown increasingly tough in the climate of "cold war." In this new trend, with its

rearrangement of the boundaries between civil liberty and public safety, some critics have indeed seen an ominous departure from the American tradition of free trade in ideas.

The Mundt Bill was devised by the House Committee on Un-American Activities, a body which has since 1938 devoted its main energies to the investigation and exposure of alleged Communists and "Communist-front" activities. Approved by the House of Representatives in May, 1948, the bill failed of adoption in the Senate.

A. THE BILL[1]

SHORT TITLE

SECTION 1. This Act may be cited as the "Subversive Activities Control Act, 1948." . . .

DEFINITIONS

SEC. 3 For the purposes of this Act—

(1) The term "person" means an individual or an organization.

(2) The term "organization" means an organization, corporation, company, partnership, association, trust, foundation, or fund; and includes a group of persons, whether or not incorporated, permanently or temporarily associated together for joint action on, or advancement of views on, any subject or subjects.

(3) The term "communist political organization" means any organization in the United States having some, but not necessarily all, of the ordinary and usual characteristics of a political party, with respect to which, having regard to some or all of the following considerations:

(A) the extent and nature of its activities, including the expression of views and policies,

(B) the extent to which its policies are formulated and carried out and its

activities performed, pursuant to directives or to effectuate the policies, of the foreign government or foreign governmental or political organization in which is vested, or under the domination or control of which is exercised, the direction and control of the world communist movement referred to in section 2 of this Act,

(C) the extent to which its views and policies are the same as those of such foreign government or foreign organization,

(D) the extent to which it supports or advocates the basic principles and tactics of communism as expounded by Marx and Lenin,

(E) the extent to which it receives financial or other aid, directly or indirectly, from or at the direction of such foreign government or foreign organization,

(F) the extent to which it sends members or representatives to any foreign country for instruction or training in the principles, policies, strategy, or tactics of such world communist movement,

(G) the extent to which it reports to such foreign government or foreign organization or to its representatives,

(H) the extent to which its members

1. H.R. 5852 (Mundt-Nixon Bill) (80th Cong., 2d sess. [April 30, 1948]).

or leaders are subject to or recognize the disciplinary power of such foreign government for foreign organization or its representatives,

(I) the extent to which (i) it fails to disclose, or resists efforts to obtain information as to, its membership (by keeping membership lists in code, by instructing members to refuse to acknowledge membership, or by any other method); (ii) its members refuse to acknowledge membership therein; (iii) it fails to disclose, or resists efforts to obtain information as to, records other than membership lists; (iv) its meetings are secret; and (v) it otherwise operates on a secret basis, and

(J) the extent to which its members consider the allegiance they owe to the United States as subordinate to their obligations to such foreign government or foreign organization,

it is reasonable to conclude (i) that it is under the control of such foreign government or foreign governmental or political organization, or (ii) that it is one of the principal instrumentalities utilized by the world communist movement in carrying out its objectives.

(4) The term "communist-front organization" means any organization in the United States (other than a communist political organization and other than an organization having substantially all the ordinary and usual characteristics of a political party) with respect to which, having regard to some or all of the following considerations:

(A) the identity of the persons who are active in its management, direction, or supervision, whether or not holding office therein,

(B) the sources from which an important part of its support, financial or otherwise, is derived,

(C) the use made by it of its funds, resources, or personnel, and

(D) the position taken or advanced by it from time to time on matters of policy,

it is reasonable to conclude (i) that it is under the control of a communist political organization, or (ii) that it is primarily operated for the purpose of giving aid and support to a communist political organization, a communist foreign government, or the world communist movement referred to in section 2, or (iii) that its views and policies are in general adopted and advanced because such views or policies are those of a communist political organization, a communist foreign government, or such world communist movement.

(5) The term "communist organization" means a communist political organization or a communist-front organization.

(6) the term "publication" means any circular, newspaper, periodical, pamphlet, book, letter, postcard, leaflet, or other publication.

(7) The term "United States," when used in a geographical sense, includes the several States, Territories, and possessions of the United States, the District of Columbia, and the Canal Zone.

(8) The term "interstate or foreign commerce" means trade, traffic, commerce, transportation, or communication (A) between any State, Territory, or possession of the United States (including the Canal Zone), or the District of Columbia, and any place outside thereof, or (B) within any territory or possession of the United States (including the Canal Zone) or within the District of Columbia.

(9) The term "final order of the Attorney General" means an order issued by the Attorney General under section 13 of this Act, which has become final as provided in section 14 of this Act, requiring an organization to register under section 8 of this Act as a communist political organization or a communist-front organization.

CERTAIN PROHIBITED ACTS

SEC. 4. (a) It shall be unlawful for any person—

(1) To attempt in any manner to establish in the United States a totalitarian

dictatorship the direction and control of which is to be vested in, or exercised by or under the domination or control of, any foreign government, foreign organization, or foreign individual;

(2) To perform or attempt to perform any act with intent to facilitate or aid in bringing about the establishment in the United States of such a totalitarian dictatorship;

(3) Actively to participate in the management, direction, or supervision of any movement to establish in the United States such a totalitarian dictatorship;

(4) Actively to participate in the management, direction, or supervision of any movement to facilitate or aid in bringing about the establishment in the United States of such a totalitarian dictatorship;

(5) To conspire to do anything made unlawful by this subsection.

(b) Any person who violates any of the provisions of subsection (a) of this section shall, upon conviction thereof, be punished by a fine of not more than $10,000 or imprisonment for not more than 10 years, or both such fine and imprisonment.

(c) Any offense punishable under this section may be prosecuted at any time without regard to any statute of limitations. . . .

EMPLOYMENT OF MEMBERS OF COMMUNIST POLITICAL ORGANIZATIONS

SEC. 6. (a) It shall be unlawful for any member of a communist political organization, knowing or believing, or having reasonable grounds for knowing or believing, that the organization is a communist political organization—

(1) to seek or accept any office or employment under the United States without revealing that he is a member of such organization; or

(2) after thirty days after the date of the enactment of this Act, to hold any nonelective office or employment under the United States.

(b) It shall be unlawful for any officer or employee of the United States to appoint or employ any individual as an officer or employee of the United States, knowing or believing that such individual is a member of a communist political organization.

DENIAL OF PASSPORTS TO MEMBERS OF COMMUNIST POLITICAL ORGANIZATIONS

SEC. 7. (a) It shall be unlawful for any member of a communist political organization, knowing or believing, or having reasonable grounds for knowing or believing, that the organization is a communist political organization—

(1) to make application for a passport, or the renewal of a passport, to be issued or renewed by or under the authority of the United States; or

(2) after sixty days after the date of the enactment of this Act, to use or attempt to use a passport theretofore issued.

(b) It shall be unlawful for any officer or employee of the United States to issue a passport to, or renew the passport of, any individual knowing or believing that such individual is a member of a communist political organization.

REGISTRATION AND ANNUAL REPORTS OF COMMUNIST ORGANIZATIONS

SEC. 8. (a) Each communist political organization (including any organization required, by a final order of the Attorney General, to register as a communist political organization) shall, within the time specified in subsection (c) of this section, register with the Attorney General, on a form prescribed by him by regulations, as a communist political organization.

(b) Each communist-front organization (including any organization required, by a final order of the Attorney General, to register as a communist-front organization) shall, within the time specified in subsection (c) of this section, register with the Attorney General, on a form prescribed by him by regulations, as a communist-front organization.

(c) The registration required by subsection (a) or (b) shall be made—

(1) in the case of an organization which is a communist political organization or a communist-front organization on the date of the enactment of this Act, within thirty days after such date;

(2) in the case of an organization becoming a communist political organization or a communist-front organization after the date of the enactment of this Act, within thirty days after such organization becomes a communist political organization or a communist-front organization, as the case may be; and

(3) in the case of an organization which by a final order of the Attorney General is required to register, within thirty days after such order becomes final.

(d) The registration made under subsection (a) or (b) shall be accompanied by a registration statement, to be prepared and filed in such manner and form as the Attorney General shall by regulations prescribe, containing the following information:

(1) The name of the organization.

(2) The name and last-known address of each individual who is at the time of the filing of such registration statement, and of each individual who was at any time during the period of twelve full calendar months preceding the filing of such statement, an officer of the organization, with the designation or title of the office so held, and with a brief statement of the duties and functions of such individual as such officer.

(3) An accounting, in such form and detail as the Attorney General shall by regulations prescribe, of all moneys received and expended (including the sources from which received and the purposes for which expended) by the organization during the period of twelve full calendar months preceding the filing of such statement.

(4) In the case of a communist political organization, the name and last-known address of each individual who was a member of the organization at any time during the period of twelve full calendar months preceding the filing of such statement.

(e) It shall be the duty of each organization registered under this section to file with the Attorney General on or before February 1 of the year following the year in which it registers, and on or before February 1 of each succeeding year, an annual report, prepared and filed in such manner and form as the Attorney General shall by regulations prescribe, containing the same information which by subsection (d) is required to be included in a registration statement, except that the information required with respect to the twelve-month period referred to in paragraph (2), (3), or (4) of such subsection shall, in such annual report, be given with respect to the calendar year preceding the February 1 on or before which such annual report must be filed.

(f) It shall be the duty of each organization registered under this section to keep, in such manner and form as the Attorney General shall by regulations prescribe—

(1) accurate records of the names and addresses of the members of such organization and of persons who actively participate in the activities of such organization; and

(2) accurate records and accounts of moneys received and expended (including the sources from which received and the purposes for which expended) by such organization.

(g) It shall be the duty of the Attorney General to send to each individual listed in any registration statement or annual report, filed under this section, as a member of the organization in respect of which such registration statement or annual report was filed, a notification in writing that such individual is so listed; and such notification shall be sent at the earliest practicable time after the filing of such registration statement or annual report.

(h) In the case of failure on the part of any organization to register or to file any registration statement or annual report as required by this section, it shall be the duty of the executive officer (or individual performing the ordinary and usual duties of an executive officer) and of the secretary (or individual performing the ordinary and usual duties of a secretary) of such organization, and of such officer or officers of such organization as the Attorney General shall by regulations prescribe, to register for such organization, to file such registration statement, or to file such annual report, as the case may be.

KEEPING OF REGISTER; PUBLIC INSPECTION; REPORTS TO PRESIDENT AND CONGRESS

SEC. 9. (a) The Attorney General shall keep and maintain in the Department of Justice a register of all organizations which are registered under section 8, and such register shall be known as the "Register of Communist Organizations." Communist political organizations and communist-front organizations shall be listed separately in such register.

(b) Such register, together with the registration statements and annual reports filed under section 8, shall be kept and maintained in such manner as to be open for public inspection.

(c) The Attorney General shall submit to the President and to the Congress annually (and at any time when requested by either House by resolution) a report with respect to the carrying out of the provisions of this Act, including the names of the organizations listed in such register and of the data (including the names and addresses of the individuals listed as members of such organizations) contained in registration statements and annual reports filed under section 8.

MEMBERSHIP IN CERTAIN COMMUNIST POLITICAL ORGANIZATIONS

SEC. 10. It shall be unlawful for any individual to become or remain a member of a communist political organization, knowing or believing, or having reasonable grounds for knowing or believing, that it is a communist political organization, if (1) such organization is not registered pursuant to section 8, and (2) the period of time designated in section 8 for registration by such organization has expired.

USE OF THE MAILS AND INSTRUMENTALITIES OF INTERSTATE OR FOREIGN COMMERCE

SEC. 11. It shall be unlawful for any organization which is registered under section 8, or for any organization with respect to which there is in effect a final order of the Attorney General requiring it to register under section 8, or for any person acting for or on behalf of such organization—

(1) to transmit or cause to be transmitted, through the United States mails or by any means or instrumentality of interstate or foreign commerce, any publication which is intended to be, or which it is reasonable to believe is intended to be, circulated or disseminated among two or more persons, unless such publication and any envelope, wrapper, or other container in which it is mailed or otherwise circulated or transmitted bears the following, printed in such manner as may be provided in regulations prescribed by the Attorney General, with the name of the organization appearing in lieu of the blank: "Disseminated by ———, a communist organization"; or

(2) to broadcast or cause to be broadcast any matter over any radio station in the United States, unless such matter is preceded by the following statement, with the name of the organization being stated in place of the blank: "The following program is sponsored by ———, a communist organization."

DENIAL OF TAX DEDUCTIONS AND EXEMPTION

SEC. 12. (a) Notwithstanding any other provision of law, no deduction for Federal income tax purposes shall be allowed in the case of a contribution to or for the use of any organization if at the time of the making of such contribution (1) such organization is registered under section 8, or (2) there is in effect a final order of the Attorney General requiring such organization to register under section 8.

(b) No organization shall be entitled to exemption from Federal income tax, under section 101 of the Internal Revenue Code, for any taxable year if at any time during such taxable year (1) such organization is registered under section 8, or (2) there is in effect a final order of the Attorney General requiring such organization to register under section 8.

CERTAIN ADMINISTRATIVE DETERMINATIONS

SEC. 13. (a) Whenever—

(1) in the case of any organization which is not registered under section 8 of this Act, the Attorney General has reason to believe that such organization is a communist political organization or a communist-front organization (or the Attorney General is requested, by resolution of either House of Congress, to investigate whether such organization is a communist political organization or a communist-front organization), or

(2) the Attorney General receives from any organization registered under section 8 an application that he make a finding that the organization is not a communist political organization or a communist-front organization, as the case may be, and by order cancel its registration and relieve it from the requirement of making further annual reports, and such organization, in support of such application, presents evidence which, in the opinion of the Attorney General, makes a prima facie showing that the organization is not a communist political organization or a communist-front organization, as the case may be,

it shall be his duty forthwith to institute and conduct a full and complete investiga-

tion to determine whether such organization is in fact a communist political organization or a communist-front organization, as the case may be. The Attorney General shall not make such a determination with respect to any organization without first affording to it, after timely notice, an opportunity for a hearing.

(b) For the purposes of such investigation the Attorney General, or any officer of the Department of Justice authorized by him, may hold hearings, administer oaths and affirmations, may examine witnesses and receive evidence at any place in the United States, and may require by subpena the attendance and testimony of witnesses and the production of books, papers, correspondence, memoranda, and other records deemed relevant to the matter under inquiry. Subpenas may be signed and issued by the Attorney General or any such authorized officer. Such attendance of witnesses and the production of such documentary evidence may be required from any place in the United States at any designated place of hearing. Witnesses summoned shall be paid the same fees and mileage that are paid witnesses in the district courts of the United States. In case of disobedience to a subpena the Attorney General may invoke the aid of any court of the United States in requiring the attendance and testimony of witnesses and the production of documentary evidence. Any of the district courts of the United States within the jurisdiction of which such inquiry is carried on may, in case of contumacy or refusal to obey a subpena issued to any person, issue an order requiring such person to appear (and to produce documentary evidence if so ordered) and give evidence relating to the matter in question; and any failure to obey such order of the court may be punished by such court as a contempt thereof. All process in any such case may be served in the judicial district whereof such person is an inhabitant or wherever he may be found.

(c) The testimony in any hearing conducted under this section shall be reduced to writing and filed in the office of the Attorney General.

(d) If upon an investigation pursuant to clause (1) of subsection (a) of this section the Attorney General determines that the organization is a communist political organization or a communist-front organization, as the case may be, he shall make a report in writing in which he shall state his findings as to the facts and shall issue and cause to be served on such organization an order requiring such organization to register as such under section 8 of this Act.

(e) If upon an investigation pursuant to clause (2) of subsection (a) of this section the Attorney General determines that the organization is not a communist political organization or a communist-front organization, as the case may be, he shall make a report in writing in which he shall state his findings as to the facts and shall by order cancel the registration of such organization and relieve it from the requirement of further annual reports. A copy of such order shall be sent to such organization.

(f) If upon an investigation pursuant to clause (2) of subsection (a) of this section the Attorney General determines that the organization is a communist political organization or a communist-front organization, as the case may be, he shall make a report in writing in which he shall state his findings as to the facts and shall issue and cause to be served on such organization an order refusing to cancel the registration of such organization and to relieve it from the requirement of further annual reports

JUDICIAL REVIEW

Sec. 14. (a) Such organization may obtain a review of an order issued under subsection (d) or (f) of section 13 in the United States Court of Appeals for the District of Columbia by filing in the court, within sixty days from the date of service upon it of such order, a written petition praying that the order of the Attorney General be set aside. A copy of such petition shall be forthwith served upon the Attorney General, and thereupon the Attorney General shall certify and file in the court a transcript of the entire record in the proceeding, including all evidence taken and the report and order of the Attorney General. Thereupon the court shall have jurisdiction of the proceeding and shall have power to affirm or set aside the order of the Attorney General. The findings of the Attorney General as to the facts, if supported by substantial evidence, shall be conclusive. If either party shall apply to the court for leave to adduce additional evidence, and shall show to the satisfaction of the court that such additional evidence is material and that there were reasonable grounds for failure to adduce such evidence in the proceeding before the Attorney General, the court may order such additional evidence to be taken before the Attorney General and to be adduced upon the proceeding in such manner and upon such terms and conditions as to the court may seem proper. The Attorney General may modify his findings as to the facts, by reason of the additional evidence so taken, and he shall file such modified or new findings, which, if supported by substantial evidence, shall be conclusive, and his recommendations, if any, with respect to action in the matter under consideration. If the court sets aside an order issued under subsection (f) of section 13 it may enter a judgment canceling the registration of the organization and relieving it from the requirement of further annual reports. The judgment and decree of the court shall be final, except that the same shall be subject to review by the Supreme Court upon certiorari, as provided in section 240 of the Judicial Code, as amended (U.S.C., 1940 edition, title 28, sec. 347).

(b) Any order of the Attorney General issued under subsection (d) of section 13 shall become final—

(1) upon the expiration of the time allowed for filing a petition for review, if no such petition has been duly filed within such time; or

(2) upon the expiration of the time allowed for filing a petition for certiorari, if the order of the Attorney General has been affirmed or the petition for review dismissed by the United States Court of Appeals for the District of Columbia, and no petition for certiorari has been duly filed; or

(3) upon the denial of a petition for certiorari, if the order of the Attorney General has been affirmed or the petition for review dismissed by the United States Court of Appeals for the District of Columbia; or

(4) upon the expiration of ten days from the date of issuance of the mandate of the Supreme Court, if such Court directs that the order of the Attorney General be affirmed or the petition for review dismissed.

PENALTIES

SEC. 15. (a) Any person failing to register or to file any registration statement or annual report as required by section 8 of this Act shall, upon conviction thereof, be punished by a fine of not less than $2,000 and not more than $5,000; except that in case such failure is on the part of the executive officer (or individual performing the ordinary and usual duties of an executive officer) or secretary (or individual performing the ordinary and usual duties of a secretary), or any other officer, of an orgaization required to register under such section 8, the punishment for such failure shall be a fine of not less than $2,000 and not more than $5,000, or imprisonment for not less than two years and not more than

five years, or both such fine and imprisonment. For the purposes of this subsection, if there is in effect with respect to an organization a final order of the Attorney General requiring it to register under section 8, each day of failure to register, whether on the part of the organization or any individual, shall constitute a separate offense.

(b) Whoever, in a registration statement or annual report filed under section 8 of this Act, willfully makes any false statement or willfully omits to state any fact which is required to be stated, or which is necessary to make the statements made or information given not misleading, shall, upon conviction thereof, be punished by a fine of not less than $2,000 and not more than $5,000, or by imprisonment for not less than two years and not more than five years, or by both such fine and imprisonment.

(c) Any person violating any provision of this Act for violation of which no penalty is provided by section 4 or by subsection (a) or (b) of this section shall, upon conviction thereof, be punished by a fine of not more than $5,000, or by imprisonment for not more than two years, or by both such fine and imprisonment.

SEPARABILITY OF PROVISIONS

SEC. 16. If any provision of this Act, or the application thereof to any person or circumstance, is held invalid, the remaining provisions of this Act, or the application of such provision to other persons or circumstances, shall not be affected thereby.

B. THE REPORT[2]

NECESSITY FOR LEGISLATION

The need for legislation to control Communist activities in the United States cannot be questioned.

2. "Protecting the United States against Un-American and Subversive Activities," submitted by Rep. Karl Mundt, from the Committee on Un-American Activities (House Report No. 1844 [80th Cong., 2d sess. (April 30, 1948)]), pp. 2–7.

Ten years of investigation by the Committee on Un-American Activities and by its predecessors have established: (1) That the Communist movement in the United States is foreign-controlled; (2) that its ultimate objective with respect to the United States is to overthrow our free American institutions in favor of a Communist totalitarian dictatorship to be controlled from abroad; (3) that its activities are carried on by secret and conspiratorial methods; and (4) that its activities, both because of the alarming march of Communist forces abroad and because of the scope and nature of Communist activities here in the United States, constitute an immediate and powerful threat to the security of the United States and to the American way of life.

The conclusion that the Communist movement constitutes a threat to the security of the United States and to the American way of life is not the cry of alarmists.

The Communist program of conquest through treachery, deceit, infiltration, espionage, sabotage, corruption, and terrorism has been carried out in country after country and is an ever-growing threat in other countries. There is ample evidence that one of the primary objectives of the world Communist movement, directed from within the most powerful existing Communist totalitarian dictatorship, is to repeat this pattern in the United States.

There is incontrovertible evidence of the fact that the Communist Party of the United States is dominated by such totalitarian dictatorship and that it is one of the principal instrumentalities used by the world Communist movement, directed from within that totalitarian dictatorship, in its ruthless and tireless endeavor to advance the world march of communism.

The findings, which support these conclusions, and the vast quantity of evidence on which they are based, are set forth in detail in the numerous reports which this committee and its predecessors have printed and circulated. Corroboration has been supplied by independent and exhaustive research by other committees of Congress.

Concern over this threat is not limited to the legislative branch of our Government. On March 17, 1948, the President asked the Congress to appropriate several billions of dollars to build up American defenses against the potential threat of the world Communist conspiracy, of which the Communist movement in the United States is a constituent element. Previously, on February 5, the Attorney General, in testifying before the Legislative Subcommittee of the Committee on Un-American Activities, had stated that present laws were inadequate to deal with the subversive activities of Communist threat in the United States. To resist Communist aggression abroad and ignore it at home would be an utterly inconceivable pattern of procedure.

Concern over the Communist threat is not limited to the United States. It is mounting throughout that part of the world which still remains free. For confirmation we have only to look at the recent unprecedented steps taken by the leading nations of western Europe toward banding together in a union, political as well as economic, which will be powerful enough to resist the Communist onslaught. In this hemisphere the nations assembled at Bogotá, on April 22, 1948, unanimously adopted a resolution declaring that the "present world situation demands urgent measures to safeguard peace and defend mutual respect among states" and recommending that each participating nation "adopt within their respective territories and in accord with their constitutional precepts, necessary measures to prevent and uproot activities directed, assisted, or instigated by foreign governments, organizations, or individuals." The Congress of the United States, by adopting the legislation here proposed, can set the pattern for controlling in each country the foreign-directed Communist conspiratorial activities which threaten the existence of free institutions, not only here, but throughout the world. . . .

ANALYSIS OF THE PROBLEM

In considering the merits of the various proposals before it, the committee found that it was confronted with a most perplexing and difficult problem, one of which the framers of the Constitution could have had little conception, and one which required the most comprehensive analysis and study.

The committee approached the problem with care and restraint because it is believed essential that any legislation recommended be strictly in accordance with our constitutional traditions. How to protect freedom from those who would destroy it without infringing upon the freedom of all our people presents a question fraught with constitutional and practical difficulties. We must not mortally wound our democratic framework in attempting to protect it from those who threaten to destroy it.

There are no doubt some, whose opposition to communism is beyond question, who contend that no legislation should be adopted because of the grave constitutional questions involved. The committee believes, however, that the Constitution does not deny to the Congress the power to enact laws which will defend the Nation from those who would use liberties guaranteed by the Constitution to destroy it.

In considering the problem, the committee found it necessary at the outset to distinguish those features of Communist activity against which legislation cannot and should not be directed, from those in the case of which legislative restraints are clearly practicable and necessary. Communism as an economic, social, and political theory is one thing. Communism as a secret conspiracy, dedicated to subverting the interests of the United States to that of a foreign dictatorship, is another.

The committee holds no brief for the economic, social, and political theories which the Communists advocate, but we contend that, under our constitutional system, ideas must be combated with ideas and not with legislation. If communism in the United States operated in the open, without foreign direction, and without attempting to set up a dictatorship subservient to a foreign power, legislation directed against them would neither be justified nor necessary. This, however, is not the case. A careful analysis of the strategy and tactics of communism in the United States discloses activities by reason of which the committee has concluded that legislation can and should be directed toward—

(1) Making unlawful all activity which has as its purpose setting up a totalitarian government in the United States under foreign control.

(2) In view of its foreign-directed character, requiring the Communist movement in the United States to operate in the open rather than underground.

(3) Cutting the threads which bind the international Communist conspiracy together by restricting travel of members of the American section of the world Communist movement.

(4) Protecting the integrity of the Government itself by denying Government employment to members of the American section of the world Communist movement.

As will appear from a reading of the bill and the section-by-section explanation set forth below, the legislation herewith reported to the House contains provisions designed to accomplish the four objectives listed in the preceding paragraph.

INADEQUACY OF EXISTING LEGISLATION

Congress has passed several laws which were directed specifically at curbing the subversive activities of communism in the United States, but they have proved largely ineffectual in accomplishing their purpose.

The Alien Registration Act of 1940 made it a crime to advocate the overthrow of the Government of the United States by force and violence. While force and violence is without doubt a basic principle to which all Communist Party members subscribe, the present line of the party, in order to evade existing legislation, is to avoid wherever possible the open advocacy of force and violence. Consequently, the act has not been an effective instrument in dealing with Communist activity.

The McCormack Act of 1938 required registration of individuals who are acting as agents of a foreign principal. The Voorhis Act required the registration of organizations which are agents of foreign principals. Though these acts were directed against both Nazis and Communists, they have proved ineffective against the latter, due in part to the skill and deceit which the Communists have used in concealing their foreign ties. The Attorney General pointed out some technical weaknesses in these acts in his testimony before the committee, and his recommendations have been incorporated in the registration provisions of the committee bill.

The Attorney General, together with a great majority of the expert witnesses who appeared before the committee during its legislative hearings, agreed that existing laws were inadequate to deal with the Communist threat and that new legislation was essential.

REJECTED PROPOSALS

The committee gave serious consideration to the many well-intentioned proposals which were before it which attempted to meet the problem by outlawing the Communist Party. Proponents of this approach differed as to what they desired. Some wanted to bar the Communist Party from the ballot in elections. Others would have made membership in the Communist Party illegal per se.

The committee believes that there are several compelling arguments against the outlawing approach. There are grave constitutional questions involved in attempting to interfere with the rights of the States to declare what parties and individuals may qualify for appearance on the ballot. To make membership in a specifically designated existing organization illegal per se would run the risk of being held unconstitutional on the ground that such an action was legislative fiat.

Among the policy considerations which militate against this type of approach are the following:

1. Illegalization of the party might drive the Communist movement further underground, whereas exposure of its activities is the primary need.

2. Illegalization has not proved effective in Canada and other countries which have tried it.

3. We cannot consistently criticize the Communist governments of Europe for suppressing opposition political parties if we resort to the same totalitarian methods here.

4. If the present Communist Party severs the puppet strings by which it is manipulated from abroad, if it gives up its undercover methods, there is no reason for denying it the privilege of openly advocating its beliefs, in the way in which other political parties advocate theirs. In politics as well as sports, there are certain rules of the game which must be obeyed. Daggers are out of order on the American playing field. Undercover methods and foreign direction cannot be tolerated on the political field.

This legislation does not constitute a fiat. The Communist Party of the United States is not made guilty of any offense by reason of the enactment of the provisions of this act. If, however, the Communist Party of the United States or any other party now in existence or to be formed operates in such a way that it comes within the definitions and performs activities which are proscribed under the act then the legislation will apply to it. If such party changes its characteristics then the objectives sought by the committee will have been accomplished.

CONCLUSION

The committee wishes to emphasize that this legislation alone is not a complete answer to the Communist problem in the United States.

An attack must be made upon the Communist problem on all fronts if we are to meet it successfully. It is imperative that the American people understand the true character, aims, and techniques of the

Communist conspiracy. The many patriotic and fraternal organizations in the United States can be of tremendous service in developing a program of education which will inform the people of this threat. In the words of one of the outstanding witnesses before our committee:

"The people should be informed, accurately and fully and continuously, about the nature, activities, strategy, and tactics of communism. This educational task can be in part accomplished by qualified and concerned private citizens."

The committee has intentionally not recommended legislation which will deal with so-called theoretical communism in the United States. We are seeking rather to strike a body blow at the American cadre of the foreign-directed Communist conspiracy. We believe that if its criminal activities are prosecuted, its false fronts exposed, and its foreign assistance and direction cut away, the movement in the United States, standing alone for what it is, will be overwhelmingly defeated. We are willing to permit the theories of communism and democracy to clash in the open market place of political ideas in America, but we insist that communism not be allowed to have the unfair advantages in this conflict of the unrestricted use of illegal means, the cloak of secrecy and fraud, and the assistance and direction of a foreign Communist dictatorship. . . .

8. ACADEMIC FREEDOM AND COMMUNISM[1]

By Sidney Hook

Editors' Note.—Congress and many state legislatures have been considering proposed laws to protect the state against communism. The problem of loyalty has become so serious in the minds of many citizens that they are attempting to decide what are the limits, if any, to civil liberty. The review of loyalty of all federal employees has been one aspect of this trend. Several states have passed laws to restrict Communists from teaching and political action. It is under these conditions that the issue of academic freedom is argued by two men distinguished as authors, educators, and philosophers: Sidney Hook (1902——), formerly chairman of the Department of Philosophy, now professor, at New York University, and Alexander Meiklejohn (1872——), former president of Amherst College.

The academic community throughout the United States is currently being disturbed by the perennial issue of the nature and limits of academic freedom. The specific event which has precipitated intense interest and discussion, not only in college classrooms but in all circles interested in

1. Sidney Hook, "Should Communists Be Permitted To Teach?" New York Times Magazine, February 27, 1949. By permission of the author and the New York Times. This article appears here under the title "Academic Freedom and Communism" instead of under the original title at the request of Mr. Hook. The appended letters, not previously published, are reprinted here at his request from copies provided by Mr. Hook.

education, is the expulsion of some professors from the University of Washington for being members of the Communist party. The arresting thing about this case is that for the first time in the history of education the grounds given for the expulsion of the professors is that they have been guilty of violating the principles of academic freedom, and therefore of "conduct unbecoming a teacher."

Here is certainly a startling reversal which reflects the emergence of new problems in culture and education not dreamed of when John Dewey and Arthur T. Lovejoy organized the American Association of

University Professors to further the interests of their profession and defend academic freedom and tenure.

Because the decision may set an important precedent in higher education, it invites a reconsideration of first principles in the light of the facts.

If, as Cardinal Newman has observed, the function of a university is the discovery and publication of the truth in all branches of knowledge, then academic freedom is essential to its very life. For without the freedom to inquire, to challenge and to doubt, truth cannot be well-grounded or error refuted. Since not everything which has been accepted is true, nor everything which is newly proposed is false, the result of inquiry sometimes undermines the customary and supports the novel. When this takes place in noncontroversial areas, it is recognized as the natural operation of the discipline of scientific inquiry; when it affects controversial issues, vested interests and emotions are often aroused and attempts are made to safeguard some special doctrine and conclusion from the consequences of critical scrutiny.

Anything may be regarded as a controversial subject, from the heliocentric hypothesis and the theory of evolution to the causes of World War II and the wisdom of the Marshall Plan. That is why universities from the time of their origin have been compelled to fight the battle for academic freedom over and over again. Although in the West, in matters of pure science, there are no longer powerful special interests that can be outraged by the progress of inquiry, in the social studies, arts and philosophy, convictions are not so clearly a function of evidence. Conclusions in these fields touch on issues of contemporary political or social concern in relation to which almost everyone believes he is something of an authority. One man's truth is often another man's propaganda.

Nonetheless no distinction in principle can be drawn between noncontroversial and controversial themes, especially if we recognize that all human judgments are fallible. The presumption is that university professors engaged in the search for truth are qualified by their professional competence. The judges of their competence can only be their intellectual peers or betters in their own fields. If this is denied, the university loses its *raison d'être* as an institution, not only for free research but critical teaching.

In consequence, any doctrinal impositions, no matter what their source, which set up limits beyond which the professor cannot go, affect him both as a scholar and a teacher. As a scholar, he loses professional standing in the intellectual community if it is suspected that his findings must fit the predetermined conclusions and prejudices of those whose first loyalty is not to the objective methods of seeking the truth. As a teacher, he cannot engage in the honest presentation and reasoned investigation of all relevant *alternatives* to the theories and policies he is considering. He runs the risk of forfeiting the respect of his students, who look to him for candid evaluation and intellectual stimulus, if they believe that he is time-serving or prudent beyond the call of scientific evidence.

If in the honest exercise of his academic freedom an individual reaches views which bring down about his head charges of "Communist," "Fascist" or what not, the academic community is duty bound to protect him irrespective of the truth of the charges. And since these words are often epithets of disparagement rather than of precise description, there is all the more reason why the university must stand firm. It places its faith in the loyalty of its teachers to the ethics and logic of scientific inquiry. The heresies of yesterday are often the orthodoxies of today. In the interests of winning new truths, it is better to err on the side of toleration than of proscription.

This means that the professor occupies a position of trust not only in relation to the university and his student, but to the democratic community which places its faith and hope in the processes of education. ("If a nation expects to be ignorant and free, in a state of civilization," wrote Jefferson, "it expects what never was and what never will be.") Academic freedom therefore carries with it duties correlative with rights. No professor can violate them under the pretext that he is exercising his freedom. That is why the graduate faculty of the New School of Social Research explicitly declares that in the interests of academic freedom, "no member of the faculty can be a member of any political party or group which asserts the right to dictate in matters of science or scientific opinion."

So far the analysis of principles can take us. There remains the important question of fact. Is a member of the Communist party, so long as he remains a member, free to exercise his rights and fulfill his duties as an objective scholar and teacher? To answer this question we must look at what the Communist party itself teaches, its conditions of membership, and what has come to light about the actual behavior of known members of the Communist party. We are not dealing now with the right to hold Communist *beliefs* but with what is entailed by the *act* of membership in the Communist party as it affects educational practice.

First of all, it is important to recognize that there are no "sleepers" or passive members of the Communist party. The statutes of membership define a party member as one who not only "accepts the party program, attends the regular meetings of the membership branch of his place of work" but "who is *active* in party work." Inactivity as well as disagreement with the decisions of any party organization or committee are grounds for expulsion. The concluding sentence of the pledge which the member inducted into the Communist party takes since 1935 reads: "I pledge myself to remain at all times a vigilant and firm defender of the Leninist line of the party, the only line that insures the triumph of Soviet power in the United States" (*Daily Worker*, April 2, 1936).

The "place of work" of the Communist party teacher is the school or university. How is a Communist party member active in party work at the university? Here are some directives from the official organ of the Communist party (*The Communist*, May, 1937):

Party and Y.C.L. fractions set up within classes and departments must supplement and combat by means of discussions, brochures, etc., bourgeois omissions and distortions in the regular curriculum. *Marxist-Leninist analysis must be injected into every class.*

Communist teachers must take advantage of their positions, without exposing themselves, to give their students to the best of their ability working-class education.

To enable the teachers in the party to do the latter, the party must take careful steps to see that all teacher comrades are given thorough education in the teaching of Marxism-Leninism. Only when teachers have really mastered Marxism-Leninism will they be able skillfully to inject it into their teaching at the least risk of exposure and at the same time conduct struggles around the schools in a truly Bolshevik manner.

Two things are significant here. The first is the injunction to cooperate with Communist party fractions among students in order—I am still quoting from official sources—"*to guide and direct that spirit of rebelliousness which already exists.*" The practice, many years ago, was to organize Communist students and teachers in the same cells, but since this led to exposure when students dropped out, teachers and students are now separately organized and meet only through carefully selected committees.

The second noteworthy thing is that Communist party teachers are fearful of exposure and quite aware that their practices violate accepted notions of academic freedom and responsibility. That is why when literature appears under their imprint it is anonymous. Since no one takes personal responsibility, what is said about things and persons, including non-Communist colleagues, is not likely to be scrupulous or accurate. Sometimes it is downright scurrilous.

How is it possible for the Communist party to control the thinking of its members who teach in so many different fields? What have literature, philosophy, science and mathematics got to do with its political program? The answer is to be found in the fact that according to the Communist party itself politics is bound up, through the class struggle, with every field of knowledge. On the basis of its philosophy of dialectical materialism, a party line is laid down for every area of thought from art to zoology. No person who is known to hold a view incompatible with the party line is accepted as a member. For example, if he is a historian he cannot become a member if he teaches that the economic factor is not the most decisive factor in history or, if a political scientist, that the state is not the executive committee of the ruling class or that the Soviet Union is not a democracy. Individuals have been denied membership in the Communist party because they did not believe in "dialectics" in nature.

If a philosopher, to cite cases from my own field, accepts the theories of Mach or Carnap or Husserl or Alexander or Dewey or T. H. Green or G. E. Moore, upon joining the Communist party he will criticize the doctrines he had espoused previously. He cannot ever criticize dialectical materialism or the theories of Lenin and Stalin whom he now regards as great philosophers. If a physicist or mathematician becomes a member of the Communist party he is required, wherever it is possible for him to do so, to relate his subject to the growth of technology, its impact upon social divisions, the class uses to which discovery is put, and the liberating role it can play in a Communist economy. The general theme is: science under capitalism makes for death and poverty; under communism, science makes for life and abundance.

The party line, however, is not constant in all fields. It changes with political exigencies. The life of a Communist party teacher, therefore, is not a happy one, since he may have to prove the opposite of what he once so fervently taught. His difficulties are mitigated by the fact that in different terms he faces different students whose memories are apt to be short in any event. But English teachers who have been members of the Communist party during the last few years have had to reverse their judgments about the same novelists, and sometimes even about the same books, e.g., Malraux's *Man's Fate*, Dos Passos' *U.S.A.*, Wright's *Native Son*, because of changes in the party line toward these authors.

In the social sciences, Communist party teachers taught in 1934 that Roosevelt was a Fascist; in 1936, during the Popular Front, a progressive; in 1940, during the Nazi-Stalin Pact, a warmonger and imperialist; in 1941, after Hitler invaded the Soviet Union, a leader of the oppressed peoples of the world.

Whether with respect to specific issues Communist teachers have been right or wrong in these kaleidoscopic changes is not the relevant question. What is relevant is that their conclusions are not reached by a free inquiry into the evidence. To stay in the Communist party, they must believe and teach what the party line decrees. If anyone doubts this we have the objective evidence provided by Granville Hicks in his public letter of resignation from the Communist party. Hicks resigned because he was refused even the right *to suspend judgment* on the Nazi-Stalin pact. "If the party," he writes, "had left any room for doubt, I could go along with it. . . . But they made it clear that if I eventually found it impossible to defend the pact, and defend it in their terms, there was nothing for me to do but resign" (*New Republic*, October 4, 1939).

It is argued by some civil libertarians, who are prepared to grant the foregoing, that this is still not sufficient evidence to impugn the integrity of teachers who are members of the Communist party. They must be judged by their individual actions in the classroom; they must, so to speak, be "caught in the act" of inculcating the party line in the minds of their students.

This has two fatal difficulties. It would require spying in every classroom to detect the party line, and disorganize or intimidate not only Communist party members but the entire faculty, since a member of the Communist party admits membership only when faced with a charge of perjury, and not always then. The academic community would wrathfully and rightfully repudiate any such practice.

Second, it would be very difficult to determine when a teacher was defending a conclusion because he honestly believed it followed from the evidence, and when he was carrying out his task as a good soldier in the party cause.

Those who contend that membership in the Communist party is *prima facie* evidence that a teacher does not believe in or practice academic freedom, insist that such membership is an *act*, not merely an expression of opinion. They deny that they are invoking the principle of guilt by association, for no one who joins and remains a member of the Communist party could be ignorant of what classroom practices are required of him. If he were ignorant, the Communist party itself would drop him for "inactivity."

It is interesting to note that this position is independent of the questions whether a teacher has a right to be a member of a legal party or whether the Communist party is or should be a legal organization. Paraphrasing Justice Holmes' famous remark about the Boston policeman, a man may have a constitutional right to be a member of the Communist party but he has no constitutional right to be a college professor unless he is free to accept the duties as well as rights of academic freedom. Anyone is free to join or leave the Communist party: but once he joins and remains a member, he is not a free mind.

Some administrative authorities have taken the position that they would not knowingly engage members of the Communist party, otherwise thought competent, but that they would not discharge them after they discovered the fact of their membership. This is obviously inconsistent. The reason which explains their reluctance to take on a member of the Communist party, if valid, still operates when he has already joined the faculty. If on educational grounds a Communist party member is objectionable *before* he has begun working for the party line, is he any less objectionable when he is actually in action? If anything, a person, known from the very outset as a member of the Communist party, may be assigned to a post where he can do far less damage than someone who has successfully concealed the fact of his membership.

There remains the question as to whether expulsion on grounds of membership in the Communist party does not set a dangerous precedent. Communists under fire in a sudden accession of concern for Catholics, express fear lest this threaten the tenure of teachers who are members of the Catholic Church.

As one who cannot be taxed with undue sympathy for Thomist doctrine, I should maintain there is no evidence whatsoever of the operation of Catholic cells in nonsectarian universities which impose a party line in all the arts and sciences that must be followed by all Catholic teachers on pain of excommunication. The comparison is a red herring. The danger to free inquiry in education from Catholic quarters comes not from teachers but from outside pressure groups.

If any other organization exists which operates like the Communist party, its members should be treated equitably with the members of the Communist party. Members of the Nazi party were under similar discipline. But in their case, before and after the Stalin-Hitler alliance, the Communists demanded their peremptory dismissal.

The problem of the "fellow-traveler" is

even a more difficult and involved question. But its solution, paradoxical as it may appear, is simple. It must be left entirely to the enlightened good sense of the academic community, which can apply various sanctions short of dismissal. The term "fellow-traveler" is hopelessly vague. "Fellow-travelers" come and go. They are of all varieties. No one is wise enough to pick out the dumb, innocent sheep from the cunning and dishonest goats. So long as they are not under the discipline of the Communist party, they may still be sensitive to the results of honest inquiry. Whatever harm they do is incomparably less than the harm that would result from any attempt to purge them. Without the steel core of the Communist party fraction on the campus to magnetize them, they will fly off in all the directions their scattered wits take them.

Although the exclusion of Communist party teachers from the academic community seems justified in *principle*, this by itself does not determine whether it is a wise or prudent action in *all* circumstances. Sometimes the consequences of removing an unmitigated evil may be such as to make its sufferance preferable. If removal of Communist party members were to be used by other reactionary elements as a pretext to hurl irresponsible charges against professors whose views they disapprove, a case might be made for suspending action. On the other hand, failure to act in a situation where the academic process has been flagrantly suborned may lead to public suspicion and reprisals that injure innocent and guilty alike.

How to protect the innocent, as well as those who have genuinely broken with the Communist party, from dangers attending a policy justified in principle is too large a theme to explore here. But I am confident that *if the execution of the policy were left to university faculties themselves*, and not to administrators and trustees who are harried by pressure groups, there would be little ground for complaint. In the last analysis there is no safer repository of the integrity of teaching and scholarship than the dedicated men and women who constitute the faculties of our colleges and universities.

THREE LETTERS ON ACADEMIC FREEDOM

I

March 7, 1949

DEAR ——

If the Communist Party *were* like the Episcopalian church, you would be justified in demanding proof of individual acceptance of its tenets. But the Communist Party is emphatically *not* like the Episcopalian Church in this regard or any other organization you know. That you should even compare it to the Episcopalian Church gives me pause. I begin to appreciate how great is the task of making clear what the *facts* are.

First, the Episcopalian Church not so long ago declared officially that it was not necessary to subscribe to *all* 39 articles in order to receive communion. Dean Inge has for years publicly criticized some of these articles as absurd. If you can find since 1929 one single Communist—anywhere—who ever criticized one single item in the close to 390 articles of Communist Party faith without being expelled forthwith, I shall grant you your point. If you can find one philosopher who is a member of the Communist Party who ever wrote that Lenin was wrong in his belief that ideas are images—even though they hold beliefs that are incompatible with the correspondence-image theory of truth—I shall grant you your point. If any Communist Party philosopher did, the Agit-Prop director would visit him to show him the error of his ways and give him a chance to recant. If he didn't recant, out he would go.

2. The Communist Party is a unique organization. The nearest I can come to suggesting what it is like is to say that it is

something of a cross between an army and a Jesuit order except that the Jesuits are not so monolithic ideologically. Incidentally, there is nothing in the Communist Party like the divergencies between the Augustinian and Thomistic traditions in the Catholic Church. Were the Catholics to become a majority in the country, the Church would *begin* to approach the position of the Party.

3. There is a vast literature on how the C.P. is organized and how it functions. Cf. the books by Gitlow on the United States, Ruth Fisher on Germany, Tosca on France, Krivitsky on Europe. Same story everywhere.

4. Every member of the C.P. is instructed when he joins about the way the Party is organized, what his tasks and duties are. He cannot remain innocent and he cannot remain inactive. Meetings are held periodically to ascertain what members have been inactive, and why. If the reason for inactivity is invalid, the member is expelled. The C.P. no more accepts resignations than an army does. The record shows that the C.P. cell on the University of Washington campus held meetings to determine who was active and who not.

5. Communist Party members are required not only to teach the Party line when they can but to recruit for party organizations and to distribute party literature. The anonymous cell paper on the campus is gotten out as a collective project. Every member is supposed to do *something* in relation to it, at the very least mailing or personal distribution, *in order that everyone be involved as a measure of protection for everyone else.*

6. Have you ever seen some of these campus shop papers? I haven't seen any from the coast but here in the East professors who are non-Communists have been libelled and slandered; branded as plagiarists and thieves; accused of diverting college property to their own use and of padding payrolls. In one case indirect responsibility for death was charged to college authorities. I need not list at length the dishonorable epithets from the Communist litany of denunciation like "spy," "Fascist," "anti-Semite" hurled promiscuously at colleagues.

If such charges were made openly they would lay the persons who made them open to criminal prosecution.

These publications are distributed not only to faculty members but to students. All this is no help to teaching and learning.

That Communist Party members on the campus are bound by party rules, beliefs, dogmas, is a matter of fact which I am confident can be established once American professors can find its *possibility* credible. Until now, like most of their fellow citizens, they have been unable to understand what politics based on *Weltanschauung* means.

The main question which troubles not only you but others is not one of fact but one of procedure and policy. Even if the above is true, mustn't we actually bring home to the door of the individual *his* specific act of wrongdoing? If it were a matter of sending a man to jail, I would agree, but what is involved is dissociating him from the profession on grounds of violation of *professional* standards.

Perhaps an analogy can make this clearer. Suppose you sit down with a person to play a game of cards under given rules. You then discover he has a sleeve full of aces which he is obviously planning to use. Must you catch him in the act of drawing his ace before you are justified in telling him off and sending him packing? It seems to me that in *principle*, although we may not enforce the rule for some special reason, we are not obligated to wait until we detect the Communist Party member in the act of subverting academic freedom. He has already declared his intentions and read himself out of the community of honest investigators and/or teachers.

(Incidentally, I don't know the specific facts about Washington, although I expect to read the entire record if I can find the time. But I read in the newspapers that

Phillips claims to have informed his class that he was "a Marxist" when he discussed social and political philosophy. A "Marxist" may mean anything. Harold Laski is a Marxist; so am I after a fashion. The point is that you can be certain that Phillips *didn't* tell his class "I'm a member of the Communist Party," which is what, in all honesty, he should have done if he wanted to put them on guard against his own bias. And, further, there is no evidence that he told his classes that he was a Marxist until the last year or two when things got hot.)

There are also some other considerations that should be mentioned. Every Communist Party member who is in a science department is expected to report on all new work or experiments to someone who is introduced to him by the cell-leader who himself receives orders from the leader of the next highest group. All these reports are channelled through a special agency to one particular person on the Central Committee of the party who is contacted by a liaison man from abroad. I know of the existence of the apparatus through General Krivitsky, whom I knew after he broke with the Soviet Union. I have no way of knowing, however, whether and what information was transmitted. But since the Communist Party has already given notice what it expects to do if there is an outbreak of hostilities, sheer prudence would dictate caution in permitting Communist Party members, except under special circumstances, access to laboratories.

One final point which recapitulates all. In 1924 or 1925 when a member of the Masons joined the Communist Party, he would resign from the Lodge because it was understood that he could honor no oath of secrecy as a member of the Communist Party. But he resigned—and this was an honorable act. Ten years later if a member of the Masons or any other secret fraternal order joined the Communist Party, he was instructed to remain and organize a cell or fraction within the organization.

Sincerely,
SIDNEY HOOK

P.S. I see I should have written "penultimate" point instead of final point.

But this footnote has a bearing on one of your questions. There are two cultural magazines published by the Communist Party in this country. One is *New Masses and Main Stream*, the other is *Science and Society*. Observe the following: After the condemnation of the Mendelian geneticists by the Soviet Union, both magazines suddenly appeared with articles endorsing the government action and upholding Lysenko. I am confident myself that not one of the Editors of these magazines really believes in Lysenko's doctrines. Why, then, you may ask, do they print these articles? The answer is because of their total commitment to the Soviet Union.

The Communist teacher's "integrity" is expressed in this *total* commitment. In virtue of it, he refuses to criticize the party line on any special point, even when he personally disagrees with it. He squares this to himself with the reflection that the point on which he feels the party line is wrong is comparatively unimportant. But it is precisely this subordination to his total commitment, and his evaluation of what is important or unimportant in the light of a political objective, which makes it impossible for him to exercise the *free criticism* he would naturally engage in were he loyal to the principles of scientific inquiry. The Communist Party teachers in this respect remind me of some Nazi Party members whom I knew who, because they accepted the general outlook of the Nazi Party, refused to criticize, when circumstances were relevant, the Nazi myth about the existence and moral inferiority of the Jewish race, even when *personally* they acknowledged it was nonsense.

II

March 9, 1949

DEAR ———

As you probably know, for years I have been ardently combating all forms of totalitarianism, including the Catholic variety (cf. the chapter on Maritain in my book *Reason, Social Myths, and Democracy*).

As a result of my researches on the Catholic philosophy and practices, I have come to the conclusion that the church has two positions, which as a matter of fact have papal sanction. One position holds for situations in which the Catholics constitute a majority of the community. This position is totalitarian even though it permits a much wider variation in approach and detail to dogma than the Communist position. For example, there was nothing in Communist theory which allows divergencies as great as those that exist between the Augustinian and Thomistic traditions in the Catholic church.

The second position has been worked out for situations in which the Catholics constitute a minority of the population, and in which Catholics, according to one of the Encyclicals, must suffer other people's conceptions of freedom. In such situations Catholics have papal justification to live under and even enforce certain laws which run *counter* to Catholic dogma. For example, Catholic judges on the bench in New York State grant divorces even to Catholics and recognize that they have a duty both to the standards of their profession and to the laws of the state, insofar as it is not a Catholic law or a Catholic state under which they live. The same "absolution" is granted to Catholic teachers who are good members of the church insofar as they are members of non-Catholic institutions. They are supposed to fulfill their obligations and duties as a member of the non-Catholic academic community and prescribe readings, for example, for their students which are on the Catholic index even when their students are Catholics. Dean Carman of Columbia University is a good Catholic, but he is very proud of the Columbia Contemporary Civilization and Humanities courses in which students read many works that are on the Catholic index. Of course, in Catholic institutions, the church dogma is the decisive matter.

There has been wide interest aroused in the Catholic aspect of the issue, and although there is nothing like the urgency involved, as is the case with the Communist issue on some campuses, perhaps it would be an excellent notion for some scholars to explore that phase of the subject further.

Sincerely yours,
SIDNEY HOOK

III

A LETTER FROM A STUDENT—TYPICAL
OF MANY OTHERS

[Address given]
Professor Sidney Hook
Chairman, Department of Philosophy
Washington Square College
New York University
New York City
DEAR PROFESSOR:

In connection with your recent article which appeared in last Sunday's *Times* discussing the desirability of Communists as instructors, I feel that the following information might be of some little use to you.

The other day in discussing the English statesman and orator, Edmund Burke, I suddenly discovered how many misconceptions and untruths I had carried away from a basic College Composition Course. I referred to Burke as a "fascistic sycophant" and was astounded to discover how wrong I had been. After I had devoured the evidence on the subject of Burke and came to a rational conclusion, I wondered what other thoughts and fallacies I had carried away from that class.

Burke was "fascistic" because he opposed the French Revolution. General Marshall's *Report to the Nation* was a "fabrication and a pack of lies" because he had failed to give Russia its proper place in the winning of the war. These are only two of the subjects I remember which were discussed and analyzed from the Instructor's viewpoint. This viewpoint seems to me now as decidedly biased.

It is true that we discussed the styles of the writing of the men involved but when we came to the context of their writings or political convictions, we were presented distorted versions from the Instructor's Party Line leanings. The remarkable aspect of these teachings was that the Instructor had such an engaging personality and warm sense of humor that those few members of the class who saw fit to disagree with his contentions and assumptions, found themselves disagreeing not only with him but with the majority of the entire class. His subtle misrepresentations of certain facts, his personal, colored interpretations of the material under discussion were so forceful and effective that I went out of the course believing many things to be true which were actually false. I assume from class discussion that many others were similarly impressed.

During the course of that term, at the suggestion of the Instructor, I wrote a paper on the topic, "Idealism versus Materialism." Looking back now I realize how ridiculous an essay this really was, but at the time, under the influence of this man, and helped by a suggested reference, Stalin's *Historical and Dialectical Materialism*, I attacked the problem crudely but enthusiastically. The result was a hodgepodge of adolescent gibberish.

Another memory which I carry with me as a result of this Freshman Course is a rather unpleasant one. One evening, during a class discussion, members of the class (apparently with the permission of the Instructor—because he did not object) circulated an enrollment petition for an or-

ganization which stated as its purpose support for Civil Rights, Price Controls, Veteran's Housing and an imposing list of similar benefits. The name of the organization was the "American Youth for Democracy." I signed the membership list. This group, as we now know, was later revealed to be a front for the Communist Party. Due to my ignorance and gullibility, today my name is contained on the scrolls along with those of the other one-time members of this organization, and although I never attended any meetings— never was active in *any* sense of the word, if this knowledge comes into the hands of future employers, my position might be jeopardized. I wonder how many others were duped in the same manner? I say duped, because I have never seen that procedure carried out in any other classroom.

Fortunately, in the course of my education, I came in contact with other instructors as a result of accident who not only weren't dogmatic but who gave me the necessary techniques and methods for approaching problems myself—rationally and intelligently. And so I have been able to overcome the disadvantage of this first impression, which, although it wasn't etched in my mind was nonetheless effective for a time. I wonder if the other students were as "accidentally" fortunate as I was. If their education had been devoid of these instructors, then they probably still hold these same biased and untruthful ideas. I fervently hope that the other young, pliable students who were like me, quite definitely swayed, have also learned how to think for themselves. That, I feel, should be the prime purpose of an education which has for its basis, academic freedom.

Sincerely yours,

[*Signed*]

9. PROFESSORS ON PROBATION[1]

By Alexander Meiklejohn

The president and regents of the University of Washington have dismissed three professors and have placed three others on probation. That statement fails to mention the most significant feature of what has been done. The entire faculty is now on probation. Every scholar, every teacher, is officially notified that if, in his search for the truth, he finds the policies of the American Communist party to be wise, and acts on that belief, he will be dismissed from the university.

In one of the dismissal cases, the evidence is not clear enough to enable an outsider to measure the validity of the decision. But the other five cases force an issue on which everyone who cares for the integrity and freedom of American scholarship and teaching must take his stand. Cool and careful consideration of that issue should be given by all of us, whether or not we agree with the teachers in question, but especially if we do not agree with them.

The general question in dispute is that of the meaning of academic freedom. But that question has three distinct phases. The first of these has to do with the organization of a university. It asks about the rights and duties of the faculty in relation to the rights and duties of the administration. And the principle at issue corresponds closely to that which, in the Government of the United States, is laid down by the First Amendment to the Constitution. Just as that Amendment declares that "Congress shall make no law abridging the freedom of speech," so, generally, our universities and colleges have adopted a principle which forbids the administra-

tion to abridge the intellectual freedom of scholars and teachers. And, at this point, the question is whether or not the president and regents at Washington have violated an agreement, made in good faith, and of vital importance to the work of the university.

The principle of academic freedom was clearly stated by Sidney Hook in the *New York Times Magazine* of February 27, 1949. After noting that "administrators and trustees" are "harried by pressure groups," Mr. Hook concluded his argument by saying, "In the last analysis there is no safer repository of the integrity of teaching and scholarship than the dedicated men and women who constitute the faculties of our colleges and universities." On the basis of that conviction, the Association of University Professors has advocated, and most of our universities, including Washington, have adopted, a "tenure system." That system recognizes that legal authority to appoint, promote, and dismiss teachers belongs to the president and regents. But so far as dismissals are concerned, the purpose of the tenure agreement is to set definite limits to the exercise of that authority.

This limitation of their power, governing boards throughout the nation have gladly recognized and accepted. To the Association of University Professors it has seemed so important that violations of it have been held to justify a "blacklisting" of a transgressor institution—a recommendation by the association that scholars and teachers refuse to serve in a university or college which has thus broken down the defenses of free inquiry and belief.

It is essential at this point to note the fact that the fear expressed by the tenure system is a fear of action by the president and regents. Since these officers control the status and the salaries of teachers, it is only through them or by them that effective external pressure can be used to limit

1. Alexander Meiklejohn, "Should Communists Be Allowed To Teach?" *New York Times Magazine*, March 27, 1949. By permission of the author and the *New York Times*. This article appears here under the title "Professors on Probation" instead of under the original title at the request of Mr. Meiklejohn.

faculty freedom. To say, then, as we must, that the explicit purpose of the tenure system is to protect freedom against the president and regents, is not to say that these officials are more evil than others. It says only that they are more powerful than others. Theirs is the power by which, unless it is checked by a tenure system, evil may be done.

Under the excellent code adopted at the University of Washington, it is agreed that, after a trial period in which the university makes sure that a teacher is competent and worthy of confidence, he is given "permanence" of tenure. This means that he is secure from dismissal unless one or more of five carefully specified charges are proved against him. And the crucial feature of this defense of freedom is that the holding of any set of opinions, however unpopular or unconventional, is scrupulously excluded from the list of proper grounds for dismissal. The teacher who has tenure may, therefore, go fearlessly wherever his search for the truth may lead him. And no officer of the university has authority, openly or by indirection, to abridge that freedom.

When, under the Washington code, charges are made against a teacher, it is provided that prosecution and defense shall be heard by a tenure committee of the faculty, which shall judge whether or not the accusations have been established. In the five cases here under discussion, the only charge made was that of present or past membership of the American Communist party. Specific evidence of acts revealing unfitness or misconduct in university or other activities was deliberately excluded from the prosecution case. And, further, since the alleged fact of party membership was frankly admitted by the defense, the only question at issue was the abstract inquiry whether or not such membership is forbidden under the five provisions of the tenure code.

Upon that issue, the faculty committee decided unanimously that, in the cases of the ex-members of the Communist party,

there were, under the code, no grounds for dismissal. And, by a vote of eight to three, the same conclusion was reached concerning the two men who were still members of the party. In the discussions of the committee, the suggestion was made that the code should be so amended that party membership would give ground for dismissal. But that action was not recommended. In its capacity as the interpreter of the code which now protects academic freedom, the committee, in all five cases, declared the charges to be not supported by the evidence presented.

In response to this judgment upon teachers by their intellectual peers, the regents, on the recommendation of the president, dismissed the two party members. And, second, going beyond the recommendation of the president, they placed the three ex-members "on probation" for two years. These actions are clearly a violation of the agreement under which faculty members have accepted or continued service in the university. They deserve the condemnation of everyone who respects the integrity of a covenant, of everyone who values faculty freedom and faculty responsibility for the maintaining of freedom.

The second phase of the general question goes deeper than the forms of university organization. It challenges the wisdom of the tenure code as it now stands. It may be that, though the regents are wrong in procedure, they are right in principle. Here, then, we must ask whether President Allen is justified in saying that a teacher who is "sincere in his belief in communism" cannot "at the same time be a sincere seeker after truth which is the first obligation of the teacher." In a press interview, Mr. Allen is quoted as saying, "I insist that the Communist party exercises thought control over every one of its members. That's what I object to." Such teachers, he tells us, are "incompetent, intellectually dishonest, and derelict in their duty to find and teach the truth." Can those assertions be verified? If so, then the tenure code should be amended. If not, then the action of the university should be immediately and decisively reversed.

No one can deny that a member of the American Communist party accepts a "discipline." He follows a party "line." As the policies of the party shift, he shifts with them. That statement is in some measure true of all parties, whose members agree to work together by common tactics toward a common end. But the Communist discipline, it must be added, is unusually rigid and severe. Our question is, then, whether submission to that discipline unfits for university work men who, on grounds of scholarship and character, have been judged by their colleagues to be fitted for it.

For the judging of that issue we must examine the forces by means of which the discipline of the American Communist party is exercised. It is idle to speak of "thought control" except as we measure the compulsions by which that control is made effective. What, then, are the inducements, the dominations which, by their impact upon the minds of these university teachers, rob them of the scholar's proper objectivity?

So far as inducements are concerned, good measuring of them requires that we place side by side the advantages offered to a scholar by the Communist party and those offered by the president and regents of a university. On the one hand, as seen in the present case, the administration can break a man's career at one stroke. It has power over every external thing he cares for. It can destroy his means of livelihood, can thwart his deepest inclinations and intentions. For example, in very many of our universities it is today taken for granted that a young scholar who is known to be a Communist has not the slightest chance of a faculty appointment. He is barred from academic work. And, as against this, what has the American Communist party to offer? Its "inducements" are the torments of suspicion, disrepute, insecurity, personal and family disaster.

Why, then, do men and women of scholarly training and taste choose party membership? Undoubtedly, some of them are, hysterically, attracted by disrepute and disaster. But, in general, the only explanation which fits the facts is that these scholars are moved by a passionate determination to follow the truth where it seems to lead, no matter what may be the cost to themselves and their families. If anyone wishes to unearth the "inducements" which threaten the integrity of American scholarship he can find far more fruitful lines of inquiry than that taken by the administration of the University of Washington.

But Communist controls, we are told, go far deeper than "inducements." The members of the party, it is said, "take orders from Moscow"; they are subject to "thought control by a foreign power." Now, here again, the fact of rigid party discipline makes these assertions, in some ambiguous sense, true. But, in the sense in which President Allen and his regents interpret them, they are radically false.

Let us assume as valid the statement that, in the American Communist party "orders" do come from Moscow. But by what power are those orders enforced in the United States? In the Soviet Union, Mr. Stalin and his colleagues can, and do, enforce orders by police and military might. In that nation their control is violent and dictatorial. But by what form of "might" do they control an American university? What can they do to him? At its extreme limit, their only enforcing action is that of dismissal from the party. They can say to him, "You cannot be a member of this party unless you believe our doctrines, unless you conform to our policies." But, under that form of control, a man's acceptance of doctrines and policies is not "required." It is voluntary.

To say that beliefs are required as "conditions of membership" in a party is not to say that the beliefs are required by force, unless it is shown that membership in the party is enforced. If membership is free, then the beliefs are free.

Misled by the hatreds and fears of the cold war, President Allen and his regents are unconsciously tricked by the ambiguities of the words, "control," and "require," and "free," and "objective." The scholars whom they condemn are, so far as the evidence shows, free American citizens. For purposes of social action, they have chosen party affiliation with other men, here and abroad, whose beliefs are akin to their own. In a word, they do not accept Communist beliefs because they are members of the party. They are members of the party because they accept Communist beliefs.

Specific evidence to support the assertion just made was staring President Allen and his regents in the face at the very time when they were abstractly denying that such evidence could exist. Three of the five men whom they condemned as enslaved by party orders had already, by their own free and independent thinking, resigned from the party. How could they have done that if, as charged, they were incapable of free and independent thinking? Slaves do not resign.

At the committee hearings, these men explained, simply and directly, that, under past conditions, they had found the party the most effective available weapon for attack upon evil social forces but that, with changing conditions, the use of that weapon seemed no longer advisable. Shall we say that the decision to be in the party gave evidence of a lack of objectivity while the decision to resign gave evidence of the possession of it? Such a statement would have no meaning except as indicating our own lack of objectivity.

In these three cases, as in the more famous case of Granville Hicks who, some years ago, resigned party membership with a brilliant account of his reasons for doing so, the charge made cannot be sustained. The accusation as it stands means nothing more than that the president and regents are advocating one set of ideas and are banning another. They are attributing to their victims their own intellectual sins. And the tragedy of their action is that it has immeasurably injured the cause which they seek to serve and, correspondingly, has advanced the cause which they are seeking to hold back.

The third phase of our question has to do with the wisdom, the effectiveness, of the educational policy under which teachers have been dismissed or put on probation. And, on this issue, the evidence against the president and regents is clear and decisive. However good their intention, they have made a fatal blunder in teaching method.

As that statement is made, it is taken for granted that the primary task of education in our colleges and universities is the teaching of the theory and practice of intellectual freedom, as the first principle of the democratic way of life. Whatever else our students may do or fail to do, they must learn what freedom is. They must learn to believe in it, to love it, and most important of all, to trust it.

What, then, is this faith in freedom, so far as the conflict of opinions is concerned? With respect to the world-wide controversy now raging between the advocates of the freedom of belief and the advocates of suppression of belief, what is our American doctrine? Simply stated, that doctrine expresses our confidence that whenever, in the field of ideas, the advocates of freedom and the advocates of suppression meet in fair and unabridged discussion, freedom will win. If that were not true, if the intellectual program of democracy could not hold its own in fair debate, then that program itself would require of us its own abandonment. That chance we believers in self-government have determined to take. We have put our faith in democracy.

But the president and regents have, at this point, taken the opposite course. They have gone over to the enemy. They are not willing to give a fair and equal hearing to those who disagree with us. They are convinced that suppression is more effective as an agency of freedom than is freedom itself.

But this procedure violates the one basic principle on which all teaching rests. It is impossible to teach what one does not believe. It is idle to preach what one does not practice. These men who advocate that we do to the Russians what the Russians, if they had the power, would do to us are declaring that the Russians are right and that we are wrong. They practice suppression because they have more faith in the methods of dictatorship than in those of a free self-governing society.

For many years the writer of these words has watched the disastrous educational effects upon student opinion and attitude when suppression has been used, openly or secretly, in our universities and colleges. The outcome is always the same. Dictatorship breeds rebellion and dissatisfaction. High-spirited youth will not stand the double-dealing which prates of academic freedom and muzzles its teachers by putting them "on probation."

If we suggest to these young people that they believe in democracy, then they will insist on knowing what can be said against it as well as what can be said for it. If we ask them to get ready to lay down their lives in conflict against an enemy, they want to know not only how strong or how weak are the military forces of that enemy, but also what he has to say for himself as against what we are saying for ourselves.

Many of the students in our colleges and universities are today driven into an irresponsible radicalism. But that drive does not come from the critics of our American political institutions. It comes chiefly from the irresponsible defenders of those institutions—the men who make a mockery of freedom by using in its service the forces of suppression.

Underlying and surrounding the Washington controversy is the same controversy as it runs through our national life. The most tragic mistake of the contemporary American mind is its failure to recognize the inherent strength and stability of free institutions when they are true to themselves. Democracy is not a weak and unstable thing which forever needs propping up by the devices of dictatorship. It is the only form of social life and of government which today has assurance of maintaining itself.

As contrasted with it, all governments of suppression are temporary and insecure. The regimes of Hitler and Mussolini flared into strength, and quickly died away. The power of the Soviet Union cannot endure unless that nation can find its way into the practices of political freedom. And all the other dictatorships are falling, and will fall, day by day. Free self-government alone gives promise of permanence and peace. The only real danger which threatens our democracy is that lack of faith which leads us into the devices and follies of suppression.

UNIT XIII
RECENT FOREIGN POLICY

IN THE past decade American foreign policy has undergone a revolutionary transformation. From being
a nation which in 1939 still cultivated
the Washingtonian tradition of isolationism, America in 1949 is committed
to the deliberate exercise of political
power over the greater part of the
globe. Admittedly, it is power which
the Russian sphere of influence repudiates and against which other nations are able to assert, in varying degrees, the claims of "independence."
But, whatever the limitations, the fact
remains that Americans are now
pledged to a policy of world leadership
around which the formulas of isolationism can no longer be stretched.

The recent problem has been to
find an American foreign policy which
will deal with three facts of international life. First, the fact that whereas
in 1938 there were seven great powers
—or six, if the courtesy is withdrawn
from Italy—there are now only two in
the top rank. Second, the fact that in
a world which modern technology has
made inescapably interdependent and
hideously dangerous the reasons for
seeking peace and agreement are more
compelling than ever. Third, the fact
that the two dominant powers, together with their associates and satellites, have reached no agreement about
the kind of world they can live in.

How has this happened? What has
been the official American policy?
What are the grounds for criticism?

No doubt there were many factors
in the prewar period which were involving America more deeply in world
affairs. Expanding power—measured
in terms of population, industrial efficiency, national wealth, and military
potential—forces responsibility on the
politicians who represent such nations
in the world community whether they
welcome it or not. It alters the shifting
balance of world power. It attracts
dependents and provokes enmity. It
incurs commitments. There is sufficient evidence that American policy
in the interwar years was being affected by these familiar consequences
of growth; and there were serious misgivings, as the thirties advanced,
about the drift of German, Italian, and
Japanese policy, the weakness of the
western European powers, and the
likelihood of war. However, this new
concern with world affairs was largely
neutralized by the determination of
American opinion to avoid entanglement. The supreme example of this
isolationism was the neutrality legislation of 1935–37—the ripened fruit of
heated reflection on the entanglements
of World War I. There has been some
question as to the extent to which the
initiative of the administration had to

be restricted by this mentality, but undoubtedly the major task of educating the American people in the realities of world politics was left to the painful pressure of events.

In September, 1939, Germany invaded Poland, and Britain and France declared war. The modification of the neutrality legislation in favor of the western powers began early. In the spring of 1940 western Europe was overrun by Germany (which was then joined by Italy), and Britain remained for one year the sole military opponent. The American intervention during this period took the form of substituting every assistance short of war for the remnants of neutrality. The national resources were mobilized, and immense supplies began to be diverted into the British war effort in the form of Lend-Lease. In June, 1941, Germany turned eastward and invaded Russia—an event which united Britain and Russia in common resistance to Germany and brought Russia within the scope of American aid. In December, 1941, prolonged tension between America and Japan reached its climax in the attack on Pearl Harbor. Thereafter the war was fought by an alliance of America and Britain against Japan and by an alliance of America, Britain, and Russia against Germany and Italy. Germany surrendered unconditionally in May, 1945. The Japanese war, which Russia entered at the last moment under the terms of an Allied agreement, was brought to an abrupt end when American pressure on Japan culminated in the atomic bombardment.

This war left European affairs—for the first time in European history—under the decisive influence of two powers one of which was wholly and the other partly non-European. German and Italian power was obliterated. French power was prostrate after five years of enemy occupation. British power was seriously impaired by six years of war. Western Europe was incapable of organizing its own economic recovery.

The end of the war found Russia mauled and bloody but with opportunities for expansion which exceeded the wildest ambitions of the czars and with irresistible inducements to seize them. The territories lost in World War I were within reach. The vacuum created by the disappearance of German power in eastern Europe could be filled by Russian power. The British security system, extending from the Balkans to the Far East and forming in the past a massive counterpoise to Russian ambition, might be made to contract under pressure. The elimination of Japanese influence in Asia offered similar opportunities for Russian and Communist expansion.

America, alone among the major combatants, was left with an increased industrial production and without a single battle scar across the whole of her sheltered land. Armed with economic might and atomic weapons, dominant in Japan and the Pacific, indispensable to Britain and to western Europe, established with armies of occupation in Germany, Austria, and Italy—however benevolent in her own eyes, she constituted a formidable threat to any suspicious competitor.

The Roosevelt policy seems to have been intended to disarm suspicion. While the war was being fought, and the latent antagonisms were masked by common strategy and sacrifice, the ground was prepared for a great effort of constructive peacemaking at the war's end. American war aims had been stated in the Four Freedoms, the Atlantic Charter, and the propaganda for "One World." Plans for a division of influence, for a settlement with the enemy powers, and for the organization of a world assembly had been discussed in wartime conferences with Great Britain and Russia. A charter for the United Nations had been drawn up at San Francisco before the fighting was finished. Broadly speaking, it was expected that the problems of the peace would be attacked simultaneously on two fronts. The diplomatic representatives of the great powers would negotiate the peace treaties, the evacuation of armies, and the settlement of a workable balance of power to underpin the new world. Meanwhile the United Nations, in which great and small were represented, would attempt to succeed where the League of Nations had failed.

Whispers of the coming storm had been heard at San Francisco. The foreign ministers held their first meeting in the fall of 1945; the United Nations, in January, 1946. Neither opening was at all encouraging. In the course of the four years which have elapsed, the foreign ministers have negotiated trea-

ties for Italy and the satellite powers. The attempt to frame a settlement for Germany has broken down in complete failure, and Germany is partitioned between two hostile systems of military occupation. There is no treaty for Austria and none for Japan. The Security Council, the General Assembly, the Atomic Energy Commission, and every other agency of the United Nations on which high hopes had been built has been either divided into antagonistic blocs or boycotted by the Soviet representatives. The United Nations exists and has its uses. But it inspires no confidence as a framework for a world community while the entire world is involved in a "cold war" between East and West.

American policy has passed through a phase of optimism and good will into a mood of calculated resistance to Russian expansion. Its authors believe that the American effort to co-operate in the reconstruction of a shattered world was met with obstruction, bad faith, and naked aggression. They have taken, and are taking, countermeasures. The spread of communism has been denounced. Military responsibilities have been assumed in Greece and Turkey. A western German state is being organized. A gigantic scheme of financial aid is promoting the economic recovery of sixteen European countries. A system of military security, underwritten by the American colossus, is taking shape among the nations of the Atlantic community. The wreckage of Western influence in China is being watched with meditative hostility. Nor is this exertion of material power the sole preoccupation of the national policy. It is accompanied, and fully justified in the eyes of most Americans, by a determined attempt to demonstrate the moral superiority of Western democracy to Russian communism.

It is true that support for the United Nations, and a readiness to revert to co-operation with the eastern sphere of influence, remains the official policy; but the American countermeasures have not been confined within the framework of the United Nations, nor is grace to be bestowed on Russia before it is earned by repentance and good works.

This official policy has been supported by both the major parties. It has also, on most occasions, secured the support of a numerical majority among the member states of the United Nations. But there has been no lack of controversy. A selection from the topical literature of the subject is presented here to enable the student to form his own opinion.

How far is the breakdown of co-operation to be attributed to the system of power politics within which independent states are obliged to conduct their relations? In a world in which anarchy is only tempered by prudence, as distinct from being controlled by law, great powers have developed habits of self-protection which cannot be conjured away by professions of good will. From this standpoint, Soviet expansion offers few novelties to the student of czarist Russia, nor can Americans be reasonably surprised if the spectacle of American expansion arouses fear abroad as well as friendship. It has further been argued that the League of Nations and the United Nations, considered as attempts to escape from this system, were doomed by their very nature to futility.

How far have the failures been due to an ideological conflict? The two contenders for world domination represent the extremes of communism and democratic capitalism. In the eyes of the Communist, capitalism sacrifices the welfare of the masses to the rights of property; it is involved in contradictions from which it vainly endeavors to escape through imperialism and war; it is certain sooner or later to collapse in violent convulsions from which the proletariat will advance toward their preordained triumph. In the eyes of democratic capitalists this potent theory is the offspring of misery and ignorance, false in theory and vicious in practice. The conflict of ideas transcends national frontiers. It distracts the loyalties of Europeans, ramifies throughout the Asiatic and colonial worlds, and raises the ghouls of disloyalty and sedition here in America. Much of the mutual recrimination is no doubt absurd; but beneath the fog of partisan denunciation there are deep-seated differences which range over the whole field of social policy. In the opinion of some observers, this fact alone makes co-operation impossible.

It has been urged in opposition to both these views that neither national nor ideological prejudices ought to deflect diplomacy from its traditional tasks. Nations do not have to love one another; they need only agree to respect one another. The world cannot be altered overnight; it is unlikely to destroy itself as quickly as the sensationalists predict. From this standpoint, the practical duty is to seek a workable balance of power between East and West which will safeguard the national interest while leaving the door open for a gradual construction of a better world order. If the latter prospect seems more remote in 1949 than it did four years ago, it is held that America's present task is to bring Russia to reason by measures which she cannot ignore.

Can the responsibility for the deadlock be fairly placed on Russia? There has been much difference of opinion in America about the tactics of our policy but substantial support for the contention that the burden of responsibility lies on the other side. Views which dissociate themselves from this assumption, in varying degrees, are reflected here by Frederick Schuman, Henry Wallace, and Mr. Vishinsky. Have we broken our wartime agreements? Have we sabotaged the United Nations? Were the Baruch proposals for the international control of atomic energy as magnanimous as they seemed? Are we really imperialist, in the invidious meaning of the word?

Finally, there are the extreme representatives of American nationalism and internationalism. Is it America's mission to become the new Rome, persuading where she can, coercing where she must, and building her regime of order out of the ruin of her enemies? Or must she promote a government of the world, in which all are promised justice and might submits to right?

It is over three centuries since Western civilization, expanding out of its European birthplace, planted its first colonies on North American shores. Today this civilization, which embraces the world in its triumphs and its failures, has yielded a decisive share of its political leadership into American hands. The virtues of American values, the stability of the American economy, and the quality of American statesmanship have never been as important to as many peoples as they are now. Upon the wisdom of American decisions depends not only the national welfare but much also that may make the difference between the survival of civilized life at the level which the West has known and its disruption in violence. This is a responsibility which no citizen of a democratic country can evade.

SECTION A. PREWAR POLICY

1. THE QUARANTINE SPEECH, 1937[1]

By FRANKLIN D. ROOSEVELT

EDITORS' NOTE.—The dominant American opinon had reacted to the aggressive policies of Japan, Germany, and Italy by showing a strenuous determination to avoid entanglement in any new war. This isolationist sentiment, fostered by such investigations as the Nye inquiry into the part played by industrial and financial interests in involving the United States in the first World War, had reached a climax with the passage of the neutrality legislation of 1935–37. It seemed, however, by October, 1937, that the growing hostility to the methods and purposes of the totalitarian powers, combined with a new concern for America's own security in such a world, might call for a different policy. Neutrality was bringing aid and comfort to America's enemies. It was in this atmosphere that President Roosevelt canvassed the possibility of co-operative action against the dictators in his famous "Quarantine Speech" at Chicago. American advocates of collective security acclaimed the speech, but the mass response was discouraging. In the following month a resolution which sought to make entry into war conditional on a popular referendum was only narrowly defeated in the House of Representatives.

I am glad to come once again to Chicago and especially to have the opportunity of taking part in the dedication of this important project of civic betterment.

On my trip across the continent and back I have been shown many evidences of the result of common sense cooperation between municipalities and the Federal Government, and I have been greeted by tens of thousands of Americans who have told me in every look and word that their material and spiritual well-being has made great strides forward in the past few years.

And yet, as I have seen with my own eyes, the prosperous farms, the thriving factories and the busy railroads, as I have seen the happiness and security and peace which covers our wide land, almost inevitably I have been compelled to contrast our peace with very different scenes being enacted in other parts of the world.

It is because the people of the United States under modern conditions must, for the sake of their own future, give thought to the rest of the world, that I, as the responsible executive head of the Nation, have chosen this great inland city and this gala occasion to speak to you on a subject of definite national importance.

The political situation in the world, which of late has been growing progressively worse, is such as to cause grave concern and anxiety to all the peoples and nations who wish to live in peace and amity with their neighbors.

Some fifteen years ago the hopes of mankind for a continuing era of international peace were raised to great heights

1. *Development of United States Foreign Policy: Addresses and Messages of Franklin D. Roosevelt* (77th Cong., 2d sess.; Senate Doc. No. 188, Serial No. 10676 [Washington, 1942]), pp. 21–24.

when more than sixty nations solemnly pledged themselves not to resort to arms in furtherance of their national aims and policies. The high aspirations expressed in the Briand-Kellogg Peace Pact and the hopes for peace thus raised have of late given way to a haunting fear of calamity. The present reign of terror and international lawlessness began a few years ago.

It began through unjustified interference in the internal affairs of other nations or the invasion of alien territory in violation of treaties; and has now reached a stage where the very foundations of civilization are seriously threatened. The landmarks and traditions which have marked the progress of civilization toward a condition of law, order and justice are being wiped away.

Without a declaration of war and without warning or justification of any kind, civilians, including vast numbers of women and children, are being ruthlessly murdered with bombs from the air. In times of so-called peace, ships are being attacked and sunk by submarines without cause or notice. Nations are fomenting and taking sides in civil warfare in nations that have never done them any harm. Nations claiming freedom for themselves deny it to others.

Innocent peoples, innocent nations, are being cruelly sacrificed to a greed for power and supremacy which is devoid of all sense of justice and humane considerations.

To paraphrase a recent author "perhaps we foresee a time when men, exultant in the technique of homicide, will rage so hotly over the world that every precious thing will be in danger, every book and picture and harmony, every treasure garnered through two millenniums, the small, the delicate, the defenseless—all will be lost or wrecked or utterly destroyed."

If those things come to pass in other parts of the world, let no one imagine that America will escape, that America may expect mercy, that this Western Hemisphere will not be attacked and that it will continue tranquilly and peacefully to carry on the ethics and the arts of civilization.

If those days come, "there will be no safety by arms, no help from authority, no answer in science. The storm will rage till every flower of culture is trampled and all human beings are leveled in a vast chaos."

If those days are not to come to pass— if we are to have a world in which we can breathe freely and live in amity without fear—the peace-loving nations must make a concerted effort to uphold laws and principles on which alone peace can rest secure.

The peace-loving nations must make a concerted effort in opposition to those violations of treaties and those ignorings of humane instincts which today are creating a state of international anarchy and instability from which there is no escape through mere isolation or neutrality.

Those who cherish their freedom and recognize and respect the equal right of their neighbors to be free and live in peace must work together for the triumph of law and moral principles in order that peace, justice and confidence may prevail in the world. There must be a return to a belief in the pledged word, in the value of a signed treaty. There must be recognition of the fact that national morality is as vital as private morality.

A bishop wrote me the other day: "It seems to me that something greatly needs to be said in behalf of ordinary humanity against the present practice of carrying the horrors of war to helpless civilians, especially women and children. It may be that such a protest might be regarded by many, who claim to be realists, as futile, but may it not be that the heart of mankind is so filled with horror at the present needless suffering that that force could be mobilized in sufficient volume to lessen such cruelty in the days ahead. Even though it may take twenty years, which God forbid, for civilization to make effective its corporate protest against this barbarism, surely strong voices may hasten the day."

There is a solidarity and interdependence about the modern world, both technically and morally, which makes it impossible for any nation completely to isolate itself from economic and political upheavals in the rest of the world, especially when such upheavals appear to be spreading and not declining. There can be no stability or peace either within nations or between nations except under laws and moral standards adhered to by all. International anarchy destroys every foundation for peace. It jeopardizes either the immediate or the future security of every nation, large or small. It is, therefore, a matter of vital interest and concern to the people of the United States that the sanctity of international treaties and the maintenance of international morality be restored.

The overwhelming majority of the peoples and nations of the world today want to live in peace. They seek the removal of barriers against trade. They want to exert themselves in industry, in agriculture and in business, that they may increase their wealth through the production of wealth-producing goods rather than striving to produce military planes and bombs and machine guns and cannon for the destruction of human lives and useful property.

In those nations of the world which seem to be piling armament on armament for purposes of aggression, and those other nations which fear acts of aggression against them and their security, a very high proportion of their national income is being spent directly for armaments. It runs from thirty to as high as fifty percent. We are fortunate. The proportion that we in the United States spend is far less—eleven or twelve percent.

How happy we are that the circumstances of the moment permit us to put our money into bridges and boulevards, dams and reforestation, the conservation of our soil and many other kinds of useful works rather than into huge standing armies and vast supplies of implements of war.

I am compelled and you are compelled, nevertheless, to look ahead. The peace, the freedom and the security of ninety percent of the population of the world is being jeopardized by the remaining ten percent who are threatening a breakdown of all international order and law. Surely the ninety percent who want to live in peace under law and in accordance with moral standards that have received almost universal acceptance through the centuries can and must find some way to make their will prevail.

The situation is definitely of universal concern. The questions involved relate not merely to violations of specific provisions of particular treaties; they are questions of war and of peace, of international law and especially of principles of humanity. It is true that they involve definite violations of agreements, and especially of the Covenant of the League of Nations, the Briand-Kellog Pact and the Nine Power Treaty. But they also involve problems of world economy, world security and world humanity.

It is true that the moral consciousness of the world must recognize the importance of removing injustices and wellfounded grievances; but at the same time it must be aroused to the cardinal necessity of honoring sanctity of treaties, of respecting the rights and liberties of others and of putting an end to acts of international aggression.

It seems to be unfortunately true that the epidemic of world lawlessness is spreading.

When an epidemic of physical disease starts to spread, the community approves and joins in a quarantine of the patients in order to protect the health of the community against the spread of the disease.

It is my determination to pursue a policy of peace. It is my determination to adopt every practicable measure to avoid involvement in war. It ought to be inconceivable that in this modern era, and in the face of experience, any nation could be so foolish and ruthless as to run the risk of plunging the whole world into war by invading and violating, in contravention of solemn treaties, the territory of other nations that have done them no real harm and are too weak to protect themselves adequately. Yet the peace of the world and the welfare and security of every nation, including our own, is today being threatened by that very thing.

No nation which refuses to exercise forbearance and to respect the freedom and rights of others can long remain strong and retain the confidence and respect of other nations. No nation ever loses its dignity or its good standing by conciliating its differences, and by exercising great patience with, and consideration for, the rights of other nations.

War is a contagion, whether it be declared or undeclared. It can engulf states and peoples remote from the original scene of hostilities. We are determined to keep out of war, yet we cannot insure ourselves against the disastrous effects of war and the dangers of involvement. We are adopting such measures as will minimize our risk of involvement, but we cannot have complete protection in a world of disorder in which confidence and security have broken down.

If civilization is to survive, the principles of the Prince of Peace must be restored. Trust between nations must be revived.

Most important of all, the will for peace on the part of peace-loving nations must express itself to the end that nations that may be tempted to violate their agreements and the rights of others will desist from such a course. There must be positive endeavors to preserve peace.

America hates war. America hopes for peace. Therefore, America actively engages in the search for peace.

2. A FOREIGN POLICY FOR AMERICA[1]

By CHARLES A. BEARD

EDITORS' NOTE.—The second World War confronted the United States with a challenge to determine what foreign policy was consistent with our interests, obligations, and resources. One policy was represented in Roosevelt's "Quarantine Speech" (p. 725). In opposition to this policy of intervention or internationalism, a policy of isolation or, in Beard's vocabulary, "continentalism" was strongly advocated. To the intense public debate of September 1, 1939, to December 7, 1941, over United States neutrality, Charles A. Beard (1874–1948) made a considerable contribution; his central ideas are revealed in this reading.

1. Charles A. Beard, *A Foreign Policy for America* (New York, 1940), pp. 134, 140, 149–54. By permission of the Alfred A. Knopf Company.

Beard was educated at DePauw, Oxford, and Columbia universities. He was professor of politics at Columbia University (1907–17) until he resigned in protest over the discharge of his colleagues Cattell and Dana because of their opposition to American participation in the first World War. He acted in defense of academic freedom, not in defense of the ideas of Cattell and Dana. Beard favored American participation in the first World War. In 1918, with Thorstein Veblen, John Dewey, and James Harvey Robinson, he founded the New School for Social Research in New York. He was president of the American Political Science Association in 1926 and president of the American Historical

Association in 1933. He was the author of a great many books on history and politics, including the *Economic Interpretation of the Constitution* (1913) and the *Rise of American Civilization* (1927).

PERSISTENCE OF CONTINENTAL AMERICANISM

As an outcome of the historical heritage, American foreign policy became a loose intermingling of conflicting elements —continentalism, imperialism, and internationalism. Each of the three programs was supported, more or less, by specific interests and portions of the intelligentsia. At every crisis in world affairs, as the running fire of debate on foreign events continued in the United States, each school maneuvered for possession of the American mind and the direction of policy, through propaganda and the varied use of communication agencies. In the polls of public opinion, the winds of doctrine veered and twisted.

Yet at repeated tests, taken in formal elections and congressional battles, the principal body of that opinion was found consistently on the side of continentalism. Despite temporary victories, politicians who tried to swing the United States off its continental center of gravity toward imperialism or internationalism were never completely successful. To their efforts the nation at large always showed a strong resistance and, after each display of eccentricity, it revealed a powerful tendency to recover its balance and return to its geographical base. . . .

. . . [I]n 1937, when professional peace advocates tried to use President Roosevelt's "quarantine" doctrine as a slogan for driving the nation into some kind of collective action, the spirit of continentalism overwhelmed them. The protests against that doctrine which flooded into Washington by wire and mail were so numerous and so strong that even Roosevelt refrained from repeating it. Although Congress, after a vitriolic debate, passed his naval expansion bill the following year, members of his own party took occasion, during the discussion, to repudiate all taint of quarantinism. The chorus of praise set up by internationalists after they read the President's Chicago address died away and disappeared in an empty echo. Again it was made evident that the people of the United States wanted nothing to do with quarantinism, that their continentalist attachment was still dominant, and that using the power of the United States in efforts to impose any system on the world was to be blocked whenever proposed. . . .

Twice in American history the governing élite had turned the American nation away from its continental center of gravity into world adventures, ostensibly in a search for relations with the other countries or regions that would yield prosperity for American industry and a flowering of American prestige. First, in 1898; second, in 1917. But each time the main body of the people had resisted the populsion, had found delusions in the false promises, and had returned to the continental orbit. Imperialism had failed to bring either profits, glory, or security. Internationalism had been wrecked at Versailles—by the struggle for power under the League of Nations, by the revelations of war propaganda, and by other brutal events which could not be erased from the record.

Again and again the fundamental resolve of the country against imperialism and internationalism had been revealed; in provisions for withdrawing from the Philippine area; in the surrender of specious rights to engage in trade where great nations were fighting for their lives; in neutrality acts keeping American ships and travelers out of war zones; in the refusal of Congress to transform Guam into a great naval base; in an evident unwillingness to engage in a major war over the petty commerce of China; and in persistent efforts to overcome, by domestic measures, the cri-

sis in domestic economy, without wholesale resort to artificial devices for dumping
American "surpluses" abroad, that is, giving them to foreigners.

After all the illusory adventures in policy based on the Cobden-Bright conception of "free international exchange," the
American nation confronted, not a growing freedom of that kind, but a steady increase in the number of countries operating on difference principles. At best free
international exchange had been merely
partial; and the tendencies in that direction
had been reversed.

Germany, Italy, Russia, and Japan went
over to controlled economies of a totalitarian character. France, Great Britain,
and other powers turned in the direction of
management and "regimentation." Even if
the United States had labored with might
and main to force commerce on these
countries and widen the channels of its foreign traffic, it could have made little headway against the apparently irresistible determination of other governments—capitalist, fascist, and communist—to grapple
with their problems of living by direct
action at home. By sheer necessity, American civilization was turned back upon
itself.

Slowly, but with increasing force, it
was realized that the "foreign outlet" doctrines of imperialism and internationalism
were illusions. This did not mean that foreign commerce was deprecated or deemed
undesirable. Indeed such commerce was
fully recognized as desirable within the
limits of American needs for products not
available at home. But it did mean that the
potentials of buying power indispensable
to keeping American industry and agriculture running at a high tempo lay right here,
in the creation of new wealth at home;
that three or four billions of foreign commerce were relatively small as compared
with the twenty or thirty billions annually
wasted in idle plants, idle labor, and idle
resources at home; that the frontiers for
the expansion of American enterprise were
within this continent, not in the fabled

Indies or on the Rhine, the Danube, or the
Vistula; that all about us, right here, lay
the materials for a magnificent civilization; and that the principal task was the
concentration of intelligence, the cultural
forces of men and women, upon the problem of putting science, technology, inventive ingenuity, private energies, and public
enterprise to work in making real the vision of a civilization that rose before the
mind as a goal to be attained by majestic
effort on this continent, without recourse
to empire or entanglements in the age-long
coalitions of Europe and Asia.

This continentalism did not seek to
make a "hermit" nation out of America.
From the very beginning under the aus-
pices of the early Republic, it never had
embraced that impossible conception. It
did not deny the obvious fact that American civilization had made use of its European heritages, was a part of western
civilization, and had continuous contacts
with Occidental and Oriental cultures. It
did not deny the obvious fact that wars in
Europe and Asia "affect" or "concern"
the United States. It did not mean "indifference" to the sufferings of Europe or
China (or India or Ethiopia). In truth, in
all history, no people ever poured out
treasure more generously in aid of human
distresses in every quarter of the globe—
distresses springing from wars, famines,
revolutions, persecutions, and earthquakes.

With reference to such conflicts and
sufferings, continentalism merely meant a
recognition of the limited nature of American powers to relieve, restore, and maintain life beyond its own sphere of interest
and control—a recognition of the hard fact
that the United States, either alone or in
any coalition, did not possess the power to
force peace on Europe and Asia, to assure
the establishment of democratic and pacific governments there, or to provide the
social and economic underwriting necessary to the perdurance of such governments. In respect of morality continental-
ists did not deny the existence of responsibilities to other nations and peoples. On

the contrary they favored discharging such responsibilities, always with due regard for the physical, economic, and political limits on the powers of the United States and for the solemn obligation of protecting the Republic against misadventures headed in the direction of disaster. If this conception fell short of the selfless sacrifice required by an absolute morality, it could claim worthiness in the presence of other examples set by the family of nations.

Besides forcing a concentration of attention, energy, and intelligence on overcoming the grave economic and social crisis at home and on strengthening American civilization in all its best features, continentalism, strictly construed, meant a return to the correct and restrained diplomacy of an earlier time. The freedom of the people and the press to discuss foreign affairs and favor foreign nations, parties, factions, and causes, within the limits of neutrality laws was accepted as axiomatic. Equally axiomatic, if America was to keep its peace, was the duty of public officials, especially the President and Secretary of State, speaking in the name of the whole nation, to abstain from denouncing and abusing foreign states, good or bad, with

which diplomatic relations are maintained and the United States is at peace.

Correct policy likewise commanded such public officials to avoid vain and verbose dissertations on the manners and morals of other countries; to couch protests in the language of dignity; to speak and write as briefly and courteously as possible in necessary dealings with foreign governments; to make no boasts which the army and navy could not enforce with a reasonable prospect of success; to carry on international relations with restraint, and in the subdued style of approved diplomatic usage—speaking softly, keeping the powder dry, withholding wrath except when war is intended as a last resort. Such official conduct would enable the Government of the United States to escape innumerable hatreds abroad, offer its services and cooperation to troubled peoples with authority on proper occasions, and win respect, even affection and esteem, throughout the earth.

This policy, consistently followed by the United States, would favor, not hinder, the coming of peace to other nations of the world.

3. U.S. FOREIGN POLICY[1]

By WALTER LIPPMANN

EDITORS' NOTE.—Walter Lippmann (1889——) graduated from Harvard University as a student in philosophy. In 1917 he was assistant to the Secretary of War. He was secretary of the committee headed by E. M. House to make preparations for the Versailles Peace Conference and was attached to the American Mission To Negotiate Peace in Paris in 1919. He has been editor of the *New Republic* and of the *New York World*, author of several studies on the theory and practice of modern politics, and an active commentator on current affairs in the columns of the national press. He has made a special reputation as an analyst of American foreign policy.

CHAPTER I

THE SUBJECT OF THIS BOOK

As the climax of the war finds the people of the United States approaching a national election, we must face the fact that for nearly fifty years the nation has not had a settled and generally accepted

1. Walter Lippmann, *United States Foreign Policy: Shield of the Republic* (Boston, 1943), pp. 3–10, 27–49, 119–36. Reprinted by permission of Little, Brown and Company.

foreign policy. This is a danger to the Republic. For when a people is divided within itself about the conduct of its foreign relations, it is unable to agree on the determination of its true interest. It is unable to prepare adequately for war or to safeguard successfully its peace. Thus its course in foreign affairs depends, in Hamilton's words, not on reflection and choice but on accident and force.

The country, as I shall try to demonstrate, had a secure foreign policy toward the great powers from the decade after the end of the War of 1812 to the end of the war with Spain in 1898. In that long period it was true that politics stopped at the water's edge, and that the people were not seriously divided on our relations with the Old World. But in the election of 1900 the nation became divided over the consequences of the war with Spain, and never since then has it been possible for any President of the United States to rely upon the united support of the nation in the conduct of foreign affairs.

The consequences have been grave. The war with Spain left the United States with commitments in the Pacific 7000 miles west of California. The lack of a settled foreign policy made it impossible for the United States to liquidate the commitment by withdrawing from the Far Pacific or to fulfill the commitment by assuring the defense of the Philippines. The outbreak of the first World War in Europe precipitated an internal controversy in the United States about America's rights and its interests, its duties and its obligations. As a result of that division of opinion the country was unable to prepare for that war even when American participation had become probable, and it was unable to consolidate the victory which it helped to win. During the twenty years which followed there was unending domestic controversy over foreign policy. This made the American government as ineffective in preventing the second World War as it was in preparing for it. Now, under the spell cast by the coming elections of 1944, the country again finds itself unable to think clearly and to decide firmly what policy it will follow in the settlement of the war.

The spectacle of this great nation which does not know its own mind is as humiliating as it is dangerous. It casts doubt upon the capacity of the people to govern themselves. For nowhere else on earth, and never before in all history, has any people had conditions so favorable as they are in the United States to proving their capacity for self-government. It will be a profound humiliation, therefore, if once again we fail to form a national policy, and the acids of this failure will be with us for ages to come, corroding our self-confidence and our self-respect. Our failure now to form a national policy will, though we defeat our enemies, leave us dangerously exposed to deadly conflict at home and to unmanageable perils from abroad. For the return from a state of total war to a state of peace which no one trusts will raise catastrophic issues in our midst. Rent by domestic controversy, for want of a settled foreign policy we shall act not upon reflection and choice but under the impulse of accidents and the impact of force.

In pondering our failure to form a foreign policy in the twentieth century, we must remember that each of us is himself susceptible to the partisanship which is the cause of that failure. Therefore, we must shun the temptation to explain on the ground that they are stupid, ambitious, or self-regarding the opposition of those who have differed with us.

Candor, as Hamilton said in beginning his argument for the adoption of the Constitution, will oblige us to admit that, in this half century of controversy, "wise and good men have been on the wrong as well as on the right side of questions of the first magnitude to society," and that "we are not always sure that those who advocate the truth are influenced by purer principles than their antagonists," and that "ambition, avarice, personal animosity and party opposition, and many other motives not more laudable than these, are apt to operate as well upon those who support, as upon those who oppose, the right side of a question."

More than charity of mind and humility of soul dictates this approach to the settlement of our national division. An objective study of our foreign relations in the past fifty years will, I believe, show that our national failure to form a foreign policy is due to an historic circumstance. For about eighty years—from the promulgation of the Monroe Doctrine to the end of the war with Spain—there was no need for the American people to form a foreign policy. In that long period the very nature of foreign policy, of what it consists and how it is formed, was forgotten. Thus, when events compelled us once again to attend to foreign relations, we had lost the art of shaping a policy, and could not find a policy because we no longer knew what we needed.

This is the reason why good and patriotic Americans have differed so sharply and so long without reaching a common view. They have forgotten the compelling and, once seen, the self-evident common principle of all genuine foreign policy—the principle that alone can force decisions, can settle controversy, and can induce agreement. This is the principle that in foreign relations, as in all other relations, a policy has been formed only when commitments and power have been brought into balance. This is the forgotten principle which must be recovered and restored to the first place in American thought if the nation is to achieve the foreign policy which it so desperately wants.

Without the controlling principle that the nation must maintain its objectives and its power in equilibrium, its purposes within its means and its means equal to its purposes, its commitments related to its resources and its resources adequate to its commitments, it is impossible to think at all about foreign affairs. Yet the history of our acts and of our declarations in the past fifty years will show that rarely, and never consistently, have American statesmen and the American people been guided by this elementary principle of practical life.

No one would seriously suppose that he had a fiscal policy if he did not consider together expenditure and revenue, outgo and income, liabilities and assets. But in foreign relations we have habitually in our minds divorced the discussion of our war aims, our peace aims, our ideals, our interests, our commitments, from the discussion of our armaments, our strategic position, our potential allies and our probable enemies. No policy could emerge from such a discussion. For what settles practical controversy is the knowledge that ends and means have to be balanced: an agreement has eventually to be reached when men admit that they must pay for what they want and that they must want only what they are willing to pay for. If they do not have to come to such an agreement, they will never except by accident agree. For they will lack a yardstick by which to measure their ideals and their interests, or their ways and means of protecting and promoting them.

If we survey, as we shall in the course of the argument, our own course since the war with Spain, we shall find that there has been no serious and sustained conviction that American commitments and interests and ideals must be covered by our armaments, our strategic frontiers, and our alliances. In fact we shall find that we have been the victims of a blinding prejudice—that concern with our frontiers, our armaments, and with alliances, is immoral and reactionary.

Yet now that the Philippines have been lost, now that we have been attacked by a combination of exceedingly dangerous enemies, we must see how awful is the price we must pay because in our foreign relations for nearly half a century the United States has been insolvent. This is the time of the reckoning. We are liquidating in sweat and blood and tears, and at our mortal peril, the fact that we made commitments, asserted rights, and proclaimed ideals while we left our frontiers unguarded, our armaments unprepared, and our alliances unformed and unsustained.

CHAPTER II

The Fundamental Principle of a Foreign Policy

Before we examine the history of our insolvent foreign relations we must be sure that we know what we mean by a foreign commitment and by the power to balance it.

I mean by a *foreign commitment* an obligation, outside the continental limits of the United States, which may in the last analysis have to be met by waging war.

I mean by *power* the force which is necessary to prevent such a war or to win it if it cannot be prevented. In the term *necessary* power I include the military force which can be mobilized effectively within the domestic territory of the United States and also the reinforcements which can be obtained from dependable allies.

The thesis of this book is that a foreign policy consists in bringing into balance, with a comfortable surplus of power in reserve, the nation's commitments and the nation's power. The constant preoccupation of the true statesman is to achieve and maintain this balance. Having determined the foreign commitments which are vitally necessary to his people, he will never rest until he has mustered the force to cover them. In assaying ideals, interests, and ambitions which are to be asserted abroad, his measure of their validity will be the force he can muster at home combined with the support he can find abroad among other nations which have similar ideals, interests and ambitions.

For nations, as for families, the level may vary at which a solvent balance is struck. If its expenditures are safely within its assured means, a family is solvent when it is poor, or is well-to-do, or is rich. The same principle holds true of nations. The statesman of a strong country may balance its commitments at a high level or at a low. But whether he is conducting the

affairs of Germany, which has had dynamic ambitions, or the affairs of Switzerland which seeks only to hold what it already has, or of the United States, he must still bring his ends and means into balance. If he does not, he will follow a course that leads to disaster. . . .

CHAPTER IV

The Bankruptcy of American Foreign Relations
(1898–1941)

I. PRESIDENT THEODORE ROOSEVELT'S FOREIGN POLICY

The period of unending domestic controversy over American foreign relations began in January 1899 when the Treaty of Paris, which concluded the war with Spain, was submitted to the Senate for ratification. The debate was held in Executive Session and was unreported. But Senator Henry Cabot Lodge described it as the "closest, hardest fight I have ever known." The opposition to the annexation of the Philippines was led by his colleague, Senator Hoar of Massachusetts. The vote was taken on February 6, 1899, and it was the belief of Theodore Roosevelt that the treaty would have been rejected if the Filipino insurrection, which broke out on February 4, had not been looked upon as a challenge to American prestige. That the outcome was uncertain is clear. A motion to promise the Filipinos ultimate independence was defeated only by the vote of the Vice President, and ratification was obtained by only one vote more than the required two thirds.

The wisdom of the immense commitment to superimpose upon the Monroe Doctrine what Mahan called "Asiatic dominion" was hotly debated not only in the Senate, but in the McKinley-Bryan elections of 1900. It is too late to debate it now. What cannot be gainsaid, however, is that the subsequent foreign policy of the United States has never been equal to the size of the commitment. From the day when Admiral Dewey sailed into Manila

Bay until the day when General Wainwright surrendered Corregidor, the United States never made a sustained and prudent, or remotely adequate, effort to bring its obligations and its power into balance.

President Theodore Roosevelt, who, with Senator Lodge and Captain Mahan, was the principal promoter of the commitment, did realize that the new departure called for new measures. He saw that we had assumed vast responsibilities in the two oceans. So he insisted upon digging the Panama Canal in order that the navy could be concentrated rapidly in either ocean. He persuaded Congress and the people to support the construction of an enlarged and modern navy.

In his own mind he went further, though he never explained it to the nation or made it a matter of avowed national policy. He knew that in 1900 Germany had staked out her claim to world power by deciding to build a navy so large that it compelled Great Britain "to set about the reduction of her outlying squadrons with a view to mustering her full strength in home waters." He knew that Germany was jealous of the American annexation of the Philippines, and had ordered Admiral von Diederichs to Manila to watch Admiral Dewey. He knew that two days before the battle of Manila Bay, John Hay had sent a telegram from London saying of Germany, "*Voilà l'ennemi* in the present crisis."

Theodore Roosevelt realized that to support our commitments we needed not only the Panama Canal and a strong navy, but also friends and virtual allies—allies against the rising imperialism of Japan. For that reason President Roosevelt and his Secretary of State, John Hay, never allowed disputes about financial concessions in China to alienate the United States from Great Britain. For the same reason he intervened quickly in the Moroccan Affair of 1905 in order to prevent a European war which, he realized, would leave the United States alone with its vast commitment.

Theodore Roosevelt had, therefore, the elements of a genuine foreign policy. Aware of the American commitments, he sought to develop—though tentatively, unsurely, and without making the matter plain to the nation—the elements of American power: our strategic position by constructing the Panama Canal, our armaments by enlarging the navy, our alliances by adhering to those powers who were our friends and the opponents of our opponents. But these rudimentary beginnings of a true foreign policy were not carried forward by Theodore Roosevelt's successors.

2. THE PERSISTING ILLUSION

In the long period from 1823 to 1898 the nation had lived in a state of illusory isolation: it was committed to the Monroe Doctrine, which rested upon the support of British sea power, without having been made to understand that the defense of the Western Hemisphere did in fact require the support of British sea power.

The illusion had been confirmed because the Monroe Doctrine had been seriously challenged only by the Maximilian affair in Mexico, which was easily forgotten. After her defeat by Prussia in 1870 France was never again capable of entertaining Napoleonic designs. Until about 1900 Germany, though powerful on land, had no navy with which to threaten the Western Hemisphere or to reach out into the Pacific. When in 1900 Germany did begin to build a navy, it was obvious that she would first have to dispose of the British navy before she could look further. Thus for about fifty years after Napoleon III had flagrantly breached the Monroe Doctrine, and had proved that it had been a mistake not to make binding and clear the British support of the commitment, circumstances made it appear falsely that our foreign commitments rested securely upon our geography, our inherent virtues, and our own isolated military strength.

Successive generations of Americans lived, therefore, in the illusion that our position and our commitments were inviolable. The mental habits of Theodore Roosevelt's immediate successors—Taft and Wilson—were formed in that period of illusory isolation which had lasted from 1823 to 1898. Both were idealists who habitually rejected the premises of the politics of power. Both disliked armaments. In them the idealism which prompts Americans to make large and resounding commitments was combined with the pacifism which causes Americans to shrink from the measures of force that are needed to support the commitments. Neither promoted the preparation of armaments in time of peace. Both accepted reluctantly and tardily the need to arm. Both abhorred as inherently vicious and unnecessary, and as contrary to American principles, the formation of alliances. But both favored a League of Nations in which the United States assumed the obligation to enforce peace.

Thus the seeds of a genuine foreign policy, which Theodore Roosevelt planted, never matured. A national understanding of what is a foreign policy was never inculcated into the minds of the later American generations. When the long-expected war in Europe broke out in 1914, the United States had no foreign policy which enabled the nation to determine its interests in the conflict. President Wilson had no foreign policy, accepted by the nation, which gave him the means of judging whether, why, when, where, how, and to what end, the United States must take its position in the war.

From 1914 to 1916 Wilson vacillated between the assertion of American rights and reluctance to face the consequences of asserting them, between dread of a German victory and dread of a war to prevent a German victory. Thus he took a zigzag course, now one way because the British blockade infringed the American doctrine of the freedom of the seas, now the other way because German ruthlessness outraged American sensibilities. Lacking a foreign policy, and with leaders whose training was wholly in domestic politics,

the nation had no means of ascertaining its true interests. The verbal battle of the propagandists, of which so much was made in later years, was fought in this vacuum of the American mind. It was fought because the American nation lacked even the rudiments of a settled foreign policy which could make clear whose victory and what kind of victory would best serve the vital interests of the United States.

Because of this vacuum, the United States went to war in April 1917 for reasons which were never willingly or accurately avowed. And so they were never clearly recognized.

3. PRESIDENT WILSON'S FOREIGN POLICY

The occasion for going to war was Germany's unrestricted use of the submarine against American merchant shipping on the Atlantic routes from North America to the British Isles and France. But the substantial and compelling reason for going to war was that the cutting of the Atlantic communications meant the starvation of Britain and, therefore, the conquest of Western Europe by Imperial Germany.

President Wilson avoided this explanation of his decision to intervene, choosing instead to base his decision upon the specific legal objection to unrestricted submarine warfare and upon a generalized moral objection to lawless and cruel aggression. But these superficial reasons for the declaration of war would never have carried the day if a majority of the people had not recognized intuitively, and if some Americans had not seen clearly, what the threatened German victory would mean to the United States. Though there was lacking the tradition of a foreign policy which made the matter self-evident, many Americans saw in 1917 that if Germany won, the United States would have to face a new and aggressively expanding German empire which had made Britain, France, and Russia its vassals, and Japan its ally. They saw that in such a position the defense of the Western Hemisphere would require immense armaments over and above those needed in the Pacific, and that America would have to live in a perpetual state of high and alert military preparedness. It was in this very concrete and practical sense, though unhappily President Wilson preferred not to particularize, that a German victory in 1917 would have made the world unsafe for the American democracies from Canada to the Argentine.

This in brief was the undeclared, and only partially realized, foreign policy which determined the participation of the United States in the first German World War. The sinking of merchant ships without visit and search, and without provision for the safety of crews and passengers, would not in itself have been the *casus belli* if the German submarines had caused less destruction. Sporadic sinkings would have continued to lead to protests, as they did in 1915 and 1916, and probably to reprisals. But they would not have led to war if by 1917 the submarine had not become so destructive as to make it seem probable that Germany would starve out Britain and isolate France.

Nor did the United States go to war to make the world safe for all democracies: if it had seemed probable that Germany would be defeated by Czarist Russia, the United States would have remained neutral because its vital interests in the North Atlantic would have remained secure. The war was certainly not engaged to overthrow the Kaiser and to make Germany a democratic republic: if the Germans had not broken into the Atlantic and threatened the whole structure of our Atlantic defenses, private citizens would still have made faces at the Kaiser, but the nation would not have made war upon him.

The United States did not go to war because it wished to found a League of Nations; it went to war in order to preserve American security. And when the war was over, the nation would almost certainly have accepted in some form or other the scheme of the League of Nations if President Wilson had been able to demonstrate to the people that the League would perpetuate the security which the military victory had won for them. Mr. Wilson failed to make this demonstration. He failed because in leading the nation to war he had failed to give the durable and compelling reasons for the momentous decision. The reasons he did give were legalistic and moralistic and idealistic reasons, rather than the substantial and vital reason that the security of the United States demanded that no aggressively expanding imperial power, like Germany, should be allowed to gain the mastery of the Atlantic Ocean.

Because this simple and self-evident American interest was not candidly made explicit, the nation never understood clearly why it had entered the war. As time went on, the country was, therefore, open to every suggestion and insinuation that the nation had fought for no good reason at all, that its victory was meaningless, that it had been maneuvered into a non-American war by the international bankers and the British diplomats. And so, having failed to make plain that the war was waged for a vital American interest, President Wilson had no way of proving to the nation that his settlement of the war really concerned the United States. The war had been fought without a foreign policy, and neither President Wilson nor the nation had the means, therefore, of judging whether the League was merely a foreign or was also an American interest.

Thus the longer the Senate debated the Treaty of Versailles with its covenant, the more the people felt that there was no compelling connection between their vital interests and the program which President Wilson offered them. They saw that the League imposed upon the United States the unprecedented commitment to help enforce the peace of Europe. They saw only what they were asked to contribute. For they had not been taught to understand what British and French power meant to the security of America's vital interests all over the world.

They had not had it demonstrated to

them how much the defense of the Western Hemisphere depended upon having friendly and strong partners in the British Isles, in the French ports on the Atlantic, at Gibraltar and Casablanca and Dakar; or how much the defense of the Philippines depended upon French Indo-China, and upon British Hong Kong, Malaya, and Burma, and upon the attitude and the strength of Russia and upon China in Eastern Asia. The legalistic, moralistic, idealistic presentation of the war and of the League obscured the realities—caused it to appear that for what we were asked to give to our allies, we were to receive nothing from them. It was made to seem that the new responsibilities of the League flowed from President Wilson's philanthropy and not from the vital necessity of finding allies to support America's vast existing commitments in the Western Hemisphere and all the way across the Pacific to the China Coast.

Not until twenty years later, not until France had fallen and Britain was in mortal peril, not until the Japanese had surrounded the Philippines, did it become possible for the nation to perceive the hidden but real structure of America's strategic position in the world.

4. THE COLLAPSE OF U.S. FOREIGN POLICY

As I have tried to show, the nation had no foreign policy to guide it during the historic half century in which the United States has waged three wars. President McKinley, who made the momentous commitment in the Philippines, asked at first only for the island of Luzon, then for the whole archipelago, and also for one island in the Ladrones, which turned out to be Guam. But in 1899 he let Spain sell the rest of the Ladrones and the Marianas and the Carolines to Germany.

These islands which are the barrier between the Philippines and Hawaii were seized by Japan in 1914. At the Peace Conference in Paris, President Wilson agreed to let Japan retain them under a theoreti-

cal and unenforceable mandate from the League of Nations. From these islands the attack on Pearl Harbor was launched. Because Japan held these islands it was impossible to reinforce General MacArthur. Such a neglect of American interest, such a failure to see the value of these islands, would have been impossible if Americans had had the habit of maintaining a foreign policy. The Japanese, who had a foreign policy, even if it was a pernicious policy, knew why they wanted the strategic islands. We, who had no foreign policy, did not know enough to care about the islands.

Still larger consequences flowed from our national failure to develop a foreign policy. After the rejection of Wilson's settlement, American foreign relations were conducted for twenty years without any indication that the nation had any conception of its commitments. In 1922 we reduced our naval strength to a ratio which gave Japan naval superiority in the Western Pacific. We agreed also not to improve the fortifications of Corregidor, Cavite, and Guam, which lay under the guns of the Japanese fleet. At the same time we renewed our commitment to oppose Japanese imperialism in Asia and to encourage Chinese resistance to it. Thus at the very time when we were reducing our power we renewed and even enlarged our commitments.

Knowing that Japan was the only possible enemy we had to consider in the Pacific, we nevertheless turned upon our natural partners, Britain and France, and treated them as rivals whose armaments it was a diplomatic triumph to reduce. Though we observed scrupulously our own promise not to fortify Guam or to reinforce the defenses of the Philippines, we submitted to the Japanese refusal to let us know what she was doing in her islands. But the more we disarmed ourselves and our natural allies in the coming Pacific war, the more vehemently we committed ourselves to oppose Japanese expansion.

The climax of this unbelievably reckless conduct was reached in the summer of 1939, two months before the outbreak of the second German World War. In July of that summer a majority of the Senate Committee on Foreign Relations took two decisions. One was to advise the State Department to declare economic war against Japan by abrogating the Commercial Treaty. The treaty was abrogated and Japan was put on notice that we were her avowed antagonists. The Committee's second decision was to refuse to lift the arms embargo which prevented Britain and France from buying arms here to resist Germany—the Germany which had been allied with Japan since 1936!

It would be hard to find a more perfect example of total incompetence in guiding the foreign relations of a people. The Senate Committee invited a war in the Pacific while it deliberately refused to take measures to fortify our ancient defenses in the Atlantic. This monstrous imprudence was what passed for American foreign policy at the outbreak of the present war.

5 · PRESIDENT FRANKLIN D. ROOSEVELT'S PRE-WAR POSITION

It was then that the emasculation of American foreign policy reached its extreme limit—the limit of total absurdity and total bankruptcy. The events of the perilous thirties, which were inaugurated by the Japanese conquest of Manchuria and the rise of Hitler, had led inexorably to a world war waged from Europe and from Asia against our vital interests and our inescapable commitments. At this juncture we found ourselves opposed to our future enemies but with our exposed possessions undefended, without allies, isolated from our friends, and yet committed over the length of the Western Hemisphere and across the vast expanse of the Pacific. At the zenith of our commitments we were at the nadir of our precautions.

Eventually there is a reckoning for nations, as for individuals, who have obligations that are not covered by their re-

sources. Between 1931 and 1937 it had become manifest that the time of that reckoning had come. Japan's seizure of Manchuria had proved that the collective opinion of mankind, which all our statesmen loved to invoke, was no deterrent to the aggressor. The Italian conquest of Abyssinia in 1935, the successful intervention of Germany and Italy in Spain, the rearmament of Germany, the reoccupation of the Rhineland, the Anti-Comintern Pact which in fact allied Germany with Japan, and the invasion of China proper in 1937—these events made it unmistakably clear that Germany and Japan and Italy were on the march and that they would dominate the world if they were not successfully resisted.

From 1937, when he made his "quarantine" speech in Chicago until the Japanese attack on Pearl Harbor, President Roosevelt struggled with the problem of making our bankrupt foreign position solvent. As early as 1937 it was clear that the American situation demanded an immediate, intensified expansion of our armed forces, the fortification of our strategic commitments in Alaska, Guam, the Philippines, and Panama, and the formation of arrangements for mutual aid with Great Britain, France, and China—our obvious allies in an attack which was being prepared against them and against us alike. But this prudent course was held to be politically imprudent. This is another way of saying that the American people would not agree to protect their vital interests because they had no foreign policy which disclosed their vital interests.

Thus from 1937 to 1940 President Roosevelt moved anxiously and hesitantly between his knowledge of what ought to be done and his estimate of how much the people would understand what ought to be done. I shall not attempt to answer the question whether he could have made the people understand how great was their peril because their commitments were totally unbalanced. The illusions of a century stood in the way of their understanding, and it may be that no words, but only the awful experience of total war, could even partially dispel the illusion.

In any event the fact is that Mr. Roosevelt did not succeed in persuading the nation to attend effectively to the American interest. Though he understood it himself, though he realized the peril, in action he followed events, taking small measures to repair great disasters which were undermining the American position in all the strategic areas of the world. Thus he did not insist on greater armaments until after the Japanese had conquered the coast of China, had encircled the Philippines, and were poised for the attack on Singapore, Burma, and the Netherlands Indies. Not until after France had fallen and had left exposed the bulge of Africa, where it juts out against the bulge of Brazil, not until Britain was threatened with invasion and her fleet with destruction or capture, did he feel able to move at all.

He did not feel able to do what was needed because of the series of furious controversies which divided the nation between 1937 and 1941—over the repeal of the arms embargo, over the transaction of the over-age destroyers and the bases, over conscription, over lend-lease, and over the repeal of the Neutrality Act. None of these costly controversies would have taken the form it did take if the President had been able to present it to a people which realized how serious were their commitments and had acquired the habit of covering their commitments.

Thus almost none of the so-called isolationists declared that the commitments of the United States should be reduced—that the Monroe Doctrine should be revoked, that the Philippines should not be defended, that Japan should be given the free hand in China which she demanded as the price of peace. The isolationist party adhered, on the whole, to our vast trans-oceanic commitments. They devoted their efforts to opposing the alliances which, as is now obvious, we needed in order to validate the commitments. They argued

that only by doing nothing to save our present allies from defeat would we be able to stay out of war. This was the ground on which they opposed the repeal of the arms embargo, the transfer of the destroyers, and lend-lease. They took this view because they felt confident that continental United States could not be invaded, and they chose to ignore as a disagreeable anomaly the fact that American obligations extended to South America and to islands 7000 miles west of the coast of California. Isolationism, in other words, was based on a failure to appreciate the long-established trans-oceanic commitments of the United States.

The case of the "interventionists" rested on a correct appreciation of the situation—that alone and without allies the United States could not sustain its commitments against the combined power of the totalitarian alliance. Yet not until only the British Isles and the armies of General Chiang Kai-shek were left did the President feel it expedient in domestic politics to avow openly this self-evident truth. Even then it was still regarded as the Roosevelt policy rather than as the American national policy.

And even now, as we approach the climax of the struggle, it is still by no means certain that a settled American policy can be established against the abiding illusions of more than a century of inexperience in the realities of foreign policy.

CHAPTER V
MIRAGES

The habits of a century have fostered prejudices and illusions that vitiate our capacity to think effectively about foreign relations. The elementary means by which all foreign policy must be conducted are the armed forces of the nation, the arrangement of its strategic position, and the choice of its alliances. In the American ideology of our times these things had come to be regarded as militaristic, imperialistic, reactionary, and archaic; the proper concern of right-minded men was held to be peace, disarmament, and a choice between non-intervention and collective security.

We not only ignored the development of the means to achieve our ends: we chose as the ends of our efforts a set of ideals which were incompatible with all the means of achieving any ideals. The ideal of peace diverted our attention from the idea of national security. The ideal of disarmament caused us to be inadequately armed. The apparently opposed ideals of non-intervention on the one hand, and of collective security on the other, had at bottom the same practical result in that they inhibited us from forming our necessary alliances. Thus for nearly half a century after our vast commitments in the Pacific had been superimposed upon our immense commitment in the Western Hemisphere, we have had to conduct our pre-war diplomacy verbally—by promises, threats, and exhortations; we have had to wage war three times without being prepared to fight; and we have twice made peace without knowing what we wanted.

These spendthrift habits have led us to the bankruptcy of a total war in which we have suffered humiliating initial disasters at the hands of the Japanese; and our very independence was for a time in jeopardy. The habits of mind of Americans of our generation are quite alien to those of the Founders of the Republic. Washington, Hamilton, Jefferson, Madison, Monroe, entertained none of the basic illusions and prejudices which have dominated the later generations of Americans. They did not regard peace as more important than the national security. Though Jefferson had some odd ideas about the navy, the Founders never thought of making unpreparedness for war a national ideal. And though they spoke against "entangling" alliances, they never hesitated to seek the support of other powers, as in the case of the Louisiana Purchase and the declaration of the Monroe Doctrine, when they saw that directly or indirectly the help of an ally could promote the national interest.

The idealistic objections to preparedness, to strategic precautions, and to alliances came to dominate American thinking in the hundred years which followed Monroe's declaration. The objections flourished, and became a national ideology, owing to the historical accident that in that period Asia was dormant, Europe divided, and Britain's command of the sea unchallenged. As a result, we never had to meet our obligations in this hemisphere and in the Pacific, and we enjoyed a security which in fact we took almost no measures to sustain.

This unearned security during a long century had the effect upon our national habits of mind which the lazy enjoyment of unearned income so often has upon the descendants of a hard-working grandfather. It caused us to forget that man has to earn his security and his liberty as he has to earn his living. We came to think that our privileged position was a natural right, and then to believe that our unearned security was the reward of our moral superiority. Finally we came to argue, like the idle rich who regard work as something for menials, that a concern with the foundations of national security, with arms, with strategy, and with diplomacy, was beneath our dignity as idealists. . . .

CHAPTER VII
THE ATLANTIC COMMUNITY

3. THE BRITISH-AMERICAN CONNECTION

The question then is on the formation of an American alliance with the British Commonwealth and its Empire, and with the Soviet Union.

Let us examine first the project of a British-American alliance.

When we consider the region which the United States must defend, we find that Britain is established within that region as well as outside of it. The defensive region, we must remind ourselves, lies within a line from Greenland to Brazil, and from Alaska to the Philippines.

The Dominion of Canada, with which we have a common land frontier three thousand miles long, is in the geographic center of this region. The only land highway to Alaska passes through Canada. All the short airways to Europe and Asia pass over Canada. To fly to the United Kingdom and to Iceland, to Scandinavia, to Berlin and Moscow, to Siberia, Japan, and China, the shortest airways are over Canada. Thus the geography of air power links the leading dominion in the British Commonwealth of Nations inseparably with the United States.

But no matter how boldly we allow ourselves to imagine the range and carrying capacity and striking power of the aircraft of the future, two limitations are unalterable.

The first is that aircraft taking off in North America must for civilian purposes be able to land outside of North America—somewhere in Europe, Africa, and Asia. A flight is between two airfields on the ground. For military purposes it is just theoretically conceivable that planes could be built which took off in the United States, attacked in Europe or Asia, and returned to the United States without coming to the ground. But such flights would for the practical future be of no military importance against well-defended objectives across the oceans. So we must conclude that without the use of advanced air bases across the oceans, American air power cannot be developed effectively.

At the utmost, American air power, with assured use of air bases only in North America, would be condemned to the strategy of the passive defense—to waiting for the enemy to strike if, when, and where he chooses. We have already examined the fatal disadvantages of the passive defensive. We need only remind ourselves here that all the positions we have to defend are exposed salients—Greenland and the bulge of Brazil, Alaska and the Philippines. All of them are nearer by air and by sea to some great power of the Old World than they are to the arsenals, training grounds, and recruiting centers of the United States.

The second limitation which we must for the practical future regard as controlling is that American air power cannot be effective without sea power. For it is not practicable by means of the air alone to establish, construct, supply and defend overseas air bases.

Thus Alaska is no doubt destined to be one of the greatest centers of the air power of the future. But no conceivable development of cargo and transport planes could alone develop and maintain the installations of air power in Alaska. The use of the land highway across Canada and the command of the seas from our Pacific Coast to Alaska are absolutely indispensable.

In regard to Greenland, or a more advanced air base in Iceland, the support of American air power depends upon sea communications. These communications must pass through the North Atlantic ocean passage. On one side of that passage lie the Dominion of Canada and the British colony of Newfoundland, and on the other side of it lie the British Isles. It follows that the security of the northern approaches to the American continent is inseparably related to the sea and air power of Britain. In 1940 when the British Isles were in mortal peril, it was self-evident that the United States could not have held its position in Greenland against German submarines and aircraft established in a conquered Britain. In 1941 it was equally self-evident that Iceland could not be held against a determined attack from German-held Norway without the assured support of British sea and air power. And if Iceland and then Greenland had fallen into enemy hands, the North American continent would have been gravely threatened.

In the South Atlantic, on the approaches to South America, the maintenance of strong sea and air bases on the bulge of Brazil is essential. These bases cannot be maintained by Brazil alone. For Brazil is not an arsenal. The Brazilians have, therefore, to be supported from the United States. But there are no land communications with Brazil. And therefore the strategic defense of the whole South American continent as it faces the Atlantic is dependent upon sea and air communications.

With respect to the arsenal and the primary industrial centers of the world, Brazil is, for commerce and in war, an island. Moreover, it is an island lying nearer to the Old World than to the New. From New York to Belém it is 2975 sea miles. From New York to Pernambuco it is 3698 sea miles. Now, the distances from South America to all important points under European control are no greater, and to the strategic outposts of European power in Africa they are shorter. Thus the distance from Pernambuco to French Dakar, or from Belém to British Gibraltar or Bathurst or Freetown, is at least a thousand miles shorter than, is not two thirds so far as, the distance to any comparable strong point of the United States. And if we examine the island outposts of Europe in the South Atlantic—the Spanish Canaries, the Portuguese Cape Verdes, and Britain's Ascension Island—it is evident that the European states are inside the close approaches to South America. We are no nearer than Trinidad, a base useful to the defense of the Panama Canal and the Caribbean, but awkwardly placed and much too distant to be used in the defense of the vast and populous region of South America. Trinidad is a British island, where we have been granted the lease of land for a base because in 1940 we had the sense to realize that the defense of Britain and the defense of America are inseparably a combined undertaking.

Yet even if our sea communications with the bulge of Brazil were assured, we should still be only better prepared to conduct the passive defense. Our bases, including those leased by Britain in 1940, are good only for our passive defense: they cannot be used for the active defense of South America. The jumping-off places for the invasion of South America would still be numerous and so far beyond our reach that we could not snuff out an attack before it was mounted. Here again we find the British power founded on the United Kingdom and projected to Gibraltar and to Bathurst and Freetown in West Africa, and to Capetown in South Africa. The British Isles command the northern entrance to the Atlantic. Gibraltar commands the Mediterranean entrance. Capetown commands the southern entrance from the Indian Ocean. The Falkland Islands command the southern entrance from the Pacific Ocean around Cape Horn. Thus the region we must defend can be attacked only from the region over which Britain commands all the approaches by sea.

Moreover, because the defense of Canada, the greatest of all the British dominions, is inextricably bound up with the defense of the Western Hemisphere, the British vital interest and the American vital interest are complementary and inseparable. Britain must go to the defense of the Americas or the British Commonwealth of Nations would dissolve. America must go to the defense of the United Kingdom and its positions on the other side of the Atlantic, or run the mortal risk of letting a hostile power establish itself in the near approaches to the Western Hemisphere.

The reality of this bond between Britain and America has been tested and demonstrated for more than a century. It compelled Britain in her own interest, it compelled the three Virginian Presidents who had twice been at war with England, to form that concert upon which the Monroe Doctrine has always rested. It compelled both Canada and the United States to enter the two great wars of the twentieth century because in each war the survival of the British power, and therefore the strategic security of the Americas, was at stake.

4. THE BRITISH-AMERICAN CONNECTION
IN THE PACIFIC

Once it is clear how indispensable is a British-American alliance in the Atlantic, where our most fundamental interests lie, it will also become clear that the alliance is necessary to the defense of the Pacific. American naval power in the Pacific must, in order to be fully effective, hold securely a chain of bases extending from continental United States through Hawaii, Wake, Guam, and the Japanese mandated islands to the Philippines. It is, however, a line which cannot easily be held securely unless there is an anchor at the other end of this barrier chain of bases. This anchor can be provided only by China. For we must remember that this American line is a very long salient thrust out into Asia. Inevitably, therefore, it is weakest at the end of the salient in the Philippines, and therefore vulnerable if it stands alone.

Our war with Japan has proved how vulnerable it is. For everything from Wake west has been lost. Moreover, even if we acknowledge that the unpreparedness of December 7, 1941, will never be permitted to exist again, it is still the fact that the isolated defense of such a long salient cannot be guaranteed. When we lost the American line in the winter of 1941–1942, what would we have done if we had had no allies? What would we have done if China, Britain, Australia, the Netherlands, and Fighting France had been neutrals in the Japanese-American war? The whole campaign of the South Pacific is conducted from British and French bases. The possibility of any direct attack upon Japan herself depends upon having China as an ally, and for its full success it depends also upon having Russia as an ally.

We shall examine our relations with Russia in the next chapter. Let us note here, however, that we are powerless alone to open the ports of China. Our sea power is insufficient. The Chinese armies and American air forces in China can be built up and maintained only because India is an ally of China and of the United States. It is from India that supplies reach China by air. It is only from India that Burma can be reconquered and the Burma Road reopened. But nothing whatever could be done from India if the British in the United Kingdom were not able to keep open the sea communications through the Indian Ocean. Much more can be done from India when the shorter passage through the Mediterranean, past the British strong positions at Gibraltar, Malta, and Suez, is again open to us.

Is it not undeniable that American commitments in the Atlantic and the Pacific dictate the need for an alliance with the British Commonwealth of Nations and with the Empire?

It has been the geography and the history of North America which have made the British-American connection the crucial point in American foreign relations. To imagine that the connection was invented by schemers and financiers and munitions-makers, and promoted by propagandists, is to deny the facts of geography and the inexorable lessons of historic experience. The real trouble, if we look objectively at our situation and at our history, is not, as some pretend, that American statesmen have been seduced by the British. It is that they have not seen clearly enough and advocated boldly enough the critical and enduring necessity of what Monroe called the concert by agreement—in the plain unadorned language of the obvious truth, of a British-American alliance. As for the propagandists, the trouble with them has been that they have tried to circumvent prejudice and the lack of an understanding of the facts of life by devious, indirect, furtive, emotional circumlocutions. It is better to proclaim frankly that the alliance is necessary, and then to demonstrate the need for it to the common sense of the British, the Canadian, and the American people.

Granting that all alliances have their risks and their inconveniences, is it not a fact that an avowed alliance, an open covenant openly arrived at, is a far healthier relation than a connection which is concealed and denied in time of peace, and then imperatively acted upon under the pressure of catastrophic peril in time of war? No doubt there are, between the British and Americans, conflicting commercial interests at some points, and there are some unhappy memories, and there are social difficulties. But the more openly avowed is the bond of our vital interests, the more clearly we shall see in their true perspective the points of friction and antagonism.

In order to defend the vital interests of both peoples, to make sure that each will survive, responsible men have been compelled since 1914 to gloss over the conflicts of interests which are not vital. Those who emphasize the conflicts—often genuine and important—are in the position of men who irresponsibly risk the greater interest for the sake of the lesser. Only by making sure that the vital common interest in security is invincibly settled can the lesser conflicts of interest be dealt with safely by open discussion and by negotiation. Only when it is certain that the two great systems of states—the British Commonwealth and the American republics—will not go to war with each other, and that neither will permit the other to be destroyed, will there exist the security within which they can safely work out their differences.

5. THE MEMBERS OF THE ATLANTIC COMMUNITY

The special characteristic of British-American relations is that the British Commonwealth is both inside and outside the area of America's defensive commitments. Canada lies in the midst of it; Australia and New Zealand within it. Thus the overthrow of the American position in the world would mean the break-up of the British Commonwealth. At the same time the citadel of British power is the United Kingdom and the outlying strong points from Gibraltar to Singapore are at the strategic frontiers of the Americas. Thus the overthrow of the British position in the world would mean a revolutionary change in the system of defense within which the American republics have lived for more than a century.

There are twenty American republics and there are, counting Eire and South Africa, six British nations within this community. All of these twenty-six states are self-governing. Though some are much more powerful than others, the sovereignty of their independence is attested by the fact that Eire within the British Commonwealth and the Argentine and Chile within the Pan-American system have been free to remain neutral. They have been free to stay out of the war, even though the war is fought to preserve the system of security which enables them to make this sovereign choice. This is the proof that in fact the British Commonwealth is a commonwealth and not an empire, that the association of American republics is not the façade of United States imperialism.

London was so obviously unable to give orders to the dominions to go to war that no such order was even contemplated, that none, as we see in the case of Eire, was given. Washington gives no orders to its neighbor republics, the proof being that they have freely decided for themselves the time, the degree, and the modes of their neutrality, their non-belligerency, or their adherence to the alliance.

It is the demonstrated fact that London cannot and does not dominate so small, so near, so weak, and so strategically important a dominion as Eire, but must treat with it as a sovereign independent state. It has been demonstrated that the United States cannot and does not dominate on the crucial issue of war and peace American republics like the Argentine and Chile. How insubstantial then is the fear that Britain could dominate a powerful nation like the United States, or be dominated by the United States. Can it then be denied that the British-American connection is, through the facts of geography and the results of historic experience, a community of interest and not a plan of domination or a scheme of empire?

Nor is it, nor can it be, a plan for the combined domination of the world by the English-speaking nations. We shall see this when we turn to Russia and China. We can see this when we fix our attention upon the other nations which, like Britain, have their vital interests both within and outside the New World. The first of these is France. For a hundred years the only enemy of France has been Germany, and the one frontier France had to defend was her frontier facing Germany. But when France is unable to defend that frontier, as seemed possible in 1917 and was the fact in 1940, it is immediately evident in the New World that the security of France is indispensable to the security of the New World.

The fall of France in 1940 was a conclusive demonstration that France is a member of the great defensive system in which the American republics live. The fall of France laid Spain and Portugal open to the possibility of invasion and domination. This in turn opened up the question of the security of the Spanish and Portuguese island stepping-stones in the Atlantic. The fall of France gave Germany the sea and air bases from which Britain was beseiged and American shipping along our Eastern shore and in the Caribbean subjected to a devastating raid. The fall of France uncovered the West Coast of Africa from above Casablanca to Dakar, and opened up the threat, in the event of a German victory in Europe, of a sea-borne and air-borne invasion of South America. The fall of France had equally momentous consequences in the Pacific. The surrender of French Indo-China to Japan completed the envelopment of the Philippines, and provided the base from which Japan conquered Burma and closed the Burma Road and thus cut off China from her allies.

It follows that France, though a state in continental Europe, is primarily a member of the same community to which the United States belongs. The security of France is an American interest, and the security of the American position is a French interest. The same holds true, and for the same reasons, of Spain and Portugal. The vital interests of the British nations, the American nations, and of the Latin nations on both sides of the Atlantic, and across the Pacific, are so enmeshed by geography, by strategic necessity, and by historic formation that their paramount interests are, when tested in the fires of total war, inseparable. They can fall separately. None of them, not the most powerful, not the two most powerful among them combined —namely the United Kingdom and the United States—can stand comfortably and securely without the others. The proof that clinches the demonstration is that the British nations and the American nations are compelled for their own survival to liberate France and to foster the restoration of the power of France.

Other nations are vitally involved in the system of security to which we belong. The Netherlands is a small state in Europe with a great empire overseas in the Pacific and with important colonies in the New World. The Netherlands is also one of the outer bastions of both France and Britain. The same is true of Belgium, which has an empire on the Atlantic and is also an outer bastion. Another member of the Atlantic Community is Denmark, which only very recently retired from her colonial possessions in the West Indies, which on the northern approaches to the American continent holds Greenland as a colony and, until recently, was related to Iceland because both had the same king. Norway, too, is a member. For Norway is a country which in relation to Europe is strategically an island lying on the outer limits of the Atlantic world.

Thus the violation of Denmark and Norway, as of the Netherlands and Belgium, was instantly recognized in the Americas and in Britain as a breach in their defenses, and in Norway and in Denmark, as in the Netherlands and Belgium, it was instantly recognized that liberation and restoration depended upon the victory of the British and American nations. Thus when we say that they are members of the same community of interest, we are making an avowal which has been put to the acid test and is no mere amiable generalization.

6. THE INLAND SEA

If we re-examine the catalogue of nations which are involved in the same system of security, we come upon an interesting and, I believe, a very significant fact. It is that the nations of the New World are still vitally related to precisely those nations of the Old World from which they originated. The settlement of the New World after 1492 was a movement from East to West. The British, the French, the Dutch, the Danes, and we may add the Swedes, moved from the northerly part of the Old World to the northerly part of the New. In the course of their movement they fought many imperialistic wars with one another. But the net result was that the upper part of North America stems from the English and French, and contains important vestiges in New York of the Dutch settlements. The rest of the Americas were settled from the Iberian peninsula, and the two languages of Central and South America are Spanish and Portuguese.

At the end of the eighteenth and the beginning of the nineteenth century most of the nations of the New World won their sovereign independence from the parent nations in the Old World. But the separation, though it is absolute in the realm of self-government, has never existed in the realm of strategic security. The original geographic and historic connections across the Atlantic have persisted. The Atlantic Ocean is not the frontier between Europe and the Americas. It is the inland sea of a community of nations allied with one another by geography, history, and vital necessity.

The members of this community may not all love one another, and they have many conflicting interests. But that is true of any community except perhaps a community of the saints. The test of whether a community exists is not whether we have learned to love our neighbors but whether, when put to the test, we find that we do act as neighbors. By that test all the centuries of experience since the discovery of the Americas have shown that there is peace and order on this side of the Atlantic only when there is peace and order among our neighbors on the other side of the Atlantic. Whenever they have been involved in great wars, the New World has been involved. When they have had peace from great wars, as they did have from Waterloo to the first invasion of Belgium, there have been no great international wars that concerned the Americas.

Not what men say, nor what they think they feel, but what in fact when they have to act they actually do—that is the test of community. By that test there is a great community on this earth from which no member can be excluded and none can resign. This community has its geographical center in the great basin of the Atlantic.

The security of this community turns upon the relations of the two great powers —Britain and the United States. In this area and at this phase of historic time, they have the arsenals and the military formations necessary to the waging of war. And therefore their alliance is the nucleus of force around which the security of the whole region must necessarily be organized, to which, when their alliance is firm, the other members of the community will in their own interest freely adhere. . . .

4. THE PROPOSED BASIS FOR AGREEMENT BETWEEN THE UNITED STATES AND JAPAN, NOVEMBER, 1941[1]

EDITORS' NOTE.—This notable communication of November 26, 1941, was handed to Japanese Ambassador Nomura by Secretary of State Cordell Hull. This note had been preceded by ten days of conferences between Ambassadors Nomura and Kurusu and Hull and Roosevelt. Ambassador Kurusu stated that the situation in Japan was very pressing and wanted the United States to abandon the July, 1941, regulations freezing Japanese credits in the United States. After making an attempt to defend the Tripartite Pact, in which Japan was allied with Germany and Italy, Kurusu pointed out the desire of the Japanese to secure oil and to maintain peaceful relations with the United States; then they could both secure needed commodities from the Netherlands East Indies; finally, with this change in policy, Japan would expect America to withdraw its support of the Chinese government then at war with Japan. Hull and Roosevelt argued that America felt endangered by Japanese membership in the Tripartite Pact, that the Japanese formula of a new order in Greater East Asia was but another name for a program to dominate the Pacific, that the American people were angry with the statements by Japanese officials, and that the following proposal was as far as the United States would go in reference to the Japanese requests. Secretary Hull stated to Ambassador Kurusu that "there was so much confusion among the public that it was necessary to bring about some clarification; that we have reached a stage when the public has lost its perspective and that it was therefore necessary to draw up a document which would present a complete picture of our position by making provision for each essential point involved. . . . [On] the oil question . . . public feeling was so acute on that question that he might almost be lynched if he permitted oil to go freely to Japan . . . they [the Japanese] did not know what tremendous injury they were doing to us by keeping immobilized so many forces in countries neighboring Indochina . . . we are primarily out for our permanent futures, and the question of Japanese troops in Indochina affects our direct interests." A few critics say that Roosevelt and Hull managed diplomacy with Japan so that no alternative was left in the end except war. Most observers believe that the war resulted from Japanese aggression and the American determination to restrain it.

SECTION I

DRAFT MUTUAL DECLARATION OF POLICY

The Government of the United States and the Government of Japan both being solicitous for the peace of the Pacific affirm that their national policies are directed toward lasting and extensive peace throughout the Pacific area, that they have no territorial designs in that area, that they have no intention of threatening other

1. U.S. Department of State, *Papers Relating to Foreign Relations, Japan, 1931–1941* (Washington, 1943), II, 768–70.

countries or of using military force aggressively against any neighboring nation, and that, accordingly, in their national policies they will actively support and give practical application to the following fundamental principles upon which their relations with each other and with all other governments are based:

(1) The principle of inviolability of territorial integrity and sovereignty of each and all nations.

(2) The principle of non-interference in the internal affairs of other countries.

(3) The principle of equality, including equality of commercial opportunity and treatment.

(4) The principle of reliance upon international cooperation and conciliation for the prevention and pacific settlement of controversies and for improvement of international conditions by peaceful methods and processes.

The Government of Japan and the Government of the United States have agreed that toward eliminating chronic political instability, preventing recurrent economic collapse, and providing a basis for peace, they will actively support and practically apply the following principles in their economic relations with each other and with other nations and peoples:

(1) The principle of non-discrimination in international commercial relations.

(2) The principle of international economic cooperation and abolition of extreme nationalism as expressed in excessive trade restrictions.

(3) The principle of non-discriminatory access by all nations to raw material supplies.

(4) The principle of full protection of the interests of consuming countries and populations as regards the operation of international commodity agreements.

(5) The principle of establishment of such institutions and arrangements of international finance as may lend aid to the essential enterprises and the continuous development of all countries and may permit payments through processes of trade consonant with the welfare of all countries.

SECTION II

STEPS TO BE TAKEN BY THE GOVERNMENT OF THE UNITED STATES AND BY THE GOVERNMENT OF JAPAN

The Government of the United States and the Government of Japan propose to take steps as follows:

1. The Government of the United States and the Government of Japan will endeavor to conclude a multilateral non-aggression pact among the British Empire, China, Japan, the Netherlands, the Soviet Union, Thailand and the United States.

2. Both Governments will endeavor to conclude among the American, British, Chinese, Japanese, the Netherland and Thai Governments an agreement whereunder each of the Governments would pledge itself to respect the territorial integrity of French Indochina and, in the event that there should develop a threat to the territorial integrity of Indochina, to enter into immediate consultation with a view to taking such measures as may be deemed necessary and advisable to meet the threat in question. Such agreement would provide also that each of the Governments party to the agreement would not seek or accept preferential treatment in its trade or economic relations with Indochina and would use its influence to obtain for each of the signatories equality of treatment in trade and commerce with French Indochina.

3. The Government of Japan will withdraw all military, naval, air and police forces from China and from Indochina.

4. The Government of the United States and the Government of Japan will not support—militarily, politically, economically—any government or regime in China other than the National Government of the Republic of China with capital temporarily at Chungking.

5. Both Governments will give up all extraterritorial rights in China, including rights and interests in and with regard to

international settlements and concessions, and rights under the Boxer Protocol of 1901.

Both Governments will endeavor to obtain the agreement of the British and other governments to give up extraterritorial rights in China, including rights in international settlements and in concessions and under the Boxer Protocol of 1901.

6. The Government of the United States and the Government of Japan will enter into negotiations for the conclusion between the United States and Japan of a trade agreement, based upon reciprocal most-favored-nation treatment and reduction of trade barriers by both countries, including an undertaking by the United States to bind raw silk on the free list.

7. The Government of the United States and the Government of Japan will, respectively, remove the freezing restrictions on Japanese funds in the United States and on American funds in Japan.

8. Both Governments will agree upon a plan for the stabilization of the dollar-yen rate, with the allocation of funds adequate for this purpose, half to be supplied by Japan and half by the United States.

9. Both Governments will agree that no agreement which either has concluded with any third power or powers shall be interpreted by it in such a way as to conflict with the fundamental purpose of this agreement, the establishment and preservation of peace throughout the Pacific area.

10. Both Governments will use their influence to cause other governments to adhere to and to give practical application to the basic political and economic principles set forth in this agreement.

SECTION B. PLANS FOR "ONE WORLD"

1. THE FOUR FREEDOMS SPEECH, 1941[1]

By Franklin D. Roosevelt

EDITORS' NOTE.—This message to the Seventy-seventh Congress followed an election campaign in which both President Roosevelt and his Republican opponent, Wendell L. Willkie, had indorsed the policy of giving aid "short of war" to the Allies. The Lend-Lease Bill—President Roosevelt's device for converting the United States into an "arsenal of democracy"

—had been prepared since the election and was ready for presentation to Congress. Isolationist sentiment, though highly vocal and well organized, was not strong enough to prevent the adoption of Lend-Lease in the subsequent congressional debates. The enunciation of the "Four Freedoms" was a challenging contribution to the discussion of American peace aims.

I address you, the Members of the Seventy-seventh Congress, at a moment unprecedented in the history of the Union. I use the word "unprecedented," because at no previous time has American security been as seriously threatened from without as it is today.

Since the permanent formation of our Government under the Constitution, in 1789, most of the periods of crisis in our history have related to our domestic affairs. Fortunately, only one of these—the four-year War between the States—ever threatened our national unity. Today, thank God, one hundred and thirty million Americans, in forty-eight States, have forgotten points of the compass in our national unity.

It is true that prior to 1914 the United States often had been disturbed by events in other Continents. We had even engaged in two wars with European nations and in a number of undeclared wars in the West Indies, in the Mediterranean and in the

Pacific for the maintenance of American rights and for the principles of peaceful commerce. But in no case had a serious threat been raised against our national safety or our continued independence.

What I seek to convey is the historic truth that the United States as a nation has at all times maintained clear, definite opposition, to any attempt to lock us in behind an ancient Chinese wall while the procession of civilization went past. Today, thinking of our children and of their children, we oppose enforced isolation for ourselves or for any other part of the Americas.

That determination of ours, extending over all these years, was proved, for example, during the quarter century of wars following the French Revolution.

While the Napoleonic struggles did threaten interests of the United States because of the French foothold in the West Indies and in Louisiana, and while we engaged in the War of 1812 to vindicate our right to peaceful trade, it is nevertheless clear that neither France nor Great Britain, nor any other nation, was aiming at domination of the whole world.

1. *Development of United States Foreign Policy: Addresses and Messages of Franklin D. Roosevelt* (77th Cong., 2d sess.; Senate Doc. No. 188, Serial No. 10676 [Washington, 1942]), pp. 81–87.

In like fashion, from 1815 to 1914—ninety-nine years—no single war in Europe or in Asia constituted a real threat against our future or against the future of any other American nation.

Except in the Maximilian interlude in Mexico, no foreign power sought to establish itself in this Hemisphere; and the strength of the British fleet in the Atlantic has been a friendly strength. It is still a friendly strength.

Even when World War broke out in 1914, it seemed to contain only small threat of danger to our own American future. But, as time went on, the American people began to visualize what the downfall of democratic nations might mean to our own democracy.

We need not overemphasize imperfections in the Peace of Versailles. We need not harp on failure of the democracies to deal with problems of world reconstruction. We should remember that the Peace of 1919 was far less unjust than the kind of "pacification" which began even before Munich, and which is being carried on under the new order of tyranny that seeks to spread over every continent today. The American people have unalterably set their faces against that tyranny.

Every realist knows that the democratic way of life is at this moment being directly assailed in every part of the world—assailed either by arms, or by secret spreading of poisonous propaganda by those who seek to destroy unity and promote discord in nations that are still at peace.

During sixteen long months this assault has blotted out the whole pattern of democratic life in an appalling number of independent nations, great and small. The assailants are still on the march, threatening other nations, great and small.

Therefore, as your President, performing my constitutional duty to "give to the Congress information of the state of the Union," I find it, unhappily, necessary to report that the future and the safety of our country and of our democracy are overwhelmingly involved in events far beyond our borders.

Armed defense of democratic existence is now being gallantly waged in four continents. If that defense fails, all the population and all the resources of Europe, Asia, Africa and Australasia will be dominated by the conquerors. Let us remember that the total of those populations and their resources in those four continents greatly exceeds the sum total of the population and the resources of the whole of the Western Hemisphere—many times over.

In times like these it is immature—and incidentally, untrue—for anybody to brag that an unprepared America, single-handed, and with one hand tied behind its back, can hold off the whole world.

No realistic American can expect from a dictator's peace international generosity, or return of true independence, or world disarmament, or freedom of expression, or freedom of religion—or even good business.

Such a peace would bring no security for us or for our neighbors. "Those, who would give up essential liberty to purchase a little temporary safety, deserve neither liberty nor safety."

As a nation, we may take pride in the fact that we are soft-hearted; but we cannot afford to be soft-headed.

We must always be wary of those who with sounding brass and a tinkling cymbal preach the "ism" of appeasement.

We must especially beware of that small group of selfish men who would clip the wings of the American eagle in order to feather their own nests.

I have recently pointed out how quickly the tempo of modern warfare could bring into our very midst the physical attack which we must eventually expect if the dictator nations win this war.

There is much loose talk of our immunity from immediate and direct invasion from across the seas. Obviously, as long as the British Navy retains its power, no such danger exists. Even if there were no British Navy, it is not probable that any enemy would be stupid enough to attack us by landing troops in the United States from across thousands of miles of ocean, until it had acquired strategic bases from which to operate.

But we learn much from the lessons of the past years in Europe—particularly the lesson of Norway, whose essential seaports were captured by treachery and surprise built up over a series of years.

The first phase of the invasion of this Hemisphere would not be the landing of regular troops. The necessary strategic points would be occupied by secret agents and their dupes—and great numbers of them are already here, and in Latin America.

As long as the aggressor nations maintain the offensive, they—not we—will choose the time and the place and the method of their attack.

That is why the future of all the American Republics is today in serious danger.

That is why this Annual Message to the Congress is unique in our history.

That is why every member of the Executive Branch of the Government and every member of the Congress faces great responsibility and great accountability.

The need of the moment is that our actions and our policy should be devoted primarily—almost exclusively—to meeting this foreign peril. For all our domestic problems are now a part of the great emergency.

Just as our national policy in internal affairs has been based upon a decent respect for the rights and the dignity of all our fellow men within our gates, so our national policy in foreign affairs has been based on a decent respect for the rights and dignity of all nations, large and small. And the justice of morality must and will win in the end.

Our national policy is this:

First, by an impressive expression of the public will and without regard to partisanship, we are committed to all-inclusive national defense.

Second, by an impressive expression of the public will and without regard to partisanship, we are committed to full support of all those resolute peoples, everywhere, who are resisting aggression and are thereby keeping war away from our Hemisphere. By this support, we express our determination that the democratic cause shall prevail; and we strengthen the defense and the security of our own nation.

Third, by an impressive expression of the public will and without regard to partisanship, we are committed to the proposition that principles of morality and considerations for our own security will never permit us to acquiesce in a peace dictated by aggressors and sponsored by appeasers. We know that enduring peace cannot be bought at the cost of other people's freedom.

In the recent national election there was no substantial difference between the two great parties in respect to that national policy. No issue was fought out on this line before the American electorate. Today it is abundantly evident that American citizens everywhere are demanding and supporting speedy and complete action in recognition of obvious danger.

Therefore, the immediate need is a swift and driving increase in our armament production.

Leaders of industry and labor have responded to our summons. Goals of speed have been set. In some cases these goals are being reached ahead of time; in some cases we are on schedule; in other cases there are slight but not serious delays; and in some cases—and I am sorry to say very important cases—we are all concerned by the slowness of the accomplishment of our plans.

The Army and Navy, however, have made substantial progress during the past year. Actual experience is improving and speeding up our methods of production with every passing day. And today's best is not good enough for tomorrow.

I am not satisfied with the progress thus far made. The men in charge of the program represent the best in training, in ability and in patriotism. They are not satisfied with the progress thus far made. None of us will be satisfied until the job is done.

No matter whether the original goal was set too high or too low, our objective is quicker and better results.

To give you two illustrations:

We are behind schedule in turning out finished airplanes; we are working day and night to solve the innumerable problems and to catch up.

We are ahead of schedule in building warships but we are working to get even further ahead of that schedule.

To change a whole nation from a basis of peacetime production of implements of peace to a basis of wartime production of implements of war is no small task. And the greatest difficulty comes at the beginning of the program, when new tools, new plant facilities, new assembly lines, and new ship ways must first be constructed before the actual matériel begins to flow steadily and speedily from them.

The Congress, of course, must rightly keep itself informed at all times of the progress of the program. However, there is certain information, as the Congress itself will readily recognize, which, in the interests of our own security and those of the nations that we are supporting, must of needs be kept in confidence.

New circumstances are constantly begetting new needs for our safety. I shall ask this Congress for greatly increased new appropriations and authorizations to carry on what we have begun.

I also ask this Congress for authority and for funds sufficient to manufacture additional munitions and war supplies of many kinds, to be turned over to those nations which are now in actual war with aggressor nations.

Our most useful and immediate role is to act as an arsenal for them as well as for ourselves. They do not need man power, but they do need billions of dollars worth of the weapons of defense.

The time is near when they will not be able to pay for them all in ready cash. We cannot, and we will not, tell them that they must surrender, merely because of inability to pay for the weapons which we know they must have.

I do not recommend that we make them a loan of dollars with which to pay for these weapons—a loan to be repaid in dollars.

I recommend that we make it possible for those nations to continue to obtain war materials in the United States, fitting their orders into our own program. Nearly all their matériel would, if the time ever came, be useful for our own defense.

Taking counsel of expert military and naval authorities, considering what is best for our own security, we are free to decide how much should be kept here and how much should be sent abroad to our friends who by their determined and heroic resistance are giving us time in which to make ready our own defense.

For what we send abroad, we shall be repaid within a reasonable time following the close of hostilities, in similar materials, or, at our option, in other goods of many kinds, which they can produce and which we need.

Let us say to the democracies: "We Americans are vitally concerned in your defense of freedom. We are putting forth our energies, our resources and our organizing powers to give you the strength to regain and maintain a free world. We shall send you, in ever-increasing numbers, ships, planes, tanks, guns. This is our purpose and our pledge."

In fulfillment of this purpose we will not be intimidated by the threats of dictators that they will regard as a breach of international law or as an act of war our aid to the democracies which dare to resist their aggression. Such aid is not an act of war, even if a dictator should unilaterally proclaim it so to be.

When the dictators, if the dictators, are ready to make war upon us, they will not wait for an act of war on our part. They did not wait for Norway or Belgium or the Netherlands to commit an act of war.

Their only interest is in a new one-way international law, which lacks mutuality in its observance, and, therefore, becomes an instrument of oppression.

The happiness of future generations of Americans may well depend upon how effective and how immediate we can make our aid felt. No one can tell the exact character of the emergency situations that we may be called upon to meet. The Nation's hands must not be tied when the Nation's life is in danger.

We must all prepare to make the sacrifices that the emergency—almost as serious as war itself—demands. Whatever stands in the way of speed and efficiency in defense preparations must give way to the national need.

A free nation has the right to expect full cooperation from all groups. A free nation has the right to look to the leaders of business, of labor, and of agriculture to take the lead in stimulating effort, not among other groups but within their own groups.

The best way of dealing with the few slackers or trouble makers in our midst is, first, to shame them by patriotic example, and, if that fails, to use the sovereignty of Government to save Government.

As men do not live by bread alone, they do not fight by armaments alone. Those who man our defenses, and those behind them who build our defenses, must have the stamina and the courage which come from unshakeable belief in the manner of life which they are defending. The mighty action that we are calling for cannot be based on a disregard of all things worth fighting for.

The Nation takes great satisfaction and much strength from the things which have been done to make its people conscious of their individual stake in the preservation of democratic life in America. Those things have toughened the fibre of our people, have renewed their faith and strengthened their devotion to the institutions we make ready to protect.

Certainly this is no time for any of us to stop thinking about the social and economic problems which are the root cause of the social revolution which is today a supreme factor in the world.

For there is nothing mysterious about the foundations of a healthy and strong democracy. The basic things expected by our people of their political and economic systems are simple. They are:

Equality of opportunity for youth and for others.

Jobs for those who can work.

Security for those who need it.

The ending of special privilege for the few.

The preservation of civil liberties for all.

The enjoyment of the fruits of scientific progress in a wider and constantly rising standard of living.

These are the simple, basic things that must never be lost sight of in the turmoil and unbelievable complexity of our modern world. The inner and abiding strength of our economic and political systems is dependent upon the degree to which they fulfill these expectations.

Many subjects connected with our social economy call for immediate improvement.

As examples:

We should bring more citizens under the coverage of old-age pensions and unemployment insurance.

We should widen the opportunities for adequate medical care.

We should plan a better system by which persons deserving or needing gainful employment may obtain it.

I have called for personal sacrifice. I am assured of the willingness of almost all Americans to respond to that call.

A part of the sacrifice means the payment of more money in taxes. In my Budget Message I shall recommend that a greater portion of this great defense program be paid for from taxation than we are paying today. No person should try, or be allowed, to get rich out of this program;

and the principle of tax payments in accordance with ability to pay should be constantly before our eyes to guide our legislation.

If the Congress maintains these principles, the voters, putting patriotism ahead of pocketbooks, will give you their applause.

In the future days, which we seek to make secure, we look forward to a world founded upon four essential human freedoms.

The first is freedom of speech and expression—everywhere in the world.

The second is freedom of every person to worship God in his own way—everywhere in the world.

The third is freedom from want—which, translated into world terms, means economic understandings which will secure to every nation a healthy peacetime life for its inhabitants—everywhere in the world.

The fourth is freedom from fear—which, translated into world terms, means a world-wide reduction of armaments to such a point and in such a thorough fashion that no nation will be in a position to commit an act of physical aggression against any neighbor—anywhere in the world.

That is no vision of a distant millennium. It is a definite basis for a kind of world attainable in our own time and generation. That kind of world is the very antithesis of the so-called new order of tyranny which the dictators seek to create with the crash of a bomb.

To that new order we oppose the greater conception—the moral order. A good society is able to face schemes of world domination and foreign revolutions alike without fear.

Since the beginning of our American history, we have been engaged in change—in a perpetual peaceful revolution—a revolution which goes on steadily, quietly adjusting itself to changing conditions—without the concentration camp or the quick-lime in the ditch. The world order which we seek is the cooperation of free countries, working together in a friendly, civilized society.

This nation has placed its destiny in the hands and heads and hearts of its millions of free men and women; and its faith in freedom under the guidance of God. Freedom means the supremacy of human rights everywhere. Our support goes to those who struggle to gain those rights or keep them. Our strength is our unity of purpose.

To that high concept there can be no end save victory.

2. THE ATLANTIC CHARTER, AUGUST, 1941[1]

EDITORS' NOTE.—The Atlantic Charter was released in Washington and London on August 14, 1941, after a three-day conference between the American President and the British prime minister at a secret rendezvous in the Newfoundland Bight. It represents a further stage in the development of Anglo-American collaboration and in the specification of their

Joint declaration of the President of the United States of America and the Prime Minister, Mr. Churchill, representing His Majesty's government in the United

common program for the postwar world. One of Britain's chief aims at this conference was to obtain strong American pressure against Japan, but in this they were not successful. Plans were also concerted at this meeting for sending supplies to Russia, which had been invaded by Germany six weeks before.

Kingdom, being met together, deem it

1. United States Department of State, *Toward the Peace: Documents* (Publication 2298 [Washington, 1945]), p. 1.

right to make known certain common principles in the national policies of their respective countries on which they base their hopes for a better future for the world.

First, their countries seek no aggrandizement, territorial or other;

Second, they desire to see no territorial changes that do not accord with the freely expressed wishes of the people concerned;

Third, they respect the right of all peoples to choose the form of government under which they will live; and they wish to see sovereign rights and self-government restored to those who have been forcibly deprived of them;

Fourth, they will endeavor, with due respect for their existing obligations; to further the enjoyment by all States, great or small, victor or vanquished, of access, on equal terms, to the trade and to the raw materials of the world which are needed for their economic prosperity;

Fifth, they desire to bring about the fullest collaboration between all nations in the economic field with the object of securing, for all, improved labor standards, economic advancement and social security;

Sixth, after the final destruction of the Nazi tyranny, they hope to see established a peace which will afford to all nations the means of dwelling in safety within their own boundaries, and which will afford assurance that all the men in all the lands may live out their lives in freedom from fear and want;

Seventh, such a peace should enable all men to traverse the high seas and oceans without hindrance;

Eighth, they believe that all of the nations of the world, for realistic as well as spiritual reasons must come to the abandonment of the use of force. Since no future peace can be maintained if land, sea or air armaments continue to be employed by nations which threaten, or may threaten, aggression outside of their frontiers, they believe, pending the establishment of a wider and permanent system of general security, that the disarmament of such nations is essential. They will likewise aid and encourage all other practicable measures which will lighten for peace-loving peoples the crushing burden of armaments.

3. ONE WORLD[1]

By WENDELL L. WILLKIE

EDITORS' NOTE.—Wendell L. Willkie (1892–1944), Wall Street lawyer and president of the Commonwealth and Southern Corporation (a holding company in utilities), had been nominated Republican candidate in the presidential election of 1940. To his strong popular following he was a vigorous, constructive leader favoring liberalism at home and internationalism abroad— policies which were not popular with the old guard of the party. His support for American intervention in world affairs continued after his electoral defeat and was a valuable reinforcement to the administration in the debates over Lend-Lease and Selective Service. On August 26, 1942, some eight months after Pearl Harbor, he left New York on a global survey in a United States Army plane, returning forty-nine days later. While enjoying presidential approval for his mission, Willkie claimed and exercised full liberty of judgment and comment. The publication of *One World* was a landmark in the emancipation of American opinion from the century-old tradition of isolationism.

1. Wendell L. Willkie, *One World* (New York, 1943), pp. 71–80. Reprinted by permission of Simon and Schuster.

THIS IS A WAR OF LIBERATION

This war that I saw going on all around the world is, in Mr. Stalin's phrase, a war of liberation. It is to liberate some nations from the Nazi or the Japanese Army, and to liberate others from the threat of those armies. On this much we are all agreed. Are we yet agreed that liberation means more than this? Specifically, are the thirty-one United Nations now fighting together agreed that our common job of liberation includes giving to *all* peoples freedom to govern themselves as soon as they are able, and the economic freedom on which all lasting self-government inevitably rests?

It is these two aspects of freedom, I believe, which form the touchstone of our good faith in this war. I believe we must include them both in our idea of the freedom we are fighting for. Otherwise, I am certain we shall not win the peace, and I am sure we cannot win the war.

In Chungking, on October 7, 1942, I made a statement to the Chinese and foreign press in which I tried to state some of the conclusions I had reached on my trip around the world. In part, this is what I said:

I have traveled through thirteen countries. I have seen kingdoms, soviets, republics, mandated areas, colonies, and dependencies. I have seen an almost bewildering variety of ways of living and ways of ruling and of being ruled. But I have found certain things common to all the countries I have visited and to all the ordinary people in those countries with whom I have talked:

They all want the United Nations to win the war.

They all want a chance at the end of the war to live in liberty and independence.

They all doubt, in varying degree, the readiness of the leading democracies of the world to stand up and be counted for freedom for others after the war is over. This doubt kills their enthusiastic participation on our side.

Now, without the real support of these common people, the winning of the war will be enormously difficult. The winning of the peace will be nearly impossible. This war is not a simple, technical problem for task forces. It is also a war for men's minds. We must organize on our side not simply the sympathies but the active, aggressive, offensive spirit of nearly three fourths of the people of the world who live in South America, Africa, eastern Europe, and Asia. We have not done this, and at present are not doing this. We have got to do it. . . .

Men need more than arms with which to fight and win this kind of war. They need enthusiasm for the future and a conviction that the flags they fight under are in bright, clean colors. The truth is that we as a nation have not made up our minds what kind of world we want to speak for when victory comes.

Especially here in Asia the common people feel that we have asked them to join us for no better reason than that Japanese rule would be even worse than Western imperialism. This is a continent where the record of the Western democracies has been long and mixed, but where people—and remember there are a billion of them—are determined no longer to live under foreign control. Freedom and opportunity are the words which have modern magic for the people of Asia, and we have let the Japanese—the most cruel imperialists the modern world has known—steal these words from us and corrupt them to their own uses.

Most of the people in Asia have never known democracy. They may or may not want *our* type of democracy. Obviously all of them are not ready to have democracy handed to them next Tuesday on a silver platter. But they are determined to work out their own destiny under governments selected by themselves.

Even the name of the Atlantic Charter disturbs thoughtful men and women I have been talking to. Do all of those who signed it, these people ask, agree that it applies to the Pacific? We must answer this question with a clear and simple statement of where we stand. And we must begin to sweat over our common problem of translating such a statement into plans which will be concrete and meaningful to the lives of these millions of people who are our allies.

Some of the plans to which such a statement would lead are already clear, I deeply believe, to most Americans:

We believe this war must mean an end to the empire of nations over other nations. No foot of Chinese soil, for example, should be or can be ruled from now on except by the people who live on it. And we must say so *now*, not after the war.

We believe it is the world's job to find some system for helping colonial peoples who join the United Nations' cause to become free and independent nations. We must set up firm time-tables under which they can work out and train governments of their own choosing, and we must establish ironclad guarantees, administered by all the United Nations jointly, that they shall not slip back into colonial status.

Some say these subjects should be hushed until victory is won. Exactly the reverse is true. Sincere efforts to find progressive solutions now will bring strength to our cause. Remember, opponents of social change always urge delay because of some present crisis. After the war, the changes may be too little and too late.

We must develop between nations trade and trade routes strong enough to give all peoples the same vested interest in peace which we in America have had.

In the United States, we are being asked to give up temporarily our individual freedom and economic liberty in order to crush the Axis. We must recover this freedom and this liberty after the war. The way to make certain we do recover our traditional American way of life with a rising standard of living for all is to create a world in which all men everywhere can be free.

This statement caused a good deal of comment. Some of it was angry, but for the most part the reaction cheered me greatly. For it confirmed my feeling that the deep drift of public opinion, which works quietly but powerfully, has already moved ahead of many of our leaders on these questions and that it will, before long, push us into the open acknowledgment, before the world, of the beliefs we hold most firmly.

The temptation is great, in all of us, to limit the objectives of a war. Cynically, we may hope that the big words we have used will become smaller at the peace table, that we can avoid the costly and difficult readjustments which will be required to establish and defend real freedom for all peoples.

Many men and women I have talked with from Africa to Alaska asked me the question which has become almost a symbol all through Asia: what about India?

Now I did not go to India. I do not propose to discuss that tangled question. But it has one aspect, in the East, which I should report. From Cairo on, it confronted me at every turn. The wisest man in China said to me: "When the aspiration of India for freedom was put aside to some future date, it was not Great Britain that suffered in public esteem in the Far East. It was the United States."

This wise man was not quarreling with British imperialism in India when he said this—a benevolent imperialism, if you like. He does not happen to believe in it, but he was not even talking about it. He was telling me that by our silence on India we have already drawn heavily on our reservoir of good will in the East. People of the East who would like to count on us are doubtful. They cannot ascertain from our attitude toward the problem of India what we are likely to feel at the end of the war about all the other hundreds of millions of Eastern peoples. They cannot tell from our vague and vacillating talk whether or not we really do stand for freedom, or what we mean by freedom.

In China, students who were refugees a thousand miles from their homes asked me if we were going to try to take back Shanghai after the war. In Beirut, Lebanese asked me if their relatives in Brooklyn—one third of all the Lebanese in the world live in the United States—would help to persuade the British and French occupying forces to leave Syria and the Lebanon after the war and let them run their own country.

In Africa, in the Middle East, throughout the Arab world, as well as in China and the whole Far East, freedom means the orderly but scheduled abolition of the colonial system. Whether we like it or not, this is true.

The British Commonwealth of Nations is the world's most spectacular example of such an orderly process. And the success of that great experiment should be immensely encouraging to the United Nations in working out the problems of self-government that lie ahead. For large sections of the world are still governed by the colonial system. Despite the Commonwealth, Great Britain still has numerous colonies, remnants of empire, with little or no self-rule, though the English people, millions of them, at home and throughout the Commonwealth, are working selflessly and with great skill toward reducing these remnants, toward extending the Commonwealth in place of the colonial system.

The English are by no means the only colonial rulers. The French still claim empire in Africa, in Indo-China, in South America, and in islands throughout the world. The Dutch still regard themselves as rulers of large parts of the East Indies and of territories in the West. The Portuguese, the Belgians, and other nations have colonial possessions. And we ourselves have not yet promised complete freedom to all the peoples in the West Indies for whom we have assumed responsibility. Furthermore, we have our domestic imperialisms.

But the world is awake, at last, to the knowledge that the rule of people by other peoples is not freedom, and not what we must fight to preserve.

There will be lots of tough problems ahead. And they will differ in different mandates and different colonies. Not all the peoples of the world are ready for freedom, or can defend it, the day after tomorrow. But today they all want some date to work toward, some assurance that the date will be kept. For the future, they do not ask that we solve their problems for them. They are neither so foolish nor so fainthearted. They ask only for the chance to solve their own problems with economic as well as political co-operation. For the peoples of the world intend to be free not only for their political satisfaction, but also for their economic advancement.

OUR IMPERIALISMS AT HOME

I mentioned among the imperialisms of the world our own domestic imperialisms.

This war has opened for us new horizons —new geographical horizons, new mental horizons. We have been a people devoted largely to home enterprise. We have become a people whose first interests are beyond the seas. The names of Russian, Burmese, Tunisian, or Chinese towns command primary attention in our newspapers. The most eagerly seized letters coming into our homes are from our young men in Australia, New Guinea, Guadalcanal, Ireland, or North Africa. Our interests go with their interests, and we may feel certain that when they have battled over the world, they will not return home as provincial Americans. Nor will they find us so. What does all this mean? It means that though we began to grow up with the earlier World War, we are only now changing completely from a young nation of domestic concerns to an adult nation of international interests and world outlook.

A true world outlook is incompatible with a foreign imperialism, no matter how high-minded the governing country. It is equally incompatible with the kind of imperialism which can develop inside any nation. Freedom is an indivisible word. If we want to enjoy it, and fight for it, we must be prepared to extend it to everyone, whether they are rich or poor, whether they agree with us or not, no matter what their race or the color of their skin. We cannot, with good conscience, expect the British to set up an orderly schedule for the liberation of India before we have decided for ourselves to make all who live in America free.

In this war we are allied with four hundred million people of China and we count as our friends three hundred million people of India. Fighting with us are the Filipinos and the natives of Java and the East Indies and of South Africa. Together, these peoples comprise almost half of the world's population. With none of them have the majority of Americans any ties of race. But we are learning in this war that it is not racial classifications nor ethnological considerations which bind men together; it is shared concepts and kindred objectives.

We are learning that the test of a people is their aim and not their color. Even Hitler's high racial wall has been breached by the recognition of a common purpose with those "honorary Aryans," the Japanese. We, too, have our natural allies. We must, now and hereafter, cast our lot as a nation with all those other peoples, whatever their race or color, who prize liberty as an innate right, both for themselves and for others. We must, now and hereafter, together with those peoples, reject the doctrine of imperialism which condemns the world to endless war.

Let me emphasize once more that race and color do not determine what people are allies and what people are enemies in this struggle. In the East, we have a plain example. Japan is our enemy because of her wanton and barbaric aggression upon weaker nations and because of the imperialistic doctrine by which she seeks to rule and enslave the world. Japan is our enemy because of the treacherous and unprovoked attacks by which she has launched each of her assaults in carrying forward her scheme of conquest.

China is our friend because like us she nourishes no dream of conquest and because she values liberty. She is our ally because, first among the nations, she resisted aggression and enslavement. . . .

It has been a long while since the United States had any imperialistic designs toward the outside world. But we have practiced within our own boundaries something that amounts to race imperialism. The attitude of the white citizens of this country toward the Negroes has undeniably had some of the unlovely characteristics of an alien imperialism—a smug racial superiority, a willingness to exploit an unprotected people. We have justified it by telling ourselves that its end is benevolent. And sometimes it has been. But so sometimes have been the ends of imperialism. And the moral atmosphere in which it has

existed is identical with that in which men —well-meaning men—talk of "the white man's burden."

But that atmosphere is changing. Today it is becoming increasingly apparent to thoughtful Americans that we cannot fight the forces and ideas of imperialism abroad and maintain any form of imperialism at home. The war has done this to our thinking.

Emancipation came to the colored race in America as a war measure. It was an act of military necessity. Manifestly it would have come without war, in the slower process of humanitarian reform and social enlightenment. But it required a disastrous, internecine war to bring this question of human freedom to a crisis, and the process of striking the shackles from the slave was accomplished in a single hour. We are finding under the pressure of this present conflict that long-standing barriers and prejudices are breaking down. The defense of our democracy against the forces that threaten it from without has made some of its failures to function at home glaringly apparent.

Our very proclamations of what we are fighting for have rendered our own inequities self-evident. When we talk of freedom and opportunity for all nations, the mocking paradoxes in our own society become so clear they can no longer be ignored. If we want to talk about freedom, we must mean freedom for others as well as ourselves, and we must mean freedom for everyone inside our frontiers as well as outside. During a war, this is especially important.

The threat to racial and religious, even to political, minority groups springs in wartime from two things—an overzealous mass insistence upon general conformity to majority standards, and the revival under emotional strains of age-old racial and religious distrusts. Minorities then are apt to be charged with responsibility for the war itself, and all the dislocations and discomforts arising from it. They are jealously subjected to scrutiny to determine if they are the recipients of special advantages.

We are all familiar with the process by which, in a war psychology, the unusual is distrusted and anything unorthodox is associated by some people with enemy intriguing. Chauvinists are likely to spring up in any community. There is the instance in our War of 1812 of a young man arrested and held for espionage on the suspicious circumstances that "he carried a long whip and wore an unusual number of buttons on his pantaloons." When affairs go wrong the public, by ancient custom, demands a scapegoat, and the first place to seek one is from a minority.

All this would appear ridiculous in our modern age were it not for the examples of bigotry and persecution we see in countries once presumed to be enlightened, and, even more seriously, were it not for the fact that we are already witnessing a crawling, insidious anti-Semitism in our own country. It will be well to bear in mind continuously that we are fighting today against intolerance and oppression, and that we shall get them in abundance if we lose. If we allow them to develop at home while we are engaging the enemy abroad, we shall have immeasurably weakened our fighting arm.

Our nation is composed of no one race, faith, or cultural heritage. It is a grouping of some thirty peoples possessing varying religious concepts, philosophies, and historical backgrounds. They are linked together by their confidence in our democratic institutions as expressed in the Declaration of Independence and guaranteed by the Constitution for themselves and for their children.

The keystone of our union of states is freedom—freedom for the individual to worship as he chooses, to work as he chooses, and to live and rear his children as he chooses. Liberty, if it is to be for all, must be protected by basic safeguards intended to give it the most general diffusion attainable, and none can expect privileges which encroach upon the rights of others.

Despite the functionings of our mischievous bureaucracies, and our sometimes excessively enterprising legislatures, and—in deplorable but fortunately isolated instances—the flaring of mob law, we have obtained here in America, in the course of little more than a century and a half of experience and adjustment, the most reasonable expression of freedom that has yet existed in history.

Our success thus far as a nation is not because we have built great cities and big factories and cultivated vast areas, but because we have promoted this fundamental assurance of freedom upon which all our material development has depended, and have tolerated, and learned to use, our diversities.

We remain a relatively new nation. As recently as fifty years ago, more than half our mining and a third of our total manufacturing were carried on by immigrants. More than half of the farm population of some of our leading agricultural states was alien-born. In the formative period of the nation, between 1820 and 1890, more than 15,000,000 newcomers reached our shores, and a still greater number were yet to arrive in the twenty-four years preceding the outbreak of the last war. In other words, we have had two hundred years of reinvigorating immigration which has brought us new blood, new experiences, new ideas. Here was a vast assembly of minority groups which have gone into the welding of a nation. We have created a strong nation because these new arrivals did not have the distractions, under our form of government, of continually opposing and battling one another, but entered as partners into the general upbuilding and consolidation. The height of our civilization, it seems to me, has been reached not by our assembly lines, our inventions, or any of our great factitious development, but by the ability of peoples of varying beliefs and of different racial extractions to live side by side here in the United States with common understanding, respect, and helpfulness.

If we want to see the opposite of this American system, we have merely to look at the military despotism of Hitler and the autocracy of Japan, and the fading dictatorship of Fascist Italy. The story of Germany for the last ten years has been one of racial and religious intolerance that provided a mask behind which a peace-professing dictator lured the people first to minority persecution, then to war. This intolerance gave the German nation the momentary strength of complete regimentation. Actually, it has undermined and weakened the social structure so that when the tide of war turns, collapse is likely to be sudden and complete.

It has always impressed me that, quite apart from any reasons of humanitarianism or justice or any sentiment regarding the protection of the weak by the strong, it is only common sense to safeguard jealously the rights of minorities. For minorities are rich assets of a democracy, assets which no totalitarian government can afford. Dictatorships must, of necessity, fear and suppress them. But within the tolerance of a democracy, minorities are the constant spring of new ideas, stimulating new thought and action, the constant source of new vigor.

To suppress minority thinking and minority expression would tend to freeze society and prevent progress. For the majority itself is stimulated by the existence of minority groups. The human mind requires contrary expressions against which to test itself.

For now more than ever, we must keep in the forefront of our minds the fact that whenever we take away the liberties of those whom we hate, we are opening the way to loss of liberty for those we love.

Our way of living together in America is a strong but delicate fabric. It is made up of many threads. It has been woven over many centuries by the patience and sacrifices of countless liberty-loving men and women. It serves as a cloak for the protection of poor and rich, of black and white, of Jew and gentile, of foreign- and native-born.

Let us not tear it asunder. For no man knows, once it is destroyed, where or when man will find its protective warmth again.

ONE WORLD

It was only a short time ago—less than a quarter of a century—that the allied nations gained an outstanding victory over the forces of conquest and aggression then led by imperial Germany.

But the peace that should have followed that war failed primarily because no joint objectives upon which it could be based had been arrived at in the minds of the people, and therefore no world peace was possible. The League of Nations was created full-blown; and men and women, having developed no joint purpose, except to defeat a common enemy, fell into capricious arguments about its structural form. Likewise, it failed because it was primarily an Anglo-French-American solution, retaining the old colonial imperialisms under new and fancy terms. It took inadequate account of the pressing needs of the Far East, nor did it sufficiently seek solution of the economic problems of the world. Its attempts to solve the world's problems were primarily political. But political internationalism without economic internationalism is a house built upon sand. For no nation can reach its fullest development alone.

Our own history furnishes, I believe, another clue to our failure. One of our most obvious weaknesses, in the light of what is going on today, is the lack of any continuity in our foreign policy. Neither major party can claim to have pursued a stable or consistent program of international co-operation even during the relatively brief period of the last forty-five years. Each has had its season of world outlook—sometimes an imperialistic one —and each its season of strict isolationism, the Congressional leadership of the party out of power usually, according to accepted American political practice, opposing the program of the party in power, whatever it might be.

For years many in both parties have recognized that if peace, economic prosperity, and liberty itself were to continue in this world, the nations of the world must find a method of economic stabilization and co-operative effort.

These aspirations at the end of the first World War, under the presidency of Woodrow Wilson, produced a program of international co-operation intended to safeguard all nations against military aggression, to protect racial minorities, and to give the oncoming generation some confidence that it could go about its affairs without a return of the disrupting and blighting scourge of war. Whatever we may think about the details of that program, it was definite, affirmative action for world peace. We cannot state positively just how effective it might have proved had the United States extended to it support, influence, and active participation.

But we do know that we tried the opposite course and found it altogether futile. We entered into an era of strictest detachment from world affairs. Many of our public leaders, Democratic and Republican, went about the country proclaiming that we had been tricked, that our ideals had been betrayed, that never again should we allow ourselves to become entangled in world politics which would inevitably bring about another armed outbreak. We were blessed with natural barriers, they maintained, and need not concern ourselves with the complicated and unsavory affairs of an old world beyond our borders.

We shut ourselves away from world trade by excessive tariff barriers. We washed our hands of the continent of Europe and displayed no interest in its fate while Germany rearmed. We torpedoed the London Economic Conference when the European democracies, with France lagging in the rear, were just beginning to recover from the economic depression

that had sapped their vitality, and when the instability of foreign exchange remained the principal obstacle to full revival. And in so doing, we sacrificed a magnificent opportunity for leadership in strengthening and rehabilitating the democratic nations, in fortifying them against assault by the forces of aggression which at that very moment were beginning to gather.

The responsibility for this does not attach solely to any political party. For neither major party stood consistently and conclusively before the American public as either the party of world outlook or the party of isolation. If we were to say that Republican leadership destroyed the League of Nations in 1920, we must add that it was Democratic leadership that broke up the London Economic Conference in 1933. . . .

I am satisfied that the American people never deliberately and intentionally turned their backs on a program for international co-operation. Possibly they would have preferred changes in the precise Versailles covenant, but not complete aloofness from the efforts of other nations. They were betrayed by leaders without convictions who were thinking in terms of group vote catching and partisan advantage.

If our withdrawal from world affairs after the last war was a contributing factor to the present war and to the economic instability of the past twenty years—and it seems plain that it was—a withdrawal from the problems and responsibilities of the world after this war would be sheer disaster. Even our relative geographical isolation no longer exists.

At the end of the last war, not a single plane had flown across the Atlantic. Today that ocean is a mere ribbon, with airplanes making regular scheduled flights. The Pacific is only a slightly wider ribbon in the ocean of the air, and Europe and Asia are at our very doorstep.

America must choose one of three courses after this war: narrow nationalism, which inevitably means the ultimate loss of our own liberty; international imperialism, which means the sacrifice of some other nation's liberty; or the creation of a world in which there shall be an equality of opportunity for every race and every nation. I am convinced the American people will choose, by overwhelming majority, the last of these courses. To make this choice effective, we must win not only the war, but also the peace, and we must start winning it now.

To win this peace three things seem to me necessary—first, we must plan now for peace on a world basis; second, the world must be free, politically and economically, for nations and for men, that peace may exist in it; third, America must play an active, constructive part in freeing it and keeping its peace.

When I say that peace must be planned on a world basis, I mean quite literally that it must embrace the earth. Continents and oceans are plainly only parts of a whole, seen, as I have seen them, from the air. England and America are parts; Russia and China, Egypt, Syria and Turkey, Iraq and Iran are also parts. And it is inescapable that there can be no peace for any part of the world unless the foundations of peace are made secure throughout all parts of the world.

This cannot be accomplished by mere declarations of our leaders, as in an Atlantic Charter. Its accomplishment depends primarily upon acceptance by the peoples of the world. For if the failure to reach international understanding after the last war taught us anything it taught us this: even if war leaders apparently agree upon generalized principles and slogans while the war is being fought, when they come to the peace table they make their own interpretations of their previous declarations. So unless today, while the war is being fought, the people of the United States and of Great Britain, of Russia and of China, and of all the other United Nations, fundamentally agree on their purposes, fine and idealistic expressions of hope such as those of the Atlantic Charter

will live merely to mock us as have Mr. Wilson's Fourteen Points. The Four Freedoms will not be accomplished by the declarations of those momentarily in power. They will become real only if the people of the world force them into actuality.

When I say that in order to have peace this world must be free, I am only reporting that a great process has started which no man—certainly not Hitler—can stop. Men and women all over the world are on the march, physically, intellectually, and spiritually. After centuries of ignorant and dull compliance, hundreds of millions of people in eastern Europe and Asia have opened the books. Old fears no longer frighten them. They are no longer willing to be Eastern slaves for Western profits. They are beginning to know that men's welfare throughout the world is interdependent. They are resolved, as we must be, that there is no more place for imperialism within their own society than in the society of nations. The big house on the hill surrounded by mud huts has lost its awesome charm.

Our Western world and our presumed supremacy are now on trial. Our boasting and our big talk leave Asia cold. Men and women in Russia and China and in the Middle East are conscious now of their own potential strength. They are coming to know that many of the decisions about the future of the world lie in their hands. And they intend that these decisions shall leave the peoples of each nation free from foreign domination, free for economic, social, and spiritual growth.

Economic freedom is as important as political freedom. Not only must people have access to what other peoples produce, but their own products must in turn have some chance of reaching men all over the world. There will be no peace, there will be no real development, there will be no economic stability, unless we find the method by which we can begin to break down the unnecessary trade barriers hampering the flow of goods. Obviously the sudden and uncompromising abolition of tariffs after the war could only result in disaster. But obviously, also, one of the freedoms we are fighting for is freedom to trade. I know there are many men, particularly in America, where our standard of living exceeds the standard of living in the rest of the world, who are genuinely alarmed at such a prospect, who believe that any such process will only lessen our own standard of living. The reverse of this is true.

Many reasons may be assigned for the amazing economic development of the United States. The abundance of our national resources, the freedom of our political institutions, and the character of our population have all undoubtedly contributed. But in my judgment the greatest factor has been the fact that by the happenstance of good fortune there was created here in America the largest area in the world in which there were no barriers to the exchange of goods and ideas.

And I should like to point out to those who are fearful one inescapable fact. In view of the astronomical figures our national debt will assume by the end of this war, and in a world reduced in size by industrial and transportation developments, even our present standard of living in America cannot be maintained unless the exchange of goods flows more freely over the whole world. It is also inescap-

ably true that to raise the standard of living of any man anywhere in the world is to raise the standard of living by some slight degree of every man everywhere in the world.

Finally, when I say that this world demands the full participation of a self-confident America, I am only passing on an invitation which the peoples of the East have given us. They would like the United States and the other United Nations to be partners with them in this grand adventure. They want us to join them in creating a new society of independent nations, free alike of the economic injustices of the West and the political malpractices of the East. But as partners in that great new combination they want us neither hesitant, incompetent, nor afraid. They want partners who will not hesitate to speak out for the correction of injustice anywhere in the world.

Our allies in the East know that we intend to pour out our resources in this war. But they expect us now—not after the war—to use the enormous power of our giving to promote liberty and justice. Other peoples, not yet fighting, are waiting no less eagerly for us to accept the most challenging opportunity of all history—the chance to help create a new society in which men and women the world around can live and grow invigorated by independence and freedom.

4. CHARTER OF THE UNITED NATIONS, JUNE, 1945[1]

EDITORS' NOTE.—It was agreed at the Moscow Conference of October, 1943, the first political conference of the "Big Three" powers, that "a general international organization, based on the sovereign equality of all peace-loving states" would be established as soon after the war as possible. A repre-

sentative of China joined those of the United States, Great Britain, and Russia in a four-power declaration to this effect. Delegates of these powers met at Dumbarton Oaks in 1944 and prepared a tentative outline of the Charter for the United Nations. At the Yalta Conference of February, 1945, the United States proposed the device of the veto as a means of pro-

[1]. United States Department of State, *Charter of the United Nations* (Publication 2353, "Conference Series," No. 74 [Washington, 1945]).

tecting the dominant position of the great powers in the world organization. On this critical issue of veto rights in the Security Council, President Roosevelt, Prime Minister Churchill, and Marshall Stalin thought that they had reached agreement; they then arranged for a conference of the United Nations to assemble at San Francisco on April 25. Delegates of fifty nations attended the proceedings, which lasted until June 26. President Roosevelt had died two weeks before the date of assembly; the war in Germany ended on May 7; the Japanese war was not concluded until August, by which time the Charter had been completed. The implications of atomic energy consequently formed no part in these discussions.

The Charter was ratified by the United States Senate on July 28, 1945, by a vote of 89 to 2. The initial meetings of the General Assembly and the Security Council were held in London in January, 1946.

We the peoples of the United Nations determined

to save succeeding generations from the scourge of war, which twice in our lifetime has brought untold sorrow to mankind, and

to reaffirm faith in fundamental human rights, in the dignity and worth of the human person, in the equal rights of men and women and of nations large and small, and

to establish conditions under which justice and respect for the obligations arising from treaties and other sources of international law can be maintained, and

to promote social progress and better standards of life in larger freedom,

and for these ends

to practice tolerance and live together in peace with one another as good neighbors, and

to unite our strength to maintain international peace and security, and

to ensure, by the acceptance of principles and the institution of methods, that armed force shall not be used, save in the common interest, and

to employ international machinery for the promotion of the economic and social advancement of all peoples,

have resolved to combine our efforts to accomplish these aims.

Accordingly, our respective Governments, through representatives assembled in the city of San Francisco, who have exhibited their full powers found to be in good and due form, have agreed to the present Charter of the United Nations and do hereby establish an international organization to be known as the United Nations.

Chapter I

PURPOSES AND PRINCIPLES

ARTICLE I

The Purposes of the United Nations are:

1. To maintain international peace and security, and to that end: to take effective collective measures for the prevention and removal of threats to the peace, and for the suppression of acts of aggression or other breaches of the peace, and to bring about by peaceful means, and in conformity with the principles of justice and international law, adjustment or settlement of international disputes or situations which might lead to a breach of the peace;

2. To develop friendly relations among nations based on respect for the principle of equal rights and self-determination of peoples, and to take other appropriate measures to strengthen universal peace;

3. To achieve international cooperation

in solving international problems of an economic, social, cultural, or humanitarian character, and in promoting and encouraging respect for human rights and for fundamental freedoms for all without distinction as to race, sex, language, or religion; and

4. To be a center for harmonizing the actions of nations in the attainment of these common ends.

ARTICLE 2

The Organization and its Members, in pursuit of the Purposes stated in Article 1, shall act in accordance with the following Principles.

1. The Organization is based on the principle of the sovereign equality of all its Members.

2. All Members, in order to ensure to all of them the rights and benefits resulting from membership, shall fulfil in good faith the obligations assumed by them in accordance with the present Charter.

3. All Members shall settle their international disputes by peaceful means in such a manner that international peace and security, and justice, are not endangered.

4. All Members shall refrain in their international relations from the threat or use of force against the territorial integrity or political independence of any state, or in any other manner inconsistent with the Purposes of the United Nations.

5. All Members shall give the United Nations every assistance in any action it takes in accordance with the present Charter, and shall refrain from giving assistance to any state against which the United Nations is taking preventive or enforcement action.

6. The Organization shall ensure that states which are not Members of the United Nations act in accordance with these Principles so far as may be necessary for the maintenance of international peace and security.

7. Nothing contained in the present Charter shall authorize the United Nations to intervene in matters which are essentially within the domestic jurisdiction of any state or shall require the Members to submit such matters to settlement under the present Charter; but this principle shall not prejudice the application of enforcement measures under Chapter VII.

CHAPTER II
MEMBERSHIP

ARTICLE 3

The original Members of the United Nations shall be the states which, having participated in the United Nations Conference on International Organization at San Francisco, or having previously signed the Declaration by United Nations of January 1, 1942, sign the present Charter and ratify it in accordance with Article 110.

ARTICLE 4

1. Membership in the United Nations is open to all other peace-loving states which accept the obligations contained in the present Charter and, in the judgment of the Organization, are able and willing to carry out these obligations.

2. The admission of any such state to membership in the United Nations will be effected by a decision of the General Assembly upon the recommendation of the Security Council.

ARTICLE 5

A Member of the United Nations against which preventive or enforcement action has been taken by the Security Council may be suspended from the exercise of the rights and privileges of membership by the General Assembly upon the recommendation of the Security Council. The exercise of these rights and privileges may be restored by the Security Council.

ARTICLE 6

A Member of the United Nations which has persistently violated the Principles contained in the present Charter may be expelled from the Organization by the General Assembly upon the recommendation of the Security Council.

Chapter III

ORGANS

ARTICLE 7

1. There are established as the principal organs of the United Nations: a General Assembly, a Security Council, an Economic and Social Council, a Trusteeship Council, an International Court of Justice, and a Secretariat.

2. Such subsidiary organs as may be found necessary may be established in accordance with the present Charter.

ARTICLE 8

The United Nations shall place no restrictions on the eligibility of men and women to participate in any capacity and under conditions of equality in its principal and subsidiary organs.

Chapter IV

THE GENERAL ASSEMBLY

COMPOSITION

ARTICLE 9

1. The General Assembly shall consist of all the Members of the United Nations.

2. Each Member shall have not more than five representatives in the General Assembly.

FUNCTIONS AND POWERS

ARTICLE 10

The General Assembly may discuss any questions or any matters within the scope of the present Charter or relating to the powers and functions of any organs provided for in the present Charter, and except as provided in Article 12, may make recommendations to the Members of the United Nations or to the Security Council or to both on any such questions or matters.

ARTICLE 11

1. The General Assembly may consider the general principles of cooperation in the maintenance of international peace and security, including the principles governing disarmament and the regulation of armaments, and may make recommendations with regard to such principles to the Members or to the Security Council or to both.

2. The General Assembly may discuss any questions relating to the maintenance of international peace and security brought before it by any Member of the United Nations, or by the Security Council, or by a state which is not a Member of the United Nations in accordance with Article 35, paragraph 2, and, except as provided in Article 12, may make recommendations with regard to any such questions to the state or states concerned or to the Security Council or to both. Any such question on which action is necessary shall be referred to the Security Council by the General Assembly either before or after discussion.

3. The General Assembly may call the attention of the Security Council to situations which are likely to endanger international peace and security.

4. The powers of the General Assembly set forth in this Article shall not limit the general scope of Article 10.

ARTICLE 12

1. While the Security Council is exercising in respect of any dispute or situation the functions assigned to it in the present Charter, the General Assembly shall not make any recommendation with regard to that dispute or situation unless the Security Council so requests.

2. The Secretary-General, with the consent of the Security Council, shall notify the General Assembly at each session of any matters relative to the maintenance of international peace and security which are being dealt with by the Security Council and shall similarly notify the General Assembly, or the Members of the United Nations if the General Assembly is not in session, immediately the Security Council ceases to deal with such matters.

ARTICLE 13

1. The General Assembly shall initiate studies and make recommendations for the purpose of:

a. promoting international cooperation in the political field and encouraging the progressive development of international law and its codification;

b. promoting international cooperation in the economic, social, cultural, educational, and health fields, and assisting in the realization of human rights and fundamental freedoms for all without distinction as to race, sex, language, or religion.

2. The further responsibilities, functions, and powers of the General Assembly with respect to matters mentioned in paragraph 1 (b) above are set forth in Chapters IX and X.

ARTICLE 14

Subject to the provisions of Article 12, the General Assembly may recommend measures for the peaceful adjustment of any situation, regardless of origin, which it deems likely to impair the general welfare or friendly relations among nations, including situations resulting from a violation of the provisions of the present Charter setting forth the Purposes and Principles of the United Nations.

ARTICLE 15

1. The General Assembly shall receive and consider annual and special reports from the Security Council; these reports shall include an account of the measures that the Security Council has decided upon or taken to maintain international peace and security.

2. The General Assembly shall receive and consider reports from the other organs of the United Nations.

ARTICLE 16

The General Assembly shall perform such functions with respect to the international trusteeship system as are assigned to it under Chapters XII and XIII, including the approval of the trusteeship agreements for areas not designated as strategic.

ARTICLE 17

1. The General Assembly shall consider and approve the budget of the Organization.

2. The expenses of the Organization shall be borne by the Members as apportioned by the General Assembly.

3. The General Assembly shall consider and approve any financial and budgetary arrangements with specialized agencies referred to in Article 57 and shall examine the administrative budgets of such specialized agencies with a view to making recommendations to the agencies concerned.

VOTING

ARTICLE 18

1. Each member of the General Assembly shall have one vote.

2. Decisions of the General Assembly on important questions shall be made by a two-thirds majority of the members present and voting. These questions shall include: recommendations with respect to the maintenance of international peace and security, the election of the non-permanent members of the Security Council, the election of the members of the Economic and Social Council, the election of members of the Trusteeship Council in accordance with paragraph 1 (c) of Article 86, the admission of new Members to the United Nations, the suspension of the rights and privileges of membership, the expulsion of Members, questions relating to the operation of the trusteeship system, and budgetary questions.

3. Decisions on other questions, including the determination of additional categories of questions to be decided by a two-thirds majority, shall be made by a majority of the members present and voting.

ARTICLE 19

A member of the United Nations which is in arrears in the payment of its financial contributions to the Organization shall have no vote in the General Assembly if the amount of its arrears equals or exceeds the amount of the contributions due from it for the preceding two full years. The General Assembly may, nevertheless, permit such a Member to vote if it is satisfied that the failure to pay is due to conditions beyond the control of the Member.

PROCEDURE

ARTICLE 20

The General Assembly shall meet in regular annual sessions and in such special sessions as occasion may require. Special sessions shall be convoked by the Secretary-General at the request of the Security Council or of a majority of the Members of the United Nations.

ARTICLE 21

The General Assembly shall adopt its own rules of procedure. It shall elect its President for each session.

ARTICLE 22

The General Assembly may establish such subsidiary organs as it deems necessary for the performance of its functions.

CHAPTER V

THE SECURITY COUNCIL

COMPOSITION

ARTICLE 23

1. The Security Council shall consist of eleven Members of the United Nations. The Republic of China, France, the Union of Soviet Socialist Republics, the United Kingdom of Great Britain and Northern Ireland, and the United States of America shall be permanent members of the Security Council. The General Assembly shall elect six other Members of the United Nations to be nonpermanent members of the Security Council, due regard being specially paid, in the first instance to the contribution of Members of the United Nations to the maintenance of international peace and security and to the other purposes of the Organization, and also to equitable geographical distribution.

2. The non-permanent members of the Security Council shall be elected for a term of two years. In the first election of the non-permanent members, however, three shall be chosen for a term of one year. A retiring member shall not be eligible for immediate re-election.

3. Each member of the Security Council shall have one representative.

FUNCTIONS AND POWERS

ARTICLE 24

1. In order to ensure prompt and effective action by the United Nations, its Members confer on the Security Council primary responsibility for the maintenance of international peace and security, and agree that in carrying out its duties under this responsibility the Security Council acts on their behalf.

2. In discharging these duties the Security Council shall act in accordance with the Purposes and Principles of the United Nations. The specific powers granted to the Security Council for the discharge of these duties are laid down in Chapters VI, VII, VIII, and XII.

3. The Security Council shall submit annual and, when necessary, special reports to the General Assembly for its consideration.

ARTICLE 25

The Members of the United Nations agree to accept and carry out the decisions of the Security Council in accordance with the present Charter.

ARTICLE 26

In order to promote the establishment and maintenance of international peace and security with the least diversion for armaments of the world's human and economic resources, the Security Council shall be responsible for formulating, with the assistance of the Military Staff Committee referred to in Article 47, plans to be submitted to the Members of the United Nations for the establishment of a system for the regulation of armaments.

VOTING

ARTICLE 27

1. Each member of the Security Council shall have one vote.

2. Decisions of the Security Council on

procedural matters shall be made by an affirmative vote of seven members.

3. Decisions of the Security Council on all other matters shall be made by an affirmative vote of seven members including the concurring votes of the permanent members; provided that, in decisions under Chapter VI, and under paragraph 3 of Article 52, a party to a dispute shall abstain from voting.

PROCEDURE
ARTICLE 28

1. The Security Council shall be so organized as to be able to function continuously. Each member of the Security Council shall for this purpose be represented at all times at the seat of the Organization.

2. The Security Council shall hold periodic meetings at which each of its members may, if it so desires, be represented by a member of the government or by some other specially designated representative.

3. The Security Council may hold meetings at such places other than the seat of the Organization as in its judgment will best facilitate its work.

ARTICLE 29

The Security Council may establish such subsidiary organs as it deems necessary for the performance of its functions.

ARTICLE 30

The Security Council shall adopt its own rules of procedure, including the method of selecting its President.

ARTICLE 31

Any Member of the United Nations which is not a member of the Security Council may participate, without vote, in the discussion of any question brought before the Security Council whenever the latter considers that the interests of that Member are specially affected.

ARTICLE 32

Any Member of the United Nations which is not a member of the Security Council or any state which is not a Member of the United Nations, if it is a party to a dispute under consideration by the Security Council, shall be invited to participate, without vote, in the discussion relating to the dispute. The Security Council shall lay down such conditions as it deems just for the participation of a state which is not a Member of the United Nations.

CHAPTER VI
PACIFIC SETTLEMENT OF DISPUTES
ARTICLE 33

1. The parties to any dispute, the continuance of which is likely to endanger the maintenance of international peace and security, shall, first of all, seek a solution by negotiation, enquiry, mediation, conciliation, arbitration, judicial settlement, resort to regional agencies or arrangements, or other peaceful means of their own choice.

2. The Security Council shall, when it deems necessary, call upon the parties to settle their dispute by such means.

ARTICLE 34

The Security Council may investigate any dispute, or any situation which might lead to international friction or give rise to a dispute, in order to determine whether the continuance of the dispute or situation is likely to endanger the maintenance of international peace and security.

ARTICLE 35

1. Any Member of the United Nations may bring any dispute, or any situation of the nature referred to in Article 34, to the attention of the Security Council or of the General Assembly.

2. A state which is not a Member of the United Nations may bring to the attention of the Security Council or of the General Assembly any dispute to which it is a party if it accepts in advance, for the purposes of the dispute, the obligations of pacific settlement provided in the present Charter.

3. The proceedings of the General As-

sembly in respect of matters brought to its attention under this Article will be subject to the provisions of Articles 11 and 12.

ARTICLE 36

1. The Security Council may, at any stage of a dispute of the nature referred to in Article 33 or of a situation of like nature, recommend appropriate procedures or methods of adjustment.

2. The Security Council should take into consideration any procedures for the settlement of the dispute which have already been adopted by the parties.

3. In making recommendations under this Article the Security Council should also take into consideration that legal disputes should as a general rule be referred by the parties to the International Court of Justice in accordance with the provisions of the Statute of the Court.

ARTICLE 37

1. Should the parties to a dispute of the nature referred to in Article 33 fail to settle it by the means indicated in that Article, they shall refer it to the Security Council.

2. If the Security Council deems that the continuance of the dispute is in fact likely to endanger the maintenance of international peace and security, it shall decide whether to take action under Article 36 or to recommend such terms of settlement as it may consider appropriate.

ARTICLE 38

Without prejudice to the provisions of Articles 33 to 37, the Security Council may, if all the parties to any dispute so request, make recommendations to the parties with a view to a pacific settlement of the dispute.

CHAPTER VII
ACTION WITH RESPECT TO THREATS TO THE PEACE, BREACHES OF THE PEACE, AND ACTS OF AGGRESSION

ARTICLE 39

The Security Council shall determine the existence of any threat to the peace,

breach of the peace, or act of aggression and shall make recommendations, or decide what measures shall be taken in accordance with Articles 41 and 42, to maintain or restore international peace and security.

ARTICLE 40

In order to prevent an aggravation of the situation, the Security Council may, before making the recommendations or deciding upon the measures provided for in Article 39, call upon the parties concerned to comply with such provisional measures as it deems necessary or desirable. Such provisional measures shall be without prejudice to the rights, claims, or position of the parties concerned. The Security Council shall duly take account of failure to comply with such provisional measures.

ARTICLE 41

The Security Council may decide what measures not involving the use of armed force are to be employed to give effect to its decisions, and it may call upon the Members of the United Nations to apply such measures. These may include complete or partial interruption of economic relations and of rail, sea, air, postal, telegraphic, radio, and other means of communication, and the severance of diplomatic relations.

ARTICLE 42

Should the Security Council consider that measures provided for in Article 41 would be inadequate or have proved to be inadequate, it may take such action by air, sea, or land forces as may be necessary to maintain or restore international peace and security. Such action may include demonstrations, blockade, and other operations by air, sea, or land forces of Members of the United Nations.

ARTICLE 43

1. All Members of the United Nations, in order to contribute to the maintenance of international peace and security, under-

take to make available to the Security Council, on its call and in accordance with a special agreement or agreements, armed forces, assistance, and facilities, including rights of passage, necessary for the purpose of maintaining international peace and security.

2. Such agreement or agreements shall govern the numbers and types of forces, their degree of readiness and general location, and the nature of the facilities and assistance to be provided.

3. The agreement or agreements shall be negotiated as soon as possible on the initiative of the Security Council. They shall be concluded between the Security Council and Members or between the Security Council and groups of Members and shall be subject to ratification by the signatory states in accordance with their respective constitutional processes.

ARTICLE 44

When the Security Council has decided to use force it shall, before calling upon a Member not represented on it to provide armed forces in fulfillment of the obligations assumed under Article 43, invite that Member, if the Member so desires, to participate in the decisions of the Security Council concerning the employment of contingents of that Member's armed forces.

ARTICLE 45

In order to enable the United Nations to take urgent military measures, Members shall hold immediately available national air-force contingents for combined international enforcement action. The strength and degree of readiness of these contingents and plans for their combined action shall be determined, within the limits laid down in the special agreement or agreements referred to in Article 43, by the Security Council with the assistance of the Military Staff Committee.

ARTICLE 46

Plans for the application of armed force shall be made by the Security Council with the assistance of the Military Staff Committee.

ARTICLE 47

1. There shall be established a Military Staff Committee to advise and assist the Security Council on all questions relating to the Security Council's military requirements for the maintenance of international peace and security, the employment and command of forces placed at its disposal, the regulation of armaments, and possible disarmament.

2. The Military Staff Committee shall consist of the Chiefs of Staff of the permanent members of the Security Council or their representatives. Any Member of the United Nations not permanently represented on the Committee shall be invited by the Committee to be associated with it when the efficient discharge of the Committee's responsibilities requires the participation of that Member in its work.

3. The Military Staff Committee shall be responsible under the Security Council for the strategic direction of any armed forces placed at the disposal of the Security Council. Questions relating to the command of such forces shall be worked out subsequently.

4. The Miltary Staff Committee, with the authorization of the Security Council and after consultation with appropriate regional agencies, may establish regional subcommittees.

ARTICLE 48

1. The action required to carry out the decisions of the Security Council for the maintenance of international peace and security shall be taken by all the Members of the United Nations or by some of them, as the Security Council may determine.

2. Such decisions shall be carried out by the Members of the United Nations directly and through their action in the appropriate international agencies of which they are members.

ARTICLE 49

The Members of the United Nations shall join in affording mutual assistance in carrying out the measures decided upon by the Security Council.

ARTICLE 50

If preventive or enforcement measures against any state are taken by the Security Council, any other state, whether a Member of the United Nations or not, which finds itself confronted with special economic problems arising from the carrying out of those measures shall have the right to consult the Security Council with regard to a solution of those problems.

ARTICLE 51

Nothing in the present Charter shall impair the inherent right of individual or collective self-defense if an armed attack occurs against a Member of the United Nations, until the Security Council has taken the measures necessary to maintain international peace and security. Measures taken by Members in the exercise of this right of self-defense shall be immediately reported to the Security Council and shall not in any way affect the authority and responsibility of the Security Council under the present Charter to take at any time such action as it deems necessary in order to maintain or restore international peace and security.

Chapter VIII
REGIONAL ARRANGEMENTS

ARTICLE 52

1. Nothing in the present Charter precludes the existence of regional arrangements or agencies for dealing with such matters relating to the maintenance of international peace and security as are appropriate for regional action, provided that such arrangements or agencies and their activities are consistent with the Purposes and Principles of the United Nations.

2. The Members of the United Nations entering into such arrangements or constituting such agencies shall make every effort to achieve pacific settlement of local disputes through such regional arrangements or by such regional agencies before referring them to the Security Council.

3. The Security Council shall encourage the development of pacific settlement of local disputes through such regional arrangements or by such regional agencies either on the initiative of the states concerned or by reference from the Security Council.

4. This Article in no way impairs the application of Articles 34 and 35.

ARTICLE 53

1. The Security Council shall, where appropriate, utilize such regional arrangements or agencies for enforcement action under its authority. But no enforcement action shall be taken under regional arrangements or by regional agencies without the authorization of the Security Council, with the exception of measures against any enemy state, as defined in paragraph 2 of this Article, provided for pursuant to Article 107 or in regional arrangements directed against renewal of aggressive policy on the part of any such state, until such time as the Organization may, on request of the Governments concerned, be charged with the responsibility for preventing further aggression by such a state.

2. The term enemy state as used in paragraph 1 of this Article applies to any state which during the Second World War has been an enemy of any signatory of the present Charter.

ARTICLE 54

The Security Council shall at all times be kept fully informed of activities undertaken or in contemplation under regional arrangements or by regional agencies for the maintenance of international peace and security.

Chapter IX

INTERNATIONAL ECONOMIC AND SOCIAL COOPERATION

ARTICLE 55

With a view to the creation of conditions of stability and well-being which are necessary for peaceful and friendly relations among nations based on respect for the principle of equal rights and self-determination of peoples, the United Nations shall promote:

a. higher standards of living, full employment, and conditions of economic and social progress and development;

b. solutions of international economic, social, health, and related problems; and international cultural and educational cooperation; and

c. universal respect for, and observance of, human rights and fundamental freedoms for all without distinction as to race, sex, language, or religion.

ARTICLE 56

All Members pledge themselves to take joint and separate action in cooperation with the Organization for the achievement of the purposes set forth in Article 55.

ARTICLE 57

1. The various specialized agencies, established by intergovernmental agreement and having wide international responsibilities, as defined in their basic instruments, in economic, social, cultural, educational, health, and related fields, shall be brought into relationship with the United Nations in accordance with the provisions of Article 63.

2. Such agencies thus brought into relationship with the United Nations are hereinafter referred to as specialized agencies.

ARTICLE 58

The Organization shall make recommendations for the coordination of the policies and activities of the specialized agencies.

ARTICLE 59

The Organization shall, where appropriate, initiate negotiations among the states concerned for the creation of any new specialized agencies required for the accomplishment of the purposes set forth in Article 55.

ARTICLE 60

Responsibility for the discharge of the functions of the Organization set forth in this Chapter shall be vested in the General Assembly and, under the authority of the General Assembly, in the Economic and Social Council, which shall have for this purpose the powers set forth in Chapter X.

Chapter X

THE ECONOMIC AND SOCIAL COUNCIL

COMPOSITION

ARTICLE 61

1. The Economic and Social Council shall consist of eighteen Members of the United Nations elected by the General Assembly.

2. Subject to the provisions of paragraph 3, six members of the Economic and Social Council shall be elected each year for a term of three years. A retiring member shall be eligible for immediate re-election.

3. At the first election, eighteen members of the Economic and Social Council shall be chosen. The term of office of six members so chosen shall expire at the end of one year, and of six other members at the end of two years, in accordance with arrangements made by the General Assembly.

4. Each member of the Economic and Social Council shall have one representative.

FUNCTIONS AND POWERS

ARTICLE 62

1. The Economic and Social Council may make or initiate studies and reports with respect to international economic,

social, cultural, educational, health, and related matters and may make recommendations with respect to any such matters to the General Assembly, to the Members of the United Nations, and to the specialized agencies concerned.

2. It may make recommendations for the purpose of promoting respect for, and observance of, human rights and fundamental freedoms for all.

3. It may prepare draft conventions for submission to the General Assembly, with respect to matters falling within its competence.

4. It may call, in accordance with the rules prescribed by the United Nations, international conferences on matters falling within its competence.

ARTICLE 63

1. The Economic and Social Council may enter into agreements with any of the agencies referred to in Article 57, defining the terms on which the agency concerned shall be brought into relationship with the United Nations. Such agreements shall be subject to approval by the General Assembly.

2. It may coordinate the activities of the specialized agencies through consultation with and recommendations to such agencies and through recommendations to the General Assembly and to the Members of the United Nations.

ARTICLE 64

1. The Economic and Social Council may take appropriate steps to obtain regular reports from the specialized agencies. It may make arrangements with the Members of the United Nations and with the specialized agencies to obtain reports on the steps taken to give effect to its own recommendations and to recommendations on matters falling within its competence made by the General Assembly.

2. It may communicate its observations on these reports to the General Assembly.

ARTICLE 65

The Economic and Social Council may furnish information to the Security Council and shall assist the Security Council upon its request.

ARTICLE 66

1. The Economic and Social Council shall perform such functions as fall within its competence in connection with the carrying out of the recommendations of the General Assembly.

2. It may, with the approval of the General Assembly, perform services at the request of Members of the United Nations and at the request of specialized agencies.

3. It shall perform such other functions as are specified elsewhere in the present Charter or as may be assigned to it by the General Assembly.

VOTING

ARTICLE 67

1. Each member of the Economic and Social Council shall have one vote.

2. Decisions of the Economic and Social Council shall be made by a majority of the members present and voting.

PROCEDURE

ARTICLE 68

The Economic and Social Council shall set up commissions in economic and social fields and for the promotion of human rights, and such other commissions as may be required for the performance of its functions.

ARTICLE 69

The Economic and Social Council shall invite any Member of the United Nations to participate, without vote, in its deliberations on any matter of particular concern to that Member.

ARTICLE 70

The Economic and Social Council may make arrangements for representatives of the specialized agencies to participate, without vote, in its deliberations and in those of the commissions established by it, and for its representatives to participate in the deliberations of the specialized agencies.

ARTICLE 71

The Economic and Social Council may make suitable arrangements for consultation with non-governmental organizations which are concerned with matters within its competence. Such arrangements may be made with international organizations and, where appropriate, with national organizations after consultation with the Member of the United Nations concerned.

ARTICLE 72

1. The Economic and Social Council shall adopt its own rules of procedure, including the method of selecting its President.

2. The Economic and Social Council shall meet as required in accordance with its rules, which shall include provision for the convening of meetings on the request of a majority of its members.

CHAPTER XI

DECLARATION REGARDING NON-SELF-GOVERNING TERRITORIES

ARTICLE 73

Members of the United Nations which have or assume responsibilities for the administration of territories whose peoples have not yet attained a full measure of self-government recognize the principle that the interests of the inhabitants of these territories are paramount, and accept as a sacred trust the obligation to promote to the utmost, within the system of international peace and security established by the present Charter, the well-being of the inhabitants of these territories, and, to this end:

a. to ensure, with due respect for the culture of the peoples concerned, their political, economic, social, and educational advancement, their just treatment, and their protection against abuses;

b. to develop self-government, to take due account of the political aspirations of the peoples, and to assist them in the progressive development of their free political institutions, according to the particular circumstances of each territory and its peoples and their varying stages of advancement;

c. to further international peace and security;

d. to promote constructive measures of development, to encourage research, and to cooperate with one another and, when and where appropriate, with specialized international bodies with a veiw to the practical achievement of the social, economic, and scientific purposes set forth in this Article; and

e. to transmit regularly to the Secretary-General for information purposes, subject to such limitation as security and constitutional considerations may require, statistical and other information of a technical nature relating to economic, social, and educational conditions in the territories for which they are respectively responsible other than those territories to which Chapters XII and XIII apply.

ARTICLE 74

Members of the United Nations also agree that their policy in respect of the territories to which this Chapter applies, no less than in respect to their metropolitan areas, must be based on the general principle of good-neighborliness, due account being taken of the interests and well-being of the rest of the world, in social, economic, and commercial matters.

CHAPTER XII

INTERNATIONAL TRUSTEESHIP SYSTEM

ARTICLE 75

The United Nations shall establish under its authority an international trusteeship system for the administration and supervision of such territories as may be placed thereunder by subsequent individual agreements. These territories are hereinafter referred to as trust territories.

ARTICLE 76

The basic objectives of the trusteeship system, in accordance with the Purposes of the United Nations laid down in Article 1 of the present Charter, shall be:

a. to further international peace and security;

b. to promote the political, economic, social, and educational advancement of the inhabitants of the trust territories, and their progressive development towards self-government or independence as may be appropriate to the particular circumstances of each territory and its peoples and the freely expressed wishes of the peoples concerned, and as may be provided by the terms of each trusteeship agreement;

c. to encourage respect for human rights and for fundamental freedoms for all without distinction as to race, sex, language, or religion, and to encourage recognition of the interdependence of the peoples of the world; and

d. to ensure equal treatment in social, economic, and commercial matters for all Members of the United Nations and their nationals, and also equal treatment for the latter in the administration of justice, without prejudice to the attainment of the foregoing objectives and subject to the provisions of Article 80.

ARTICLE 77

1. The trusteeship system shall apply to such territories in the following categories as may be placed thereunder by means of trusteeship agreements:

a. territories now held under mandate;

b. territories which may be detached from enemy states as a result of the Second World War; and

c. territories voluntarily placed under the system by states responsible for their administration.

2. It will be a matter for subsequent agreement as to which territories in the foregoing categories will be brought under the trusteeship system and upon what terms.

ARTICLE 78

The trusteeship system shall not apply to territories which have become Members of the United Nations, relationship among which shall be based on respect for the principle of sovereign equality.

ARTICLE 79

The terms of trusteeship for each territory to be placed under the trusteeship system, including any alteration or amendment, shall be agreed upon by the states directly concerned, including the mandatory power in the case of territories held under mandate by a Member of the United Nations, and shall be approved as provided for in Articles 83 and 85.

ARTICLE 80

1. Except as may be agreed upon in individual trusteeship agreements, made under Articles 77, 79, and 81, placing each territory under the trusteeship system, and until such agreements have been concluded, nothing in this Chapter shall be construed in or of itself to alter in any manner the rights whatsoever of any states or any peoples or the terms of existing international instruments to which Members of the United Nations may respectively be parties.

2. Paragraph 1 of this Article shall not be interpreted as giving grounds for delay or postponement of the negotiation and conclusion of agreements for placing mandated and other territories under the trusteeship system as provided for in Article 77.

ARTICLE 81

The trusteeship agreement shall in each case include the terms under which the trust territory will be administered and designate the authority which will exercise the administration of the trust territory. Such authority, hereinafter called the administering authority, may be one or more states or the Organization itself.

ARTICLE 82

There may be designated, in any trusteeship agreement, a strategic area or areas which may include part or all of the trust territory to which the agreement applies, without prejudice to any special agreement or agreements made under Article 43.

ARTICLE 83

1. All functions of the United Nations relating to strategic areas, including the approval of the terms of the trusteeship agreements and of their alteration or amendment, shall be exercised by the Security Council.

2. The basic objectives set forth in Article 76 shall be applicable to the people of each strategic area.

3. The Security Council shall, subject to the provisions of the trusteeship agreements and without prejudice to security considerations, avail itself of the assistance of the Trusteeship Council to perform those functions of the United Nations under the trusteeship system relating to political, economic, social, and educational matters in the strategic areas.

ARTICLE 84

It shall be the duty of the administering authority to ensure that the trust territory shall play its part in the maintenance of international peace and security. To this end the administering authority may make use of volunteer forces, facilities, and assistance from the trust territory in carrying out the obligations towards the Security Council undertaken in this regard by the administering authority, as well as for local defense and the maintenance of law and order within the trust territory.

ARTICLE 85

1. The functions of the United Nations with regard to trusteeship agreements for all areas not designated as strategic, including the approval of the terms of the trusteeship agreements and of their alteration or amendment, shall be exercised by the General Assembly.

2. The Trusteeship Council, operating under the authority of the General Assembly, shall assist the General Assembly in carrying out these functions.

Chapter XIII

THE TRUSTEESHIP COUNCIL

COMPOSITION

ARTICLE 86

1. The Trusteeship Council shall consist of the following Members of the United Nations:

a. those Members administering trust territories;

b. such of those Members mentioned by name in Article 23 as are not administering trust territories; and

c. as many other Members elected for three-year terms by the General Assembly as may be necessary to ensure that the total number of members of the Trusteeship Council is equally divided between those Members of the United Nations which administer trust territories and those which do not.

2. Each member of the Trusteeship Council shall designate one specially qualified person to represent it therein.

FUNCTIONS AND POWERS

ARTICLE 87

The General Assembly and, under its authority, the Trusteeship Council, in carrying out their functions, may:

a. consider reports submitted by the administering authority;

b. accept petitions and examine them in consultation with the administering authority;

c. provide for periodic visits to the respective trust territories at times agreed upon with the administering authority; and

d. take these and other actions in conformity with the terms of the trusteeship agreements.

ARTICLE 88

The Trusteeship Council shall formulate a questionnaire on the political, economic, social, and educational advancement of the inhabitants of each trust territory, and the administering authority for each trust territory within the competence of the General Assembly shall make an annual report to the General Assembly upon the basis of such questionnaire.

VOTING

ARTICLE 89

1. Each member of the Trusteeship Council shall have one vote.

2. Decisions of the Trusteeship Council shall be made by a majority of the members present and voting.

PROCEDURE

ARTICLE 90

1. The Trusteeship Council shall adopt its own rules of procedure, including the method of selecting its President.

2. The Trusteeship Council shall meet as required in accordance with its rules, which shall include provision for the convening of meetings on the request of a majority of its members.

ARTICLE 91

The Trusteeship Council shall, when appropriate, avail itself of the assistance of the Economic and Social Council and of the specialized agencies in regard to matters with which they are respectively concerned.

Chapter XIV
THE INTERNATIONAL COURT OF JUSTICE

ARTICLE 92

The International Court of Justice shall be the principal judicial organ of the United Nations. It shall function in accordance with the annexed Statute, which is based upon the Statute of the Permanent Court of International Justice and forms an integral part of the present Charter.

ARTICLE 93

1. All Members of the United Nations are *ipso facto* parties to the Statute of the International Court of Justice.

2. A state which is not a Member of the United Nations may become a party to the Statute of the International Court of Justice on conditions to be determined in each case by the General Assembly upon the recommendation of the Security Council.

ARTICLE 94

1. Each Member of the United Nations undertakes to comply with the decision of the International Court of Justice in any case to which it is a party.

2. If any party to a case fails to perform the obligations incumbent upon it under a judgment rendered by the Court, the other party may have recourse to the Security Council, which may, if it deems necessary, make recommendations or decide upon measures to be taken to give effect to the judgment.

ARTICLE 95

Nothing in the present Charter shall prevent Members of the United Nations from entrusting the solution of their differences to other tribunals by virtue of agreements already in existence or which may be concluded in the future.

ARTICLE 96

1. The General Assembly or the Security Council may request the International Court of Justice to give an advisory opinion on any legal question.

2. Other organs of the United Nations and specialized agencies, which may at any time be so authorized by the General Assembly, may also request advisory opinions of the Court on legal questions arising within the scope of their activities.

Chapter XV
THE SECRETARIAT

ARTICLE 97

The Secretariat shall comprise a Secretary-General and such staff as the Organization may require. The Secretary-General shall be appointed by the General Assembly upon the recommendation of the

Security Council. He shall be the chief administrative officer of the Organization.

ARTICLE 98

The Secretary-General shall act in that capacity in all meetings of the General Assembly, of the Security Council, of the Economic and Social Council, and of the Trusteeship Council, and shall perform such other functions as are entrusted to him by these organs. The Secretary-General shall make an annual report to the General Assembly on the work of the Organization.

ARTICLE 99

The Secretary-General may bring to the attention of the Security Council any matter which in his opinion may threaten the maintenance of international peace and security.

ARTICLE 100

1. In the performance of their duties the Secretary-General and the staff shall not seek or receive instructions from any government or from any other authority external to the Organization. They shall refrain from any action which might reflect on their position as international officials responsible only to the Organization.

2. Each Member of the United Nations undertakes to respect the exclusively international character of the responsibilities of the Secretary-General and the staff and not to seek to influence them in the discharge of their responsibilities.

ARTICLE 101

1. The staff shall be appointed by the Secretary-General under regulations established by the General Assembly.

2. Appropriate staffs shall be permanently assigned to the Economic and Social Council, the Trusteeship Council, and, as required, to other organs of the United Nations. These staffs shall form a part of the Secretariat.

3. The paramount consideration in the employment of the staff and in the determination of the conditions of service shall be the necessity of securing the highest standards of efficiency, competence, and integrity. Due regard shall be paid to the importance of recruiting the staff on as wide a geographical basis as possible.

CHAPTER XVI
MISCELLANEOUS PROVISIONS

ARTICLE 102

1. Every treaty and every international agreement entered into by any Member of the United Nations after the present Charter comes into force shall as soon as possible be registered with the Secretariat and published by it.

2. No party to any such treaty or international agreement which has not been registered in accordance with the provisions of paragraph 1 of this Article may invoke that treaty or agreement before any organ of the United Nations.

ARTICLE 103

In the event of a conflict between the obligations of the Members of the United Nations under the present Charter and their obligations under any other international agreement, their obligations under the present Charter shall prevail.

ARTICLE 104

The Organization shall enjoy in the territory of each of its Members such legal capacity as may be necessary for the exercise of its functions and the fulfillment of its purposes.

ARTICLE 105

1. The Organization shall enjoy in the territory of each of its Members such privileges and immunities as are necessary for the fulfillment of its purposes.

2. Representatives of the Members of the United Nations and officials of the Organization shall similarly enjoy such privileges and immunities as are necessary for the independent exercise of their functions in connection with the Organization.

3. The General Assembly may make

recommendations with a view to determining the details of the application of paragraphs 1 and 2 of this Article or may propose conventions to the Members of the United Nations for this purpose.

CHAPTER XVII
TRANSITIONAL SECURITY ARRANGEMENTS

ARTICLE 106

Pending the coming into force of such special agreements referred to in Article 43 as in the opinion of the Security Council enable it to begin the exercise of its responsibilities under Article 42, the parties to the Four-Nation Declaration, signed at Moscow, October 30, 1943, and France, shall, in accordance with the provisions of paragraph 5 of that Declaration, consult with one another and as occasion requires with other Members of the United Nations with a view to such joint action on behalf of the Organization as may be necessary for the purpose of maintaining international peace and security.

ARTICLE 107

Nothing in the present Charter shall invalidate or preclude action, in relation to any state which during the Second World War has been an enemy of any signatory to the present Charter, taken or authorized as a result of that war by the Governments having responsibility for such action.

CHAPTER XVIII
AMENDMENTS

ARTICLE 108

Amendments to the present Charter shall come into force for all Members of the United Nations when they have been adopted by a vote of two thirds of the members of the General Assembly and ratified in accordance with their respective constitutional processes by two thirds of the Members of the United Nations, including all the permanent members of the Security Council.

ARTICLE 109

1. A General Conference of the Members of the United Nations for the purpose of reviewing the present Charter may be held at a date and place to be fixed by a two-thirds vote of the members of the General Assembly and by a vote of any seven members of the Security Council. Each Member of the United Nations shall have one vote in the conference.

2. Any alteration of the present Charter recommended by a two-thirds vote of the conference shall take effect when ratified in accordance with their respective constitutional processes by two thirds of the Members of the United Nations including all the permanent members of the Security Council.

3. If such a conference has not been held before the tenth annual session of the General Assembly following the coming into force of the present Charter, the proposal to call such a conference shall be placed on the agenda of that session of the General Assembly, and the conference shall be held if so decided by a majority vote of the members of the General Assembly and by a vote of any seven members of the Security Council.

CHAPTER XIX
RATIFICATION AND SIGNATURE

ARTICLE 110

1. The present Charter shall be ratified by the signatory states in accordance with their respective constitutional processes.

2. The ratifications shall be deposited with the Government of the United States of America, which shall notify all the signatory states of each deposit as well as the Secretary-General of the Organization when he has been appointed.

3. The present Charter shall come into force upon the deposit of ratifications by the Republic of China, France, the Union of Soviet Socialist Republics, the United Kingdom of Great Britain and Northern Ireland, and the United States of America, and by a majority of the other signatory

states. A protocol of the ratifications deposited shall thereupon be drawn up by the Government of the United States of America which shall communicate copies thereof to all the signatory states.

4. The states signatory to the present Charter which ratify it after it has come into force will become original Members of the United Nations on the date of the deposit of their respective ratifications.

ARTICLE III

The present Charter, of which the Chi-

nese, French, Russian, English, and Spanish texts are equally authentic, shall remain deposited in the archives of the Government of the United States of America. Duly certified copies thereof shall be transmitted by that Government to the Governments of the other signatory states.

IN FAITH WHEREOF the representatives of the Governments of the United Nations have signed the present Charter.

DONE at the city of San Francisco the twenty-sixth day of June, one thousand nine hundred and forty-five.

5. EXTRACTS FROM THE PROCEEDINGS OF THE UNITED NATIONS COMMISSION ON HUMAN RIGHTS, 1947[1]

EDITORS' NOTE.—The signatories of the Charter of the United Nations stated that one of the purposes of the organization was "to reaffirm faith in fundamental human rights." A Commission on Human Rights, associated with other commissions under the Economic and Social Council, was established to formulate a Declaration of

Human Rights. The following statements were selected from the discussions in the first session of the Commission, January 27–February 10, 1947. A Universal Declaration of Human Rights was eventually drafted by the Commission and approved by the United Nations General Assembly on December 6, 1948.

GENERAL ROMULO (Philippines): History records the long and violent struggle that preceded the recognition of the rights of man, the centuried conflict between plebian and patrician, commoner and nobility, alien and citizen, subject and king, worker and capitalist, the individual and the State—in all conceivable situations where the factor of inherited or acquired wealth or power or position arrayed men or groups of men, one against the other, in relations of inevitable opposition.

1. *Extracts from the Proceedings of the United Nations Commission on Human Rights,* selected from the verbatim records by Anne Winslow for the Commission To Study the Organization of Peace. The extracts quoted here have been selected from the various speeches made by each delegate during the session rather than from any one speech made by him. Reprinted by permission of the Commission To Study the Organization of Peace.

It is perhaps true to affirm that in the state of nature man is born free and equal, and it is certainly a comforting doctrine to proclaim that men are endowed with certain inalienable rights, among which are the right to life, liberty and the pursuit of happiness. Yet the experience of the human race, living in communities together or in separate nations and states, shows that history has played with man and with groups of men, much as a logician might play with theses and antitheses, in continual conflict with one another, in positions of unequal rights and privileges that have nothing to do with their God-given endowments.

We have seen that men have been disinherited of rights regarded as inborn, or deprived of rights considered as inalienable. It is the glaring disparity between sound doctrine and unsound practice, between perfect ideal and imperfect fact which has served as the toxin of revolution through the centuries. . . .

The principle that man is endowed by nature with certain inherent and inalienable rights harks back to the ancient Greeks and Romans. The enthronement of this principle in the laws and constitutions of most modern States dates from a century and a half ago. What is new is the principle that these natural human rights need to be safeguarded by some authority more potent than the sovereignty of the State by an instrument of common consent more stable and efficacious than the law of nations as we know it today. It is to the task of fashioning such an instrument which shall lie outside and above the State that this Commission is dedicated. . . .

We are here to prepare the way for a Bill of Rights that shall be for all races and conditions of men regardless of whether they are today in a position to enjoy each separate guarantee or any given benefit that may accrue therefrom. We hold that the postulation of fundamental human rights and freedoms is an act of conscience that has positive value in itself, apart from any practical and profitable use to which the specific rights and freedoms may be put by any given community at any given time. By postulating these rights and freedoms, we fix them permanently in the minds and hearts of men everywhere. On the one hand, we set certain inviolable limits to the possible encroachments of oppression and exploitation, despotism and tyranny. And on the other, we set the goals for the backward peoples to strive after. Education, economic progress, the advance of scientific knowledge, and the political consequences of all these different forces will do the rest. . . .

We would favour a Bill of Rights sufficiently ample in its dispositions that it will cover the needs of men who are now free as well as of men who are still to be freed. . . .

I wish to go on record on behalf of my Government that we hold to the familiar Jeffersonian maxim that governments derive their just powers from the consent of the governed, that the natural rights of men are anterior to the authority of the state, that the people are sovereign, and the state merely the instrument of their sovereign will. We hold that no state can exercise powers in excess of those prerogatives which the citizens have conferred upon it of their own free will and volition. It is the natural state of man to strive after perfection and the fullest development of personality and the principal function of the state is to safeguard the individual in his observance of this primordial law of being. . . .

Mr. Ribnikar (Yugoslavia): The first declarations of human rights that originated in the eighteenth century, expressed the social and political ideal of young revolutionary bourgeoisie. The first of these principles with which the bourgeoisie started its historical fight was for individual liberty, and it is especially this principle that was fought for. It was quite natural, because in that time the young bourgeoisie had an acute necessity to push aside all the obstacles that were in her way, under a form of feudal privileges, and so forth. To achieve freedom of enterprise, it opposed liberalism to absolutism; to the privileges of the classes, it opposed free competition in the economic life. The fight for the liberation from the feudal chains was logically concentrated in the request for individual liberty. Later on, the individualist psychology was especially characteristic for the nineteenth century. It had as a result, the creation and the spreading of the conception that was very often developed to an extreme. It was contrary to the nature itself of the human being. I am speaking now of conception of certain animosity between the individual and the society.

In societies there are divided classes. The ruling class has used this psychology of individualism as a tool in its fight against the aspirations of working classes, in spreading this ideology of individualism, with one purpose, to save its prerogatives. They have just put the poison of dislocation and of disruption among the different classes. . . .

The new conditions of the economic, social and national life of our time have tended to develop the spirit of collectivity, and the conscience, and the solidarity of the popular masses. We are more and more aware that real individual liberty can be reached only in perfect harmony between the individual and the collectivity. It becomes quite obvious that this common interest is more important than the individual interest, and that man can liberate himself only when the mass of a population is free.

In our time the social principle comes first. It has one purpose, to create conditions necessary to the fulfilment of the interest of every individual. The social ideal is the ideal of the enormous majority of the world and it is in the identity of the interest of society and of the individual. Therefore, when we desire to speak today of the rights of man, of modern men, we must not think of the social ideal or of a political ideal of another age. This ideal belongs to the past, and if it remains in some countries, it is the ideal of one class only of a society. . . .

To establish a modern declaration of human rights, we must look for the realities of the contemporary world and we must find, in these realities, the social principles that have validity for our age, ideals that, in the judgment of many sociologists, are now embodied in an age of transition, a revolutionary age. Our task would be perfectly illusory and our work perfectly incomplete if we would limit ourselves to reproduce, with some minor changes, the declarations of human rights that were created in other ages, that is, about two centuries ago. It would be, on our part, a gross error as history would never forgive. . . .

The social picture of the contemporary world presents very different aspects. The social ideal, the political, and national ideals, are very different in the different countries, and from one social class to another.

Before going on in our task, we must know, in a very definite way, what we would like to embody in the declaration that we are about to make. Should we consider only the rights that the ruling classes are defending, that is, the rights in countries where there exists an antagonism among the classes, or are we going to start with the rights that men have conquered in countries where a socialist regime is existing, or are we going to note the aspirations of peoples that have not reached the stage of national independence?

First of all, I think we must agree on this point. Should we make a declaration that will have a universal character for our time or should we limit this declaration to a certain extent only? In that case, it would have only very relative meaning. For my part, I think it is quite necessary for us to try to reach this universal character of declaration. In this case the declaration would not only be the logical proceeding and the logical development of rights of citizens and chosen in the constitution of one or another country, but it would contain the principles that are in agreement with the general aspirations of the popular masses of the entire world.

If we set the goal, I think—and this is obvious by the nature of my declaration, the rights of modern man, for the reason of diversity of the social structures and of political regimes in the world, can never be a formal obligation for all Member States. The form of this declaration that will be established cannot be an international convention, neither an annex to the Charter. It could only have the form of a resolution of the General Assembly of the United Nations. Only this form and only if this declaration has a universal character, could this declaration have the importance of a historical document, and it would have a far-reaching moral significance that will correspond to the spirit of the Charter of the United Nations.

DR. MALIK (Lebanon): . . . our concern in my country is primarily in the field of liberty and of equality. What is paramount to us more than anything else is the freedom of thought and conscience. But here I would like to stress an important point which is often lost sight of; namely, that it is not enough to formulate the rights of man in static terms. They must rather be expressed in what I would call dynamic terms.

So, it would not be enough to say that we will grant the right of freedom of thought and freedom of conscience, leaving it in that static form, but I would suggest that we must emphatically state that a man has a right to change his mind and change his fundamental convictions of conscience whenever his mind and conscience so dictate to him in the best light that he knows. . . .

Then I wish further to say that the very phrase, "human rights" obviously refers to man, and by "rights," you can only mean that which belongs to the essence of man, namely, that which is not accidental, that which does not come and go with the passage of time and with the rise and fall of fads and styles and systems. It must be something belonging to man as such. We are, therefore, raising the fundamental question, what is man? And our differences will reflect faithfully the differences in our conceptions of men, namely, of ourselves. . . .

The individual human being, you and I, today may not be in need of protection against the despotism of the individual. The day of individual dictators and tyrants may be passed. But if man is no longer in need of protection against the tyranny of kings and dictators, he is, Madam Chairman, desperately in need of protection against another kind of tyranny, in my opinion equally grievous.

There has been rising in the last few decades a new tyranny, the tyranny of the masses, which seems to have an inevitable tendency of ultimately embodying itself in what I might call the tyranny of the state.

If there is any danger to fundamental human rights today, it is certainly from that direction.

The Charter speaks in the preamble of the worth and dignity of man, Madam Chairman. The states, governments, colonies, and non-self-governing territories—all these have other organs to plead their rights for them. They have other agencies to plead their rights. We here in this Commission represent and defend the individual man in his conscience and in his individual freedom, and there is no other body in the United Nations to do that. We must defend him against any tyranny, against the tyranny of the state and the tyranny of systems, because man has other loyalties than his loyalty to the state. He has his loyalty to his family, to his religion, to his profession; he has his loyalty to science and to truth. These loyalties are equally exacting as the loyalty to the state. And, in my opinion, the fight for freedom today consists primarily in asserting the rights of these intermediate institutions, between the individual and the state against the overwhelming claims of the state. Unless we succeed in embodying in our proposed Bill of Rights something of this fight, of the lonely human individual against the all-encompassing danger of the state, I am afraid we will have missed our greatest opportunity. . . .

My contention is that whatever human dignity and worth may mean, it certainly means the possibility of freedom of choice, freedom, real freedom, of choice without recriminations. . . .

The real danger of the present age is that social claims are in danger of snuffing out any real personal liberty. It is not social security and responsibility that are not going to find advocates and therefore expression in our bill. It is rather the questions which relate to personal values and freedoms.

May I express that what I ultimately mean is this. I am not setting an artificial antithesis between the individual and the State. I am asking this question. Which is for the sake of the other? Is the State for the sake of the human person or is the human person for the sake of the State? That, to me, is the ultimate question of the present day. I believe the State is for the sake of the person and therefore our Bill of Rights must express that for the sake of which everything else exists, including the States.

MR. DUKES (United Kingdom): My Government wishes to emphasize our faith in the dignity and worth of the human person, as stated in the preamble of the Charter. We say, right here, that we attach the greatest importance to world-wide acceptance and practice of human rights and fundamental freedoms. Our society is founded on what might be called in one word "tolerance." We feel that tolerance is not only the essence of democracy but it is also the essence of civilization. We believe that, as a fundamental principle, every human person should be able to think, speak and worship as he pleases and be able to act in accordance with his beliefs, provided that the rights of others are equally recognized and provided the preservation of an ordered society is not endangered thereby. These freedoms of the individual can only be satisfactorily reconciled with these two provisos, through the existence of an independent judiciary and by the rule of law. We believe that every human person in the world has the right to have access to full information about what is happening in the world and that his capacity for right judgment should not be impeded by lack of knowledge, whether through censorship or through faulty machinery of information. This freedom of information is a necessary condition both in order to enable the individual to be in a position to form judgments in full knowledge of the facts, and, what is very important, in order to make possible international action to secure the observance of human rights generally. We cannot know what is the position regarding human rights in various parts of the world if our knowledge of parts of the

world is blacked out. Many of the rights which we will publish in our bill will be ideals to be aimed at. We must be realists and not expect to get them accepted all at once. The Charter already compels Member Governments to promote and encourage respect for human rights and for fundamental freedom for all without distinction as to race, sex, language or religion. We must concentrate our work first of all in defining what are the rights we believe in, and then attempt to elaborate machinery whereby their enjoyment can be secured and protected. At the present moment there are no standards of rights under the Charter, and it is largely a matter for individual States to determine. We hope that these rights can soon be defined and machinery created by the United Nations to which appeals might be directed, if it were considered that the minimum standard laid down were not being observed.

It is desired by his Majesty's Government that ultimately—I cannot say when, but I hope it will be soon—some body should be set up to which appeals can be made so that the full floodlight of publicity, the full weight of international conscience can be brought to bear on all relevant facts, so that any violation of human rights would be arraigned before the bar of international opinion. . . .

There is no such a thing as complete personal freedom. We must pay the price for the advantages that result from our calling upon the state to safeguard our liberties, both in the sense of personal freedoms and also in the direction of a minimum degree of economic security . . . the state is not some mythical body. The state is composed of the people, all fully conscious of the freedom to change those governments if they do not comply with what may be regarded as the common will and the common obligation. . . . Therefore, we have got to try to produce a bill of rights which must carry with it, step by step as it proceeds along that road, the right and freedom of the individual to play his part in molding the society in which he lives and the right to change that society or to change its form of government if he disapproves of what is being done, which I regard as one of the highest freedoms. . . .

The state exists and so does the individual. Higher civilization, as I conceive of it, can only be enjoyed by the impact of those two things one upon the other. And I am convinced that if we are to hold out any reasonable prospects of a developing civilization, we must provide for the minimum requirements of life, without which freedom becomes a meaningless thing—a very meaningless thing, unless we are going to develop along the roads for ensuring these minimums that we are seeking now to formulate and to recognize that the individual, as an individual, is in the majority of cases incapable of doing it without assistance from the state. . . .

DR. CHANG (China): There is a history to all this—the declaration of human rights and rights of the citizen, especially in European thought, from the eighteenth century on.

Let us go back to that period and see how this word "human" was added, how it was used. There was the divine right of kings, and naturally there needed to be asserted the human rights of the citizen, and so the human rights have been used from the eighteenth century down to the present time. All the discussions so far have been on the word "rights"—rights, rights, rights. And, of course, that is due to the fact that there have been so many wrongs, wrongs, wrongs. There are still wrongs, and they need to be righted. So, we will have to have rights. . . .

I am not arguing against the rights, but I think the time has come for us to pay some attention to the word "human."

You see, at first, there was a reaction against the conception of certain divine rights of certain titles, and then there came this assertion of certain human rights. That is historically correct in terms of eighteenth century thought. From the middle of the nineteenth century, especially the famous year, I think, of 1859, the

publication of a certain book that emphasized the struggle for existence in the *Origin of Species*, we have been proving ever since then down to the present day—up-to-the-minute studies of psychology prove that human beings are animals. It has taken a lot of time to show that we are animals . . . this recognition of man being not so far from animals is in all philosophies, but especially realized in the Chinese philosopher Mencius. He recognized that very clearly, and then he gave a definition of civilization or human effort, I think, which is very good, realizing the difference between animal and man, a man and animal, is very, very little. Yet, it is the effort of man to make that difference firm and to enlarge it.

We should pay attention to that little bit of difference. It seems as though, ever since 1859, the whole idea has been to minimize that. That is all right—to say that, after all, we are animals. But, after all, there is that little bit of difference, and to make firm that difference and to enlarge that difference is the whole effort of human civilization and of human life, if human life is interpreted in the sense of being worth while, not simply to get food, clothing and other things.

MR. CASSIN (France): In the eighteenth century, declarations of rights were generally proposed by men who were reacting against tyranny, particularly that of the divine right of kings. But this was not true in every instance. The American declaration of rights constituted not so much an attack on the divine right of kings as an effort to apply the principle of the creation of a society based upon the common welfare.

However, in the present state of our civilization we cannot forget that there was a time when human society narrowly escaped destruction by another divine pretender. This time it was not threatened by religious dogmas but by a concept of race, of the nation, state or *Volk* organized as such. I do not like to say that a single people are guilty of evil instincts. But, the fact remains that these men destroyed the international community, denied the rights of other nations, and, at the same time, denied the rights of man as an individual.

We are now ready to distinguish between man as an individual and man as a member of the community. There may be important intermediaries such as the state, but I do not think there is a single civilized nation which does not recognize the rights of man as such. . . . We have the right, even the duty . . . to affirm the reappearance of man as an individual in the presence of the universality of mankind. . . .

The individual, the human being, is above all a social creature whose life and development and whose progress have been made possible only because he could lean upon his neighbors. And, by the same token, there is no social group, no state, not even this international community which could exist without the support of human beings with every characteristic nature gave to them. And we are forced since we live on this earth to try to solve in a practical way these two aspects of the problem.

There is no doubt that the international community—not only of the mythical plan but even on the legal political level, which is now represented by the United Nations—that this international community now gives us possibilities which did not exist before.

Should we give to the individual certain rights and state in our bill that these rights are unconditional? No. We know very well that, unfortunately, it is sometimes necessary, as in the case of crime, for society to take upon itself the right of eliminating criminals. . . . When the state is in danger, the nation is. When the reasons for the existence of society are threatened, we ourselves call upon human beings to sacrifice their lives for something even more sacred than life itself. Therefore, even the very right of life is not an unconditional right. But if a highly organized state should say that if there were too many children, 20,000,000, 20,000 should

be killed, our conscience would not admit it. Therefore, we can easily say that there are certain fundamental rights which all human consciences will support and which must be considered as the pillars of human society. . . . We place in the highest rank the inherent right of man, not as an animal, but as a creature and a creature capable of ideas. . . .

I do not think that those who are entrusted with the drafting of this bill should attack the problem of a declaration of the rights of man on the international plane in the same way as they would a national declaration of rights. The two are very closely connected, no doubt, but they are not exactly the same. As a human being, man may have certain rights and duties which do not correspond completely with those which he has as a member of a particular society, within the narrower confines of a state. I do not think that any national declaration of rights exists which specifies, as it ought to, the right of a human being to a nationality. I do not say to nationalities but to a national territorial group, and we have this scandalous situation that in the last twenty years, but principally in the last ten, there has been an enormous floating mass of human beings who, in an international society founded mainly upon states, had no longer any territorial attachment because they had not nationality. That is a fundamental problem which no declaration of the rights of man can avoid.

I think we ought to ask those who draft the Bill of Rights when they come to the problem of the actual contents of this Bill that they not only take into account a classification of the rights both by their nature, but also according to the ideas to which they pertain, and finally, according to the effective sanction which can be given to them and also as regards the commitments which they imply, far more precise for the international community than for any individual nation.

Mr. Lebeau (Belgium): . . . the Industrial Revolution of the nineteenth century has brought about certain changes which the philosophers of the eighteenth century could not possibly foresee. The rhythm of production, for instance, has passed from, say one to a thousand or a hundred thousand, or in some cases, one million.

The main difficulty which we have to conquer is not production in itself, but the distribution of production in order that each individual may have the benefit of this production. Distribution is modified and influenced by the fluctuation of prices and if the sale price of any commodity falls under the price of production, production itself comes down and, therefore, the individual finds himself without work, without the normal means of earning his livelihood. That, as I say, could not be foreseen by the philosophers of the eighteenth century and that is a point which we must deal with.

I agree with the representative of Yugoslavia that we must state the rights of the individual to participate in the general economy without running the risk of being a victim of the various dangers which lie in this economy, that is, the dangers of unemployment and other dangers. And I do not agree with the representative of Yugoslavia when he says we should make, as a starting point of our Bill, the protection of the collectivity or of the mass. I think our starting point must be the human person, the human being. . . .

The representative from Lebanon said and we also agree with that, that there are two main dangers which nowadays threaten human beings. The first is in our minds, the domination of the collectivity or of the mass of the state. I think we only have to look back in the last ten or fifteen years to see what terrible havoc can be wrought by such conceptions as that of the totalitarian state. I will not insist upon that point any more. It has been sufficiently stressed.

The second danger is the overdevelopment of industrial life, the dangers of mass production, the dangers of very large cities, in which the human being finds himself completely crushed. I think we can see a striking example very close to where we are now of what becomes of the human being when he is crushed by houses which are too high, streets which are too many, telephone wires, I might say, which are too numerous, everything, finally, which would contribute to destroy him as a personality, as an individual. I think the main point is that we should in our Bill assert that we intend to protect the human being from those two dangers.

MRS. ROOSEVELT (United States of America): It seems to me that . . . the rights of the individual are extremely important. It is not exactly that you set the individual apart from his society, but you recognize that within any society the individual must have rights that are guarded. . . .

Many of us believe that an organized society in the form of a government, exists for the good of the individual; others believe that an organized society in the form of a government, exists for the benefit of a group. We may not have to decide that particular point, but I think we do have to make sure, in writing a bill of human rights, that we safeguard the fundamental freedoms of the individual. If you do not do that, in the long run, it seems to me, that you run the risk of having certain conditions which we have just tried to prevent at great cost in human life, paramount in various groups.

MR. TEPLIAKOV (U.S.S.R.): . . . we are living as individuals in a community and a society, and we are working for the community and the society. The community has provided the material substance for our existence, first of all. . . .

Equality of rights is recognized as equality, irrespective of nationality or race in all spheres of economic, state, cultural, social, and political life. Any direct or indirect restriction of the rights of, or conversely, any establishment of direct or indirect privileges for citizens, on account of their race or nationality, as well as any advocacy of racial or national exclusiveness or hatred or contempt, is, or must be, punishable by law.

MR. MORA (Uruguay): ... Man today moves between two spheres, two sets of rules, one of which comes from national law and the other one comes from international law. I believe that we ought to complete this right of citizenship so that human beings might receive a certain degree of what we might almost call world citizenship. ...

The traditional bills of rights have a national character. It seems to me that in the twentieth century we must emphasize the international human rights, the international rights of the man. ...

The classic doctrine says that only states are subject to international laws. We need now to declare that man is the most important element of any kind of law, national or international.

I hope that in the future the United Nations will set up international tribunals of justice, or any kind of court of appeal for the individual, as for the states. But, for the moment, in the name of the Government of Uruguay, I want to make a proposition to enlarge the rights of citizenship, in order to establish the right of citizens to participate not only in their Government but also in the organization of the international community of states, that the right be granted to any man to have access to the United Nations.

6. UNIVERSAL DECLARATION OF HUMAN RIGHTS, 1948[1]

PREAMBLE

WHEREAS recognition of the inherent dignity and of the equal and inalienable rights of all members of the human family is the foundation of freedom, justice and peace in the world, and

WHEREAS disregard and contempt for human rights have resulted in barbarous acts which have outraged the conscience of mankind, and the advent of a world in which human beings shall enjoy freedom of speech and belief and freedom from fear and want has been proclaimed as the highest aspiration of the common people, and

WHEREAS it is essential, if man is not to be compelled to have recourse, as a last resort, to rebellion against tyranny and oppression that human rights should be protected by the rule of law, and

WHEREAS it is essential to promote the development of friendly relations between nations, and

WHEREAS the peoples of the United Nations have in the Charter reaffirmed their faith in fundamental human rights, in the

1. United Nations, General Assembly, *Universal Declaration of Human Rights*, Doc. A/811 (16 December 1948), approved by the General Assembly at its plenary meeting on December 6, 1948.

dignity and worth of the human person and in the equal rights of men and women, and determined to promote social progress and better standards of life in larger freedom, and

WHEREAS the Member States have pledged themselves to achieve, in cooperation with the United Nations, the promotion of universal respect for and observance of human rights and fundamental freedoms, and

WHEREAS a common understanding of these rights and freedoms is of the greatest importance for the full realization of this pledge,

Now therefore,

THE GENERAL ASSEMBLY

PROCLAIMS this Declaration of Human Rights as a common standard of achievement for all peoples and all nations, to the end that every individual and every organ of society, keeping this declaration constantly in mind, shall strive by teaching and education to promote respect for these rights and freedoms and by progressive measures, national and international, to secure their universal and effective recognition and observance, both among the peoples of member states themselves and among the peoples of territories under their jurisdiction.

ARTICLE 1. All human beings are born free and equal, in dignity and rights. They are endowed with reason and conscience, and should act towards one another in a spirit of brotherhood.

ART. 2. Everyone is entitled to all the rights and freedoms set forth in this declaration, without distinction of any kind, such as race, colour, sex, language, religion, political or other opinion, national or social origin, property, birth or other status.

Furthermore, no distinction shall be made on the basis of the political, jurisdictional or international status of the country or territory to which a person belongs, whether it be independent, Trust, Non-Self-Governing or under any other limitation of sovereignty.

ART. 3. Everyone has the right to life, liberty and security of person.

ART. 4. No one shall be held in slavery or servitude; slavery and the slave trade shall be prohibited in all their forms.

ART. 5. No one shall be subjected to torture or to cruel, inhuman or degrading treatment or punishment.

ART. 6. Everyone has the right to recognition everywhere as a person before the law.

ART. 7. All are equal before the law and are entitled without any discrimination to equal protection of the law. All are entitled to equal protection against any discrimination in violation of this Declaration and against any incitement to such discrimination.

ART. 8. Everyone has the right to an effective remedy by the competent national tribunals for acts violating the fundamental rights granted him by the Constitution or by law.

ART. 9. No one shall be subjected to arbitrary arrest, detention or exile.

ART. 10. Everyone is entitled in full equality to a fair and public hearing by an independent and impartial tribunal, in the determination of his rights and obligations and of any criminal charge against him.

ART. 11. 1. Everyone with a penal offence has the right to be presumed innocent until proved guilty according to law in a public trial at which he has had all the guarantees necessary for his defence.

2. No one shall be held guilty of any penal offence on account of any act or omission which did not constitute a penal offence, under national or international law, at the time when it was committed. Nor shall a heavier penalty be imposed than the one that was applicable at the time the penal offence was committed.

ART. 12. No one shall be subjected to arbitrary interference with his privacy, family, home or correspondence, nor to attacks upon his honour and reputation. Everyone has the right to the protection of the law against such interference or attacks.

ART. 13. 1. Everyone has the right to freedom of movement and residence within the borders of each state.

2. Everyone has the right to leave any country, including his own, and to return to his country.

ART. 14. 1. Everyone has the right to seek and to enjoy in other countries asylum from persecution.

2. This right may not be invoked in the case of prosecutions genuinely arising from non-political crimes or from acts contrary to the purposes and principles of the United Nations.

ART. 15. 1. Everyone has the right to a nationality.

2. No one shall be arbitrarily deprived of his nationality nor denied the right to change his nationality.

ART. 16. 1. Men and women of full age, without any limitation due to race, nationality or religion, have the right to marry and to found a family. They are entitled to equal rights as to marriage, during marriage and at its dissolution.

2. Marriage shall be entered into only with the free and full consent of the intending spouses.

3. The family is the natural and fundamental group unit of society and is entitled to protection by society and the State.

Art. 17. *1.* Everyone has the right to own property alone as well as in association with others.

2. No one shall be arbitrarily deprived of his property.

Art. 18. Everyone has the right to freedom of thought, conscience and religion; this right includes freedom to change his religion or belief, and freedom, either alone or in community with others and in public or private, to manifest his religion or belief in teaching, practice, worship and observance.

Art. 19. Everyone has the right to freedom of opinion and expression; this right includes freedom to hold opinions without interference and to seek, receive and impart information and ideas through any media and regardless of frontiers.

Art. 20. *1.* Everyone has the right to freedom of peaceful assembly and association.

2. No one may be compelled to belong to an association.

Art. 21. *1.* Everyone has the right to take part in the Government of his country, directly or through freely chosen representatives.

2. Everyone has the right of equal access to public service in his country.

3. The will of the people shall be the basis of the authority of government; this will shall be expressed in periodic and genuine elections which shall be by universal and equal suffrage and shall be held by secret vote or by equivalent free voting procedures.

Art. 22. Everyone, as a member of society, has the right to social security and is entitled to the realization, through national effort and international co-operation and in accordance with the organization and resources of each state, of the economic, social and cultural rights indispensable for his dignity and the free development of his personality.

Art. 23. *1.* Everyone has the right to work, to free choice of employment, to just and favourable conditions of work and to protection against unemployment.

2. Everyone, without any discrimination, has the right to equal pay for equal work.

3. Everyone who works has the right to just and favourable remuneration insuring for himself and his family an existence worthy of human dignity, and supplemented, if necessary, by other means of social protection.

4. Everyone has the right to form and to join trade unions for the protection of his interests.

Art. 24. Everyone has the right to rest and leisure, including reasonable limitation of working hours and periodic holidays with pay.

Art. 25. *1.* Everyone has the right to a standard of living adequate for the health and well-being of himself and of his family, including food, clothing, housing and medical care and necessary social services, and the right to security in the event of unemployment, sickness, disability, widowhood, old age or other lack of livelihood in circumstances beyond his control.

2. Motherhood and childhood are entitled to special care and assistance. All children, whether born in or out of wedlock, shall enjoy the same social protection.

Art. 26. *1.* Everyone has the right to education. Education shall be free, at least in the elementary and fundamental stages. Elementary education shall be compulsory. Technical and professional education shall be made generally available, and higher education shall be equally accessible to all on the basis of merit.

2. Education shall be directed to the full development of the human personality and to the strengthening of respect for human rights and fundamental freedoms. It shall promote understanding, tolerance and friendship among all nations, racial or religious groups, and shall further the activities of the United Nations for the maintenance of peace.

3. Parents have a prior right to choose the kind of education that shall be given to their children.

ART. 27. *1*. Everyone has the right freely to participate in the cultural life of the community, to enjoy the arts and to share in scientific advancement and its benefits.

2. Everyone has the right to the protection of the moral and material interests resulting from any scientific, literary or artistic production of which he is the author.

ART. 28. Everyone is entitled to a social and international order in which the rights and freedoms set forth in this declaration can be fully realized.

ART. 29. *1*. Everyone has duties to the community in which alone the free and full development of his personality is possible.

2. In the exercise of his rights and freedoms, everyone shall be subject only to such limitations as are determined by law solely for the purpose of securing due recognition and respect for the rights and freedoms of others and of meeting the just requirements of morality, public order and the general welfare in a democratic society.

3. These rights and freedoms may in no case be exercised contrary to the purposes and principles of the United Nations.

ART. 30. Nothing in this declaration may be interpreted as implying for any state, group or person, any right to engage in any activity or to perform any act aimed at the destruction of any of the rights and freedoms set forth herein.

SECTION C. POSTWAR CONFLICT: ANALYSES AND PROPOSALS

1. POWER POLITICS[1]

By Martin Wight

EDITORS' NOTE.—The Royal Institute of International Affairs, a non-political body founded in Great Britain in 1920 to promote the scientific study of international questions, published at the close of the recent war a series of pamphlets under the general title "Looking Forward." The following analysis of power politics has been selected from one of these studies.

9. THE BALANCE OF POWER

The central principle in what we might call the "mechanics" of power politics is that of the Balance of Power, which describes the way Powers group themselves in a state of international anarchy. The Balance of Power is a phrase with two distinct meanings. It can be used either objectively or subjectively—to describe either a "law" or principle of international politics (a general statement of how Powers in fact behave), or a policy which may be adopted by a particular Power.

In the first sense, as a principle of international relations, the Balance of Power is an application of the fundamental law of self-preservation. If there are three Powers, of which the first attacks the second, the third cannot afford to see the second so decisively crushed that it becomes threatened itself; therefore if it is far-sighted enough it supports the second. When one Power grows dangerously strong, other Powers combine against it. The Balance of Power thus comes into play each time that a Dominant Power has tried to gain mastery of the world. The Dominant Power usually has a small entourage of vassal-states which are more frightened of defending their independence than of collaborating, and of jackal-states which have

private local interests to pursue; but arrayed against them there arises a grand coalition of superior strength which finally wins. This is the extreme illustration of the Balance of Power.

The Balance of Power develops through various phases. First there can be a multiple balance, i.e., a balance similar to a chandelier. This was the normal state of Europe in the eighteenth century. In Western Europe and overseas there was the balance between Britain, France and Spain; in Central and Eastern Europe there was the balance between Austria and Prussia, Russia and Turkey. The balances interacted, and were completed by the smaller Powers. The Great Powers changed partners when their interests shifted as in a quadrille: in 1740 Britain and Austria were allied against France and Prussia, in 1756 Britain and Prussia were allied against France and Austria. The multiple balance broke down, first with the War of American Independence, and then decisively with the Revolutionary and Napoleonic War. The Vienna Settlement tried to restore it: Britain had unchallengeable supremacy outside Europe, Russia took Poland, Austria was predominant in Italy, Prussia was given the Rhineland, and all together in the Quadruple Alliance formed a counterpoise against the recovery of France. But the multiple balance can only last so long as

1. Martin Wight, *Power Politics* ("Looking Forward" [London: Royal Institute of International Affairs, 1946]).

there is international tranquillity and no vital issues arise to split the Great Powers. When this sooner or later occurs, the Great Powers divide into opposite camps, and the multiple balance is replaced by a *simple* balance: it is no longer a chandelier but a pair of scales. This was what happened in Europe with the creation of the Franco-Russian Alliance in 1893 against the Triple Alliance of Germany, Austria-Hungary and Italy; and again with the creation of the Berlin-Rome Axis in 1936 against the League Powers. The period of the simple balance is marked by heightened tension, a race between the two groups in armaments, and uneasy oscillations which we know as *crises*. Mr. Churchill has brilliantly described a crisis, writing of the pre-1914 Balance of Power:

The great Powers marshalled on either side, preceded and protected by an elaborate cushion of diplomatic courtesies and formalities, would display to each other their respective arrays. In the forefront would be the two principal disputants, Germany and France, and echeloned back on either side at varying distances and under veils of reserves and qualifications of different density, would be drawn up the other parties to the Triple Alliance and to what was already now beginning to be called the Triple Entente. At the proper moment these seconds or supporters would utter certain cryptic words indicative of their state of mind, as a consequence of which France or Germany would step back or forward a very small distance or perhaps move slightly to the right or to the left. When these delicate rectifications in the great balance of Europe, and indeed of the world, had been made, the formidable assembly would withdraw to their own apartments with ceremony and salutations and congratulate or condole with each other in whispers on the result.

It was the same with the crises of the 1930's, except that the courtesies had worn thinner and the power was more naked—the Italian journalists hissing and catcalling when Haile Selassie rose to address the League Assembly in June 1936; Greiser, the president of the Danzig Senate, giving the Nazi salute and cocking a snook as he marched out of the League Council a few days later; Ribbentrop giving the Nazi salute when he was presented to Edward VIII in 1937; Hitler's public threats and rages in 1938–39. And in due course the manoeuvrings for position cannot be prolonged, and the Balance of Power overbalances into war.

But there is not only the distinction between a multiple and a simple balance. We must also consider the confusion arising from the fact that the word balance itself has two meanings: it can mean equilibrium, and it can also mean preponderance, as when we say we have a balance in the bank—i.e. a plus, not an equality between assets and debits. This is the distinction between the objective and the subjective view of the Balance of Power. The historian will say that there is a balance when the opposing groups seem to him to be equal in power. The statesman will say that there is a balance when he thinks that his side is stronger than the other. And he will say that his country *holds* the balance, when it has freedom to join one side or the other according to its own interests. To hold the balance is a policy specially suited to a Sea Power that is partly detached from Europe: it has been the classic policy of Britain. The earliest known use of the phrase Balance of Power in English is, very appropriately, in a book dedicated to Queen Elizabeth in 1579: "God hath put into your hands the balance of power and justice, to appease and counterpoise at your will the actions and counsels of all the Christian kingdoms of your time." Since the day when Elizabeth broke the Anglo-Spanish alliance and threw England on the side of France and the Dutch rebels against the Dominant Power of Spain, the Balance of Power has been the traditional British foreign policy. In 1727 the phrase "the preservation of the balance of Power in Europe" was introduced into the preamble of the annual Mutiny Act, as one of the objects of the British army, and it remained there, off and on, until 1867. "Splendid isolation" is only a phase of that policy; it meant retaining freedom of action so long as it seemed unnecessary for

Britain to commit itself. American isolationism had the same character, though the Americans deluded themselves to a greater extent into thinking that their freedom of action was a permanent attribute, instead of something purely temporary.

Politics, as Bismarck said, is not an exact science, and there are no "laws" of politics without any exceptions. The Balance of Power is as nearly a fundamental law of politics as it is possible to find: it is easy to see from history that it is the way most Powers have pursued self-preservation in most cases. But rulers often make mistakes in their forecasts of power, and sometimes have other motives besides the interests of the state they rule. A good example of bungling the Balance of Power is provided by Italy in 1940. The German conquest of Western Europe immediately put Italy, like Britain, in mortal danger. In that crisis Italy might have chosen to throw itself on the side of Britain and the other resisting states, in order to preserve a balance against the Dominant Power. It did the reverse, because Mussolini was so fettered by his previous policy and by his hatred of Great Britain that he gladly anticipated its defeat. But it is unlikely that he had any illusions about the nature of his voracious ally. By not combining with Great Britain to form a real balance, he was driven into the futile policy of trying to establish a private balance between Italy and Germany. He accordingly made his ridiculous and contemptible invasion of Southern France, in order to buy prestige with as many casualties as he could manage before France surrendered, and thus to be able to meet Germany more as an equal. The result was that while Great Britain survived, Italy was occupied and ruined. This has been the usual fate of jackal Powers; the history of Prussia's relations with Napoleon before the battle of Jena provides another example. For we may notice that the law of the Balance of Power is the more true of states according to their strength, confidence and internal cohesion. Weak and corrupt states, and especially those ruled by an unrepresentative despotism or clique, tend to gravitate *towards* the Dominant Power; it is popular states without deep social cleavages (whether their governments be parliamentary democracy or a mass-party dictatorship) that tend to gravitate *away from* the Dominant Power.

10. COMPENSATION

There are three chief ways in which the Balance of Power operates: by compensation, by intervention, and by the establishment of buffer states. Let us glance briefly at each of these in turn.

In its simplest form compensation means giving a state the equivalent of something of which you deprive it: as when Russia takes from Poland the territory east of the Curzon Line and offers it most of East Prussia, Pomerania and Upper Silesia instead. This applies, of course, only to victorious Powers and their satellites; defeated Powers are usually deprived of territory without compensation. But in its more developed form, compensation means that one state cannot afford to see another increase its power without obtaining a proportionate increase, i.e. equality of aggrandizement. This was the principle on which, in the nineteenth century, the Great Powers approached the Eastern Question, partitioned Africa, and established spheres of influence in the Far East. At the Berlin Congress of 1878, for example, Russia got Rumanian Bessarabia with the control of the mouths of the Danube, Austria-Hungary got Bosnia-Herzegovina, Britain got Cyprus, and France three years later got Tunis. The same principle was seen at work in China. In 1897–98 Germany seized Kiaochow as a coaling-station. In quick succession Russia took Port Arthur, France took Kwangchow, and Britain took Weihaiwei, each at first alarmed by the other's aggrandizement, and then (as the Russian foreign minister said) "grateful to Germany" for giving the opportunity for general aggrandizement at China's expense in the name of compensation.

By the principle of compensation, a

Power can be forced to take part in an international transaction against its will. The classic example is the First Partition of Poland in 1772. Frederick the Great of Prussia and Catherine the Great of Russia had agreed on the partition; Maria Theresa of Austria could not afford to be left out. She opposed it on moral grounds, but her ministers did not, and reasons of state were paramount. "Elle pleurait, et prenait toujours," said Frederick cynically. A similar thing occurred when in August 1918 America joined the Allies in intervention in Russia. Wilson had steadily opposed intervention; but Britain, France and Japan forced his hand by sending troops themselves. America could not afford to allow the Japanese a free run in Siberia; Wilson at once reversed his policy and dispatched American troops, at the same time issuing a statement of the moral objections to intervention which was the Wilsonian equivalent of Maria Theresa's tears. It is the principle of compensation that made Russia join in the Second World War against Japan after the defeat of Germany; whatever the Russian desire for rest and recuperation, Stalin could not afford to see his allies settle the Pacific without an equal say himself.

II. INTERVENTION

Intervention means interference by a Power in the internal affairs of another Power. We may classify it as either defensive or offensive, according to whether it aims at preserving or at altering the Balance of Power. The principle of defensive intervention might be stated thus: no Power can allow the Balance of Power to be decisively altered in its disfavour by a change of régime or policy in another state. Allied intervention in Russia in 1918–20 was of this kind; British intervention in Iraq in 1941 in order to frustrate Rashid Ali's coup d'état provides a more dramatic and compelling instance. British intervention in Greece in 1944 probably also comes under this head. Offensive intervention is a technique of penetration and expansion, aimed at provoking a change of régime in another state or even at destroying its independence altogether. The Eastern Question in the nineteenth century arose out of Russia's practice of such intervention to protect the Christian inhabitants of the Turkish Empire. It was the method used by Piedmont to overthrow the other Italian governments and establish a United Italy in 1859–60, and by Germany and Italy to overthrow the government of Spain in the Spanish Civil War (1936–39). Russia's use of the Communist International in the early nineteen twenties and Nazi Germany's use of the fifth column represent the organization of this technique to an extent previously unknown; it is interesting to contrast the almost uniform lack of success achieved by Russia at that time with the formidable successes of Germany.

There is also non-intervention. Non-intervention, like neutrality, requires unassailable confidence and strength to be an effective policy, and a non-intervening Power is liable to have its hand forced if it cannot make other Powers follow non-intervention as well, as we have seen in the case of Wilson in 1918. Thus non-intervention is itself usually a positive, not a negative policy: a holding of the ring with a subtle bias in favour of one of the combatants, as Britain held the ring in favour of Garibaldi's expedition which overthrew the legitimate government of Naples in 1859–60. Hence the truth of Talleyrand's sardonic remark, that "non-intervention is a political term meaning virtually the same thing as intervention." The Non-Intervention Committee during the Spanish Civil War gave a crowning and tragic illustration.

Intervention is frequent in the relations between a Great Power and its satellites. The classic example is the relations between the United States and Latin America. The United States proclaimed the Monroe Doctrine in 1823 to prevent intervention by the European Powers in Latin America; but as it grew in strength it turned the Doctrine inside out to justify intervention in Latin America on its own part. It intervened usually to protect its investments and commercial interests, a policy which became known as "dollar imperialism"; sometimes for strategic reasons, as when it encouraged the revolt of Panama against Colombia in 1900 in order to acquire the future Canal Zone from the newly formed Panamanian republic. In the early twentieth century it sought increasingly to present its interventions in moral terms, as aimed at overthrowing unconstitutional dictatorships and upholding democracy. Franklin Roosevelt when he became president saw that United States security and American solidarity were being endangered by the intense resentment caused by this tradition of financial imperialism. He therefore initiated what has come to be called the Good Neighbour policy, which means above all that the United States has abandoned its practice of intervention and that the Monroe Doctrine is once more facing outwards against the world.

Intervention is the point at which domestic and international politics intersect, and there are particular opportunities for it in a period of conflicting ideologies; vertical national loyalties, so to speak, are then confused by horizontal loyalties. Most of the general wars have had a national civil war as a principal feature. If, as seems possible, the ideological passions of the past thirty years die out and are replaced increasingly by the hard and sober loyalties evoked by the constellations of the great World Powers, the extreme form of revolutionary intervention through fifth columns and "internationals" will probably decline. But intervention of the ordinary kinds is still likely to be apparent in the no-man's-land of weak states that separates the World Powers.

12. BUFFER ZONES

A buffer zone is an area occupied by a weaker Power or Powers between two or more stronger Powers. It will be the vital interest of each stronger Power to prevent the other from controlling the buffer zone, and each will pursue this interest in one of two ways, according to its strength: either by seeking to establish its own control over the buffer zone, transforming it into a protectorate or a frontier province, or by maintaining its neutrality and independence. Buffer states can therefore be roughly divided into neutral states and protectorates. Neutral states are states without an active foreign policy at all; protectorates are states whose foreign policy is controlled by another Power.

The most obvious and familiar examples of the buffer state are the Small Powers that have become established along the main line of political cleavage and strife in Western Europe, the Franco-German frontiers: Switzerland, a buffer state between France, Germany and the Austrian Empire; Luxemburg, a buffer state between France and Germany; and Holland and Belgium, buffer states between Britain, France and Germany.

Each of the Dominant Powers in Europe at the height of its power has absorbed a buffer state, whose independence has been re-established as vital to the general interests of Europe after the Dominant Power has been defeated. Philip II attained the summit of his success when in 1581 he seized the crown of Portugal. In 1640, when war with France and a revolution in Catalonia had made Spain's position desperate, Portugal revolted with French assistance and resumed its independence. It immediately concluded a treaty with England, "the oldest of European alliances," and Portugal has ever since remained for Britain an indispensable sea-board buffer whose independence guarantees the safety of the Atlantic routes (as well as having been the bridgehead for Wellington's expedition on the Continent against Napoleon). What Portugal was to Spain, Belgium was to France. One of the chief aims of the coalitions against first Louis XIV, and then Revolutionary France and Napoleon, was to prevent France from absorbing the Belgian Netherlands. This was achieved by joining Belgium to Holland in 1815; and when in 1830 Belgium revolted, by erecting it into an independent state under international guarantee. And what Belgium was to France, modern Austria is to Germany. After 1918 Austria became the buffer state between Germany, Italy and the Little Entente (i.e. Czechoslovakia, Yugoslavia and Rumania). The conquest of Austria in 1938 was the great stroke that opened the way for Germany to the Mediterranean and the Black Sea; it made Czechoslovakia indefensible, which made Poland indefensible, which in its turn made all South-Eastern Europe and the Ukraine indefensible; and at the same time it turned Italy into a German vassal. Germany has national claims to include Austria, as France had national claims to include Belgium; but in either case the interests of the Balance of Power are paramount.

The most important buffer zone in the world is that dividing Russia from the British Empire. Russia lies in the long curve of the British Empire rather like an egg in a spoon, but the two are separated by a layer of weak states stretching from the Near to the Far East: Turkey, Persia, Afghanistan, and China with its autonomous dependencies, Tibet and Manchuria. Britain's great anxiety throughout the nineteenth century was to keep this layer intact. There were four points along it at which a Russian breakthrough was especially feared: through Turkey to the Straits and the Mediterranean, through Persia to the Persian Gulf and the Indian Ocean, through Afghanistan to the Punjab, and through Manchuria to the China Seas. This zone illustrates all the different kinds of buffer state. Britain's historic policy in the Eastern Question was to preserve Turkey's *independence* as a bulwark against Russia; hence the Crimean War (1854–56). Persia, on the other hand, was *partitioned into spheres of influence* by Britain and Russia in agreement (1907). Afghanistan, an outpost of the Indian Empire, became a *protectorate* through the Second Afghan War (1878–80), conceding to Britain the control of its foreign policy; this was renounced after the Third Afghan War (1919), at the time when Rus-

sia had ceased to be a Great Power. Tibet, nominally under Chinese suzerainty, was *neutralized* in 1907, the two Powers agreeing not to send representatives to Lhasa, the Tibetan capital (it is interesting to note that Tibet was thus a buffer state without even having a common frontier with Russia). China itself was too vast to be absorbed or made a protectorate; it was a great arena in which the Powers shadow-boxed and staked out claims. Britain's traditional policy here was to maintain China's *independence coupled with the Open Door to all commerce;* but in the end the Chinese policy of all the Western Powers was reduced to a scramble for concessions on the compensation principle, which might have led to partition if the First World War had not intervened.

This great buffer belt from the Mediterranean to the Pacific will have even more importance in the coming century than it had in the last; for it is now the mingling place of the interests of America as well as of Russia and Britain. The Middle East is one vital area, not only as the strategic land-bridge between Europe, Asia and Africa but also because of its oil resources. Here already a single neutral buffer is faintly emerging in the Arab League of 1945. The Far East is the other vital area, where in proportion to the growing strength of China a multiple Balance of Power is likely to come into being between Russia, China, America and Britain, with perhaps Japan as a makeweight. Since China itself began to be a Power through its national resurgence, a buffer zone has appeared along its continental frontier: Manchuria and Inner Mongolia, which have been Japanese vassal states; Outer Mongolia and Tannu-Tuva, which are Soviet protectorates; and Sinkiang, a Chinese frontier province. Manchuria and Korea are the Belgium and Holland of the Far East, the buffers between Japan, Russia and China; and Manchuria is of peculiar importance by reason of its industrial wealth. If a stable Balance of Power is established after the defeat of Japan, Manchuria may be given some kind of autonomy under international guarantee; if not it will probably continue to gravitate towards the strongest of the three Powers as it has done for the past century.

It is broadly true that politics, like nature, abhor a vacuum; and buffer states cannot achieve stability and security on their own. This was the great weakness of the belt of East European Powers between Germany and Russia under the Versailles Settlement—the Middle Zone. It came into existence while Germany and Russia had temporarily ceased to be Great Powers, but it could not be maintained without relation to them; least of all could it be, as the Allies seem to have hoped, a wall to hem them both in. As soon as the two had resumed their strength they moved into this vacuum again, as the prelude to conflict between themselves. But the Second World War, by destroying Germany, France and Italy as Great Powers, has turned the whole of Europe into the buffer zone between Russia and Anglo-America. In Eastern Europe Russia is building up a frontier belt of friendly and satellite states, a glacis against invasion; the West European seaboard, with Britain as the great outpost, is equally vital to America. In between lies the vacuum of defeated Germany; and it is in its partition into spheres of influence, its neutralization, or its movement into the orbit of one or other of the victorious Great Powers, that we shall trace the shifting or stabilization of the Balance of Power in the next twenty or thirty years.

13. THE LEAGUE OF NATIONS

We have seen that the Balance of Power is inherently unstable, because Powers are not static societies, but are constantly growing or declining in relation to one another. The Balance of Power is essentially competitive. It leads to rivalry of power, which leads to war, as a consequence of which one side is temporarily eliminated and the other has a temporary monopoly of power.

In one of his famous speeches of 1918 Wilson referred to "the great game, now for ever discredited, of the Balance of Power." The League of Nations was an attempt to transform the Balance of Power into a system at once more effective and more rational, whereby it worked automatically against any aggressor. Every Power was to recognize it as its vital interest to prevent aggression against every other power as well as against itself, on the principle that the prevention of anarchy is a collective responsibility, and that the only true security is collective security. The Balance of Power was to be broadened and institutionalized into what Wilson called a "community of Power."

But far more influential than the purpose of the League was the pattern of power politics that made its establishment possible and conditioned its working. The three great factors in this were the defeat of Germany, the absence of Russia through the Bolshevik Revolution, and the withdrawal of America. The isolation of America was the least important, because the heart and test of the League system was Europe, where America had never been a regular Power. The absence of Russia was extremely important, because without Russian co-operation there could be no stable European balance; and by the time it entered the League it was too late (1934). But the defeat of Germany was perhaps the decisive factor, because it had been sealed by the Versailles Treaty; and the League, whose Covenant was Part I of the Treaty, was thus involved to its discredit in the irrelevant (though important) controversy as to whether the Treaty was just or unjust.

From the outset, therefore, the League was the product of peculiar and temporary conditions. Not only did it fail to transcend the Balance of Power, as Wilson had hoped, but it was involved in an extraordinarily unstable balance. As had always happened before when the overriding common interest of defeating the Dominant Power had been removed, the Allies fell apart after victory. America repudiated the League and sank into isolation; Italy, dissatisfied with its spoils, embarked on the Fascist Revolution; Britain dissolved its alliance with France, abandoned the Versailles Treaty as unjust, and regarded the League as an insurance requiring no premium. Only France, clear-sighted in its weakness, made a sustained attempt to keep the ends of international politics in view and to provide the necessary means during those tragic years. The League was destroyed, not by Germany over the question of revising the Versailles Treaty, but by the dissatisfied victors of Germany. The initial blow at it came from Japan, with the conquest of Manchuria in 1931–32; the second and decisive blow came from Italy with the conquest of Abyssinia in 1935–36. It was only after this that Germany took the first great step in its plans for conquest, by remilitarizing the Rhineland (March 1936) and so sealing off Western from Eastern Europe.

It is very difficult to sum up the intricate question of the League's failure—intricate in terms both of morality and of statesmanship—in a few sentences. It is true that Britain and France did not prevent the Italian conquest of Abyssinia through fear of Germany's taking the opportunity of an Anglo-Franco-Italian war in the Mediterranean to revise the Versailles Settlement by force in Europe. If we say, in Wilsonian terms, that the search for orderly methods of revising the law presupposes the intention first of all to uphold the existing law, and that for victor Powers to uphold the existing law presupposes their obedience to it and enforcement of it among themselves, we simply are underlining the inability of the Great Powers to base their policy upon the obligations of the League. Yet perhaps the lesson does emerge, that in establishing an international order you have got to start somewhere, and that the best point to start is where you are now, and not a couple of years hence when you hope that both your ex-ally Italy and your ex-enemy Germany will have become satisfied and law-abiding. That decision meant to drift steadily farther from a possible starting-point. When we are tempted to ask, what else could Britain and France have done? we must not lose sight of the fact that whatever they might have done could not have been more disastrous to international order than what they actually did.

The system later known as "appeasement" had already begun functioning behind the facade of the League. It was the old system of the Concert of Europe, whereby the Great Powers settled matters by private bargains among themselves at the expense of Small Powers. The first instance was when in 1923 Italy used a dispute with Greece to bombard and occupy Corfu. The Great Powers, anxious to secure the evacuation of Corfu and the restoration of the Balance of Power in the Mediterranean, appeased Italy by preventing the League from handling the dispute and agreeing to Italy's extortion of a large indemnity from Greece. In 1933 Mussolini tried to institutionalize the system by his proposal for a Four Power Pact, under which the four European Great Powers (excluding Russia) were to undertake the revision of the Peace Settlement, with the implication that they would impose their views on minor Powers. This was frustrated for the moment by the Little Entente. There followed the Laval-Hoare Plan (1935) to bring the Italo-Abyssinian War to an agreed end by partitioning Abyssinia: the establishment of the Non-Intervention Committee in London (1936) which removed the issues of the Spanish Civil War out of the hands of the League; the Anglo-Italian Agreement of April 1938, which adjusted Anglo-Italian interests in the Mediterranean and the Near East at the price of British recognition of the Italian conquest of Abyssinia; and the fulfilment at last of the idea of the Four Power Pact at Munich (September 1938), where the Four Powers agreed to the partitioning of Czechoslovakia by Germany (with Poland and Hungary coming in as jackal-states) in order to preserve peace.

Up to this point the Four Power directorate had excluded Russia, to whom all the Four Powers (except in some degree France) were inflexibly opposed on ideological grounds. Thus Russia, which was the last Great Power to seem to champion the League system, was driven into isolation, and itself resorted to appeasement. The Soviet-German Pact of August 1939 was Russia's Munich. The second article of the Pact stated that if either Power "should become the object of warlike action on the part of a third Power," the other would in no way support the third Power. Germany forthwith became the object of warlike action on the part of Poland and of most of the self-defending nations of Europe, while Russia hastened to transform the Baltic States into frontier provinces, and became the object of warlike action on the part of the self-defending Finns. The same method of arriving at international settlement by agreement between Great Powers over the heads of the Small Powers affected, was seen at Yalta in 1945, when the Polish question was settled by the three Allied Great Powers without Polish representation, as the Czechoslovak question had been settled in 1938 without Czechoslovak representation. These instances of appeasement are of course by no means all on the same moral level. Germany's aggressions sponsored by the Soviet-German Pact of 1939 were predatory; Russia's were defensive. But what we are here concerned to note is that the method throughout was the same: the Great Powers acting as a directorate. This is the system that has always obtained hitherto in power politics, and which the League of Nations failed to supersede.

14. THE UNITED NATIONS

The Charter for a world organization to be called the United Nations, which was drafted at Dumbarton Oaks in 1944 and completed at San Francisco in 1945, is an attempt to marry the League system with the system of the Great Power directorate. In its external characteristics—its Security Council and General Assembly—it is clearly the child of the League, and has improvements which are the fruit of League experience. For instance, the powers at the disposal of the Security Council for applying economic and military sanctions against an aggressor are detailed and precise, and far more adequate than were those of the League Council. To this extent it is true that it "puts teeth into" the League. But in other respects more has been taken out of the League than has been put into it, and it is clear that the United Nations is an organization of a different kind.

The first contrast is in the subordination of the Small Powers to the Great Powers. The old Assembly had almost equal powers with the Council, and in fact it increased its authority vis-a-vis the Council as time went on. The new Assembly is only a debating society; executive powers are concentrated in the hands of the Security Council, and on the Security Council the Great Powers (i.e. the five permanent members, as against the six non-permanent members) have a commanding position. Decisions of the Council in all matters of importance, including threats to the peace or acts of aggression, are to require a vote of seven members *including the permanent members;* that is to say, any Great Power can veto such a decision. This means that a Great Power can prevent international action against itself, or against a satellite Power whom it chooses to protect. It places the Great Powers outside the organization in all matters which they regard as their vital interests; and their relations with one another will be regulated as of old by the Balance of Power.

The second contrast is in the subordination of the world organization to regional organizations. The Charter enjoins the Security Council to encourage settlement of local disputes through regional arrangements, and such arrangements have in fact been coming into existence before the world organization itself has been set up. Russia is basing its future policy on a series of bilateral regional treaties: the Anglo-Soviet Alliance of 1942, the Czechoslovak-Soviet Alliance of 1943, the Franco-

Soviet Alliance of 1944, and the Alliances with Yugoslavia and Poland of 1945. These alliances provide for automatic action to suppress any new threat from Germany, in anticipation of and irrespective of the decisions of the world organization (though there is a provision in the Anglo-Soviet Treaty for its possible termination by mutual agreement when the world organization has been established). The Pan-American Conference at Mexico City in 1945 agreed on the Act of Chapultepec, which sets up a Pan-American regional system for outlawing aggression, but relates it more specifically to the framework of a world organization. It is noteworthy how each of the two regional systems that have so far come into existence is in essence an almost self-contained unit composed of a World Power with many Small Powers. This gives them their reality and prospect of being effective; but it also resembles the institutionalization of appeasement, in the sense that if the Security Council is to encourage the settlement of local disputes through such regional arrangements, a dispute between the United States and Mexico may be liable to be settled by the United States, or a dispute between Russia and Rumania by Russia. The exclusiveness of these two great groupings is broken by the Russian alliances with Britain and France, which prolong the encirclement of Germany into the post-War period, and by the community (almost identity) of interest between Britain and France and America, proved by two general wars, and taken too much for granted to need recognition in formal treaties. Britain and France thus form the bridge or link between America and Russia, and it is on their alliances with Russia that the decisive stress of the power politics of the next half century will fall.

The true parentage of the United Nations is thus, not the League, but the Concert of Europe. The Great Powers will impose the law, but are themselves above it. The emphasis of the Charter is on the maintenance of security, that ambiguous word, not on justice or a rule of law. And it is founded to a far greater extent than was the League on the assumption that the only threats to security will come from the defeated enemy. It is unlikely that Germany and Japan are going to be able a second time to confuse and divide the victor Powers by a clamour for "revision." But the main lesson of the League's failure, that the victor Powers, if they are to remain united, need to accept a rule of law themselves, is less clearly apparent in the organization of the United Nations.

15. BEYOND POWER POLITICS

In the study of international politics we are dogged by the insistent problem, whether the relations between Powers are in fact more than "power politics" in the popular sense of the term, and whether they can become more. From one point of view, the central question is how far Powers can be said to have interests in common. We have seen that the international anarchy is restrained and to some extent systematized in practice by two opposing kinds of common interest, pulling alternately to and fro. The first is the common interest of all Powers in their freedom, of which they are faintly conscious in peace, and assert at the eleventh hour in war by an armed coalition against a common danger. The second is the kind of common interest represented by successive Dominant Powers. For their predominance has generally safeguarded real values, and offered real benefits, for other nations, and sometimes they have wielded an international ideology as their most potent weapon—as the Hapsburg Powers were the protagonists of the Counter-Reformation, as Napoleonic France was the carrier of the French Revolution throughout feudal Europe, as Britain in the nineteenth century was the champion of liberalism. In the same way Russia in the twentieth century has represented the ideal of socialism. A Dominant Power that is thus able to give its policies the added momentum of an international ideal becomes a tremendous force, whose limits are reached only if it provokes the counter-interest of general freedom. Nor is it impossible that Powers may henceforward increasingly regard their deepest common interest as being the prevention of war and liberation from anarchy, and that this will only prove obtainable by acquiescence in a common government provided by the strongest Power.

But the idea of common interest can never have much vitality if it is separated from the idea of common obligation, and here we touch a more fundamental issue. There has always existed a theory of international relations which asserts the primacy of common conceptions of justice, right and law. There was an ancient tradition, dating back through the jurists and theologians of the Middle Ages to the jurists and philosophers of antiquity, of Natural Law or the Law of Nature. It taught that man is a rational and social animal, that there is a moral order in the universe to which his rational nature bids him always and everywhere to conform, that the true interests of human societies therefore do not conflict, and that they are bound together by obligations of law and morality. This tradition was the source of international law, which was developed in the seventeenth century to restrain the anarchy into which the states of Europe had fallen, and which used to appeal to "the common standard of right prevailing throughout the Christian world." But it was eclipsed by the new revolutionary creed of progress at the end of the eighteenth century, just at the time when the European Powers, as a consequence of the industrial revolution, were beginning to establish a material unification of the world.

The expansion of Europe itself weakened the tradition of Natural Law, by admitting states that had not been schooled in it to the international community. Of the two new Great Powers of the eighteenth century, Prussia was at the extreme limit of Western Christendom, and had been in many ways scarcely touched by its characteristic culture; and Russia is the heir and champion of the very different traditions of Byzantine Christendom. In the nineteenth century international intercourse was extended far beyond the Christian world, at the same time that Christian political theory was at a greater discount inside the Christian world than it had ever been before. In 1856, at the conclusion of the Crimean War, Turkey was admitted for the first time to the community of nations; but it was a passive and not an active member; and it is from the emergence of Japan as a Great Power—the first Great Power that was wholly non-European and non-Christian in its traditions— that we may date the effective transformation of the international community from one based on a common ethos to one whose principle is inclusiveness. Attempts have been made since the French Revolution to find an alternative common ethos in political creed instead of moral tradition. The Vienna Settlement was based on the principle of legitimacy; the Versailles Settlement was based on the principle of self-determination; the Yalta Declaration of 1945 enshrined the principle of "democracy." But in each case these formulae have reflected only a transient moment on the surface of affairs, concealing differences rather than expressing "a common standard of right," and they have soon dissolved and been superseded. It may indeed be asked whether an effective common ethos is likely to grow up again without an effective common government.

Though the tradition of an international community with a common standard of obligation and justice has faded, however, it has not altogether disappeared. It is the main influence that has modified, and can yet modify, the operations of power politics, and it still gleams faintly in the preamble to the Charter of the United Nations. In countries whose culture and politics are favourable to its survival, it can create a "moral climate" of opinion that will affect politicians who are quite ignorant of any traditional political theories. The extent to which it may do so in practice is highly controversial, and every historical example that may be brought forward in this light will lead to the kind of argument in which there can be no clear-cut and final conclusion, because it depends not on the establishment of facts but on the exercise of moral insight and political judgment.

It is sufficient to instance two statesmen whose beliefs were saturated with conceptions of Natural Law, and whose politics were grounded on its traditions, Gladstone in nineteenth-century England, and Franklin Roosevelt in twentieth-century America; nor is it any accident that each of these men in his generation had a moral ascendancy and a power over the public opinion of the world, evoking a trust and loyalty far beyond his own country, which was unapproached by any other contemporary political figure. (The devotion inspired abroad in the intervening generation by the supreme revolutionary statesman, Lenin, was perhaps more passionate in its quality, but it was limited and sectional by comparison in its range.) This is not to say that Gladstone and Roosevelt were not assiduous, subtle and far-sighted power-politicians. But their politics had overtones that are absent from the politics of a Theodore Roosevelt or a Cecil Rhodes, a Lloyd George or a Clemenceau, a Bismarck or a Cavour. When we consider the foreign policies of the latter we think in terms of patriotism, of grandeur of conception, of brilliance, of virtuosity, above all of success or failure. Most people would agree that Gladstone's Irish policy or Roosevelt's Latin-American policy (like in another way, Lincoln's Civil War policy) were different in quality from these, the fruit of a richer conception of politics, which made power an instrument and not an end, and subordinated national interest to public justice.

Nevertheless it is always well to be sceptical of statesmen, and as Lord Acton insisted, to "suspect power more than vice." It is particularly necessary to guard against the notion that morality in politics is a flower that blooms especially or exclusively in Anglo-Saxon gardens. The first thing to remember about the policies of Gladstone and Franklin Roosevelt is that Gladstone's Britain and Roosevelt's America were Dominant Powers. This will remind us of the great truth that morality in international politics is not simply a matter of civilized tradition, but is equally the result of security. If British policy in the nineteenth century showed in general perhaps a greater degree of enlightened self-interest than that of any other Great Power in modern history, it was because Britain then enjoyed perfect security. "We could afford the luxury of gentleness," as Mr. Harold Nicolson has said, "because we were completely unafraid."

Once security is destroyed, all the higher objects of politics are swallowed up in the struggle for self-preservation, a tendency seen in every war. "A great and civilized Power like England," said a distinguished writer before the War, "should strive for a margin of security big enough to make a certain bias in favour of an ideal policy possible, a bias that may never show itself in any specific political action but will inform the manner or spirit of her international conduct." Yet since it ceased to be Dominant Power, Britain's margin of security has shrunk, and the possibility of an independent ideal policy has correspondingly dwindled. This is the vicious circle of power politics: morality is the fruit of security, but lasting security as between many Powers depends on their observing a certain common standard of morality. The League of Nations in theory transformed it into a virtuous circle, by making collective security a moral obligation. But the solution presupposed a degree of enlightened self-interest among the Great Powers that did not exist.

The modern substitute for the Law of Nature might be called the Law of Common Material Interest. Contemporary writers on international politics are increasingly driven to place their hopes for future peace on the universal demand for social justice and a rising standard of living, which implies the growth of new economic and social relationships between peoples, and co-operation between Powers "for the planned development of the economies of geographical areas and groups of nations." The reality of this common interest is profound, but it does not touch the problem of power. The world community is still an anarchy, lacking a common superior, and international politics are still power politics. Every Power has an interest greater than welfare, an interest on which it believes that welfare depends and to which welfare must in the last resort be sacrificed—the maintenance of power itself.

It is true that there was equally anarchy in the period when men talked in terms of the Law of Nature, so that its influence upon politics was tenuous and remote. Yet in the long run the idea of a common moral obligation is probably a more fruitful social doctrine than the idea of a common material interest. As the French philosopher

Julien Benda has said, mankind has always betrayed its obligations, but so long as it continues to acknowledge and believe in them, the crack is kept open through which civilization can creep. Powers will continue to seek security without reference to justice, and to pursue their vital interests irrespective of common interests, but in the fraction that they may be deflected lies the difference between the jungle and the traditions of Europe. The outstanding contrast between the mood of 1945 and the mood of 1918, which is reflected in the contrast between the United Nations Charter and the League Covenant, is the absence of optimism, the greater realism. Realism can be a very good thing: it all depends whether it means the abandonment of high ideals or of foolish expectations.

2. AMERICAN POLICY TOWARD RUSSIA

By HENRY A. WALLACE

EDITORS' NOTE.—After serving as Vice-President of the United States from 1941 to 1945, Henry A. Wallace (p. 602) became Secretary of Commerce in Franklin Roosevelt's fourth-term cabinet. He continued in that position when Harry Truman became President on Roosevelt's death. Wallace's opposition to what he considered the reversal of Roosevelt's policy of friendship with the Soviet Union was

at first confined within the administration. Before making his views public at Madison Square Garden, he had presented a copy of his speech to President Truman, who apparently could find nothing he considered objectionable in it. After its delivery, however, Truman, probably at the demand of Secretary of State Byrnes, requested and received Wallace's resignation from the cabinet.

A. LETTER TO PRESIDENT TRUMAN[1]

On September 17, Secretary Wallace released the following letter that he had written to President Truman on July 23, saying that he was doing so in view of the fact that it had already fallen into the hands of a newspaper-man.

July 23, 1946

The President
The White House

MY DEAR MR. PRESIDENT:

I hope you will excuse this long letter. Personally I hate to write long letters, and

I hate to receive them.

My only excuse is that this subject is a very important one—probably the most important in the world today. I checked with you about this last Thursday and you suggested after the Cabinet meeting on Friday that you would like to have my views.

I have been increasingly disturbed about the trend of international affairs

1. Reprinted from the *New York Times*, September 18, 1946.

since the end of the war, and I am even more troubled by the apparently growing feeling among the American people that another war is coming and the only way that we can head it off is to arm ourselves to the teeth. Yet all of past history indicates that an armaments race does not lead to peace but to war. The months just ahead may well be the crucial period which will decide whether the civilized world will go down in destruction after the five or ten years needed for several nations to arm themselves with atomic bombs. Therefore I want to give you my views on how the present trend toward conflict might be averted.

You may think it strange, in reading further, that I should express so much concern at this particular time, just after the Foreign Ministers' conference at which real progress was made on peace treaties for several Eastern European countries and for Italy. Others have expressed a feeling of increased optimism that still further progress could be made through continued negotiations on the same basis, even though the remaining European issues are much more difficult than those on which a measure of agreement has already been reached. I am fully appreciative of the efforts that have been made and the patience that has been exercised by our various representatives who have carried on negotiations with the Russians during the last few years. I am conscious of the aggravations they have put up with and of the apparent inconsistencies on the part of Russian representatives. On the other hand, I feel these very difficulties make it necessary for some of us who, from the outside, are watching the course of events to voice our opinions.

Incidentally, as Secretary of Commerce I talk to a good many businessmen, and I find them very much concerned over the size of the Federal budget and the burden of the national debt. For the next fiscal year, and for the year immediately ahead, by far the largest category of Federal spending is the national defense.

For example, the total recommended Federal appropriations for the fiscal year 1947 submitted to the Congress in the official budget amounted to about $36 billion. Of the total budget some $13 billion was for the War and Navy Departments alone. An additional $5 billion was for war liquidation activities. Ten billion represented interest on the public debt and veterans' benefits, which are primarily the continuing costs of past wars. These items total $28 billion, or about 80 per cent of the total recommended expenditures.

Clearly, a large reduction in the Federal budget would require a cut in military appropriations. These appropriations are now more than ten times as great as they were during the thirties. In the 1938 budget appropriations for national defense were less than a billion dollars, compared with $13 billion for the present fiscal year. Thus, even from a purely dollars and cents standpoint, American business and the American people have an interest in organizing a peaceful world in which the completely unproductive expenditures on national defense could be reduced.

Of course, dollars and cents are not the most important reason why we all want a peaceful world. The fundamental reason is that we do not wish to go through another war—and especially an atomic war which will undoubtedly be directed primarily against civilian populations and may well mean the end of modern civilization.

Yet are we really concentrating all our efforts on a program to build a lasting peace? There can be no doubt that the American people want and expect that their leaders will work for an enduring peace. But the people must necessarily leave to their leaders the specific ways and means to this objective. I think that at the moment the people feel that the outlook for the elimination of war is dark, that other nations are wilfully obstructing American efforts to achieve a permanent peace.

How do American actions since V-J Day appear to other nations? I mean by actions the concrete things like $13 billion for the War and Navy Departments, the

Bikini tests of the atomic bomb and continued production of bombs, the plan to arm Latin America with our weapons, production of B-29s and planned production of B-36s, and the effort to secure air bases spread over half the globe from which the other half of the globe can be bombed. I cannot but feel that these actions must make it look to the rest of the world as if we were only paying lip service to peace at the conference table.

These facts rather make it appear either (1) that we are preparing ourselves to win the war which we regard as inevitable or (2) that we are trying to build up a predominance of force to intimidate the rest of mankind. How would it look to us if Russia had the atomic bomb and we did not, if Russia had 10,000-mile bombers and air bases within a thousand miles of our coastlines, and we did not?

Some of the military men and self-styled "realists" are saying: "What's wrong with trying to build up a predominance of force? The only way to preserve peace is for this country to be so well armed that no one will dare attack us. We know that America will never start a war."

The flaw in this policy is simply that it will not work. In a world of atomic bombs and other revolutionary new weapons, such as radioactive poison gases and biological warfare, a peace maintained by a predominance of force is no longer possible.

Why is this so? The reasons are clear:

First. Atomic warfare is cheap and easy compared with old-fashioned war. Within a very few years several countries can have atomic bombs and other atomic weapons. Compared with the cost of large armies and the manufacture of old-fashioned weapons, atomic bombs cost very little and require only a relatively small part of a nation's production plant and labor force.

Second. So far as winning a war is concerned, having more bombs—even many more bombs—than the other fellow is no longer a decisive advantage. If another nation had enough bombs to eliminate all of our principal cities and our heavy industry, it wouldn't help us very much if we had 10 times as many bombs as we needed to do the same to them.

Third. And most important, the very fact that several nations have atomic bombs will inevitably result in a neurotic, fear-ridden, itching-trigger psychology in all the peoples of the world, and because of our wealth and vulnerability we would be among the most seriously affected. Atomic war will not require vast and time-consuming preparations, the mobilization of large armies, the conversion of a large proportion of a country's industrial plants to the manufacture of weapons. In a world armed with atomic weapons, some incident will lead to the use of those weapons.

There is a school of military thinking which recognizes these facts, recognizes that when several nations have atomic bombs, a war which will destroy modern civilization will result and that no nation or combination of nations can win such a war. This school of thought therefore advocates a "preventive war," an attack on Russia *now* before Russia has atomic bombs.

This scheme is not only immoral, but stupid. If we should attempt to destroy all the principal Russian cities and her heavy industry, we might well succeed. But the immediate countermeasure which such an attack would call forth is the prompt occupation of all Continental Europe by the Red Army. Would we be prepared to destroy the cities of all Europe in trying to finish what we had started? This idea is so contrary to all the basic instincts and principles of the American people that any such action would be possible only under a dictatorship at home.

Thus the "predominance of force" idea, and the notion of a "defensive attack" are both unworkable. The only solution is the one which you have so wisely advanced and which forms the basis of the Moscow statement on atomic energy. That solution consists of mutual trust and confidence among nations, atomic disarmament and an effective system of enforcing that disarmament.

There is, however, a fatal defect in the Moscow statement, in the Acheson report and in the American plan recently presented to the United Nations Atomic Energy Commission. That defect is the scheme, as it is generally understood, of arriving at international agreements by "easy stages," of requiring other nations to enter into binding commitments not to conduct research into the military uses of atomic energy and to disclose their uranium and thorium resources while the United States retains the right to withhold its technical knowledge of atomic energy until the international control and inspection system is working to our satisfaction.

In other words, we are telling the Russians that if they are "good boys" we may eventually turn over our knowledge of atomic energy to them and to the other nations. But there is no objective standard of what will qualify them as being "good" nor any specified time for sharing our knowledge.

Is it any wonder that the Russians did not show any great enthusiasm for our plan? Would we have been enthusiastic if the Russians had a monopoly of atomic energy, and offered to share the information with us at some indefinite time in the future at their discretion if we agreed now not to try to make a bomb and give them information on our secret resources of uranium and thorium? I think we would react as the Russians appear to have done. We would have put up counter-proposals for the record, but our real effort would go into trying to make a bomb so that our bargaining position would be equalized. That is the essence of the Russian position, which is very clearly stated in the *Pravda* article of June 24, 1946.

It is perfectly clear that the "step-by-step" plan in any such one-sided form is not workable. The entire agreement will have to be worked out and wrapped up in a single package. This may involve certain steps or stages, but the timing of such steps must be agreed to in the initial master treaty. Realistically, Russia has two cards which she can use in negotiating with us: (1) our lack of information on the state of her scientific and technical progress on atomic energy and (2) our ignorance of her uranium and thorium resources. These cards are nothing like as powerful as our cards—a stockpile of bombs, manufacturing plants in actual production, B-29s and B-36s, and our bases covering half the globe. Yet we are in effect asking her to reveal her only two cards immediately—telling her that after we have seen her cards we will decide whether we want to continue to play the game.

Insistence on our part that the game must be played our way will only lead to a deadlock. The Russians will redouble their efforts to manufacture bombs, and they may also decide to expand their "security zone" in a serious way. Up to now, despite all our outcries against it, their efforts to develop a security zone in Eastern Europe and in the Middle East are small change from the point of view of military power as compared with our air bases in Greenland, Okinawa and many other places thousands of miles from our shores. We may feel very self-righteous if we refuse to budge on our plan and the Russians refuse to accept it, but that means only one thing—the atomic armament race is on in deadly earnest.

I am convinced therefore that if we are to achieve our hopes of negotiating a treaty which will result in effective international atomic disarmament we must abandon the impractical form of the "step-by-step" idea which was presented to the United Nations Atomic Energy Commission. We must be prepared to reach an agreement which will commit us to disclosing information and destroying our bombs at a specified time or in terms of specified actions by other countries, rather than at our unfettered discretion. If we are willing to negotiate on this basis, I believe the Russians will also negotiate seriously with a view to reaching an agreement.

There can be, of course, no absolute assurance the Russians will finally agree to a workable plan if we adopt this view. They may prefer to stall until they also have bombs and can negotiate on a more equal basis, not realizing the danger to themselves as well as the rest of the world in a situation in which several nations have atomic bombs. But we must make the effort to head off the atomic bomb race. We have everything to gain by doing so, and do not give up anything by adopting this policy as the fundamental basis for our negotiation. During the transition period toward full-scale international control we retain our technical know-how, and the only existing production plants for fissionable materials and bombs remain within our borders.

The Russian counter-proposal itself is an indication that they may be willing to negotiate seriously if we are. In some respects their counter-proposal goes even farther than our plan and is in agreement with the basic principles of our plan, which is to make violations of the proposed treaty a national and international crime for which individuals can be punished.

It will have been noted that in the preceding discussion I have not mentioned the question of the so-called "veto." I have not done so because the veto issue is completely irrelevant, because the proposal to "abolish the veto," which means something in the general activities of the Security Council, has no meaning with respect to a treaty on atomic energy. If we sign a treaty with other nations, we will all have agreed to do certain things. Until we arrive at such a treaty, we as well as the other major powers will have the power to veto. Once the treaty is ratified, however, the question of the veto becomes meaningless. If any nation violates the treaty provision, say of permitting inspection of suspected illegal bomb-making activities, what action is there that can be vetoed? As in the case of any other treaty violation, the remaining signatory nations are free to take what action they feel is necessary, including the ultimate step of declaring war.

I believe that for the United States and Russia to live together in peace is the most important single problem facing the world today. Many people, in view of the relatively satisfactory outcome of the recent Paris Conference, feel that good progress is being made on the problem of working out relations between the Anglo-Saxon powers and Russia. This feeling seems to me to be resting on superficial appearances more productive of a temporary truce than of final peace. On the whole, as we look beneath the surface in late July of 1946, our actions and those of the Western Powers in general carry with them the ultimate danger of a third world war—this time an atomic world war. As the strongest single nation, and the nation whose leadership is followed by the entire world, with the exception of Russia and a few weak neighboring countries in Eastern Europe, I believe that we have the opportunity to lead the world to peace.

In general there are two over-all points of view which can be taken in approaching the problem of the United States–Russian relations. The first is that it is not possible to get along with the Russians and therefore war is inevitable. The second is that war with Russia would bring catastrophe to all mankind, and, therefore, we must find a way of living in peace. It is clear that our own welfare as well as that of the entire world requires that we maintain the latter point of view. I am sure that this is also your opinion, and the radio address of the Secretary of State on July 15 clearly indicates that he is prepared to negotiate as long as may be necessary to work out a solution on this basis.

We should try to get an honest answer to the question of what the factors are which cause Russia to distrust us, in addition to the question of what factors lead us to distrust Russia. I am not sure that we have as a nation or an Administration found an adequate answer to either question, although we have recognized that both questions are of critical importance.

Our basic distrust of the Russians, which has been greatly intensified in recent months by the playing up of conflict in the press, stems from differences in political and economic organization. For the first time in our history defeatists among us have raised the fear of another system as a successful rival to democracy and free enterprise in other countries and perhaps even our own. I am convinced that we can meet that challenge as we have in the past by demonstrating that economic abundance can be achieved without sacrificing personal, political and religious liberties. We cannot meet it as Hitler tried to by an anti-Comintern alliance.

It is perhaps too easy to forget that despite the deep-seated differences in our cultures and intensive anti-Russian propaganda of some twenty-five years' standing, the American people reversed their attitudes during the crisis of war. Today, under the pressure of seemingly insoluble international problems and continuing deadlocks, the tide of American public opinion is again turning against Russia. In this reaction lies one of the dangers to which this letter is addressed.

I should list the factors which make for Russian distrust of the United States and of the Western world as follows. The first is Russian history, which we must take into account because it is the setting in which Russians see all actions and policies of the rest of the world. Russian history for over a thousand years has been a succession of attempts, often unsuccessful, to resist invasion and conquest—by the Mongols, the Turks, the Swedes, the Germans and the Poles. The scant thirty years of the existence of the Soviet Government has in Russian eyes been a continuation of their historical struggle for national existence. The first four years of the new regime, from 1917 through 1921, were spent in resisting attempts at destruction by the Japanese, British and French, with some American assistance, and by the several White Russian armies encouraged and financed by the Western powers. Then, in 1941, the Soviet State was almost conquered by the Germans after a period during which the Western European powers had apparently acquiesced in the rearming of Germany in the belief that the Nazis would seek to expand eastward rather than westward. The Russians, therefore, obviously see themselves as fighting for their existence in a hostile world.

Second, it follows that to the Russians all of the defense and security measures of the Western powers seem to have an aggressive intent. Our actions to expand our military security system—such steps as extending the Monroe Doctrine to include the arming of the Western Hemisphere nations, our present monopoly of the atomic bomb, our interest in outlying bases and our general support of the British Empire—appear to them as going far beyond the requirements of defense. I think we might feel the same if the United States were the only capitalistic country in the world, and the principal socialistic countries were creating a level of armed strength far exceeding anything in their previous history. From the Russian point of view, also, the granting of a loan to Britain and the lack of tangible results on their request to borrow for rehabilitation purposes may be regarded as another evidence of strengthening of an anti-Soviet bloc.

Finally, our resistance to her attempts to obtain warm-water ports and her own security system in the form of "friendly" neighboring states seems, from the Russian point of view, to clinch the case. After twenty-five years of isolation and after having achieved the status of a major power, Russia believes that she is entitled to recognition of her new status. Our interest in establishing democracy in Eastern Europe, where democracy by and large has never existed, seems to her an attempt to re-establish the encirclement of unfriendly neighbors which was created after the last war, and which might serve as a springboard of still another effort to destroy her.

If this analysis is correct, and there is ample evidence to support it, the action to improve the situation is clearly indicated. The fundamental objective of such action should be to allay any reasonable Russian grounds for fear, suspicion and distrust. We must recognize that the world has changed and that today there can be no "One World" unless the United States and Russia can find some way of living together. For example, most of us are firmly convinced of the soundness of our position when we suggest the internationalization and defortification of the Danube or of the Dardanelles, but we would be horrified and angered by any Russian counter-proposal that would involve also the internationalizing and disarming of Suez or Panama. We must recognize that to the Russians these seem to be identical situations.

We should ascertain from a fresh point of view what Russia believes to be essential to her own security as a prerequisite to the writing of the peace and to co-operation in the construction of a world order. We should be prepared to judge her requirements against the background of what we ourselves and the British have insisted upon as essential to our respective security. We should be prepared, even at the expense of risking epithets of appeasement, to agree to reasonable Russian guarantees of security. The progress made during June and July on the Italian and other treaties indicates that we can hope to arrive at understanding and agreement on this aspect of the problem.

We should not pursue further the question of the veto in connection with atomic energy, a question which is irrelevant and should never have been raised. We should be prepared to negotiate a treaty which will establish a definite sequence of events for the establishment of international control and development of atomic energy. This, I believe, is the most important single question, and the one on which the present trend is definitely toward deadlock rather than ultimate agreement.

We should make an effort to counteract the irrational fear of Russia which is being systematically built up in the American people by certain individuals and publications. The slogan that communism and capitalism, regimentation and democracy, cannot continue to exist in the same world is, from a historical point of view, pure propaganda. Several religious doctrines, all claiming to be the only true gospel and salvation, have existed side by side with a reasonable degree of tolerance for centuries. This country was for the first half of its national life a democratic island in a world dominated by absolutist governments.

We should not act as if we too felt that we were threatened in today's world. We are by far the most powerful nation in the world, the only Allied nation which came out of the war without devastation and much stronger than before the war. Any talk on our part about the need for strengthening our defenses further is bound to appear hypocritical to other nations.

We should also be prepared to enter into economic discussion without demanding that the Russians agree in advance to discussion of a series of what are to them difficult and somewhat unrelated political and economic concessions. Although this is the field in which my Department is most directly concerned, I must say that in my opinion this aspect of the problem is not as critical as some of the others, and certainly is far less important than the question of atomic-energy control. But successful negotiation in this field might help considerably to bridge the chasm that separates us.

The question of a loan should be approached on economic and commercial grounds and should be disassociated as much as possible from the current misunderstandings which flow from the basic differences between their system and ours. You have already clearly disassociated yourself and the American people from the expressions of anti-Soviet support for the British loan. If we could have followed up your statement on signing the British loan bill with a loan to U.S.S.R. on a commercial basis, and on similar financial terms, I believe that it would have clearly demonstrated that this country is not attempting to use its economic resources in the game of power politics. In the light of the present Export-Import Bank situation, it is now of the greatest importance that we undertake general economic discussions at an early date.

It is of the greatest importance that we should discuss with the Russians in a friendly way their long-range economic problems and the future of our co-operation in matters of trade. The reconstruction program of the U.S.S.R. and the plans for the full development of the Soviet Union offer tremendous opportunities for American goods and American technicians.

American products, especially machines of all kinds, are well established in the Soviet Union. For example, American equipment, processes and methods are standard in coal mining, iron and steel, oil and nonferrous metals.

Nor would this trade be one-sided. Although the Soviet Union has been an excellent credit risk in the past, eventually the goods and services exported from this country must be paid for by the Russians by exports to us and to other countries. Russian products which are either definitely needed or which are noncompetitive in this country are various nonferrous metal ores, furs, linen products, lumber products, vegetable drugs, paper and pulp, and native handicrafts.

I feel that negotiations on the establishment of active trade might well help to clear away the fog of political misunderstanding. Such discussions might well be initiated while we are endeavoring to reach a common ground on security issues, and if conducted in an understanding manner, could only serve to make that problem easier. In the memorandum which I sent to you in March, and which I suggested should be given to General [Walter Bedell] Smith to take to Moscow, I made certain suggestions for trade discussions and a trade mission. In preference to proposed discussions in this country, I want to renew my original proposal and urge the appointment of a mission to Moscow.

Such a mission might have as its objective the drafting of a proposal involving Russian reconstruction and collaboration with Russia in the industrial and economic development of areas in which we have joint interests, such as the Middle East.

As I stated at that time, I am prepared to make suggestions for the composition of the mission and some of the specific economic questions to be discussed. The Department of Commerce has already arranged, with the co-operation of the State Department, to send two representatives to Moscow for the months of July and August for preliminary discussions of a much more limited scope.

I think it is very significant that most of the more optimistic reports about the possibilities of getting along with the Russians have come from American observers who were businessmen. I have in mind such men as Wendell Willkie, Eric Johnston and former Ambassador Joe Davies. The Russians seem to be friendly to, and seem to have respect for, capitalist businessmen.

A number of observers have reported that the Soviet leaders are "isolationists," and appear to be lacking a true insight into the principles, motives, and ways of thinking in other nations. We must admit, however, that they pointed out the symptoms and the way to prevent World War II in their promotion of the concept of collective security.

And aside from that, it seems to me we should try to do something constructive about their isolationism and ignorance, and I believe the aforementioned trade mission could accomplish much in that direction. I gather, too, that is part of what you had had in mind in inviting Premier Stalin to visit America.

Many of the problems relating to the countries bordering on Russia could more readily be solved once an atmosphere of mutual trust and confidence is established and some form of economic arrangements are worked out with Russia. These problems also might be helped by discussions of an economic nature. Russian economic penetration of the Danube area, for example, might be countered by concrete proposals for economic collaboration in the development of the resources of this area, rather than by insisting that the Russians should cease their unilateral penetration and offering no solution to the present economic chaos there.

This proposal admittedly calls for a shift in some of our thinking about international matters. It is imperative that we make this shift. We have little time to lose. Our post-war actions have not yet been adjusted to the lessons to be gained from experience of Allied co-operation during the war and the facts of the atomic age.

It is certainly desirable that, as far as possible, we achieve unity on the home front with respect to our international relations; but unity on the basis of building up conflict abroad would prove to be not only unsound but disastrous. I think there is some reason to fear that in our earnest efforts to achieve bipartisan unity in this country we may have given way too much to isolationism masquerading as tough realism in international affairs.

The real test lies in the achievement of international unity. It will be fruitless to continue to seek solutions for the many specific problems that face us in the making of the peace and in the establishment of an enduring international order without first achieving an atmosphere of mutual trust and confidence. The task admittedly is not an easy one.

There is no question, as the Secretary of State has indicated, that negotiations with the Russians are difficult because of cultural differences, their traditional isolationism, and their insistence on a visible *quid pro quo* in all agreements. But the task is not an insuperable one if we take into account that to other nations our foreign policy consists not only of the principles that we advocate but of the actions we take.

Fundamentally, this comes down to the point discussed earlier in this letter, that even our own security, in the sense that we have known it in the past, cannot be preserved by military means in a world armed with atomic weapons. The only type of security which can be maintained by our own military force is the type described by a military man before the Senate Atomic Energy Committee—a security against invasion after all our cities and perhaps 40 million of our city population have been destroyed by atomic weapons. That is the best that "security" on the basis of armaments has to offer us. It is not the kind of security that our people and the people of the other United Nations are striving for.

I think that progressive leadership along the lines suggested above, would represent and best serve the interests of the large majority of our people, would reassert the forward-looking position of the Democratic Party in international affairs, and finally, would arrest the new trend towards isolationism and a disastrous atomic world war.

B. THE PRICE OF PEACE[2]

Tonight I want to talk about peace— and how to get peace. Never have the common people of all lands so longed for peace. Yet, never in a time of comparative peace have they feared war so much.

Up till now peace has been negative and unexciting. War has been positive and exciting. Far too often, hatred and fear, in-

tolerance and deceit have had the upper hand over love and confidence, trust and joy. Far too often, the law of nations has been the law of the jungle; and the constructive spiritual forces of the Lord have bowed to the destructive forces of Satan.

During the past year or so, the significance of peace has been increased immeasurably by the atom bomb, guided missiles and airplanes which soon will travel as fast as sound. Make no mistake

2. Henry A. Wallace, *The Fight for Peace* (New York, 1946), pp. 17–22. Reprinted by permission of Reynal and Hitchcock.

about it—another war would hurt the United States many times as much as the last war. We cannot rest in the assurance that we invented the atom bomb—and therefore that this agent of destruction will work best for us. He who trusts in the atom bomb will sooner or later perish by the atom bomb—or something worse.

I say this as one who steadfastly backed preparedness throughout the thirties. We have no use for namby-pamby pacifism. But we must realize that modern inventions have now made peace the most exciting thing in the world—and we should be willing to pay a just price for peace. If modern war can cost us $400,000,000,000, we should be willing and happy to pay much more for peace. But certainly, the cost of peace is to be measured not in dollars but in the hearts and minds of men.

The price of peace—for us and for every nation in the world—is the price of giving up prejudice, hatred, fear and ignorance.

Let's get down to cases here at home.

First we have prejudice, hatred, fear and ignorance of certain races. The recent mass lynching in Georgia was not merely the most unwarranted, brutal act of mob violence in the United States in recent years; it was also an illustration of the kind of prejudice that makes war inevitable.

Hatred breeds hatred. The doctrine of racial superiority produces a desire to get even on the part of its victims. If we are to work for peace in the rest of the world, we here in the United States must eliminate racism from our unions, our business organizations, our educational institutions, and our employment practices. Merit alone must be the measure of man.

Second, in payment for peace, we must give up prejudice, hatred, fear and ignorance in the economic world. This means working earnestly, day after day, for a larger volume of world trade. It means helping undeveloped areas of the world to industrialize themselves with the help of American technical assistance and loans.

We should welcome the opportunity to help along the most rapid possible industrialization in Latin America, China, India, and the Near East. For as the productivity of these peoples increases, our exports will increase.

We all remember the time, not so long ago, when the high-tariff protectionists blindly opposed any aid to the industrialization of Canada. But look at our exports to Canada today. On a per capita basis, our Canadian exports are seven times greater than our exports to Mexico.

I supported the British loan of almost four billion dollars because I knew that without this aid in the rehabilitation of its economy, the British Government would have been forced to adopt totalitarian trade methods and economic warfare of a sort which would have closed the markets of much of the world to American exports.

For the welfare of the American people and the world it is even more important to invest $4,000,000,000 in the industrialization of undeveloped areas in the so-called backward nations, thereby promoting the long-term stability that comes from an ever-increasing standard of living. This would not only be good politics and good morals. It would be good business.

The United States is the world's great creditor nation. And low tariffs by creditor nations are a part of the price of peace. For when a great creditor demands payment, and at the same time adopts policies which make it impossible for the debtors to pay in goods—the first result is the intensification of depression over large areas of the world; and the final result is the triumph of demagogues who speak only the language of violence and hate.

There are those who have expressed themselves as favoring an alliance of mutual defense with Great Britain as the key to our foreign policy. This may sound attractive because we both speak the same language and many of our customs and traditions have the same historical background. Moreover, to the military men, the British Isles are our advanced air base against Europe.

Certainly we like the British people as individuals. But to make Britain the key to our foreign policy would be, in my opinion, the height of folly. We must not let reactionary leadership force us into that position. We must not let British balance-of-power manipulations determine whether and when the United States gets into war.

Make no mistake about it—the British imperialistic policy in the Near East alone, combined with Russian retaliation, would lead the United States straight to war unless we have a clearly defined and realistic policy of our own.

Neither of these two great powers wants war now, but the danger is that whatever their intentions may be, their current policies may eventually lead to war. To prevent war and insure our survival in a stable world, it is essential that we look abroad through our own American eyes and not through the eyes of either the British Foreign Office or a pro-British or anti-Russian press.

In this connection, I want one thing clearly understood. I am neither anti-British nor pro-British—neither anti-Russian nor pro-Russian. And just two days ago, when President Truman read these words, he said that they represented the policy of his Administration.

I plead for an America vigorously dedicated to peace—just as I plead for opportunities for the next generation throughout the world to enjoy the abundance which now, more than ever before, is the birthright of man.

To achieve lasting peace, we must study in detail just how the Russian character was formed—by invasions of Tartars, Mongols, Germans, Poles, Swedes and French; by the czarist rule based on ignorance, fear and force; by the intervention of the British, French and Americans in Russian affairs from 1919 to 1921; by the geography of the huge Russian land mass situated strategically between Europe and Asia; and by the vitality derived from the rich Russian soil and the strenuous Russian climate. Add to all this the tremendous emotional power which Marxism and Leninism gives to the Russian leaders—and then we can realize that we are reckoning with a force which cannot be handled successfully by a "get tough with Russia" policy.

"Getting tough" never bought anything real and lasting—whether for schoolyard bullies or businessmen or world powers. The tougher we get, the tougher the Russians will get.

Throughout the world there are numerous reactionary elements which had hoped for Axis victory—and now profess great friendship for the United States. Yet, these enemies of yesterday and false friends of today continually try to provoke war between the United States and Russia. They have no real love of the United States. They only long for the day when the United States and Russia will destroy each other.

We must not let our Russian policy be guided or influenced by those inside or outside the United States who want war with Russia. This does not mean appeasement.

We most earnestly want peace with Russia—but we want to be met halfway. We want co-operation. And I believe that we can get co-operation once Russia understands that our primary objective is neither saving the British Empire nor purchasing oil in the Near East with the lives of American soldiers. We cannot allow national oil rivalries to force us into war. All of the nations producing oil, whether inside or outside of their own boundaries, must fulfill the provisions of the United Nations Charter and encourage the development of world petroleum reserves so as to make the maximum amount of oil available to all nations of the world on an equitable peaceful basis—and not on the basis of fighting the next war.

For her part, Russia can retain our respect by co-operating with the United Nations in a spirit of open-minded and flexible give and take.

The real peace treaty we now need is between the United States and Russia. On our part, we should recognize that we have no more business in the *political* affairs of Eastern Europe than Russia has in the *political* affairs of Latin America, Western Europe and the United States. We may not like what Russia does in Eastern Europe. Her type of land reform, industrial expropriation, and suppression of basic liberties offends the great majority of the people of the United States. But whether we like it or not the Russians will try to socialize their sphere of influence just as we try to democratize our sphere of influence. This applies also to Germany and Japan. We are striving to democratize Japan and our area of control in Germany, while Russia strives to socialize Eastern Germany.

As for Germany, we all must recognize that an equitable settlement, based on a unified German nation, is absolutely essential to any lasting European settlement. This means that Russia must be assured that never again can German industry be converted into military might to be used against her—and Britain, Western Europe and the United States must be certain that Russia's Germany policy will not become a tool of Russian design against Western Europe.

The Russians have no more business in stirring up native Communists to political activity in Western Europe, Latin America and the United States than we have in interfering in the politics of Eastern Europe and Russia. We know what Russia is up to in Eastern Europe, for example, and Russia knows what we are up to. We cannot permit the door to be closed against our trade in Eastern Europe any more than we can in China. But at the same time we have to recognize that the Balkans are closer to Russia than to us—and that Russia cannot permit either England or the United States to dominate the politics of that area.

China is a special case and although she holds the longest frontier in the world with Russia, the interests of world peace demand that China remain free from any sphere of influence, either politically or economically. We insist that the door to trade and economic development opportunities be left wide open in China as in all

the world. However, the open door to trade and opportunities for economic development in China are meaningless unless there is a unified and peaceful China—built on the co-operation of the various groups in that country and based on a hands-off policy of the outside powers.

We are still arming to the hilt. Our excessive expenses for military purposes are the chief cause of our unbalanced budget. If taxes are to be lightened we must have the basis of a real peace with Russia—a peace that cannot be broken by extremist propagandists. We do not want our course determined for us by master minds operating out of London, Moscow or Nanking.

Russian ideas of social-economic justice are going to govern nearly a third of the world. Our ideas of free-enterprise democracy will govern much of the rest. The two ideas will endeavor to prove which can deliver the most satisfaction to the common man in their respective areas of political dominance. But by mutual agreement, this competition should be put on a friendly basis and the Russians should stop conniving against us in certain areas of the world, just as we should stop scheming against them in other parts of the world. Let the results of the two systems speak for themselves.

Meanwhile, the Russians should stop teaching that their form of communism must, by force if necessary, ultimately triumph over democratic capitalism—while we should close our ears to those among us who would have us believe that Russian communism and our free-enterprise system cannot live, one with another, in a profitable and productive peace.

Under friendly peaceful competition the Russian world and the American world will gradually become more alike. The Russians will be forced to grant more and more of the personal freedoms; and we shall become more and more absorbed with the problems of social-economic justice.

Russia must be convinced that we are not planning for war against her and we must be certain that Russia is not carrying on territorial expansion or world domination through native Communists faithfully following every twist and turn in the Moscow party line. But in this competition, we must insist on an open door for trade throughout the world. There will always be an ideological conflict—but that is no reason why diplomats cannot work out a basis for both systems to live safely in the world side by side.

Once the fears of Russia and the United States Senate have been allayed by practical regional political reservations, I am sure that concern over the veto power would be greatly diminished. Then the United Nations would have a really great power in those areas which are truly international and not regional. In the worldwide, as distinguished from the regional field, the armed might of the United Nations should be so great as to make opposition useless. Only the United Nations should have atomic bombs, and its military establishment should give special emphasis to air power. It should have control of the strategically located air bases with which the United States and Britain have encircled the world. And not only should individual nations be prohibited from manufacturing atomic bombs, guided missiles and military aircraft for bombing purposes, but no nation should be allowed to spend on its military establishment more than perhaps 15 per cent of its budget.

Practically and immediately, we must recognize that we are not yet ready for World Federation. Realistically, the most we can hope for now is a safe reduction in military expense and a long period of peace based on mutual trust between the Big Three.

During this period, every effort should be made to develop as rapidly as possible a body of international law based on moral principles and not on the Machiavellian principles of deceit, force and distrust—which, if continued, will lead the modern world to rapid disintegration.

In brief, as I see it today, the World Order is bankrupt—and the United States,

Russia and England are the receivers. These are the hard facts of power politics on which we have to build a functioning, powerful United Nations and a body of International Law. And as we build, we must develop fully the doctrine of the rights of small peoples as contained in the United Nations Charter. This law should ideally apply as much to Indonesians and Greeks as to Bulgarians and Poles—but practically, the application may be delayed until both British and Russians discover the futility of their methods.

In the full development of the rights of small nations, the British and Russians can learn a lesson from the Good Neighbor policy of Franklin Roosevelt. For under Roosevelt, we in the Western Hemisphere built a workable system of regional internationalism that fully protected the sovereign rights of every nation—a system of multilateral action that immeasurably strengthened the whole of world order.

In the United States an informed public opinion will be all-powerful. Our people are peace-minded. But they often express themselves too late—for events today move much faster than public opinion. The people here, as everywhere in the world, must be convinced that another war is not inevitable. And through mass meetings such as this, and through persistent pamphleteering, the people can be organized for peace—even though a large segment of our press is propagandizing our people for war in the hope of scaring Russia. And we who look on this war-with-Russia talk as criminal foolishness must carry our message direct to the people—even though we may be called Communists because we dare to speak out.

I believe that peace—the kind of a peace I have outlined tonight—is the basic issue, both in the congressional campaign this fall and right on through the presidential election in 1948. How we meet this issue will determine whether we live not in "one world" or "two worlds"—but whether we live at all.

3. SOURCES OF SOVIET CONDUCT[1]

By X

EDITORS' NOTE.—This anonymous article appeared in the quarterly journal *Foreign Affairs* for July, 1947. The author was promptly identified by Washington correspondents as George F. Kennan, an officer of the foreign service who had recently served in Moscow and whom Secretary Marshall had made director of the Policy Planning Staff of the State Department. The attribution was not denied, and the article received wide publicity as a semiofficial statement of the calculations upon which current American policy was being formulated.

The political personality of Soviet power as we know it today is the product of ideology and circumstances: ideology inherited by the present Soviet leaders from the movement in which they had their political origin, and circumstances of the power which they now have exercised for nearly three decades in Russia. There can be few tasks of psychological analysis more difficult than to try to trace the interaction of these two forces and the relative rôle of each in the determination of official Soviet conduct. Yet the attempt must be made if that conduct is to be understood and effectively countered.

It is difficult to summarize the set of ideological concepts with which the Soviet leaders came into power. Marxian ideology, in its Russian-Communist projection, has always been in process of subtle evolution. The materials on which it bases itself are extensive and complex. But the outstanding features of Communist thought as it existed in 1916 may perhaps be summarized as follows: (*a*) that the central factor in the life of man, the factor which determines the character of public life and the "physiognomy of society," is the system by which material goods are produced and exchanged; (*b*) that the capitalist system of production is a nefarious one which

inevitably leads to the exploitation of the working class by the capital-owning class and is incapable of developing adequately the economic resources of society or of distributing fairly the material goods produced by human labor; (*c*) that capitalism contains the seeds of its own destruction and must, in view of the inability of the capital-owning class to adjust itself to economic change, result eventually and inescapably in a revolutionary transfer of power to the working class; and (*d*) that imperialism, the final phase of capitalism, leads directly to war and revolution.

The rest may be outlined in Lenin's own words: "Unevenness of economic and political development is the inflexible law of capitalism. It follows from this that the victory of Socialism may come originally in a few capitalist countries or even in a single capitalist country. The victorious proletariat of that country, having expropriated the capitalists and having organized Socialist production at home, would rise against the remaining capitalist world, drawing to itself in the process the oppressed classes of other countries." It must be noted that there was no assumption that capitalism would perish without proletarian revolution. A final push was needed from a revolutionary proletariat movement in order to tip over the tottering structure. But it was regarded as in-

[1]. "Sources of Soviet Conduct," *Foreign Affairs*, XXV (July, 1947), 566–69, 571–82.

evitable that sooner or later that push be given. . . .

The circumstances of the immediate post-revolution period—the existence in Russia of civil war and foreign intervention, together with the obvious fact that the Communists represented only a tiny minority of the Russian people—made the establishment of dictatorial power a necessity. The experiment with "war Communism" and the abrupt attempt to elimi nate private production and trade had unfortunate economic consequences and caused further bitterness against the new revolutionary régime. While the temporary relaxation of the effort to communize Russia, represented by the New Economic Policy, alleviated some of this economic distress and thereby served its purpose, it also made it evident that the "capitalistic sector of society" was still prepared to profit at once from any relaxation of governmental pressure, and would, if permitted to continue to exist, always constitute a powerful opposing element to the Soviet régime and a serious rival for influence in the country. Somewhat the same situation prevailed with respect to the individual peasant who, in his own small way, was also a private producer. . . .

Now the outstanding circumstance concerning the Soviet régime is that down to the present day this process of political consolidation has never been completed and the men in the Kremlin have continued to be predominantly absorbed with the struggle to secure and make absolute the power which they seized in November 1917. They have endeavored to secure it primarily against forces at home, within Soviet society itself. But they have also endeavored to secure it against the outside world. For ideology, as we have seen, taught them that the outside world was hostile and that it was their duty eventually to overthrow the political forces beyond their borders. The powerful hands of Russian history and tradition reached up to sustain them in this feeling. Finally, their own aggressive intransigence with respect

to the outside world began to find its own reaction; and they were soon forced, to use another Gibbonesque phrase, "to chastise the contumacy" which they themselves had provoked. It is an undeniable privilege of every man to prove himself right in the thesis that the world is his enemy; for if he reiterates it frequently enough and makes it the background of his conduct he is bound eventually to be right.

Now the maintenance of this pattern of Soviet power, namely, the pursuit of unlimited authority domestically, accompanied by the cultivation of the semi-myth of implacable foreign hostility, has gone far to shape the actual machinery of Soviet power as we know it today. Internal organs of administration which did not serve this purpose withered on the vine. Organs which did serve this purpose became vastly swollen. The security of Soviet power came to rest on the iron discipline of the Party, on the severity and ubiquity of the secret police, and on the uncompromising economic monopolism of the state. The "organs of suppression," in which the Soviet leaders had sought security from rival forces, became in large measure the masters of those whom they were designed to serve. Today the major part of the structure of Soviet power is committed to the perfection of the dictatorship and to the maintenance of the concept of Russia as in a state of siege, with the enemy lowering beyond the walls. And the millions of human beings who form that part of the structure of power must defend at all costs this concept of Russia's position, for without it they are themselves superfluous.

As things stand today, the rulers can no longer dream of parting with these organs of suppression. The quest for absolute power, pursued now for nearly three decades with a ruthlessness unparalleled (in scope at least) in modern times, has again produced internally, as it did externally, its own reaction. The excesses of the police apparatus have fanned the potential opposition to the régime into something far greater and more dangerous than it could have been before those excesses began.

But least of all can the rulers dispense with the fiction by which the maintenance of dictatorial power has been defended. For this fiction has been canonized in Soviet philosophy by the excesses already committed in its name; and it is now anchored in the Soviet structure of thought by bonds far greater than those of mere ideology.

So much for the historical background. What does it spell in terms of the political personality of Soviet power as we know it today?

Of the original ideology, nothing has been officially junked. Belief is maintained in the basic badness of capitalism, in the inevitability of its destruction, in the obligation of the proletariat to assist in that destruction and to take power into its own hands. But stress has come to be laid primarily on those concepts which relate most specifically to the Soviet régime itself: to its position as the sole truly Socialist régime in a dark and misguided world, and to the relationships of power within it.

The first of these concepts is that of the innate antagonism between capitalism and Socialism. We have seen how deeply that concept has become imbedded in foundations of Soviet power. It has profound implications for Russia's conduct as a member of international society. It means that there can never be on Moscow's side any sincere assumption of a community of aims between the Soviet Union and powers which are regarded as capitalist. It must invariably be assumed in Moscow that the aims of the capitalist world are antagonistic to the Soviet régime, and therefore to the interests of the peoples it controls. If the Soviet Government occasionally sets its signature to documents which would indicate the contrary, this is to be regarded as a tactical manoeuvre permissible in dealing with the enemy (who is without

honor) and should be taken in the spirit of *caveat emptor*. Basically, the antagonism remains. It is postulated. And from it flow many of the phenomena which we find disturbing in the Kremlin's conduct of foreign policy: the secretiveness, the lack of frankness, the duplicity, the wary suspiciousness, and the basic unfriendliness of purpose. These phenomena are there to stay, for the foreseeable future. There can be variations of degree and of emphasis. When there is something the Russians want from us, one or the other of these features of their policy may be thrust temporarily into the background; and when that happens there will always be Americans who will leap forward with gleeful announcements that "the Russians have changed," and some who will even try to take credit for having brought about such "changes." But we should not be misled by tactical manoeuvres. These characteristics of Soviet policy, like the postulate from which they flow, are basic to the internal nature of Soviet power, and will be with us, whether in the foreground or the background, until the internal nature of Soviet power is changed.

This means that we are going to continue for a long time to find the Russians difficult to deal with. It does not mean that they should be considered as embarked upon a do-or-die program to overthrow our society by a given date. The theory of the inevitability of the eventual fall of capitalism has the fortunate connotation that there is no hurry about it. The forces of progress can take their time in preparing the final *coup de grâce*. Meanwhile, what is vital is that the "Socialist fatherland"— that oasis of power which has been already won for Socialism in the person of the Soviet Union—should be cherished and defended by all good Communists at home and abroad, its fortunes promoted, its enemies badgered and confounded. The promotion of premature, "adventuristic" revolutionary projects abroad which might embarrass Soviet power in any way would be an inexcusable, even a counter-revolutionary act. The cause of Socialism is the support and promotion of Soviet power, as defined in Moscow.

This brings us to the second of the concepts important to contemporary Soviet outlook. That is the infallibility of the Kremlin. The Soviet concept of power, which permits no focal points of organization outside the Party itself, requires that the Party leadership remain in theory the sole repository of truth. For if truth were to be found elsewhere, there would be justification for its expression in organized activity. But it is precisely that which the Kremlin cannot and will not permit.

The leadership of the Communist Party is therefore always right, and has been always right ever since in 1929 Stalin formalized his personal power by announcing that decisions of the Politburo were being taken unanimously.

On the principle of infallibility there rests the iron discipline of the Communist Party. In fact, the two concepts are mutually self-supporting. Perfect discipline requires recognition of infallibility. Infallibility requires the observance of discipline. And the two together go far to determine the behaviorism of the entire Soviet apparatus of power. But their effect cannot be understood unless a third factor be taken into account: namely, the fact that the leadership is at liberty to put forward for tactical purposes any particular thesis which it finds useful to the cause at any particular moment and to require the faithful and unquestioning acceptance of that thesis by the members of the movement as a whole. This means that truth is not a constant but is actually created, for all intents and purposes, by the Soviet leaders themselves. It may vary from week to week, from month to month. It is nothing absolute and immutable—nothing which flows from objective reality. It is only the most recent manifestation of the wisdom of those in whom the ultimate wisdom is supposed to reside, because they represent the logic of history. The accumulative effect of these factors is to give to the whole

subordinate apparatus of Soviet power an unshakeable stubbornness and steadfastness in its orientation. This orientation can be changed at will by the Kremlin but by no other power. Once a given party line has been laid down on a given issue of current policy, the whole Soviet governmental machine, including the mechanism of diplomacy, moves inexorably along the prescribed path, like a persistent toy automobile wound up and headed in a given direction, stopping only when it meets with some unanswerable force. The individuals who are the components of this machine are unamenable to argument or reason which comes to them from outside sources. Their whole training has taught them to mistrust and discount the glib persuasiveness of the outside world. Like the white dog before the phonograph, they hear only the "master's voice." And if they are to be called off from the purposes last dictated to them, it is the master who must call them off. Thus the foreign representative cannot hope that his words will make any impression on them. The most that he can hope is that they will be transmitted to those at the top, who are capable of changing the party line. But even those are not likely to be swayed by any normal logic in the words of the bourgeois representative. Since there can be no appeal to common purposes, there can be no appeal to common mental approaches. For this reason, facts speak louder than words to the ears of the Kremlin; and words carry the greatest weight when they have the ring of reflecting, or being backed up by, facts of unchallengeable validity.

But we have seen that the Kremlin is under no ideological compulsion to accomplish its purposes in a hurry. Like the Church, it is dealing in ideological concepts which are of long-term validity, and it can afford to be patient. It has no right to risk the existing achievements of the revolution for the sake of vain baubles of the future. The very teachings of Lenin himself require great caution and flexibility in the pursuit of Communist purposes.

Again, these precepts are fortified by the lessons of Russian history: of centuries of obscure battles between nomadic forces over the stretches of a vast unfortified plain. Here caution, circumspection, flexibility and deception are the valuable qualities; and their value finds natural appreciation in the Russian or the oriental mind. Thus the Kremlin has no compunction about retreating in the face of superior force. And being under the compulsion of no timetable, it does not get panicky under the necessity for such retreat. Its political action is a fluid stream which moves constantly, wherever it is permitted to move, toward a given goal. Its main concern is to make sure that it has filled every nook and cranny available to it in the basin of world power. But if it finds unassailable barriers in its path, it accepts these philosophically and accommodates itself to them. The main thing is that there should always be pressure, unceasing constant pressure, toward the desired goal. There is no trace of any feeling in Soviet psychology that that goal must be reached at any given time.

These considerations make Soviet diplomacy at once easier and more difficult to deal with than the diplomacy of individual aggressive leaders like Napoleon and Hitler. On the one hand it is more sensitive to contrary force, more ready to yield on individual sectors of the diplomatic front when that force is felt to be too strong, and thus more rational in the logic and rhetoric of power. On the other hand it cannot be easily defeated or discouraged by a single victory on the part of its opponents. And the patient persistence by which it is animated means that it can be effectivaly countered not by sporadic acts which represent the momentary whims of democratic opinion but only by intelligent long-range policies on the part of Russia's adversaries—policies no less steady in their purpose, and no less variegated and resourceful in their application, than those of the Soviet Union itself.

In these circumstances it is clear that the main element of any United States policy toward the Soviet Union must be that of a long-term, patient but firm and vigilant containment of Russian expansive tendencies. It is important to note, however, that such a policy has nothing to do with outward histrionics: with threats or blustering or superfluous gestures of outward "toughness." While the Kremlin is basically flexible in its reaction to political realities, it is by no means unamenable to considerations of prestige. Like almost any other government, it can be placed by tactless and threatening gestures in a position where it cannot afford to yield even though this might be dictated by its sense of realism. The Russian leaders are keen judges of human psychology, and as such they are highly conscious that loss of temper and of self-control is never a source of strength in political affairs. They are quick to exploit such evidences of weakness. For these reasons, it is a *sine qua non* of successful dealing with Russia that the foreign government in question should remain at all times cool and collected and that its demands on Russian policy should be put forward in such a manner as to leave the way open for a compliance not too detrimental to Russian prestige.

In the light of the above, it will be clearly seen that the Soviet pressure against the free institutions of the western world is something that can be contained by the adroit and vigilant application of counter-force at a series of constantly shifting geographical and political points, corresponding to the shifts and manoeuvres of Soviety policy, but which cannot be charmed or talked out of existence. The Russians look forward to a duel of infinite duration, and they see that already they have scored great successes. It must be borne in mind that there was a time when the Communist Party represented far more of a minority in the sphere of Russian national life than Soviet power today represents in the world community.

But if ideology convinces the rulers of Russia that truth is on their side and that they can therefore afford to wait, those of us on whom that ideology has no claim are free to examine objectively the validity of that premise. The Soviet thesis not only implies complete lack of control by the west over its own economic destiny, it likewise assumes Russian unity, discipline and patience over an infinite period. Let us bring this apocalyptic vision down to earth, and suppose that the western world finds the strength and resourcefulness to contain Soviet power over a period of ten to fifteen years. What does that spell for Russia itself?

The Soviet leaders, taking advantage of the contributions of modern technique to the arts of despotism, have solved the question of obedience within the confines of their power. Few challenge their authority; and even those who do are unable to make that challenge valid as against the organs of suppression of the state.

The Kremlin has also proved able to accomplish its purpose of building up in Russia, regardless of the interests of the inhabitants, an industrial foundation of heavy metallurgy, which is, to be sure, not yet complete but which is nevertheless continuing to grow and is approaching those of the other major industrial countries. All of this, however, both the maintenance of internal political security and the building of heavy industry, has been carried out at a terrible cost in human life and in human hopes and energies. It has necessitated the use of forced labor on a scale unprecedented in modern times under conditions of peace. It has involved the neglect or abuse of other phases of Soviet economic life, particularly agriculture, consumers' goods production, housing and transportation.

To all that, the war has added its tremendous toll of destruction, death and human exhaustion. In consequence of this, we have in Russia today a population which is physically and spiritually tired. The mass of the people are disillusioned, skeptical and no longer as accessible as they once were to the magical attraction which

Soviet power still radiates to its followers abroad. The avidity with which people seized upon the slight respite accorded to the Church for tactical reasons during the war was eloquent testimony to the fact that their capacity for faith and devotion found little expression in the purposes of the régime.

In these circumstances, there are limits to the physical and nervous strength of people themselves. These limits are absolute ones, and are binding even for the cruelest dictatorship, because beyond them people cannot be driven. The forced labor camps and the other agencies of constraint provide temporary means of compelling people to work longer hours than their own volition or mere economic pressure would dictate; but if people survive them at all they become old before their time and must be considered as human casualties to the demands of dictatorship. In either case their best powers are no longer available to society and can no longer be enlisted in the service of the state.

Here only the younger generation can help. The younger generation, despite all vicissitudes and sufferings, is numerous and vigorous; and the Russians are a talented people. But it still remains to be seen what will be the effects on mature performance of the abnormal emotional strains of childhood which Soviet dictatorship created and which were enormously increased by the war. Such things as normal security and placidity of home environment have practically ceased to exist in the Soviet Union outside of the most remote farms and villages. And observers are not yet sure whether that is not going to leave its mark on the over-all capacity of the generation now coming into maturity.

In addition to this, we have the fact that Soviet economic development, while it can list certain formidable achievements, has been precariously spotty and uneven. Russian Communists who speak of the "uneven development of capitalism" should blush at the contemplation of their own national economy. Here certain branches of economic life, such as the metallurgical and machine industries, have been pushed out of all proportion to other sectors of economy. Here is a nation striving to become in a short period one of the great industrial nations of the world while it still has no highway network worthy of the name and only a relatively primitive network of railways. Much has been done to increase efficiency of labor and to teach primitive peasants something about the operation of machines. But maintenance is still a crying deficiency of all Soviet economy. Construction is hasty and poor in quality. Depreciation must be enormous. And in vast sectors of economic life it has not yet been possible to instill into labor anything like that general culture of production and technical self-respect which characterizes the skilled worker of the west.

It is difficult to see how these deficiencies can be corrected at an early date by a tired and dispirited population working largely under the shadow of fear and compulsion. And as long as they are not overcome, Russia will remain economically a vulnerable, and in a certain sense an impotent, nation, capable of exporting its enthusiasms and of radiating the strange charm of its primitive political vitality but unable to back up those articles of export by the real evidences of material power and prosperity.

Meanwhile, a great uncertainty hangs over the political life of the Soviet Union. That is the uncertainty involved in the transfer of power from one individual or group of individuals to others.

This is, of course, outstandingly the problem of the personal position of Stalin. We must remember that his succession to Lenin's pinnacle of preëminence in the Communist movement was the only such transfer of individual authority which the Soviet Union has experienced. That transfer took twelve years to consolidate. It cost the lives of millions of people and shook the state to its foundations. The attendant tremors were felt all through the

international revolutionary movement, to the disadvantage of the Kremlin itself.

It is always possible that another transfer of preëminent power may take place quietly and inconspicuously, with no repercussions anywhere. But again, it is possible that the questions involved may unleash, to use some of Lenin's words, one of those "incredibly swift transitions" from "delicate deceit" to "wild violence" which characterize Russian history, and may shake Soviet power to its foundations.

But this is not only a question of Stalin himself. There has been, since 1938, a dangerous congealment of political life in the higher circles of Soviet power. The All-Union Party Congress, in theory the supreme body of the Party, is supposed to meet not less often than once in three years. It will soon be eight full years since its last meeting. During this period membership in the Party has numerically doubled. Party mortality during the war was enormous; and today well over half of the Party members are persons who have entered since the last Party congress was held. Meanwhile, the same small group of men has carried on at the top through an amazing series of national vicissitudes. Surely there is some reason why the experiences of the war brought basic political changes to every one of the great governments of the west. Surely the causes of that phenomenon are basic enough to be present somewhere in the obscurity of Soviet political life, as well. And yet no recognition has been given to these causes in Russia.

It must be surmised from this that even within so highly disciplined an organization as the Communist Party there must be a growing divergence in age, outlook and interest between the great mass of Party members, only so recently recruited into the movement, and the little self-perpetuating clique of men at the top, whom most of these Party members have never met, with whom they have never conversed, and with whom they can have no political intimacy.

Who can say whether, in these circumstances, the eventual rejuvenation of the higher spheres of authority (which can only be a matter of time) can take place smoothly and peacefully, or whether rivals in the quest for higher power will not eventually reach down into these politically immature and inexperienced masses in order to find support for their respective claims? If this were ever to happen, strange consequences could flow for the Communist Party: for the membership at large has been exercised only in the practices of iron discipline and obedience and not in the arts of compromise and accommodation. And if disunity were ever to seize and paralyze the Party, the chaos and weakness of Russian society would be revealed in forms beyond description. For we have seen that Soviet power is only a crust concealing an amorphous mass of human beings among whom no independent organizational structure is tolerated. In Russia there is not even such a thing as local government. The present generation of Russians have never known spontaneity of collective action. If, consequently, anything were ever to occur to disrupt the unity and efficacy of the Party as a political instrument, Soviet Russia might be changed overnight from one of the strongest to one of the weakest and most pitiable of national societies.

Thus the future of Soviet power may not be by any means as secure as Russian capacity for self-delusion would make it appear to the men in the Kremlin. That they can keep power themselves, they have demonstrated. That they can quietly and easily turn it over to others remains to be proved. Meanwhile, the hardships of their rule and the vicissitudes of international life have taken a heavy toll of the strength and hopes of the great people on whom their power rests. It is curious to note that the ideological power of Soviet authority is strongest today in areas beyond the frontiers of Russia, beyond the reach of its police power. This phenomenon brings to mind a comparison used by

Thomas Mann in his great novel "Buddenbrooks." Observing that human institutions often show the greatest outward brilliance at a moment when inner decay is in reality farthest advanced, he compared the Buddenbrook family, in the days of its greatest glamour, to one of those stars whose light shines most brightly on this world when in reality it has long since ceased to exist. And who can say with assurance that the strong light still cast by the Kremlin on the dissatisfied peoples of the western world is not the powerful afterglow of a constellation which is in actuality on the wane? This cannot be proved. And it cannot be disproved. But the possibility remains (and in the opinion of this writer it is a strong one) that Soviet power, like the capitalist world of its conception, bears within it the seeds of its own decay, and that the sprouting of these seeds is well advanced.

It is clear that the United States cannot expect in the foreseeable future to enjoy political intimacy with the Soviet régime. It must continue to regard the Soviet Union as a rival, not a partner, in the political arena. It must continue to expect that Soviet policies will reflect no abstract love of peace and stability, no real faith in the possibility of a permanent happy coexistence of the Socialist and capitalist worlds, but rather a cautious, persistent pressure toward the disruption and weakening of all rival influence and rival power.

Balanced against this are the facts that Russia, as opposed to the western world in general, is still by far the weaker party, that Soviet policy is highly flexible, and that Soviet society may well contain deficiencies which will eventually weaken its own total potential. This would of itself warrant the United States entering with reasonable confidence upon a policy of firm containment, designed to confront the Russians with unalterable counter-force at every point where they show signs of encroaching upon the interests of a peaceful and stable world.

But in actuality the possibilities for American policy are by no means limited to holding the line and hoping for the best. It is entirely possible for the United States to influence by its actions the internal developments, both within Russia and throughout the international Communist movement, by which Russian policy is largely determined. This is not only a question of the modest measure of informational activity which this government can conduct in the Soviet Union and elsewhere, although that, too, is important. It is rather a question of the degree to which the United States can create among the peoples of the world generally the impression of a country which knows what it wants, which is coping successfully with the problems of its internal life and with the responsibilities of a World Power, and which has a spiritual vitality capable of holding its own among the major ideological currents of the time. To the extent that such an impression can be created and maintained, the aims of Russian Communism must appear sterile and quixotic, the hopes and enthusiasm of Moscow's supporters must wane, and added strain must be imposed on the Kremlin's foreign policies. For the palsied decrepitude of the capitalist world is the keystone of Communist philosophy. Even the failure of the United States to experience the early economic depression which the ravens of the Red Square have been predicting with such complacent confidence since hostilities ceased would have deep and important repercussions throughout the Communist world.

By the same token, exhibitions of indecision, disunity and internal disintegration within this country have an exhilarating effect on the whole Communist movement. At each evidence of these tendencies, a thrill of hope and excitement goes through the Communist world; a new jauntiness can be noted in the Moscow tread; new groups of foreign supporters climb on to what they can only view as the band wagon of international politics; and Russian pressure increases all along the line in international affairs.

It would be an exaggeration to say that American behavior unassisted and alone could exercise a power of life and death over the Communist movement and bring about the early fall of Soviet power in Russia. But the United States has it in its power to increase enormously the strains under which Soviet policy must operate, to force upon the Kremlin a far greater degree of moderation and circumspection than it has had to observe in recent years, and in this way to promote tendencies which must eventually find their outlet in either the break-up or the gradual mellowing of Soviet power. For no mystical, Messianic movement—and particularly not that of the Kremlin—can face frustration indefinitely without eventually adjusting itself in one way or another to the logic of that state of affairs.

Thus the decision will really fall in large measure in this country itself. The issue of Soviet-American relations is in essence a test of the over-all worth of the United States as a nation among nations. To avoid destruction the United States need only measure up to its own best traditions and prove itself worthy of preservation as a great nation.

Surely, there was never a fairer test of national quality than this. In the light of these circumstances, the thoughtful observer of Russian-American relations will find no cause for complaint in the Kremlin's challenge to American society. He will rather experience a certain gratitude to a Providence which, by providing the American people with this implacable challenge, has made their entire security as a nation dependent on their pulling themselves together and accepting the responsibilities of moral and political leadership that history plainly intended them to bear.

4. THE CHALLENGE TO AMERICANS[1]

By Henry L. Stimson

EDITORS' NOTE.—Henry L. Stimson (p. 337) continued his interest in public policy after his resignation from the War Department in 1945. In addition to this article, he has written other articles on public policy and his important autobiography, *On Active Service.*

We Americans today face a challenging opportunity, perhaps the greatest ever offered to a single nation. It is nothing less than a chance to use our full strength for the peace and freedom of the world. This opportunity comes when many of us are confused and unready. Only two years ago we triumphantly ended the greatest war in history. Most of us then looked forward eagerly to the relative relaxation of peace. Reluctantly we have now come to understand that victory and peace are not synonymous. Over large areas of the world we have nothing better than armed truce; in some places there is open fighting; everywhere men know that there is yet no stable settlement. Close on the heels of victory has loomed a new world crisis.

Particularly to Americans the appearance of disquieting facts and possibilities has been upsetting. We are having our first experience of constant, full-scale activity in world politics. Other nations have lived for years as principals in the give-and-take of diplomacy. Until now we have been, except in wartime, on the fringe. It is no wonder that, when suddenly placed in the center of the alarms and excursions of international affairs, we are abnormally sensitive. And, of course, it does not help to find ourselves selected as chief target for the abuse and opposition of a very bad-mannered group of men who take their orders from the Kremlin. It is not surprising, then, that many of us are confused and unhappy about our foreign relations, and

that some are tempted to seek refuge from their confusion either in retreat to isolationism or in suggested solutions whose simplicity is only matched by their folly. In the main, our difficulties arise from unwillingness to face reality.

It must be admitted that the elements of the new unrest appear to be unusually complex and trying. The war-shattered world must be rebuilt; the problem of atomic energy insistently demands solution; the present policy of Russia must be frustrated. But it is my belief that the American people have it well within their power to meet and resolve all of these problems. The essential test is one of will and understanding. We require a skilful foreign policy, of course, but we may have confidence that the farsighted and experienced men now in charge of our State Department know how to frame a policy. In outline the President and the Secretary of State have already set their course. They can develop their policy with success, however, only if they have the understanding support, on basic principles, of the American people.

First, and most important, Americans must now understand that the United States has become, for better or worse, a wholly committed member of the world community. This has not happened by conscious choice; but it is a plain fact, and our only choice is whether or not to face it. For more than a generation the increasing interrelation of American life with the life of the world has out-paced our thinking and our policy; our refusal to catch up

1. Henry L. Stimson, "The Challenge to Americans," *Foreign Affairs*, XXVI (October, 1947), 5–14.

with reality during these years was the major source of our considerable share of the responsibility for the catastrophe of World War II.

It is the first condition of effective foreign policy that this nation put away forever any thought that America can again be an island to herself. No private program and no public policy, in any sector of our national life, can now escape from the compelling fact that if it is not framed with reference to the world, it is framed with perfect futility. This would be true if there were no such thing as nuclear fission, and if all the land eastward from Poland to the Pacific were under water. Atomic energy and Soviet Russia are merely the two most conspicuous present demonstrations of what we have at stake in world affairs. The attitude of isolationism—political or economic—must die; in all its many forms the vain hope that we can live alone must be abandoned.

As a corollary to this first great principle, it follows that we shall be wholly wrong if we attempt to set a maximum or margin to our activity as members of the world. The only question we can safely ask today is whether in any of our actions on the world stage we are doing enough. In American policy toward the world there is no place for grudging or limited participation, and any attempt to cut our losses by setting bounds to our policy can only turn us backward onto the deadly road toward self-defeating isolation.

Our stake in the peace and freedom of the world is not a limited liability. Time after time in other years we have tried to solve our foreign problems with halfway measures, acting under the illusion that we could be partly in the world and partly irresponsible. Time after time our Presidents and Secretaries of State have been restrained, by their own fears or by public opinion, from effective action. It should by now be wholly clear that only failure, and its follower, war, can result from such efforts at a cheap solution.

We have fresh before us the contrary example of our magnificent success in wartime, when we have not stopped to count the cost. I have served as Secretary of State in a time of frightened isolationism, and as Secretary of War in a time of brave and generous action. I know the withering effect of limited commitments, and I know the regenerative power of full action. I know, too, that America can afford it—as who does not know it, in the face of our record in the last seven years?

It is altogether fitting and proper, of course, that we should not waste our substance in activity without result. It is also evident that we cannot do everything we would like to do. But it would be shriveling timidity for America to refuse to play to the full her present necessary part in the world. And the certain penalty for such timidity would be failure.

The troubles of Europe and Asia are not "other people's troubles"; they are ours. The world is full of friends and enemies; it is full of warring ideas; but there are no mere "foreigners," no merely "foreign" ideologies, no merely "foreign" dangers, any more. Foreign affairs are now our most intimate domestic concern. All men, good or bad, are now our neighbors. All ideas dwell among us.

A second principle, and one which requires emphasis as a necessary complement to any policy of full participation, is that we are forced to act in the world as it is, and not in the world as we wish it were, or as we would like it to become. It is a world in which we are only one of many peoples and in which our basic principles of life are not shared by all our neighbors. It has been one of the more dangerous aspects of our internationalism in past years that too often it was accompanied by the curious assumption that the world would overnight become good and clean and peaceful everywhere if only America would lead the way. The most elementary experience of human affairs should show us all how naïve and dangerous a view that is.

The most conspicuous present examples of this sort of thinking are to be found among those who refuse to recognize the strong probability that one of our great and powerful neighbor nations is at present controlled by men who are convinced that the very course of history is set against democracy and freedom, as we understand those words. A very large part of what I believe to be the mistaken thinking done by my friend Henry Wallace about Soviet Russia results simply from a good-hearted insistence that nobody can dislike us if we try to like them.

We have been very patient with the Soviet Government, and very hopeful of its good intentions. I have been among those who shared in these hopes and counseled this patience. The magnificent and loyal war effort of the Russian people, and the great successful efforts at friendliness made during the war by President Roosevelt, gave us good reason for hope. I have believed—and I still believe—that we must show good faith in all our dealings with the Russians, and that only by so doing can we leave the door open for Russian good faith toward us. I cannot too strongly express my regret that since the early spring of 1945—even before the death of Mr. Roosevelt—the Soviet Government has steadily pursued an obstructive and unfriendly course. It has been our hope that the Russians would choose to be our friends; it was and is our conviction that such a choice would be to their advantage. But, for the time being, at least, those who determine Russian policy have chosen otherwise, and their choice has been slavishly followed by Communists everywhere.

No sensible American can now ignore this fact, and those who now choose to travel in company with American Communists are very clearly either knaves or fools. This is a judgment which I make reluctantly, but there is no help for it. I have often said that the surest way to make a man trustworthy is to trust him. But I must add that this does not always apply to a man who is determined to make you his dupe. Before we can make friends with the Russians, their leaders will have to be convinced that they have nothing to gain, and everything to lose, by acting on the assumption that our society is dying and that our principles are outworn. Americans who think they can make common cause with present-day Communism are living in a world that does not exist.

They are not alone. An equal and opposite error is made by those who argue that Americans by strong-arm methods, perhaps even by a "preventive war," can and should rid the world of the Communist menace. I cannot believe that this view is widely held. For it is worse than nonsense; it results from a hopeless misunderstanding of the geographical and military situation, and a cynical incomprehension of what the people of the world will tolerate from *any* nation. Worst of all, this theory indicates a totally wrong assessment of the basic attitudes and motives of the American people. Even if it were true that the United States now had the opportunity to establish forceful hegemony throughout the world, we could not possibly take that opportunity without deserting our true inheritance. Americans as conquerors would be tragically miscast.

The world's affairs cannot be simplified by eager words. We cannot take refuge from reality in the folly of black-and-white solutions.

In dealing with the Russians, both uncritical trust and unmitigated belligerence are impossible. There is a middle course. We do not yet know surely in what proportion unreasonable fears and twisted hopes are at the root of the perverted policy now followed by the Kremlin. Assuming both to be involved, we must disarm the fears and disappoint the hopes. We must no longer let the tide of Soviet expansion cheaply roll into the empty place left by war, and yet we must make it perfectly clear that we are not ourselves expansionist. Our task is to help threatened peoples to help themselves.

This is not easy. It is quite possible, indeed, that the blind reaction of some anti-Communist governments may succeed to some extent in nullifying our labors. We must make every effort to prevent such a result. Success in this task depends so much on men and circumstances that I do not venture to prescribe a theoretical solution. It is an undertaking that demands a bold and active policy, combined with skilful and understanding execution. In such an undertaking, it is only the exceptionally well-informed who may properly give advice from the sidelines.

But our main answer to the Russians is not negative, nor is it in any sense anti-Russian. Our central task in dealing with the Kremlin is to demonstrate beyond the possibility of misunderstanding that freedom and prosperity, hand in hand, can be stably sustained in the western democratic world. This would be our greatest task even if no Soviet problem existed, and to the Soviet threat it is our best response.

Soviet intransigence is based in very large part on the hope and belief that all non-Communist systems are doomed. Soviet policy aims to help them die. We must hope that time and the success of freedom and democracy in the western world will convince both the Soviet leaders and the Russian people now behind them that our system is here to stay. This may not be possible; dictators do not easily change their hearts, and the modern armaments they possess may make it hard for their people to force such a change. Rather than be persuaded of their error, the Soviet leaders might in desperation resort to war, and against that possibility we have to guard by maintaining our present military advantages. We must never forget that while peace is a joint responsibility, the decision for war can be made by a single Power; our military strength must be maintained as a standing discouragement to aggression.

I do not, however, expect the Russians to make war. I do not share the gloomy fear of some that we are now engaged in the preliminaries of an inevitable conflict. Even the most repressive dictatorship is not perfectly unassailable from within, and the most frenzied fanaticism is never unopposed. Whatever the ideological bases of Soviet policy, it seems clear that some at least of the leaders of Russia are men who have a marked respect for facts. We must make it wholly evident that a nonaggressive Russia will have nothing to fear from us. We must make it clear, too, that the western non-Communist world is going to survive in growing economic and political stability. If we can do this, then slowly—but perhaps less slowly than we now believe—the Russian leaders may either change their minds or lose their jobs.

The problem of Russia is thus reduced to a question of our own fitness to survive. I do not mean to belittle the Communist challenge. I only mean that the essential question is one which we should have to answer if there were not a Communist alive. Can we make freedom and prosperity real in the present world? If we can, Communism is no threat. If not, with or without Communism, our own civilization would ultimately fail.

The immediate and pressing challenge to our belief in freedom and prosperity is in western Europe. Here are people who have traditionally shared our faith in human dignity. These are the nations by whose citizens our land was settled and in whose tradition our civilization is rooted. They are threatened by Communism—but only because of the dark shadows cast by the hopelessness, hunger and fear that have been the aftermath of the Nazi war. Communism or no Communism, menace or no menace, it is our simple duty as neighbors to take a generous part in helping these great peoples to help themselves.

The reconstruction of western Europe is a task from which Americans can decide to stand apart only if they wish to desert every principle by which they claim to live. And, as a decision of policy, it would be the most tragic mistake in our history. We must take part in this work; we must take our full part; we must be sure that we do enough.

I must add that I believe we should act quickly. The penalty of delay in reconstruction is to increase the size of the job and to multiply difficulties. We require a prompt and large-scale program. The government must lead the way, but we who are private citizens must support that leadership as men in all parties supported help to our Allies in 1941. The sooner we act, the surer our success—and the less it will cost us.

The need of Europe is a challenge partly to our generosity and partly to our good sense. We have ample justification for action on either ground. It is an opportunity for the best that is in America, a chance for us to show the practical idealism on which we have with reason learned to pride ourselves.

This is the way to disappoint the Russians. But it is not anti-Russian. This is a course which must be followed not because we fear the Russians, but simply because we have confidence in ourselves.

As we take part in the rebuilding of Europe, we must remember that we are building world peace, not an American peace. Freedom demands tolerance, and many Americans have much to learn about the variety of forms which free societies may take. There are Europeans, just as there are Americans, who do not believe in freedom, but they are in a minority, and—as the Editor of this review so clearly explained in its last issue—we shall not be able to separate the sheep from the goats merely by asking whether they believe in our particular economic and political system. Our coöperation with the free men of Europe must be founded on the basic principles of human dignity, and not on any theory that their way to freedom must be exactly the same as ours. We cannot ask that Europe be rebuilt in the American im-

age. If we join in the task of reconstruction with courage, confidence and goodwill, we shall learn—and teach—a lot. But we must start with a willingness to understand.

The reconstruction of western Europe is the immediate task. With it we have, of course, a job at home. We must maintain freedom and prosperity here. This is a demanding task in itself, and its success or failure will largely determine all our other efforts. If it is true that our prosperity depends on that of the world, it is true also that the whole world's economic future hangs on our success at home. We must go forward to new levels of peacetime production, and to do this we must all of us avoid the pitfalls of laziness, fear and irresponsibility. Neither real profits nor real wages can be permanently sustained—and still less increased—by anything but rising production.

But I see no reason for any man to face the American future with any other feeling than one of confident hope. However grave our problems, and however difficult their solution, I do not believe that this country is ready to acknowledge that failure is foreordained. It is our task to disprove and render laughable that utterly insulting theory. Our future does not depend on the tattered forecasts of Karl Marx. It depends on us.

In counseling against policies which ignore the facts of the world as it is, I do not, of course, mean to argue that we can for a moment forget the nature of our final goal.

Lasting peace and freedom cannot be achieved until the world finds a way toward the necessary government of the whole. It is important that this should be widely understood, and efforts to spread such understanding are commendable. The riven atom, uncontrolled, can be only a growing menace to us all, and there can be no final safety, short of full control throughout the world. Nor can we hope to realize the vast potential wealth of atomic energy until it is disarmed and rendered harmless. Upon us, as the people who first harnessed and made use of this force, there rests a grave and continuing responsibility for leadership in turning it toward life, not death.

But we cannot have world government or atomic control by wishing for them, and we cannot have them, in any meaningful sense, without Russia. If in response to our best effort there comes no answer but an everlasting "NO," then we must go to work in other fields to change the frame of mind that caused that answer. We cannot ignore it.

It is a part of any practical policy that it must keep our principles out in the open. In the imperfect, veto-ridden United Nations there is now incarnate the hope of people everywhere that this world may become one in spirit as it is in fact. No misconceived idea of "realism" should induce us to ignore this living hope or abate in its pursuit. We should be foremost among those who seek to make the United Nations stronger; if the Russians will not help us, let them be forced to make their opposition clear. As a starting-point, we might simply ask for a clear ruling that there shall be no veto on the right of investigation and report.

Because the United Nations can at present be hamstrung by the obstruction of a single major Power, we will probably find ourselves sometimes forced to act outside its system. So far as possible, we should avoid this course, and we should so conduct our operations as to make it wholly clear to all the world that it is not we who choose to make the United Nations weak, and that when we act outside it we are still acting in harmony with its declared objectives. It must be our constant endeavor to conduct our policy with full and deep respect for our signed and ratified adherence to this new league which we have done so much to build. Our insistence upon world coöperation must be unremitting; only so can we deserve and win the confidence of those who, caring nothing for

the politics of power, now see only the over-riding need for peace. Both policy and principle bind us to the support of the United Nations.

It is clear, then, that in this country we are still free to maintain our freedom. We are called to an unprecedented effort of coöperation with our friends in every country. Immediately, we are called to act in the rebuilding of civilization in that part of the world which is closest to us in history, politics and economics. We are required to think of our prosperity, our policy and our first principles as indivisibly connected with the facts of life everywhere. We must put away forever the childishness of parochial hopes and un-American fears.

We need not suppose that the task we face is easy, or that all our undertakings will be quickly successful. The construction of a stable peace is a longer, more complex and greater task than the relatively simple work of war-making. But the nature of the challenge is the same. The issue before us today is at least as significant as the one which we finally faced in 1941. By a long series of mistakes and failures, dating back over a span of more than 20 years, we had in 1941 let it become too late to save ourselves by peaceful methods; in the end we had to fight. This is not true today. If we act now, with vigor and understanding, with steadiness and without fear, we can peacefully safeguard our freedom. It is only if we turn our backs, in mistaken complacence or mistrusting timidity, that war may again become inevitable.

How soon this nation will fully understand the size and nature of its present mission, I do not dare to say. But I venture to assert that in very large degree the future of mankind depends on the answers to this question. And I am confident that if the issues are clearly presented, the American people will give the right answer. Surely there is here a fair and tempting challenge to all Americans, and especially to the nation's leaders, in and out of office.

5. SOVIET FOREIGN POLICY AND ITS IMPLICATIONS[1]

By Frederick L. Schuman

EDITORS' NOTE.—Frederick L. Shuman was born in Chicago in 1904. After receiving his Ph.D. from the University of Chicago in 1927, he joined the political science department of that university. In 1936 he became a member of the faculty of Williams College, where today he is Woodrow Wilson Professor of Government. During the war (1942–43) he was a political analyst of foreign broadcasting intelligence for the Federal Communication Commission. Among his many books on international relations are *International Politics*, published in 1933 and now in its third edition, and *Soviet Politics*, published in 1946.

Mr. Chairman, Fellow-Citizens, and Fellow-Chicagoans:

I take my text today from my usual source. "Now," said Alice, "if you will only attend, Kitty, and not talk so much, I'll tell you all my ideas about Looking-glass House. First, there's the room you can see through the glass—that's just the same as our drawing-room, only the things go the other way. I can see all of it when I get upon a chair—all but the bit just behind the fireplace. Oh! I do so wish I could see that bit!"

Like Alice, we are living in two worlds, and since the two are really one—although we cannot possibly now admit that—we are also, like Alice, somewhat schizophrenic. Lewis Carroll says little about what the people beyond the looking glass thought of our world. Alice found their world fascinating and beautiful, if somewhat topsy-turvy. But we and the Russians, as we look at one another in the mirror of our fears and hates, see only evil. We see a menacing monster aiming at dominating the world. We believe it to be Russia, but it may perhaps be a reflection of ourselves. The Russians see a monstrous

menace aiming at world domination. They believe it to be America, but it may possibly be a reflection of themselves. And like apes, we bellow at the image in the mirror, and we may well break our heads by some day charging at the enemy through the looking glass.

Intolerance and fanaticism are on the march. Westbrook Pegler, in his inimitably genial way, has predicted "strange, dramatic things" in America, such as concentration camps for all actors, writers, lawyers, teachers, labor leaders and speakers, including Henry Wallace, who have "indicated a tolerance for Russia." Well, I expect to be there. I'll see Henry, and I'll even see Bertie McCormick there—if he doesn't get killed first in his new atomic bomb shelter under the Tribune Tower.

I am reminded by the spirit of the times of the words written by a great American almost fifty years ago, on the eve of another war. He wrote:

The loud little handful—as usual—will shout for the war. The pulpit will—warily and cautiously—object—at first; the great, big, dull bulk of the nation will rub its sleepy eyes and try to make out why there should be a war and will say, earnestly and indignantly, "It is unjust and dishonorable and there is no necessity for it." Then the handful will shout louder. . . . And now the whole nation—pulpit and all

1. Frederick L. Schuman, *Soviet Foreign Policy and Its Implications* (Chicago, 1947), pp. 1–21. By permission of the Chicago Council on Foreign Relations.

—will take up the war-cry and shout itself hoarse, and mob any honest man who ventures to open his mouth, and presently such mouths will cease to open. Next the statesmen will invent cheap lies, putting the blame upon the nation that is attacked, and every man will be glad of those conscience-soothing falsities . . . and . . . will by and by convince himself that the war is just and will thank God for the better sleep he enjoys after this process of grotesque self-deception.

Those bitter words were written by Mark Twain. He saw nothing funny in the resolve of political demagogues and yellow press magnates to plunge the nation into war. He would see nothing funny in such efforts now, but only unspeakable tragedy.

No sane discussion of Soviet foreign policy is possible, as the Chairman has suggested, within a context of "we" or "they," where "we" means virtue and "they" means sin. And since most Americans, like most Russians, are now completely committed to this dichotomy on both sides of the looking glass, I have little hope that any sanity in the matter is still possible. Nevertheless, I shall venture upon a brief analysis of Soviet foreign policy and American-Soviet relations, which may still offer a slight hope.

If one asks how did these two giant powers, once strangers at opposite ends of the earth, and more recently allies in a desperate common struggle for survival, become rivals and potential enemies, the short-run answer is rather simple—although relatively few people seem to be much concerned with it. It has very little to do with conflicting ideologies or social systems or with liberty vs. totalitarianism, communism vs. capitalism, Soviet imperialism vs. the "American Century." These symbols are but the shadows of reality, no matter how much we mistake them for the substance. The reality itself with which we are concerned is a problem of power politics, and it can be understood only within the context of power politics.

My thesis, in brief, is this: Every Great Power in a world community lacking government inevitably seeks to maximize its own power and to minimize the power of potential enemies and dangerous rivals. During the past decade the greatest threat to both America and Russia was Nazi Germany. Against that threat, America and Russia almost inevitably became allies, even as Rome and Carthage were originally allies against King Pyrrhus of Epirus, and Athens and Sparta were once allies against Persia. But in the common enterprise of liquidating a common menace, the Soviet Union played a very much larger military role than did America and Britain. "It is the Russian army," said Winston Churchill in the summer of 1944, "that has done the main work of tearing the guts out of the German army." Churchill doubtless regretted that fact, since it was he who urged, in vain, upon Roosevelt and Marshall a strategy of attack on Germany through Italy and the Balkans, partly as a means of preventing Soviet expansion. As matters turned out, it was the Soviet army that drove the Nazis out of Warsaw, Bucharest, Sofia, Belgrade, Budapest, Vienna, Prague and Berlin.

The Soviet Union, having by a very wide margin paid the largest share of the cost of victory, and by far the most tragic and ghastly share, decided to reap the fruits of victory. That decision, as I see it, was not a product of Russian perversity or Slavic greed or Bolshevik sin. It was a product of a calculation of national self-interest, which is the prime motivation of all Great Powers in our civilization, including the United States.

Moscow's definition of victory was quite simple—perhaps too simple. Victory over Hitler was to mean the end of Fascism everywhere, and the reduction of Germany to permanent military impotence. Victory was to mean a new pan-Slavism and the end of a thousand years of Slavic disunity in the face of Teutonic, Magyar and Turkish aggression. Victory was to mean a reversal of the results of Russian defeat and weakness in 1904 and

1905, and again between 1916 and 1921, and hence the reincorporation into Muscovy of most of the territories then lost, with the exception of Finland and Poland proper. Victory was to mean the organization of all of Slavic Europe, including its Hungarian and Rumanian enclaves, into a security area under Muscovite direction.

All of these objectives had, and still have, almost nothing to do with Marxism, but only with the historical experiences of Slavdom and with the imperatives of power politics. The rulers of Russia, I believe, would have defined the interests of their state in almost exactly the same terms if, instead of being Marxists they had been Methodists, Moslems, Mormons, or Mennonites, though perhaps in this case we should fear and hate them less. In striving for these objectives the Soviet Government practiced what it regarded as moderation. I grant that Soviet definitions of moderation are often equivalent to American definitions of bloody murder, and *vice versa*, depending upon whose ox is being gored. But in speaking of Soviet moderation, I mean that the U.S.S.R. in 1944 and 1945 had sufficient military power, if it chose to use it, to extend the Communist ideology and the Soviet economic and social system in undiluted form over all of the border states and into all of the Balkans. The men of the Kremlin refrained from so doing in the expectation that self-restraint would make possible a workable post-war compromise and balance of power with Britain and America.

Stalin made a bargain with Roosevelt and Churchill at Yalta in February, 1945. It was foreshadowed at Moscow and Teheran in the autumn of 1943. It was completed at San Francisco and Potsdam between April and July of 1945. Apart from its important Asiatic provisions, which I haven't time to mention even, the essence of the bargain was that America and Britain sanctioned Soviet annexation of northern East Prussia, they accepted the Curzon and Oder-Neisse lines as new frontiers for Poland, they abandoned the anti-Soviet Polish and Yugoslav governments-in-exile, they accepted Soviet views of territorial and political settlement in eastern Europe and the Balkans. They definitely gave Moscow the impression—despite controversial phrases about democratic governments, free elections, and suppression of all remnants of Fascism—that they acknowledged Soviet hegemony north of Greece and east of the Stettin-Trieste line. They also agreed to a world organization, the central principle of which was to be a concert of the Great Powers, all of which would act together, none of which was to coerce another, each of which was to have the power to prevent action against it by the others. The *quid pro quo* was that the Kremlin acknowledged Anglo-American hegemony in central and western Germany, in Italy, in the Mediterranean and in Greece, where the bitter civil war in the winter of 1944–45, precipitated by British military support of the Greek monarchists, evoked protest from Washington but not a word of protest from Moscow, and where at that time not an iota of aid to the Partisans came from Albania or Yugoslavia or Bulgaria.

Here, then, was a formula for European and world equilibrium among the Big Three which promised stability and peace. Stability and peace we should doubtless have had if the Yalta-Potsdam bargain had been kept. It was not kept, and because it was not kept we are now on the road to war. Some members of the State Department, if you now ask them, will tell you that no bargain was ever made. Others will argue that the bargain was a mistake on Roosevelt's part, that it should not have been made, and that all efforts now, as Senator Taft recently argued, to undo the bargain are justified. Still others, including a good many Congressmen and journalists, want to have their cake and eat it too. They say there wasn't any bargain and that the Soviet leaders are unmitigated scoundrels for having broken it. All of you know, of course, since you have heard it and read it on the highest authority a thousand times and ten thousand times, that whether there was a bargain or not the Soviet Union broke it at once by enslaving the satellites, crushing democracy, spreading Communism, reaching out greedily in all directions, and undertaking by force and fraud to conquer all of the great globe itself.

Now anyone who throws doubt on this familiar solution of the new problem of war-guilt is currently regarded as an appropriate subject for a psychiatrist or the F.B.I. or the House Un-American Committee. Yet that is precisely what I must do, and you will have to think of me what you like. If you will look into the documents and the dates and facts, which of course nobody ever bothers to do, you will discover that the Yalta and Potsdam conferences framed what looks like, and was then currently interpreted as, an accord at the very top level; and that in the spring and summer of '45 the Soviet Union did not break the bargain. It did not impose Communist regimes on any eastern European state. It did not make any political or territorial claims anywhere in the Anglo-American sphere, and it most certainly did not launch any program of communization or conquest of Europe.

The later breakdown of friendly relations is not exclusively a Soviet responsibility. It is in part an American responsibility, and in saying this I am fully aware of the fact that Soviet diplomats are most difficult to deal with, that they are shamefully lacking in any appreciation of American opinion, and that some of them, like some of ours, delight in obfuscation and obstructionism, and cherish visions of limitless power which are utterly mad and maddening. But let me reconstruct in a few words the beginning of the breakdown of the bargain.

On the 18th day of August, 1945, four months after the death of Roosevelt, twelve days after the first use of the atomic bomb in war, and four days after V-J Day, Secretary of State Byrnes, seconded two days later by Bevin, opened a major diplomatic campaign which has gone on almost uninterruptedly ever since. The ostensible purpose of the campaign was to promote democracy in eastern Europe. That purpose, soberly considered, was doubtless noble in motive, but it is also, as Alice would say, "curiouser and curiouser." The actual purpose of the campaign, as Sir Henry Maitland Wilson, a blunt and honest soldier, said in September of 1945, was to undermine and terminate the political and military power of the Soviet Union in the Balkans. During the intervening two years the American and British notes of protest about the suppression of democracy in Bulgaria, Rumania, Hungary and Poland have been almost as numerous as the sands of the sea or the leaves of trees that fall every autumn on the barren ground.

The most important thing, I suggest to you, about this campaign is that it has failed completely of its purpose, both its ostensible purpose and its actual purpose. It has produced not more democracy, but less, and not less Soviet influence, but more, on the other side of the looking glass. The blessings of the State Department and Downing Street on opposition leaders in these areas have been a kiss of death. American spokesmen, including the President, have shouted "tyranny," "outrage," "travesty," "murder," with the result that all of their friends in eastern Europe have developed the habit of disappearing. This proves Russian wickedness. This also proves, I submit, American political ineptitude.

How can we account for so abysmal a failure of American policy? If we shared the cynical views of the vitriolic Mr. Vishinsky, we might assume that the objective was not to rescue the oppressed from their oppressors, but to prepare a plausible moral pretext for World War III. But perish the thought! In government, as in all things human, stupidity is much more common than deviltry. Government by generals and bankers, I very much fear, is not and cannot be government characterized by very much statesmanship, because statesmanship requires a grasp of the relationship between political means and ends, a sense of the facts of social change and political power, a knowledge of alternatives and consequences in world politics, a feeling for destiny, a comprehension of the fate of man. And I am very much afraid that these things are beyond the purview of most of the professional soldiers and investment bankers who have been making our national policies since Roosevelt died. These little men have preferred to revert to a kind of primitive tribalism, to repudiate Yalta, to challenge Russia in the name of moral platitudes, to pursue fatuously the will-of-the-wisp of Balkan democracy, to make diplomatic protests, to utter appeals to the gallery, to preach a new crusade against Communism —all to no effect whatever except to sow the seeds of probably irreparable tragedy.

In the face of this dismal and pathetic failure of leadership the views of George H. Earle, former Governor of Pennsylvania, American Minister to Austria and Bulgaria and a confirmed Russophobe as you know, assume the dignity of realism. Arriving in Boston in March of 1946, Mr. Earle declared that "The United States should deliver an ultimatum to Russia to get back to their own territory and if they refuse I would use the atomic bomb on them while we have it and before they get it." And a little while later Mr. Earle said that "America must prepare to wipe out every city, town and village in Russia." Mr. Earle is a realist. He is entirely right. If the United States is determined to push Russia out of Eastern Europe and the Balkans for reasons of national self-interest— which nobody has ever explained—then our government obviously should not write diplomatic notes. It should threaten Moscow with an atomic Blitzkrieg. Such a decision might have in the past, and might even now, put an end to the Soviet hegemony over eastern Europe and the Balkans which Stalin believes Roosevelt

and Churchill accepted at Yalta. I say "might" because I am not sure that the Kremlin would yield to such an ultimatum. But American diplomats, unfortunately, are addicted to self-righteousness as much as to delusions of grandeur and ignorance of *Realpolitik*. The Kremlin is fully aware of that fact. The members of the Politburo have never feared, and do not now fear, any such American ultimatum. Therefore the whole program of evicting the Soviet Union from eastern Europe and the Balkans was doomed to failure from the beginning. And the more flagrant and obvious has become the failure, the more insistently and passionately have the little men in Washington pursued the program.

All psychologists know that failure breeds frustration, and frustration breeds aggression. After eighteen months of failure President Truman and his advisers dreamed up a new departure last March. The so-called Truman Doctrine was promulgated, appropriately, a year after Mr. Truman applauded Mr. Churchill's appeal in Fulton, Missouri, for a grand alliance against Russia. The U.N., of course, was completely by-passed. Under the Truman-Marshall dispensation the U.N. is regarded as a minor division of the American State Department, to be ignored when inconvenient and to be used, when convenient, to mobilize against Russia the mythical entity called "world public opinion" and to line up against Russia all the votes of all the governments of all the world which look to America for handouts. This great crusade to "contain" so-called Soviet aggression, rightly described by Walter Lippmann as a "booby trap," is now in its sixth month. Don't look now, but it is also a failure. Turkey is less secure than ever, less democratic than ever, and wants more American money than ever. Greece has become a bottomless pit. Into the Greek rabbithole have gone a billion dollars since liberation. The government in Athens complains that it isn't enough, it needs a hundred million more at once, and still more later. There were only 13,000 armed guerrillas resisting the Athens government last March, when President Truman came to the rescue. The tiny Greek army of 130,000 men was quite incapable of coping with them, since in these matters a margin of 10-to-1 is really nothing. Therefore, the Greek army must be doubled at our expense. But now there are 25,000 armed rebels resisting the Athens government. So, you see, there is no end to the process. I suggest that if and when American troops go into action in Greece, it is quite possible that there will be 50,000 armed rebels, or 100,000 armed rebels. The prospects are quite jolly.

The Truman Doctrine is perhaps an admirable device to win the election of '48, since all Republican leaders, without exception, feel obliged to shout "Me, too! Down with Communism! Me, too!" which, of course, spells the reelection of the Administration in power. But the Truman Doctrine, I greatly fear, makes no sense whatever in world politics, except to convince the Russians that the United States is preparing to attack them.

It has, therefore, had to be supplemented by the Marshall Plan, the exact import of which is very obscure. This is not strange, because in fact there is no Plan, and Marshall had very little to do with it, and the whole thing is a kind of accident. For a brief moment Molotov thought that this represented a change of American policy. Here, too, the U.N. was completely by-passed. And it soon became apparent to Moscow, Warsaw and Prague, that the chief purpose, if any, of the Marshall Plan, was to restore Germany, in violation of the Yalta and Potsdam agreements, as a bulwark against Russia. Molotov went home and the western European governments are left in the ignominious position of saying to Washington "Save us from Communism. We want 30 billion dollars. But Will Clayton says that's too much, so we will settle for 22 billions, if you hurry."

The harsh and outrageous judgments

which I have just expressed—insofar as they have any validity—may help you to understand some aspects of the Soviet response to the Truman-Marshall challenge. I am sure that you have been surprised and angered by that response. You will remember that two years ago—one year ago—six months ago—all sorts of eminent and highly respected Americans, including probably many who have spoken from this platform, were assuring you very earnestly: "Get tough with Russia and the Russians will back down and do what we want them to do, as soon as we decide what that is. We don't want to fight, but by jingo if we do we've got the bomb, we've got the planes, we've got the money too!" So it follows clearly that if we flex our muscles and brandish our might the Russians will quiver and quake, shiver and shake, and abjectly do what we say.

The Russians, of course, do nothing of the kind, as anybody would know who knew anything whatever about Russian psychology, Slavic psychology, Soviet psychology, Communist psychology. How can we have so soon forgotten the Battle for Moscow, the sieges of Leningrad and Sevastopol, the epic of Stalingrad? Those who get tough with the Russians, from Teutonic knights, Frederick the Great and Napoleon to Churchill, Mussolini, Hitler and Truman, invariably discover that the Russians are tougher than they. At no point whatever have the Russians backed down before American threats. At every point alas—and I deplore this—they have struck back. If 20 vetoes are not enough to prevent Washington from using the U.N. as a tool of anti-Soviet diplomacy, Gromyko will be happy to supply 30 or 40 vetoes, or as many vetoes as you like. If sympathy and modest aid to the Greek rebels infuriates the Truman Administration, the Kremlin and its allies will be happy to supply large-scale aid. If Soviet non-intervention in the Chinese civil war is to be accompanied by continuing, albeit ambivalent, American aid to Chiang, Moscow will be delighted to supply a little of the "non-intervention" of the type practiced in the Spanish civil war. And if America is determined, through Norman Schwarzkopf, George Allen, and the oil companies, to maintain the Anglo-American monopoly of Persian oil and to make Iran a base against Russia, the Russians will be quite willing and able to make threats and stir up unrest.

All this, of course, is a monstrous exhibition of intolerable and contumacious insolence. Because we all know that while it is virtuous for us to act in terms of national self-interest, however strangely defined, it is indescribably sinful for the Russians to do likewise. In terms of the old French proverb, "This animal is wicked: when attacked, he defends himself."

How, then, can the struggle be ended? I have no formula to offer. To offer a formula now would be academic, and to be "academic" in America means to be irrelevant, trivial, inconsequential and crackpot. I offer you only a few predictions. I beg you not to believe them, but I beg you also to remember them in years ahead—if you're still alive. There will be no Soviet capitulation to the United States. There will be no change in the Kremlin's view that Soviet safety depends upon Muscovite hegemony over eastern Europe and the Balkans. Should that hegemony, by some improbable miracle of a return to common sense, be acknowledged by America and no longer challenged from Washington, then it is possible in time—I should say probable—that it would be exercised less nakedly and brutally and that Moscow might cease to challenge Anglo-American interests in the Mediterranean, western Europe, eastern Asia. But I say that apart from this one prospect (which, however, is important and hopeful), there will be no change in Soviet policy as a result of American pressure. The greater the pressure, the greater will be Soviet resistance. If, then, those Americans have their way who say that war is inevitable unless there is a change of Soviet policy, then undoubtedly there will ultimately be war.

Despite America's overwhelming material and military superiority, America will not win that war. In the course of it America will renounce its heritage and embrace Fascist intolerance and totalitarianism. Neither will the Soviet Union win that war, though its armies occupy all of Europe and Asia. Its cities will be vaporized and their inhabitants incinerated by the new crusaders for Christianity and capitalism. If you believe that American cities will not be vaporized and their inhabitants will not be incinerated, then you are living in a dream-world which will turn into a ghastly nightmare. Even Colonel McCormick knows better. In such a struggle the U.S.S.R. will lose whatever potentialities for freedom and democracy may exist in Soviet society (and I happen to believe that some exist), just as America will lose its legacy of liberty. England will be neutral. The Vatican will be neutral. Canada will try to be neutral. In Germany, France, Italy and Spain, India, the Near East and China, there will be savage civil strife before these lands are occupied by Soviet armies. There may again, later, be savage civil strife when American expeditionary forces attempt to make landings.

No one will win this war. With despair in their hearts and anguish in their souls, the atomic scientists have been trying to tell us for two years there must never be another war. But we do not listen, because we love our hates and our fears too much. Therefore, the war may come and at its end, if it ever ends, there will be no issues whatever of freedom vs. tyranny, liberty vs. totalitarianism, capitalism vs. communism. There will be in the end only the dark silence of the dead and blasted cities, and the laments and the violence of miserable bands of refugees in the countryside, seeking in vain a haven which is forever lost. This may be our destiny.

But I submit it is not inevitably our destiny. The final choice, I believe, is happily still before us. The great crisis lies in the future. Some time in 1948, or 1949 at the latest, that crisis will come. It will come with the convergence, or arrival in series, of three events which are now as inevitable as any human events can be. The first is the bankruptcy of the Truman Doctrine. The second is the failure of the Marshall Plan. The third is the coming American depression. When these dark days of failure come there will arise two terrifying dangers and one hopeful opportunity. The first danger is that the political and military leaders of the United States will seize upon the occasion to cover up their failure and to restore full production and employment through war. I pray that our people and their leaders, whoever they may then be, will flee from this temptation. The second danger is that the leaders of the Soviet Union will seize upon the occasion to extend their power over western Europe and eastern Asia. If they do, the result will be war. I pray that they will exercise patience and self-restraint. The opportunity before us will be one of changing the fatal course upon which we have been led, returning to the settlements of Yalta and Potsdam, embarking anew upon peace-making in the spirit of Franklin Roosevelt and Wendell Willkie, and joining forces with Russia in tolerance and compromise to restore a stable balance of power, to heal the wounds of war, to work toward government through the U.N., to foster pacific and creative competition between a democratic capitalism increasingly aware in a world at peace of social responsibilities, and a Soviet Communism increasingly aware in a world at peace of the value of freedom.

Only a blind optimist will now assume that we shall avoid the dangers which spell suicide and seize the opportunity which, if used, could open a new golden age for all the world. Upon all of us, Russians and Americans alike, are the sin of Adam, the brand of Cain, the primitive black magic of hot anger, panic—fear, and quick violence. We stand, as never before in the history of our civilization, in the presence of the problem confronting John Bunyan's Christian in his *Pilgrim's Progress:*

As I walked through the wilderness of this world . . . I saw a Man clothed with rags, standing in a certain place, with his face from his own house, a Book in his hand, and a great Burden upon his back. I looked, and saw him open the Book, and read therein; and as he read, he wept and trembled; and not being able longer to contain, he brake out with a lamentable cry, saying . . . "I am for certain informed, that this our City will be burned with fire from Heaven; in which fearful overthrow, both myself, with thee my wife, and you my sweet babes, shall miserably come to ruin, except (the which yet I see not) some Way of escape may be found, whereby we may be delivered. . . ." And as he read, he burst out . . . crying, "What shall I do to be saved?"

That is for you to answer. That is for me and all of us, Russians and Americans alike, to answer. May we find the way to the gate. May we be delivered from temptation. May we enter into the kingdom which we have abundant powers to build if only we will but use them with wisdom and good will. May we strive to seek to find, and not to yield, the means of saving our civilization from self-destruction and winning salvation for ourselves and all mankind.

Question: If the United States should work through the United Nations for European economic recovery instead of through the Marshall Plan, do you think it would be possible again to secure Soviet cooperation?

Mr. Schuman: I think the best comment to be made on that question is that when the so-called Marshall Plan first saw the light of day, quite inadvertently really, in the Secretary of State's speech at Harvard on the fifth of June, there was in existence, as you all know, the United Nations European Economic Commission; which has among its members all the member states on the Continent, including the Soviet Union. That Commission was set up for the constructive purposes, if any, supposed to be served by the Marshall Plan, to make studies, to make analyses, to coordinate efforts at reconstruction. The

Secretary of State preferred to ignore completely the European Economic Commission and adopted a course which has led to the results you are quite familiar with. If you ask me now: do I believe if there were any way of going back to the European Economic Commission and working through that, we would obtain Soviet collaboration, I don't know. Much water has gone under the bridge. There are some things that are not so easily reversible. When you spend two years pursuing a course of policy which ends in dismal failure and prospective disaster, to go back and reverse that and begin anew, after you have inspired fear, hatred and suspicion among hundreds of millions of people, is no simple thing to do. So I don't know.

Question: Does Mr. Schuman believe that there has been inspired in Russia fear and hatred as a result of our two years' past conduct? I was just wondering on which foot is the shoe. It had been my impression that it is a bit the other way around.

Mr. Schuman: The answer to the question is yes—and *vice versa*. We are operating in what I believe is usually called a vicious circle. We are operating in a context of a struggle for power in which each move on each side is represented as a defensive move against threatened aggression on the other side; in which each move on each side inspires fear and hatred on the other side. But if your question is: would I say that fear and anxiety and hatred have been inspired in the Soviet Union by American policies of the last two years, the answer of course is, why certainly, they have been inspired. Why not?

Question: I would like to ask Mr. Schuman whether Vishinsky's speech over which there is so much controversy is actually what we were told it was. There was no Chicago newspaper that carried the text of that speech.

Mr. Schuman: . . . The Vishinsky speech was a vitriolic masterpiece of invective. It named names. It cited facts.

On a few facts it was somewhat off the beam; on one or two, completely off the beam. But most of the facts cited were facts, they were not fictions. They were facts, whatever you think of the interpretation placed upon them. And it was all done quite deliberately, not in anger, very calmly, very collectedly, to make it quite clear, in case any of us still don't understand, that for every blow we deliver, whether verbally or in any other way, Russia will deliver a blow back. Russians are tough. Russians do not yield to threats and pressure. And if our current policy is based upon the assumption, as it is, that if we only get tough enough and make enough threats and exert enough pressure, then the Russians are going to yield things which they regard as indispensable components of their national security, then I say this policy is wrong.

Question: Does that mean that we must back down because Russians are tough?

Mr. Schuman: There is no way to answer that unless you talk about it in terms of specific issues. Would you like to do that? If you would like to, I would be glad to.

If you talk, for example, about Korea, what do you mean by saying we must back down? If the Russians keep troops in northern Korea, we say that is a Soviet plot. If they propose that all troops withdraw, we say it's a Soviet plot. In any case, it's a Soviet plot. Of course, if you approach the problem in that spirit, which is a very convenient way of avoiding the necessity of thinking about issues, there is no hope.

Question: I wonder whether you could say a few words on the implications of the Russian use of the veto.

Mr. Schuman: I think one cannot say anything very useful about that without embarking upon a somewhat detailed analysis of the first and central principle of the U.N., which you have no doubt discussed here before and will do again.

I would only say that Secretary General Trygve Lie said only a few days ago, that the question of the veto is not a cause of any difficulty or weakness in the U.N. The question of the veto is a symptom. It is a symptom of a conflict, a schism, a cleavage within the U.N. The veto, so-called, as you all know, is the corollary of the principle of the unanimity of the Great Powers with regard to important substantive questions and some procedural ones, and above all with regard to coercion. And when you have no longer unanimity of the Great Powers and when, in addition to that, you have our own government seeking over and over again to bring questions to a vote in the Security Council when it has been made perfectly clear that the Soviet Union will not accept the American view, then you have the veto problem. There is no solution of the veto problem by amending the Charter or adopting new rules, or even thinking or talking about the veto problem. The veto problem is a minor manifestation of the fact that America and the Soviet Union are on the road to war; and if we get America and the Soviet Union off the road to war, the veto problem will take care of itself.

Question: Do you think that there is any possibility of maintaining peace in the long run in the absence of a world government capable of enforcing law on individuals?

Mr. Schuman: I see no possibility in the long run without a world law, made within a defined and limited area by some kind of world government and enforceable, not through the coercion of sovereign states, but enforceable on individuals through local, national and international courts. Without that I see no possibility whatever in the long run of enduring peace or order or justice in the world. But the run is very long. The immediate problem is to restore the United Nations to the expectations of its original founders and to work through the United Nations, as I see it, toward that kind of world government. The problem of restoring the United Nations to some utility is a problem of somehow putting an end, by compromise

on both sides, to the present struggle for power in the world between the United States and the Soviet Union. Without a restoration of a stable balance and without a restoration of a sufficient degree of accord to make possible fruitful collaboration, I can see no possibility of any progress in this direction at all. . . .

Question: . . . I would like to know how the speaker reconciles his statement—and I am no authority on Marx—but he says in his book that capitalistic democracy and Communism can never be friends. Sooner or later one must overthrow the other. If this is all one-sided, if America is such a bad boy—how can you explain that?

Mr. Schuman: I think the best comment to be made on that is simply to notice what Joseph Stalin told Harold Stassen in their now famous interview. They were discussing related questions. Stalin said, "Marx and Engels could not have foreseen at the time of their deaths what the world would be like forty years later." One might add to that something which we apparently tend to forget constantly. Or if we remember it, we remember it for strange purposes. One might add that the Communist International was dissolved on the 22nd of May, 1943. That was a "fraud," of course, it obviously must be a "fraud," in our view. One might add that the last Congress of the Communist International was held in August of 1935, which is 12 years ago. And if you will take the trouble to see what was said and done there (but of course nobody does, it is so much more interesting to remember the minutes of the earlier Congresses), you will have the answer to your question. The answer, in brief, was that under contemporary conditions the breakdown of capitalism in highly developed countries does not and cannot mean proletarian revolution of the type that Marx and Engels anticipated. It can only mean Fascism. Therefore, there must be a united front of all anti-Fascists on an international and a national scale, against the Fascist danger.

Just one more point. The gravest single crisis in Soviet politics—the gravest crisis confronting the Soviet State in the thirty years of its existence—was the crisis precipitated by the conflict between the followers of Trotsky, who insisted upon world revolution as the prime objective and the followers of Stalin, who took the view that Socialism—and ultimately Communism—in one country was the goal. If you remember that conflict at all, you will remember that it led to crime and punishment, to executions and imprisonments and purges on an immense scale. If we remember that conflict at all, most of us remember it only for the sake of shouting from the housetops "Bloody Murder! See what scoundrels these Bolsheviks are, they have executed all the virtuous Christian Trotskyites." You know who prevailed in that contest. But if you want to sweep all this away, argue that this has no meaning, and that the leaders of the Soviet Union, in spite of all they have done and said, are still thinking in terms of Communist world revolution, proletarian dictatorship in America, and the like —then of course you are quite at liberty to do so, as almost all Americans are doing. But in this, there is no hope. If national policies are based on untruths, those policies can lead only to failure or disaster.

Question: I would like to ask this question. I think a great many Americans are perceiving a parallelism between our relations with Russia today and our relations with Hitler ten years ago. I think that parallelism has a good deal of influence on American policy. I wonder if Mr. Schuman would be able to tell the main respects in which he thinks the policy of Stalin and the background of Russia differs from that of Hitler and Germany in the previous period.

Mr. Schumann: . . . Totalitarianism is totalitarianism, we are assured. . . .

Are the results not the same? Are the results not to be equated one with another? The answer is no, if you ask the questions, "What were the objectives in the way of social and economic change aimed at in the Soviet Union, and in a very large measure achieved?" and "What were the social and economic changes to which the Fascist dictatorship in Italy and the Nazi dictatorship in Germany were committed?" At that point I think you begin to perceive some differences which, in my judgment, are decisive differences. The differences are that the Soviet Union has created an economic order which—whatever its weaknesses and defects—is nonetheless viable and is not afflicted with periodical crises and mass unemployment and breakdown and bankruptcy. Their economy has stability and potentialities for growth in a stable way, whatever else it has. And I'm not idealizing it at all, I'm just saying these are some of its attributes. Italy's economy under Mussolini and Germany's economy under Hitler, on the other hand, had none of these characteristics whatever. In terms of class structure, the actual effective political power under Fascism rests with moneyed industrialists and the landed aristocrats, and the technique of Fascism to restore full production and full employment was in each case a technique of vast public spending on armaments, war and conquest as a means of preventing the political and social breakdown within the body of the Fascist society which otherwise would have taken place. I am trying to say that in class structure, in economic organization, in internal dynamics, and external conduct, there are vast differences between Fascist totalitarianism and Communist totalitarianism —and I'm not praising one at the expense of the other. Fascist totalitarianism, at least in a highly industrialized state, inevitably means imperialism and war and conquest and barbarism and breakdown. It cannot be otherwise. Communist totalitarianism does not necessarily mean those things, and need not mean them at all, in my judgment. If, however, we choose to continue to think, or to refuse to think, by using the familiar term of "Red Fascism" and basing our attitudes and policies on this false analogy, then we shall all together, I suppose, get what we deserve.

6. THE STRUGGLE FOR THE WORLD[1]

By James Burnham

EDITORS' NOTE.—Born in Chicago in 1905 and educated at Princeton and Oxford, James Burnham has been a member of the department of philosophy at New York University since 1929. He published in 1941 *The Managerial Revolution*, in which he propounds a theory that modern society is passing through a social revolution, comparable to the displacement of feudalism by capitalism, in which the bourgeoisie is being superseded by the "managerial class."

A recognition of the fact that the survival of Western Civilization, and perhaps of mankind, depends upon the early establishment of a monopoly control over atomic weapons usually leads, we have noted, to the conclusion that a "World Government" must be formed. The World Government would exercise supreme world sovereignty. In it the atomic monopoly would be vested. Since there would no longer be independent, sovereign nations, international war would "by definition" become impossible, and mankind would thus be saved from the general atomic destruction which another war would make probable. . . .

The achievement of a World Government is not impossible. We cannot correctly argue that because there has never been a World Government, one therefore can never be. Because, for tens of thousands of years, no human society exceeded a few thousand souls, it did not follow that no future society could comprise many scores of millions. Inferences from the past can be drawn only when they also take into account new material and social factors that were not present in the past. On the other hand, it is even more grossly fallacious to argue that because a certain solution is desirable or "needed," therefore it will come about. There is nothing whatsoever in either individual or social experience to suggest that men will get out of their difficulties in the way which, rationally considered, is best for them. Pointing out to an alcoholic that alcohol is bad for him does not stop him from drinking, any more than a lesson on the general evils of inflation will lead a farmer to sell his grain below the market price. A World Government would be the best solution to the present crisis. But this truth, even if it were far more generally accepted, is not enough to bring a World Government into being.

If we judge by facts and not by wishes, we cannot escape the following conclusion: within the given time limits, the free and voluntary establishment of a World Government is historically impossible. It is impossible because the necessary historical pre-conditions do not exist.

A World Government means world political unity. Historical experience shows that political unity is achieved by cultural diffusion plus military conquest, or simply by conquest. The Roman legions plus the Roman educators and architects and language could unify Gaul and Italy; the soldiers and priests of Ancient Egypt could unite, politically, the valley of the Nile; *Kultur* plus diplomacy plus the best trained soldiers of Europe could bring together the small German states; by direct conquest, without cultural penetration, the Ottoman Turks could unite the various Byzantine states of Asia Minor and the Balkans. But we find in history almost no examples of the political unification of hitherto separate autonomous communi-

1. James Burnham, *The Struggle for the World* (New York, 1947), pp. 42, 45–51, 53–55. Reprinted by permission of the John Day Company.

ties brought about by deliberate, voluntary decision.

The seemingly voluntary unification of separate communities shows, on more careful examination, two conditions always present: a pre-existing cultural unity shared by the communities; and the actuality or strong threat of an external force directed against the communities which unite. . . .

It is above all in the founding of the United States that the believers in World Government seek their precedents. There, they hold, is a positive example, by following which we could, today, voluntarily and peacefully, set up and maintain a unified government of the world. Analysis can easily show, however, that this analogy, so persuasive at first hearing, breaks down at every relevant point.

The thirteen colonies, to begin with, shared not only the common Western culture, but, for the most part, the specifically English form of that culture, including the English language. As all dependencies of a single great power, they were accustomed to think of themselves together politically, as united in a common political fate; and they had no tradition of separate sovereign existence. Spatial continuity with each other and isolation from the rest of the world, with the vast sea to one side and the vast wilderness to the other, imposed on them a geographical unity. They had fought together the long, difficult revolutionary war, and had together conquered. In the war, though their unity had been far from complete, though in many respects it was fought as a coalition of independent powers, they had come to possess in common many symbols and traditions of unity: a single Congress, no matter how limited in power; united and often thrilling Declarations; joint victories and defeats and treaties; national heroes. Influential classes of the population stood to gain by unity, and to lose much by separatism. Moreover, the very real threat of external force was by no means removed through victory in the War of Independence. Almost all of the leading statesmen of the colonies understood that the failure to become a strongly united nation would surely open the road to constant intrigue by the great European powers, playing off one set of States against others, with the long-term aim of re-establishing European domination.

Even all of this was not enough to bring about a free, deliberate decision to unite. What was in reality a minority *coup* was in addition required. The Philadelphia Convention had to violate its specific instructions which limited it to the mere amendment of the Articles of Confederation. The new Constitution itself contained a blatant threat of coercion through the provision that the new government would come into being after the adherence of only nine of the States. In the doubtful States, the bold campaign for adoption joined open intimidation to rational argument and demagogy. New York City's declared intention to secede from the State doubtless weighed as much at Poughkeepsie as Hamilton's speeches. And, finally, the unity was sealed only with the blood of one of the most terrible of Civil Wars.

Even, then, if we were to grant the American precedent, it hardly suggests a soft slide into World Government. The precedent itself, however, is plainly inapplicable. In the world as a whole there is not cultural unity, but cultural plurality, and, in addition, the superimposed fracture into totalitarian and non-totalitarian segments. Western Civilization is itself harshly divided into separate communities, with the inertial weight of centuries reinforcing the divisions. By the nature of the case, at any rate until the era of interplanetary wars begins, there can be no external force prompting a move toward world unity. The evidence of experience is unambiguous. We can have no reason to believe that the people of the world will, in the predictable future, establish, through any form of free, deliberate decision, a World Government.

We have been considering the prospects of a World Government achieved by free and deliberate decision. If, however, we shift the locus of the problem, and consider, not such a World Government, but rather a World Empire, established at least partly through force and the threat of force, the evidence from historical experience no longer dictates the same negative conclusion.

There has, of course, never been a World Empire in the sense of an Empire the dominion of which comprised literally the entire earth. What Toynbee calls "Universal Empires" have, however, come into being many times; and are, indeed, a usual stage—the next to final stage—in the history of civilizations. In the instances of those civilizations of which we have knowledge, what seems usually to happen is more or less this: Each civilization expands gradually from its original, comparatively limited home, by diffusion, colonization and conquest. It becomes articulated into a number of independent (sovereign) political communities. At some point in the development there occurs a long series of catastrophes and crises—named by Toynbee the "Time of Troubles." At the culmination of the Time of Troubles, some one state succeeds in eliminating all rivals and founding a Universal Empire, the extent of which coincides roughly with the sphere of cultural influence attained previously by the civilization. The Universal Empire, in its turn, has so far always been followed by the breakup and destruction of the civilization in question. . . .

We who belong to Western Civilization are, with a natural provincialism, best acquainted with the Roman Empire, since it was in the breakup of that Empire that the seeds of our own civilization were fertilized. For the sake of a possible analogy to our own present situation, we may recall the general form of the development of the Roman Empire.

Following the breakup of the Minoan Society, Hellenic Civilization had its origin along the littoral, and on the islands, of the Aegean. From this source, for a number of centuries it gradually expanded. Politically, it was for the most part articulated into independent small city-states, many of them with various sorts of colonies. After the victory over Persia during the first part of the fifth century B.C., two great coalitions arose, under the leadership of Athens and Sparta. One or the other of these might have succeeded in unifying the Hellenic world; but, as it turned out, the long clash between them, in the Peloponnesian Wars at the end of the fifth century, ended with a mutual exhaustion from which the original homeland of the civilization never recovered. The mother cities lost the creative initiative.

The problem of unification remained, however. Its challenge was taken up by the "semi-barbarian super-states of the periphery," as Toynbee calls them. For nearly three centuries, with intervals of relative quiet, Macedonia, Carthage, and Rome struggled to deliver "the knock-out blow." War took on a new meaning, vastly enlarged in scope and fierceness, with limited specific aims transformed into the objective of annihilation—*Carthago delenda est*. These wars merged into gigantic class and social struggles, revolutions and civil wars. Spartacus, the Gracchi, Sulla, Marius, Pompey, Julius, Antony, Octavius fought in cross-tides over the entire area of the civilization, purged their own followers, overthrew the old social forms, proscribed and slaughtered the ranks of the defeated, until the definitive victory of Octavius established the Empire as a functioning and universal fact.

How close is the parallel? The source of Western Civilization is in the western half of the European peninsula. Political separatism, becoming ever more intense since the Renaissance, poses more and more inescapably the problem of political unification. From within the homeland, first France, under Napoleon, attempts to meet the challenge, and fails. Then Germany tries twice, with an intervening collapse of all proposals for peaceful union.

In the recently concluded second attempt, for the first time in Western history, anhihilation of the defeated becomes the objective of war. The lists of the proscribed are drawn up in advance. The social and revolutionary wars cut across the lines of the international battles. The homeland has failed. There remain the two mighty, semibarbarian super-states of the periphery, the American and the communist. If either of these succeeds, the resultant Universal Empire of Western Civilization, unlike the Universal Empires of other civilizations, will also be a World Empire. This will follow because, though Western Civilization is not culturally world-wide, its political influence and material power dominate the world.

Toynbee nowhere commits himself to acceptance of a positive analogy between Hellenic and Western history, although he outlines it in details that go much beyond the political scheme into parallels of philosophy, literature, moral attitudes and emotional moods. It is not, however, necessary to derive our forecast of world political developments from analogies based on past civilizations, the laws of which are, it may be admitted, very doubtfully known. The over-all nature of the present world political situation, the tendencies therein observably at work, can make sufficiently plain what, in general, is happening, and what is going to happen.

It is now apparent to everyone that the pre-1939 world political division into a comparatively large number of independent, sovereign nations is finished. Two of the great independent powers have been destroyed by the war. Smaller nations are no longer serious independent factors in world politics. The United Nations Charter drops even the fiction of the equality of small nations, which would be incompatible with the veto rules and the assignment of permanent seats on the Security Council....

Whether we approach the problem from the point of view of the general pattern of history, or from that of a more or less Marxian analysis of socio-economic needs and possibilities, or from that of the potentialities of the new military weapons, or from that of the existing division of the world into the two major power spheres, we are led to a single conclusion. A World Empire has become possible, and the attempt will be made to establish a World Empire. A World Empire would, moreover, solve the problem of atomic weapons, within the terms set in Chapter 3. That is, it would institute a monopoly control over such weapons.

I wish to clarify the distinction which I have made between the terms "World Government" and "World Empire." The former I have been using in the sense which I believe is given to it by those who regard themselves as advocates of World Government. It means a world state set up by peaceful means, through some sort of constitutional or democratic processes, and in which the various peoples of the world would have, more or less, political equality. It is such a state that I regard as impossible for the next historical period.

By a World Empire I mean a state, not necessarily world-wide in literal extent but world-dominating in political power, set up at least in part through coercion (quite probably including war, but certainly the threat of war), and in which one group of peoples (its nucleus being one of the existing nations) would hold more than its equal share of power.

Let us suppose that the United States had been founded not through acceptance by all the States of the Philadelphia Constitution, but in some such way as follows. New York and Pennsylvania, convinced that the unity of the colonies was necessary, and despairing of getting it in time through peaceful agreement, determined to force it. Through a combination of negotiation, threats, concessions, bribes, and perhaps some actual fighting, they succeeded; and brought all the colonies under the jurisdiction of a government so constituted that a predominant (though not necessarily exclusive) power over certain key questions, such as foreign affairs and the army, was guaranteed to New York–Pennsylvania. Then, in the sense I am giving, the result would have been an "Empire."

The world "Empire" has, for Americans, connotations of extreme tyranny and despotism which are historically unjustified. There have been many kinds and degrees of Empire, and I shall discuss later (in Chapter 17) some of these variations. An Empire is not incompatible with democracy in the imperial power—indeed, Athens and England, two of the greatest imperial powers in history, are the two most democratic governments so far known. The British Empire, as well as other lesser Empires, prove also that democracy can exist and develop within the subordinate realms of the Empire. The relations between the imperial power and the subordinate realms need not in all cases be the same, but may vary all the way from the harshest exploitation to nearly equal partnership.

The imperial power need not be totalitarian—that is, intervening in all phases of social activity. It can be restricted to what is necessary in order to maintain the integrity of the empire. There is, in fact, only one absolutely essential world task of the possible World Empire of tomorrow: the preservation of the monopoly of atomic (and comparable) weapons. The fulfillment of the central task is compatible with much looseness of the imperial structure in other fields.

It goes without saying that the attempt at World Empire will not be carried out under the open slogan of "World Empire." More acceptable phrases, such as "World Federation," "World Republic," "United States of the World," "World Government," or even "United Nations" will be used. But in this book, I am concerned with realities, not with words. The truth is that the growing belief in, and propaganda for, various sorts of World Government are in historical actuality both a symptom of the need for a World Empire, a support

for the attempt to achieve such an Empire, and a psychological preparation for its acceptance, if it comes. A similar longing, similarly expressed, was widespread throughout the Hellenic world during the century preceding the foundation of the Roman Empire. It is like a bachelor who begins to prepare himself for the restrictions of matrimony by discoursing on the beauties of "true love."

Finally, it should be noted that there is not, historically speaking, an absolute opposition between World Empire and World Government. Rather is it the case that World Empire is the only means through which genuine World Government might be achieved. World Empire might, it is true, be at the outset, or evolve into, a world totalitarian tyranny. But such a development is not inevitable. The believers in a free world government, if they are politically serious, if their beliefs are more than dreams whereby they compensate for the grimness of actual experience and their own weakness, are in practice committed to an acceptance of the perspective of World Empire, because through that alone is there a chance for the realization of their more ultimate ideal.

We may now summarize the result, up to this point, of our analysis:

The discovery of atomic weapons has brought about a situation in which Western Civilization, and perhaps human society in general, can continue to exist only if an absolute monopoly in the control of atomic weapons is created. This monopoly can be gained and exercised only through a World Empire, for which the historical stage had already been set prior to and independently of the discovery of atomic weapons. The attempt at World Empire will be made, and is, in fact, the objective of the Third World War, which, in its preliminary stages, has already begun.

It should not require argument to state that the present candidates for leadership in the World Empire are only two: the Soviet Union and the United States.

7. THE CONSTITUTIONAL FOUNDATIONS
OF WORLD ORDER[1]

By Robert M. Hutchins

EDITORS' NOTE.—The following article was first presented on October 13, 1947, in a series of lectures on "Foundations for World Order," arranged by the Social Science Foundation of the University of Denver. Its author is chancellor of the University of Chicago. Mr. Hutchins (1899——) is president of the Committee To Frame a World Constitution, which was conceived in the aftermath of the atomic bombardment of Hiroshima. This committee submitted a draft of a world constitution in the March, 1948, number of its monthly publication, *Common Cause*.

We have a mystical notion that all the issues that perplex us are going to be settled by improvements in transportation. They will give us one world. A colleague of mine has asked, one world, but whose? We may also inquire, one world, but how long? And one world, but what kind? One world which brings in closer contact the sparks of greed and ambition is sure to be in constant explosion. One world under one tyrant, or one association of tyrants, would be worse than many. In many worlds there is at least the chance of escape from one to the other.

But let us suppose that by one world we mean one good world. Will we stop to ask what one good world involves? It involves, unless we propose to kill them all, such people as the Russians. The proposal to kill them all seems to be gaining in popularity. If we are going to do that we had better do it at once. Now we have a monopoly of the atomic bomb.

There are two propositions about the atomic bomb that are worth remembering. There is no secret. There is no defense. Since there is no secret, other nations will have the bomb almost any day. Since there is no defense, we cannot use the bomb after our monopoly ends to kill other people without being killed ourselves.

In a war in which both sides have atomic bombs the cities of both sides will be destroyed. Since one to ten atomic bombs can reduce any city in the world to ashes, superiority in atomic bombs will not give material advantage to the side possessing it. Superiority in land, sea, and air forces will mean little. The atomic bomb is a weapon directed against civilians. The economy which supports the military can be wiped out before the military can get started. As General Groves said in Chicago a few weeks ago, "I do not see how it will be possible to supply large armies in the field." When two nations have the atomic bomb, it will be impossible for either of them to win a war. The day of force as the determining factor in world affairs ends with the end of our monopoly of the atomic bomb.

Yet just as the day of force is waning, the official American attitude is to rely on it more than ever. In the greatest moral crisis in history we do not say, "Let us be good." We say, "Let us be powerful—and then we can compel other people to be good." Instead of saying, "Let us use our knowledge and our resources for the benefit of all mankind," we say, "Let us use our knowledge to make more terrifying weapons of destruction; and let us use our resources to usher in the American Century, in which we shall dominate the world." Instead of saying, "Let us feed the

1. Robert M. Hutchins, "The Constitutional Foundations of World Order," *Common Cause*, I (December, 1947), 201–8.

starving because all men are brothers," we say, "Let us feed the starving, if we feed them at all, so that they will not vote the Communist ticket." Instead of saying, "Let us have moral education in the United States," we say, "Let us have military training."

Three weeks ago the Chairman of the Federal Reserve Board said that we had spent 25 billions on military forces in the first two post-war fiscal years, compared with 16 billions spent on foreign aid in that period.

Yet even before the atomic bomb it is possible that General Montgomery was right in saying, as he did the other day, that it is not weapons or large armies that win victories, but the character, that is, the education, of the people. A tremendous military establishment can be, and usually is, a Frankenstein; and all history confirms the doctrine that those who rely upon the sword shall perish by it. Power corrupts. A false sense of superiority leads to a false sense of security. Behind an impressive facade the building falls into ruins. The building can be no better than the character of the people who inhabit it.

Force is absolutely amoral, and therefore has no role, except in support of law, in a world that has any title to be called good. Force is almost certain to be immoral. The essence of fascism is pushing other people around; you frighten them into doing what you want them to do. A country composed of people who want to push other people around is a fascist country; a government which pursues a fascist policy will eventually produce a lot of fascist citizens. It will produce a population of immoral individuals who regard other individuals as means to their ends and who will seek the power to make other individuals serve their ends. Such a country cannot long remain strong; such a population cannot be happy. If the official American attitude is to rely upon force, it follows that the power and the happiness of America have already passed their zenith.

And, if the official policy of America is to rely upon force, it follows that the security of America cannot be guaranteed by force after the day of force is over. The day of force can last only a moment longer. There are only two possibilities: to use the bomb at once, or to create a situation in which nobody can ever use it.

Of these two possibilities, we hear more and more about the first and less and about the second. The first possibility is a preventive war on Russia. If we seriously entertain this possibility, we ought first to make our apologies to the Nazis we hanged at Nuremberg.

If we are concerned to create a situation in which the bomb will not be used, we must recognize that international agreements for the control of atomic energy will simply mean that the next war will end with atomic bombs instead of beginning with them. The minute war breaks out, every nation that knows how will start making atomic bombs.

The *New York Times*, in its editorial on the second anniversary of the bomb, says that the ultimate protection against it can only be the abolition of war itself. The *Times* suggests that the final success of efforts to abolish war can be realized only in an ultimate World Government.

I do not understand the use of the word "ultimate" in this connection. We have now arrived at the ultimate stage in history. We cannot do something intermediate now and ultimately do something ultimate. What is ultimately required of us is required of us now. If what is ultimately required of us is the abolition of war through a World Government, then we had better set about trying to get war abolished through World Government now.

Any proposal for a world atomic authority is a proposal for World Government. Such an authority must have a monopoly of atomic bombs, which means that every nation would be at its mercy, and it must have the right to enter, inspect, and destroy atomic installations anywhere in the world. No nation could call itself sovereign in any usual sense under such conditions.

The major premise of all discussions looking toward agreements for the control of atomic energy has been that the nations retain their sovereignty. Hence, these discussions have not succeeded and cannot succeed. Either we have World Federal Government and real atomic control, or we have no agreements, or agreements that are meaningless, and eventually atomic war.

It will be said, of course, that if nations will not collaborate in an alliance or debating society or propaganda forum like the United Nations, they cannot be expected to come together or stay together in a World State. The American states could not or would not collaborate under the Articles of Confederation before 1787, but they did come together, and, with the exception of one period, they stayed together under the Constitution.

It may be admitted that there were ties which united them which do not unite the nations today. Moreover, they were remote from the rest of the world. Both their enemies and their friends were too preoccupied to bother them. They had the safety valve of a new country and the western lands. On the other hand, we should not forget that many differences deeply divided the American states, so much so that, three months before the Constitutional Convention, Madison wrote that he "trembled for the issue."

Mr. Hooker has lately shown in the magazine *Common Cause* how serious the divisions among the states in the Confederation were. Virginia had twelve times as many people as Delaware. Georgia claimed a hundred times as many square miles as Rhode Island. There were so many Germans in Pennsylvania that Franklin feared they might make German the language of the state. It was impossible to get along in some sections of New York without knowing Dutch. The trip from Boston to New York, which now takes less than an hour, took four days to a week along the finest road, or longer than it takes now to go round the world.

Gouverneur Morris thought that a federal tax was impossible because of the extent of the country; and one member of the Convention asked, "How can it be supposed that this vast country, including the western territory, will, one hundred and fifty years hence, remain one nation?"

When Washington took charge of the armies surrounding Boston, he wrote that the New Englanders were exceedingly dirty and nasty people. On the other hand, Ephraim Paine of Vermont complained that the southern members of Congress regarded themselves as a superior order of animals. Tariffs were levied by New York, Pennsylvania, and Maryland on the goods of other states; and New Jersey taxed the New York lighthouse on Sandy Hook. New York, New Hampshire, and Massachusetts quarreled about Vermont, and Pennsylvanians battled Virginians on the Upper Ohio. It is no wonder that when the Constitution was completed by the Convention, the principal attack upon it was that it was utopian, a visionary project, an indigestible panacea.

And it barely was accepted. In the conventions in the critical states it just squeaked through. In Massachusetts it carried by twenty-nine votes; in Virginia by ten; and in New York by only three.

What we are talking about is the relation between world community and world law. Reinhold Niebuhr, whom I greatly admire, takes the view that we cannot discuss World Government because we have no world community to support it. The discussion of World Government, he thinks, may even retard the development of world community and hence retard World Government.

It is true that one good world presupposes a world community. In one good world every man is our neighbor, because every man is our fellow citizen. The commands of the political community supplement the demands of charity. Three or four years ago the Council of the American Federation of Labor, in response to the suggestion that China was our ally, voted to reaffirm its support of the Chinese Exclusion Act. Mr. William Green took the occasion to announce that "A Chinaman is still a Chinaman." If this is so, the one good world at which Mr. Green doubtless aims is still far off.

Our traditional attitude toward the rest of the world has been expressed in the old question, "Should foreigners be abolished, or should we save some to sell things to?" We have been dedicated to a policy of high tariffs and no immigration. Twenty years ago we regarded national relief of the unemployed as revolutionary socialism. Our system of social security is only twelve years old. We are not yet committed to give national aid to the education of underprivileged American children. And yet, in one good world, we should be called on to support, to educate, to buy from, and to receive as fellow citizens, men of every race, creed, and color, at every economic level, and at every stage of ignorance or enlightenment.

One good world requires more than the sacrifice of ancient prejudices. It requires the formulation and adoption of common principles and common ideals. It requires that this be done on a world-wide basis. A world organization cannot be held together simply by fear. Not transportation but communication lies at the foundation of any durable community. By communication I do not refer to the means of communication, but to a common understanding of what is communicated. The extraordinary development of the telegraph, the telephone, the radio, the motion picture, and air mail in our time has done as much as any single factor to disrupt international relations and exacerbate wounded feelings throughout the world. A vice-president of the General Electric Company has lately commented on the benefits to civilization from television. He said that, since the principal market for television sets was taverns, what this triumph of technology

had meant to society was more booze, less fresh air, and the same old ball game. It would have been very fortunate if almost every speech made by representatives of great powers in the last two years, from Mr. Truman's Navy Day Address of October, 1945 to Mr. Vishinsky's recent outpourings, could have been heard or read only by their own people, and a very small fraction of them. Confucius remarked that men cannot work together unless they have common principles. Common principles are essential to communication.

Here it will not do to say that common principles cannot be found. They must be found. And they can be found in the common humanity of all mankind. By patience, tolerance, and good will we can come to understand other human beings, because they are human beings like ourselves. The most salutary reflection about the Russians in which we can indulge is to imagine how we would feel about the United States if we were Russians. And it would do the Russians no harm to consider how Mr. Vishinsky's speeches would affect them if they were Americans. By patience, tolerance, and good will we can come to understand one another; understanding is essential to communication. Communication is the basis of community. Transportation hastens consolidation; there can be no doubt about that. In the last century it has hastened consolidation of the most unstable and disagreeable kind, consolidation by conquest. One good world presupposes that the moral, intellectual, and spiritual foundations of the community have been laid. Otherwise the improvement of transportation must simply mean more frequent and terrible wars leading to the despotism of that power which discovers how best to apply the latest inventions to the destruction of its neighbors.

But I am afraid that Mr. Niebuhr exaggerates the state of perfection which world community must achieve before World Government can be considered. Before the atomic bomb we could take World Government or leave it. We could rely on the long process of evolution to bring world community and World Government hand in hand. Any such program today means another war, and another war means the end of civilization. The slogan of our faith today must be, World Government is necessary, and therefore possible.

Furthermore, those who oppose discussion of World Government on the ground that a world community must precede a World Government overlook the interaction between the two. This is what the Greeks had in mind when they said that law was an educational force and that the city educates the man. The Constitution of the United States has educated the people of this country to believe in and support the Constitution of the United States. We are so used to thinking of law as repressive and constitutions as the embodiment of pre-existing agreement that we neglect the tremendous force which any constitution and any system of law exerts in behalf of its own acceptance and perpetuation. Anybody who has studied the relation between the political institutions of a state and its educational system, for example, must agree with Aristotle that politics is the architectonic science. One of the reasons Aristotle gives for this conclusion is that politics determines what is studied in the state.

The way to promote world community is to have World Government. But since we cannot establish a World Government here tonight the next best thing we can do to promote world community is to talk about World Government. World discussion of World Government, far from disrupting the world, may have some chance of uniting it; for the consideration of what is necessary to unite the world, the discussion of a common problem of overwhelming importance, should lead to a growing sense of community among all peoples.

An important reason for talking about World Government is that nobody knows what it is. Should a World Government aim at limited measures designed to maintain what is called security, or is security itself dependent on the pursuit of broader purposes? Should a World State be federal or unitary, or should it, perhaps, contain the best features of each? What should be the relation of the World Government to the citizens of extant states? What taxing powers shall the World State have, and what order of military forces, if any? This list of questions can be prolonged indefinitely, and there are countless possible answers to each of them. Yet people go around saying World Government is wonderful or World Government is impossible. It may be that many forms of World Government would be something less than wonderful; and it may be that some form of World Government is possible. The only way to find out whether any form of World Government is possible and practicable in our time is to work at it and talk about it.

Such discussion cannot legitimately be interpreted as an attack upon the United Nations. We must support the United Nations; it is all we have. We support it, not because it can guarantee peace, but because it is a highly tentative first step toward World Government and world law. To say that the discussion of World Government is a criticism of the United Nations is like saying that to talk about buying an automobile is an attack on the baby-carriage industry. The notion that if only we don't say anything about it the United Nations will in some way, while nobody is looking, turn gradually into an effective World Government is surely naive. Constitution framing is a highly technical problem. The organization of sentiment for a new constitution is a matter of time, thought, and effort. And when the task must be carried forward on a global scale we must realize that no matter how soon we start we may be too late.

Mr. Molotov defends the United Nations and proposes as a remedy for the ills of the world what he calls the peaceful competition of states and social systems. This is certainly better, if it may be taken at face value, than the stirring calls issued by our statesmen for the largest army, navy, and air force in the world. But Mr. Molotov overlooks or suppresses the fact that between states and social systems there cannot in the long run be peaceful competition unless peace is enforced by law. The history of our own country from the Gold Rush to the Chicago newspaper wars shows that competition between individuals can be made peaceful only with some difficulty, and then only within a framework of law. The competition of sovereign states is competing anarchy. It is peaceful only so long as all nations want it to be. When one nation thinks that its competitive position would be improved if it stopped being peaceful, it will engage in warlike, instead of peaceful, competition, and there is no way for other nations to stop this process except to abandon peaceful competition, too. The United Nations is composed of independent, sovereign states. Their competition must be anarchical. Therefore, in the long run it cannot be peaceful.

Every alteration in the constitution of the United Nations looking toward making it a World Government is to the good. But any important limitation on the powers of sovereign states means that the whole theory of the United Nations is changed. To allege that anybody who insists on the basic theory of the United Nations is in some way an enemy of world peace is unfair. This applies, for example, to criticism on constitutional grounds of the use of the veto. Such criticism assumes that the United Nations is a World Government and assails Russia on the ground that it does not recognize this obvious fact. Actually, the United Nations was not designed to put an end to the competing anarchy of sovereign states, but to perpetuate it.

Does anybody imagine that the United States would consent to any modification of the veto which would endanger our present majority position? Suppose that we were in a minority in the United Nations. Would we part with the veto, which

would be the only weapon with which we could protect ourselves against the majority? Does anybody imagine that we would consent to effective inspection by an international body of atomic installations in this country? The United Nations is and is by its charter declared to be an association of independent, sovereign states. How can we complain if one of the members insists on asserting its independent sovereignty?

Tinkering with the United Nations will not help us, if we agree with the *New York Times* that our only hope is in the ultimate abolition of war through an ultimate World Government. An entirely different constitutional foundation is required. A new set of commitments must be made. Commitments to an alliance can be transformed into allegiance to a government only by a change of heart, reflected in a fundamental constitutional reform.

The most futile of all the things we can do is to speculate about the intentions of the Politburo. Even if we were sure at some given moment that we knew what these gentlemen were planning, we could not be positive that they would adhere to these plans for more than a few minutes. What we should be thinking about is what America should stand for, regardless of what other nations may have in mind. If that policy fails, we shall at least have the satisfaction of knowing that we have done the best we could and that the catastrophe cannot be laid at our door. The policies we have been following—peace by intimidation and peace by purchase—do not seem to be succeeding very well; and, if the catastrophe comes, we shall be unable to evade a large share of the responsibility for it.

The policy of peace by intimidation, otherwise known as "getting tough with Russia," has produced Mr. Vishinsky, who proclaims a policy of peace by vilification, which is the *reductio ad absurdum* of peace by intimidation. Peace by vilification is that version of peace by intimidation which can be adopted by powerful and remote nations who do not yet have the atomic bomb, but who, since they are powerful and remote, can respond to attempts to intimidate them by showing in as rude and noisy a fashion as possible that two can play at that game. The policy of peace by purchase may succeed temporarily in those portions of the world which are purchasable. In those areas it will last as long as the purchase price is being paid or as long as no other bidder will offer more or until the nations bought come to value their independence more than more food, clothing, and houses. But we have really made no attempt to buy peace. We have been attempting to buy allies for the next war. Yet we cannot contemplate another war. Another war will mean the end of civilization. We have reached the point where we cannot have war and civilization, too.

If peace through intimidation and peace through purchase are failing and in the nature of things are bound to fail, we might try peace through justice. Justice means giving every man his due; it means not doing to others what you are unwilling to have them do to you. Justice is suggested to us by a well-known American document which states that all men are created equal. Justice is the cement which holds a political organization together.

If we will grant that what we want is peace, and that justice is the only way to peace, then we may begin dimly to perceive both the outlines of a policy for the present and the constitutional foundations of a future world order. We are required to abandon a policy of power and purchase and pursue a policy of justice at home and abroad.

In order to pursue this policy we have to make certain moral and intellectual commitments, commitments that threaten to take us, in fact, into the realm of metaphysics. We have to admit that men are different from the other animals and that their moral, rational, and spiritual qualities are the qualities that make them men. These characteristics prevent us from dealing with men as we are free to deal with other animals. Human dignity forbids us to apply force to men, except by law. It forbids us to regard other men as means to our ends, for every man is an end in himself. The prospects of a human community result from our common humanity.

To give every man his due, therefore, is to treat every man as a man, black or white, British or Russian, rich or poor, ignorant or educated. And we may remember, as John Stuart Mill pointed out long ago, that we cannot expect the slave to show the virtues of the free man unless we first make him free. To say that certain men cannot be treated as men means simply that they have never had a chance to be men, and they must be given that chance.

To give every man his due is to give him the Rights of Man. This means that he must be free from want as long as he is willing to work. It means that he must be free from the fear of tyranny, oppression, and exploitation. It means that his claims to life, liberty, and the dignity of the human person are inalienable. It means that the necessities of life must be the common property of the human race, and that the management of the necessities of life by individual owners is a trusteeship which such owners hold subject always to the common good. It means that a World Government must be a democracy, because only democracy gives every man his due.

It will be said that a World Government which is founded on justice goes further than World Government has to go and that we should limit ourselves to those objects as to which there can be no debate, the principal one of which is security. It will be said that nobody wants war and that all that a World Government should do is to try to prevent war. This it can do by securing a monopoly of arms. Why talk about justice, the rights of man, and the law of nature when all we want is peace?

The answer is that men will fight until

they get their rights. The minimum structural requirements of World Government are plain enough. A World Government must have a monopoly of arms. It must be a federal government, so as to preserve the cultural values that now exist in the states and regions of the world. It must be a government which acts directly on the individual, wherever he may be; for otherwise it is merely a league of sovereign, and hence ultimately warlike states. But those are minimum structural requirements. There are minimum moral and spiritual requirements, too; and these may be summed up in the single word justice. The advancement of man in spiritual excellence and physical welfare is the common goal of mankind. Universal peace is the prerequisite for the pursuit of that goal. Justice in turn is the prerequisite of peace. Peace and justice stand or fall together. Men will fight until they get their rights.

These are hard sayings; for if we are going to promote justice throughout the world we shall have to rely largely on the power of example. We shall have to start doing justice at home, and shall have to sacrifice many ancient prejudices that are very dear to us. And if we are to have a World Government based on justice, we, as the most prosperous and powerful nation of the earth, shall have to give up many economic and political advantages. We shall have to give up also the notion that there are some people in the world who are subhuman and not qualified to participate in any government that will hold sway over us. If we are going to have peace we must pay for it; and the price of peace is justice. If it will cost us a good deal to have World Government, it will cost us far more to have war.

We are in no present danger from Russia. We have the atomic bomb. We have the industrial power. We are in no present danger from communism. The people of this country could be made communistic only by conquest, and probably not then. At present we are our own worst enemy. The present danger to us lies in our own hysteria and inertia. Our hysteria means that we will not face the facts of life, and our inertia means that we will not do anything about them. We hysterically build up tremendous military preparations, oblivious to the fact that while we have a monopoly of the atomic bomb we do not need these preparations, and when other nations have the bomb these preparations will do us no good. These preparations are, in fact, a danger to us for they can be used to convince other nations that we are out to dominate the world. Because of our inertia we will not recognize that our first obligation is to make our own system work until it must command the admiration and imitation of the world. We will not see that the atomic bomb puts all further talk of force out of the question and that the hope of civilization is in World Government. The Pax Romana existed before the atomic bomb. The atomic bomb makes a Pax Americana a romantic dream. The attempt to get a Pax Americana will give us not one Rome, but two Carthages.

The task of this generation is to establish peace. Gibbon in a celebrated chapter seeks to relieve the fears of Europe by assuring his contemporaries that there can never be another barbarian conqueror. The reason is simple. War is now so far advanced and requires the knowledge of so many arts and sciences that only highly educated men can hope to wage war successfully. The inference is that if men are highly educated they will not be so stupid or so vulgar as to wage war. But the last war was the most barbarous in history precisely because so much knowledge was at the disposal of those who waged it; and the atomic bomb is the final refutation of Gibbon's comforting theory. It can be little consolation to the Japanese who died at Hiroshima and Nagasaki that they were killed by Ph.D's.

The crisis of our time may be summed up in the proposition that our knowledge now exceeds our capacity to use it for good. The solution is not to reduce our knowledge, or to halt the progress of science, but to make our moral stamina equal to it. We have now reached the point where the bad character, or even the momentary carelessness, of the human race may lead to its extermination by the tremendous discoveries which the human intellect has achieved. The problem of preserving our civilization is a moral problem. Our difficulty is not to get more knowledge or more goods, but to do the right thing with them when we get them. Today we are confident that every scientific question will in time be answered. We know that every material deficiency of mankind can with good will be supplied. The problem is obtaining the good will. This is a moral problem.

The task of our generation is to establish peace. We cannot establish it by power or by purchase. We can establish it only by justice which begins at home and extends throughout the world. If you ask, what good will it do for us to be just if other nations are unjust, I reply as Plato did 2500 years ago, that the unjust man and the unjust state bear within themselves the seeds of their own destruction; and as General Montgomery did the other day, that the character of a person is its best defense. Character implies moral and intellectual conviction. We must know, understand, and believe in what we are defending. What we are defending is not the American Way of Life, by which we usually seem to mean All the Comforts of Home. We are defending the cause of suffering humanity everywhere. This is justice, which is the foundation of any constitutional order and the basis of one good world.

8. ADDRESS BEFORE THE UNITED NATIONS GENERAL ASSEMBLY, 1947[1]

By ANDREI VISHINSKY

EDITORS' NOTE.—Andrei Vishinsky, now commissar of foreign affairs of the Soviet Union, was born in 1883. He joined the Russian revolutionary movement in 1905 while a law student at the University of Kiev. During the 1920's Vishinsky was professor of law and rector of the University of Moscow, and he is generally credited with a leading role in the organization of the Soviet judicial system. He first came into international prominence as public prosecutor in the trials of the Trotskyist-Zinoviev factions, who were charged in the 1930's

1. Andrei Y. Vishinsky, "Speech Delivered at the General Assembly of the United Nations, September 18, 1947" (Washington: Embassy of Union of Soviet Socialist Republics, 1947), pp. 3–38. This speech as printed in the *New York Times*, September 19, 1947, is a rougher translation than the one reprinted here.

with conspiring with Nazi Germany to overthrow the Soviet government.

The address printed below was delivered at a meeting of the United Nations General Assembly in answer to a speech made the day before by United States Secretary of State George Marshall. In that speech Marshall called for the organization of an interim committee of the Assembly, in which the Soviet Union and its supporters would be a minority, demanded an investigation of Balkan aid to Greek revolutionaries, attacked Russian policy in northern Korea, and hinted that, if Russia would not accept the American proposals for the control of atomic energy, the United States would set up a control agency without her.

A year has passed since the First Session of the General Assembly. It is necessary to cast a retrospective glance on the road traversed, and to make an analysis of the work performed during this time by the Organization of the United Nations, to summarize certain results, and to outline possible perspectives. . . .

Casting its retrospective glance, the Soviet Union delegation must note that during the period covered by the Report there were serious setbacks in the activity of the United Nations. These setbacks should be disclosed and identified with all determination and consistency. They have been expressed mainly in a departure from the most important principle on which this Organization is founded, and also, in some cases, in a direct violation of a number of important decisions of the General Assembly. These setbacks have been, to a large extent, the result of a tendency on the part of such influential members of the United Nations as the United States of America, and also the United Kingdom, to utilize the Organization in the interests of their small group, without any regard for international cooperation on the basis of the principles set forth in the Charter.

The policy of individual states in using this Organization for the purpose of achieving their own selfish and narrowly conceived interests leads to the undermining of the Organization's prestige, just as took place in the case of the League of Nations of grievous memory.

On the other hand, the unsatisfactory state of affairs in the United Nations Organization, which has a telling negative effect upon its prestige, is a result of ignoring the Organization of the United Nations by the states mentioned above, which are attempting to carry out a number of practical measures outside the framework of the United Nations and with a lack of due regard for it.

It is necessary to draw serious attention to the menace thus created to the United Nations Organization by such a policy, which is incompatible with the principles of the Charter and with the aims and purposes contemplated by the United Nations when they established the Organization.

I. THE U.S.A. AND GREAT BRITAIN ARE OPPOSED TO THE REDUCTION OF ARMAMENTS

Among the most important setbacks in the activities of the United Nations Organization, one should mention, in the first place, the unsatisfactory fulfilment of the Assembly's decision of December 14, 1946, with regard to the universal reduction of armaments. . . .

The representatives of the United States and the United Kingdom, at the time attempts were being made to outline within the framework of the Security Council and the Commission of Conventional Armaments practical measures for the realization of the General Assembly's decision on the universal regulation and reduction of armaments, proposed such terms for the reduction of armaments as could only result in failure to realize the above-mentioned decision of the Assembly. The whole activity of the United States and United Kingdom delegations in the Commission for Conventional Armaments testifies to the fact that the United States and the United Kingdom are unwilling to disarm and that they are putting a brake on the realization of disarmament, which gives reason for anxiety among the peace-loving nations of the world.

The statement of Mr. Bevin, made in Southport, to the effect that he was not going to further disarmament, serves as a convincing answer to the question about the reasons for the unsatisfactory state of affairs with regard to the realization of the Assembly's decision on the reduction of armaments. The recent statement by the President of the United States, Mr. Truman, in Petropolis, in which the President emphasized that the United States military forces are to be maintained, while saying not a single word about the obligation to make a reduction of armed forces assumed by the United Nations in accordance with the General Assembly's decisions, speaks of the same. . . .

. . . This undermines the faith in the sincerity of peaceful declarations and statements on the determination to make future generations free from the hardships and horrors of war.

II. THE UNITED STATES OF AMERICA DISRUPTS THE OUTLAWING OF ATOMIC WEAPONS

The unsatisfactory state of affairs with regard to the outlawing of atomic and other principal types of weapons of mass extermination gives rise to particular anxiety on the part of millions of common people. The anxiety is all the more justified for the reason that atomic weapons are weapons of attack and aggression. After one and a half years of work by the Atomic Energy Commission, none of the tasks set before it by the General Assembly's resolution of January 24, 1946, has been completed, nor has there been the slightest progress in the fulfilment of those tasks. . . .

. . . The United States of America, believing that it will continue to exercise a monopoly with regard to atomic weapons, resists any attempts to dismantle the existing stock of atomic bombs and outlaw their further production. At the same time the United States of America systematically increases the production of such bombs. The disagreement among the Commission members in this respect hinders the work of the Commission and paralyzes all efforts directed to the successful solution of the task set before the Commission.

At the same time there is no doubt whatever that many of these disagreements could have been eliminated, provided there had been displayed a more objective approach to the question on the part of some delegations, the American delegation included. For instance, it could have been possible to eliminate the disagreement that arose in connection with the Soviet delegation's proposal on de-struction of atomic bomb stocks upon the coming into force of the convention outlawing atomic weapons. As is known, the majority in the Commission agreed in principle that it is necessary to destroy the stock of atomic weapons and use their nuclear energy only for peaceful aims. Only one delegation, to wit, the delegation of the United States of America, continues to object to the destruction of the stock of atomic bombs, thus obstructing a decision on the question approved by the majority of the Commission.

One's attention is attracted by the situation that has been created with regard to the question of inspection. The American delegation previously was stressing the particular significance of inspection. In the Soviet delegation's proposals inspection also is the main issue after the outlawing of atomic weapons.

At present, the American delegation has unexpectedly begun to lessen the importance of inspection, putting into first place other questions, such as the transfer of atomic enterprises to the ownership of an international body, management, issuance of licenses and so forth. At the same time, the American delegation does not want the opinions of authoritative men of science to be taken into account. For instance, in the memorandum of the British Council of Atomic Scientists Association, which includes such prominent scientists as Rudolf Peierls, Oliphant, Moon and others, that memorandum objects to the ownership of the means of production of atomic energy by an international control body. As is known, the British scientists emphasize in this memorandum that transfer to this international control body of the means of production "into its full ownership, in the usual sense of this word, would give rise to difficulties, since this ownership would give the control body the right to decide whether this or that country is entitled to construct atomic energy plants and the right to prevent the use of energy manufactured by such plants and to set the terms for supplying such energy."

The British scientists, criticizing the thesis defended by the American delegation since the time of Mr. Baruch's activity, justly state: "Such a restriction would make it possible to intervene in the economic life of each country to an extent not necessary for preventing the use of atomic energy for destructive purposes." . . .

The Soviet Union proposed in the interests of universal peace to conclude a convention outlawing the use of atomic weapons in all circumstances whatever. This proposal made by the Soviet Union found a warm response and support in all countries. "Such a convention," says the memorandum of the British Association of Scientific Workers, "appears to us to be highly desirable, and it is difficult to justify the reluctance on the part of the United Kingdom and the United States of America to agree to it." . . .

The Soviet Union stands for strict international control over atomic energy plants but such control, however, which should not be transformed into interference with those branches of national industry and with those questions that are not connected with atomic energy. Here again, the British atomic scientists are right, because in the memorandum covered on January 23 of this year they state "that the right of inspection should be limited as far as possible and should not serve to satisfy excessive curiosity with regard to legitimate industry and other forms of activity."

The British scientists in this memorandum published in August, 1947, once more point to the necessity of restricting to certain limits the rights of inspection, which should not serve the aims of organized economic and military espionage. The memorandum states: "The United States and other supporters of the Baruch plan should be encouraged to formulate safeguards to ensure that any inspection scheme should not develop into an elaborate system of espionage." . . .

The previously quoted memorandum of the British scientists does not conceal the fact that the United States plan for the organization of control over atomic energy provides for measures which, as stated in the memorandum, "can be interpreted as a support of the United States dominance in the province of atomic energy. . . ."

The Soviet delegation is opposed to such a thesis and will remain opposed to it in future, trying to achieve not the dominance of a single nation in the international control body but equality of all participants in this body in all its activities.

It should be recalled in this connection that the United States representatives on the Atomic Energy Commission stubbornly oppose the simultaneous establishment of control over atomic industry in all its stages, from the extraction of raw material up to the output of finished products.

The United States representatives propose to postpone indefinitely the establishment of control over the most dangerous final stages of atomic manufacturing, stages in which the United States considers itself at the present time to be holding a monopoly. At the same time, the United States insists that control over the initial stage—extraction of the raw material—should be immediately introduced. It is abundantly clear that the American position cannot be otherwise interpreted but as a position according to which control is not to be extended to the United States of America while all other countries should immediately come under international control. . . .

The conscience of the nations cannot tolerate such a state of affairs when, notwithstanding the appeal of the United Nations Organization to eliminate atomic weapons and other principal types of mass extermination of human beings, the manufacturing of such means not only continues but even increases more and more.

IV. THE PLANS OF TRUMAN AND MARSHALL ARE NOT COMPATIBLE WITH THE PRINCIPLES OF THE UNITED NATIONS ORGANIZATION

The so-called "Truman Doctrine" and "Marshall Plan" are particularly striking instances of the violation of the principles of the United Nations Organization, and of the ignoring of the Organization.

The experience of the past few months has proved that the proclamation of this doctrine meant that the United States Government openly gave up the principles of international cooperation and concerted action of the great powers, and passed to attempts to dictate its will to other independent nations, utilizing at the same time the economic means allotted as relief for individual countries in need for open political pressure. This has been sufficiently illustrated by the measures undertaken by the United States Government in Greece and Turkey outside the framework of the United Nations Organization, and in evasion of it, as well as by the measures planned for Europe in accordance with the so-called "Marshall Plan." This policy is in deep contradiction to the principle proclaimed by the General Assembly in its resolution of December 11, 1946, that assistance to other countries "should never be used as a political weapon."

The "Marshall Plan" is in fact, as it is perfectly clear now, only another version of the "Truman Doctrine" adjusted to the conditions of postwar Europe. The United States Government, when putting forward this "Plan," apparently expected, with the cooperation of the British and French Governments, to make the European countries that are in need of relief face the necessity of giving up their inalienable rights to dispose of their own economic resources, to plan their own national economy as they see fit, just as the United States Government expected to make all those countries directly dependent on the interests of American monopolies which are seeking to avoid the impending crisis by accelerated export to Europe of accumulated commodities and capital. . . .

It is becoming more clear to everybody that the implementation of the "Marshall Plan" would mean the subjugation of European countries to economic and political control exercised by the United States of America, and direct interference on its part in the internal affairs of those countries.

At the same time this "Plan" is an attempt to break Europe into two camps and to complete, with the assistance of the United Kingdom and France, the formation of a bloc of a number of European countries, hostile to the interests of the democratic states of Eastern Europe, and first of all, to the interests of the Soviet Union. The tendency to set up a bloc of a number of Western European countries, Western Germany included, as against the countries of Eastern Europe is an important feature of this "Plan." At the same time, it is intended to use Western Germany and German heavy industry (the Ruhr) as one of the principal economic bases for United States expansion in Europe, in spite of the national interests of the countries which have been victims of German aggression.

It suffices to recall these facts to show indisputably the full incompatibility of such a policy of the United States as well as the policies of the French and United Kingdom Governments which support the United States, with the basic principles of the United Nations Organization.

V. THE VIOLATIONS OF THE UNITED NATIONS ORGANIZATION'S DECISIONS

Neither can one consider as normal such a situation with regard to the relations among the members of the United Nations Organization where foreign armed forces continue to remain on the territories of the members of the Organization, such armed forces being instruments of political interference in their internal affairs and thus creating unequal and subordinate relations among the states, contradictory to the Charter. British troops still remain in Egypt against the will of that country. Troops still remain in Greece in violation of her State Constitution, and in Transjordan which applied for membership in the United Nations. United States troops continue to remain in China. This by no means contributes to the establishment of internal peace in that country. The presence of foreign troops on the territory of non-enemy states should not take place unless such presence is connected with the protection of communications with ex-enemy territories during their occupation. The strengthening of universal peace and mutual confidence among the nations demands an urgent and positive solution of the question of the evacuation from the territories of the non-enemy states of foreign troops when they are not engaged in guarding the communications of their countries with former enemy states.

One should point out also the failure on the part of some members of the Organization to put into effect important decisions of the Assembly: on the Spanish question (Argentina); on the question of discrimination against Indians in South Africa, and the establishment of a trusteeship over the former mandated territory of Southwest Africa (Union of South Africa).

The General Assembly cannot pass by such actions of some individual members of the Organization who disrupt the achievement of the aims set out by the decisions of the Assembly, and who weaken the prestige of the United Nations Organization.

In this connection, we cannot but dwell on the developments which have taken place in Indonesia. These events cannot be qualified otherwise than as an act of aggression perpetrated against the people of Indonesia by a member state of the United Nations. The unprovoked military attack by the Netherlands against the Indonesian Republic has caused the justified indignation of all honest people throughout the world. Well, did the United Nations render due assistance and defense to the Indonesian people? We all know that this was not the case. As the result of the consideration of the Indonesian question by the Security Council, certain states made no small effort to minimize the importance and significance of developments in In-

donesia, and made no small effort to foist upon the Security Council a decision which can by no means be regarded as sufficient to protect the legitimate interests of the Indonesian Republic, which has become a victim of military attack. It is clear that such decisions cannot but undermine the prestige of the United Nations, which is specifically called upon to secure the maintenance of peace among the nations. . . .

Touching upon the subject of the Trusteeship Council, the Soviet Union delegation also considers it necessary to note the following:

At the meeting of the General Assembly of December 13, 1946, the delegation of the Union of Soviet Socialist Republics criticized the agreements on trusteeship over the ex-mandated territories submitted for the approval of the Assembly, for the reason that the very preparation of those agreements and some of their articles did not correspond to what was required by the appropriate Articles of the Charter of the United Nations. . . .

The unsatisfactory state of affairs with regard to the work of the United Nations Organization is not an accident, but it is a direct result of an attitude toward the Organization on the part of a number of member nations of the Organization, particularly the United States and the United Kingdom. . . .

As regards the Soviet Union, its policy with regard to the United Nations Organization is a policy of strengthening the Organization; it is a policy of broadening and strengthening international cooperation; a policy of steady, consistent observance of the Charter and of the implementation and fulfillment of its principles.

The strengthening of the United Nations Organization is only possible on the basis of a respectful attitude toward the political and economic independence of nations, on the basis of a respectful attitude toward the sovereign equality of nations, as well as of a consistent and unconditional observance of one of the most important principles of the United Nations Organization, that is, the principle of unanimity and accord among the great powers in making decisions on the most important problems dealing with the maintenance of international peace and security. This is in full accord with the special responsibility of these powers for the maintenance of universal peace, and is a guarantee of the protection of the interests of all the members of the United Nations Organization, great and small.

The Soviet Union feels that it is its duty to struggle resolutely against any attempts to shake this principle, no matter under what motives or guises these attempts might be made.

It is only left for me to say a few words with regard to the address of the Honorable Secretary of State of the United States of America, Mr. Marshall. . . .

The charges leveled by the United States delegation against Yugoslavia, Bulgaria and Albania are utterly arbitrary and without any proof. These charges go much further than the conclusions of the majority of the Commission, which were not supported by almost one half of the members of that Commission and which do not stand criticism if one is to take any serious approach to the data on which the conclusions are based. It will not be difficult to prove that the so-called Report of the Balkan Investigating Commission is full of contradictions and gross exaggerations which deprive its conclusions of any importance or significance whatsoever.

Now, as to the question of Korea. Having arbitrarily outlined the situation in such a way that the futility of the work of the Soviet-American Commission on Korea is attributed to the Soviet Union, Mr. Marshall makes a proposal which is in direct violation of the Moscow Agreement on Korea reached by the Foreign Ministers in December, 1945. According to this Agreement, the United States of America and the Union of Soviet Socialist Republics undertook the responsibility of preparing a joint solution to the problem of the unification of Korea into one independent democratic state. The new proposal made by Mr. Marshall is a violation of the obligations assumed by the United States of America, and for that reason is not right or acceptable. The United States Government, instead of undertaking arrangements for carrying out adopted measures according to the Moscow Agreement on Korea in December, 1945, and submitting them to the consideration of the Governments of the United States of America, the Union of Soviet Socialist Republics, the United Kingdom and China, prefers to violate its undertakings by attempting to conceal, under the prestige of the General Assembly, its own unilateral and completely unjustifiable actions. The Soviet Government cannot accept such a violation of the agreement on Korea and will insist that the proposal made by Mr. Marshall be rejected for the reason that it is contrary to the obligations assumed under the tripartite agreement by the three powers on Korea.

Now, as to the question of the Interim Committee. Mr. Marshall proposes the establishment of a Standing Committee of the General Assembly under the title of the "Interim Committee on Peace and Security," which would pay constant attention to the work of the General Assembly and its continuing problems. In spite of the reservations in the United States proposal to the effect that the Committee would not impinge on matters which are the primary responsibility of the Security Council or its special commissions, there is not the slightest doubt that the attempt to create an Interim Committee is nothing but a badly concealed scheme to substitute for and to bypass the Security Council. The functions of this Committee, whose task it would be to consider "situations and disputes that impair friendly relations" among nations, are nothing more than the functions of the Security Council as provided for by Article 34 of the Charter. . . .

The Soviet Union delegation believes it necessary to raise before the General Assembly a very important question concerning measures against the propaganda of a new war steadily increasing in a number of countries. . . .

We wish to be sure that the severe lesson given to the aggressive states during the Second World War has not passed away leaving no traces, and that the fate of the severely punished aggressors of the last war will serve as a stern warning to those who, disregarding their obligations to develop friendly relations among the nations and to strengthen peace and security in the whole world, are preparing both secretly and openly for a new war. A war psychosis which is instigated by the efforts of the militarist and expansionist circles of certain countries—the United States occupying the foremost place among them—is continually spreading and assuming an all the more threatening character.

A furious campaign in the press, mainly in the United States press and in the press of the countries obediently following the example of the United States, like Turkey, has been spread for a considerable time for the purpose of coaxing world public opinion in favor of a new war. All means of psychological influence have been used—newspapers, magazines, radio and films.

This propaganda of a new war is being carried on under various flags and pretexts. But no matter how much the flags and pretexts differ, the essence of the whole propaganda remains the same: to justify the furious armament race which is being carried on by the United States, including atomic weapons; to justify the limitless desires of the influential circles in the United States to fulfill their expansionist plans, the keystone of which is a senseless idea of world domination. Torrents of the propaganda of a new war and appeals to prepare for it better and more expediently flow from the pages of the press of the United States.

A number of newspapers and magazines, mostly American, cry every day and in every way about a new war, systematically promoting this baneful psychological coaxing of the public opinion of their countries. The war-mongers indulge in propaganda under a smokescreen of cries about the strengthening of national defense and the so-called necessity to fight against a war danger which allegedly comes from other countries. The war-mongering propagandists try by hook and crook to frighten people poorly versed in politics by fables and vicious fabrications and slanders about alleged preparations on the part of the Soviet Union to attack the United States. They certainly know only too well that they are telling lies and slanders, that the Soviet Union is not threatening in any way an attack on any country; that the Soviet Union is devoting all its forces to the cause of rehabilitation of the areas that either were destroyed by the war or which suffered general damage in the course of the war; that the Soviet Union is devoting all its efforts to the cause of rehabilitation and further development of its national economy. . . .

The Soviet Union is engaged in the work of peaceful reconstruction, is peacefully laboring, having much to do in the field of rehabilitation of areas damaged by the war, and in that of strengthening and further development of its national economy which suffered from the heavy blows of the war imposed upon the Soviet Union by the Hitlerite bandits. . . . Should any person in the Soviet Union make a statement, even in infinitesimal degree resembling the above-mentioned statements which are full of criminal greediness for a new manslaughter, such a statement would meet with a severe rebuff and public disapproval as a socially dangerous act leading to serious harm.

Nevertheless, the gentlemen who make their profession the baiting of the Soviet Union and other democratic eastern European countries, and the baiting of consistent democrats and antagonists of a new war in other countries as well, never lack false and slanderous insinuations manufactured by these provocateurs and war-mongers and spread all over the world through numerous information channels.

They stubbornly preach that a new war is inevitable and even necessary, under the pretext that it is necessary to forestall the alleged aggressive policy of the Soviet Union and other eastern European countries. Really, this is to lay the fault at another man's door. Truly, as a Russian proverb says: though it is he who flogs, he cries out in the pretence of pain. . . .

As one can judge by a number of signs, the preparation for a new war has already passed the stage of sheer propaganda, psychological coaxing and war of nerves. Numerous facts prove that in some countries—and this is particularly the case in the United States of America—the war psychosis is being warmed up by putting into effect practical measures of a military and strategic character, together with such organizational and technical measures as the construction of new military bases, relocation of armed forces in accordance with the plans of future military operations, expansion of manufacture of new armaments, and feverish work for the purpose of improving existing weapons.

Simultaneously, military blocs, military agreements on so-called mutual defense are being formed and concluded, measures for the unification of armaments are being elaborated, and the general headquarters plans for a new war are being worked out. The American journalist Leon Pearson, in a recent broadcast, had reason to admit that "American military officers slowly and carefully are preparing for the next world war, in which the enemy will be Russia."

This is the way in which the warmongers and propagandists of a new war are acting. Being afraid of a new crisis, they are instigating a new war, expecting to remove by such means the approaching menace of collapse and loss of their profits. . . .

The most active role in the promotion of this propaganda is assumed by the representatives of American capitalist mo-nopolies, by representatives of the largest enterprises and the leading branches of American industry, by representatives of banking and financial groups. These are the groups that have received from the Second World War great profits and accumulated vast capital, as was the case in the First World War.

Comparing the five prewar years, 1935 to 1939 inclusive, with the five years of the Second World War, 1940 to 1944, inclusive, we find that the profits of all American corporations for the five prewar years amounted, after payment of taxes, to 15.3 billion dollars, and for the five years of the Second World War those profits amounted, after payment of taxes, to 42.3 billion dollars. According to the data of the Department of Commerce the net profit of those corporations for six years of the war—1940 to 1945 inclusive—amounted to 52 billion dollars. . . .

Thus, in certain countries, the war is not so hateful after all to those groups of society which skillfully utilize the hardships of wartime for the purpose of their own enrichment. Therefore, it is not by accident that James Allen in his book *International Monopolies and Peace* states that in capitalist countries economy suffers so-called "loss of balance" and "radical disruption," and quotes from the report of a governmental body engaged in the research of this particular problem some extracts which lead to the conclusion that "only under the conditions of war is the modern economic system able to secure approximately full employment." Any comments on this frank confession are hardly needed. It speaks eloquently for itself.

It should be noted that the capitalist monopolies, having secured a decisive influence during the war, have retained this influence on the termination of the war, skillfully utilizing for this purpose governmental subsidies and grants of billions of dollars, as well as the protection which they enjoyed and are still enjoying from the various governmental agencies and organizations. This is facilitated by the close connection of the monopolies with senators and members of governments, many of whom often are either officials or partners in the monopolistic corporations.

This situation affects also the industrial scientific-technical activity concentrated in the laboratories of various large corporations.

The same can be said with regard to the research field in the use of atomic energy. Such capitalist monopolies as Dupont chemical trust, Monsanto Chemical Company, Westinghouse company, General Electric, Standard Oil, and others are most closely connected with this research work, being complete masters in the field. Before the war they maintained the closest cartel connections with German trusts, and many cartel agreements contained a clause to the effect that there would be a renewal of the exchange of information after the termination of the war.

All these facts suffice to explain the extreme interest of the various capitalist monopolies in the manufacture of atomic weapons. One can find in these facts an explanation for the stubborn resistance to the justified demands to outlaw the manufacture of atomic weapons and destroy the stock of atomic bombs, in the manufacture of which tremendous sums are invested. The rush for profits on the part of the capitalist monopolies, their endeavor to maintain by all means and to develop further those branches of war industry which yield large profits, cannot but influence foreign policy, strengthening militaristic, expansionist and aggressive tendencies to satisfy the ever-increasing appetite of the influential monopolistic circles.

WHO IS INCITING THE NEW WAR?

Such is the soil in the United States of America that feeds the propaganda of a new war. The promoters of this propaganda are not only prominent representatives of American influential industrial and military circles, influential organs of the press and prominent politicians, but also official representatives of the American Government as well. It is by no means accidental that the particularly violent warmongers among them are those who are closely connected already with commercial, industrial and financial trusts, concerns and monopolies. There is no need to name too many names; it is sufficient to name some of them, having in view certainly not their personalities, personal convictions, personal merits, and so on, but mainly those social groups, enterprises, industrial, technical and scientific societies and firms whose views and interests these persons represent.

1. Dorn, Member of the House of Representatives. On May 7 when the House of Representatives discussed the proposed relief assistance for the Greek and Turkish Governments, he made a cynical statement worthy of an experienced war-monger to the effect that "the Soviet Union cannot be halted by four hundred million dollars." "But this can be done," he said, "with the aid of a big air force and the bombing of potential industrial centers of the Soviet Union, the Ural Mountains industrial area, and other vital places." This was said from the floor of the House of Representatives of the United States of America by a man who considers himself to be a representative of the people of the United States of America.

2. Jordan, the President of the National Industrial Conference Board. He made a slanderous statement concerning the Soviet Union. According to Jordan, the above-named Jordan, for whom the sky is the limit, the United States of America should manufacture many atomic bombs and quickly release them whether there is or is not any reason to believe that the country concerned is manufacturing armaments.

3. Earle, a former United States Minister in Bulgaria, who was testifying before the Committee on Un-American Activities of the House of Representatives, stated in a provocative manner that the United States of America should immedi-

ately use atomic bombs against the country which refuses to agree with the American draft inspection system. Frightening his listeners with stories of Soviet "reactive bombs released from submarines," he insisted that "the most terrible weapons should be secretly perfected," and that "the Russians should be informed that when the first bomb is dropped on us" (the United States of America) "we will destroy every village in Russia."

4. Eaton, Chairman of the Committee on Foreign Affairs of the House of Representatives, published in the *American Magazine* an article in which he stated that "we are still able to block Russia psychologically; if we fail in this we should rout Russia by the force of weapons. . . ."

Where has it been said? It has been said in the *American Magazine*. By whom has it been said? By the Chairman of the Committee on Foreign Affairs. What kind of policy can one expect from such a Chairman of the Committee on Foreign Affairs?

5. Senator McMahon, former Chairman of the Joint Congressional Committee on Atomic Energy, stated in Congress that the "United States should be the first to drop atom bombs if the atom war is inevitable." . . .

6. Senator Brooks, from Illinois, in his speech in the Senate on March 12, 1947, did not hesitate to declare quite cynically that had the United States listened to the advice the Republican Party offered before the war, and "had the Germans eaten up Russia," the present Truman program would have been unnecessary. He added that in wartime the United States rendered assistance to the Soviet Union, and now, said Brooks, the United States might be compelled to wage war against the Soviet Union.

7. General Deane, the former head of the United States Military Mission in the Soviet Union, writes in his book that the United States military program should be designed to meet specialized situations which war with the Soviet Union would entail.

8. Harwood, Vice-President of the industrial firm of Cutler-Hammer, Incorporated, according to the *Milwaukee Journal*, said that the atom bomb is a poor weapon because instead of exterminating human beings only it destroys excessive amounts of property as well. This Mr. Harwood cynically said at the conference of the American Inter-Professional Institute of Milwaukee: "Though it sounds cruel, still the type of weapon we should possess if we are to wage war is such a one that will kill only human beings. Such a weapon will eliminate during the next war the necessity to rehabilitate countries and material property on such a broad and expensive scale."

9. Finally, I must name a name which is well-known to all of us, Mr. John Foster Dulles who in a speech delivered on February 10, 1947, in Chicago urged a tough foreign policy toward the Soviet Union, declaring that if the United States of America does not take such a course, counting on the possibility of reaching a compromise with the Soviet Union, then war is inevitable. In the same speech Mr. Dulles boasted that since the collapse of the Roman Empire no nation ever possessed such great superiority of material power as the United States and urged the United States to utilize this power to promote its ideals. This is good advice indeed, from a member of the United States delegation to the General Assembly of the United Nations.

The meaning of these statements is clear—in some cases they are open and in some cases they are poorly camouflaged instigation for war against the Union of Soviet Socialist Republics. This is a provocative attempt to divert attention from the true war-mongers and to camouflage their war-mongering activities with slanderous demagogy about a "social revolution in the whole world," and other rot, expecting the simpletons to believe it. . . .

Numerous organs of the American reactionary press, which are in the hands of such newspaper magnates as Morgan, Rockefeller, Ford, Hearst, McCormick and others do not lag behind the reactionary political statesmen who busy themselves with war-mongering. As is known, Morgan controls the following magazines: *Time*, *Life*, and *Fortune*, published by the well-known publishing corporation, Time Incorporated, the largest shareholder being, by the way, Brown Brothers, Harriman and Company.

It is well-known that the richest American capitalists own or control large organs of the press—magazines, newspapers, bulletins; they have their own publishing houses inundating the book market with specific publications. By the order of their bosses all these publications are waging sharp propaganda for unleashing a new war, using all possible insinuations and forgeries fabricated in a certain way with the view to provoking hatred toward the Soviet Union and other Eastern European nations of a new democracy. Provocative appeals for an attack on other nations which allegedly threaten the security of the United States are being daily trumpeted from the pages of these newspapers and magazines, although these organs of the press, as well as their bosses, are well aware of the fact that nobody is going to attack the United States in this respect. . . .

But the main thing to be pointed out is not the fact that such statements take place, but the fact that they do not encounter the necessary rebuff, thus only encouraging further provocations on their part. . . .

It may be said with confidence, however, that the American people, as well as the peoples of the other democratic countries, are against a new war while the scars made by the last war have not yet healed on their bodies. But in most cases it is impossible for the people to speak of their needs and wishes in books, magazines and newspapers published in millions of copies. This, of course, facilitates the work of the propagandists and instigators of a new war who take advantage of their

privileged position against the interests of peace-loving peoples.

I cannot but add a few words with regard to the propaganda of a new war on the part of various scientific institutions and universities in the United States. In this connection, one cannot but mention the works recently published by Yale University under the title *The Absolute Weapon*, in which a group of scientists, speaking of the atomic weapon and the control of the use of atomic energy, found nothing better than to come to the conclusion that "the most effective existing means of preventing war is the ability to launch war literally in no time."

Under the mask of scientific objectivity, this book treats different variants of atomic war, and says that if the United States air forces "succeed in using bases in northern Canada, the towns of the Soviet Union will be within a much shorter distance," and thus "it will be possible to destroy, operating from their own bases, the majority of the large cities of any other power." . . .

How far has gone the propaganda for a new war, accompanied by demands for the production of the deadliest types of weapons, might be seen from the report published in the magazine *Chemical and Engineering News*, of Mr. Merck, where in the section under the title "Science and Civilization," all the deadly advantages of bacterial warfare are openly advocated. Just the same direction is also taken in an article in the *Army Ordnance*, concerning a new toxin, the development of which, according to this magazine, cost 50 million dollars, which expenses, however, to use the author's words, "are fully justified," because one ounce of this toxin is quite sufficient to kill 180 million people.

When reading all this so-called quasi-scientific literature, one feels what a satanic energy is being developed by the war-mongers and propagandists of a new war in order to create a suitable atmosphere capable of poisoning the people's minds with war madness. . . .

This information coincides with the material in the journal *Newsweek*, which published an article of the editor of the foreign section of this magazine, Mr. Kern, who recently returned from Japan. Mr. Kern says that in Japan the American generals are systematically agitating the Japanese militarists in the direction of the inevitability and necessity of war against the Soviet Union. . . .

Thus for a long time in the United States of America war propaganda has been systematically carried on, with the following main trends:

1. Fear of the Soviet Union, as a mighty power allegedly seeking world domination and preparing an attack on the United States of America, is propagated and inspired in every way. While doing so, slanderous fictions and provocative attacks of all possible kinds are used against the Soviet Union most shamelessly.

2. Open propaganda is being carried on for the increase of armaments and further perfection of atomic weapons, while any attempt to limit or to prohibit the use of atomic weapons is rejected.

3. Statements openly calling for an immediate attack against the Soviet Union are made, using provocative intimidations with the military strength of the Soviet Union on the one hand, and stressing the necessity of taking advantage of the present situation when, in the war-mongers' opinion, the Soviet Union is weak militarily, not having fully recovered after the Second World War.

Thus we have a shameless propaganda of fear against the power of the so-called Polar Bear, the Soviet Union; and on the other hand it is stated that the Polar Bear should be taken fast while he is not yet strong enough and while his wounds are not yet healed.

4. The war-hungry psychosis is stimulated in every way among the American public, excited and fanned by militarists and expansionist circles of the United States of America.

American progressive persons are aware of this situation and are making efforts to expose the preparation for war, which is now carried on in America, and to sober the minds of those affected with a war madness. These progressive persons in the United States of America and the progressive elements of the American press expose the military preparation which is carried on in the United States, instigated by military groups and various reactionary organizations. . . .

From the above, it follows quite obviously that American reactionary circles who reckon only with their own selfish interests and are ready for the sake of these interests to plunge humanity into a new exterminating world war, are the main inciters in the field of propaganda and instigation of a new war.

The American reactionaries, however, are not alone in these efforts of theirs. They are supported by their adherents in some other countries who are busy knocking together military-political and simply political Western, Northern and other blocs. In this connection it is deemed necessary to mention the statements made by certain British politicians who, it is true, are acting not so resolutely as their United States adherents, but mostly in an underhanded way—yet in the same alarmist spirit.

Everybody remembers Churchill's speech at Fulton, Missouri. . . .

In this connection one also ought to point out the fact that the Anglo-American Combined Chiefs of Staff in Washington are continuing to function. It is known that Great Britain is represented on the Combined Chiefs of Staff by the military mission headed by General Morgan, and that the United States is represented by a military mission headed by Admiral Leahy. This Anglo-American Combined Chiefs of Staff was set up to coordinate military operations against Germany and Japan and still continues to exist, and it is not known for what purpose, in spite of the fact that the war ceased two years ago. . . .

THE PROPOSALS OF THE SOVIET UNION

The Government of the Soviet Union feels that the conscience of the nations who carried the whole burden of the recently terminated Second World War, who paid for that war imposed on them with their own blood, suffering and ruins, cannot reconcile itself with such a state of affairs.

The delegation of the Soviet Union, on instruction of the Government of the Soviet Union, declares that the Union of Soviet Socialist Republics considers as a matter of urgency the adoption by the United Nations of measures directed against the propaganda of a new war; propaganda which is being carried out at present in some countries, and particularly in the United States of America. To this end the Soviet Union delegation suggests that the following resolution be adopted:

1. The United Nations Organization condemns the criminal propaganda of a new war which is being carried on by reactionary circles in a number of countries, particularly in the United States, Turkey and Greece by means of spreading all kinds of insinuations through radio, press, cinema and public statements and which contains an open appeal for an attack on peace-loving democratic countries.

2. The United Nations Organization considers the tolerance, and more so the support, of such propaganda of a new war, that would inevitably be transformed into a third world war, as a violation of the obligations undertaken by the members of the United Nations Organization, whose Charter provides for an obligation "to develop friendly relations among nations based on respect for the principle of equal rights and self-determination of peoples and to take other appropriate measures to strengthen universal peace" so "that international peace and security and justice are not endangered." (Article I, Paragraph 2; Article II, Paragraph 3.)

3. The United Nations Organization considers it necessary to urge the governments of all countries on pain of criminal punishment to prohibit war propaganda in any form whatever and to take measures for the prevention and suppression of war propaganda as a socially dangerous activity threatening the vital interests and welfare of the peace-loving nations of the world.

4. The United Nations Organization reaffirms the necessity for the speediest implementation of the decision of the General Assembly of December 14, 1946, with regard to the reduction of armaments and the decision of the General Assembly of January 24, 1946, on the exclusion from national armaments of atomic weapons and all other principal types of weapons designed for mass extermination, and considers that the implementation of these decisions meets the interests of all the peace-loving nations and would be the heaviest blow upon the propaganda and the instigators of a new war.

Generalissimo Stalin, in his welcome to Moscow, on the occasion of celebrating the eight hundredth anniversary of the foundation of Moscow, indicated that Moscow was the herald of the fight for peace and friendship among nations. . . .

1. PROPOSALS FOR THE CONTROL OF ATOMIC ENERGY, 1946[1]

By BERNARD M. BARUCH

EDITORS' NOTE.—Proposals for the international control of atomic energy were initiated by the United States of America, Great Britain, and Canada in November, 1945, and approved by Russia in the Moscow Conference of December, 1945. Under the sponsorship of these powers, the United Nations Atomic Energy Commission was created by the General Assembly of the United Nations in its opening session of January, 1946. Bernard M. Baruch, American representative on the above commission, made the following official proposals to his fellow-commissioners in June, 1946. In the interval between January and June the formulation of American policy had been assisted by the preparation of the Acheson-Lilienthal report on the control of atomic energy.

American proposals were countered by Russian proposals, and the controversy over international control within this area became part of the wider, and so far unsolved, controversy between East and West. As the political differences have hardened, the effort of the Atomic Energy Commission to fulfil its assignment, like that of the United Nations Organization as a whole, has been steadily stultified.

Bernard M. Baruch (1870——), elder statesman, was prominently associated with the organization of war production and postwar planning in both world wars. In the earlier period he was chairman of the War Industries Board and economic adviser to the American Peace Commission. In the latter he acted as adviser to James F. Byrnes, director of war mobilization (1943–45).

My Fellow Members of the United Nations Atomic Energy Commission, and My Fellow Citizens of the World:

We are here to make a choice between the quick and the dead.

That is our business.

Behind the black portent of the new atomic age lies a hope which, seized upon with faith, can work our salvation. If we fail, then we have damned every man to be the slave of Fear. Let us not deceive ourselves: We must elect World Peace or World Destruction.

Science has torn from nature a secret so vast in its potentialities that our minds cower from the terror it creates. Yet terror is not enough to inhibit the use of the atomic bomb. The terror created by weapons has never stopped man from employing them. For each new weapon a defense has been produced, in time. But now we face a condition in which adequate defense does not exist.

1. United States Department of State, *The United States and the United Nations* ("Report Series," No. 7 [Washington, 1947]), pp. 169–78.

Science, which gave us this dread power, shows that it *can* be made a giant help to humanity, but science does *not* show us how to prevent its baleful use. So we have been appointed to obviate that peril by finding a meeting of the minds and hearts of our people. Only in the will of mankind lies the answer.

It is to express this will and make it effective that we have been assembled. We must provide the mechanism to assure that atomic energy is used for peaceful purposes and preclude its use in war. To that end, we must provide immediate, swift, and sure punishment of those who violate the agreements that are reached by the nations. Penalization is essential if peace is to be more than a feverish interlude between wars. And, too, the United Nations can prescribe individual responsibility and punishment on the principles applied at Nurnberg by the Union of Soviet Socialist Republics, the United Kingdom, France, and the United States—a formula certain to benefit the world's future.

In this crisis, we represent not only our governments but, in a larger way, we represent the peoples of the world. We must remember that the peoples do not belong to the governments but that the governments belong to the peoples. We must answer their demands; we must answer the world's longing for peace and security.

In that desire the United States shares ardently and hopefully. The search of science for the absolute weapon has reached fruition in this country. But she stands ready to proscribe and destroy this instrument—to lift its use from death to life—if the world will join in a pact to that end.

In our success lies the promise of a new life, freed from the heart-stopping fears that now beset the world. The beginning of victory for the great ideals for which millions have bled and died lies in building a workable plan. Now we approach fulfilment of the aspirations of mankind. At the end of the road lies the fairer, better, surer life we crave and mean to have.

Only by a lasting peace are liberties and democracies strengthened and deepened. War is their enemy. And it will not do to believe that any of us can escape war's devastation. Victor, vanquished, and neutrals alike are affected physically, economically, and morally.

Against the degradation of war we can erect a safeguard. That is the guerdon for which we reach. Within the scope of the formula we outline here there will be found, to those who seek it, the essential elements of our purpose. Others will see only emptiness. Each of us carries his own mirror in which is reflected hope—or determined desperation—courage or cowardice.

There is a famine throughout the world today. It starves men's bodies. But there is a greater famine—the hunger of men's spirit. That starvation can be cured by the conquest of fear, and the substitution of hope, from which springs faith—faith in each other, faith that we want to work together toward salvation, and determination that those who threaten the peace and safety shall be punished.

The peoples of these democracies gathered here have a particular concern with our answer, for their peoples hate war. They will have a heavy exaction to make of those who fail to provide an escape. They are not afraid of an internationalism that protects; they are unwilling to be fobbed off by mouthings about narrow sovereignty, which is today's phrase for yesterday's isolation.

The basis of a sound foreign policy, in this new age, for all the nations here gathered, is that anything that happens, no matter where or how, which menaces the peace of the world, or the economic stability, concerns each and all of us.

That, roughly, may be said to be the central theme of the United Nations. It is with that thought we begin consideration of the most important subject that can engage mankind—life itself.

Let there be no quibbling about the duty and the responsibility of this group and of the governments we represent. I was moved, in the afternoon of my life, to add my effort to gain the world's quest, by the broad mandate under which we were created. The resolution of the General Assembly, passed January 24, 1946 in London, reads:

SECTION V. TERMS OF REFERENCE OF THE COMMISSION

The Commission shall proceed with the utmost despatch and enquire into all phases of the problems, and make such recommendations from time to time with respect to them as it finds possible. In particular the Commission shall make specific proposals:

a) For extending between all nations the exchange of basic scientific information for peaceful ends;

b) For control of atomic energy to the extent necessary to ensure its use only for peaceful purposes;

c) For the elimination from national armaments of atomic weapons and of all other major weapons adaptable to mass destruction;

d) For effective safeguards by way of inspection and other means to protect complying States against the hazards of violations and evasions.

The work of the Commission should proceed by separate stages, the successful completion of each of which will develop the necessary confidence of the world before the next stage is undertaken. . . .

Our mandate rests, in text and in spirit, upon the outcome of the Conference in Moscow of Messrs. Molotov of the Union of Soviet Socialist Republics, Bevin of the United Kingdom, and Byrnes of the United States of America. The three Foreign Ministers on December 27, 1945 proposed the establishment of this body.

Their action was animated by a preceding conference in Washington on November 15, 1945, when the President of the United States, associated with Mr. Attlee, Prime Minister of the United Kingdom, and Mr. Mackenzie King, Prime Minister of Canada, stated that international control of the whole field of atomic energy was immediately essential. They proposed the formation of this body. In examining

that source, the Agreed Declaration, it will be found that the fathers of the concept recognized the final means of world salvation—the abolition of war. Solemnly they wrote:

We are aware that the only complete protection for the civilized world from the destructive use of scientific knowledge lies in the prevention of war. No system of safeguards that can be devised will of itself provide an effective guarantee against production of atomic weapons by a nation bent on aggression. Nor can we ignore the possibility of the development of other weapons, or of new methods of warfare, which may constitute as great a threat to civilization as the military use of atomic energy.

Through the historical approach I have outlined, we find ourselves here to test if man can produce, through his will and faith, the miracle of peace, just as he has, through science and skill, the miracle of the atom.

The United States proposes the creation of an International Atomic Development Authority, to which should be entrusted all phases of the development and use of atomic energy, starting with the raw material and including—

1. Managerial control or ownership of all atomic-energy activities potentially dangerous to world security.

2. Power to control, inspect, and license all other atomic activities.

3. The duty of fostering the beneficial uses of atomic energy.

4. Research and development responsibilities of an affirmative character intended to put the Authority in the forefront of atomic knowledge and thus to enable it to comprehend, and therefore to detect, misuse of atomic energy. To be effective, the Authority must itself be the world's leader in the field of atomic knowledge and development and thus supplement its legal authority with the great power inherent in possession of leadership in knowledge.

I offer this as a basis for beginning our discussion.

But I think the peoples we serve would

not believe—and without faith nothing counts—that a treaty, merely outlawing possession or use of the atomic bomb, constitutes effective fulfilment of the instructions to this Commission. Previous failures have been recorded in trying the method of simple renunciation, unsupported by effective guarantees of security and armament limitation. No one would have faith in that approach alone.

Now, if ever, is the time to act for the common good. Public opinion supports a world movement toward security. If I read the signs aright, the peoples want a program not composed merely of pious thoughts but of enforceable sanctions—an international law with teeth in it.

We of this nation, desirous of helping to bring peace to the world and realizing the heavy obligations upon us arising from our possession of the means of producing the bomb and from the fact that it is part of our armament, are prepared to make our full contribution toward effective control of atomic energy.

When an adequate system for control of atomic energy, including the renunciation of the bomb as a weapon, has been agreed upon and put into effective operation and condign punishments set up for violations of the rules of control which are to be stigmatized as international crimes, we propose that—

1. Manufacture of atomic bombs shall stop;

2. Existing bombs shall be disposed of pursuant to the terms of the treaty; and

3. The Authority shall be in possession of full information as to the know-how for the production of atomic energy.

Let me repeat, so as to avoid misunderstanding: My country is ready to make its full contribution toward the end we seek, subject of course to our constitutional processes and to an adequate system of control becoming fully effective, as we finally work it out.

Now as to violations: In the agreement, penalties of as serious a nature as the nations may wish and as immediate and certain in their execution as possible should be fixed for—

1. Illegal possession or use of an atomic bomb;

2. Illegal possession, or separation, of atomic material suitable for use in an atomic bomb;

3. Seizure of any plant or other property belonging to or licensed by the Authority;

4. Wilful interference with the activities of the Authority;

5. Creation or operation of dangerous projects in a manner contrary to, or in the absence of, a license granted by the international control body.

It would be a deception, to which I am unwilling to lend myself, were I not to say to you and to our peoples that the matter of punishment lies at the very heart of our present security system. It might as well be admitted, here and now, that the subject goes straight to the veto power contained in the Charter of the United Nations so far as it relates to the field of atomic energy. The Charter permits penalization only by concurrence of each of the five great powers—the Union of Soviet Socialist Republics, the United Kingdom, China, France, and the United States.

I want to make very plain that I am concerned here with the veto power only as it affects this particular problem. There must be no veto to protect those who violate their solemn agreements not to develop or use atomic energy for destructive purposes.

The bomb does not wait upon debate. To delay may be to die. The time between violation and preventive action or punishment would be all too short for extended discussion as to the course to be followed.

As matters now stand several years may be necessary for another country to produce a bomb, *de novo*. However, once the basic information is generally known, and the Authority has established producing plants for peaceful purposes in the several countries, an illegal seizure of such a plant might permit a malevolent nation to produce a bomb in 12 months, and if preceded by secret preparation and necessary facilities perhaps even in a much shorter time. The time required—the advance warning given of the possible use of a bomb—can only be generally estimated but obviously will depend upon many factors, including the success with which the Authority has been able to introduce elements of safety in the design of its plants and the degree to which illegal and secret preparation for the military use of atomic energy will have been eliminated. Presumably no nation would think of starting a war with only one bomb.

This shows how imperative speed is in detecting and penalizing violations.

The process of prevention and penalization—a problem of profound statecraft—is, as I read it, implicit in the Moscow statement, signed by the Union of Soviet Socialist Republics, the United States, and the United Kingdom a few months ago.

But before a country is ready to relinquish any winning weapons it must have more than words to reassure it. It must have a guarantee of safety, not only against the offenders in the atomic area but against the illegal users of other weapons—bacteriological, biological, gas—perhaps—why not?—against war itself.

In the elimination of war lies our solution, for only then will nations cease to compete with one another in the production and use of dread "secret" weapons which are evaluated solely by their capacity to kill. This devilish program takes us back not merely to the Dark Ages but from cosmos to chaos. If we succeed in finding a suitable way to control atomic weapons, it is reasonable to hope that we may also preclude the use of other weapons adaptable to mass destruction. When a man learns to say "A" he can, if he chooses, learn the rest of the alphabet too.

Let this be anchored in our minds:

Peace is never long preserved by weight of metal or by an armament race. Peace can be made tranquil and secure only by understanding and agreement fortified by sanctions. We must embrace international cooperation or international disintegration.

Science has taught us how to put the atom to work. But to make it work for good instead of for evil lies in the domain dealing with the principles of human duty. We are now facing a problem more of ethics than of physics.

The solution will require apparent sacrifice in pride and in position, but better pain as the price of peace than death as the price of war.

I now submit the following measures as representing the fundamental features of a plan which would give effect to certain of the conclusions which I have epitomized.

1. *General*. The Authority should set up a thorough plan for control of the field of atomic energy, through various forms of ownership, dominion, licenses, operation, inspection, research, and management by competent personnel. After this is provided for, there should be as little interference as may be with the economic plans and the present private, corporate, and state relationships in the several countries involved.

2. *Raw Materials*. The Authority should have as one of its earliest purposes to obtain and maintain complete and accurate information on world supplies of uranium and thorium and to bring them under its dominion. The precise pattern of control for various types of deposits of such materials will have to depend upon the geological, mining, refining, and economic facts involved in different situations.

The Authority should conduct continuous surveys so that it will have the most complete knowledge of the world geology of uranium and thorium. Only after all current information on world sources of uranium and thorium is known to us all can equitable plans be made for their production, refining, and distribution.

3. *Primary Production Plants*. The Authority should exercise complete managerial control of the production of fissionable materials. This means that it should

control and operate all plants producing fissionable materials in dangerous quantities and must own and control the product of these plants.

4. *Atomic Explosives.* The Authority should be given sole and exclusive right to conduct research in the field of atomic explosives. Research activities in the field of atomic explosives are essential in order that the Authority may keep in the forefront of knowledge in the field of atomic energy and fulfil the objective of preventing illicit manufacture of bombs. Only by maintaining its position as the best-informed agency will the Authority be able to determine the line between intrinsically dangerous and non-dangerous activities.

5. *Strategic Distribution of Activities and Materials.* The activities entrusted exclusively to the Authority because they are intrinsically dangerous to security should be distributed throughout the world. Similarly, stockpiles of raw materials and fissionable materials should not be centralized.

6. *Non-dangerous Activities.* A function of the Authority should be promotion of the peacetime benefits of atomic energy.

Atomic research (except in explosives), the use of research reactors, the production of radioactive tracers by means of non-dangerous reactors, the use of such tracers, and to some extent the production of power should be open to nations and their citizens under reasonable licensing arrangements from the Authority. Denatured materials, whose use we know also requires suitable safeguards, should be furnished for such purposes by the Authority under lease or other arrangement. Denaturing seems to have been overestimated by the public as a safety measure.

7. *Definition of Dangerous and Non-dangerous Activities.* Although a reasonable dividing line can be drawn between dangerous and non-dangerous activities, it is not hard and fast. Provision should, therefore, be made to assure constant reexamination of the questions and to permit revision of the dividing line as changing conditions and new discoveries may require.

8. *Operations of Dangerous Activities.* Any plant dealing with uranium or thorium after it once reaches the potential of dangerous use must be not only subject to the most rigorous and competent inspection by the Authority, but its actual operation shall be under the management, supervision, and control of the Authority.

9. *Inspection.* By assigning intrinsically dangerous activities exclusively to the Authority, the difficulties of inspection are reduced. If the Authority is the only agency which may lawfully conduct dangerous activities, then visible operation by others than the Authority will constitute an unambiguous danger signal. Inspection will also occur in connection with the licensing functions of the Authority.

10. *Freedom of Access.* Adequate ingress and egress for all qualified representatives of the Authority must be assured. Many of the inspection activities of the Authority should grow out of, and be incidental to, its other functions. Important measures of inspection will be associated with the tight control of raw materials, for this is a keystone of the plan. The continuing activities of prospecting, survey, and research in relation to raw materials will be designed not only to serve the affirmative development functions of the Authority but also to assure that no surreptitious operations are conducted in the raw-materials field by nations or their citizens.

11. *Personnel.* The personnel of the Authority should be recruited on a basis of proven competence but also so far as possible on an international basis.

12. *Progress by Stages.* A primary step in the creation of the system of control is the setting forth, in comprehensive terms, of the functions, responsibilities, powers, and limitations of the Authority. Once a charter for the Authority has been adopted, the Authority and the system of control for which it will be responsible will require time to become fully organized and effective. The plan of control will, therefore,

have to come into effect in successive stages. These should be specifically fixed in the charter or means should be otherwise set forth in the charter for transitions from one stage to another, as contemplated in the resolution of the United Nations Assembly which created this Commission.

13. *Disclosures.* In the deliberations of the United Nations Commission on Atomic Energy, the United States is prepared to make available the information essential to a reasonable understanding of the proposals which it advocates. Further disclosures must be dependent, in the interests of all, upon the effective ratification of the treaty. When the Authority is actually created, the United States will join the other nations in making available the further information essential to that organization for the performance of its functions. As the successive stages of international control are reached, the United States will be prepared to yield, to the extent required by each stage, national control of activities in this field to the Authority.

14. *International Control.* There will be questions about the extent of control to be allowed to national bodies, when the Authority is established. Purely national authorities for control and development of atomic energy should to the extent necessary for the effective operation of the Authority be subordinate to it. This is neither an endorsement nor a disapproval of the creation of national authorities. The Commission should evolve a clear demarcation of the scope of duties and responsibilities of such national authorities.

And now I end. I have submitted an outline for present discussion. Our consideration will be broadened by the criticism of the United States proposals and by the plans of the other nations, which, it is to be hoped, will be submitted at their early convenience. I and my associates of the United States Delegation will make available to each member of this body books and pamphlets, including the Acheson-Lilienthal report, recently made by the United States Department of State, and the McMahon Committee Monograph No. 1 entitled *Essential Information on Atomic Energy* relating to the McMahon bill recently passed by the United States Senate, which may prove of value in assessing the situation.

All of us are consecrated to making an end of gloom and hopelessness. It will not be an easy job. The way is long and thorny, but supremely worth traveling. All of us want to stand erect, with our faces to the sun, instead of being forced to burrow into the earth, like rats.

The pattern of salvation must be worked out by all for all.

The light at the end of the tunnel is dim, but our path seems to grow brighter as we actually begin our journey. We cannot yet light the way to the end. However, we hope the suggestions of my Government will be illuminating.

Let us keep in mind the exhortation of Abraham Lincoln, whose words, uttered at a moment of shattering national peril, form a complete text for our deliberation. I quote, paraphrasing slightly:

We cannot escape history. We of this meeting will be remembered in spite of ourselves. No personal significance or insignificance can spare one or another of us. The fiery trial through which we are passing will light us down in honor or dishonor to the latest generation.

We say we are for Peace. The world will not forget that we say this. We know how to save Peace. The world knows that we do. We, even we here, hold the power and have the responsibility.

We shall nobly save, or meanly lose, the last, best hope of earth. The way is plain, peaceful, generous, just—a way which, if followed, the world will forever applaud.

My thanks for your attention.

2. THE TRUMAN DOCTRINE, 1947[1]

By Harry S. Truman

EDITORS' NOTE.—Much of the background of the Truman Doctrine may be read in and between the lines of the message. The end of the war found the Near and Middle East—key zones of big-power rivalry—exposed to the pressures of Russian, British, and American power and convulsed by internal disorders. A favorable platform for the extension of Russian power had been created by the Soviet victories: notably in the Balkans, where all but the Grecian tip of the peninsula had passed into the sphere of Russian influence. Russian pressure on Greece, Turkey, and Iran had aroused growing misgivings among the weaker powers. The big power immediately interested in the equilibrium of this area had been Britain, traditionally dominant in its maritime zones and redeployed in the same regions throughout the war. It was the sharp contraction of British power, the result of war strain and near-bankruptcy, which forced Britain to reduce her commitments and so obliged America to define her own position.

The gravity of the situation which confronts the world today necessitates my appearance before a joint session of the Congress.

The foreign policy and the national security of this country are involved.

One aspect of the present situation, which I wish to present to you at this time for your consideration and decision, concerns Greece and Turkey.

The United States has received from the Greek government an urgent appeal for financial and economic assistance. Preliminary reports from the American economic mission now in Greece and reports from the American Ambassador in Greece corroborate the statement of the Greek government that assistance is imperative if Greece is to survive as a free nation.

I do not believe that the American people and the Congress wish to turn a deaf ear to the appeal of the Greek government.

Greece is not a rich country. Lack of sufficient natural resources has always forced the Greek people to work hard to make both ends meet. Since 1940 this industrious and peace-loving country has suffered invasion, four years of cruel enemy occupation and bitter internal strife.

When forces of liberation entered Greece they found that the retreating Germans had destroyed virtually all the railways, roads, port facilities, communications and merchant marine. More than a thousand villages had been burned. Eighty-five per cent of the children were tubercular. Livestock, poultry and draft animals had almost disappeared. Inflation had wiped out practically all savings.

As a result of these tragic conditions, a militant minority, exploiting human want and misery, was able to create political chaos which, until now, has made economic recovery impossible.

Greece is today without funds to finance the importation of those goods which are essential to bare subsistence. Under these circumstances the people of Greece cannot make progress in solving their problems of reconstruction. Greece is in desperate need of financial and economic assistance to enable it to resume purchases of food, cloth-

1. *Congressional Record*, XCIII (March 12, 1947), 1999–2000.

ing, fuel and seeds. These are indispensable for the subsistence of its people and are obtainable only from abroad. Greece must have help to import the goods necessary to restore internal order and security so essential for economic and political recovery.

The Greek government has also asked for the assistance of experienced American administrators, economists and technicians to insure that the financial and other aid given to Greece shall be used effectively in creating a stable and self-sustaining economy and in improving its public administration.

The very existence of the Greek state is today threatened by the terrorist activities of several thousand armed men, led by Communists, who defy the government's authority at a number of points, particularly along the northern boundaries. A commission appointed by the United Nations Security Council is at present investigating disturbed conditions in northern Greece on the one hand and Albania, Bulgaria and Yugoslavia on the other.

Meanwhile, the Greek government is unable to cope with the situation. The Greek army is small and poorly equipped. It needs supplies and equipment if it is to restore the authority of the government throughout Greek territory.

Greece must have assistance if it is to become a self-supporting and self-respecting democracy.

The United States must supply that assistance. We have already extended to Greece certain types of relief and economic aid but these are inadequate.

There is no other country to which democratic Greece can turn.

No other nation is willing and able to provide the necessary support for a democratic Greek government.

The British government, which has been helping Greece, can give no further financial or economic aid after March 31. Great Britain finds itself under the necessity of reducing or liquidating its commitments in several parts of the world, including Greece.

We have considered how the United Nations might assist in this crisis. But the situation is an urgent one requiring immediate action, and the United Nations and its related organizations are not in a position to extend help of the kind that is required.

It is important to note that the Greek government has asked for our aid in utilizing effectively the financial and other assistance we may give to Greece, and in improving its public administration. It is of the utmost importance that we supervise the use of any funds made available to Greece, in such a manner that each dollar spent will count toward making Greece self-supporting, and will help to build an economy in which a healthy democracy can flourish.

No government is perfect. One of the chief virtues of a democracy, however, is that its defects are always visible and under democratic processes can be pointed out and corrected. The government of Greece is not perfect. Nevertheless it represents 80 per cent of the members of the Greek Parliament who were chosen in an election last year. Foreign observers, including 692 Americans, considered this election to be a fair expression of the views of the Greek people.

The Greek government has been operating in an atmosphere of chaos and extremism. It has made mistakes. The extension of aid by this country does not mean that the United States condones everything that the Greek government has done or will do. We have condemned in the past, and we condemn now, extremist measures of the Right or the Left. We have in the past advised tolerance, and we advise tolerance now.

Greece's neighbor, Turkey, also deserves our attention.

The future of Turkey as an independent and economically sound state is clearly no less important to the freedom-loving people of the world than the future of Greece.

The circumstances in which Turkey finds itself today are considerably different from those of Greece. Turkey has been spared the disasters that have beset Greece. And during the war the United States and Great Britain furnished Turkey with material aid. Nevertheless, Turkey now needs our support.

Since the war, Turkey has sought financial assistance from Great Britain and the United States for the purpose of effecting that modernization necessary for the maintenance of its national integrity.

That integrity is essential to the preservation of order in the Middle East.

The British government has informed us that, owing to its own difficulties, it can no longer extend financial or economic aid to Turkey.

As in the case of Greece, if Turkey is to have the assistance it needs, the United States must supply it. We are the only country able to provide that help.

I am fully aware of the broad implications involved if the United States extends assistance to Greece and Turkey, and I shall discuss these implications with you at this time.

One of the primary objectives of the foreign policy of the United States is the creation of conditions in which we and other nations will be able to work out a way of life free from coercion. This was a fundamental issue in the war with Germany and Japan. Our victory was won over countries which sought to impose their will, and their way of life, upon other nations.

To insure the peaceful development of nations, free from coercion, the United States has taken a leading part in establishing the United Nations. The United Nations is designed to make possible lasting freedom and independence for all its members. We shall not realize our objectives, however, unless we are willing to help free people to maintain their free institutions and their national integrity against aggressive movements that seek to impose upon them totalitarian regimes. This is no more than a frank recognition that totalitarian regimes imposed on free peoples, by direct or indirect aggression, undermine the foundations of international peace and hence the security of the United States.

The peoples of a number of countries of the world have recently had totalitarian regimes forced upon them against their will. The government of the United States has made frequent protests against coercion and intimidation, in violation of the Yalta agreement, in Poland, Rumania and Bulgaria. I must also state that in a number of other countries there have been similar developments.

At the present moment in world history nearly every nation must choose between alternative ways of life. The choice is too often not a free one.

One way of life is based upon the will of the majority, and is distinguished by free institutions, representative government, free elections, guaranties of individual liberty, freedom of speech and religion and freedom from political oppression.

The second way of life is based upon the will of a minority forcibly imposed upon the majority. It relies upon terror and oppression, a controlled press and radio, fixed elections and the suppression of personal freedoms.

I believe that it must be the policy of the United States to support peoples who are resisting attempted subjugation by armed minorities or by outside pressures.

I believe that we must assist free peoples to work out their own destinies in their own way.

I believe that our help should be primarily through economic and financial aid which is essential to economic stability and orderly political processes.

The world is not static, and the status quo is not sacred. But we cannot allow changes in the status quo in violation of the charter of the United Nations by such methods as coercion, or by such subterfuges as political infiltration. In helping free and independent nations to maintain their freedom, the United States will be giving effect to the principles of the charter of the United Nations.

It is necessary only to glance at a map to realize that the survival and integrity of the Greek nation are of grave importance in a much wider situation. If Greece should fall under the control of an armed minority, the effect upon its neighbor, Turkey, would be immediate and serious. Confusion and disorder might well spread throughout the entire Middle East.

Moreover, the disappearance of Greece as an independent state would have a profound effect upon those countries in Europe whose peoples are struggling against great difficulties to maintain their freedoms and their independence while they repair the damages of war.

It would be an unspeakable tragedy if these countries, which have struggled so long against overwhelming odds, should lose that victory for which they sacrificed so much. Collapse of free institutions and loss of independence would be disastrous not only for them but for the world. Discouragement and possibly failure would quickly be the lot of neighboring peoples striving to maintain their freedom and independence.

Should we fail to aid Greece and Turkey in this fateful hour, the effect will be far-reaching to the West as well as to the East.

We must take immediate and resolute action.

I therefore ask the Congress to provide authority for assistance to Greece and Turkey in the amount of $400,000,000 for the period ending June 30, 1948. In requesting these funds, I have taken into consideration the maximum amount of relief assistance which would be furnished to Greece out of the $350,000,000 which I recently requested that the Congress authorize for the prevention of starvation and suffering in countries devastated by the war.

In addition to funds, I ask the Congress to authorize the detail of American civilian and military personnel to Greece and Turkey, at the request of those countries, to assist in the tasks of reconstruction, and for the purpose of supervising the use of such financial and material assistance as may be furnished. I recommend that authority also be provided for the instruction and training of selected Greek and Turkish personnel.

Finally, I ask that the Congress provide authority which will permit the speediest and most effective use, in terms of needed commodities, supplies and equipment, of such funds as may be authorized.

If further funds, or further authority, should be needed for purposes indicated in this message, I shall not hesitate to bring the situation before the Congress. On this subject the executive and legislative branches of the government must work together.

This is a serious course upon which we embark.

I would not recommend it except that the alternative is much more serious.

The United States contributed $341,000,000,000 toward winning World War II. This is an investment in world freedom and world peace.

The assistance that I am recommending for Greece and Turkey amounts to little more than one-tenth of 1 per cent of this investment. It is only common sense that we should safeguard this investment and make sure that it was not in vain.

The seeds of totalitarian regimes are nurtured by misery and want. They spread and grow in the evil soil of poverty and strife. They reach their full growth when the hope of a people for a better life has died.

We must keep that hope alive.

The free peoples of the world look to us for support in maintaining their freedoms.

If we falter in our leadership, we may endanger the peace of the world—and we shall surely endanger the welfare of our own nation.

Great responsibilities have been placed upon us by the swift movement of events.

I am confident that the Congress will face these responsibilities squarely.

3. THE MARSHALL PLAN, 1947[1]

EDITORS' NOTE.—The European Recovery Program, initiated in the spring of 1948, began with the invitation to the European nations issued by Secretary of State Marshall on June 5, 1947, in a memorable Harvard address. The devastation of World War II and the continued instability of European economies were to be hurdled by grants from America, which possessed 40 per cent of the world's income and 7 per cent of the world's population. This would solve the dollar famine and increase European productivity, with the eventual goal of European economic health. All the nations of Europe met in conference at Paris to determine how much economic aid was needed for European recovery. Molotov attended the conference as the Russian delegate but withdrew and denounced the project as a device to make Europe a colonial slum run by the United States. In 1948 Congress voted approval of the appropriation for the first year of a four-year Marshall Plan aiding sixteen participating nations and western Germany. It was felt, and events have shown, that the Marshall Plan is of major importance in checking communism in western Europe. About four and one-half billion dollars was spent in the first year of the plan (1948–49). The hope is to make Europe economically able to solve the dollar-shortage problem by 1952–53. Critics are afraid that the Marshall Plan is a WPA operation, with western Europe becoming a permanent pensioner of the United States. There are difficult problems of the degree of interference in European economic state planning and the degree of American ability to spend four or five billion dollars in the face of changes in the American business cycle.

General George C. Marshall (1880——), educated at Virginia Military Institute, began his army career in 1901. In the army his important assignments included those of aide-de-camp to General Pershing (1919–21), deputy chief of staff (1938), and chief of staff during the second World War. He went to China in November, 1945, as a special representative of the President to mediate to halt the Chinese civil war. He became Secretary of State in January, 1947, and served until his resignation because of illness in January, 1949.

I need not tell you, gentlemen, that the world situation is very serious. That must be apparent to all intelligent people. I think one difficulty is that the problem is one of such enormous complexity that the very mass of facts presented to the public by press and radio make it exceedingly difficult for the man in the street to reach a clear appraisement of the situation. Furthermore, the people of this country are distant from the troubled areas of the earth and it is hard for them to comprehend the plight and consequent reactions of the long-suffering peoples, and the effect of those reactions on their governments in connection with our efforts to promote peace in the world.

1. *New York Times*, June 6, 1947.

In considering the requirements for the rehabilitation of Europe the physical loss of life, the visible destruction of cities, factories, mines and railroads was correctly estimated, but it has become obvious during recent months that this visible destruction was probably less serious than the dislocation of the entire fabric of European economy. For the past ten years conditions have been highly abnormal.

The feverish preparation for war and the more feverish maintenance of the war effort engulfed all aspects of national economies. Machinery has fallen into disrepair or is entirely obsolete. Under the arbitrary and destructive Nazi rule, virtually every possible enterprise was geared into the German war machine. Longstanding commercial ties, private institutions, banks, insurance companies and shipping companies disappeared, through loss of capital, absorption through nationalization or by simple destruction.

In many countries, confidence in the local currency has been severely shaken. The breakdown of the business structure of Europe during the war was complete. Recovery has been seriously retarded by the fact that two years after the close of hostilities a peace settlement with Germany and Austria has not been agreed upon. But even given a more prompt solution of these difficult problems, the rehabilitation of the economic structure of Europe quite evidently will require a much longer time and greater effort than had been foreseen.

There is a phase of this matter which is both interesting and serious. The farmer has always produced the foodstuffs to exchange with the city dweller for the other necessities of life. This division of Labor is the basis of modern civilization. At the present time it is threatened with breakdown. The town and city industries are not producing adequate goods to exchange with the food-producing farmer. Raw materials and fuel are in short supply. Machinery is lacking or worn out.

The farmer or the peasant cannot find the goods for sale which he desires to purchase. So the sale of his farm produce for money which he cannot use, seems to him an unprofitable transaction. He, therefore, has withdrawn many fields from crop cultivation and is using them for grazing. He feeds more grain to stock and finds for himself and his family an ample supply of food, however short he may be on clothing and the other ordinary gadgets of civilization. Meanwhile, people in the cities are short of food and fuel. So the governments are forced to use their foreign money and credits to procure these necessities abroad. This process exhausts funds which are urgently needed for reconstruction. Thus a very serious situation is rapidly developing which bodes no good for the world. The modern system of the division of labor upon which the exchange of products is based is in danger of breaking down.

The truth of the matter is that Europe's requirements for the next three or four years of foreign food and other essential products—principally from America—are so much greater than her present ability to pay that she must have substantial additional help, or face economic, social and political deterioration of a very grave character.

The remedy lies in breaking the vicious circle and restoring the confidence of the European people in the economic future of their own countries and of Europe as a whole. The manufacturer and the farmer throughout wide areas must be able and willing to exchange their products for currencies, the continuing value of which is not open to question.

Aside from the demoralizing effect on the world at large and the possibilities of disturbances arising as a result of the desperation of the people concerned, the consequences to the economy of the United States should be apparent to all. It is logical that the United States should do whatever it is able to do to assist in the return of normal economic health in the world, without which there can be no political stability and no assured peace.

Our policy is directed not against any country or doctrine but against hunger, poverty, desperation and chaos. Its purpose should be the revival of a working economy in the world so as to permit the emergence of political and social conditions in which free institutions can exist. Such assistance, I am convinced, must not be on a piecemeal basis as various crises develop. Any assistance that this Government may render in the future should provide a cure rather than a mere palliative.

Any government that is willing to assist in the task of recovery will find full cooperation, I am sure, on the part of the United States Government. Any government which maneuvers to block the recovery of other countries cannot expect help from us. Furthermore, governments, political parties or groups which seek to perpetuate human misery in order to profit therefrom politically or otherwise will encounter the opposition of the United States.

It is already evident that, before the United States Government can proceed much further in its efforts to alleviate the situation and help start the European world on its way to recovery, there must be some agreement among the countries of Europe as to the requirements of the situation and the part those countries themselves will take in order to give proper effect to whatever action might be undertaken by this Government. It would be neither fitting nor efficacious for this Government to undertake to draw up unilaterally a program designed to place Europe on its feet economically. This is the business of the Europeans. The initiative, I think, must come from Europe. The role of this country should consist of friendly aid in the drafting of a European program and of later support of such a program so far as it may be practical for us to do so. The program should be a joint one, agreed to by a number, if not all European nations.

An essential part of any successful action on the part of the United States is an understanding on the part of the people of America of the character of the problem and the remedies to be applied. Political passion and prejudice should have no part. With foresight, and a willingness on the part of our people to face up to the vast responsibility which history has clearly placed upon our country, the difficulties I have outlined can and will be overcome.

4. STATEMENT ON THE MARSHALL PLAN[1]

By JAMES E. FORRESTAL

EDITORS' NOTE.—Secretary of Defense James Forrestal in this testimony before the Senate Committee on Foreign Relations argued that recovery of the European community, which the proposed European Recovery Program would assist, was necessary for the security of the United States. Forrestal (1892–1949) was born in New York, entered the investment business, and by 1940 had become president of the Dillon, Read Company. In that year he entered the government service as an administrative assistant to President Roosevelt and later in the year was appointed Undersecretary of the Navy, responsible for the great procurement program during the second World War. Upon the death in 1944 of Frank Knox, Forrestal became Secretary of the Navy, and, after the unification of the three armed services, he was in July, 1947, made the first Secretary of Defense. He resigned in March, 1949.

1. United States Senate Committee on Foreign Relations, *Hearings on U.S. Assistance to European Recovery, 1948,* Part I, pp. 477–81.

SECRETARY FORRESTAL: Mr. Chairman, the Secretary of State, in supporting before your committee the program of United States assistance known as the European recovery program, outlined three basic questions in connection with this legislative proposal.

"Why does Europe need help?"

"How much help is needed?"

"How much help should be given?"

His answers to those questions were clear, and in their broad aspects, supported the recommendations of the executive branch of the Government as placed before you by the President in his message to the Congress of December 19. What I have to say I consider to be an extension of views already presented, except with this difference: That I am speaking from the somewhat more limited point of view of our military security.

All of you are familiar with, and some of you have seen, the conditions in Europe that make necessary the proposals embodied in the European recovery program. The instinctive generosity and humane impulses of Americans would ordinarily move us to aid our neighbors in distress. I think that without any complacency we can say that we are a generous people, and in keeping with that tradition, we have already made vast contributions to the alleviation of distress on the European Continent. There is, however, another and fully as compelling a reason for us to do our utmost to bring about recovery in Europe.

As Secretary of Defense my concern is directed particularly toward the considerations of national security. And so in answering the question which General Marshall posed, "Why does Europe need help?" I shall address myself principally to the factors affecting the security of the United States.

SENATOR WILEY: You are talking to the point of what we might get out of it?

SECRETARY FORRESTAL: Yes, sir.

As in most other periods of history, there is a conflict of world politics taking place in Europe today. There is nothing more unusual about this political conflict, viewed in the long light of history, than there is about political differences in our own country, with this one exception: That we are living in a world today in which there is imbalance—a world in which, broadly speaking, there are two great powers, the Union of Soviet Socialist Republics and the United States. There is a vacuum in middle and western Europe as a result of the destruction caused by, and visited upon, Hitler's Germany. In most political differences a balance of power is exercised by moderate influence in the form of men or nations who are able to contribute the good offices of compromise and amelioration.

Today, however, because of the vacuum in Europe, the nation-components of what would otherwise be the balance of power find their position impaired by economic instability, political unrest, and consequent military ineffectiveness.

In these circumstances we are seeking to redress the balance of Europe by helping the western nations to get on their feet. Our purpose in doing this is not to forge an iron ring around any nation or to set up an aggressive military threat to any other nation. Our purpose and object is totally and exclusively to prevent another war by the creation of political and economic and social equilibrium which is requisite to the maintenance of peace.

Without our aid it is by no means certain that the western European nations can save themselves from economic collapse and political disintegration. In spite of great difficulties and tremendous handicaps, certain of these nations have already made an extraordinary start toward recovery, and I have in mind Belgium, Holland, and Luxemburg.

Recently, France and Italy have also given indications of a renascence of national vitality and national will. Two leaders have risen in the persons of Mr. Schuman, of France, and Mr. de Gasperi, of

Italy, who have shown the capacity for the exercise of leadership without any corresponding effort to grab for totalitarian power. And in Great Britain there is substantial evidence that the great resilience and moral fiber which served that nation so well when she stood alone against Hitler are again asserting themselves.

Coal production in that country has failed by only a small margin of hitting the goal set for 1947 and while the problem of exchange and currency is still a continuing source of concern the British have recognized the fact that work and production are the foundations of an adequate standard of living; in other words, that political science as asserted by Bentham, Ricardo, and Adam Smith still has a validity that Marx assumed was gone forever.

The 16 nations which associated themselves in Paris last summer with the plan for European recovery comprise a great workshop with 270,000,000 of inhabitants. Should that workshop be integrated, with all its industrial and military potential, with its great business complex, into a coalition of totalitarian states, it is possible that we in time would find ourselves isolated in a hostile world. That situation would, in my opinion, be a threat to world peace, to our economic and political position, and, in fact, to the very existence of the United States.

You are familiar with Hitler's success in the middle and late 1920's in exploiting both the economic distress which existed in Germany just after the last war and the inequities which he declared were imposed on Germany by the Versailles Treaty. With every device of political demagoguery, he beguiled and seduced his people with promises of food, employment, and redress of grievances, and with these he laid the foundation for the political movement embraced in the National Socialist Party of Germany. It was these events which led to the tragedy and destruction of World War II. Today, conditions similar to those in which Hitler's evil doctrines fell upon politically susceptible ears might be recreated, not merely in Germany, but in other countries in Europe as well.

Our hope and our effort is to prevent such a recurrence by the acceleration of a healthy European recovery, where the processes of trade, of business, and a free exchange of goods, commodities, services, and individuals can again give men the foundations of hope.

After World War I, the United States, France, and Great Britain, together with other capitalistic countries of Europe, participated in the restoration of the economic stability of Germany. I am one of those who feel that this restoration of economic stability could have laid the foundations for an ultimate republican regime in Germany. It was aborted by the economic crisis of 1929, accompanied by the abrupt cutting off of external credits to Germany, precipitating that chain of events which led to the rise of Hitler.

As in all other countries in times of political and economic difficulty, the moderates and the liberals of Germany fell between the pincers of Bolshevism on the one hand and Hitler's Nazis on the other. It is my hope that throughout Europe what we are now proposing to do will restore hope and courage in this great central bloc of ordinarily decent and peace-loving people in every country.

The result can be, and I believe will be, that these nations, if they recover their true sovereignty and their true positions in the society of western Europe, will reassert those principles of individual freedom and determination to live in a free society, which form such a large part of our own inheritance.

Central in that pattern are, of course, Great Britain and France. From both of these nations we have derived great lessons in political wisdom, in spiritual and cultural values. I believe that none of us today can accurately picture the effect upon our minds and our hopes for the future if we had to witness the surrender of France to a totalitarian authority or the economic collapse of Britain.

And yet if I did not believe that there was a vigor and a vitality in both nations which are capable of surviving, I should not be supporting the program which your committee is considering. Despair is a disease which is easily communicated, but we must not forget that what I call the epidemic of hope is an even more powerful motivating force in man.

The example of an industrious and hard-working Belgium, Luxemburg, and Holland, which is reflected in the now well-known Benelux trade agreements, had repercussions throughout Europe and evoked admiration here. I firmly believe that there are similar reservoirs of energy, resourcefulness, and strength in Europe, which can be stirred to beneficial and constructive action by the catalyst of American aid.

Europe is essentially a trading, manufacturing, and commercial continent. The skill and knowledge of business are still in existence and will be vigorously reasserted if we can re-create the background against which trade can flourish; namely, stable currencies, the elimination of commercial barriers, and the withdrawal of restraints upon free enterprise.

Peace and security are not to be viewed merely in terms of great military power or wealth in the hands of the United States. France had its Maginot line, Hitler had his blitzkrieg, and, further back in history, Philip II of Spain had great wealth and possessions, and ancient Rome had her legionnaires, but none of these gave real security. In each case there were conditions which insured the failure of an apparently impervious formula. In our own case the security of our Nation has to be viewed not merely in the light of our military strength but in the light of the restoration of balance throughout the world.

The essential requirements of our own people are, of course, the first charge against United States resources. However, the conclusions of three special committees—with the results of which you are, of course, familiar—that is, the committees of Harriman, Krug, and Dr. Nourse—are in agreement that our economy in general and our financial capacity in particular are able to support the proposed program.

The cost of that program for the reconstruction of Europe will be high. It will be idle to say—and I do not say—that it will not mean sacrifice, self-denial, and hard work for all of us, but it is a sound investment in the attainment of world order.

It contributes to insurance against war, and, combined with the maintenance of a substantial military power at home, will be far less expensive than standing isolated and alone in an unfriendly world.

It is always dangerous to try to draw exact analogies or parallels between periods of history, but it seems to me that the position in which we find ourselves today is not unlike that of Britain after the Napoleonic wars. Britain, after she had spent 20 years and much of her resources in defeating the attempt of Napoleon to conquer Europe, was anxious to withdraw from that continent. She found great difficulty in doing so, however, without exposing Europe and eventually herself to a recurrence of the very threat of which she had just disposed at such a high cost. So England had to stay in order to make an effective contribution to the maintenance of the balance of power in Europe.

In my opinion, however, England was neither plotting nor planning solely for her own particular advantage; her statesmen were merely wise enough to understand the terrible cost of world-wide conflict and the necessity for localizing those conflicts that did occur. And, as we all know, there were a substantial number of such local conflicts that did occur in the nineteenth century.

Britain, through the exercise of her influence, was able to keep relative peace and stability throughout Europe for a century. There were, to be sure, many wars, both in Europe and in other parts of the world—but those conflicts were always kept localized. They did not result, incidentally, in vast injury to, or destruction of, the economic machinery of Europe. I think it can be said, therefore, that British policy in the nineteenth century was successful.

Our own objective in the present recovery program for Europe is the prevention of war. Neither this program nor our national defense expenditures are designed as a threat against any nation nor as an effort to restrain the legitimate purposes of any nation nor to dominate a group of nations.

The policy of the United States, as I see it, is directed to the single end that free nations shall be allowed to select their own governments, and that no one country or political concept shall be permitted by force to conquer the world.

We need to maintain here substantial military power, but I would rate the need for the restoration of the European community as equally strong.

5. THE NORTH ATLANTIC PACT, 1949

EDITORS' NOTE.—The North Atlantic Pact, April 4, 1949, is a treaty for mutual defense against aggression signed by twelve nations: the United States, Canada, Great Britain, France, Belgium, The Netherlands, Luxembourg, Norway, Italy, Portugal, Denmark, and Iceland. Five of these nations, confronted by the weakness of the United Nations in the face of the growing East-West tension and the Communist seizure of Czechoslovakia (February, 1948), had established the Western European Union in the Brussels Pact, March 17, 1948. The Vandenberg Resolution of June 11, 1948, advocating American co-operation with regional defense associations which should be formed within the principles and provisions of the United Nations sanctioned United States informal collaboration with the Western European Union. This gave a sharp impetus to the development of the more extensive North Atlantic Alliance. The North Atlantic Pact was first publicly advocated the following September by the Canadian minister for external affairs, Louis St. Laurent, and secret talks about the pact were begun that month in London. These

discussions continued until agreement had been reached, when the treaty was made public and signed. On July 21, 1949, the United States Senate ratified the North Atlantic Pact by a vote of 82 to 13.

On the night of March 18, 1949, when the treaty was published, Secretary of State Dean Acheson explained and justified the pact on the radio in the speech reprinted below. He was born in 1893 in Connecticut, received his general and law education at Yale University, and, after serving first in the navy and then as private secretary to Mr. Justice Brandeis, practiced law in New York until 1941, except 1933-34, when he served as Undersecretary of the Treasury. He was Assistant Secretary of State from 1941 to 1947. In this period he was chairman of the Secretary of State's Commission on Atomic Energy, whose report was the basis of the United States proposal for the international control of atomic energy presented by Bernard Baruch, June, 1946, to the United Nations Commission (p. 874). Acheson was appointed Secretary of State in January, 1949.

The North Atlantic Pact was signed

for France by Robert Schuman, the French foreign minister. Born in 1886, he began his law practice in 1912. As a member of the cabinet in 1940, he was imprisoned in Germany until he escaped in 1942 to unoccupied France and worked during the remainder of the war in the underground movement. In 1946 he was elected to the National Assembly as a member of the Mouvement Républicain Populaire, a new party formed in the underground, a party standing midway between De Gaulle's party on the right and the Communists on the left.

On March 18, when the pact was made public, the Soviet government sent a memorandum to the seven original sponsors denying the defensive intentions of the treaty and its legality under the United Nations. This memorandum, as reported in the American press, is reprinted here (pp. 901–3).

A. THE PACT[1]

PREAMBLE

The parties to this treaty reaffirm their faith in the purposes and principles of the Charter of the United Nations and their desire to live in peace with all peoples and all governments.

They are determined to safeguard the freedom, common heritage and civilization of their peoples, founded on the principles of democracy, individual liberty and the rule of law.

They seek to promote stability and well-being in the North Atlantic Area.

They are resolved to unite their efforts for collective defense and for the preservation of peace and security.

They therefore agree to this North Atlantic Treaty:

ARTICLE I

The parties undertake, as set forth in the Charter of the United Nations, to settle any international disputes in which they may be involved by peaceful means in such a manner that international peace and security, and justice, are not endangered, and to refrain in their international relations from the threat or use of force in any manner inconsistent with the purposes of the United Nations.

1. *New York Herald Tribune*, March 19, 1949.

ARTICLE 2

The parties will contribute toward the further development of peaceful and friendly international relations by strengthening their free institutions, by bringing about a better understanding of the principles upon which these institutions are founded, and by promoting conditions of stability and well-being. They will seek to eliminate conflict in their international economic policies and will encourage economic collaboration between any or all of them.

ARTICLE 3

In order more effectively to achieve the objectives of this treaty, the parties, separately and jointly, by means of continuous and effective self-help and mutual aid, will maintain and develop their individual and collective capacity to resist armed attack.

ARTICLE 4

The parties will consult together whenever, in the opinion of any of them, the territorial integrity, political independence or security of any of the parties is threatened.

ARTICLE 5

The parties agree that an armed attack against one or more of them in Europe or North America shall be considered an attack against them all; and consequently they agree that, if such an armed attack occurs, each of them, in exercise of the right of individual or collective self-defense recognized by Article 51 of the Charter of the United Nations, will assist the party or parties so attacked by taking forthwith, individually and in concert with the other parties, such action as it deems necessary including the use of armed force, to restore and maintain the security of the North Atlantic Area.

Any such armed attack and all measures taken as a result thereof shall immediately be reported to the Security Council. Such measures shall be terminated when the Security Council has taken the measures necessary to restore and maintain international peace and security.

ARTICLE 6

For the purpose of Article 5 an armed attack on one or more of the parties is deemed to include an armed attack on the territory of any of the parties in Europe or North America, on the Algerian Departments of France, on the occupation forces of any party in Europe, on the islands under the jurisdiction of any party in the North Atlantic Area north of the Tropic of Cancer or on the vessels or aircraft in this area of any of the parties.

ARTICLE 7

This treaty does not affect, and shall not be interpreted as affecting, in any way the rights and obligations under the Charter of the parties which are members of the United Nations, or the primary responsibility of the Security Council for the maintenance of international peace and security.

ARTICLE 8

Each party declares that none of the international engagements now in force between it and any other of the parties or any third state is in conflict with the provisions of this treaty, and undertakes not to enter into any international engagement in conflict with this treaty.

ARTICLE 9

The parties hereby establish a Council, on which each of them shall be represented, to consider matters concerning the implementation of this treaty. The Council shall be so organized as to be able to meet promptly at any time. The Council shall set up such subsidiary bodies as may be necessary; in particular it shall establish immediately a Defense Committee which shall recommend measures for the implementation of Articles 3 and 5.

ARTICLE 10

The parties may, by unanimous agreement, invite any other European state in a position to further the principles of this treaty and to contribute to the security of the North Atlantic Area to accede to this treaty. Any state so invited may become a party to the treaty by depositing its instrument of accession with the Government of the United States of America. The Government of the United States of America will inform each of the parties of the deposit of each such instrument of accession.

ARTICLE 11

This treaty shall be ratified and its provisions carried out by the parties in accordance with their respective constitutional processes. The instruments of ratification shall be deposited as soon as possible with the Government of the United States of America, which will notify all the other signatories of each deposit. The treaty shall enter into force between the states which have ratified it as soon as the ratifications of the majority of the signatories, including the ratifications of Belgium, Canada, France, Luxemburg, the Netherlands, the United Kingdom and the United States, have been deposited and shall come into effect with respect to other states on the date of the deposit of their ratifications.

ARTICLE 12

After the treaty has been in force for ten years, or at any time thereafter, the parties shall, if any of them so requests, consult together for the purpose of reviewing the treaty, having regard for the factors then affecting peace and security in the North Atlantic Area, including the development of universal as well as regional arrangements under the Charter of the United Nations for the maintenance of international peace and security.

ARTICLE 13

After the treaty has been in force for twenty years, any party may cease to be a party one year after its notice of denunciation has been given to the Government of the United States of America, which will inform the governments of the other parties of the deposit of each notice of denunciation.

ARTICLE 14

This treaty, of which the English and French texts are equally authentic, shall be deposited in the archives of the Government of the United States of America. Duly certified copies thereof will be transmitted by that government to the governments of the other signatories.

In witness whereof, the undersigned plenipotentiaries have signed this treaty.

B. ON THE NORTH ATLANTIC PACT[2]

By Dean Acheson

I think the American people will want to know the answers to three principal questions about the pact: How did it come about and why is it necessary? What are its terms? Will it accomplish its purpose?

The paramount purposes of the pact are peace and security. If peace and security can be achieved in the North Atlantic area, we shall have gone a long way to assure peace and security in other areas as well.

The achievement of peace and security means more than that in the final outcome we shall have prevented war and brought about the settlement of international disputes by peaceful means. There must be conviction of people everywhere that war will be prevented and that disputes will be settled peacefully. In the most practical terms, true international peace and security require a firm belief by the peoples of the world that they will not be subjected to unprovoked attack, to coercion and intimidation, to interference in their own affairs. Peace and security require confidence in the future, based on the assurance that the peoples of the world will be permitted to improve their conditions of life, free from fear that the fruits of their labor may be taken from them by alien hands.

These are goals of our own foreign pol-

2. *St. Louis Post-Dispatch*, April 1, 1949.

icy which President Truman has emphasized many times, most recently in his inaugural address when he spoke of the hope that we could help create "the conditions that will lead eventually to personal freedom and happiness for all mankind." These are also the purposes of the United Nations, whose members are pledged "to maintain international peace and security" and to promote "the economic and social advancement of all peoples."

These purposes are intimately related to the origins of the United Nations. As the second World War neared its end, the peoples who bore the brunt of the fighting were sick of the horror, the brutality, the tragedy of war. Out of that revulsion came the determination to create a system that would go as far as humanly possible in insuring international peace and security.

The United Nations seeks to maintain peace and security by enjoining its members from using force to settle international disputes. Moreover, it insists that they acknowledge tolerance and cooperation as the guiding principles for the conduct of nations.

The members are expected to settle differences by the exercise of reason and adjustment, according to the principles of justice and law. This requires a spirit of tolerance and restraint on the part of all the members.

But, as in any other institution which presupposes restraint, violence or obstruction can be used to defeat the basic undertaking. This happens in personal relations, in families, communities, churches, politics, and everywhere in human life. If the system is used in ways it was not intended to be used, there is grave danger that the system will be disrupted.

That applies to the United Nations. The system is not working as effectively as we hoped because one of its members has attempted to prevent it from working. By obstructive tactics and the misuse of the veto, the Soviet Union has seriously interfered with the work of the Security Council in maintaining international peace and security.

But the United Nations is a flexible instrument. Although the actions of the Soviet Union have disturbed the work of the United Nations, it is strong enough to be an effective instrument for peace. It is the instrument by which we hope world peace will be achieved. The Charter recognizes the importance of regional arrangements consistent with the purposes and principles of the Charter. Such arrangements can greatly strengthen it.

The Atlantic pact is a collective self-defense arrangement among the countries of the North Atlantic area. It is aimed at coordinating the exercise of the right of self-defense especially recognized in Article 51 of the United Nations Charter. It is designed to fit precisely into the framework of the United Nations and to assure practical measures for maintaining peace and security in harmony with the Charter.

It is the firm intention of the parties to carry out the pact in accordance with the provisions of the United Nations Charter and in a manner which will advance its purposes and principles.

Already one such arrangement under the Charter has been established with United States participation. The twenty-one American republics in reorganizing their regional system have specifically brought it within the framework of the United Nations Charter. We are now joining in the formation of a second arrangement, pertaining to the North Atlantic area, likewise within the framework of the United Nations.

It is important to keep in mind that the really successful national and international institutions are those that recognize and express underlying realities. The North Atlantic community of nations is such a reality. It is based on the affinity and natural identity of interests of the North Atlantic powers.

The North Atlantic treaty which will formally unite them is the product of at least 350 years of history, perhaps more. There developed on our Atlantic Coast a community, which has spread across the continent, connected with Western Europe by common institutions and moral and ethical beliefs. Similarities of this kind are not superficial, but fundamental. They are the strongest kind of ties, because they are based on moral conviction, on acceptance of the same values in life.

The very basis of Western civilization, which we share with the other nations bordering the North Atlantic, and which all of us share with many other nations, is the ingrained spirit of restraint and tolerance. This is the opposite of the Communist belief that coercion by force is a proper method of hastening the inevitable. Western civilization has lived by mutual restraint and tolerance. This civilization permits and stimulates free inquiry and bold experimentation. It creates the environment of freedom, from which flows the greatest amount of ingenuity, enterprise and accomplishment.

These principles of democracy, individual liberty and the rule of law have flourished in this Atlantic community. They have universal validity. They are shared by other free nations and find expression on a universal basis in the Charter of the United Nations; they are the standards by which its members have solemnly agreed to be judged. They are the elements out of which are forged the peace and welfare of mankind.

Added to this profoundly important basis of understanding is another unifying influence—the effect of living on the sea. The sea does not separate people as much as it joins them, through trade, travel, mutual understanding and common interests.

For this second reason, as well as the first, North America and Western Europe have formed the two halves of what is in reality one community, and have maintained an abiding interest in each other.

It is clear that the North Atlantic Pact is not an improvisation. It is the statement of the facts and lessons of history. We have learned our history lesson from two world wars in less than half a century. That experience has taught us that the control of Europe by a single aggressive, unfriendly power would constitute an intolerable threat to the national security of the United States. We participated in those two great wars to preserve the integrity and independence of the European half of the Atlantic community in order to preserve the integrity and independence of the American half. It is a simple fact, proved by experience, that an outside attack on one member of this community is an attack upon all members.

We have also learned that if the free nations do not stand together, they will fall one by one. The strategem of the aggressor is to keep his intended victims divided, or better still, set them to quarreling among themselves. Then they can be picked off one by one without arousing unified resistance. We and the free nations of Europe are determined that history shall not repeat itself in that melancholy particular.

As President Truman has said: "If we can make it sufficiently clear, in advance, that any armed attack affecting our national security would be met with overwhelming force, the armed attack might never occur."

The same thought was expressed by the Foreign Relations Committee of the Senate last year in its report recommending approval of Senate Resolution 239. "The committee is convinced," the report said, "that the horrors of another world war can be avoided with certainty only by preventing war from starting. The experience of World War I and World War II suggests that the best deterrent to aggression is the certainty that immediate and effective counter-measures will be taken against those who violate the peace." That resolution, adopted by an overwhelming vote of the Senate, expressly encourages the development of collective self-defense and regional arrangements within the United Nations framework and the participation of the United States in these arrangements.

What are the principal provisions of the North Atlantic Pact? I should like to summarize them.

First, the pact is carefully and conscientiously designed to conform in every particular with the Charter of the United Nations. This is made clear in the first article of the pact, which reiterates and reaffirms the basic principle of the Charter. The participating countries at the very outset of their association state again that they will settle all their international disputes, not only among themselves but with any nation, by peaceful means, in accordance with the provisions of the Charter. This declaration sets the whole tone and purpose of this treaty.

The second article is equally fundamental. The associated countries assert that they will preserve and strengthen their free institutions, and will see to it that the fundamental principles upon which free institutions are founded are better understood everywhere. They also agree to eliminate conflicts in their economic life and to promote economic cooperation among themselves. Here is the ethical essence of the treaty—the common resolve to preserve, strengthen and make understood the very basis of tolerance, restraint and freedom—the really vital things with which we are concerned.

This purpose is extended further in Article 3, in which the participating countries pledge themselves to self-help and mutual aid. In addition to strengthening their free institutions, they will take practical steps to maintain and develop their own capacity and that of their partners to resist aggression. They also agree to consult together when the integrity or security of any of them is threatened. The treaty sets up a council, consisting of all the members, and other machinery for consultation and for carrying out the provisions of the pact.

Successful resistance to aggression in the modern world requires modern arms and trained military forces. As a result of the recent war, the European countries joining the pact are generally deficient in both requirements. The treaty does not bind the United States to any arms program. But we all know that the United States is now the only democratic nation with the resources and the productive capacity to help the free nations of Europe to recover their military strength.

Therefore, we expect to ask the Congress to supply our European partners some of the weapons and equipment they need to be able to resist aggression. We also expect to recommend military supplies for other free nations which will co-operate with us in safeguarding peace and security.

In the compact world of today the security of the United States cannot be defined in terms of boundaries and frontiers. A serious threat to international peace and security anywhere in the world is of direct concern to this country. Therefore it is our policy to help free peoples to maintain their integrity and independence, not only in Western Europe or in the Americas, but wherever the aid we are able to provide can be effective. Our actions in supporting the integrity and independence of Greece, Turkey and Iran are expressions of that determination. Our interest in the security of these countries has been made clear, and we shall continue to pursue that policy.

In providing military assistance to other countries, both inside and outside the North Atlantic Pact, we will give clear priority to the requirements for economic recovery. We will carefully balance the military assistance program with the capacity and requirements of the total economy, both at home and abroad.

But to return to the treaty, Article 5 deals with the possibility, which unhappily cannot be excluded, that the nations joining together in the pact may have to face the eventuality of an armed attack. In this article, they agree that an armed attack on any of them, in Europe or North America, will be considered an attack on all of them. In the event of such an attack, each of them will take, individually and in concert with the other parties, whatever action it deems necessary to restore and maintain the security of the North Atlantic area, including the use of armed force.

This does not mean that the United States would be automatically at war if one of the nations covered by the pact is subjected to armed attack. Under our Constitution, the Congress alone has the power to declare war. We would be bound to take promptly the action which we deemed necessary to restore and maintain the security of the North Atlantic area. That decision would be taken in accordance with our constitutional procedures. The factors which would have to be considered would be, on the one side, the gravity of the armed attack; on the other, the action which we believed necessary to restore and maintain the security of the North Atlantic area. That is the end to be achieved. We are bound to do what in our honest judgment is necessary to reach that result. If we should be confronted again with a calculated armed attack such as we have twice seen in the Twentieth Century, I should not suppose that we would decide any action other than the use of armed force effective either as an exercise of the right of collective self-defense or as necessary to restore the peace and security of the North Atlantic area. That decision will rest where the Constitution has placed it.

This is not a legalistic question. It is a question we have frequently faced, the question of faith and principle in carrying out treaties. Those who decide it will have the responsibility for taking all appropriate action under the treaty. Such a responsibility requires the exercise of will— a will disciplined by the undertaking solemnly contracted to do what they decide is necessary to restore and maintain the peace and security of the North Atlantic area. That is our obligation under this Article 5. It is equally our duty and obligation to the security of our own country.

All of these provisions of the pact are subject to the overriding provisions of the United Nations Charter. Any measure for self-defense taken under the treaty will be reported to the Security Council of the United Nations. These measures will continue only until the Security Council, with its primary responsibility, takes the necessary action to restore peace and maintain security.

The treaty has no time limit, but after it has been in effect twenty years any member can withdraw on one year's notice. It also provides that after it has been in existence ten years, it will be reviewed in the circumstances prevailing at that time. Additional countries may be admitted to the pact by agreement of all the parties already signatories.

These are the principal provisions of the treaty.

Will the pact accomplish its purpose?

No one can say with certainty. We can only act on our convictions. The United States Government and the Governments with which we are associated in this treaty are convinced that it is an essential measure for strengthening the United Nations, deterring aggression, and establishing the sense of security necessary for the restoration of the economic and political health of the world.

The nations joining in the pact know that war does not pay. Others may not be as deeply convinced of this as we are. The North Atlantic treaty should help convince them also that war does not pay.

It seems absurd that it should be necessary in this era of popular education and highly developed communications, to deal with allegations which have no relation to to the truth and could not stand even the crudest test of measurement against realities. Nevertheless, the power and persistence with which the lie is today employed as a weapon of international policy is such that this cannot always be avoided.

I refer here to the allegations that this treaty conceals aggressive designs on the part of its authors with respect to other countries. Anyone with the most elementary knowledge of the processes of democratic government knows that democracies do not and cannot plan aggressive wars. But for those from whom such knowledge may have been withheld I must make the following categoric and unequivocal statement, for which I stand with the full measure of my responsibility in the office I hold:

This country is not planning to make war against anyone. It is not seeking war. It abhors war. It does not hold war to be inevitable. Its policies are devised with the specific aim of bridging by peaceful means the tremendous differences which beset international society at the present time.

Allegations that aggressive designs lie behind this country's signature of the Atlantic pact can rest only on a malicious misrepresentation or a fantastic misunderstanding of the nature and aims of American society. It is hard to say which of these attitudes is more irresponsible and more dangerous to the stability of international life. For misunderstanding on a question so vital to world progress and so easily susceptible of clarification could only be willful or the product of a system that imprisons the human mind and makes it impervious to facts. It is the duty of all those who seriously and realistically wish for peace to refuse to be misled by this type of falsehood and to prevent it from poisoning the atmosphere in which the quest of a happier world must be conducted.

This treaty is designed to help toward the goal envisioned by President Truman when he said: ". . . As our stability becomes manifest, as more and more nations come to know the benefits of democracy and to participate in growing abundance, I believe that those countries which now oppose us will abandon their delusions and join with the free nations of the world in a just settlement of international differences."

To bring that time to pass, we are determined, on the one hand, to make it unmistakably clear that immediate and effective counter measures will be taken against those who violate the peace, and on the other, to wage peace vigorously and relentlessly.

Too often peace has been thought of as a negative condition—the mere absence of war. We know now that we cannot achieve peace by taking a negative attitude. Peace is positive, and it has to be waged with all our thought, energy and courage, and with the conviction that war is not inevitable.

Under the leadership of President Truman the United States is waging peace with a vigor and on a scale without precedent. While the war was being fought this country took the initiative in the organization of the United Nations and related agencies for the collective and cooperative conduct of international affairs. We withdrew our military forces, except those required for occupation duties, and quickly reduced our military establishment to about one-tenth its wartime size. We contributed generously to post-war relief and rehabilitation.

When events called for firmness as well as generosity the United States waged peace by pledging its aid to free nations threatened by aggression, and took prompt and vigorous action to fulfill that pledge. We have actively sought and are actively seeking to make the United Nations an effective instrument of international cooperation. We proposed, and, with the eager cooperation of sixteen other nations, put into effect a great concerted program for the economic recovery and spiritual reinvigoration of Europe. We joined the other American republics, and we now join with Western Europe, in treaties to strengthen the United Nations and insure international peace and security.

The United States is waging peace by promoting measures for the revival and expansion of world trade on a sound and beneficial basis. Continuance of the reciprocal trade agreements program and ratification by the United States of the Charter of the International Trade Organization are essential to the success of our foreign trade policies. We are preparing to carry out an energetic program to apply modern skills and techniques to what President Truman has called the "primitive and stagnant" economies of vast areas, so that they will yield a better and richer life for their people.

The United States is waging peace by throwing its full strength and energy into the struggle, and we shall continue to do so.

We sincerely hope we can avoid strife, but we cannot avoid striving for what is right. We devoutly hope we can have genuine peace, but we cannot be complacent about the present uneasy and troubled peace.

A secure and stable peace is not a goal we can reach all at once and for all time. It is a dynamic state, produced by effort and faith with justice and courage. The struggle is continuous and hard. The prize is never irrevocably ours.

To have this genuine peace we must constantly work for it. But we must do even more. We must make it clear that armed attack will be met by collective defense, prompt and effective.

That is the meaning of the North Atlantic pact.

C. ON THE NORTH ATLANTIC PACT[3]

By ROBERT SCHUMAN

The history of contemporary France is a succession of aggressions she has endured and of attempts she has made to avoid them.

Three times in seventy years she has been invaded. The first time, she was the sole victim of the aggressor. From 1914 to 1918, half of our continent was submerged under the wave of aggression. And the last war overflowed Europe; the invasion became transcontinental, not only because of alliances, but also because of the immensity of the means of action. Invasion crosses neutral frontiers; neither distance nor natural obstacles can stop it any longer.

In the past, the peoples menaced by it too often allowed themselves to be surprised by it. The teaching of experience has led them to draw together. They have placed their confidence in international organization for peace and security. France has constantly supported these efforts and nurtured this great hope. She remains fervently attached to it because she is convinced that in the end humanity will submit to the exigencies of solidarity.

But she is obliged also to recognize that collective organizations, as they function today, have not yet acquired the necessary efficacy. The Charter envisages the possibility of regional pacts. It authorizes its members to organize individually or collectively for self-defense in conformity with the principles of the Charter.

France ardently desires that the United Nations may become one day strong enough to assure by itself peace and security in the world, thus rendering any individual initiative unnecessary.

But, meanwhile, the Governments which bear the fearsome responsibility of guarding the independence of their countries have no right to put their trust in partial guarantees. It would be criminal for them

3. *New York Herald Tribune*, March 19, 1949.

to neglect a single opportunity, or a possible aid, for the preservation of peace.

The exclusive concern of France is to make impossible any invasion of her own territory or of the territory of peace-loving nations. Our aim cannot be restricted to the winning of a war which might be forced upon us, a war which, even if we win it, would leave Europe ravaged and depopulated. We want to avoid such a war by becoming, together, strong enough, together to safeguard peace.

Who, in justice, could reproach us for such an attempt? What sincere friend could take offense at it? In the past, France has been sufficiently respectful of her obligations and true to her friendships, sufficiently alerted also by dreadful experience, to be beyond all suspicion.

There is no contradiction between two treaties when both have as their object to guarantee the security of the same country but are concluded with different guarantors. The multiplicity of possible risks necessitates a multiplicity of precautions. This answer we gave to Germany when, in 1935, she took objection to the Franco-Russian treaty, incompatible, according to her, with the Locarno pact. Today, we give it to the U.S.S.R. with whom we remain bound by a defense pact against a possible German menace and by the obligation we accepted never to associate ourselves with any threat directed against her. We shall scrupulously honor this obligation. When we expand the network of our friendships, old and new, do we in fact repudiate a friendship which does not satisfy all our need for security? Is it a threat to anyone when we take out insurance against all risks, when we organize a system of common defense against any attack, whatever its nature?

We are uniting, with the intention of providing a common and reciprocal protection. We want to discourage in advance any aggression, by making it more dangerous for the aggressor. Only a potential aggressor could legitimately consider it aimed at him. Our conscience is clear. In signing this pact, France solemnly proclaims her absolute determination to maintain peace. It is not for herself alone that France wants peace, for she knows that peace has become the indivisible property of all, and that, by allowing it to be compromised by one of us, we would all lose it together.

Nations are more and more convinced that their fates are closely bound together, that their salvation and their welfare can no longer be based upon an egotistical and aggressive nationalism, but must rest upon the progressive application of human solidarity.

D. SOVIET COMMENT ON THE PACT[4]

On March 18 the State Department of the United States published the text of the North Atlantic Treaty which the governments of the United States of America, Great Britain, France, Belgium, The Netherlands, Luxembourg and Canada intend to sign within the next few days.

The North Atlantic Treaty fully confirms what was said in the declaration of the Ministry of Foreign Affairs of the U.S.S.R. of Jan. 29 this year which is being attached hereto both as regards the aggressive aims of this treaty and the fact that the North Atlantic Treaty contradicts the principles and aims of the United Nations organization and commitments which the governments of the United States of America, Great Britain and France have assumed under other treaties and agreements.

Statements contained in the North Atlantic Treaty that it is designated for defense and that it recognizes the principles of the United Nations organization serve aims which have nothing in common either with the tasks of self-defense of the parties to the treaty or with the real recognition of the aims and principles of the United Nations organization. Such great powers as the United States, Great Britain and France are parties to the North Atlantic Treaty. Thus the treaty is not directed either against the United States of America, Great Britain or France.

Of the great powers, only the Soviet

4. *New York Times*, April 5, 1949.

Union is excluded from among the parties to this treaty which can be explained only by the fact this treaty is directed against the Soviet Union. The fact that the North Atlantic Treaty is directed against the U.S.S.R. as well as against the countries of the people's democracy was definitely pointed out also by official representatives of the United States of America, Great Britain, and France.

To justify the conclusion of the North Atlantic Treaty, references are being made to the fact the Soviet Union has defensive treaties with countries of the peoples' democracy. These references, however, are utterly untenable.

All the treaties of the Soviet Union on friendship and mutual assistance with the countries of the peoples' democracy are of a bilateral nature and they are directed solely against a possible repetition of German aggression, of which danger no single peace-loving state can forget. The possibility of interpreting them as treaties which are in any degree aimed against the allies of the U.S.S.R. in the late war, against the United States or Great Britain or France, is absolutely precluded.

Moreover, the U.S.S.R. has similar treaties against the repetition of German aggression not only with the countries of the peoples' democracy but also with Great Britain and France.

In contradistinction, this North Atlantic Treaty is not a bilateral but a multilateral treaty which creates a closed grouping of states and what is particularly important absolutely ignores the possibility of a repetition of German aggression not having consequently as its aim prevention of a new German aggression. And inasmuch as of the great powers which comprised the anti-Hitlerite coalition only the U.S.S.R. is not a party to this treaty the North Atlantic Treaty must be regarded as a treaty directed aganst one of the chief allies of the United States, Great Britain and France in the late war, against the U.S.S.R.

Participants in the North Atlantic Treaty are effecting extensive military measures which can in no way be justified by interests of self-defense of these countries. Extensive military measures carried out by the United States of co-operation with Great Britain and France under the present peacetime conditions including the increase in all types of armed forces, the drafting of a plan for utilization of the atomic weapon, the stockpiling of atom bombs which are purely an offensive weapon, and the building of a network of air and naval bases, etc.—by no means bear a defensive character.

Preservation in Washington of a combined Anglo-American staff organized during the second world war and the recent establishment of a military staff of the so-called Western Union in Fontainbleau (France) as well as the intention immediately to set up a defense committee envisaged by the North Atlantic Treaty is by no means an invitation of peace-loving or defensive aims of the participants of the treaty but together with other numerous military preparations contributes to the intensifying anxiety and alarm and to whipping up of a war hysteria in which all sorts of instigators of a new war are so interested.

The North Atlantic pact is designed to daunt the states which do not agree to obey the dictate of the Anglo-American grouping of the powers that lay claim to world domination though the untenability of such claims was once again affirmed by the second world war which ended in the debacle of Fascist Germany which also laid claim to world domination.

Among the participants in the North Atlantic Treaty are also the countries whose governments expect to benefit at the expense of the richer parties to this treaty and make various plans with regard to obtaining new credits and other material advantages.

At the same time one cannot but see the groundlessness of anti-Soviet motives of the North Atlantic Treaty inasmuch as it is known to all the Soviet Union does not intend to attack anyone and in no way threatens the United States of America, Great Britain or the other parties to the treaty.

The conclusion of the North Atlantic Treaty and establishment of a new grouping of powers is motivated by the weakness of the United Nations organization. It is perfectly evident, however, that the North Atlantic Treaty does not serve the cause of consolidating the United Nations organization but on the contrary leads to the undermining of the very foundation of this international organization because establishment of the above grouping of powers is far from corresponding to the aims and principles of the United Nations organization and runs counter to the charter of this organization.

Parties to the North Atlantic Treaty maintain that this treaty allegedly represents a regional arrangement envisaged by Article 52 of the United Nations Charter. But such references are utterly groundless and untenable. There can be no question whatsoever of any regional character of this treaty inasmuch as the union provided for by this treaty embraces states located in both hemispheres of the globe and has not as its aim settlement of any regional issues. This is also confirmed by the fact as has already been announced that states which are not members of the United Nations organization (Italy and Portugal) are being drawn into participation in the North Atlantic Treaty though Article 52 of the United Nations Charter has in view conclusion of regional arrangements only among members of the United Nations organization.

Nor can establishment of a North Atlantic grouping of states be justified by the right of each member of the United Nations to an individual or collective self-defense in conformity with Article 51 of the Charter. Suffice it to say such a right under the Charter of the United Nations can arise only in case of an armed attack against a member of the organization; yet as is known to all neither the United States of America, Britain, France nor other parties to the pact are threatened by any armed attack.

It is clear references to Articles 51 and 52 of the United Nations charter are untenable and designed merely to cover up the real aggressive aims of a military grouping of states which are being set up by the conclusion of the North Atlantic Treaty.

No one can deny that the North Atlantic Treaty and the first and foremost Article 5 of this treaty directly contradict the charter of the United Nations organization. The text of Article 53 of the charter which speaks of enforcement actions under regional arrangements states directly that "no enforcement action shall be taken on the strength of regional arrangements or by regional agencies without authorization of the Security Council" with the exception of special measures provided with regard to former enemy states.

This notwithstanding Article 5 of the North Atlantic pact envisages employment of armed force by the parties to the treaty without any authorization of the Security Council. Thus even if the North Atlantic Treaty were to be considered a regional arrangement Article 5 of this treaty is incompatible with the United Nations Charter. This shows once more how unfounded are all references of the North Atlantic Treaty to the recognition of the principles and aims of the Charter of the United Nations organization.

On the basis of the above said the Soviet Government arrives at the following conclusions:

1. The North Atlantic Treaty has nothing in common with the aims of self-defense of states who are parties to the treaty, who are threatened by no one, whom no one intends to attack. On the contrary this treaty has an obviously aggressive character, is aimed against the U.S.S.R., which fact is not concealed even by the official representatives of the states —parties to the treaty in their public pronouncements.

2. The North Atlantic Treaty not only does not contribute to the consolidation of peace and international security which is the duty of all members of the United Nations organization, but it directly runs counter to the principles and aims of the United Nations Charter and leads to the undermining of the United Nations organization.

3. The North Atlantic Treaty runs counter to the treaty between Great Britain and the Soviet Union signed in 1942 under which both states assumed the obligation to co-operate in the maintenance of peace, international security and "not to conclude any alliances and not to participate in any coalitions directed against the other high contracting party."

4. The North Atlantic Treaty runs counter to the treaty between France and the Soviet Union signed in 1944 under which both states assumed an obligation to co-operate in the maintenance of peace and international security and "not to conclude any alliance and not to take part in any coalition directed against one of the high contracting parties."

5. The North Atlantic Treaty runs counter to agreements between the Soviet Union, the United States of America and Great Britain concluded at the Yalta and Potsdam conferences as well as at other conferences of representatives of these powers held both during and after the second world war under which the United States of America and Great Britain like the Soviet Union assumed the obligation to co-operate in consolidation of general peace and international security and to the consolidation of the United Nations organization.

6. ORGANIZATION OF THE AMERICAN STATES, 1948[1]

EDITORS' NOTE.—The Organization of the American States, part of whose charger is reprinted below, is at the same time a regional security organization under the United Nations and the culmination of a long Pan-American development. This development began with the Monroe Doctrine, became increasingly co-operative instead of unilateral under the Good Neighbor policy initiated in 1933, and was brought to its culmination by the agreements reached in the Act of Chapultepec, 1945, and the Treaty of Reciprocal Assistance, 1947. The Ninth International Conference of the American States at Bogotá, Colombia, March 30–May 2, 1948, attended by representatives of twenty-one republics, adopted the Organization of the American States.

The organization has been provisionally established pending the required ratifications by two-thirds of the signatory states. By May 1, 1949, the United States had not ratified the agreement to establish the organization, and only three states (Costa Rica, Dominican Republic, Mexico) had ratified it.

CHARTER OF THE ORGANIZATION OF AMERICAN STATES

IN THE NAME OF THEIR PEOPLES, THE STATES REPRESENTED AT THE NINTH INTERNATIONAL CONFERENCE OF AMERICAN STATES,

CONVINCED that the historic mission of America is to offer to man a land of liberty, and a favorable environment for the development of his personality and the realization of his just aspirations;

CONSCIOUS that that mission has already inspired numerous agreements, whose essential value lies in the desire of the American peoples to live together in peace, and, through their mutual understanding and respect for the sovereignty of each one, to provide for the betterment of all, in independence, in equality and under law;

CONFIDENT that the true significance of American solidarity and good neighborliness can only mean the consolidation on this continent, within the framework of democratic institutions, of a system of individual liberty and social justice based on respect for the essential rights of man;

PERSUADED that their welfare and their contribution to the progress and the civilization of the world will increasingly require intensive continental cooperation;

RESOLVED to persevere in the noble undertaking that humanity has conferred upon the United Nations, whose principles and purposes they solemnly reaffirm;

CONVINCED that juridical organization is a necessary condition for security and peace founded on moral order and on justice; and

In accordance with Resolution IX of the Inter-American Conference on Problems of War and Peace, held at Mexico City,

HAVE AGREED UPON THE FOLLOWING CHARTER OF THE ORGANIZATION OF AMERICAN STATES

PART ONE

CHAPTER I

NATURE AND PURPOSES

Article 1

The American States establish by this Charter the international organization that

1. United States Department of State, *Ninth International Conference of American States* ("International Organization and Conference Series," Vol. II; Pub. 3263 [Washington, 1948]), pp. 166–75.

they have developed to achieve an order of peace and justice, to promote their solidarity, to strengthen their collaboration, and to defend their sovereignty, their territorial integrity and their independence. Within the United Nations, the Organization of American States is a regional agency.

Article 2

All American States that ratify the present Charter are Members of the Organization.

Article 3

Any new political entity that arises from the union of several Member States and that, as such, ratifies the present Charter, shall become a Member of the Organization. The entry of the new political entity into the Organization shall result in the loss of membership of each one of the States which constitute it.

Article 4

The Organization of American States, in order to put into practice the principles on which it is founded and to fulfill its regional obligations under the Charter of the United Nations, proclaims the following essential purposes:

a) To strengthen the peace and security of the continent;

b) To prevent possible causes of difficulties and to ensure the pacific settlement of disputes that may arise among the Member States;

c) To provide for common action on the part of those States in the event of aggression;

d) To seek the solution of political, juridical and economic problems that may arise among them; and

e) To promote, by cooperative action, their economic, social and cultural development.

CHAPTER II

PRINCIPLES

Article 5

The American States reaffirm the following principles:

a) International law is the standard of conduct of States in their reciprocal relations;

b) International order consists essentially of respect for the personality, sovereignty and independence of States, and the faithful fulfillment of obligations derived from treaties and other sources of international law;

c) Good faith shall govern the relations between States;

d) The solidarity of the American States and the high aims which are sought through it require the political organization of those States on the basis of the effective exercise of representative democracy;

e) The American States condemn war of aggression: victory does not give rights;

f) An act of aggression against one American State is an act of aggression against all the other American States;

g) Controversies of an international character arising between two or more American States shall be settled by peaceful procedures;

h) Social justice and social security are bases of lasting peace;

i) Economic cooperation is essential to the common welfare and prosperity of the peoples of the continent;

j) The American States proclaim the fundamental rights of the individual without distinction as to race, nationality, creed or sex;

k) The spiritual unity of the continent is based on respect for the cultural values of the American countries and requires their close cooperation for the high purposes of civilization;

l) The education of peoples should be directed toward justice, freedom and peace.

CHAPTER III

FUNDAMENTAL RIGHTS AND DUTIES
OF STATES

Article 6

States are juridically equal, enjoy equal rights and equal capacity to exercise these rights, and have equal duties. The rights of each State depend not upon its power to ensure the exercise thereof, but upon the mere fact of its existence as a person under international law.

Article 7

Every American State has the duty to respect the rights enjoyed by every other State in accordance with international law.

Article 8

The fundamental rights of States may not be impaired in any manner whatsoever.

Article 9

The political existence of the State is independent of recognition by other States. Even before being recognized, the State has the right to defend its integrity and independence, to provide for its preservation and prosperity, and consequently to organize itself as it sees fit, to legislate concerning its interests, to administer its services, and to determine the jurisdiction and competence of its courts. The exercise of these rights is limited only by the exercise of the rights of other States in accordance with international law.

Article 10

Recognition implies that the State granting it accepts the personality of the new State, with all the rights and duties that international law prescribes for the two States.

Article 11

The right of each State to protect itself and to live its own life does not authorize it to commit unjust acts against another State.

Article 12

The jurisdiction of States within the limits of their national territory is exercised equally over all the inhabitants, whether nationals or aliens.

Article 13

Each State has the right to develop its cultural, political and economic life freely and naturally. In this free development, the State shall respect the rights of the individual and the principles of universal morality.

Article 14

Respect for and the faithful observance of treaties constitute standards for the development of peaceful relations among States. International treaties and agreements should be public.

Article 15

No State or group of States has the right to intervene, directly or indirectly, for any reason whatever, in the internal or external affairs of any other State. The foregoing principle prohibits not only armed force but also any other form of interference or attempted threat against the personality of the State or against its political, economic and cultural elements.

Article 16

No State may use or encourage the use of coercive measures of an economic or political character in order to force the sovereign will of another State and obtain from it advantages of any kind.

Article 17

The territory of a State is inviolable; it may not be the object, even temporarily, of military occupation or of other measures of force taken by another State, directly or indirectly, on any grounds whatever. No territorial acquisitions or special advantages obtained either by force or by other means of coercion shall be recognized.

Article 18

The American States bind themselves in their international relations not to have recourse to the use of force, except in the case of self-defense in accordance with existing treaties or in fulfillment thereof.

Article 19

Measures adopted for the maintenance of peace and security in accordance with existing treaties do not constitute a violation of the principles set forth in Articles 15 and 17.

CHAPTER IV

PACIFIC SETTLEMENT OF DISPUTES

Article 20

All international disputes that may arise between American States shall be submitted to the peaceful procedures set forth in this Charter, before being referred to the Security Council of the United Nations.

Article 21

The following are peaceful procedures: direct negotiation, good offices, mediation, investigation and conciliation, judicial settlement, arbitration, and those which the parties to the dispute may especially agree upon at any time.

Article 22

In the event that a dispute arises between two or more American States which, in the opinion of one of them, cannot be settled through the usual diplomatic channels, the Parties shall agree on some other peaceful procedure that will enable them to reach a solution.

Article 23

A special treaty will establish adequate procedures for the pacific settlement of disputes and will determine the appropriate means for their application so that no dispute between American States shall fail of definitive settlement within a reasonable period.

CHAPTER V

COLLECTIVE SECURITY

Article 24

Every act of aggression by a State against the territorial integrity of the inviolability of the territory or against the sovereignty or political independence of an American State shall be considered an act of aggression against the other American States.

Article 25

If the inviolability or the integrity of the territory or the sovereignty or political independence of any American State should be affected by an armed attack or an act of aggression that is not an armed attack, or by an extra-continental conflict, or by a conflict between two or more American States, or by any other fact or situation that might endanger the peace of America, the American States, in furtherance of the principles of continental solidarity or collective self-defense, shall apply the measures and procedures established in the special treaties on the subject. . . .

Article 32

The Organization of American States accomplishes its purposes by means of:

a) The Inter-American Conference;

b) The Meeting of Consultation of Ministers of Foreign Affairs;

c) The Council;

d) The Pan American Union;

e) The Specialized Conferences; and

f) The Specialized Organizations.

Article 33

The Inter-American Conference is the supreme organ of the Organization of American States. It decides the general action and policy of the Organization and determines the structure and functions of its Organs, and has the authority to consider any matter relating to friendly relations among the American States. These functions shall be carried out in accordance with the provisions of this Charter and of other inter-American treaties. . . .

Article 35

The Conference shall convene every five years at the time fixed by the Council of the Organization, after consultation with the government of the country where the Conference is to be held. . . .

Article 39

The Meeting of Consultation of Ministers of Foreign Affairs shall be held in order to consider problems of an urgent nature and of common interest to the American States, and to serve as the Organ of Consultation. . . .

Article 43

In case of an armed attack within the territory of an American State or within the region of security delimited by treaties in force, a Meeting of Consultation shall be held without delay. Such Meeting shall be called immediately by the Chairman of the Council of the Organization, who shall at the same time call a meeting of the Council itself.

Article 44

An Advisory Defense Committee shall be established to advise the Organ of Consultation on problems of military cooperation that may arise in connection with the application of existing special treaties on collective security. . . .

Article 48

The Council of the Organization of American States is composed of one Representative of each Member State of the Organization, especially appointed by the respective Government, with the rank of Ambassador. The appointment may be given to the diplomatic representative accredited to the Government of the country in which the Council has its seat. During the absence of the titular Representative, the Government may appoint an interim Representative.

STATISTICAL APPENDIX[1]

LIST OF CHARTS AND TABLES

[1] To secure the latest statistics for these charts and tables, see the source cited, or, for a more accessible compilation, see the latest *Statistical Abstract of the United States*, *World Almanac*, or *Information Please Almanac*. Many other useful statistics, as well as the source of many of these, are to be found in U.S. Bureau of the Census, *Historical Statistics of the United States, 1789–1945* (Washington, D.C., 1949).

1. POPULATION GROWTH IN THE UNITED STATES, 1790-1949

By Urban-Rural Residence and by Farm Residence since 1910

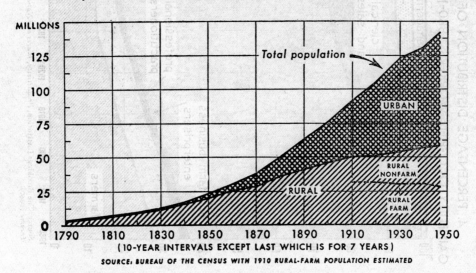

MILLIONS

Total population

URBAN

RURAL NONFARM

RURAL

RURAL FARM

1790 1810 1830 1850 1870 1890 1910 1930 1950

(10-YEAR INTERVALS EXCEPT LAST WHICH IS FOR 7 YEARS)

SOURCE: BUREAU OF THE CENSUS WITH 1910 RURAL-FARM POPULATION ESTIMATED

2. UNITED STATES POPULATION AND IMMIGRATION, 1790–1950

Year	Population (Millions)	Increase over Preceding Census		Population per Square Mile	Immigration in Preceding Decade (Millions)	Immigration as Per Cent of Population Increase	Immigrants Arriving after 1840 and Their Descendants	Per Cent Urban Population (Millions)*
		Millions	Per Cent					
1790	3.9	1.1	41.3	4.5				5.1
1800	5.3	1.4	35.1	6.1				6.1
1810	7.2	1.9	36.4	4.3				7.3
1820	9.6	2.4	33.1	5.5				7.2
1830	12.9	3.2	33.5	7.3	0.15	4.4		8.8
1840	17.0	4.2	32.7	9.7	0.6	14.3		10.8
1850	23.2	6.1	35.9	7.9	1.7	27.9	1.9	15.3
1860	31.4	8.3	35.6	10.6	2.6	31.3	4.9	19.8
1870	39.8	8.4	26.6	13.4	2.3	27.4	7.8	25.7
1880	50.2	10.3	26.0	16.9	2.8	27.2	12.2	28.2
1890	62.9	12.8	25.5	21.2	5.2	40.6	20.0	35.1
1900	76.0	13.0	20.7	25.6	3.7	28.5	28.0	39.7
1910	92.0	16.0	21.0	30.9	8.8	55.0	41.0	45.7
1920	105.7	13.7	14.9	35.5	5.7	27.0	53.0	51.2
1930	122.8	17.1	16.1	41.2	4.1	18.7	64.0	56.2
1940	131.7	8.9	7.2	44.2	0.5	− 0.4	67.0	56.5
1950 (est.)	150.0	18.3	13.8					59.0

Source: Bureau of the Census.

* Cities and other incorporated places having 2,500 inhabitants or more.

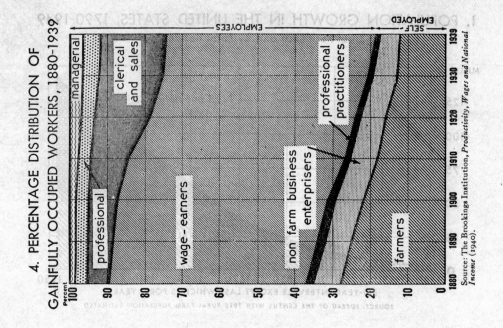

4. PERCENTAGE DISTRIBUTION OF GAINFULLY OCCUPIED WORKERS, 1880–1939

Percent

managerial

professional

clerical and sales

wage-earners

professional practitioners

non farm business enterprisers

farmers

EMPLOYEES

SELF EMPLOYED

1880 1890 1900 1910 1920 1930 1939

100 90 80 70 60 50 40 30 20 10 0

Source: The Brookings Institution, *Productivity, Wages and National Income* (1940).

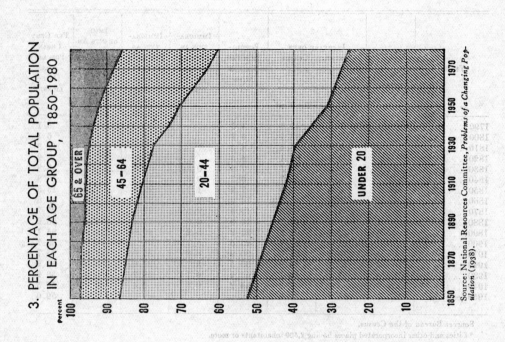

3. PERCENTAGE OF TOTAL POPULATION IN EACH AGE GROUP, 1850–1980

Percent

65 & OVER

45–64

20–44

UNDER 20

1850 1870 1880 1910 1930 1950 1970

100 90 80 70 60 50 40 30 20 10

Source: National Resources Committee, *Problems of a Changing Population* (1938).

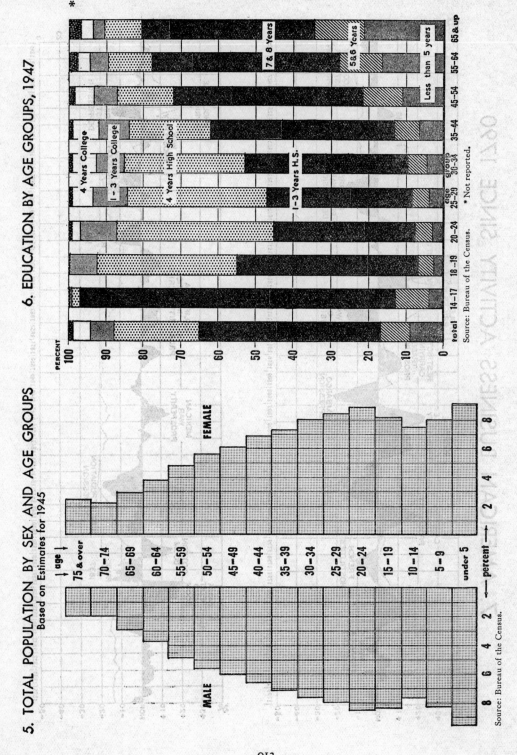

5. TOTAL POPULATION BY SEX AND AGE GROUPS
Based on Estimates for 1945

6. EDUCATION BY AGE GROUPS, 1947

Source: Bureau of the Census.

Source: Bureau of the Census.

7. AMERICAN BUSINESS ACTIVITY SINCE 1790

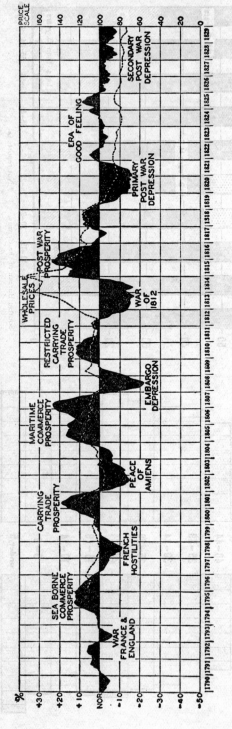

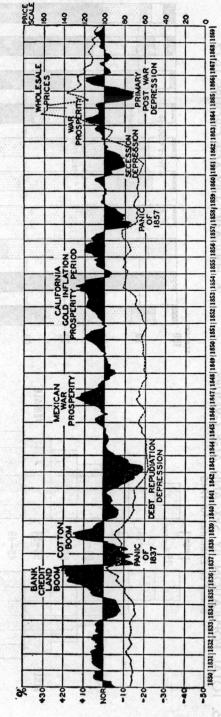

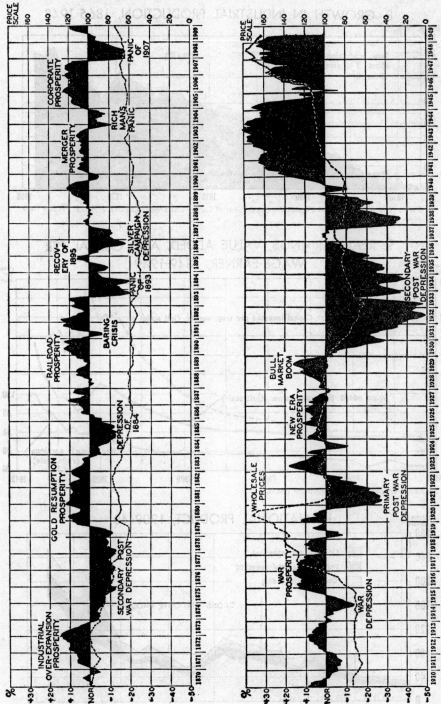

The Cleveland Trust Company

8. GROWTH IN INDUSTRIAL PRODUCTION, 1865-1948

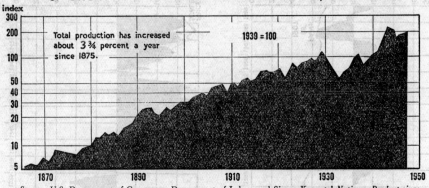

Total production has increased about 3 ¾ percent a year since 1875.

1939 = 100

Source: U.S. Department of Commerce, Department of Labor, and Simon Kuznets' *Nationa Product since 1869*.

9. REAL EARNINGS, VALUE ADDED, AND CAPITAL PER WAGE-EARNER, 1849-1949

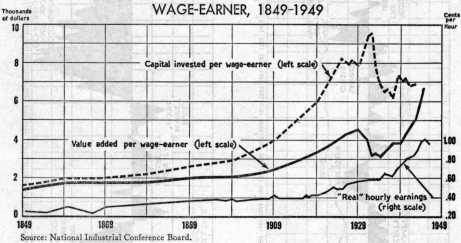

Capital invested per wage-earner (left scale)

Value added per wage-earner (left scale)

"Real" hourly earnings (right scale)

Source: National Industrial Conference Board.

10. NATIONAL PRODUCT, 1909-48

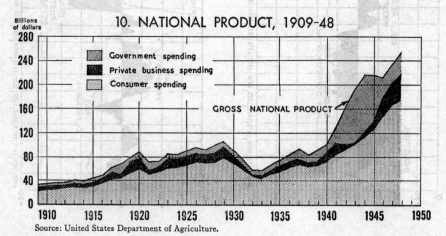

Government spending
Private business spending
Consumer spending

GROSS NATIONAL PRODUCT

Source: United States Department of Agriculture.

11. GROWTH OF AMERICAN LABOR UNIONS, 1900-1949

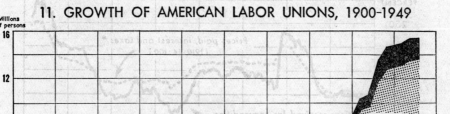

Millions of persons

16

12

8

4

Independent

AFL

CIO

1900   1910   1920   1930   1940   1950

Source: United States Department of Labor and the Bureau of Labor Statistics.

12. FACTORY WORKERS' WAGES SINCE 1913
In Dollars and Purchasing Power

Dollars

50
40
30
20
10
0

Weekly wages – actual dollars

Real weekly wages – in dollars of 1913 purchasing

1913   1920   1925   1930   1935   1940   1945   1950

Source: Bureau of Labor Statistics.

13. LABOR FORCE AND UNEMPLOYMENT, 1900-1948

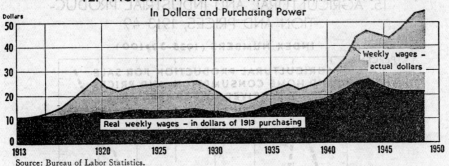

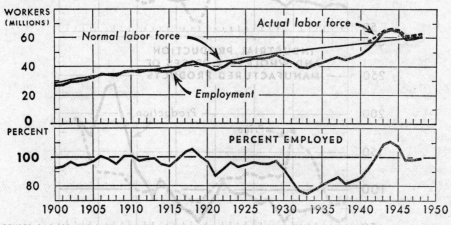

WORKERS (MILLIONS)

60
40
20
0

Normal labor force

Actual labor force

Employment

PERCENT

100

80

PERCENT EMPLOYED

1900 1905 1910 1915 1920 1925 1930 1935 1940 1945 1950

SOURCE: BAE, BLS, AND BUREAU OF THE CENSUS   1948 DATA PARTLY ESTIMATED   U.S. DEPARTMENT OF AGRICULTURE

14. PRICES RECEIVED AND PAID BY FARMERS, 1910-48

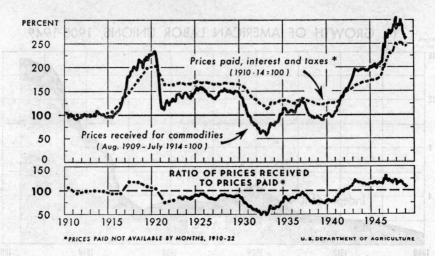

PERCENT

Prices paid, interest and taxes *
(1910-14 = 100)

Prices received for commodities
(Aug. 1909 - July 1914 = 100)

RATIO OF PRICES RECEIVED
TO PRICES PAID *

*PRICES PAID NOT AVAILABLE BY MONTHS, 1910-22   U. S. DEPARTMENT OF AGRICULTURE

15. AGRICULTURAL AND INDUSTRIAL PRODUC-
TION AND PRICES, 1913-49

INDEX NUMBERS (1935-39=100)

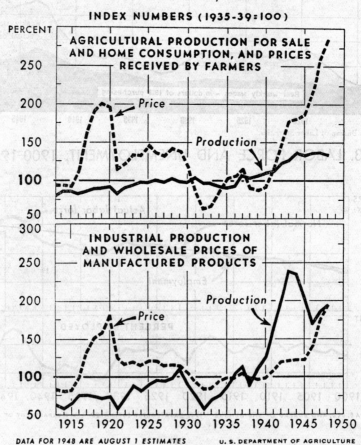

PERCENT

AGRICULTURAL PRODUCTION FOR SALE
AND HOME CONSUMPTION, AND PRICES
RECEIVED BY FARMERS

Price

Production

INDUSTRIAL PRODUCTION
AND WHOLESALE PRICES OF
MANUFACTURED PRODUCTS

Price

Production

DATA FOR 1948 ARE AUGUST 1 ESTIMATES   U. S. DEPARTMENT OF AGRICULTURE

16. WHOLESALE PRICES, 1749-1949

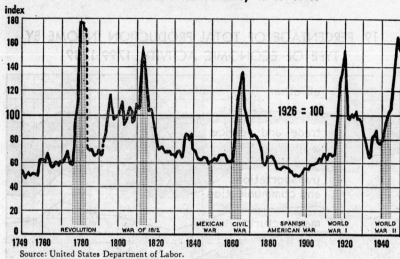

1926 = 100

REVOLUTION — WAR OF 1812 — MEXICAN WAR — CIVIL WAR — SPANISH AMERICAN WAR — WORLD WAR I — WORLD WAR II

Source: United States Department of Labor.

17. COST OF LIVING, 1913-49

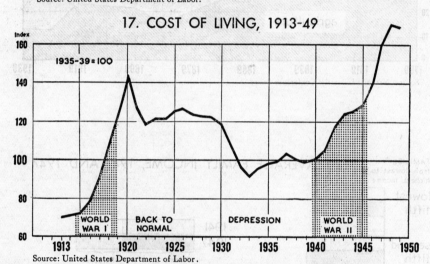

1935-39 = 100

WORLD WAR I — BACK TO NORMAL — DEPRESSION — WORLD WAR II

Source: United States Department of Labor.

18. STOCK-MARKET PRICES, 1915-48

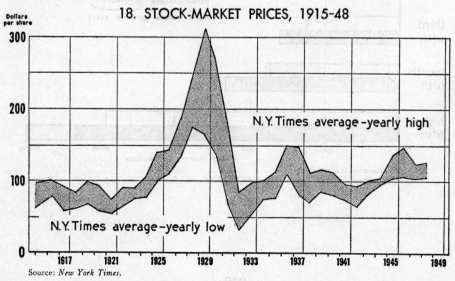

N.Y. Times average – yearly high

N.Y. Times average – yearly low

Source: *New York Times.*

19. PERCENTAGE OF TOTAL PRODUCTION INCOME BY TYPE OF ECONOMIC ACTIVITY, 1799-1939

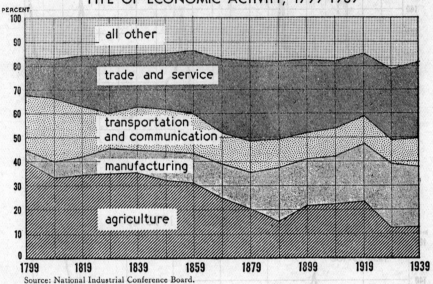

all other

trade and service

transportation and communication

manufacturing

agriculture

Source: National Industrial Conference Board.

20. AVERAGE FAMILY INCOME, 1941 AND 1947

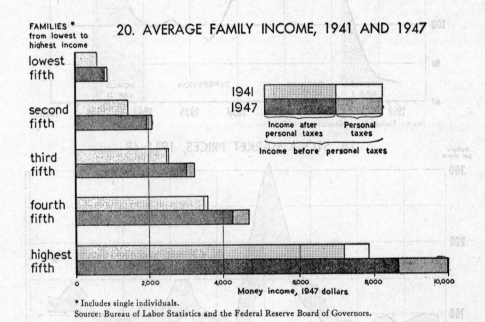

FAMILIES *
from lowest to
highest income

lowest fifth

second fifth

third fifth

fourth fifth

highest fifth

1941
1947

Income after personal taxes   Personal taxes

Income before personal taxes

Money income, 1947 dollars

* Includes single individuals.
Source: Bureau of Labor Statistics and the Federal Reserve Board of Governors.

21. ANNUAL AVERAGE PER CAPITA INCOME BY STATES, 1947

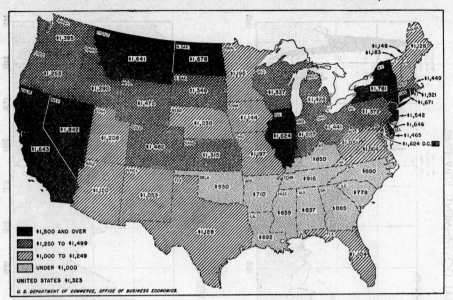

Legend:
- $1,500 AND OVER
- $1,250 TO $1,499
- $1,000 TO $1,249
- UNDER $1,000

UNITED STATES $1,323

U. S. DEPARTMENT OF COMMERCE, OFFICE OF BUSINESS ECONOMICS.

22. NATIONAL INCOME BY DISTRIBUTIVE SHARES, 1929–48
(Billions of Dollars)

Period	Total National Income*	Compensation of Employees†	Proprietors' and Rental Income — Total	Business and Professional	Farm	Rental Income of Persons	Corporate Profits and Inventory Valuation Adjustment — Total	Corporate Profits — Profits before Tax	Corporate Profits — Tax Liability	Corporate Profits — Profits after Tax	Inventory Valuation Adjustment	Net Interest
1929...	87.4	50.8	19.7	8.3	5.7	5.8	10.3	9.8	1.4	8.4	0.5	6.5
1930...	75.0	46.5	15.7	7.0	3.9	4.8	6.6	3.3	0.8	2.5	3.3	6.2
1931...	58.9	39.5	11.8	5.3	2.9	3.6	1.6	− 0.8	0.5	− 1.3	2.4	5.9
1932...	41.7	30.8	7.4	3.2	1.7	2.5	− 2.0	− 3.0	0.4	− 3.4	1.0	5.4
1933...	39.6	29.3	7.2	2.9	2.3	2.0	− 2.0	0.2	0.5	− 0.4	−2.1	5.0
1934...	48.6	34.1	8.7	4.3	2.3	2.1	1.1	1.7	0.7	1.0	−0.6	4.7
1935...	56.8	37.1	12.1	5.0	4.9	2.3	3.0	3.2	1.0	2.3	−0.2	4.5
1936...	64.7	42.7	12.6	6.1	3.9	2.7	4.9	5.7	1.4	4.3	−0.7	4.5
1937...	73.6	47.7	15.4	6.6	5.6	3.1	6.2	6.2	1.5	4.7	......	4.4
1938...	67.4	44.7	14.0	6.3	4.4	3.3	4.3	3.3	1.0	2.3	1.0	4.3
1939...	72.5	47.8	14.7	6.8	4.5	3.5	5.8	6.5	1.5	5.0	−0.7	4.2
1940...	81.3	51.8	16.3	7.7	4.9	3.6	9.2	9.3	2.9	6.4	−0.1	4.1
1941...	103.8	64.3	20.8	9.6	6.9	4.3	14.6	17.2	7.8	9.4	−2.6	4.1
1942...	136.5	84.7	28.1	12.1	10.6	5.4	19.8	21.1	11.7	9.4	−1.3	3.9
1943...	168.3	109.1	32.1	14.1	11.8	6.2	23.7	24.5	14.2	10.4	−0.8	3.4
1944...	182.4	121.1	34.1	15.4	11.9	6.7	24.0	24.3	13.5	10.8	−0.3	3.1
1945...	181.7	122.9	36.0	16.8	12.3	7.0	19.8	20.4	11.6	8.7	−0.6	3.0
1946...	179.3	117.3	41.8	20.4	14.6	6.7	16.8	21.8	9.0	12.8	−5.0	3.4
1947...	202.5	127.5	46.0	23.2	15.6	7.1	24.7	29.8	11.7	18.1	−5.1	4.3
1948...	224.0	137.8	50.7	25.2	18.0	7.6	30.7	34.0	13.2	20.8	−3.3	4.7

Source: Department of Commerce.

* National income is the total net income earned in production by individuals or businesses. The concept of national income currently used differs from the concept of gross national product (cf. Chart 10) in that it excludes depreciation charges and other allowances for business and institutional consumption of durable capital goods.

† Includes wage and salary receipts and other labor income and employer and employee contributions for social insurance.

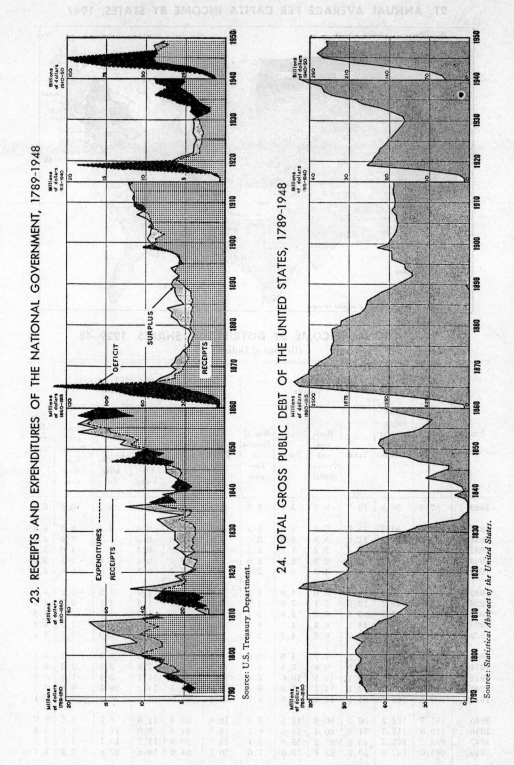

23. RECEIPTS AND EXPENDITURES OF THE NATIONAL GOVERNMENT, 1789-1948

Source: U.S. Treasury Department.

24. TOTAL GROSS PUBLIC DEBT OF THE UNITED STATES, 1789-1948

Source: Statistical Abstract of the United States.

25. THE TARIFF SINCE 1789

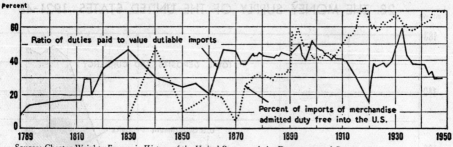

Source: Chester Wright, *Economic History of the United States*, and the Department of Commerce.

26. PER CAPITA EXPORTS AND IMPORTS, 1790-1940

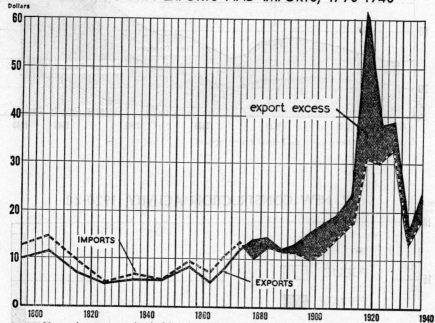

1791–1860, yearly average per decade (plotted at midpoint); 1861–1940, yearly average per five-year period (plotted at midpoint).
Source: Department of Commerce.

27. EXPORTS AND IMPORTS BY TYPE, 1820-1940

1820–60, yearly average per decade (plotted at midpoint); 1861–1940, yearly average per five-year period (plotted at midpoint).
Source: Department of Commerce.

28. THE MONEY SUPPLY OF THE UNITED STATES, 1921-48

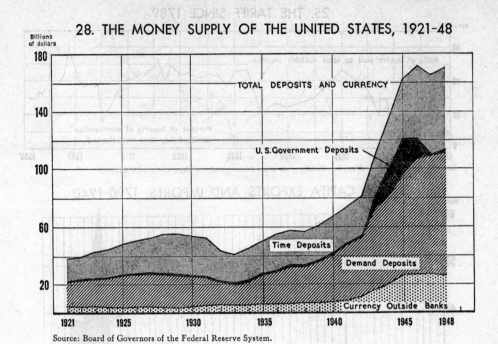

Source: Board of Governors of the Federal Reserve System.

29. NEW CONSTRUCTION ACTIVITY, 1920-48

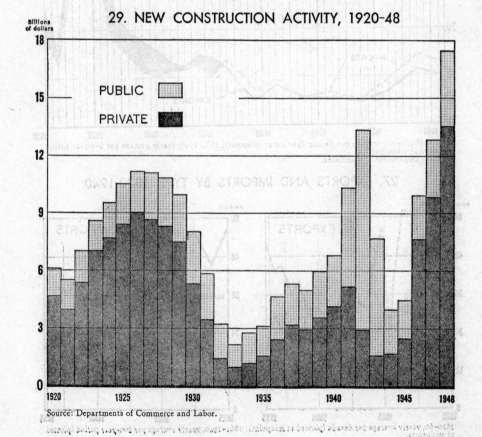

Source: Departments of Commerce and Labor.

30. PER CENT CHANGES IN PRICES AND PRODUCTION
1929–32 AND 1932–37
(All Per Cents Are of 1929 Level)

INDUSTRY GROUP	PER CENT DROP, 1929–32				PER CENT RECOVERY 1932–37	
	Prices	Production	Man-Hours	Hourly Wages	Prices	Production
Motor vehicles............	−12	−74	−64	− 9	+ 2	+64
Agricultural implements......	−14	−84	−84	−18	+ 9	+84
Cement.....................	−16	−55	−62	−19	+20	+24
Iron and steel...............	−16	−76	−70	−20	+20	+67
Automobile tires.............	−25	−42	−60	− 7	+27	+24
Leather and products........	−33	−18	−30	−14	+29	+27
Petroleum products.........	−36	−17	−35	− 3	+21	+27
Textile products.............	−39	−28	−40	−20	+24	+24
Food products..............	−39	−10	−29	−11	+24	− 1
Agricultural commodities......	−54	− 1	....	....	+36	+ 8

General Economic Activity	Changes from 1929 to 1932 (Per Cent)	Changes from 1932 to 1937 (Per Cent)	Costs of Production	Changes from 1929 to 1932 (Per Cent)	Changes from 1932 to 1937 (Per Cent)
National or individual income...................	−52	+38	Postal rates.............	+16	+ 7
Employment.............	−29	+16	Railroad freight rates....	+ 2	− 4
Cost of living...........	−20	+ 4	Factory building costs....	−11	+16
Wholesale prices.........	−31	+22	Electricity..............	−12	−12
Industrial production	−48	+50	Wages and salaries in manufacturing............	−16	+20

COMMODITIES	PER CENT CHANGE 1929–33		COMMODITIES	PER CENT CHANGE 1929–33	
	Average Wholesale Price	Amount Available for Consumption		Average Wholesale Price	Amount Available for Consumption
Nondurable goods:			*Semidurable goods—Cont.*		
Corn..................	−37	− 3	Rayon................	−51	+64
Wheat................	−28	+ 1	Silk (raw, Japan)......	−67	−23
Steers................	−57	+28	Rubber (plantation)...	−71	−27
Hogs.................	−61	− 2			
Milk.................	−39	+ 4	*Durable goods:*		
Tobacco..............	−42	− 4	Harvester (thresher)...	− 2	−99
Bread...............	− 7	−16	Plows................	0	−61
Beef (fresh)...........	−51	+ 6	Structural		
Sugar (granulated)......	−15	− 6	steel...............	−15	−76
Coal (bituminous).....	− 9	−37	Passenger cars........	−16	−64
Petroleum............	−54	−15	Copper (ingot)........	−61	−88
Fertilizers (mixed).....	−34	−45	Tin (pig).............	−13	−28
Cigarettes.............	− 9	− 1	Bathtubs.............	−26	−69
			Brick (front)..........	− 7	−87
Semidurable goods:			Cement..............	− 6	−63
Cotton................	−33	− 7	Lumber (oak)........	−22	−77
Hides (steer)..........	−43	−14	Crushed stone.........	−11	−51
Suits (men's)..........	−11	−40	Washing machines (electric).............	−47	+ 8
Print cloth............	−28	+ 2			
Cotton yarn (carded)...	−23	−23			

Sources: National Resources Committee, Bureau of Labor Statistics, and Bureau of Agricultural Economics.

31. PRODUCTION AND PRICES OF ADMINISTERED AND MARKET-PRICE COMMODITIES, 1925–35

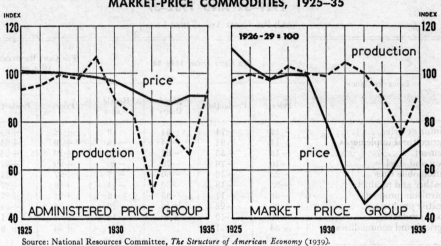

Source: National Resources Committee, *The Structure of American Economy* (1939).

32. TOTAL ASSESSED VALUATION OF STATES (1937) COMPARED WITH ASSETS OF THIRTY BILLION-DOLLAR CORPORATIONS (1935)

	In Billions		In Billions
New York	$25.70	Louisiana	$1.34
Pennsylvania	12.40	Bank of America	1.27
Ohio	8.80	Mutual Life Ins. Co. of N.Y.	1.24
California	7.80	Oklahoma	1.22
Massachusetts	6.30	Commonwealth & Southern Corp.	1.17
Michigan	6.20	Great Northern Ry. Co.	1.15
New Jersey	6.20	Continental Illinois Nat. Bank & Trust	
Illinois	5.20	Co.	1.14
Indiana	5.10	Northern Pacific R.R. Co.	1.13
Wisconsin	4.80	Associated Gas & Electric Co.	1.12
Metropolitan Life Ins. Co.	4.23	Baltimore & Ohio R.R. Co.	1.11
American Tel. & Tel. Co.	3.99	City Service Co.	1.11
Missouri	3.80	Colorado	1.10
Texas	3.20	Atchison, Topeka & Santa Fe R.R. Co.	1.09
Iowa	3.20	Washington	1.08
Prudential Ins. Co.	3.12	Northwestern Mutual Life Ins. Co.	1.07
Connecticut	2.90	Union Pacific R.R. Co.	1.07
Pennsylvania R.R. Co.	2.86	Georgia	1.06
Kansas	2.70	North American Co.	1.04
Maryland	2.60	South Dakota	1.03
Kentucky	2.40	Banker's Trust Co.	1.03
New York Central R.R. Co.	2.35	Alabama	.92
Chase National Bank	2.33	Oregon	.89
New York Life Ins. Co.	2.22	Maine	.66
North Carolina	2.20	Florida	.60
Nebraska	2.10	New Hampshire	.58
Minnesota	2.00	Utah	.52
Standard Oil Co.	1.89	North Dakota	.49
National City Bank of N.Y.	1.88	Mississippi	.44
Guaranty Trust Co.	1.84	Arkansas	.43
Equitable Life Ass. Co.	1.82	Idaho	.38
U.S. Steel Corp.	1.82	Arizona	.36
District of Columbia	1.78	South Carolina	.36
West Virginia	1.74	Montana	.33
Allegheny Corp.	1.73	Vermont	.32
Southern Pacific R.R. Co.	1.67	Delaware	.31
General Motors Corp.	1.49	New Mexico	.29
Tennessee	1.47	Wyoming	.28
Consolidated Edison Co. of N.Y., Inc.	1.38	Nevada	.18
Rhode Island	1.36		

Source: Bureau of Foreign and Domestic Commerce and Senate Judiciary Committee.

926

33. DISTRIBUTION OF EMPLOYEES AND EMPLOYERS BY SIZE OF BUSINESS CONCERN, 1937

Employers of the Following Number of Employees	Amounted to the Following Percentage of All Firms	And Employed the Following Percentage of All Employees
1 only	25	1.2
1–9 inclusive	75	11.0
10–99	22	26.5
100 and over	3	73.5
300 and over	1	47.0
1,000 and over	0.2	32.0
10,000 and over	0.011	12.3

Source: Adapted from *Social Security Bulletin*.

34. OWNERSHIP OF AMERICAN ENTERPRISES BY FORM OF ORGANIZATION, 1904–39

Year	Per Cent of Manufacturers Which Were—		Per Cent of Wage-Earners Working for—		Per Cent of Value of Manufactured Products by—	
	Corporations	Others	Corporations	Others	Corporations	Others
1904	23.6	76.4	70.6	29.9	73.7	26.3
1909	25.9	74.1	75.6	24.4	79.0	21.0
1914	28.3	71.7	80.3	19.7	83.2	16.8
1919	31.5	68.5	86.9	13.4	87.7	12.3
1929	48.3	51.7	89.9	10.1	92.1	7.9
1939	51.5	48.5	89.4	10.6	92.6	7.4

Source: Census of Manufactures.

35. PERCENTAGE DISTRIBUTION OF TOTAL NATIONAL INCOME PRODUCED BY CORPORATIONS OF VARIOUS TOTAL ASSETS CLASSED BY MAJOR DIVISIONS OF ECONOMIC ACTIVITY, 1933

Economic Activity	Per Cent of Total National Income for Each Group Produced by—				
	Unincorporated Enterprises	Corporations with Total Assets of—			
		Less than $1 Million	$1–5 Millions	$5–50 Millions	$50 Millions and Over
Agriculture	94	3.1	2.9	....	....
Mining and quarrying	4	19.8	15.4	60.8	....
Manufacturing	8	24.3	14.3	20.0	33.4
Construction	67	23.4	5.0	4.6	....
Transport and utilities	14	6.5	2.9	11.1	65.5
Trade	37	37.0	9.5	9.1	7.4
Service	67	19.3	5.0	8.7	....
Finance	44	16.0	9.0	14.0	17.0
Miscellaneous	62	28.2	9.8	....	....
All economic activity	43	20.1	7.9	10.6	18.4
All economic activity, govt. excluded	38	21.8	8.6	11.6	20.0

Source: U.S. Census.

36. IMMIGRATION TO THE UNITED STATES FROM PRINCIPAL COUNTRIES OF ORIGIN, 1820-1923

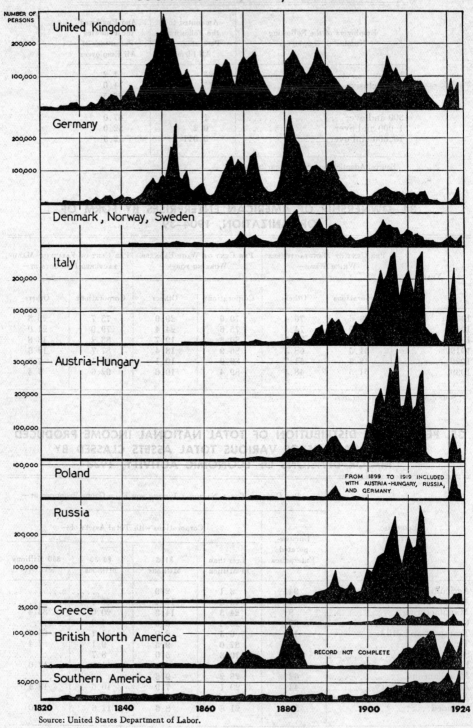

Source: United States Department of Labor.

| YEAR | CANDIDATE AND PARTY | POPULAR VOTE | | ELECTORAL VOTE |
		In Thousands	Per Cent	
1789........	Washington (No party)			69
	John Adams (No party)			34
	Scattering (No party)			35
1792........	Washington (Federalist)			132
	John Adams (Federalist)			77
	George Clinton (Anti-Federalist)			50
	Jefferson (Anti-Federalist)			4
	Burr (Anti-Federalist)			1
1796........	John Adams (Federalist)			71
	Jefferson (Democratic-Republican)			68
	Thomas Pinckney (Federalist)			59
	Burr (Democratic-Republican)			30
	Scattering (No party)			48
1800........	Jefferson* (Democratic-Republican)			73
	Burr (Democratic-Republican)			73
	John Adams (Federalist)			65
	C. C. Pinckney (Federalist)			64
	Jay (Federalist)			1
1804........	Jefferson (Democratic-Republican)			162
	C. C. Pinckney (Federalist)			14
1808........	Madison (Democratic-Republican)			122
	C. C. Pinckney (Federalist)			47
	George Clinton (Democratic-Republican)			6
1812........	Madison (Democratic-Republican)			128
	DeWitt Clinton (Federalist)			89
1816........	Monroe (Democratic-Republican)			183
	King (Federalist)			34
1820........	Monroe (Democratic-Republican)			231
	J. Q. Adams (Independent)			1
1824........	J. Q. Adams† (No party)	114	32	84
	Jackson (No party)	153	42	99
	Crawford (No party)	47	13	41
	Clay (No party)	47	13	37
1828........	Jackson (Democratic)	647	56	178
	J. Q. Adams (National Republican)	508	44	83
1832........	Jackson (Democratic)	688	55	219
	Clay (National Republican)	530	42	49
	Floyd (Independent [no party]) }	33	3	11
	Wirt (Anti-Masonic) }			7
1836........	Van Buren (Democratic)	763	51	170
	W. H. Harrison (Whig) }			73
	White (Whig) }	736	49	26
	Webster (Whig) }			14
	Mangum (Ind. [no party]) }			11
1840........	W. H. Harrison (Whig)‡	1,275	53	234
	Van Buren (Democratic)	1,129	47	60
	Birney (Liberty)	7	0.4	....
1844........	Polk (Democratic)	1,337	50	170
	Clay (Whig)	1,299	48	105
	Birney (Liberty)	62	2	....
1848........	Taylor (Whig)§	1,360	47	163
	Cass (Democratic)	1,221	43	127
	Van Buren (Free Soil)	291	10	....

Sources: *1789–1924:* Edward Stanwood, *A History of the Presidency from 1788 to 1897.* Revised by Charles Knowles Bolton (Boston and New York: Houghton Mifflin Co., 1928), pp. 27–568; Edward Stanwood, *A History of the Presidency from 1897 to 1916.* Additions and revisions to 1928 by Charles Knowles Bolton (Boston and New York: Houghton Mifflin Co., 1928), pp. 75–472. *1928–1948: The World Almanac, 1949* (New York: New York World Telegram, 1949), p. 48; *The World Almanac, 1944* (New York: New York World Telegram, 1944), pp. 427–29.

* The election went to the House of Representatives, where Thomas Jefferson was chosen President.

† The election went to the House of Representatives, where John Quincy Adams was chosen President.

‡ Vice-President John Tyler became President upon Harrison's death on April 4, 1841.

§ Vice-President Millard Fillmore became President upon Taylor's death on July 9, 1850.

YEAR	CANDIDATE AND PARTY	POPULAR VOTE		ELECTORAL VOTE
		In Thousands	Per Cent	
1852........	Pierce (Democratic)	1,601	51	254
	Scott (Whig)	1,387	44	42
	Hale (Free Soil)	157	5	....
1856........	Buchanan (Democratic)	1,838	45	174
	Frémont (Republican)	1,341	33	114
	Fillmore (American or Know-Nothing)	875	22	8
1860........	Lincoln (Republican)	1,866	40	180
	Douglas (Democratic)	1,377	29	12
	Breckinridge (Democratic)	850	18	72
	Bell (Constitutional Union)	589	13	39
1864........	Lincoln (Union)‖	2,214	55	212
	McClellan (Democratic)	1,802	45	21
1868........	Grant (Republican)	3,013	53	214
	Seymour (Democratic)	2,703	47	80
1872........	Grant (Republican)	3,597	56	286
	Greeley (Democratic)	2,834	44	#
1876........	Hayes (Republican)	4,034	48	185
	Tilden (Democratic)	4,286	51	184
	Cooper (Greenback)	82	1	....
1880........	Garfield (Republican)**	4,454	48	214
	Hancock (Democratic)	4,445	48	155
	Weaver (Greenback)	309	3	....
1884........	Cleveland (Democratic)	4,875	49	219
	Blaine (Republican)	4,852	48	182
	Butler (Greenback)	175	1.3	
	St. John (Prohibition)	150	1.5	....
1888........	Benjamin Harrison (Republican)	5,440	48	233
	Cleveland (Democratic)	5,540	49	168
	Streeter (Union Labor)	147	1.3	
	Fisk (Prohibition)	250	2.2	
1892........	Cleveland (Democratic)	5,557	46	277
	Benjamin Harrison (Republican)	5,176	43	145
	Weaver (Populist)	1,041	8.5	22
	Bidwell (Prohibition)	256	2.2	....
1896........	McKinley (Republican)	7,112	51	271
	Bryan (Democratic)	6,509	47	176
	Levering (Prohibition)	131	1	
	Palmer (National Democratic)	135	1	....
1900........	McKinley (Republican)††	7,220	52	292
	Bryan (Democratic)	6,359	46	155
	Woolley (Prohibition)	209	1.5	
	Debs (Social Democrat)	95	0.7	....
1904........	Theodore Roosevelt (Republican)	7,629	56	336
	Parker (Democratic)	5,084	38	140
	Debs (Socialist)	403	3	....
	Swallow (Prohibition)	259	2	....
1908........	Taft (Republican)	7,678	52	321
	Bryan (Democratic)	6,408	43	162
	Debs (Socialist)	421	2.8	....
	Chafin (Prohibition)	253	1.7	....
1912........	Wilson (Democratic)	6,293	42	435
	Theodore Roosevelt (Progressive)	4,120	27	88
	Taft (Republican)	3,485	23	8
	Debs (Socialist)	902	6	
	Chafin (Prohibition)	208	1.4	....

‖ Vice-President Andrew Johnson became President upon Lincoln's death, April 15, 1865.

Greeley died on November 29, 1872, and his electoral votes were scattered among minor candidates.

** Vice-President Chester A. Arthur became President upon Garfield's death, September 19, 1881.

†† Vice-President Theodore Roosevelt became President upon McKinley's death, September 14, 1901.

37. PRESIDENTIAL VOTE, 1789-1948—*Continued*

Year	Candidate and Party	Popular Vote		Electoral Vote
		In Thousands	Per Cent	
1916........	Wilson (Democratic)	9,130	49	277
	Hughes (Republican)	8,538	46	254
	Benson (Socialist)	585	3.2	....
	Hanly (Prohibition)	221	1.2	....
1920........	Harding (Republican)‡‡	16,152	61	404
	Cox (Democratic)	9,147	35	127
	Debs (Socialist)	920	3.5	....
1924........	Coolidge (Republican)	15,725	54	382
	Davis (Democratic)	8,386	29	136
	La Follette (Progressive)	4,826	17	13
1928........	Hoover (Republican)	21,392	58	444
	Smith (Democratic)	15,016	41	87
1932........	F. D. Roosevelt (Democratic)	22,822	57	472
	Hoover (Republican)	15,762	40	59
	Thomas (Socialist)	885	2.5	....
1936........	F. D. Roosevelt (Democratic)	27,477	61	523
	Landon (Republican)	16,680	36	8
	Lemke (Union)	882	2	....
1940........	F. D. Roosevelt (Democratic)	27,243	54	449
	Willkie (Republican)	22,305	44	82
1944........	F. D. Roosevelt (Democratic)§§	25,603	52	432
	Dewey (Republican)	22,006	46	99
1948........	Truman (Democratic)	24,105	50	304
	Dewey (Republican)	21,969	46	189
	Thurmond (States' Rights)	1,169	2	36
	Wallace (Progressive)	1,157	2	....

‡‡ Vice-President Calvin Coolidge became President upon Harding's death, August 2, 1923.
§§ Vice-President Harry S. Truman became President upon Roosevelt's death, April 12, 1945,

38. PRESIDENTIAL POPULAR VOTE SINCE 1912

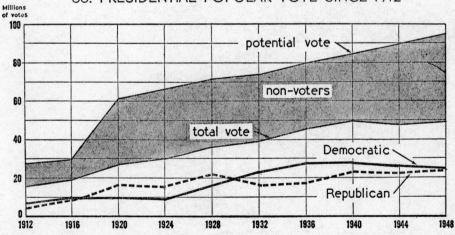

38. PRESIDENTIAL POPULAR VOTE SINCE 1912

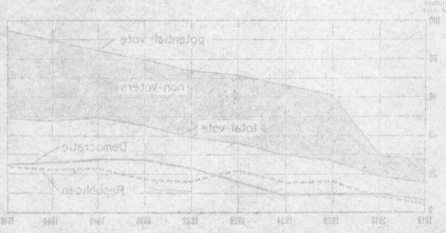